AAK-9913

PSYCHOLOGY AND ITS ALLIED DISCIPLINES

Volume I: Psychology and the Humanities
Volume II: Psychology and the Social Sciences
Volume III: Psychology and the Natural Sciences

WITHDRAWN

Edited by
MARC H. BORNSTEIN
NEW YORK UNIVERSITY

 LAWRENCE ERLBAUM ASSOCIATES, PUBLISHERS
1984   Hillsdale, New Jersey   London

Lawrence Erlbaum Associates, Inc., Publishers
365 Broadway
Hillsdale, New Jersey 07642

Library of Congress Cataloging in Publication Data

Main entry unter title:

Psychology and its allied disciplines.

Includes bibliographical references and index.
Contents: v. 1. Psychology and humanities—v. 2.
Psychology and the social sciences—v. 3. Psychology
and the natural sciences.
1. Psychology and the humanities. 2. Social sciences
and psychology. 3. Science and psychology.
I. Bornstein, Marc H.
BF38.P786 1984   150   84-13565
ISBN 0-89859-318-2 (set)
ISBN 0-89859-319-9 (pbk.: set)
ISBN 0-89859-320-4 (vol. 1)
ISBN 0-89859-321-1 (vol. 2)
ISBN 0-89859-322-0 (vol. 3)

Printed in the United States of America
10 9 8 7 6 5 4 3 2 1

Three books on psychology
for
Four men of psychology

Lawrence Erlbaum
William Kessen
Lawrence Marks
Hanuš Papoušek

CROSSCURRENTS IN CONTEMPORARY PSYCHOLOGY

A series of volumes edited by Marc H. Bornstein
New York University

1979   PSYCHOLOGICAL DEVELOPMENT FROM INFANCY:
       Image to Intention
       BORNSTEIN AND KESSEN

1980   COMPARATIVE METHODS IN PSYCHOLOGY
       BORNSTEIN

1984   PSYCHOLOGY AND ITS ALLIED DISCIPLINES
       BORNSTEIN
       Volume I: Psychology and the Humanities
       Volume II: Psychology and the Social Sciences
       Volume III: Psychology and the Natural Sciences

       THE SEGMENTATION OF BEHAVIOR *(In preparation)*
       BORNSTEIN

       THE CRITICAL PERIOD: Interdisciplinary Perspectives *(In preparation)*
       BORNSTEIN

Series Prologue

CROSSCURRENTS IN CONTEMPORARY PSYCHOLOGY

Contemporary psychology is increasingly diversified, pluralistic, and specialized, and most psychologists tend to venture beyond the confines of their narrow subdiscipline only rarely. Yet psychologists with different specialties encounter similar problems, ask similar questions, and share similar concerns. Unfortunately, there are far too few forums for the expression or exploration of what is common in psychology. This series, *Crosscurrents in Contemporary Psychology,* is intended to serve as such a forum.

The chief aim of this series is to provide integrated perspectives on supradisciplinary themes in psychology. The first volume in the series was devoted to a consideration of *Psychological Development from Infancy;* the second volume to *Comparative Methods in Psychology;* volumes three, four, and five examine relations between psychology and allied disciplines in the humanities, the social sciences, and the natural sciences; future volumes will focus on the segmentation of behavior and critical periods. Each volume in the series thus treats a different issue and is self-contained, yet the series as a whole endeavors to interrelate psychological subdisciplines bringing new or shared perspectives to bear on a wide variety of issues in psychological thought and research. As a consequence of this structure and the flexibility and scope it affords, volumes in the *Crosscurrents in Contemporary Psychology* series will appeal, individually or as a group, to psychologists with diverse interests. Reflecting the nature and intent of this series, contributing authors are drawn from a broad spectrum of humanities and sciences—anthropology to zoology—but representational emphasis is placed on active contributing authorities to the contemporary psychological literature.

Crosscurrents in Contemporary Psychology is a series whose stated intent is to explore a broad range of supradisciplinary issues. In its concern with such issues, the series is devoted to promoting interest in the interconnectedness of research, method, and theory in psychological study.

MARC H. BORNSTEIN
Editor

Contributors to This Volume

William P. Alston, *Department of Philosophy, Syracuse University, Syracuse, New York 13210*

Kurt W. Back, *Department of Sociology, Duke University, Durham, North Carolina 27706*

Benjamin Beit-Hallahmi, *Department of Psychology, Haifa University, Haifa, Israel 31999*

Ned Block, *Department of Linguistics and Philosophy, Massachusetts Institute of Technology, Cambridge, Massachusetts 02139*

Marc H. Bornstein, *Department of Psychology, New York University, New York, New York 10003*

Alphonse Chapanis, *Communications Research Laboratory, The Johns Hopkins University, Baltimore, Maryland 21204*

Clyde H. Coombs, *Department of Psychology, University of Michigan, Ann Arbor, Michigan 48109*

Diana Deutsch, *Center for Human Information Processing, University of California at San Diego, La Jolla, California 92093*

Alan C. Elms, *Department of Psychology, University of California at Davis, Davis, California 95616*

Hans J. Eysenck, *Institute of Psychiatry, London, England SE5 8AF*

John L. Fuller, *P.O. Box 543, York, Maine 03909*

David C. Glass, *Department of Psychology, State University of New York Stony Brook, New York 11794*

Philip N. Johnson-Laird, *MRC Applied Psychology Unit, Cambridge, England CB2 2EF*

Conan Kornetsky, *Division of Psychiatry, School of Medicine, Boston University, Boston, Massachusetts 02118*

David S. Krantz, *Uniform Services University of the Health Sciences, School of Medicine, Bethesda, Maryland 20014*

Robert Jay Lifton, *Department of Psychiatry, School of Medicine, Yale University, New Haven, Connecticut 06519*

Martin S. Lindauer, *Department of Psychology, State University of New York, Brockport, New York 14420*

Sharone Maital, *Haifa School Psychological Services, Haifa, Israel 32000*

Shlomo Maital, *Faculty of Industrial Engineering, Technion, Haifa, Israel 32000*

Lawrence E. Marks, *J. B. Pierce Foundation Laboratory, New Haven, Connecticut 06519*

Douglass R. Price-Williams, *Department of Psychiatry, School of Medicine, University of California at Los Angeles, Los Angeles, California 90024*

Charles B. Strozier, *History Program, Sangamon State University, Springfield, Illinois 62708*

William R. Uttal, *Institute for Social Research, University of Michigan, Ann Arbor, Michigan 48106*

Joanna P. Williams, *Department of Psychology, Teachers College, Columbia University, New York, New York 10027*

Joachim F. Wohlwill, *Division of Man-Environment Relations, The Pennsylvania State University, University Park, Pennsylvania 16802*

Contents

Contents

Contents

Preface

It is natural for intellectual disciplines to ally with one another. Of course, linkages between disciplines can be few or many, direct or indirect, common or exotic, intimate or distant. In its central concern with the mind and soul, psychology, among all fields of interest, is impressive in the number and diversity of other disciplines to which it is allied. Psychology seems naturally to contact, to contribute to, and to benefit from the greatest possible variety of other disciplines. Many psychologists actually work at the intersection of psychology and some other discipline; most psychologists at least touch another discipline regularly.

What relations exist between psychology and disciplines allied to it? How are the boundaries between psychology and its affiliated disciplines defined and constructed? How do mutual contributions between psychology and associated disciplines function and balance? In *Psychology and Its Allied Disciplines,* scholars whose intellectual interests and research efforts lie at the interface of psychology and other disciplines in the humanities, social sciences, and natural sciences explore, analyze, discuss, and appraise those affiliations. Each essay is structured to include, first, a brief historical review of the association between psychology and another discipline, second, theoretical evaluations and interpretations of the bases of these associations, third, discussions of major issues and advances psychology has brought to affiliated disciplines and *vice versa,* and, fourth, directions that future research between psychology and associated other disciplines are likely to follow to mutual advantage. The principal purposes of these essays are, therefore, to reflect on psychology, to assess psychology's relations to its allied disciplines, and to guide further cooperation between psychology and other disciplines.

The essays in *Psychology and Its Allied Disciplines* are formally organized into three volumes associated with different knowledge domains. Volume I treats *Psychology and the Humanities,* including art, linguistics, literature, music, philosophy, and religion. Volume II treats *Psychology and the Social Sciences,* including anthropology, behavior therapy, economics, education, environmental disciplines, history, political science, and sociology. Volume III treats *Psychology and the Natural Sciences,* including biology, engineering, genetics, mathematics, medicine, pharmacology, and physics. These three volumes are preceded by brief introductory observations and commentary on the two major orientations to knowledge in psychology, on early interdisciplinary integration and later fragmentation of modern psychology, on the statuses of psychology amongst intellectual domains, on the variety of styles of association between psychology and affiliated disciplines, and, finally, on mutual contributions between psychology and other related disciplines.

Several words can be shared about the selection and style of essays included in this collection. Even though connections between psychology and twenty-one related disciplines are documented across these three volumes, psychology is allied to even more; the decision to omit some connections—notably between psychology and law—was not active but regrettable. Additionally, contemporary psychology is sophisticated, so that some essays which appear here are different from ones originally solicited—psychology and pharmacology *rather* than chemistry is a notable example. Further, psychology is pluralistically related to different disciplines, requiring rational, informed, and commonsensical decisions about what relational aspect(s) to highlight; in one case, psychology's relation to the academic institution not its social cognate is emphasized—thus, psychology and political science *rather* than politics—but in another case just the opposite decision is appropriate—thus, psychology and religion *rather* than theology. Finally, some contributors to these volumes identify themselves principally with psychology while others identity with the "other" discipline; all of the contributors are prominent figures, doubly knowledgeable as they work at the intersection of intellectual fields. It is fortunate for this endeavor that a group of outstanding scholars could be enlisted to summarize, examine, interpret, and evaluate psychology's relations to their allied discipline.

Psychology and Its Allied Disciplines encompass three collections of essays that attempt to place psychology in perspective relative to its intellectual neighbors specifically and to domains of knowledge generally. As a whole, these volumes fit the theme of their parent series, *Crosscurrents in Contemporary Psychology,* in that they are devoted to examination of a supradisciplinary issue that traditionally distinguishes subdisciplines of psychology.

Several individuals aided in preparation of these volumes. Among them, I would like especially to thank Iona Aibel, Helen Bornstein, Kay Ferdinand-sen, Evelyn Hu, Art Lizza, Janet Mindes, Mary Ann Opperman, Madeleine Tress, and Martha Vibbert.

Marc H. Bornstein

Psychology's Relations With Allied Intellectual Disciplines: An Overview

Marc H. Bornstein
New York University

Psychology maintains a special, and arguably unique, status among the humanities, the social sciences, and the natural sciences. However these domains of knowledge are themselves organized—as autonomous or overlapping, as hierarchical or democratic—since its inception and through modern times psychology has forged and sustained strong, integral, and pervasive alliances with each. The chief aim of the essays in *Psychology and Its Allied Disciplines* is to examine the nature of psychology and its relations with the many subdisciplines of these major domains of knowledge.

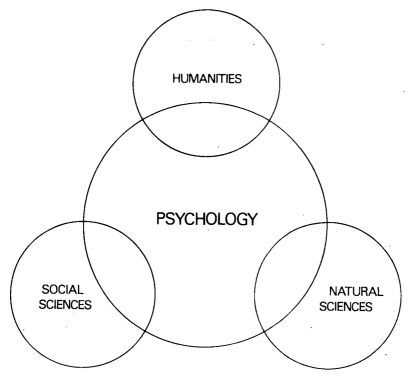

FIG. 1   Psychology amongst the three domains of knowledge. This schematic represents the structure developed in these volumes—*psychology's relations to the humanities, the social sciences, and the natural sciences.* (In reality all domains of knowledge are at once autonomous and interrelated; the humanities, social sciences, and natural sciences are separated here for effect.)

These volumes have two premises. The first is that psychology occupies a privileged position among different knowledge domains. The human individual is the natural unit of analysis in psychology and the starting point for the study of knowledge: Smaller units, the province of physics, genetics, biology, and other natural sciences, as well as larger units, the province of anthropology, history, sociology, and other social sciences, derive meaning in relation to individual psychology. The humanities are, of course, products of human psychology. Psychology therefore pervades all domains of knowledge. The second premise (perhaps a corrollary of the first) is that to understand human beings, the principal goal of psychology, psychologists must comprehend a great many phenomena that are primarily of interest to specialists in other disciplines.

The *Oxford English Dictionary* defines Psychology as "the science of the nature, functions, and phenomena of the human soul or mind." This central task of psychology encompasses humanities, social sciences, and natural sciences. Only through exchange with each has psychology historically pursued its study of the soul or mind. To achieve its aim, psychology has followed two fundamentally different paths associated with different domains of knowledge. One has developed into a "scientific psychology," and the other into a "humanistic psychology."

Scientific psychology embraces the positivist program of the natural sciences. In this empirical approach, psychology proposes preliminary hypotheses, narrows and fixes experimental conditions, manipulates specific variables, and refines results and deduces logic from those results. It then seeks objective verifications and, finally, constructs theories. The program of proper science so defined is, first, to derive general laws of behavior by analyzing complex phenomena into smaller comprehensible units and, then, to synthesize those units into the larger pattern of behavior. Humanistic psychology, by contrast, adopts quite a different strategy. Its approach is private, intuitive, subjective, and wholistic rather than analytical; it is concerned with the individual rather than the general—with idiographic rather than nomothetic understanding; it stresses individual history, ethnography, and biography as opposed to empirically-derived generalization. Here seemingly lurks a disquieting schism in psychology: one psychology of the laboratory and a different psychology of life. The former adopts Cartesian mechanics as an appropriate metaphor of human functioning and directs itself toward explanation; the latter sees living beings as organisms ever adapting to their environment and interests itself in interpretation. The former upholds biology, physics, and ultimately mathematics as ideal sciences to emulate; the latter looks toward the immediate knowledge of art, literature, and philosophy or the personal knowledge of ethnography, history, or psychiatry.

Scientific and humanistic psychology represent two ways of knowing, both deep and penetrating. One endeavors to unearth universal principles with the design that they will prove valuable eventually in understanding the individual; the other assays the individual in the belief that this orientation will inevitably prove valuable in elucidating general truths. In its adventure to comprehend the nature, functions, and phenomena of the human soul and mind, psychology has explored, exploited, and extolled both approaches. Indeed, psychology has not only survived this internal schism, it has thrived if not profited from these distinct contributions to its task. As a consequence, the vast and varied subject matters psychology touches require more flexible and disparate approaches than any single view admits. After all, who can say whether our psychological understanding of the soul or mind is better informed by reading William James or Henry James?

Psychology is therefore in principle pluralistic and by nature interdisciplinary. The volumes that comprise *Psychology and Its Allied Disciplines* concern themselves with these central aspects of psychology, and the goals of this introduction are to raise and to review some of the principal issues that emerge in considering how psychology articulates with different domains of knowledge. Particular themes echo across essays in the three volumes that construct this collection. This introduction is structured to provide a setting for these themes as well as to open them to examination. First, the integrated interdisciplinary character of early psychology is overviewed through a brief consideration of the contributions of three prominent founders of psychology, and that integration is then contrasted with the intellectual fragmentation that characterizes contemporary relations between psychology and other knowledge domains. Next, the nature of psychology's relations with other disciplines is examined through an extended metaphor of family relations. In particular, symmetries and asymmetries of influence between psychology and other fields are evaluated. These considerations lead, finally, to a brief summary of the content of essays in these volumes.

Although the schism of lab and life in contemporary psychology seems today to loom large, it did not always. A quick glance back is convincing that a more integrated view not long ago prevailed in psychology and in knowledge.

MODERN PSYCHOLOGY'S BEGINNINGS: A CONFLUENCE OF INTERESTS

When modern psychology was founded, toward the close of the nineteenth century, it identified with several different domains of knowledge. *Psychology was demonstrably one of the humanities.* Psychology was originally concerned with pivotal philosophical questions—Helmholtz had construed early psychology as an empirical force in epistemological study—and modern psychology was not only fostered initially by philosophers, it even grew out of traditional academic departments of philosophy. Today, in addition to its continuing link with philosophy, psychologies of art, linguistics, literature, and music each has strong adherents. *Psychology was manifestly a social science.* For many influential early psychologists, like Freud, major phenomena that defined the psyche could be properly analyzed or comprehended only from the point of view of social experience. From its beginnings through the present day, quite naturally culture, history, and sociology have persistently influenced psychological science. *Psychology was patently a natural science.* Many of the original psychological investigators, like Wundt, concerned themselves substantively with the physiological analysis of sensory processes, drawing directly on traditions of biology, physics, and mathematics. Spiritually, early psychology modelled itself after these laboratory sciences and has since maintained its embrace with the experimental rigor and the nomothetic goals of the natural sciences. Merely to reraise these points here serves both to convey the reader back to a time when they constituted meaningful and serious issues about the fundamental nature of psychology and to remind the reader of the contemporary legitimacy of psychology's pluralistic temper.

Of course, at the moment of psychology's birth, the Weltanschauungen of philosophy and of science were more coordinated and considerably different from today. For the most part, an idealism reigned in the philosophy of knowledge, and, far from contemporary specialization, contradiction, or conflict among different domains of knowledge, each was conceived to contribute harmoniously, coherently, and complementarily to a whole of knowledge. Three case studies of the lives of individuals who began formatively to practice psychology at the turn of the century help further to support this historical lesson.

When Wilhelm Wundt (1832–1920) established the first laboratory of experimental psychology in Leipzig, Germany, in 1879, he modelled it and his new science in the tradition of the natural sciences. Wundt had studied chemistry in Bunsen's laboratory and physiology in Müller's and Helmholtz's laboratories. Simultaneously, however, Wundt was lecturing on the "Natural History of Man" and writing his 10-volume masterwork, *Völkerpsychologie* (1900–1920), a seminal contribution to cultural anthropology. In the laboratory, Wundt studied the construction of perceptions from sensations; however, in his cultural researches Wundt argued that social phenomena, like language and customs, were not reducible to more elementary psychological processes but originated and were maintained at a social plane.

At about the same time but half a world away, at Harvard University in Cambridge, Massachusetts, William James (1842–1910) was preparing his benchmark *Principles of Psychology* (1890). James first taught physiology and anatomy at Harvard and only later philosophy and psychology. Epistemologies of both invade his *Principles:* Chapter 7 of Volume I, "The Methods and Snares of Psychology," presents an insightful and rigorous demonstration of psychology's stature and value as a natural experimental science divorced from the poverty of fallacy, introspection, and error; Chapter 10, "The Consciousness of Self," however, analyzes and defines the psychological realm of the self nonexperimentally and in essentially social terms. James, the son of a Swedenborgian theologian, exemplified psychology's pluralism in his life: He trained as a physician, explored the Amazon in the company of the zoologist-geologist Louis Agassiz, and studied painting with the Barbizon portrait and landscape artist William Morris Hunt, before advancing his own influential Pragmatic philosophy. Such catholicity of psychological interests and confluences in these founders of psychology compels us to keep in the forefront of our minds that Wundt's and James's acceptable and comfortable heterodoxy was as much a product of their times as our orthodoxy is of ours.

Our third historical persona was a contemporary of the first two, Sigmund Freud (1856–1939). It may be appropriate to linger longer on Freud since, as cursory or perusing readers of *Psychology and Its Allied Disciplines* will recognize, Freud's presence hovers over all different facets of psychology. Even sophisticated devotees of Feudiana may be surprised to find Freud so often, so formally, and even so warmly acknowledged by authors whose specialities range across humanities, social sciences, and natural sciences. It may also be profitable to dwell on Freud since he so clearly personifies past protean psychology.

Formative professional influences clearly provided Freud with impetus to see and to apply his ideas over the broadest possible sweep. Freud's most influential medical science teachers included Theodor Billroth, Ernst Brücke, Theodor Meynert, and Herman Nothnagel. Each of these men was preeminently accomplished in his specialty science as well as in the humanities, thereby setting clear goals for young Freud. Billroth, from whom Freud learned surgical technique, was a musician and fast friends with Johannes Brahms who premiered scores in Billroth's home. Brücke, who was a founder of modern physiology and in whose Physiology Institute Freud initially conducted research, came from a family of painters, himself painted, and authored three academic treatises on art. Meynert, Freud's great nineteenth-century Viennese neuroanatomy professor, was the son of a drama critic and a singer; Nothnagel, under whom Freud studied internal medicine, was an amateur classicist. Prior to beginning his medical studies with these greats, three other teachers, Franz Brentano, the philosopher, Carl Claus, the zoologist, and Lorenz von Stein, the economist, all intimately touched Freud's life: At Brentano's invitation, the 23-year-old Freud made the first German translation of J. S. Mills's *Essays*; at Claus's zoological experimental station in Trieste, Freud conducted original anatomical and physiological research; and Freud married Martha Bernays whose father was von Stein's principal assistant. Later, Freud's postgraduate studies were complemented by the continuing close influence of figures like Sigmund Exner, from whom he learned sensory physiology, Ernst von Fleischl-Marxow, from whom he learned higher mathematics, and Jean-Martin Charcot, from whom he learned to marry literature and medicine.

Freud's own professional accomplishments span a dazzling diversity of fields, exemplifying his intellectual range and versatility and attesting to the influences of his educators, his peers, and his disciples. Freud made original contributions in nearly every natural science, from anatomy to zoology: His chemistry and histology led him to develop a valuable brain dye, his physiology confirmed the location of the gonads of the eel and delimited functioning of nervous tissue in crayfish, and his pharmacology eventuated in objective evaluation of the effects of materia medica (especially cocaine) on motor power and reaction time. Freud employed physical metaphors brilliantly to describe psychic forces. Most significantly, of course, Freud broke the tradition of materialism prevailing in Helmholtz's school of medicine, suggesting boldly how the mind might cause its own malfunction. In the social sciences, Freud contributed in *Totem and Taboo* a theory of the origins of law and social culture; he advised on Róheim's anthropological expedition to test psychoanalytic theories in exotic parts of the world; he employed sociological and economic argumentation knowledgeably and persuasively, as for example demonstrating why hysteria manifested itself more often among women than among men; he wrote about ascertaining truth in courts of law; he collaborated with Albert Einstein in an epistolary exchange, *Why War?,* which was published simultaneously in German, French, and English by the League of Nations; he coauthored with W. C. Bullitt, President Roosevelt's Ambassador to Paris, a psychological study of President Wilson; and in 1925 he even found himself the object of William Randolph Hearst's extravagant entreaties to travel to the U.S. to psychoanalyze Leopold and Loeb. Freud's interests and activities in the humanities are no less awe inspiring even in equivalent précis. He was an avid art collector and wrote a psychobiography of Leonardo as well as an essay on Michelangelo's "Moses." Freud translated J. S. Mill and J.-M. Charcot into German and was reputedly at home in Greek, Latin, Hebrew, French, Italian, Spanish, and English, above his native German. He used his deep knowledge of archaeological excavation to construct the basic metaphor for analytic examination of the psyche, authored papers and books on humor, and integrated the classics into his own work, recognizing Sophocles and Shakespeare as original explorers of the unconscious, even as he himself was criticizing novels and assessing associations between creative writing and day-dreaming. Freud's link to religion was more ambiguous, though not less passionate: He relegated religion to the status of an illusion whose raison d'être was wish fulfillment, yet he also developed a general theory of monotheism in his *Moses* book (originally subtitled, "A Historical Novel"). Freud's psychoanalysis had so great an impact on the humanities, even during his own lifetime, that Thomas Mann delivered an eightieth birthday appreciation of Freud that was endorsed by H. G. Wells, Virginia Woolf, and nearly 200 other prominent artists and critics of the time. Sigmund Freud was nominated for the Nobel Prize in Literature as well as Physiology and Medicine; his prose style won him the Goethe Prize in Literature.

Though Freud was originally trained in the natural sciences—so in evidence in his laborious and precise microscopic studies of the medulla oblongata—he saw clearly the virtues of the humanities and social sciences. Indeed, this clinician transformed medical science into a healing art (albeit, in the view of some, an art that constructs and invents). For Freud, science provided no more convincing evidence for the origins of sexual desire than could be found in Plato's "Symposium." Art and literature provided Freud insights into human character, as anthropological prehistory provided an understanding of human nature, laws, and culture. *Imago,* a nonmedical interdisciplinary journal, was founded remarkably early in the development of psychoanalysis as an outlet for anthropological, political, and economic as well as artistic and literary explorations in Freud's technique. In these ways, Freud's psychology was as close to the scholarship of archaeology as it was to the materialism of physics. In "A Difficulty in the Path of Psychoanalysis," Freud himself characterized his brainchild as a discipline somewhere between medicine and philosophy. It was well recognized as such even at the beginning: William James, the philosopher and psychologist, Franz Boas, the anthropologist, and James Putnam, the neurologist, all trekked from Harvard in Cambridge to Clark in Worcester in 1909 to attend Freud's extempore *Five Lectures on Psycho-Analysis.*

Even in this brief catalogue, we find roots in Sigmund Freud of a multiplicity of original and creative accomplishments in psychology to which the several contributors to *Psychology and Its Allied Disciplines* pay ecomium. Essays in *Psychology and the Humanities* separately echo the early development and appreciation of psychoanalysis as one of few comprehensive theories of human behavior to address art, literature, philosophy, and religion. Essays in *Psychology and the Social Sciences* acknowledge a central contribution of Freudian psychodynamics to understanding cultural, economic, historical, and political socialization. Essays in *Psychology and the Natural Sciences* expressly recognize Freud's critical role in identifying psychological and ideational origins of disease states and laud the biological, chemical, and physical models Freud so artfully applied to elucidating dynamics of the human soul and mind. Thus, Freud's prodigious and variegated accomplishments built opportunely upon firm foundations of humanities, social sciences, and natural sciences and contributed centrally toward the burgeoning twentieth-century science of psychology.

In summary, in Wundt, in James, and in Freud, we find the founders of modern psychology completely at home with their discipline's epistemic pluralism. There appears to have been little internal contradiction or conflict in these rigorous yet highly diversified intellectual minds. Since their time, specialization and fragmentation in psychology have transpired and unfortunately conspire in our modern heritage. Yet, the scientific and humanistic traditions so vibrant in psychology at the opening of the twentieth century are still vital as this century draws to a close. No one tradition has dominated since psychology's founding, and it would appear that structurally none could . . . nor will. Psychology resonates humanism and science, is by nature multivocal, and articulates equally and effectively with humanities, social sciences, and natural sciences. The purposes of *Psychology and Its Allied Disciplines* are to scrutinize, deliberate, and evaluate similarities and differences in philosophy, epistemology, methodology, and progress between psychology and a diversity of other naturally allied fields from these different knowledge domains.

THE UNIQUE POSITION OF PSYCHOLOGY IN THE CONTEMPORARY FRAGMENTATION OF KNOWLEDGE

At the beginning of this century, knowledge was far from an Aristotelian vision of unity; nevertheless, it possessed a certain cohesion and coherence. The intellectual lives of three of psychology's principal progenitors impress us how, not long ago, one individual could contribute positively to thought and to research in vast and varied subject areas of our discipline. Specialization and expertise compelling the fragmentation of knowledge have since rendered such accomplishments less conceivable.

It is outside the scope of these introductory observations to compare or to contrast the separate requisites, philosophies, and goals of humanities, social sciences, and natural sciences. It is pertinent, however, to evaluate how select aspects of each interrelate with psychology and hence to clarify psychology's exceptional position at the intersection of different fields of knowledge. Though sometimes troubled by this confluence of different interests in its makeup, psychology seems openly to accept and to accommodate diverse traditions and even to derive certain strength from its inherent pluralism, if not from the reconciliation of divergencies that arise within it.

Consider, for example, the nature of explanation in the humanities and in the sciences. The two cultures disagree so on the criteria that constitute explanation that, in Snow's view, they inhabit diametric poles. Scientists are empirical, skeptical, material, and analytic; humanists are intuitive, subjective, private, and instinctive. Evidence the one accepts the other rejects, thereby fostering mutual disregard. Psychology has settled a terrain intermediate between the two, accepting and building on customs and traditions of both. For example, some philosophers recognize an ordering among humanities and sciences from proximate to ultimate cause. In this hierarchic reductionism, aggregate phenomena are dissected into more elementary phenomena to permit more direct examination. However, while it is true that larger units may be constructed of smaller units—sociological of psychological and psychological of biological—and understanding smaller units may contribute to understanding larger ones, it is also true that smaller units accrete meaning in the context of larger units. Therefore, critics of reductionism emphasize that smaller units must be studied in the context of larger ones. Perhaps in ways that reflect its history, psychology coopts attributes of both humanities and sciences to explain soul and mind. At the same time that some psychologists are laboratory reductionists, controlling variables to reject hypotheses and analyze origins, parameters, and dimensions of different phenomena in the best tradition of the natural sciences, other psychologists distant from the laboratory are content to glimpse their phenomena privately and apply humanistic principles to satisfy descriptive needs. Not infrequently as well, these psychologists are studying the same phenomena (thus another source of internal contemporary conflict in psychology is that the psychologists involved are often different).

Insofar as scientists and humanists go about defining, collecting, and evaluating evidence in vastly different ways, psychology draws eclectically on diverse traditions in its own interpretation of necessary and sufficient explanation. It therefore occupies a pivotal juncture between major levels of epistemological analysis, trading with some disciplines "above" it and some "below" it in terms of an implicit ladder of reductionist explication. In proffering inquiry or explanation of some humanist issue or institution, psychology's relevance has been avowed and esteemed (though, to be sure, it has also been demeaned and denigrated). Vis-à-vis natural sciences, psychological explanation (though sometimes accused of insufficient penetration) is often praised for the insight and relevance that it bears to mind and soul. Significantly for psychology, those in the chain who admit analysis from the top downward—as, for example, in "explaining" art or literature—stop with psychology and do not usually truck penetration beyond it; likewise, those who entertain explanation from the bottom upward only very infrequently or with great trepidation venture beyond psychology—witness the cutural tension engendered by sociobiology.

Consider another point of comparison between humanities and sciences, viz. their respective units of analysis. In the humanities, the individual (or an individual creation) seems most naturally to constitute the meaningful unit of analysis. Among the social sciences at large, the unit changes to a higher aggregate level, that is to individuals in groups. In the natural sciences, lower-level cells and organs predominate as the principal units of analysis. Again accommodating internal conflict, psychology interests itself in and attempts to reconcile all three levels of analysis. Psychology fosters the careers of clinician as well as neuropsychopharmacologist. This robustness accrues power to psychology's mission, rather than diluting it.

Consider, further, the different levels at which individuals are believed to be motivated to think, feel, or act. From the point of view of many social sciences, individual conduct is conceived primarily to derive from social or cultural forces. From the point of view of the natural sciences, by contrast, individual behavior of the viewed to be compelled by biological, and ultimately by chemical and physical determinants. Consequently, the origins and motives of individual soul and mind are often perceived by social and natural sciences from mutually exclusive perspectives. Intelligence, aggression, and gender are genetic and biological or cultural and environmental. Psychologists embrace all these divergent viewpoints but, again, not without some internal conflict.

Beyond these several considerations, the paths which professionals in diverse fields of knowledge travel to reach an understanding of human soul or mind differ, though psychologists assimilate these differences as well. Humanists and some social scientists tend to follow the narrow and winding idiographic way, seeking to describe individual phenomena through unique occurrences and historical analyses; other social scientists and natural scientists drive the broad and straight nomothetic avenue, seeking to describe more general phenomena through empiricism and statistical generalization. Psychologists are eclectic in this regard; they pursue (though not without difficulty) this divergency of means among their allies.

In modern times psychology has turned increasingly to empiricism and tipped its internal balance toward the scientific side of its Janusian character. Experimentation constitutes the method of choice today, and in some subdisciplines of psychology, especially those closer to the natural sciences, empiricism has manifestly progressed scientific psychology. When the balance thus alters, however, it exposes psychology to unexpected dangers that only the true dual nature of the discipline can check. A major premise of analytical, scientific psychology is that simple processes aggregate into complex phenomena, and a second premise is that understanding simple processes will ineluctably lead to understanding the more complex phenomena that interested psychologists in the first place. Of course, neither promise is certain. Is individual psychology an aggregation of materialistic elements, or is individual psychology epiphenomenal social interaction? At which level are psychological phenomena most fruitfully analyzed? In the minds of some, the strategy to control variables in order to isolate basic processes artificially simplifies psychology to a focus on facets of phenomena that stray far from their natural color, drama, complexity, and intensity. Though not transcendent today, humanistic psychology still thrives, for its parent discipline encompasses both orientations.

Thus, history informs. As the troika of personalities invoked earlier reminds us, modern psychology was fathered at the beginning of this century—by Wundt ca. 1879, by James ca. 1890, and by Freud ca. 1900—as a ·pluralistic discipline. In the first century of its growth, psychology has influenced and been influenced by a host of different disciplines from the humanities, from the social sciences, and from the natural sciences. Today psychology has matured into a major field of knowledge that is still highly pluralistic. The 1982 directory of the American Psychological Association lists fully 47 "major fields" in psychology. Aside from its rapid and extensive personal and internal development, psychology has also maintained its unique position among traditional knowledge domains: Psychology draws on, shares with, and contributes to humanities, social sciences, and natural sciences. *How*?

INTERACTIONS AMONG INTELLECTUAL DISCIPLINES: "FAMILY INTERRELATIONS"

Despite currents that favor specialization and fragmentation in the pursuits of knowledge, intellectual disciplines are not solitary entities. Nor do they merely coexist, like academic departments, one simply adjoining another. Intercourse among intellectual disciplines is natural, though degrees of relatedness, intimacy, and alliance may vary among them widely. Curiously, the nature of interdisciplinary relationships is almost never systematically examined, and the consequences of interdisciplinary activity for either partner discipline or for knowledge generally are only infrequently evaluated. *Psychology and Its Allied Disciplines* is about psychology but, especially, about psychology's relations with the variety of intellectual disciplines affiliated to it. One purpose of these books is self-examination of interdisciplinary activity and its consequences for psychology.

When disciplines ally they create a kind of family atmosphere. Perhaps it will be helpful to pursue the extended metaphor of family dynamics (as every reader will be familiar with) in order to explore some salient characteristics of relations among disciplines. The descriptions and examples employed in the brief discussion that follows mainly derive from the essays in *Psychology and Its Allied Disciplines.* Though they may to some extent reflect the individual perspectives of their authors, they express the variety of relationships logically endemic to interdisciplinary marriages generally.

Consider the "parents" of an interdiscipline. Individuals may be more or less mature, secure, etc. in their own lives in advance of marriage, a status sure to affect the nature of their commitment. They may have the same or different motives for marrying, they may have the same or different reasons to maintain their marriage, and they may espouse the same or different goals for their marriage. Has each entered into the alliance willingly? Does each contribute equally, or is one dominant? Has their courtship or engagement been longstanding? Is their relationship open and explicit, or has their relationship been tacit and implicit, curiously or necessarily clandestine? Is the relationship a serious alliance or mere dalliance? Are the disciplines permanently united, or are they merely cohabiting? Is there passion to their embrace? (Does it matter?)

Some interdisciplinary relationships are based on a variety of shared interests; between psychology and religion, for example, the meaning of phenomenal experiences, the nature of death, the assessment of attitudes and beliefs, and catharsis wed interests of the two. Some relationships share many fewer mutual interests; cognition and personality, for example, form the primary bonds between psychology and anthropology. For a few couples, one point of interest serves as the magnet of attraction, as stress seems to currently between psychology and medicine, auditory perception between psychology and music, and choice between psychology and economics. If one member of the disciplinary dyad has more than a single significant facet in its own personality, one, both, or all may attract a partner: Some spouses share their personal and professional lives, others share only their personal lives or only parts of their personal lives. Economics is partitioned into macroeconomics and microeconomics, but micro relates to psychology more intimately than does macro. Of course, some more common or general interest, like children, might transcend in many interdisciplinary relationships; creativity is one likely candidate of this category between psychology and a myriad of other disciplines.

Consider, next, the "marriage" itself. The intensity, intimacy, and immediacy of all relationships wax and wane. So psychology's relations with some affiliated disciplines have known better times; some are today reaching maturity; while still others hold only the promise of future bliss. Three examples: Though once intimate, psychology and religion are estranged today and entertain only very dim prospects for any future reconciliation; psychology and pharmacology have displayed increasing affection since their initial mutual appeal; and psychology and economics, which once flirted briefly but have more recently had altogether too little to do with one another formally, seem now destined for a future of better times. As in many personal associations as well, a match between disciplines may not be perfect, though it maintains. Psychology and sociology, for example, are closely tied to one another though the two vie constantly (and often argue bitterly) over innumerable consequential issues: Psychology says that science ought to be value free, while sociology maintains that science can never be value free; psychology promotes individual determinism, while for sociology individual motives are essentially epiphenomena of larger cultural forces; etc.

A complete discussion of determinants of the rise and fall of inter-disciplinary associations lies beyond the scope of this introduction. However, it is possible to suggest some salient characteristics that excite or inhibit psychology's alliances to other disciplines. We are constantly reminded that intellectual advances are achieved as often along cross roads as along main roads, that real gains in understanding are bound up inherently with taking risks over new territory, and that the arbitrary, stubborn defense of disciplinary boundaries from neighbors, though sociopolitically wise, is costly to the general growth of knowledge. Disciplines remain ignorant, fearful, or bashful of one another when they should converse and fraternize. Philosophers and linguists commonly psychologize, historians and political scientists often posit psychological views of man, and geneticists and biologists constantly propose psychological theories to explain behavior: Those who are ignorant of psychology proper perforce practice naive psychology. If a philosophy or a political science or a biology remains too distant from psychology, it loses practical impact.

From an historical vantage, we have also learned that disciplinary differences are artificial at least and false at worst. Maintaining disciplinary autonomy in the face of increasing specialization is self-defeating. For these reasons, some scholarly suitors intentionally cross intellectual boundaries, some stray, while others are unwillingly seduced. The quality of the consequences varies accordingly. For some, interdisciplinary association is ever superficial dialogue; for others it comes to mean deep and sincere communication. The attraction of allied systems of thought, the recognition that natural connections exist among different systems, and the belief that interdisciplinary knowledge may be especially rewarding promote interdisciplinary initiatives in the minds of most intellectuals and militate against disciplinary xenophobia. Jealousy, too, in its own way curiously sustains interdisciplinary associations: As psychology increasingly emulates the doctrines and methods of natural sciences like physics and chemistry, it seems more than ever attracted to them, just as new strides in understanding cognitive processes promise new vigor in overtures of psychology to art, music, and economics.

Consider, too, the "birth" of a new interdiscipline. Who or what motivates the union? When did the mating occur? At whose insistence? The reasons to procreate an interdiscipline are manifold; sometimes they involve personalities, sometimes larger issues. A "Great Man" theory can hold when the personality involved is clearly perceived to possess firm expertise in both subject areas. Lasswell seems essentially to have created political psychology, for example. More frequently, however, the rationale for initially crossing disciplinary boundaries is less personal, as applies for instance in theory testing. One strong impetus to the birth of psychological anthropology was the desire to ascertain whether Freud's theory of psychosocial development could apply in understanding dynamics of different cultures; in anthropological psychology Piaget inaugurated the *International Journal of Psychology* with a plea to test the generality of his cognitive developmental theory cross-culturally.

Consider, finally, the "development" of an interdiscipline. We know that a new interdiscipline, like a new child, may grow up in the shadow of one or both of its parents; neither psychological anthropology nor cross-cultural psychology has reached the stature of anthropology or of psychology. Children can also be very different from parents; oxygen and hydrogen alone are inactive gases while their combination is a life-sustaining liquid. Likewise, parent disciplines together can create new entities with new characters and new qualities, as is the case in psychopharmacology. Interdisciplinary offspring can be reared as genuinely new and generative brainchildren of their devoted parents, as has occurred in psycholinguistics, cross-cultural psychology, and psychobiology. Alternatively, they may represent the sterile grafting of two very separate intellectual endeavors cohabiting. In this case, new offspring may not always be welcome. Does biology or politics want biopolitics?

What path(s) does a new interdiscipline follow to develop an identity of its own? Which parent ought to take responsibility for rearing an interdisciplinary offspring and for fostering its development? In some instances, socialization must clearly be shared between parent disciplines: A cognitive anthropologist must today be trained in both psychology and anthropology. In other cases, such as the neurosciences, it would appear (for good or ill) that one parent dominates the socialization process. More mundanely, in explicit or implicit hyphenations which comes first and why? Is psychohistory more satisfactory than historiopsychology for reasons other than ease of pronunciation? By contrast, biopsychology seems to be interchangeable with psychobiology.

As in human families, the nature of the parents' styles of socialization conditions the child's independence and contributes to the strength of its character. For some psycholinguistic problems, psychological experimentation does a fine job of analysis and explication, but for others linguistic argument may be more telling than empirical findings. Perhaps the attitudes or perceptions of one or the other parent discipline determine the stature of interdisciplinary offspring. For example, in the reductionist view, the more material the science the more basic: Psychophysics emphasizes understanding perceptual processes first in terms of biological, then chemical, and eventually physical processes (ultimately in mathematical terms).

Once grown, new interdisciplines can be attributed independent character. Are successful new disciplines maintained by personalities or by issues? In some psychological alliances, individuals or schools of thought associated with them have mattered a great deal, as in educational psychology where Dewey, Thorndike, Hull, Piaget, and Skinner have each succeeded. In other psychological interdisciplines, issues dominate as, for example, is true of the nature of belief systems in psychology and religion or anthropology.

In constitution, interdisciplinary offspring may be singular, or they may be multiple, "fraternal twins" so to speak, equal but clearly different. Two kinds of interdisciplinary twin relationships are noteworthy. In one, the children are independent but each resembles one parent quite distinctly. Sociological social psychology (being more sociological) sees social psychology as concerned with the social conditions that define human nature, whereas psychological social psychology (being more psychological) conceives social psychology as concerned with the ways social phenomena function as stimulus variables. In the second kind of twin relationship, emphasis alone seems to matter: Cross-cultural psychology has pressed historically for experimental manipulation (almost) without regard for culture, while psychological anthropology has emphasized exploration of similar subject matter with only the highest regard for culture.

Just as parents affect children, children affect parents and can potentially alter the nature of their parents. The study of psychology and medicine has demonstrated that people fall ill and die today as often for behavioral reasons (diet, exercise, care and treatment of the environment) as for purely physiological reasons; this fact must transform medicine in the future. Similarly, education has served as a kind of test ground for psychological theories of learning, and the relative successes within education of Piagetian versus information-processing views, for example, have altered psychology.

Someone once said that cross-disciplinary study in many ways resembles the weather: People tend more to talk about it than to do anything about it, and when they do something their efforts are often as ephemeral as the seasons. *Why?*

There are too many obvious reasons why interdisciplinary intercourse is taboo. Different disciplines harbor intrinsically different motivations, interests, philosophies, and methodologies, not to mention their vastly different professional rites of passage. For most investigators, mastery of one field is sufficiently effortful that it suffices to make (or take) a career. For

many, successfully evolving a paradigm or excelling in one subfield promotes a kind of intellectual conservatism. Some initially hearty investigators who venture across disciplinary boundaries soon confront
dangers inherent in the foreign discipline's idiosyncrasies, complexities, and
esoterica—or sooner still are undone by the new discipline's hostility to out-
siders—that their conservatism is reinforced. Sophistication and learning in
the crossdisciplinary investigator must extend to the new subject domain at
least as well as it does to the investigator's home territory. As every tactician
knows, crossroads positions are easy to take, invaluable to hold, but difficult to defend. Further, disciplinary parochialism is often so entrenched as
to reinforce boundaries. Where practitioners in the environmental
disciplines, like architects, see the need for concrete solutions to problems
of the effective use of space, for example, social psychologists in the same
problem area adopt other agenda and are on the look out for mechanisms
underlying territoriality in individuals or groups. Thus, psychologists define
research problems, conceive of research designs relevant to those problems,
and conduct that research quite differently from the ways their non-
psychologist professional associates do.

Sometimes, just submitting a "real world" question to psychological
analysis is sufficient to engender disdain from nonpsychologists; for them,
the laboratory study of many phenomena is synonymous with displacing
those phenomena from reality. A psychological approach to art through
analytic-constructivist "aesthetics from below", for example, is for some
humanists antithetical or irrelevant to aesthetic understanding. Many professionals in literature and religion similarly interpret psychologizing pe-
joratively—that is, as an inappropriate if not obscene kind of reductionism.

Similar differences of theory or of praxis impede collaborations between
psychologists and professionals in many related disciplines. Perhaps
economics and psychology have not been drawn to one another in the past
because economics concerns itself with error-free prediction whereas
psychology is often interested in error variance. Historically, psychology
has been theory-driven and oriented to normal behavior and states of well-
being, whereas medicine has been problem oriented and focused on biology
and pathological states. It is hardly surprising, therefore, that there is intellectual tension between psychology and medicine, nor is it surprising that
that tension has been so detrimental to the development of medical
psychology. It is now clearly recognized that chronic disease states are influenced by biological as well as by behavioral and social factors. However,
medical and behavioral models are at variance in theorizing about the
causes of disease, and hence the two often prescribe complementary
therapeutic solutions; the two are still not easily reconciled either. In these
situations, as elsewhere, problems must be worked out for the welfare of
each family member.

Finally, different disciplines, like family members, interact and influence the course of one another's development. This aspect of the family relationship between psychology and other fields merits separate treatment.

SYMMETRIES AND ASYMMETRIES OF INFLUENCE BETWEEN PSYCHOLOGY AND OTHER DISCIPLINES

Several themes emerge from an overview of psychology's relations with disciplines allied to it. One is the extraordinary diversity of fields with which psychology seems naturally associated. A second theme is the varied ways in which psychology may relate to other fields. Between psychology and other fields at some times there pervades (more or less) symmetrical influence; at other times, either psychology is conceived to exert control or, alternatively, to be influenced in asymmetrically determinative ways. Examining these three states of interdependence informs as to psychology's authority and limitations amongst its disciplinary neighbors.

Symmetries of Influence

Between symmetry and asymmetry in psychology's relations with other disciplines, symmetries seem to be less frequent and more difficult to discern. Symmetries of association that are apparent usually assume one of a limited number of forms: They may include simultaneous mutual contributions of disciplines to particular research questions or to theory, serial mutual influence between disciplines over time, or complementary contributions of two disciplines to one intellectual subdiscipline. One example of the first is between psychology and engineering, where early valuable information about the course of human learning arose from the collaboration of two investigators with very different specialities, one a psychologist (Bryan) and the other a railway telegrapher (Harter); a second example is the cofounding of culture and personality by an anthropologist (Linton) and a psychologist (Kardiner). Between psychology and music is an example of serial influence: Theses of Berlioz, the composer, about the significance of the physical locations of instruments to the musical effect of a composition led to empirical studies of Deutsch, a psychoacoustician, on the influence of space on musical attributes in perception that in turn led to analyses of Butler, a music theoretician, on matching effects of free-sound fields in musical production of Tchaikovsky. Psychology and anthropology coexist in the third kind of symmetry: The two disciplines centrally share two main interests, cognition and personality, and within each interest the two disciplines provide complementary knowledge—for example, in cognition, psychology focuses on mental processes and anthropology on mental content. Psychology and pharmacology are inextricably entwined in yet a different symmetry: Behavior is always definable in terms of state, and individuals always exist in one or another psychopharmacological state.

Of course, there is a variety of less practical and more theoretical ways by which psychology and other knowledge domains, particularly those with applied goals, symmetrically influence one another. As psychology is empirical it builds on data collection toward theory and eventually toward explanation by plying between laboratory and field as well as between application and evaluation. From this viewpoint educational practice, environmental design, and medical treatment all proceed in step with psychology.

Asymmetries of Influence

More frequently, psychology dominates or is dominated in its associations with other disciplines; some influences are relatively strong, others are weak. When the influence of one discipline in another is too liberal and change is frequent or pervasive, loss of identity threatens. Conversely, if conservatism and resistance to change reign, real growth and development are threatened.

Psychology influencing.   The advent and conduct of psychology have had continuing, emphatic, and penetrating effects on some related disciplines. Religion is one: Psychologists—Freud, Hall, James, Skinner—have submitted religious attitudes and beliefs to (sometimes excoriating) psychological examination; pastoral counseling has coopted men of the cloth to new psychologically-oriented work; and, most significantly, the very existence, growth, and success of psychology (read: relativistic social knowledge) have challenged the foundations of religion and religious claims. Psychology's historical associations with education and anthropology have in many ways been equally controlling though not so intentionally detrimental. When the psychology of learning was Hullian, so was education; as psychology moved on to Piaget, education advanced concomitantly; and as psychology today embraces cognition and information processing along follows education. Likewise, anthropology first adopted dynamic interpretations from psychology, later it took up behaviorism, and today culture is construed in many quarters as a kind of cognitive organization. More extremely, human endeavors as diverse as art and linguistics have been characterized by some as subfields of psychology. Recently medical concerns have shifted sharply away from a monistic determinism of the influence of physiologic diseases on morbidity and mortality to a wider view that suffers an influence of behavior. Psychology is also realizing an impact on the conduct of law and political science: Increasingly, considera-

tions about juries and their decision making are being drawn into the purview of psychology, and more and more psychology is providing data and
clarifying insights about voters and about the self-esteem, achievement
motivation, and affiliative tendencies of elected officials. These are examples of domain relationships in which psychology previously or currently
exercises influence. In a few other interesting cases, psychology has come to
rival or supersede another discipline for authority in a third: Where
mathematics and physics long guided the path to music, perception now
shows the way, and where impersonal mathematical modelling was once the
main tool in economics, cognitive decision making is now beginning to rectify and to infuse that "dismal" science with a human élan.

   But psychology's status vis-à-vis other disciplines is not always flattering
or leading. To be accused of "psychologizing" is insulting to critics in
literature and art, to historians and political scientists, and to biologists and
geneticists. Freud's thoroughgoing social and intellectual impact has caused
practitioners in many disciplines to be especially wary of psychology, if not
outright psychophobic or reactionary toward perceived psychological imperialism. Indeed, the pervasiveness of psychodynamics has cost psychology a legitimate level of explanation in two key ways. First,
psychodynamic analysis, as is well known, is facilely applied, once its lingo
is mastered; however, it is often heard as superficially glib, and many professionals are manifestly offput by its transparency. "Sometimes a cigar *is*
just a cigar." Second, Freudian analyses have eclipsed the value of other
psychological approaches to neighboring knowledge domains. Freud and
Jones both psychoanalyzed "Hamlet" (with interesting success), but this
does not mean that every dramatic persona can or ought to be analyzed, nor
does it excuse students of literature from ignorance or distortion of
psychological experiments on literary creativity, reader perceptions, etc.
These facts and the lack of balanced input from literature have eventuated
in a lopsided, weak, and internally inconsistent interdiscipline, the
psychology of literature.

   Psychology influenced.   Reciprocally, psychology has been the direct
object of influence and has been changed, in some ways fundamentally, by
its alliances with other disciplines. Insofar as cultures and ecologies provide
a laboratory for testing psychological theories and for assessing the universality of psychological effects, anthropology has influenced psychology.
Moreover, the entire notion of cultural conditioning has risen in status
among psychology's concerns sui generis on account of anthropological
sensitization. Likewise, education's availability for pragmatic tests of
psychological theories and sociology's emphasis on interpretation in context
have markedly influenced much of contemporary psychology. Perhaps
more conspicuous, however, are the asymmetric influences of engineering,

mathematics, and physics on psychology. Not only does psychology practically exist as an experimental science because of advances in engineering methods and technologies, but in every age psychological conceptions of man have been modelled on the machines man in that age manufactured. In psychology's association with mathematics, a similar strong truth holds: Mathematics has influenced psychological practice and accomplishment directly through the development of measurement systems and statistical reasoning and procedures; mathematics captures deep psychological truths about behavior; and mathematics is constantly held up as a theory language for psychological ratiocination. Physics, as much or more than any other discipline, has dominated in its association with psychology. The earliest psychological studies were conducted by physicists, and contemporary psychological philosophy—from metaphors and models of man to fundamental conceptions, including operationalism, the empirical ethic, and ultimately the quantitative scientific method—derives from physics. Physics comprises the standards of scientific spirit and procedures de rigueur psychology emulates.

A "Great Man" theory can also be applied to understand how one or another discipline has influenced psychology. Among early philosophers-turned-psychologists may be counted Dewey, Hall, and Titchener; among engineers, Hull, Boring, Thurstone, Tolman, and Hunter; among physicians, Young, Wundt, James, Gesell, and Freud; among physiologists, Pavlov. Psychology has received more influential disciplinary defectors than, perhaps, vice versa, and if these names are indicative, psychology has benefitted.

The discussion of asymmetries between psychology and other disciplines invites a comparison of more general patterns of mutual influence. These patterns tend intriguingly to mirror the reductionist viewpoint first proposed by the categorizer Aristotle and echoed across centuries of the philosophy of science by Comte, Spencer, and others. In the dynamics of knowledge of humanities, social sciences, and natural sciences, psychology—fortunately or unfortunately—tends often to exercise influence over humanities, tends to engage the social sciences in more mutual and egalitarian exchange, and tends often to be influenced by natural sciences. To wit: Psychology has contributed in diverse ways to intellectual examinations of art, literature, and religion more than is oppositely true. (This relationship even holds in philosophy; though the modern philosophy of psychology is much like traditional philosophy, contemporary psychological science actively informs philosophy.) But, psychology has been influenced practically and theoretically more by biology, mathematics, pharmacology, and physics than vice versa. Against the social sciences, psychology either maintains a democratic intellectual status, as with anthropology (where largely positive give and take have prevailed) or with sociology (where fundamental philosophical pitched battle rages), or maintains virtually no relation, as has been true until recently with economics. By this logic of functional association, developments within psychology are likely to affect humanities and social sciences with greater probability than they are natural sciences; reciprocally, developments in the natural sciences are likely to affect psychology deeply.

PSYCHOLOGY AND ITS ALLIED DISCIPLINES

Psychology stands at the nexus of humanities, social sciences, and natural sciences. It contains each, it exchanges with each, and it complements each. *Psychology and Its Allied Disciplines* examines relations and interactions between psychology and diverse other intellectual disciplines with which it is naturally affiliated.

Psychology and the Humanities

Volume I treats psychology and art, linguistics, literature, music, philosophy, and religion. Psychology's chief aims in the humanities have been to clarify our understanding of the object, the creator, and the experiencer of art, language, literature, music, philosophy, and religion. To these ends, the thoughts, feelings, and motives of actor and audience have been subjected to psychological scrutiny and analysis. To date, scientific psychology has been less frequently followed in approaching these goals than has humanistic psychology (particularly depth psychologies, whose abuse as well as use is great). Thus, the foci of most explorations between psychology and humanities have tended toward the emotional, the intuitive, the aesthetic, and the idiographic, and the data base for these explorations tends largely, though not exclusively, to draw on historical analyses, biographical accounts, and experiential self- or other-reports. From the beginnings of modern psychology, however, an empirical approach has sputtered along in art, literature, and music—a so-called psychological "aesthetics from below"—and in recent years empirical study has increasingly infiltrated between psychology and linguistics, philosophy, and religion. Though artistic experimentation holds out extraordinary potential, the general relationship between artistic and experimental sentiments is traditionally so antithetical and oxymoronish that creative individuals virtually never experiment (in the traditional sense) to produce perceptions or emotions—unless by their "successes" and "failures". They are usually reluctant to submit themselves or they only reluctantly condone submitting their work to psychological analysis. Interestingly, students of art, music, and literature, just like students of linguistics, philosophy, and religion, seem to express little compunction when borrowing psychological constructs or explanations, however vague and imprecise they may be. Creativity, which is important (and shared) in this group, is a good example; the relationship of cognition to emotion or affect is another. Today, empiricism is bringing a new set of psychological principles to humanistic interests, as the essays in Volume I attest.

Psychology and the Social Sciences

Volume II treats psychology's relations to anthropology, economics, education, environmental disciplines, history, political science, and sociology. Many of these disciplines are behavioral sciences which speak the same language and share many topics and concepts with psychology. Not all social sciences partake of the same modes of analysis or move toward the same goals as psychology does, however. Some social sciences question whether social or cultural processes exist that could not be psychological at base, whereas others argue oppositely (and vehemently) that social and cultural processes originate and function exclusive of the psychological relevance of the individual. It has also been argued, albeit narrowly, that social sciences (economics, education) have more practical value to human meaning than do humanities (art, literature), which are often cast as epiphenomena of human existence. Social sciences define external differences and external settings for the conduct of human behavior. Unlike the more reductionist dictatorial influence psychology seems to hold vis-à-vis the humanities, its lateral and more nearly democratic affiliations with the social sciences betray much greater variance and are (as is always true of democracies) often much more socially difficult. The complexity and tension of psychology's relations to other social sciences is captured readily in the articulation of two key questions: Does individual behavior actually aggregate to social and cultural behavior? Can aggregate-level social and cultural behavior help to explain individual conduct? Tensions between these two levels are not easily resolved.

Psychology and the Natural Sciences

Volume III treats psychology's relations to biology, engineering, genetics, mathematics, medicine, pharmacology, and physics. Vis-à-vis these disciplines, in contrast to the humanities, psychology largely receives rather than gives. In the natural sciences, logic, analysis, determinism, precision, and operationalism hold; they represent principles which modern psychology holds in so great esteem that the discipline has virtually modelled itself on them. Experimental physics, for example, is 350 years old, experimental psychology is 100, and emulation of the older by the younger science is pervasive, extending into theoretical, methodological, and practical domains. Thus, experimental interest in cause-effect relations represents a fundamental theoretical focus in physics, and it is to a like ambition that psychology aspires; much of psychology mimics analysis and persistence on the elementary, a reductionist hallmark of natural sciences; the development of axioms, laws, postulates, and empirical regularities, the very foundations of the experimental sciences, constitute models of methodology for scientific psychology; and, daily, psychology is practicably influenced by developments in the physical and life sciences. In particular, psychology has adopted the fundamental outlook preferred by the natural sciences, including the experimental attitude of physics, the materialism of biology, and the logic of mathematics.

CONCLUSIONS

Nature is complex, not easily parsed, and seems to know nothing of academic departments: Nature *naturally* expects and encourages interdisciplinary study. Psychology, though specifically a human science, is centrally situated among the major domains of knowledge. These facts together warrant high signficance of psychology. As intellectual disciplines have evolved toward specialization, increasingly fragmenting knowledge, they are also ever more jealous of their autonomy. Yet, the movement toward specialization, fragmentation, and autonomy is in many ways antithetical to the growth and development of knowledge in general. It is from this perspective that psychology's contribution is to be most appreciated. Psychology's centrality among domains of knowledge means that it articulates meaningfully with humanities, with social sciences, and with natural sciences. Though it functions on many levels—evolutional, cellular and organic, individual, social and cultural, historical—psychology is definitionally concerned with human soul and mind, which means that it may cross disciplinary boundaries diplomatically and with equanimity.

Many scholars have astutely observed that all knowledge—humanities, social sciences, and natural sciences—turns on psychology. Psychology endeavors to explain humans and human activities, and it is humans—answerable to psychology—who engage in humanities, social sciences, and natural sciences and endeavor, in turn, to explain them. Psychology thereby challenges the autonomy of diverse domains of knowledge. Knowledge, the access to knowledge, and the organization of knowledge are inherently human endeavors, and the natural, logical, and meaningful unit in psychology is the human being. This view of psychology and its charge lends great credence to Pope's dictum that "the proper study of manking is man."

Psychology's relations to other disciplines are clearly not simple, though in this introduction I have simplified them. Moreover, psychological connections to other fields are often constrained by how psychology is oriented. If scientific psychology is ascendant, then connections where experimentation is not feasible, tractable, or useful are not worthy; if psychology is only empirical, then the sweep of humanity and the complexity of life is lost to it. If psychology is only humanistic, it chances idiosyncrasies and false generalizations. A narrowly inward looking and preoccupied psychology of either kind will surely surrender its relevance to other fields and lose reciprocity with those fields. Examples and results are equally worthy, and rational commonsense is as valuable as analytic systematization. Psychology can ill afford to neglect philosophy, sociology, and history; in the same way it cannot deny biology, physics, and mathematics.

There is clear value in holding the center, as psychology does; but there is also jeopardy. Insofar as diverse humanities, social sciences, and natural sciences contribute to defining psychology, and so far as psychology derives meaning from its allied disciplines, psychologists must keep at the forefront of their own endeavors as well as remain vigilant to evolution in other fields. Other disciplines' conflicts are psychology's, just as is their harmony; other disciplines' intellectual contradictions are psychology's, just as are their intellectual advances. Interrelations among intellectual disciplines are critical to the growth of knowledge, and psychology can be construed to hold a privileged central position among them all. Hence the importance for psychology to reflect on and to examine its relations with those intellectual disciplines allied to it.

1

Psychology and Art

Marc H. Bornstein
New York University

INTRODUCTION

One can suppose that the psychology of art began when the first Magdalenian peoples entered the grottos of Lascaux to discover there elaborate
realistic wall paintings. How were these people *affected* by what they
saw, and what did those images *mean* to them? Intriguingly, some
Paleolithic animal drawings show signs of having been struck with blunt
objects, as if in ritualistic killing. Or, one can suppose that the psychology
of art began somewhat earlier when the same peoples actually painted on
those cave walls. Why and how did these painters *create* such art works?
Doubtlessly, prehistoric art served religious and social functions, but the
quality and surety of these depictions and the fact that some gallery
drawings are superimposed on earlier etchings suggest that artistry for its
own sake was also involved. Or, perhaps, the psychology of art began
when those same painters first *thought* to depict their ideas or subjects
from life around them.

The questions that these earliest art works provoke are the same that
arise today when we wander through the Metropolitan Museum of Art in
New York City, the British Museum in London, or the Louvre in Paris.
We wonder what works of art mean to their audience and how works of
art affect an audience. We wonder too how and why artists create works
that fire our imagination and quicken our feelings. We also wonder what
purposes art serves. These questions define and motivate a psychology of
art, and the psychological questions art provokes constitute the foci
around which this essay is organized.

There are no definitive answers to these questions, however. Art is a
mystery. And so the chief aims of this essay are to reraise these questions
in the reader's mind and to organize and discuss psychological opinions
about them. The central questions of art endure.

1

Art is a curious and in many ways paradoxical aspect of life. Humans expend great energy and resources on art, though it seems to be of little biological necessity or relevance. Unlike many things, art must be experienced first-hand—to be told about a painting, a building, or a sculpture is wholly unsatisfying. Art is conveyed in form and content, but the experience of art transcends both; moreover, the subject theme and materials matter, but attention specifically drawn to them can detract from their very effect. Art is private and often wholly idiosyncratic, but it is also largely public—opinion and preference vary in art as much or more than anywhere in human experience, but there is also surprisingly wide consensus. Further, emotion and understanding in art may be coincident or not—one may understand and enjoy a painting, be moved in the absence of comprehension, have insight without feeling, or neither apprehend nor emote in the presence of works of art. The psychology of art must be concerned with all of these contradictory and mysterious dimensions of the art experience.

Outside of art theory and art history and the internal analyses to which they give rise, there are two main intellectual avenues to art and to artistic appreciation or aesthetics. Since aesthetics is defined as a branch of philosophy specifically concerned with the nature of the *beautiful,* aesthetics is first and prominently identified with philosophy, both in the artistic world and in the lay mind. Philosophical aesthetics is the self-contained study of beauty that derives from speculation, opinion, and judgment based on experience and scholarship. This is an "aesthetics from above" and is the creation of philosophers who grapple with questions about the metaphysical meaning of fine art, the definition, appraisal, and evaluation of beauty, and the language of criticism. However, the constructs it has built on, including shared feeling (Tolstoy, 1898/1962), morality, ethics, sentimentality (Ruskin, 1907), emotion, expression, imagination (Collingwood, 1938/1958), symbolism (Goodman, 1968), and the like (see Croce, 1909/1972; Margolis, 1962), have for the most part defied operationalism. Doubtlessly, art embraces elements of all of these qualities; it is just that it is difficult to see how the ascription of any one in particular has advanced our thinking about the central questions art provokes.

The major alternative approach to art and to aesthetics, again outside of art theory and art history proper, is through diverse social science disciplines, especially psychology. Psychology is the closest science to art. Broadly, art and aesthetics directly invoke personality, creativity, mentation, and perception—as much as they do theme, style, and technique. Simply put, the art object could not exist without its creator or meaningfully exist without its perceiver. Further, painting is not just a photographic reproduction, but is always a uniquely human interpretation. Finally, painters are unremittingly fascinated with other humans: Stroll through a museum and the salient fact will emerge that portraiture has been the secular obsession of artists. Construed thus, art, artist, audience, and aesthetics clearly fall in the purview of psychology; indeed, art is inextricably entwined with psychology.

Out of its own pluralistic nature, psychology itself has delimited two principal approaches to creativity, aesthetics, and meaning in the arts: One orientation is *scientific* and concerns itself centrally with perceptual and cognitive aspects of art, and the other is *humanistic* and is concerned with emotional and motivational components of art. The two comprise a complementary "aesthetics from below" and represent comprehensive orientations to art. Both are relatively young, having developed as has psychology in the twentieth century. Sigmund Freud (1856–1939) established the humanistic orientation. Freud's insights in art were broad and sweeping; he endeavored to bring art under a general psychological theory of personality. Gustav Fechner (1801–1887) originated the scientific tradition. Fechner's views about art were focused and narrow; he thought to submit art to experimental analytic investigation in the laboratory. Though these two different paths have led to seemingly different perspectives on art, a panorama of the psychology of art is more detailed and richly textured for their joint efforts.

> The *oeuvre* of the Belgian Surrealist René Magritte (1898–1967) is perfused with pictorial ambiguity and is preoccupied with themes of presence-absence and life-death. Understanding some of his compositions can be informed by clinical knowledge of the artist's enduring melancholia ascribable to the early death of his mother [Wolfenstein, 1973].

> The human mind has a special affinity for pictures. Not only do infants, children, and adults shown pictures for the first time recognize familiar objects [Bornstein, 1984a], but adults can expertly recognize over 2000 different images days after they have seen each only once for one second [Standing, Conezio, & Haber, 1970].

The psychological enterprise in art—humanistic *or* scientific—is predicated on the utility, acceptability, and meaningfulness of explanation or interpretation in art. Clearly, not everyone subscribes to the idea that understanding art can be advanced through psychological ratiocination. If explanation were not meaningful, then the psychological "enterprise," as I have called it, would amount to a useless exercise. But I think that it is not, and, as I endeavor to show, in the *very* short time since psychology was established, the psychology of art has made substantial contributions to elucidating motivation and meaning as well as the effects of formal properties of art. Works of art need to be understood, and they need to be approached via many avenues; art does not undergo diminution when it is

FIG. 1.   Sigmund Freud (1856–1939) and Gustav Fechner (1801–1887). (National Library of Medicine, Washington, DC)

submitted to analysis. Psychologists, of course, have been strong on this point; Freud, for example, maintained that "what has not been understood has been inaccurately perceived or reproduced [1914/1963, p. 83]." But artists and connoisseurs too have compellingly argued the case of psychological analysis. Analysis has always proved valuable to artistic fidelity, quality, and creativity. As Pablo Picasso admitted:

> Paintings are but research and experiment. I never do a painting as a work of art. All of them are researches [quoted by Arnheim, 1962, p. 13].

And, the affect and the meaning of art works are augmented, not reduced, by knowledge of the mental and emotional processes they excite. As the respected critic Max J. Friedländer observed:

> Art being a thing of the mind, it follows that any scientific study of art will be psychology. It may be other things as well, but psychology it will always be [1946, p. 128].

This essay is formally arranged around the major psychological orientations toward art. Psychologies of art—scientific and humanistic—are difficult to disentangle from psychologies of the artist and of the audience. For this reason, I have not attempted to separate art, artist, and audience in discussing different psychological traditions in art. In the first two sections, I introduce, discuss, and evaluate the humanistic and scientific approaches to psychological theories and data about art, artist, and audience. In each of these main stopping points in the psychology of art we discover a developmental dimension: development of the artist and development of the audience. In the third section of the essay, I review progress in the developmental psychology of art. In the fourth section, I discuss the historical development of Western art from a psychological vantage; and I raise the possibility of a psychologically universal aesthetic. The essay concludes with a discussion of future productive directions between psychology and art.

In this essay I am concerned with psychological viewpoints and do not broach philosophical, sociological, anthropological, or other related orientations to art. *Art* is limitless in conception and scope, and no one could argue that the political statement of Goya's *2 May and 3 May 1808*, the social compassion of Orozco's *Slave,* or the impact of the call of an anonymous Chinese poster are any less *psychological* than the pregnant moment captured by Vermeer in *The Love-Letter,* the intense gloom and anguish of Munch's *Jealousy,* or the pure and direct formalism in any Mondrian *Composition.* The word "art" itself invokes very different images and ideas in different individuals. This being the case, it is necessary to place limits on the conception and scope of our endeavor here, and this essay is therefore circumscribed to a psychological introduction to humanism, science, and development in the visual fine arts of the West—especially to painting—though the psychological principles discussed presumably extend to sculpture, architecture, photography, cinema, and theater.

THE HUMANISTIC TRADITION OF ART, ARTIST, AND AUDIENCE

The humanistic tradition in the psychology of art has tended to focus on the motivation to create art and on the meaning of themes in art, and has attended, albeit to a lesser degree, to reciprocal psychological responses of the audience to those motivations and themes. In this perspective art is an outlet for the artist and a conduit for the audience. Psychologists in the humanistic tradition have been especially attracted to the interrelated problems of *creativity* and *artistic personality*.

The question of whether artistic personality is special has classical roots. Plato proclaimed an Idealist view—the artist as divinely inspired;

Aristotle proclaimed a Realist view—the artist as acute observer and interpreter of nature. However different, artistic personality has nearly always been characterized by an "otherness" from personality styles in the general population. Wittkower and Wittkower (1963) brought historical and sociological analysis to bear on this question and concluded that, from classical times until the present, three separate interpretations of eccentricity of artistic temperament have been entertained: "first, Plato's *mania*, the sacred madness of enthusiasm and inspiration; secondly, insanity or mental disorders of various kinds; and thirdly, a rather vague reference to eccentric behavior [p. 101]." Hard data on the question of whether the artistic personality deviates significantly from the normal range, though sparse, suggest that it does not. Nonetheless, the "otherness" of artists has been a conception widely subscribed to by art historians, by psychologists, and by the lay public alike. This view reached ascendency with the dominance of emotion over intellect and reason in nineteenth-century Romanticism. The mainstream movement in art during this period popularly presented as subject matter basic feelings and emotional situations of life (Goldwater, 1967). The art of the Norwegian painter Edvard Munch (1863–1944), which itself sometimes bordered on neurotic or hysterical, is characteristic of this time (Figure 2). Out of this *Weltanschauung* the most influential psychological movement in art, psychoanalytic theory, was introduced.

Freud was the modern fountainhead of the humanistic approach, and, like most of his opinions, Freud's insights into art and the artistic temperament derived from self-analysis and from his studies and interpretations of abnormal character. Freud, it so happens, was also an art connoisseur and avid collector (Spector, 1972).

In spite of the thoroughgoing impact that Freud's theory has had in the cultural domain—Lionel Trilling once observed that Freud "ultimately did more for our understanding of art than any other writer since Aristotle [1947/1953, p. 160]"—Freud's original essays in the fine arts were infrequent, severely limited, and highly tentative. Freud seems to have used art more to explore the breadth of his brainchild psychoanalysis and less to provide exegesis of specific works of art. In one major effort Freud psychoanalyzed Leonardo to examine the influence of childhood experiences on mature personality, and in a second Freud analyzed Michelangelo's *Moses* to show the intent of the unconscious in the parapraxes of the everyday life of an artist.

Freud observed that art works exerted an especially "powerful effect" on him, and he wondered why. He eventually arrived at the interpretation that art represents a socially acceptable sphere for redirection and release of otherwise taboo instinctual energies and sexual wishes, and he hypothesized that art constitutes substitute gratification for the artist and

FIG. 2. *The Scream* (1893) by Edvard Munch (1863–1944).

One evening I was walking along a path—on one side lay the city and below me the fjord. I was tired and ill—I stopped and looked out across the fjord—the sun was setting—the clouds were dyed red like blood.

I felt a scream pass through nature; it seemed to me that I could hear the scream. I painted this picture—painted the clouds as real blood.—The colors were screaming [Munch, quoted by Messer, n.d., p. 84].

Munch's starkly expressionist style intended to convey through pictorial equivalents the basic themes of life. Here inner terror arising from alienation from reality is captured in the selection of this nightmarish image and visualized in the long wavy lines which heighten the intensity of the sound waves and echo the emotional pitch of the scream into every part of the landscape. (Nasjonalgalleriet, Oslo) vicarious fulfillment for the audience. Freud opined that the creation as well as the appreciation of art have common roots in sexual excitation (albeit *Vorlust*), and it was in this way that Freud drew art (and artistry) into his general psychological theory.[1]

Freud's most famous case study in this arena was developed in an historical psychobiography, *Leonardo da Vinci and a Memory of His Childhood* (1910/1964). Freud used Leonardo as a showpiece for the general theory that aspects of mature personality could be understood from specific childhood experiences. Freud argued that Leonardo, who was illegitimate and who early in life lived exclusively with his natural mother, developed a strong and precocious sexual attitude toward her which was thwarted when in middle childhood he was removed permanently to his father's house and the care of a stepmother. Freud supposes that Leonardo afterward rechannelled powerful Oedipal desires into a creative surge, sublimating sexual expression into artistic productivity—without, as Freud endeavored to show, much consummation in the sexual or artistic sphere. To crystallize this analysis of the artist, Freud added to his 1910 manuscript a critical discussion of Leonardo's painting of the *Madonna and Child with Saint Anne*. According to Freud, one can plainly see in this picture unconscious fulfillment of Leonardo's wish to be nurtured by both youngish mothers. Painting is regression to and expression of primary process thinking—unconscious thought directed by the id to obtain satisfaction of libidinous or other instinctual wishes—and this painting provided Leonardo (and continues to provide its audience), however unconsciously, with partial gratification of the demand for nurturance.[2]

---

[1]Waelder (1965) has pointed out that art actually services all three levels in Freud's psychodynamic system: for the Id, art preserves the pleasure principle; for the Ego, art represents economy of solutions (see the discussion of problem-solving in the section on The Scientific Tradition); and for the Super-Ego, art accomplishes a transcendence of nature.

[2]It is not possible to recount the story of this classic psychoanalysis of an artist and his work and omit its starting point—and one of the most famous footnotes in the psychology of art history. Leonardo recorded the following fragment of his childhood in his *Notebooks;* it is reputedly one of the sole records of the artist's youth:

I recall as one of my very earliest memories that while I was in my cradle a vulture came down to me, and opened my mouth with its tail, and struck me many times with its tail against my lips [Freud, 1910/1964, p. 32].

Freud added the following footnote to the second (1919) edition of his *Leonardo* book:

A remarkable discovery has been made in the Louvre picture by Oskar Pfister, which is of undeniable interest, even if one may not feel inclined to accept it without reserve. In Mary's curiously arranged and rather confusing drapery he has discovered the *outline of a vulture* and he interprets it as an *unconscious picture-puzzle:*—

"In the picture that represents the artist's mother *the vulture, the symbol of motherhood,* is perfectly clearly visible.

Freud's intention in this exercise was as much inductive as it was idiographic, for he wished to illustrate that the personalities and creativity of artists (and scientists alike) could be explicated by appealing to a theory of psychosexual dynamics. Of course, Freud's was also among the first (and has been among the strongest) versions of this kind of theorizing about art and artist or about creativity, and its reception was mixed. According to the art historian Kenneth Clark (1939/1958, p. 20), Freud's "conclusions [were] rejected with horror by the majority of Leonardo scholars." Freud's historiography and his assumptions about Leonardo's personal life have been faulted, and personal bias and overinterpretation built into psychoanalytic exposition have been reproved (see, for example, Schapiro, 1955–1956, 1956; Wittkower & Wittkower, 1963; and see, too, Lifton & Strozier, in Volume II). However, Clark, who was also the renowned Leonardo scholar of his time, himself held Freud's efforts and message in esteem:

[Freud's study] helps our conception of Leonardo's character by insisting that he was abnormal. We must remember the undercurrent when examining the surface of his . . . work [p. 20],

and Clark introduced his own discussion of the Louvre *Madonna and Child,* stating:

"In the length of blue cloth, which is visible around the hip of the woman in front and which extends in the direction of her lap and her right knee, one can see the vulture's extremely characteristic head, its neck and the sharp curve where its body begins. . . ."

At this point the reader will not, I feel sure, grudge the effort of looking at the accompanying illustration, to see if he can find in it the outlines of the vulture seen by Pfister. The piece of blue cloth, whose border marks the edges of the picture-puzzle, stands out in the reproduction as a light grey field against the darker ground of the rest of the drapery.

Pfister continues: "The important question however is: How far does the picture-puzzle extend? If we follow the length of cloth, which stands out so sharply from its surroundings, starting at the middle of the wing and continuing from there, we notice that one part of it runs down the woman's foot, while the other part extends in an upward direction and rests on her shoulder and on the child. The former of these parts might more or less represent the vulture's wing and tail, as it is in nature; the latter might be a pointed belly and—especially when we notice the radiating lines which resemble the outlines of feathers—a bird's outspread tail, whose right-hand end, *exactly as in Leonardo's fateful childhood dream* [sic], *leads the mouth to the child, i.e. of Leonardo himself.*"

Although Freud himself accepted the observation with "reserve"—and, to be sure, there are difficulties with it: the Italian in Leonardo's *Notebooks* is *"nibio"* (kite) which Freud translated as *"Geier"* (vulture)—it is compelling; as Pfister suggested:

"hardly any observer whom I have confronted with my little find has been able to resist the evidence of this picture-puzzle [pp. 65–66]."

FIG. 3. *Madonna and Child with Saint Anne* (1503–1507) by Leonardo da Vinci (1452–1518). This painting has been used as a psychoanalytic clue to decipher the enigmatic character of the artist. (Louvre, Paris)

I cannot resist quoting the beautiful, and I believe profound, interpretation which Freud has put on this picture [p. 137].

In his other notable essay into the visual arts, Freud brought Michelangelo Buonarroti's *Moses* (S. Pietro in Vincoli, Rome) under the power of his analytic microscope. Whereas art historians and critics might interpret such a sculpture in terms of its historical, religious, or artistic stature (as do the many scholars Freud cites), Freud approached the statue with psychological questions—What did the artist intend to convey?—to which he applied psychological interpretations—*Moses* is a "character study" whose secrets are to be divined by exposing hitherto "unconsidered and unnoticed details" that betray the significance of the artist's intent. Freud spells out the rationale for his psychological exercise quite clearly:

why should the artist's intention not be capable of being communicated and comprehended in words like any other fact of mental life? Perhaps where great works of art are concerned this would never be possible without the application of psychoanalysis. The product itself after all must admit of such an analysis, if it really is an effective expression of the intentions and emotional activities of the artist. To discover his intention, though, I must first find out the meaning and content of what is represented in his work; I must, in other words, be able to *interpret* it. It is possible, therefore, that a work of art of this kind needs interpretation, and that until I have accomplished that interpretation I cannot come to know why I have been so powerfully affected [Freud, 1914/1963, p. 81].

Freud's ensuing interpretation of the *Moses* capitalized on the mental detective work he had developed a decade earlier in *The Psychopathology of Everyday Life*. Freud concentrates on the loop of Moses's divided beard, the pressure of his index finger there, and the disoriented, unsupported Tables to illuminate Michelangelo's meaning and intent in the statue. But Freud is also modest in the endeavor and sensitive to its potential shortcomings: "may not these minute particulars mean nothing in reality, and may we not be racking our brains about things which were of no moment to their creator? [p. 94]" In the end, however, Freud's essay succeeded both for psychology and for art history for he refocused viewers' attention on a hidden set of details, and his analysis eventuated in a revolutionary interpretation of attitude in the *Moses*.[3]

---

[3]Although Freud is acknowledged as the founder of a major tradition in the psychology of art, his publishers at first made the *Leonardo* book available only to members of the medical profession on account of its sexual orientation. Further, Freud originally published his study

Freud's two essays illustrate essentially what psychoanalysis can and cannot do in art. Psychoanalysis has successfully illuminated some inner meanings of art works—though it is widely recognized that psychoanaly- tic interpretations are not exclusive of other meanings. And, psychoanalysis has certainly also had a persistent romantic attraction in explicating the temperament of individual artists. In these ways, in par- ticular, psychoanalysis is commonly regarded to have enriched our grasp and appreciation of the arts. But in Freud's hands, psychoanalysis as a general theory of artistic culture remained incomplete (Kuhns, 1983). It was not applied to explicating artistic technique, and Freud's aesthetic has often also been criticized as notably lacking in a system of perception. Psychoanalysis found no application to elucidating the nature of artistic gifts. Freud also appears to have been more interested in analysis of historical than living artists, relying heavily on inference from the exami- nation of symbols. In addition, Freud isolated individual works from art- ists' *oeuvres* and from their cultural context, he failed satisfactorily to reconcile primary and secondary process thinking in art, and he neglected details of the artist-art-audience nexus.

The vigor and rewards of the Freudian orientation toward art attracted many adherents from within psychology. Though the contributions of neo-Freudians to explicating meaning and character in the arts have not significantly superseded Freud's own, loyal disciples added individual fillips or closed lacunae in the basic theory. Thus, Ehrenzweig (1965, 1967) supplemented his teacher by concentrating on the genesis of draw- ing in children and on perception. He opined that childhood's polymorph- ous perversity finds first expression in "libidinous scribblings [1965, p. 178]" and later in the apprehension of certain forms that appeal to unconscious sexual motives: "I follow Freud in assuming that the esthetic pleasure transmuted a sexual (visual or acoustic) voyeurism [1965, p. 258]." Kris (1952/1964), another student, took up issues of control of the unconscious in artistic production and artist-audience communica- tion. Kris theorized that artists possess the ability to tap the unconscious without necessarily losing control, an ability he constructively labeled "regression in the service of the ego." Kris further proposed a psychologi- cal aesthetic built on the artist's communication with his audience: "Es- thetic creation is aimed at an audience: only that self-expression is

of the *Moses* of Michelangelo in *Imago* anonymously, and his own ambivalences perfuse the manuscript. The printed version was prefaced by the following editorial note:

Although this paper does not, strictly speaking, conform to the conditions under which contributions are accepted for publication in this Journal, the editors have decided to print it, since the author, who is personally known to them, belongs to psychoanalytical circles, and since his model of thought has in point of fact a certain resemblance to the methodology of psychoanalysis [Freud, 1914/1963, p. 80].

esthetic which is communicated (or communicable) to others . . . what is made common to artist and audience is the esthetic experience itself, not a pre-existent content [1952/1964, p. 254]." Kris's further excursions into the arts of schizophrenics are classic (see below).

Not all who followed Freud's humanism followed Freud. Characteristically, Freud (1930/1961, p. 30) maintained that art constituted an expression of sexuality: "All that seems certain is [beauty's] derivation from the field of sexual feeling." But the psychoanalytic revisionist Carl Gustav Jung (1875–1961) held alternatively that art expressed emotions arising from archetypes of the collective unconscious of the race of man and were not necessarily sexual in origin. The reappearance of certain symbolic forms (like the *mandala*) in the arts of different cultures and of different epochs as well as in the art of very young children lent support, Jung (e.g., 1966) argued, to notions of aesthetic universality deep in the unconscious of men. Truths of the Jungian depth-psychology of art in turn attracted adherents within psychoanalysis (e.g., Neumann, 1959/1966) and within art history (e.g., Abell, 1957/1966; Read, 1960a, 1960b).

The intellectual premise of these humanistic inquiries in the arts is essentially Newtonian; Freud subscribed to the dualistic view that an important psychical reality lurks behind the physical reality discernible by the senses, but that that psychical reality is ultimately accessible to scrutiny through an inferential science like psychoanalysis. Freud then pursued art in the way he did dreams; the manifest content of art is only the starting point toward understanding the hidden, significant, and meaningful latent content. The manifest content conveys unconscious, universal, and timeless emotions, ideas, and desires whose open expression is socially unacceptable but whose latent presence is recognized, appeals to, and satisfies an audience. Freud concluded that art deals with the same problems he encountered in his clinical work. Certain psychologically significant ideas are commonly repressed, or turned away from consciousness, and therefore repression *(Verdrängung)* is an all-important mechanism in artistic expression and appreciation. "Objects created by humans, responded to by humans, will exhibit the force of repression in both the content of the objects and in the processes of response to the objects. In general this means that objects still possess a latent content whose translation to manifest content will be at once sought and resisted [Kuhns, 1983, p. 28]." The artist's acuity lies in his ability to raise and to express latent ideas; viewers' perceptions and responses are, in turn, shaped by those ideas. "It is as if works of art have the power to transport certain thoughts from the unconscious to the preconscious though their having been, as it were, 'aestheticized.' The whole complex activity of art-making and art-using can be understood as a cultural loosening of the ordinarily rigid boundaries of the unconscious and the conscious [p. 18]."

Freud's insight into the impact and value of art borrowed from Aristotle the notion that art serves safely to release universal pent-up emotions through catharsis and from Lipps the notion that audiences may empathize with external sources of satisfaction. Thus, art is esteemed and excites and gratifies because it meets the emotional needs of the audience through vicarious wish fulfillment. Given this premise, several problems of art unravelled for Freud: Attraction to certain artists betrayed their ability to rechannel or release instinctual demands in audiences successfully; pleasure in art derived from sexual motives that the work of art could meet or from wishes that the manifest content of the work could gratify; etc.

It stands for the psychodynamic school that insofar as the creation of works of art acts to relieve psychic tension by transforming instinctual energies (sexual or aggressive) that may otherwise be symptomatogenic, creativity in art—*qua* unconscious gratification—should be therapeutic (e.g., Kramer, 1971; Naumburg, 1950). Art therapy with the delinquent, emotionally disturbed, and physically handicapped has been founded and has grown (though not flourished) on this logic. Resolution of questions of training, of evaluation, and most importantly, of empirical support for the actual therapeutic value of this endeavor is thus far wanting. Most keenly it seems that no one has grappled with the (inherent) contradiction that the saturnine dispositions and the sanity of great artists (Michelangelo, Caravaggio, van Gogh) seem not to have been helped by their considerable labors in art.

It stands also for Freudians that insofar as works of art are products of the unconscious they may be a "window on the unconscious." Among those who have examined the manifest content of the art works of psychotics with this in mind is Kris (1952/1964) whose *Psychoanalytic Explorations in Art* submitted to analysis the creations of schizophrenics (a favorite among psychotic-artist types). Kris's treatment of the works of the eighteenth-century sculptor Franz X. Messerschmidt (1736–1784) is especially notable for its fusion of art historical and psychological scholarship. The art of schizophrenics tends to be formulaic in certain respects—characterized by dense ornamentation, repetitious detail, and a lack of compositional integration—and the art of psychotics generally does not give the impression that it is oriented toward (unambiguous) communication (Plokker, 1965). Psychoanalytic interpreters suggest that the schizophrenic artist's regression to purely primary process thinking helps to explain his mysterious outpourings. Although cataloguing schizophrenic art by particular criteria may not provoke incredulity—indeed there is evidence that these criteria possess some cross-cultural validity (Billig & Burton-Bradley, 1978)—the accuracy of blind observers actually to diagnose schizophrenia on the basis of art works would probably not fare well.

Nevertheless, several investigators have followed the logic of the psychodynamic system suggesting that it should be possible to trace the course of deterioration or improvement in neuroses and psychoses through the art work of mental patients (e.g., Bettelheim, 1959; Plokker, 1965). Support for these claims varies. Further curious happenstances for this field of application include the eventual psychotic breakdown of established artists, like van Gogh. (Van Gogh's life has received especial attention from psychologists because of the voluminous expressive and insightful letters he left behind; see, for example, Graetz, 1963; Heiman, 1976; Nagera, 1967.) Although van Gogh's style altered (in dynamism mainly) and his productivity increased (amazingly) after the first signs of his emotional disorder appeared *circa* 1885, his art cannot be described readily with any simple recipe; nor apparently did the flurry of work he created while in the asylums at Arles and S. Remy near the end of his life constitute meaningful therapy (see Figure 4).

Freud and the humanistic tradition in art he founded travel well—from the urge to create, to what is created, to how that creation is perceived and received. The dynamic effects of unconscious motivations in sexuality, aggression, or other personality constructs are nearly universally recognized today as foundations of art theory. Freudianism has affected both the appreciation and the creation of art in profound ways. Freud was among the first to connect an artist's personal life with the analysis of his works, a practice which now is not only popular in art historical and psychological scholarship (e.g., Liebert, 1983; Wolfenstein, 1973), but constitutes a lesson for these diverse fields that cannot practicably be put aside. Thus, professional art critics and historians have been much influenced by the analytic tradition (e.g., Friedländer, 1946; Gombrich, 1954; Read, 1960a; Schapiro, 1956; Stokes, 1961; Trilling, 1947/1953; see too, Phillips, 1963, and Sterba, 1940). Significantly, Freud's interpretations have illuminated art works that came before him (that is, in the light of his theory) and have influenced those which came after him (e.g., Surrealism; see below).

Nevertheless, Freud claimed never to have solved all of the puzzles of art: "Before the problem of the creative artist analysis must, alas, lay down its arms [Freud, 1928/1963, p. 274]." Freud's dictum is telling, for while the humanistic tradition he founded has concerned art and the artist, Freud himself seems to have been less interested in art and artists than in creation and genius. (It has not passed unnoticed that Freud's choices of artists—Leonardo, Michelangelo—and subjects in art—the scientist-artist, the law giver—were mostly influenced by his personal quest for

FIG. 4. *A Man Mourning* painted by Vincent Van Gogh (1853–1890) in the year of his suicide. (Rijksmuseum Kröller-Müller, Otterlo, Holland)

self-identity with select historical personae and roles.) It is not surprising, then, that the humanistic tradition has also emphasized creativity. One of the most inventive of the neo-Freudians interested in this aspect of art was Otto Rank (1884–1937) who, like Jung, broke with Freud on the centrality of sexuality as a motivating force. For Rank, creativity was not sublimination of biological drives, but represented the development of a strong, assertive, and willful sense of self in the world. Creativity was not the byproduct of unresolved Oedipal dynamics in the nuclear family, but was the positive outcome of an independent break from parental authority. Creativity was synonymous with ego strength. Based on their personal experiences, Rank (1932) asserted, artists have a message, have a mission to communicate that message, the self-confidence to communicate it, and an attractiveness to audiences in that their message evokes deep and meaningful responses.

> Creativity is not something which happens but once, it is the constant continuing expression of the individual will [Rank, 1945, p. 276].

Empirical studies of creativity have attracted a cohort of personality psychologists. While creativity *per se* remains rather an elusive concept (MacKinnon, 1968), the characteristics of artistically creative persons lend themselves to general profile that articulates surprisingly well with Rank's views. MacKinnon (1965), for example, compared personality characteristics among architects nominated by experts as most creative, architects only professionally associated with the creative group, and architects selected at random; all were given a battery of psychological questionnaries, tests, and inventories. Individuals in the creative group proved to be high in ego strength and will, independence and self-confidence, and self-centeredness and autonomy; far from neurotic complicatedness, creative individuals tended to manifest candor and spontaneity, even if embedded in complex, rich, and unconventional personalities (e.g., Barron, 1972; MacKinnon, 1965, 1968; Roe, 1975). Further, MacKinnon found that creativity taps analysis and reasoning (convergent thinking) as well as richness and novelty of ideas (divergent thinking), but that beyond a certain degree of intelligence creativity is not necessarily correlated with IQ. Creative individuals are, however, high in need for achievement. Architects in the most creative group also scored the highest in perceptiveness, aesthetic sensitivity, and preference for complexity; these are characteristics that echo concerns of the scientific tradition of a psychology of art, and we shall turn to consider them in the next section.

In the end we have come full circle to ask again whether artistic personality is special, whether it deviates meaningfully from the range of personalities of nonartistic people. The mythology of the artistic personality as different in some way is ancient and enduring. The Renaissance characterized artists as "saturnine." Though Freud was personally passionate and respectful of art and artist, Freudianism can be (and has been) read as derogatory or hostile to artist and art. Early influential psychoanalytic theory implied that of the two ways to deal with harsh

FIG. 5.   Detail from the *School of Athens* (1509–1511) by Raphael Sanzio (1483–1520). This crouching figure of Heraclitus has been identified as a portrait of Michelangelo. Raphael represented his rival in the traditional pose of *Melancholy*, wrapped in brooding solitary thought. (Stanza della Segnatura, Vatican City, Rome)

18

reality—the healthy and positive *versus* the sick and negative—the artist, like the neurotic, adopts the latter in efforts to escape. Inherent in this position therefore is a kind of "contempt" for art. But the studies of Leonardo and of Michelangelo, published in 1910 and 1914 respectively, are early Freud. In his later years, when Freud returned to cultural things, he attempted to rectify psychoanalysis's negative interpretations in the arts. The intellectual development of ego psychology has reinforced this view. In these later positivistic constructions, the genius is seen as in command of his fantasies and is distinguished from the neurotic who is possessed by his. Indeed, Freud himself paid tribute to artists for their clarity of vision: He demurred the attribution that he was discoverer of the unconscious but credited this accomplishment to artists.

In a witty, scholarly, and exhaustive review of the character and conduct of artists since antiquity, Wittkower and Wittkower (1963) also warn against the tendency to stereotype. Many artists, they point out, have been melancholic (Michelangelo, Carracchi), suicidal (Bassano, Borromini, van Gogh), alcoholic (Toulouse-Lautrec), licentious (Raphael, Tasso—See Footnote 8), homosexual (Bazzi, Leonardo, Michelangelo), criminal (Cellini), or spendthrifty (Holbein, Reni), but many have also been models of dignity and gentility (Titian, Bernini, Rubens, Reynolds). Modern psychological studies lend no empirical support to the link Lombroso and Kretschmer propounded between genius and madness either, and though many critics (e.g., Trilling, 1947/1953), following late-Freud, have endeavored to lay the fascinating tradition of the *genus irritabile* to rest, it obstinately persists. After all, it is a myth fostered by those hostile to the arts, by those partisan to the arts, and by artists themselves; a little reflection shows that the myth has distinct advantages for each.

THE SCIENTIFIC TRADITION OF ART, ARTIST, AND AUDIENCE

The humanistic tradition in the psychology of art is organized around a global, rational, and speculative aesthetics; it addresses large questions of creativity and meaning based on intuition, insight, and idiographic induction, and it emphasizes primarily art in terms of the artist and secondarily art in terms of the audience. The scientific tradition in the psychology of art, by contrast, is organized around a local, analytic, and empirical aesthetics; it addresses circumscribed questions of specific effects based on experiment, analysis, and nomothetic deduction, and it emphasizes, again not exclusively, art in terms of the audience. Gustav Fechner originated the modern scientific study of the psychology of art in 1876 with his publication of *Vorschule der Ästhetik*. Briefly, Fechner propounded the doctrine that artistic effects could be evaluated experimentally, even in the laboratory, by following the traditional scientific formula in which comprehensible elements are first isolated, their molecular consequences appraised, and those effects eventually synthesized into a molar aesthetic. This orientation construes art psychology as a psychophysics between art and audience, as opposed to a personality theory of the artist, and so theories of artistic representation in experimental aesthetics easily devolve into theories of perception and cognition. Experimental aesthetics submits to academic study the aesthetic consequences of formal properties of art and invites perception and cognition from psychology to partake in the analysis of works of art, their generation, and their effect.

Fechner founded this psychological orientation toward art and aesthetics, he worked out the basics of its major experimental and observational methodologies, and he began research in several substantive areas of experimental aesthetics still of interest today. Fechner brought to aesthetics his experience in sensory psychophysics, the experimental study of relations between physical stimuli and events in the world and the sensations they provoke, and he adapted methodologies developed in psychophysics to study art. For example, two techniques for an experimental aesthetics Fechner proposed parallel basic psychophysical methods: In the method of choice observers select or rank stimuli in order of preference, and in the method of production observers alter stimuli in order to enhance preferred qualities. As emerges readily from a consideration of these methods, Fechner interpreted psychological aesthetics to imply the study of *preference*.

Fechner's own experients using these methods are still noteworthy; two are sufficient to represent his originality and classic and enduring concerns. In one, Fechner (1865) asked observers to rank in order of preference a variety of rectangles drawn so that their sides varied in relative proportion to one another. He found that subjects most preferred the rectangle that possessed dimensions of about 1:.62. Fechner also observed that many common rectangles—playing cards, windows, books, writing pads—possessed approximately the same dimensions. This proportion, it so happens, constitutes the famous "golden section"—wherein the smaller part is to the larger as the larger is to the whole—whose mathematical significance and aesthetic virtue have been speculated about since Pythagoras and Euclid (Berlyne, 1971; Huntley, 1970; Zusne, 1970): With its triangular pediment intact, the façade of the Parthenon, for example, almost exactly fits the golden rectangle, and the aesthetics of the golden section have been formally acknowledged in the writings of many artists (e.g., Le Corbusier, 1954). In a second study, Fechner (1876) observed the behaviors of museum-goers whose preference he sought for paintings, for example two versions of Holbein's *Madonna with Bur-*

gomaster Meyer hanging side by side. Fechner found that paintings could be judged meaningfully in this way, but only with difficulty and at the expense of experimental control over factors that contribute to the judgment in the first place.

In the century since Fechner first conducted his studies, psychologists have enlarged the experimental aesthetician's armamentarium with sophisticated methods of data collection and analysis (including multivariate analyses, scaling, and content analysis). However, the underlying premise of experimental aesthetics has not transcended Fechner's original design, nor have the substantive interests or general orientations of the experimental aesthetician deviated very far from Fechner's own original themes. Aesthetics as a "theory of pleasing and displeasing [Fechner, 1876, p. 1]" is still the prominent concern; laboratory studies are still contrasted with observations of gallery behavior; and elements of aesthetic works are still isolated, judged, and mathematically compared with each other and with judgments of whole works. Indeed, many of Fechner's particular interests have been subjected to continuing scrutiny (e.g., Benjafield & Adams-Webber, 1976; Martin, 1906; Svensson, 1977; Thorndike, 1917).

Fechner's main contribution was, therefore, to found and direct a movement in aesthetics away from idiosyncratic judgment and authoritative pronouncement, toward analysis and nomothetic understanding in art. For vague reasons, this orientation is antithetical to and often derogated by the two other traditional approaches to art and aesthetics, philosophy and humanistic psychology. Philosophical and humanistic aestheticians alike balk especially at the dissection of whole works to concentrate on elements, at statistical averaging and population inference, and at other fundamentals and assumptions of the empirical approach, and they often negate the scientific psychology of art as artificial at best or irrelevant at worst. Aesthetics from above has a place in the philosophy of art. However, aesthetics from below has its legitimate place in the psychology of art. Indeed, it is often not recognized that many artists, art historians, and art connoisseurs themselves have practiced, promoted, and even promulgated experimental aesthetics, and theory and writing in art provide ample identifiable precedents for this psychological approach. In advance of discussing the scientific tradition, it may be valuable to digress momentarily to consider the documentation and authorization that art historical sources supply an aesthetics from below.

Giorgio Vasari (1511–1574), the first art historian, observes in the Introduction to the Third Part of his 1550 *Lives of the Most Eminent Painters, Sculptors, and Architects* that there is "grace exceeding measurement," but he plainly states that successful techniques of artists were built on an analytic-synthetic orientation to aesthetics. "Manner," he says, "then attained to the greatest beauty from the practice which arose of constantly copying these most beautiful objects and joining together these most beautiful things, hands, heads, bodies, and legs so as to make a figure of the greatest possible beauty [1550/1912/1958, p. 26]." (Though nowhere to my knowledge given credit, in the same passage Vasari puts forward the technique of paired comparisons, Michelangelo against the Greeks and Romans.) A somewhat later and more vehement advocate of the same point of view was Roger de Piles (1635–1709), one of the most influential art historians and theoreticians to succeed Vasari. In his *Principles of Painting with a Balance of Painters* (1708/1743/1958), de Piles put color and composition on a plane with drawing and expression in analyzing art works, and to show their aesthetic value, de Piles created a "balance" in which he compared sixty-odd painters on these four "most essential points of his art"—composition, drawing, color, and expression. De Piles then assigned each painter "of established reputation" a value between 0 and 20 on each dimension.[4] "By collecting all the parts, as they appear in each painter's work," de Piles argued, "one might be able to judge how much the whole weighs [p. 183]." Characteristically, Leonardo and Raphael scored high on composition, drawing, and expression but low on color; Rembrandt and Titian high on color but lower on the other three dimensions. De Piles recognized that "opinions are too various . . . to let us think that we alone are in the right" in such judgment; however, he continued:

> I must give notice, that in order to criticize judiciously, one must have a perfect knowledge of all the parts of a piece of painting, and of the reasons which make the whole good; for many judge of a picture only by the part they like, and make no account of those other parts which either they do not understand, or do not relish [pp. 184–185].

Vasari and de Piles are among the oldest and most venerated academic sources in the history of art.

Art historians, critics, and connoisseurs typically approach the study of art through academic considerations of artists, themes, documents, periods, and genres, but they also delight in the analysis of parts and of wholes, of composition and of style, and of intrinsic aesthetic character independent of subject matter, morality, sentimentality, or ethics in their

---

[4]De Piles adopted a psychometrically curious 20-point scale:

The twentieth degree is the highest, and implies *sovereign perfection;* which no man has fully arrived at. The nineteenth is the highest degree that we know, but which no person has yet gained. And the eighteenth is, for those who, in my opinion, have come nearest to perfection; as the lower figures are for those who appear to be further from it [De Piles, 1708/1743/1958, p. 184].

efforts to interpret underlying principles of what is aesthetic. For example, Kenneth Clark's (1956) book on *The Nude* is an historical study of
ideal form; Roger Fry's (1956) collection *Vision and Design* makes plain
the connection between formal composition and the underlying structure
of nature as aesthetic, most evident in Fry's (1927/1958) own earlier
championing of *Cézanne* for the artist's penetration to the essence of form
beneath appearance; likewise, Clive Bell's (1913/1958) essay on *Art*
praised "significant form" as relations among line, color, and volume.

More importantly, in every century since the Renaissance, the most
prominent artists who have written about art have consistently recognized intrinsic aesthetics in the formal elements of their work. The earliest
articulations of this perspective appeared in Leon Battista Alberti's
(1404?–1472) quattrocento treatise *On Painting:*

> Painting, then, is nothing other than a cross-section of a visual pyramid upon
> a certain surface, artificially represented with lines and colors at a given
> distance, with a central stance established and light arranged [p. 209]. . . . I
> would say the business of a painter is this: to draw with lines and dye with
> colors, on whatever panel or wall is given, . . . [1435/1726/1957, p. 215],

and in Leonardo da Vinci's (1452–1519) cinquecento *Trattato della Pittura,* including *"Paragone," or First Part of the Book on Painting:*

> what makes the beauty of the world, namely, light, shade, colour, body,
> figure, position, distance, nearness, motion, and rest—these ten ornaments
> of nature [n.d./1817/1957, p. 278].

In the seventeenth century, Nicolas Poussin (1594–1665) wrote in his
Observations on Painting:

> The idea of beauty does not infuse itself into matter which is not prepared to
> the utmost. This preparation consists of three things: order, mode, and form
> or *species*. Order means the spacing of parts; mode has to do with quantity;
> species [form] consists in line and colors [1672/1911/1958, p. 144];

in the eighteenth century, William Hogarth (1697–1764) observed in *The
Analysis of Beauty:*

> In this manner of attending to forms, they will be found whether *at rest* or *in
> motion,* to give *movement* . . . or, more properly speaking, to the eye itself,
> affecting it *thereby* more or less *pleasingly,* according to their different
> *shapes* and *motions* [1753/1958, p. 272];

and, in the nineteenth century, Eugène Delacroix (1798–1863) recorded
on 20 October 1853 in his *Journal:*

looking upon the spectacle of created things, we have here the satisfaction
given by beauty, proportion, contrast, harmony of color, and everything that
the eye looks upon with so much pleasure in the outer world—one of the
great needs of our nature [1923/1948/1966, p. 166].

In modern times, Piet Mondrian (1872–1944) wrote in "Plastic Art and
Pure Plastic Art":

Thus we see in every work of figurative art the desire, objectively to represent beauty, solely through form and color, in mutually balanced relations,
and, at the same time, an attempt to express that which these forms, colors,
and relations arouse in us [1937/1964, p. 115],

and Wassily Kandinsky (1866–1944) expounded the same opinion this
way in his declaration *Point and Line to Plane:*

Aside from its scientific value, which depends upon an exact examination of
the individual art elements, the analysis of the art elements forms a bridge to
the inner pulsation of a work of art [1947/1979, p. 17].

Thus artists themselves seem always to have regarded and esteemed aesthetics of the elemental in art. Indeed, this perspective reflects a fundamental way of seeing among artists: Whistler (1834–1903) called his
portrait of his own mother *An Arrangement in Grey and Black* (1871),
Matisse (1869–1954) called his portrayal of Mme. Matisse, *The Green
Line* (1905), and, when Camille lay in her death bed, Monet (1840–1926)
lamented that all he could see were changing colors in her face. In point of
fact, psychologists developing an experimental aesthetics have intuitively
stuck remarkably close to what artists and art connoisseurs, art critics,
and art historians through the ages have judged to be of principal importance in art, *viz.* aesthetics from below.

Four branches of a scientific psychology of art have sprouted and
spread since Fechner's seminal contribution; unlike neo-Freudian movements, which can be seen as more than less homogeneous, developments
in the scientific tradition have been considerably more heterogeneous in
spirit. They include orientations associated with the Gestalt school, with
mathematical information theory, with applied perceptual theory and experimentation, and with the "new" experimental aesthetics. The four still
have many common roots in Fechner; for example, many experimental
psychologists have followed Fechner's concentration on preference in
assessing aesthetic experience, judgment, or effect, and many have used
Fechner's methods in doing so, usually measuring expressed verbal opinions (to which some have added physiological responses, including heart

rate, galvanic skin response, and evoked brain potentials). Other experimental psychologists, particularly in the first half of this century, concentrated on other problems in the psychology of art, including, for example,
the perception of depth. An honor role of experimental psychologists who
have expressed a professional interest in art at one or another time in their
careers in this period (and later) would have high recognition value:
Ames, Bruner, Burt, Dennis, Ellis, Eysenck, Gibson, Guilford, Jastrow,
Koffka, Luria, Münsterberg, Sully, Thorndike, and Vygotsky. Valentine
(1925), Beebe-Center (1932), Hogg (1969), Berlyne (1971), Child (1972,
1973, 1978), Pickford (1972), and O'Hare (1982) have reprinted significant
papers or provided summary evaluations of diverse contributions to experimental aesthetics. There are also extensive bibliographies of experimental aesthetics (e.g., Chandler & Barnhart, 1938; Hammond, 1933),
and by now there are even bibliographies of bibliographies (e.g., Shields,
1974). Let us turn to consider the four approaches, and even more contemporary cognitive considerations that have invaded the scientific psychology of art.

Gestalt psychology posits a perceptual theory from which a theory of
aesthetics derives. Koffka (1935) demonstrated the necessary role of general Gestalt principles to "reading" art in his famous text, *Principles of
Gestalt Psychology*. He showed an ambiguous figure—a jumble of lines
which make sense *only* when perceived as a face—from which he simply
and correctly pointed out "how on pure psychological grounds we must
acknowledge that there are proper and improper ways of apprehending a
work of art [p. 352]." The laws of Gestalt psychology constitute one
proper way to organize perceptual materials as prerequisite to aesthetic
reaction.

Rudolf Arnheim (1972, 1974, 1982) has been the chief modern psychologist to translate Gestalt perceptual principles in terms of aesthetic reactions, notably in his *Art and Visual Perception* (1974). In Gestalt
aesthetics, particular elements of composition (balance, shape, form,
space, color, movement, dynamics) are read as aesthetic by viewers,
automatically transforming information into meaning, and they are taken
to project and to convey expression or mood directly. That is, artists are
believed to be capable of setting up psychophysical correspondences between compositional elements in art works and audience perception and
reaction. Specific Gestalts excite pleasure by their "goodness," for example. Symmetry is such a Gestalt, and symmetry's undeniable aesthetic
appeal also satisfies dictates of Gestalt economy. Human beings are ex-
quisitely sensitive to visual symmetries, and symmetry appears in art
works of nearly every culture and period (Bornstein, 1984b). Indeed, the
physicist Hermann Weyl has written thus about symmetry's ubiquity:

Symmetry, as wide or as narrow as you may define its meaning, is one idea
by which man through the ages has tried to comprehend and create order,
beauty, and perfection [1952, p. 5].

By way of explanation of these phenomena, Arnheim invoked Lipps's
empathy theory, the same to which Freud himself had earlier appealed. It
is apparently implicit in the belief structure of many artists (at least since
Leonardo) that formal qualities of art can sometimes directly express or
invoke in their audience particular emotions. Expressionism, which advocated stylistic simplification and exaggeration of line and color, developed as a twentieth-century movement sympathetic to this view.
Expressionism has many well-known examples: Picasso's *Old Guitarist*
(1903) is thought to convey the intention of the artist's Blue Period in the
color, line, and mood of the canvas; Expressionism reached some sort of
apex in Munch (Figure 2). The intent is that pictorial elements and composition—colors, static lines, or dynamic forces—convey emotion and
meaning on inspection without necessarily calling reflective analysis into
play. In these ways, interestingly, the scientific and the humanistic traditions connect with art: Denis (1912) and Fry (1956) among art theoreticians and critics, Ehrenzweig (1965) and Rose (1980) among
psychoanalysts, and Hogarth's "line of beauty" and Gauguin's "synthet-
ism" all refer explicitly to structural universals in art thought to contribute
isomorphically to meaning; these are the targets of experimental aestheticians.

Undeniably Gestalts are aesthetically appealing. Unfortunately, Gestalt
has not succeeded (better than any other perceptual psychophysics) to
clarify exactly what "good form" is (Eysenck, 1968; Zusne, 1970), nor has
it grappled adequately with the false implication that good form alone
dictates aesthetic (Kreitler & Kreitler, 1972; Peckham, 1965). It is also
ironic that Gestalt aesthetics concentrate on formal elements, when a
central proposition of Gestalt—and art—is that the effect of the whole is
greater than any value of the elements combined.

Information theory has provided a more specific and limited scientific
psychological approach to art. In this realm, the accomplishments of two
investigators are particularly noteworthy. In *Aesthetic Measure* the
mathematician George Birkhoff (1933) attempted a quantitative theory of
aesthetics. Birkhoff posited that aesthetic value *(M)* in an art work is a
function of the relation between order *(O)* and complexity *(C)*, two factors
thought traditionally to contribute to aesthetics, and he expressed their
relationship in the formula:

$$M = O/C.$$

In these terms, aesthetic value strictly increases with order (e.g., symmetry) and decreases with complexity (e.g., density). Independent of

whence order and complexity arise—whether "in the stimulus" or "in the perceiver"—order eases or facilitates perception, whereas complexity necessitates effortful cognition. Birkhoff applied this aesthetic measure in two spheres, to geometrical patterns (simple polygons, decorations on ornaments, and tiles) and to Greek and Chinese vases, and his formula gave differential aesthetic rankings to diverse art works.

Insofar as Birkhoff infused psychological aesthetics with mathematical thinking his contributions were seminal to the advancement of experimental aesthetics, and several theorists have elaborated on them. In particular, Abraham Moles introduced information theory into the scientific psychology of art through his book *Information Theory and Aesthetic Perception* (1958/1966). Information theory is concerned with accuracy, efficiency, and effectiveness in communications. It deals with whether symbols convey their intended meaning, how extraneous noise introduces error into communication, and whether all portions of a message are equally necessary. Insofar as elements of a pattern are related or interdependent, for example, their structure (order) is high and their information value low; they are, therefore, readily communicable and easy to assimilate. To some degree, this is aesthetic. In information theory, audience and artist play critical reciprocal roles mediated by the informational structure of works of art.

The application of mathematical techniques to aesthetic judgment is appealing to some because of its patent potential for objectivity and rigor. In Birkhoff, in Moles, et in al., mathematical approaches reached an early asymptote in terms of any comprehensive explication of art works, however. Birkhoff's ratings were based on his own judgments of the significant dimensions of patterns, and the spheres of art in which he and Moles chose to apply their thinking have proved to be too narrow. First, polygons that measured high in aesthetic quality are not at all necessarily those independent observers have judged to be aesthetically appealing (e.g., Beebe-Center & Pratt, 1937; Davis, 1936; Eysenck, 1941a, 1968). Second, mathematical information theory has achieved greater applicability in music than in other arts. This is not to imply a uselessness to this approach: Information theory broadened the contribution of mathematics to artistic measure. Attneave (1959), for example, applied information theory to the analysis of select visual patterns and found that a few structures (notably, symmetry) actually met the information definition as well as the artistic criterion. Clearly, aesthetic effects consist of more than ratios on an order-complexity dimension or of simple information value so that efforts in mathematical aesthetics, like the effort of the Gestalt school, have in the end been viewed, oxymoronishly, as sophisticated yet naive.

Gestalt and information theories of art are at base theories of percep-

FIG. 6. *Girl from the Volga* (1959) photographed by S. Fridlyand. Viewers scan the most interesting features of pictures, and so their gaze patterns (over 3 minutes) nearly recreate features of the picture itself. (From the cover of *Ogonek;* reprinted as Figure 115 in A. L. Yarbus, 1967. Copyright Plenum Publishing Corporation. Reprinted by permission.)

tion applied to art: Aptly, since the word "aesthetics" derives etymologi-
cally from the Greek, *aisthagomai,* meaning "to perceive." Moreover,
these theories adhere to the scientific pursuit of analysis then synthesis,
and they grope toward understanding the aesthetic of works as wholes via
audience perceptual evaluation of parts. In the same general spirit, diverse other perceptual theories and modes of perceptual analysis have
been applied to pictorial representation.

  Since we acquire information about the world actively by orienting our
senses to that information, many perceptual psychologists have argued
that the study of eye movements must illuminate perceptual processing of
pictures (e.g., Buswell, 1935; Mackworth & Bruner, 1970; Noton &
Stark, 1971; Yarbus, 1967). While it is true that complex stimuli are
sampled over time, vision is not simply moving a searchlight over a pattern; and while it has proved true that visual scan patterns unveil features
of particular interest to viewers (Figure 6), it is also true that much of the
information in visual scenes is apprehended in units of time considerably
shorter than even one eye movement requires. Moreover, it is also true
that viewing is not determinative of interestingness or pleasingness. Finally, with the exception of the *trompe-l'oeil,* pictures require purposive
perceptual investment beyond mere visual investigation; besides, it also
helps if inconsistent areas of pictures are not simultaneously compared
(e.g., Pirenne, 1970). As a consequence, "looking at looking" can be
informative but is not altogether revealing of what may be the critical
processes in picture perception.

  Traditional perceptual theory says that as we look at the world we first
focus on and analyze parts and afterward integrate and synthesize them
into meaningful wholes. This straightforward theory is immediately, easily, and frequently applied to art. Moreover, artists sometimes purpose-
fully distort elements, as in the subtle bowing of the stylobate (main floor)
or columns of the Parthenon, in ways that contribute to the harmony of
the whole of their works; reciprocally, audiences perceptually compensate for such artistic distortions. In many senses, therefore, aesthetics
entails perception, and many experimental aestheticians have profitably
gone about the business of applying traditional perceptual analysis to
explicating works of art as well as the aesthetics therein (e.g., Berlyne,
1974, 1975; Bornstein, 1975, 1983; Gross & Bornstein, 1978; Jameson &
Hurvich, 1975; Konečni & Sargent-Pollock, 1977; Oppé, 1944; Teuber,
1974). Such an approach is equally compatible with art history (e.g.,
Rosand, 1975). Other perceptual theories deviate from the traditional
view that perceiving is the mental elaboration of sensory data. One such
influential radical alternative was propounded by J. J. Gibson in perception (1950, 1979a) as well as in art (1971). According to Gibson, whole
patterns or structures, not elements, convey information directly to the

FIG. 7.   *Man Drawing a Lute* (1525) by Albrecht Dürer (1471–1528). The woodcut shows the use of "Leonardo's Window." Since light waves converge they form a pyramid whose base is the object and whose apex is at the eye. Intercepting this pyramid allows the painter to create perspective, that is accurately to represent three dimensionality two-dimensionally. As the person on the left moves the string over the lute, the person on the right places corresponding points on the paper in the window thus rendering an image in perspective. (Public Library, New York City)

senses. These patterns consist, not of static features whose effects must be analyzed apart from the general dynamic array, but of higher-order correspondences (perceptual invariances, texture gradients) and optical information perceived directly. Pictures deceive the eye as to the world. The focal point may be situated in the picture, as in the revolutionary success of Leonardo's method of recreating three-dimensional information two-dimensionally so that pictures provide viewers with textured and structured information equivalent to real life (Figure 7). Or, the focal point may be situated in the eye, as in the equally revolutionary success of Monet's impressionist method (recall Cézanne: *"Monet n'est pas qu'un oeil—mais quel oeil!"*). As the epistemology of perceptual theory is debated today (e.g., Hochberg, 1978), so are its applications to art (see, for example, the continuing debate in *Leonardo* among Arnheim, 1979; Gibson, 1975, 1976, 1979b; and Pickford, 1976, 1979). The contemporary status of perceptual psychology's contributions to looking at pictures is summed up nicely in three recent books: Kennedy's (1974) *A Psychology of Picture Perception,* Nodine and Fisher's (1979) *Perception and Pictorial Representation,* and Hagen's (1980) *The Perception of Pictures: Alberti's Window* (Volume 1) and *Dürer's Devices* (Volume 2). An enlarged psychological aesthetic sorely missing, but one whose time is ripe, would embrace dynamic perceptions, not just of cinema (e.g., Arnheim, 1969; Hochberg & Brooks, 1978), but of the dynamic in static art (Braque's Cubism, Duchamp's Futurism) and kinetic art (Bornstein, 1975; Calder, 1966).

In the 1960s, Daniel Berlyne revived the more traditional experimental aesthetics of Fechner. In his book *Aesthetics and Psychobiology,* Berlyne (1971) gathered forces from several related and developing lines of psychological investigation to synthesize a "new" experimental aesthetics. First, Berlyne drew on information theory approaches to how expressive, semantic, and syntactic elements specify the aesthetic in works of art. Second, Berlyne drew on developments in behavior theory which showed that exploration and perceptual stimulation seem to be intrinsically motivating and rewarding activities and that certain classes of stimuli naturally provoke organisms to seek and to process information in the environment. Stimuli which prompt exploration in this way, which contain variability, and which reward search with moderate levels of information are pleasurably arousing (possess a positive hedonic value), and Berlyne termed them "collative." Collative properties of stimuli therefore include novelty, surprisingness, incongruity, and ambiguity; art, Berlyne observed, is collative in virtually all these respects. (If Fechner's was a sensory aesthetics, Berlyne's was a perceptual one.) Third, Berlyne drew on developments in the psychophysiology of motivation and emotion, particularly arousal and self-reward for exploration and stimulation, to provide his theory with a generalist biological underpinning.

So equipped, Berlyne parametrically explored psychophysiological (heart rate, galvanic skin potential, electroencephalography), behavioral (exploratory looking or listening time, choice), and verbal (ratings of pleasingness, interestingness) measures to tap judgments of hedonic arousal and aesthetic appeal. Berlyne (e.g., 1971, 1974) worked through the complex relationship between hedonic value (preference) and arousal, re-invoking the "Wundt curve" (Figure 8) by way of descriptive explanation. (Wilhelm Wundt, 1874, who established the first laboratory of experimental psychology, had developed general mathematical notions relating stimulus intensity to pleasingness nearly a century earlier; see also Coombs, in Volume III.) For several dimensions of arousal (intensity, complexity, novelty), hedonic judgment of a stimulus above threshold (L_a) first increases from indifference to reach a peak at a moderate level of arousal (X_1), but hedonic value decreases from that peak and eventually passes through indifference (at X_2) so that persistent "over-

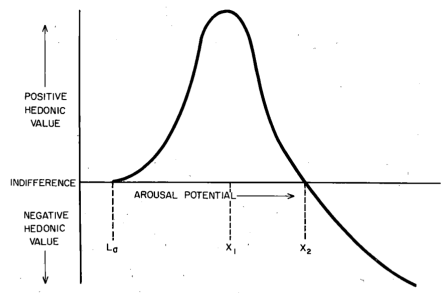

FIG. 8.   The Wundt curve. (From D. E. Berlyne, 1971. Copyright Appleton-Century-Crofts. Reprinted by permission.)

stimulation" is experienced as unpleasant. Berlyne's formulation thus retained the scientific attitude and mathematical base of its predecessors but justly supplanted aesthetically simplistic linear formulations of hedonic effects with an appropriate curvilinear one.

Berlyne truly captained this new tack. He personally reinvigorated the only extant journal in the field, *Sciences de l'Art,* which he reconstituted as the short-lived *Scientific Aesthetics.* Many generously read his last efforts, *Studies in the New Experimental Aesthetics* (1974), a collection of student, colleague, and personal papers that originated in what Berlyne called his "Laboratory of Aplopathematic and Thelematoscopic Pneumatology,"[5] as the pangs of rebirth; they turned out to be the death throes of his untimely passing. However, a validity has emerged from this approach to aesthetics: Experimental, cross-cultural, developmental, and cross-cultural developmental data have now lent support to some of its claims. Systematic empirical studies in this tradition indicate that—far from the lay and uninformed opinion that preference is highly individualized, wholly fashionable, or ineradicably esoteric—many preferences are made quickly, consistently, and self-confidently and many preferences tend toward remarkable regularity and order in many spheres

---

[5]Berlyne (1974, p. 5) derived the terms from Bentham; they "denote the aims of unraveling the determinants of hedonic processes and unraveling the role of hedonic processes in the determination of behavior."

of aesthetic judgment. These claims do not detract from the idiosyncrasies of artistic temperament or individuality, but nevertheless indicate
that some aesthetic judgments seem to be universal in that they demonstrably transcend sex, age, and culture. For example, Eysenck (e.g.,
1940, 1941a, 1941b) who has concentrated on elements in compositions
has found consistent preference across diverse populations for certain
(abstract geometric) patterns—notably good Gestalts (like symmetry);
and Child (1973) who has used whole representational works of art has
also found general agreements (when familiarity with representational
arts is taken into account). Whether common human neurological functions or common cultural experiences underpin such universalities, these
studies show wide agreement in certain hedonic judgments of aesthetic
affects (see, too, Francès, 1968).

Much of this line of inquiry has been motivated to answer the question,
What is liked? Paul Gauguin (1848–1903) probably best articulated the
artist's bewilderment about "the curious and mad public which demands
of the painter the greatest possible originality and yet only accepts him
when he calls to mind other painters." Now and again, psychologists have
believed themselves to have identified a "general factor" of aesthetic
appreciation in the public. However, Pickford (1972, p. 144), otherwise a
champion of experimental aesthetics, recounts the following telling and
humbling 1962 study. Five different groups of thirty observers, including
children, English, French, and Indian university students, and art students, rank ordered sixteen paintings from four sources, unaware of the
sources—Picasso, P. Reid (a young painter "of some recognition"), 10-
year-old retardates, and Congo (D. Morris's, 1962, chimpanzee). No
group ordered the pictures as intuitively predicted. Perhaps we can reach
an aesthetic of elements, but agreement or understanding in terms of a
general aesthetic will be more elusive.

Berlyne's new experimental aesthetics encompassed many psychological constructs and thereby made a start at a more generic scientific aesthetics. By the 1970s, however, experimental psychology proper had
turned away from these kinds of issues and toward cognition, and it
became involved with other questions in art. Cognitive psychology today
is pluralistic, and its extension to art has not had opportunity to develop a
unified direction nor any single champion of Berlyne's stature. Some clear
directions can be discerned, however. For example, cognitive psychology
has rechannelled what information-processing currents there were in experimental aesthetics toward new landfalls, such as problem solving, as
well as toward more exotic ones, such as problem finding. Needless to
say, with these developments the scientific psychology of art has reached
new and provocative levels of analysis.

Consider, for example, the following summary task analysis of viewing art: A representational picture conveys the artist's interpretation of a three-dimensional scene in two dimensions that the audience reads as three-dimensional but knows to be two-dimensional. This analysis has two key components: The first is the artist's "interpretation," and second is the audience's "reading." Historically, as we have seen, the scientific psychology of art concerned itself principally with the psychology of the perceiver, and, hence, aesthetics from below (not unreasonably) transmuted into psychologies of perception: The scientific psychology of art was narrowly construed as a perceptual task for the audience. In the main tradition of experimental aesthetics, from the psychophysical to the Gibsonian discussed earlier, picture perception is considered more or less direct (mimicking perception in everyday life), and perceivers need add little to the process beyond sensory and perceptual mechanisms and principles they already possess to derive meaning from pictures, much as they do from perceptual events in everyday life. The new view elevates this psychology of art to higher perceptual and cognitive considerations simultaneously, and though they may be new in their application to art proper the facts this approach entails are not at all esoteric in perception. Since Helmholtz, psychology has maintained that individuals construct (or cognitively re-construct) their perceptions. In this view, information arriving at the senses is conceived to be inherently ambiguous or unorganized or uninformed and must be worked on to be correctly interpreted by the observer. Perception is based on, filtered through, and constructed by experiences. A modern and influential exponent of the constructivist view in the psychology of art is Gombrich (1960). For Gombrich, reading a picture is not a sensory or purely perceptual process, but rather calls into play the viewer's cognitive conventions, knowledge, and expectations.

If we accept this point of view, we are forced to re-admit a series of nontrivial psychological considerations to our understanding of art. The importance of the *image* and, behind the image, the *concept* are exemplary here. Artists in representational as well as nonrepresentational arts are in the business of rendering their private images public. When Michelangelo undertook to portray God on the Sistine Chapel ceiling he also undertook to interpret and to render private images publicly. Imagery has always played dual essential roles in art (e.g., Mandelbrojt, 1970). One is straightforwardly iconographic: what is selected for depiction and what is conveyed (e.g., Mâle, 1913/1958; Panofsky, 1939/1962). The other is more psychological: the artist's conception of how a thing shall be rendered and how it is meant to be read. The second connotation of imagery in art, the one we are concerned with here, has classical roots. The English portrait painter and first president of the Royal Academy Sir Joshua Reynolds (1723–1792) reinvoked in this connection in his presidential *Discourses* Proclus's words about Phidias, the favorite artist of antiquity. Phidias, it was believed, ascended to heaven to furnish his mind with the perfect idea of beauty:

> He who takes for his model such forms as nature produces, and confines himself to an exact imitation of them, will never attain to what is perfectly beautiful. For the works of nature are full of disproportion, and fall very short of the true standard of beauty. So that Phidias, when he formed his Jupiter, did not copy any object ever presented to his sight; but contemplated only that image which he had conceived in his mind from Homer's description [1768/1797/1958, pp. 274–275].

This conception reflects Aristotelian ideals of rendering, and it maintained prominence in artistic practice through the Renaissance. Donatello (1386–1466), the first sculptor of the Renaissance, is reputed to have described his art thus:

> Sculpture is an art which, by removing all that is superfluous from the material under treatment, reduces it to that form designed in the artist's mind.

And, for the second expanded 1568 edition of the *Lives*, Vasari added to his introductory chapter on painting a passage that re-emphasized the relevance of images in drawing:

> proceeding from the intellect [drawing] extracts from many things a universal judgment, like a form or idea of all the things in nature. . . . From this knowledge there proceeds a certain idea or judgment, which is formed in the mind, and this idea to which expression is given by the hands is called drawing. It can therefore be concluded, that this drawing is simply a visible expression and manifestation of the idea which exists in our mind, and which others have formed in their mind and created in their imagination [quoted by Blunt, 1940, p. 100].

The selfsame approach has guided artists since the Renaissance; indeed, Romanticism took imagination as the point of departure for artistic creation. But, scientific study since tells us that images so relied upon for rendering may be influenced by expectation and are oftentimes misled . . . sometimes in curious directions (Figure 9).

The image is central to artistic perception and creation. But without a conception of the image in the first place, there is no art work. Rewriting and updating opinions of the painter de Kooning, the art theoretician and critic Wollheim (1968) observed that "nothing is positive about art except that it is a concept [p. i]." Like the humanistic tradition, the scientific tradition in the psychology of art has therefore concerned itself with determinants and expressions of conceptual development in artistic

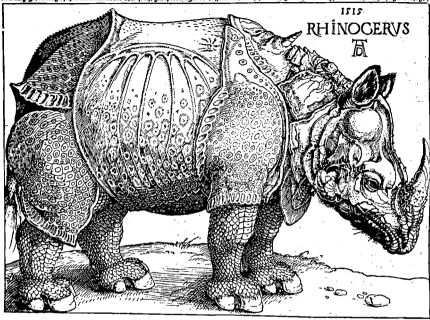

FIG. 9. *Rhinoceros* (1515) by Albrecht Dürer. This woodcut is the rendering of a mental image, and not "from the life," since it was based on second-hand reports about overlapping plates of armor and was patently embellished by Dürer's imagination; Dürer had never personally seen such a beast. (Public Library, New York City)

creativity—today's catch words are "problem solving" and "problem finding." However, scientific psychology offers learning and cognitive alternatives to psychodynamic explanations for creative artistic activity. The learning theorist's view is that creative behaviors differentiate because divergent responses are reinforced. As interpreted by Skinner (1970, p. 64), for example, forces that operate on artistic expression are predictable and clear: "The artist puts paint on canvas and is or is not reinforced by the result. If he is reinforced, he goes on painting." This view of the creative process in art has not attracted large numbers of adherents.

Cognitive theorists have approached creativity in artistry from a variety of different perspectives. One has been to assess the relationships among psychometric intelligence, creativity, and artistic success. Among the most influential psychometric theoreticians of creativity is Guilford (1965) who has argued that creativity is a multicomponent construct consisting of fluency (the number of responses produced), flexibility (the variety of

FIG. 10. *Summer* (on the left) and *Winter* (on the right) of the Seasons cycle (1563) by Guiseppe Arcimboldo (1527–1593). The series plays on the phases of a man's life. (Kunsthistorisches Museum, Vienna)

responses), and originality (the novelty of responses). While intelligence or creativity (so defined) has *prima facie* validity, attempts to assess the relationship between divergent thinking which characterizes creativity and intelligence and later artistry have not met with notable success (see Getzels & Csikszentmihalyi, 1976). There can be no doubt, however, about some contribution of intelligence in artistic accomplishment.

The cognitive view of creative activity—seeking good problems and searching for better solutions (which artistry does) need not necessarily be related to conventional notions of intelligence or creativity (which artistry is not). Problem solving and problem finding commingle indistinguishably and inextricably in the arts for it is the essence the of appellations "aesthetic" and "artistic" to seek as well as to solve problems in immediately impressive ways. What is the right moment and spirit to capture? How does one know when a work is finished? How well does the completed art work match and convey the original conception? Aesthetic and artistic responses to these questions are diverse. We all recognize beauty in art works as an achievement, but Arcimboldo Arcimboldi's (1527–1593) *Seasons* is esteemed more for its conceit than for its artistic execution (Figure 10), and Pablo Picasso's (1881–1973) *Guernica* is hardly

FIG. 11.   *Guernica* (1937) by Pablo Ruiz y Picasso (1881–1973). An artistic statement of the first order that is hardly aesthetic in the traditional or conventional sense. (Prado, Madrid)

aesthetic by conventional standards but unquestionably constitutes a dramatic artistic statement (Figure 11).

Howard Gardner (1971, 1973) has been at the forefront of the cognitive movement in the psychology of art. He has reasoned that artists face a unique problem situation: Artists must not only find their own problems, they do not know beforehand what a solution will consist of, they do not know if or when they have actually achieved a solution, and their solutions for problems are not replicable in any traditional sense. Matisse's historical answer to this Zenoan paradox is simple: "The great painter is the one who finds a personal and enduring idiom in which to express his vision."

An empirical fashion in which this new view has been investigated has been to follow artistic creativity and accomplishment on-line, so to speak. Picasso is reported to have suggested one mode:

> It would be very interesting to preserve photographically, not the stages, but the metamorphoses of a picture. Possibly one might discover the path followed by the brain in materializing a dream. But there is one very odd thing—to notice that basically a picture doesn't change, that the first vision remains almost intact, in spite of appearances [quoted by Arnheim, 1962, p. 31].

Two years after he made this statement Picasso issued the *Guernica* (1937), and years later Arnheim (1962) traced the development of this mural through drafts and sketches of the piece for, by happy coincidence, Picasso had numbered and dated all his preliminary efforts. In Arnheim's view, Picasso's preparatory drawings tell us that the artist had a goal consistently in mind and that he moved on a definable trajectory toward that goal. When a painter changes his mind and alters the canvas in some way, eventually *pentimenti* ("repentent ghosts") will show through, revealing in an aging canvas old conceptions replaced by later choices. *Pentimenti* reappear in many of the works of the Old Masters, just as they do in Mondrian's unfinished *Victory Boogie Woogie* (1943–1944). It may be possible, therefore, to assess various artists' conceptions and reconceptions retrospectively. Certainly *cartoons, designos,* and other forms of sketches for major works are available to scrutiny and to study artistic creativity.[6] More recently, Perkins (1981) developed a fresh technique, asking individuals involved in creative processes to describe the process as their work unfolded. Perkins's assessments match Arnheim's conclusions reasonably closely: At least a major part of the creative process evolves in small, quick, logical, and comprehensible steps toward a fixed goal. The question not answered by any of these cognitive approaches is one that echoes Lashley (1951), *viz.* that in art, the hand knows something the mind does not.

Though abstract, this problem-oriented view jibes well with current vogue in cognitive psychology and in philosophy that art works are actually ways of knowing and understanding. Perhaps the perennial view of the artist as *avante garde* accurately characterizes a segment of society that is persistently at the frontier (or fringe). From the viewpoint of this new tradition, the original impetus for the scientific study of art, to assess the origins of pleasingness, is achieved anyway through the mastery and knowledge gained in artistic accomplishment or intellectual penetration; these developments also jibe with post-Modern, purely cerebral movements in art (see below).

The scientific tradition in the psychology of art has sustained critical attack from within and from without since its inception just a century ago, and its intellectual life has been imperiled many times. Not only have nonartistic systems that are intended to "explain" art always been suspect, but major intellectual traditions outside of art though presumably given over to art, like philosophy, have traditionally rejected any value to an aesthetics based on elemental analysis. Moreover, many an eminent psychologist has sided with the philosopher-humanist's skepticism. Having returned one February evening in 1914 from a soirée spent with an artist, Sigmund Freud wrote disapprovingly to Ernest Jones: "Meaning is but little to these men; all they care for is line, shape, agreement of

---

[6] For example, Raphael's final *cartoon* (Ambrosiana, Milan) for the fresco of *The School of Athens* (Vatican City, Rome) conspicuously omits the brooding Michelangelo who was at the time working nearby on the Sistine Chapel ceiling; neither does it include, however, the self-portrait Raphael was eventually to paint on the stanza wall.

contours." This was the year that Freud wrote his *Moses* essay in which he reiterated: "The subject-matter of works of art has a stronger attraction for me than their formal and technical qualities, though to the artist their value lies first and foremost in the latter [1914/1963, p. 80]." And, William James (1842–1910), who himself trained as a painter with the renowned Barbizon artist William Morris Hunt (1824–1879), had essentially nothing to say about "aesthetics" in his *Principles* of 1890; but, elsewhere he once wrote:

> It strikes me that no good will ever come to Art as such from the analytic study of Aesthetics—harm rather, if the abstraction could in any way be made the basis of practice. The difference between the first and second best things in art absolutely seem to escape verbal definition—it is a matter of a hair, a shade, an inner quiver of some kind—yet what miles away in points of persuasiveness. . . . Absolutely the same verbal formula applied to the supreme success and to the thing that just misses and yet the verbal formulas are all that your aesthetic will give [H. James, 1920, pp. 86–87].

Finally, even experimental aestheticians from Fechner to Berlyne have had to approach art with caution because of the difficulty in specifying the independent variable when whole works are involved; their typical strategy has been to isolate simpler forms in the laboratory in the hope of first indexing elemental aesthetics toward a fusion of complex art forms in the context of the real world. In view of some, a magnificent synthesis; in the view of others, a patchwork Shelleyan Frankenstein.

Despite such attacks, the experimental psychology of art continues to progress. Though it has gone through better and worse times during its century-long career, it is doubtlessly better off now than when it started—or, perhaps, at any time in between. Indeed, scientific psychological aesthetics now embraces and appraises all sorts of issues from psychophysics to perception to cognition to social cognition, bringing more and more subject matter relevant to the proper understanding of art into its purview.

DEVELOPMENTAL PSYCHOLOGY AND ART

Art must have its creator and its perceiver: Even if the interpretation of art objects could be accomplished wholly internally—through the analysis of common themes, shared styles, or evidence from documents—artist and audience both would still be necessary for art. Following this logic further inevitably points up the significance of *development* for art. Obviously, the art object has its tradition; but so too do artists and audiences mature, and as a consequence, iconography—the meaning attached to *objets d'art*—must have developmental dimensions.

How do artists and audiences mature, and *why* do art and artists change? In this section, I turn to consider some of the principal psychological theories and data on artistic and aesthetic development that address these two questions. Much of the discussion focuses on children and art.[7] In the next section, I take up the separate question of whether the history of Western art itself can perhaps be interpreted as having followed any regular pattern of "psychological" development. Both the history of Western art and the ontogeny of artists provoke similar questions about the mechanisms and motives of artistic change.

Ever since children first put pen to paper, psychologists peering over

---

[7]The roles children have played in fine art are provocative and diverse. Here are some samples. In *The Commentaries*, one of the earliest known autobiographies of an artist, the painter Lorenzo Ghiberti (1378–1455) tells the following story about Cimabue (ca. 1240–1302?), his pupil Giotto (1266/7–1337), and the history of modern painting:

> The art of painting began to arise in Etruria in a village called Vespignano, near the city of Florence. There was born a boy of wonderful talent, who was drawing a sheep from life [when] the painter Cimabue, passing by on the road to Bologna, saw the lad seated on the ground, drawing on a slab of rock. Struck with great admiration for the boy, who, though so young, did so well, and perceiving his skill came from nature, Cimabue asked him what he was named. The lad answered, "I am called by the name Giotto. . . ." Cimbue, who had a distinguished appearance, went with Giotto to his father. He asked the father, who was very poor, for the boy. He gave the lad to Cimabue, who took him with him. Giotto was a disciple of Cimabue, who held to the Greek manner [of painting] and had acquired very great fame in Etruria for this style. Giotto made himself great in the art of painting [n.d./1912/1957, p. 153].

The story is significant since Cimabue and Giotto have been put at the beginning of modern art for introducing imagination and naturalism into stale Byzantine formulae. This part of the child and childhood in artistic originality has been echoed time and again by art historian and artist alike. Listen to John Ruskin (1819–1900), the first professor of art in England, from *Modern Painters:*

> It is a fact more universally acknowledged than enforced or acted upon, that all great painters, of whatever school, have been great only in their rendering of what they had seen and felt from early childhood, and that the greatest among them have been the most frank in acknowledging this [1873/1966, p. 120],

or to Henri Matisse (1869–1954) who said:

> the artist . . . [has] to look at life as he did when he was a child and, if he loses that faculty, he cannot express himself in an original . . . way [Ziegfeld, 1953, p. 21],

or to Picasso, who was of course well-known to have held a similar view:

> Once I drew like Raphael, but it has taken me a whole lifetime to learn to draw like children [de Meredieu, 1974, p. 13].

Children have also played a critical role in discovering art: In 1940, it was four young boys from Montignac in Périgord who actually found the galleries in Lascaux, just as half a century earlier, in 1879, it was the young daughter of Don Marcelino S. de Sautuola, the Spanish archaeologist, who first noticed painted bulls on the vaulted ceiling at Altamira.

their shoulders have used children's drawings to enter children's minds. The list of interested investigators is impressive: from Baldwin, Binet, Burt, and Claparède to Shinn, Stern, Sully, and Thorndike. A catalogue that includes what child psychologists have been interested in is similarly telling: Gesell used children's drawings to trace the course of maturation; Arnheim to relate the development of visual perception in children to visual thinking; Piaget to estimate the stage of children's cognitive progress; Goodenough and Harris to assay children's intelligence; Freeman to evaluate information processing capacities in children; Lowenfeld to assess levels of emotional development in children; and Bettelheim to track one child's recovery during psychotherapy. As this accounting suggests, child art has been approached from a myriad of conceivable angles: There is, however, no formal study of child art apart from the child.

There are two main orientations to child art and child artists, therefore. One is concerned with the development of artistic expression in children, and the other is concerned with the growth of perception and cognition interlocking with art. Is child art "art," or an inchoate supplement to perception, thought, and emotion? Do children draw what they see, what they know, or what they feel?

The Child as Artist

Art is natural play in young children. This fact is so manifest and impressive to adults that we marvel at the consistency with which art first arises in childhood and wonder why such a spontaneous and joyful act virtually disappears as children grow up. The first question has been easier to tackle than the second.

Normal development. It is the everyday work of developmental psychologists to trace growth and to chart stability and change of function. One of the more delightful (but no less challenging) tasks which developmental psychologists take up must be analysis of children's art since their subjects are so willing (Goodnow, 1977). Two punctilious observational studies of how drawing develops in children are Kellogg (1969) and Golomb (1973, 1981). A summary of the main developmental trends these astute observers discovered is as follows. Given the opportunity, even very young children (1–2-year-olds) spontaneously scribble, adopting from the very beginning an attitude which is at once active and carefree (as in their flagrant lack of regard for colors, which are picked up and put aside arbitrarily) but also confined (as in their usual careful regard for the boundaries of the page). In cataloguing young children's scribbles, Kellogg defined the appearance in virtually all children of 20 separate elements; more conservatively, Golomb later differentiated two simpler

FIG. 12. A variety of children's drawings of the human figure. (From N. H. Freeman, 1980. Copyright Academic Press. Reprinted by permission.)

classes, straightedged parallels and loops, circles, and whorls. Next, rudimentary design considerations and greater control emerge in children's methods (as when, for example, 2–3-year-olds join up individual scribbles). Though at this stage children seem to give little or no thought to representation they nonetheless begin to give evidence that they are on an inevitable trajectory toward it. The first signs appear to be "wishful" (3–4-year-olds typically label their hopelessly unrealistic depictions as if thereby to endow them with meaning: "This is mummy!"). Later, children's representations begin to follow convention and are more directly "readable" by the impartial observer (4–8-year-olds' drawings consciously represent, adopting accepted conventions of spatial organization, color, etc.). Even if they achieve representation in adolescence, for better or worse, the vast majority of normal children, it seems, rather abruptly arrest in artistic development.

The period of representation has captured the attention of most psychological investigators, particularly because of the very queer images young children initially produce. Contemplating Figure 12, Freeman has asked

"What should we conclude: that some of the children are confused, or that some intend deliberately to produce monstrosities, or that the task is a very difficult one for which many strategies are possible, not all of which will pay off? [1980, p. 2]" Freeman's musings become the commonly asked competence-performance question (see Johnson-Laird, in this volume): That is, what do children know *versus* what do children do? Minimally, correct representation implies fine eye-hand coordination, accurate perception, cognitive understanding, and sophisticated decision-making and planning. Perhaps young children simply lack the skill to represent properly; perhaps they see the world in a unique way; perhaps their mental representations of things and relationships in the world are deficient; perhaps their strategies of representing three-dimensionality two-dimensionally are wanting; or, perhaps they choose to represent in their own ways, and children's drawings are "deficient" only by adult standards and conventions.

Different views from this entire panoply of possibilities have been proposed and defended by developmentalists. For example, Piaget (1961/1969), the epistemological and cognitive developmental theorist, attributed children's representations to their "childish beliefs." If asked to draw the top of the liquid in a container which is tilted at a 45° angle, young children tend not to represent the liquid by a line parallel to the true horizontal, but instead draw the line representing the liquid as parallel to the top of its container. Of course, no child could ever have seen liquid in a container that appeared so. This drawing therefore cannot reflect the child's own worldly experience, Piaget argued, but must represent the child's understanding of what he sees. Conjure a prototypical juvenile drawing of a house with the chimney top drawn parallel to its angled roof rather than to the ground. In a task designed to assess Piaget's conclusions more closely, Golomb (1973) separated competence from performance, asking children of different ages to draw a person themselves, to assemble a person out of pieces they were given, to draw a person as the experimenter instructed them, to tell the experimenter how to draw a person, to copy a drawing of a person, and to choose among several examples the best representation of a person. In general, children's mental competence far outstrips their performance: The representations children directed and selected were more detailed and realistic than those they drew. Golomb's results suggest that the visual statements children opt to draw are not based on "childish beliefs" but may, rather, reflect developing stages of fine eye-hand coordination (Connolly & Bruner, 1974). Perhaps, in some cases children's creations are as intentionally bold as we imagine.

The advent of representational realism in children has been traced elegantly by close analysis of the recognition of perspective in their drawings. Willats (1977) found that the development of perspective follows six

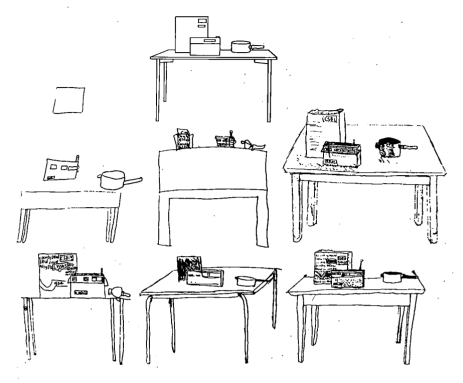

FIG. 13.   Children between about 5 and 17 years of age were asked to draw an arrangment situated in front of them: a table and the objects on top of it (top). The youngest children (5–8 years) draw essentially two-dimensional representations (left column); older children (9–14 years) add depth by depicting the table's surface (middle column); and the oldest children (15–17 years) draw in more and more accurate perspective (right column). (After J. Willats, 1977. Copyright Plenum Publishing Corporation. Reprinted by permission.)

identifiable stages in children between approximately 5 and 17 years of age. He sat children in front of a table and asked them to draw it and the objects situated on it. Figure 13 shows the developmental progression that obtained. Children at first fail to give evidence that they possess any system of projection: They draw a rectangular table top and represent objects on it as above it, or, moving on to an orthographic system of projection, they draw the table top on the horizontal and put objects on the surface. Children next graduate in two stages to projections that admit the table's surface, drawing the table top as rectangular with parallel sides and then drawing the top as a parallelogram. Finally, children represent true perspective, at first incorrectly, but eventually as geometrically accurate. In Willats's view, this progression reflects the child's increasing competency at problem solving.

Whether the route to representation in all children is marked by so clearly definable "stages" is uncertain. It is natural, however, to discern in the competences seen at one time the competences of previous efforts, as though later, advanced stages in drawing integrate over earlier, less accomplished ones. At minimum, we can safely agree with the psychologist–art historians Schaefer-Simmern (1948) and Arnheim (1974) that, like many other features of ontogenesis (e.g., Werner, 1957), the development of drawing by children proceeds from simple global forms to complex differentiated ones.

Some special populations of children. The "stages" through which normal children naturally pass in the development of drawing seem not to be fundamentally perturbed amongst most special populations, whether they are advanced or delayed. Evidence suggests that deaf and retarded children, for example, negotiate the same stages, only more slowly, and that gifted children (those later recognized as artists) seem also to proceed through the same stages, only more quickly (Gardner, 1980; Selfe, 1983).

All children draw, but are artists born or made? Michelangelo was definitively a prodigy (Figure 14), and, though the story may be apocryphal that Picasso's father who was himself a painter laid down his brushes forever when he saw his 14-year-old son work at the canvas, Picasso, who was admitted to the prestigious Royal Academy at Barcelona at 15, was demonstrably a prodigy as well. While youthful genius seems to emerge on a rather regular basis in music and in mathematics, prodigy in the fine arts is rather rare. Views on whether artists are born or made, however, mimic "nature-nurture" controversies in developmental psychology and themselves have classical roots. Two central figures of the Renaissance, who bothered to record their views, took opposing positions. On the one hand, Vasari propounded a kind of nativist doctrine in the *Lives,* conceding that beauty and facility derive from a natural gift which cannot be acquired by pains or by tutorial: "Very great is the obligation that is owed to Heaven and to Nature by those who bring their works to birth without effort and with a certain grace which others cannot give to their creations either by study or by imitation [quoted by Blunt, 1940, p. 96]." On the other hand, Leonardo, Vasari's contemporary art theoretician and master, asserted an empiricist view, ruminating in his *Notebooks* that youthful painters must necessarily study and copy works of the masters as requisite early training to achievement. Sixteen centuries earlier, however, in Chapter I of the first of *The Ten Books on Architecture,* devoted aptly to "The Education of the Architect," Vitruvius took the middle road:

[The architect] ought, therefore, to be both naturally gifted and amenable to instruction. Neither natural ability without instruction nor instruction without natural ability can make the perfect artist [1st Century B.C./1914, p. 5].

FIG. 14. *Michelangelo as a Child* by Zocchi. (Galleria Palatina, Florence)

Leonardo, Vasari, and their successors also advocated that young artists begin by imitating—a sentiment which psychologists have lately recognized (e.g., Gardner, 1980)—but also abjure imitation in maturity in order to cultivate their own natural talents and proclivities.

Gardner (1980) has observed that prodigies like Picasso, about whose particular childhood production we possess definite information, seem to pass through the same stages as do normal and other artistic though less talented children, but, to be sure, they do so more rapidly and with greater profundity and sensitivity than usually encountered. In brief, the study of prodigy may prove worthwhile on several counts: to inform an understanding of the origins of artistic ability (Paine, 1982), to document the nature of early expressions of creativity (Barron, 1972), and, as well, to unravel the conundrum of dismaying but blatant sex differences in the realm of artistic expression[8] (Petersen & Wilson, 1976).

Is this regularity in development sufficient to imply that axioms govern the growth of artistic representation? Not necessarily. One counterexample is the case of an extraordinarily gifted autistic girl, Nadia; Selfe (1977a) has documented the sophisticated productions of this odd prodigy, who either skipped immature stages or passed through them at an extremely rapid rate. Compare the representations of a man on horseback by a typical 6½-year-old and by Nadia at approximately the same age (Figure 15).[9]

Further, does such regularity imply that experience cannot influence children's artistic development? How does the child from a pictureless culture represent the world? Fortes (1940) gave unschooled Tallensi children (and adults) their first pencil. In the beginning, they scribbled à la Kellogg, but the Tallensi also drew figures more advanced than Kellogg's children's first drawings. Tallensi school children do much better, of course (Figure 16). Clearly experience matters. We ought to remember, however, that the many apprentices who worked in Ghirlandaio's fresco atelier and in Bertoldo's sculpture garden alongside Michelangelo actively contributed to the glory of Medici Florence while still preteens.

The regularity of children's passage through stages of composition

---

[8] Petersen and Wilson (1976) have documented the lives of women artists. Many, they observe, were daughters of artists. Notable Renaissance examples include Antonia Uccello, daughter of Paolo (1396/7–1475), Marietta Tintoretto, daughter of Jacopo (1518–1594), and Artemesia Gentileschi, daughter of Orazio (1563–1639); a more modern example is Jane Stuart, daughter of Gilbert (1755–1828). The stories about each fascinate: Uccello disappeared; Tintoretto was only permitted to work on the backgrounds of her father's huge canvases; Gentileschi was raped by her father's studio collaborator Tasso and was later preoccupied with the Judith and Holofernes theme; and Stuart supported her family after her father's death by copying his *Athenaeum Head* of George Washington.

[9] Nadia's artistic abilities declined precipitously soon after she developed language.

FIG. 15. *Man on a Horse* drawn by a typical 6½-year-old child (on the left) and *Man on a Horse* drawn by Nadia, an autistic 6-year-old (on the right). (After L. Selfe, 1977b. Copyright Plenum Publishing Corporation. Reprinted by permission.)

makes deviant representations reasonably good diagnostic indexes of emotional disorders or retardation (e.g., Di Leo, 1970, 1973). Moreover, children seem to express themselves more freely and openly in drawing than in conversation (Levick, 1983). Thus, how children in crisis represent themselves can be illuminating: In the celebrated case of Joey, the "mechanical boy," Bettelheim (1959) used self-portraits to assess the mental status and to track the recovery of this autistic child.

The Child in the Audience

The participation of children in art depends on entwined cognitive and emotional capacities to understand and to appreciate, and they in turn await the development of perception, cognition, and social cognition. Any opinion that the youngest child understands and appreciates art upon inspection must be suspect. Although experimental studies suggest that

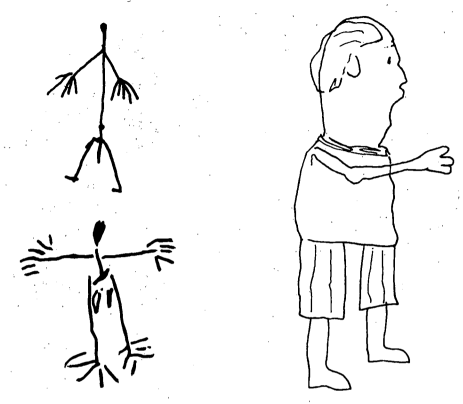

FIG. 16.   Drawings of men by African Tallensi whose culture is pictureless. Drawings by Tallensi children who have never drawn before (on the left) and a drawing by a Tallensi schoolboy (on the right). (After Fortes, 1940.)

many rudimentary components to perceiving art—like reading two-dimensional representations as equivalent to three-dimensional—are present even in very young children (Bornstein, 1984a), cognitive and emotional components of audience participation (e.g., "the willing suspension of disbelief," grasp of composition, knowledge of subject matter, and empathy with the expressive or emotive aspects of art works) require time to develop or need to be learned. There is considerable research related to the development of cognitive requisites of artistic understanding because such research addresses general issues of cognitive development as much as they do artistic development; there is substantially less research related to issues of appreciation, however. It seems clear that in most but not all situations cognitive understanding presupposes aesthetic appreciation.

During late childhood and early adolescence, the basis of children's aesthetic judgments seems to shift in three stages, first from a focus on the

content of depictions or on formal composition, next to an emphasis on
realism, and ultimately to evaluation relative to artistic intention or personal preference (Machotka, 1966). These steps in the growth of evaluative orientation parallel but lag developments in cognition. Aesthetic
preferences for certain elements of composition and style appear to be
reasonably uniform across the lifespan and across cultures, and there is
considerable experimental evidence that universals of judgment in this
realm probably relate to universal characteristics of the human sensory
systems (as, for example, of color preference or the perception of symmetry; see Bornstein, 1975, 1984b).

   Children's sensitivities to composition, mood, and style in fine art implicate their perceptual and cognitive capacities, and these sensitivities
have been studied using methods from contemporary cognitive psychology. Much of the extant research in these realms we owe to Howard
Gardner's original and programmatic studies. Three experiments will illustrate progress in this area. In one study, Gardner and Gardner (1973)
investigated development of sensitivity to composition in children from 5
to 19 years of age. They presented children with four pictures at a time,
organized experimentally so that pairs of pictures could be matched on
subject matter or on composition of elements, and the investigators asked
the children simply to sort the pictures into pairs. Younger children
tended to classify paintings by subject matter, older children by composition. In a second study, Carothers and Gardner (1979) investigated development of the child's sensitivity to mood in pictures. They asked
children 7 and 10 years of age to complete pictures that depicted a happy
person or a sad person by adding to the picture an upright and blooming
tree or a drooping and wilted tree. Younger children did not match on
expression; older children did so consistently. In a third set of studies,
Gardner (1970, 1972) investigated children's sensitivity to style. In one
experiment, he showed children 6 to 14 years of age six pictures, including two original images of the same content by the same artist, and four
test comparisons, one by the same artist but of different content, one of
the same content but by a different artist, and two of different contents by
different artists. Children were asked to pick among the test comparisons
the picture by the painter of the two original images. Even the oldest
children persisted in selecting by color or by content rather than by style.
Other studies have shown that children are not altogether blind to style,
and although more manifest properties of pictures dominate youthful sensitivities, children may be trained to recognize style (see, too, Child, 1962,
1965). As with any psychological experiments, aspects of methods (questions asked, materials used, paradigms adopted) can affect the results.
Nevertheless, development of artistic appreciation seems to proceed from
concentration on formal properties or representational content to compo-

sition to mood and eventually to style. Cognitive competences in children seem to set lower limits on aesthetic appreciation, whereas methodological factors seem to affect timing rather than order in development.

Children constitute a curious audience. As Gardner (1973, p. 152) notes:

> When children attending the theatre cover their eyes until the hero has been saved, they reveal that they have not yet achieved the status of an informed audience member. . . . Aesthetic maturity involves an increase of distance between the perceiver and the aesthetic object, so that the perceiver can discriminate between "real" and "pretend" and appreciate the work as the product of another individual working in a symbolic medium.

So children need aesthetic education, yet exactly how, when, and with what should children be introduced to art? Some pedagogues have advocated school curricula built around art (Read, n.d.). Some museums (like the Frick Collection in New York) do not admit children, while others (like the Pompidou Center in Paris) go out of their way to entice them.

Summary and Interlude

Young children will draw spontaneously and unceasingly it seems, stopping only if they are deprived of visual feedback. Startlingly, only very few adults draw. Play that does not come to artistry is widely surrendered—and often scorned—in favor of passive modes of aesthetic participation.

For more than a century, psychologists have studied drawing systems and devices, representations and expressions, meanings and symbols in the genesis of children's art forms. Indeed, developmental psychology's main connection to art has been that art opens a major avenue to perceiving, thinking, and feeling in children. Time and again, however, children at their coloring books have sent developmental psychologists to the drawing board, for developmental studies suggest that children traverse more or less definable stages in their production and perception of art works, and that these changing phases of interaction with the world of art reflect children's changing cognitive status and service their changing needs. Independent of quibbles about the grammar of scribbles or the universality of stage theories underpinning growth toward representation, developmentalists are convinced, first, that all children spontaneously pick up crayons to make their mark and, second, that virtually all children eventually set those same crayons down. Simply put, there seem to be regular stages of growth toward artistry, and all children who will draw seem to traverse those same stages. Some do so more slowly and hesitatingly; some more quickly and with greater self-assurance.

Though it has traced the evolution of art-play reasonably successfully, developmental psychology is stymied about the normal and nearly ubiquitous devolution of artistic creativity. Children seem all too ready to give up the artist in them to join the audience. Does artistic imagination dwindle of its own accord, do we get lazy, or do verbal and written modes of expression simply supersede? Gardner (1973) has reasoned through the following terms of a paradox. First, to be an artist does not require lengthy or elaborate cognitive development—indeed, the advent of formal operations may actually be inimical to artistic development since abstraction, task conformity, systematicity, and comprehensiveness move the child away from original primitive expressions and away from his native media. Second, the roles of audience and especially discriminating, evaluative critic and connoisseur are only sustained through formal operations. The facts that children, "primitives," retardates, and even chimpanzees produce art and that most art is accessible to the population at large seem to confirm Gardner's two intuitions. Though I think relevant, these observations do not explain the underdevelopment of artistry in adults, or how or why some children escape developmental arrest and the descent from creativity; they only pique our interest further. It is probable, however, unfortunate, that the child's everyday dialectic with society sucks dry natural creativity, a further discontent of civilization. Personality theorists have lamented that:

> By the time the children are nine or ten years of age they have, as a rule, been so thoroughly infused with the need for reproducing exactly what they see that their own natural modes of self-expression have been blocked off and the earlier impulse to paint and express themselves from within have very largely been stifled [Alschuler & Hattwick, 1969, p. 9].

Perhaps, we shall have to turn to historiography and the insights of dynamic or individual psychologies to explain why only such a rare number of individuals persevere and attain true artistry. In this connection, the artistic achievements of old age merit attention (e.g., Münsterberg, 1982).

The development of art and aesthetics in children provokes us to consider several curious psychological parallels to the history of art. Are the nonrepresentational arts of children, modern artists, and so-called "primitives" of a kind? For example, children, like ancient Egyptians, draw composite multiple perspectives of a single object or person. Are these depictions driven by common misunderstandings of the single point of view, by a common grammar of representation, or by a common desire to show each part of a person or object as it appears most characteristically?

Why is true perspective not a part of children's art until they reach 9 or 10 years of age, and why was it not a part of Western art until the Renaissance? How are the motives for children to develop through artistic stages different from those that drive mature artists to change styles? If children of both sexes equally delight in art play, why have most artists been male? Has the history of art itself evolved through identifiable "developmental stages"? Is aesthetic ephemeral fashion, or are there universals of aesthetic appreciation?

PSYCHOLOGICAL HISTORIES OF ART

A Diachronic Developmental Psychology of Art?

Art excites pleasure of the senses and inflames the imagination. But, art is, as we have seen, also an attempt to represent one's perceptual or conceptual world for others to share. The urge in humans to represent has persisted from etching in the bedrock of the Lascaux caves to drawing on the sidewalk of Sixth Avenue in New York City. Can we say that in this time art itself has *developed?* As child psychologists are prone to see growth, or even stages, in ontogenesis, many art historians have likewise perceived unfolding patterns in local styles as well as in the historical sweep of man's prodigious invention in the arts. For some scholars, therefore, discerning diachronicity in the history of art is as compelling as is meaning in Mondrian or plan in Pollock; it is fair to say, however, that for others there is nothing there. The case for a progressive history of art is difficult to prove, partly because the origins and purposes of such development are so obscure, diverse, and complex. Nevertheless, broad historical phases in the history of representation can be divined.

Over twenty-four centuries ago Egyptian rock carvers developed pictorial conventions that mixed perspectives (not unlike the manner of young children described earlier). They drew heads and feet in profile, but torsos in a fronto-parallel plane, for example. Clearly these artists (like children) were not depicting what they saw, but instead appear to have preferred to project *mental representations* of characteristic features of the world: heads in side view, bodies in full view. Gothic art was spiritually similar, informed by and concerned with *mysticism* and *symbolism* rather than exactness in representation. The Renaissance moved away from mental projection to adopt *scientific canons of nature*. The systematic application of laws of perspective by scientist-artists of the time enhanced coherence of aspect and the fidelity of two-dimensional representation. Although Mannerism, Baroque, and other post-Renaissance movements played with Renaissance "laws," none really broke with this new tradition until Impressionism in the nineteenth century. The French school rejected academic orientations that embodied fixed projections of reality on the sensory apparatus and opted for an art whose goals were to grasp and to reflect *experience*. The development of Impressionism and Neo-Impressionism also paralleled advances in science (e.g., Jameson & Hurvich, 1975; Richardson, 1971; Vitz, 1979; Waddington, 1970); for example, a knowledge of how the visual system integrates separate sensations over space permitted Impressionists and their successors, Pointillists and Divisionists, to infuse the otherwise frozen canvas with spirit sufficient to endow movement and action. This focus on the eye and on perception was followed in the twentieth century by proliferating movements concerned with the inner eye, with imagination, and with symbolism, conveying "aesthetic" backward, beyond the Egyptians, to value the *idea* in an art work for itself. Cubism replaced visual effects with conceptions; Surrealism concentrated on true processes of thought; Conceptual Art dispensed with the object altogether. Tom Wolfe (1976, pp. 108–109) has summarized the post-Modern demise of representation, concluding his book, *The Painted Word*, with these swirling sentiments:

And there, at last, it was! No more realism, no more representational objects, no more lines, colors, forms, and contours, no more pigments, no more brush strokes, no more evocations, no more frames, walls, galleries, museums, . . . no more audience required, just a "receiver" that may or may not be a person or may or may not be there at all, no more ego projected, just "the artist," in the third person, who may be anyone or no one at all, for nothing is demanded of him, nothing at all, not even existence, for that got lost in the subjunctive mode—and in that moment of absolutely dispassionate abdication, of insouciant withering away, Art made its final flight, climbed higher and higher in an ever-decreasing tighter-turning spiral until, with one last erg of freedom, one last dendritic synapse, it disappeared up its own fundamental aperture . . . and came out the other side as Art Theory!

From this history-of-art-in-a-paragraph emerge gross outlines of a kind of progressive-regressive evolution, and there is at least an element of truth even to this simplistic caricature. Movements in art seem always to reflect modes of interpretation, and artistic and audience interpretations now are not what they were five or twenty-five centuries ago. Further, though art seems initially to have moved toward and later away from depicting realism, it has at the same time moved consistently toward engaging its audience more actively and aggressively. The Egyptian artist appears to us to have been careless of the viewer's perspective or understanding; the Medieval artist appears to have presumed viewer knowledge; the Renaissance artist appears to have fixed the viewer stationary and passive; the Impressionist artist seems to have desired to draw the viewer into an experience; and, the Modern artist seems to require the viewer actively to figure out, fill in, correct, or even imagine the art work altogether. The aesthetic effects of audience participation in art are yet largely unexplored; however, we do know that "people ran like madmen to this new and more lifelike beauty [of the Renaissance], for it seemed to them quite certain that nothing better could ever be done [Vasari, 1550/ 1912/1958, p. 28]," while three centuries later the Salons of Paris greeted each new development in art with a new derisive term—"Impressionism," "Cubism," "Fauvism"—and a century after that the most historically apt characterization of modern art's popular reception is still *The Shock of the New* (Hughes, 1980).

These developments in the history of art constitute more than slight modifications of style; rather, they define diacritical shifts of conceptual orientation. But this history is descriptive, and developmental psychology—whatever the particular domain—must also be concerned with explanation. Traditional answers to the question why style changes in art history (or in the histories of individual artists) have adopted a "nature-nurture" flavor reminiscent of that typical of developmental psychology's approach to its own perennial questions. Consider the views of some prominent art historians. The social historian Hauser (1959) and psychologically-minded historian Gombrich (1960) have argued that cultural conventions condition artistic conventions of each period and change between periods. It is Gombrich's position, for example, that artists and audiences always see and interpret the world in terms of contemporary knowledge. Movements that define the history of art, on this account, consist of successive stages of interpretation reflecting the growth of knowledge—hence the close association of changes in art with advances in science. The painter Georges Seurat (1859–1891), on the other hand, took a somewhat narrower, and dimmer, social view: "The more we are, the less originality we will have, and the day when everyone makes use of our technique, it will have no value and people will start looking for something new."

Against these "external" theories, the art historian Wölfflin (1915/n.d.) and the artist and art critic Gablik (1976) have proposed "internal" theories. Wölfflin, in a Hegelian tradition, hypothesized that development transpires across art historical periods in continuous cyclic reactions among several dimensions of representation, one against the other.

In a challenging treatise of a related sort, Gablik proposed a rather novel developmental account of the history of art based on psychological and structuralist principles. She argued that the history of art betrays an intrinsic development of unfolding rational psychological processes that have moved, not teleologically toward a fixed and specific goal, but nonetheless ineluctably toward higher, more differentiated and conceptual forms of organization. In specific, Gablik closely followed the genetic epistemology of Piaget hypothesizing that Western art progressed over three distinct periods—Ancient and Medieval, Renaissance, and The Modern—from less to more complex logical structures and coherent relationships, from less to more perspective in representation and pure mentation, and from less to more infusion of scientific rationalism. Gablik's thesis demurs on any notion of an aesthetic hierarchy among these periods though, importantly, it emphasizes mental progress in art. In her view, ancient and medieval painters, like Piaget's preoperational children, could only represent scenes as static and subjectively organized; for example, distance between objects in these periods is depicted by simple proximity between them in a two-dimensional plane. Quattrocento and cinquecento painters, like concrete operational children, supplanted planometric with recessional Euclidian perspective and the coordinate organization of spatial representation, but were still tied to a single static point of view. The moderns, like formal operational children, are mentally independent, dynamic, and logical—no longer restrained by static unitary representation or, for that matter, by representation at all. Though such bold theorizing is, of course, open to questions of irregularities in the historical record or in individual systems, of the selectivity of examples, and, at base, of implicit evaluation, Gablik's application of genetic epistemology to art history is appealing, provocative, and engrossing.

I have described grand movements on the cultural plane. Do they translate in any way to the level of the individual? After all, cultures are constituted of individuals, movements of individual artists. Put succinctly, the developmental argument has been advanced on one side that culture influences artists; the older, and more romantic, argument is, of course, that artists influence culture. If the history of art can be viewed developmentally, what of the history of artists? The mechanism of developmental change is crucial in any scheme of ontogenesis, but it has also proved to be one of the most elusive and difficult issues of developmental psychology (e.g., Kuhn, 1984). One of the commonplace observations about artists is change; perhaps more than any other, Picasso's development prototypifies artistic trajectory over successive, separate, identifiable periods. Why and how do artists change? Diverse psychological theories posit different motivations for individual change: maturation, imitation, contingent reinforcement, adaptation, or disequilibrium. Let us consider each, even if we may not provide a definitive answer to the question.

Though early drawing is natural and talent is distributed in the population at large, it is doubtful that mature artistry is simply a product of unfolding biology; certainly, maturation per se could not account for particular alterations in style (Picasso's Blue to Rose Periods) that occur in

maturity, change in artistry is not universal, etc. Nor could imitation
account for change, since the invention of new styles (Picasso's Cubism)
by definition could not be imitated. If creativity generally were rewarded
in an artist, that artist might be prone to change; though the direction of
change would depend on mutation. If a particular artistic practice brought
rewards, as each of Picasso's did, reinforcement theory would dictate a
lower probability of change. This is not necessarily the outcome. Adaptation or habituation reflects exposure and boredom and hence is likely to
motivate change in artists—particularly in artists not being reinforced for
their current style or those practicing one style for a long time. To continue the example at hand, neither condition was true in Picasso's case;
moreover, adaptation does not adequately account for why stylistic revolutions adopt particular directions. Disequilibrium theory posits motivation born of dissatisfaction with limitations of current cognitive strategies
(based on feedback from the exercise of those strategies) and emphasizes
the construction of new more adequate (and elaborate) strategies marked
by higher levels of equilibrium between organism and environment. If
disequilibrium motivates change, why did Renaissance artists not progress: Was Leonardo not a mature, inventive, creative, or formal operational thinker? While these major candidate explanations compete, none
accounts satisfactorily for ontogenetic development in art. To explain
change and lack of it, art, it would appear, must borrow again from the
developmental perspective and move on to a theory of transaction—the
individual interacting with the environment over time. It would not be
inappropriate for a future psychology of art to begin with studies of Giotto
(1266/7–1337) and of Édouard Manet (1832–1883) who at separate inter-
sections of tradition and personal development played pivotal roles in the
psychological development of art.

A Transcendental Aesthetics?

Change typifies the arts and more than most qualities characterizes the
history of the fine arts. Each generation seems to project its own ways of
representing and its own aesthetic. Amidst this constant flux, are there
qualities, styles, or elements that maintain aesthetic value? Aesthetics is,
as we have learned, definitionally concerned with beauty and with the
affordance of pleasure to the senses. Are standards of beauty wholly
conditioned culturally and hence doomed to idiosyncrasy, or can we identify an aesthetic that is "transcendental" in the Kantian sense? That is, are
there components of beauty universally conditioned by the human mind
which transcend both space and time?

For example, whatever the fashion of a given age, all ages since the fifth
century B.C. have agreed that Classical beauty is timeless, and as the

English Romantic poet John Keats (1795–1821) foretold in "Ode On A Grecian Urn" (1819/1963) all ages into the future would continue to regard it so:

> O Attic shape! Fair attitude! . . .
> When old age shall this generation waste,
> Thou shalt remain, . . .
> . . . a friend to man, to whom thou say'st,
> Beauty is truth, truth beauty,—that is all
> Ye know on earth, and all ye need to know.

Perhaps, however, aesthetic ideals since Greece have in some way been historically conditioned by Classicism. Would non-Western peoples naive to this Classical aesthetic appreciate Greco-Roman beauty in the same ways that successive generations of Westerners have? Would those Magdalenian painters of Lascaux have esteemed the paintings of Apelles, the sculpture of Myron and Phidias, and the architecture of Ictinus and Callicrates? There is another way to ask the question: Has a non-Classical aesthetic developed since the fifth century B.C. which would be equally admired by those Greeks?

These are at base psychological questions and may be interpreted as empirical and concerned with submitting aesthetic judgment in different cultures at different times to psychological scrutiny and analysis. Put the case that such a "transcendental aesthetic" exists for all cultures and all times. Whence would such a universal appeal originate, and of what could it be constituted? It is likely, on logical grounds, that such an aesthetic would be restricted by a common denominator of simple biologically conditioned facts. That is, anything that could be universally appreciated and valued must appeal to characteristics of humanity which are equally universal. Prominently, the human nervous system meets this criterion.[10] It may be, therefore, that formal properties of art—form and color, for example—qualify since these properties hold the potential of direct psychophysiological appeal, whereas many alternative aspects of art—morality, ethics, sentimentality, symbolism, which at one or another time have been identified as "aesthetic"—are subject to cultural interpretation, transmutation, and relativism. I am simply echoing Keats here in emphasizing the role of a timeless sensuousness in aesthetic.

---

[10] By nervous system I mean to include, of course, natural aspects of the physical environment in the context of which it has evolved. I do not include here social universals, such as those Freud posited, because of their cultural base and uncertain status as universal. However, other social-biological events, such as birth and death, constitute candidate universals. For an opposite view of the basis for aesthetic, see Kreitler and Kreitler (1972) and Peckham (1965).

Can the case of universal appeal be made for color and for form? The answer, I think, is yes. The vast literature on perception and preference for formal elements in art strongly indicates that certain colors (blues and reds) and certain dimensions of color (particularly saturation) and that certain forms (Gestalts, especially symmetry, and ogival curves) in certain orientations (especially vertical, then horizontal) nearly universally provoke aesthetic responses in human beings (Bornstein, 1975, 1984b). Further, these properties show direct psychophysiological correspondences, and studies of nervous system function reveal special sensitivities to them. Perhaps there is something in the psychophysical isomorphism of empathy theories so popular with both humanistic and scientific psychological aestheticians. Finally, if particular stimulus properties were aesthetic because they appealed in some way to biological substrates and, hence, if they were universal, then human beings and other animals not influenced by culture ought to value the same properties as "aesthetic." In support of this deduction, studies of human infants and of infrahuman species confirm the psychological specialty of the same properties of color and form.

The identification of components of a transcendental aesthetic points up a hidden value of "aesthetics from below" since it would not have been possible to identify any true aesthetic universal in the absence of widespread experimentation in art. Certainly this possibility gives impetus to scientific psychology to begin synthesizing local aesthetic effects into a global experimental aesthetics (see Bornstein, 1979). Can this approach successfully reach the universal idiom of Mondrian or Moore?

CONCLUSIONS

If we reflect on the questions first raised in this essay, we find that psychology offers some critical ways of thinking about art. Certainly, art has served pragmatic and ceremonial ends since its inception, just as chromaticity, idealization of curve, and economy of line confirm that *l'art pour l'art* has always been a substantial human motive.[11] But, aesthetic decoration and human expression testify that even from its earliest beginnings (Figure 17) art has met additional psychological needs unconnected with the immediate material requirements of life. Prominently, art communicates information and expresses emotion, and art both pleases and entertains.

But language, not art, is the principal mode of communication among

---

[11]Lyons (1967) and Kennedy and Silver (1974) provide discussions of the psychological aesthetics of cave art.

FIG. 17.   *Reindeer* (*ca.* 15,000 B.C.) by unknown Magdalenian peoples. (Font-de-Gaume Cave, Dordogne, France)

human beings. And art is not the most pleasing or entertaining pastime; for most, it is far surpassed by sex, sport, games, and many other human activities. Nevertheless, art has persisted as a special human endeavor, cultivated through the centuries, and it has captured the interest and imagination of generations of students of human behavior. Significantly, throughout its history art has been conceived to reflect the myriad workings of the human mind. This rationale alone qualifies psychology as the closest science to art, as I have labored to show in this essay. Not detailed in this compressed and selective treatment, art's many other motivations and associations reinforce this special relationship.[12]

Two major traditions in the psychology of art have evolved. The humanistic tradition originated in clinical observation and has approached art principally through intuitive, subjective, and rational investigations of

---

[12] I have unfortunately had to slight many highly relevant considerations. One example is how artists' vision or neurological integrity may affect their portrayals; interesting discussions are to be found in Trevor-Roper (1970), Pickford (1972), Gardner (1975), and Lee (1981), but the interested reader is also urged to consult Sir Peter Medawar's incisive discussion (1979, p. 9). Another example is the comparative contributions of allied disciplines to the same issues, as for example from sociology (e.g., Albrecht, Barnett, & Griff, 1976; Creedy, 1970; Duvignaud, 1967/1972; Fischer, 1963; Kavolis, 1968; Sorokin, 1962).

the artist. The scientific tradition originated in empirical investigation and has approached art principally through objective and analytic evaluation of art and of audience. Comparisons and contrasts of these two traditions show that while the epistemologies they promulgate differ considerably their domains of interest are not mutually exclusive. More importantly, the two together open a wide panorama of psychological opinion, theory, and research progress on virtually all of the major issues embraced by a psychology of art.

How have psychology and art contributed to one another? In fact, psychology and art co-exist in an unnaturally asymmetric relationship. By and large, the fine arts have contributed only very little to psychology— solidly in terms of material and illustration, of course, but only marginally in terms of substance (consider the status of the therapeutic utility of artistic expression). If we distinguish between lay psychology and academic psychology, we can say that artists are perennial and inveterate lay psychologists. Leonardo da Vinci, who was among the most influential and articulate of early art theoreticians, stated that: "The good painter must paint principally two things, which are man and the ideas in man's mind. The first is easy, the second difficult, because they can only be expressed by means of gestures and the movements of the limbs [quoted by Blunt, 1940, p. 34]." It was for this reason that Leonardo developed a theory of expression. Many artists must subscribe to this view since much secular art is portraiture. But the contribution of the arts and of such psychologies born of art have not endured in psychology. Of course, to the degree psychoanalysis has merit, the study of cultural artefacts holds untapped promise for revealing much about the human unconscious.

Formal psychology has been applied to description, analysis, and explanation in art as this chapter has shown. But both traditions in psychology have profoundly influenced art. In fact, Leonardo instigated one tradition through his direct infusion of principles of visual perception and perspective into artistic practice. "Those who become enamored of the practice of art without having previously applied themselves to the diligent study of the scientific part of it," he wrote in the Trattato della Pittura, "may be compared to mariners, who put to sea in a ship without rudder or compass and, therefore, cannot be certain of arriving at the wished-for port." The nineteenth century reinforced this scientific influence: The color and form researches of Michel Eugène Chevreul, Ogden N. Rood, Paul Signac, and Charles Henry, for example, fostered the development of Impressionism and Neo-Impressionist movements (Argüelles, 1972). The twentieth century has confirmed it: The relativist physics of Einstein and the visual science of Wheatstone have influenced the development of photography in Eadweard Muybridge and the development of Cubism in Braque and Picasso (Vitz, 1979; Waddington,

1970); the Gestalt psychology of Koffka has influenced new applications of perceptual representation in the likes of Maurits Escher (Teuber, 1974); and the information theory of MacKay has influenced the development of Op Art in, for example, Bridget Riley (Parola, 1969). An equally compelling psychological influence on art derived from the humanistic tradition and, in particular, from psychoanalysis. Psychoanalysis impelled movements in twentieth-century art (e.g., Symbolism, Expressionism, Surrealism) providing them with a secular mythology to replace the failing religious mythology traditional in the fine arts. Following Freud, irony, ambiguity, and symbolism supplanted form, style, and realism as the modern aesthetic. Indeed, the end point of this trajectory—Conceptual Art—continues the Freudian tradition in its concern with mind behind the work rather than the work itself.[13] Psychoanalytic interpretations are double-edged, however: While they expose inner meaning, they are also mythological and not determinative; while they are interminable, they are ever adaptive.

Yet, withal, numerous questions in the psychology of art, artist, and audience endure. Many will be familiar and few surprising. What, if anything, differentiates artistic personality and intellect from nonartistic personality and intellect? Does artistic creativity lend itself to analysis? What motivates new artistic styles, and why do new styles emerge in different individuals and at different historical periods? Why have artists in different ages represented the world—which is, after all, mostly constant—in such different ways? Why are children so spontaneously motivated to draw, and why do they so easily give art up? Why is fashion aesthetic initially only to a select few, why does the public eye eventually come to accept new fashion as aesthetic so completely, and why is accommodation to new fashion easy in youth but so difficult in old age? Can findings of an experimental aesthetics be bound to a coherent theoretical framework? Are aesthetic standards destined always to be subjective, or can there ever be a universal aesthetic?

These questions essentially formulate an agendum for any future psychology of art. On the scientific side, new approaches and new categories are needed to analyze works of art and their development; these categories should be informed in larger degree by the opinions and insights of art critics, of art connoisseurs, and of art historians as well as of artists

---

[13] Two interesting paradoxes arise in this connection. First, Freud himself rejected these contemporaneous developments in art as trivial, characterizing Impressionism as merely "a feast for the eye" and Cubism as "arid." Second, the modern movements which psychoanalysis inspired and on which it exerted so great influence are themselves ill-suited to psychoanalytic interpretation; psychoanalysis requires rather a classical tableau into which artists paint hidden ideas exposing the unconscious.

themselves in order properly to enhance the validity of future psychological assessments. On the humanistic side, closer investigation of motivations for engaging in art ought to proceed in conjunction with evaluations of productivity and the personal evolution of practicing artists. Development in both traditions then ought to be applied systematically to children's artistic productivity and to the early development of practicing artists. Far too often the psychology of productive artists has been retrospective (and heir to all of the shortcomings of retrospective analysis); prospective study is in order. Further, relationships among dexterity, cognition, and temperament ought to be explored in children who do and do not become artists as well as in artists who are acknowledged to be successful or unsuccessful. Finally, psychological studies of artists and art have been distanced, if not wholly divorced, from the realities of the art world; we ought to study the insights of critics like Émile Zola who prematurely recognized the merit in Manet and the opinions of connoisseurs like Bernard Berenson who set style and defined taste. In short, one future direction psychology ought to pursue vis-à-vis art is simply to move closer to art. At the same time, psychology ought also to embrace different arts. While psychology has made overtures in the direction of cinema (e.g., Arnheim, 1969; Hochberg & Brooks, 1978; Münsterberg, 1916/1970), architecture (e.g., Arnheim, 1977; Hooper, 1978), and other fine arts, the advancement and generality of psychological principles in art will await further development in these visual domains as well as expansion to other arts (see Wohlwill, in Volume II).

A second direction psychology ought to follow is one which effects a closer reconciliation of its own two traditions. The humanistic and scientific psychologies of art contrast with one another in several ways and here and there are fundamentally at odds. The humanistic tradition, respecting its clinical origins, has construed art to fall within the framework of a rationality and a logic buried deep in the psyche; art is a product of the human unconscious, just as it appeals to the unconscious. The scientific tradition, on the other hand, respecting its experimental origins, has placed art within a framework of rationality and logic close to surface behavior; art is a product of human consciousness, just as it appeals to the conscious. Although the humanistic tradition in psychology has tended to emphasize the artist and the scientific tradition the audience, the two are not so exclusively focused; the two traditions share many important interests such as creativity in the artist and empathy in the audience. Further rapprochement of these traditions, however difficult or awkward at the beginning, can only serve to fortify psychology's contributions to and prestige in art.

Is the psychology of art confused because it assumes such diametric postures? Psychology thinks that art is emotional and cerebral, accidental and deliberate, unconscious and conscious, inspired and serene, spontaneous and planned. But art is each of these. And the beauty and mystery of art are that it is each. There is aesthetic in respite and symmetry, in excitement and complexity, in tension-then-release and in unity-in-variety. Short of reconciling these divergent and powerful motives, the psychology of art accretes to itself greater repute and respect insofar as it can accommodate and can embrace the inherent mysteries and paradoxes that make art.

In this essay I have presented an overview of psychological approaches to fine art. Psychology's two traditions, the humanistic and the scientific, contribute much to our understanding of what is artistic and aesthetic, but plainly the whole of art *is* more than the sum of its parts. In assessing psychology's contribution, we ought to keep in mind also that the psychology of art is only as old as is modern psychology itself, about a century, and therefore it only encompasses perhaps three or four generations of thinkers. The humanistic and scientific approaches can in no way be conceived of as complete or comprehensive. Rather, they are traditions; what we have inherited from them constitute prolegomena to any future psychology of art.

For Evelyn Hu—scientist, humanist, and friend.

REFERENCES

Abell, W. *The collective dream in art: A psycho-historical theory of culture based on relations between the arts, psychology, and the social sciences.* New York: Schocken Books, 1966. (Originally published, 1957.)

Alberti, L. B. [*On painting*] (G. Leoni, trans.). London: n.p., 1726. (Originally published, 1435.) [Reprinted in E. G. Holt (Ed.), *A documentary history of art* (Vol. 1). New York: Anchor Books, 1957.]

Albrecht, M. C., Barnett, J. H., & Griff, M. *The sociology of art and literature: A reader.* New York: Praeger Publishers, 1976.

Alschuler, R., & Hattwick, L. W. *Painting and personality: A study of young children.* Chicago, IL: University of Chicago Press, 1969.

Ames, A. Depth in pictorial art. *Art Bulletin,* 1925, *8,* 5–24.

Argüelles, J. A. *Charles Henry and the formation of a psychophysical aesthetic.* Chicago, IL: University of Chicago Press, 1972.

Arnheim, R. *The genesis of a painting: Picasso's Guernica.* Berkeley, CA: University of California Press, 1962.

Arnheim, R. *Film as art.* Berkeley, CA: University of California Press, 1969.

Arnheim, R. *Toward a psychology of art.* Berkeley, CA: University of California Press, 1972.

Arnheim, R. *Art and visual perception.* Berkeley, CA: University of California Press, 1974.

Arnheim, R. *The dynamics of architectural form*. Berkeley, CA: University of California Press, 1977.

Arnheim, R. Some comments on J. J. Gibson's approach to picture perception. *Leonardo*, 1979, *12*, 121–122.

Arnheim, R. *The power of the center*. Berkeley, CA: University of California Press, 1982.

Attneave, F. *Application of information theory to psychology*. New York: Holt, 1959.

Barron, F. *Artists in the making*. New York: Seminar Press, 1972.

Beebe-Center, J. G. *The psychology of pleasantness and unpleasantness*. New York: Van Nostrand, 1932.

Beebe-Center, J. G., & Pratt, C. C. A test of Birkhoff's aesthetic measure. *Journal of General Psychology*, 1937, *17*, 335–350.

Bell, C. *Art*. New York: G. P. Putnam's Sons, 1958. (Originally published, 1913.)

Benjafield, J., & Adams-Webber, J. The golden section hypothesis. *British Journal of Psychology*, 1976, *67*, 11–15.

Berlyne, D. E. *Aesthetics and psychobiology*. New York: Appleton-Century-Crofts, 1971.

Berlyne, D. E. (Ed.). *Studies in the new experimental aesthetics: Steps toward an objective psychology of aesthetic appreciation*. New York: Wiley, 1974.

Berlyne, D. E. Dimensions of perception of exotic and pre-Renaissance paintings. *Canadian Journal of Psychology*, 1975, *29*, 151–173.

Bettelheim, B. Joey: A "mechanical boy." *Scientific American*, 1959, *200*, 116–127.

Billig, O., & Burton-Bradley, B. *The painted message*. Cambridge, MA: Schenkman, 1978.

Birkhoff, G. D. *Aesthetic measure*. Cambridge, MA: Harvard University Press, 1933.

Blunt, A. *Artistic theory in Italy: 1450–1600*. Oxford, England: The Clarendon Press, 1940.

Bornstein, M. H. On light and the aesthetics of color: Lumia kinetic art. *Leonardo*, 1975, *8*, 203–212.

Bornstein, M. H. Review essay of *A Common Taste in Art* by S. Sandström. *The Journal of Aesthetics and Art Criticism*, 1979, *31*, 485–489.

Bornstein, M. H. *Piet Mondrian and psychological determinism*. Unpublished manuscript, New York University, 1983.

Bornstein, M. H. Perceptual development. In M. H. Bornstein & M. E. Lamb (Eds.), *Developmental psychology*. Hillsdale, NJ: Lawrence Erlbaum Associates, 1984. (a)

Bornstein, M. H. *Symmetry: Psychology and aesthetics*. Unpublished manuscript, New York University, 1984. (b)

Burt, C. The psychology of art. In C. Burt, E. Jones, & W. Moodie, *How the mind works*. London: Allen & Unwin, 1933.

Buswell, G. T. *How people look at pictures*. Chicago, IL: University of Chicago Press, 1935.

Calder, A., & Davidson, J. *Calder: An autobiography with pictures*. New York: Random House, 1966.

Carothers, T., & Gardner, H. When children's drawings become art: The emergence of aesthetic production and perception. *Developmental Psychology*, 1979, *15*, 570–580.

Chandler, A. R., & Barnhart, E. N. *A bibliography of psychological and experimental aesthetics, 1864–1937*. Berkeley, CA: University of California Press, 1938.

Child, I. L. Personal preferences as an expression of aesthetic sensitivity. *Journal of Personality*, 1962, *30*, 496–512.

Child, I. L. Personality correlates of aesthetic judgment in college students. *Journal of Personality*, 1965, *33*, 476–511.

Child, I. L. Esthetics. *Annual Review of Psychology*, 1972, *23*, 669–694.

Child, I. L. *Humanistic psychology and the research tradition: Their several virtues*. New York: Wiley, 1973.

Child, I. L. Aesthetic theories. In E. C. Carterette & M. P. Friedman (Eds.), *Handbook of perception (Vol. 10): Perceptual ecology*. New York: Academic Press, 1978.

Clark, K. *Leonardo da Vinci: An account of his development as an artist*. Baltimore, MD: Penguin Books, 1958. (Originally published, 1939.)

Collingwood, R. *The principles of art*. Oxford, England: Oxford University Press, 1958. (Originally published, 1938.)

Connolly, K. J., & Bruner, J. S. (Eds.). *The growth of competence*. London: Academic Press, 1974.

Creedy, J. (Ed.). *The social context of art*. London: Tavistock Publications, 1970.

Croce, B. *[Aesthetic]* (D. Ainslie, trans.). New York: Farrar, Straus & Giroux, 1972. (Originally published, 1909.)

Davis, R. C. An evaluation and test of Birkhoff's aesthetic measure formula. *Journal of General Psychology*, 1936, *19*, 231–240.

Delacroix, E. *[The journal of Eugène Delacroix]* (W. Patch, trans.). New York: Crown, 1948. (Originally published, 1923.) [Reprinted in E. G. Holt (Ed.), *A documentary history of art* (Vol. 3). New York: Anchor, 1966.]

Denis, M. *Théories: 1890–1910*. Paris: L'Occident, 1912.

Dennis, W. Goodenough scores, art experience, and modernization. *Journal of Social Psychology*, 1966, *68*, 211–228.

Di Leo, J. *Young children and their drawings*. New York: Brunner/Mazel, 1970.

Di Leo, J. *Children's drawings as diagnostic aids*. New York: Brunner/Mazel, 1973.

Duvignaud, J. *[The sociology of art]* (T. Wilson, trans.). New York: Harper & Row, 1972. (Orignally published, 1967.)

Ehrenzweig, A. *The psychoanalysis of artistic vision and hearing*. New York: Braziller, 1965.

Ehrenzweig, A. *The hidden order of art: A study in the psychology of artistic imagination*. Berkeley, CA: University of California Press, 1967.

Ellis, H. The psychology of red. *Popular Science Monthly*, 1900, *57*, 365–375, 517–526.

Ellis, H. The psychology of yellow. *Popular Science Monthly*, 1906, *68*, 456–463.

Eysenck, H. J. The general factor in aesthetic judgments. *British Journal of Psychology*, 1940, *31*, 94–102.

Eysenck, H. J. The empirical determination of an aesthetic formula. *Psychological Review*, 1941, *48*, 83–92. (a)

Eysenck, H. J. Psychological aspects of colour measurement. *Nature*, 1941, *147*, 682–683. (b)

Eysenck, H. J. An experimental study of aesthetic preference for polygonal figures. *Journal of General Psychology*, 1968, *79*, 3–17.

Fechner, G. T. Über die Frage des goldnen Schnitts. *Archiv für die zeichnenden Künste*, 1865, *11*, 100–112.

Fechner, G. T. *Vorschule der Ästhetik*. Leipzig: Breitkopf & Härtel, 1876.

Fischer, E. *[The necessity of art]* (A. Bostock, trans.). Harmondsworth, England: Penguin Books, 1963.

Fortes, M. Children's drawings among the Tallensi. *Africa*, 1940, *13*, 239–295.

Francès, R. *Psychologie de l'esthétique*. Paris: Presses Universitaires de France, 1968.

Freeman, N. H. *Strategies of representation in young children: Analysis of spatial skills and drawing processes*. London: Academic Press, 1980.

Freud, S. *[Leonardo da Vinci and a memory of his childhood]* (A. Tyson, trans.). New York: Norton, 1964. (Originally published, 1910.)

Freud, S. [Dostoevsky and parricide] (D. F. Tait, trans.). In P. Rieff (Ed.), *Sigmund Freud: Character and culture*. New York: Collier, 1963. (Originally published, 1928.)

Freud, S. *[Civilization and its discontents]* (J. Strachey, trans.). New York: Norton, 1961. (Originally published, 1930.)

Freud, S. The Moses of Michelangelo. In P. Rieff (Ed.), *Sigmund Freud: Character and culture*. New York: Collier, 1963. (Originally published, 1914.)

Friedländer, M. J. *Von Kunst und Kennerschaft*. Oxford, England: Oxford University Press, 1946.

Fry, R. *Vision and design*. New York: Meridian Books, 1956.

Fry, R. *Cézanne: A study of his development*. New York: Farrar, Straus & Giroux, 1958. (Originally published, 1922.)

Gablik, S. *Progress in art*. New York: Rizzoli, 1976.

Gardner, H. Children's sensitivity to painting styles. *Child Development*, 1970, *41*, 813–821.

Gardner, H. Problem-solving in the arts and sciences. *Journal of Aesthetic Education*, 1971, *5*, 93–113.

Gardner, H. The development of sensitivity to figural and stylistic aspects of paintings. *British Journal of Psychology*, 1972, *63*, 605–615.

Gardner, H. *The arts and human development: A psychological study of the artistic process*. New York: Wiley, 1973.

Gardner, H. *The shattered mind*. New York: Knopf, 1975.

Gardner, H. *Artful scribbles: The significance of children's drawings*. New York: Basic Books, 1980.

Gardner, H., & Gardner, J. Developmental trends in sensitivity to form and subject matter in paintings. *Studies in Art Education*, 1973, *14*, 52–56.

Getzels, J. W., & Csikszentmihalyi, M. *The creative vision: A longitudinal study of problem finding in art*. New York: Wiley, 1976.

Ghiberti, L. *[The commentaries]*. In J. von Schlosser, *Lorenzo Ghibertis Denkwürdigkeiten (I. Commentarii)*. Berlin: n.p., 1912. [Reprinted in E. G. Holt (Ed.), *A documentary history of art* (Vol. 1). New York: Anchor Books, 1957.]

Gibson, J. J. *The perception of the visual world*. Boston, MA: Houghton-Mifflin, 1950.

Gibson, J. J. The information available in pictures. *Leonardo*, 1971, *4*, 27–35.

Gibson, J. J. Pickford and the failure of experimental aesthetics. *Leonardo*, 1975, *8*, 319–321.

Gibson, J. J. Comment on Professor Pickford's letter. *Leonardo*, 1976, *9*, 173.

Gibson, J. J. *The ecological approach to visual perception*. Boston, MA: Houghton-Mifflin, 1979. (a)

Gibson, J. J. Note. *Leonardo*, 1979, *12*, 135 and 174. (b)

Goldwater, R. *Primitivism in modern art*. New York: Random House, 1967.

Golomb, C. Children's representation of the human figure: The effects of models, media, and instruction. *Genetic Psychology Monographs*, 1973, *87*, 187–251.

Golomb, C. *Young children's sculpture and drawing: A study in representational development*. Cambridge, MA: Harvard University Press, 1974.

Golomb, C. Representation and reality: The origins and determinants of young children's drawings. *Review of Research in Visual Arts Education*, 1981, *14*, 36–48.

Gombrich, E. H. Psychoanalysis and the history of art. *International Journal of Psychoanalysis*, 1954, *35*, 1–11.

Gombrich, E. H. *Art and illusion: A study in the psychology of pictorial representation*. Princeton, NJ: Princeton University Press, 1960.

Goodman, N. *Languages of art*. Indianapolis, IN: Bobbs-Merrill, 1968.

Goodnow, J. *Children's drawing*. London: Fontana/Open Books, 1977.

Graetz, H. R. *The symbolic language of Vincent Van Gogh*. New York: McGraw-Hill, 1963.

Gross, C. G., & Bornstein, M. H. Left and right in science and art. *Leonardo*, 1978, *11*, 29–38.

Guilford, J. P. There is a system in color preferences. *Journal of the Optical Society of America*, 1940, *30*, 455–459.

Guilford, J. P. A psychometric approach to creativity. In H. H. Anderson (Ed.), *Creativity in childhood and adolescence: A diversity of approaches*. Palo Alto, CA: Science and Behavior Books, 1965.

Hagen, M. A. (Ed.). *The perception of pictures (Vol. 1): Alberti's widow: The projective model of pictorial information*. New York: Academic Press, 1980.

Hagen, M. A. (Ed.). *The perception of pictures (Vol. 2): Dürer's devices: Beyond the projective model of pictures*. New York: Academic Press, 1980.

Hammond, W. A. *A bibliography of aesthetics and the philosophy of the fine arts from 1900 to 1932*. New York: Longmans, Green, 1933.

Hauser, A. *The philosophy of art history*. New York: Knopf, 1959.

Heiman, M. Psychoanalytic observations on the last painting and suicide of Vincent van Gogh. *International Journal of Psychoanalysis*, 1976, *57*, 71.

Hochberg, J. Art and perception. In E. C. Carterette and M. P. Friedman (Eds.), *Handbook of perception (Vol. 10): Perceptual ecology*. New York: Academic Press, 1978.

Hochberg, J., & Brooks, V. The perception of motion pictures. In E. C. Carterette & M. P. Friedman (Eds.), *Handbook of perception (Vol. 10): Perceptual ecology*. New York: Academic Press, 1978.

Hogarth, W. *The analysis of beauty*. London: n.p., 1753. [Reprinted in E. G. Holt (Ed.), *A documentary history of art* (Vol. 2). New York: Anchor Books, 1958.]

Hogg, J. (Ed.). *Psychology and the visual arts: Selected readings*. Baltimore, MD: Penguin Books, 1969.

Hooper, K. Perceptual aspects of architecture. In E. C. Carterette & M. P. Friedman (Eds.), *Handbook of perception (Vol. 10): Perceptual ecology*. New York: Academic Press, 1978.

Hughes, R. *The shock of the new*. London: BBC, 1980.

Huntley, H. E. *The divine proportion: A study in mathematical beauty*. New York: Dover, 1970.

James, H. (Ed.). *The letters of William James* (Vol. 2). Boston, MA: Atlantic Monthly Press, 1920.

James, W. *The principles of psychology*. New York: Henry Holt, 1890.

Jameson, D., & Hurvich, L. M. From contrast to assimilation: In art and in the eye. *Leonardo*, 1975, *8*, 125–131.

Jastrow, J. The popular aesthetics of color. *Popular Science Monthly*, 1897, *50*, 361–368.

Jung, C. G. *[The spirit in man, art, and literature]* (R. F. C. Hull, trans.). Princeton, NJ: Princeton University Press, 1966.

Kandinsky, W. *Point and line to plane*. New York: Dover, 1979. (Originally published, 1947.)

Kavolis, V. *Artistic expression: A sociological analysis*. Ithaca, NY: Cornell University Press, 1968.

Keats, J. Ode on a Grecian urn. In W. H. Marshall (Ed.), *The major English Romantic poets*. New York: Washington Square Press, 1963. (Originally published, 1819.)

Kellogg, R. *Analyzing children's art*. Palo Alto, CA: National Press Books, 1969.

Kennedy, J. M. *A psychology of picture perception*. San Francisco, CA: Jossey-Bass, 1974.

Kennedy, J. M., & Silver, J. The surrogate functions of lines in visual perception: Evidence from antipodal rock and cave artwork sources. *Perception*, 1974, *3*, 313–322.

Koffka, K. *Principles of Gestalt psychology*. New York: Harcourt, Brace, 1935.

Koffka, K. Problems in the psychology of art. In R. Bernheimer, R. Carpenter, K. Koffka, & M. C. Nahm (Eds.), *Art: A Bryn Mawr symposium*. Lancaster, PA: Lancaster Press, 1940.

Konečni, V. J., & Sargent-Pollock, D. Arousal, positive and negative affect, and preference for Renaissance and 20th-century paintings. *Motivation and Emotion*, 1977, *1*, 75–93.

Kramer, E. *Art as therapy with children*. New York: Schocken Books, 1971.

Kreitler, H., & Kreitler, S. *Psychology of the arts*. Durham, NC: Duke University Press, 1972.

Kris, E. *Psychoanalytic explorations in art*. New York: Schocken Books, 1964. (Originally published, 1952.)

Kuhn, D. Cognitive development. In M. H. Bornstein & M. E. Lamb (Eds.), *Developmental psychology*. Hillsdale, NJ: Lawrence Erlbaum Associates, 1984.

Kuhns, R. *Psychoanalytic theory of art: A philosophy of art on developmental principles*. New York: Columbia University Press, 1983.

Lashley, K. S. The problem of serial order in behavior. In L. A. Jeffries (Ed.), *Cerebral mechanisms in behavior*. New York: Wiley, 1951.

Le Corbusier. *Modulor*. London: Faber & Faber, 1954.

Lee, T. C. Van Gogh's vision: Digitalis intoxication? *Journal of the American Medical Association*, 1981, *245*, 727–729.

Levick, M. F. *They could not talk and so they drew: Children's styles of coping and thinking*. New York: Charles C. Thomas, 1983.

Liebert, R. S. *Michelangelo: A psychoanalytic study of his life and images*. New Haven, CT: Yale University Press, 1983.

Luria, A. R. The development of constructive activity in the preschool child. In M. Cole (Ed.), *The selected writings of A. R. Luria*. New York: M. E. Sharpe, 1978. (Originally published, 1948.)

Lyons, J. Paleolithic aesthetics: The psychology of cave art. *Journal of Aesthetics and Art Criticism*, 1967, *27*, 107–114.

MacKinnon, D. Personality and the realization of creative potential. *American Psychologist*, 1965, *20*, 273–281.

MacKinnon, D. Creativity: Psychological aspects. In D. L. Sills (Ed.), *International encyclopedia of the social sciences*. New York: Macmillan-Free Press, 1968.

Mackworth, N. H., & Bruner, J. S. How adults and children search and recognize pictures. *Human Development*, 1970, *13*, 149–177.

Machotka, P. Aesthetic criteria in childhood: Justifications of preference. *Child Development*, 1966, *37*, 877–885.

Mâle, E. *The Gothic image: Religious art in France in the thirteenth century*. New York: Harper & Row, 1958. (Originally published, 1913.)

Mandelbrojt, J. On mental images and their pictorial representation. *Leonardo*, 1970, *3*, 19–26.

Margolis, J. *Philosophy looks at the arts*. New York: Scribners, 1962.

Martin, J. L. An experimental study of Fechner's principles of aesthetics. *Psychological Review*, 1906, *13*, 142–219.

Medawar, P. B. *Advice to a young scientist*. New York: Harper & Row, 1979.

de Meredieu, F. *Le dessin d'enfant*. Paris: Editions Universitaires Jean-Pierre de Large, 1974.

Messer, T. M. *Edvard Munch*. New York: H. N. Abrams, n.d.

Moles, A. [*Information theory and aesthetic perception*] (J. E. Cohen, trans.). Urbana, IL: University of Illinois Press, 1966. (Originally published, 1958.)

Mondrian, P. Plastic art and pure plastic art. In R. L. Herbert (Ed.), *Modern artists on art*. Englewood Cliffs, NJ: Prentice-Hall, 1964. (Originally published, 1937.)

Morris, D. *The biology of art: A study of the picture-making behaviour of the Great Apes and its relationship to human art*. London: Methuen, 1962.

Münsterberg, H. *The film: A psychological study*. New York: Dover, 1970. (Originally published, 1916.)

Münsterberg, H. *The crown of life: Artistic creativity in old age*. New York: Harcourt, Brace, Jovanovich, 1982.

Nagera, H. *Vincent van Gogh: A psychological study*. New York: International Universities Press, 1967.

Naumburg, M. *Schizophrenic art: Its meaning in psychotherapy*. New York: Grune & Statton, 1950.

Neumann, E. [*Art and the creative unconscious*] (R. Manheim, trans.). New York: Harper Torchbooks, 1966. (Originally published, 1959.)

Nodine, C. F., & Fisher, D. F. (Eds.). *Perception in pictorial representation*. New York: Praeger, 1979.

Noton, D., & Stark, L. Scanpaths in saccadic eye movements while viewing and recognizing patterns. *Vision Research*, 1971, *11*, 929–942.

O'Hare, D. (Ed.). *Psychology and the arts*. Atlantic Highlands, NJ: Humanities Press, 1982.

Oppé, A. P. Right and left in Raphael's cartoons. *Journal of the Warburg and Courtauld Institutes*, 1944, *7*, 82–94.

Paine, S. *Six children draw*. New York: Academic Press, 1982.

Panofsky, E. *Studies in iconology: Humanistic themes in the art of the Renaissance*. New York: Harper & Row, 1962. (Originally published, 1939.)

Parola, R. *Optical art: Theory and practice*. New York: Beekman House, 1969.

Peckham, M. *Man's rage for chaos: Biology, behavior, and the arts*. Philadelphia, PA: Chilton Books, 1965.

Perkins, D. N. *The mind's best work*. Cambridge, MA: Harvard University Press, 1981.

Petersen, K., & Wilson, J. J. *Women artists: Recognition and reappraisal from the early middle ages to the twentieth century*. New York: New York University Press, 1976.

Phillips, W. (Ed.). *Art and psychoanalysis*. New York: Meridian Books, 1963.

Piaget, J. [*The mechanisms of perception*] (G. N. Seagrim, trans.). London: Routledge & Kegan Paul, 1969. (Originally published, 1961.)

Pickford, R. W. *Psychology and visual aesthetics*. London: Hutchinson, 1972.

Pickford, R. W. Gibson and the success of experimental aesthetics. *Leonardo*, 1976, *9*, 56–57.

Pickford, R. W. Note. *Leonardo*, 1979, *12*, 135 and 174.

de Piles, R. [*Principles of painting with a balance of painters*] (A. Painter, trans.). London: n.p., 1743. (Originally published, 1708.) [Reprinted in E. G. Holt (Ed.), *A documentary history of art* (Vol. 2). New York: Anchor Books, 1958.]

Pirenne, M. H. *Optics, painting, & photography*. New York: Cambridge University Press, 1970.

Plokker, J. R. *Art from the mentally disturbed*. Boston, MA: Little, Brown, 1965.

Poussin, N. [*Observations on painting*] (D. J. Jansen, trans.). In Ch. Jouanny (Ed.), *Correspondance de Nicolas Poussin*. Paris: n.p., 1911. (Originally published, 1672.) [Reprinted in E. G. Holt (Ed.), *A documentary history of art* (Vol. 2). New York: Anchor Books, 1958.]

Rank, O. *Art and artist*. New York: Knopf, 1932.

Rank, O. *Will therapy and truth and reality*. New York: Knopf, 1945.

Read, H. *Education through art*. New York: Pantheon, n.d.

Read, H. *Art now*. New York: Pittman, 1960. (a)

Read, H. *The forms of things unknown*. London: Faber & Faber, 1960. (b)

Reynolds, J. *Discourses*. In E. Malone (Ed.), *The works of Sir Joshua Reynolds*. London: n.p., 1797. (Originally published, 1768.) [Reprinted in E. G. Holt (Ed.), *A documentary history of art* (Vol. 2). New York: Anchor Books, 1958.]

Richardson, J. A. *Modern art and scientific thought*. Urbana, IL: University of Illinois Press, 1971.

Roe, A. Painters and painting. In I. A. Taylor & J. W. Getzels (Eds.), *Perspectives in creativity*. Chicago, IL: Aldine, 1975.

Rosand, D. Titian's light as form and symbol. *The Art Bulletin*, 1975, *57*, 58–64.

Rose, G. J. *The power of form: A psychoanalytic approach to aesthetic form*. New York: International Universities Press, 1980.

Ruskin, J. *The seven lamps of architecture*. London: J. M. Dent & Sons, 1907.

Ruskin, J. *Modern painters*. In E. G. Holt (Ed.), *A documentary history of art* (Vol. 3). New York: Anchor, 1966. (Originally published, 1893.)

Schaefer-Simmern, H. *The unfolding of artistic activity*. Berkeley, CA: University of California Press, 1948.

Schapiro, M. Two slips of Leonardo and a slip of Freud. *Psychoanalysis*, 1955–1956, *2*, 3–8.

Schapiro, M. Leonardo and Freud: An art-historical study. *Journal of the History of Ideas*, 1956, *17*, 147–178.

Selfe, L. *Nadia: A case of extraordinary drawing ability in an autistic child*. London: Academic Press, 1977. (a)

Selfe, L. A single case study of an autistic child with exceptional drawing ability. In G. Butterworth (Ed.), *The child's representation of the world*. New York: Plenum, 1977. (b)

Selfe, L. *Normal and anomalous representational drawing ability in children*. New York: Academic Press, 1983.

Shields, A. *A bibliography of bibliographies in aesthetics*. San Diego, CA: San Diego State University Press, 1974.

Skinner, B. F. Creating the creative artist. In *On the future of art* (A Symposium at the Solomon R. Guggenheim Museum). New York: Viking, 1970.

Sorokin, P. A. *Social and cultural dynamics (Vol. 1): Fluctuations of forms of art*. New York: Bedminster Press, 1962.

Spector, J. J. *The aesthetics of Freud: A study in psychoanalysis and art*. New York: Praeger Publishers, 1972.

Standing, L., Conezio, J., & Haber, R. N. Perception and memory for pictures: Single-trial learning of 2500 visual stimuli. *Psychonomic Science*, 1970, *19*, 73–74.

Sterba, R. The problem of art in Freud's writings. *Psychoanalytic Quarterly*, 1940, *9*, 256–268.

Stokes, A. *Three essays on the painting of our time*. London: Tavistock, 1961.

Sully, J. Harmony of colors. *Mind*, 1879, *4*, 172–191.

Svensson, L. T. Note on the golden section. *Scandinavian Journal of Psychology*, 1977, *18*, 79–80.

Teuber, M. L. Sources of ambiguity in the prints of Maurits C. Escher. *Scientific American*, 1974, *231*, 90–104.

Thorndike, E. L. Individual differences in judgments of the beauty of simple forms. *Psychological Review*, 1917, *24*, 147–153.

Tolstoy, L. [*What is art?*] (A. Maude, trans.). New York: Oxford University Press, 1962. (Originally published, 1898.)

Trevor-Roper, P. *The world through blunted sight: An inquiry into the influence of defective vision on art and character*. Indianapolis, IN: Bobbs-Merrill, 1970.

Trilling, L. Art and neurosis. In L. Trilling, *The liberal imagination: Essays on literature and society*. New York: Doubleday, 1953. (Originally published, 1947.)

Valentine, C. W. *The experimental psychology of beauty*. London: T. C. & E. C. Jack, 1925.

Vasari, G. [*Lives of the most eminent painters, sculptors, and architects*] (G. du C. de Vere, trans.). London: n.p., 1912. (Originally published, 1550. Revised second edition, 1568.) [Reprinted in E. G. Holt (Ed.), *A documentary history of art* (Vol. 2). New York: Anchor Books, 1958.]

da Vinci, L. [*"Paragone," or, the first part of the book on painting.*] In G. Manzi (Ed.), *Trattato della pittura di L. da V.* Rome: n.p., 1817. [Reprinted in E. G. Holt (Ed.), *A documentary history of art* (Vol. 1). New York: Anchor Books, 1957.]

Vitruvius, M. [*The ten books on architecture*] (M. H. Morgan, trans.). Cambridge, MA: Harvard University Press, 1914. (Originally published, 1st century B.C.)

Vitz, P. Visual science and modernist art: Historical parallels. In C. F. Nodine & D. F. Fisher (Eds.), *Perception and pictorial representation*. New York: Praeger, 1979.

Vygotsky, L. S. *The psychology of art*. Cambridge, MA: MIT Press, 1971.

Waddington, C. H. *Behind appearance: A study of the relations between painting and the natural sciences in this century*. Cambridge, MA: MIT Press, 1970.

Waelder, R. *Psychoanalytic avenues to art.* New York: International Universities Press, 1965.

Werner, H. *Comparative psychology of mental development*. New York: International Universities Press, 1957.

Weyl, H. *Symmetry*. Princeton, NJ: Princeton University Press, 1952.

Willats, J. How children learn to represent three-dimensional space in drawings. In G. Butterworth (Ed.), *The child's representation of the world*. New York: Plenum, 1977.

Wittkower, R., & Wittkower, M. *Born under Saturn*. New York: Norton, 1963.

Wölfflin, H. [*Principles of art history*] (M. D. Hottinger, trans.). New York: Dover, n.d. (Originally published, 1915.)

Wolfe, T. *The painted word*. New York: Bantam Books, 1976.

Wolfenstein, M. The image of the lost parent. *Psychoanalytic Study of the Child*, 1973, *28*, 433–456.

Wollheim, R. *Art and its objects: An introduction to aesthetics*. New York: Harper Torchbooks, 1968.

Wundt, W. M. *Grundzüge der physiologischen Psychologie*. Leipzig: Engelmann, 1874.

Yarbus, A. L. [*Eye movements and vision*] (B. Haigh, trans.). New York: Plenum, 1967.

Ziegfeld, E. (Ed.). *Education and art*. Paris: UNESCO, 1953.

Zusne, L. *Visual perception of form*. New York: Academic Press, 1970.

2 Psychology and Linguistics

P.N. Johnson-Laird
MRC Applied Psychology Unit
Cambridge, England

INTRODUCTION

Psychology is related to linguistics in a way that is unlike its relations to any other discipline: *Many linguists have taken the view that their subject is a branch of psychology.* This view is by no means recent, though it has received a fresh impetus from the revolution in linguistics inspired by Noam Chomsky. Certainly, for over a century psychologists and linguists have been treading on each other's toes, and this "special relation" creates difficulties for assessing the mutual relations of the two disciplines. The aims of the present essay are accordingly to outline the principal developments in modern linguistics and to relate them to the concurrent study of psycholinguistics. This direction of influence reflects the main methodological question to be confronted: Why is it that arguments about the psychology of language based on linguistic considerations have tended to outweigh arguments based on psychological findings?

The essay begins with a survey of the foundations of modern psychology and linguistics. It then turns to Chomsky's transformational generative grammar—its radical conception of linguistic theory, its early impact on psychologists, its subsequent reformulations, and its disintegration into competing schools. The next section of the essay is devoted to meaning. It outlines the major linguistic theories of meaning and includes an account of the "model-theoretic" methods embodied in Montague (1974) grammar. These developments are contrasted with what has happened in psychology and, in particular, with the major experimental phenomena and the modified version of linguistic theories that have been proposed to account for them. The crux of this section is a confrontation of two divergent underlying philosophies of meaning. One philosophy, which owes much to de Saussure (1960), takes the view that meanings are mental entities. The other philosophy, which can be traced back to Frege (1892) and ultimately to Plato, holds that meanings are independent of psychological considerations. The essay closes with a section on current issues in the two disciplines, including a radical proposal about syntactic theory that makes possible a shift towards a psychologically realistic theory of language.

THE ORIGINS OF MODERN PSYCHOLOGY AND LINGUISTICS

There is no obvious point in time at which modern psychology and linguistics may be said to have begun. They both, however, have their roots in the nineteenth century, and perhaps a significant historical datum is the arrival of Wilhelm Wundt and Ferdinand de Saussure at the University of Leipzig in 1875. Wundt, who was to open the first laboratory of experimental psychology, dealt at length with the role of the mind in language and speech (e.g., Wundt, 1900). De Saussure, who was a young student of linguistics, went on to become the key figure in the development of Structuralism and modern linguistics. He established the principle that language could be studied independently of its historical origins, contrary to the lore of the philologists, and the principle that the significance of a sign depends on what other signs are in the system (de Saussure, 1960). In this era, there was no marked distinction between the psychology of language and linguistic theory. There were psychologists who considered that linguistics was an essential prerequisite to understanding the mind; there were linguists who argued that the methods of experimental psychology were indispensable to elucidating grammar. Both disciplines were internally divided along various lines, including the familiar split between Empiricists and Rationalists, but even when psychologists and linguists fell out with each other they still talked freely of the mind and readily entertained mentalistic hypotheses.

The flavor of linguistic speculations in the late nineteenth and early twentieth centuries can best be captured by a few quotations. The German linguist, Hermann Paul, remarked: "All linguistic activity involves the formation of sentences. The sentence is the linguistic expression, or symbol, which indicates that several ideas or groups of ideas have been joined in the mind of the speaker. It is the means for reproducing the same linking of ideas in the mind of a listener . . . [from Paul, 1886, as cited and translated by Blumenthal, 1970]." Michel Bréal (1897) argued: "It cannot be a matter of indifference to us to note, above the seeming chance that

governs the words and form of language, the appearance of laws corresponding in each case to an advance of the mind." On occasion, linguists
would write like speculative psychologists: ". . . negative words express a
feeling of resistance as opposed to logical negation—that is, this writer
believes that negative words do not express ideas, but feeling states [Van
Ginneken, 1907]." On occasion, their ideas were startlingly prescient.
Alfred D. Sheffield (1912) in a work, titled significantly, *Grammar and
Thinking,* discussed the process of speaking in a wholly mentalistic fashion. In analyzing sentences semantically, he used the notion of a conceptual unit, and then ulitized tree diagrams to indicate the relation of
conceptual units from one sentence to another in the structure of paragraphs—a method of analysis that has a distinctly modern touch to it
(Kintsch, 1974).

There was one decisive problem with all these early psycholinguistic
speculations. Theorists lacked a formalism in which their ideas could be
expressed with precision, and in consequence much of what they had to
say lacked any clear empirical content. The inadequacy of the theoretical
machinery was similarly masked from theorists themselves by the
vagueness of its formulation. There was a barren controversy between
Wundt and Paul over the role of analogy in the production and comprehension of speech. There was another prolonged and equally futile
debate over the existence of *Bewusstseinslagen*—thoughts which, according to the psychologists of the Würzburg school, have no underpinning of mental imagery and which are particularly prevalent in verbal
reasoning. Such arguments prepared the ground for the radical Behaviorism of J.B. Watson (1914). This doctrine eschewed talk of mental entities
and abandoned speculative psychology along with, in principle, any topic
that could not be reduced to observable phenomena. Hence, the meanings
of words are simply the objects in the world with which they become
associated; they come to stand for their corresponding object in the same
way that in classical conditioning a conditioned stimulus such as a bell
comes to elicit the same response of salivation as did the original unconditioned stimulus of food.

In America, psychology rapidly became Behavioristic, and its adherents sought the principles by which external stimuli controlled overt responses—a search that was supposed to begin and end in the laboratory
with the rigorous manipulation of experimental variables and the objective recording of human and animal responses. In the rest of the world,
there was a variety of schools of thought, most of which were influenced
by Behaviorism, either positively or negatively, but none of which was so
conspicuously hostile to the theoretical discussion of mental events and
processes.

This broad pattern was mirrored by the state of affairs that prevailed in linguistics. In the United States, Bloomfield (1926) abandoned his earlier mentalism and embraced many aspects of Behaviorism, including the doctrine of meaning as a conditioned reflex. He inaugurated an empiricist methodology for American structural linguistics that prevailed until the mid-1950s. But, elsewhere different schools of thought flourished, though they were influenced by Bloomfieldian precepts to some extent. Much of the linguistic work in Europe continued the Structuralism of de Saussure and laid down the foundations of theories that still claim followers today. Thus, Trubetzkoy (1939) and Jakobson (1962), who were both members of the Prague school of linguists, elaborated the concept of *distinctive features,* i.e. (binary) contrasts in sound quality that distinguish the phonemes of a language, and this idea forms the basis of modern phonological theory (e.g., Chomsky & Halle, 1968). Moreover, European linguists were not afraid of mental entities. The works of Otto Jespersen (e.g., 1924), for example, abound with psychological insights, many of which are remarkably modern and highly relevant to current work in psycholinguistics (e.g., Johnson-Laird, 1977a). He remarked characteristically: "Psychology should assist us in understanding what is going on in the mind of speakers, and more particularly how they are led to deviate from previously existing rules in consequence of conflicting tendencies each of them dependent on some facts in the structure of the language concerned [Jespersen, 1924]."

During the years since World War II, the global pattern of the two disciplines has shifted. In psychology, Behaviorism and the old schools have progressively declined in their influence. They have been replaced by ideas drawn from information theory, cybernetics, control theory, and computer science. There is a consensus that investigation should be pursued experimentally, and the majority of practitioners has absorbed the terminology, if not the theoretical commitments, of information processing. Images, intentions, and the mind, are no longer taboo topics.

In linguistics, the scene is more variegated. Noam Chomsky (1957) introduced a radically new approach to the subject, which has attracted a new sort of scholar. The modern linguist is just as likely to have a background in logic or computer science as in the more traditional humanities. In fact, the new approach relies, not on computer programming and information theory, but on some of the techniques of formal logic and the theory of computation. The more traditional schools of linguistics continue to exist, but their influence has waned—and with only a few exceptions they have had scant effects on psychology. In order to understand modern psycholinguistics, it is accordingly necessary to grasp Chomsky's contributions to linguistic theory.

PSYCHOLINGUISTICS AND GENERATIVE GRAMMAR

Chomsky's Conception of Linguistics

Chomsky (1957) brought to linguistics three radical ideas: a novel conception of the goals of linguistic theory, a new notion of what a language is and of what counts as linguistic evidence, and, perhaps most important, the use of formal mathematical techniques in theorizing about grammar. None of these ideas was wholly original, but their amalgam in the doctrines of transformational generative grammar was unique and exerted a powerful intellectual shock on linguistics. Let us briefly explore each of the three ideas.

First, for Chomsky, a linguist's initial goal should be to frame rules of a language that are at least descriptively adequate, i.e. that will characterize the sentences in the language together with their correct structures. Only then can the linguist try to formulate an explanatorily adequate theory and attempt to account for how children can construct a grammar for their language from the utterances that they hear. Chomsky accordingly draws a line between linguistic competence—what an individual knows tacitly about the rules of the language—and linguistic performance—how the individual puts this knowledge to work in speaking and understanding. Grammar in the widest sense is thus a mental faculty; and linguistics, the study of grammar, is a branch of psychology. The proper study of linguistics, however, is the study of competence, not performance.

Second, Chomsky believes that, although languages differ superficially, their underlying form is universal and innately determined. Only this supposition can explain children's ability to construct a grammar from the fragmentary evidence of the utterances they hear. Linguists had customarily treated written texts or recorded discourse as their primary evidence, but the fundamental data for linguistics concern what is, and what is not, in the language. Hence, linguists can rely on their own intuitions about their native tongues in order to construct theories. As native speakers they can judge, for example, that *platch, snorp,* and *brell* are in accordance with the rules governing the sounds of possible English words, whereas *tchpla, spnor,* and *blree* are not. Likewise, they can judge that a string of words such as, "They saw the swimmer dive into the pool," is in accordance with the rules of English syntax, whereas "They know the swimmer dive into the pool" is not.

Third, at the back of Chomsky's concern with rules lies a mathematical or formal conception of language. From this standpoint, a language can be thought of as a set of sentences (or strings) defined over some vocabulary of signs. The set of all possible strings that can be formed from a given

vocabulary is countably infinite, i.e. it can be put into a one-to-one correspondence with the integers. A language is a subset of this set. It is easy to
show that the set of all subsets of a countably infinite set is *not* itself
countably infinite, but still larger (see Boolos & Jeffrey, 1974). Hence, the
set of *all* possible languages is more than merely countably infinite. When
one confronts this mathematical consequence with the reasonable psychological requirement that any grammar of a language should be finitely
representable then a striking conclusion emerges. There are more possible languages than there are possible grammars (Hopcroft ,& Ullman,
1969). The conclusion follows from the fact that whatever a finite representation of a grammar is, it is plainly something that can be written down
in a finite number of symbols, and there are only a countably infinite
number of such representations. The argument is no mere speculation but
can be readily proved, granted the assumptions about language on which
it is based.

The effects of the mathematical approach to linguistic theory have been
profound. They have also subtly influenced the relations between linguistics and psychology. On the one hand, the characterization of a language
as a set of sentences naturally leads linguists to think about structures
rather than processes. Thus, grammatical rules are treated as a way of
specifying the members of a set rather than as governing the mental
processes by which human beings produce or understand sentences. Linguists have accordingly largely ignored psycholinguistic findings obtained
in the laboratory. On the other hand, when a claim about a natural language can be proved mathematically it naturally exerts a decisive effect
on the whole field. Since psycholinguists have taken the view that any
adequate model of linguistic performance must be related to a theory of
linguistic competence, they have not been able to retreat completely into
the laboratory but have been forced to keep an anxious eye on the latest
developments in linguistic theory. This asymmetry in the way in which
the two disciplines regard each other is well entrenched and may well
have had a deleterious effect on both of them (see Johnson-Laird, 1977b).

The most influential of Chomsky's proofs concerns the impossibility of
characterizing the grammar of a natural language by way of what is known
as a finite state device. To understand what such a device is, imagine a
matrix which has its rows and columns labelled with the names of the
English parts of speech. Each entry in the matrix contains either 1 or 0,
depending on whether or not in grammatical English the part of speech
labelling the row is followed by the part of speech labelling the column.
(The entries could be accurate probabilities, but the argument applies just
the same.) Such a device would be a very rudimentary description of the
language. It would be very much improved by increasing the number of
words that are taken into account prior to a transition. If the rows were

labelled with the grammatical categories of all acceptable adjacent *pairs* of words, e.g., noun-verb, adjective-noun, etc., then the entries in a row could represent the acceptability of that particular pair being followed by each of the different parts of speech. Obviously, there are many different acceptable pairs of sorts of word, and so the array would have to have many rows, and the labor of completing it accurately would be considerable. Nevertheless, there is no reason to settle for a context of just a pair of words, and theorists had generally believed that if the amount of context taken into account were increased to some relatively large number of words, then the resulting device would eventually converge upon the language. This view is certainly implicit in the neo-Behaviorists' assumption that grammar consists of a habit-family hierarchy of responses for each word position in a sentence. Such an assumption is entirely equivalent to a finite state device.

Chomsky demolished this line of thought by showing that no matter how large the number of words taken into account prior to transitions, a finite state device could never converge upon English. His argument rests on the fact that a grammatical structure can be interrupted by another grammatical structure of the same sort, which, in turn, can be interrupted in the same way, and so on, ad infinitum. Consider the sequence of self-embedded sentences:

The affair ends the marriage.
The affair the story describes ends the marriage.
The affair the story the author wrote describes . . . ends the marriage.

Although this sequence of sentences gets progressively harder to understand as the number of embeddings increases, each of its members is grammatical, and there is, as in many other sorts of sentence, no limit on the number of embedded structures that can intervene between the subject of the sentence, "the affair," and its main verb, "ends," which must agree in grammatical number. It follows, with one caveat, that there is no end to the amount of context that a finite state device would have to take into account, but, because it is finite, it obviously cannot do so. The one caveat is crucial. Suppose that there were no constraints on the order of words in English, and that any order would make up a sentence. It would follow that embedded structures would occur in the set of English sentences, along with all the other possibilities. Yet, a finite state device certainly suffices to generate any order of words. What therefore has to be shown about real English in order for Chomsky's proof to work is that "a certain change in the sentences of a self-embedding subset [of sentences] must always be accompanied by a certain other change, on pain of grammaticality [Levelt, 1974, p. 25]." Thus, for example, a change in the actual number of embedded noun phrases must be accompanied by a corresponding change in the number of verbs. In fact, Chomsky was somewhat cavalier about this aspect of the proof. Nevertheless, it seemed irresistible and was almost universally accepted.

It is rare that psychologists are able to marshall a case of comparable force to a linguistic argument, but it so happens that just such an argument was made against finite state devices by Miller, Galanter, and Pribram (1960). They pointed out that if children are to acquire the mental embodiment of a finite state device, then they will have to learn the appropriate transitional probabilities from one syntactic category to another within the sequences of words making up sentences. They point out that on average there are about four alternative choices for the syntactic category of the next word in a sentence. Hence, in order to handle a one-word context, children need to learn 4^2 transitional probabilities. In order to handle transitions from two-word contexts to a third word, they need to learn $4^2 \times 4$ transitional probabilities. It follows that if they are to master a device that accommodates, say, the modest amount of context of 15 words, then they need to know 4^{15} probabilities. This number is far too large to be feasible: 4^{15} is roughly equal to 10^9, and childhood lasts only 10^8 seconds.

In order to handle self-embedded sentences, Chomsky showed that a grammar must contain *recursive* rules. Perhaps the simplest way to grasp the important feature of recursion is in computational terms. Let us suppose that you wish to formulate an algorithm that will compute the factorial of any integer, e.g., the factorial of 3, which is symbolized 3!, is $3 \times 2 \times 1 = 6$, and the factorial of 0 is stipulated to be 1. A simple algorithm would multiply the number, n, by $n - 1$, then multiply the product by $(n - 1) - 1$, and so on, until the repeated subtractions reduce n to 1. This procedure involves a simple *iteration,* i.e. the procedure loops round and round, carrying out here the same computations until the number it begins with is reduced to unity. There is another way of computing a factorial, which can be represented by the following procedure:

Factorial n;
If $n = 0$ then 1;
Else $n \times$ Factorial$(n - 1)$.

The first line of the procedure names it "Factorial" and specifies that it takes a single argument, n. The second line stipulates that the factorial of 0 equals 1. The third line is required if n is not equal to 0, and here something interesting happens: The procedure calls itself by name. If you follow this algorithm in computing the factorial of 3, then you go through the following steps:

3! = 3 × (Factorial(2) which equals:
      2 × (Factorial(1) which equals:
           1 × (Factorial(0) which equals:
                (1)))).

Only when you get to the last step of recovering the factorial of 0 can you carry out the actual multiplication: $3 \times 2 \times 1 \times 1$. A procedure that calls itself in this way is recursive.

To call a grammatical rule "recursive" is not the same as saying that computationally it would demand the power of recursion, but there is a close relation between the two notions. A grammatical rule is defined as "recursive" if the same symbol occurs on both sides of it, e.g., $A \rightarrow a\ A$, which specifies that the symbol "A" can be rewritten as "a A". Such a rule can be applied to its own output ad infinitum to generate strings of the form, "a A," "a a A," "a a a A," and so on. In fact, this process of generation does not require the computational power of recursion and can be handled by a finite state device using iteration. However, recursive rules that generate self-embedded structures do require the full power of recursion. An example of such a rule is: $A \rightarrow a\ A\ b$, which applied to its own output generates an arbitrarily large number of self-embeddings of the form, "aaaAbbb," in which each *a* is mirrored by its corresponding *b*. Rules of this sort cannot be handled by a finite state device. One way of introducing the required power into a grammar for natural language is illustrated in Table 1. This solution was *not* the one that Chomsky advocated in 1957—though he did come to adopt it subsequently—since he then preferred to make use of transformational rules.

The Case for Transformational Rules

There is an important distinction between the weak generative power and the strong generative power of a grammar. The weak power of a grammar concerns solely the set of sentences that it specifies. Thus, a finite state device, or rather its corresponding grammar, does not have sufficient weak generative power to specify English. Strong generative power, however, concerns the specification of the set of sentences *and* their syntactic structures. Chomsky has always taken the view that linguistic theory must concern itself with syntactic structure and accordingly with strong generative capacity.

It seemed intuitively obvious to Chomsky (1957) that phrase structure rules of the sort illustrated in Table 1 could not give an adequate description of a natural language. Such rules seemed unlikely to possess sufficiently strong generative capacity to cope with the description of

TABLE 1
A simple example of a phrase structure grammar containing recursive rules.

1. Sentence   → Noun phrase   Verb phrase
2. Verb phrase → Verb·   Noun phrase
3. Noun phrase → Determiner   Nominal
4. Nominal   → Adjective   Nominal
5. Nominal   → Nominal   Sentence
6. Nominal   → Noun

Rule 1 specifies that the symbol "Sentence" can be rewritten as "Noun phrase" followed by "Verb phrase." Rules 2 and 3 allow for the category "Verb phrase" to be further specified. Rule 4 is recursive since it allows "Nominal" to be rewritten as two symbols, one of which is "Nominal" itself. This rule and Rule 6 generate such *tree structures* as:

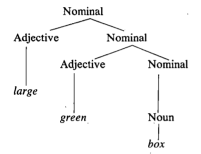

Rule 5 is also recursive: Both the symbols on its right-hand side, "Nominal" and "Sentence," occur on the left-hand side of rules. It generates tree structures that can ultimately underlie embedded relative clauses such as, "The guests who like the hotel . . .":

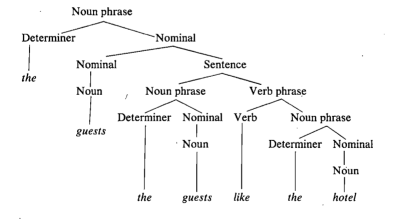

syntactic structure. One problem is that the rules themselves have no way of specifying contextual constraints. For example, if a verb is transitive then it can take a direct object, whereas if it is intransitive it cannot. A simple way to capture this fact is to introduce a new sort of phrase structure rule:

Verb → Transitive-verb / __Noun phrase
Verb → Intransitive-verb/ __#

These *context-sensitive rules* subcategorize verbs into two sorts: transitive verbs, which occur in a constituent in which they are followed by a noun phrase, as is indicated by the context "__Noun phrase" following the slash in the rule; and intransitive verbs, which occur in a constituent in which there is no such noun phrase, as is indicated by "__#." Chomsky (1959) proved that grammars containing context-sensitive rules are more powerful in terms of weak generative capacity than those containing only context-free rules. However, although he has always admitted that context-sensitive rules may have the weak generative capacity required for natural language, he has maintained that a still more powerful sort of rule is required to do justice to syntactic structures (Chomsky, 1965, 1977).

What is required are *transformational rules,* which, instead of merely rewriting one symbol in terms of others, map whole tree structures (of the sort specified by a phrase structure grammar) onto new tree structures. It was into these transformational rules that Chomsky (1957) built the recursive power of his grammar. Phrase structure rules produced tree structures, and transformational rules transformed them and could take one tree structure and embed it within another.

The case for transformational rules is one of the most crucial aspects of modern linguistic theory. It merits close inspection.

Chomsky (1957) advanced a number of essentially aesthetic objections to phrase structure grammar: Its syntactic descriptions are inelegant. It provides only a clumsy treatment of conjunctions involving deletions, such as, "The liner sailed down and the tugboat sailed up the river," and of discontinuous constituents such as the auxiliary verb *be* and its related affix *-ing* that is added to the main verb. It fails to capture the obvious relations between sentences, such as an active and its corresponding passive. Other authors advanced still stronger arguments against phrase structure grammar. Postal (1964) argued that context-free grammar lacked the weak generative capacity required for the grammar of Mohawk, and that no known context-sensitive grammar could cope, either. Mohawk, he claimed, contains an infinite subset of sentences of the form:

$$a_1 \, a_2 \, \ldots \, a_n \, b_1 \, b_2 \, \ldots \, b_n$$

where the corresponding pairs $a_1\ b_1,\ a_2\ b_2,\ \ldots,\ a_n\ b_n$ must contain the same grammatical stem. It had been proved that a language composed entirely of such strings requires a grammar with a weak generative capacity greater than that of context-free rules. Bar-Hillel and Shamir (1960), said Postal (1964), had also noted that English constructions using *respectively* have the same property of requiring a potentially infinite series of agreements between corresponding strings of words, e.g., "Tom, Dick, Harry . . . respectively require a gin, a scotch, a cognac. . . ." The case against phrase structure grammar seemed so overwhelming that Postal's main endeavor was to show that grammars in the American structural tradition, including those proposed by Rulon Wells (1947), Charles Hockett (1954), and Sydney Lamb (1966), were merely variations on the phrase structural theme and could accordingly be dismissed outright. If phrase structure grammars were eliminated, then their natural replacements were transformational grammars. They had the weak generative capacity to cope with languages such as Mohawk, and they had the strong generative capacity to overcome Chomsky's aesthetic qualms.

The case for transformations was not, in fact, decisive, and the reasons why will be described presently. What matters is that the case *seemed* to be overwhelming at the time. It encountered no challenge from either linguists or psycholinguists.

Psycholinguistics and Transformational Grammar

Modern psycholinguistics began with a collaboration between Noam Chomsky and George Miller, who worked together on a number of topics, including finite state devices and the implications of the formal approach to syntax for psychological theory. The appeal of transformational grammar lay not only in the fact that it brushed away all the old theories based on transitional probabilities—and seemed to do the same to the American Structuralists' theories—but also in the subtle analyses of syntax that it offered. They might readily explain a number of aspects of linguistic performance. The initial psycholinguistic experiments carried out by Miller (1962) and his colleagues were concerned with whether there are mental processes that correspond to transformations, particularly those transformations that take simple active declarative structures, the so-called "kernel" structures underlying such sentences as, "The horse ate the apple," and transform them into passives, negatives, interrogatives, or other such sentences. The early results were encouraging. It looked as though the reason that a sentence such as, "Wasn't the apple eaten by the horse?" was harder to understand than the sentence, "The horse ate the apple," was because the first requires three transformations in its specification that are not required in the second. Likewise, it seemed that people remember a sentence by storing its kernel together with a series of "footnotes" about the transformations that it involves (see, e.g., Mehler, 1963; Savin & Perchonock, 1965). Few investigators were concerned with the psychological status of the rules in the phrase structure grammar or with the fact that there were certain transformations that seemed to make sentences easier to understand, e.g., the deletion of the underlying subject of a passive sentence, as in, "The apple was eaten." However, as experimentation burgeoned, psycholinguists gradually realized that something was wrong; transformational complexity was not a reliable guide to psychological complexity. It might still predict the order in which children mastered the structures of their native tongue, but it was a poor index for other aspects of performance. Meanwhile, there were growing pains and growing changes in linguistic theory.

The "Standard" Theory and Perceptual Heuristics

Influenced in part by the ideas of Jerry Katz, Jerry Fodor, and Paul Postal, Chomsky (1965) proposed what is now known as the "standard theory" of transformational grammar in his book, *Aspects of the Theory of Syntax*. This account embodied a number of changes; most notably, Chomsky now located the recursive power of the grammar in the phrase structure rules, roughly along the lines illustrated in Table 1. This manoeuvre made it possible to treat the tree structures generated by the phrase structure rules as *deep structures* that specify all the syntactic information required for recovering the meaning of a sentence. The transformation rules convert such deep structures into the surface structures of actual sentences, and hence the same underlying meaning can be expressed by a variety of sentences differing in their surface forms. Once again, the linguistic arguments in favor of this arrangement seemed convincing. What turned out to be the root of many subsequent disagreements, however, was the introduction of semantic considerations into the organization of grammar. A more immediate psychological problem was to give an account of linguistic performance that was compatible with the standard theory.

A collaboration at M.I.T., among a philosopher, a linguist, and a psychologist—Jerry Fodor, Tom Bever, and Merrill Garrett—yielded the most influential psycholinguistic theory of the early 1970s. They carried out a series of experiments that showed the importance of underlying deep-structure clauses in the perception of syntactic structure. Their paradigm experiment examined the perception of clicks that were presented to one ear while a tape-recorded sentence was being played to the other ear. In this task, subjects characteristically made errors in reporting the location of the click; they tended to re-locate it to a position where it no longer interrupted a word or grammatical constituent. In particular, the click would migrate to a position between underlying clauses even when there was no corresponding boundary between them in the surface structure of the sentence, e.g., into the position marked by the slash in "John expected / Bill to leave" (see Fodor, Bever, & Garrett, 1974, p. 338). Fodor and his colleagues concluded that a crucial step in the perception of sentences is the active recovery of deep structure clauses. This claim was paradoxical because, of course, deep structure is related to surface structure by a series of grammatical transformations, but there was no longer any case to be made for mental processes akin to transformations. It was as though the roles played by the different characters were drawn from linguistic theory, but the actual plot that they enacted was not. The investigators at M.I.T. accordingly proposed a number of perceptual heuristics whose function was to fill the gap left by the nonexistent role for transformations. One such heuristic treated any sequence of the form noun–verb–noun as a putative underlying clause, and another specified that the first noun corresponded to the subject, the second noun corresponded to the object, and the verb corresponded to the main verb of the clause. The notion was plausible because when such an analysis turns out to be erroneous, as in "The horse raced past the barn fell," the sentence seems to have led the reader up the garden path. Likewise, self-embedded sentences may be hard to understand because they, too, are susceptible to the same misreading. "The affair the story the author wrote described ended the marriage" plays havoc with the proposed parsing heuristics.

The search for perceptual cues led to the invention of a number of ingenious experimental techniques that have subsequently been put to other uses. Foss (1969) introduced a procedure in which subjects have to respond as soon as they detect the presence of a target phoneme that occurs at the start of a word in a recorded sentence. The latencies of response in this "phoneme-monitoring" task are affected by a variety of variables, including syntactic cues, but it now appears that there are at least two different ways in which the target phoneme is recognized: one that consists of a purely phonological process, and one that involves the identification of the word bearing the target phoneme (see Cutler & Norris, 1979). Forster (1970) devised a technique in which the words of a sentence are superimposed one after the other in a rapid serial visual presentation—the "RSVP" procedure. The accuracy of subjects' perceptions of sentences presented in this way is also affected by their syntactic structure.

There was certainly no lack of experimental ingenuity in pursuit of perceptual heuristics. However, the trouble with the theory, as Gough (1971) remarked, was that it did not suffer from premature formalization;

it was never specified in a way that constituted an effective procedure, perhaps because psycholinguists have seldom achieved the same degree of explicitness and precision that linguists cherish. The development of computer programs for parsing, both for compiling high-level programming languages (see Aho & Ullman, 1972) and for analyzing natural language (see Thorne, Bratley, & Dewar, 1968; Winograd, 1972; Woods, 1970) has led to a number of more specific proposals about the psychology of syntactic analysis (Kaplan, 1972; Wanner & Maratsos, 1978).

Generative Semantics and CASE Grammar

There was another difficulty with the theory of perceptual heuristics, which its authors acknowledged. Because deep structure is a basic syntactic "blueprint" for obtaining the meaning of a sentence from the meanings of its constituents, any evidence suggesting a role for deep structure in psychological processes could equally well be interpreted as evidence in favor of a role for semantic representation. Moreover, there were findings in the literature on memory that implied that people generally recall the meaning of a sentence, *not* its deep structure. They readily confuse such clauses as "John bought the picture from the duchess" and "The duchess sold the picture to John," which have similar meanings, but in which the same noun phrases play very different roles in deep structure. The status of deep structure in psychological processes became somewhat suspect (see Johnson-Laird, 1974). And these suspicions were nothing in comparison to those of certain linguists.

On the one hand, the so-called "generative semanticists," such as Lakoff (1971), McCawley (1968), and Ross (1970), argued that sentences should be transformationally derived from an underlying *semantic* representation. This derivation, they claimed, captured generalizations that were outside the scope of the standard theory, such as the obvious relation between:

Cain killed Abel

and:

Abel died.

But, this approach was incompatible with the existence of deep structure as an independent and unitary level of syntactic representation; at no point in the derivation of a sentence from a semantic representation did such a structure exist.

On the other hand, Fillmore (1968) proposed a theory of "case grammar," which had a considerable influence on psychologists. His thesis was that each noun phrase associated with a verb in a clause occurred in a different "case," corresponding to its underlying semantic role. Thus, for example, the similarity between:

John bought the picture from the duchess

and:

The duchess sold the picture to John

is a reflection of the case structure of the two sentences, since in both of them "John" is in the *goal* case, and "the duchess" is in the *source* case.

Neither generative semantics nor case grammar has outlived its useful initial lessons. They both suffered from vagueness and lack of precision. For instance, although case grammar provided a useful informal taxonomy of the major semantic roles that can occur in a sentence, no explicit and exhaustive formulation of all the different cases was ever satisfactorily devised. Similarly, there was no decisive evidence to suggest that the phenomena that the theories drew attention to could not be accommodated by more orthodox means. A comprehensive account of syntax and semantics might readily allow that a noun phrase could play a different syntactic role in two different sentences and yet combine with the semantics of their respective verbs so as to yield the same meaning for both sentences.

Chomsky and his associates reacted to the challenge from generative semantics by proposing a succession of revisions to the standard theory and by arguing that deep structure was a purely syntactic object that provided only *some* of the information needed for semantic interpretation (Chomsky, 1971). There were indeed many syntactic phenomena that stood in urgent need of explanation. Transformations that moved a constituent of a tree from one place to another had long been invoked—and had long been known to require certain constraints, yet no explanatorily adequate theory had been proposed for movement transformations.

By the late 1970s, the erstwhile unity of generative grammar had split into a bewildering set of schisms, whose proponents often disagreed on the goals of linguistics and the nature of the evidence relevant to the evaluation of theories. Psycholinguists had developed sufficient autonomy to continue their investigations while they waited to see how the linguistic controversies would be settled, but in both experimental and developmental studies interest shifted away from syntax and towards semantics. Indeed, psychologists have usually been interested in meaning and how it is communicated, to a greater extent than their linguist colleagues.

SEMANTIC THEORY AND THE PSYCHOLOGY OF MEANING

The Theory of Semantic Markers

Meaning has always been too important to be left to a single intellectual discipline; philosophers, logicians, psychologists, and anthropologists have all contributed to semantic theory. However, after Bloomfield's (1926) interdiction on the topic, it did not re-enter the mainstream of linguistics until the work of Katz and Fodor (1963). Their theory had an immediate impact on both linguistics and psycholinguistics because it appeared to be a natural development of transformational grammar. They assumed that the semantic interpretation of a sentence is obtained by replacing its words with their semantic representations, which are then combined according to the deep syntactic structure of the sentence. They also held that the semantic representation of a word comprises a structured set of elements, or "semantic markers," which decompose the meaning of the word into its more primitive semantic constituents. Underlying the meaning of *woman,* for example, are the fundamental concepts of human, female, and adult. Since a word may have several distinct meanings, the process of combining the meanings of words is sensitive to the constraints, the so-called "selectional restrictions," that one word may place upon the meanings of others with which it is to be combined. One sense of *handsome,* for instance, is restricted to human beings and artifacts, and another sense is restricted to conduct. Hence, neither *a handsome price* nor *a handsome act* is ambiguous because each noun meets the selectional restrictions of only one sense of *handsome.*

The theory of semantic markers inspired a considerable amount of empirical work in psycholinguistics. What proved to be particularly attractive was the notion of decomposing the meaning of a word into its more fundamental conceptual elements. This analysis was used to explain many of the phenomena of word association (H. Clark, 1970; Marshall, 1969). It led plausibly to the hypothesis that a child learns the meaning of a word by gradually acquiring its underlying semantic markers—a notion that has been most systematically explored by E. Clark (1973). It also offered accounts of how the mental lexicon is organized and how information is retrieved from it in the evaluation of sentences. A characteristic experimental finding is that a sentence such as "A poodle is a dog" is evaluated faster than a sentence such as "A poodle is an animal"; whereas a sentence such as "A poodle is a cat" is evaluated as false slower than a sentence such as "A poodle is a fruit." It seems that the greater the overlap of the semantic markers of the subject and predicate nouns, the easier it is to respond true and the harder it is to respond false (see, e.g., Schaeffer & Wallace, 1969; Smith, Shoben, & Rips, 1974). However, the notion of a semantic network in which words are linked according to the semantic relations between them offers a comparable explanation of the phenomenon (see Collins & Quillian, 1972; Hollan, 1975).

Despite the successes of semantic marker theory, there remain some obstinate problems with it. A crucial psychological difficulty is that the semantic decomposition of words turns out to be a process that is virtually unobservable. The greater the amount of decomposition, the longer it ought to take to understand a sentence. The sentence, "The priest lifted the bible," ought to take longer to understand than, "The man moved the book," because *priest* is more complex than *man, lift* is more complex than *move,* and *bible* is more complex than *book.* (Whenever one word such as *priest* implies another such as *man,* but not vice versa, then the first word must include as a proper subset all the semantic markers of the second word.) There does not appear intuitively to be any great difference in the ease of understanding such sentences. No experiments have yet established any reliable differences of this sort, though when subjects are required to *verify* sentences there are results which suggest that lexical semantics can have a reliable effect. H. Clark and his colleagues have established in a striking series of experiments that an implicitly negative relation such as *below* takes reliably longer to verify than the equivalent affirmative relation *above* (see Clark & Clark, 1977, for a review of these experiments). However, if decomposition occurs during comprehension alone—and there is no reason to suppose that it is invariably necessary for understanding—it would seem to be carried out by some sort of mechanism that operates either in parallel or too rapidly for the sensitivity of orthodox experimental techniques to detect.

A linguistic difficulty with the theory, which was anticipated by Wittgenstein (1953), is that many terms in natural language have no necessary and sufficient conditions for their correct application. This difficulty was pointed out most forcefully by Putnam (1975), who argued that "natural kind terms" such as *lemon, gold,* and *tiger,* lack such conditions for their application, and that what a speaker relies on in giving an account of their meanings is a theory about the prototypical, or stereotypical, members of the natural kind. There is much empirical evidence for the existence of prototypes in the minds of both adults (see, e.g., Rosch, 1973) and children (see Bornstein, 1981; Bowerman, 1977); they may well exist even for terms that have necessary and sufficient conditions.

Attempts have been made to patch up the psychological versions of semantic marker theory so as to meet these various difficulties. Certain theorists, however, have argued that the decompositional doctrine should be abandoned in favor of the approach to be described next.

The Meaning Postulate Theory

A very different conception of meaning, which gives up both semantic decomposition and dictionary entries, was independently proposed by Kintsch (1974) and Fodor, Fodor, and Garrett (1975). The theory relies on the formal device of "meaning postulates," which were originally introduced by Carnap (1956) in order to stipulate that certain semantic relations held between the predicates of a formal calculus. To establish that it is necessarily true that all bachelors are unmarried, the following meaning postulate is added to the calculus:

For any x, if x is a bachelor then x is unmarried.

According to the psychological theory, the first stage of understanding a sentence in a natural language is to translate it into a mental language in which there are tokens corresponding to each of the lexical items in the sentence. The entailments of the sentence can then be recovered, if need be, by applying the relevant meaning postulates to this relatively superficial representation. The fact that "The priest lifted the bible" implies "The man moved the book" can be inferred from the following meaning postulates:

For any x, if x is a priest then x is a man.
For any x, y, if x lifts y then x moves y.
For any x, if x is a bible then x is a book.

The major advantage of the meaning postulate theory is that it posits no process of decomposition during initial comprehension, and it is therefore entirely compatible with the failure to demonstrate such effects in the laboratory. Its proponents also claim that it easily accommodates predicates that lack necessary and sufficient conditions, since it can readily capture the necessary entailments of a term without being committed to the view that it must have an exhaustive analysis. If something is *a tiger* then indeed it is *an animal*. Unfortunately, however, the stereotypical tiger has stripes, a tail, four legs, and many other characteristics which, though neither necessary nor sufficient for the application of the term, should be captured in some way by a psychological theory of meaning. The meaning postulate theory lacks any machinery for this job. A stereotype demands the existence of values that can be assumed by default, that is, they can be taken for granted unless there are grounds to the contrary. This idea can be traced back to Wittgenstein's notion of a *criterion* for the application of a term, and it has been rendered explicit in Minsky's (1975) concept of a "default value."

One final omission in both the meaning postulate and the semantic marker theories needs to be pointed out. They are both primarily theories designed to account for semantic properties, such as ambiguity and anomaly, and for semantic relations between expressions, such as synonymy and entailment; they have nothing to say about how words relate to the world. They assume implicitly that a plausible theory of the semantic properties and relations of expressions can be constructed without regard to the referents of such expressions. This approach may be feasible for linguistic theory, but there are grounds for supposing that it will not work for psychological theories of meaning (see Johnson-Laird, 1980). The problem of relating language to the world has been dealt with only by theories of meaning deriving from formal semantics, and it is to those theories that we now turn.

Realism and Psychologism: The Traditions of Frege and de Saussure

The distinction between what an expression *means* and what it *refers to* goes back at least to the work of the great German logician, Gottlob Frege, and particularly the paper he published on sense and reference (Frege, 1892/1952). He distinguished between the reference of an expression, i.e. the object it designates, and the sense of an expression, i.e. the way in which it makes the designation. The terms *extension* and *intension* have come to be used in place of reference and sense. To take Frege's example, the two expressions "The Morning Star" and "The Evening Star" have the same extension in our universe, namely, the planet Venus, but different intensions since one means the star observed in the morning and the other means the star observed in the evening. Frege argued that the extension of an assertion is its truth value, and its intension is the proposition that it expresses. In an ideal language, such as the predicate calculus of formal logic, which Frege invented, the extension of an expression can be built up compositionally from the extension of its constituents according to their syntactic organization. However, in natural language, as Frege pointed out, this principle cannot hold. The *intension* of an expression can certainly be built up compositionally in this way, and here Frege anticipated the central assumption of the theory of semantic markers, but the principle fails for *extensions*. As he pointed out, the assertion "Copernicus believed that the planetary orbits are circles" is true even though, of course, the assertion "the planetary orbits are circles" is false.

Frege's insight into the compositional workings of natural language was in advance of his time. It had a negligible effect on linguistic theory, perhaps in part because of Frege's philosophical doctrine of Realism. He took great pains to distinguish both sense and reference from the *idea* associated with a sign. He wrote:

> If the reference of a sign is an object perceivable by the senses, my idea of it is an internal image, arising from memories of sensory impressions which I have had and acts, both internal and external, which I have performed. Such an idea is often saturated with feeling; the clarity of its separate parts varies and oscillates. The same sense is not always connected, even in the same man, with the same idea. The idea is subjective: one man's idea is not that of another. There results, as a matter of course, a variety of differences in the ideas associated with the same sense. A painter, a horseman, and a zoologist will probably connect different ideas with the name 'Bucephalus'. This constitutes an essential distinction between the idea and the sign's sense, which may be the common property of many and therefore is not part of the individual mind. For one can hardly deny that mankind has a common store of thoughts which is transmitted from one generation to another [Frege, 1892/ 1952 p. 59].

This doctrine, that there is the real sense of a sign, distinct from an individual's idea of it, which somehow society is able to grasp and to pass down to the next generation, probably derives from Frege's concern with the language of mathematics.

A very different doctrine of meaning was promulgated by de Saussure. He took the view in his lectures (1907–1911) at the University of Geneva (see de Saussure, 1960) that a sign consists of a form (the "signifier") that is mentally associated with a concept (the "signified"). In language, the actual sound-form that is bound to a particular concept is arbitrary, that is, there is no natural connection between them except in the few cases of onomatopoeia. However, the particular value that a concept has depends on what other concepts exist. Indeed, de Saussure insists that it is impossible to define a concept positively, but only in terms of its relations to other concepts. (He made the same point about phonemes—an assumption that lies behind the notion of distinctive features.) Thus, the French word *mouton* and the English word *sheep* can have the same signification because they can both be used in talking about sheep, but they differ in value because English contains the word *mutton* for talking about meat, whereas French has no such counterpart. The concepts for which there are signs plainly differ from one language to another. They are by no means immutable but can change from one generation to another. Hence, while de Saussure takes the same view as Frege about the fact that language goes beyond what occurs in an individual's mind, he does not adopt the philosophy of Platonic Realism in which there is some objective realm of meanings where every term has necessary and sufficient conditions. On the contrary, de Saussure recognized that language is a mental and social product—the associations between words and concepts bear the stamp of societal approval—and that the lexicon is relationally organized.

Model-theoretic Semantics

The development of Frege's ideas has until recently been largely the work of logicians. They showed how to develop a compositional semantics for a formal language in terms of a *model*. A model consists of a function from the well-formed expressions of the language to elements in some specified *model structure* such as a set of individuals, integers, or other mathematical objects. The function that assigns such interpretations depends on two sorts of semantic rules. There are rules that provide an interpretation for the basic lexical items of the language: They pick out the appropriate individual in the model structure for a proper name, the appropriate set of individuals for a common noun, and so on. There are also structural rules that build up the interpretation of complex expressions from the interpretations of their constituents: These rules are contrived to operate in parallel with the syntactic rules governing what counts as a well-formed expression. They provide the semantics for those lexical items, such as *and* and *or,* that are not basic. There will be, for instance, a syntactic rule governing how to form a conjunction in the language and a corresponding semantic rule that specifies the interpretation of a conjunction as a function of the interpretations of its separate conjuncts.

The extension of "model-theoretic" methods to natural language was made possible by two major developments. First, Tarski (1956), in defining the notion of *truth* for a formal language, showed how to cope with sentences such as, "Every mother has a child who loves her," where the constituent, "who loves her," unlike a clause in a conjunction, cannot have a truth value in isolation. Tarski's solution was to introduce a more general notion, *satisfaction,* which applies to such constituents, and to use it in turn to define truth. An ordered pair of individuals in a model structure, say, James and Mary, satisfies the expression, "who loves her," just in case the pair is in the set of ordered pairs assigned as the interpretation of the two-place relation, *loves,* by the basic semantic rules. Second, Kripke (1963) showed how to formulate a model-theoretic semantics for the so-called "modal" logics governing the notions of necessity and possibility. The fundamental Leibnizian assumptions are that a proposition that is necessary is true in all possible states of affairs and that a proposition that is possible is true in at least some possible states of affairs. Logicians talk of "possible worlds" rather than the more cumbersome "possible states of affairs;" the real world is of course a member of the set of possible worlds. What Kripke introduced was the notion of an accessibility relation between possible worlds; an assertion is necessarily true in a particular world if and only if it is true in all possible worlds that are accessible to that world. Different assumptions can be made about the logical properties of the accessibility relation, and depending on them so the resulting semantics corresponds to different modal logics.

The introduction of possible worlds into the model structures of formal semantics has illuminated Frege's distinction between sense (intension) and reference (extension). The intension of a sentence—the proposition that it expresses—can be treated as a function from the set of possible worlds onto the set of truth values (true and false); the extension of the sentence is its truth value with respect to the particular "possible world" under consideration. Hence, the difference between the obvious truism, "The Morning Star is identical to the Morning Star," and the true but informative assertion, "The Morning Star is identical to the Evening Star," is that the first is true in all possible worlds, whereas the second is true only in some possible worlds (including the real one). The two assertions accordingly have different intensions but the same extension in our world. As a matter of fact, this account is an oversimplification because the proposition expressed by a sentence in ordinary language depends on the context in which it occurs—the time and place, the speaker and listener, and the circumstances of the utterance. It is therefore more appropriate to think of one set of possible worlds as representing the context of a sentence's utterance and to treat the meaning of the sentence as a function from contexts to a proposition, and the proposition in turn as a function from possible worlds to a truth value (see, e.g., Stalnaker, 1978).

Montague Grammar

The application of model-theoretic semantics to natural language by Montague (1974), and other like-minded theorists, has relied on the use of "possible worlds" semantics in order to cope with expressions whose extensions cannot be built up compositionally from the extensions of their constituents, e.g., sentences expressing modal propositions, assertions about propositional attitudes such as wants or beliefs, and terms like *alleged* that cannot be treated in a simple extensional manner. Montague, in particular, extended the apparatus of formal semantics in order to analyze various "fragments" of English, and he established an elegant system of different semantic *types* that were constructed to work in parallel with the different grammatical categories of his theory. There are two basic types: *e,* expressions that denote individuals, and *t,* expressions that denote truth values, but complex types build up recursively to designate any function from one type to another. For example, a property designated by an adjective such as *tall* or an intransitive verb such as *sneezes* is interpreted in the model structure as a set of individuals, which is defined by its characteristic function. This function returns the value true or false for each individual in the model structure depending on whether or not that individual has the property in question. Hence, terms designating a property are of the type $\langle e,t \rangle$ since they are interpreted as functions from individuals to truth values. Strictly speaking, the value of the characteristic function for *sneezes* will change from one moment to the next, but I am assuming here that the model structure represents just a single moment of time and a single possible world.

The fundamental simplicity of Montague's scheme is masked by several factors, in addition to his somewhat rebarbative notation. In his analysis of noun phrases, Montague uses an approach which, though familiar to logicians, is different from the one that is found in logic texts. The idea is to treat all the different sorts of noun phrase, such as *every woman, John, a boy, no one,* in the same uniform way. Since a property is interpreted as a set of individuals, then each of, say, John's properties consists of a set of individuals, included in each of which, of course, is John himself. However, only one person, John, will be a member of all of these sets, because if two individuals have all their properties in common they must be identical. This consideration allows Montague to interpret the noun phrase, *John,* as a set of sets, viz., the set of all of John's properties, or, in other words, the set of all sets of which John is a member. This way of interpreting a proper noun as a set of sets can be extended to deal with any sort of noun phrase. Thus, the interpretation of *every woman* consists of all the sets (formed from the individuals and entities in the model structure) that contain every woman; the interpretation of *a boy* consists of all the sets that contain at least one boy; the interpretation of *no one* consists of all the sets that contain no persons (they will contain the other animate and inanimate entities in the model structure). This way of proceeding may seem mystifying at first, but it is perfectly sensible, and it has several advantages over the more traditional approach since it can also cope with quantifiers, such as *most women* and *few people,* and with noun phrases with relative clauses, such as *every woman who has had a child.* The reason that it works depends on the way in which the structural rules assign a truth value to a sentence (with respect to the model structure). A sentence such as *John sneezes* is true if the set of individuals comprising the interpretation of *sneezes* is a member of the set comprising the interpretation of *John.* Thus, the expression *John* denotes a function that takes *sneezes* as an argument and returns a truth value. Once again, this way of proceeding may seem counterintuitive, but a moment's thought should clarify matters. If one of John's properties is that he sneezes at the moment of time embodied in the model structure, then one of the sets comprising the interpretation of *John* will consist of all the individuals sneezing at that time. Hence, the set comprising the interpretation of the verb, *sneezes,* will indeed be a member of the set comprising the interpretation of the noun phrase, *John.* This principle holds equally for the interpretation of the other sorts of noun phrase, as the reader may readily check by experimenting with a model structure containing only a few individuals.

There are several further layers of complexity in Montague's approach. Clearly, a model cannot usefully represent just a single moment of time in a single world: It is necessary to adapt the "possible worlds" approach and to have a separate model structure representing each moment of time. Likewise, in order to ensure the greatest possible generality, Montague initially treats all expressions intensionally; if a construction is extensional then there are meaning postulates that will capture that aspect of it. In his treatment of quantification, Montague showed how to translate natural language into a formal language—a tensed intensional logic, for which he provided a "possible worlds" interpretation. However, there is really no need for such a translation into an intermediate language since a model-theoretic semantics can be provided for natural language directly, as Montague did for the fragment characterized in his paper on English as a formal language (see, Montague, 1974).

There are a number of important methodological differences between model-theoretic semantics and the theories of meaning propounded within the immediate tradition of transformational grammar. The crucial division, perhaps, is over the assumption that the rules of semantic interpretation should run in parallel with the rules of syntax. Chomsky established the need for recursive rules in order to capture the grammar of a language. There is a similar need for recursive rules in order to capture the meanings of sentences. Montague assumed that the two sets of rules should parallel one another—in this way each constituent of a well-formed sentence receives a semantic interpretation, and the interpretation of the sentence is built up compositionally (at least insofar as intensions are concerned). Chomsky (1977), however, has argued for the autonomy of syntax: Syntax is not simply a means for ensuring the proper composition of meaning-bearing elements; a syntactic analysis is justified by the extent to which it can account for syntactic phenomena other than those that motivated it. Despite Chomsky's rejection of the crucial methodological assumption of Montague grammar, increasing numbers of generative linguists are adopting its principles (see, e.g., Bach, 1979; Dowty, 1976; Partee, 1975, 1976).

The machinery of formal semantics provides linguists with the most powerful techniques so far developed for the analysis of the structural or compositional aspects of the meanings of sentences. There is clearly a relation between the concept of 'mental models' canvassed by some psychologists and the model-structures of formal semantics (see Johnson-Laird, 1979, for a discussion of this relation), and there is plenty of scope for psychologists to explore Stanley Peters's unpublished ecumenical principle: Formal semantics should characterize *what* is computed when a sentence is understood, and psychological semantics should characterize *how* it is computed.

CURRENT ISSUES IN LINGUISTICS AND PSYCHOLOGY

Syntax and Parsing

Linguistic arguments have often proved more decisive than the empirical findings obtained by psychologists. The reason for this asymmetry is that linguists have been able to prove theorems based on certain assumptions about language. The power of proofs can cut both ways, however, for the exact nature of those assumptions may elude investigators and the proof accordingly mislead them in a more profound and prolonged manner than any argument based on an appeal to data. Few theorists working within the generative framework challenged the case for transformational rules, for instance, and it was not until recently that there was any recognition that perhaps that case, which was summarized earlier, had been over-stated. A number of independent developments were necessary before there was any scepticism about transformations on the part of those who appreciated the power of the mathematical approach to syntax.

First, Peters and Ritchie (1973a) established that a transformational grammar is in principle as powerful as a Turing machine. Turing machines are abstract automata that form the basis of the theory of computation, and, as far as anyone knows, any procedure that can be spelt out in the form of an explicit algorithm can be computed by a Turing machine. However, there can be no general and effective method for determining whether or not a Turing machine eventually halts once it has started computing on the basis of input data (see Boolos & Jeffrey, 1974). That a grammar should be this powerful is embarrassing because it implies that the property of sentence-hood is not a decidable matter, that the underlying phrase structure grammar on whose output the transformations operate can be entirely arbitrary, and that the grammar may in principle be unlearnable.

Second, one by one, the various arguments that Chomsky and his associates had put forward to support the need for transformations have appeared to be less than decisive. In particular, Postal's data on Mohawk were not published, and it was unclear whether he had taken into account what structures were ruled out by the grammar of the language—a critical factor because a weaker grammar, such as one admitting all possible sequences of words, would obviously also admit the relevant infinite subset of sentences. Likewise, the English constructions using *respectively* seemed to be better accounted for semantically than syntactically, since *respectively* has the force of the deictic expression *in that order* (de Cornulier, 1973).

Third, Peters and Ritchie (1973b) proved a theorem which showed that a seemingly innocuous assumption about the interpretation of context-sensitive grammars had a striking consequence. The orthodox interpretation of a phrase structure rule is that it specifies how one symbol can be *rewritten* in terms of others. An alternative interpretation, which had seemed to be equivalent, is to treat rules as a specification of what is an acceptable *analysis* of an already given tree structure. The tree structure shown in Table 2 is certainly analyzable by the grammar shown there, because each node in the tree satisfies a rule of the grammar. What Peters and Ritchie demonstrated, however, is that when a context-sensitive grammar is interpreted in this alternative way, it possesses only the (weak generative) power of a context-free grammar. The reader can intuitively grasp the difference between the two interpretations of grammatical rules by checking that although the grammar in Table 2 analyzes the tree there, it cannot in fact generate it when the rules are interpreted as rewriting one symbol in terms of others: S can be expanded to A B, but then the rewriting process blocks because the rule for rewriting A requires the context generated by the rule for rewriting B, and vice versa. The important consequence of this theorem is that rules that take context into account in analyzing sentences do not exceed the weak generative power of context-free grammar.

A number of linguists are currently exploring various ways in which constraints can be placed on the power of transformations (see, e.g., Chomsky, 1977). Others are reducing the number of transformations employed by the grammar and shifting the burden of work into the underlying phrase structure rules or the machinery for semantic interpretation (see, e.g., Bresnan, 1978). And, from within the generative tradition, there have been at least three independent proposals to give up transformations altogether, by Brame (1978), by Peters (personal communication), and by Gazdar (in press). What is important about these last two studies is that they propose to treat English as a context-free language and that they include an account of how sentences should be semantically interpreted along model-theoretic lines. Hence, there is a prima facie case that they give a satisfactory description of both sentences and their syntactic structures, that is, they are meeting Chomsky's demand for strong generative capacity.

TABLE 2
A simple context-sensitive grammar interpreted, not as rewriting rules, but
as conditions on the admissibility of a tree structure.

The grammar:
 1. S → A B
 2. A → a / __ b
 3. B → b / a __

The tree structure:

This tree can be analyzed by the grammar: the S-node in the tree is analyzed as an A and B according to Rule 1; the A-node is analyzed as an a in the context __ b according to Rule 2; the B-node is analyzed as a b in the context a __ according to Rule 3.

There are a number of theoretical advantages that follow from charac-terizing language as context free. Studies of context-free grammars from a computational standpoint have established a variety of parsing algorithms for them based on the idea of a push-down store—a memory which can cope with recursive rules and which works on the principle of a stack in which the most recently stored item has to be recalled first. It has been proved that any context-free language can be parsed within a time propor-tional to n^3, where n is the length of an input string (see Hopcroft & Ullman, 1969). No such bounds have been established for transforma-tional grammars, which may well turn out in general to require a non-deterministic parser that takes an exponential amount of time proportional to k^n, where k is a constant and n is the length of the input string. Such a parsing could not in general be carried out on a computer (Garey & Johnson, 1978)—it would take far too long—and the implication is obviously that it would not be tractable for the human mind, either.

There are also many psychological advantages inherent in the notion that natural languages are context free. It has long seemed plausible that the comprehension mechanism builds up an immediate interpretation of a sentence without the need to construct an intermediate syntactic repre-sentation (see, e.g., Steedman & Johnson-Laird, 1976). This conjecture has received considerable experimental support from an outstanding series of experiments conducted by Marslen-Wilson and his colleagues. One of their procedures requires subjects to repeat aloud a tape-recorded passage in which there are deliberate mistakes. Subjects in this "shadow-ing" task often spontaneously correct these mistakes without even noticing them. By an ingenious manipulation of the nature of the deliberate mistakes, Marslen-Wilson has shown that subjects appear to interpret discourse virtually completely almost as soon as they hear it, on a word-by-word basis (see Marslen-Wilson, Tyler, & Seidenberg, 1978). The production of speech can likewise be envisaged as a direct mapping from a semantic representation to the words expressing it. One exciting possibility, proposed by Ades and Steedman (personal communication), is that the mental parser does indeed rely on a push-down store and that the intrinsic nature of its operations constrains the possible word orders that can be embodied in natural language.

The pattern of much current theoretical work reflects a growing concern on the part of linguists and psycholinguists that grammars should be plausible psychologically (see Halle, Bresnan, & Miller, 1978). A major problem for this approach is to give an account of the comprehension of dislocated constituents such as those noun phrases that movement transformations had been hitherto invoked to explain. In *WH*-questions, such as: "What do you have after dinner?" there is plainly a constituent, "you have after dinner," which has a gap in it and which would be grammatical if the missing noun phrase were replaced, as in "you have mint chocolates after dinner." There is a similar relation between the relative pronoun and the gap in a relative clause, "The chocolates you have after dinner are from Dundee." What is impressive about current attempts to analyze such sentences is the interplay between psychological and linguistic considerations (e.g., Fodor, 1978; Frazier & Fodor, 1978; Wanner & Maratsos, 1978). This interplay is likely to continue in studies of syntax and parsing.

Semantics: Models and Procedures

Current developments in model-theoretic semantics reflect the fundamental contributions of a number of individuals. Frege contributed the sense-reference distinction and the idea of the compositionality of the meanings of sentences. Chomsky established the need for recursive rules of syntax. Montague stressed the advantage of syntactic and semantic rules that operate in tandem. The one major influence on linguistics yet to be incorporated into model theory is that of de Saussure, who pointed out that the semantic value of a lexical sign depends on its relations to other signs. The lack of any sustained analyses of lexical meanings in model theory (cf., Dowty, 1979) is the major reason for its negligible influence so far on the psychology of meaning.

Psychologists need to account for the relation between words and the world and for how this relation is mediated by the mind. The heart of the problem is indeed in lexical semantics. Miller and Johnson-Laird (1976) have made a detailed analysis of the structure of the mental lexicon, and of the content and form of its lexical entries, in order to try to elucidate both the way in which words mentally relate to one another and the way in which they mentally relate to the world. Neither the semantic marker theory nor the meaning postulate theory have anything significant to contribute to the problem of reference and extension since they are primarily intensional theories. Hence, Miller and Johnson-Laird turned to the "procedural semantics" developed within artificial intelligence (see, e.g., Davies & Isard, 1972; Woods, 1967). They argued that the meaning of a word could not be reduced to the ability, often limited, to identify instances of the corresponding object, property, or relation. The procedures underlying this ability were only one component of semantics. Nevertheless, it is possible to treat the mental lexicon on a wider procedural basis; the meaning of a word can be treated as a procedure that by itself can do nothing but that can enter into the general procedures for describing states of affairs, asking questions or answering them, making requests, verifying assertions, and so on. A task for the future is to try to implement a working simulation of such a system and to integrate it, with suitable modifications (see Cushing, 1979), into an appropriate compositional treatment of sentences.

The mental representation of the world is analogous to a model-structure of formal semantics, but there are a number of important differences between the two. First, the mental interpretation of a lexical item is likely to be a partial function. Language is vague and "open textured" in that in many cases it is impossible to draw a clear line between those entities that satisfy a predicate and those that do not. Recourse to *fuzzy set theory* perhaps solves this problem but only at the cost of raising another one, since it becomes impossible to cope with the compositional aspects of semantics correctly (see Kamp, 1975), though this problem has deterred neither linguists (e.g., Lakoff, 1972) nor psychologists (e.g., Hersh & Caramazza, 1976). Second, the primary use of language is communication, which often goes beyond what is linguistically given. Although the need for an inferential component in comprehension was long overlooked, its importance has been well established in the psychological laboratory (see, e.g., Bransford & McCarrell, 1975). It is plainly necessary to cope with indirect reference (Nunberg, 1979), as when a waiter remarks to his replacement: "The ham sandwich is sitting at table 20." It is also required to provide the sense of denominal verbs (Clark & Clark, 1979), as when a speaker invents the following sort of neologism: "He Nixonized the tapes." Of course, no description can pin down a model of the world unequivocally, and so the model that a listener constructs may diverge from the model that the speaker had in mind.

What these discrepancies bring out is the fact that the model structures of formal semantics are too precise, too explicit, and too complete to provide an adequate basis for a psychology of communication. Mental models can somehow function efficiently even though they are vague, indeterminate, and incomplete. Hence, an important psychological puzzle to be solved is to show how vagueness and indeterminacy are mentally represented. Likewise, a plausible account is needed of pronominal reference and of other anaphoric phenomena (cf., Sag, 1979). Both problems seem likely to require a combined attack by linguists and psychologists.

Language Acquisition

The psychological study of how children acquire their native tongues has been largely inspired by the theoretical ideas of linguists. Chomsky's (1965) speculations about the "language acquisition device" stimulated workers to investigate syntactic development (e.g., McNeill, 1970). Fillmore's (1968) case grammar provided a useful conceptual tool for the analysis of children's mastery of semantics (e.g., Bloom, 1971; Brown, 1973; Schlesinger, 1971). Halliday's (1975) systemic grammar, his own empirical observations, and the influence of "speech act" philosophers have inspired more recent studies of the acquisition of pragmatics (e.g., Bates, 1976; Dore, 1975). As each successive wave of investigations has subsided, what it has left behind is a progressively stronger impression of the difficulty of finding out how children learn to speak. The crucial developments are mental; they do not manifest themselves very tangibly in what children say or do. A good index of the gap between theory and obtainable data concerns the learnability of syntax.

A number of mathematical studies, initiated by Gold (1967), have dealt with the design of algorithms that could learn a grammar of a known class (finite state, context free, context sensitive, transformational). Given only a finite number of sentences in a language, then there will always be many—infinitely many—different grammars that could specify those sentences. An abstract strategy for coping with this problem was formulated by Gold: Enumerate every possible grammar of the relevant class, start with the first grammar and as soon as it fails to cope with the data abandon it in favor of the next grammar on the list, and so on. Sooner or later, this procedure will encounter the correct grammar, and thenceforth it will never encounter sentences that it cannot accommodate. The strategy can only work, however, if the data include information about both grammatical sentences and ungrammatical sequences of words. Obviously, a string of words must either be accepted or rejected by each grammar in the enumeration. The worrisome nature of the proof that transformational grammars are equivalent to Turing machines is precisely that there can be no effective procedure for determining whether or not any arbitrarily selected Turing machine will ever cease computing when presented with an input string. Hence, one reason for seeking to reduce the power of transformational rules is to break their equivalence with Turing machines and thereby ensure that in principle they are learnable. Culicover, Wexler, and Hamburger have established a series of theorems on this issue (for a review, see Culicover, 1976), and they have shown how to introduce constraints on transformational grammars that guarantee learnability. However, if the conjecture that natural languages are context free turns out to be correct, then the task of proving learnability will be considerably easier.

Psycholinguists have generally assumed that the meanings of expressions, which can be independently known to a child, play a large part in helping the child to figure out the rules of syntax. Thus, Anderson's (1976) computer program, which can acquire certain fragments of English, has recourse to semantic representations and to constraints on the relations between them and syntactic structures. However, the problem is to formulate a psychologically plausible theory of semantic representations. As several commentators have noted (e.g., Pinker, 1979), there is a great danger that the theorist simply chooses a semantic representation that is little different from the syntactic structure to be learnt. Perhaps model-theoretic semantics could play a useful part here. Several theorists, including Anderson, employ tree structures to represent meanings, but such trees have nothing to do with the extensions of expressions, and it is at least arguable that children initially acquire an extensional knowledge of the words. Hence, in order to exploit the intuition that meaning plays a role in acquiring grammar, it would be a useful working principle to assume only that children relate linguistic expressions to their extensions in mental models rather than that they translate them into an internalized intensional language (whose syntax just happens to mirror that of the natural language to be learned).

The remoteness of these theories of language acquisition from what can be observed empirically is as obvious as it is regrettable. Developmental psycholinguists have established beyond doubt that children do not learn their language by being reinforced for speaking grammatically (Brown, 1973). They have also collected many observations about the nature of both the language that children speak and the language that is spoken to them. Yet, more than one warning has been recently sounded to the effect that the field may collapse under the weight of inconsistent and inexplicable data. The best hope for avoiding this fate is a renewed attempt to devise theories of acquisition that have obvious observational consequences.

CONCLUSIONS

There is a fine irony in the way in which, in the past, generative grammarians have ignored psychological phenomena, since its proponents generally argue that linguistics is a branch of psychology. What are the main psychological phenomena? The most important ones are so obvious that they are seldom noticed:

Speaking and understanding language depend on processes almost entirely outside conscious awareness.

It is impossible to discover anything of importance about grammatical rules or semantic representations by introspection.

The most frequently used words are precisely those that are the most ambiguous, and thus their interpretation depends on an ability to make inferences from linguistic context.

Utterances invariably depend on the circumstances in which they are uttered for their correct interpretation, and thus in turn on an ability to make inferences from those circumstances.

It is these phenomena that maintain the existence of both theoretical linguistics and experimental psycholinguistics. Neither subject would exist if you could recover the rules of your language, and the mental processes that underlie your use of them, without ever stirring from an introspective posture.

Modern psycholinguistics arose from a combination of linguistic theories and psychological experiments. After a promising beginning, a hiatus occurred because the mathematical conception of grammar pulled in one direction and the experimental facts pulled in another. It now seems that perhaps the mathematical pull was not entirely along the right lines. If this conjecture proves to be correct, then the way is clear once more for a mutual attack upon the problems of language. Certainly, this approach is needed. What the phenomena above undoubtedly imply is that the most powerful mental machinery for coping with language is profoundly hidden and highly inferential.

ACKNOWLEDGMENTS

This essay was prepared while I was in receipt of a research grant from the Social Science Research Council (GB). I am grateful to many colleagues and friends at Sussex University, Stanford University, and the University of Texas at Austin for numerous insights into the nature of language. Part of the essay was indeed written while I was visiting Stanford on a Sloan Foundation fellowship. Both Gerald Gazdar and the editor very kindly read an earlier draft of the essay and pointed out a number of inadequacies. They are not to blame for those that remain.

REFERENCES

Aho, A. V., & Ullman, J. D. *The theory of parsing, translation, and compiling (Vol. 1: Parsing)*. Englewood Cliffs, NJ: Prentice-Hall, 1972.

Anderson, J. *Language, memory and thought*. Hillsdale, NJ: Lawrence Erlbaum Associates, 1976.

Bach, E. Control in Montague grammar. *Linguistic Inquiry*, 1979, *10*, 515–531.

Bar-Hillel, Y., & Shamir, E. Finite-state languages: Formal representations and adequacy problems. *The Bulletin of the Research Council of Israel*, 1960, *8F* (No. 3).

Bates, E. *Language and context: The acquisition of pragmatics*. New York: Academic Press, 1976.

Bloom, L. Why not pivot grammar? *Journal of Speech and Hearing Disorders*, 1971, *36*, 40–50.

Bloomfield, L. A set of postulates for the science of language. *Language*, 1926, *2*, 153–164.

Blumenthal, A. L. *Language and psychology: Historical aspects of psycholinguistics*. London: Wiley, 1970.

Boolos, G., & Jeffrey, R. *Computability and logic*. Cambridge: Cambridge University Press, 1974.

Bornstein, M. H. Two kinds of perceptual organization near the beginning of life. In W. A. Collins (Ed.), *Minnesota symposium on child psychology* (Vol. 14). Hillsdale, NJ: Lawrence Erlbaum Associates, 1981.

Bowerman, M. The acquisition of word meaning: An investigation of some current concepts. In N. Waterson & C. Snow (Eds.), *Development of communication: Social and pragmatic factors in language acquisition*. New York: Wiley, 1977.

Brame, M. K. *Base generated syntax*. Seattle, WA: Noit Amrofer, 1978.

Bransford, J. D., & McCarrell, N. S. A sketch of a cognitive approach to comprehension: Some thoughts about understanding what it means to comprehend. In W. B. Weimar & D. S. Palermo (Eds.), *Cognition and the symbolic processes*. Hillsdale, NJ: Lawrence Erlbaum Associates, 1975.

Bréal, M. *Essai de sémantique*. Paris: Hachette, 1897.

Bresnan , J. A realistic transformational grammar. In M. Halle, J. Bresnan, & G. A. Miller (Eds.), *Linguistic theory and psychological reality*. Cambridge, MA: M.I.T. Press, 1978.

Brown, R. *A first language: The early stages*. Cambridge, MA: Harvard University Press, 1973.

Carnap, R. *Meaning and necessity: A study in semantics and modal logic* (2nd ed.). Chicago, IL: University of Chicago Press, 1956.

Chomsky, N. *Syntactic structures*. The Hague: Mouton, 1957.

Chomsky, N. On certain formal properties of grammars. *Information and Control*, 1959, *2*, 137–167.

Chomsky, N. *Aspects of the theory of syntax*. Cambridge, MA: M.I.T. Press, 1965.

Chomsky, N. Deep structure, surface structure, and semantic interpretation. In D. D. Steinberg & L. A. Jakobovits (Eds.), *Semantics: An interdisciplinary reader in philosophy, linguistics, and psychology*. Cambridge: Cambridge University Press, 1971.

Chomsky, N. *Essays on form and interpretation*. New York: North-Holland, 1977.

Chomsky, N., & Halle, M. *The sound pattern of English*. New York: Harper and Row, 1968.

Clark, E. V. What's in a word? On the child's acquisition of semantics in his first language. In T. E. Moore (Ed.), *Cognitive development and the acquisition of language*. New York: Academic Press, 1973.

Clark, E. V., & Clark, H. H. When nouns surface as verbs. *Language*, 1979, *55*, 767–811.

Clark, H. H. Word associations and linguistic theory. In J. Lyons (Ed.), *New horizons in linguistics*. Harmondsworth, Middlesex, England: Penguin, 1970.

Clark, H. H., & Clark, E. V. *Psychology and language: An introduction to psycholinguistics*. New York: Harcourt, Brace and Jovanovich, 1977.

Collins, A. M., & Quillian, M. R. Experiments on semantic memory and language comprehension. In L. W. Gregg (Ed.), *Cognition in learning and memory*. New York: Wiley, 1972.

Culicover, P. W. *Syntax*. New York: Academic Press, 1976.

Cushing, S. Lexical functions and lexical decomposition: An algebraic approach to lexical meaning. *Linguistic Inquiry*, 1979, *10*, 327–345.

Cutler, A., & Norris, D. Monitoring sentence comprehension. In W. E. Cooper & E. C. T. Walker (Eds.), *Sentence processing: Studies in honor of Merrill Garrett*. Hillsdale, NJ: Lawrence Erlbaum Associates, 1979.

Davies, D. J. M., & Isard, S. Utterances as programs. In D. Michie (Ed.), *Machine intelligence, 7*. Edinburgh: Edinburgh University Press, 1972.

de Cornulier, B. But if 'respectively' meant something? *Papers in Linguistics*, 1973, *6*, 131–134.

de Saussure, F. *Course in general linguistics*. (Edited posthumously from students' notes by C. Bally, A. Sechehaye, & A. Reidlinger; W. Baskin, trans.). London: Peter Owen, 1960.

Dore, J. Holophrases, speech acts and language universals. *Journal of Child Language*, 1975, *2*, 21–39.

Dowty, D. Montague grammar and the lexical decomposition of causative verbs. In B. Partee (Ed.), *Montague grammar*. New York: Academic Press, 1976.

Dowty, D. *Word meaning in generative semantics and Montague grammar*. Dordrecht: Reidel, 1979.

Fillmore, C. J. The case for case. In E. Bach & R. T. Harms (Eds.), *Universals in linguistic theory*. New York: Holt, Rinehart and Winston, 1968.

Fodor, J. A., Bever, T. G., & Garrett, M. F. *The psychology of language: An introduction to psycholinguistics and generative grammar*. New York: McGraw-Hill, 1974.

Fodor, J. D. Parsing strategies and constraints on transformations. *Linguistic Inquiry*, 1978, *9*, 427–473.

Fodor, J. D., Fodor, J. A., & Garrett, M. F. The psychological unreality of semantic representations. *Linguistic Inquiry*, 1975, *4*, 515–531.

Forster, K. I. Visual perception of rapidly presented word sequences of varying complexity. *Perception and Psychophysics*, 1970, *8*, 215–221.

Foss, D. J. Decision processes during sentence comprehension: Effects of lexical item difficulty and position upon decision times. *Journal of Verbal Learning and Verbal Behavior*, 1969, *8*, 457–462.

Frazier, L., & Fodor, J. D. The sausage machine. *Cognition*, 1978, *6*, 291–325.

Frege, G. On sense and reference. In P. T. Geach & M. Black (Eds.), *Translations from the philosophical writings of Gottleb Frege*. Oxford: Blackwell, 1952. (Originally published, 1892.)

Garey, M. R., & Johnson, D. S. *Computers and intractability: A guide to the theory of NP [nondeterministic polynomial]–completeness*. San Francisco, CA: Freeman, 1978.

Gazdar, G. Phrase structure grammar. In G. K. Pullum & P. Jacobson (Eds.), *The nature of syntactic representation*. London: Croom Helm, in press.

Gold, E. Language identification in the limit. *Information and Control,* 1967, *16*, 447–474.

Gough, P. B. Experimental psycholinguistics. In W. O. Dingwall (Ed.), *A survey of linguistic science*. Baltimore, MD: University of Maryland Press, 1971.

Halle, M., Bresnan, J., & Miller, G. A. (Eds.). *Linguistic theory and psychological reality*. Cambridge, MA: M.I.T. Press, 1978.

Halliday, M. A. K. *Learning how to mean: Explorations in the development of language*. London: Arnold, 1975.

Hersh, H. M., & Caramazza, A. A fuzzy set approach to modifiers and vagueness in natural language. *Journal of Experimental Psychology: General,* 1976, *105*, 254–276.

Hockett, C. F. Two models of grammatical description. *Word,* 1954, *10*, 210–233.

Hollan, J. D. Features and semantic memory: Set-theoretic or network model? *Psychological Review,* 1975, *82*, 154–155.

Hopcroft, J. E., & Ullman, J. D. *Formal languages and their relation to automata*. Reading, MA: Addison-Wesley, 1969.

Jakobson, R. *Selected writings I: Phonological studies*. The Hague: Mouton, 1962.

Jespersen, O. *The philosophy of grammar*. London: Allen & Unwin, 1924.

Johnson-Laird, P. N. Experimental psycholinguistics. *Annual Review of Psychology,* 1974, *25*, 135–160.

Johnson-Laird, P. N. The passive paradox: A reply to Costermans and Hupet. *British Journal of Psychology,* 1977, *68*, 113–116. (a)

Johnson-Laird, P. N. Psycholinguistics without linguistics. In N. S. Sutherland (Ed.), *Tutorial essays in psychology* (Vol. 1). Hillsdale, NJ: Lawrence Erlbaum Associates, 1977. (b)

Johnson-Laird, P. N. Formal semantics and the psychology of meaning. Paper presented at the Symposium on *Formal semantics and natural language,* University of Texas at Austin, 1979.

Johnson-Laird, P. N. Mental models in cognitive science. *Cognitive Science,* 1980, *4*, 71–115.

Kamp, J. A. W. Two theories about adjectives. In E. Keenan (Ed.), *Formal semantics of natural language*. Cambridge: Cambridge University Press, 1975.

Kaplan, R. M. Augmented transition networks as psychological models of sentence comprehension. *Artificial Intelligence,* 1972, *3*, 77–100.

Katz, J. J., & Fodor, J. A. The structure of a semantic theory. *Language,* 1963, *39*, 170–210.

Kintsch, W. *The representation of meaning in memory*. Hillsdale, NJ: Lawrence Erlbaum Associates, 1974.

Kripke, S. Semantical considerations on modal logic. *Acta Philosophica Fennica,* 1963, *16*, 83–94.

Lakoff, G. On generative semantics. In D. D. Steinberg & L. A. Jakobovits (Eds.), *Semantics: An interdisciplinary reader in philosophy, linguistics, and psychology*. Cambridge: Cambridge University Press, 1971.

Lakoff, G. Hedges: A study of meaning criteria and the logic of fuzzy concepts. *Papers from the Eighth Regional Meeting of the Chicago Linguistic Society*. Chicago, IL: Chicago Linguistic Society, 1972.

Lamb, S. M. *Outline of stratificational grammar*. Washington, DC: Georgetown University Press, 1966.

Levelt, W. J. M. *Formal grammars in linguistics and psycholinguistics (Vol. 2: Applications in linguistic theory)*. The Hague: Mouton, 1974.

Marshall, J. Psychological linguistics: Psychological aspects of semantic structure. In A. R.

Meetham (Ed.), *Encyclopedia of linguistics, information and control*. London: Pergamon, 1969.

Marslen-Wilson, W., Tyler, L. K., & Seidenberg, M. Sentence processing and the clause boundary. In W. J. M. Levelt & G. B. Flores d'Arcais (Eds.), *Studies in the perception of language*. Chichester, England: Wiley, 1978.

McCawley, J. D. The role of semantics in grammar. In E. Bach & R. T. Harms (Eds.), *Universals in linguistic theory*. New York: Holt, Rinehart, and Winston, 1968.

McNeill, D. *The acquisition of language: The study of developmental psycholinguistics*. New York: Harper and Row, 1970.

Mehler, J. Some effects of grammatical transformations on the recall of English sentences. *Journal of Verbal Learning and Verbal Behavior*, 1963, *2*, 250–262.

Miller, G. A. Some psychological studies of grammar. *American Psychologist*, 1962, *17*, 748–762.

Miller, G. A., Galanter, E., & Pribram, K. *Plans and the structure of behavior*. New York: Holt, Rinehart, and Winston, 1960.

Miller, G. A., & Johnson-Laird, P. N. *Language and perception*. Cambridge, MA: Harvard University Press, 1976.

Minsky, M. Frame-system theory. In P. N. Johnson-Laird & P. C. Wason (Eds.), *Thinking: Readings in cognitive science*. Cambridge: Cambridge University Press, 1977.

Montague, R. *Formal philosophy*. (R. H. Thomason, Ed.). New Haven, CT: Yale University Press, 1974.

Nunberg, G. The non-uniqueness of semantic solutions: Polysemy. *Linguistics and Philosophy*, 1979, *3*, 143–184.

Partee, B. Montague grammar and transformational grammar. *Linguistic Inquiry*, 1975, *6*, 203–300.

Partee, B. (Ed.). *Montague grammar*. New York: Academic Press, 1976.

Paul, H. *Prinzipien der Sprachgeschichte*. Halle: Niemeyer, 1886.

Peters, P. S., & Ritchie, R. W. On the generative power of transformational grammars. *Information Sciences*, 1973, *6*, 49–83. (a)

Peters, P. S., & Ritchie, R. W. Context-sensitive immediate constituent-analysis: Context-free languages revisited. *Mathematical Systems Theory*, 1973, *6*, 324–333. (b)

Pinker, S. Formal models of language learning. *Cognition*, 1979, *7*, 217–283.

Postal, P. *Constituent structure: A study of contemporary models of syntactic description*. Bloomington, IN: Research Center for Language Sciences of Indiana University, 1964.

Putnam, H. The meaning of "meaning". In K. Gunderson (Ed.), *Language, mind and knowledge: Minnesota studies in the philosophy of science* (Vol. 7). Minneapolis, MN: University of Minnesota Press, 1975.

Rosch, E. On the internal structure of perceptual and semantic categories. In T. Moore (Ed.), *Cognitive development and the acquisition of language*. New York: Academic Press, 1973.

Ross, J. R. On declarative sentences. In R. A. Jacobs & P. S. Rosenbaum (Eds.), *Readings in English transformational grammar*. Waltham, MA: Blaisdell, 1970.

Sag, I. A. The nonunity of anaphora. *Linguistic Inquiry*, 1979, *10*, 152–164.

Savin, H., & Perchonock, E. Grammatical structure and the immediate recall of English sentences. *Journal of Verbal Learning and Verbal Behavior*, 1965, *4*, 348–353.

Schaeffer, B., & Wallace, R. Semantic similarity and the comparison of word meanings. *Journal of Experimental Psychology*, 1969, *82*, 343–346.

Schlesinger, I. M. Production of utterances and language acquisition. In D. I. Slobin (Ed.), *The ontogenesis of grammar: Some facts and several theories*. New York: Academic Press, 1971.

Sheffield, A. D. *Grammar and thinking*. New York: Putnam, 1912.

Smith, E. E., Shoben, E. J., & Rips, L. J. Comparison processes in semantic memory. *Psychological Review*, 1974, *81*, 214–241.

Stalnaker, R. C. Assertion. In P. Cole (Ed.), *Syntax and semantics (Vol. 9: Pragmatics)*. New York: Academic Press, 1978.

Steedman, M. J., & Johnson-Laird, P. N. A programmatic theory of linguistic performance. In P. Smith & R. Campbell (Eds.), *Advances in the psychology of language: Formal and experimental approaches*. New York: Plenum Press, 1976.

Tarski, A. *Logic, semantics, metamathematics*. Oxford: Clarendon Press, 1956.

Thorne, J. P., Bratley, P., & Dewar, H. The syntactic analysis of English by machine. In D. Michie (Ed.), *Machine intelligence* (Vol. 3). Edinburgh: Oliver and Boyd, 1968.

Trubetzkoy, N. S. *Grundzüge der Phonologie*. Prague: Cercle Linguistique de Prague, 1939.

Van Ginneken, J. *Principes de linguistique psychologie*. Paris: Riviére, 1907.

Wanner, E., & Maratsos, M. An ATN approach to comprehension. In M. Halle, J. Bresnan, & G. A. Miller (Eds.), *Linguistic theory and psychological reality*. Cambridge, MA: M.I.T. Press, 1978.

Watson, J. B. *Behavior: An introduction to comparative psychology*. New York: Holt, 1914.

Wells, R. S. Immediate constituents. *Language*, 1947, *23*, 81–117.

Winograd, T. *Understanding natural language*. New York: Academic Press, 1972.

Wittgenstein, L. *Philosophical investigations*. Oxford: Blackwell, 1953.

Woods, W. A. *Semantics for a question-answering system*. (Mathematical Linguistics and Automatic Translation Report NSF-19). Cambridge, MA: Harvard Computational Laboratory, 1967.

Woods, W. A. Transition network grammars for natural language analysis. *Communications of the Association for Computing Machinery*, 1970, *13*, 591–606.

Wundt, W. *Die Sprache*. Leipzig: Engelmann, 1900.

3 Psychology and Literature: An Empirical Perspective

Martin S. Lindauer
State University of New York, College at Brockport

INTRODUCTION

The psychology of literature covers a very wide field. Included are studies of authors and their creativity, investigations of readers and their reactions to literature, and analyses of literary texts for their psychological referents. Psychological content, whether explicit or implicit, occurs in such diverse literary forms as poetry, the short story, the play, and the novel. The latter offers numerous possibilities: According to Burgess (1978), there are about 30 different types of novels, but the most direct reference to mental life is found in the psychological novel. This form highlights the introspections, streams of consciousness, inner and personal experiences, and feelings and emotions of a few literary characters.

The psychological novel is a fairly recent form. Boccaccio, writing in the fourteenth century, was its first exponent. The earliest "literary psychology" is attributed to a group of unknown authors from ancient Greece (Jastrow, 1915; Mackinnon, 1944; Roback, 1968). Their "psychological portraits" are brief literary sketches of personality types like the fool, the flatterer, and the virtuous woman. Early psychological analyses in literary contexts are also found in discussions of creativity and catharsis in Plato and in Aristotle (Strelka, 1976).

Psychological content, whatever literary form it takes, can be represented thematically or symbolically; and it may be contained in units of language as small as the metaphor. Psychological analysis is not only directed to the content of literary forms, but also toward a work's structure—the time, place, action, plot, and characterization; and in the case of poetry, to such elements as metre and rhythm. Even the subtleties of a work's style (e.g., romanticism or realism) could be the focus of psychological attention. Aside from psychology's concentration on the work, whatever direction it may take, analyses can be appreciably expanded by a consideration of the author and the reader (as well as the social context in which a work takes place).

The psychology of literature is complicated even further by several definitional considerations. The boundaries are blurred between literature and other art forms. Thus, drama can be read as literature; and films are made from novels (see Bornstein, in this volume). Distinctions have also been drawn between the classics ("literary art") and best sellers (popular art). Other issues include the status of oral and folk literature, songs and librettos, autobiographies and diaries; and whether history and philosophy can also qualify as literature. These concerns are the province of literary criticism (some of which can itself be classified as literature).

In short, literary material of psychological relevance is itself diverse and can be examined from several points of view. An extensive analysis of literature can also be found in several other disciplines (not only in psychoanalysis, psychiatry, literary criticism and history, and philosophical aesthetics, but also in sociology). Because of the great amount of material and perspectives available, this review must be selective.[1]

This essay examines the major ties between psychology and literature, discusses several of the important ways in which this interchange has been fulfilled (or not), and offers some possibilities for furthering the relationship.[2] However, the essay is guided by the logic of scientific inquiry and the methodology of empiricism. The assumption is made that literature is a source of observable data which can be systematically analyzed and quantitatively expressed. Most other approaches to literature and psychology, in contrast to the present orientation, have taken a speculative view. That is, their analyses are personal, intuitive, and indi-

---

[1] There is a large amount of material on the relationship between psychology and literature. The section on psychological (mainly psychoanalytical) themes in Dudley's (1968) bibliography of literature and science for the period 1930–1967 has over 450 entries by critics and over 1300 entries by writers. (Five additional bibliographies have since been published.) Given the volume of material, several general sources for the last few years were scanned. These included the *Essay and General Literature Index* (1970 to 1977); *Humanities Index* (1974 to 1977); *Reader's Guide* (1969 to 1978); and the *Social Science and Humanities Index* (1970 to 1974). Secondary sources of special value were Hay (1973), Huxley (1963), Patterson (1976), Richards (1925, 1926, 1950), Wellek and Warren (1942), and Walsh (1972).

[2] Other perspectives on the relationship between psychology and literature from a psychological perspective are found in Lindauer (1974), McCurdy (1968), and Martindale (1978b). Swartz (1979) has sensitively discussed the difficulties in relating the two fields. Views of psychology from the standpoint of literature are well represented in Nixon (1928) and Richards (1925, 1926, 1950). An attempt to combine psychology and literary criticism may be found in Maier and Reninger (1933). Literature's place in the psychology of the arts is briefly indicated in general reviews by Child (1969, 1972, 1977, 1978), Pratt (1961), and Valentine (1962). An original analysis of aesthetics based mainly on examples from literature is found in Vygotsky (1925/1971).

vidualistic. Thus, the exchange between literature and psychology is largely marked by polemical pronouncements and rhetorical arguments that either favor or oppose exchange between the fields. Another serious limitation to the usual approach taken by psychological analyses of literature is that only the single author or work is examined. This exclusivity prevents valid generalizations.

Discussions of literature and psychology are not only dominated by speculative accounts, they also omit scientific versions of psychology by taking a perspective which either emphasizes literary issues (Taylor, 1969) or psychoanalytic concerns (Holland, 1968). These viewpoints are familiar to most informed readers by dint of their abundance. But the scientific approach to literature is not very well known, and the advantages, accomplishments, and limitations of psychology's scientific study of literature are not familiar to most scholars.

This essay begins by reviewing the psychoanalytic approach and, in addition, six other psychological approaches to literature which fall within an empirical framework. Illustrative studies (where available) are included, along with critical comments. The overview of these seven approaches is followed by a discussion of the two major ways in which literature is used in psychology, namely, as illustration or as a source of information. Another section examines the relatively minor status of the psychology of literature in psychology, and perhaps more surprisingly, in the psychology of the arts. Some of the reasons for this neglect are discussed. Even though literature is scarcely represented in scientific psychology, there are reasons for being optimistic about an increase in its presence. Suggestions for improvement, along both methodological and substantive lines, are outlined in another section. In the concluding section, the position is taken that an empirical psychology of literature can help draw the sciences and the humanities closer together.

PSYCHOLOGICAL APPROACHES TO LITERATURE

Psychoanalysis

Most psychological excursions into literature have been psychoanalytic. (Psychoanalysis is broadly defined to include not only Freud, but Jung, Adler, and other neo- and non-Freudians.) Psychoanalytically-oriented articles account for about 80% of the entries under the category "psychology and literature" in recent bibliographies (e.g., Kiell, 1963; Perloff, 1974).

Freud (1928/1950, 1908/1960) is the direct inspiration for most of these efforts, as authors either extend his work or react against it in part or in whole. Freud's first work on literature was published in 1908; and even earlier references (in 1900) were made to Sophocles's *Oedipus*. Other versions of psychoanalysis are amply represented (Baird, 1976; Baudry, 1977; Paris, 1974). These generally retain a Freudian core while modifying certain aspects, e.g., the relative importance of the conscious ego over the unconscious id (Friedman, 1978). Proponents of a tie between literature and psychoanalysis, of whatever variety, are found in numerous sources (Edel, 1959; Holland, 1966, 1968; Lucas, 1957; Mindess, 1967; Shupe, 1976).

Representing most of the essential themes of psychoanalysis is Jones's (1949) analysis of Shakespeare's *Hamlet*. It is a classic illustration of Freudian as well as related approaches to literature. Jones argues that Hamlet's indecision arises because previously repressed murderous and incestuous thoughts about his parents were aroused. These childhood wishes were re-awakened by the death of Hamlet's father and the remarriage of his mother. Thus, in Jones's view, the key to the play is the Oedipus conflict. The play's timelessness and universal acclaim by audiences and critics, Jones surmises, stems from the play's capacity to provide a safe release ("catharsis") from unconscious Oedipal forces shared with its observers and readers. The play, like the dream, is a safe way of expressing childhood fantasies without raising defenses against their recall. Jones also argues that the creative origins of the play lie in Shakespeare's own life history, namely, the death of his father (and later his patron) and the loss of his mistress. Furthermore, Jones notes that the presence of the Hamlet (Oedipus) theme in legends and myths of other peoples and times historically and culturally validates its import. For psychoanalysis, then, the audience's response to literature—and to all the arts (and indeed to life's events in general)—is the result of the "working out" of the unconscious events of childhood. For the artist, this process fortuitously results in a creative product (Martindale, 1975).

Psychoanalytic approaches to literature have not gone unchallenged. The literary critic Burgess (1978), for example, points out that "the greatest disclosures about human motivation have been achieved more by intuition and introspections of novelists and dramatists than by more systematic clinicians [p. 286]." Crews (1975) has some serious reservations about the reductionism of this approach. Clinicians themselves question the legitimacy of a secondhand psychoanalysis of a nonparticipating author (or literary character), and many doubt the usefulness of such secondary and fragmented information. Scientists' evaluations of the psychoanalytical approach are even more critical (Eysenck, 1958). They argue that the evidence, at best, is incomplete, and what remains is intuitive and qualitative. Thus, there is little if any possibility for quantification or public verification, since a sample size of one cannot be the basis for generalizing to other works, authors, and audiences. It is pointed out that a scientific use of biographical information (discussed later) requires the quantitative analysis of hundreds (if not thousands) of biographies in order to achieve reliable findings and to have any hope of reaching valid generalizations. In reply to the scientists' charges, psychoanalysts retort that the richness of the individual case is lost when laced with quantitative detail. Furthermore, psychoanalysts argue that their purpose in examining biographies is different from that of scientists (e.g., it is done in order to identify unifying themes.).

Despite the objections of literary critics, clinicians, and scientists, psychoanalysis remains a robust and attractive theory of literature to many. Among social scientists, political scientists and historians use psychoanalytically oriented psychobiographies and psychohistories, inspired in large part by Erikson's (1958, 1969) success with Luther and Ghandi (see Elms and Lifton & Strozier in Volume II). For the general reader and theatergoer, and for many critics, psychoanalysis offers a revelatory kind of proof. The psychoanalytic exegesis of a work and one's experience with that work are joined, resulting in new, provocative, and challenging levels of understanding and appreciation. Psychoanalytic efforts, despite their flaws, therefore act as a sort of foil against which personal (and other types of) analysis are tried out in an expanding and perhaps deepening circle of explication and reaction. The vast and continually increasing amount of psychoanalytic studies about literature leave little doubt that this approach has fulfilled an important role for many.

Nevertheless, the psychoanalytical approach is limited to personal and speculative analyses of literature. Its greatest value, from an empirical point of view, is as a source of ideas. These can be an impetus to more rigorous efforts. Psychoanalysis provides hypotheses about authors' motives, literary characters' conflicts, and readers' reactions. These suggestions, however, remain to be empirically tested. Some of these psychoanalytical starting points can be found in the clinical-objective approach, discussed next.

Clinical-Objective

The impressionistic sweep of psychoanalysis cannot easily be captured by the rigorous requirements of empirical psychology. However, coming closest is the clinical-objective approach, a scientific orientation toward the study of personality and creativity in artistic contexts (MacKinnon, 1975). Information about the personal qualities of authors and the origins of their creativity are inferred from the work (as is true of the psychoanalytic approach), or less frequently, based on interviews with or tests of living authors. But the clinical-objective approach, unlike psychoanalysis, is more systematic in its observations; data are collected and findings are couched in quantitative terms.

Thus, McCurdy (1947, 1949, 1961) used frequency tallies of themes in samples of passages from several classical works (e.g., the Brontë sisters and Shakespeare) to illustrate, corroborate, and expand on Freudian notions of motivation. Freud's concepts of primary and secondary processes (corresponding to unconscious and conscious, respectively) together with Kris's "regression in the service of the ego" (a kind of sophisticated yet child-like quality) were used by Martindale (1973, 1977, 1978a), in conjunction with statistical descriptions of the characteristics of several generations of English and French poets and their poetry, objective counts of peer and audience demands, and prevalent patterns of social change. Martindale's extensive analysis showed how poets were able to use childhood fantasies in a constructive way. Helson (1973, 1977, 1977-78, 1978) took a Jungian orientation toward works of fantasy written for children. Judges objectively categorized the archetypes in children's literature (e.g., the hero), and authors of different works were interviewed or completed questionnaires. Helson's complex picture of the role of the author's personality in literary creativity also touches on the role of the critic, the nature of the child as a reader, and the way in which shifts in cultural values (e.g., in sex roles) are represented in literature. Barron (1969, pp. 13-14; 1972) used both clinical interviews and tests (e.g., the MMPI) to provide a detailed statistical description of the major personality traits of student and professional writers; he also included qualitative case studies. Another highly statistical procedure (the Q-sort) was applied by Kohlberg (1963) to passages in Dostoevsky's novels. He was able quantitatively to establish the recurrence of a few types among 34 major characters (such as "the double" and the "Christ figure").

The research of Sears (1976) and his colleagues (Sears & Lapidus, 1973; Sears, Lapidus, & Cozzens, 1978) provides a good example of the psychoanalytically oriented but empirically strengthened approach to literature. Their interest was in the personal events of Mark Twain's childhood and adulthood and their effect on his writing. The first step was to examine objectively (with the aid of judges) biographical material (i.e., letters and diaries) on Twain. Nine characteristic personal themes were extracted (e.g., loneliness and denial). Twain's novels were then objectively divided (again by judges) into independent episodes. These were scored on the nine personal themes previously established. For example, on the basis of Twain's childhood relationship to his mother, Sears concluded that he feared a loss of love. This "separation anxiety" theme recurred at several points in Twain's adulthood (for example, with the birth of each of his children). Sears was able to show that contemporary events in Twain's life reawakened earlier personal conflicts. These, Sears argued, helped to explain otherwise inexplicable sections in *Tom Sawyer*, the rewriting of *Hucklebury Finn*, and the pessimistic shift in Twain's last work, *The Mysterious Stranger*.

The research of the clinical-objective group illustrates that qualitative and quantitative analyses can be combined so as to help clarify the relationship between an author and his work. Furthermore, an objective examination of one author's novels demonstrates that the scientific method can do justice to the single case. Empirical criteria and statistical techniques need not destroy the uniqueness of the individual author or work, an argument often made by literary scholars, literary critics, and psychoanalysts. A rigorously empirical study of literature does not destroy the work of art, distort the literary experience, or demean the talents of an author. These studies may not (yet) impress professional students of literature with their literary insights. But they do convincingly demonstrate that empirical analysis is relevant to both psychological and literary interests.

Experimental Aesthetics

The rigor with which the scientific approach can be applied to the arts is most clearly illustrated by experimental aesthetics. Founded by Fechner (1897), experimental aesthetics was the first scientific way of studying the arts and remains its most vigorous proponent. While mainly represented in the visual arts (see Bornstein, in this volume), it is also found elsewhere, e.g., in music (Deutsch, 1978, and in this volume) and even in architecture (Hooper, 1978). Like psychoanalysis, experimental aesthetics has both advocates (e.g., Berlyne, 1971) and detractors (e.g., Lindauer, 1973). Like psychoanalysis, it too has played a dominant and pervasive role in contemporary psychological contributions to the arts. Considering the "softness" with which research in the arts is viewed by some scientists, it is ironic to note that Fechner is also the "father" of psychophysics, one of the most exact and quantitative of scientific psychology's accomplishments.

Experimental aesthetics, in essence, seeks predictable and mathematical relationships between artistic stimuli and preferential or aesthetic judgments of these stimuli. To accomplish this goal, an extremely physicalistic and reductionistic approach to the artistic situation is taken. Hevener (1937), for example, attempted to capture the affective meaning of poetry by obtaining preferential ratings for vowels, consonants, and syllables. Birkhoff's (1933) concept of aesthetic measure (M), as applied to "good" literature, used counts of the length of lines and the number of syllables in words as indicators of order (O) and complexity (C). When placed into the formula $M = O/C$, the best balance of elements is indicated by approximation to the value "1" (unity).

The most influential version of experimental aesthetics, because of its applicability to non-artistic situations, is Berlyne's (1971). He argued that we are attracted to, sustain our interest in, and seek stimuli which have a certain amount of novelty, complexity, and heterogeneity. These stimuli provide new or higher sources of stimulation, thereby fulfilling a basic biological need for exploration and the satisfaction of curiosity. For example, we dislike the very simple (it is too boring) as well as the very complex (it is too confusing) and instead prefer moderate or intermediate degrees of complexity. The non-monotonic relationship between preference and complexity is complicated by the type of material used (e.g., whether the complex is familiar or unfamiliar). Further, the optimum preferential level will shift up or down depending on the background and experience of the observer (e.g., artists vs. non-artists). Despite these complexities, predictions regarding a U-shaped relationship between preference and complexity have been confirmed many times, e.g. Kammann's (1966) study of poetry. Unfortunately, there have actually been very few experiments with literary materials, whether inspired by experimental aesthetics or not (Arcamore & Lindauer, 1974; Halasz, 1978, 1980) because the requirements of the experimental method—the manipulation of literary prose under controlled conditions—have been difficult to fulfill. The units of literature, unlike the colors and forms in art, for example, are difficult to specify: Are they letters, words, sentences, or paragraphs?

Even if the relevant units of literature could be operationally defined and then experimentally manipulated, the reading response is difficult to capture. Reading unfolds over time. Unlike the response to art or music, which can be taken in at a glance or in less than a minute, literary experience follows a more extended temporal course. Cognitive processes alone include perception, as well as memory, imagination, and judgment. It is difficult to separate and then study each of these components of the literary experience.

Forced thereby to simplify the literary situation, experimentalists have used very simple surrogates for literary prose (e.g., Hevener, 1937). While the study of vowels and syllables may be pertinent to some aspects of the study of poetry, such fragments are hardly relevant to other literary forms, such as the novel, or to broader literary concerns, such as the effects of literature on the reader. Strict definitional and methodological criteria are needed for experimental manipulation and laboratory control. But the unfortunate consequence of such necessary simplifications, as illustrated by experimental aesthetics, is that art and our reaction to it are translated into surrogates that are artistically unrecognizable. Art, for example, becomes color patches and geometrical forms (e.g., "the golden section"), and the aesthetic experience is given by ratings of liking (Lindauer, 1981). Whether one can have an experimental psychology of literature, of the experimental aesthetics variety or otherwise, remains problematical.

Factor-Analysis

Statistical procedures also play a large part in the factor-analytic approach to the arts. Factor-analysis is essentially a correlational technique which allows the investigator to simplify, through statistical groupings ("factors"), responses to art (or to any stimulus). Usually, no more than three or four factors emerge from the quantitative reduction of what would otherwise be great masses of unrelated data.

Research in the arts, for the factor analysts, is guided by the search for an aesthetic factor (see Birkhoff, 1933, above). The hope is to discover a common denominator which underlies all the different types of and responses to art. A mathematical description of the fundamental factors in art would demonstrate, in an empirical and precise manner, a phenomenon as subjective and subtle as "the aesthetic." An objective confirmation of aesthetic phenomena sharply contrasts with the more typical philosophical or intuitive types of analyses.

Factor-analytic researchers (e.g., Eysenck, 1940) believe that they have found such a general aesthetic factor. They also note the presence of one or two more specific factors. To these have been applied such bipolar names as complex-simple, technical-emotional, and form-content. These labels, unfortunately, often vary in name (and number) because they rely on the imaginativeness with which "fits" can be made with neutral statistical groupings. Decisions of this sort are a source of contention between factor-analysts and with their critics.

Factor-analytic research also includes an examination of the relationships between general and specific factors on the one hand and other variables (Gunn, 1951, 1952) which include the respondents' preferences for art and colors, their sex and age, and intelligence.

Aesthetic preferences are frequently correlated with personality, especially extraversion-introversion. For example, Eysenck (1940) had 32 poems preferentially rated by sophisticated judges. Factor-analysis of the intercorrelations between the sets of ratings disclosed the existence of two bipolar factors. The first factor, simplicity-complexity, pertained to the poetry's content and form; the second factor, sentimental-restricted, distinguished the readers' emotional response to the poetry. Thus, only two factors apparently account for a good proportion of readers' reactions to poetry, e.g., the difference between a Yeats and a Joyce. (However, most of the readers' response to poetry could not be statistically accounted for.) In the second part of the same study, Eysenck found a fairly high correlation (.61) between liking of simpler poems and extraversion. Eysenck (1940) speculated that the "the extravert is quick to assess [the poem's] value but also quick to turn away to something else; he is hasty, impulsive, and to some extent, superficial [p. 165]." In contrast, Eysenck concludes that the introvert "takes his time, he consults his feelings and is slow to give a judgment. When he makes up his mind, he may judge less spontaneously, but perhaps more profoundly [p. 165]." A similar emphasis on personality, but with somewhat different results (perhaps because it was not based only on poetry), characterizes the study by Williams, White, and Woods (1938). They found that introverts preferred objective, classical, formal, and conventional literature, while extraverts preferred subjective, romantic, wild, and irrational literature.

Factor-analysis has aroused considerable controversy over the proper way to perform the mathematical functions, as well as the merits of the whole approach regardless of how the analysis is done. There are concerns over the sorts of materials and the types of responses that determine the factors and, once obtained, how best to label as well as interpret them. The absence of explanation has also been criticized. To call a particular set of literary works "aesthetic" does not indicate why they are aesthetic or explain their relationship to other variables (e.g., personality). However, some of these concerns are intrinsic to any correlational study.

These issues point out that answers to causal questions about literature (e.g., why certain literature is liked or why certain people prefer a particular kind of literature) can only be given by the experimental approach. Yet literary material is not tractable to the experimental approach, at least as it is presently applied to the arts. A similar dilemma, this time pertaining to inferring causes (of literary creativity) from the historical record, is also faced by the biographical method, discussed next.

Biography

The biographical approach, first systematically and quantitatively pursued by Galton (1869), holds our interest for four reasons. First, biographies are a major literary form; second, among the many types of biographies, those by literary figures are relatively prominent; third, the approach demonstrates a reliable method of handling prose material that is equally applicable to non-biographical forms of literature; and fourth, auto-biographical statements, as for example about the stages of creativity (Wallas, 1926), among other suggestions, have been used to illustrate as well as to guide research. There are also some interesting parallels between Galton and Fechner. Both of these early major figures of psychology, unlike many of their contemporaries, were quite open to the research possibilities of aesthetic material. In addition, Galton like Fechner helped to found some of psychology's most quantitative and rigorous branches, psychometrics and statistics. (This historical note suggests that there are no inherent methodological reasons for shying away from the apparent subjective pitfalls of artistic material.)

Galton's main objective in studying the biographies of 1000 geniuses (among whom were a number of novelists and poets) was to investigate the role of hereditary and environmental influences on their talents. His main finding was that the number of eminent relatives of geniuses declined as consanguinity became more remote. For example, literary geniuses had 16 eminent fathers, 14 eminent brothers, and 17 eminent sons—but only a handful of eminent uncles, nephews, and cousins. Galton concluded that heredity was therefore the major determinant of genius. Unfortunately, despite Galton's own genius, he overlooked the confounding effects of environment. Closeness of kinship is not only hereditary, but also likely to be tied to similar home influences.

Galton's method but not his theory was continued by Cox (1926) and White (1931). Biographical entries indicated, for example, that poets and novelists were accomplished in 6.7 fields. This number is fairly close to the top groups, statesmen and scholars at 7.5, and higher than scientists and musicians at 4.0 and 2.7, respectively. Among the 23 fields in which versatility was recorded, poetry ranked third, far ahead of drama (13th) and fiction (18th); art and music ranked 14th and 15th, respectively.

A more circumscribed aspect of the biographical record is productivity. Because it can be so easily measured (simply by counting accomplishments), productivity has emerged as a major way of looking at creativity. Lehman (1937, 1953) found that literary productivity, like that of most professions, generally peaked in authors' late 30s or early 40s. In comparison, mathematicians produced earlier and philosophers later in life. However, age distinctions among types of literature were also found. Most types of poetry were produced at the earliest ages (25–30 years); short stories and comedies, as well as satiric and religous poetry, fell at the next age group (30–35); tragedies occurred somewhat later (35–40); and novels were produced at the latest years (40–45). Simonton (1975) expanded Lehman's sample of biographies so as to span several thousand years and many cultures. He also found that poets produced at an earlier age than other writers (novelists and biographers). Dennis (1966) used a different kind of sample, long-lived people. The productivity of writers (considered together with artists) declined faster than either scholars or scientists. Dennis speculated that artists, unlike other professions who rely more on assistants, are unable to compensate for declining energies in their old age.

Simonton (1975, 1978) has carried out an impressive series of biographical studies using a sophisticated assortment of statistical techniques. He applied these to the productivity records of thousands of universally recognized writers and other creative persons (artists, composers, philosophers, and scientists) who lived between 700 B.C. and 1900 A.D. Their output was related to similarly quantitative treatments of the social, cultural, economic, political, and historical forces at work during their lives. Consider examples of findings for men of letters: Productive poets and novelists were likely to be contemporaries of each other (rather than flourishing at different periods) and to have had their highest periods of productivity at irregular periods (rather than in a cyclical manner). Writers were generally contemporaries of scientists, philosophers, and composers (rather than painters, sculpters, or architects). Political instability affected the productivity of the generation which followed that period (i.e., political unrest did not inhibit the creative writers living at that time).

The biographical approach provides a broad temporal and cultural perspective and an abundance of information that is relatively easily measured. Hence, it is an attractive and useful way of studying writers and other creative persons (Simonton, 1976). However, its emphasis on frequency counts, no matter how brilliantly treated, overlooks the content of the works it is counting as well as readers' reactions to the works. (The latter could be reflected, for example, in critical reviews in newspapers of their time.) Another shortcoming of the biographical approach is its inherent inability to examine directly, through either observation or testing, the psychological processes at work in an author (for an exception, see Martindale, 1975).

The biographical approach thus needs to be supplemented by the study of living authors. Although the clinical-objective approach has the potential for doing this, it usually neglects the biographical record of the authors it studies. This tendency for an approach to emphasize one aspect of literature to the exclusion of other aspects is not, however, unique to the biographical approach.

Developmental Psychology

One approach that is especially marked by its isolation from general literary interests is the developmental one, the study of the child-as-reader, as story-teller, and as writer. Children's reading and writing habits contribute to an understanding of the growth of language and symbol formation (Gardner, 1973), educational practice (Koch, 1970), and cognitive development (Botvin & Sutton-Smith, 1977; Perkins & Leondar, 1977). But their contribution to the psychology of literature lies mainly in demonstrating that highly sophisticated experimental research can be carried out with literary material. The importance of this has not been fully appreciated by those who follow the experimental approach with its penchant for simple surrogates for literature.

Consider these examples of experimental research with children. Gardner, Kircher, Winner, and Perkins (1975) presented children (some of whom were as young as three years) with several versions of incomplete stories. The children had to select one of several endings, each of which differed in literalness, conventionality, and appropriateness. The choices indicated that children were able to understand metaphors at a very young age. To take another example, Gardner and Lohman (1975) had children examine prose and poetry selections. They were later given brief portions of either the original or altered material. The success with which the material was assigned to the original sources revealed young children's awareness of style. These examples illustrate that experimental research, despite the obvious difficulties of control, could be designed for adult readers of classical literature. Indeed, the research noted above merits replication with adults.

The insularity of the approaches from one another, already noted earlier, is apparent in developmental studies which do not trace the growth of the child-as-writer (or -reader) to the adult-as-writer (or -reader). Yet several approaches already discussed (psychoanalysis, the clinical-objective, and biography) are interested in the child, but only indirectly. That is, they depend on adult recollections, inferences drawn from children's books and fairy tales, or on tallies of biographical accounts of childhood. Consequently, there are developmental questions of literary importance that have not yet been empirically studied among adults.

For example, have those children who showed literary talents at an early age fulfilled their promise? There are obvious practical difficulties in longitudinal research, i.e., tracking a person over a 20-year span or more. Perhaps a more realistic strategy is to study a more circumscribed age span. Thus, literature majors could be studied during their undergraduate years (as Barron, 1972, did for art majors); or writers could be studied during their early professional years after school so as to note how they get established (as Getzels & Csiksentmihalyi, 1976, did for artists). Other developmental questions include the age at which an interest in classical literature emerges and if there are shifts with age to different forms of literature. Finally, do these preferences endure?

Observation

There are other basic questions that might be asked of writers. One that has not yet been posed is what they actually do when they work. Arnheim (1948) has suggested that a poet's "creative trail" might be traced through early drafts. The corrections, he suggests, might shed light on the author's struggle for structure and order. Descriptive research of this fundamental sort (as well as of the reader's experience) may have gone wanting because it is less exciting than hypothesis-testing research.

The classic example of the observational approach to literary creativity is embodied in the work of Patrick (1935, 1937). She studied recognized writers at work under relatively controlled conditions. Each writer received a common scene (a landscape) to write about. Upon gaining the writer's confidence and after the writer became used to her presence, Patrick unobtrusively observed the writer's behavior and recorded spontaneous comments. The authors were also interviewed in depth. The results for writers were compared with other creative groups (e.g., artists) and to non-creative control subjects matched in age, sex, race, and IQ, all of whom responded to the same scene.

Patrick was interested in whether creative people displayed four stages of creativity (preparation, incubation, insight, and verification) often noted in autobiographies and self-reports (e.g., Vinacke, 1974; Wallas, 1926). Patrick found that the stages were neither as sequential nor as overt as previously believed. There were also many similarities between the way writers and other creative people worked and, surprisingly, between creative and non-creative people. Thus, all groups showed some evidence for the various stages (although they were qualitatively different). From a methodological point of view, it is reassuring to learn that Patrick's participants did not report being negatively affected by the brief, restricted, and artificial conditions under which they were studied. Neither was the work they produced judged to be inferior. These are encouraging signs that writers can be directly observed under structured but fairly naturalistic conditions.

Despite Patrick's early success, observational studies are rare in the study of artists. Also infrequent are tests of writers. Their skills, unlike those of musicians and artists for whom there is a variety of music and art aptitude tests, are usually not assessed. There is only Stumberg's (1928) pioneering effort. He tested poets' and non-poets' abilities in a number of areas related to writing (e.g., rhyming, associating, imaging, sentence completion). As might be expected, poets as a group were superior on most tests. But unexpectedly, poets were not superior on several measures related to poetry (e.g., sense of rhythm, imaging, and affective reactions to words). Thus, it cannot be assumed that writers are highly skilled on dimensions relevant to writing (even if we were sure which are the relevant dimensions). Both the observational approach and more standardized approaches which use tests of abilities deserve to be pursued among writers more than they have been.

Summary

Psychology takes many diverse approaches to literature. Because of the various possibilities, no one approach by itself is sufficient. The ideal psychological study of literature would have to touch on several different forms of literature, e.g., the poem as well as the novel. The ideal study would also focus on the author and the work, as well as on the reader and the critic. And to be complete, the social-historical setting in which writing and reading take place should also be included. Investigators should at least be cognizant of, if not illuminated by, ideas that span psychoanalysis and experimental aesthetics, be alert to the methodological possibilities of factor-analysis, and consult observational and developmental sources.

Rothenberg's (1976) composite approach comes closest to approximating the ideal. A clinician well versed in the arts and sciences generally, and in mythology particularly, he interviewed poets and novelists and a comparable group of prominent (but not as creative) writers. Rothenberg also conducted an experiment on the role of free associations in creative thinking. He also examined one author's life and one of his works in detail (O'Neill's *The Iceman Cometh*). Rothenberg's varied background, combined with the investigations he carried out, led to an original conception of creativity, the "Janusian" mode of thinking, defined as the ability to carry out oppositional ways of thinking simultaneously. The power of the model is suggested by similar conceptions independently developed by Koestler (1964) and Guilford (1970) from quite different starting points.

However, the typical approach to the psychology of literature has been much more circumscribed than Rothenberg's. No one approach in the psychology of literature can be realistically expected to manage the required analysis and synthesis suggested by the above ideal. The scope of literature makes it unlikely that one approach can encompass the diversity of the field: hence, the existence of and the need for many different approaches. By emphasizing what the others omit, each supplements the other. Therefore there cannot be one approach which can represent *the* psychology of literature, although some may write as if that were the case.

The isolation of the approaches from one another, although necessary, discourages a view of the field as a whole and leaves larger issues unexamined. Two of these broader concerns, discussed next, are the ways in which literature is used in psychology generally and the place of a psychology of literature within the larger boundaries of the psychology of art.

THE USES OF LITERATURE IN PSYCHOLOGY

Psychology takes many and varied approaches to literature. Nevertheless, psychology's use of literature is relatively restricted. The most dominant approach of all those reviewed, that of psychoanalysis, lifts examples from literature in order to illustrate clinical concepts. The other approaches, for the most part, use literary materials to extend findings already established with non-literary materials in non-aesthetic settings. Literature is illustrative of what is already known, but in an aesthetic context. Literature-as-illustration cannot provide psychology with new or interesting ideas. The relatively unimaginative uses of literature are discussed below in more detail.

Literature as Illustration

The most frequent (and least controversial) way in which psychology uses literature is as an illustration of psychological phenomena. Examples from literature can dramatically exemplify what is known about personality, neurosis, childhood development, memory, and any other psychological topics. Robert Frost (in Nemerov, 1978) explained the author's role as exemplifier as follows: "It is our job to get people to say, 'Oh yes, I know what you mean.' It is not to tell them what they didn't know, but something they had thought of and hadn't thought of saying [p. 602]." Case studies from literature can make otherwise abstruse and abstract information more real and concrete, give implicit and vague ideas more substance, and bring coherence to scattered and unorganized facts and concepts. Psychological phenomena have the possibility of being refined and sharpened through the experiencing of literature, through the "filter" of an author's writing, or by the characterizations drawn by literary figures. Swartz's (1978) detailed study of Proust is a good example of the author's power to elucidate a psychological process (in this case, of cognition). (Mythology's similarly illuminative function has been discussed by Maddi, 1978.)

The typical place in which to find literature's illustrative function is in collections of classical and popular (e.g., science fiction) writing. Their large number attests to the popularity of this genre (Beck, 1976; Buhrich & McConaghy, 1976; Chapko & Lewis, 1975; Fernandez, 1972; Haimowitz & Haimowitz, 1966; Katz, Warrick, & Greenberg, 1974; Kegan, 1975; Kiell, 1974; Levitas, 1963; Mcmahon, 1976; Melvin, Brodsky, & Fowler, 1977; Peterson & Karnes, 1976; Shrodes, Gundy, & Husband, 1943). Psychology is not alone in this pedagogical technique, as similar collections are found in sociology and anthropology (Albrecht, Barnett, & Griff, 1970; Shumaker, 1960; Spradley & McDonough, 1973). In these selections, each literary piece is prefaced by an introduction which contains the "real" psychological facts taken from the clinic (or more rarely, from the laboratory). The emphasis is usually on psychopathology (Rabkin, 1966; Silberger, 1973; Stone & Stone, 1966), and psychoanalysis is the approach most often represented.

Literature as illustration is therefore, at most, a supplement to psychology rather than a primary source of information. Overlooked is the possibility that literary illustrations themselves are data. These could be systematically examined for the light they might throw on important questions. A tabulation of the topics covered in these collections and elsewhere might suggest whether certain types of literature, literary periods, or authors best portray certain psychological phenomena. The same analysis might inform us as to what has been neglected in literature as well as in psychology (Lindauer, 1969b). These statistical profiles could offer suggestive leads to be followed up by either critical essays or empirical studies. A more basic research question is to examine the presumed effectiveness of literary illustrations on learning. For example, does learning proceed faster or is memory better for knowledge which is dramatically illustrated? Literature's educational function has usually been taken for granted, and its effects assumed rather than demonstrated by empirical test.

Literature as a Primary Source of Information

Literature is not just a storehouse of psychological examples. Literature also provides material with which most psychological approaches reviewed earlier can test hypotheses. However, literature also serves as a testing ground for ideas that have their sources elsewhere (e.g., experimental aesthetic's arousal model of affect originated in the laboratory). The possibility that literature might contain original and untapped material of psychological importance has hardly been recognized by any of the approaches reviewed above.

The belief that literature might be a place to look for new concepts and undisclosed facts is based on the reputation authors have for acute powers of observation and a superb ability to communicate sensitively these observations. Authors, if we are to believe literary scholars, "hold human experience and life up to examination" so as to present us with "psychological truths" through the exercise of their "poetic vision."

Hospers (1960, pp. 45–46) puts the case quite strongly. "Many writers have believed themselves, and with good reason, to be commentators on and interpreters of human behavior and the social situation in their time." Further, continues Hospers, literature contains characters who are "true to human nature, and events described in literature are . . . true to history or actual sequences of events in this world." Hospers also believes that the "characters described by the novelist behave, feel and are motivated the way people in real life behave, feel, and are motivated." Hospers recognizes that literature also falsifies, distorts, and modifies. Nevertheless, he feels that literature remains essentially true. "Human nature, as described in works of literature, is anchored in human nature as it exists outside of works of literature." This view is supported by Huxley (1963): "Literature gives a form to life, helps us to know who we are, how we feel, and what is the point of the whole unutterly rummy business [p. 71]."

A neglected role of literature may therefore be to point the way toward otherwise unknown or vaguely known facts about people, their experiences and motives, and other little studied human phenomena of psychological relevance. It is possible that literary content anticipates facts and concepts that will eventually be discovered, studied, and proven by scientific means. Were scientific investigators alert to these clues in literature, new research directions might be initiated. Literature could also serve to confirm otherwise untestable or inaccessible (at least for the moment) facts about, for example, the motives of historical persons and the social forces at work in earlier times.

Literary hunches may be invaluable when science is ignorant, at a loss as how to proceed, or stands in unresolvable disagreement. After all, not every fact has been uncovered, and the facts we now have are often in doubt, unreconciled, or limited. Literature, if taken seriously by scientific investigators, could at least hint at what psychology has missed, where to look next, and what needs to be reconsidered.

So grand a view of literature, as a source of scientifically reliable and valid information, contains a number of difficulties. Fact-gathering or hypotheses-generating are not goals of the humanities. It is not an author's purpose to present us with evidence, nor is it the reader's goal necessarily to find such evidence. Consequently, literary critics have objected to the use of literature as data. To do so, they argue, is to commit "the literary fallacy." This is to assume wrongly that literature is self-validating, that is, really representative of life.

The writer does not give us facts, argues Evans (1954), "but he can *interpret* whatever is valuable within human experience, extending beyond the range of the observed to all the imagination can achieve [p. 98; emphasis added]." Literary (or aesthetic) truth, continues Evans, is irrelevant to scientific truth; other criteria (entertainment, personal growth, and revelation) are more important. Walsh (1972) also maintains that literature need not have any practical or intellectual relevance to life or to problems and issues of our time. Nor should it be used that way by the reader, teacher, or even the author. In fact, Walsh continues literature's "humanistic insights" and "aesthetic character" can only be realized if the reader approaches a work with a "self-forgetful aesthetic detachment that makes him openly receptive to its expressive import [p. 29]."

Despite these sources of contention, it might be worth the effort at least to try to treat literature as a primary source of information. In order to begin, appropriate literary selections have to be chosen. The search for psychologically useful passages from literature is subject to more than the usual amount of personal and other idiosyncratic biases. What is moving to one reader may be trite to another. Hence, it is imperative that consensual judgments about passages of psychological significance be obtained. This could be done by a group of literary experts acting as judges. They might be asked, for example, to submit what they consider to be the most moving passages they have encountered in literature. When the collection stage is completed, the most frequently cited passages would then be chosen. The danger of this reductionistic process is that it may result in statements which are trivial, or appear more like clichés than literary insights. (Clichés were once considered to be profound statements though; Lindauer, 1968a.) It is at this point that consensual judgments by psychologists are needed on the usefulness of these passages. Literary extracts, despite their impressive origins, may be irrelevant, uninteresting, or already known by ordinary scientific procedures. If true, there of course would be no reason to examine further the psychological significance of the phenomenon alluded to in the passage.

A start has been made in the attempt to extract original hypotheses from literature. Nadel and Altrocchi (1969) carefully read such major works as Melville's *Billy Budd,* Shakespeare's *Othello,* Dostoevsky's *Crime and Punishment,* and E. Bronté's *Wuthering Heights.* The authors were able to come up with several possible motives that could account for the attribution of hostile intent to others (a problem of interpersonal perception). These possibilities, however, were not empirically tested.

Despite the rarity with which the hypothesis-generating function has been applied to literature, there are reasons to be optimistic about its increasing use in the future. Throughout this essay, literature has been shown to be susceptible to objective analysis and amenable to statistical descriptions. These encouraging signs, along with literature's use in empirical studies that call for prose material, are discussed next.

Literature and the social sciences. Social scientists, aside from psychologists, have long looked to literature as an important source of information (e.g., Davies, 1968; Escarpit, 1968; Lowenthal, 1961; Wilson, 1973). The literature they refer to, however, is the popular variety (e.g., short stories in mass circulation magazines, best sellers, and TV drama). The large audience appeal of popular works is taken as a valid reflector of the social forces at work in society. These might not otherwise be noted or noted as well by the usual sources of information relied upon by investigators. The power of literature, for sociologists, lies in its use as propaganda, as an agent for social change, and as a reinforcer of the status quo. These beliefs are affirmed by the suppression,and censorship of literature at various times and places by government.

Literature is treated like any other archival, historical, or post hoc type of data (e.g., speeches, diaries, and newspaper accounts). Literary content has been systematically and quantitatively examined so as to reflect, parallel, corroborate, and anticipate social facts (e.g., sex role changes, trends, and comparisons). Content analysis (Holsti, 1969) is the technique used to tabulate the frequency of occurrence of coded categories.

McClelland's (1961) studies of earlier civilizations are outstanding examples of content analysis in a social psychological framework that used literary materials. In order to measure need for achievement in ancient Greece, coders were trained to count instances in ballads, epics, poems, speeches, and odes at different time periods. The motivational patterns which emerged were related to profiles of economic indices. The relationships between the two measures confirmed McClelland's theory about the rise and decline of society as a function of early patterns of childhood upbringing (i.e., independence training). McClelland has also used a similar approach and materials to examine other inaccessible cultures like the Incan, Aztecan, and Minoan.

Most psychologists, however, have been reluctant to ask empirically oriented questions of historical materials, including literature. Such accounts, despite (or because of) their origins in naturalistic observation, are less favored than laboratory and similarly controlled observations. The success of sociologically oriented investigators with popular literature may encourage psychologists to accept classical literature as a primary source of data.

The statistical analysis of literature.   The susceptibility of literature to statistical analysis is evident in the empirical studies reviewed above. There are several areas of research in which statistical analyses of literature play a primary role.

Quantitative techniques play a large part in answering questions about disputed authorship ("Who really wrote Shakespeare?"). These rely on extensive tabulations and sophisticated types of comparisons of grammatical elements, content, or images taken from samples of literary passages (Lindauer, 1974, pp. 154–155). Literary (and other) prose selections have also been subject to readability and interest measures expressed in formulae (Flesch, 1948). These depend on word counts, sentence length, and pronoun use. Other kinds of material taken from literary sources (quotes, clichés, titles, characters' names) have been tabulated in studies of emotions (Lindauer, 1968b), attitudes (Lindauer, 1969a), perception (Bodman, Mincher, Williams, & Lindauer, 1979), and thinking (Lindauer, 1968a). The success with which quantitative analyses have been applied to literature indicates that as "special" as it may be in many important respects, literature can nevertheless be systematically treated.

Literary prose as stimulus material. Studies of learning, remembering, and thinking usually depend on non-literary prose, such as lists of real and nonsense words. Rarely found are even simple sentences or made-up paragraphs. However, there are a few studies in cognition which have instead used more complex material. Although not exactly literary, they suggest future possibilities of an experimental psychology of literature.

Bartlett (1932) used fables in his classic studies of memory. A few contemporary studies of reconstructive processes in memory continue the tradition of studying meaningful, quasi-literary prose. Sulin and Dooling (1974) used short biographical passages, and Thorndike (1977) relied on simple stories whose organization (plot structure) could be manipulated in time and location.

Other areas of psychology are also beginning to depend on more interesting prose material. Creativity measures often use stories to which the subject assigns a title or chooses one from among several options. (Some also use endings.) The originality or cleverness of the choice is then scored (e.g., Wilson, Guilford, & Christensen, 1953). Proverbs and epigrams are found in diagnostic tests of personality (Friedman & Manaster, 1973; Marzolf, 1974). Passages from the *Declaration of Independence* were read in Asch's (1952) social psychological studies of prestige.

These examples hint at the eventual likelihood of substituting literary for ordinary prose. Material which has aesthetic appeal, compared to non-literary prose, is inherently more interesting, is dramatic, and has style. Perhaps for these reasons, Johnson and Zerbolio (1964) claimed that complex prose examples would "make greater intellectual demands and presumably have more significance [to the phenomenon under study] [p. 99]." Systematic, quantitative, and controlled analyses in a wide array of studies of different phenomena in various investigative contexts attest to literature's possibilities as an empirical source of objective and reliable data. Yet whenever prose has been required, psychologists have opted for simpler and neutral material. In contrast, visual art has fared much better than literature as a substitute for simpler material. Thus, paintings have replaced lines and geometric forms in some studies of perception (Lindauer, 1973). Indeed, literature in general has not received as much attention from psychology as have the other arts. The reasons for the psychologist's reluctance to study literature and the psychologist's relatively greater interest in other art forms are discussed next.

THE STATUS OF THE PSYCHOLOGY OF LITERATURE

When compared to the other arts, and in particular painting (Bornstein, in this volume; Hochberg, 1978) and music (Deutsch, 1978, in this volume), literature has received little attention from scientific psychology, and among literary scholars, the psychoanalytic approach, far more than any other, has almost exclusively dominated. The low profile of the psychology of literature, and some of the factors responsible, are discussed here; suggestions for improving this situation are outlined subsequently.

The Psychology of Literature and the Psychology of the Arts

Most texts and reviews on "psychology and the arts" (or aesthetics) are mainly about the visual arts (with music ranking second). Child's (1972) treatment is typical, with about 10% of his coverage given to literature. In general, whenever the arts are related to science and technology, it is usually the visual arts which are meant (e.g., the journal *Leonardo*).

Empirical psychology's neglect of literature can be ascribed to certain definitional uncertainties over the status of literature as material suitable for analysis. Literature, as complex prose, does not lend itself to the kind of sensory and perceptual concreteness found in art and music. Experimental study of these domains can therefore at least begin with the manipulation of light and sound. But literature-as-a-stimulus cannot be as easily captured as, for example, the lines, shapes, and colors of a painting. Arnheim (1969, 1970, 1976) is almost alone in attempting to treat both art and poetry along similarly perceptual lines. Words, like shapes, argues Arnheim, are visual patterns or shapes which contain thoughts and meanings. "Words are a species of pure shapes [Arnheim, 1976, p. 109]."

The response to literature is also difficult to pin down. Literary responses, more than reactions to art and music, take a relatively longer time to unfold. The reading of literature requires a series of processes which range from the perceptual to the cognitive to the affective. In contrast, the thematic content of art and even music (in its opening chords) can be minimally grasped within seconds. The immediacy of response to art and music helps to specify the processes at work. Thus, it is perception rather than memory or imagination which defines our first glance of art or the opening chord of music. To capture the immediacy of the response to literature requires a molecular analysis of letters, words, and similarly short and quasi-literary fragments which may no longer hold any literary referent.

But in art and music, specifiable stimulus and response components allow for controlled experimental attack and exact quantitative analysis. Hence the attractiveness of the arts other than literature to rigorous investigations. It is perhaps for these reasons that Child (1977) suggested that the study of literature fits better within the framework of literary criticism and among scholars "rather than [among] psychologists [p. 290]." Wilson (1973) reached a similarly pessimistic conclusion regarding the possibility of reaching scientifically acceptable facts about writers. These studies, Wilson said, "have been on the whole unconvincing, beset by conflicting and scattered evidence [and] have not proven valuable to psychology because they do not advance generalization [p. 12]."

Literature is therefore relatively more intractable to methodologically rigorous research designs than are the other major forms of art. Hence, the paucity of experiments, and instead, the abundance of historical analyses, biographical accounts, and self-reports.

The Psychology of Literature and Literary Scholarship

However small the contribution of empirical psychology may be to literature, literary scholars remain largely unaware of it. Psychology as a science is generally unknown, misunderstood, or distorted among most literary critics, scholars, aestheticians, and historians of the arts. Ignorance of the scientific method and an insufficient appreciation of objective facts, however, have not prevented literary experts from making some rather harsh judgments about psychology's role in literature.

Psychology is accused of being "imperialistic," that is, of attempting to explain away or "psychologize" literature. Psychology seems to have the reputation of taking a "nothing but" attitude, which is to treat literature as if it were nothing but a psychological case study. These fears have led to an exaggerated concern over the place of psychology in literature. This, in turn, has resulted in either a misguided skepticism or an inappropriate hostility toward psychological investigations of literature.

These apprehensions are not unusual. They occur whenever the relationship between science and art is discussed (see below). The two disciplines have been antithetical for nearly 200 years (Hay, 1973). "Distrust, suspicion, and even contempt are common enough between members of both the humanities and behavioral sciences [Peckham, 1976, p. 48]," but among literary scholars the view of scientific psychology seems to be worse than it is elsewhere. Peckham (1976) finds that literature's psychological interpretations and explanations are "platitudes and old wive's tales. I have rarely observed any effort to support the probability of statements [on psychological matters] by an appeal to the literature of psychology, except to psychoanalysis [p. 49]." Peckham wonders how many literature students are familiar with research in creativity, even though he ruefully notes that they are always using the concept. Vagueness and imprecision, Peckham concludes, characterize the use of many psychological terms (e.g., reinforcement) in literary writing.

The poor esteem in which scientific psychology is held by many literary scholars is at least partially due to an extraordinary and unfortunate confusion over the term "psychology." All psychology, including empirical and non-empirical variants, are treated as if they were synonymous with psychoanalysis (which in turn is treated as equivalent to all depth psychologies). Consequently, empirical approaches, ranging from clinical-objective to observation, have somehow been lost within the immense bulk of psychoanalytic speculations. The dominant position of speculative psychology has effectively masked literary experts' awareness (and appreciation, if not intelligent criticism) of other kinds of psychology.

Thus, Strelka (1976) is only referring to psychoanalysis (without using that term) when he claims that "psychologically [sic] oriented methods have added invaluable insights to the body of knowledge of literary criticism [p. viii]." Similarly, his cautions about the excesses of psychology are solely directed toward depth psychologies. It would be, Strelka says, "the greatest error on the part of literary critics . . . to reduce a work's literary aspects to psychological [sic] means and ends, to psychologize it completely [p. vii]." Wellek (cited in Strelka, 1976) makes the same sort of mistake when he ignores most of contemporary psychology by reporting that psychoanalysis (mainly Freudian) and the depth psychology of Jung have had a "tremendous" influence on literary analysis. Wellek makes only passing mention of behaviorism (it "proved to have almost no influence [p. viii]"), but he is here referring to a school of thought some 30 years old rather than contemporary versions (e.g., Skinner). Phenomenological psychology is approvingly mentioned by Wellek as having had more influence than behaviorism, but we are not told exactly what its contribution is.

Literature's parochialism has been criticized by literary scholars as well. Eastman (1969), for example, chastized literary experts for their general ignorance of scientific information. They "are fighting for the right . . . to talk loosely and yet be taken seriously in a scientific age [p. 16]." In Martindale's (1978c) appraisal of the field of poetics (the study of literary and non-literary texts), we find a similarly negative judgment. "The rather long history of scientific poetics is in large part composed of books and articles claiming that such a science is (or is not) possible [p. 278]." The reason for this, concludes Martindale, is that literary scholars are not trained to test hypotheses or to ask questions susceptible to quantitative attack.

Literary analysis could profit from the kind of rigor and precision exemplified by scientific psychology. As the critic Crews (1978) put it, "objective knowledge is a desirable end" in literary criticism. Criticism, Crews continues, has to be empirical, even technical in nature, for "whatever can lead to an understanding of the work or the author's intent should be used." Objectivity, he adds, would be "an antidote to personal, private, and intuitive engagements with literature [p. 1040]." Crews would like to believe that "the recourse to scientific authority and method is the outstanding trait of 20th century criticism [p. 1041]." However, not much of this trait is readily apparent in the references literary scholars make to psychology.

Part of the indifference of literary scholars to empirical psychology is also ascribable to deficiencies in the research techniques used in its investigations of literature, as well as a certain narrowness in the literary questions it studies. Methodological and substantive improvements in psychological investigations of literature might bring them to the attention of literary scholars. These changes might also place the psychology of literature within the mainstream of the psychology of the arts.

NEW DIRECTIONS FOR A PSYCHOLOGY OF LITERATURE

Literature directly refers to psychological matters. Literary content is explictly about human experience, motives and feelings, interpersonal relations, conflicts, behaviors of all kinds, and a host of other psychological topics. And as a bonus, these are presented in dramatic fashion. We might learn more than we have from literature if we could expand our methods so as to extract these psychological phenomena and if we looked more closely at some overlooked areas.

Improvements in Methodology

Content analysis is the most appropriate technique for the examination of prose material (Gottschalk, 1978; Holsti, 1969). It has successfully been applied by social scientists to narrative and historical material, and there is no reason why it should not become increasingly more popular in scientific investigations of literature (e.g., Sears & Lapidus, 1973). Several other new, revived, or modified methodologies can also add to the empirical approach to literature.

A renewed interest in the introspective method (see Lieberman, 1979) should encourage greater attention to literature. Writers have something to teach us about the introspective method—if we would ask them. They rely on introspection in their work, not only in self-examination, but in the reflections of their characters. A related methodological development is the increased use of phenomenology. The importance of a full description of people and events in as unbiased a manner as possible has been discussed in relation to the arts in general (Lindauer, 1981) and literature specifically (Ruthrof, 1974). There have also been several relatively informal phenomenological studies of literature, the writer, and the reader (Collier & Kuiken, 1977; Sardello, 1978).

Another recent development has been the championing of qualitative data as an alternative to the narrowing and exclusive dependence on quantitative data (Bogdan & Taylor, 1975; Filstead, 1970). A loosening of the quantitative criterion is of benefit to research in literature. Literature is like participant and naturalistic observation, two of the better-known sources of qualitative information. Literature offers a first-hand and intimate source of information; it maintains the wholeness, unity, and context in which events occur and people behave. As Eisner (1978) puts it, a qualitative approach "emphasize[s] the importance of context in understanding . . . that pieces cannot be understood aside from their relationship to the whole in which they participate [p. 198]." Eisner encourages the greater use of the qualitative language of the literary critic in order better to convey quantitative information. Literary criticism, Eisner argues, is a language proficient in the art of disclosure; it is capable of entering a work. Through qualitative language, a researcher can "create, render, portray, and disclose in a way that the reader [can] emphatically participate in the events described [and to use] emotion in knowing [and to] exploit the potential of language in order to further human understanding [p. 199]."

There are, however, real concerns about how one exactly does and uses qualitative research, the reliability of the data, and in particular its relationship to traditional quantitative approaches (Elms, 1979). Are qualitative data supposed to supplement or replace quantitative data? How much does qualitative data add to what otherwise might be overlooked by quantification? And how do we resolve contradictions between the two types of data?

The study of literature could contribute to these methodological questions. Both qualitative and quantitative types of information are already available in the psychology of literature (i.e., depth and empirical psychologies), but they have not yet been systematically compared in methodological terms. The opportunity for scientists to combine both "hard" and "soft" technologies in the study of the arts has only occasionally been pursued (see, for example, Roe, 1975).

Qualitative data, the acceptance of introspection, and the use of phenomenology are useful methodological additions to the empirical study of literature. They probably have their greatest relevance, though, at the exploratory stages of inquiry, that is, in providing ideas or hypotheses that could be developed or tested by more traditional research methods. They might also be useful in situations where more rigorous methods would be inappropriate (e.g., interviews of authors).

But the method of choice, when rigor is demanded and explanation is the goal, is the experimental method. Yet we have already noted that the precision and power of the experimental method have rarely been applied to literature. Poetry has been the most frequently used literary form in experimental aesthetics because its brevity lends itself to experimental control and manipulation.

But other literary or quasi-literary forms can also be placed within experimental designs. These include epigrams, plot summaries, fables, and short stories. Brief literary pieces or extracts can be relatively easily matched with one another or non-literary prose (e.g., in such things as familiarity, content, and emotionality) and altered in purposeful ways (e.g., in titles, tense, endings, and plot structure). Thus, experimental variations are possible while unwanted variables can be controlled. Extensive research on the metaphor (Billow, 1977; Ortony, Reynolds, & Arter, 1978), although not pursued in a literary context, attests to the ways in which short prose materials can be studied experimentally. Experimental research conducted with children, reviewed earlier, also indicates how the experimental method can be imaginatively used with quasi-literary material.

Literature will remain a minor part of the empirical psychology of the arts if more creative and rigorous methods are not increasingly relied upon. Otherwise, the psychology of literature will continue to be dominated by literary illustrations and psychological speculations. Such interesting but limited accomplishments will not change the narrow and skeptical appraisal of the psychology of literature now held by most literary scholars, nor will it change the indifference and neglect of psychological investigators who demand a more rigorous brand of psychology.

Study of the Reader

The status of empirical psychology in the study of literature could also be strengthened by a shift in the topics emphasized. Research has mostly been on authors or literary texts, with little on the less glamorous subject of the reader. Why does literature bring us feelings of pleasure, excitement, fun, satisfaction, entertainment, and perhaps even escape (Shafer, 1965)? An understanding of the reader is fundamental. In the final analysis, the choice of which author, work, or literary character to study is often decided by what has attracted and sustained a readership. Futhermore, the reader is the target of and hence the ultimate measuring rod of the effects of literature.

There is an abundance of views on the experiential and behavioral influences of literature. While often confusing, they may provide the researcher with clues on what aspects of the reader to study. Thus, literary critics speculate about the reader's "state of readiness" or "reciprocity," and they refer to the "willing suspension of disbelief." Similarly provocative suggestions are made by authors on the effects of literature. "All great artists," said de Maupassant (in Wijsen, 1978), "are those who can make other men see their own particular illusion [p. 160]." A related assertion is that writers "bring new perceptions that allow other men to create new illusions [Wijsen, 1978, p. 160]." A somewhat different but even more cryptic view of the reader's perceptual experience is that of William James (in Wijsen, 1978), who said that literature allows us to "watch . . . consciousness float by [p. 149]." These comments suggest a possibly more empirical question, namely, whether the reader reconstructs the author's experience or whether the two sets of experiences are as distinct as their origins.

A widely promoted view of what reading does, taken mainly from philosophers, is that it evokes a special and unique kind of experience, the aesthetic experience. The reader is said to be elevated, transformed, inspired, moved, and detached. The aesthetic experience not only increases our awareness of the self, but also that of others and of larger social forces beyond the self. Hospers (1978) amplifies: "Literature is unique in its stimulation of the imagination. . . . The reader is carried beyond the confines of the narrow world . . . into a world of thought and feeling more profound and more varied than his own [where he can] share experiences of human beings . . . who are far removed from him in space and time and in attitudes and way of life . . . to enter directly the affective processes of other human beings, and having done this [find and appreciate] the common ties of human nature [p. 54]." Literature works, according to Hospers, because it provides images and fantasies, and these contain thoughts and feelings not otherwise expressable in ordinary language or accessible to everyday experiences.

A well-known psychological but still speculative belief is that reading literature is cathartic. It releases the inhibitions, restrictions, and tensions of normal living (with different types of literature presumably serving different types of people at different times and places). Kreitler and Kreitler (1972) hold that literature is more effective than the other arts in releasing tensions, and good literature compared to ordinary literature is even better. "Of all the arts, literature is oftenest associated with the principle of tension and relief. [T]ension and relief are an integral element of the dramatic nucleus of every literary art [pp. 251-252]."

Even conditioning principles might be applied to the reading of literature. Selective reading habits are sustained because they have been associated in the past with "good things" (reinforcers); or looked at from another conditioning perspective, "good things" (like esteem and status from knowing who the best sellers and great authors are) follow from reading literature. More cognitive is the information-processing approach. The so-called "challenge of literature" is our straining for meaning, which if pursued is the source of literature's attractiveness. Falling somewhere between conditioning and cognitive theories is Berlyne's (1971) position that literature is a source of novelty and unfamiliarity (as are play, humor, and the other arts). Hence, literature offers the reader a moderate kind of diversity and complexity. These are removed from usual experience yet not so strange as to be stressful or uncomfortable. Thus, literature satisfies a need for stimulation whose optimal level varies for different persons depending on their experience and training.

There are therefore many ways in which literature might affect the reader. Having had "a literary experience," though, is the reader thereby changed? Hospers (1978) is cautious: "Those who read great literature . . . are [not] necessarily more tolerant or sympathetic to human beings." But Hospers is nevertheless optimistic about the power of literature to influence people as they become "more understanding of other people's conflicts and . . . have more sympathy with their problems and [can] empathize more [p. 54]." Auden (1962) adds that literature's effectiveness can be increased with the help of the critic who serves to translate the author's intent and the work's meaning.

If changes result from the literary experience, the question then becomes how change is accomplished. A number of suggestions have been made. Literature may provide surrogate solutions to problems or present models of action. These guide and in this way modify the reader's behavior. Changes might also occur because the reader has become more sensitive to real-life events which are similar to those that have been read about. In specifying exactly how these changes come about, terms like identification, projection, and empathy (with key characters and crucial events) are loosely (and interchangeably) referred to. Whatever the process may be and however it is labelled, it is still unclear whether literature is most effective when it supplements or complements the reader's personality.

There is therefore a plethora of ideas on the effects of literature on the reader. But what kind of support has been marshalled to advance any particular argument? Foremost is personal testimony, that is, people attest to literature's vital place in their lives; they hold that the reading of literature has changed their thoughts, feelings, and actions. Indirect support of these claims is found among educators and therapists. Teachers of literature expect the reading of literature to result in some kind of positive outcome. They hope that good reading habits will develop and be sustained, and they believe that some transfer and generalization from the classroom to real-life will happen. Even greater benefits are presumed to occur through poetry therapy (Buck & Kramer, 1974) and "bibliotherapy" (Freedman, 1974). By writing or reading one's own (or others') prose or verse, the capacity to express or communicate in general is presumably increased as well.

There are only a few empirical studies on the effects of literature. The evidence, warns Wilson (1973), is "remarkable for its rarity." Wilson contributed his own informal study. He found that the memorability of positive and negative fictional characters depended upon the reader's personality. "Interesting correspondences were found between the student's own personality configuration in the identity of ego-ideal or ego-alien figures in their remembered reading [p. 15]." A more quantitative approach was taken by Ebersole (1974) who tabulated and classified readers' recollections of their responses to literature. A small number (about 7%) of his college sample reported that a literary work had resulted in a bahavioral effect; a somewhat larger number (about 18%) indicated there had been an aesthetic effect; and about the same number reported no effect of literature at all. But the largest response (about 57%) indicated that literature had led to cognitive and experiential effects. Literature, this group said, strenghtened existing views, led to new philosophical or ideological thinking, and prompted more thinking about important personal concerns. This kind of research should be extended, but with more specificity. It is important to relate the different types of responses to the kind and amount of literature read and even to the ages at which the reading took place.

However, recollections of reading experiences that occurred some time ago are subject to all sorts of omissions and distortions. Thus, more immediate and hence more reliable measures of the consequences of reading are needed. There are few direct studies of the effects of reading.

Thayer and Pronko (1958) gave college students brief excerpts from fiction and asked them to give their impression of the central character. While the readers sharply differed in their feelings and interpretations about the characters (which is not surprising), they agreed on the physical and psychological descriptions. Patrick (1939) asked college students to talk aloud about their reactions to good and bad poems (the former by "outstanding" authors, the latter by "authors who entirely lacked poetic talent [p. 255]"). These reports, along with interviews and ratings of the poems, indicated that as many as 11 factors characterized the good poems. For example, they involved more thought changes and images, and they took longer to respond to. Recently, Klinger (1978) studied the effects of literary extracts which were altered to fit readers' personal concerns. "Readers will pay more attention, have better recall for, and have more thoughts about literary passages that touch on their current concerns [p. 195]." Klinger tied these results to the success of certain authors: "Authors who address influential current concerns, then, will have the most absorbed readers. To be effective, authors must understand which set of their readers' needs they seek to fullfill and suit their imagery to the particular response at hand [pp. 195–196]."

These studies, while mainly exploratory, serve to encourage the possibility of further research about the reader. There are other important questions to be empirically studied. Are there different kinds of readers? How do readers respond to different types of literature? And what are the best ages at which to introduce great literature to young readers?

An understanding of the literary experience might profitably begin with the study of readers' imagery (Lindauer, 1977). The place of imagery in the responses of readers to literature and the kind of prose which is most evocative of different kinds of imagery (e.g., visual or auditory) are issues that deserve to be seriously investigated. The mediating role of imagery in the observer's reaction, mainly to art and music, has been attested to in self-reports and biographical accounts (e.g., Ghiselin, 1952). Unfortunately, there are few studies of imagery in literature (Lindauer & Leonard, 1973). Wheeler's (1923) work, although old, suggests how imagery might influence literary appreciation. He obtained reports of readers' imagery while they read poetry, and he found two kinds of readers: "spontaneous" and "forced" (that is, where the reader either unintentionally or intentionally tried to call forth images). Spontaneous imagery appeared to be more beneficial to appreciation, although its effectiveness depended on both the content and rhythm of the poetry.

There are a number of interesting characteristics about the reader and the reading of literature whose factual status has been assumed by literary scholars and educators. However, nearly all assertions remain untested by scientific procedures. Aside from the few exploratory and descriptive efforts reviewed above, and the occasional studies of the reader found here and there among the seven psychological approaches to literature discussed earlier, the reader of literature has not been investigated with any thoroughness. There is therefore a sense of inbalance to the psychology of literature, in which the author and work have taken precedence.

Neglecting the reader also works against the seriousness with which literary scholars can be expected to view psychology.

CONCLUSION

Literature is best at describing the human condition in dramatic form, while psychology's strength lies in investigating human behavior in systematic ways. Both literature and psychology examine the human experience and those actions which express our thoughts, feelings, and motives. Each discipline, in its own way, highlights a different approach to the understanding of human phenomena.

Given psychology and literature's common interest in humankind, one might expect to find a high degree of shared communication between them. Yet, at least from the perspective of scientific empiricism, the status of the psychology of literature is uncertain in relation to humanistic scholarship. Nor is its status in relation to the psychology of the arts or to psychology in general much better. Serious conceptual, methodological, and substantive questions exist, and of those that have been recognized, research has barely begun to provide answers.

The various psychological approaches to literature have achieved some success, and directions for improvement have been identified. But when these are weighed against the vast scope of the literary domain and its possibilities, psychological efforts are quite limited. Psychological investigations are usually exploratory, fragmentary in their accomplishments, and too often superficial. Studies of the literary work, the author, or the reader can, with some justification, be accused of being irrelevant to the concerns of both psychology and literature. There is little, for example, that psychologists contribute to an understanding of the processes which underlie the aesthetic experience of the reader.

However, given the self-corrective, accumulative, and progressive nature of science, we can expect the situation in psychology to improve. It is less certain whether we can be as optimistic about clarifying the often distorted and limited perspective taken by literary experts on psychology. Any change there is probably dependent on first improving psychology's position in literature.

The estrangement between psychology and literature is the result of several factors. There are real and sharp differences in what each is trying to do and how their goals are pursued. In contrast to psychology, literature deals with judgmental matters of value, meaning, and significance; it is receptive to private, visionary, and prophetic intuitions and revelations; it is avowedly personal, subjective, and selective; and its language

is intentionally aesthetic. Because of these profound differences in working style, literary experts are too frequently not listening to whatever
psychologists are trying to say about literature, although admittedly
garbled and stumbling at times.

An antipathy between psychology and literature also stems from a
larger conflict, that between science and the humanities. There has been a
long and often bitter debate, seemingly more exacerbated in literature
than elsewhere, over the "two cultures and their conflict" (Cornelius &
Vincent, 1964). "Between [literary intellectuals and the scientific commu-
nity] there is little communication and instead of fellow-being, something
like hostility [Snow, 1963/1964, p. 61]." Even stronger is the view of the
poet Blake (cited in Evans, 1954): "Science is the enemy and destroyer of
imagination [p. 13]." An equally negative view among scientists is represented by Darwin (cited in Evans, 1954). After noting that he enjoyed
poetry until he was around 30, Darwin voiced this complaint: "But now
for many years I cannot endure to read a line of poetry. I have tried lately
to read Shakespeare and found it so intolerably dull that it nauseated me
[p. 90]." (Darwin voiced similar complaints about paintings and music.)
But usually omitted from these frequently cited remarks is Darwin's
evaluation of his rejection of the arts: "This [is a] curious and lament-
able . . . loss of the higher aesthetic traits. If I had to live my life again, I
would have made it a rule to read poetry and listen to some music at least
once every week [and thereby perhaps prevent this loss] [p. 91]."

The balance between science and the humanities has been tipping in
favor of the former in recent years. The importance of literature has been
declining and that of science has been increasing to the point of almost
overwhelming the humanities. Even the critic Eastman (1969) noted that
"the business which made literary critics great and important in times
gone by—the business of understanding human nature—has been taken
over by experts and left them with empty minds and hands [p. 260]."
"Critics of literary art [are] very little troubled by the advance of science
and *very little troubling it* [p. 265, emphasis added]."

These antipathies between science and art were not always the case.
Until fairly recently, literary men were also usually scientists, scholars, or
more generally, philosophically oriented investigators of nature; and
many scientists were deliberately literary in the expression of their intellectual pursuits (e.g., Aristotle, Plato, Machiavelli, Locke, Bacon, and
Kepler, to name just a few). Indeed, many poets (e.g., Whitman, Shelley,
Donne, and others) deliberately tried to incorporate the scientific discoveries of their time into their work (Hay, 1973; Jerome, 1969; McDaniel
1974; Nicolson, 1962/1976;   Sinsheimer, 1977; Sussman, 1968). "Poets
greeted the advancements of science with enthusiasm [Jones, 1966, p. 1]."

"The ideas represented by scientists . . . were repeated in poetry during the eighteenth century with profuse variations [p. 27]." But such mutually beneficial interchanges are rare today.

The apparently irreconcilable positions held by the humanities and science overlooks indisputable similarities between the two. Most visible and important are the parallel ways in which different disciplines conceptualize and solve problems (Gardner, 1971) or, in more general terms, depend on the same creative process. Thus, Bronowski (1974a), himself a scientist and poet, said that "poetry is a wonderful topic constantly to bear in mind when talking about scientific ideas because it reminds you that you can communicate truth in a way that carries intellectual conviction without setting up equations about it [p. 396]." Creative work in the best of literature and science (e.g., Shakespeare and Blake, Copernicus and Planck), Bronowski continues, touches on the unity, likeness, and patterns discovered in nature. "A man becomes creative, whether he is an artist or a scientist, when he finds a new unity in the variety of nature [Bronowski, 1974b, p. 98]."

A scientifically oriented psychology of literature could be a common ground between science and the humanities (Putnam, 1976). The methods of empirical psychology, with their insistence on reliable data, can be joined with the expertise of literary scholars, with their sensitivity toward the messages communicated by prose. Were tangible research on topics of humanistic concern the result of an interchange between psychology and literature, it would move discussion beyond exhortation or polemics over the possibility of such an exchange. Research outcomes could concretely demonstrate the advantages (or limitations) of a closer tie between science and the humanities (Jennings, 1970; Lindauer, 1978). Psychological research in literature might convincingly demonstrate, in a public and verifiable manner, the frequently heard about but rarely demonstrated "bridge" between science and the humanities (Friedman & Puetz 1974; Fritz-Bailey & Buckalew, 1976). If it is true that science has the cerebral, intellectual, and analytical skills (and a tendency to dehumanize) and the humanities have the visceral, intuitive, and holistic sensibilities (and a tendency to sentimentalize), then both used together can complement each other's strengths and offset the other's weaknesses.

Freud and Jung both reacted with awe and humility when they turned to the study of the arts. Both expressed a sense of futility in trying to understand such phenomena. "Psychoanalysis must lay down its arms before the problem of the poet" said Freud. "The creation of art . . . must forever elude our understanding" said Jung (cited in Wilson, 1973, p. 12). Despite these protestations, both Freud and Jung (and a host of their students) unhesitatingly attempted to solve the riddle of the arts. Empirical psychologists have an equal if not greater possibility of solving the riddle. But psychology and literature will have to work more closely with one another than they have in the past if progress is to be made. "The sciences of life . . . have need of the artist's intuitions and conversely, the artist has need of all that these sciences can offer him in the way of new materials on which to exercise his creative power [Huxley, 1963, p. 79]."

REFERENCES

Albrecht, M. C., Barnett, J. H., & Griff, M. (Eds.). *The sociology of art and literature: A reader*. New York: Praeger, 1970.
Arnheim, R. Psychological notes on the poetical process. In R. Arnheim, K. Shapiro, & D. A. Stauffer (Eds.), *Poets at work*. New York: Harcourt, Brace, 1948.
Arnheim, R. *Visual thinking*. Berkeley, CA: University of California Press, 1969.
Arnheim, R. Words in their place. *Journal of Typographic Research*, 1970, *4*, 199–212.
Arnheim, R. Visual aspects of concrete poetry. In J. P. Strelka (Ed.), *Literary criticism and psychology*. College Park, PA: The Pennsylvania State University Press, 1976.
Arcamore, A., & Lindauer, M. S. Concept learning and the identification of poetic style. *Psychological Reports*, 1974, *35*, 207–210.
Asch, S. E. *Social psychology*. Englewood Cliffs, NJ: Prentice-Hall, 1952.
Auden, W. H. *The dyer's hand and other essays*. New York: Random House, 1962.
Baird, J. Jungian psychology in criticism: Theoretical problems. In J. P. Strelka (Ed.), *Literary criticism and psychology*. College Park, PA: The Pennsylvania State University Press, 1976.
Barron, F. *Creative person and creative process*. New York: Holt, Rinehart & Winston, 1969.
Barron, F. *Artists in the making*. New York: Seminar Press, 1972.
Bartlett, F. C. *Remembering*. Cambridge: Cambridge University Press, 1932.
Baudry, F. Literature and psychoanalysis. In B. B. Wolman (Ed.), *International encyclopedia of psychiatry, psychology, psychoanalysis, and neurology* (Vol. 6). New York: Aesculapius-Van Nostrand, 1977.
Beck, S. J. *The Rorschach test: Exemplified in classics of drama and fiction*. New York: Stratton Intercontinental Medical Book Corp., 1976.
Berlyne, D. E. *Aesthetics and psychobiology*. New York: Appleton-Century-Crofts, 1971.
Billow, R. M. Metaphor: A review of the psychological literature. *Psychological Bulletin*, 1977, *84*, 81–92.
Birkhoff, G. D. *Aesthetic measure*. Cambridge, MA: Harvard University Press, 1933.
Bodman, P. I., Mincher, M., Williams, C., & Lindauer, M. S. What's in a name? Evaluations of literary names in context and in isolation. *Poetics*, 1979, *8*, 491–496.
Botvin, G. J., & Sutton-Smith, B. The development of structural complexity in children's fantasy narratives. *Developmental Psychology*, 1977, *13*, 377–388.
Bogdan, R., & Taylor, S. J. *An introduction to qualitative research methods: A phenomenological approach to the social sciences*. New York: Wiley, 1975.
Bronowski, J. Science, poetry, and human specificity: Interview with J. Bronowski by G. Derfer. *American Scholar*, 1974, *43*, 386–404.(a)
Bronowski, J. Experience of creation. *Diogenes*, 1974, *86*, 94–100.(b)
Buck, L. A., & Kramer, A. Poetry as a means of group facilitation. *Journal of Humanistic Psychology*, 1974, *14*, 57–71.
Buhrich, N., & McConaghy, N. Transvestite fiction. *Journal of Nervous & Mental Disease*, 1976, *163*, 420–427.

148   LINDAUER

Burgess, A. The novel. In *New encyclopedia Britannica* (15th ed., Vol. 13). Chicago, IL: Encyclopedia Britannica, 1978.

Chapko, M. K., & Lewis, M. H. Authoritarianism and All in the Family. *Journal of Psychology,* 1975, *90,* 245–248.

Child, I. L. Esthetics. In G. Lindzey & E. Aronson (Eds.), *Handbook of social psychology* (Vol. 3). Reading, MA: Addison-Wesley, 1969.

Child, I. L. Esthetics. *Annual Review of Psychology,* 1972, *23,* 669–694.

Child, I. L. Aesthetics. In B. B. Wolman (Ed.), *International encyclopedia of psychiatry, psychology, psychoanalysis, and neurology* (Vol. 1). New York: Aesculapius-Van Nostrand, 1977.

Child, I. L. Aesthetic theories. In E. C. Carterette & M. P. Friedman (Eds.), *Handbook of perception* (Vol. 10). New York: Academic Press, 1978.

Collier, G., & Kuiken, D. A phenomenological study of the experience of poetry. *Journal of Phenomenological Psychology,* 1977, *7,* 209–225.

Cornelius, D. K., & Vincent, E. S. (Eds.). *Cultures in conflict: Perspectives on the Snow-Leavis controversy.* Chicago, IL: Scott, Foresman, 1964.

Cox, C. M. *The early mental traits of three hundred geniuses.* Stanford, CA: Stanford University Press, 1926.

Crews, F. C. *Out of my system.* New York: Oxford University Press, 1975.

Crews, F. C. Literary criticism. In *New encyclopedia Britannica* (15th ed., Vol. 10). Chicago, IL: Encyclopedia Britannica, 1978.

Davies, J. C. Political fiction. In D. L. Sills (Ed.), *International encyclopedia of the social sciences* (Vol. 9). New York: Macmillan-Free Press, 1968.

Dennis, W. Creative productivity between the age of 20 and 80 years. *Journal of Gerontology,* 1966, *21,* 1–8.

Deutsch, D. The psychology of music. In E. C. Carterette & M. P. Friedman (Eds.), *Handbook of perception* (Vol. 10). New York: Academic Press, 1978.

Dudley, F. A. *The relations of literature and science: A selected bibliography 1930–1967.* Ann Arbor, MI: University Microfilms, 1968.

Eastman, M. *The literary mind: Its place in an age of science.* New York: Octagon, 1969.

Ebersole, P. Impact of literary works upon college students. *Psychological Reports,* 1974, *34,* 1127–1130.

Edel, L. *The modern psychological novel.* New York: Grove, 1959.

Eisner, E. W. Humanistic trends and the curriculum field. *Curriculum Studies,* 1978, *10,* 197–204.

Elms, A. C. *Biographical studies of creative artists: The psychologist's contribution.* Paper presented at the 87th Annual Convention of the American Psychological Association, New York, 1979.

Erikson, E. H. *Young man Luther.* New York: Norton, 1958.

Erikson, E. H. *Ghandi's truth.* New York: Norton, 1969.

Escarpit, T. The sociology of literature. In D.L. Sills (Ed.), *International encyclopedia of the social sciences* (Vol. 9). New York: Macmillan-Free Press, 1968.

Evans, I. *Literature and science.* London: Allen & Unwin, 1954.

Eysenck, H. J. Some factors in the appreciation of poetry. *Character & Personality,* 1940, *9,* 160–167.

Eysenck, H. J. *Sense and nonsense in psychology.* Baltimore, MD: Pelican, 1958.

Fechner, G. T. *Vorschule der Aesthetik.* Leipzig: Breithopf & Haerted, 1897.

Fernandez, T. (Ed.). *Social psychology through literature.* New York: Wiley, 1972.

Filstead, W. J. *Qualitative methodology: Firsthand involvement with the social world.* Chicago, IL: Markham, 1970.

Flesch, R. A new readability yardstick. *Journal of Applied Psychology,* 1948, *32,* 221–233.

Freedman, B. J. Cognitive disturbances in schizophrenia. *Archives of General Psychiatry,* 1974, *30,* 330–340.

Freud, S. Dostoevsky and parricide. In *Collected papers* (Vol. 5). London: Hogarth, 1950. (Originally published, 1928.)

Freud, S. The relation of the poet to daydreaming. In *Collected papers* (Vol. 4). New York: Basic Books, 1960. (Originally published, 1908.)

Friedman, A. J., & Puetz, M. Science as metaphor: Thomas Pynchon and Gravity's Rainbow. *Contemporary Literature,* 1974, *15,* 345–359.

Friedman, N. Psychology and literary form: Toward a unified approach. *Psychocultural Review,* 1978, *2,* 75–95.

Friedman, S.T., & Manaster, G. Internal-external control: Studied through the use of proverbs. *Psychological Reports,* 1973, *33,* 611–615.

Fritz-Bailey, S., & Buckalew, M.W. Alfred Korzybski and Marcel Duchamp: A study in science and art. *Etc.,* 1976, *33,* 380–384.

Galton, F. *Hereditary genius: An inquiry into its laws and consequences.* London: MacMillan, 1869.

Gardner, H. Problem-solving in the arts and sciences. *Journal of Aesthetic Education,* 1971, *5,* 93–113.

Gardner, H. *The arts and human development: A psychological study of the artistic process.* New York: Wiley, 1973.

Gardner, H., Kircher, M., Winner, E., & Perkins, D. Children's metaphoric productions and preferences. *Journal of Child Language,* 1975, *2,* 125–141.

Gardner, H., & Lohman, W. Children's sensitivity to literary styles. *Merrill-Palmer Quarterly,* 1975, *21,* 113–126.

Getzels, J.B., & Csiksentmihalyi, M. *The creative vision: A longitudinal study of problem solving in art.* New York: Wiley, 1976.

Ghiselin, B. (Ed.). *The creative process.* New York: Mentor-New American Library, 1952.

Gottschalk, L. A. *The content analysis of verbal behavior: Further studies.* Somerset, NJ: Halsted-Wiley, 1978.

Guilford, J. P. Creativity: Retrospect and prospect. *Journal of Creative Behavior,* 1970, *4,* 149–168.

Gunn, D. G. Factors in the appreciation of poetry. *British Journal of Educational Psychology,* 1951, *21,* 96-104.

Gunn, D. G. Further observations on factors in the appreciation of poetry. *British Psychological Society Bulletin,* 1952, *3,* 24–26.

Haimowitz, M. L., & Haimowitz, N. R. (Eds.). *Human development: Selected readings.* New York: Thomas Y. Crowell, 1966.

Halasz, L. *Reader's information processing of a literary work.* Paper Presented at 19th International Congress of Applied Psychology, Munich, West Germany, 1978.

Halasz, L. Organization of judgments of works of art and psychological characteristics of value recognition. In L. Kardos (Ed.), *Attitudes, interaction, personality.* Budapest, Hungary: Publisher unknown, 1980.

Hay, D. Learning and literature. In J. Buchanan-Brown (Ed.), *Cassell's encyclopedia of world literature* (Vol. 1). New York: William Morrow, 1973.

Helson, R. Through the pages of children's books. *Psychology Today,* 1973, *7,* 107–117.

Helson, R. The creative spectrum of fantasy. *Journal of Personality,* 1977, *45,* 310–326.

Helson R. Experiences of authors in writing fantasy: Two relationships between creative process and product. *Journal of Altered States of Consciousness,* 1977–78, *3,* 235–248.

Helson, R. The imaginative process in children's literature: A quantitative approach. *Poetics,* 1978, *7,* 135–153.

Hevener, K. An experimental study of the affective nature of sounds in poetry. *American Journal of Psychology*, 1937, *49*, 419–434.

Hochberg, J. Art and perception. In E. C. Carterette & M. P. Friedman (Eds.), *Handbook of perception* (Vol. 10). New York: Academic Press, 1978.

Holland, N. N. *Psychoanalysis and Shakespeare*. New York: McGraw-Hill, 1966.

Holland, N. N. *The dynamics of literary response*. New York: Oxford, 1968.

Holsti, O. R. *Content analysis for the social sciences and humanities*. Reading, MA: Addison-Wesley, 1969.

Hooper, K. Perceptual aspects of architecture. In E. C. Carterette & M. P. Friedman (Eds.), *Handbook of perception* (Vol. 10). New York: Academic Press, 1978.

Hospers, J. Implied truth in literature. *Journal of Aesthetics and Art Criticism*, 1960, *19*, 37–46.

Hospers, J. Philosophy of art. In *New encyclopedia Britannica* (15 ed. Vol. 2), Chicago, IL: Encyclopedia Britannica, 1978.

Huxley, A. *Literature and science*. New York: Harper & Row, 1963.

Jastrow, S. The antecedents of the study of character and temperament. *Popular Science Monthly*, 1915, *86*, 590–613.

Jennings, E. M. (Ed.). *Science and literature: New lens for criticism*. Garden City, NY: Anchor, 1970.

Jerome, J. Poetry: How and why: science and poetry. *Writers Digest*, 1969, *49*, 26–31.

Johnson, D. M., & Zerbolio, D. J. Relations between productions and judgments of plot-titles. *American Journal of Psychology*, 1964, *77*, 99–105.

Jones, E. *Hamlet and Oedipus*. New York: Norton, 1949.

Jones, W. P. *The rhetoric of science: A study of scientific ideas and imagery in eighteenth-century English poetry*. Berkeley, CA: University of California Press, 1966.

Kammann, R. Verbal complexity and preferences in poetry. *Journal of Verbal Learning & Verbal Behavior*, 1966, *5*, 536–540.

Katz, H. A., Warrick, P., & Greenberg, M. H. (Eds.). *Introductory psychology through science fiction*. Chicago, IL: Rand-McNally, 1974.

Kegan, D. Paperback images of encounter. *Journal of Humanistic Psychology*, 1975, *15*, 31–37.

Kiell, N. (Ed.). *Psychoanalysis, psychology, and literature: A bibliography*. Madison, WI: University of Wisconsin, 1963.

Kiell, N. *The adolescent through fiction*. New York: International Universities Press, 1974.

Klinger, E. The flow of thought and its implications for literary communication. *Poetics*, 1978, *7*, 191–205.

Koch, K. *Wishes, lies, and dreams: Teaching children to write poetry*. New York: Chelsea, 1970.

Koestler, A. *The act of creation*. New York: Dell, 1964.

Kohlberg, L. Psychological analysis and literary form: A study of the doubles in Dostoevsky. *Daedalus*, 1963, *92*, 345–362.

Kreitler, H., & Kreitler, S. *Psychology and the arts*. Durham, NC: Duke University Press, 1972.

Lehman, H. C. The creative years: Best books. *Scientific Monthly*, 1937, *85*, 67–76.

Lehman, H. C. *Age and achievement*. Princeton, NJ: Van Nostrand, 1953.

Levitas, G. B. (Ed.). *The world of psychology* (Vol. 1 & 2). New York: George Braziller, 1963.

Lieberman, D. A. Behaviorism and the mind: A (limited) call for a return to introspection. *American Psychologist*, 1979, *34*, 319–333.

Lindauer, M. S. The nature and use of the cliché. *Journal of General Psychology*, 1968, *78*, 133–143. (a)

Lindauer, M. A. Pleasant and unpleasant emotions in literature: A comparison with the affective tone of psychology. *Journal of Psychology*, 1968, *70*, 55–67. (b)

Lindauer, M.S. Historical and contemporary attitudes toward numbers. *Journal of Psychology*, 1969, *71*, 41–43. (a)

Lindauer, M. S. Quantitative analyses of psychoanalytic studies of Shakespeare. *Journal of Psychology*, 1969, *72*, 3–9. (b)

Lindauer, M. S. Toward a liberalization of experimental aesthetics. *Journal of Aesthetics and Art Criticism*, 1973, *31*, 459–465.

Lindauer, M. S. *The psychological study of literature*. Chicago, IL: Nelson-Hall, 1974.

Lindauer, M. S. Imagery from the point of view of psychological aesthetics, the arts, and creativity. *Journal of Mental Imagery*, 1977, *1*, 343–362.

Lindauer, M. S. Psychology as a humanistic science. *Psychocultural Review*, 1978, *2*, 139–145.

Lindauer, M. S. Aesthetic experience: A neglected topic in the psychology of the arts. In D. O'Hare (Ed.), *Psychology and the arts*. Sussex: Harvester, 1981.

Lindauer, M. S., & Leonard, G. Aesthetic participation and imagery arousal. *Perceptual & Motor Skills*, 1973, *36*, 977–978.

Lowenthal, L. *Literature, popular culture, and society*. Englewood Cliffs, NJ: Prentice-Hall, 1961.

Lucas, F. L. *Literature and psychology*. Ann Arbor, MI: University of Michigan Press, 1957.

MacKinnon, D. W. The structure of personality. In J. McV. Hunt (Ed.), *Personality and the behavior disorders* (Vol. 1). New York: Ronald, 1944.

MacKinnon, D. W. IPAR's contribution to the conceptualization and study of creativity. In I. A. Taylor & J. W. Getzels (Eds.), *Perspectives in creativity*. Chicago, IL: Aldine, 1975.

Maddi, S. R. *Myth and personality*. Paper presented at the 86th annual convention of the American Psychological Association, Toronto, 1978.

Maier, N. R. F., & Reninger, H. W. *A psychological approach to literary criticism*. New York: Appleton, 1933.

Martindale, C. An experimental simulation of literary change. *Journal of Personality & Social Psychology*, 1973, *25*, 319–326.

Martindale, C. *Romantic progression: The psychology of literary history*. New York: Halsted-Wiley, 1975.

Martindale, C. Creativity, consciousness, and cortical arousal. *Journal of Altered States of Consciousness*, 1977, *3*, 69–87.

Martindale, C. The evolution of English poetry. *Poetics*, 1978, *7*, 231–248. (a)

Martindale, C. Preface: Psychological contributions to poetics. *Poetics*, 1978, *7*, 121–133. (b)

Martindale, C. Sit with statisticians and commit a social science: Interdisciplinary aspects of poetics. *Poetics*, 1978, *7*, 273–282. (c)

Marzolf, S. Common sayings and 16 PF traits. *Journal of Clinical Psychology*, 1974, *30*, 202–204.

McClelland, D. C. *The achieving society*. Princeton, NJ: Van Nostrand, 1961.

McCurdy, H. G. A study of the novels of Charlotte and Emily Brontë as an expression of their personalities. *Journal of Personality*, 1947, *16*, 109–152.

McCurdy, H. G. Literature as a resource in personality study: Theory and methods. *Journal of Aesthetics and Art Criticism*, 1949, *8*, 42–46.

McCurdy, H. G. *The personal world*. New York: Harcourt, Brace & World, 1961.

McCurdy, H. G. The psychology of literature. In D. L. Sills (Ed.), *International encyclopedia of the social sciences* (Vol. 9). New York: Macmillan-Free Press, 1968.

McDaniel, J. Wallace Stevens and the scientific imagination. *Contemporary Literature,* 1974, *15,* 221–237.

McMahon, C. E. Psychosomatic concepts in the works of Shakespeare. *Journal of the History of the Behavioral Sciences,* 1976, *12,* 275–282.

Melvin, K. B., Brodsky, S. L., & Fowler, R. D. Jr. (Eds.). *Psy-fi one: An anthology of psychology in science fiction.* New York: Random House, 1977.

Mindess, A. A psychologist looks at the writer. *Psychology Today,* 1967, *1,* 40–55.

Nadel, B. S., & Altrocchi, J. Attribution of hostile intent in literature. *Psychological Reports,* 1969, *25,* 747–763.

Nemerov, H. Poetry. In *New encyclopedia Britannica* (15th ed., Vol. 14). Chicago, IL: Encyclopedia Britannica, 1978.

Nicolson, M. *Science and imagination.* Ithaca, NY: Great Seal Books, 1976. (Originally published, 1962.)

Nixon, H. K. *Psychology for the writer.* New York: Harper, 1928.

Ortony, A., Reynolds, R. E., & Arter, J. A. Metaphor: Theoretical and empirical research. *Psychological Bulletin,* 1978, *85,* 919–943.

Paris, B. J. *A psychological approach to fiction: Studies in Thackeray, Stendhal, George Elliot, Dostoevsky, and Coward.* Bloomington, IN: Indiana University Press, 1974.

Patrick, C. Creative thought in poets. *Archives of Psychology,* 1935, *26,* No. 178.

Patrick, C. Creative thought in poets. *Journal of Psychology,* 1937, *4,* 35–73.

Patrick, C. How responses to good and poor poetry differ. *Journal of Psychology,* 1939, *8,* 253–283.

Patterson, M. C. *Literary research guide.* Detroit, MI: Gale, 1976.

Peckham, M. Psychology in literature. In J. P. Strelka (Ed.), *Literary criticism and psychology.* University Park, PA: The Pennsylvania State University Press, 1976.

Perkins, D., & Leondar, B. (Eds.). *The arts and cognition.* Baltimore, MD: The Johns Hopkins University Press, 1977.

Perloff, E. A selected bibliography on psychology and literature: Psychological Abstracts, 1960–1969. *JSAS Catalog of Selected Documents in Psychology,* 1974, *4,* 68.

Peterson, D. A., & Karnes, E. L. Older people in adolescent literature. *Gerontologist,* 1976, *16,* 225–231.

Pratt, C. C. Aesthetics. *Annual Review of Psychology,* 1961, *12,* 71–92.

Putnam, H. Literature, science, and reflection. *New Literary History,* 1976, *7,* 483–491.

Rabkin, L. Y. (Ed.). *Psychopathology and literature.* San Francisco, CA: Chandler, 1966.

Richards, I. A. *Principles of literary criticism.* New York: Harcourt, Brace, 1925.

Richards, I. A. *Science and poetry.* London: Kegan, Paul, Trench, Trubner, 1926.

Richards, I. A. *Practical criticism,* New York: Harcourt, Brace, 1950.

Roback, A. A. The psychology of literature. In A. A. Roback (Ed.), *Presentday psychology.* New York: Greenwood, 1968.

Roe, A. Painters and painting. In I. A. Taylor & J. W. Getzels (Eds.), *Perspectives in creativity.* Chicago, IL: Aldine, 1975.

Rothenberg, A. The process of Janusian thinking in creativity. In A. Rothenberg & C. R. Hausman (Eds.), *The creativity question.* Durham, NC: Duke University Press, 1976.

Ruthrof, H. G. Reading works of literary art. *Journal of Aesthetic Education,* 1974, *8,* 75–90.

Sardello, R. An empirical-phenomenological study of fantasy, with a note on J. R. R. Tolkien and C. S. Lewis. *Psychocultural Review,* 1978, *2,* 203–220.

Sears, R. R. Episodic and content analysis of Mark Twain's novels. In J. P. Strelka (Ed.), *Literary criticism and psychology.* College Park, PA: The Pennsylvania State University Press, 1976.

Sears, R. R., & Lapidus, D. Episodic analysis of novels. *Journal of Psychology,* 1973, *85,* 267–276.

Sears, R. R., Lapidus, D., & Cozzens, C. Content analysis of Mark Twain's novels and letters as a biographical method. *Poetics,* 1978, *7,* 155–175.

Shafer, R. E. The reading of literature. *Journal of Reading,* 1965, *8,* 345–349.

Shrodes, C., Gundy, J. V., & Husband, R. W. (Eds.). *Psychology through literature: An anthology.* New York: Oxford, 1943.

Shumaker, W. *Literature and the irrational: A study in anthropological backgrounds.* New York: Prentice-Hall, 1960.

Shupe, D. R. Representation versus detection as a model for psychological criticism. *Journal of Aesthetics and Art Criticism,* 1976, *34,* 432–440.

Silberger, J. Using literary material to teach psychiatry. *Seminars in Psychiatry,* 1973, *5,* 275–285.

Simonton, D. K. Age and literary creativity: A cross-cultural and trans-historical survey. *Journal of Cross-Cultural Psychology,* 1975, *6,* 259–277.

Simonton, D. K. Biographical determinants of archival eminence: A multivariate approach to the Cox data. *Journal of Personality & Social Psychology,* 1976, *33,* 218–226.

Simonton, D. K. Time series analysis of literary creativity: A potential paradigm. *Poetics,* 1978, *7,* 249–259.

Sinsheimer, R. L. Humanism and science. *Leonardo,* 1977, *10,* 59–62.

Snow, C. P. *The two cultures: And a second look.* Cambridge: Cambridge University Press, 1964. (Originally published, 1963.)

Spradley, J. P., & McDonough, L. (Eds.). *Anthropology through literature: Cross-cultural perspectives.* Boston, MA: Little, Brown, 1973.

Stone, A. A., & Stone, S. S. (Eds.). *The abnormal personality through literature.* Englewood Cliffs, NJ: Prentice-Hall, 1966.

Strelka, J. P. (Ed.). *Literary criticism and psychology.* College Park, PA: The Pennsylvania State University Press, 1976.

Stumberg, D. Poetic talent. *Journal of Experimental Psychology,* 1928, *11,* 219–234.

Sulin, R. A., & Dooling, D. J. Intrusion of a thematic idea in retention of prose. *Journal of Experimental Psychology,* 1974, *103,* 255–262.

Sussman, H. L. *Victorians and the machine: The literary response to technology.* Cambridge, MA: Harvard University Press, 1968.

Swartz, P. Marcel Proust and the problem of time and place. *Psychological Reports,* 1978, *34,* 291–297.

Swartz, P. On the relevance of literature for psychology. *Perceptual & Motor Skills,* 1979, *48,* 1023–1045.

Taylor, G. O. *The passages of thought: Psychological representation in the American novel, 1879–1900.* New York: Oxford, 1969.

Thayer, L. O., & Pronko, N. N. Some psychological factors in the reading of fiction. *Journal of Genetic Psychology,* 1958, *93,* 113–117.

Thorndike, P. W. Cognitive structure in comprehension and memory of narrative discourse. *Cognitive Psychology,* 1977, *9,* 77–110.

Valentine, C. W. *The experimental psychology of beauty.* London: Methuen, 1962.

Vinacke, W. E. *The psychology of thinking* New York: McGraw-Hill, 1974.

Vygotsky, L. S. *The psychology of art.* Cambridge, MA: The M.I.T. Press, 1971. (Originally published, 1925.)

Wallas, G. *The art of thought.* New York: Harcourt, Brace, 1926.

Walsh, D. The question of relevance in literature. *Journal of Aesthetic Education,* 1972, *6,* 29–38.

Wellek, R., & Warren, A. *Theory of literature.* New York: Harcourt, Brace, 1942.

Wheeler, O. A. An analysis of literary appreciation. *British Journal of Psychology,* 1923, *13,* 229–242.

White, R. K. The versatility of genius. *Journal of Social Psychology,* 1931, *2,* 460–489.

Wijsen, L. M. P. T. From text to symbol: The cognitive and affective response to literature. *Psychocultural Review,* 1978, *2,* 147–163.

Williams, E. D., White, L., & Woods, J. M. Tests of literary appreciation. *British Journal of Educational Psychology,* 1938, *8,* 265–284.

Wilson, R. C., Guilford, J. P., & Christensen, P. R. The measurement of individual differences in originality. *Psychological Bulletin,* 1953, *50,* 362–370.

Wilson, R. N. *The sociology and psychology of art.* Morristown, NJ: General Learning Press, 1973.

4 Psychology and Music

Diana Deutsch
University of California, San Diego

INTRODUCTION

The relationship between psychology and music is characteristic of that between a new science and an established discipline. Western music theory has a very old tradition, dating at least from the time of Pythagoras; and the philosophical underpinnings of this tradition that were established in ancient times still exist today. Most characteristic of this tradition is its rationalism. In contrast with the scientific disciplines, the development of music theory over the last few hundred years has not been characterized by a growth in the empirical method. Rather, while composers have constantly experimented with new means of expression, music theorists have on the whole been system builders who sought to justify existing compositional practice or to prescribe new practice on numerological grounds. Further, when an external principle has been invoked as an explanatory device, most commonly such a principle was taken from physics. The concept of music as essentially the product of our processing mechanisms and therefore related to psychology has only rarely been entertained.

There are several reasons why this rationalistic stance was adopted, most of which no longer apply. One reason was a paucity of knowledge concerning the nature of sound. It is understandable that the inability to characterize a physical stimulus should have inhibited the development of theories concerning how this stimulus is processed. A related reason was poor stimulus control, which made experimentation difficult. A third reason was the lack of appropriate mathematical techniques with which to study probabilistic phenomena. However, another reason, which is still with us today, lies in the peculiar nature of music itself. There are no external criteria for distinguishing between music and nonmusic, or between good music and bad music. Further, it is clear that how we perceive

155

music depends at least to some extent on prior experience. Thus the relevance of psychological experimentation to music theory requires careful definition.

In this chapter I first review major developments in music theory from an historical point of view. Following this I explore various issues that are currently being studied both by music theorists and by psychologists. Finally, I discuss the role of psychology in music theory.

HISTORICAL PERSPECTIVE

Speculations concerning music may be traced back to very ancient times (Hunt, 1978), but the foundations of Western music theory are generally held to have been laid by Pythagoras (ca. 570–497 B.C.). Pythagoras was concerned mostly with the study of musical intervals. He is credited with identifying the musical consonances of the octave, fifth, and fourth with the numerical ratios 1:2, 2:3, and 3:4. He is also credited with establishing by experiment that the pitch of a vibrating string varies inversely with its length. However, Pythagoras and his followers ultimately lost faith in the empirical method and instead attempted to explain all musical phenomena purely in terms of numerical relationships. As Anaxagoras (ca. 499–428 B.C.) declared: "Through the weakness of the sense-perceptions, we cannot judge truth [Freeman, 1948, p. 86]." And later Boethius, the leading music theorist of the Middle Ages and a strong follower of Pythagoras, wrote in *De Institutione Musica:*

> For what need is there of speaking further concerning the error of the senses when this same faculty of sensing is neither equal in all men, nor at all times equal within the same man? Therefore anyone vainly puts his trust in a changing judgement since he aspires to seek the truth [Boethius, 1967, p. 58].

The view that music ought to be investigated solely by contemplation of numerical relationships has characterized most music theory since Pythagorean times. On this view, the world of mathematics is held to provide an ideal which the world of sense-perception can only imitate. Experimental procedures are therefore held to be irrelevant: If the results of experiments are in accordance with theory, then they are redundant; if the results conflict with theory, then they must have been ill-conceived in the first place. Also stemming from the mathematical approach of the Pythagoreans have been the numerous attempts to build entire musical systems by mathematical deduction from a minimal number of established musical facts. Essentially this approach derives from a false analogy with geometry (Russell, 1945). Euclidean geometry begins with a few axioms which are held to be self-evident, and from these axioms arrives by deduction at theorems that are not in themselves self-evident. However, it is a logical error to assume that we can proceed *by deduction* from one musical fact to another musical fact. Properly, musical facts can only be used as a basis for the formulation of *hypotheses* about further musical facts, which require empirical verification.

Another strong influence on music theory which stemmed from the Pythagoreans was the belief that the ultimate explanation of musical phenomena lies in physics. Until the Copernican revolution, this belief took the form of assuming that music serves as a reflection of sounds produced by the heavenly bodies. As described by Aristotle in *De Caelo,* it was thought:

> that the motion of bodies of that [astronomical] size must produce a noise, since on our earth the motion of bodies far inferior in size and in speed of movement has that effect. Also, when the sun and the moon, they say, and all the stars, so great in number and size, are moving with so rapid a motion, how should they not produce a sound immensely great? Starting from this argument, and from the observation that their speeds, as measured by their distances, are in the same ratio as musical concordances, they assert that the sound given forth by the circular movement of the stars is a harmony [Aristotle, 1930, p. 290].

Figure 1 shows the Pythagorean view of the universe, in which the relative distances of the heavenly bodies to each other are displayed, together with the musical intervals formed thereby. It can be seen that the distance between the Earth and the Moon formed a whole tone, from the Moon to Mercury a semitone, from Mercury to Venus a semitone, from Venus to the Sun a tone and a half, from the Sun to Mars a whole tone, from Mars to Jupiter a semitone, from Jupiter to Saturn a semitone, and finally from Saturn to the Supreme Heaven, a semitone. Notice further that the entire distance between Earth and the Supreme Heaven formed an Octave.

The theory of the Harmony of the Spheres was an attractive one, since it provided answers to several fundamental questions about music. One question was why music exists in the first place; and the answer provided was that it serves as a reflection of the Divine Harmony. A second question was why certain musical intervals (the consonances) strike us as pleasing while others do not; and the answer here was that the consonances are those intervals that are present in this Divine Harmony. The theory even had a normative value, since it provided boundary conditions for separating music from non-music.

The main problem with the theory that puzzled the ancient Greeks (as well as those who followed) was why, if the heavenly bodies do indeed produce this harmony, we cannot hear it. One answer, suggested by Censorinus, was that loudness of the sound is so great as to cause deafness[1] (Hawkins, 1853/1963). An alternative view, described by Aristotle (who did not in fact endorse it), was that since this sound is with us since birth, and since sound is perceived only in contrast to silence, we are not aware of its presence. However, neither of these views was considered satisfactory.

At all events, the theory of the Harmony of the Spheres provided a strong link among the studies of music, astronomy, and mathematics, with the result that the scientific part of the program of higher education developed into the *Quadrivium* of the "related studies" of astronomy, geometry, arithmetic, and music. The Quadrivium persisted through to the end of the sixteenth century and was responsible for much interaction between the disciplines.

In general, the later Greek theorists adhered to the numerological approach of the Pythagoreans. There was, however, a notable exception. Aristoxenus (ca. 320 B.C.), originally a pupil of the Pythagoreans and later of Aristotle, saw clearly that music cannot be understood by contemplation of mathematical relationships alone. He argued that the study of music should be considered an empirical science and that musical

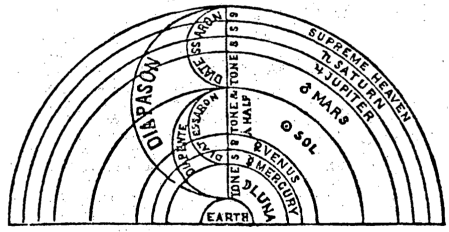

FIG. 1.   Pythagorean view of the universe in musical intervals. (From Hawkins, 1853/1963.)

---

[1] This view inspired Butler's lines in *Hudibras* (Part II):

> Her voice, the music of the spheres,
> So loud it deafens mortal ears,
> As wise philosophers have thought,
> And that's the cause we hear it not.
> [Butler, 1973, p. 122].

phenomena were basically perceptual and cognitive in nature. For example, in the *Harmonic Elements* he wrote:

> The order that distinguishes the melodious from the unmelodious resembles that which we find in the collocation of letters in language. For it is not every collocation but only certain collocations of any given letters that will produce a syllable.

And later:

> It is plain that the apprehension of a melody consists in noting with both the ear and intellect every distinction as it arises in the successive sounds—successive, for melody, like all branches of music, consists in a successive production. For the apprehension of music depends on these two faculties, sense-perception and memory; for we must perceive the sound that is present and remember that which is past. In no other way can we follow the phenomenon of music [Aristoxenus, 1902, pp. 192–194].

But Aristoxenus was not understood by his contemporaries, nor by the music theorists of the Middle Ages and early Renaissance, who continued to adhere to the numerological approach. Most of his works were lost to posterity, though fortunately two books of his *Harmonic Elements* and fragments of his *Elements of Rhythmics* were preserved.

In violation of prevailing theoretical constraints, medieval polyphony employed intervals other than the pure consonances of the octave, fifth, and fourth allowed by the Pythagoreans. It therefore fell to the theorists of the fifteenth and sixteenth centuries to justify existing practice in the context of the Pythagorean doctrine. This was achieved by Zarlino (1517–1590) who argued that the number six had various metaphysical properties. For example, it is the first perfect number $(1 + 2 + 3 = 1 \times 2 \times 3 = 6)$. Zarlino proposed that the realm of the consonances be extended to combinations produced by ratios formed by the first six numbers. This justified the use of the major third (5:4), minor third (6:5), and major sixth (5:3). (The minor sixth was also admitted somehow, although its ratio is 8:3.) In his heavily numerological and theological treatise, *Istituzioni Armoniche* (1558/1950), Zarlino developed rules of composition based on the concept of the first six numbers as a divinely ordained sanctuary containing the consonances (the *scenario*) outside of which the composer can wander only under severe restrictions. Thus theoretical approval was given to existing musical practice on numerological grounds, and a new set of boundary conditions for music was established (Palisca, 1961).

The scientific revolution of the sixteenth and seventeenth centuries had a profound effect on music theory. First, advances in astronomy forced theorists to abandon the view that the universe was a harmony, and with it the view that musical consonances reflect this harmony. Second, advances in understanding the properties of vibrating strings led to a reevaluation of the role of number in musical explanation: Numerical ratios were now considered meaningful in that they applied to the properties of sounding bodies. Discovery of the overtone series, of the relationship between pitch and frequency, and of the physical correlates of consonance and dissonance inclined some thinkers to adopt a more empirical approach to musical issues in general (Palisca, 1961).

Notable among the musical empirists of the sixteenth century were Giovanni Battista Benedetti (1530–1590) and Vincenzo Galilei (1520–1591).[2] Beneditti was perhaps the first to relate the sensations of pitch and consonance to rates of vibration. Galilei demonstrated by experiment that the association of the consonant intervals with simple numerical ratios held only when their terms represented pipe or string lengths and also when other factors were held constant. For example, these relationships did not hold for relative weights of hammers, nor for volumes enclosed in bells. He also argued that disputes concerning tuning systems were futile, since the ear cannot detect the small pitch differences under debate. He proposed a new theory of counterpoint based on existing musical practice, rather than on appeal to extra-musical phenomena, and he argued strongly for the empirical method in studying music. However, thinkers such as Galilei were very much in the minority, and the prevailing theoretical stance continued to be heavily rationalistic.

In parallel with scientific advances concerning the physical properties of sound,[3] composers of the late sixteenth and the seventeenth centuries were particularly active in experimenting with new techniques. There thus arose a need for a new theoretical synthesis to justify prevailing musical practice and to link this with newly obtained scientific knowledge. This was achieved by the composer and music theorist Jean-Philippe Rameau (1683–1764). Rameau's systematization forms the basis of traditional harmonic theory as we know it today. By analyzing the compositions of his predecessors and contemporaries and by joining to these analyses the results of his own musical investigations, Rameau arrived at important fundamental laws and concepts such as the invertibility of chords, the generation of a chord by its root, the root progression of chords, and so on.

In one sense, Rameau's synthesis can be regarded as a great psychological achievement, in which he used as his body of data the music of

[2]Galilei was the father of Galileo.
[3]Many noted scientists of the seventeenth century addressed themselves to issues concerning sound and music, notably in the areas of pitch and interval relationships. These included Galileo, Mersenne, Descartes, Kepler, and Huygens.

common practice to formulate a viable theory of the abstract structure of music. However, Rameau did not regard music as essentially the product of our perceptual and cognitive mechanisms; rather, true to tradition, he felt the need to justify his system in terms of a single physical principle. He found this in the recently discovered phenomenon of the overtone series, and so he invoked it as the "self-evident principle" from which he attempted to derive an entire musical system by mathematical deduction. As he wrote:

> Music is a science which ought to have certain rules; these rules ought to be derived from a self-evident principle; and this principle can scarcely be known to us without the help of mathematics [Rameau, 1722/1950, p. 566].

Although his attempts to manipulate the numerical ratios failed and involved him in a mass of inconsistencies and contradictions, Rameau's approach laid the groundwork for a new musical numerology in which the overtone series replaced the Harmony of the Spheres as the ultimate explanatory device (Palisca, 1961).

Perhaps the greatest music theorist of the nineteenth century was Hermann von Helmholtz (1831–1894), whose book *On the Sensations of Tone* (1885/1954) makes important reading even today. Helmholtz saw clearly that musical phenomena require explanation in terms of the processing mechanisms of the listener. He carried out important experimental work on issues such as the perception of pitch, combination tones, beats, and consonance and dissonance. He also speculated concerning the nature of high-level cognitive mechanisms underlying music perception, though he lacked the technical resources to investigate these mechanisms experimentally.

Technological advances of the end of the last century and the beginning of this one enabled scientists for the first time to investigate auditory phenomena under strictly controlled conditions (see Marks, in Volume III). The science of psychoacoustics was thus established. However, the sound stimuli that could be precisely generated were very limited in scope. It became possible, for example, to perform careful measurements on auditory threshold phenomena and to devise psychophysical scales of pitch and loudness. However, it was still prohibitively difficult to construct sequences of tones under controlled conditions or to generate tones with specified time-varying spectra. Thus, the issues to which psychoacousticians addressed themselves were not of much concern to musicians, who found the perceptual properties of simple auditory stimuli in isolation of little theoretical interest.

Matters were made worse by certain conclusions from psychoacoustics which musicians felt were at variance with their experience and intuitions. One notable example is the mel scale for pitch (Stevens & Volkmann, 1940). As shown on Figure 2, this scale designates as equal,

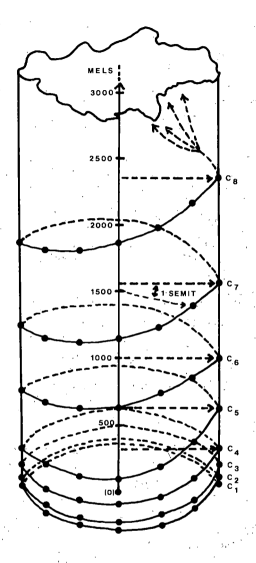

FIG. 2.   Pitch as scaled in mels and in octaves. (From Ward & Burns, 1982.)

intervals which are unequal on the musical scale; and conversely, equal
musical intervals are designated as unequal on the mel scale. Thus, it
seemed to many musicians that, however carefully controlled
psychoacoustical experiments were, they were leading to incorrect conclusions. Rather than criticizing these conclusions on home ground, musicians regarded them as evidence that scientific methodology was
inappropriate for the study of music.

At the same time as the science of psychoacoustics was developing with its focus on narrow stimulus parameters, music theorists were finding themselves faced with a vast increase in the complexity of the music that they were attempting to explain. The development of chromaticism in the music of the nineteenth and early twentieth centuries, for example in the music of Wagner, Debussy, Moussorgsky, and Mahler, forced a fundamental change in the concept of harmony. First the concept of tonality developed into the concept of extended tonality to accommodate these new complexities. However even this latter concept had to be abandoned, since it became dubious whether the notion of a tonic served as a useful explanatory concept for the new compositions. Music theorists therefore began to search for an entirely new theoretical framework within which they could compose.

The framework which became the most influential was the twelve—tone system, originally developed by Schoenberg. This system, which is described below, has inspired much theoretical work on equivalence relations between sets of pitches. However, twelve-tone theorists did not deem it appropriate to determine experimentally whether the equivalence relations of their system were perceptually relevant. Rather, in line with Pythagorean tradition, they considered the intrinsic plausibility of the basic axioms of the system, together with its internal consistency, as sufficient justification for its use in compositional practice.

Just as the technological advances of the first part of this century tended to create a rift between scientists and musicians, so have recent technological advances over the last decade created an era of collaboration between the disciplines. With the aid of computer technology, psychologists are now able to generate complex auditory stimuli with precision and so to examine musical issues in a controlled experimental setting. At the same time, composers have been increasingly interested in the computer as a compositional tool. However, in order to make effective use of this new technology, they need to obtain answers to questions in perceptual and cognitive psychology. As a result of these developing interests from both disciplines, there is not only a rapid expansion of empirical work on music perception and cognition, but, perhaps more importantly, increasing collaboration between psychologists and musicians. We can confidently predict that over the next decade psychology will have a firmly established place in the music theory.

SOME CURRENT ISSUES

I now turn to consider various issues concerning music perception and cognition that are currently being studied both by music theorists and by psychologists. These are likely to be the focus of future work. This review is not intended to be exhaustive, but rather illustrative of the ways in which findings from psychology can usefully be applied to music.

Music and Composed Sounds

In the music of the seventeenth, eighteenth, and early nineteenth centuries, the timbre or sound quality of an instrument was generally treated as a carrier of melodic motion, rather than as a primary compositional attribute in itself. However, the decline of tonality opened the way for new compositional uses of timbre. Composers began experimenting with complex sound structures that resulted from several instruments playing simultaneously, such that the individual instruments lost their identifiability and fused to produce a single sound impression. Debussy in particular made extensive use of chords that approached timbres. Early in this century composers such as Schoenberg, Webern, Stravinsky, and particularly Varese frequently employed such highly individualized sound structures, termed by Varese "sound masses." Such experimentation led composers to explore the characteristics of sound that were conducive to perceptual fusion (Erickson, 1975, 1982).

Developing interest in musical timbre also led composers to experiment with sound sequences involving rapid timbral changes. Such sequences, known as *Klangfarbenmelodien,* or melodies composed of timbres, were used early in this century by composers such as Schoenberg and Webern, and later by composers such as Boulez. This led to speculation concerning the rules governing orderly transitions between timbres. As Schoenberg (1911) wrote:

> If it is possible to make compositional structures from sounds which differ according to pitch, structures which we call melodies, sequences producing an effect similar to thought, then it must also be possible to create such sequences from the timbres of that other dimension from what we normally and simply call timbre. Such sequences would work with an inherent logic, equivalent to the kind of logic which is effective in melodies based on pitch. All this seems a fantasy of the future, which it probably is. But I am firmly convinced that it can be realized [470–471].

In essence, Schoenberg was proposing that timbres are psychologically represented in an orderly fashion and that the structure of this representation can be exploited compositionally.

Interest is understanding the psychological representation of timbre was accelerated by the development of electronic and computer music (Mathews, 1969). With the aid of new technology, composers became able for the first time to generate any sounds they wished, free from constraints imposed by the physics of natural instruments or by the capabilities of the human performer. But this very freedom presented fundamental problems in perceptual psychology which required solution. As the music theorist and composer Robert Erickson (1975) wrote:

> A composer who wishes to carve out certain sounds from this infinity of possibilities must decide: which ones? He may attempt to create "an instrument," meaning some sort of unified selection of sounds from the infinity of possibilities. . . . Or he may go at things more abstractly, thinking in terms of contrast, similarity, sound classes. . . . It may be true that we are on the edge of being able to produce any sound we can imagine, just as it is true that we can produce any pitch we can imagine. The infinity of sounds in the universe may be objectively real to physics and measuring instruments; if it is unrealizable in music then the difficulty must be related to human limitations and to the limitations imposed by musical discourse [p. 9].

Three related questions concerning timbre perception are here examined. First, what are the acoustical parameters underlying perception of instrumental timbre? Second, what parameters give rise to the perception of unitary sound images, and what give rise to the perception of multiple simultaneous sound images? Third, how do timbres behave when juxtaposed in time? It is clear that these questions all have implications not only for music, but also for auditory perception in general.

The identification of timbre. It is remarkable that the sound of a musical instrument can be identified under a wide range of conditions, regardless of its pitch, its loudness, and so on. The sound spectrograms produced by the same instrument under different conditions vary considerably. What are the features underlying such perceptual constancy?

Classically, the issue of timbre perception has been concerned with tones in the steady state. According to Helmholtz (1885/1954), differences in the timbre of complex tones depend on the strengths of their various harmonics. He claimed that simple tones sound pleasant, but dull at low frequencies; complex tones whose harmonics are moderately strong sound richer but still pleasant; tones with strong upper harmonics sound rough and sharp; and complex tones consisting only of odd harmonics sound hollow. More recently, Plomp and his collaborators have argued that the critical band[4] plays an imortant role in timbre perception (Plomp, 1964, 1970; Plomp & Mimpen, 1968). Evidence was obtained that harmonics falling within the same critical band fuse is their effect. Other experiments have been addressed to the question of whether perceived timbre is based on the relationships formed by the fundamental frequency and the

---

[4]The critical band is that frequency band within which the loudness of a band of sound of constant sound pressure level is independent of bandwidth.

frequency region of a formant, or on the absolute level of the formant. In general the results favor a modified fixed-formant model of timbre percep- tion (Plomp & Steeneken, 1971; Slawson, 1968).

Recently, the investigation of timbre has concerned itself with tones produced by natural instruments. Such tones are held to consist of three temporal segments: the attack, the steady state, and the decay. The attack segment has been found to be of particular importance to timbre identification (Berger, 1964; Grey, 1975; Saldanha & Corso, 1964; Wedin & Goude, 1972; Wessel, 1973, 1978); the steady state segment contributes more to timbre identification if it varies in time; and the decay segment appears of little consequence (Saldanha & Corso, 1964).

An important technique in the study of timbre perception was pioneered by Risset and Mathews (1969). Samples of natural instrument tones are digitized and analyzed by computer, a set of physical parame- ters is extracted from this analysis, and tones are then synthesized by computer in accordance with these parameters. This technique enables the experimenter to vary systematically any parameters, and so to ex- amine the perceptual effects of these variations. It has been shown using this technique, for instance, that when tones are resynthesized with a line- segment approximation to the time-varying amplitude and frequency function for the partials, there is very little loss of characteristic percep- tual quality, though considerable information reduction may thus be pro- duced (Grey & Moorer, 1977).

Also using this technique, geometric models of subjective timbral space have been generated. Instrument sounds that are judged as similar are positioned close together in this space; sounds that are judged as dissimi- lar are positioned far apart. Such models have been provided by Wessel (1973, 1978) and by Grey (1975) for string and wind instrument tones that were equated for pitch, loudness, and duration. At least two dimensions have been unveiled: The first appears to relate to the spectral and distribu- tion of sound energy, and the second to temporal features such as details of the attack.

With such representations, it has proved possible to draw trajectories through a given timbral space and so to create interpolated sounds that are consistent with the geometry of the space. For example, Grey (1975) created a series of tones which traversed his multidimensional space in small steps, so that the listener first perceived one instrument (such as a clarinet) and at some point in the series realized that he was now hearing a different instrument (such as a cello). Yet the perceptual transition be- tween instruments appeared completely smooth. Thus Schoenberg's vi- sion of composing with timbres that are arranged along an orderly continuum appears realizable. However, before these models can be used flexibly they will require considerable elaboration to accommodate the invariance of timbre under pitch and loudness changes, as well as effects of context. (See also Risset & Wessel, 1982.)

Spectral fusion and separation. A fundamental task for auditory theory is to define the relationships between components of an ongoing acoustic spectrum that result in the perception of a unitary sound image, and those that result in the perception of several simultaneous but distinct sound images. These processes of fusion and separation are of basic importance, since without them there would be no intelligible listening at all. Presumably, we have evolved mechanisms that lead us to fuse together elements of the spectrum that are likely to be emanating from the same source, and to separate out those that are likely to be emanating from different sources. This view of perception as a process of "unconscious inference" was originally proposed by Helmholtz (see Helmholtz, 1909–1911/1925) and has recently been invoked to explain various findings in perceptual psychology, both in vision (e.g., Gregory, 1970; Hochberg, 1974; Sutherland, 1973) and in hearing (e.g., Bregman, 1978; Deutsch, 1975a, 1979; Warren, 1974).

With specific regard to music, Helmholtz (1885/1954) posed the question of how, given the rapidly changing, complex spectrum resulting from several instruments playing simultaneously, we are able to reconstruct our musical environment so that some components of the spectrum give rise to a unitary sound image, and others give rise to several distinct but simultaneous sound images. Thus, he wrote:

Now there are many circumstances which assist us first in separating the musical tones arising from different sources, and secondly, in keeping together the partial tones of each separate source. Thus when one musical tone is heard for some time before being joined by the second, and then the second continues after the first has ceased, the separation in sound is facilitated by the succession of time. We have already heard the first musical tone by itself, and hence know immediately what we have to deduct from the compound effect for the effect of this first tone. Even when several parts proceed in the same rhythm in polyphonic music, the mode in which the tones of different instruments and voices commence, the nature of their increase in force, the certainty with which they are held and the manner in which they die off, are generally slightly different for each . . . but besides all this, in good part music, especial care is taken to facilitate the separation of the parts by the ear. In polyphonic music proper, where each part has its own distinct melody, a principal means of clearly separating the progression of each part has always consisted in making them proceed in different rhythms and on different divisions of the bars.

And later:

> All these helps fail in the resolution of musical tones into their constituent ·
> partials. When a compound tone commences to sound, all its partial tones
> commence with the same comparative strength; when it swells, all of them
> generally swell uniformly; when it ceases, all cease simultaneously. Hence
> no opportunity is generally given for hearing them separately and indepen-
> dently [Helmholtz, 1885/1954, pp. 59–60].

One factor proposed by Helmholtz as promoting fusion was onset syn-
chronicity of spectral components. This has recently been shown to be
important in several studies. Rasch (1978) investigated the threshold for
perception of a high tone when this was accompanied by a low tone. He
found that when the onset of the low tone was delayed relative to the high
tone there was a substantial lowering of threshold. In addition, the percept when the tones were asynchronous was very different from the percept when the tones were synchronous; in the former case, two distinct
tones were clearly perceived, but in the latter case, they fused to produce
a single percept. Bregman and Pinker (1978) employed a paradigm in
which a simultaneous two-tone complex was presented in alternation with
a third tone. With increasing asynchrony between the simultaneous tones
there was an increased likelihood that one of these would form a melodic
stream with the third tone. Both sets of authors interpret their findings
along the lines advanced by Helmholtz. A related study on the effects of
asynchrony was performed by Deutsch (1979) using spatially separated
tones (see p. 170).

A second factor proposed by Helmholtz to promote fusion is coordinated modulation in the steady state. McNabb and Chowning have
shown informally that with a harmonic tone complex whose spectrum
corresponds to a vowel the impression of a voice is strongly enhanced
when a small amount of coordinated frequency modulation, which can be
either periodic (vibrato) or random (shimmer), is superimposed on all
components simultaneously. McAdams and Wessel have informally investigated the effect of imposing two different modulation functions on
the odd or even partials of a complex tone and report that this produced
the impression of two simultaneous sounds (see McAdams, 1981).

A third factor that has been hypothesized to promote fusion is harmon-
icity of the components of a complex spectrum. Stringed and blown instruments, which tend to produce strongly fused images, have partials
that are harmonic or nearly harmonic. However bells and gongs, which
produce diffuse images, have partials that are nonharmonic (Mathews &
Pierce, 1980). De Boer (1976) has shown that harmonic complexes tend to
produce unitary and unequivocal pitch sensations, whereas various kinds

of nonharmonic complexes produce multiple pitch sensations. Again, this is expected on the assumption that our auditory mechanisms have evolved so as to make the most probable interpretations in terms of sound sources, since most forced vibration systems such as the voice have partials whose frequencies are harmonic or close to harmonic.

Perception of sequences of timbres.   As noted above, twentieth-century composers have become interested in the production of sound sequences involving rapid changes of timbre. This raises the question of how sequences of contrasting timbres are perceived. An effect of central interest here was first reported by Warren, Obusek, Farmer, and Warren (1969) in a paper entitled (rather ironically): "Auditory sequence: Confusions of patterns other than speech or music." These authors constructed repeating sequences of four unrelated sounds: a high tone (1000 Hz), a hiss (2000 Hz octave band noise), a low tone (796 Hz), and a buzz (4000 Hz square wave). Each sound lasted for 200 msec, and the different sounds followed each other without pause. Listeners were found to be quite unable to name the orders of such repeating sounds. The duration of each sound had to be increased to over 500 msec for correct ordering to be achieved.

The "Warren effect" probably has two bases. The first is that listeners tend to organize sounds into separate streams on the basis of sound type; and auditory streaming produces difficulty in forming temporal relationships across streams (see p. 173). Indeed, the threshold for ordering two acoustic events is higher when these events are dissimilar than when they are similar (Hirsh, 1959; Hirsh & Sherrick, 1961). Second, Warren (1974) has hypothesized that unfamiliarity with such a sound sequence contributes to difficulty in ordering. At all events, this type of study shows that with rapid contrasting sounds the listener may be unable to obtain the impression of a coherent sequence and may instead perceive multiple sequences in parallel.

Another effect of context was studied by Bregman and Pinker (1978). In conditions where a two-tone complex alternates with a third tone, if one of the tones in the complex is similar in frequency to the third tone, this component may detach itself perceptually so as to form a melodic stream with the third tone. When this happens there is an alteration in perceived timbre for the two-tone complex. Thus, the timbre of any given sound is likely to vary depending on the sequential context in which this sound is embedded.

In summary, the study of timbre perception is a particularly good example of fruitful collaboration between psychologists and musicians. Most of the questions so far raised in this area have been by musicians who were concerned with solving compositional problems; however, these questions are fundamental to the understanding of sound perception in general. Progress toward answering these questions probably could not have been achieved without the use of experimental techniques developed by psychologists.

Music and the Performing Space

Composers have long been concerned with spatial aspects of music; however interest in this area has developed particularly since Berlioz (1806–1869) who argued that the disposition of instruments in space should be considered an essential part of a composition. In his *Treatise on Instrumentation,* Berlioz wrote:

> I want to mention the importance of the different points of origin of the tonal masses. Certain groups of an orchestra are selected by the composer to question and answer each other; but this design becomes clear and effective only if the groups which are to carry on the dialogue are placed at a sufficient distance from each other. The composer must therefore indicate in his score their exact disposition. For instance, the drums, bass drums, cymbals and kettledrums may remain together if they are employed, as usual, to strike certain rhythms simultaneously. But if they execute an interlocutory rhythm, one fragment of which is given to the bass drums and cymbals, the other to kettledrums and drums, the effect would be greatly improved and intensified by placing the two groups of percussion instruments at the opposite ends of the orchestra, i.e., at a considerable distance from each other [Berlioz, 1948, p. 407].

Later composers such as Ives, Brant, and Stockhausen paid particular attention to the positioning of instruments and instrument groups and carried out informal experiments to investigate the effects of different spatial arrangements on the way music is perceived (see, e.g., Brant, 1966).

In a controlled experimental setting, spatial relationships have been shown to interact with other musical attributes in systematic ways. Earphone listening provides a particularly well-defined situation for examining the effects of spatial separation; and results obtained under these conditions can later be tested for generality in free sound-field environments (Deutsch, 1982a).

Deutsch (1975a, 1975b) examined the perceptual effects of presenting two simultaneous sequences of tones, one to each ear. The following question was raised. Does the listener, under these conditions of extreme spatial separation, perceive the sequence emanating from one side of space or the other; or, does the listener instead form perceptual configurations on a different basis?

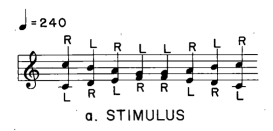

a. STIMULUS

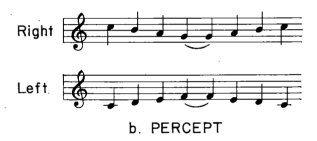

b. PERCEPT

FIG. 3. (A) Configuration giving rise to the scale illusion. (B) Illusion most commonly produced. (From Deutsch, 1975a.)

The stimulus pattern employed to examine this issue is shown in Figure 3A. It consisted of a major scale, presented simultaneously in both ascending and descending form, such that when a tone from the ascending scale was in one ear, a tone from the descending scale was in the other ear, and successive tones in each scale alternated from ear to ear. No listener perceived the sequence of tones presented to one side of space or to the other. Instead, most listeners obtained the percept shown in Figure 3B. This consisted of two melodic lines, one formed by the higher tones and the other by the lower tones. Further, the higher tones all appeared to emanate from one earphone, and the lower tones from the other. A minority of listeners perceived instead a single melodic line that corresponded to the higher tones, and they perceived little or nothing of the lower tones. Thus for all listeners, the formation of perceptual configurations on the basis of pitch proximity was so strong as to override completely the effects of spatial separation and often to produce striking localization illusions. The tones were perceptually reorganized in space to be consistent with pitch proximity.

Further findings concerned localization patterns for the higher and lower tones, and their handedness correlates. Righthanders showed a pronounced tendency to hear the higher tones as on the right and the lower tones as on the left, regardless of their true locations. However, lefthanders did not show this tendency. Since the left hemisphere is dominant in most righthanders, this pattern of results indicates that we tend to hear the higher tones as coming from the side of space that is contralateral to the dominant hemisphere, and the lower tones as from the other side (Deutsch, 1975a, 1975b).

This study was followed up by the music theorist Butler (1979a) who was concerned with determining the generality of these findings in natural musical situations. He presented the scale configuration through loudspeakers in a free sound-field environment and asked music students to notate separately the sequence that they heard coming from the speaker on the right and the sequence that they heard coming from the speaker on the left. In some conditions piano tones were used as stimuli. Despite these differences, essentially the same pattern of results emerged: Virtually all listeners heard the higher tones as emanating from one speaker and the lower tones as from the other. The effects were also explored of introducing differences in loudness and timbre between the stimuli coming from the two speakers. This resulted in a change in tone quality, however the new sound was heard as though coming simultaneously from both speakers. Thus, not only were the spatial locations of the tones perceptually rearranged to accommodate pitch proximity, but their timbres and loudnesses were rearranged also. Butler also devised different contrapuntal patterns which were played to listeners through earphones or spatially separated loudspeakers. Essentially the same results were obtained: The patterns were perceptually reorganized so that a higher melodic line appeared to be emanating from one earphone or speaker, and a lower melodic line from the other.

Such effects are found in performed music. For example, the last movement of Tschaikowsky's Sixth Symphony (the "Pathetique") begins with a passage in which the theme and accompaniment are distributed between two violin parts. However, the theme is heard as coming from one set of violins and the accompaniment as from the other (Butler, 1979b). This is true even with the orchestra arranged in nineteenth century fashion, with the first violins on one side and the second violins on the other side. Thus spatial separation by no means guarantees that music will be perceived in accordance with the positioning of the instruments. Rather, groupings may be formed on the basis of some other attribute such as pitch, and this may in turn cause the listener to mislocalize the components of the musical configuration in accordance with such groupings. It also appears that other attributes such as loudness and timbre may be perceptually reorganized in this fashion.

Such findings, apart from their musical relevance, are of general interest to perceptual psychology, since they show that subjective grouping is
not simply a matter of linking different stimuli together. Rather, this may
involve a process in which the different stimulus attributes are dissociated
and recombined so that illusory percepts result.

The experiments just described involved two musical sequences that
were simultaneous or near-simultaneous. What happens when temporal
differences are introduced? To examine this issue, Deutsch (1979) presented listeners with two melodic patterns, and they identified on each
trial which one they had heard. Four conditions were employed. In the
first, the melody was presented simultaneously to both ears, and here the
level of identification performance was very high. In the second condition, the component tones of the melody switched between the ears, and
here identification performance was considerably poorer. Subjectively in
this condition the listener felt impelled to attend to the signal arriving at
one ear or the other, and could not integrate the two sets of signals into a
single perceptual stream. In the third condition, the component tones of
the melody still switched between the ears; however the melody was
accompanied by a drone. Whenever a component of the melody was in
the right ear the drone was in the left ear, and whenever a component of
the melody was in the left ear the drone was in the right ear. Thus the two
ears again received input simultaneously, even though the melody to be
identified still switched between the ears. This simultaneity of input produced a dramatic rise in identification performance. In the fourth condition, a drone was again presented; but this time to the same ear as the ear
receiving the melody component (rather than the contralateral ear). Thus
input was again to only one ear at a time. Here identification performance
was again very low.

This experiment demonstrates that the tones emanating from different
spatial locations, temporal relationships between them are important determinants of grouping. When signals are delivered to both ears simultaneously, it is easy to integrate the information into a single perceptual
stream. But when the signals delivered to the two ears are clearly separated in time, subjective grouping by spatial location is so powerful as to
prevent the listener from combining the signals to produce an integrated
percept.

This finding leads one to ask what happens in the intermediate case,
where the tones arriving at the two ears are not simultaneous, but rather
overlapping in time. In a further experiment this intermediate case was
found to produce intermediate results. Identification of the melody in the
presence of the contralateral drone was poorer when the melody and
drone were asynchronous than when they were strictly synchronous, but
better than when there was no accompanying drone (Deutsch, 1979).

We can conclude from these studies that when a rapid sequence of tones is distributed between spatially separated instruments, and a clear temporal separation exists between the sounds produced by these instruments, the listener may be unable to integrate the sequence into a single coherent stream. However, a certain amount of overlap among the different instruments will facilitate such integration. Yet there is a tradeoff: the greater the amount of overlap, the greater will be the loss of spatial distinctiveness; and as simultaneity is approached, spatial illusions may occur.

We now turn to the question of how perception of two simultaneous sequences of tones may be affected by whether the higher tones are presented to the right and the lower tones to the left, or whether this configuration is reversed. We noted earlier that, in the scale illusion, righthanders tend to perceive higher tones as on the right and lower tones as on the left, regardless of their actual locations. Thus simultaneous tone pairs of the "high-right/low-left" type tend to be well localized, and pairs of the "high-left/low-right" type tend to be mislocalized. This finding has been confirmed in more general settings (Deutsch, 1983).

We may then enquire whether pitch perception might also be affected by such spatial considerations. In an experiment to investigate this question, musically trained listeners were asked to notate two sequences of tones which were simultaneously presented, one to each ear. Tone pairs of which the higher was on the right and the lower on the left were notated significantly more accurately than tone pairs of which the higher was on the left and the lower on the right. This was found true with sequences organized in several different ways (Deutsch, 1983).

The above findings explain certain patterns of ear advantage which have been obtained for musical materials, and which have been thought to reflect patterns of hemispheric asymmetry in processing such materials. In addition, they have implications for the question of optimal seating arrangements for orchestras. In general, contemporary arrangements are such that, from the performers' point of view, instruments with high registers tend to be to the right, and instruments with low registers to the left. Figure 4 shows, for example, a seating arrangement of the Chicago symphony orchestra. From the above findings we can assume that this "high-right/low-left" disposition has evolved by trial and error because it is conducive to optimal performance. However, this leaves us with a paradox: From the viewpoint of the audience this configuration is mirror-imaged reversed, and so is such as to cause perceptual difficulties. There is no easy solution to this paradox for the case of concert hall listening (see Deutsch, in press, for a discussion). However, we may assume that reversing this disposition in multitrack recording should result in enhanced perceptual clarity.

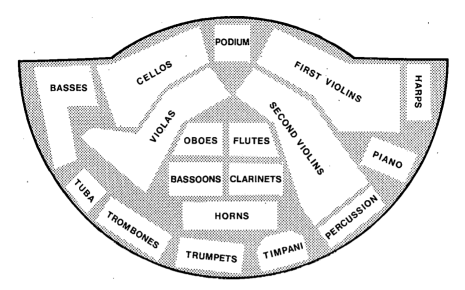

FIG. 4.   Chicago Symphony seating plan from the viewpoint of the orchestra. (Adapted from Machlis, 1977.)

Another issue concerning music and the performing space involves the aesthetic effects of different auditory environments. As implied in Berlioz's statement "There is no such thing as music in the open air," the enclosed space of the concert hall contributes much to the aesthetic quality of music, through the complex sound reflections that are produced in this environment. The phenomenological effects of these reflections have frequently been discussed by musicians at an informal level, and recently they have been the subject of controlled experimental investigation. The physicist Schroeder and his associates have conducted a series of studies in which recordings of music were made in numerous European concert halls by means of two microphones placed at the ears of a "dummy." These recordings were then played to listeners in an anechoic chamber, enabling a realistic recreation of the acoustics of the concert hall at the ears of the "dummy." The method of paired comparisons was used to obtain preference ratings, and the individual scores were subjected to multidimensional scaling, thus producing a "preference space." Analyses of the correlations between various physical parameters of a concert hall and its coordinates in this "preference space" led to the conclusion that the greater the similarity of the signals arriving at the two ears, the lower the preference. This conclusion was reinforced by further studies in which the recorded signals were modified so as to increase binaural dissimilarities by adding lateral reflections. This manipulation had the expected effect of increasing preference ratings. It was concluded that wide halls with low ceilings (which tend to be constructed today for economic considerations) are associated with less listener enjoyment than narrow halls with high ceilings (more typical of older concert halls); since the latter type of design emphasizes early lateral reflections (Schroeder, 1980).

The study of spatial aspects of music is another area where the concerns of composers and of scientists have combined to very useful effect. Apart from their relevance to music, experiments on the effects of spatial separation have served to elucidate the nature of fundamental mechanisms involving stimulus integration and separation.

The Law of Stepwise Progression and the Principle of Proximity

In textbooks on tonal music we generally encounter the "law of stepwise progression," which states that melodic progression should be by steps (a half step or a whole step) rather than by skips (more than a whole step), since stepwise progression is considered "stronger" or "more binding." What is left unspecified is why this law should be obeyed: The reader is supposed either to accept the law uncritically or to recognize its truth in some way by introspection.

To the psychologist, this law appears as an example of the Gestalt principle of proximity, which states that we tend to group together elements that are proximal along some dimension and to separate those that are spaced further apart (Wertheimer, 1923). Presumably, we have evolved mechanisms that produce such perceptual grouping, since this is conducive to an effective interpretation of our environment. Thus in the case of vision, proximal elements are more likely to belong together than elements that are spaced further apart. In the case of hearing, sounds that are similar in frequency spectrum are likely to emanate from the same source, and sounds that are dissimilar are likely to come from different sources.

Consideration of the "law of stepwise progression" therefore leads us to enquire specifically into the ways in which the principle of proximity manifests itself when applied to pitch. Not only is this question of interest to perceptual psychology, but such enquiry also serves to provide the "law of stepwise progression" with a rational basis, by demonstrating the adverse effects to be expected when it is violated. Further, by characterizing the ways in which such effects behave under parametric manipulation, we can determine the conditions under which the law may be violated with relative impunity, and those under which its violation produces strongly adverse effects on perception and memory.

In an experimental setting, the impression of connectedness produced

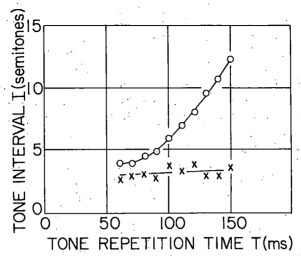

FIG. 5. Boundaries for perception of a sequence of tones as a connected series as a function of pitch proximity and tempo. (o) Listener attempting to hear a a connected series. (x) Listener attempting to hear a disconnected series. (From Van Noorden, 1975.)

by a sequence of tones depends in a complex fashion on the pitch relationships involved, and also on their interaction with other factors (Deutsch, 1982a). One such factor is tempo. The higher the rate of presentation, the greater is the tendency for tones that are disparate in pitch to be heard as separate rather than as a single connected series (Schouten, 1962). A second factor is attentional set. When presented with a sequence of two alternating tones, the listener may attempt to hear these either as a single connected series or as two disjoint series. As shown in Figure 5, when the listener is attempting to hear a single series, the impression of connectedness depends very strongly on presentation rate. However, when the listener is attempting to hear the tones as disconnected, temporal factors appear unimportant (Van Noorden, 1975). A third factor is the length of sequence presented. For an impression of connectedness to be obtained, a larger decrease in tempo is required for long sequences than for two-tone sequences (Van Noorden, 1975).

One adverse effect of violating the principle of proximity, at least at fast tempi, is that temporal relationships between adjacent tones become difficult to judge. For example, when a rapid sequence of tones is presented, and these are drawn from two different pitch ranges, judgment of the orders of these tones is very difficult. However this problem disappears when the tones are brought close together in pitch (Bregman & Campbell, 1971). When the presentation rate is slowed down, so that order perception is readily accomplished, there is still a gradual breakdown of temporal resolution as the pitch disparity in a sequence of alternating tones increases. For example, it becomes increasingly difficult to detect a rhythmic irregularity in such a sequence. This effect is also more pronounced with long sequences than with short ones (Van Noorden, 1975).

A further loss of perceptual accuracy that results from violating the principle of proximity involves the situation where two simultaneous sequences of tones are presented, each in a different spatial location. As described earlier, there is a tendency to reorganize such sequences perceptually in accordance with pitch proximity, so that a sequence formed by tones in one pitch range appears to be coming from one spatial location and a sequence formed by tones in a different pitch range appears to be coming from the other location (Butler, 1979a; Deutsch, 1975a, 1975b, 1979). This phenomenon is also related to another musical rule which forbids the crossing of voices in counterpoint. If the composer attempts to produce a crossing of voices, there is a risk that the listener will synthesize voices in accordance with pitch proximity rather than in accordance with the composer's intentions. This perceptual phenomenon holds true also when only a single spatial location is involved (though the illusion that tones in one pitch range are emanating from one spatial location and tones in another pitch range from a different location is of course not produced).

Finally, pitch proximity can be shown to affect the ability to recognize individual tones in a sequence. Deutsch (1978a) employed the following paradigm. Listeners compared the pitches of two tones when these were separated by a time interval during which a sequence of extra tones was interpolated. They were asked to ignore the interpolated tones and to judge whether the test tones were the same or different in pitch. Accuracy of pitch recognition was found to increase as the average size of the intervals formed by the interpolated tones decreased. It was concluded that the interpolated sequence provides a framework of pitch relationships in which the test tones are embedded and that the more proximal these relationships the stronger the framework.

The perceptual separation that occurs between tones that are disparate in pitch can be exploited to musical advantage. If a composer wishes the listener to perceive two simultaneous melodic lines, this can be greatly facilitated by presenting the two lines in different pitch ranges. A particularly interesting technique that exploits this phenomenon was used extensively by the Baroque composers and is known as pseudopolyphony. Here an instrument plays a rapid sequence of single tones which are drawn from two different pitch ranges; as a result the listener perceives two melodic lines in parallel. Dowling (1973) has demonsrated the strength of this perceptual effect in a formal experiment. He presented listeners with two well-known melodies, which were interleaved in time.

The listeners' were asked to identify the melodies. When these were drawn from the identical pitch range the task was very difficult, since temporally adjacent tones were perceptually combined into a single stream. However as one of the interleaved melodies was gradually transposed, so that the pitch ranges of the two melodies diverged, identification became increasingly more easy.

The above studies demonstrate the usefulness of the experimental technique in understanding the basis of musical rules which have developed by trial and error. The conclusions from these studies could not have been arrived at by examination of musical examples alone, and many of them are not apparent from introspection.

Musical Shape Analysis and the Theory of Twelve-Tone Composition

Present-day interest in shape analyzing mechanisms has stemmed largely from the work of the Gestalt psychologists at the end of the last century and the beginning of this one. The Gestaltists were concerned with characterizing the ways in which shapes may be transformed without losing their perceptual identities. For example, the identities of visual shapes are not destroyed when they are changed in size or translated to a different position in the visual field (Sutherland, 1973).

The large majority of work on shape analysis has been concerned with vision. However, it may be noted that Von Ehrenfels (1890) in his influential paper "Uber Gestaltqualitaten" gave melody as an example of a Gestalt. He pointed out that a melody when transposed retains its essential form, the *Gestaltqualitat,* provided that the relations among individual tones are unaltered. In this respect, he argued, melodies are like visual shapes.

Largely unknown to psychologists, the theory of twelve-tone composition, developed early in this century by Schoenberg, is based on a theory of shape analysis for pitch structures. This theory is in turn based on an intermodal analogy in which one dimension of visual space is mapped into pitch and another into time. Describing his system of composition as "not a mere technical device" but as of the "rank and importance of a scientific theory," Schoenberg justifies it in the following way:

THE TWO-OR-MORE DIMENSIONAL SPACE IN WHICH MUSICAL IDEAS ARE PRESENTED IS A UNIT. . . . The elements of a musical idea are partly incorporated in the horizontal plane as successive sounds, and partly in the vertical plane as simultaneous sounds. . . . *The unity of musical space demands an absolute and unitary perception.* In this space . . . there is no absolute down, no right or left, forward or backward. . . . To the imagina- .

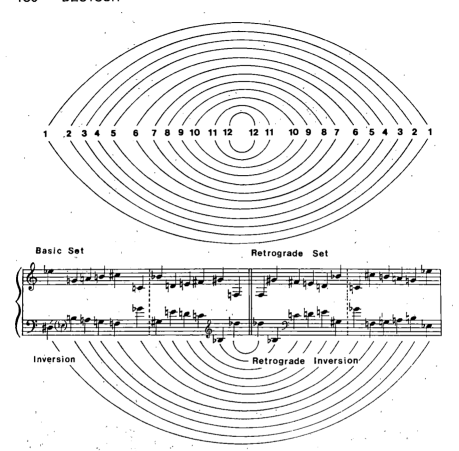

FIG. 6. Schoenberg's illustration of his theory of equivalence relations between pitch structures. The musical example is taken from the Wind Quartet, Op. 26. (From Schoenberg, 1951.)

tive and creative faculty, relations in the material sphere are as independent from directions or planes as material objects are, in their sphere, to our perceptive faculties. Just as our mind always recognizes, for instance, a knife, a bottle or a watch, regardless of its position, and can reproduce it in the imagination in every possible position, even so a musical creator's mind can operate subconsciously with a row of tones, regardless of their direction, regardless of the way in which a mirror might show the mutual relations, which remain a given quantity [Schoenberg, 1951, pp. 220–223].

Figure 6 illustrates Schoenberg's use of his theory in compositional practice. As he wrote: "The employment of these mirror forms corresponds to the principle of *the absolute and unitary perception of musical space* [p. 225]."

Schoenberg thus proposed that a tone row, defined as a particular linear ordering of the twelve tones of the chromatic scale, retains its perceptual identity under the following transformations: when it is transposed to a different pitch range ("transposition"), when all ascending intervals become descending intervals and vice versa ("inversion"), when it is presented in reverse order ("retrogression"), and when it is transformed by both these operations ("retrograde-inversion"). Further, Schoenberg proposed that, given the strong perceptual similarity between tones than are separated by octaves, the identity of a tone row is preserved when the individual tones in the row are placed in different octaves.

Schoenberg's theory provided the basis for much sophisticated system building around the middle of the century. Foremost here is the work of Babbitt and his followers in interpreting the twelve-tone system as a group. The elements of the group are twelve-tone sets, represented as permutations of pitch or order numbers; the operation is the multiplication of permutations (Babbitt, 1960, 1961). This system has been used extensively in compositional practice (see also Perle, 1972, 1977).

The question may be raised of whether the equivalence relations defined in twelve-tone theory are indeed utilized by the perceptual system. We may note that Schoenberg's intermodal analogy, although interesting, is rather forced. It makes sense to assume that we have evolved mechanisms that enable us to recognize an object when it is presented in a different orientation relative to the observer. However, it does not make sense in the same way to assume that we will recognize a sound sequence when this is reversed in time, or when its pitch relationships are turned upside-down: In our natural environment we are never required to do this. Further, it has been shown in the case of vision that some formal relationships that exist within a configuration are readily perceived, others are perceived with difficulty, and yet others are not perceived at all (Garner, 1974).

Concerning the perceptual identity of a tone row under retrogression and inversion, two studies in the psychological literature may be cited. White (1960) used a long-term recognition paradigm to study the ability of listeners to identify well-known melodies when these were played in retrogression. Some recognition was obtained; however, performance was no better than when the melody was played in a monotone with rhythm as the only cue. Further, better recognition was obtained when the intervals within the melody were randomly permuted than when the orders of the tones were strictly reversed. This indicates that the listeners were recognizing the retrograde sequences on the basis of the set of intervals involved, rather than on their orderings.

Dowling (1972) used a short-term paradigm to study recognition of a sequence of tones under retrogression, inversion, and retrograde-inversion. He presented listeners with a standard five-tone sequence, followed by a comparison sequence. The comparison was either unrelated to the standard, or it was an exact transposition, or it was transformed by retrogression, inversion, or retrograde-inversion. In another set of conditions, the comparison sequence was further distorted so that its contour was preserved but the exact intervals were not. Although the listeners performed above chance on these tasks, they were unable to distinguish between exact transformations and those that preserved contour alone. Dowling (1978) later provided evidence that exact interval recognition was being masked by the listeners' projecting the pitch information onto the highly over-learned scales of our tonal system. Whether extensive exposure to twelve-tone music could overcome such a masking effect is a matter that requires further investigation.

Another issue raised by twelve-tone theory is whether a sequence of tones retains its perceptual identity when its components are placed in different octaves. For single tones in isolation, there is a strong perceptual similarity between tones that stand in octave relation. Psychologists have noted this equivalence and refer to tones that are an octave apart as having the same "tone chroma" (Bachem, 1954; Meyer, 1904, 1914; Revesz, 1913; Ruckmick, 1929; Shepard, 1964; Ward & Burns, 1982). Further, traditional music theory recognizes the equivalence of such tones in simultaneous structures through the rules governing chord progressions (Rameau, 1722/1950). However, where melodies or successive pitch structures are concerned, octave equivalence does not obviously hold, since we do not interchange octaves in successive contexts in the same way as we do in simultaneous contexts.

According to twelve-tone theory, tones that are separated by octaves are considered to be in the same "pitch class," and their equivalence is assumed to be a perceptual invariant. It is therefore held that intervals (both simultaneous and successive) retain their perceptual identities when the tones forming these intervals are placed in different octaves; such intervals are held to be in the same "interval class." However, the hypothesized equivalence relation of interval class is not a necessary consequence of interval equivalence together with octave equivalence. Deutsch (1969) proposed a neural network for the abstraction of pitch combinations in which the perceptual equivalence of transposed intervals and chords is mediated by one channel, and the perceptual equivalence of tones that are separated by octaves, together with the invertibility of chords, is mediated by a separate and parallel channel. This network gives rise to octave equivalence for single tones in isolation and in a harmonic or simultaneous context, but not in a melodic or successive context.

In an experiment designed to examine the issue of octave equivalence in a successive context, the tune "Yankee Doodle" was presented to listeners in several versions (Deutsch, 1972). One version was untransformed. In a second version, the tones were in their correct positions within the octave, but the octaves in which they were placed varied randomly; thus interval class was preserved even though the intervals were altered. In a third version, the pitch information was removed entirely. Each version was played to a different group of listeners. Although the untransformed version was recognized by everyone, recognition of the randomized octaves version was no better than of the version where the pitch information was removed entirely. This finding is as predicted from the two-channel model of Deutsch (1969), and it shows that interval class cannot be treated as a perceptual invariant.

When the listeners in this study were later informed of the identity of the melody and heard it again, many found that they could now follow it to a large extent and confirm that each note was indeed correctly placed within its octave. Thus the listeners were able to use octave equivalence to confirm a hypothesized melodic shape, though they were unable to recognize this shape in the absence of strong cues on which the hypothesis might be based. We can conclude that interval class can be perceived in a successive context under certain conditions, but that such perception does not result from a passive process. Rather, it may be regarded as an example of "top-down" shape analysis; i.e., as the result of hypothesis-testing by the listener.

Further studies support this argument. Dowling and Hollombe (1977) presented listeners with melodies whose individual tones were placed in different octaves, and they found that recognition performance was better for melodies whose contours were preserved than for melodies with altered contours. This finding is in accordance with the present line of reasoning. Since melodies can be recognized on the basis of their contours alone (Werner, 1925; White, 1960), contour should act as a powerful cue for hypothesis-testing. Similar findings were obtained by Idson and Massaro (1978) and Kallman and Massaro (1979). Second, it has been found that when listeners were presented with a small set of melodies many times and were asked to identify each melody from a small list of alternatives, recognition performance was considerably better than when such melodies were presented only once with no cues concerning their identity (House, 1977; Idson & Massaro, 1978). In the former case ample opportunity was given for hypothesis testing, so that again enhanced recognition would be expected (Deutsch, 1978b).

Returning to twelve-tone theory, we can conclude that interval class may be perceived, but only under conditions of reasonably high expectancy. The ability of a listener to recognize a tone row under octave displacement should depend critically on such factors as prior familiarity with the row and whether or not the relationships formed by earlier tones in the row are such as to produce clear expectations for the later tones (see also Deutsch, in 1982b).

Hierarchical Structure in Music

It may generally be stated that we tend to encode and retain information in the form of hierarchies when given the opportunity to do so. For example, programs of behavior tend to be retained as hierarchies (Miller, Galanter, & Pribram, 1960) and goals in problem solving as hierarchies of subgoals (Ernst & Newell, 1969). Visual scenes appear to be encoded as hierarchies of subscenes (Hanson & Riseman, 1978; Navon, 1977; Palmer, 1977; Winston, 1973). The phrase structure of a sentence lends itself readily to hierarchical interpretations (Chomsky, 1963; Johnson-Laird, in this volume; Miller & Chomsky, 1963; Yngve, 1960). When presented with artificial serial patterns which may be hierarchically encoded, we readily form encodings that reflect pattern structure (Kotovsky & Simon, 1973; Restle, 1970; Restle & Brown, 1970; Simon & Kotovsky, 1963; Vitz & Todd, 1967, 1969). Such findings have given rise to the development of sophisticated models of serial pattern representation in terms of hierarchies of operators (Greeno & Simon, 1974; Leewenberg, 1971; Restle, 1970; Simon, 1972; Simon & Kotovsky, 1963; Simon & Sumner, 1968; Vitz & Todd, 1967, 1969).

In considering how we most naturally form hierarchies, however, theories have generally been constrained by the nature of the stimulus material under consideration. For example, visually perceived objects are naturally formed out of parts and subparts. The hierarchical structure of language must necessarily be constrained by the logical structure of events in the world. The attainment of a goal is generally arrived at by an optimal system of subgoals. And so on.

This problem is just as severe for theories based on experiments utilizing artificial serial patterns devised by the experimenter. To take a concrete example, Restle's (1970) theory of hierarchical representation of serial patterns evolved from findings based on the following experimental paradigm. Subjects were presented with a row of six lights, which turned on and off in repetitive sequence, and they were required on each trial to predict which light would come on next. The sequences were structured as hierarchies of operators. For example, given the basic subsequence X = (1 2), then the operation R ('repeat of X') produces the sequence 1 2 1 2; the operation M ('mirror-image of X') produces the sequence 1 2 6 5, and the operation T ('transposition + 1 of X') produces the sequence 1 2 2 3. Through recursive application of such operations, long sequences can be generated which have compact structural descriptions. Thus M(T(R(T(1)))) describes the sequence 1 2 1 2 2 3 2 3 6 5 6 5 5 4 5 4.

Restle and Brown (1970), using sequences constructed in this fashion, found compelling evidence that subjects encoded them in accordance with their hierarchical structure. However, it should be noted that the sequences were constructed so as to allow for only one hierarchical interpretation. Thus it is difficult to estimate the generalizability of this model to situations where alternative hierarchical realizations are possible.

Given these problems, the hierarchical structure of established music is of particular interest to cognitive psychology, since such music is solely the product of human processing mechanisms, unfettered by external constraints. Further, music can reasonably be considered to have evolved so as to make optimal use of these mechanisms.

Long before cognitive psychologists became seriously interested in hierarchical structure, the music theorist Schenker proposed a hierarchical system for tonal music that has points of similarity with the system proposed by Chomsky for language (Chomsky, 1957, 1965). (In fact, Schenker acknowledged that his ideas were inspired by C. P. E. Bach whose *Essay on the True Art of Playing Keyboard Instruments* details the processes by which a simple musical event may be replaced by a more elaborate musical event which expresses the same basic content.) In Schenker's system, music is regarded as a hierarchy in which notes at any given level are considered "prolonged" by a sequence of notes at the next-lower level. Three basic levels are distinguished. First there is the *fore-ground,* or surface representation; second there is the *middleground;* and third there is the *background,* or *Ursatz.* The *Ursatz* is itself considered a prolongation of the triad (Schenker, 1956, 1973).

Schenker's work, though largely unrecognized in his time, has had a profound influence on music theory since the late 1950s (see, e.g., Forte, 1974; Salzer, 1962; Westergaard, 1975; Yeston, 1977). Most Schenkerian analysis, however, is purely descriptive in nature and is generally regarded as an end in itself. Furthermore, the assumptions of Schenkerian analysis are at basis rather inexplicit.

The collaborative work of the music theorist Lerdahl and the psycholinguist Jackendoff (1977) represents an attempt to explicate the structure of Schenker's system and to interpret this structure as a form of internal representation. Their approach makes use of tree diagrams that resemble in some respects those used in transformational grammar. However, the authors are careful to emphasize the very real differences that exist between language and music. For example, linguistic trees represent "is-a" relations: A noun phrase that is followed by a verb phrase *is a* sentence, and so on. In contrast, musical trees do not involve grammatical categories. Rather, the fundamental relationship that they express is that of the elaboration of a single pitch event by a sequence of pitch events. Their theory also emphasizes the importance of psychological grouping phenomena in the formation of musical hierarchies.

Schenker's theory is essentially "top-down" in nature, in that the *Ursatz* acts as a "kernel" from which the middleground and foreground structures are derived. (This is analogous to transformational grammar, which relies on "kernel" sentences to generate linguistic structures.) The foreground levels are held to be generated from above, from levels at which the actual notes are not themselves present. The music theorist Narmour (1977) has argued that this constitutes a serious difficulty for Schenker's theory. He shows by numerous examples that patterns of relationship between notes that are not necessarily adjacent at the foreground level contribute importantly to musical structure. He proposes alternatively that a given representation is generated "bottom-up" and that Schenker's terminal symbols (the actual notes on the page of the composition) be conceived not as the result of mappings onto a lower level from middleground structures and the background kernel, but rather as the initiating structure from which higher-level structures are built. He also argues that foreground structures create multiple alternative representations (or implications), so that musical pieces should be conceptualized not as tree structures, but rather as interlocking networks.

Narmour's work was inspired by that of the music theorist Meyer (1956, 1960, 1973), who argues that musical structure should be viewed in terms of implications generated by pitch events that are realized by further pitch events. Such implications and their realizations are considered to occur at all hierarchical levels. Further, a sequence of pitch events often has multiple implications, only some of which are realized.

Deutsch and Feroe (1981) have advanced a formal theory for the representation of pitch sequences in tonal music which falls into the class of those developed by Restle, Simon, and others in that it proposes a specific language or notation for describing serial patterns, and this language is considered to reflect specific encodings. However, the concerns of music theorists were also considered in developing the formalism. Basically pitch sequences are assumed to be retained as hierarchical networks. Elements that are present at each hierarchical level are elaborated by further elements at the next-lower level, until the lowest level is reached. At each level of the hierarchy, elements are organized as structural units in accordance with laws of figural goodness. The basic architecture of this system can also be applied to the internal representation of other types of information, such as visual scenes (Lynch, 1960).

Hierarchical structure in music provides a rich field for experimental investigation, which has so far been largely untapped. Two recent studies may be mentioned. The psychologist Rosner in collaboration with the music theorist Meyer (1982) addressed the following question: Frequently, melodies appear to be hierarchically structured in such a way that the type of patterning exhibited by a given melody changes from one hierarchical level to the next. For example, a melody at one level may be characterized by a linear pattern; at another level by a gap-fill pattern;[5] and so on. The authors further hypothesized that melodies are classified by the listener in terms of the organization at the highest level at which significant closure is created. In a test of this hypothesis, musically untrained listeners were asked to categorize melodies in a concept identification task. The melodies had previously been categorized by musical analysis as either gap-fill or non-gap-fill at the appropriate hierarchical level. It was found that listeners classified the melodies in accordance with theoretical expectations.

In another study, Deutsch (1980) compared memory for tonal sequences that were hierarchically structured with those that were not. Musically trained listeners were presented with sequences which they recalled in musical notation. Half of the sequences were hierarchically structured such that a higher-level subsequence of three elements acted on a lower-level subsequence of four elements. The remaining sequences were unstructured. Recall was found to be considerably superior for the structured than for the unstructured sequences. It was concluded that listeners readily detect hierarchical organization in tonal sequences and can utilize this organization so as to produce parsimonious encodings.

In summary, hierarchical structure in music is an area of study which has strong dividends for both music theory and psychology. Since music is the product of our processing mechanisms and since traditional music may be taken to have evolved so as to make optimal use of these mechanisms, understanding the structure of tonal music and how it is processed is likely to have broad implications for theories of human cognition.

CONCLUSIONS: MUSIC THEORY AND PSYCHOLOGY

In the Introduction I referred to fundamental problems in determining the relationship of findings in psychology to music theory. It is with a discussion of these problems that I shall conclude this essay.

Psychology contributes to the understanding of music by characterizing

---

[5] A gap-fill pattern is characterized by two elements: (a) a skip or succession of skips that move in the same direction and (b) a succession of steps which fill the gap, that move in the opposite direction.

the processing mechanisms of the listener. What is worrisome to some music theorists is the possibility that findings from psychology might be taken as a basis for arguing what music *ought* to be. Much work in perceptual and cognitive psychology has to do with determining limits: limits to the amount of information that can be retained, limits of discriminability, and so on. Taking such "scientifically established limits" too seriously, it is feared, might serve to stultify musical development by creating artificial boundary conditions for acceptable music. For the limitations determined by such experiments might not in fact be fixed but might rather be a function of the type of music to which the listener has been exposed.

To place this concern in historical perspective, the development of Western music may be viewed as a constant struggle between innovative composers on the one hand and establishment critics on the other, who have argued against various innovations on the grounds that they are unacceptable to the listener. Some examples of "new" music that were considered unacceptable would surprise a modern audience. For example, J. S. Bach was considered in his time to have "confused the congregation with many peculiar and foreign tunes [Portnoy, 1954, p. 144]." Another composer who was censured by his contemporaries was Monteverdi. The distinguished music critic and theorist Artusi wrote of his music:

> Insofar as it introduced new rules, new modes, and new turns of phrase, these were harsh and little pleasing to the ear, nor could they be otherwise, for as long as they violate the good rules—in part founded by experience, the mother of all things, in part observed by nature, and in part by demonstration—we must believe them to be deformations of the nature and propriety of true harmony, far removed from the object of music [Artusi, 1600/1950, p. 394].

Yet the works of Bach and of Monteverdi appear to us as outstanding examples of traditional cultivated music. Clearly, the way that music affects the listener is at least to some extent a function of experience.

It should be stated that in the past, arguments against new music have been aesthetic in nature and were not based on controlled experiments demonstrating processing limitations. The possibility remains, however, that the typical listener of Monteverdi's time might have displayed a different set of processing limitations than those displayed by the typical listener of our time. One could plausibly regard the development of Western music as in part an extensive long-term field study in which generations of audiences have been exposed to various types of music and their processing mechanisms have been shaped and reshaped as a result of such exposure. It is this line of reasoning that causes some theorists to insist that when laboratory studies show that listeners do not perceive equivalences that exist formally in a musical system, this provides no argument against the ultimate viability of the system.

However, to dismiss the findings of psychology because of such concerns does not constitute a solution. If a music theory is to be scientifically justified, such justification must lie in its relationship to the processing mechanisms of the listener. To take an extreme example, no one would seriously consider composing in a musical system that employs only sounds outside the range of hearing. Central processing limitations are no less real than those of our peripheral hearing apparatus; the only difference is that while peripheral limitations are fixed, some central limitations are fixed and some are plastic.

There remains the question of determining which of our musical processing mechanisms can be shaped by experience. To me it appears that no clear answer can be obtained by laboratory experimentation. We can expose subjects to intensive training on a given system and determine whether or not they can learn to use its rules. But negative results would not be conclusive, since it could always be argued that long-term exposure, particularly during early childhood, might have produced positive results instead. We can, however, make some inspired guesses as to which processing characteristics are likely to be fixed. Those characteristics which are most useful in making sense of our auditory environment are prime candidates. These include the tendency to fuse together components of a sound spectrum that are in harmonic relationship; the tendency to form sequential configurations on the basis of frequency proximity; the tendency to attend on the basis of spatial location; and so on. Such mechanisms are likely either to be hardwired or, if acquired through experience, to continue to be acquired as a result of experience with our nonmusical auditory environment. Amongst other candidates for fixed processing characteristics are those that lead to parsimony of encoding and other measures of encoding efficiency.

To conclude, it must remain the prerogative of the composer to experiment with any new rules that he wishes; psychology cannot provide prescriptive answers and can only explain how existing music is perceived. However, by the same token, music theory cannot provide prescriptive answers either. As Aristoxenus (1902, p. 195) wrote over two millennia ago: "We shall advance to our conclusions by strict demonstration." If there is no strict demonstration, then there can be no conclusions.

ACKNOWLEDGMENT

This work was supported by United States Public Health Service Grant MH–21001. The concluding section of this essay first appeared, with minor differences, as an editorial in *Music Perception*, 1983, *1*, 1–2.

REFERENCES

Aristotle. [*De caelo*] (J. L. Stocks, trans.). In *The works of Aristotle* (Vol. 2). Oxford: Oxford University Press, 1930.

Aristoxenus. [*The harmonics of Aristoxenus*] (H. S. Macran, trans.). Oxford: Clarendon Press, 1902.

Artusi. *L'Artusi, ovvero, Delle imperfezioni della moderna musica*. In O. Strunk (Ed.), *Source readings in music history*. New York: Norton, 1950. (Originally published, 1600.)

Babbitt, M. Twelve-tone invariants as compositional determinants. *The Musical Quarterly*, 1960, *46*, 246–259.

Babbitt, M. Set structure as a compositional determinant. *Journal of Music Theory*, 1961, *5*, 73–94.

Bach, C. P. E. [*Essay on the true art of playing keyboard instruments*] (W. J. Mitchell, Ed. and trans.). New York: W. W. Norton, 1949.

Bachem, A. Time factors in relative and absolute pitch determination. *Journal of the Acoustical Society of America*, 1954, *26*, 751–753.

Berger, K. W. Some factors in the recognition of timbre. *Journal of the Acoustical Society of America*, 1964, *36*, 1888–1891.

Berlioz, H. [*Treatise on instrumentation*] (R. Strauss, Ed. & T. Front, trans.). New York: E. F. Kalmus, 1948.

Boethius. [*Boethius' the principles of music*] (C. M. Bower, trans.). Ann Arbor, MI: University of Michigan Press, 1967.

Brant, H. Space as an essential aspect of musical composition. In E. Schwartz & B. Childs (Eds.), *Contemporary composers on contemporary music*. New York: Holt, Rinehart and Winston, 1966.

Bregman, A. S. The formation of auditory streams. In J. Requin (Ed.), *Attention and performance VII*. Hillsdale, NJ: Lawrence Erlbaum Associates, 1978.

Bregman, A. S., & Campbell, Jr. Primary auditory stream segregation and perception of order in rapid sequence of tones. *Journal of Experimental Psychology*, 1971, *89*, 244–249.

Bregman, A. S., & Pinker, S. Auditory streaming and the building of timbre. *Canadian Journal of Psychology*, 1978, *32*, 20–31.

Butler, S. *Hudibras, parts I and II, and selected other writings* (J. Wilders & H. de Quehen, Eds.). Oxford: Clarendon Press, 1973.

Butler, D. A further study of melodic channeling. *Perception and Psychophysics*, 1979, *25*, 264–268. (a)

Butler, D. Melodic channeling in a musical environment. *Research Symposium on the Psychology and Acoustics of Music*, Kansas, 1979. (b)

Chomsky, N. *Syntactic structures*. The Hague: Mouton, 1957.

Chomsky, N. Formal properties of grammars. In R. D. Luce, R. R. Bush, & E. Galanter (Eds.), *Handbook of mathematical psychology* (Vol. 2). New York: Wiley, 1963.

Chomsky, N. *Aspects of the theory of syntax*. Cambridge, MA: M.I.T. Press, 1965.

de Boer, E. On the "residue" and auditory pitch perception. In W. D. Keidel & W. D. Neff (Eds.), *Handbook of sensory physiology* (Vol. V/3). Wein: Springer-Verlag, 1976.

Deutsch, D. Music recognition. *Psychological Review,* 1969, *76,* 300–307.

Deutsch, D. Octave generalization and tune recognition. *Perception and Psychophysics,* 1972, *11,* 411–412.

Deutsch, D. Musical illusions. *Scientific American,* 1975, *233,* 92–104. (a)

Deutsch, D. Two-channel listening to musical scales. *Journal of the Acoustical Society of America,* 1975, *57,* 1156–1160. (b)

Deutsch, D. Delayed pitch comparisons and the principle of proximity. *Perception and Psychophysics,* 1978, *23,* 227–230. (a)

Deutsch, D. Octave generalization and melody identification. *Perception and Psychophysics,* 1978, *23,* 91–92. (b)

Deutsch, D. Binaural integration of melodic patterns. *Perception and Psychophysics,* 1979, *25,* 399–405.

Deutsch, D. The processing of structured and unstructured tonal sequences. *Perception and Psychophysics,* 1980, *28,* 381–389.

Deutsch, D. Grouping mechanisms in music. In D. Deutsch (Ed.), *The psychology of music.* New York: Academic Press, 1982. (a)

Deutsch, D. The processing of pitch combinations. In D. Deutsch (Ed.), *The psychology of music.* New York: Academic Press, 1982. (b)

Deutsch, D. Dichotic listening to musical sequences: Relationship to hemispheric specialization of function. *Journal of the Acoustical Society of America,* 1983, *74,* S79–80.

Deutsch, D. Musical space. In W. R. Crozier & A. J. Chapman (Eds.), *Cognitive processes in the perception of art.* Amsterdam: North Holland, in press.

Deutsch, D., & Feroe, J. The internal representation of pitch sequences in tonal music. *Psychological Review,* 1981, *88,* 503–522.

Dowling, W. J. Recognition of melodic transformations: Inversion, retrograde, and retrograde-inversion. *Perception and Psychophysics,* 1972, *12,* 417–421.

Dowling, W. J. The perception of interleaved melodies. *Cognitive Psychology,* 1973, *5,* 322–337.

Dowling, W. J. Scale and contour: Two components of a theory of memory for melodies. *Psychological Review,* 1978, *85,* 342–354.

Dowling, W. J., & Hollombe, A. W. The perception of melodies distorted by splitting into several octaves: Effects of increasing proximity and melodic contour. *Perception and Psychophysics,* 1977, *21,* 60–64.

Ehrenfels, C. Von. Uber Gestaltqualitaten. *Vierteljahrschrift fur Wissenschaftliche Philosophie,* 1890, *14,* 249–292.

Erickson, R. *Sound structure in music.* Berkeley: University of California Press, 1975.

Erickson, R. New music and psychology. In D. Deutsch (Ed.), *The psychology of music.* New York: Academic Press, 1982.

Ernst, G. W., & Newell, A. *GPS: A case study in generality and problem solving.* New York: Academic Press, 1969.

Forte, A. *Tonal harmony in concept and practice.* New York: Holt, Rinehart and Winston, 1974.

Freeman, K. *Ancilla to the pre-Socratic philosophers.* Cambridge, MA: Harvard University Press, 1948.

Garner, W. R. *The processing of information and structure.* New York: Wiley, 1974.

Greeno, J. G., & Simon, H. A. Processes for sequence production. *Psychological Review,* 1974, *81,* 187–196.

Gregory, R. L. *The intelligent eye.* New York: McGraw-Hill, 1970.

Grey, J. M. *An exploration of musical timbre.* Unpublished doctoral dissertation. Stanford University, 1975.

Grey, J. M., & Moorer, J. A. Perceptual evaluation of synthesized musical instrument tones. *Journal of the Acoustical Society of America*, 1977, *62*, 454–462.

Hanson, A. R., & Riseman, E. M. (Eds.). *Computer vision systems*. New York: Academic Press, 1978.

Hawkins, Sir J. A. *General history of the science and practice of music* (Vol. 1). London: Dover, 1963. (Originally published, 1853.)

Helmholtz, H. Von. [*Helmholtz's physiological optics*] (J. P. C. Southall, Ed. and trans.). Rochester, New York: Optical Society of America, 1925. (Originally published, 1909–1911.)

Helmholtz, H. von. *On the sensations of tone as a physiological basis for the theory of music*. New York: Dover, 1954. (Originally published, 1885.)

Hirsh, I. J. Auditory perception of temporal order. *Journal of the Acoustical Society of America*, 1959, *31*, 759–767.

Hirsh, I. J., & Sherrick, C. E. Perceived order in different sense modalities. *Journal of Experimental Psychology*, 1961, *62*, 423–432.

Hochberg, J. Organization and the Gestalt tradition. In E. C. Carterette & M. P. Friedman (Eds.), *Handbook of perception* (Vol. 1). New York: Academic Press, 1974.

House, W. J. Octave generalization and the identification of distorted melodies. *Perception and Psychophysics*, 1977, *21*, 586–589.

Hunt, F. V. *Origins in acoustics*. New Haven, CT: Yale University Press, 1978.

Idson, W. L., & Massaro, D. W. A bidimensional model of pitch in the recognition of melodies. *Perception and Psychophysics*, 1978, *24*, 551–565.

Kallman, H. J., & Massaro, D. W. Tone chroma is functional in melody recognition. *Perception and Psychophysics*, 1979, *26*, 32–36.

Kotovsky, K., & Simon, H. A. Empirical tests of a theory of human acquisition of concepts for sequential events. *Cognitive Psychology*, 1973, *4*, 399–424.

Leewenberg, E. L. A perceptual coding language for visual and auditory patterns. *American Journal of Psychology*, 1971, *84*, 307–349.

Lerdahl, F., & Jackendoff, R. Toward a formal theory of music. *Journal of Music Theory*, 1977, *21*, 111–172.

Lynch, K. *The image of the city*. Cambridge, MA: Harvard University Press, 1960.

Machlis, J. *The enjoyment of music*. New York: Norton, 1977.

McAdams, S. Spectral fusion and the creation of auditory images. In M. Clynes (Ed.), *Music, mind and brain*. New York: Plenum Press, 1981.

Mathews, M. V. *The technology of computer music*. Cambridge, MA: M.I.T. Press, 1969.

Mathews, M. V., & Pierce, J. R. Harmony and nonharmonic partials. *Journal of the Acoustical Society of America*, 1980, *68*, 1252–1257.

Meyer, L. B. *Emotion and meaning in music*. Chicago, IL: University of Chicago Press, 1956.

Meyer, L. B. *Music, the arts and ideas*. Chicago, IL: University of Chicago Press, 1960.

Meyer, L. B. *Explaining music: Essays and explorations*. Berkeley, CA: University of California Press, 1973.

Meyer, M. On the attributes of the sensations. *Psychological Review*, 1904, *11*, 83–103.

Meyer, M. Review of G. Revesz, "Zur Grundleguncy der Tonpsychologie." *Psychological Bulletin*, 1914, *11*, 349–352.

Miller, G. A., & Chomsky, N. Finitary models of language users. In R. D. Luce, R. R. Bush, & E. Galanter (Eds.), *Handbook of mathematical psychology* (Vol. 2). New York: Wiley, 1963.

Miller, G. A., Galanter, E. H., & Pribram, K. H. *Plans and the structure of behavior*. New York: Holt, Rinehart and Winston, 1960.

Narmour, E. *Beyond Schenkerism*. Chicago: University of Chicago Press, 1977.

Navon, D. Forest before trees: The precedence of global features in visual perception. *Cognitive Psychology*, 1977, *9*, 353–383.

Palisca, C. V. Scientific empiricism in musical thought. In H. H. Rhys (Ed.), *Seventeenth century science in the arts*. Princeton, NJ: Princeton University Press, 1961.

Palmer, S. E. Hierarchical structure in perceptual representation. *Cognitive Psychology*, 1977, *9*, 441–474.

Perle, G. *Serial composition and atonality*. Berkeley, CA: University of California Press, 1972.

Perle, G. *Twelve-tone tonality*. Berkeley, CA: University of California Press, 1977.

Plomp, R. The ear as frequency analyzer. *Journal of the Acoustical Society of America*, 1964, *36*, 1628–1636.

Plomp, R. Timbre as a multidimensional attribute of complex tones. In R. Plomp & G. F. Smoorenburg (Eds.), *Frequency analysis and periodicity detection in hearing*. Sijthoff: Leiden, 1970.

Plomp, R., & Mimpen, A. M. The ear as frequency analyzer II. *Journal of the Acoustical Society of America*, 1968, *43*, 764–767.

Plomp, R., & Steeneken, H. J. M. *Pitch versus timbre*. Paper presented at the Seventh International Congress on Acoustics, Budapest, 1971.

Portnoy, J. *The philosopher and music*. New York: The Humanities Press, 1954.

Rameau, J.-P. *Traite de l'harmonie reduite a ses principes naturels*. In O. Strunk (Ed.), *Source readings in music history*. New York: Norton, 1950. (Originally published, 1722.)

Rasch, R. A. The perception of simultaneous notes such as in polyphonic music. *Acustica*, 1978, *40*, 1–72.

Restle, F. Theory of serial pattern learning: Structural trees. *Psychological Review*, 1970, *77*, 481–495.

Restle, F., & Brown, E. Organization of serial pattern learning. In G. H. Bower (Ed.), *The psychology of learning and motivation* (Vol. 4). New York: Academic Press, 1970.

Revesz, G. *Zur Grundleguncy der Tonpsychologie*. Leipzig: Feit, 1913.

Risset, J.-C., & Mathews, M. V. Analysis of musical instrument tones. *Physics Today*, 1969, *22*, 23–30.

Risset, J.-C., & Wessel, D. L. Exploration of timbre by analysis and synthesis. In D. Deutsch (Ed.), *The psychology of music*. New York: Academic Press, 1982.

Rosner, B. S., & Meyer, L. B. Melodic processes and the perception of music. In D. Deutsch (Ed.), *The psychology of music*. New York: Academic Press, 1982.

Ruckmick, C. A. A new classification of tonal qualities. *Psychological Review*, 1929, *36*, 172–180.

Russell, B. *A history of Western philosophy*. New York: Simon and Schuster, 1945.

Saldanha, E. L., & Corso, J. F. Timbre cues for the recognition of musical instruments. *Journal of the Acoustical Society of America*, 1964, *36*, 2021–2026.

Salzer, F. *Structural hearing*. New York: Dover, 1962.

Schenker, H. *Neue musikalische theorien und phantasien: Der freie satz*. Vienna, Austria: Universal Edition, 1956.

Schenker, H. [*Harmony*] (O. Jonas, Ed. & E. M. Borgese, trans.). Cambridge, MA: M.I.T. Press, 1973.

Schoenberg, A. *Harmonielehre*. Leipzig and Vienna: Universal Edition, 1911.

Schoenberg, A. *Style and idea*. London: Williams and Norgate, 1951.

Schouten, J. F. On the perception of sound and speech: Subjective time analysis. *Fourth International Congress on Acoustics, Copenhagen Congress Report II*, 1962, 201–203.

Schroeder, M. R. Acoustics in human communications: Room acoustics, music, and speech. *Journal of the Acoustical Society of America*, 1980, *68*, 22–28.

Shepard, R. N. Circularity in judgments of relative pitch. *Journal of the Acoustical Society of America,* 1964, *36,* 2345–2353.

Simon, H. A. Complexity and the representation of patterned sequences of symbols. *Psychological Review,* 1972, *79,* 369–382.

Simon, H. A., & Kotovsky, K. Human acquisition of concepts for sequential patterns. *Psychological Review,* 1963, *70,* 534–546.

Simon, H. A., & Sumner, R. K. Pattern in music. In B. Kleinmuntz (Ed.), *Formal representation of human judgment.* New York: Wiley, 1968.

Slawson, A. W. Vowel quality and musical timbre as functions of spectrum envelope and fundamental frequency. *Journal of the Acoustical Society of America,* 1968, *43,* 87–101.

Stevens, S. S., & Volkmann, J. The relation of pitch to frequency: A revised scale. *American Journal of Psychology,* 1940, *53,* 329–353.

Strunk, O. (Ed.). *Source readings in music history.* New York: Norton, 1950.

Sutherland, N. S. Object recognition. In E. C. Carterette & M. P. Friedman (Eds.), *Handbook of pereception* (Vol. 3). New York: Academic Press, 1973.

Van Noorden, L. P. A. S. *Temporal coherence in the perception of tone sequences.* Unpublished doctoral thesis, Technische Hogeschool, Eindhoven, Holland, 1975.

Vitz, P. C., & Todd, T. C. A model of learning for simple repeating binary patterns. *Journal of Experimental Psychology,* 1967, *75,* 108–117.

Vitz, P. C., & Todd, T. C. A coded element model of the perceptual processing of sequential stimuli. *Psychological Review,* 1969, *76,* 433–449.

Ward, W. D., & Burns, E. M. Absolute pitch. In D. Deutsch (Ed.), *The psychology of music.* New York: Academic Press, 1982.

Warren, R. M. Auditory temporal discrimination by trained listeners. *Cognitive Psychology,* 1974, *6,* 237–256.

Warren, R. M., Obusek, C. J., Farmer, R. M., & Warren, R. P. Auditory sequence: Confusions of patterns other than speech or music. *Science,* 1969, *164,* 586–587.

Wedin, L., & Goude, G. Dimension analysis of the perception of instrumental timbre. *Scandinavian Journal of Psychology,* 1972, *13,* 228–240.

Werner, H. Uber Mikromelodik und Mikroharmonik. *Zeitschrift fur Psychologie,* 1925, *98,* 74–89.

Wertheimer, M. Untersuchungen sur Lehre von der Gestalt, II. *Psychologische Forschung,* 1923, *4,* 301–350.

Wessel, D. L. Psychoacoustics and music. *Bulletin of the Computer Arts Society,* 1973, *1,* 30–31.

Wessel, D. L. *Low dimensional control of timbre.* IRCAM Report No. 12, 1978, Paris.

Westergaard, P. *An introduction to tonal theory.* New York: Norton, 1975.

White, B. Recognition of distorted melodies. *American Journal of Psychology,* 1960, *73,* 100–107.

Winston, P. H. Learning to identify toy block structures. In R. L. Solso (Ed.), *Contemporary issues in cognitive psychology: The Loyola symposium.* Washington, DC: Winston, 1973.

Yeston, M. (Ed.). *Readings in Schenker analysis and other approaches.* New Haven, CT: Yale University Press, 1977.

Yngve, V. H. A model and an hypothesis for language structure. *Proceedings of the American Philosophical Society,* 1960, *104,* 444–466.

Zarlino, G. *Instituzioni armoniche* (Book 3). In O. Strunk (Ed.), *Source readings in music history.* New York: Norton, 1950. (Originally published, 1558.)

5 Psychology and Philosophy

Ned Block
Massachusetts Institute of Technology

William P. Alston
Syracuse University

INTRODUCTION

This essay aims at explaining what philosphers do under the banner of "philosophy of psychology." Psychology groups together subject matters that but for historical accident might have ended up in different academic disciplines. Philosophy of psychology is similarly fragmented. One could define philosophy of psychology as the study of conceptual problems in psychology, but any really informative account of philosophy of psychology is better conveyed by illustration than by definition.

What follows is an overview of the field, plus sixteen "MODULES," each describing a specific problem area. The overview can be read on its own, but it is also intended to function as a guide to the modules. To use it as a guide to the modules, the reader should start reading the overview, turning to each module as it is mentioned in the overview.

PHILOSOPHY OF PSYCHOLOGY OVERVIEW

Philosophy of psychology, as understood in this overview, is a subject that includes traditional philosophy of mind plus the foundations of empirical psychology and also various conceptual problems in empirical psychology. Until the 1970s, philosophers who studied the mind worked on *the* metaphysical problem of mind, namely the mind-body problem, or else on analyses of individual mental concepts, e.g., pleasure or jealousy. (For example, an analysis of jealousy might tell you that in order for someone to be jealous of x, x must exist—so no one can *really* be jealous of Santa Claus.) Other endeavors were often included in the domain of philosophy of mind, for example, the problem of other minds (How do I know that all the bodies around me are not really the bodies of mindless robots?), but these problems are more closely related to other areas of philosophy—the general problem of justifying knowledge, in the case of the problem of other minds. In this period, empirical psychology was widely considered to be irrelevant to the problems of mind that had interested philosophers. (Oxford undergraduates had a program in which they could "double major" in philosophy and psychology, but the two subjects were taught separately, and no one succeeded in putting them together.) For reasons having to do with changes in the separate courses of psychology (mainly the advent of cognitive psychology) and philosophy, philosophers interested in the mind began to take a serious interest in psychology. The result is that there is now a considerable amount of philososphical work that attempts to describe, articulate, and criticize the theoretical presuppositions of research in psychology and related sciences such as artificial intelligence and linguistics. There is also a good deal of work on an important set of specific conceptual issues; they include: whether mental images are pictorial or descriptional representations; whether there is inference in perception; whether the object of study of linguistics is mental (or whether linguistics has an abstract subject matter in the manner of mathematics); whether work on people whose brains have been cut in two shows that a typical body's left hemisphere is the brain of a different person from the person whose brain is the corresponding right hemisphere; what it is to have a concept (an image, a set of procedures, or a list of features?); what differences may exist between rule-governed and rule-described action; whether there are innate ideas; and whether people are ultimately mechanical entities.

Many of the problems dealt with by contemporary philosophy of psychology are strikingly similar to traditional issues in philosophy. A philosopher of long ago would not be baffled by the appearance in this list of the issue of innate ideas or by the question of whether there is inference in perception. By contrast, Aristotle would find utterly unintelligible most of the issues of concern to contemporary philosophy of physics, e.g., whether the psi function of quantum mechanics is a probability wave. The difference is that advances in physics have involved strikingly new concepts (and thus new conceptual issues) while psychology is still at a relatively primitive stage.

This being said, it should also be noted that the old issues typically appear in new and often more tractable forms. Indeed, some of the old issues are hardly recognizable in their new guises. For example, the issue of whether the subject matter of grammar is rules in the mind has been considerably altered by advances in transformational-generative grammar (see Johnson-Laird, in this volume). The issues in current discussions of innate ideas involve new ideas from biology (see Uttal, in Volume III). And new *data* have transformed discussions of mental imagery, unity of consciousness, and inference in perception. Moreover, since psychology does contain *some* new theoretical apparatus, new issues arise in connection with that apparatus, for example, the philosophical issues concerning Freudian theory (Wollheim, 1974) and formal learning theory (Wexler & Culcover, 1980). Also, new experimental techniques sometimes reveal previously unrecognized human capacities about which philosophical questions arise. For example, the experimental techniques of psychophysics reveal that people can make a series of verbal judgements of relative brightness of lights that are stable and coherent and that allow experimenters to conclude that perceived brightness is a certain function of a physical parameter (intensity). But this result raises the questions of what sort of magnitude brightness is and what it means for one light to be twice as bright as another (see Marks, in Volume III; Savage, 1970). The claims of psychometricians to measure intelligence, personality, and so on, have also attracted the attention of philosophers (Block & Dworkin, 1974). What makes this issue of interest to a philosopher (aside from its moral and political implications) is, first, that arguments for the claim that the tests test innate intelligence have typically gone unformulated and unexamined, and it is a typically philosophical task to examine and formulate arguments and, second, that psychometric practice and ideology appear to presuppose philosophical doctrines such as operationalism.

In what follows in this overview, we shall first examine the traditional mind-body problem. The relevance of the mind-body problem to the day-to-day concerns of psychologists is far from obvious. But as we shall see, the issues raised in discussion of the mind-body problem tend to crop up again and again in work on foundational issues that are more directly related to experimental psychology. Next, we turn to discuss attempts philosophers have made to clarify the foundations of psychology, especially cognitive psychology. Finally, we examine a scattering of topics raised by research in various areas of psychology.

THE MIND-BODY PROBLEM

Work on the mind-body problem has been motivated by two distinct but closely related questions. On the one hand, philosophers have asked a *metaphysical* question: What is it that pains (or beliefs that the world is round) have in common in virtue of which they are pains (or beliefs that the world is round)? On the other hand, we have an *ontological* question (a question about what there is in the world): Are pains (or beliefs) just states of the brain? Or are they behavioral entities? Or are they non-physical altogether? Attempts to answer the ontological and metaphysical questions can be organized into four categories corresponding roughly to the doctrines of dualism, behaviorism, physicalism, and functionalism. A fifth category, eliminativism, comprises a variety of doctrines that in one way or another deny that mental states exist at all. See Rorty (1965) and Dennett (1979) for different types of eliminativism. (Before turning to an examination of these theories of mind, the reader who wants to see a more detailed overview should consult Fodor, 1982 or Dennett, 1978a.) Turn now to the module DUALISM (p. 202).

Dualism has not been a very popular theory of mind among philosophers, chiefly because it seems incompatible (in many of its forms) with the world view of modern physics. Curiously, the major adherents of dualism have been neurophysiologists (such as Sir John Eccles). The controversies in philosophy have been mainly concerned with the advantages and difficulties of various non-dualistic materialistic theories of mind. For many years, the most discussed candidate was a philosophical variety of behaviorism sometimes called "logical behaviorism." Logical behaviorism differs from the other "isms" to be discussed in being a theory of the *meaning* of mental terms. The term "pain," for example, is supposed to be analyzable in terms of behavioral tendencies, such as a tendency to scream or say "ouch" under certain circumstances. Dualism and physicalism, by contrast, are not supposed to be theories of what "pain" *means,* but rather what pain *is.* Turn now to the module BEHAVIORISM (p. 203).

As we have just seen, one of the most serious defects of behaviorism is that it did not allow mental states to be real causes and effects. Philosophers who are impressed by these defects have been attracted to physicalism and functionalism. Physicalism is an old doctrine which, in its weakest form, might be put as follows: A person is decomposable without remainder into material particles. Contemporary physicalism gives this idea a somewhat technical twist, deploying the notion of identity. First formulated by Place (1956) and Smart (1959) in the 1950s, the doctrine is that pain (for example) *is* a state of the brain. Turn now to the module REDUCTIONISM AND PHYSICALISM (p. 205).

The difficulties in behaviorism and physicalism mentioned in the last two modules have attracted philosophers to a doctrine that purports to avoid the pitfalls of behaviorism and physicalism while also capturing the insights of machine theories of mind: functionalism. In one version, functionalism just is the doctrine that the mind is to be understood as a machine. In another version, mental states are regarded as best characterized by their causal roles, their syndromes of typical causes and effects. So pain might be characterized in part by its tendency to be caused by damage to the body and in part by its tendency to cause distress and the desire for its cause to be removed.

It is important to note that functionalism is concerned in the first instance with mental state *types*, not tokens—with *pain*, for example, and not with particular *pains*. (For more on this distinction, see Boyd, 1980, and Fodor, 1974.) Most functionalists are willing to grant what is often called "token physicalism": that each particular pain is a physical event or state. But functionalism is incompatible with *type* physicalism, the doctrine that pain, for example, is a brain state type. (Note, incidentally, that type physicalism is more of a stalking horse invented by functionalists than a doctrine defended by flesh and blood philosophers.) Where functionalism differs from type physicalism is on the question of what is in *common* to all pains in virtue of which they are pains. Functionalism says the something in common is functional, while type physicalism says it is physical (behaviorism says it is behavioral, and dualism says it is ectoplasmic). Thus the disagreement between functionalism and type physicalism is *metaphysical* without being *ontological*. Functionalists can be physicalists (token physicalists, that is) in allowing that all the entities (things, states, events, and so on) that exist in the world are physical entities. Where functionalists differ with physicalists is that functionalists insist that what binds metal things together into *kinds* is not a physical property. Turn now to the module FUNCTIONALISM (p. 208).

One difficulty common to the last three "isms" discussed is their failure to accommodate the fact of consciousness. (In our opinion, dualism does no better: Dualism's apparent success with consciousness derives from the fact that dualism makes all aspects of mentality mysterious, and consciousness is one aspect of mentality which one hasn't dealt with if one doesn't make room for the fact that it is remarkably and mysteriously resistant to investigation.) Turn now to the module CONSCIOUSNESS AND QUALIA (p. 210).

PHILOSOPHY OF EMPIRICAL PSYCHOLOGY

We now leave traditional philosophy of mind, turning to issues more directly related to empirical psychology. We begin with motivation. Philosophers have discussed many issues about the springs of action. Do reasons, desires, and purposes ever cause actions? Are all actions selfish? More specifically, are all actions aimed at the agent's pleasure? If so, what is the upshot for morality? Are there different motivational systems (e.g., "higher" and "lower" desires)? Turn now to the module MOTIVATION (p. 211).

In the module on logical behaviorism, we noted that belief, desire, and pain cannot be analyzed in terms of dispositions to emit certain responses in certain stimulus situations. But *some* aspects of mind—for example, traits such as domineeringness, persistence, and cooperativeness—are analyzable roughly in this way. The distinction between mental concepts that are analyzable as behavioral dispositions and those that are not is of crucial importance to the psychology of personality. Now read the module PERSONALITY (p. 214).

We now move on to examine the foundations of cognitive science. If you want to examine the foundations of cognitive science, you are ahead if you know what cognitive science is. Philosophers have not attempted to define "cognitive science" (as might have been the approach of a previous generation). Rather, they have attempted to make explicit the presuppositions behind a line of thought and research that has generally been associated with the title. Turn now to the module THE IDEOLOGY BEHIND COGNITIVE SCIENCE (p. 218).

Now that we understand what the program of cognitive science is, we are in a position to ask whether it is likely to succeed. Dreyfus (1972) and, more recently, Haugeland (1978) and Searle (1980) have argued forcefully that the program of cognitive science is subject to grave difficulties. Now read the module IS COGNITIVE SCIENCE POSSIBLE? (p. 220).

We now turn to an examination of the key concept of cognitive science, mental representation. The reader will be in a better position to understand the issues raised about mental representation if he is aware of general issues about beliefs, desires, and other propositional attitudes. A highly readable account is to be found in the first half of Dennett (1982). According to contemporary cognitive science, our thoughts are written in our heads in a symbolic system, *mentalese*. On a crude but particularly useful version of this view, what it is to believe that water is wet is to have a sentence that expresses the proposition that water is wet literally written down in a particular area of the brain, the "belief box."

There are a number of serious puzzles associated with this idea. For one thing, the meanings of our English sentences clearly are intimately tied up with the *intentions* with which we standardly use them. For example, "There is a mosquito on your nose," would standardly be used with the intention of communicating a certain idea, and this fact is clearly closely tied to the meaning of the sentence (though of course there are differences among different theorists about which is the *primary* bearer of meaning, the intention or the sentence). But it doesn't seem obvious that we have *intentions* regarding the sentences in our heads at all, even according to the theories current in cognitive science. These sentences are the field of a set of computational procedures, not things *we use* at all,

much less use intentionally. Turn now to the module MENTAL REPRE-
SENTATION (p. 221).

We have now seen the representationalist perspective of cognitive science spelled out. A natural question is: If it is true that we have symbol
strings in our heads that have semantic properties, to what extent are
these semantic properties relevant to the investigation of the computational processes that operate on them? Do the semantic properties of
mental representations *affect* the computations? If the answer is "no," is
it nonetheless important for the theorist to *know* about the semantic properties of mental representations in order to investigate the mental representations? These issues are covered in the module METHODOLOGICAL
SOLIPSISM (p. 223).

Another natural question about mental representations is: If they have
semantic properties, what gives them these semantic properties? One
answer appeals to the causal relations between the representations and
the world. Another appeals to an idealized correspondence between representations functioning as beliefs, and states of affairs in the world.
Another answer appeals to the ways that the representations function
inside the head. Another appeals to the mental states that the representations are associated with. Turn now to the module THE SEMANTICS OF
MENTAL REPRESENTATION (p. 225).

One particular type of mental representation that has been the source of
particular controversy is the type of representation involved in mental
imagery. One school of thought, pictorialism, takes these representations
to represent in the manner of *pictures* (e.g., a picture of Reagan being
shot). The competing school of thought, descriptionalism, takes the representations of imagery to represent in the manner of *language* (e.g., as in
the sentence "Reagan was shot."). Many of the general issues about mental representations are encountered here, along with issues about just
what the pictorial/descriptional distinction really comes to, what the relation is between the representations of imagery and of perception, and to
what extent introspection can provide a source of information about internal representation. Turn now to the module CONCEPTUAL PROBLEMS
ABOUT IMAGERY (p. 226).

OTHER ISSUES IN THE PHILOSOPHY OF
PSYCHOLOGY

We have now covered the basic ideology of cognitive science, and we
have also examined in detail the most important and troublesome concept
in contemporary cognitive science, that of mental representation. This

completes the *systematic* part of our discussion of conceptual issues in empirical psychology. There are many important issues outside our current focus on *cognitive* science including some already mentioned such as issues in Freudian theory and the question of whether IQ tests measure intelligence. There are also interesting issues about the extent to which aspects of the mind really are cognitive; for example, one controversial theory of emotion holds that emotions share a common "excitational" state, and where they differ is in the subject's cognitive state. Another important issue is the relevance of psychology to epistemology (see Goldman 1978). There are far too many important conceptual issues in empirical psychology to discuss here. So what we have done is to choose a few topics as much on the basis of intrinsic interest as for the purpose of illustrating general categories of problems that play an important role in current discussion of philosophy of psychology.

Now turn to the remaining modules. They are not very closely related, so they can be covered in any order: SPLIT BRAINS AND THE UNITY OF CONSCIOUSNESS (p. 228, IQ AND INTELLIGENCE (p. 230), and THE NATIVISM—EMPIRICISM DEBATE (p. 231)

MODULES[1]

DUALISM

Dualism comes in many forms. We highlight two. "Cartesian Dualism" (incorrectly so-called, according to some Descartes scholars) is the doctrine that mental properties and physical properties are properties of two different *substances* and that these two substances causally interact with one another. Much of Descartes's argumentation is quite cogent and still convinces eminent readers. Consider, for example, his argument that the inconceivability of a mechanistic account of creative human intelligence forces us to consider extraphysical causes of; for example, human speech. (See the selections from Descartes in Rosenthal, 1971.)

One of the most powerful arguments against Cartesian dualism has been the claim that it is incompatible with modern physics. If the mind has *effects* on the body, then those effects cannot be explained by physics, and this is incompatible with a principle often alleged to be implicit in modern physics, a principle to the effect that physics can in principle

---

[1] Alston wrote the modules on MOTIVATION and PERSONALITY; Block is responsible for the rest. Curricular information on philosophy of psychology overlapping with this article is available from The Council for Philosophical Studies, San Francisco State University, 1600 Holloway Ave., San Francisco, CA 94132.

supply a causal account of any event that occurs. Sir John Eccles (Popper & Eccles, 1977) has propounded a form of dualism that is designed to avoid this difficulty. He argues that the mind affects the brain in just those instances where quantum-mechanical indeterminacies are such that no more or less deterministic explanation in terms of physics could be found. We have a *cause,* but the cause could equally well have produced an effect quite different from the one it did produce. Eccles makes heavy use of the fact that tiny neurophysiological differences can be magnified in the brain and result in large behavioral differences (a fact that he deserves much of the credit for discovering). Read Savage (1976) and Eccles's reply (1976).

Another form of dualism is "epiphenomenalism"; it differs from Cartesian dualism in disallowing effects of the mind on the material world. According to epiphenomenalism, the mind is totally passive. It is acted on by the world, but when it appears that it acts on the world (say, when your intention seems to cause you to act) what is really going on is that a brain state correlated with your intention is causing the action. (For a modern attempt to defend dualism, consult Puccetti & Dykes, 1978, and the criticisms published together in the same journal issue.)

BEHAVIORISM

There are two quite different kinds of behaviorism, "methodological behaviorism" and "logical behaviorism." Methodological behaviorism is the doctrine that mental talk is illegitimate in scientific psychology except as shorthand for behavioral talk. Logical behaviorism is the view that mental terms can be analyzed in behavioral terms. The two are related mainly in that the latter is often a reason for following the former methodological practice. Since our focus at the moment is mainly philosophical theories of the mind, we give only brief attention to methodological behaviorism.

The most eminent exponent of methodological behaviorism in recent times is B. F. Skinner (1953). Skinner's best argument is a dilemma: Either talk of mental entities is eliminable, in which case it is superfluous; or else talk of mental entities is not eliminable, in which case it is illegitimate. (Now read Skinner, 1953, pages 27–35, 62–66, and 87–90. These passages are reprinted in Block, 1980a.) Chomsky (1959) provides the classic refutation; see, too, Dennett (1979).

As mentioned above, logical behaviorism holds that mental terms are behaviorally analyzable. For example, a typical logical behaviorist view is that a mental term such as "pain" or "desire" can be analyzed in terms of a set (usually thought to be infinite or at least indefinitely large) of conditionals which specifies what response will tend to be contingent on a given stimulus (sometimes the stimulus includes a variety of contextual conditions). For example, the desire for an ice cream cone might be analyzed in part by a conditional that states that if an ice cream cone is placed in front of the face, it will tend to be grasped.

There are two quite different rationales for logical behaviorism. One derives from the logical positivist desire to rationally reconstruct the ideas of science in terms of observables. Mental terms were held by many of the logical positivists not to be observational terms, and therefore suspect. This line of thought was influenced considerably by the impressive success of Russell and Whitehead (1910–1913) in giving a rational reconstruction of talk of numbers in terms of talk of sets. Early behaviorists such as Hempel (1972—originally published in French in 1935) and Carnap (1932/1959) hoped for a similar success in replacing mental talk with behavioral talk. Many philosophers read Turing (1950) as expressing much the same view.

A somewhat different cast of mind leading to basically the same doctrine was the view of Oxford analytical philosophers that the meaning of mental terms as they are now (not as they would be in a rational reconstruction of ordinary language) can be analyzed behaviorally.

One of the difficulties opponents find with behaviorism is that it does not take mental causation seriously enough. According to behaviorism, to say that someone has a pain is just to say what he is disposed to do. Explaining screaming by appeal to causation by pain, according to Ryle (1949), is like explaining a glass breaking by appeal to its brittleness. Brittleness, on Ryle's analysis, is just the fact of breaking easily. This "fictionalism" about mental causation cannot be used against behaviorists, however, since they embrace it; they simply decide that in the realists' sense of "cause," there are no mental causes. (Alternatively, behaviorists who are realists about causation say that whatever the causes of screams are, they do not include events or states of pain.) The basic criticism of logical behaviorism, due independently to Chisholm (1957) and to Geach (1957), is that what behavioral dispositions a mental state issues in depends on the other mental states the person has. For example, if I want an ice cream cone and one is placed in front of my face, I won't grasp it if I think it is a tube of axle grease, or even if I know full well it is an ice cream cone, if I would rather not incur an obligation to return the favor. Hence, any analysis of wanting an ice cream cone must appeal to other mental states, not just inputs and outputs. The same is true for all mental states, not just wanting an ice cream cone. The Chisholm-Geach criticism of logical behaviorism leads naturally to the construction of a class of "perfect pretender" counterexamples, particularly incisive discussion of which is to be found in Putnam (1965).

The Chisholm-Geach criticism and the perfect pretender counterexamples do not work so neatly on the very general mental property of posses-

sing the ability to think and reason. This problem with the arguments against behaviorism and a way of extending the arguments are discussed in connection with the "Turing Test" in Block (1981b).

The version of behaviorism just discussed is an ideal type existing in the literature mainly in the works of the doctrine's critics (such as Chisholm, Geach, and Putnam). The value of spelling out and criticizing the stark form is that the subtle quasi-behaviorist views that are held by real people can (arguably) be felled by variants of the arguments that hold against the ideal type. To get a sense of the subtlety of actual behaviorists (and their deviation from the ideal type) read Ryle (1949) or a work by a "Wittgensteinian" such as Malcolm (1954).

REDUCTIONISM AND PHYSICALISM

The basic question of reductionism is whether social phenomena, mental phenomena, and the phenomena of life are anything over and above physico-chemical phenomena. Philosophers have produced an analysis of such questions in terms of two conditions: definability and derivability. The definability condition: Biology is *definable* in terms of physics and chemistry just in case every term of biological theory is definable in terms of physico-chemical theory. The derivability condition: Biology is *derivable* from physics and chemistry just in case every law of biology is derivable from physico-chemical laws. Hempel (1966) provides a lucid account of this sort of analysis. It should be noted that the definability-derivability analysis of reduction substitutes talk of theories for the talk in the original questions of *phenomena*. There is reason to believe that this replacement leaves out a good part of what we originally wanted to know in asking the basic questions mentioned above. A good account of these difficulties is given in Hempel (1970).

Are the special sciences (social sciences, psychology, biology, and other sciences above the level of physics and chemistry) reducible to physics and chemistry? There is an old argument to the effect that they are not. Consider money. In some societies, large stones are used for money; in others, feathers; in others, pelts. How could there be anything physico-chemical in common to all these forms of money that would distinguish them from things that are not money. It seems that almost anything could be used as money in *some* social setting. Conclusion: No *definition* of money in physico-chemical terms can be given, and so the definability condition (described above) cannot be met. Fodor (1974) supplies an exposition of this and other considerations against reduction of the special sciences; Causey (1977, pp. 142–159) supplies a critique of Fodor.

There is, however, a simple objection to the multiple realizability argument of the last paragraph. Why not treat money as a *relational* term like "weighs more than"? No one would say that "weighs more than" is not definable in physico-chemical terms just because things as disparate as feathers and stones and pelts can weigh more than one another. But money is just such a relative term. What makes something money is its relation to social practices, its role in human activity. And the fact that things as disparate as feathers, stones, and pelts can all bear that relation to something is a very poor reason to reject the definability of "money" in physico-chemical terms.

So the multiple realizability argument in its standard form may not work. However, there *is* a version of it which can avoid the objection. Consider a simple finite automaton such as the one described in Block (1978) and Block (1980). Could there be a physico-chemical description of what all and only realizations of this simple automaton have in common? The answer certainly seems to be "no"—and for exactly the same reason, there seems little hope of a physico-chemical characterization of such properties as having a certain program. If we are creatures whose mental nature is given by a program or by a machine table, then the argument just given will militate against the reduction of psychology to physics and chemistry.

Reductionism with respect to the special sciences is not so popular now as it once was, partly because of the force of multiple realizability arguments and partly because of the widespread realization that one need not believe in reductionism in order to be a materialist. (This point is spelled out in Fodor, 1974, and in Boyd, 1980.)

There has been a great deal of discussion in recent years of the "ontological" (having to do with what exists) aspect of the question of whether psychology is reducible to physics and chemistry: viz., are mental phenomena anything over and above physical phenomena? Place (1956) and Smart (1959) introduced the *identity* formulation of this thesis in the 1950s. The question in their terms becomes: Is pain (or any other mental state) *identical* with a brain state? This way of seeing the matter allows an assimilation of physicalism to other identity claims in science, such as the claim that water is H_2O and that temperature is mean molecular kinetic energy. (See Nagel, 1965, for further discussion.)

For many years, discussion of the mind-body identity claim centered on whether it could be vanquished by a very simple sort of argument based on Leibniz's Law (sometimes called the indiscernability of identicals): If $x = y$, then every property of x is a property of y. A pain can have the property of being in my arm, but no brain state has this property. Similarly, afterimages can be red and green striped, but no brain state has that property. Conversely, brain states have electrochemical properties that are not properties of any mental state. Worse, it is sometimes claimed, brain states have properties which are not exactly *false* of mental states, but which yield *nonsense* when applied to mental states. Does it make sense, for example, to speak of the location of a wish? Many physicalists have replied to such objections. Smart (1959) argued that there are no such things as afterimages; what there actually are, he said, are experiences of afterimages. These are never red or green, and it is these that are identical to brain states. Kim (1966) later applied such a move to all the Leibniz's Law difficulties. (See also Nagel, 1965, and Fodor, 1968a.)

Leibniz's Law (and also its special case, the symmetry of identity) tells us that pains are just as real as brain states. If a pain is identical to brain state B, and B is real, then the pain is real too. Some philosophers of a materialistic bent prefer to give up the identity claim in favor of what is sometimes called eliminative materialism or the disappearance theory. On this view, pains are *not* real; only brain states are. If we knew which brain states to talk about, we would be correct to talk of these brain states instead of pains, desires, wishes, and so forth. On this view, our mental talk is like talk of phlogiston, ether, and caloric in the heyday of those theories: a convenient way of talking, but one that is to be superseded, with subsequent rejection of the entities that this talk appeared to commit one to (see Rorty, 1965, and Churchland, 1981). (See also Dennett, 1978b, and other articles in Dennett, 1979.)

Supposing that distinct brain states are correlated with distinct mental states in the fashion that Smart supposes, what positive reason is there for supposing that the mental states and the brain states are *identical?* Smart argued that the identity thesis has the same scientific status as our rejection of Gosse's hypothesis that the universe was created only 5000 years ago complete with fossils, appropriate radioactivity for carbon dating, and other evidence of an age in the billions of years. According to Smart, the argument against Gosse and the argument for the identity thesis both make use of a kind of scientific simplicity principle. Kim (1966) and others have objected. According to Kim, one can *observe* the correlation between pain and brain state B, but the further claim that pain is brain state B does not have the same kind of scientific status that the correlation claim has. Kim's objection is rebutted in Block (1979). Yet another view on this matter is that championed by Lewis (1972) and by Armstrong (1977) and widely followed by Australian materialists. According to Lewis, "pain" is defined as the state with a certain causal role; brain state B may have that causal role as a matter of fact, and if so, it will follow that pain is brain state B. No appeal to simplicity is required, and since the identity claim follows from scientific and logical considerations alone, its scientific credibility is as strong as the scientific credibility of the description of the causal role, contra Kim.

Kripke (1972) showed that if "a" and "b" function in a certain sort of namelike way (if they are "rigid designators," in Kripke's terminology), then if "a = b" is true, it is necessarily true. Kripke went on to argue that "pain" and "c-fiber stimulation" (used as a sample brain state term) are rigid designators, and that there could be a pain without a corresponding c-fiber stimulation or a c-fiber stimulation without a corresponding pain. The claim that a given pain, a, is a c-fiber stimulation, b, is therefore not a necessary truth, and by Kripke's principle, it is not a truth at all. So the mind-body identity thesis is false. By contrast, Kripke argues, scientific identity claims (e.g., temperature = mean-molecular kinetic energy) are not subject to this kind of difficulty. Feldman (1980) argued that Kripke's reasoning depended on the claim that each pain is necessarily painful, i.e., that it couldn't have existed without having had a painful "feel" to it. Feldman argues that this is not an obvious truth and that Kripke owes us some reason to believe it. (See also Lycan, 1974.) McGinn (1977) objects against Kripke's use of the intuition that this very pain might have occurred without c-fiber stimulation. Says McGinn, this intuition could be construed as an intuition about a pain qualitatively like this one, but not identical to it. Indeed, as McGinn points out, this way of disarming an objection to an identity is used by Kripke himself in supporting other identity claims. Finally, Boyd (1980) argues that when one looks carefully at the intuitions that Kripke appeals to, one sees that they involve apparatus for detecting c-fiber stimulations and that one could as well to construe Kripke's intuitions as intuitions about possible worlds in which brain-scanning apparatus does not work properly.

FUNCTIONALISM

"Functionalism" is used in three distinct ways in philosophy of psychology. In the first two of the three senses to be considered, functionalism is not a theory of the nature of the mind of a sort corresponding to dualism, behaviorism, and physicalism. But these senses of the term are important, and they are closely related to functionalism as a theory of the mind, so we shall briefly examine them.

Functional analysis. In this sense of the term, functionalism is a research strategy, the strategy of looking for functional *explanations*. A functional explanation is one that relies on a decomposition of a system into its component parts; such an explanation shows how the system works by appeal to the capacities of the parts and the ways the parts are integrated with one another. For example, we can explain how a factory can produce refrigerators by appealing to the capacities of the various assembly lines, their workers, and machines, and the organization of these components (see Cummins, 1975, and Fodor, 1968b).

Computation-representation functionalism. In this sense of the term, "functionalism" applies to an important special case of functional explanation as defined above, namely to psychological explanation seen as akin to providing a computer program for the mind. Whatever mystery our mental life may initially seem to have, it is dissolved by functional analysis of mental processes to the point where they are seen to be composed of computations as mechanical as the primitive operations of a digital computer. Psychological states are seen as systematically representing the world via a language of thought akin to the "machine language" of a computer, and psychological processes are seen as computations involving those representations (see Fodor, 1968b, and Dennett, 1975a).

Metaphysical functionalism. This is the sense of the term in which "functionalism" is a theory of the nature of the mind, a competitor to dualism, behaviorism, and physicalism. Metaphysical functionalists are concerned not with how mental states account for behavior, but rather with what mental states are. The functionalist answer to "What are mental states?" is simply that mental states are functional states.

One way of defining functional states is in terms of states of a Turing machine. Putnam (1967a) supplies an exposition of this view; Block and Fodor (1972) supply a critique of it. Another way of defining functional states is via causal roles: causal relations to sensory inputs, behavioral outputs, and other mental states. For example, the causal role of pain might involve pain's tendency to be caused by tissue damage, by its tendency to cause the desire to be rid of it, and by its tendency to produce action designed to separate the damaged part of the body from what is thought to cause the damage. Via a technique adapted from the work of Ramsey and Carnap by Lewis (1972), these causal role definitions of mental state terms can be stated without use of any other mental state terms. So mental terms can be defined entirely in terms of input-output language (plus logical apparatus). This feature has attracted many who liked the eliminative feature of logical behaviorism but who were dissatisfied with behaviorism's "fictionalism" about the mental.

Another advantage of functionalism (as mentioned in the Overview) is that functionalists can be physicalists in claiming that each particular "token" pain is a physical state or event. (A token is a concrete object, while a type is the abstract property that knits a category of tokens together; the following inky blob, "together," contains two tokens of the type "t".) Where functionalists and physicalists (that is, *type* physicalists, those who think that the *type* pain can be identified with a physical type) disagree is with regard to the question of what is in common to pains in virtue of which they are pains. Discussions of what functionalism is can be found in Block (1980b) and in Shoemaker (1981a).

The main weakness of functionalism is easy to see. Functionalism identifies mental states with abstract causal structures. The trouble is that it seems so clearly conceivable that something could have such an abstract causal structure, yet not have the corresponding mental state. This point seems especially persuasive if one considers *qualitative* mental states such as pain, and if one considers systems such as whole countries that have the causal organization that functionalists attribute to us. This sort of critique is elaborated in Block (1978) and criticized in Lycan (1980) and Churchland and Churchland (1981).

CONSCIOUSNESS AND QUALIA

Three quite different categories of phenomena are invoked by the term "consciousness." In one sense of the term, conscious information or belief contrasts with unconscious information or belief. The distinction has something to do with *access*. Unconscious beliefs can influence one's actions, but they are not available for reasoning to the same degree; they are not inferentially promiscuous, in Stich's terminology. In another sense of the term, to be conscious is to be aware of oneself, to be able to reflect on one's own mental activities. In a final sense of the term, your consciousness has to do with "what it's like" to be you. Consciousness in this sense is denoted by technical terms such as "qualitative content," "qualia," "immediate phenomenological quality," "raw feel," and the like. Thus far, this module has attempted to explain the third sense of consciousness using technical terms (suggestive ones, but still only technical terms). Another approach is to invoke the familiar inverted spectrum hypothesis: Perhaps the way things we both call green look to you is the same as the way things we both call red look to me. If so, the sensation you get from green things has the same *qualitative content* as the sensation I get from red things (see Shoemaker, 1982).

One focus of discussion about consciousness in this third sense has been its relevance to the various theories of the mind that we have been discussing. Nagel (1974) argues that consciousness poses serious problems for any "objective" theory of the mind. Much of the discussion about consciousness has been directed towards its relevance to functionalism. Shoemaker (1975) modifies functionalism so as to allow the possibility of inverted spectra. Block (1978) argues that the possibility of what might be called an "absent spectrum" defeats functionalism. (Other articles in the debate are Block, 1980, Lycan, 1980, and Shoemaker, 1981a.)

One approach to consciousness in the third sense is to deny its existence. According to Dennett, consciousness in this sense is something like a myth. Dennett's view of consciousness is like Hume's view of causation. According to Dennett, the typically cited features of consciousness in this sense are the result of illusions that people create and fall for (Dennett 1978c, 1978b, in press-a, in press-b).

MOTIVATION

Motivation comprises processes that lead to behavior. Thus the study of motivation is the study of the determinants of, or influences on, behavior. Since the reconception of psychology as the "science of behavior" in the early decades of the twentieth century, this problem has been at the center of psychology's self-conception. To be sure, the proportion of research time devoted specifically to motivation has not matched this official concern; but one need only think of the mid-century motivational models of Hull (1943), Tolman (1932), and Skinner (1938), together with all the research devoted to applying, supporting, or attacking them, to realize that the study of motivation has been a significant part of twentieth-century psychology. More recently, problems of specifically human motivation have received considerable attention, both within social psychology and elsewhere (e.g., Atkinson & Birch, 1970; Atkinson & Feather, 1966; Harré & Seacord, 1972).

Philosophers have been concerned with motivation since the beginnings of philosophical thought. To be sure, one must exercise caution in reading current disciplinary divisions into pre-nineteenth century thought; the thought of Plato, Aristotle, Descartes, Locke, Spinoza, et al. on motivation might with equal justice be reckoned to the history of psychology. But by taking problems that are currently recognized as philosophical we can see how concern with these problems has led, and continues to lead, philosophers into the study of motivation.

We all have a strong inclination to think of ourselves as, in some sense, autonomous authors of our actions, as opposed to merely being conduits of causation. This view is deeply rooted in our sense of what we are doing when we act, and in our sense that we are morally responsible for our actions. But how can this be squared with the modern scientific view that everything that happens, including human actions, is uniquely determined by its causal antecedents: In grappling with this issue philosophers have been forced to consider how human actions might possibly be causally determined—by what kinds of factors and by what kinds of processes involving those factors. In seeking to preserve the possibility of free will, some have cut the Gordian knot by maintaining that the relation of reasons, purposes, desires, intentions, etc., to actions is not a *causal* relationship, so that insofar as an agent does what he does because of what he wants or intends, or because of his reasons for doing it, the "because" is not a causal "because"; and so the possibility of his action being causally

determined does not arise (Kenny, 1963; Melden, 1961; Peters, 1958).
Purely habitual actions or those done in a blind rage may be causally
determined, but not deliberate actions done for a reason. Theorists of this
stripe have various suggestions as to how an intention (or whatever) is
related to an action, if not causally. The most popular alternative is that
the specification of the intention or reason "rationalizes" the action,
makes it intelligible that the agent should do it, rather than specifying
what causally produced it. Contra-causal theorists typically acknowledge
that bodily movements are causally determined physiologically, but they
insist on a distinction between, for example, the fact that Jones signed a
check and the fact that Jones moved his hand in a certain physically
describable manner (see Brand, 1970; Care & Landesman, 1968). Other
philosophers have vigorously criticized this contra-causal position and
have maintained that the relation of intentions and desires to actions can
only be understood causally. Such thinkers have made a contribution to
the development of a model of motivation that emphasizes the wants and
beliefs of the agents as crucial determinants of action, thus making contact with psychologists who have been elaborating such models (e.g.,
Brandt & Kim, 1963; Davidson, 1963; Goldman, 1970). Still others take
the position that though intentions, desires, and other "psychological"
factors are causal influences on action, when a person acts freely the
action is caused not by some psychological process or state of the agent,
but by the agent herself (e.g., Chisholm, 1964, 1969; Taylor, 1963, 1966).
In taking this position they are hearkening back to an older, Aristotelian
conception of causality, according to which a cause is always some substance exercising its powers; their claim is that free, responsible human
action cannot be understood on the more modern conception of "event
causality" and that, even if the Aristotelian conception is outmoded in
physics, it is indispensable for the understanding of human behavior.

Consider conscience, a sense of right and wrong, the recognition that
one ought or ought not to do something, the recognition that a proposed
action falls under a moral principle that enjoins or forbids it. Can such
factors have any effective role in the motivation of behavior? Is it ever
true that someone does something because it is the right thing to do? Or is
this always a rationalization of subterranean emotional or appetitive
forces that really determine what is done? This issue is paradigmatically
represented by the opposition between Hume, who held that "reason is
and ought to be the slave of the passions," and Kant, who held that
"respect for the moral law" is a powerful motivating force. In thinking
about this issue one is forced to become more explicit about the nature of
conscience, the sense of right and wrong, or "respect for the moral law,"
and the relation of such factors to various sorts of wants, desires, and
attitudes. Is a tendency to obey the moral law simply another desire,
differing from the desire for food only in its object, or is it a different kind

of psychological factor that operates according to different dynamics? Is conscience a fairly sharply differentiated motivational system, as Freudians and others suppose?

Moral philosophers have sometimes sought to support fundamental moral principles by appeal to the psychology of motivation. This usually takes the form of arguing that a certain kind of goal has to be recognized as supremely good or worthwhile, just because it is the only ultimate goal for human action. Perhaps the most famous example of this line of argument is Mill's (1863) attempt to ground ethical hedonism on psychological hedonism. That is, Mill argued that no one, in the end, desires anything but pleasure, that anything one desires other than pleasure is desired for the sake of pleasure one supposed it to contain or to lead to. He inferred from this that we all recognize, in practice, that pleasure is the only thing that is good for its own sake. Mill's contention unleashed torrents of philosophical argumentation that is still continuing and that makes obvious contact with hedonistic psychological theories of motivation.

A phenomenon that poses special problems for theories of motivation is what we may call "self-intervention," a deliberate attempt by an agent to get himself to do (refrain from doing) something he would not do (would do) apart from that intervention. Thus I may try to get myself to write a letter I am reluctant to write, or try to get myself to refrain from watching a tennis match on television so that I can finish some work. The reason this phenomenon poses special problems is the following. Let us suppose that at the point of intervention my dominant tendency was to watch the tennis match. In these cases we often suppose that, but for the intervention, we would do (or refrain from doing) what it is we are intervening to get ourselves not to do (to do). And presumably we are sometimes correct about this. But the intervention is undertaken because of a dominant tendency to refrain from watching the match. Hence at the same time we have both a dominant tendency to watch the match and a dominant tendency to refrain from doing so. In order to avoid contradiction, we have to distinguish different motivational systems, systems which are related hierarchically. The system involved in self-intervention is a system for motivating actions that are directed to the other, "lower-level" system. The history of philosophy is full of attempts to make such distinctions. One thinks of Plato's tripartite division of the soul into rational, appetitive, and "spirited" elements. Innumerable philosophers have distinguished the will from the appetites and/or passions, allotting what we have been calling "self-intervention" to the will. Freudian psychology is a more modern example of a tripartition of motivational systems, a scheme that is designed to handle this problem among others. Several analytical philosophers have recently taken up the gauntlet, distinguishing "higher-level" and "lower-level" systems, desires, and so on (e.g., Alston, 1977; Frankfurt, 1971). Most recent psychology that is concerned with self-intervention in one or another guise, "resistance to temptation," "self-control," or "delay of gratification," has not really come to terms with the need for distinguishing and interrelating different motivational systems (e.g., Aaronfreed, 1968; Bandura & Walters, 1963; Mischel, 1966, 1973).

All this strongly suggests both that philosophers and psychologists have overlapping concerns in the area of motivation and that they can be mutually helpful to each other. As for the latter point, practitioners of the two disciplines are trained to be sensitive to different aspects of the subject matter. Psychologists are professionally committed to keeping in mind the biological roots of human motivation, the continuity with motivation in the lower animals, and the need for objective empirical tests of speculative hypotheses. Philosophers are preoccupied with understanding the human person as a moral agent; they feel free to think about aspects of motivation, such as the phenomenon of self-intervention or the possibility of doing one's duty for its own sake, that are not currently amenable to experimental investigation; and they are accustomed to trying to see the "big picture."

PERSONALITY

Personality is the organization of the relatively stable characteristics of the person with respect to which she differs from (many) other persons and which influence the person's behavior. As so construed, the psychology of personality is the most difficult branch of psychology, largely because it is ideally the integration of all of psychology into a single study. If we think of the psychology of (human) perception, memory, learning, etc., as the study of psychological functions that are common to all normal human beings, then all of that is presupposed by the personologist in his study of the ways in which one person's tendencies with respect to those and other functions differ from the tendencies of other persons. But fortunately, personology has not always aimed so high, or it may not have gotten off the ground at all. The particular characteristics featured by one or another theorist of personality have generally been determined by factors that must appear accidental in the light of the big picture just adumbrated. Such concerns as the needs of personnel selection, the availability of measuring instruments, the requirements of therapy, and the interest in occupational efficiency have to a large extent dictated the aspects of personality that have been selected for study. As a result, different theorists have organized the field in radically different ways among which there are no obvious manuals of translation. Freudians think in terms of defense mechanisms, strengths of libido investments, etc.; Murray in terms of needs; Cattell in terms of various sorts of factors; many thinkers stress the traits putatively measured by questionnaires, projective tests, and so on. From a theoretical perspective the field presents an undeniably chaotic appearance (see Hall & Lindzey, 1957; Maddi, 1972).

Philosophy has infrequently been concerned with personality in just the way this is thought of in psychology. Nevertheless, philosophers have thought a lot about various psychological factors that are prime candidates for components of personality. Moral philosophy has long been concerned with understanding virtues, vices, and other habits of behavior. The module on MOTIVATION should have made it clear that philosophy has been much concerned with desires, interests, likes, preferences, purposes, needs, and other such prominent components of motivation. Moral philosophers have had a standing interest in what it is for a person to "accept" or "be committed to" a moral principle and what it is for a person to internalize a value or a standard. With the twentieth century development of "emotivism" in ethics, the view that moral judgments are simply expressions of emotions and/or attitudes, philosophers have perforce paid greater attention to these matters. In particular, the nature of attitudes and their relation to belief, judgment, emotion, and behavior has recently become a topic of concern (e.g., Alston, 1968; Audi, 1972). Philosophical concern with dispositions and dispositional concepts in general has spilled over into a concern with personality traits, moral and otherwise (see Alston, 1970; Brandt, 1970).

These considerations suggest the possibility of fruitful cooperation between the psychologist and the philosopher in the area of personality. The psychologist, of course, has the empirical data, the command of measuring instruments, and the concrete concerns of application. The philosopher, for her part, possesses a surer grasp of conceptual structure and conceptual distinctions and a better sense of the structure and evaluation of theories. The philosopher who is willing to acquaint himself with the relevant psychological material and who is possessed of the requisite philosophical skills can perform a valuable service by way of straightening out the conceptual kinks psychologists sometimes develop and by way of setting out and interrelating conceptual alternatives for personality theory. Consider, for example, an important distinction between types of personality characteristics (see Alston, 1970, 1975).

One side of the distinction is represented by a definition many personologists take to be applicable to all personality characteristics.

A trait is a tendency to react in a defined way in response to a defined class of stimuli [Cronbach, 1960, p. 449].

Making some terminological changes, we may say that a concept that conforms to this definition is a concept of a *disposition to emit responses of a certain category (R), when in a situation that belongs to a certain category (S).* We may call such dispositions "T"s (for "traits"). Some familiar T-concepts, each with its distinctive S- and R-categories are the following.

Domineeringness—(R) takes advantage of (S) opportunities to control the behavior of others.

Persistence—(R) continues an activity (S) in the face of difficulties.

Cooperativeness—(R) complies with (S) requests.

However, many concepts employed in personality description do not conform to the T-model; these include desires, needs, interests, attitudes, and abilities. Call these characteristics "PC-concepts," for reasons to be brought out shortly.

The most obvious deviation of PCs from the T-model has to do with determinants of strength. T-strength is a function of the frequency with which the person emits Rs of the appropriate category in a wide spread of Ss of the appropriate category.[2] It could not be correct to call a person *very* domineering unless, given a large number of opportunities, he actually made many attempts to control the activities of others. But PC strength does not necessarily vary with the frequency of typical manifestations. If a person has a strong need, or desire, to dominate others, we would expect him to:

(1) seek to control the behavior of others;

(2) feel elated when he succeeds in doing so; and

(3) frequently think of dominance-related matters.

Nevertheless one can have a strong desire for dominance without frequently emitting such Rs. One's tendencies to control others may be inhibited by fear of rejection. Thoughts of dominance may be excluded from consciousness if it would be too painful to entertain them. And so on. And all this is compatible with having a strong need or desire for dominance.

How, then, are desires, needs, and the like to be conceived? In one view they spring from a familiar model of motivation, what we may call the "purposive-cognitive (PC) model".[3] In stark outline, this model features three basic types of psychological determinants of action: *desires,* which mark out certain states of affairs as goals; *beliefs,* which select certain lines of action as ways of reaching these goals; and *abilities,* which determine the response repertoire from which the desire-belief combinations make their selections. Typically more than one desire is activated at

---

[2] For simplicity of exposition we ignore variables other than the number of Rs (e.g., the strength of each R) that would have to be included in an adequate account.

[3] For elaborations of this model by psychologists, see Tolman (1954), Edwards and Tversky (1967), and Atkinson and Birch (1970). For elaborations by philosophers, see Goldman (1970) and Brandt (1979).

a given moment, and for any given goal typically more than one means is envisaged. Hence there is often conflict as to which of several lines of action is to be pursued at a given moment. These facts require the insertion of a "field" of "tendencies" between the activated desires and beliefs on the one hand, and the actual responses on the other. Where there is competition we may think of each belief-desire pair as giving rise to a *tendency* to a certain response, which will issue in that response unless inhibited by a stronger contrary tendency. Thus, out of the interaction within a field of tendencies some response finally emerges.

If we think of a PC, like a desire, as what plays a certain role in motivational processes, as depicted by the PC model, we can see why it is possible to have, for example, a strong desire without frequent manifestations. Whether the tendencies to which a desire is a disposition are actually carried out depends not only on its strength but also on the competition those tendencies encounter in the current psychological field. A strong desire will necessarily give rise to strong tendencies, but those tendencies may still be inhibited if confronted with even stronger contrary tendencies. That is why the strength of a PC, unlike the strength of a T, is not a simple function of frequency of response.

Now consider briefly some implications of this distinction for the psychology of personality. First, consider the validation of measures. A distinction is often made between validation against a "criterion" and "construct validation." Partisans of one or the other take it that their chosen type is equally appropriate for all personality characteristics. However, our distinction is crucial here; criterion validation is possible for Ts but not for PCs. Since a given T is conceived in terms of a particular S-R frequency, there is a uniquely direct and decisive way of measuring the degree of T-possession. Observe the subject in a wide spread of Ss and note the proportion of Rs. We can't mean what we do by "cooperativeness" and still doubt that a person who has acceded frequently over a wide spread of requests is a very cooperative person. With PCs, on the other hand, it is a different story. We have seen that a desire or a need can be very strong without spawning frequent manifestations. Hence, frequency of manifestations is not an adequate measure of strength. Here construct validation is the only possibility.

Second, consider the use of personality characteristics in general hypotheses. More specifically, consider the influence of such characteristics on behavior. Here the basic difference of Ts and PCs is this: Each T is, by its conceptual structure, fitted to be used in isolation for the prediction of a restricted range of Rs, while a given PC, by its conceptual structure, is fitted rather to enter with other variables into an indefinitely large number of combinations that can be used to predict and explain Rs of many different sorts.

In attributing a high degree of some T (e.g., aggressiveness) to a person,

P, we are commiting ourselves to P's emitting a large number of aggressive responses in a wide spread of opportunities. Therefore that attribution, just by virtue of its content, puts us in a position to predict such Rs. Just by virtue of what is meant by "aggressiveness" we are justified in supposing that a very aggressive person will be likely to take vigorous steps to defend himself if charged with a criminal violation, will protest vigorously if someone tries to get ahead of him a queue, and so on. PC-concepts, on the contrary, carry no such predictive power in isolation. If all we know about a person is that he has a very strong desire for recognition, that will not, by itself, give us a strong basis for predicting that he will frequently seek recognition. We have to consider what other strong needs, aversions, or fears he has (e.g., a strong fear of failure) and whether the desire for recognition might be overborne by some of those. By way of compensation, however, a PC-concept is fitted to enter with other factors into a wide variety of explanations of a wide variety of Rs. We conceptualize a desire, for example, as a state that combines with beliefs in a certain way to produce action tendencies, combines with beliefs in another way to produce affective reaction tendencies, and so on. Since a PC is embedded in this kind of systematic matrix, it contains, so to say, plugs and sockets for making connections with other factors for the complex determination of an indefinitely wide range of responses. Knowledge that P has a strong need for recognition gives us innumerable leads as to how further features can combine with this to produce a wide variety of responses. When this need is activated and combined with the belief that the most likely route to recognition is publishing carefully worked papers in his field, P will develop a strong tendency to try to do so; combined with another belief, that recognition is best secured by making himself agreeable to powerful individuals, a strong tendency to that will be engendered. Whether such tendencies will actually be carried out depends on their competition; and so the model directs us to look for possible competitors (e.g., a fear of having papers rejected) and to make an estimate of their strength. There is virtually no kind of R that might not be explained by this need in combination with various factors. Thus the very thing that prevents a PC from being useful in isolation is the source of its unlimited potential for entering into systematic explanations.

THE IDEOLOGY BEHIND COGNITIVE SCIENCE

Cognitive science has two basic presuppositions. The first is that our mental states have content in virtue of a system—or perhaps a number of systems—of neurological structures, at least some of which have syntax and semantics roughly akin to those of familiar natural and artificial languages. Computers use on-off states of binary elements to do this, but no one has any idea how it is done in the brain. However the brain does it, there is a finite alphabet of elementary structures. Complex structures— "words" and "sentences"—are built up out of elementary structures. The word and sentence structures have meaning, and the meanings of sentences are determined by the meanings of words plus syntax. Cognitive science is committed to these descriptional internal representations, but it is not committed to the absence of nonlinguistic, pictorial representations. (A good introductory account of this matter is to be found in Hills, 1980. This topic is covered in detail in a later module MENTAL REPRESENTATION.)

The second presupposition of cognitive science is that there is a system of levels of neural processors that operate on the representations. Furthermore, these processors operate only on their physical properties. Thus, though the structures have meaning, the processors can take account of meaning only to the extent that it is reflected in the physical properties. Some processors may search lists of representations; others may compare representations, checking for matching; others may transform representations in various ways. The processors are sometimes described as "black boxes," sometimes more imaginatively as "homunculi." The task of cognitive science is seen as one of modeling human thought by constructing networks of homunculi that examine and change representations and send messages to one another. Each homunculus is decomposed into further networks until the whole system is grounded in processors whose operation is to be explained neurophysiologically rather than in terms of operations on representations.

The ultimate aim is to "discharge" the homunculi, in Dennett's (1975a) apt phrase. The first step is to give an account of an homunculus in terms of another network of homunculi and *their* representations, if this can be done. But in the end, discharging depends on finding homunculi that cannot be explained in this way, but only in a different way— nomologically—that is, in terms of laws of nature or their consequences.

The bottom level processors, the ones whose operation can only be explained nomologically, can be called *primitive* processors. For example, a cognitive science theory of, say, language understanding may take the form of a flow chart which contains a box labeled "Decide if input is a word." This processor can send a "yes" to another box (or rather to the processor symbolized by the box) or a "no" to still another box. But determining whether a given form is a word is a poor candidate for a primitive processor. So a deeper level theory is called for in which the "Decide if input is a word" box is replaced by a network of other boxes with their own representations. One of the lower level processors might contain a dictionary from which it fetches words one at a time; another processor might check whether a fetched word matches the target form;

and so on. The discharging of homunculi is done when all the postulated processors can be reduced to processors whose only explanation is in physiology, and which cannot be explained by further decomposition.

The decompositional picture was first sketched in Fodor (1968a) and later by Dennett (1975b). This picture is placed in a wider context of functional explanation by Cummins (1975). These readings do not touch on the representationalist presupposition. For a complete picture, including representationalism, see Pylyshyn (1980) and Haugeland (1978). Note that Haugeland assumes that cognitive science representations must be descriptional rather than pictorial. Thus, what he describes is really a descriptionalist school *within* cognitive science (one that is more representative of artificial intelligence than cognitive psychology) rather than cognitive science proper.

IS COGNITIVE SCIENCE POSSIBLE?

There has been a great deal of controversy in the literature about whether the program of cognitive science is based on a mistake. The main objectors to cognitive science have been philosophers influenced by the continental tradition in philosophy: Dreyfus (1972), Haugeland (1978), and Searle (1980). All three share the fundamental view that it is questionable whether there is a coherent level of explanation of behavior between the ordinary common sense level and the physiological level. Information processing psychology, artificial intelligence, and other cognitive science approaches attempt to occupy such an "intermediate" level, and so, according to the critics, they are misguided.

A good place to start is with the "Potentially Serious Hurdles" section of Haugeland (1978). Here Haugeland finds difficulties for cognitive science in phenomena involving moods, skills, and insight or understanding. The best critique is Rey (1978). A somewhat different tack is to be found in Dreyfus and Haugeland (1974). There, they argue on the basis of physiological evidence that the brain is very likely an *analog* system, and since cognitive science assumes digital models, cognitive science is mistaken. (See also Dreyfus, 1972.)

Quite a different tack is taken in Searle (1980). Searle relies on a rather compelling example: He imagines a monolingual speaker of Chinese who implements a program for understanding English. The idea is that whatever program he implements (by following rules in Chinese) *he* will not thereby understand English, and neither will the system that consists of him *plus* his rule books and input and output devices. The critics have tended to focus on the very last conjunction, the idea that even if the Chinese speaker does not understand English, nonetheless the system of which he is a part *does*. (This is what Searle calls the "systems" reply in his original article.)

MENTAL REPRESENTATION

The crude idea behind the mental representation hypothesis is that all of our propositional attitude states involve sentences in our heads. For example, we believe that grass is green just in case we have a sentence that says that grass is green in a part of our brain that we might call the "belief box." This is certainly crude, but how do we go about being more sophisticated? Fodor's (1975b) formulation is: We believe that grass is green just in case we bear a certain relation to a formula that expresses the proposition that grass is green. Now "formula" differs from "sentence" in this context only in being more vague. What about the "certain relation"? Well, the only example Fodor gives of the sort of relation he has in mind is when he says that remembering that p is *storing* a formula that expresses p. In this case, he says, we actually know the relation, but in other cases (such as believing) we will have to wait for cognitive science to tell us the relation. However, storing can't be quite right for Fodor's purpose (since, for example, one could store something but not remember its message, because one had no access to what one had stored). But the present point is mainly that the sophisticated account differs from the crude one in containing a promissory note to be filled in by future science.

Functionalism and mental representation. Many authors, including Stalnaker (1976), for example, suppose that functionalism and the view that thoughts are sentences in the head are competitors. The idea seems to be that if we had an account of a creature's beliefs or thoughts in terms of functional states, we would no longer have any motivation to hypothesize internal sentences. Field (1978) argues that this is a mistake. Functionalism identifies the belief that grass is green with a certain causal role. It says that what it is to have the belief that grass is green is to have a state with that causal role. This gives us an account of what it would be for *any* creature to have that belief. But what if we also want an account of what occupies this causal role in us? This is where the internal sentence story enters in. It is not meant as a *universal* account, but as only an account of what belief is in *us*. As Field argues convincingly, the two types of accounts, functional and representational, fit together nicely. The representational account gives us the realizations of the functional account, that is the things (internal sentences) that play the functional roles the functionalist talks about.

Arguments for mental representation. The main argument for the mental representation hypothesis is that, as Fodor says, it's the only president we've got. We seem to have the ability to produce distinct thoughts limited only by constraints such as mortality and our finite memories. The only hypothesis that anyone has ever come up with about how finite beings could produce such a range of thoughts is that their thoughts are expressed in a combinatorial system with a finite base. Another point in favor of this hypothesis appeals to the computer metaphor. To the extent that computers can have thought-like states, it is via an internal representational system. If the computer metaphor is the right track for congitive science, then so is the internal sentence story.

Advocates of internal representation also claim that there is real empirical support for the view. Work done assuming internal representation yields results about the format of the representations. A paradigm that yields coherent results gives us reason to believe in presuppositions. (This applies to Skinnerian behaviorism's *real* presuppositions too; see the later chapters of Fodor, 1975b.) Some good examples are to be found in the psycholinguistics literature: For example, Fromkin's (1971) and Garrett's (1982) studies have yielded many types of speech errors which can be explained rather neatly by supposing that we represent sentences at levels corresponding to the levels linguists have postulated for independent reasons. An example: A person who meant to say "Rosa always dated shrinks" said instead "Rosa always date shranks." Fromkin's explanation: The "past element" that was attached to "date" somehow became attached to "shrinks." Since "shrink" is also a verb, this resulted in the normal tense change in the verb.

Doubts about mental representation. One doubt about mental representation was expressed by Nagel (1969). He argued that nothing should be regarded as mental unless it is accessible to consciousness "from the inside." (This would allow Freudian unconscious beliefs to be mental since one can recover them through psychoanalysis.) On this criterion, the unconscious representations and reasoning processes of cognitive psychology would not be mental. But this is really a terminological matter. We could satisfy this objection at no real cost by using "internal representation" instead of "mental representation" (and indeed this is common enough terminology).

A number of criticisms of the internal sentence story are made by Dennett (1975a, 1979). One of Dennett's points is that we have too many beliefs for them all to be in our heads. For example, we all have the belief that zebras don't wear underpants in the wild, and many other "negative" beliefs of this sort. One representationalist reply is that we don't actually have the zebra belief until we think such thoughts (which we only do rarely, on occasions such as reading this paragraph). Another line of reply is suggested by Dennett himself: Reconstruct the ordinary notion of belief in terms of the scientific representationalist notion by defining the things we believe as those that are explicitly represented—core beliefs—plus those that follow from the core beliefs in some simple way.

Here is another problem raised by Dennett. Suppose a future neurosurgon inserts in your head the mentalese sentence that says "I have a brother in Cleveland." That doesn't *give* you the belief that you have a brother in Cleveland, since if asked questions such as "What's his name?" your story starts to crumble. One representationalist reply here is that the "relation" one must be in to a sentence in order for it to be believed is not so simple as "being in the belief box," but rather requires a degree of connection to other sentences to which one is in this relation as well.

Another line of representationalist reply would be based on the claim that belief is a natural kind. If belief is a natural kind, then we should expect the possibility of genuine beliefs that do not fit the standard "criteria," just as we expect the possibility of lemons that are not yellow or that are as big as a grapefruit.

Another quite common objection to internal representation is the one mentioned in the Overview, viz. that what gives a representation its meaning is our intentions towards it, and we have *no* intentions towards our internal representations, indeed we don't even know about them until cognitive scientists tell us. The representationalist has no easy reply to this sort of objection. All he can do is to produce a theory of the semantics of mental representations which allows us to see how they can have a semantics even though we have no intentions towards them. This matter is discussed further in the module THE SEMANTICS OF MENTAL REPRESENTATION.

METHODOLOGICAL SOLIPSISM

Fodor (1980) argues that no two representations can differ in their semantic properties unless they also differ in "form" or "shape." In other words, there can't be ambiguity in the language of thought. For if two words in the language of thought could differ in form while having the same semantic properties, then they would be ambiguous.

This doctrine has two motivations. First, one of the roles of the language of thought is to be the *language of disambiguation* of external language. The idea is that whenever what one *says* is ambiguous, this is because one's thought is expressed in ambiguous language, not because one has an ambiguous thought, for how could there be such a thing? When one hears an ambiguous sentence, one knows it is ambiguous precisely because one "finds" alternative translations into the language of thought. The second motivation is mechanism. If the processors that operate on symbols in the head could react to semantic properties "directly," we would have a first class mystery on our hands. Mechanism requires that to the extent that computations take account of the semantic properties of the representations that they compute over, they do so only by operating on the *forms* of the representations. So if internal processors are to have access to semantic properties of representations, this can only be because these semantic properties are *reflected* in the forms themselves. If there were any semantic properties *not* reflected in the forms, they would make no difference to the internal processing and thus would be irrelevant to thought.

Critics object to both of these arguments. With regard to the first line of argument, one might reasonably wonder *why* a thought cannot be ambiguous. Before the child learns the difference among weight, volume, and mass, he uses the term "more" as ambiguous between more weight, more volume, and more mass. We see his ambiguity with respect to a more articulated terminology all right, but the more articulated terminology is not one that he possesses.

With regard to the second point, the critics argue that mechanism requires only that processors react to *physical* properties of representations, not that they react only to form. Suppose, for example, that a language-understanding machine stores information about rivers in one place and information about financial matters in another. In a conversation which it determines to be about financial matters, it activates the local financial interpretations of ambiguous words such as "bank." However, if it had antecedently determined that the conversation was about rivers, it would have activated a different area and hence a different reading of "bank." So one and the same representation, "bank," can mean two things in two different contexts. There is no violation of mechanism here, since what the machine does is determined by a physical property of a representation, its location.

There is an important larger question raised by Fodor. In doing cognitive science, need the researcher attend to anything outside the head of the person whose cognitive machinery is under investigation? In terms of Putnam's twin earth example (described by Fodor), is there any difference between doing cognitive science on earth and on twin earth. Putnam (1983) argues cogently that solipsistic psychology is misconceived. He argues that cognitive science as it is now conceived requires a notion of sameness of content and that any such notion requires appeal to the real referents of terms in the world. (See also Burge, 1979.)

THE SEMANTICS OF MENTAL REPRESENTATION

The cognitivist perspective assumes that we have symbol strings in our heads that are manipulated by processors—processors that attend only to the "shapes" (or other physical properties) of the symbol strings. To the extent that the semantic properties of the internal representations have any *influence* on computation, it is because they are reflected in the "shapes" of the representations. But *do* the internal representations have semantic properties at all? Stich (1980, 1983) and Rey (1980) argue that since all the generalizations of cognitive science can be stated in terms of *shapes* of the representations, there is no need for cognitive science to recognize *semantic* properties of the representations. The counterargument (see Fodor, 1978) is that some generalizations *do* require reference to semantic properties. For example, if I have an experience that I take to be of a pink elephant, then I typically come to believe that there is at least one pink elephant. This generalization appeals to semantic contents. Stich (1983) replies that the corresponding "shape" generalization can capture the same facts while also indicating the cases in which the semantic generalization fails, and why.

Among theorists who ascribe semantic properties to internal representations, there are two quite different schools of thought about where these semantic properties come from. One school of thought holds that representations get their semantic contents from mental states. Grice (1975) long ago advocated the view that the semantic content of natural language derives from the *intentions* (intentions being mental states) with which the language is used, and Shiffer (1981) and Loar (1981) see the meaning of internal language as deriving from mental states.

Another school of thought sees things the other way around: The semantic properties of internal representations are basic, and the content of mental states derives from this more basic kind of content. The mental state of believing that some elephants are pink gets its content from an internal symbol structure that *means* that elephants are pink. But how is it that the internal symbol structure has this meaning? Three types of view have been advocated.

Conceptual role semantics. In its crudest version, this view amounts to the familiar logical positivist idea that the meaning of a sentence is given by its method of verification. This view is still often championed today in artificial intelligence circles under the banner "Procedural Semantics." A much more sophisticated version has been advocated by Harman (1975, 1982) and by Field (1977, 1978), though Field, as a proponent of the two-factor theory described below, takes conceptual role to determine only part of meaning. Harman identifies the meaning of a symbol structure with its patterns of use in reasoning, thought, and interaction with the world.

Referential semantics. This view takes the relation between internal symbols and the world as primary. Following the famous causal theory of reference, the semantic properties of the mentalese word corresponding to "tiger" are held to derive from its causal connection to tigers. Devitt (1981) attempts to include the insight of the conceptual role perspective in a causal account by regarding the conceptual role of the mentalese word for tiger as part of its causal relation to tigers.

Two-factor theory. This view combines elements of the previous two views. It says that there is an *internal* determinant of meaning of internal symbols, namely their internal conceptual role, and an *external* referential determinant as well. The internal conceptual role includes the use of internal terms in reasoning, etc., but not their use in contact with the world as in Harman's view. The external referential determinant includes (in some versions) the causal relation to the world, but not the internal causal role as on Devitt's view. The two-factor view is described (though not with special attention to internal language) in McGinn (1982); also consult Field (1977).

Recent writing by Fodor (in press), Dretske (1980), and Stampe (1979) developed a rather different version of the second (referential) factor. On Fodor's version, the view is that the referential component can be characterized by a certain idealized correspondence—a correspondence between mentalese sentences in the "belief box" and states of affairs in the world. The state of affairs in the world that makes a mentalese sentence true is the one that obtains just in case the sentence is in the "belief box" under certain highly idealized conditions which Fodor attempts to spell out. This formulation characterizes truth in terms of a relation between internal sentence and the world; a corresponding definition purports to characterize reference via a similar relation between words and things. What is crucial in both cases is that truth and reference are characterized in non-semantic terms.

CONCEPTUAL PROBLEMS ABOUT IMAGERY

Recent experimental work on mental imagery has raised a number of fascinating conceptual issues in rather new forms. A good short introduction is to be found in Brown and Herrnstein (in Block, 1981a). Much more detailed accounts are to be found in Shepard and Cooper (1982) and Kosslyn (1980).

The pictorialism-descriptionalism debate. This debate is about whether mental images represent in the manner of pictures (as, e.g., the sentence "Reagan was shot."). Much of the controversy about imagery has been generated by this issue: See Fodor (1975a), Kosslyn, Pinker, Schwartz, and Smith (1979), Pylyshyn (1980, 1981), Kosslyn (1981), Anderson (1978), and Block (1983).

The "no see 'em" argument. One argument against mental images being pictorial is that if you look inside people's heads you do not see any pictures. But this argument would equally well count against descriptionalism, since if you look inside people's heads, you do not see sentences either. Of course, one would not expect to see sentences, since one knows that in order to see a sentence one has to know the code. The spy arranges a 500 word message in his hair to be read by his contact with the KGB, his barber. But *you* do not see the message, even when you look at his hair. What holds for descriptional representation also holds for pictorial representation. You cannot recognize either type of representation just by looking. You have to know the system of representation. (See Schwartz, 1982, for a discussion of how pictures and descriptions represent; a more detailed discussion can be found in Goodman, 1968.)

Imagery and perception. The rotation and scanning experiments that motivate the pictorialist perspective are often taken to support a supposedly alternative hypothesis: that the representations and processes of imagery are like the representations and processes of perception. Actually, there is a different group of experiments that supports this latter hypothesis much more strongly. For example, it is known that visual acuity for vertical stripes is better than for oblique stripes. This is called the "oblique effect." If the experimenter holds up a grating and slowly moves it away, asking subjects to indicate when the stripes blur, subjects report the vertical stripes beginning to blur further away than the oblique stripes. Amazingly, the oblique effect occurs when the subjects are asked to *imagine* a grating moved slowly away from them. If the imagined grating is vertical, blurring occurs at a greater subjective distance than if it is oblique.

Many perceptual phenomena such as the oblique effect have been found to occur with imagery. While the experimental literature does not distinguish as clearly as one would like between the effects of representations and the effects of the processes that manipulate representations, the evidence is strong that the representations of imagery and perception are of the same kind. (See Finke, 1980, Kosslyn, 1980, and Shepard, 1978, for a description of many of these experiments.)

But the claim that the representations of imagery and perception are of the same kind is not an *alternative* to a pictorialist or a descriptionalist interpretation of image scanning and rotation experiments. The representations of imaging and perceiving should be lumped together as either both pictorial or both descriptional. But we still want to know which!

The "striped tiger." Dennett (1969) argues against pictorialism by noting that there do not seem to be a definite number of stripes on my image of a tiger. He says that a picture of a tiger would have to have a definite number of stripes, and therefore the mental image is not pictorial. Fodor (1975a) gives a reply in which he argues, among other things, that a picture need not be determinate under such descriptions as "number of stripes."

Tacit knowledge. Pylyshyn (1981) argues that the phenomena that appear to support pictorialism can actually be explained much more simply by supposing that what subjects are trying to do when they are told, for example, to find a tree on their image of a map, is to reproduce the experiences they would have if they were finding the tree on the real map. According to Pylyshyn, the data from map scanning experiments and the like are due to the fact that the subjects have tacit knowledge of features of perceptual interactions and they are simply trying to mimic the features of perceptual interactions. However, Finke and Pinker (1983) show that subjects in a scanning experiment exhibit a pattern of *errors* predicted by pictorialist theory. It is hard to believe that these errors could be a product of tacit knowledge.

SPLIT BRAINS AND THE UNITY OF CONSCIOUSNESS

In recent years, research on a small group of patients whose brains have been cut into two halves (by severing the corpus callosum, the fiber bundle that connects the two hemispheres) has fueled a controversy about the unity of the self. Sperry (1977) describes these experimental results. There is some reason to think that the left hemisphere of the split brain patient is the brain of one person, while the right hemisphere is the brain of another. What impresses Sperry is that information that gets into one hemisphere through the senses does not get into the other hemisphere and, further, that output organs controlled by the hemisphere that has the information will express it, while output organs controlled by the other hemisphere will not.

Puccetti (1973) gives us a more detailed argument for the double consciousness conclusion and then goes further: He applies the same conclusion to normals. Let us look at Puccetti's first argument. He describes the type of case where one word (say "key") is presented to the right hemi-

sphere (via the left visual field) while another word ("case") is presented
to the left hemisphere (via the right visual field). If asked what word was
seen, the speech system (controlled by the left hemisphere) says "case."
But if the instruction is "What word did you see?—indicate by pointing
with your left hand," the result is that the left hand points to the other
word, "key." Puccetti argues that if we assume these responses issue
from one and the same person, we have a contradiction:

(1) The person believes he saw "key" (as indicated by his pointing),
    and
(2) It is not the case that the person believes he saw "key" (as indicated
    by the fact that he says he saw "case" and, if questioned further,
    will say he did not see "key").

So, Puccetti concludes, to avoid contradiction we must suppose there are
two people involved, each hemisphere being the brain of a different person.

Now the critic of Puccetti might want to allow that Puccetti is right
about (1) but not (2). What the person's denying he saw "key" would
show is not (2), but only (2'):

(2') The person believes he did not see "key."

Here we have *contradictory beliefs* assigned to the unfortunate patient,
but we can believe that he has contradictory beliefs without accepting a
contradiction ourselves. (1) and (2) are contradictory, but (1) and (2') are
not.

Still, the critic owes us something. Can we really accept the idea that
there is one person in the experiment with contradictory beliefs? Can we
assimilate this case to uncontroversial cases of contradictory beliefs (as
when a mathematician discovers a contradiction in a mathematical system
he has believed for years)? Suppose the critic says that this is just a case
where the person knows that he saw "key" but does not *know that he
knows* (as indicated by what he would say if you were to ask him whether
he knows he saw "key"). Will this line of thought pan out? To see that it
won't, it suffices to note that one might be able to produce evidence from
behavior of the left hand that the person who controls that left hand *does*
know that he knows.

Quite a different point of view is presented in Nagel (1971). He argues
that we have no way of understanding these results while retaining our
ordinary conception of a person. The fragmentation is enough to conclusively rule out one person; the unity is enough to conclusively rule out
two people; so there is no fact of the matter about how many people are

embodied in a split-brain body. Is the ordinary conception of a person of which Nagel speaks *really* the ordinary conception or a philosopher's construction? Do you know the capitol cities of all 50 states? Perhaps you will say "no," but when you sit down to list them, perhaps you'll get them all. Does your ordinary conception of a person allow for times when you don't "feel like yourself," when you depart substantially from your normal patterns? Is this sort of consideration relevant?

A much more detailed consideration of the split brain results and the positions discussed in this module is to be found in Marks (1980).

IQ AND INTELLIGENCE

Ever since the first uses of proto-IQ tests on immigrants at Ellis Island around the turn of the century, there has been a raging debate about whether they measure an important cognitive capacity worthy of being thought of as intelligence and whether whatever they measure is innate. Those who want to see a good example of the debate in its early stages should now read the *New Republic* articles by Lippman and Terman reprinted in Block and Dworkin (1976).

Herrnstein (1971) summarizes the case for IQ tests as measures of innate intelligence. He concludes with his famous "syllogism," arguing that as our society equalizes opportunity, we will move towards a genetically based caste system in which unemployment will run in families as surely as bad teeth does now.

Block and Dworkin (1974) argue that IQ tests contain a hodgepodge of items which tap family background, test-taking skills, personality traits, such as persistence and tendency to check back for errors, confidence (as opposed to the tendency to give up on hard questions), as well as genuine cognitive skills. McClelland (1973) discusses the utility of IQ tests in predicting occupational success.

We now turn to the issue of the heritability of IQ and whether racial differences are genetically caused. Jensen (1978) summarizes recent evidence from a hereditarian perspective. More detail is to be found in Jensen (1969), though the description of the data in this article is now quite out of date. Jensen (1969) describes evidence that IQ is heritable in white populations and that the average difference between blacks and whites is mainly genetic in origin. Lewontin (1970) has criticized Jensen (1969), by noting, in effect that Argument I below is valid, though Argument II, which seems to amount to the same reasoning, is invalid.

Argument I.   Roses are genetically red.
              Violets are genetically blue.
              Therefore, the color difference is due to a genetic difference.

Argument II. IQ is heritable in whites.
IQ is heritable in blacks.
Therefore, the black-white difference is due to a genetic
difference.

When we say roses are genetically red, we mean that their redness is coded in and caused by their genes. This is basically the sense of "innate" as used in the module THE EMPIRICISM-NATIVISM DEBATE. When we say IQ is heritable in whites, on the other hand, we are saying that IQ *differences* among whites are caused by genetic differences.

Herrnstein and Jensen argue that if IQ is highly heritable, then, since most of the variance in IQ is genetically caused, most of the variance in IQ will remain, even if all inequality of opportunity is eliminated, and even if everyone is given the *same* environment. If differences are mainly genetically caused, they say, then equalizing environment will not have much effect on the differences. In "The Analysis of Variance and the Analysis of Cause," Lewontin points out that heritability statistics give a "local" analysis that holds only under the circumstances that prevail in the populations being measured and do not allow prediction of what will happen in a population in which different circumstances prevail, even the same population at a different time.

THE EMPIRICISM-NATIVISM DEBATE

The form of arguments for innateness by developmental psychologists is simply that if such and such knowledge or ideas or capacities appear at a time when the child did not have the experience requisite to have learned them, they are probably innate. (See Bower, 1975, for a number of examples.) The most impressive cases are the ones where a bit of knowledge or a capacity is exhibited in the first hour of life, when it would seem that the child has had little opportunity to have learned anything. An example: Newborns were given pacifiers of an unusual shape (cubical, pyramidal, spherical) and simultaneously shown pictures of various shapes. It was found that the babies gazed at the shape of the pacifier they happened to be sucking far more often than the other shapes. The conception of innateness presupposed by developmental psychologists is roughly: coded in the genes. A characteristic is taken to be coded in the genes if it appears before it could have been acquired from the environment.

A different nativism-empiricism debate appears in Plato's *Meno* and the Locke-Leibniz debate in Stich (1975). Stich's introduction argues that Plato's conception of innateness is quite different from the one presupposed in the Locke-Leibniz debate, and both, according to him, are different from the one deployed in current scientific controversies. Plato's conception of innateness, as Stich points out, is a "triggering" conception. The slave boy never would have discovered any mathematical truths without the "triggering" of Socrates's clever questions. By contrast, says Stich, the conception of innateness common to both Locke and Leibniz has to do with a natural unfolding. For them, something is innate if there is a tendency for it to appear in the natural course of things.

So we appear to have three quite different ideas of innateness: the modern one of being coded in the genes, and two historical ones, triggering and natural unfolding. Is it a mistake to talk of *the* nativism-empiricism debate?

Chomsky (1975) argues that knowledge of language must come in large part from *within the child,* rather than from the environment, on the ground that the child has much more information about language than he could have received from the environment. The idea of Chomsky's argument is the same as that of the developmental psychologists discussed at the beginning of this module. Information in the child is judged probably innate if it is unlikely to have come from the environment. Now this theme allows us to see an important commonality with Plato and with Locke and Leibniz. When knowledge is "triggered," there is more information in the knowledge than is present in the trigger (otherwise, it is *learning,* not triggering). Turning to natural unfolding, the reason an item of knowledge has a tendency to unfold in the natural course of things is that the source of the information is within the person and appears more or less independently of the information in the environment. All that is required of the environment is that it provide a minimal level of stimulation. (What is *not* required of the environment is that it provide all of the information that the child comes to have.) Proponents of nativism about language rely on the following:

(1) Given the degenerate character of the data the child has available for language learning, and the complexity of the grammar the child acquires, unless the language acquisition device comes equipped with a great deal of information built into it, language learning would be a mystery;

(2) Language universals;

(3) Within broad limits, diversity of linguistic data causes very little variation in the language abilities acquired;

(4) The child's mistakes in language learning form a surprisingly limited class; in particular, the child makes no structure independent mistakes;

(5) Critical periods:
   a. Second languages become harder to learn around puberty;

    b. At the same time, the kind and degree of recovery from aphasia changes; and

    c. At the same time, mental retardates reach their maximal language ability;

(6) Language is independent of general learning abilities:

    a. Chimps seem very similar to 3-year-old children in general learning ability, yet no one has succeeded in teaching a chimp a language that approaches in complexity the language of 3-year-old humans; and

    b. Very large differences among humans in general learning do not seem to be reflected in differences among internalized grammars;

(7) Syntactic and phonological training has no lasting effect; and

(8) Imitation has no effect in language learning, as is indicated by:

    a. What imitation there is does not seem to be progressive;

    b. When children repeat what adults say, they often alter it in the direction of "baby talk"; and

    c. Since language is productive, imitation could not possibly account for the acquisition of language.

Putnam (1967b) argues that phenomena such as the eight just listed can be explained in terms of powerful general learning abilities plus features of human life—such as our need for ways of referring to objects and to avoid inefficient methods of communication. Chomsky's (1969) reply is noteworthy. (See also Putnam, 1980a, Chomsky's reply, 1980, and Putnam's rejoinder, 1980b. Another line of attack on the nativist position questions its very intelligibility, e.g., Goodman, 1967.)

A far more extreme version of nativism than those described above is to be found in Fodor (1975b). Fodor's argument in essence is this:

(1) We can learn an English term (e.g., "tiger") only by defining it in terms already known (including terms of Mentalese);

(2) The history of attempts to define terms "decompositionally" has been a dismal failure. This suggests that most terms of English simply cannot be so defined; and

(3) Therefore, single terms with the meaning of "tiger" (and most other English terms) must already be present in Mentalese.

Proponents of conceptual role semantics would reply to Fodor by denying his first premise. They say that we learn an English term by learning how it fits into patterns of use in thought, reasoning, etc. Of course the *description* of these patterns of use would require a system of internal representation (according to representationalists), some of which would have to be innate. But the innate language would not have to be nearly so rich as what Fodor argues for.

REFERENCES

Aaronfreed, J. *Conduct and conscience: The socialization of internalized control over behavior.* New York: Academic Press, 1968.

Alston, W. P. Moral attitudes and moral judgements. *Nous,* 1968, *2,* 1–23.

Alston, W. P. Toward a logical geography of personality: Traits and deeper lying personality characteristics. In M. K. Munitz (Ed.), *Mind, science, and history.* Albany, NY: State University of New York Press, 1970.

Alston, W. P. Traits, consistency and conceptual alternatives for personality theory. *Journal for the Theory of Social Behavior,* 1975, *5,* 17–48.

Alston, W. P. Self-intervention and the structure of motivation. In T. Mischel (Ed.), *The self: Psychological and philosophical issues.* Oxford: Basil Blackwell, 1977.

Anderson, J. R. Arguments concerning representations for mental imagery. *Psychological Review,* 1978, *85,* 249–277.

Armstrong, D. The causal theory of the mind. *Neue Heft fuer Philosophie,* 1977, *11,* 82–95.

Atkinson, J. W., & Birch, D. *The dynamics of action.* New York: Wiley, 1970.

Atkinson, J. W., & Feather, N. T. *A theory of achievement motivation.* New York: Wiley, 1966.

Audi, R. On the conception and measurement of attitudes in contemporary Anglo-American psychology. *Journal for the Theory of Social Behavior,* 1972, *2,* 179–203.

Bandura, A., & Walters, R. *Social learning and personality development.* New York: Holt, Rinehart & Winston, 1963.

Block, N. Troubles with functionalism. In C. W. Savage (Ed.), *Perception and cognition: Issues in the foundations of psychology* (Minnesota Studies in the Philosophy of Science, Vol. 9). Minneapolis, MN: University of Minnesota Press, 1978.

Block, N. Reductionism. *Encyclopedia of bioethics.* New York: Macmillan, 1979.

Block, N. Are absent qualia impossible? *Philosophical Review,* 1980, *89,* 257–274.

Block, N. (Ed.). *Readings in the philosophy of psychology.* Cambridge, MA: Harvard University Press, 1980. (a)

Block, N. What is functionalism? In N. Block (Ed.), *Readings in the philosophy of psychology (Vol. 1).* Cambridge, MA: Harvard University Press, 1980. (b)

Block, N. (Ed.). *Imagery.* Cambridge, MA: MIT Press, 1981. (a)

Block, N. Psychologism and behaviorism. *Philosophical Review,* 1981, *91,* 5–43. (b)

Block, N. Mental pictures and cognitive science. *Philosophical Review,* 1983, *92,*

Block, N., & Dworkin, G. IQ, heritability, and inequality. *Philosophy and Public Affairs 3,* 1974, 331–409, *4, 1,* 40–99.

Block, N., & Dworkin, G. *The IQ controversy.* New York: Pantheon, 1976.

Block, N., & Fodor, J. What psychological states are not. *Philosophical Review,* 1972, *81,* 159–181.

Bower, T. *Development in infancy.* San Francisco, CA: Freeman, 1975.

Boyd, R. Materialism without reductionism: What physicalism does not entail. In N. Block (Ed.), *Readings in the philosophy of psychology (Vol. 1).* Cambridge, MA: Harvard University Press, 1980.

Brand, M. (Ed.). *The nature of human action.* Glenview, IL: Scott, Foresman, 1970.

Brandt, R. B. Traits of character: A conceptual analysis. *American Philosophical Quarterly,* 1970, *7,* 23–37.

Brandt, R. B. *A theory of the good and the right*. Oxford: Clarendon Press, 1979.

Brandt, R. B., & Kim, J. Wants as explanations of actions. *Journal of Philosophy*, 1963, *60*, 425–435.

Burge, T. Individualism and the mental. In P. A. French, et al. (Eds.), *Midwest studies in philosophy IV: Studies in metaphysics*. Minneapolis, MN: University of Minnesota Press, 1979.

Care, N. S., & Landesman, C. (Eds.). *Readings in the theory of action*. Bloomington, IN: Indiana University Press, 1968.

Carnap, R. Psychology in physical language. *Erkenntnis*, 1932, *3*, 107–142. (Reprinted in A. J. Ayer (Ed.), *Logical positivism*. New York: Free Press, 1959.)

Causey, R. *The unity of science*. Dordrecht: Reidel, 1977.

Chisholm, R. *Perceiving*. Ithaca, NY: Cornell University Press, 1957.

Chisholm, R. M. *Human freedom and the self*. Lawrence, KS: University of Kansas Press, 1964.

Chisholm, R. M. Freedom and action. In K. Lehrer (Ed.), *Freedom and determinism*. New York: Random House, 1969.

Chomsky, N. Review of B. F. Skinner's *Verbal Behavior*. *Language*, 1959, *35*, 26–58.

Chomsky, N. Reply to Putnam: From linguistics and philosophy. In S. Hook (Ed.), *Language and philosophy*. New York: New York University Press, 1969.

Chomsky, N. On cognitive capacity. In N. Chomsky *Reflections on language*. New York: Pantheon, 1975.

Chomsky, N. Discussion of Putnam's comments. In M. Piatelli-Palmirini (Ed.), *Language and learning: The debate between Jean Piaget and Noam Chomsky*. Cambridge, MA: Harvard University Press, 1980.

Churchland, P. M. Eliminative materialism and the propositional attitudes. *The Journal of Philosophy*, 1981, *78*, 67–90.

Churchland, P. M., & Churchland, P. S. Functionalism, qualia, and intentionality. *Philosophical Topics*, 1981, *12*, 1.

Cronbach, L. J. *Essentials of psychological testing*. New York: Harper & Row, 1960.

Cummins, R. Functional analysis. *Journal of Philosophy*, 1975, *72*, 741–765.

Davidson, D. Actions, reasons, and causes. *Journal of Philosophy*, 1963, *60*, 685–700.

Dennett, D. *Content and consciousness*. London: Routledge, 1969.

Dennett, D. Why the law of effect won't go away. *Journal for the Theory of Social Behavior*, 1975, *5*, 169–187.(a)

Dennett, D. Brain-writing and mind reading. In K. Gunderson (Ed.), *Language, mind, and knowledge* (Minnesota Studies in the Philosophy of Science, Vol. 7). Minneapolis, MN: University of Minnesota Press, 1975.(b)

Dennett, D. Current issues in the philosophy of mind. *American Philosophical Quarterly*, 1978, *15*, 249–261.(a)

Dennett, D. Why you can't make a computer that feels pain. *Synthese*, 1978, *38*, 415–456.(b)

Dennett, D. A cognitive theory of consciousness. *Minnesota studies in the philosophy of science* (Vol. 9). Minneapolis, MN: University of Minnesota Press, 1978.(c)

Dennett, D. A cure for the common code? In D. Dennett, *Brainstorms*. Montgomery, VT: Bradford Books, 1979.(a)

Dennett, D. Skinner skinned. In D. Dennett, *Brainstorms*. Montgomery, VT: Bradford Books, 1979.(b)

Dennett, D. Beyond belief. In A Woodfield (Ed.), *Thought and object*. Oxford: Oxford University Press, 1982.

Dennett, D. Quining qualia. In press-a.

Dennett, D. How to study consciousness empirically or nothing comes to mind. In press-b

Dennett, D., & Hofstadter, D. *The mind's I*. New York: Basic Books, 1981.

Dretske, K. *Knowledge and the flow of information.* Cambridge: MIT Press, 1980.

Dreyfus, H. *What computers can't do.* New York: Harper & Row, 1972.

Dreyfus, H., & Haugeland, J. The computer as a mistaken model of the mind. In S. C. Brown (Ed.), *Philosophy of psychology.* London: Macmillan, 1974.

Eccles, J. Reply to Savage. In G. Globus (Ed.), *Consciousness and the brain.* New York: Plenum, 1976.

Edwards, W., & Tversky, A. (Eds.). *Decision making.* Baltimore, MD: Penguin Books, 1967.

Feldman, F. Identity, necessity, and events. In N. Block (Ed.), *Readings in the philosophy of psychology.* Cambridge, MA: Harvard University Press, 1980.

Field, H. Logic, meaning and conceptual role. *Journal of Philosophy,* 1977, *74,* 79–409.

Field, H. Mental representation. *Erkenntnis,* 1978, *13,* 9–61.

Finke, R. A. Levels of equivalence in imagery and perception. *Psychological Review,* 1980, *87,* 113–139.

Finke, R. A., & Pinker, S. Directional scanning of remembered visual patterns. *Journal of Experimental Psychology: Learning, Memory and Cognition.* 1983.

Fodor, J. A. Materialism. In J. Fodor, *Psychological explanation.* New York: Random House, 1968.(a)

Fodor, J. A. The appeal to tacit knowledge in psychological explanation. *Journal of Philosophy,* 1968, *65,* 627–640.(b)

Fodor, J. A. Special sciences, or The disunity of science as a working hypothesis. *Synthese,* 1974, *28,* 97–115.

Fodor, J. A. Imagistic representation. In J. Fodor, *The language of thought.* New York: Crowell, 1975.(a)

Fodor, J. A. *The language of thought.* New York: Crowell, 1975.(b)

Fodor, J. A. Methodological solipsism as a research strategy in cognitive psychology. *The Behavioral and Brain Sciences,* 1980, *3,* 63–72.

Fodor, J. A. The mind-body problem. *Scientific American,* 1981, *244,* 124–133.

Fodor, J. A. Psychosemantics. In press.

Fodor, J. A., Bever, T., & Garrett, M. The specificity of language skills. In N. Block (Ed.), *Readings in the philosophy of psychology.* Cambridge, MA: Harvard University Press, 1980.

Frankfurt, H. Freedom of the will and the concept of a person. *Journal of Philosophy,* 1971, *68,* 5–20.

Fromkin, V. The non-anomalous nature of anomalous utterances. *Language,* 1971, *47,* 27–52.

Garrett, M. Production of speech: Observations from normal and pathological language. In A. Ellis (Ed.), *Normality and pathology in cognitive functions.* London: Academic Press, 1982.

Geach, P. *Mental acts.* London: Routledge, 1957.

Globus, G. (Ed.). *Consciousness and the brain.* New York: Plenum, 1976.

Goldman, A. I. *A theory of human action.* Englewood Cliffs, NJ: Prentice-Hall, 1970.

Goldman, A. I. Epistemics: The regulative theory of cognition. *The Journal of Philosophy,* 1978, *75,* 509–23.

Goodman, N. The epistemological argument. *Synthese,* 1967, *17,* 23–28.

Goodman, N. *Languages of art.* Indianapolis, IN: Bobbs-Merrill, 1968.

Grice, H. P. Logic and conversation. In D. Davidson & G. Harman (Eds.), *The logic of grammar.* Dickenson: Encino, 1975.

Hall, C. S., & Lindzey, G. *Theories of personality.* New York: Wiley, 1957.

Harman, G. Language, thought and communication. In K. Gunderson (Ed.), *Language, mind, and knowledge* (Minnesota studies in the philosophy of science, Vol. 6). Minneapolis, MN: University of Minnesota Press, 1975.

Harman, G. Conceptual role semantics. *The Notre Dame Journal of Formal Logic*, 1982, *23*, 242–256.

Harré, R., & Secord, P. F. *The explanation of social behavior.* Totowa, NJ: Rowman & Littlefield, 1972.

Haugeland, J. The nature and plausibility of cognitivism. *The Behavioral and Brain Sciences*, 1978, *2*, 215–225.

Hempel, C. G. *Philosophy of natural science.* Englewood Cliffs, NJ: Prentice-Hall, 1966.

Hempel, C. G. Reduction: Ontological and linguistic facets. In S. Morgenbesser, P. Suppes, & M. White (Eds.), *Essays in honor of Ernest Nagel.* New York: St. Martin's Press, 1970.

Hempel, C. G. The logical analysis of psychology. In A. Marras (Ed.), *Intentionality, mind, and language.* Urbana, IL: University of Illinois Press, 1972.

Herrnstein, R. J. IQ. *Atlantic Monthly,* 1971, *227*, 43–64.

Hills, D. Introduction: Mental representations and languages of thought. In N. Block (Ed.), *Readings in the philosophy of psychology.* Cambridge, MA: Harvard University Press, 1980.

Hull, C. L. *The principles of behavior.* New York: Appleton-Century-Crofts, 1943.

Jensen, A. R. Can we raise IQ and scholastic achievement. *Harvard Educational Review,* 1969, *39*, 1–123.

Jensen, A. R. The current status of the IQ controversy. *Australian Psychologist,* 1978, *13*, 1.

Kenny, A. *Action, emotion, and will.* London: Routledge & Kegan Paul, 1963.

Kim, J. On the psycho-physical identity theory. *American Philosophical Quarterly,* 1966, *3*, 227–235.

Kosslyn, S. M. *Image and mind.* Cambridge, MA: Harvard University Press, 1980.

Kosslyn, S. M. The medium and the message in mental imagery: A theory. *Psychological Review,* 1981, *88*, 46–66.

Kosslyn, S. M., Pinker, S., Smith, G. E., & Schwartz, S. P. On the demystification of mental imagery. *The Behavioral and Brain Sciences,* 1979, *2*, 535–581.

Kripke, S. Naming and necessity. In D. Davidson & G. Harman (Eds.), *Semantics and natural language.* Dordrecht: Reidel, 1972.

Leibniz, G. The Locke-Leibniz debate. In S. Stich (Ed.), *Innate ideas.* Berkeley, CA: University of California Press, 1975.

Lewis, D. Psychophysical and theoretical identifications. *Australasian Journal of Philosophy,* 1972, *50*, 249–258.

Lewontin, R. Race and intelligence. *Bulletin of the Atomic Scientists,* 1970, 2–8.

Loar, B. *Mind and meaning.* Cambridge, MA: Cambridge University Press, 1981.

Locke, J. The Locke-Leibniz debate. In S. Stich, *Innate ideas.* Berkeley, CA: University of California Press, 1975.

Lycan, W. Kripke and materialism. *Journal of Philosophy,* 1974, *71*, 677–689.

Lycan, W. Form, function and feele. *Journal of Philosophy,* 1980, *78*, 24–50.

Maddi, S. R. *Personality theories: A comparative analysis.* Homewood, IL: Dorsey Press, 1972.

Malcolm, N. Wittgenstein's philosophical investigations. *Philosophical Review,* 1954, *63*, 530–559.

Marks, C. E. *Commisurotomy, consciousness and unity of mind.* Cambridge, MA: MIT Press and Bradford Books, 1980.

McClelland, D. Testing for competence rather than for 'intelligence'. *American Psychologist,* 1973, *29*.

McGinn, C. Anomalous monism and Kripke's cartesian intuitions. *Analysis,* 1977, *37*, 78–80.

McGinn, C. The structure of content. In A. Woodfield (Ed.), *Thought and object.* Oxford: Oxford University Press, 1982.

Melden, A. I. *Free action*. London: Routledge & Kegan Paul, 1961.

Mill, J. S. *Utilitarianism*. London: J. M. Dent & Sons, 1863.

Mischel, W. Theory and research on the antecedents of self-imposed delay of reward. In B. A. Maher (Ed.), *Progress in experimental personality research*. New York: Academic, 1966.

Mischel, W. Processes in delay of gratification. In L. Berkowitz (Ed.), *Advances in social psychology* (Vol. 7). New York: Academic Press, 1973.

Nagel, T. Physicalism. *The Philosophical Review*, 1965, *74*, 339–356.

Nagel, T. Linguistics and epistemology. In S. Hook (Ed.), *Language and Philosophy*. New York: New York University Press, 1969.

Nagel, T. Brain bisection and the unity of consciousness. *Synthese*, 1971, *22*, 396–413.

Nagel, T. What is it like to be a bat? *Philosophical Review*, 1974, *83*, 435–450.

Peters, R. S. *The concept of motivation*. London: Routledge & Kegan Paul, 1958.

Place, U. T. Is consciousness a brain process? *British Journal of Psychology*, 1956, *67*, 44–50.

Popper, K., & Eccles, J. *The self and its brain*. New York: Springer, 1977.

Puccetti, R. Brain bisection and personal identity. *British Journal of Philosophy of Science*, 1973, *24*, 330–355.

Puccetti, R., & Dykes, R. Sensory cortex and the mind-brain problem. *The Behavioral and Brain Sciences*, 1978, *1*, 337–375.

Putnam, H. Brains and behavior. In R. J. Butler (Ed.), *Analytical philosophy*. Oxford: Blackwell, 1965.

Putnam, H. The nature of mental states. In W. H. Capitan & D. D. Merrill (Eds.), *Art, mind, and religion*. Pittsburgh: University of Pittsburgh Press, 1967.(a)

Putnam, H. The innateness hypothesis and explanatory models in linguistics. *Synthese*, 1967, *17*, 12–22.(b)

Putnam, H. Comment on Chomsky's reply. In M. Piatelli-Palmirini (Ed.), *Language and learning: The debate between Jean Piaget and Noam Chomsky*. Cambridge, MA: Harvard University Press, 1980.(a)

Putnam, H. What is innate and why. In M. Piatelli-Palmirini (Ed.), *Language and learning: The debate between Jean Piaget and Noam Chomsky*. Cambridge, MA: Harvard University Press, 1980.(b).

Putnam, H. Computational psychology and interpretation theory. In *Realism and reason*. Cambridge: Cambridge University Press, 1983.

Pylyshyn, Z. Computation and cognition: Issues in the foundation of cognitive science. *The Behavioral and Brain Sciences*, 1980, *3*, 111–169.

Pylyshyn, Z. The imagery debate: Analog media vs. tacit knowledge. *Psychological Review*, 1981, *88*, 16–45.

Pylyshyn, Z. *Computation and cognition*. Cambridge, MA: MIT Press, in press.

Rey, G. Worries about Haugeland's worries. *The Behavioral and Brain Sciences*, 1978, *1*, 246–248.

Rorty, R. Mind-body identity, privacy, and categories. *The Review of Metaphysics*, 1965, *19*, 24–54.

Rosenthal, D. M. (Ed.). *Materialism and the mind-body problem*. Englewood Cliffs, NJ: Prentice-Hall, 1971.

Russell, B., & Whitehead, A. N. *Principia mathematica*. Cambridge: Cambridge University Press, 1910–1913.

Ryle, G. *The concept of mind*. London: Hutchinson, 1949.

Savage, C. W. *The measurement of sensation*. Berkeley, CA: University of California Press, 1970.

Savage, C. W. An old ghost in a new body. In G. Globus (Ed.), *Consciousness and the brain*. New York: Plenum, 1976.

Schwartz, R. Imagery—There's more to it than meets the eye. In P. Asquith & R. Giere (Eds.), *PSA 1980* (Vol. 2). East Lansing, MI: Philosophy of Science Association, 1982.

Searle, J. Minds, brains and programs. *The Behavioral and Brain Sciences*, 1980, *3*, 417–459.

Shepard, R. The mental image. *American Psychologist*, 1978, *33*, 123–137.

Shepard, R., & Cooper, L. *Mental images and their transformations*. Cambridge, MA: MIT Press, 1982.

Shiffer, S. Truth and the theory of content. In H. Parret & J. Bouveresse (Eds.), *Meaning and understanding*. Berlin: de Bruyter, 1981.

Shoemaker, S. Functionalism and qualia. *Philosophical Studies,* 1975, *27*, 291–315.

Shoemaker, S. Absent qualia are impossible: A reply to Block. *Philosophical Review*, 1981, *90*, 581–589.(a)

Shoemaker, S. Some varieties of functionalism. *Philosophical Topics*, 1981, *12*, 93–120.(b)

Shoemaker, S. The inverted spectrum. *Journal of Philosophy*, 1982, *79*, 357–381.

Skinner, B. F. *The behavior of organisms*. New York: Appleton-Century-Crofts, 1938.

Skinner, B. F. *Science and human behavior*. New York: Macmillan, 1953.

Smart, J. J. C. Sensations and brain processes. *Philosophical Review*, 1959, *68*, 141–156.

Sperry, R. W. Forebrain commisurotomy and conscious awareness. *Journal of Medicine and Philosophy*, 1977, *2*, 101–126.

Stalnaker, R. Propositions. In A. Machay & D. Merrill (Eds.), *Philosophy of language*. New Haven, CT: Yale University Press, 1976.

Stampe D. Toward a causal theory of linguistic representation. In P. A. French (Eds.), *Contemporary perspectives in the philosophy of language*. Minneapolis, MN: University of Minnesota Press, 1979.

Stich, S. (Ed.). *Innate ideas*. Berkeley, CA: University of California Press, 1975.

Stich, S. Paying the price for methodological solipsism. *The Behavioral and Brain Sciences,* 1980, *3*, 1.

Stich, S. (Ed.), *The case against belief*. Cambridge, MA: MIT Press, 1983.

Taylor, R. *Metaphysics*. Englewood Cliffs, NJ: Prentice-Hall, 1963.

Taylor, R. *Action and purpose*. Englewood Cliffs, NJ: Prentice-Hall, 1966.

Tolman, E. C. *Purposive behavior in animals and men*. New York: Appleton-Century-Crofts, 1932.

Tolman, E. C. A psychological model. In T. Parsons & E. A. Shils (Eds.), *Toward a general theory of action*. Cambridge, MA: Harvard University Press, 1954.

Turing, A. M. Computing machinery and intelligence. *Mind*, 1950, *59*, No. 236.

Wexler, K., & Culicover, P. W. *Formal principles of language acquisition*. Cambridge, MA: MIT Press, 1980.

Wollheim, R. (Ed.). *Freud*. New York: Doubleday, Anchor, 1974.

6

Psychology and Religion

Benjamin Beit-Hallahmi
University of Haifa

INTRODUCTION

Discussions of the relationships between psychology and religion in the context of the relations of psychology with other academic disciplines have to be informed first by the unique nature of religion. Unlike biology, economics, or sociology, the term "religion" does not bring to mind an academic discipline, but a social institution. This social institution also has its own "academic discipline," namely theology, which cannot be put in the same category as typical academic disciplines. Thus, the discussion of the relationship between psychology and religion has to recognize both academic and non-academic aspects. (The situation is somewhat similar in the case of political science, for example; see Elms, in Volume II.)

The non-academic aspects will include the effects of psychology as a field of knowledge and as a recognized discipline on religion as an institution and the effects of psychology on theology and religious studies. Secular science has long been regarded as a competition and a threat to religion, with good reason, and psychology has been viewed as a special competitor and a special threat. Institutional religion has reacted to the challenge by creating its own institutional forms of psychological theory and practice. One such phenomenon is the emergence of pastoral counseling and pastoral psychology. Another one is the psychologizing of theology. In historical perspective, one might say that the process of secularization is expressed in the relegation of the religious to a private, psychological realm. Trends in contemporary theology reflect the view of religion as a private psychological experience. Liberal theology draws many of its ideas from the same climate of thought that has given rise to "humanistic psychology."

The academic aspects of the relationship between psychology and religion include the contributions of psychology to understanding the phenomenon of religion and the contributions of psychology to other academic disciplines involved in the study of religion. Psychology as a discipline has made attempts to explain the phenomena of religion both individually and socially. The success of these attempts may be judged on the basis of their congruence with the rest of psychology or on the basis of their value for scholars in other disciplines studying religion, such as historians and sociologists. Before such a judgment is made, however, the body of knowledge produced by psychology in regard to religious beliefs and religious behaviors has to be discussed.

This essay reviews this body of knowledge and then attempts to evaluate it from the perspective of psychological theory. The understanding of religion is viewed as both an attempt at cultural analysis and an attempt to understand certain universal psychological characteristics of humanity. This essay limits itself to the English speaking world, and to the United States in particular.

BACKGROUND CONSIDERATIONS

A Working Definition of Religion

Since the relationship between psychology and religion is not one between two disciplines, but the relationship of an academic discipline (psychology) to its subject matter (religion), this subject matter should be defined and delineated. Offering a psychological working definition of religion is to present both the products of social science scholarship and a direction for the rest of the essay.

Following Alatas (1977), religion may be defined as a sphere of human activity which includes seven principal elements:

(1) Belief in a supernatural being or beings and belief that human beings will establish a personal relationship with that being or beings.
(2) Certain rites and beliefs, in addition to those in (1), which are sanctioned by supernatural reality.
(3) The division of life into the sacred and the profane.
(4) Belief that the supernatural world communicates through human messengers.
(5) The attempt to order life in harmony with supernatural designs.
(6) The belief that revealed truth supersedes other human efforts at understanding the world.
(7) The practice of creating a community of believers.

While this list may still be too narrow to include some religious traditions, it is broad enough to cover what to most human beings is connoted by religion through their concrete experience. There is a large gap between religion, as it is recognized directly in the culture, and the definitions of religion offered by theologians and philosophers. The psychological definition of religion has to be close to that which real people experience and recognize immediately, and such substantive definitions are in line with the traditions of scholarship in the study of religion.

Durkheim (1915) observed that all religions ". . . presuppose a classification of all things . . . into two classes of opposed groups . . . *profane and sacred* [p. 37]," and from this observation he went on to define religion: "A religion is a unified system of beliefs and practices relative to sacred things, that is to say, things set apart and forbidden—beliefs and practices which unite into one single moral community called a Church, all those who adhere to them [p. 47]." Similarly, William James (1956), in his lesser known definition of religion, describes a separation of the visible and the invisible worlds, which parallels the separation between scared and profane:

> Religion has meant many things in human history; but when from now onward I use the word I mean to us it in the supernaturalist sense, as declaring that the so-called order of nature, which constitutes this world's experience, is only one portion of the total universe, and that there stretches beyond this visible world an unseen world of which we now know nothing positive, but in its relation to which the true significance of our present mundane life consists. A man's religious faith . . . means for me essentially his faith in the existence of an unseen order of some kind in which the riddles of the natural order may be found explained [James, 1956, p. 51].

And if we believe in the existence of the unseen world, then religion as a social institution is for us the mediator between the invisible supernatural world and the visible human and natural world, but that institution, with the behaviors tied to it, does not exist without the belief in the supernatural.

> It is the premise of every religion—and this premise is religion's defining characteristic—that souls, supernatural beings, and supernatural forces exist. Furthermore, there are certain minimal categories of behavior, which, in the context of the *supernatural premise,* are always found in association with one another and which are the substance of religion itself [Wallace, 1966, p. 52].

The problem of defining religion is not only scholarly or theoretical (e.g., Bowser, 1977). A psychological definition of religion, as opposed to a legal one, attempts to delineate what is universal in all the concrete experiences and behaviors of humans which are recognized as relating to religion. The working definition of religion used here (Argyle & Beit-Hallahmi, 1975) is the ". . . straightforward, everyday, limited definition of religion as a system of beliefs in divine or superhuman power, and practices or worship or other rituals directed towards such a power [p. 1]." This definition, while being "conservative" for some tastes, has the advantages of being concrete, historical, and close to the direct experience of the common believer.

What Is Unique to Religious Actions and Ideas?

There is no intrinsically religious meaning in anything. Any object, person, time, or place may be imbued with holiness and thus gain religious meaning. Holiness is a realm of psychological content, rather than psychological function or structure. Religious actions are defined by their relation to the psychological realm of holiness and not by anything else. Religious rituals have the capacity to induce ecstasy or at least excitement in the participants. This ecstasy can objectively be defined as measureable physiological arousal, but such arousal is not unique to religious occasions and cannot be regarded as identifying religious activities. There is no objective difference between physiological (and psychological) arousal during a religious ceremony and similar arousal during a *Rolling Stones* concert. The differences may be in the stimulus. Emotional arousal may seem like the most "objective" basis for a psychological definition of religion, but it becomes clear that this is not a unique aspect of religious actions.

Religions not only state the *supernatural premise* in an abstract, general way, but also present many specific and elaborate ideas about the supernatural world and its inhabitant entities. Religious belief systems include also a philosophical anthropology (the "nature of man") tied to, but not limited to, the supernatural world and psychological claims regarding human beings in this world. These claims most often refer to the existence of a "soul" and less often to human "free will." As Tylor (1871) suggested, the theory of the soul offers an explanation for two puzzling questions for primitive science: What happens to consciousness during sleep? What happens to consciousness after death? There is, of course, no necessary logical connection between the psychological part of religious beliefs (i.e., belief in free will and the soul) and the supernatural part. It may be possible to separate the two parts of the system, i.e., to believe in the soul or in free will, without believing in the world of spirits. The idea of the soul is usually tied to the idea of immortality. The soul is immortal and survives physical death, and this claim of religion is one of the most important, culturally and individually. As William James (1902) put it: "Religion, in fact, for the great majority of our own race, *means* immortality, and nothing else [p. 406]."

The Task of Psychology

Religion seems to be an ideal subject matter for the psychologist. It is a system which is defined solely by the existence of beliefs and fantasies, which is a unique product of human cognitive capacities, and which is a reflection of human flexibility and creativity. The basic question for the psychologist of religion is how to explain the existence of religious beliefs, their sources, and their cultural manifestations, using psychological concepts, i.e. concepts dealing with the mental abilities and processes of human beings. It is quite readily assumed that psychology does not, and can not, offer explanations for every manifestation of religion as a human activity. Other disciplines may be called upon to offer explanations for various aspects of religion.

Psychology, as a branch of systematic human knowledge, has two components: a set of problems, topics, or questions, and a range of methods by which these are investigated. The psychology of religion, in relation to other areas of psychology, can be defined through its set of problems, which sets it apart from the rest of psychology. If we want to look at the psychology of religion from the perspective of other disciplines dealing with religion, then the definition of the area is slightly different. What is the task of the psychology of religion, and what answers does it have to provide? What is it about religion that cannot be answered by other disciplines? One definition of the psychology of religion may be negative: It will include those issues not dealt with by other disciplines.

The question that the psychology of religion attempts to answer is the question of religious motivation. Why do people engage in religious acts? This is the question put before the psychologist of religion, as varied from the questions put before the historian or the sociologist of religion. The boundaries between any two disciplines studying religion may become irrelevant or may become a hindrance to pursuing significant questions; issues do not define themselves according to boundaries among disciplines. Religion as a phenomenon has been studied by history, sociology, philosophy, and anthropology. One significant difference between the study of religion in the traditional human science disciplines and the work done in psychology is that the traditional disciplines are historical, while modern academic psychology is not.

HISTORICAL PERSPECTIVES

The cliché popular with writers of psychology textbooks applies here: The relationship between psychology and religion is that between a young science and an old tradition. The rise of systematic psychology as an independent discipline has been correlated, and not by accident, with the decline of religion. This statement summarizes best what has happened over the past 200 years. When discussing the psychological aspects of modernization, Inkeles and Smith (1974) noted that "Religion ranks with the extended family as the institution most often identified both as an obstacle to economic development and as a victim of the same process [p. 21]." Secularization, the decline of religion as a social institution, has been connected with the rise of sciences: Since the days of Giordano Bruno and Galileo, the natural sciences have demolished the religious cosmology, and the biological sciences have demolished the religious view of man in the natural world. But it was left to the social sciences and psychology to examine the nature of religious beliefs, their development, and their relativity, and in this way to deal a final blow to the credibility of religious claims (Cattell, 1938). Moreover, the decline of religion is especially tied to the social sciences' examination of the social order, often legitimized by religion. Thus, the social sciences have very clearly followed the Comtean model replacing religious traditions with new, rational, and systematic science. The social sciences especially threaten religion because they take religion as an object of study and not as a representation of a special reality or a special mode of knowledge. The social sciences study changes in culture over time and space and show that beliefs and customs, including religious ones, are relative and culturally conditioned (Glock & Stark, 1965) against traditional religious claims of universal validity. Psychology, as the discipline that deals directly with the nature of human beliefs, presents a most direct threat; first, it challenges and rejects the notions of the soul and free will, which are integral to religious traditions, and, second, it is part of the historical rise of science which challenges and makes less tenable the supernatural premise.

Modern psychology, as Allport (1950) put it, is rather proud of being "a psychology without a soul," thus representing a direct departure from religious tradition. Actually, the development of modern psychology would not have been possible without rejecting the ideal of the soul. The development of a scientific psychology has meant the naturalization and secularization of the soul, and finally its disappearance (Kantor, 1969).

The process of psychologizing religion has paralleled the historical process of secularization. Religion is becoming more psychological (or psychologistic) in two senses. The first sense is that of emphasizing personal experience and personal faith rather than communal experiences or meanings. It is the individual who is being offered salvation in modern religion (and modern psychology; cf. Beit-Hallahmi, 1974a) rather than the community or society as a whole. Religion has become an individual matter, with its tenets becoming more abstract. Instead of clear cosmological claims and world transformation, religion now offers believers individual psychological change. The second sense in which religion is becoming psychologized is that of its rapproachement with applied and clinical psychology.

In historical perspective, the effects of religion on psychology seem obvious and preeminent. Psychology is the successor to religion in both scientific functions and social functions. Primitive theories of conscious-ness were a part of religion, until they were replaced by modern psychol-ogy. In their social and applied functions, modern psychological theories have acted to provide individuals with a secular meaning system, filling the "ecological niche" emptied by the decline of religion. Religion and psychology have remained competing, alternative meaning systems for some individuals even today. Many individuals in need of advice about personal difficulties turn first to their clergymen, rather than to the secular "helping professionals" (Gurin, Veroff, & Feld, 1960). The competition between religion and psychology as meaning systems, expressed in the scholarly work of psychologists, will be described below.

THE PSYCHOLOGICAL STUDY OF RELIGION: HISTORICAL PERSPECTIVE

The history of the psychological study of religion is complex and paradox-ical. Some of the best minds in the history of psychology have devoted considerable amounts of intellectual energy to the subject matter of reli-gion, including Cattell (1938), Freud (1927/1961), Guntrip (1968), Hall (1904), James (1902), Maslow (1964), Mowrer (1961), Skinner (1953), and Watson (1924). Wilhelm Wundt (1912/1916), universally considered the progenitor of the laboratory paradigm of psychology, was also an early pioneer of the psychology of culture and the psychology of religion and mythology: His *Volkerpsychologie* included three volumes on religion and mythology.

What is most often noted in discussions of the history of the psychologi-cal study of religion is that the area enjoyed a period of enormous activity and attention at the end of the nineteenth century and at the beginning of the twentieth (Beit-Hallahmi, 1974b), only to decline greatly afterward in terms of research activity and publications. We are able to speak of a "psychology of religion" movement existing roughly between 1880 and 1930; its history is enlightening and important for what has happened to the psychological study of religion since then.

During the last decade of the nineteenth century and the first quarter of this one, American psychologists pioneered and led a "psychology of religion" movement (e.g., Page, 1951; Pratt, 1908; Schaub, 1922, 1924, 1926a, 1926b). Beginning in the middle 1890s, books and articles dealing with religious behavior were common on the American psychological scene. The first study of conversion (Leuba, 1896) was followed three years later by publication of the first book entitled *The Psychology of Religion* (Starbuck, 1899). In 1902 James published his epoch-making *The Varieties of Religious Experience*.

Schaub (1924), describing this movement, wrote: "When we consider such problems as conversion, revival phenomena, normal religious growth, or the influence of adolescence upon religious life, the American primacy is indisputable [p. 117]." Psychology of religion as a field was started in the U.S. because most fields of psychology started in the U.S.

As we consider the literature of this era, four individuals stand out. Two provided theoretical impetus and practical encouragement: G. S. Hall and W. James. Two others did most of the work and took over the leadership from the first generation: J.H. Leuba and E.D. Starbuck. Although James is usually credited with most of the influence on the psychological study of religion in the U.S., a closer scrutiny of the historical facts reveals that Hall was more instrumental in bringing about psychological studies of religion. Leuba and Starbuck, the real pioneers, were Hall's students, and they published their first studies in the 1890s, before the "revival" caused by the publication of the *Varieties* in 1902. J.B. Pratt (1908) describes Hall as the guiding influence in this area, being the founder of the "Clark school of religious psychology." Early in the 1880s, Hall lectured and wrote on the "moral and religious training of children and adolescents" as part of his general interest in developmental psychology. The publication of Hall's article on the above subject in 1882 marked the beginning of the new movement, and Hall's interest in adolescence brought about empirical studies of religious "conversion," later studied by Clark (1929), Coe (1916), Hall (1904), Leuba (1896), and Starbuck (1899).

Leuba was the most active of Hall's students. His numerous articles and books (e.g., 1896, 1901, 1912, 1917, 1926a, 1926b, 1934) made him the leader of this movement as long as it existed. Starbuck was a student of James at Harvard before moving to Clark University to study with Hall. In 1890 he was stirred by Max Muller's (1870) *Introduction to the Science of Religion* and decided to study the area systematically. In 1893, at Harvard, he put out two questionnaires (or "circulars," as they were called then), one on "conversion" and the other on "gradual growth." According to James (1899), Starbuck's basic aim in starting his studies was to bring conciliation into the feud between science and religion.

Conklin's (1929) *The Psychology of Religious Adjustment* was the swan song of this group's activity. Other books by E. T. Clark (1929) and G. Betts (1929) showed similar decline. Why did this movement arise in the first place, and why did it end?

Schaub (1924) has described the rise of this movement in a way that provides some insight into the *Zeitgeist* that produced it: "The dawn of the twentieth century witnessed the rise of a new approach to the study of religion . . . psychological investigations along strictly empirical and scientific lines [p. 113]." As we go back to Starbuck (1899), a positivistic approach is clear: "Science has conquered one field after another, until it is now entering the most complex, the most inaccessible and, of all, the most sacred domain—that of religion [p. 1]." The psychology of religion movement was undoubtedly influenced by the growth in the academic study of religion in the nineteenth century and by the rise of the history of religion and comparative religion as academic "movements." Philosophy has always dealt with questions of belief and religion; psychology as a legitimate heir and descendant of philosophy took upon itself the chore of objectively studying subjects that formerly belonged to philosophy. The pioneers of the empirical-experimental approach to human bahavior saw religion as a subject fit to study and eagerly wanted to prove that even this area of study could be studied "scientifically." Great advances were being made in the sociology of religion and in anthropology as studies of primitive religion by Frazer (1951) and by Tylor (1871) aroused much interest and theorizing. Given this background, the pioneers in the movement may have felt that the time was right for a positivistic approach to religion in psychology.

Following the traditional view of religion as something necessary to human society, the references to religion itself in the writings of James, Hall, Leuba, and Starbuck show an attitude of deference and reverence to basic religious dogmas. Publication of psychological articles in religious and theological journals shows the spirit of cooperation and contribution to religion that prevailed in the movement. Why then did this movement decline?

The rapid decline and final demise of the movement were reflected in the disappearance in 1933 of the annual reviews of the psychology of religion which had been published in the *Psychological Bulletin* since 1904. The last review (Cronbach, 1933) contained mostly material taken from German and French sources, showing the loss of interest in the area in the U.S. Also, a survey on courses in psychology offered by undergraduate colleges (Henry, 1938) showed the decline of interest, compared with the previous decade (see Schaub, 1924): Out of 154 colleges surveyed, only 24 offered psychology of religion courses. Thus, in a little over three decades after its birth, the psychology of religion movement was dead.

Douglas (1963) offered the following reasons for the decline: the psychology of religion failed to separate itself from theology, philosophy of religion, and the general dogmatic and evangelistic tasks of religious institutions, and, in the desperate effort to be recognized as "scientific," there was an emphasis on collecting discrete facts, without integrating them into a comprehensive theory, while the use of data collection methods and explanations was often uncritical and incompetent. "Subjective" phenomena were avoided by this developing social science, which tried to be "empirical" and "objective." The climate of public opinion was changing away from religion and toward a behavioristic and positivistic world view, and the study of religion was conflictual for both researcher and subject, because of their own personal investment in religion.

Strunk (1957) regarded the following factors as crucial: first, theological interest in the field introduced speculative and apologetic tendencies, which hampered advancement; second, psychoanalytic approaches to the study of religion attracted more attention and efforts since they seemed more promising; and third, the influence of behaviorism led to the neglect of complex human behaviors as the focus of attention in academic psychology.

As illustrated above, the philosophical-mystical approach could not have gained much respect for a psychology of religion among younger and more critical scholars. Despite the publication of several impressive studies (e.g., Coe, 1916; Leuba, 1896; Starbuck, 1899), such a naive theoretical approach limited the impact of the movement on general psychology and separated it from the mainstream of academic research. Inside academic psychology in the 1920s and 1930s, interest in religious behavior came to be perceived as unscientific. The theoretical and ideological bases of the movement showed that the psychology of religion was basically a residue of the philosophical tradition in psychology. This was probably the most severe limitation of the movement and may ultimately have caused its decline.

In addition to the reasons suggested above, other factors can be identified. One is the growth and development of other areas of academic psychology, introducing new "fads" which won interest, energy, and students. Another may be social pressure, or lack of support from the outside. Thurstone and Chave's book (1929) signalled a new stage in the development of social psychology that coincided with the decline in the psychology of religion. Objective methods of attitude measurement boosted the study of social and poltical behavior. Though social psychology could incorporate the study of religious attitudes, and thus transfer the study of religion into a new stage, it did not.

The issue of social pressure is rarely discussed in connection with the psychology of religion. However, as Glock and Stark (1965) show, any serious systematic study of religion must be a threat to religious institutions. The threat posed by the psychology of religion movement was responded to by taking the movement over. The second generation in the movement (including Pratt, Coe, Ames, and Johnson), as Strunk (1957) points out, were theologians first and psychologists second.

In another interpretation of the decline of the movement, Homans (1970) claims that this decline " . . . coincided with beginnings of both theological existentialism and psychoanalysis [p. 99]." Another coincidence noted by Homans is the one between the appearance of pastoral psychology and the decline of the movement. Homans suggests that the pastoral counseling process is heir to the conversion experience described by the early psychologists of religion.

Neutralizing the threat of the movement by taking it under the wings of religious institutions had a significant role in its decline and stagnation in psychology. No sinister, deliberate conspiracy is implied. The movement was not an unwilling victim since its friendliness to religion was widely proclaimed. The whole takeover process was a rather natural one—a combination of inherent weakness and external pressure. Pastoral counseling is thus the natural and only successor to the psychology of religion movement.

Another important social factor that seems to have influenced psychologists in their attitude toward the study of religion is what is called here "the ivory tower effect." As early as 1917 (Leuba, 1917, 1934), it was shown that scientists, and especially psychologists, were less religious than most of the American population. More recent studies show the same results (Stark, 1963). Thus, social scientists acquired the impression that religion may be "neutralized" (Adorno, Frenkel-Brunswick, Levinson, & Sanford, 1950). This misconception may also have contributed to the declining research interest in religion. Scientists in the 1930s might have felt that the long war between science and religion was won by science, and there was not much left to study in religion.

In brief, a combination of inherent, internal weaknesses and the existence of outside pressures caused religion to decline in acceptability as a focus for psychological inquiry. One possible inference is that internal weaknesses, mainly the lack of a non-religious, non-philosophical theoretical basis, doomed the movement from its inception and caused its quick demise. At the same time, outside pressures both within and without of academic psychology were considerable. The years between 1930 and 1960 were a low point for publications dealing with psychology and religion. Allport (1950) has pointed to the interesting change in the status of religion and sex as appropriate subjects of psychological study between 1930 and 1960; during those 30 years sex became a very fashionable area of research, while religion became almost a taboo subject. Since 1960, however, there has been a mild "revival" of interest in the psychology of religion (Beit-Hallahmi, 1973; Dittes, 1969).

RELIGION'S RESPONSE TO PSYCHOLOGY

Glock and Stark (1965) state that social science research is ". . . putting religion on the defensive about some of its traditional beliefs and the effect, in the long run, is likely to produce a process of accommodation parallel to that which religion experienced in its earlier confrontation with the natural sciences [p. 291]." The nature of this accommodation will be expressed in further acceptance by religion of secular ideas. The effects of the rise of psychology as a discipline and the rise of systematic secular psychological theories on the institution of religion can be viewed at three levels. First, the rise of psychology is part of the general challenge of modern science to religion. Second, it is a part of the rise of modern social science, and modern social critiques, exemplified in the work of Marx, Durkheim, and Freud. Third, there are the specific effects of psychology as an emerging scientific discipline and as an emerging technology.

Theological Responses

The one development in modern psychological theories that has received most attention from theologians is psychoanalysis (Homans, 1970). There is a voluminous literature of theological responses to psychoanalysis, both Catholic and Protestant, which can best be described as attempting a reconciliation, or a compromise, with Freud's ideas (Beit-Hallahmi, 1978). "Liberal" Protestant theology in the twentieth century has been using depth psychology and "humanistic" psychology, and psychological concepts have become part of the theological discourse. Theologicans have become amazingly fluent in the language of psychoanalysis, in its various dialects from Freud to Erikson, and in the language of client-centered psychotherapy (Homans, 1968a). While specific references to psychological writings are to be found mainly in "liberal" theology, the process of psychologizing religion is also taking place among conservative sectors of organized religion. All branches of popular theology, presented not only in scholarly publications but through the mass media, especially television, offer believers a personal and psychological kind of salvation. Religious salvation today is defined in psychological and temporal ways, such as "peace of mind" and happiness. There is less emphasis on ever-lasting life or the kingdom of heaven and more on the private and personal. It is significant that popular proselytizing in the U.S. in the 1970–1980s is based on "accepting Jesus as your personal saviour." The benefits of religion to the faithful are presented as personal and immediate. There is an obvious continuity between secular psychotherapy, with its message of private solutions to private problems, and the contemporary religious message of private salvation (Beit-Hallahmi, 1974a,

1976). The psychologizing of religion in this sense is not only a response to psychology but a reflection of the parallel roles of both religion and secular psychotherapy in social control (Beit-Hallahmi, 1976).

The Rise of Pastoral Psychology

One of the reactions of the religious establishment to the early development of psychological approaches to religion was the development of the pastoral counseling movement, in existence since the 1930s. Pastoral counseling has sought to appropriate the techniques of secular psychotherapy and integrate them into the work of the clergy.

From the viewpoint of the history of the "helping professions," pastoral counseling has been a basic part of the movement for non-medical psychotherapy. From the perspective presented by Glock and Stark (1965), the development of pastoral counseling can be seen as part of the process of accommodation and assimilation through which religion responds to technological and scientific innovations. Pastoral counseling was not just a reaction to a new technology, but also a response to specific psychological theories. Homans (1970) states that " . . . the first theological attempt to deal with psychoanalysis was made by pastoral psychology [p. 15]." Historically, the appearance of pastoral psychology is connected to the decline of the "psychology of religion" movement (Beit-Hallahmi, 1974b; Homans, 1970) and to the rise of psychoanalysis, including neo-Freudian theories and (to some extent) client-centered theory in counseling (Homans, 1970).

The journal *Pastoral Psychology,* which appeared between 1950 and 1972, is the best written record of the pastoral psychology movement. The list of contributors to its first volume included such prominent psychologists and psychiatrists as Molly Harrower, Rollo May, Carl Rogers, Karen Horney, P. Spurgeon English, William Menninger, Lawrence Kubie, Franz Alexander, Karl Menninger, and Erich Fromm. The dominant spirit of the volume can best be described as the progeny of a marriage between liberal Christian theology and liberal psychoanalysis, the progeny being characterized by considerable sophistication in psychoanalytic terms, a liberal stand on many issues of the day, and a large dose of positive thinking. From a different perspective, the pastoral psychology movement can be viewed as an integral part of the Americanization of psychoanalysis.

The institutionalization of pastoral psychology is one area where the impact of psychology on religion is rather substantial. Most clergy in the English-speaking world today have been exposed to psychological theories as part of their training in theology and, to a larger extent, in pastoral counseling. While the impact of psychology is more dominant in "liberal" theology, both "liberal" and traditional denominations train their clergy in pastoral psychology; conservative denominations use psychology for counseling techniques and not for theology.

The Impact of Psychology on Religious Studies

What are the academic reflections of religion as an institution? In the 1980s, the academic side of religion has two aspects: religious studies and theology. While departments of religious studies have come into existence in a few universities and serve to house scholarly work on religion, theology is not considered a legitimate academic discipline outside of religious institutions but is part of the institution of religion; the history of religions as a discipline is part of the secular world of academic scholarship.

Questions now surround the influence of psychology on the work of scholars in other disciplines concerned with the study of religion. The answer seems to be that the situation of psychology in relation to the academic study of religion is the same as that of psychology in relation to the humanities and social sciences in general. Any scholar in the humanities today is familiar with psychological concepts and theories, mainly those of depth psychology. There have been historical trends for greater use of psychological ideas in the traditional humanities, such as literature (see Lindauer, in this volume), and there have been attempts for formalize a new discipline of psychohistory (see Lifton & Strozier, in Volume II). All of these developments affect scholars who study religion. The criticisms directed at the uses (and abuses) of psychology in the humanities in general are also applied to the uses of psychology in the humanities when the subject matter is religion. Students of comparative religion and the history of religion are familiar with psychological interpretations of their materials, but quite often react to them critically. The methodological issues here are similar to those which arise in the psychological study of religion and will be discussed below.

PSYCHOANALYSIS AND THE PSYCHOLOGICAL STUDY OF RELIGION

Dynamic psychology in general and psychoanalysis in particular have had more to say about religious actions than other movements in conventional academic psychology. Psychoanalysis is the psychological approach to understanding religion which has had a major effect on both religion as an institution and on the study of religion in all human sciences (e.g., Kardiner & Linton, 1945; Parsons, 1951, 1960). The psychoanalytic psychology of religion can be divided into two main parts: the original writings of Freud (see Beit-Hallahmi, 1978; Pruyser, 1973) and further contributions by his students and followers, such as those by Rank (1914), Reik (1946, 1951), Jones (1951), and Erikson (1958, 1966). The best articulated contemporary presentation of the psychoanalytic approach to religion is that of La Barre (1972) which combines Freudian theory with a rich collection of cultural and historical case studies.

Psychoanalysis is the only major psychological theory which offers an explanation of religion as part of a comprehensive theory of human behavior. Religion is presented as an instance of general psychological forces in action (cf. Dittes, 1969). Freud's theoretical explanation for the origin and existence of religion is based on certain presumed universal psychological experiences and processes: the universal experience of helplessness, the tendency for compensation through fantasy, and the experience of early relations with protective figures. Every individual is psychologically prepared by these universal experiences to accept religious ideas, which are obviously culturally transmitted. The question about the world of spirits is an example: Does this world really exist "out there," and if it does not, where is it? The answer given by psychoanalysis is that it exists within, in our own mental apparatus and our own mental abilities to fantasize and project. Psychoanalytic theory explains both the origin of the supernatural premise and its specific contents. The world of spirits, the supernatural world unseen and somehow felt in religious experience, is a projection of the internal world of internalized and fantasized objects. An eloquent summary of the psychoanalytic explanation for the world of the spirits has been offered by Muensterberger (1972):

> Who are the gods who panic? Who are the monsters and werewolves, ogres and witches? Or the bogeys, vampires, and vultures who appear in dreams and mysteries and threaten one's life? Whence those fears and figments; the notion of fantastic beings and domains no human is able to fathom? We encounter them everywhere. They are an integral part of the vast repertoire of human imagination, nay, the human condition. Their supernatural craft stems from that inspiration which in one way or the other belongs inevitably to everyone's childlike sense of impending doom or disaster and only magic, ritual, or prayer can tame or dispel [p. ix].

Paradoxically, psychoanalysis is less individualistic in its biases, and this becomes clear when we look at the materials that have been used in psychoanalytic interpretations of religion (Beit-Hallahmi, 1978) and which consist mostly of mythology. Freud's theory does not suggest that the individual creates his religion *de novo* as he grows up, but that childhood experiences within the family prepare the individual for the cultural system of religion. Psychoanalysis sees every religious act, every religious belief or ritual, as the appropriate unit of analysis. There is no need for special sampling, since every unit of behavior is equally representative. The same basic method can be used to analyze a whole mythical system or one individual believer. The psychoanalytic paradigm enables us to analyze both process and content in religion (see Pruyser, 1973).

Freud's contributions are to date the most ambitious attempt to present a comprehensive non-religious interpretation of religion in Western culture and history. The topics Freud dealt with include, first, a developmental theory of religion, both phylogenetically and ontogenetically, and, second, an attempt to explain the functions and consequences of religion, for both society and the individual. In this area, as in many others, Freud's writings offer a rich variety of hypotheses regarding various religious beliefs and practices.

Some of the better-known hypotheses derived from psychoanalytic theory are the father-projection hypothesis (Beit-Hallahmi & Argyle, 1975), the super-ego projection hypothesis (Argyle & Beit-Hallahmi, 1975), and the obsessional neurosis hypothesis. These hypotheses can be interpreted both phylogenetically and ontogenetically.

Quantitatively, psychoanalysis has contributed more to the psychology of religion than any other theoretical approach. At the same time, the actual impact of the psychoanalytic approach is more limited than could be expected on the basis of quantity alone. The major qualitative characteristic of psychoanalytic interpretations of religion is that they deal more often with the substance of religious beliefs and myths and less often with function and structure. A quantitative analysis of psychoanalytic writings (see Beit-Hallahmi, 1978) shows that mythology is a major topic, while religious experience receives less attention than it gets from other theoretical approaches.

Methodologically, most psychoanalytic studies of religious phenomena can be characterized by their structure and style. "Modal articles" can be identified by several common characteristics. These include the choice of a myth or belief to be discussed, rather than individual experience, and the use of material taken from anthropology, comparative religion, or archaeology. Often clinical material is introduced after the analysis of historical material to show parallels between individual and cultural processes. The model for this way of analysis is the clinical analysis of a dream or a symptom. The religious belief or behavior is selected as the segment of human action to be analyzed in order to discover an unconscious (or at least unknown to the involved person) meaning. The assumptions behind this approach are that religious acts are always psychologically meaningful and that the same rules apply to the analysis of individual and cultural products. The psychoanalytic style of studying religion becomes then very similar to the style of clinical discussion.

One indication of the importance of the psychoanalytic interpretation of religion is the degree and the amount of reaction to it on the part of religionists and religious institutions. "If the status of depth psychology as insider or outsider has provoked the dialogue between theology and psychology we must note that the archoutsider (or -insider), Freud himself, continues to make himself felt whenever religion and theology take psychology seriously [Homans, 1968b, p. 8]."

Criticism of the psychoanalytic approach to religion has been voiced often, not only from religionists, but also from sympathetic social scientists. One of the common complaints is the psychoanalytic tendency to overinterpret and over-psychologize, while neglecting the historical and cultural components of the phenomena under analysis. Of course, such accusations of "psychological imperialism" are made against psychological approaches in general from the perspective of other disciplines, and the avoidance of such imperialism should be a basic theoretical concern to all psychologists. Another kind of criticism, which is specific to psychoanalysis, is that it uses a model of psychopathology to explain the phenomena of religion, either as a substantive approach (phenomenon X is the expression of psychopathology, be it a "trance" state or a certain religious persuasion) or as analogy (the dynamics of religious actions are identical to those of psychopathological symptoms—religion as a universal compulsive neurosis). To this criticism there are several answers. First, a dynamic approach to psychopathology means that underlying processes and forces are looked at, and they may be the same for pathological and non-pathological behavior. Second, there is a great deal of interaction between certain religious experiences and psychopathology, as clinical data indicate (e.g., Cavenar & Spaulding, 1977). Third, there may be more psychopathology in individuals and cultures than commonly realized. The Freudian emphasis on pathology teaches humility. Being neurotic is not the exception; it is the rule. And so, the use of psychopathology as a model may be more appropriate than we are ready to admit in our natural narcissism.

Within psychoanalysis itself, new theoretical developments have taken the place of emphasis on Oedipal and instinctual motives, which has been typical of the psychoanalytic study of religion. The rise of Object relations theory (Guntrip, 1968; Rizzuto, 1979; Rubenstein, 1963) and the attention given pre-Oedipal experiences have broadened the scope of the basic psychoanalytic view of personal and cultural phenomena. As a result, many early psychoanalytic studies seem obsolete or narrow in their approach. Another common source of criticism is the use psychoanalysts make of historical and archaeological findings. Still, the weaknesses of specific applications may not negate the value of the general approach.

On the positive side, psychoanalysis may be adopted as a general mode for viewing religion in the context of culture, when more attention is given to social and cultural factors. The impressive body of work inspired by psychoanalysis cannot be dismissed or ignored by the contemporary psychology of religion.

THE STUDY OF RELIGION AND ACADEMIC PSYCHOLOGY

References to religion may be found in the writings of many classical major psychologists, if diligently searched for; but most contemporary academic psychologists would be hard pressed to say anything if invited to give a 5-minute talk on "The Psychology of Religion." Systematic treatments of the subject are rare today. Among the "psychologies of . . . ," the psychology of religion is in a respectable place in terms of the number of books and articles devoted to it, but questions surround the quality of the work and its relationship to other developments in psychology. While many books on "The Psychology of Religion" can be found on library shelves, references to religion or to the psychological study of religion are rare in psychology textbooks, one way of measuring the impact and importance of the psychology of religion today.

Social psychology seems to be the natural subfield of psychology in which to study religion because religion lends itself easily to analysis in social psychological terms, such as beliefs, attitudes, values, and norms. Yet social psychologists, with a few notable and commendable exceptions (Bem, 1970; Festinger, Riecken, & Schachter, 1956; Fishbein & Ajzen, 1974; Rokeach, 1968), have not used religious beliefs as the subject matter for their research and theorizing on beliefs and attitudes. The general flight into the laboratory in social psychology and the trend away from natural social behavior have taken a toll on religion. That the psychological study of religion is of interest to only a small minority in psychology has been documented by Malony (1972). He found, in a random sample of APA members, that only 1.1% reported an interest in studying religion. In brief, the study of religion has not been integrated into mainstream contemporary academic psychology.

The Reluctance to Approach Religion as a Subject of Study

Paradoxical and contradictory forces have shaped the attitudes of psychologists toward the study of religion. Hostility to religion, support for religion, and fear of religion all combine to hamper scholarly work. There may be two sources of resistance—within psychology and within the culture. There may be in all social sciences traces of the cultural taboo against a close study of religion from a scholarly viewpoint. Religion, both as a social institution in the abstract and as concrete institutions and individuals, defends itself against close scrutiny. Psychologists involved in studying religion may be concerned about stepping on too many cultural toes. Religious beliefs still enjoy a tabooed status in Western society, and the religious establishment is not totally powerless. There may be a cultural taboo against looking at religion too closely, which is still affecting scholars in the age of secularization.

Empirical research in behavioral science does not exist in a social vacuum. It is supported, or hindered, by its social environment. Part of this environment is the academic community itself, but sources of pressure extend far beyond universities. Most psychological research projects have been supported by outside sources, especially government ones. Applicants for research grants have to defend the importance and relevance of their projects, and it is doubtful whether many psychologists have proposed projects dealing with religious behavior. From the government's side, it is also doubtful whether much encouragement would have been given those who had applied. Discussions during the uproar over invasion of privacy in psychological testing in 1965 made it clear that members of the U.S. Congress (Gallagher, 1966) considered psychological research in religion undesirable.

Though it may seem logical that religious organizations would be a natural source of support for psychologists interested in studying religion, they have sponsored only limited work. Actually, the relationship of religious organizations to research on religious behavior is ambivalent. As Glock and Stark (1965) have suggested, any seriour systematic study of religion, which follows the canons of social science, must be a threat to religious institutions and these institutions resist it. Leuba (1916) long ago wrote about the resistance to scientific studies of religious beliefs: "It is rather the old desire to protect 'Holy things' from too close scrutiny, and also the more or less unconscious antagonism of those interested in the maintenance of the status quo in religion that have stood in the way of those who might have disposed to face the difficulties of a statistical investigation of religious convictions [p. 175]."

The Study of Religion and the "Paradigm" of Academic Psychology

The psychological study of religion is outside the mainstream of academic psychology because it does not fit into the dominant paradigm in the field. If we follow James's (1907) division between the "tough minded" and the "tender minded," it is easy to see why psychology's approach to religion will be that of rejection and distance. Modern psychology is undoubtedly tough minded, and thus it will be empiricist, skeptical, and irreligious. Several biases in academic psychology work against the study of religion. Psychologists typically pursue a theoretical ideal of studying ahistorical, universal mental processes, and not mental content. The philosophical biases of academic psychology are ahistorical, acultural, asocial, and a-introspective. Thus, psychologists study memory as a process, regardless of the specific material remembered. A case may be made for the claim that there is nothing unique about religion in terms of psychological processes. What defines religion is a specific content, which is rather relative, historical, and constantly changing. Religion means specific content and not specific process.

The triumph of positivism and operationalism contributed to the desire to stay away from religion, on pain of contamination by "unscientific" attitudes. Religion reminds psychology of its "unscientific" past, with ideas of the should, absolute judgments, and untestable beliefs. Some psychologists may wish that this embarrassing relic would just disappear, since they believe that what they are engaged in signifies a triumph over old, mistaken traditions. The academic study of religion in general may be perceived as a threat to ". . . science, reason, logic, and the whole heritage of the Enlightenment [Bellah, 1970, p. 113]." This perception may be exaggerated, but it is not completely without foundation. In the case of psychology, it is true that those who study religion are also promoting it, so that the reaction to the study of religion is a reaction to religion itself. The subject of religion seems too complex and too soft for the laboratory. It is filled with much imagination and feelings, two topics which academic psychology finds hard to approach. Experimental studies of religion in humans are also frought with ethical and practical problems, and only little "experimental" or "quasi-experimental" work has been done in the psychology of religion using the dominant laboratory model in psychology (Deconchy, 1977; Osarchuk & Tate, 1973).

It is unclear whether experimentation in the psychology of religion would have been very fruitful anyway (see Batson, 1977) since it has not always been very fruitful in other areas of social behavior; but, it is certain that the lack of experimentation has contributed to the alienation of the field from mainstream psychology. The "humanistic" criticism of mainstream psychology (Hudson, 1972) seems fully justified in this case: Academic psychology seems to run away from meaningful human behaviors.

Decline in the interest which psychologists have shown in religion as an area of study also parallels the decline in the importance of religion as a social institution, which is a major fact of modern history and modern society (Argyle & Beit-Hallahmi, 1975; Wilson, 1966). Psychologists, too, may be regarded as justified in neglecting religion to some extent, especially in connection with individual dynamics. Religiosity and religious affiliation are found to be correlated with sociological variables, i.e., group traits, rather than psychological variables, i.e., individual traits.

THE STUDY OF RELIGION AND THE RELIGIOUS BELIEFS OF PSYCHOLOGISTS

The finding that scientists and academicians are less religious than the rest of the population has been amply documented (Anderson, 1968a, 1968b; Argyle & Beit-Hallahmi, 1975). Even those who have found that academicians are not totally divorced from religiosity have described them as adhering to a most secularized kind of religious creed (Faulkner & DeJong, 1972)

Stark (1963) provided a convincing illustration of the incompatibility of the scholarly ethos and religion, and he also pointed to the lack of productivity on the part of religious scholars. What has been presumed to be incompatible with the religious stance has been designated by various authors as the "scientific," "scholarly," or "intellectual" viewpoint (Campbell & Magill, 1968; Knapp & Greenbaum, 1953; Lazarsfeld & Thielens, 1958; MacDonell & Campbell, 1971; Stark, 1963) The presumed incompatibility between the scientific orientation and the religious one is supported by the fact that sectarian schools generally rank lower with respect to the quality of their educational programs, student ability, and faculty productivity (Hassenger, 1967; Pattilo & MacKenzie, 1966; Trent, 1967). The explanation is that religious commitment typically leads to compromising scholarly standards.

More detailed investigations have discovered differences in religiosity among academic disciplines. Lehman and Shriver (1968) introduced the concept of scholarly distance from religion which refers to the extent to which an academic discipline considers religion a legitimate object of study. Thus, historians would be lower in scholarly distance than biologists because religion is an accepted subject for historians to study while for biologists it is not.

These findings are especially relevant to the discussion of religious beliefs among psychologists. Psychology is, at least in principle, a "low distance" discipline, and its practitioners are likely to explore religion as they explore other human behaviors. Psychology, as a discipline, would prescribe an analytical stance toward religion and thus would make it less likely for psychologists to be religiously committed. An identical prediction regarding the religiosity of psychologists can be made from the point of view of occupational psychology (Bordin, 1966; Bordin, Nachmann, & Segal, 1963). The choice of psychology as an occupation stems from strong needs for the exploration of interpersonal and personal experiences, and scientific creativity requires skepticism and doubt (Bordin, 1966), which in psychology include skepticism about beliefs and mores. Together with other social scientists, psychologists are considered unconventional, and with some justification (Bereiter & Freedman, 1962; Roe, 1956). This lack of conventionality coupled with the attitude of skepticism that the scientist displays toward social norms should be reflected in lower religious involvement.

Studies of religious beliefs among psychologists tend to support the impression of relative irreligiosity. Leuba (1916) studied the religious beliefs of 50 "distinguished psychologists" and 57 "lesser psychologists" compared to other scientists, sociologists, and historians. He reported that the proportion of believers in "God" among the distinguished psychologists was the lowest of all the groups studied (13.2%). The percentage of believers among the "lesser" psychologists was 32.1 and among all psychologists was 24.2. These results were consistent with Leuba's hypothesis that religious personalities were less likely to be found among social scientists than among physical scientists. Very similar findings regarding psychologists and other scientists were reported by Rogers (1965).

Roe (1952) studied a group of 64 eminent scientists, including 22 psychologists and anthropologists. Most of the scientists came from a Protestant background, and a small minority were Jews. Only three members of the group were active in any church, and the rest were "indifferent" to religion. One clear limitation of the Roe study is that only eminent scientists and psychologists were included. (On the other hand, their eminence may have something to do with the embodiment of traits crucial to the fulfillment of the academic psychologist's role.) A confirmation of Roe's (1952) and Anderson's (1968a) findings came from McClelland (1964), who stated: "I can hardly think of a psychologist, sociologist, or anthropologist of my generation who would admit publicly or privately to a religious commitment of any kind. . . [p. 118]." Henry, Sims, and Spray (1971) studied a large groups of "mental health professionals"— psychologists, psychiatrists, clinical psychologists, and social workers. Almost 50% of the clinical psychologists in this study described their "cultural affinity" as Jewish. In terms of religious affiliation, as differentiated from cultural affinity, 20% of the clinical psychologists identified themselves as Protestant, 8% as Catholic, and 30% as Jewish. The rest reported various shades of nonreligiosity. This picture is, of course, striking when compared with national figures for religious affiliation (which are, roughly 69% Protestant, 25% Catholic, 3% Jewish). Henry et al. (1971) see it as part of the "social marginality" of all mental health professions (Szasz & Nemiroff, 1963). This marginality is similar to that described by Anderson (1968a) for academicians in general. Ragan, Malony, and Beit-Hallahmi (1980) found that in a random sample of APA members, 43% reported a belief in a "transcendent deity," compared to 98% of the general population. Of those APA members who reported a religious affiliation, 51% were Protestant (compared to 69% in the American population), 19% were Jewish (compared to almost 3%), and 15% were Catholic (compared to 25%). This study again confirms that in both religious beliefs and religious affiliation psychologists are far from representative of the general population, or "the real world."

Psychologists Who Study Religion

Given the findings on the indifferent or negative attitudes of most social scientists and psychologists toward religion and the lack of professional interest in it, we would expect those psychologists who are interested in religion as a topic of study to be different from most of their colleagues. The stereotype of the psychologist who is interested in religion, at least among his academic colleagues, embodies the notion of strong religious commitments or frustrated theological ambitions. This stereotype seems to have much truth to it. Ragan et al. (1980) found that members of the APA who study religion tend to be religious themselves. Commitment to religion among such scholars is clear (Allport, 1950, 1978), and many see their main contribution in terms of helping religion become better and stronger (Dittes, 1967). Many have been ordained as ministers or priests and are affiliated with divinity schools, theology schools, or departments of religious studies. Personal statements by psychologists who have been involved in writing in the area of the psychology of religion (Clark, 1978; Dittes, 1978; Gorsuch, 1978; Malony, 1978; Strunk, 1978) show quite clearly that a commitment to a religious viewpoint is an important part of the motivation for their work as psychologists.

Division 36 of the American Psychological Association was founded in 1975. Its official title is "Psychologists Interested in Religious Issues" (PIRI). This name does not reflect religion as an object of study, but only "Religious Issues". The founders of the division are clearly committed religionists. The Society for the Scientific Study of Religion (SSSR), an interdisciplinary nonsectarian organization, includes a minority of psychologists among its members, the majority of whom are sociologists, theologians, historians, and clergymen. Most SSSR members who are psychologists also have a background in religious education.

Ideological Approaches to the Psychological Study of Religion

Any discipline studying religion is forced to deal with the validity of religious claims because religion typically makes rather strong and unusual claims which often enjoy a privileged status within the individual scholar's own culture. The attitude of the psychologist toward the claims of religion has a strong bearing on the way religion is going to be studied. Religious psychologists treat their subject matter differently because they accord a special status to religion's claims, religious institutions, and individual experiences in religion. The religious psychologists will admit the similarity between religion and other belief systems, but will also emphasize the correctness of religion.

The literature on the academic psychology of religion can usefully be divided, according to its ideological bent, into the religionist and the irreligious. Searching in a university library for a book titled *The Psychology of Religion,* the naive reader is likely in most cases to find a volume which is more religious than psychological. The specific religious orientation can, in most cases, be simply deduced from the author's institutional affiliation and the publisher's identity. The religionists' contributions to the psychology of religion may contain useful insights, but they are hampered by the excess baggage of theology, which to most psychologists may seem strange. The theological language used by such authors is not likely to be shared with readers outside their particular tradition, while the psychological language may well be. Some of these books are scholarly, in the sense of demonstrating an excellent knowledge of psychological literature. However, the mélange resulting from the combination of theology and psychology is likely to be exasperating for most psychologists. An example of such writing is Oates (1973), which is a compendium of psychological theories and findings from a variety of sources, presented rather clearly but unsystematically, together with Biblical quotations and theological assertions. Anybody who tries to comprehend the book in search of a psychological theory will be sorely frustrated. Its religious message, however, is much clearer to grasp and is consistent with the fact that the author is a faculty member at the Southern Baptists Theological Seminary.

What prevails today in the writings of psychologists about religion are really three separate traditions:

(1) A religious psychology, which focuses on religious apologetics (e.g., Johnson, 1959).
(2) A psychology of religion, which focuses on the psychological explanation of religious phenomena (e.g., Spanos & Hewitt, 1979).

(3) A social psychology of religion, studying the social-psychological correlates of religion and religiosity, without taking a stand on the validity of religious claims (e.g., Argyle & Beit-Hallahmi, 1975; Beit-Hallahmi, 1973).

The difference between a religious psychology and a psychology of religion is that between defending religious beliefs and explaining them. Psychology of religion treats religion as a phenomenon for systematic psychological study, while religious psychology aims at promoting religion through the adaptation and use of psychological concepts. Our division of the literature into religious psychology, psychology of religion, and the social psychology of religion is based on works rather than individuals. The same individual psychologist can be engaged in all three, though in reality this is not often the case. Allport, for example, has contributed to all three areas. The literature of religious psychology can be identified by the inclusion of a differentiation between "good" religion and "bad" religion, presented under the psychological terms of neurotic versus mature religion (Allport, 1950) or intrinsic versus extrinsic religion (Allport & Ross, 1967). Religious psychologists are preoccupied with questions of the positive and negative effects of religious beliefs and practices, and with the effects of religion on personality functioning. The latter can be seen as the legacy of Jamesian pragmatism and the functionalist school in psychology, combined with the stand of the apologist. The differences in approaches among religious psychology, the psychology of religion, and the social psychology of religion can be best illustrated with a concrete example: the question of the correlation between religiosity and prejudice.

The history of research on this question is quite well known (Argyle & Beit-Hallahmi, 1975). There has been a great number of studies since 1945 showing that in the English-speaking world there is usually a positive correlation between conventional religiosity and the holding of various social prejudices, e.g., racial prejudice. Religious psychologists react to this finding with disappointment and distinguish between those who are deeply religious and less prejudiced and the majority of conventionally religious people, who are prejudiced (Allport & Ross, 1967). Irreligious psychologists deal with this question as part of the social psychology of religion by pointing to a variety of factors in religion as an institution and in society around it. Argyle and Beit-Hallahmi (1975) present a social psychological view, which emphasizes the correlational nature of the findings and their social context. This view is that religion does not cause prejudice, but that religiosity is, in most cases, a part of a social-psychological complex which includes overall conventionality and conservatism. Thus, the social-psychological findings remain the same:

Church-members are more prejudiced than non-church members for so-cial reasons. Religious psychologists have put much effort into showing that "good religion" is correlated with less prejudice, but "good religion" represents only a small social minority and so does not affect the general correlation.

FINDINGS, GENERALIZATIONS, AND THEORETICAL QUESTIONS

In this section I review briefly findings in the social psychology of religion on behaviors and social background correlates of religiosity and religious affiliations. More detailed reports of these findings, summarizing the re-search literature, are found in Dittes (1969) and in Argyle and Beit-Hallahmi (1975).

The Consequence of Religiosity

Glock (1962), in one of the best known and most frequently used formula-tions in social science literature on religion, proposed the following five dimensions of religiosity:

(1) Ideological, covering religious beliefs.
(2) Intellectual, covering religious knowledge.
(3) Ritualistic, covering participation in religious rituals.
(4) Experiental, covering intense religious experiences.
(5) Consequential, covering the consequences of religiosity in non-religious activities.

Later, as the result of further research, the consequential dimension was dropped, the reason given that such consequences in non-religious behavior could not be found, and only four dimensions have remained (Glock & Stark, 1965). These four dimensions are widely used. One prob-lem in the study of consequences is logical and methodological. Most of the research done on consequences is correlational and cannot indicate causality. Even when more detailed comparisons are made between groups, the question of screening out non-religious variables remains. It is always safer to assume that secular factors lead to secular behaviors, but, traditionally, religion is tied to the expectation of consequences in the secular sphere. The main reason for the expectation of consequences is that religious traditions quite explicitly predict those consequences. Reli-gion exists for many believers as a prescriptive behavior system, contain-ing specific "shoulds" and "should nots." For many believers, religion is a proscriptive, not a prescriptive, system and from the psychological viewpoint is concerned mainly with impulse control. The findings (Argyle & Beit-Hallahmi, 1975) indicate that religion does have a considerable effect on secular behavior in two areas, sexual behavior and the use of drugs, but these effects exist only where a specific proscription exists. Generalizing beyond these specific areas has been difficult.

The expectation that religiosity would lead to some kind of a general social attitude in response to the traditional moral exhortations of religious representatives has not been supported by research. Religious people are not more likely to engage in positive social actions, to be more honest, or to be more generous (Argyle & Beit-Hallahmi, 1975). The well-known findings about the positive correlation between religiosity and prejudice have been mentioned in this context, but it is hard to view them as specific consequences of religiosity. The best explanation for the correlation among religiosity and prejudice, authoritarianism, and conservatism, may be sociological rather than psychological. Religious people tend to be conservative in their general world view and to support the traditional beliefs of their cultures in non-religious areas. The question of consequences is related to the question of the religious personality which is the search for consequences on an individual personality level.

The Search for the "Religious Personality"

After sources of religious motivation are examined, a distinction is often made between genuine religious motives and secondary (external) motives. This issue has been studied by Allport and Ross (1967) and by others through the suggested intrinsic-extrinsic dimension of religious belief. Actually, this is the old tradition of differentiating the "true believer", who puts his heart and soul into his faith (or his faith into his heart and soul), and the "follower" of religion, who pays lip service to its tenets because of external considerations.

But this attractive distinction between true believers and the conventionally religious has gotten bogged down in the mire of empirical measurements. The dimension proposed by Allport and Ross (1967) has been found to be lacking in validity and consistency. One finding is clear: that is, the majority of churchgoers belong to the extrinsic category, the true believers having always been, and remain, in the minority.

Something which the layman expects of the psychologist studying religion is a psychological description of the religious person. The layman may ask, with some justification, what the religious person is like and how that person is different from the non-religious person. Religion expects the religious person to be different and tells him to be different. So one natural task of the psychology of religion is to develop a psychological profile of the religious person. The obstacles to the completion of this task have been many. Numerous studies have tried to contribute to the hoped-for psychological profile (see Beit-Hallahmi, 1973; Brown, 1973), but so far the results have been disappointing. The first obstacle, pointed out above, is that of defining the truly religious person. What we are able to conclude about the religious person in Western society today is that that person is probably more conventional, authoritarian, dogmatic, and suggestible than is the non-religious person. Dittes (1969) reflects another judgment when he states that " . . . psychological research reflects an over-whelming consensus that religion (at least as measured in the research, usually institutional affiliation or adherence to conservative traditional doctrines) is associated with awareness of personal inadequacies, either generally or in response to particular crisis or threat situations; with objective evidence of inadequacy, such as low intelligence; with a strong responsiveness to the suggestions of other persons or other external influences; and with an array of what may be called desperate and generally unadaptive defensive maneuvers [p. 616]."

Why have attempts to relate personality variables and religiosity been unsuccessful? One reason is the complexity of variables and measurements. The field of personality research in recent years has been in a state of upheaval. One extreme position suggests that stable trans-situational personality traits do not exist. Less extreme positions emphasize the ideal of the interaction, i.e. behavior is a function of both internal stable traits and external presses of the situation, and those traits or presses change over time. When this complexity is brought into the study of religious behavior, which is in itself complex and overdetermined, it is small wonder that no easy generalizations arise. Further, secularization has meant that there is less detectable influence of religion on individual personality and behavior.

One may ask the question, "Does religion, in our secularized society, make a difference in anybody's life?" This question has been asked by Bouma (1970), and his answer was that indeed we are able to prove only a marginal influence of religion in any area of modern life. Nevertheless, religion may remain useful for predicting group trends, and it may serve as a significant identity label.

Social-Psychological Findings

The following findings are summarized from Argyle and Beit-Hallahmi (1975):

(1) Religious behavior is obviously culturally and socially conditioned. This may sound like a truism, but it is an important and elementary truth which tends to be neglected quite often. Social

learning remains the best explanation for most religious actions. Actually, as we look closer at more unusual and "esoteric" religious actions, it becomes clear that they are socially learned, just like the less "esoteric" ones. To the question, "Why do people believe in God?", the best answer remains, "Because they have been taught to believe in God." The variety of religious traditions and the correspondence between the tradition of the social environment and the religion of the individual are the most obvious proofs to the validity of the social learning approach, which is also able to explain what are considered intense religious experiences (Spanos & Hewitt, 1979).

(2) In accordance with (1) above, the effects of parental beliefs are more important than any other factor in determining individual religiosity.

(3) Unmarried individuals are likely to be more involved in religious activities than married individuals.

(4) Adolescence is the period of religious "conversions," which are experiences of personal re-commitment to a familiar religious tradition and differ from true conversions, which mean the change from religious tradition A to religious tradition B, such as the cases of Thomas Merton (1948) and Alphonse Ratisbonne (James, 1902).

(5) There is a decline in religious involvement during the third decade of life.

(6) There is a rise in religious involvement after age 30 to old age.

(7) Women are higher than men on every measure of religiosity and religious involvement. They are also more likely to support para-religious, para-psychological, and pseudo-scientific beliefs (e.g., Markle, Peterson, & Wagenfeld, 1978).

(8) There is a slight negative correlation between religiosity and I.Q.

(9) Religiosity is correlated with the traits of authoritarianism, dogmatism, and suggestibility.

(10) Religiosity is positively correlated with ethnocentrism and political conservatism.

(11) Religiosity does not affect suicidal behaviors.

(12) Religiosity is negatively correlated with sexual activity, as measured by "total sexual outlet" (number of orgasms per week).

(13) Religiosity is positively correlated with better adjustment in marriage and a lower frequency of divorce.

The Historicity of Findings in The Study of Religion

An important realization in regard to research in the social psychology of religion is that answers to the questions that this field attempts to address are often historical in nature. This argument has been raised in connection with other areas of psychological research. Psychologists frequently look for universal laws and generalizations, and this search is believed to be feasible in principle and hampered only by technical difficulties. However, it is possible that this search may be more difficult than hitherto expected. A source of doubt and criticism among psychologists over the past few years has been the growing realization of the timebound nature of psychological findings; that is, psychologists have realized that more general questions in social psychology and in personality research have answers which are always tied to specific historical situations. Atkinson (1974) suggested that any empirical relationship between personality variables describes only a "modal personality" at a particular historical moment.

Notions of the transhistorical and transcultural nature of certain behaviors are especially prevalent in the study of religion. Religious beliefs and religious sentiments seem to have been in existence everywhere and in every historical period. Distinguishing the cultural and temporal from the transcultural and transhistorical may be one aim of the psychology of religion. Cultural differences in space, of which we are already aware, may be equalled by historical differences in time, of which we are now becoming increasingly conscious. The historicity of findings regarding the social psychology of religion may be realized reading any survey of such findings (Argyle & Beit-Hallahmi, 1975). It becomes clear that the psychological impact of religion in modern societies is changing and becoming more limited as a result of secularization. Psychologists of religion, while describing contemporary situations, were mainly writing the chronicles of secularization.

QUESTIONS FOR FUTURE WORK

It seems that the surface has barely been scratched in considering psychological aspects of religion as a living institution. The "classical" question in the psychological study of religion has been phrased as follows: "Does religion, or religiosity, make a difference in individual behavior and individual personality?" The question of consequences on behavior and personality has been the most common other than the question of the psychological nature of religion itself. The reason for the emphasis on consequences has been historical and cultural. Historically, religion has been thought of and described as a "moral system," concerned with the morality or immorality of specific behaviors and the definition of transgression and sin. The traditional view of religion as a prescriptive-proscriptive system, aimed at controlling individual behavior, has led to the expectation of differences in actual behavior. This expectation may have to be changed for the following reasons:

(1) Historically, the influence of religion is diminishing. Religion will make less of a difference in individual behavior, as the worldwide process of secularization continues.
(2) There are many human activities that are engaged in for themselves, without any additional consequences expected. Such activities are commonly referred to as "art" or "entertainment." We do not expect any effects in subsequent behavior when people go to museums, theaters, or athletic events; why should be expect any effects when they go to church?
(3) In light of (2), it is possible that we were looking for the wrong kinds of consequence and using the wrong kinds of instruments.

One of the functions of religion, according to "cognitive need" theories in the social sciences (Argyle & Beit-Hallahmi, 1975), is to supply both individuals and societies with a meaning system for life events. If religion is indeed a personal meaning system, the questions to be answered are, "When and how often are religious explanations used for personal or non-personal events?" If religion is a meaning system, and if religion is a system of moral guidance designed to affect individual moral decisions, how does this process take place in reality? How often do individuals ascribe religious meaning to events in their everyday life? How often is religion taken into consideration in moral decisions? Despite the fact that these concerns are a major part of religious traditions, we still know very us meaning to events in their everyday life? How often is religion taken into consideration in moral decisions? Despite the fact that these concerns are a major part of religious traditions, we still know very little about them. It is plausible to assume that religious belief systems are not used often, or only as a last resort, in modern society. If religion is indeed an individual or a social meaning system, then it is quite clear that its function as a meaning system is quite limited and does not ever include every sphere of human experience. Even in the most religious culture, there are always certain objects or occasions which are outside the realm of holiness. Otherwise, how would holiness be defined? Cultures may differ, of course, quantitatively, in the extent to which religious meaning is given to human experiences, and this may be a psychological index of secularization. What we can say is that for most humans today, the religious meaning system, if extant at all, is well circumscribed and rather narrow. The boundaries of the religious meaning system constitute an intriguing question for psychological research.

The Nature of Religious Beliefs

The nature of religious belief for the common believer has not really been investigated because notions about beliefs have been heavily influenced by theology, not psychology. Beliefs are most often expressed as fantasies. A belief is a certainty that *something happened,* that a certain story is true. This is our subject matter, and our abstractions should grow out of it, and not above it. The question to be answered is that of the human capacity to imagine and believe, as it is expressed in concrete cultural forms. How and when do religious beliefs appear in the consciousness of the believer? Do they appear in the context of "ultimate concerns" or other concerns? Do they appear in connection with ideas about death, morality, or social divisions? It may be useful to accept the dichotomy between the majority of religious persons, for whom religious commitment is rather limited and narrow, and the minority of "true believers," whose commitment to religion is deep and wide. The latter group is more interesting psychologically, and studying them may be more fruitful for answering the above questions.

Religion and Identity

The tension between the individual and the social in religion has not been recognized often enough in psychological studies. The individualistic bias in the psychology of religion can be traced back, though not exclusively ascribed, to William James and his notions that the "religions experience" is an individual experience. James (1902) once defined religion as "The feelings, acts, and experiences of individual men in their solitude, so far as they apprehend themselves to stand in relation to whatever they may consider divine [pp. 31–32]." As Reck (1967) put it, the definition "strikingly excludes institutional religion." James's separation of the private and the public in religious acts seems to echo a cultural trend, that of separating the private and the public in every aspect of behavior; but the question is open whether such a separation is possible in religion, or in any other field. Is there any religious activity which is not part of an institution? Are there any private creations in religion which reflect only an experience "in solitude," without reference to a tradition? James, and Maslow (1964) after him, have supported the myth of the lonely great founder, the individual who goes into the desert, comes back with a great vision, and then loses this vision to the forces of institutionalization. This myth is psychologically attractive, but historically far from true. Religion is a communal experience, not only an individual experience.

Religion is both personal and social, individual and cultural. The questions are, "What and how does the individual add to the cultural tradition?" The concept of identity seems to provide a bridge between the private and the public realms of religion, as an appropriate locus for that which connects the individual personality and the cultural matrix. An individual identity is made up of several subidentities, and the religious subidentity may be one of those.

Identity and subidentity are useful social-psychological concepts which provide a bridge between individual personality and social tradition. The psychology of identity, as a social-psychological concept, should contribute to understanding the so-called "persistence of religion" (Allport, 1950). Religion is preserved where social forces keep it as part of a group identity, and it is often promoted as such.

For most individuals, religion exists as part of their identity. They do not believe in a certain religious system. They are members of a religious group. They are Catholics, Jews, or Moslems. The only choice most individuals make, if they can make a choice at all regarding the dominant religious belief system in their group, is a sociometric one: whether they will follow group tradition.

CONCLUSION:
INTEGRATING THE STUDY OF RELIGION AND THE DISCIPLINE OF PSYCHOLOGY

The problem of integrating the psychology of religion within psychology in general has to do with our conceptions of the two. Today, the psychology of religion is outside the mainstream of academic psychology (Beit-Hallahmi, 1977). A changed conception of the science of psychology as the science of being human will enable such an integration. The current lack of interest on the part of academic psychology in religion, in terms of theory and research, is not that different paradigmatically from the situation in regard to other significant social behaviors. (How much attention does academic psychology give to art?) Such studies require a historical and humanistic approach and cooperation with the traditional humanities and "softer" social sciences. It may be claimed, with justification, that most research in the psychological study of religion is unsystematic and rarely guided by a general model or paradigm. Often, it takes the form of a correlational study done on a sample of convenience, through the use of a questionnaire created especially for that particular study. However, the above description fits many areas of psychology and not just the study of religion. Academic psychologists studying religion merely follow the accepted etiquette of research production. The relationship between the psychological study of religion and academic psychology in general may be assessed by the extent to which general principles of psychological theories are applied to the study of religion. The truth of the matter is that, first, we do not have many accepted general principles in psychological

theory and, second, to the extent that such principles exist, they are not
often applied to the study of religion. Research questions in the psychological study of religion are not usually formulated as a test of some
general theory or principle. More often than not they are internal to the
field.

The cry may be heard that the reason much research on the psychology
of religion is unsystematic is that the field lacks a major coherent theory.
This claim is worth examining. What do we want a psychological theory
of religion to explain? What is a good theory in the psychology of religion?
Ideally, a psychological theory of religion should be a general theory of
human actions and consciousness in which religion is but one instance of
more general principles. Universal elements in religion and culture are the
subject matter of the psychology of religion. The world of the spirits is
universal, created by universal process of the human psyche. It is projection of the internal psychical world of objects. We do have a good theory
in the psychology of religion, and that theory is psychoanalysis.

Freud and James told us that though religion may be an illusion, its
psychological sources are real and effective. Religious involvement stems
from the deepest layers of man's consciousness and experiences. One
thing we should all remember as psychologists is that emotion is the fuel
which keeps many religious flames alive. It was Freud who enabled us to
relate the strength of religious emotions in the individual to the individual's developmental history. Depth psychology gives us an answer to the
question of the universal potential for religion. If there is indeed such a
universal readiness, it must stem from the universal nature of those early
universal conflicts which religion reflects and projects. If, as Freud suggested, religion reflects the yearning and fears tied to the early objects in
the child's life, then universal experiences with these objects create the
readiness to echo religious sentiments.

What Freud emphasized, in contrast to various apologists for religion,
was that the strength of human emotions involved in religious activities
and experiences is not proof for the validity of religious beliefs. The
source of these emotions, according to psychoanalysis, is internal. They
are no indication of a response to something "out there," but an indication
of needs and anxieties within the human psyche. Freud's insights may
help us empathize with the two faces of religion as a social force—the
Eros and Thanatos of religion. It may be a force for love and brotherhood
when human beings are drawn together by a common belief and a common attachment. It may also be a force for hatred, ranging from the moral
indignation of the preacher to the lethal fanaticism of the crusader, both
guided and driven by the burning flames of a cruel super-ego, reflected
and projected in the fires of hell.

One thing that has to be remembered in connection with Freud's historical hypothesis is that explanations for the historical origins of religious acts may not be identical or relevant to the motivation for such acts at present, i.e., it is possible that a certain religious act is a sublimation and ritualization of some prehistorical event or custom, but the person follow-ing this religious custom today is not aware of this origin and may be doing it for completely different reasons. Many academic psychologists are made uneasy by the psychoanalytic emphasis on the unconscious and the invisible. But when psychologists analyze fantasies, they have to base their analysis on a theory which regards human fantasy as its subject matter. It is quite clear that behaviorism does not have much to say about religion, beyond the fact that it serves a social control function. Reading Skinner (1953) on religion is one of the best arguments for a dynamic psychology of religion. The behaviorist analysis turns out to be merely a boring and narrow description without any explanations whatsoever.

We can reach another conclusion and another answer to the question of why religion is not studied more often by psychologists. If the best avail-able theory for understanding religious phenomena, psychoanalysis, is almost banished from the groves of academic psychology, and if the whole approach of academic psychology to human actions is mainly acul-tural and ahistorical, then it is not surprising that religion is not a very appropriate topic for psychological research. The psychology of religion has to be historical and cultural, and it will flourish only with a psychology which is cultural and historical. While we cannot expect a rise in the popularity of the psychoanalytic paradigm within academic psychology, it will continue to be one of the dominant paradigms in the study of religion outside of psychology.

"Religious suffering is at the same time an expression of real suffering and a protest against real suffering. Religion is the sign of the oppressed creature, the heart of a heartless world, and the soul of soulless condi-tions. It is the opium of the people [Marx, 1964, pp. 43–44]." If Freud provides us with the basis for a depth psychology of religion, this well-known and eloquent quotation can serve as the basis for a social psychol-ogy of religion in the contemporary world. Marxian ideas are especially enlightening if we want to understand the functions of religion in a sec-ularized world. In the rationalized world of advanced industrial society, religion may be indeed the heart of the heartless world and the soul of soulless conditions. More effective kinds of opium now dominate the market, but religion still offers a shelter, a sanctuary from dehumanized reality, and a haven from alienation. The needs satisfied by religion are real and intense, while its answers are illusory and harmful. The intensity of responses to religious solutions may be one indication of real psycho-logical deprivations. The enthusiastic adherents of old and new gurus try to heal the deep wounds left in their souls by our mechanized, cruel world. Theirs may be a false consciousness, but their pain is never false (Marx, 1964; Marx & Engels, 1957). Marx offered his own theory of psychological projections as the source of religion. His view of religion in relation to the real world leads to several interesting predictions, both social and personal. If religion is indeed a projection of the mysteries and deprivations of the real world, then we can expect two things: first, more religiosity in oppressed groups and, second, more emotion in the religiosity of the oppressed. Research on the social psychology of religion has provided much support for these predictions (Argyle & Beit-Hallahmi, 1975; Photiadis & Schnabel, 1977).

Ideas for revising the philosophy of our specialized field should consider the calls for the renewal of psychology as a discipline. The movement to turn psychology into a humanistic field of inquiry will make it easier to find within it a home for the psychology of religion. Cronbach (1975) in proposing a new manifesto for psychology states: "The goal of our work . . . is not to amass generalizations atop which a theoretical tower can someday be erected. . . . The special task of the social scientist in each generation is to pin down the contemporary facts. Beyond that, he shared with the humanistic scholar and the artist in the effort to gain insight into contemporary relationships, and to realign the culture's view of man with present realities. To know man as he is, is no mean aspiration [p. 126]."

The definition of boundaries between the psychology of religion and other disciplines has been worked in practice. What happened in the field, so to speak, in the places where psychologists of religion carry out their work and present the fruits of their labor (in conferences, libraries, and scholarly journals), is that contributions to the field were not made only by psychologists. Sociologists and anthropologists have opened up the field and have made psychological contributions. Trying to keep from crossing disciplinary boundaries becomes futile since the issues do not define themselves according to the conventional boundaries, and the answers we are seeking cannot be limited by those boundaries. There are no purely psychological questions in the psychology of religion, so that there are no purely psychological answers.

Any attempt to understand religion as a human phenomenon has to be interdisciplinary; indeed, ". . . religion can best be understood from a combination of psychological and cultural points of view [Wallace, 1966, p. vii]." Psychoanalysis, while being in conflict with the dominant paradigm in academic psychology, fits well with a historical, cultural, and humanistic emphasis. While psychoanalytic theory provides the grounding for an understanding of the world of spirits as a creation of the human psyche, the specific cultural projections onto the world of spirits have to be examined in relation to anthropology and history. Psychology of religion should become part of the study of cultures, or the science of culture, which would include the shared and collective experiences of individual humans in cultural groups. In such an enterprise the concept of identity should be central for the psychological viewpoint. Instead of the behavioral sciences—ahistorical and acultural—we should have the cultural sciences, psychology, anthropology, and sociology, collaborating with the traditional humanities. Psychology of culture should cover art, literature, religion, ritual, symbols, and cultural communication. Within such a psychology of culture there will be room for the development of a humanistic psychological study of religion.

ACKNOWLEDGMENTS

I would like to acknowledge the useful ideas generously offered to me by Robert T. Anderson, Lucy Bregman, Donald Capps, W. Fred Graham, Paul M. Gustafson, Peter Homans, Lewish R. Rambo, Hendrika Vande Kemp, Alford T. Welch, and A. H. Mathias Zahniser. The views presented here have profited from their advice, but are my sole responsibility. Most of this essay was wrritten during a sabbatical leave at Michigan State University; I am grateful to the psychology department there for making this work possible.

REFERENCES

Adorno, T. W., Frenkel-Brunswick, E., Levinson, D. J., & Sanford, R. N. *The authoritarian personality*. New York: Harper, 1950.
Alatas, S. H. Problems of defining religion. *International Social Science Journal*, 1977, *29*, 213–234.
Allport, G. W. *The individual and his religion*. New York: Macmillan, 1950.
Allport, G. W. *Waiting for the Lord: 33 meditations on God and man*. New York: Macmillan, 1978.
Allport, G. W., & Ross, J. M. Personal religious orientation and prejudice. *Journal of Personality and Social Psychology*, 1967, *5*, 432–443.
Anderson, C. H. The intellectual subsociety hypothesis: An empirical test. *Sociological Quarterly*, 1968, *8*, 210–227. (a)
Anderson, C. H. Religious communality among academics. *Journal for the Scientific Study of Religion*, 1968, *7*, 87–96. (b)
Argyle, M., & Beit-Hallahmi, B. *The social psychology of religion*. London: Routledge and Kegan Paul, 1975.
Atkinson, J. W. Motivational determinants of intellective performance and cumulative achievement. In J. W. Atkinson & J. O. Raynor (Eds.), *Motivation and achievement*. Washington, DC: Winston, 1974.
Batson, C. D. Experimentation in the psychology of religion: An impossible dream. *Journal for the Scientific Study of Religion*, 1977, *16*, 413–418.

Beit-Hallahmi, B. *Research in religious behavior: Selected readings.* Belmont, CA: Brooks/Cole, 1973.

Beit-Hallahmi, B. Salvation and its vicissitudes: Clinical psychology and political values. *American Psychologist,* 1974, *29,* 124–129. (a)

Beit-Hallahmi, B. Psychology of religion, 1880–1930: The rise and fall of a psychological movement. *Journal of the History of the Behavioral Sciences,* 1974, *10,* 84–90. (b)

Beit-Hallahmi, B. On the "religious" functions of the helping professions. *Archiv für Religionpsychologie,* 1976, *12,* 48–52.

Beit-Hallahmi, B. Curiosity, doubt and devotion. The beliefs of psychologists and the psychology of religion. In H. N. Malong (Ed.), *Current perspectives in the psychology of religion.* Grand Rapids, MI: Eerdmans, 1977.

Beit-Hallahmi, B. *Psycholoanalysis and religion: A bibliography.* Norwood, PA: Norwood Editions, 1978.

Beit-Hallahmi, B., & Argyle, M. God as a father projection: The theory and the evidence. *British Journal of Medical Psychology,* 1975, *48,* 71–75.

Bellah, R. N. Response to comments on "Christianity and symbolic realism." *Journal for the Scientific Study of Religion,* 1970, *9,* 112–115.

Bem, D. J. *Beliefs, attitudes, and human affairs.* Belmont, CA: Brooks/Cole, 1970.

Bereiter, C., & Freedman, M. B. Fields of study and the people in them. In N. Sanford (Ed.), *The American college.* New York: Wiley, 1962.

Betts, G. *The beliefs of 700 ministers.* New York: Abington, 1929.

Bordin, E. S. Curiosity, compassion and doubt: The dilemma of the psychologist. *American Psychologist,* 1966, *21,* 116–121.

Bordin, E. S., Nachmann, B., & Segal, S. J. An articulated framework for vocational development. *Journal of Counseling Psychology,* 1963, *10,* 107–118.

Bouma, G. D. Assessing the impact of religion: A critical review. *Sociological Analysis,* 1970, *31,* 172–179.

Bowser, A. Delimiting religion in the constitution: A classification problem. *Valparaiso Univeristy Law Review,* 1977, *11,* 163–226.

Brown, L. B. *Psychology and religion.* Harmondsworth: Penguin, 1973.

Campbell, D. F., & Magill, D. W. Religious involvement and intellectuality among univeristy students. *Sociological Analysis,* 1968, *29,* 79–93.

Cattell, R. B. *Psychology and the religious quest.* London: Thomas Nelson and Sons, 1938.

Cavenar, J. C. Jr., & Spaulding, J. G. Depressive disorders and religious conversions. *Journal of Nervous and Mental Disease,* 1977, *165,* 209–212.

Clark, E. T. *The psychology of religious awakening.* New York: Macmillan, 1929.

Clark, W. H. A follower of William James. In H. N. Malony (Ed.) *Psychology and faith: The Christian experience of eighteen psychologists.* Washington, DC: University Press of America, 1978.

Coe, G. A. *The psychology of religion.* Chicago, IL: University of Chicago, 1916.

Conklin, E. S. *The psychology of religious adjustment.* New York: Macmillan, 1929.

Cronbach, A. The psychology of religion. *Psychological Bulletin,* 1933, *30,* 377–384.

Cronbach, L. J. Beyond the two disciplines of scientific psychology. *American Psychologist,* 1975, *30,* 116–127.

Deconchy, J. P. Regulation et signification dans un cas de "compromis" ideologique (ecclesiastiques catholiques et propositions "marxistes"). *Bulletin de Psychologie,* 1977, *30,* 436–450.

Dittes, J. E. *The Church in the way.* New York: Scribners, 1967.

Dittes, J. E. Psychology of religion. In G. Lindzey & E. Aronson (Eds.), *The handbook of social psychology* (Vol. 5). Reading, MA: Addison-Wesley, 1969.

Dittes, J. E. Christian style in academics and administration. In H. N. Malony (Ed.),

Psychology and faith: The Christian experience of eighteen psychologists. Washington, DC: University Press of America, 1978.

Douglas, W. Religion. In N. L. Farberow (Ed.), *Taboo topics.* New York: Atherton Press, 1963.

Durkheim, E. *The elementary forms of religious life.* London: Allen and Unwin, 1915.

Erikson, E. *Young man Luther.* New York: Norton, 1958.

Erikson, E. H. Ontogeny of ritualization. In R.M. Loewenstein (Ed.), *Psychoanalysis—A general psychology.* New York: International Universities Press, 1966.

Faulkner, J. E., & DeJong, G. Religion and intellectuals. *Review of Religious Research,* 1972, *14,* 15–24.

Festinger, L., Riecken, H. W., & Schachter, S. *When prophecy fails.* Minneapolis, MN: University of Minnesota Press, 1956.

Fishbein, M., & Ajzen, I. Attitudes towards objects as predictors of single and multiple behavioral criteria. *Psychological Bulletin,* 1974, *81,* 59–74.

Frazer, J. G. *The golden bough.* New York: Macmillan, 1951.

Freud, S. [*The future of an illusion*] *The standard edition of the psychological writings of Sigmund Freud* (Vol. 21). (J. Strachey, trans. and ed.). London: Hogarth Press, 1961. (Originally published, 1927.)

Gallagher, C. E. In testimony before the House Special Subcommittee on Invasion of Privacy of the Committee on Government Operations. *American Psychologist,* 1966, *21,* 404–422.

Glock, C. Y. On the study of religious commitment. *Religious Education,* 1962, *57,* S98–S109.

Glock, C. Y., & Stark, R. *Religion and society in tension.* Chicago, IL: Rand McNally, 1965.

Gorsuch, R. L. Research psychology: An indirect ministry to the ministers. In H. N. Malony (Ed.), *Psychology and faith: The Christian experience of eighteen psychologists.* Washington, DC: University Press of America, 1978.

Guntrip, H. *Schizoid phenomena, object relations and the self.* New York: International Universities Press, 1968.

Gurin, G., Veroff, J., & Feld, S. *Americans view their mental health.* New York: Basic Books, 1960.

Hall, G. S. The moral and religious training of children. *Princeton Review,* 1882, *9,* 26–45.

Hall, G. S. *Adolescence: Its psychology and its relations to physiology, anthropology, sociology, sex, crime, religion, and education.* New York: Appleton, 1904.

Hassenger, R. (Ed.). *The shape of Catholic higher education.* Chicago, IL: University of Chicago Press, 1967.

Henry, E. R. A survey of courses in psychology offered by undergraduate colleges of liberal arts. *Psychological Bulletin,* 1938, *35,* 430–435.

Henry, W. E., Sims, J. H., & Spray, S.L. *The fifth profession.* San Francisco, CA: Jossey-Bass, 1971.

Homans, P. (Ed.). *The dialogue between theology and psychology.* Chicago, IL: The University of Chicago Press, 1968. (a)

Homans, P. Introduction. In P. Homans (Ed.), *The dialogue between theology and psychology.* Chicago, IL: University of Chicago Press, 1968. (b)

Homans, P. *Theology after Freud.* Indianapolis, IN: Bobbs-Merrill, 1970.

Hudson, L. *The cult of the fact.* London: Cape, 1972.

Inkeles, A., & Smith, D. H. *Becoming modern.* Cambridge, MA: Harvard University Press, 1974.

James, W. Preface in E. D. Starbuck, *The psychology of religion.* New York: Scribners, 1899.

·James, W. *The varieties of religious experience: A study in human nature*. New York: Longmans, Green, 1902.

James, W. *Pragmatism: A new name for some old ways of thinking*. New York: Longmans, Green, 1907.

James, W. *The will to believe*. New York: Dover Publications, 1956.

Johnson, P. E. *Psychology of religion*. New York: Abingdon, 1959.

Jones, E. *Essays in applied psychoanalysis*. London: Hogarth Press, 1951.

Kantor, J. R. *The scientific evolution of psychology*. Chicago, IL: The Principia Press, 1969.

Kardiner, A., & Linton, R. *The psychological frontiers of society*. New York: Columbia University Press,1945.

Knapp, R. H., & Greenbaum, J. J. *The younger American scholar*. Chicago, IL: The University of Chicago Press, 1953.

La Barre, W. *The ghost dance*. New York: Dell, 1972.

Lazarsfeld, P., & Thielens, W., Jr. *The academic mind*. Glencoe, IL: Free Press, 1958.

Lehman, E. C., & Shriver, D. W. Academic discipline as predictive of faculty religiosity. *Social Forces*, 1968, *47*, 171–182.

Leuba, J. H. A study in the psychology of religious phenomena. *American Journal of Psychology*, 1896, *7*, 309–385.

Leuba, J. H. The contents of religious experience. *The Monist*, 1901, *4*, 11.

Leuba, J. H. *A psychological study of religion*. New York: Macmillan, 1912.

Leuba, J. H. *The belief in God and immorality*. Boston, MA: Sherman, French, 1916.

Leuba, J. H. Ecstatic intoxication in religion. *American Journal of Psychology*, 1917, *28*, 578–584.

Leuba, J. H. Psychology of religion. *Psychological Bulletin*, 1926, *23*, 714–722. (a)

Leuba, J. H. *The psychology of religious mysticism*. New York: Harcourt, 1926. (b)

Leuba, J. H. Religious beliefs of American scientists. *Harper's*, 1934, *169*, 297.

McClelland, D. C. *The roots of consciousness*. New York: Van Nostrand, 1964.

MacDonell, A. J., & Campbell, D. F. Performance and change in the religious dimensions of an intellectual elite. *Social Compass*, 1971, *18*, 609–619.

Malony, H. N. The psychologist-Christian. *Journal of the American Scientific Affiliation*, 1972, 24, 135–144.

Malony, H. N. The psychologist-Christian. In H. N. Malony (Ed.), *Psychology and faith: The Christian experience of eighteen psychologists*. Washington, DC: University Press of America, 1978.

Markle, G. E., Peterson, J. C., & Wagenfeld, M. O. Notes from the cancer underground: Participation in the Laetrile movement. *Social Science and Medicine*, 1978, *12*, 31–57.

Marx, K. *Early writings*. New York: McGraw-Hill, 1964.

Marx, K., & Engels, F. *K. Marx and F. Engels on religion*. Moscow: Foreign Languages Publishing House, 1957.

Maslow, A. H. *Religions, values, and peak experiences*. Columbus, OH: Ohio State University Press, 1964.

Merton, T. *The seven storey mountain*. New York: Harcourt, Brace, 1948.

Mowrer, O. H. *The crisis in psychiatry and religion*. Princeton, NJ: Van Nostrand, 1961.

Muensterberger, W. The sources of belief. Introduction to G. Roheim, *The panic of the gods*. New York: Harper, 1972.

Muller, M. *Introduction to the science of religion*. London: Longsman, Green, 1870.

Oates, W. A. *The psychology of religion*. Waco, TX: Word Publishers, 1973.

Osarchuk, M., & Tate, S.J. Effect of induced fear of death on belief in afterlife. *Journal of Personality and Social Psychology*, 1973, *27*, 256–260.

Page, F. H. The psychology of religion after fifty years. *Canadian Journal of Psychology*, 1951, *5*, 60–67.

Parsons, T. *The social system*. Glencoe, IL: Free Press, 1951.

Parsons, T. *Structure and process in modern society*. Glencoe, IL: Free Press, 1960.

Pattillo, M. M., & MacKenzie, D. M. *Church-sponsored higher education in the United States*. Washington, DC: American Council on Higher Education, 1966.

Photiadis, J. D., & Schnabel, J. F. Religion: A persistent institution in a changing Appalachia. *Review of Religious Research*, 1977, *19*, 32–42.

Pratt, J. B. Psychology of religion. *Harvard Theological Review*, 1908, *1*, 435–454.

Pruyser, P. W. Sigmund Freud and his legacy: Psychoanalytic psychology of religion. In C. Y. Glock & P. E. Hammond (Eds.), *Beyond the classics: Essays in the scientific study of religion*. New York: Harper and Row, 1973.

Ragan, C., Malony, H. N., & Beit-Hallahmi, B. Psychologists and religion—Professional factors and personal beliefs. *Review of Religious Research*, 1980, *21*, 208–217.

Rank, O. *The myth of the birth of the hero*. New York: Journal of Nervous and Mental Disease Publishing Company, 1914.

Reck, A. J. *Introduction to William James*. Bloomington, IN: Indiana University Press, 1967.

Reik, T. *Ritual: Psychoanalytic studies*. New York: Farrar, 1946.

Reik, T. *Dogma and compulsion*. New York: International Universities Press, 1951.

Rizzuto, A. M. *The birth of the living God*. Chicago, IL: University of Chicago Press, 1979.

Roe, A. *The making of a scientist*. New York: Dodd, Mead, 1952.

Roe, A. *The psychology of occupations*. New York: Wiley, 1956.

Rogers, D. P. Some religious beliefs of scientists and the effect of the scientific method. *Review of Religious Research*, 1965, *7*, 70–77.

Rokeach, M. *Beliefs, attitudes, and values*. San Francisco, CA: Jossey-Bass, 1968.

Rubenstein, R. L. A note on the research lag in psychoanalytic studies in religion. *Jewish Social Studies*, 1963, *25*, 133–144.

Schaub, E. L. The present status of the psychology of religion. *Journal of Religion*, 1922, *2*, 362–365.

Schaub, E. L. The psychology of religion in America during the past quarter century. *Journal of Religion*, 1924, *4*, 113–134.

Schaub, E. L. Psychology of religion. *Psychological Bulletin*, 1926, *23*, 681–700. (a)

Schaub, E. L. The psychology of religion in America. *Symposium*, 1926, *1*, 292–314. (b)

Skinner, B. F. *Science and human behavior*. New York: Macmillan, 1953.

Spanos, N. P., & Hewitt, E. C. Glossolalia: A test of the "trance" and psychopathology hypotheses. *Journal of Abnormal Psychology*, 1979, *88*, 427–434.

Starbuck, E. D. *Psychology of religion*. New York: Scribner's, 1899.

Stark, R. On the incompatibility of religion and science: A survey of American graduate students. *Journal for the Scientific Study of Religion*, 1963, *3*, 3–21.

Strunk, O., Jr. The present status of the psychology of religion. *The Journal of Bible and Religion*, 1957, *25*, 287–292.

Strunk, O., Jr. All things hold together. In H. N. Malony (Ed.), *Psychology and faith: The Christian experience of eighteen psychologists*. Washington, DC: University Press of America, 1978.

Szasz, T. S., & Nemiroff, R. A. A questionnaire study of psychoanalytic practices and opinions. *Journal of Nervous and Mental Disease*, 1963, *137*, 209–221.

Thurstone, L. L., & Chave, E. J. *The measurement of attitude*. Chicago, IL: University of Chicago Press, 1929.

Trent, J. W. *Catholics in college: Religious commitment and the intellectual life*. Chicago, IL: University of Chicago Press, 1967.

Tylor, E. B. *Primitive culture*. London: Murray, 1871.

Wallace, A. F. C. *Religion: An anthropological view*. New York: Random House, 1966.
Watson, J. B. *Behaviorism*. Chicago, IL: University of Chicago Press, 1924.
Wilson, B. R. *Religion in secular society*. London: Watts, 1966.
Wundt, W. [*Elements of folk psychology*] (E. L. Schaub, trans.). New York: The Macmillan Company, 1916. (Originally published, 1912.)

Biographical Notes

WILLIAM P. ALSTON is Professor of Philosophy at Syracuse University. He received his Ph.D. from the University of Chicago and was previously on the faculty of the University of Michigan, Rutgers University, and the University of Illinois. He has been a fellow at the Center for Advanced Study in the Behavioral Sciences at Stanford, and he is past president of the Western Division of the American Philosophical Association, the Society for Philosophy and Psychology, and the Society of Christian Philosophers. He is the author of *Philosophy of Language* and of many articles in journals and collections.

BENJAMIN BEIT-HALLAHMI is Senior Lecturer in psychology at the University of Haifa. He received his B.A. from the Hebrew University, and his M.A. and Ph.D. from Michigan State University. He has held clinical, research, and teaching positions at The University of Michigan, the University of Pennsylvania, the Hebrew University, Michigan State University, and Tel-Aviv University. His publications have focused on the clinical, social, and humanistic side of psychology. He edited *Research in Religious Behavior,* authored *Psychoanalysis and Religion: A Bibliography,* and co-authored *The Social Psychology of Religion* and *Twenty Years Later: Kibbutz Children Grow Up*.

NED BLOCK is Professor of Philosophy at the Massachusetts Institute of Technology. He spent two years at Oxford and received his doctorate from Harvard. He has been president of the Society for Philosophy and Psychology and is on the editorial boards of *Cognitive Science, Cognition and Brain Theory,* and *Cognition*. He is editor of *Imagery* and *Readings in the Philosophy of Psychology*.

283

MARC H. BORNSTEIN is Professor of Psychology and Human Development at New York University. He received a B.A. degree from Columbia College and the M.S. and Ph.D. degrees from Yale University, after which he spent one post-doctoral year at the Max-Planck-Institute for Psychiatry in Munich and a second at Yale. Bornstein has received the C. S. Ford Cross-Cultural Research Award from the Human Relations Area Files and the B. R. McCandless Young Scientist Award from the American Psychological Association; he has been a J. S. Guggenheim Fellow; and he holds a Research Career Development Award from the National Institute of Child Health and Human Development. Bornstein is editor of *The Crosscurrents in Contemporary Psychology Series,* including *Psychological Development from Infancy* (edited with W. Kessen) and *Comparative Methods in Psychology.* Bornstein sits on the editorial boards of several journals in psychology, is a member of scholarly societies in anthropology, child development, and visual science, and has published studies in human experimental, methodological, comparative, developmental, and cross-cultural psychology.

DIANA DEUTSCH is at the Center for Human Information Processing at the University of California, San Diego. She received a First Class Honors B. A. in Psychology, Philosophy, and Physiology at Oxford University and a Ph.D. in Psychology at the University of California, San Diego. She is the founding editor of the journal *Music Perception.* She has served on the *Technical Committee on Psychological and Physiological Acoustics,* *The Committee on Education in Acoustics,* and the *Nominating Committee,* and is presently serving on the *Technical Committee on Musical Acoustics* of the *Acoustical Society of America.* She is co-author of *Physiological Psychology,* co-editor of *Short Term Memory,* and editor of the *The Psychology of Music.* Her major fields of research interest are musical and auditory information processing.

PHILIP N. JOHNSON-LAIRD is a member of the scientific staff of the MRC Applied Psychology Unit, Cambridge, England. He received the Ph.D. at University College London, where he also collaborated with P. C. Wason on *The Psychology of Reasoning: Structure and Content.* In 1971–72, Johnson-Laird was a visiting member of the Institute for Advanced Study, Princeton, where he worked with George A. Miller on a study of lexical semantics that led to co-authorship of *Language and Perception.* His research interests remain primarily in the fields of language and thought. Johnson-Laird and P. C. Wason have also edited *Thinking: Readings in Cognitive Science.*

MARTIN S. LINDAUER is Professor of Psychology at the State University of New York at Brockport. He received the Ph.D. from the New School for Social Research. Lindauer is on the editorial boards of the *Journal of Mental Imagery, Scientific Aesthetics,* and *Psychocultural Review*. He is currently the Secretary-Treasurer of Division 10 (Psychology and the Arts) of the American Psychological Association. Lindauer received a Fulbright award to the Free University of Berlin, and he is the author of *The Psychological Study of Literature* and scientific publications in several fields of the arts, aesthetics, and creativity, as well as in perception and environmental psychology.

PSYCHOLOGY AND ITS ALLIED DISCIPLINES
Volume II: Psychology and the Social Sciences

1 Psychology and Anthropology

Douglass R. Price-Williams
University of California, Los Angeles

INTRODUCTION

The mutual interaction between psychology and anthropology has waxed and waned over a period of at least one hundred years. A good number of anthropologists have had considerable knowledge of psychology, and a lesser, but still substantial, number of psychologists have entered into the anthropological domain. In former times, the professional expertise of the two disciplines was not so divergent as it later became, so that concepts related to the two disciplines were equally familiar to scholars in both. Even after the two disciplines became professionally and academically independent, there has remained sufficient overlap between the two to allow two independent subdisciplines to emerge. One, from the direction of anthropology, goes by the name of "psychological anthropology," and the other, from the direction of psychology, is simply called "cross-cultural psychology." I shall discuss the nature of cross-cultural psychology later in this essay, but I ought to point out from the outset that major developments between psychology and anthropology have been stimulated from the anthropological side. Putting it another way, anthropology has drawn more on psychological concepts and methods than psychology has on anthropological ones. In fact, the development of psychological anthropology has been so invasive that it is difficult to discern with any firm boundary distinctive features of the two originating disciplines. Even before Hsu (1961/1972) formally coined the term of psychological anthropology, it was clear that in some substantive areas (such as personality) boundary lines were fuzzy. Indeed, in the second edition of

1

his *Psychological Anthropology,* Hsu (1961/1972) mentions that many of
his contributors were of the opinion that the very attempt to delineate
such boundaries would do more harm than good. While this minority
party may have been so willingly fluid, it is clear that establishment views
in social science generally, and certainly those beyond anthropology,
have historically entertained an aversion to psychological intrusion. In
turn, this aversion has given rise to reaction by more interdisciplinary
scientists. In this vein, Inkeles (1959) has commented that social scientists
spend too much time and energy defending the boundaries of their fields,
almost as if they were holy lands assailed by the heathen. Campbell (1969)
has also discussed the basic ethnocentrism of disciplines which he wished
to circumvent by using what he calls the "fish-scale model of omniscience, which would focus on the overlap of different disciplines [p. 328]."
Finally, Lewis (1977) introduced a book on symbolism in anthropology by
making a case that British anthropology, never known for any adoption of
psychological concepts, least of all psychoanalytic notions, has actually
"for long been living in sin with psychology and psychoanalysis [p. 13]."
   The principal arenas of overlap in psychological anthropology are
themselves difficult to delineate. In the introduction to his recent book
The Making of Psychological Anthropology, Spindler (1978) suggests
that: "It is in fact possible that there is no field, or subdiscipline in the
usual sense of the word. There is an implicit if not explicit psychological
element or process in almost every formulation or treatment of ostensibly
social or cultural process [p. 10]."
   We are left therefore with a spectrum of positions, or a psychology-
anthropology rapprochement *within* anthropology. At the far end of that
spectrum is the position that anthropology generates its own explanatory
concepts and needs no psychological input. Moving away from that end,
there is the position that invokes psychological concepts, but the psychology that is involved is a non-technical, everyday garden variety. Then
comes the congregation of openly psychological approaches falling under
the rubric of various substantive headings such as "culture and personality," "cognitive anthropology," and "psychiatric anthropology." These
areas of investigation differ from their counterparts in psychology and
psychiatry mainly in the weightings they give to social and cultural
parameters.

DOMAINS OF OVERLAP

We can approach the theme of domains of overlap between psychology
and anthropology in two ways. First, we can focus on specific substantive
areas that have exercised the interests of both psychologists and anthro-

pologists. Second, we can demonstrate the influence on anthropological thought of certain psychological ways of representation.

Substantive Areas of Mutual Interest

A mere listing of psychological subjects that have piqued the interest of anthropologists would be reasonably extensive. The assortment includes studies of personality, cognition, socialization (especially child-rearing), dreams, what would now be called altered states of consciousness (incorporating trance and possession), belief systems, and perception. My task here is not to itemize the substantive areas of common interest, but rather to establish a few foci. Of those mentioned, two areas are immediately highlighted: studies of personality and of cognition. They stand out in the sense that they have generated a major amount of the literature of psychological anthropology and have served as constructs in that field. In discussing these subjects further, I shall try to indicate how they serve the intent and theory of psychological anthropology.

Culture and personality. The study of personality and culture is the older of the two; it has attracted psychological anthropologists for at least four decades. Comprehensive volumes on the subject stretch from the 1940s through the 1970s. Among the most notable are Haring's (1949) *Personal Character and Cultural Milieu,* Barnouw's (1973) *Culture and Personality,* Honigmann's (1967) *Personality in Culture,* Wallace's (1961) *Culture and Personality,* LeVine's (1974) *Culture and Personality,* in addition to the editions of Hsu's (1961/1972) *Psychological Anthropology* mentioned above. Throughout this period there have been substantial clarifications and changes in the field itself. Many of these changes can be attributed directly to psychological schools of thought.

At the outset it may be important to survey what purposes the invocation of the personality construct serves in anthropology. LeVine (1973) has simplified our task by specifying that there are basically four psychological positions in the personality and culture field. First, there is the simple reductionist posture. This position states that internal, intrapsychic factors are actual causes of cultural and social behavior. The theory is deterministic and is diametrically opposed to notions that social facts are autonomous and that the study of anthropology owes nothing to psychology—the so-called culturological approach. A second position, shared by such well-known anthropologists as Margaret Mead, Ruth Benedict, and Geoffrey Gorer, LeVine calls the "personality-is-culture" school. This position states that personality and culture are basically equivalent. This school would agree with the position of the first that collective products of culture, such as myth, ritual, and art, can be interpreted psychologically, but it would disagree with the viewpoint that culture is simply reducible to individualistic considerations. The third position in LeVine's taxonomy is the personality mediation view. This position stems from the early idea of a basic personality structure or typical personality (Kardiner, 1939; Whiting & Child, 1953) that was hypothesized as a kind of intervening variable among different parts of a culture. Specifically, the link was between the maintenance systems of a society (forms of child rearing, for example) and specific cultural institutions (such as religious systems). Both the maintenance and cultural institutions are observable; personality is an inferred construct. The personality construct is thus seen as mediating between the two cultural systems, serving not only as a link but as an integrating mechanism. Fourth, LeVine notes, there is the two-systems view which regards personality and culture interacting but each having its own organization. This position advances the idea that the interaction between the two results in stability when both psychological needs of the individual and sociocultural requirements are satisfied. If these needs are not met, or only individual or cultural requirements are satisfied, then instability emerges in the total society.

Underlying all these differing attitudes towards the relationship of personality to culture is a concern with the dispositions of a person within a specific sociocultural context. As I shall mark later, it is the contextual emphasis that demarcates the psychologically oriented social scientist from the psychologist, particularly the experimental laboratory-type psychologist. The roots of interest in the concept of personality lie in dismissing the notion that culture is a process *sui generis* and accepting the thesis that it is acquired. Bidney (1953) makes this plain:

> . . . there has been a persistent though minor, tendency to regard culture realistically as referring to acquired forms of technique, behavior, feeling, and thought of individuals within society. From this point of view, culture is essentially a subjective, or personal, attribute of individuals, since it is a state or quality acquired by and attributed to individuals participating in a given cultural configuration and specific cultural institutions [p. 328].

This statement is congruent with the words of a principal psychological anthropologist, A. I. Hallowell. Taking off from the fact that one of the founders of modern anthropology, namely E. B. Taylor, had flatly emphasized that culture is acquired, Hallowell (1976) elaborated that: ". . . empirically, one culture may vary greatly from another in pattern and content. So the question is raised: what psychological significance have these facts with reference to the differential psychological structuring and behavior of one group of people as compared to another? [p. 168]"

To psychological anthropologists, the search for concepts that aid in the inquiry of acquisition of culture itself takes them directly to the domain of psychology. As noted above, the search does not have to be deterministic in principle, but that is often a necessary condition. The concept of personality has the advantages of being broad and flexible enough to carry the burden which anthropologists demand of it. It is worth noting that in the course of history, other dispositional concepts have been utilized. Early on, for example, the concept of "sentiments" was used (Radcliffe-Brown, 1922). Later, Nadel (1951) tried the notion of "inherited tendencies" to action in order to explain the kind of behavior that anthropologists studied; his scheme involved three pairs of drives underlying societal action. Both sets of concepts never really aroused the degree of general acceptance that the concept of personality has.

The basic ideas of the culture and personality school were worked out thirty to forty years ago, and their psychological dependency turned on psychological ideas of personality that preceded this period. In the course of time, a great deal of the armory that personality and culture theorists used has run into jeopardy within psychology itself, however. For example, the crucial concept of "trait" has been criticized (see Mischel, 1968), and doubt has been raised about ideas of consistency across situations or times for the same individual. Attribution theory (see Fiske, 1978) has suggested that causes affiliated with the notion of personality can be traced to the assessor of personality rather than to the person assessed. Shweder (1972) has gathered together much of the recent psychological material that bears on this point, and he judges that culture and personality theory as presently constituted is not acceptable and that the anthropologist needs to turn to cognition.

Culture and cognition. In the same manner as anthropologists have—with rare exceptions—picked on the social side of personality, the dominant issue in the study of cognition concerns the linkage of indigenous thought with social organization. Anthropologists are not, on the whole, concerned with the dynamics of cognition, in the sense of neural organization or of hypothetical models of thinking.

At the beginning of the 1980s, it appears that cognition is assuming equal prominence in anthropology as in psychology. The point of entry for the anthropologist is the study of classification. Originating with the seminal work of Durkheim and Mauss (1903), interest has now grown to the point where cognition features in chapter headings in the *Annual Review of Anthropology* (see Ember, 1977; *Laboratory of Comparative Human Cognition,* 1978). Anthropologists are less concerned with processes and inferred mechanisms of classification, topics which are left strictly for the psychologist, as with what is classified, what use is made of classifications, and with what social rules classifications are associated. Again, the focus is on classification, or cognition generically, always within a specific sociocultural context. Two recent books, by Tyler (1969) and by Spradley (1972), cover the range of topics.

It is instructive to note the rationale of cognitive anthropologists. Their starting point, as Tyler (1969) suggests, is recognition that cultures are not material phenomena, "they are cognitive organizations of material phenomena [p. 3]." The consequent procedures for finding out what these cognitive organizations consist of are to elicit and analyze the ways in which people talk about elements in their culture. The actual technique owes more to linguistics than to psychology. Generally, this so-called "ethnoscience" approach works best in finite domains, such as classification of plants, colors, kinship, and illnesses. It has been applied more liberally to the classification of planting practices, sleeping arrangements, and the ecology of hunting. Its purpose is to find out how people construct the world around them—*what* they cognize, if not *how* they cognize. As such, the intention is to get "inside the head" of informants. However, there is a marked division among anthropologists themselves in terms of end interests. One group (represented by Werner, 1972) flatly rejects this ideal and sees ethnoscience as allied with generative semantics and sociolinguistics, as studying verbal behavior per se. Another group (represented by Ember, 1977), while not rejecting this ideal, prefers a more comparative approach to just piling up native taxonomies. The middle road is to isolate a domain of interest, to show how differentiations and groupings of terms are used, and to connect these with the ecology and livelihood of the people studied. Not all anthropological works on cognition have necessarily identified themselves with ethnoscience. Hallowell's (1960) study of the world view of the Ojibwa, for example, is clearly a folk taxonomy but was not approached in any formal way with the ethnoscientific framework in mind. Other workers also are interested in cognitive matters but aim their interests at less discursive forms of thought (see, for example, Horton & Finnegan, 1973).

Influence of Psychological Schools of Thought on Anthropology

The cultivation of psychological concepts within anthropology is not totally explained by reference to subject matter alone. It has also to be explained by the prominence of psychological perspectives and the influence that they may have had on anthropologists, particularly in their formative years. Some anthropologists have actually trained in psychoanalysis; LeVine is an example. Others have adopted, either in part or whole, the armory of psychoanalytic concepts and applied these to anthropological settings. Despite the early disdain by anthropologists of Freud's (1913–1914/1938) direct contribution to anthropology with his famous *Totem and Taboo,* the influence of psychoanalytic ideas on psychological anthropology has been extensive. Early on, Seligman (1924) in a Presidential Address to the Royal Anthropological Institute of Great Britain recommended research along the lines Freud postulated as stages of child development. Although this advice was not heeded by his own countrymen, it bore fruit later with the personality and culture school in the United States. By the time this school was forming, the classical Freudian position had already been modified by prominent neo-Freudians, such as Horney and Fromm. It was more in this soil that the personality and culture school took root. For example, Kardiner, a psychiatrist, and Linton, an anthropologist, joined forces and exerted a combined powerful influence on culture and personality studies. Kardiner (1939) introduced the concept of a "basic personality structure" which Linton (1945, p. 129) later defined as "common personality elements (which) together form a fairly well-integrated configuration." The subsequent development of this idea need not concern us here; it has been well documented by Barnouw (1973). What is of interest here is that Kardiner set up a personality construct that bridged the time gap between events early in the individual's life span (such as family organization, child-rearing techniques, and subsistence practices) with belief systems of the adult individual (as reflected in religion and folklore). Belief systems then are interpreted as projections formed through early childhood experiences. The intention of making this bridge, between events in childhood and adult belief systems, is to explain religious and folklore beliefs in terms of personality; the underlying premise is the Freudian hypothesis of identification of deities with parental figures. There has been extreme modification of this early view among psychological anthropologists since, and changes that have been made are less simplistic and less reductionist in character. Moreover, early interest in child training has blossomed to a full-fledged subdiscipline of socialization. In a Festschrift for Margaret Mead, Schwartz (1976, p. ix) introduced the idea of socialization as cultural communication, seeing the early interactions of the child with parents and peers as transmitters of culture. Again, though, this returns to the dominant themes in psychological anthropology: how culture is acquired, how it is maintained, how it is transmitted. The related questions are: What are the agents of these processes? What contexts are they to be found in? What functions do they serve? Although specific different scholars may have social events and social institutions as their focus of study, they have felt the need to go outside traditional social parameters to utilize psychological concepts towards understanding social phenomena.

Focus on childhood experiences is, of course, not the only sequela of a psychoanalytic orientation. Defense mechanisms constitute a second psychoanalytic fact to which anthropologists have paid attention. For example, Wright (1956) analyzed aggressive themes found in folk tales in terms of projection and displacement; Lee (1958) noted displacement in the dreams of Zulus; and, Spiro (1965) pointed out that in some Eastern societies religious institutions as a whole could be regarded as culturally constituted defense mechanisms, to the extent that an individual avails himself of the institution and needs not resort to individual defenses. Sometimes such defense mechanisms operate at the level of idealized personal and social relationships. Pastron (1974) noted a consistent repression and denial of aggressive impulses and actions among the Tarahumara Indians of Northern Mexico, defense mechanisms directed at reconciling the conflict between the idealized norm of proper behavior and actual departures from this standard. The Oedipal situation, too, has received significant attention since Malinowski's (1937) observation that in the matrilineal kinship system of the Trobriand Islands the rivalry exists between the child and the mother's brother, who is not the *genitor* of the child but is the sociological pater. Stephens (1962) has reviewed various cross-cultural hypotheses on this matter.

While early enthusiasm for pure psychoanalytic interpretations of anthropological subject matter has no doubt waned over time, more than a residue of interest still persists. It consists of background theory, rather than a direct application of theory to data. Stein (1974), for example, in examining the phenomenon of the "evil eye," utilized psychoanalytic concepts related to jealousy and evil, but did not adopt a full-fledged psychodynamic explanation. The persistence of psychoanalytic viewpoints was evident in the founding of *The Journal of Psychological Anthropology* in 1978.

As psychoanalysis was followed by behaviorism within psychology, so it was in anthropology. Indeed, one of the early supporters of the behaviorist outlook was Malinowski (1944) who equated field work with the tenets of behaviorism: "The fundamental principle of the field worker, as well as of the behaviorist, is that ideas, emotions, and convictions never continue to lead a cryptic hidden existence within the unexplorable depths of the mind, conscious or unconscious [p. 23]."

Indeed, behaviorism finds itself in good agreement with the functionalist perspective in anthropology. This perspective is wed to the view that if mental events are to be studied at all by the anthropologist, they must be mental events in operational usage and readily observable. A good instance of the functionalist approach with respect to a psychological subject may be found in Firth's (1973) approach to symbolism:

. . . the anthropological approach (to symbolism) is comparative, obser-
vationalist, functionalist, relatively neutralist. It links the occurrence and
interpretations of symbolism to social structures and social events in specific
conditions. Over a wide range of instances, anthropologists have observed
what symbols people actually use, what they said about these things, the
situations in which the symbols emerge, and the reactions to them [p. 25].

Undoubtedly the appeal to observation, the distaste for covert mental
operations, and the emphasis on what people actually do were all behaviorist characteristics that appealed to the functionalist in anthropology. In
addition, the added emphasis on learning that behaviorism encouraged
triggered fresh perspectives in anthropology. In this there was a direct
fertilization from psychology. Barnouw (1973) notes that both Whiting
and Murdock were influenced by learning theory, having studied learning
theory with Clark Hull at Yale. Whiting (1941) invoked learning theory
extensively in *Becoming a Kwoma,* whereas in later works he fused
psychodynamic ideas with learning concepts. In an article assessing the
influence of behaviorism on psychological anthropology, LeVine (1963)
endorsed the above points. He also observed the widespread anthropological assumption that culture constitutes learned behavior; this
made the psychological emphasis on learning especially important to the
discipline in general. LeVine suggested as well that the premise underlying anthropological functionalism—that there are basic needs which must
be fulfilled for a society to survive—brings anthropology into direct line
with concepts central to learning theory.

It is possible that the approach and language of information theory
could develop into another sphere of psychological influence on anthropology which would strengthen present investigations of learning,
perception, and cognition in both disciplines. That information theory has
not yet done this in part reflects the fact that cognitive anthropology has
leaned more on linguistic sources for its underpinnings. While it does
depend on psychological principles, cognitive anthropology has sought its
bases more from individual theorists than a general school of thought. The
only prominent anthropologist to date who has seriously used information
theory as a conceptual background is Gregory Bateson (1975), but even
with him the application has been on learning in general, rather than on
cultural contexts of learning.

It has been shown that there is a considerable area of mutual interest
between the two disciplines, and that two foci particularly, those of personality and of cognition, have attracted much of the attention. The fact
that these two areas stand out in part may be due to the fact that they
serve as a bridge between institution and individuals, in part also to the

fact that both of these areas have generated considerable theory of a sufficient range to accommodate societal concerns.

UNDERLYING ASSUMPTIONS

It is now appropriate to probe more deeply into the background of thought in anthropology provided by psychology, through examining some basic philosophical assumptions that were current in the initial stages of the interaction between psychology and anthropology. To do so, it will be necessary to focus on the units of analysis that are the building blocks of their interaction.

Psychological Principles in Anthropological Thought

During the late nineteenth century and the early part of the twentieth century, two quite different psychological principles invigorated anthropological development and interest in cultural psychology. These principles were "psychic unity" and the "evolutionary development of mind," respectively. The psychic unity principle assumes that the *functions* of the mind are common to all humans, even if the *contents* vary. The evolutionary development of mind principle interprets mental growth as a function of linear development from so-called "primitivism" to civilization.

The principle of *psychic unity* can be traced to the nineteenth century figure Bastian, a medical man turned ethnographer (see Lowie, 1937), who, as an opponent of Darwinism, postulated uniform laws of growth. The principle was reinstated by Boas (1911/1938) in *The Mind of Primitive Man*. As Lowie (1937) has pointed out, Boas was less concerned with promulgating this principle as a psychological law than with stressing the lack of evidence for the opposing assumption, namely that some minds are superior to others. Nevertheless, the principle continues to operate as an underlying assumption in anthropology and, as Geertz (1973) pointed out, has not been seriously questioned. Two additional observations can be made here: The first is that psychic unity has relevance to assumptions about cognition in general and intellectual capacity in particular. It really has no relevance to emotional or psychodynamic concerns, a point which Hallowell (1976) recognized when he stated that the principle of psychic unity was "a vague concept . . . approached chiefly with questions of racial differences in mind. It [has] no reference to the dynamics of the personality structure [p. 210]." However, it is important to note further that in many anthropological studies homogeneity of personality is *assumed*. The second comment is that the question of individual differences needs to be tested in individuals, not in groups or institutions. At the time when Boas was writing (about 1911), there were few psychological data that could be brought to bear on the subject. Although the ensuing half century has produced an enormous amount of relevant data, we still must acknowledge that although considerable variance in cognitive and intellectual skills can be shown across cultures, both the nature of the variance and how it should be interpreted leave the question of psychic unity still in doubt.

The second principle, which I have termed the *evolutionary development of mind,* has depended less on actual data drawn from the study of individuals than on an identification of cultural belief systems whose assumptions are grounded in psychology. The notion of social evolution and the principle that ontogeny repeats phylogeny were foundations for this principle, and it can be traced in part to the publication of Tylor's *Anthropology* in 1881; in that seminal book, Tylor advanced the social evolutionary thesis that mankind had progressed through three stages ("savage", "barbaric," and "civilized") which were defined purely by ecological and technological criteria. This thesis in itself, of course, would have no psychological connotation were it not for Tylor's further assumption that the causal laws underlying cultural evolution were to be found in the laws of individual human nature, specifically in the laws of mental development.

Somewhat parallel to Tylor's evolutionary thesis, a French tradition (represented by Durkheim) established the preeminence of "social facts." This phrase was defined by Durkheim (1895/1938) as "every way of acting which is general throughout a given society, while at the same time existing in its own right independent of its individual manifestations [p. 13]." This view gave rise to acceptance of the principle that through its institutions, the modes of thought of a society can be discerned. Within this same tradition, the French philosopher Lévy-Bruhl (1923, 1926, 1928) drew a sharp distinction between the pre-logical nature of the collective representations of so-called "primitive" peoples and the collective representations of so-called "civilized" peoples. It is important to note that Lévy-Bruhl did not wish to be identified with the views of Tylor and Frazer (the English school) and later admitted that his use of the term "pre-logical" was misleading in this respect (see Cazaneuve, 1973). Lévy-Bruhl focused mainly on the collective belief systems of indigenous peoples, seeing in their various world-views of religion, myth, and magic an alternative logical system to that accepted in more advanced technological societies. For example, he drew attention to two cultural facts: first, that many native belief systems operated in terms of what he called a "participation mystique" with nature, in which people related themselves with animals or plants to the point of identity and, second, that they failed to distinguish between natural and supernatural phenomena. Hence, he distinguished between prescientific and scientific mentalities.

While Lévy-Bruhl's thesis was never taken up by the mainstream of anthropology—it was immediately criticized by notable field workers of the time—certain legacies of his viewpoint persist. The distinction between (the unfortunate term) "primitive" and "civilized" was eliminated. That there may be different styles of thinking in native belief systems, however, is still actively debated in the literature: It can be found in Tambiah's (1973) analysis of the use of analogy in magical thinking and in Horton's (1967) distinction of closed versus open thinking. As a matter of fact, the notion of alternative logics used in traditional belief systems has been currently resurrected in the anthropological literature (Cooper, 1975). Probably none of these authors would wish to state that examples of such thinking styles could not also be found in modern technological societies, but there does persist the idea that thought patterns can be discerned through the study of metaphysical belief systems. As a matter of history, the fusion of the idea of a primitive mentality with modified ideas of an evolutionary principle was given a more forceful push by certain psychologists. Werner's (1940/1973) *Comparative Psychology of Mental Development,* while explicitly rejecting Haeckel's law that ontogeny recapitulates phylogeny, holds to a strong principle of parallelism. · A passage from his book makes the basic point:

> Although the biogenetic principle of recapitulation is not applicable either to the mental or to the anatomical-physiological sphere, nevertheless it is still highly expedient to employ the principle of parallelism. If the peculiarly concrete thinking of the child is compared with certain forms of thinking typical of primitive peoples . . . certain striking parallels will be found. These parallels must be taken as such, as merely indicating a similar mental structure in a general and purely formal sense. In a particular and material sense, there will be irreconcilable differences in the behavior of the child and of the primitive man [Werner, 1940/1973, p. 28].

With this important distinction in mind, Werner then advanced the thesis that ontogenetic development, like phylogenetic development, progresses from the diffuse to the differentiated, from the concrete to the abstract.

To a much lesser extent the developmental theories of Jean Piaget are apt to fall into the same mold. The difference here, though, is that Piaget himself was very much aware of cultural factors which by themselves fitted into one of his four big factors of cognitive development. Also, there has been considerable experimental cross-cultural work done, using Piaget's methods (see, e.g., Bornstein, 1980). The upshot of this research belies any simple interpretation of the type hiterto discussed. (Both of these points can be found in Dasen, 1977.)

Another modified form of the evolutionary argument can be detected in the entire psychoanalytical movement as it touches anthropology. It is difficult to find explicit references to the notion that primary thought processes (substitution, condensation, reversal, etc.) are phylogenetically antecedent to secondary processes (reasoning, direction, logical order, etc.), or that the first kind of thought dominates in the belief systems of traditional peoples. However, the thesis does seem to be implicit in several notable psychoanalytical forays into anthropology, particularly for the more "classical" psychoanalysts such as Róheim (1955/1970, 1934/1974). Be that as it may, the evolutionary argument prompted Geertz (1973) to comment that "within the confines of anthropology, this thesis has been based on the assumption that it is possible simply to identify patterns of culture and modes of thought [p. 61]." The search for underlying assumptions now takes us to the target of psychological anthropology: simply, *what* is being explained?

Units of Analysis

The recurrent assumption that cultural and institutional patterns reflect psychological factors suggests that we should look more carefully at the units of analysis used in psychological anthropology. This essentially means getting into the question of method and stating some generalizations. There are at least two sets of distinctions used in psychological anthropology to note. First, there is the distinction between the individual and some collective, such as a tribe, society, or organization, as the unit of analysis. When the individual is targeted, psychological techniques are employed. When social units exclusively are invoked, the approach to psychology is through concepts or processes. The second distinction pertains to different approaches within anthropology. A descriptive approach to any one culture is contrasted with the approach of comparing two or more cultures on some given factor. Both approaches are used in anthropology and do not necessarily have any connection to psychological ideas. The comparative approach, for example, was used in an early monograph (Hobhouse, Wheeler, & Ginsberg, 1915) that related the frequency of certain social institutions to stages of economic development. Since then it has been used extensively in relation to psychological concepts and with an eye to test specific hypotheses. Frequently hypotheses are framed against data coming from the ethnographic material stored in the Human Relations Area Files (HRAF; see Jahoda, 1980). This is a collection of ethnographic reports from several hundred societies around the world which are analyzed and classified under a number of headings. Two examples will suffice to indicate how HRAF works. Lambert, Triandis, and Wolf (1959) used HRAF to test the hypothesis that supernatural figures reported in the belief systems of a large number of societies tended to be judged as more aggressive in those societies where there was pressure among the young males to be self-reliant and independent. Material for both of these factors was taken from ethnographic data in the filing system and analyzed and judged for more elaborate coding of psychological traits such as nurturance and obedience, self-reliance, and general independence. The two sets of data were then correlated statistically. What concerns us is the unit of analysis, which here is the *convention* adopted by members of these societies. Thus, in the final outcome in this study, it is the society, viewed as a collective unit, that is the unit of analysis. A second example is drawn from psychodynamic principles regarding relationships between a mother and her male infant. A number of studies have suggested that this relationship is connected with sleeping arrangements of mother and son. These suggestions led to the comparative study (see Whiting, Chasdi, Antonovsky, & Ayres, 1974) in which exclusive mother-child sleeping arrangements were contrasted to nonexclusive sleeping arrangements and these in turn to whether the same societies were high or low on sex training. The actual findings (Whiting & D'Andrade, 1959) were: Of the ten societies where the infant and mother shared a bed (the father sleeping elsewhere), eight fell above the median in the severity with which sex is punished in later childhood. Conversely, in eight instances where the father and mother slept together (the infant sleeping elsewhere), only two societies showed severe sex training.

   The exclusivity of mother-infant sleeping arrangements was then used in a more ambitious way to explain couvade practices (Munroe, Munroe, & Whiting, 1973). The couvade, an institution wherein the father goes through many of the concomitants of childbirth during the time of his wife's parturition, is recognized in many societies. This study compared those societies which recognized couvade against those that did not and in turn correlated the presence or absence of the couvade with practices in the same societies known to have exclusive sleeping arrangements of mother and infant. Matri-residence was conjoined with the sleeping arrangements, and when these two variables are observed in any society the likelihood of the society's having the couvade is great.

   The HRAF approach has entertained some success in psychological anthropology, to the extent that a society has been formed around the idea along with a house organ, *Behavior Science Research*. The HRAF are not always the exclusive data base: More first-hand studies have often been carried out. In addition, the comparative approach has been allied with the more traditional descriptive-functional approach within a single society. This conjoining is well exemplified in a series of books originated by the Whitings (Minturn & Lambert, 1964; B. B. Whiting, 1963; Whiting & Whiting, 1975). Further, the necessity of probing for data on individuals to buttress the data on social units has been recognized. In the couvade study mentioned above, data using tribes as the unit have been followed by investigations of actual individuals in a specific society. Further, a question of causation is continuously acknowledged by scholars adopting this essentially correlational approach. Nevertheless, this type of comparative approach is well within the tradition connecting psychological mechanisms with the study of institutions.

In the history of psychological anthropology there has been a tendency to infer psychological states within the individual from the study of institutions in which individuals must necessarily partake. Many of the inferences of the evolutionary arguments that we have just discussed stem just from this tendency. That is why examination of the units of analysis used in psychological anthropology is mandatory. There are appropriate units and methods required for the study of intra-individual processes; other units and methods may be required when inter-individual concerns are studied. This is especially so when the interactions between individuals coalesce into working social systems, which subsequently operate autonomously of the individuals involved in them.

METHODOLOGY

The foregoing discussion has already merged into the larger question of method. I now turn to discuss similarities and differences in the methods practiced by psychology and anthropology.

Descriptive Analysis versus Hypothesis Testing

When Campbell and Naroll (1972) wrote an article on the mutual methodological relevance between psychology and anthropology they drew attention to the difference between "the descriptive, humanistic task of one who seeks to record all aspects of a given cultural instance and the task of the abstractive and generalizing 'scientist' who wants to test the concomitant variation of two isolate factors across instances in general [p. 442]." Later, they identified anthropology in general as having more to do with the descriptive-humanistic approach, though they acknowledged that there are many anthropologists who are committed to hypothesis-testing. While I can support this distinction insofar as it bears on the methodological aspects of the two disciplines, it may be advantageous to identify the former approach with the term descriptive-analysis. Because ethnographers of single cultures tend to tease out interlocking aspects of the societies studied, the resulting holistic description is not devoid of analytic focus. Whatever the terms, clearly there is a considerable difference between this approach and that of selecting one or two factors, abstracted from the total cultural complex, and comparing them with selected factors from other cultural complexes. The descriptive emphasis in anthropology is so pervasive and fundamental to the discipline that it is important to emphasize the essential ingredient in it. A prominent psychological anthropologist (Edgerton, 1974) has, I believe, very accurately identified the issue when he considered the anthropological approach as fundamentally naturalistic: "At heart, anthropologists are naturalists whose commitment is to the phenomena themselves. Anthropologists have always believed that human phenomena can best be understood by procedures which are primarily sensitive to context, be it situational, social or cultural [pp. 63–64]."

While Edgerton contrasts this stance with direct psychological experimentation, hypothesis-testing can and has been reached through controlled observational procedures. I have already noted some examples. Indeed, Edgerton's (1971) own work in East Africa, comparing four African ecologies with certain personality clusterings, best exemplifies such selective and controlled observation. Nevertheless, anthropology typically makes far more use of contextual factors than psychology. In this connection it could be argued that traditional psychology is laboratory centered, while the traditional anthropology is field centered, as Edgerton stressed. This difference however is really not crucial. There have been many instances within the last decade where laboratory procedures were carried out in traditional indigenous settings. The crucial difference is the amount of reliance on context. I shall remark on the increased contextual reliance in *cross-cultural psychology* in a later section.

Field Work and Participant Observation

There are very few techniques as such which can be thought of as exclusively anthropological. The generic method is to immerse oneself into the language, lives, and history of the people being studied, to observe as many aspects of the society as possible, and to keep a faithful record of all these things. This approach goes by the name of "field work", conducted through participant observation. Observation, of course, is buttressed through extensive interviewing, which, unlike the formal structured interview of survey research, can become synonymous with casual conversation. Remember that the average anthropologist is a *participant* observer, and thus lives a dual existence of a quasi-member of the society and observer and note-taker of its functions. This does not mean that observations are random and that quality control is not a consideration of the anthropological observer. Observation has been made very specific. Nerlove, Roberts, Klein, Yarborough, and Habicht (1974), for example, related extremely detailed observation of Guatemalan children at work and at play to cognitive processes. Observations, as in this case, follow hypothesis and theory, in the same way they would in more formal psychological studies.

Use of Psychological Techniques

When it comes to psychological matters beyond those that could be adduced by observation, anthropology has borrowed directly from psychology. Probably the largest borrowing has been of projective tests, prompted by anthropological interest in personality. Beginning with early studies by Wallace (1952) among the Tuscarora Indians and DuBois (1944) with the Alorese, the Rorschach and Thematic Apperception Tests have been used to determine the personality make-up of individual society members. Psychological professionals have usually scored the results of the protocols. The intent of their use is clear: Inferences about the relation between culture and personality could now be backed up with evidence external to the judgment of the observer. Lindzey (1961) assessed this cross-cultural use of projective techniques by both anthropologists and cross-cultural psychologists. Briefly, Lindzey concluded from his survey that while there were serious problems involved in the cross-cultural use of projective techniques, their utilization within this field has not been without benefit for the anthropologist.

On the psychoanalytic level, there have been very few ethnographic applications of the clinical method (as distinct from clinical concepts) to individuals. Rare exceptions to this rule have been anthropological studies of shamans; these are typically cast in the more classical mode of psychoanalysis (e.g., Boyer's, 1962, work with Mescalero Indians and Devereux's, 1951, work with Plains Indians). Levy's (1973) psychodynamic interviews with Tahitians is a more recent example.

When cognitive, as distinct from linguistic, phenomena are studied, anthropological techniques are identical to those used by psychologists. Articles published in the anthropological journals on the subject of visual perception are identical to any that would be found in a psychological journal (e.g., Bornstein, 1975; Kilbride & Robbins, 1969). Although experimentation is generally not done in anthropology, cognitive experiments have been performed. Thus Shweder (1972), testing an hypothesis with Zinacanteco shamans, devised a cognitive experiment to see if shamans were more likely than fellow Indians to impose form on unstructured stimuli. Sanday (1971) has advocated direct experimentation on cognitive concerns to run *pari passu* with linguistic techniques.

A survey of anthropological opinion today would probably show that psychological techniques should be employed whenever necessary. Only the purposes for which they are used might differ among social scientists. Psychologists employ experiments to probe psychological theories, and anthropologists use them to test sociocultural assumptions, expecially those assumptions relating the culture to the individual.

The question of what method to use should not be regarded by itself. The choice depends on what question is being addressed, what units of analysis are being invoked, and what conclusions will be drawn from the application of any method. There are indeed traditional methods associated with each of the two disciplines. There are indeed problems in applying methods derived from the one discipline to the other. Sometimes these are judiciously applied, sometimes not. The logic of methodology depends on the nature of the theory to be tested and the kind of data to be gathered. The problem of methodology should not be isolated from these other concerns.

MUTUAL DEPENDENCY BETWEEN PSYCHOLOGY AND ANTHROPOLOGY

This section asks and attempts to answer two central questions. Simply put, What do anthropologists expect and demand from the science of psychology? And, vice versa, What do psychologists require of the discipline of anthropology?

Psychological Ideas Required by Anthropologists

Very much of what anthropology requires of psychology depends on the *a priori* attitude of the particular anthropologist. In his book *Man's Way*, Goldschmidt (1967) discussed the various dimensions of anthropological theory, contrasting historical explanations, sociological orientations, psychological explanations, and eclecticism. It is obvious that those anthropologists who align themselves towards the end of this list will more likely turn towards psychology than those who unilaterally favor a sociological orientation, as Leslie White (1947, 1949). What distinguishes the anthropologist using psychological concepts and techniques from the psychologist is the anthropologist's continual reference to societal events. The psychological anthropologist uses psychology not to supersede his own subject, but to complement it. There may indeed be a few anthropological theorists who would go the whole way towards a psychological reductionism, but even among them there is a continuing touchstone to social events. The uses of psychological assumptions and ideas by anthropologists depend to a large extent on the substantive area of inquiry. When there are topic areas that strongly require psychological input, like beliefs or deviancy, it is more likely that the ensuing explanation will be ex-, pressed in psychological terms. On the other hand, when topics such as demography or economics are touched on, then it is more likely that psychological explanations will be avoided. Again, this will depend on the disposition of the investigator. Some investigators invoke psychological explanations on minimal excuse; their opposite numbers are adroit in redefining what appear to be obvious candidates for psychological inquiry into societal explanations. In other words, some anthropologists happily embrace psychological explanations; others become almost casuistic in avoiding them. What really seems to be at issue is the *weighting* factor on behalf of purely social explanations or conversely purely psychological factors.

The Durkheimian approach to suicide serves as a good example. Durkheim (1897/1951) showed quite clearly that suicide rates in various geographical areas could be explained parsimoniously by reference to social and economic conditions operating in certain places and that recourse to the psychology of the actual individuals committing suicide was not needed. While this may be true, it is also true as Inkeles (1959) has brought out, that further facts about suicide can be accounted for if psychodynamic ideas are utilized (see Henry & Short, 1954). It is difficult to determine what are the exact factors involved in judging whether or not specific social phenomena need be pursued psychologically. Of the many anthropologists who have pondered this problem, Nadel (though hardly a psychological anthropologist) has not seriously considered psychological notions in terms of explanatory assumptions (see Nadel, 1951). However, he was cautious about psychology. In a seminal passage (1951, pp. 295–296), he gave serious attention to the distinction between the content and process of mental events. Nadel stipulated that inasmuch as a psychological inquiry stressed content rather than process, it would only duplicate a purely social inquiry, particularly if the object of inquiry was not behavior, but mental events (e.g., ideas, beliefs, and so forth). In this passage, Nadel seems to anticipate comments by Cole and Scribner (1974) and by Price-Williams (1978) that when anthropologists study cognition they are studying cognitive products and not cognitive processes. Nadel (1951) then goes on to say, "Clearly, if the psychological enquiries are to add relevant, novel knowledge, which social enquiry cannot attain they must relate the things visible in the latter with things and factors not so visible, that is with the *modus operandi* of the psychological processes [p. 296]."

Elsewhere in the same book, Nadel (1951, p. 407) pursued this argument in relation to the concept of personality, stating that the anthropological approach can deal only with the "surface traits," which personality theorists distinguish from "source traits." Surface traits are easily observable in everyday behavior, while source traits depend on examination of the individual. This leads Nadel to the conclusion that so long as personality typing is done through cultural observation alone, no explanatory value for the personality concept can be claimed. His conclusion is in keeping with the viewpoint that the explanatory value of psychological concepts is only operative at the level of process. Nadel's argument may point to the relationship between general statements of a law and particular instances of it. If the latter can be deduced from the former, which after all is the point of formulating laws, then there would be value in generating psychological principles that have bearing on anthropological situations. Nadel's point is that the psychological principles that he sees generated in anthropology are not this nature at all; indeed they run parallel to the particular instances which need to be explained. Hence, all that results from the exercise of employing psychological concepts is a tautology in terms of using psychological language where a social language would suffice. On the other hand is a point which Nadel did not raise: There appears to be a gap between the generation of general principles and their application to different events that interest anthropologists. This is particularly true of the findings of social psychology— the one subdiscipline of psychology often thought to have the most direct relevance to anthropological study. Social psychology has generated general principles of behavior, mainly through experimentation and sometimes from controlled observational studies, but it is by no means obvious that the psychological principles that Nadel would have seen as apposite to anthropology can be drawn from its corpus of findings. Even if they are judged so, most anthropologists would demand that application to particular problems be shown for each case. Such a demonstration is still necessary.

Nadel's remarks have launched discussions of what are the fundamental issues in the relationship between psychology and anthropology. There are deep and difficult philosophical problems here concerning the nature of explanation, particularly the weighting between necessary and sufficient explanation. At the same time, the use of psychological information by anthropologists is often a personal judgment tailored to the subject matter under consideration and is sensitive to what is to be explained in the first place. Durkheim (1897/1951) argued that suicide could be explained in purely societal terms. There was only a vague reference in his writings to psychological terminology (e.g., "needs" and a "sense of belongingness"). In other subjects of interest to anthropologists, sometimes the psychology of the situation is not denied, but the presence of cultural elements is made salient. Bourguignon (1976, pp. 53–54), for instance, does not deny that psychopathological elements are involved in possession, but she still points to purely cultural elements that cannot be explained by simple recourse to psychology or psychiatry. She points out that whereas in Protestant New England it was the spirit of the witch that possessed the victims, in Catholic France devils did, and in Jewish cases of possession the spirit of a dead person did. No general principles from the study of psychopathology will explain the particular variations that are of importance to the anthropologist. On the other hand, many psychological anthropologists would be content, first, to point to the central fact that there is the idea of an entity taking over a living body and, second, to seek psychopathological reasons for it. In the final analysis the issue may be one of choice.

Anthropological Ideas Required by Psychologists

The factual material I have presented has slanted this essay almost entirely in the direction of the psychological underpinnings of anthropology. Up to very recently there has been very little factual material to discuss in the reverse. It is true that from time to time anthropologists and psychologists have collaborated. Indeed, at the very beginning of this century the University of Cambridge scientific expedition to the Torres Straits was composed of experimental psychologists and ethnographers (see Haddon, 1901). But it was not until sixty or so years later that the field of cross-cultural psychology began to emerge, where the psychologist's overtures to anthropologists became more intimate. At this time, not only were anthropologists consulted, but the psychologist began to adopt some of the habits of the anthropologist, such as living *in situ* with informants, learning their language, etc. Having said this, however, I still have difficulty specifying what the cross-cultural psychologist requires from anthropology. One cannot say that anything is required in terms of theory and method, with the one proviso that the psychologist now adopts the loose-knit set of field-work procedures. What the psychologist derives from anthropology is a kind of perspective, which can best be formulated by placing importance on the cultural medium in which psychological processes are embedded. However, the degree to which psychologists pay attention to culture varies. Cross-cultural psychologists fixate on cultural factors to the same degree as anthropologists, as they also consider it necessary to gain some knowledge of the culture in which observations and experiments are made in order to reach appropriate conclusions. Elsewhere, I have concluded that what psychological investigation requires from the study of culture is "that amount of information which is required to render the psychological event of sufficient meaning [Price-Williams, 1975, pp. 17–18]." The appeal of contextual meaning varies from investigator to investigator, and it is not possible to make any definitive limit. Some psychologists who are interested in cognitive aspects of populations have delved as deeply as an anthropologist would into the language structure. Thus, Cole and his associates (1971) studied the classificatory system of Kpelle, and Greenfield and Childs (1977), analyzing the psychological components of kinship among the Zinacanteco Indians of Chiapas, constructed a formal ethnoscientific model of kin terms used by these people. Still other investigators have directed their attention to ecological matters. Dasen (1974), for example, related classificatory ability among Australian aborigines to certain scholastic abilities; this involved examining the Aborigines' way of life, especially noting their dependence on water holes for subsistence and locating direction. Berry (1976) has also made ecological reference the cornerstone of the theory of psychological differentiation (Witkin, Dyk, Faterson, Goodenough, & Karp, 1962) stressing the importance of food accumulation. Berry's emphasis on these points brings his theory very near to anthropological functionalism, as he himself recognizes. Many other cross-cultural psychologists have focused on subsistence skills as relevant to perceptual and cognitive processes (e.g., Adjei, 1977; Bovet, 1976; Price-Williams, Gordon, & Ramirez, 1969). Looking at this literature, Berland (1977) has suggested the term "cultural amplifiers" to indicate those social and technological skills that are thought to support certain psychological mechanisms.

A systematic treatment of the interaction of ecological and cultural factors on the one hand and psychological behavior on the other hand can be found in the contributions made by the Whitings (Harrington & Whiting, 1972; Whiting & Whiting, 1960). This orientation has had a profound influence on cross-cultural child development (see Bornstein, 1980; Munroe & Munroe, 1975; Werner, 1979). The system is complicated and represented as a system of inter-locking feed-back units, but briefly the emphasis is on so-called maintenance systems. These are defined as social, economic, and political organizations that have as their function the continuing nourishment and protection of its members. The maintenance systems are varied; they include basic subsistence patterns, means of production, and the division of labor in the community. Population pressures and types of family are important parameters that have been found to have a heavy influence on specific areas of children's behavior, such as dependency and responsibility, aggression and sociability. The detailed working out of the interaction between purely ecological and cultural systems with traditional targets of child psychology display the mutual dependency of these two disciplines.

Perhaps the most beneficial effect on psychology of anthropology is the range and variations of the populations that anthropologists study. These can be used to test hypotheses that are not possible to test with the smaller and relatively more homogenous samples that psychological laboratories are accustomed to use. Campbell and Naroll (1972) make this point a crucial nexus in the relationship between the two disciplines. In an early study on the cross-cultural method, J. W. M. Whiting (1954) emphasized the importance of studying areas of the world where weaning continues past the age where it customarily stops in Western societies for reaching conclusions about the effects of weaning. An expanded data base and an expanded contextual reference, with the meaning these have for psychological theories, are important ingredients that psychology can borrow from anthropology. I might also add, almost parenthetically, that the skills and unobtrusive measures that anthropologists utilize for data gathering are further points to be learned by psychologists.

A promising input from anthropology for psychology may lie in the developing area of sociobiology. While psychologists have undoubtedly found in anthropological studies a fruitful source of variation of human behavior, there is also there great attention given to similarities of human behavior. Recently, Lonner (1980) has summarized the search for psychological universals and has identified the quest as an important goal of cross-cultural psychology. The search for universals in psychology fits in very well with the emphasis given to the adaptive function of the individual, seen in a broad phylogenetic context. This is the contribution that sociobiology makes. It is easier to see this in wide terms of types of communities rather then by reference to individuals. Much has been made, for example, of the kinds of individuals seen in small hunting and gathering societies versus those seen in pastoral societies. Rohner's cross-cultural study (1975) of over one hundred societies, for example, correlated society with parental acceptance or rejection of children. Rohner interprets the tendency of parents in hunting and gathering groups to foster independence and initiative in their children as a selective and built-in tendency reinforced over generations. The logic of the interpretation is that these qualities in the children are the kinds that adapt best to the mode of livelihood. At the moment there is considerable debate over the validity of sociobiological interpretations. Nevertheless, it can be said that the broad evolutionary perspective is one that has always been associated with anthropology, and it is to be expected that its contribution will be felt in the psychological arena (see Fuller, in Volume III).

Anthropology has drawn from psychology concepts, theories, and methods. Psychology has begun to realize the importance and intricacies of context which anthropologists have so well delineated. In addition, anthropology has provided a wealth of material on which the success of psychological theories of behavior depend.

CONCLUSIONS

Future Directions

It is very noticeable that the possibilities for fusion between psychology and anthropology have been promoted from the direction of anthropology. With the advent and increasing popularity of cross-cultural psychology, we might anticipate a fresh impetus from the direction of psychology. After all, psychological mechanisms and cultural variables are intertwined. But even if this new impetus should prove successful, the fusion of the two disciplines would still be limited. Both cross-cultural psychology and psychological anthropology are offspring dwarfed by their respective parent disciplines. One needs to delve further into psychology to achieve a deeper link with anthropology. It is possible that this connection could be made through a more elaborate application of the concept of "situation," a concept that has been found to be salient across a number of disciplines. Cole and his colleagues (Cole, Gay, Glick, & Sharp, 1971, p. 233) considered that the variance in cognition across cultures was attributable more to the situation in which particular cognitive processes were applied than to culture itself. The concept of situation has provoked a sharp debate in the field of personality (see Magnusson & Endler, 1977) to the extent that situational variables and person variables are juxtaposed. Goffman (1961) has further contributed to the microanalysis of situations with his idea of "encounters," and Lofland (1976) has shaped the idea of situations from the interactional perspective of sociology and social psychology.

Assessment

Whether the concept of situation will be able to carry the full burden of a psychology-anthropology rapproachement is a matter of theoretical surmise. Behavioral theorists tend to be arch conservatives and cling to concepts and techniques to which they have become accustomed. Changes in perspective take a long time to develop, and when one talks of the merging of different disciplines into a more congruent framework of ideas, an even longer time frame is to be expected. The formal structure of academic disciplines and the professionalization of perspectives in the form of learned societies and specialized journals tend to maintain a status quo. In the last analysis, it lies with the personal interests of the individual investigator and scholar as to what should be studied and what kind of explanatory framework should be used. Barring the sudden emergence of an over-riding theory to guide the individual scholar, I anticipate that the relationship between anthropology and psychology will continue to be a mosaic of interdependent meeting points.

ACKNOWLEDGMENTS

Preparation of this essay was supported by NICHD Mental Retardation Grant 04612 and by the School of Medicine, University of California, Los Angeles. The author wishes to thank Professor T. Weisner for good advice on a preliminary draft.   /

REFERENCES

Adjei, K. Influence of specific maternal occupation and behavior on Piagetian cognitive development. In P. R. Dasen (Ed.), *Piagetian psychology: Cross-cultural contributions*. New York: Gardner Press, 1977.
Barnouw, V. *Culture and personality*. Homewood, IL: Dorsey Press, 1973.
Bateson, G. *Steps to an ecology of mind*. New York: Ballantine Books, 1975.
Berland, J. C. *Cultural amplifiers and psychological differentiation among Khanabadosh in Pakistan*. Unpublished doctoral dissertation, University of Hawaii, 1977.
Berry, J. W. *Human ecology and cognitive style: Comparative studies in cultural and psychological adaptation*. New York: Wiley, 1976.
Bidney, D. *Theoretical anthropology*. New York: Columbia University Press, 1953.
Boas, F. *The mind of primitive man*. New York: MacMillan, 1938. (Originally published, 1911.)
Bornstein, M. H. The influence of visual perception on culture. *American Anthropologist*, 1975, 77, 774–798.
Bornstein, M. H. Cross-cultural developmental psychology. In M. H. Bornstein (Ed.), *Comparative methods in psychology*, Hillsdale, NJ: Lawrence Erlbaum Associates, 1980.
Bourguignon, E. *Possession*. San Francisco, CA: Chandler and Sharp, 1976.
Bovet, M. C. Piaget's theory of cognitive development and individual differences. In B. Inhelder & H. W. Chipman (Eds.), *Piaget and his school: A reader in developmental psychology*. New York: Springer-Verlag, 1976.
Boyer, L. B. Remarks on the personality of shamans, with special reference to the Apaches of the Mescalero Indian Reservation. In W. Muensterberger (Ed.), *The psychoanalytic study of society* (Vol. 2). New York: International Universities Press, 1962.
Campbell, D. T. Ethnocentrism of disciplines and the fish-scale model of omniscience. In M. Sherif & C. W. Sherif (Eds.), *Interdisciplinary relationships in the social sciences*. Chicago, IL: Aldine, 1969.
Campbell, D. T., & Naroll, R. The mutual methodological relevance of anthropology and psychology. In F. L. K. Hsu (Ed.), *Psychological anthropology*. New York: Dorsey Press, 1972.
Cazaneuve, J. *Lucien Lévy-Bruhl*. New York: Harper and Row, 1973.
Cole, M., Gay, J. Glick, J. A., & Sharp, D. W. *The cultural context of learning and thinking*. New York: Basic Books, 1971.

Cole, M. & Scribner, S. *Culture and thought: A psychological introduction*. New York: Wiley, 1974.

Cooper, D. E. Alternative logic in 'Primitive Thought.' *Man*, 1975, *10*, 238–256.

Dasen, P. R. The influence of ecology, culture and European contact on cognitive development in Australian Aborigines. In J. W. Berry & P. R. Dasen (Eds.), *Culture and cognition: Readings in cross-cultural psychology*. London: Methuen, 1974.

Dasen, P. R. (Ed.). *Piagetian psychology: Cross-cultural contributions*. New York: Gardner Press, 1977.

Devereux, G. *Reality and dream: The psychotherapy of a Plains Indian*. New York: International Universities Press, 1951.

Du Bois, C. *The people of Alor*. Minneapolis, MN: University of Minnesota Press, 1944.

Durkheim, E. *The rules of sociological method* (S. A. Solvay & J. H. Mueller, trans.). Chicago, IL: Chicago University Press, 1938. (Originally published, 1895.)

Durkheim, E. *Suicide: A study in sociology* (J. A. Spaulding & G. Simpson, trans.). Glencoe, IL: Free Press, 1951. (Originally published, 1897.)

Durkheim, E., & Mauss, M. De quelques formes primitives de classification. *Année Sociologique*, 1903, *6*, 1–17. (Reprinted in R. Needham, Ed. and trans. *Primitive classification*. Chicago, IL: University of Chicago Press, 1963.)

Edgerton, R. B. *The individual in social adaptation: A study of four East African societies*. Los Angeles, CA: University of California Press, 1971.

Edgerton, R. B. Cross-cultural psychology and psychological anthropology: Two paradigms or one? *Reviews in Anthropology*, 1974, *1*, 52–64.

Ember, M. R. Cross-cultural cognitive studies. *Annual Review of Anthropology*, 1977, *6*, 33–56.

Firth, R. *Symbols: Public and private*. Ithaca, NY: Cornell University Press, 1973.

Fiske, D. W. *Strategies for personality research*. San Francisco, CA: Jossey-Bass, 1978.

Freud, S. *Totem and taboo*. Harmondsworth, England: Penguin, 1938. (Originally published, 1913–1914.)

Geertz, C. *The interpretation of cultures*. New York: Basic Books, 1973.

Goffman, E. *Encounters*. Indianapolis, IN: Bobbs-Merrill, 1961.

Goldschmidt, W. *Man's way: A preface to the understanding of human society*. New York: Holt, Rinehart and Winston, 1967.

Greenfield, P. M., & Childs, C. P. Understanding sibling concepts: A developmental study of kin terms in Zinacantan. In P. Dasen (Ed.), *Piagetian psychology: Cross-cultural contributions*. New York: Gardner Press, 1977.

Haddon, A. C. (Ed.). *Reports of the Cambridge anthropological expedition to the Torres Straits*. London: Cambridge University Press, 1901.

Hallowell, A. I. Ojibwa ontology, behavior and world view. In S. Diamond (Ed.), *Culture in history*. New York: Columbia University Press, 1960.

Hallowell, A. I. *Contributions to anthropology: Selected papers of A. Irving Hallowell*. Chicago, IL: University of Chicago Press, 1976.

Haring, D. G. (Ed.). *Personal character and cultural milieu*. Syracuse, NY: Syracuse University Press, 1949.

Harrington, C., & Whiting, J. W. M. Socialization process and personality. In F. L. K. Hsu (Ed.), *Psychological anthropology*. Cambridge, MA: Schenkman Publishing Co., 1972.

Henry, A. F., & Short, J. F. *Suicide and homicide: Some economic, sociological and psychological aspects of aggression*. New York: Free Press, 1954.

Hobhouse, L. T., Wheeler, G. C., & Ginsberg, M. *The material culture and social institutions of the simpler peoples: An essay in correlation*. London: Chapman and Hall, 1915.

Honigmann, J. J. *Personality in culture*. New York: Harper and Row, 1967.

Horton, R. African traditional thought and western science. *Africa,* 1967, *37,* 50-71, 155–187.

Horton, R., & Finnegan, R. *Modes of thought.* London: Faber and Faber, 1973.

Hsu, F. L. K. (Ed.). *Psychological anthropology: Approaches to culture and personality.* Cambridge, MA: Schenkman Publishing Co., 1972. (Originally published, 1961.)

Inkeles, A. Personality and social structure. In R. K. Merton, L. Broom, & L. A. Cottrell (Eds.), *Sociology today: Problems and prospects.* New York: Basic Books, 1959.

Jahoda, G. Cross-cultural comparisons. In M. H. Bornstein (Ed.), *Comparative methods in psychology.* Hillsdale, NJ: Lawrence Erlbaum Associates, 1980.

Kardiner, A. *The individual and society: The psychodynamics of primitive social organization.* New York: Columbia University Press, 1939.

Kilbride, P. L., & Robbins, M. C. Pictorial depth perception and acculturation among the Baganda. *American Anthropologist,* 1969, *71,* 293–301.

Laboratory of Comparative Human Cognition. Cognition as a residual category in anthropology. *Annual Review of Anthropology,* 1978, *7,* 51-69.

Lambert, W. W., Triandis, L., & Wolf, M. Some correlates of beliefs in the malevolence and benevolence of supernatural beings: A cross-cultural study. *Journal of Abnormal and Social Psychology,* 1959, *58,* 162–169.

Lee, S. G. Social influences in Zulu dreaming. *Journal of Social Psychology,* 1958, *47,* 265–283.

LeVine, R. A. Behaviorism in psychological anthropology. In J. W. Wepman & R. W. Heine (Eds.), *Concepts of personality.* Chicago, IL: Aldine, 1963.

LeVine, R. A. *Culture, behavior, and personality.* Chicago, IL: Aldine, 1973.

LeVine, R. A. *Culture and personality: Contemporary readings.* Chicago, IL: Aldine, 1974.

Levy, R. I. *Tahitians: Mind and experience in the Society Islands.* Chicago, IL: University of Chicago Press, 1973.

Lévy-Bruhl, L. *Primitive mentality.* New York: MacMillan, 1923.

Lévy-Bruhl, L. *How natives think.* London: Allen and Unwin, 1926.

Lévy-Bruhl, L. *The 'soul' of the primitive.* New York: MacMillan, 1928.

Lewis, I. (Ed.). *Symbols and sentiments: Cross-cultural studies in symbolism.* London: Academic Press, 1977.

Lindzey, G. *Projective techniques and cross-cultural research.* New York: Appleton-Century-Crofts, 1961.

Linton, R. *The cultural background of personality.* New York: Appleton-Century, 1945.

Lofland, J. *Doing social life: The qualitative study of human interaction in natural settings.* New York: Wiley, 1976.

Lonner, W. The search for psychological universals. In H. C. Triandis & W. W. Lambert (Eds.), *Handbook of cross-cultural psychology.* Boston, MA: Allyn & Bacon, 1980.

Lowie, R. H. *The history of ethnological theory.* New York: Rinehart, 1937.

Magnusson, D., & Endler, N. S. (Eds.). *Personality at the cross-roads: Current issues in interactional psychology.* New York: Wiley, 1977.

Malinowski, B. *Sex and repression in savage society.* London: Harcourt, Brace, 1937.

Malinowski, B. *A scientific theory of culture and other essays.* Chapel Hill, NC: University of North Carolina Press, 1944.

Minturn, L., & Lambert, W. W. *Mothers of six cultures: Antecedents of child rearing.* New York: Wiley, 1964.

Mischel, W. *Personality and assessment.* New York: Wiley, 1968.

Munroe, R. L., & Munroe, R. H. *Cross-cultural human development.* Monterey, CA: Brooks/Cole, 1975.

Munroe, R. L., Munroe, R. H., & Whiting, J. W. M. The couvade: A psychological analysis. *Ethos,* 1973, *1,* 30–74.

Nadel, S. F. *The foundations of social anthropology*. New York: Free Press, 1951.

Nerlove, S. B., Roberts, J. M., Klein, R. E., Yarborough, C., & Habicht, J. P. Natural indicators of cognitive development: An observational study of rural Guatemalan children. *Ethos*, 1974, 2, 387–404.

Pastron, A. G. Collective defenses of repression and denial: Their relationship to violence among the Tarahumara Indians of northern Mexico. *Ethos*, 1974, 2, 387–404.

Price-Williams, D. R. *Explorations in cross-cultural psychology*. San Francisco, CA: Chandler and Sharp, 1975.

Price-Williams, D. R. Cognition: Anthropological and psychological nexus. In G. Spindler (Ed.), *The making of psychological anthropology*. Berkeley, CA: University of California Press, 1978.

Price-Williams, D.R., Gordon, W., & Ramirez, M., III Skill and conservation: A study of pottery-making children. *Developmental Psychology*, 1969, 1, 769.

Radcliffe-Brown, A. R. *The Andaman Islanders: A study in social anthropology*. Cambridge: Cambridge University Press, 1922.

Róheim, G. *Magic and schizophrenia*. Bloomington, IL: Indiana University Press, 1970. (Originally published, 1955.)

Róheim, F. *The riddle of the sphinx of human origins*. New York: Harper and Row, 1974. (Originally published, 1934.)

Rohner, R. P. *They love me, they love me not: A universalist approach to behavioral science*. New Haven, CT: HRAF Press, 1975.

Sanday, P. Analysis of the psychological reality of American-English kin terms in an urban poverty environment. *American Anthropologist*, 1971, 73, 555–570.

Schwartz, T. (Ed.). *Socialization as cultural communication*. Berkeley, CA: University of California Press, 1976.

Seligman, C. G. Anthropology and psychology: A study of some points of contact. *Journal of the Royal Anthropological Institute*, 1924, 54, 13–46.

Shweder, R. A. Aspects of cognition in Zinacanteco shamans: Experimental results. In W. A. Lessa & E. Z. Vogt (Eds.), *Reader in comparative religion: An anthropological approach*. New York: Harper and Row, 1972.

Spindler, G. D. (Ed.). *The making of psychological anthropology*. Berkeley, CA: University of California Press, 1978.

Spiro, M. Religious systems as culturally constituted defense mechanisms. In M. Spiro (Ed.), *Context and meaning in cultural anthropology*. New York: Free Press, 1965.

Spradley, J. P. (Ed.). *Culture and cognition: Rules, maps and plans*. San Francisco, CA: Chandler, 1972.

Stein, H. F. Envy and the evil eye among Slovak-Americans: An essay on the psychological ontogeny of belief and ritual. *Ethos*, 1974, 2, 15–46.

Stephens, W. N. *The Oedipus complex: Cross-cultural evidence*. Glencoe, IL: Free Press, 1962.

Tambiah, S. J. Form and meaning of magical acts: A point of view. In R. Horton & R. Finnegan (Eds.), *Modes of thought*. London: Faber and Faber, 1973.

Tyler, S. A. (Ed.). *Cognitive anthropology*. New York: Holt, Rinehart and Winston, 1969.

Tylor, E. B. *Anthropology*. London: Watts, 1930. (Originally published, 1881.)

Wallace, A. F. C. *The modal personality of the Tuscarora Indians as revealed by the Rorschach test*. Washington, DC: Smithsonian Institute, Bureau of American Ethnology, 1952.

Wallace, A. F. C. *Culture and personality*. New York: Random House, 1961.

Werner, E. E. *Cross-cultural child development*. Monterey, CA: Brooks/Cole, 1979.

Werner, H. *Comparative psychology of mental development*. New York: International Universities Press, 1973. (Originally published, 1940.)

Werner, O. Ethnoscience 1972. *Annual Review of Anthropology*, 1972, *1*, 271–308.
White, L. Culturological vs. psychological interpretations of human behavior. *American Sociological Review*, 1947, *12*, 686–698.
White, L. *The science of culture*. New York: Farrar, Strauss, 1949.
Whiting, B. B. (Ed.). *Six cultures: Studies in child rearing*. New York: Wiley, 1963.
Whiting, B. B., & Whiting, J. W. M. *Children of six cultures: A psychocultural analysis*. Cambridge, MA: Harvard University Press, 1975.
Whiting, J. W. M. *Becoming a Kwoma*. New Haven, CT: Yale University Press, 1941.
Whiting, J. W. M. The cross-cultural method. In G. Lindzey (Ed.), *Handbook of social psychology*. Reading, MA: Addison-Wesley, 1954.
Whiting, J. W. M., Chasdi, E. H., Antonovsky, H. F., & Ayres, B. C. The learning of values. In R. A. LeVine (Ed.), *Culture and personality: Contemporary readings*. Chicago, IL: Aldine, 1974.
Whiting, J. W. M., & Child, I. L. *Child training and personality: A cross-cultural study*. New Haven, CT: Yale University Press, 1953.
Whiting, J. W. M., & D'Andrade, R. *Sleeping arrangements and social structure: A cross-cultural study*. Paper presented at the meeting of the American Anthropological Association, Mexico City, 1959.
Whiting, J. W. M., & Whiting, B. B. Contributions of anthropology to the methods of studying child rearing. In P. Mussen (Ed.), *Handbook of research methods in child development*. New York: Wiley, 1960.
Witkin, H. A., Dyk, R. B., Faterson, H. F., Goodenough, F. R., & Karp, S. A. *Psychological differentiation*. New York: Wiley, 1962.
Wright, G. O. Projection and displacement: A cross-cultural study of folk-tale aggression. *Journal of Abnormal and Social Psychology*, 1956, *49*, 523–528.

2 Psychology, Behavior Therapy, and Psychiatry

Hans J. Eysenck
Institute of Psychiatry, University of London

HISTORY OF THEIR RELATIONS

Oscar Wilde once said that England and America were separated by a common language, and the same might be said of psychology and psychiatry. To the man in the street, the two terms seem to refer to identical content, as indeed does the term psychoanalysis; he (and many academic people as well) fails to detect the very real differences between these disciplines. Those working in the field might agree to a distinction such as this: Psychology is a fundamental science of human behavior, studied in laboratories and taught in academic courses. Psychiatry is a medical discipline based on psychology, physiology, neurology, biochemistry, genetics, pharmacology, and many other sciences (see Volume III) and devoted to the diagnosis and treatment of mentally ill people. Psychoanalysis is a theory of mental activity, and at the same time it is a method of treatment for psychiatric casualties. But these definitions, although probably widely accepted, hide many difficulties. It will be the main purposes of this chapter to bring out these difficulties and to suggest what should be, as well as what are, the relations between psychology and psychiatry.

A brief historical survey suggests that psychiatry precedes psychology in point of time. Already the ancient Greeks and Romans had psychiatrists (of a kind!); but psychology, in so far as it existed at all, was in the hands of philosophers and did not become an experimental science until a bare century ago. Thus psychiatrists, even then, had to construct a psychology to fit their needs, and this "psychiatric psychology" created from

the observation of abnormal people without benefit of experimental control and without check from studies of normal persons has remained as a
rival to orthodox, academic psychology.

It should be said that then as now psychiatry was in poor repute in
medical and even lay circles. Two thousand years ago Cicero (1971) already commented on the sad state of psychiatry: "Why is it that for the
care and maintenance of the body there has been devised an art which,
because of its usefulness, has had its discovery attributed to the immortal
gods, and is regarded as sacred, while on the other hand the need of an art
of healing for the soul has not been felt so deeply before its discovery, has
not been studied so closely after becoming known, and has not been
welcomed with approval by the majority; indeed, has been regarded by
most with suspicion and hatred?" Clearly psychiatry has had a poor image
for a very long time compared with physical medicine!

The aspect of psychiatry which most often depresses its critics is the
comparative neglect of the outcome problem, i.e. the detailed, clinical
study of the effectiveness of therapy. Until fairly recently, physicians had
hardly any effective remedies at their command, and consequently they
seem to have concentrated on perfecting their skills of diagnosis and
prognosis. To paraphrase one authority, the therapeutic revolution has
since changed the physician's role entirely, but neither the medical curriculum, nor the attitude of practicing clinicians, has kept pace with the
change. Diagnosis is still regarded as the noblest medical skill, and treatment is still almost a secondary consideration. Whether this statement is
true of general medicine I am not in a position to say; however, it certainly gives a good idea of the position of psychiatry. Psychoanalysts have
been the prime culprits in this connection. Busy with patients since the
turn of the century, they have not published even a single properly designed study to demonstrate the effectiveness of the Freudian method of
treatment (Rachman, 1971). This predominance of diagnosis and prognosis in psychiatric work is particularly unfortunate because psychiatry
still lacks the knowledge on which alone a proper system of diagnosis and
prognosis can be built; thus the judgments made are not usually very
reliable nor particularly valid (Eysenck, 1973).

In actual fact the first encounter of psychiatry and psychology in the
latter part of the nineteenth century was promising. Kraepelin, who may
be regarded as the father of modern psychiatry, was a student of Wundt
and carried out many experimental psychological studies with his patients
which promised to lead to important advances (Eysenck, 1968). Unfortunately, under the influence of Freud, psychiatry reverted to its customary
neglect of academic psychology, and its adoption of theories was derived
from and based exclusively on abnormal patients. This is not the place to
note the many criticisms to which Freudian theories (Eysenck & Wilson,

1973; Rachman, 1963), and more particularly Freudian methods of treatment (Rachman, 1971), have been subjected. Let it merely be said that
instead of being based on scientific knowledge acquired in the laboratory,
psychiatric practice became more and more widely based on insubstantial
speculations of an unscientific kind. It is only in recent years, with the
arrival of behavior therapy (Kazdin, 1978), that this disastrous direction
of advance has been reversed. It should also be noted that for many years
clinical psychologists—who in theory one might have expected to bring to
bear on the problems of psychiatry their scientific training and academic
knowledge—have in fact preferred to act as lower-level psychiatrists,
using psychiatric theories and terms, applying psychiatric methods of
treatment, and subordinating themselves in every way to the dictates of
the socially more powerful medical group. Again, this trend has now been
reversed with the advent of behavior therapy, but this is a relatively
recent development. Historically, psychiatry has influenced clinical psychology much more powerfully than vice versa. In general, one may say
that modern psychiatry has tended to receive the contributions of psychology, in so far as they have been acknowledged at all, with hostility,
derision, and contempt. Seldom has an effort been made to understand
the methodologies of the studies cited, the logic of the arguments presented, or the statistical methods of analysis employed.
   Redlich and Freeman (1966), to take but one example, have written a
whole textbook on psychiatry without mentioning the importance of
genetic factors in the origin of neurosis, except for a derisory reference to
an irrelevant study by Eysenck and Prell (1951) whom they state to be the
only ones to believe in genetic causes; yet as Fieve, Rosenthal, and Brill
(1975), Rosenthal (1970), Shields (1973), and even Schepank (1974), who
writes from a psychoanalytic position similar to that of Redlich and
Freeman, make clear, the evidence is in fact overwhelming for the importance of genetic factors (see Fuller, in Volume III). Particularly important
is the fact that studies of behavioral genetics contradict firmly held
theories concerning the environmental factors supposed to be responsible
for the genesis of neurotic and psychotic disorders; contrary to such
theories (Freudian, Laingian, etc.), there is no evidence of *between family
environmental variance,* but only of *within family environmental variance*
(Fulker, 1980).
   As another example, consider the psychiatric habit of imitating the
diagnostic habits of physicians concerned with physical diseases and diagnosing patients in a qualitatively categorical manner (anxiety state, hysteria, schizophrenia), when the evidence indicates very clearly that such
methods of diagnosis are extremely unreliable and make assumptions
about continuity and discontinuity which are plainly contradicted by research evidence (Eysenck, 1955, 1970). It is not only that the psychologi-

cal findings are disregarded; so is the very existence of the problem, or the existence of statistical methods for resolving it (Eysenck, 1950).

A third example is the tardy recognition of the superiority of methods of treatment originating in modern learning theory; behavior therapy, although demonstrably superior in its effects for neurotic disorders to psychoanalysis, psychotherapy, or drug therapy, is still treated as a disreputable relative by most psychiatrists (Rachman & Hodgson, 1980; Rachman & Wilson, 1980). These examples must suffice; many others could be given.

So far we have been speaking of psychiatry in some sense as a unitary discipline. It seems that this is in fact quite erroneous. Psychiatry is not, and never has been, such a unitary discipline, and to understand the relation between psychiatry and psychology properly, we must investigate the dual nature of psychiatry. Without an understanding of this dual nature, no sensible conclusions can be reached.

THE DUAL NATURE OF PSYCHIATRY

Most medical specialties cover ground which is relatively easy to define. This is so because the specialty deals with a circumscribed part of the body (ear, nose, and throat), uses a particular technique (surgery), or is concerned with a particular disease (cancer). Psychiatry clearly cannot be defined along any of these lines, hence the considerable degree of puzzlement which most laymen (and many physicians) exhibit when the discussion turns to psychiatry. We are clearly not concerned with a particular disease. The typical textbook of psychiatry lists a truly remarkable variety of diseases which at first sight have nothing in common—from epilepsy to neurosis, from syphilis of the central nervous system to dyslexia in children, from schizophrenia to degenerative brain disorders of the aged. Neither is there any particular technique involved in treating these diverse disorders—operative procedures, drug treatment, psychotherapy, and custodial care are only some of the techniques used.

Could we say that a particular part of the body was involved, perhaps the brain and the central nervous system? But if we did so we could run foul of the neurologist who would claim that we had described his own specialty. Could we say that psychiatry deals with mental diseases, as opposed to the rest of medicine, which is concerned with physical disease? This also will not do. Epilepsy or general paralysis of the insane are physical diseases the origins of which are more or less well understood, and the treatment of which is no different from that of many other physical diseases. Here then is our first difficulty: If we do not know what we are talking about, how can we discuss it rationally, and how can we look at its relation with psychology in any reasonable fashion?

Many years ago, a famous German philosopher who was also a physician, K. Jasper, undertook to look at psychiatry from the points of view of medicine and the philosophy of science. He became an internationally known psychiatrist, and he wrote what was probably the best textbook of psychiatry of the early twentieth century. (It appeared first in 1913, and was republished in 1948; it has recently been translated into English.) Being completely nonsectarian, Jasper (1948) viewed the many existing schools with impartiality, and his views are still worth listening to. One of his major conclusions, and the one which may contain the answer to the problem of psychiatry's identity crisis, was that the medical notion of "disease" might not be relevant to most of psychiatry. In this he anticipated the shrill and vociferous group of antipsychiatry psychiatrists (e.g., Laing, 1960; Szasz, 1971) who nowadays take up in a more extreme (and unacceptable) form the less extreme and sensible ideas promoted originally by Jasper.

Another of Jasper's major conclusions, perhaps even more important and relevant, related to the existence of three psychiatries rather than one. In the first group are those psychological abnormalities which are based on physiological and neurological disorders of the brain and the central nervous system. Jaspers states that the psychiatrist appears to be rescued from the difficulties presented by the concept of "disease" in those cases where he finds a *somatic* process to be responsible for the psychological disorder, a process which is objectively demonstrable and measurable. In this connection, psychopathology is only a means to an end, namely the discovery of physical symptoms. Physiology, not psychology, is the final aim of medical research. Physicians are concerned with the body alone. Only those psychological processes are diseased which are produced by diseases of the brain. Into this category would presumably fall general paralysis of the insane, epilepsy, and the degenerative psychoses of the senium, i.e. mental disorders in old people due to physical processes in the brain. Most if not all of this group are also in the field of the neurologist, and it might be tidier to hand them over to practitioners of neurology altogether. They have no clear-cut connection with the rest of psychiatry, and many of them arrived there on the basis of clearly erroneous theories (such as G.P.I., an outstanding example).

Jasper's second group contains the so-called functional psychoses, i.e. mainly schizophrenia (or the schizophrenias—there may be several different varieties) and manic-depressive illness (which might be unipolar or bipolar—not all depressives have manic episodes). According to Jasper, these disorders do not manifest somatic disorders of a kind which would enable us to diagnose psychosis by reference to them. Consequently, the notion of disease is here primarily and exclusively related to psychological events. It is true that in many cases there occur somatic phenomena which suggest that perhaps some fundamental somatic cause may be at work and discoverable in the future. But in many cases these phenomena are absent. Hence it appears probable that certain definite somatic diseases will have to be excluded from this group and apportioned to the first group. Nevertheless, a clearly differentiated and independent group of disorders will remain, purified by this process of exclusion. Research into these disorders would be directed towards the discovery of psychological factors *(Grundfunktionen)* whose disturbance would render intelligible the manifold symptoms, rather in the same manner as in the first group.

Even now, sixty years later, biochemists and others are still struggling to discover somatic causes of schizophrenic and manic-depressive illness; there are many claims, but few replicable findings (Weil-Malherbe & Szara, 1971). Nevertheless, the evidence is very strong that these disorders *have* a somatic basis. The reasons are twofold. In the first place, there is very strong evidence (considered conclusive by most geneticists and psychiatrists with a proper training in biometrical genetics) that heredity plays an important part in the causation of these disorders (Shields, 1973). Studies on identical and fraternal twins, familial studies, work on foster children, and other lines of evidence all converge on the same verdict: Heredity is a powerful factor in causing functional psychoses, but it is not by any means all powerful. Environmental stress also plays an important part, although the precise nature of this stress has been no more clearly defined than has the biological or biochemical factor (see Krantz & Glass, in Volume III). There is some evidence that the stress involved may be more closely related to interpersonal relations than to other factors; service in the army during war time, for instance, can produce neurotic breakdown but has not been shown to increase the incidence of psychotic breakdown.

In the second place, psychotic disorders of the kind in question respond well and specifically to certain drugs whose action is beginning to be understood to some degree. Antipsychotic drugs and physical treatments like electroshock certainly truncate select types of attacks and make recurrence less likely. All is not well, of course: There are cases where no drug seems to work, and the actual prescription is often subject to trial-and-error search. Our understanding of the precise mode of action of these drugs is still woefully incomplete, and so is our ability to match the drug, the dose, and the patient. In view of the relatively recent discovery of most of these drugs and the difficulties of psychiatric research (to say nothing of the lack of finance for such research which has retarded psychiatry for such a long time), nothing else could be expected. These

difficulties notwithstanding, treatment of psychotics has undergone a tremendous change in recent years, and this change has come about by
treating these disorders as physical diseases having a somatic cause that
responds to medication. Jasper did not know of these developments, of
course, which were still very much in the future when he wrote. They
suggest that perhaps his second group will in due course be assimilated to
his first group.

Jasper's third group is quite distinct from the other two, and it involves
potentially a far greater number of cases than the other two combined.
The incidence of schizophrenia in different countries ranges from 1.6 to
2.9 in a hundred; that of manic-depressive disorder ranges from 0.4 to 2.5
in a hundred. In a typical Western country, something like 2% of the
population will be found to suffer from one or the other of these twin
scourges, although by virtue of differing criteria for diagnosis and different methods of ascertainment, these figures are by no means accurate.
Disorders in the third group are much more widespread, and much less
clearly identified. Diagnosis here is so subjective as to be almost worthless. Nevertheless, the disorders in question are recognizable and frequently demand treatment.

In Jasper's third group of disorders we find undesirable variants of
humanity *(die unerwünschten Variationen des Menschseins),* and here
there can be no question of somatic foundations for organic diseases. The
body only enters the picture as it does in relation to healthy psychological
development. Nor is the disease process something quite novel compared
with the preceding stage of health. We are dealing with fundamental properties of human existence *(Grundeigenschaften menschlichen Daseins).*
Disorders in this group would be the neuroses, the character disorders,
and criminal and other social propensities. Admittedly there are strong
genetic factors in predisposing a person towards neurotic or criminal
behavior, but these are not as specific as those involved in the functional
psychoses. Evidence suggests that probably a large number of genes is
involved here, whereas in the case of psychoses the number may be quite
small. In other words, psychotic abnormality may be more nearly qualitatively different from normality, whereas neurosis, character disorders,
criminality, and the other constituents of this third group are largely indicative of quantitative differences. We are all likely to commit antisocial or
even criminal acts given enough provocation; we are all likely to suffer a
neurotic breakdown, or at least neurotic symptoms of a minor kind, when
stress is too severe. But we are not all likely to suffer schizophrenic or
manic-depressive attacks. This is a profound difference.

My own feeling is that if Jasper had known what we know now about
the biology of schizophrenia and manic-depressive illness, he would have
tended to class them with his first group, although perhaps only tenta-

tively. This would leave him with two major groups, which may be named *organic* and *behavioral,* respectively. The medical part of psychiatry deals with the effects of tumors, lesions, infections, and other physical conditions, where the treatment is either physical (e.g., leucotomy, more general surgery, electroshock, etc.) or pharmacological. There is much similarity here to orthodox medicine, and a reasonable unification can be achieved by reference to a circumscribed part of the body, viz. the brain and central nervous system. If this throws psychiatrists and neurologists together again, so much the better; there seems little reason to have two overlapping specialties covering much the same ground. The behavioral part of psychiatry deals with disorders of behavior acquired in large part through the ordinary processes of learning, unlearning, or failure to learn. Neurotic disorders, personality disorders, and many types of criminal conduct probably come under this heading. These are not to be construed as diseases in the usual medical sense of the word, and their treatment is subject to many ethical and social considerations that are largely irrelevant to the medical disorders discussed above. We will have to consider the behavioral disorders in some detail later on; here let me simply make this important distinction between the organic and the behavioral disorders. And let me note that the subject which is fundamental to an understanding and the treatment of behavioral disorders is psychology, not medicine. This was explicitly recognized by Jasper when he wrote: "The study of psychology is indispensable for the psychopathologist as is the study of physiology for the somatic pathologist."

Psychiatry, then, is not a unitary subject in any meaningful sense; it breaks up into two (or possibly three or more) fragments which have nothing very much to do with each other. We may now formulate a diagnosis: Not only does psychiatry suffer from depersonalization and an identity crisis it also suffers from split personality, and possibly schizophrenia as well. The outlook is grave.

SOCIETY, PSYCHIATRY, AND THE MEDICAL MODEL

Many psychologists as well as psychiatrists of the "antipsychiatry" school have criticized the medical model on which psychiatry operates. We shall discuss these objections insofar as they relate to the functional psychoses later on. At least some of the objections of the antipsychiatrists are not unreasonable, and they certainly require an answer. If it should turn out that on the whole we must reject their arguments as far as the medical part of psychiatry is concerned, we must be careful not to extend this rejection to the psychological part; here it is very unlikely that a medical model has much to be said for itself. Where we are clearly not dealing with diseases, but with behavior largely determined by learning, conditioning, deconditioning, or failure to learn or condition, the disease concept (however defined) largely loses its meaning. It may be useful to illustrate the way in which physicians have sometimes attempted to use medical concepts in quite irrelevant fields by means of a quotation. In March of 1851, the Medical Association of Louisiana, at its annual meeting, received a lengthy and detailed report on "The Diseases and Physical Peculiarities of the Negro Race." This report, authored on behalf of a specially appointed committee of the Association by its chairman, Dr. Samuel Cartwright, was published soon afterwards in the then prestigious *New Orleans Medical and Surgical Journal.* This report attempts to justify Negro slavery on medical grounds and to prescribe medical remedies for types of slave behavior displeasing to the slave owner. Thus Cartwright claimed to have discovered anatomical evidence that managed to "confirm the Creator's will in regard to the negro; it declares him to be the 'submissive knee-bender' which the Almighty declared he should be. [Thus] in the anatomical conformation of his knees we see 'genu flexit' written in the physical structure [which is] more flexed or bent than any other kind of man."

Of major social importance is the use of the medical model of neurosis by psychiatrists to justify their central role in the treatment of neurotic disorders. The evidence suggests strongly that neurotic disorders are learned behavior patterns and emotional reactions, acquired according to Pavlovian conditioning model and best treated by Pavlovian extinction methods (Eysenck, 1979); retention of the medical model assigns to psychiatrists, medically trained but ignorant of the relevant psychological principles, a leading role in treatment, and it relegates psychologists, trained in the relevant psychological principles and their application to neurotic disorders and their treatment, to a secondary position as "medical auxiliaries". This is clearly absurd and constitutes an attempt to use scientific models as arguments in favor of preserving superior social status. Science should remain independent of political power struggles.

It might be answered that this example is taken from a rather old source and that surely modern psychiatrists are more cautious in their writings. But this is not so; in fact, exactly the opposite is true. Psychoanalysts in particular assure us that strikes, wars, accidents, and many other ills our flesh is heir to are in fact neurotic disorders caused by Freudian mechanisms and complexes. One example may suffice to illustrate this curious tendency. In the *Uses and Abuses of Psychology,* I quote a report made by a psychoanalytically oriented research institute to a Government Department which had asked questions about the causation of strikes in the coal industry (Eysenck, 1953). The answer was very simple: Coal miners developed complexes because they were "hacking away at mother earth;" such an ambiguous activity naturally gave rise to repressed anxiety and reawakened the Oedipus complex, which then led to strikes and other irrational activities. In other words, when miners ask for more money it is simply a "symptom" of a far more serious "disease." You must treat the disease, not the symptom—which presumably means that all coal miners must be relieved of their Oedipus complexes by a long continued, personal psychoanalysis if strikes are to be avoided. It hardly needs saying that these suppositious Oedipus complexes are about as real and meaningful as Dr. Cartwright's *drapetomania* and *synesthesia aethiopsis*. The evidence for either is nil, and the very notion that the behaviors complained about are diseases, and consequently subject to medical scrutiny, is insulting and completely unrealistic. Strikes and running away are not "diseases" in any recognized medical sense. At this writing, homosexuality is still defined as a "disease" by the American Psychiatric Association; unnatural it may be, a socially undesirable practice it certainly seems to many people, but a disease? Hardly. The medical model is clearly inappropriate to social behaviors of this kind, and efforts made by many modern psychoanalysts to extend medical practices unduly so as to embrace ordinary human behaviors should be resisted—particularly when the theories advanced are as absurd as that of miner's Oedipus complexes mentioned above.

The practice of using medical analogies for social ills is of course not new; it has existed for a long time. Writers have for many centuries declared the "body politic" to be ill. They have prescribed remedies, and they have predicted death to follow if these prescriptions were not followed. The Turk was declared in Victorian times to be "the ill man of Europe," a place now occupied by Italy and perhaps in the near future by Britain. Strikes, wars, and other social upheavals are declared to be "infectious," as are mutinies and riots. But writers using these metaphors were quite consciously using them as analogies; they were not suggesting that these eruptions were in fact "diseases" comparable to smallpox and lung cancer. They might call a political enemy's speeches and suggestions "pestilential" without implying that the behaviors produced as a consequence were in fact in any way like the bubonic plague—other than that the consequences would be very serious. *Medicine has nothing to say about the behavior and the social actions of normal people, and psychiatry as part of medicine should follow this rule and concern itself with medical disorders to which its teachings and prescriptions are relevant.* This is of course realized by the great majority of psychiatrists, who have no wish to be called upon to cure the ills of society, knowing full well that their training is quite irrelevant to any such grandiose endeavor.

We may conclude that attempts to extend the medical model of psychiatry to include social activities of the most varied sort have failed and have no substance to support them. The activities in which normal

people indulge may be hateful, deplorable, despicable, obscene, undesirable, absurd, comical, infantile, dangerous, odd, scurrilous, unusual,
queer, and outrageous; but unless they meet the clear requirements of
psychiatric diagnosis, society will have to deal with these oddities without
recourse to psychiatry. There may be in this field psychological problems
in great number, but these are the province of psychology, not of
medicine or psychiatry.

NEUROSIS AND THE MEDICAL MODEL

The previous sentence may require a good deal of amplification; as it
stands it might not be as clear as desirable. Let us by way of explication
consider Freud's attempt to subsume neurotic, criminal, psychopathic,
and other types of nonpsychotic behavior under the medical "disease"
model, and let us go on from there to the modern psychological view of
these matters. Neurotic behavior is essentially unreasonable behavior,
but with the proviso that the neurotic himself is quite aware of the fact
that his or her behavior is in fact unreasonable; where such insight is
lacking, psychosis is a more likely diagnosis. Consider a woman with a
phobia for cats; she is so afraid of encountering a cat that she does not
dare go out and is completely housebound. Yet she knows that there is no
objective danger; she is simply unable to overcome her (unreasonable)
fear. Consider a man who is suffering from an obsessive-compulsive disorder; he is afraid of dirt and contamination and compulsively washes his
hands hundreds of times each day—so often, in fact, that he cannot hold
down any job and is effectively housebound. Yet he is aware of the fact
that other people survive without washing their hands all that often and
that quite likely he too would get by after the same fashion; he is simply
unable to overcome the (unreasoning) fear which arises every time he fails
to wash his hands. Are phobias, obsessive-compulsive activities, and
quite generally unreasoning anxieties "diseases"? In the absence of any
proper definition of "disease" such a question is difficult to answer. The
dictionary simply gives alternatives, such as "sickness" or "illness,"
rather than a proper definition, and medical textbooks have too much
sense to attempt such a definition. Nevertheless, let us try.

Medicine distinguishes carefully between an illness, or disease, and the
symptoms the patient may complain of. The patient may have a fever, but
that is not the illness; we must treat the illness giving rise to the fever, not
the symptom directly. A disease is something underlying a series of symptoms, or "syndrome", and from knowledge of such syndromes, the experienced physician can often diagnose the nature of the disease giving rise
to this particular set of symptoms. Freud very cleverly made use of this

medical habit of clearly distinguishing between "disease" and "symptom" by declaring that the fears and anxieties the neurotic complained of were but the symptoms of some underlying disease, and that he proposed to treat this underlying disease by means of his new method of psychoanalysis. The symptoms, he declared, were but the outgrowths of an underlying complex; this complex originated in the early years of a child's life and derived from his interaction with his parents. Thus the Oedipus complex arose because the young boy wanted to have sexual intercourse with his mother; he was, however, afraid of his father and jealous of his powers and consequently repressed his desires into the unconscious. There it lay only to be activated whenever conflict situations reawakened this ancient conflict. The particular symptoms produced were the outcome of the struggle of the original complex to find an outlet for its energy.

If all of this were true (and of course it is not possible to give in a brief paragraph any idea of the richness of Freud's imagination and luxurious speculative capacity) then, Freud argued, the only way to treat the person in question was by concentrating on the underlying complex. Once this was cured (by long-continued attempts to make the original conflict conscious and redintegrate it with the rest of the psyche) the symptoms would vanish. This process, continued over many years of daily sessions between analyst and patient, was declared to be the only method of relieving the patient of his troubles. "Symptomatic treatment" was declared dangerous and useless because unless the complex was made conscious, and integrated with the rest of the patient's personality, the symptoms would return (relapse), or others would emerge (symptom substitution). Hence Freud produced a proper medical model of neurotic disorder, complete with disease and symptoms and with a prescription for treatment. No wonder this method was quickly adopted all over the world as an improvement over the previous set of theories of neurotic disorder (demonic possession cured by exorcism). Freud often complained that his teaching was widely rejected because of "psychological resistances," but this is not true; acceptance of new ideas is never accomplished quickly, and his views became accepted quite widely with unusual speed.

There is no evidence for any therapeutic effects of psychotherapy as a whole, or psychoanalysis in particular, when compared with the spontaneous remission that occurs without treatment in the great majority of neurotic disorders (Rachman, 1971). This fact was indeed realized by Freud himself, who towards the end of his life became deeply pessimistic about the practical usefulness of psychoanalysis (he thought it would be most useful as a method for investigating mental processes). It has also been tacitly accepted by most psychoanalysts who have changed their strident claims of being able to *cure* neurotic disorders (which were widespread in the 1930s and 1940s) to the much more modest claim that they could enable the patient to live more peacefully with his neuroses and that they could, in some mysterious way, make the patient into "a better person"—with the term "better" being left unspecified, so that any proof of such a claim became impossible. Rachman and Wilson (1980) quote recent and serious admissions of therapeutic impotence from psychoanalytic sources; there is no point in going into this question here. Let me merely state that there are very few, if any, leading psychoanalysts who would publicly state that their methods had been shown, by proper clinical trial, to give results greatly superior to those achieved by spontaneous remission (i.e. with no psychiatric treatment at all). This is not to say that it may not be fun for some rich and mildly neurotic individuals to talk about their sex lives with a sympathetic and usually intelligent and well-read psychoanalyst, or that many people who find difficulties in getting hold of a friendly listener to their tales of woe may not find it worth their while to pay an analyst to fulfill that function. But as far as the systematic, scientific theory of neurosis is concerned, and deductions from such a theory as might lead to improved methods of treatment, the Freudian theory is as dead as that attributing neurotic symptoms to demonological influences, and Freud's method of therapy is following exorcism into oblivion. And with it goes the only systematic medical model of neurosis.

An appropriate funeral oration over the grave of psychoanalytic hopes to make psychiatry a useful and effective discipline was pronounced by Sir Peter Medawar (1972) who has looked carefully into the pretensions of the Freudians. He concluded; "There is some truth in psychoanalysis, as there was in Mesmerism and in phrenology. . . . But, considered in its entirety, psychoanalysis won't do. It is an end-product, moreover, like a dinosaur or a zeppelin; no better theory can ever be erected on its ruins, which will remain forever one of the saddest and strangest of all landmarks in the history of twentieth century thought." Many laymen and administrators are still unaware that the patient, long ailing, has finally died; psychiatrists who are familiar with the literature are beginning to take off their mourning clothes and to look around for a replacement.

Medawar also explains why the failure of psychoanalysis to achieve cures in excess of spontaneous remission is so important. As he points out, "psychoanalysis has now achieved a complete intellectual closure: it explains even why some people disbelieve in it. But this accomplishment is self-defeating, for in explaining why some people do not believe in it, it has deprived itself of the power to explain why other people do. The ideas of psychoanalysis cannot both be an object of critical scrutiny and at the same time provide the conceptual background of the method by which that scrutiny is carried out." Then follows the crucial argument. "It is for this reason that the notion of *cure* is methodologically so important. It provides the only independent criterion by which the acceptability of psychoanalytic notions can be judged. This is why cure is such an embarrassment for 'cultural' psychiatry in general. No wonder its practitioners try to talk us out of it, no wonder they prefer to see themselves as the agents of some altogether more genteel ambition, e.g. to give the patient a new insight through a new deep, inner understanding of himself. . . . The lack of good evidence of the specific therapeutic effectiveness of psychoanalysis is one of the reasons why it has not been received into the general body of medical practice."

Nature abhors a vacuum, and demonstrations of the uselessness of a theory, or a method of treatment, are never sufficient to dethrone that theory or persuade people not to use that method of treatment. What is needed is an alternative, better theory and an alternative, better method of treatment. Both are now available. Behavior therapy, which is based essentially on the principles of modern learning theory and derives from properly-designed experimental studies carried out in psychological laboratories, furnishes us with both a proper theory and a set of methods for the treatment of neurotic disorders (Eysenck & Rachman, 1965). It also furnishes us with a scientific model of neurosis that is derived from laboratory investigations and academic theories of learning and conditioning (Eysenck, 1976a). This psychological model of neurosis has given rise to many different types of treatment, such as desensitization, "flooding," modeling, covert conditioning, aversion therapy, etc.; and these methods *are* based on laboratory experiments, both with animals and humans, and on academic learning theory. There is now little doubt that these methods of behavior therapy are successful well beyond the range of spontaneous remission, placebo treatment, or psychotherapy and psychoanalysis (Kazdin & Wilson, 1978). The effectiveness of the methods is one argument in favor of the theory underlying them, although it is not the only one, nor necessarily the most persuasive.

What has been said of neurosis is also true of criminality (Eysenck, 1977), sexual behavior (Eysenck, 1976b), and many other social behaviors which psychiatry and psychoanalysis once claimed for their own. The ineffectiveness of conceptualizations, predictions, and treatments of these approaches (e.g., Eysenck, 1976b, 1977; McCord, 1978) has given way to more systematic approaches based on academic psychological theories, themselves firmly based on laboratory and other empirical findings.

A DIVORCE IS BEING ARRANGED

Having now completed a brief look at certain issues which had to be gone into before we could enter into a meaningful discussion of the relation of psychiatry and psychology, we are now in a position to make certain proposals that may be to the advantage of psychiatry on the one side, and of society on the other. The first proposal is that there should be a divorce between the two incompatible halves which now go to make up psychiatry, i.e. the organic and the behavioral. I believe that these two sides are not at all closely related; that they demand quite different kinds of expertise, background knowledge, and training; that the medical model makes sense for the one, but not for the other; and that no single person or specialty can span the gulf that stretches between the two. The second proposal follows directly from the first: It is that organic psychiatry should remain largely in the hands of medically-trained persons, helped in large measure by clinical psychologists in putting into effect "token economies" and reinforcement conditioning treatments.

The behavioral side of psychiatry, however, requires radically new approaches if it is to come to grips with the problems that society is presenting to it more and more. Two rather obvious suggestions come to mind; one or the other (or even both in combination) might serve to improve the situation. The first proposal would be that psychiatrists opting to work in the behavioral field should have a quite different training from psychiatrists working in the organic field, and one quite different from that now current. This training would embody a realistic training in psychology, particularly those aspects concerned with learning, with conditioning, with personality, and with psychometrics, as well as with the principles of abnormal psychology; social psychology would also figure strongly. A limited amount of sociology (of the factual rather than the ideological and political variety) might also be useful, together with some information on anthropology (see Back and Price-Williams, in this volume). There would have to be concentrated practical work with patients using the methods of behavior therapy and gaining experience in the application of such methods to a great variety of different types of disorder. There would be a limited amount of time devoted to work with psychotic patients, largely to enable behavioral psychiatrists to recognize disorders of behavior caused by psychotic episodes. There would be no stress on methods lacking evidence of effectiveness, such as psychoanalysis; training would emphasize the scientific aspects of psychiatry and include courses on the evaluation of evidence. Training would also emphasize supervision of nurses, social workers, parents, and other family members of the patient in carrying out those parts of behavior therapy which can best be carried out by them, once the plan of treatment had been drawn up. Much of this training would of necessity be given by psychologists and other social-science experts. It is after all in their field that the behavioral psychiatrist would be working.

To what extent trainees would and should be excluded from certain traditional courses in medicine is an arguable point. Much of what the medical curriculum contains would be of little or no use to the practitioner; it is not clear how knowledge of anatomy would help in the treatment of obsessive-compulsive disorders, or of head bangers, or of phobias and anxieties. It would clearly become necessary to weigh the time taken by the training against the importance attached to the "medical" qualification of the final product: Is it really necessary that the behavioral psychiatrist be able to deliver babies, set bones, and generally possess all the competence of the family physician, having no intention of ever using that competence? These points are raised because they require discussion; no obvious solution suggests itself.

An alternative and even more radical proposal might be to hand over the behavioral side of treatment to nonmedical clinical psychologists, working together with medical psychiatrists in cases where medical problems were important in addition to behavioral ones, or where it was essential to rule out certain organic dysfunctions. This proposal is not as revolutionary as it might appear at first. Sir George Godber, former Chief Medical Officer to the Department of Health in Britian, explicitly suggested that, doctors being so scarce in relation to the demands on their services, other professional workers whose basic training was directly relevant should take over some of the work previously regarded as medical. There seems to be high regard among the medical profession for this idea. It is not of course that the divorce suggested should be in any way rancorous; what is intended is that the medical and the psychological sides should work together.

Little need be said about the proposals that psychiatry should continue to rule undisputed over the medical half of its present territory, even though psychologists might nevertheless have an important part to play in the design of suitable therapies and in their evaluation. This follows from the fact, already noted, that while psychotic disorders probably have definite biological roots, nevertheless these are not sufficient to produce the final breakdown. This is clearly seen in the fact that identical twins, although much more frequently concordant for psychosis than are fraternal twins, are nevertheless by no means always concordant. It is quite common to find one schizophrenic twin in an asylum, while his identical twin is apparently relatively normal, living a useful and reasonably happy life without any contact with psychiatry. Thus, there is much room in the etiology of psychosis for psychological determinants, and these of course are the special concern of psychology. Furthermore, many of the "symptoms" shown by psychotics immured in mental hospitals for many years are iatrogenic, i.e. produced not by their illness but rather by their treatment; these iatrogenic symptoms can be reduced by psychological methods such as "token economies." Consequently, this proposal does not suggest that psychiatry, as a medical specialty, should "go it alone"; it would still lean heavily on psychological advice and help in the design of methods of treatment, in research, and in the practical execution of those parts of the treatment which depend on psychological expertise and train-ing.

More controversy is likely to be raised concerning the second proposal, namely that behavioral disorders should be sloughed off completely to become the concern of behavioral psychiatrists or of psychologists alone. This suggestion will no doubt be criticized on the grounds that it is the task of medically trained people to look after the sick and the disabled, and that psychologists, not being so trained, have at most an ancillary role to play. There are many reasons for doubting the wisdom of such an argument, and a short discussion may clarify the issue.

In the first place, medicine does indeed deal with the treatment of diseases, but this does not get us very far. When is a disease not a disease? Is a person who has an inordinate fear of snakes "ill" in the medical sense? There are no lesions anywhere in his nervous system; there is no infection; there is nothing whatever that suggests that he is "diseased" in a meaningful manner. Does the golfer suffer from a "dis-ease" when he habitually slices his drive into the rough? Is the tennis player suffering from a "disease" when he habitually serves double faults? Is the football player suffering from a "disease" when he loses his temper, kicks an opponent, and is sent off? It is easy to extend the meaning of "disease" to undue lengths; we have already noted some examples of this in connection with the peculiar "diseases" attributed to slaves. We want to be very careful not to let erroneous notions enter into our discussion. It might be suggested that when the complaint is purely of behavioral "symptoms" (including here emotional reactions, whether conditioned or unconditioned, as is the usual practice), without demonstrable or even probable lesion or infection, then our first impulse should be to consider such a complaint nonmedical. It is certainly possible to call neurotic disorders "diseases," and it is possible to extend this appellation to crimi-nal acts, to school truancy, to mental defect, to alcoholism, to smoking cigarettes, and to all and any type of behavior of which society disap-proves, or of which the person afflicted himself complains. I would sug-gest that such an extension is completely unreasonable and goes counter to common sense, as much as to medical practice to date.

In the second place, we must look at the theories relating to the causes of the complaints made by people who are labelled "neurotic." We have seen that psychology provides a very well–grounded theory, stating in essence that neurotic "symptoms" are not in fact symptomatic of any-thing, but are simply learned (conditioned) emotional responses, together with motor responses associated or caused by these emotional reactions. Thus we may quite reasonably say that what is required is not medical treatment, but re-education; behavior therapy comes into the broad field of education rather than that of medicine. Psychiatrists who wish to retain the treatment of neuroses within the medical field usually refer back to the alleged "diseases" underlying the neurotic symptoms according to the Freudian paradigm. We have seen that there is no validity to this argument and that there is no evidence for these alleged "complexes." But we may go even further than this. As Freud himself maintained, there is no reason to restrict the practice of psychoanalysis to medically trained persons; he favored lay analysis and was displeased with the manner in which American psychoanalysts overrode his opinions on this topic. Thus even if psychoanalysis is the doctrine of choice, there would still be no reason for reserving the treatment of neurotic disorders for doctors.

In the third place, we must bear in mind the actual methods of treatment of neurotic disorders which have proved their effectiveness. These are all behavioral; they have originated from psychological theories developed by psychologists, and they find their main support in experiments performed by psychologists in psychological laboratories. The actual methods used on patients (some writers prefer the term "clients" to get away from the medical nomenclature, which prejudices the point at issue) have also largely been developed and perfected by clinical psychologists. Given all these facts, how can it be argued that psychologists are not capable of treating patients when the methods in use were in fact developed by the self-same psychologists? New deductions from learning theory are constantly being made by psychologists, and new methods of treatments, or improvements of the old methods, are also constantly being made. Occasionally psychiatrists (usually with some solid training in psychology) join in, but the major part of this work is in fact being done by psychologists.

The fourth point concerns the training of psychiatrists and psychologists, respectively. Effective behavioral methods of treatment are part and parcel of the background of the psychologist; they form little part at all of the training of the medical psychiatrist. There is no part of his medical training that is relevant to behavioral types of treatment, and those subjects which are relevant to treatment (such as learning theory, conditioning, personality theory, social psychology, etc.) he has either never been exposed to at all or else has met only in the most perfunctory manner during a short course which forms part of his later professional training. In other words, we have the odd situation where medical psychiatrists claim the right to direct and supervise the behavioral treatment of neurotic patients by psychologists when it is the latter, not the former, who have alone had the required training to understand and administer these methods properly and wisely. This situation clearly demands a change; any particular form of therapy should be carried out by those whose training has been geared specifically to the performance of these duties, not by others whose training is largely irrelevant.

Many psychiatrists argue that while these points are in many ways valid, medical responsibility must remain with the medically trained person. This leads to a halfway house position, implemented in many of the more advanced hospitals, in which patients are referred to the clinical psychologist by the consultant; the treatment is carried out by the psychologist, but responsibility remains with the consultant. Largely this responsibility is of course a useful figment of the imagination, and a reasonable psychiatrist would not dream of interfering in a treatment in which it is the psychologist, not he, who is the expert. But the position is clumsy and complex and sometimes leads to conflict. Furthermore, it makes referral much more devious than it need be, and it can often thwart the wishes of the patient. Many patients wishing to be treated by behavior therapy find themselves referred to a consultant who prefers psychoanalysis, or some other form of treatment, and under these circumstances the patient is powerless to achieve his aims. This does not seem fair and just; direct referral to a clinical psychologist would obviate this difficulty. Particularly in the field of child psychiatry there are still many old-fashioned, analytically trained doctors who refuse to refer children for treatment to psychologists, even though the record clearly shows that the children would be much better off if so referred. Parents should have knowledge of the facts and a proper choice; at the moment, they have none.

There remains one important point. Occasionally, an apparently neurotic "symptom" may mask a serious physical disease, and then the absence of medical knowledge may be dangerous. This is infrequent, but it suggests that in all those cases medical doctors should be available to undertake any necessary physical investigation and assume responsibility for purely physical disorders. This is, in practice, already the position with many psychoanalysts, particularly in the U.S.A.; they have medical training but do not practice ordinary medicine; they rely instead on non-psychiatrists to undertake the physical examination of their patients. There is thus no difficulty with this proposal. Family physicians would normally undertake a physical examination in any case before referring patients to the psychiatrist or, under the proposed scheme, to the psychologist.

In any case, the proposal is one of a friendly divorce, not an acidulated quarrel; a separation from bed and board, but without necessarily setting up two entirely separate households. What I am envisaging is rather like this: We have a large child guidance clinic, say, in which incoming patients are seen by a small panel including a psychiatrist, a clinical psychologist, an educational psychologist, and a social worker. The case is discussed and judged suitable for behavior therapy, for medical psychiatric treatment, for educational treatment, or for some combination of these. The psychiatrist or the psychologist to whom the case is referred takes on complete responsibility and reports back to the panel when success has been achieved, or when failure has become clear. When physical causes are suspected to be producing the symptoms or of interfering with the treatment, the child is sent to a consultant who specializes in the complaints suspected. The whole unit may be in the charge of a psychiatrist or a psychologist; there is no automatic administrative superiority based on medical qualifications. A similar type of unit may be envisaged with respect to adult patients; here, too, a small panel on which the various specialties concerned are represented would make decisions affecting the course of treatment for the patient—taking into account, of course, the wishes of the patient; just as in the case of children, their wishes, or those of their parents, would be taken into account. I am certainly not suggesting that patients wishing to receive psychotherapy would have behavior therapy forced on them; the alternative possibilities would be explained to them, and their wishes taken into serious consideration.

A GENERAL OVERVIEW

Psychiatry, in so far as it has claims to be scientific at all, is essentially an applied science. As I have pointed out, it splits into two major parts, a medical and a behavioral one. As far as the behavioral part is concerned, psychiatry is applied psychology; the contribution is almost wholly from psychology to psychiatry. Proper theories of neurotic disorders, their classification, their origin, and their treatment must come, and have come, from psychologists; psychiatrists have for the most part preferred to disregard these theories and to use idiosyncratic and ad hoc notions of their own, without empirical background or experimental verification and support. The failure to psychiatric nosology is notorious and well-documented (Cooper, Kendell, Gurland, Sharpe, Copeland, & Simons, 1972; Smith, 1978), yet psychiatrists persist with the faulty underlying "medical" model, rather than adopt the well-supported dimensional approach. Similarly, they persist with psychotherapeutic methods of treatment, which have been shown to be lacking in effectiveness (Rachman & Wilson, 1980), and fail to make use of methods, such as behavior therapy, which have an excellent laboratory pedigree and can be demonstrated to be superior in effectiveness to all traditional methods (Rachman & Hodgson, 1980). Psychiatry, then, is not really an applied science; it is rather a medical discipline which refuses to apply such scientific knowledge as exists. This is a curious position, and it will be interesting to see how long it can continue.

This is not to say that psychology has not benefited from its association with psychiatry. There are many phenomena which are for all practical purposes impossible to reproduce in the laboratory—for ethical if for no other reasons! The production of strong emotions is one such phenomenon; the production and extinction of conditioned emotional responses under real-life conditions is another. Modern behavior therapy has not only benefited from academic knowledge and theories in working out methods of treatment of neurotic patients, but it has in turn been able to repay academic psychology by adding to its store of knowledge and theory. The rewriting of the law of extinction (Eysenck, 1976a) is only one example of this mutual interplay.

Psychoanalysts of course see the matter in quite a different light; they would suggest that the study of personality, of abnormality, and of social life altogether (not to mention anthropology, history, and other such matters!) has been completely revolutionized and revitalized by the contributions of psychiatry (meaning by that "dynamic" psychiatry). There has certainly been a tremendous influence in this direction (e.g., Price-Williams, Strozier, & Lifton, in this volume), but this influence has been baleful rather than advantageous. Instead of furthering the scientific study of these topics, psychoanalysis has had the effect of encouraging idle speculation, the neglect of scientific proof, and the predominance of interpretive rather than causal analyses. Popper (1959) and other philosophers have done much to make clear the unscientific nature of psychoanalysis; there would be little point in doing so again here. If psychiatry had continued on the path outlined by Kraepelin around the turn of the century, its position would have been quite different. Psychology would have been recognized as the parent science for much of psychiatric research, and its methods would have been used to good effect by psychiatrists properly trained to so use them. Freud and his followers have set back psychiatry (and in part psychology, too) by some 75 years, so that at present the relation between psychology and psychiatry is not one of excessive friendliness and certainly not one in which the partners derive much benefit from each other's expertise. It is unfortunate that this should be the position, but it would not be honest to pretend otherwise.

It is impossible to predict what the future may hold as far as the relation between psychology and psychiatry is concerned. Ideally, psychiatrists would realize the dual nature of their discipline (which of course many already do), split up psychiatry into a neurological-medical section and a quite independent psychological-behavioral one, and adopt for the latter the scientific methods and theories of psychology, just as they adopt for the former the scientific methods and theories of neurology. If this were to happen, and if the education of the behavioral psychiatrists included a proper modicum of psychology (particularly learning theory, conditioning theory, and personality theory), then a most productive relation could emerge with psychology. History does not suggest that powerful groups ever voluntarily give up positions of great economic and social power and influence. The outlook therefore cannot be overly optimistic. However, certain increasing numbers of psychiatrists, won over by the obvious successes of behavior therapy, are beginning to see the advantages of acquiring some knowledge of psychology, and in time important changes in the desired direction may well take place. In that case, psychology and psychiatry may yet engage in a mutually beneficial association and achieve a relation more appropriate to both.

REFERENCES

Cicero, M. T. *Tusculanarum disputationum.* London: Heinemann, 1971.

Cooper, J. E., Kendell, R. E., Gurland, B. J., Sharpe, L., Copeland, J. R., & Simon, R. *Psychiatric diagnosis in New York and London.* London: Oxford University Press, 1972.

Eysenck, H. J. Criterion analysis: An application of the hypotheticodeductive method to factor analysis. *Psychological Review, 1950, 57,* 38–53.

Eysenck, H. J. *Uses and abuses of psychology.* London: Pelican, 1953.

Eysenck, H. J. Psychiatric diagnosis as a psychological statistical problem. *Psychological Reports, 1955, 1,* 3–17.

Eysenck, H. J. Emil Kraepelin. *International encyclopaedia of the social sciences.* New York: Macmillan, 1968.

Eysenck, H. J. A dimensional system of psychodiagnostics. In A. R. Mahrer (Ed.), *New approaches to personality classification.* New York: Columbia University Press, 1970.

Eysenck, H. J. (Ed.). *Handbook of abnormal psychology.* London: Pitman, 1973.

Eysenck, H. J. *The future of psychiatry.* London: Methuen, 1975.

Eysenck, H. J. The learning theory model of neurosis: A new approach. *Behaviour Research & Therapy,* 1976, *14,* 251–267. (a)

Eysenck, H. J. *Sex and personality.* London: Open Books, 1976.(b)

Eysenck, H. J. *Crime and personality.* London: Routledge & Kegan Paul, 1977.

Eysenck, H. J. The conditioning model of neurosis. *The Behavioral and Brain Sciences,* 1979, *2,* 175–199.

Eysenck, H. J., & Prell, D. B. The inheritance of neuroticism: An experimental study. *Journal of Mental Science,* 1951, *97,* 441–465.

Eysenck, H. J., & Rachman, S. *The causes and cures of neurosis.* London: Routledge & Kegan Paul, 1965.

Eysenck, H. J., & Wilson, G. D. *The experimental study of Freudian theories.* London: Methuen, 1973.

Fieve, R. R., Rosenthal, D., & Brill, H. (Eds.). *Genetic research in psychiatry.* London: The Johns Hopkins University Press, 1975.

Fulker, D. The genetic and environmental architecture of psychoticism, extraversion and neuroticism. In H. J. Eysenck (Ed.), *A model for personality.* New York: Springer, 1980.

Jasper, K. *Allgemeine Psychopathologie*. Berlin: J. Springer, 1948. (Originally published, 1913.)

Kazdin, A. E. *The history of behavior modification*. Baltimore, MD: University Park Press, 1978.

Kazdin, A. E., & Wilson, G. T. *Evaluation of behavior therapy*. Cambridge, MA: Ballinger, 1978.

Laing, R. D. *The divided self*. Chicago, IL: Quadrangle Books, 1960.

Mccord, J. A thirty-year follow-up of treatment effects. *American Psychologist*, 1978, *33*, 284–289.

Medawar, P. *The hope of progress*. London: Methuen, 1972.

Popper, K. R. *The logical scientific discovery*. London: Hutchinson, 1959.

Rachman, S. (Ed.). *Critical essays in psychoanalysis*. London: Pergamon, 1963.

Rachman, S. *The effects of psychotherapy*. London: Pergamon, 1971.

Rachman, S., & Hodgson, R. *Obsessions and compulsions*. Englewood Cliffs, NJ: Prentice Hall, 1980.

Rachman, S., & Wilson, T. *The effects of psychotherapy*. London: Pergamon, 1980.

Redlich, F. C., & Freeman, D. *The theory and practice of psychiatry*. New York: Basic Books, 1966.

Rosenthal, D. *Genetic theory and abnormal behavior*. New York: McGraw Hill, 1970.

Schepank, H. *Erb- und Umwelfakturen bei Neurosen*. New York: Springer, 1974.

Shields, J. Heredity and psychological abnormality. In H. J. Eysenck (Ed.), *Handbook of abnormal psychology*. London: Pitman, 1973.

Smith, R. J. The criminal insanity defense is placed on trial in New York. *Science*, 1978, *199*, 1048–1052.

Szasz, T. S. *The manufacture of madness*. London: Routledge & Kegan Paul, 1971.

Weil-Malherbe, H., & Szara, S. I. *The biochemistry of functional and experimental psychoses*. Springfield, IL: Thomas, 1971.

3

Psychology and Economics

Sharone L. Maital
Haifa School Psychological Services
Haifa, Israel

Shlomo Maital
Faculty of Industrial Engineering & Management, Technion
Haifa, Israel

INTRODUCTION

> *The proper study of mankind is Man.*
> —Alexander Pope (1733/1965)

Economics is the logic of choice. Psychology is the science of behavior. Since choice is one of the most pervasive and important types of behavior, it is self-evident that the models and methods of these two disciplines should be inextricably linked. But they are not. A generation ago, Herbert A. Simon (1959) began his survey of economics and psychology by asking, "How have psychology and economics gotten along with little relation in the past?" With some notable exceptions, Simon's question remains valid today. For that reason, this essay is largely a survey of economic phenomena that psychology could potentially illuminate, rather than a review of a large interdisciplinary literature.[1]

Why have economists been inhospitable to psychology? The answer lies, we believe, in the vastly different ways economics and psychology regard human beings and, as a consequence, the vastly different methods each discipline uses to test its theories. The following section of this essay further develops this contention and shows how economics turned away,

---

[1] A number of similar surveys were undertaken over the past three decades. Among them: Hayes (1950), Simon (1959), Simon and Stedry (1969), Katz (1972), Kagel and Winkler (1972), Katona (1975), Lea (1978), Meyer (1982), and Maital (1982).

a century ago, from its early behavior-oriented paradigm and launched itself toward the mechanical model of physics.

Economics is traditionally split into "micro" (the study of individual households and firms) and "macro" (the study of the national economy) branches. The third section of this essay surveys conventional microeconomic theories of consumers, investors, risk-takers, producers, managers and firms and suggests psychological theories and results that may prove relevant, or have already so proved.

Ordinary people generally encounter economics in its macro manifestation, in accounts of inflation, unemployment, and economic hardship. The fourth section analyzes how psychology bears upon these problems, and how behavioral science can help us understand the underlying causes of macroeconomic doldrums and suggest possible remedies.

A small but interesting body of research exists which applies economics to psychological phenomena. This work is discussed in the fifth section. The last section of the essay suggests areas for future research where economics and psychology could fruitfully join forces.

THE NATURE OF MAN IN ECONOMIC THEORY: AN HISTORICAL OVERVIEW

Psychology and economics differ widely in their concept of Man. Moreover, the gap between them has grown, rather than contracted, during the past hundred years; this explains in part why the two disciplines have had little interaction. Here, we briefly survey the history of economic thought since 1776, emphasizing economic assumptions about human nature.

In his book *The Economic Organization,* Knight (1933a) wrote that every economic system fulfills certain basic functions of social organization—deciding what to produce, how to produce it, how to distribute the output among people, and how to provide for the future needs of society. From time to time, economists shift their interest from one function to another and, inevitably, adjust the way they view Man. Modern economics dates from Adam Smith's *The Wealth of Nations* (1776/1937). The frugal Scot analyzes in this remarkable book why some societies do better than others in providing for future needs (i.e., economic growth). He finds the answer in differing penchants for accumulating wealth. *Wealth of Nations* is full of behavioral insights. Its famous "invisible hand" theorem, however, was to play a major role in banishing psychological considerations from economic theory. Adam Smith (1776/1937, p. 423) argues that an individual who "intends only his own gain" is led "by an invisible hand to promote an end which was no part of his intention. . . ."

By pursuing his own interest he frequently promotes that of society more effectually than when he really intends to promote it."[2] This is still the basic theorem of economics: Individual self-interest, freely expressed in free markets, guides us like an invisible hand to collective efficiency— provided individuals do not appreciably affect one another, favorably or unfavorably. The latter assumption may have been tenable in Smith's era; it has enabled economics to ignore the small- and large-group interactions in whose study psychology excels. But in complex, modern industrial economics, interactions cannot be assumed away; they lie at the core, rather than at the fringe, of our existence. Being some seventeen years prior to *Wealth of Nations*, Smith (1759/1976) wrote *The Theory of Moral Sentiments*, which argued that all moral feelings, without which no economy could function, are rooted in a fundamental human quality, mutual sympathy.[3] It is interesting to speculate how economics would have developed had it adopted the interactive *Moral Sentiments* view of Man, rather than the isolationist *Wealth of Nations* concept.

A generation after Smith, David Ricardo shifted attention away from growth toward how output is distributed. "To determine the laws which regulate this distribution is the principal problem in Political Economy," he wrote (Ricardo, 1817/1971, p. 49). John Maynard Keynes's father, John Neville Keynes, defined political economy as the art of choosing appropriate means to attain given ends. The economic ends, or objectives, emerge from the political system; the alliance between economics and politics continued until late in the nineteenth century. But psychology still played little role in economists' theories about income distribution. Ricardo based his theory of increasing economic inequality not on human attributes but on an attribute of land: the tendency of incremental output (the *addition* to total output) of an acre of land to decline, as increasing amounts of labor are applied to it.

In 1874, economics again changed its focus, with the publication of William Stanley Jevons's *Theory of Political Economy*. Jevons defined economics almost like a problem in Euclidean geometry: "Given, a certain population with various needs and powers of production, in possession of certain lands and other sources of material; Required, the mode of employing their labor which will maximize the utility of their produce [Jevons, 1874, p. 265]." Economics thus became primarily a study of

---

[2] William Baumol (1952) has argued persuasively that by "invisible hand" the deeply religious Smith meant the hand of God.

[3] Meyer (1982, p. 85) notes such psychological concepts and theories in *Moral Sentiments* as empathy, social comparison, reference group, conformity pressure, balance theory, self-regulatory system, and intrinsic and extrinsic motivation. *Wealth of Nations*, Meyer claims, is based on an *anonymous*, shared goal: the desire to earn more money.

resource allocation and efficiency—Knight's "what" and "how" questions. Jevons was one of the first to apply the mathematics of differential calculus to this basically *technical,* rather than *behavioral,* question.

The next, and perhaps all-important, watershed in the history of economic thought came toward the end of the nineteenth century. Two intellectual giants, Alfred Marshall and Leon Walras, offered competing models. Marshall's analog for the economic system was biology. He defined economics as "the study of men as they live and move and think in the ordinary business of life [1890/1962, p. 1]" and sprinkled his textbook *Principles of Economics* with wise observations on human behavior. At one point, in discussing what he called "deferred gratification", Marshall said we must assign to "mental science" a "post of honor" [Marshall, 1890/1962, p. 484] in order to understand fully interest rates and saving.

In the course of his varied and largely unsuccessful studies, Leon Walras acquired a knowledge of calculus and astronomy. In his *Elements of Pure Economics* (1871/1954), he claimed he intended to do for economics what Newton had done two centuries earlier for celestial mechanics, using Newton's own mathematical tools. *Elements* is one of the densest, most difficult books on the economics shelf. But with it, Walras triumphed over Marshall. As Milton Friedman once said, "We curtsy to Marshall, but we walk with Walras". As its paradigm, economics adopted physics, and as its language, mathematics.[4] Biology, and subsequently psychology, were shunted aside. This remains largely true to this day.

Walras's mathematical model helped economics make great strides in analyzing a vital, difficult problem: how economic sectors are interrelated and interdependent. By depicting the economy as a set of simultaneous equations for whose unknowns we can solve, Walras paved the way for such important tools as econometric models and input-output analysis. Paradoxically, while mathematics has made it possible to understand *technical* interrelations among goods and resources—so-called "general equilibrium theory" is the primary focus of twentieth century economics—it has led economics away from interrelations among *people,* whose subleties and complexities evade embodiment in mathematical symbols.[5]

---

[4]Ironically, Marshall was a far better mathematician than Walras. But he minimized its usefulness. "The chief use of pure mathematics in economic questions," Marshall wrote, "seems to be in helping a person to write down quickly, shortly and exactly, some of his thoughts for his own use . . . it seems doubtful whether any one spends his time well in reading lengthy translations of economic doctrines into mathematics, that have not been made by himself [1890/1962, p. ix]." For Walras, the medium of mathematics became the main message.

[5]There are noteworthy exceptions: See, for example, Kahneman and Tversky (1979) and Laffont (1980, pp. 48–57).

This century has seen economics drift away from its alliance with politics and deepen its mathematical content in an effort to attain the rigor and status of natural science. With this same objective in mind, economics has opted for normative celibacy—unwillingness to marry positive principles (statements about what *is*) with value judgments (statements about what *ought* to be). A common catchphrase in the economics literature is Pareto-efficiency—a state in which no one can be made better off without someone being made worse off (see Coombs, in Volume III). Actions or policies which improve some people's lot and worsen that of others are said to involve interpersonal comparisons and are put beyond the pale of positive economics, thereby quarantining most real-world issues. This approach found clearest expression in Lionel (now Lord) Robbins's (1935) famous essay. There, Robbins defined economics as "the science which studies human behavior as a relationship between ends and scarce means which have alternative uses [1935, p. 24]." Explicit mention by Robbins of "human behavior" in fact marked the surgical excision of behavior from the sphere of economics' interest. Modern economics has much to say about how productive resources can be efficiently combined, but it has very little to say about what motivates and energizes human resources. This is, we contend, a direct reflection of the ascendancy of the mathematics of celestial mechanics in conventional economics over the biology of changing human systems.

From Micro to Macro

Until the advent of John Maynard Keynes's theory (1936), economics confined its attention to *micro*economics: behavior of the individual household and firm. It was widely assumed that the nation-wide level of economic activity would be just sufficient to employ fully all resources and would, in a sense, take care of itself. This is often termed Say's Law, after the French economist J. B. Say. Despite long bouts of deflation and unemployment—America suffered a deep and bitter depression during 1873–1896—the full-employment assumption has been retained in microeconomic theory to this day. In *macro*economics—study of the determinants of aggregate output and employment founded by Keynes—the assumption is discarded.

The components of aggregate output and income are: private consumption, public consumption, gross capital formation, exports, and (with a minus sign) imports. Macroeconomic theory analyzes how these components are interconnected; empirical work seeks parametric characterizations of such functional relationships. For the United States, private consumption expenditures of households make up about two-thirds of gross national product and are therefore the main determinant of economic activity. For a considerably long period, empirical consumption functions were stable and enabled economists to predict what people intended to spend, without a detailed, viable theory of micro spending behavior. But this is no longer true, and a belated search has begun for appropriate micro foundations of macroeconomic theory.[6]

Two Major Errors

The foundations of the new branch of economics, macroeconomics, were laid in J. M. Keynes's *General Theory of Employment, Interest and Money* (1936). Keynes was a keen observer of behavior; his daring and successful financial speculation, both for his own purse and for King's College, verify this. Careful reading of the *General Theory* shows Keynes attached great importance to psychology in determining consumption and investment. But this did not save practitioners of his theory from a major error just after World War II. Economists furrowed their collective brow, looked at the American economy, and predicted that when war spending dried up, and with it many jobs, there would be a serious recession or depression, owing to inadequate aggregate demand. One of the few experts who said otherwise was George Katona (1975, p. 88). With a psychologist's willingness to undertake direct observation, his nationwide survey of Americans revealed huge sums of liquid assets, stored-up purchasing power saved during the shortages of war, and found Americans were ready and willing to spend it. Americans, he wrote, had both the means, and the desire, to spend. He was right. The immediate postwar problem was inflation, not deflation.

On the other side of the Atlantic, a second major predictive error occurred. Economists surveyed the terrible destruction wrought by war on Europe's plants, ports, and equipment and foresaw a long, slow road to recovery. It would take years and years to regain prewar production levels, they reasoned, with much of Europe's physical capital ruined. But the brains, muscles, and skills of European workers brought rapid economic growth, with the help of Marshall Plan aid.

The reason economists fell into this error, Theodore Schultz reasoned in his presidential address to the American Economics Association, is "because we did not have a concept of *all* capital and, therefore, failed to take account of human capital and the important part that it plays in

---

[6]FORTUNE surveyed economics professors at 55 American Universities, mostly large state institutions. Three-quarters of the respondents reported "increasing doubt about the accuracy of macroeconomic models." This has led the economics profession, FORTUNE claimed, to "a new emphasis on and interest in microeconomics . . . the way in which markets, companies, consumers and wage earners actually behave [December 31, 1978, p. 77]."

production in a modern economy [1961, p. 7]." Two major macroeconomic errors, then, arose from economists' inadequate view of people, in their roles as producers and consumers. Human capital theory,
which we discuss later, has restored, in small part, human beings to
production theory. But macroeconomics remains largely devoid of behavioral content.

When "expectations" became the focus of modern, dynamic macroeconomics, a remedy appeared at hand. The results, however, proved
disappointing.

"Rational" Expectations

In the eighteenth and nineteenth centuries, classical economics was
largely content to study states of equilibrium—"snapshots" of economic
systems. In this century, economists have focused on dynamic systems
and have built models showing "laws of motion" toward, or away from,
equilibrium, if indeed an equilibrium exists. A pioneer of economic dynamics, Sir John Hicks (1939), gave center stage in his theory to price
expectations: what people *think* about future price rises. In the post-1972
inflation, much macroeconomic theorizing has been concerned with describing the determinants and influence of inflation expectations. In such
a setting, an appeal to psychology for expertise on perception and cognition would appear inevitable. It never came, however. The dominant
assumption in recent literature has been the so-called "rational expectations"—the premise that the *mental* model people use to build their inflation expectations conforms to, or is consistent with, the *true* model.
Economics opened a window to psychology just a crack, only to slam it
shut at once.

The rational expectations models illustrate the polar divergence between economics and psychology, in defining the meaning of "rational".
To economists, rational means free of error. The handful of economic
models that treat irrational behavior usually define it as "random" (e.g.,
Becker, 1962). As one economist put it, economic theory must assume
error-free behavior, because we would otherwise need a theory of errors,
and the latter is a contradiction in terms.[7] In contrast, psychologists devote much time and effort to modeling and measuring systematic errors.
To date, some of the most valuable contributions of psychology to economics have been precisely in this area—the characterization of sys-

[7] George Stigler (1976, pp. 213-216) wrote that, for example, "waste is error, . . . and it will
not become a useful concept until we have a theory of error." But a theory of error, implying
"nonmaximizing behavior" is, he claims, "a mighty methodological leap into the unknown."
Barro and Fischer (1976) also state that "a theory of systematic mistakes" is internally
contradictory.

tematic biases in the perception of reality (Grether & Plott, 1979; Kahneman & Tversky, 1979; Slovic, 1972). But as long as this fundamental disagreement between economics and psychology remains, dialog between them will be severely constrained.

To conclude: A century ago, economics turned toward mathematics as its language and tool of analysis. Mathematics brought rigor and precision to economic models. But a price was paid for these qualities—the constricted and rather artificial view of human beings, set more by the demands of mathematics than by the dictates of reality, and the method of testing that view which shunned direct observation of individuals in controlled and natural settings. There are a growing number of research areas in economics where a richer, more complex view of Man is urgently needed—some of these areas are discussed later in this essay—along with the experimental methodology suitable for testing it. Psychology has much to contribute to such research.

Exclusion of psychological traits of individuals from macroeconomic models is sometimes justified, implicitly or explicitly, on the grounds that psychological traits of individuals or groups, when aggregated, cancel out (Maital & Maital, 1981). But as Schoemaker has asserted, "the connection between micro and macro behavior is too complex to argue that at higher levels of social aggregation, individual biases generally wash out or self-correct [1982, p. 553]."

In the next two sections, we explore, respectively, psychological aspects of microeconomics and macroeconomics. A more behavioral approach to the economic decision-making of individuals could, we contend, both strengthen microeconomics and help supply badly-needed micro foundations of macroeconomic theory (Leibenstein, 1979).

CONSUMERS, INVESTORS, AND MANAGERS: MICROECONOMICS AND PSYCHOLOGY

This section surveys the application of psychology to the economic behavior of individuals: consumers, investors, and managers. There are two basic units of analysis in microeconomics: the household and the firm. The household acquires income by supplying its labor and the services of capital to firms. Household members spend part or all of that income, as consumers. Firms, owned by shareholders and run by managers, purchase labor, capital, and raw materials from households and other firms, produce goods and services, and earn profit. Microeconomic theory analyzes the behavior of households and firms in isolation, and then, as general equilibrium theory, studies how they interact. We turn first to consumers.

Consumer Behavior

Consider the following illustration of consumer choice. A gourmet orders a meal in a fine restaurant unfamiliar to him. He requests a menu; without one, he cannot order wisely or order at all. The menu represents the "choice set," or opportunities. The gourmet notes the price of each entrée. Suppose the Dover sole is half as costly as the *coq au vin,* and only slightly cheaper than frogs' legs. He ponders his values—his subjective evaluation of each entrée and the pleasure or "utility" it would give him—and decides he dislikes fish, but likes frogs' legs nearly as much as chicken. Since chicken is much more expensive, he picks frogs' legs. In this decision process, the gourmet asks himself, for each entrée: (1) What is it worth to me? (2) What do I have to give up to get it? If he obeys the tenets of microeconomics, he will act to bring values—the answer to (1)—into equality with prices—the answer to (2).

A number of assumptions underlie this description of consumer choice. They are summarized in the following passage from a widely-used microeconomics textbook, Henderson and Quandt (1958, p. 6):

> The postulate of rationality is the customary point of departure in the theory of the consumer's behavior. The consumer is assumed to choose among the alternatives available to him in such a manner that the satisfaction derived from consuming commodities (in the broadest sense) is as large as possible. This implies that he is aware of the alternatives facing him and is capable of evaluating them. All information pertaining to the satisfaction that the consumer derives from various quantities of commodities is contained in his *utility function.*

Let us dissect these assumptions, from the standpoint of psychology.

(1) Consumers act in their own self-interest. This generally means consumers' wellbeing depends only on the amounts of goods and services they themselves consume and is independent of quantities consumed by others (Reder, 1947, p. 64). Interactions, which we believe are the core of consumer behavior, are thus assumed away at the outset. There are notable exceptions. Leibenstein (1976) has analyzed what he termed "bandwagon, snob and Veblen" effects in consumer behavior, and of course Veblen himself put the effect of a consumer's spending on *other* people at the center of his theory.[8]

---

[8] Sen (1977) recently criticized the premise that households are motivated only by narrow self-interest. He points out the importance of two additional elements: sympathy (where concern for others directly affects one's own welfare) and commitment (willingness to endure a drop in personal welfare in order to improve someone else's). Sen thinks one reason economists fail to understand Britain's economic difficulties (especially, work motivation) is "the neglect in traditional economic theory of this whole issue of commitment and the social relations surrounding it [1977, p. 334]."

Behavioral theories of consumer behavior have been proposed by Thaler (1980) and van Raaij (1977). See also Katona (1951, 1953, 1960, 1964, 1968, 1975).

(2) Self-interest is measured by "utility," a simple function of the quantity of goods and services bought. Utility functions are characterized by diminishing marginal utility (meaning that the increment to wellbeing caused by consuming one more unit of a good declines as the total amount consumed increases). An early study by Thurstone (1931) posited a log-linear utility function, supported by theory (Fechner's 1860 Law) and by experiments. Scitovsky (1976) has attacked the simplistic utility functions common to microeconomics. Relying on empirical work by such psychologists as the late D. E. Berlyne, Scitovsky reasons that our satisfaction from eating a meal depends on whether we last ate an hour, or a day, previously; when we last ate the *same* meal; and the rate at which our hunger is satisfied. He terms these effects "comfort," "novelty," and "pleasure," respectively, and uses them to explain why modern societies have more goods but less happiness. Scitovsky shows in particular how immediate satiation of wants common to societies of abundance (comfort) can rob us of greater satisfaction, through sating wants that have been allowed to grow by waiting (pleasure).

(3) Consumers act to maximize their utility. For economists, behavior which maximizes (utility, profit, output, etc.) is rational. This assumption permits use of the powerful mathematics of optimization—differential calculus, calculus of variations, mathematical programming, and optimal control—in consumer theory, but it raises the question, in Simon's words (1957), whether "this body of theory has reached a state of Thomistic refinement . . . (with) little discernible relation to the actual or possible behavior of flesh-and-blood human beings [1957, p. xxiii]." Simon himself proposed a theory of "satisficing," where consumers pick the first acceptable alternative instead of scanning the choice set for the optimal one.

(4) Consumers' tastes are stable and unchanging. A leading introductory economics textbook (Lipsey & Steiner, 1972, p. 54) states that "changes in demand that are due to changes in taste cannot be identified because taste changes often cannot be measured." A more extreme view (Stigler & Becker, 1977) holds that tastes are in fact constant over an individual's lifetime. Psychology can make a major contribution to increased realism and predictive power of consumer theory, by showing how consumer tastes, wants, values, and desires are endogenous, change over the life cycle, and can be precisely measured. The huge literature on market research—largely ignored by microeconomics—focuses on this topic.[9]

---

[9]Consumers are also assumed to have tastes that are internally consistent (transitive). If one prefers almond to butter pecan, and butter pecan to chocolate, one should also pick almond over chocolate. But inconsistencies are very common; see Tversky (1969) and Grether and Plott (1979).

Economic Man is a biological marvel—apart from his superb calculating and information-gathering capability—because at birth, he is already in his mid-twenties (Maital, 1982). Consumer theory ignores how people develop spending and saving values and habits as well as the role socialization plays in their acquisition, starting from childhood. Psychology can provide great enlightenment in this area. For a beginning, see Stacey (1982).

Consumers make two types of choices: this-or-that (at a given point in time) and now-or-later (between two points in time). Until now, we have discussed this-or-that choice and shown how psychology bears on a great many aspects of it. But if psychology is relevant to instantaneous choice, it is vitally essential for minimal understanding of intertemporal decisions.

The rate of interest is in a sense the price of time; it is the premium people attach to consuming *now,* rather than saving, waiting, and consuming *later.* For centuries, economists have tried to explain the persistence of positive interest rates, despite Biblical, canonical, and Islamic injunctions against them. Market interest rates compensate lenders for risk and for inflation, as well as for waiting. Economists call the "waiting" component of interest "pure time preference." A dominant theme in the literature on pure time preference has long been that the preference for present, immediate consumption over future, delayed consumption is irrational.[10] Moreover, it is argued that economic forces of supply and demand work to erase differences among individuals in pure time preference: If Sigmund has a five percent subjective interest rate, and Ernest a ten percent rate, Ernest will borrow from Sigmund. With his present situation ameliorated, Ernest's interest rate will fall. With his current consumption reduced (by the loan to Ernest), Sigmund's interest rate rises. The process continues until all time preference rates are equal.

Psychology's interest in time preference began with Freud's "Formulations on the Two Principles of Mental Functioning" (1911/1946) where the transition from the pleasure principle (immediate gratification) to the reality principle (ability to defer gratification) is seen as a vital step toward maturation. A brilliant series of studies by Mischel and his associates (Mischel, 1958, 1961, 1974; Mischel & Metzner, 1962) has demonstrated that ability to defer gratification is learned in childhood, increases until adolescence, can be influenced and improved by behavior modification techniques, is closely related to interpersonal trust, and varies widely from one person to another. An empirical study by Kurz, Spiegelman, and West (1973), in the context of the Denver-Seattle income mainte-

---

[10]"Pure time preference is . . . a polite expression for rapacity and the conquest of reason by passion [Harrod, 1948, p. 40]." See also Ramsay (1928) and Dobb (1960).

nance experiment, showed interpersonal differences in subjective interest rates ranging from 22 to 60 percent.

One implication of these findings is that, in the consumer theory of intertemporal choice, individual time preference rates should play an important part. For example, one theory of intergenerational transmission of economic inequality (Maital & Maital, 1977) is based on the premise that the environment of poverty breeds uncertainty, mistrust, and inability to defer gratification, making the poor unwilling to engage in income-building activities such as saving and education.

Behavior of Investors

Consumer choice may be viewed conceptually as the following logical sequence (though in fact choices are made continuously and simultaneously). First, people make the now-or-later decision about how much of their income to spend and how much to set aside as savings. Second, they make this-or-that choices for their current spending. Third, they make this-or-that choices about the physical and financial assets in which they will hold their savings. Because there are fundamental differences between choosing brands of soap or makes of car, and particular stocks or bonds, the economics of financial behavior is a large, separate literature. It addresses the question of how individuals dispose of their savings and of how firms acquire those savings by issues of common or preferred stock, sale of bonds, etc.

The economic theory of financial markets centers around how people deal with risk and uncertainty.[11] Each asset bidding for people's savings has a rate of return characterized by a known or unknown statistical distribution. The asset's riskiness is often measured by the degree of spread, or dispersion, of that distribution. It is the assumption of uncertainty which makes the choice of investment portfolios quite different from choice of consumption baskets (see Coombs, in Volume III).

Behaviors toward risk in psychology and in economics are joined by a common model, and they are separated by methodological differences. They share the expected utility model, but interpret it differently. The mathematical expectation of utility is the probability of an outcome, multiplied by the utility of that outcome, summed over all possible outcomes. This approach to choice under uncertainty was pioneered by von

---

[11] Knight (1933b) defined "risk" as a situation in which various probabilities are known and "uncertainty," where probabilities are not known. In reality, the dividing line between risk and uncertainty is blurred. People may be misinformed, unaware or incapable of making probabilistic calculations, or they may have subjective biases, even when objective probabilities are provided.

Neumann and Morgenstern (1944). Feather (1959) has shown that psychological choice theories of Kurt Lewin, E.C. Tolman, Julian Rotter, W. Edwards, and J.W. Atkinson are all variations on the expected utility model. But while economic theory presumes people use correct, objective probabilities, and have simplistic utility functions, psychology delves deeply into the nature and determinants of expectancy and "valence," or "reinforcement value."

Von Neumann and Morgenstern (1944) established a rigorous, axiomatic basis for the expected utility approach which still forms the foundation for most of the economic literature on behavior toward uncertainty. With few exceptions, in the economics literature these axioms have largely gone unchallenged for forty years.[12] Empirical research by psychologists (Kahneman, Slovic, & Tversky, 1981; Kahneman & Tversky, 1979) shows that not one of the axioms is consistent with how people really behave. Kahneman and Tversky (1979) have offered an alternate set of axioms, which they call "prospect theory", consistent with behavioral observations. Economists have been slow to revise their theories to incorporate these findings. (An exception is Shefrin & Statman, 1982, who use them to explain preferences for cash dividends.) A survey of empirical evidence on economics' expected utility models by Schoemaker (1982) concludes that "an extreme but tenable attitude is to view the EU model as an interesting theoretical construction which is useless for real-world decision-making [p. 556]."

Economic theory generally presumes that people find risk aversive. Assets that bear greater risk must therefore offer higher rates of return as compensation. Risk aversion is linked to a property of utility functions known as "diminishing marginal utility." For example, a person whose utility function had this property would decline an equal-chance bet to win or lose $1,000 because the gain in utility from an additional $1,000 would be smaller than the drop in utility from loss of $1,000. Upon embracing diminishing marginal utility and risk aversion, economists have been hard put to explain why some people engage in both gambling (risk affinity) and purchase of insurance (risk aversion). One theory (Friedman & Savage, 1948) posits undulating utility curves with alternating risk-averse and risk-affine segments. Prospect theory may offer a better explanation, based on the fact that people over*weight* small, *known* probabilities, and over*estimate* small, *unknown* probabilities, implying that rare, costly disasters are excessively feared and that rare, munificent gains are overly anticipated (Maital, 1982, p. 211).

Apart from shoring up the theory of risk taking, psychology has made

---

[12] A paradox noted by Allais (1953) is an exception.

major contributions in two other areas: the empirical measurement of risk aversion and the social psychology of risky choice. Kogan and Wallach (1964) constructed an empirical, risk aversion scale that has been related to choice under uncertainty (Filer, Maital, & Simon, 1982). A large litera- ture has been built on Stoner's (1961) finding that groups of people make riskier choices than lone individuals—the so-called risky shift. From time to time, financial markets fluctuate wildly, with soaring speculative "bub- bles" or plummeting panic crashes (Kindelberger, 1978; Plaut, 1980). No satisfactory economic theory of financial crises is possible without appeal to the psychology of small- and large-group behavior.

An efficient financial market is one where asset prices fully and accu- rately reflect existing information. Paul Samuelson (1965) and Benoit Mandelbrot (1966) independently proved the following theorem: If infor- mation-gathering is cheap, buying and selling costless, and everyone *per- ceives* information in the same way, stock prices will behave as a random walk. Profit possibilities in such an efficient market are severely limited. While strong empirical evidence has led economics to adopt the random- walk postulate—the financial equivalent of "rational expectations"—most investors, speculators, and brokers reject it. Perhaps this is a good thing; paradoxically, in order for price changes to be random, there must be many people who believe they aren't, and who therefore engage in ardu- ous information-gathering in search of profit. Perception of stock prices as random, or systematic, has been related to Rotter's internal-external locus of control scale (Filer et al., 1982). A synthesis of economic and psychological theories of the following sort appears reasonable—in any given market, there are "rational" buyers and sellers, whose actions en- able prices to reflect their "true" values, as well as participants whose perceptions and knowledge are biased, incomplete, or wrong. Behavior of markets will depend on which group is predominant and on how the two groups interact.[13]

People as Producers

Households purchase goods and services with income gained from sale of their labor and capital. Firms, the agents of production, purchase labor and capital, and face three choice decisions: what to produce, how much,

---

[13]Over the past decade, common stock prices have risen very little, though profits per share suggest they should have at least doubled (to match inflation). Modigliani and Cohn (1979) theorized that this reflects investor irrationality; specifically, investors compare real (inflation-adjusted) rates of return on stocks with high nominal interest rates *not* adjusted for inflation. In early August 1982, Modigliani said that a decline in interest rates would enable investors to correct this mistaken perception and would result in a sudden bull market. On August 17, the Dow-Jones Index of common stock prices began a rapid climb, on record volume, of nearly 150 points.

and what combination of labor, capital, and other productive resources to use. The basic underlying assumptions of the theory of the firm, again drawn from Henderson and Quandt (1958, p. 42), are:

A firm is a technical unit in which commodities are produced. Its entrepreneur (owner and manager) decides how much of and how one or more commodities will be produced, and gains the profit or bears the loss which results from his decision. An entrepreneur transforms inputs into outputs, subject to the technical rules specified by his production function. . . . The rational entrepreneur desires to maximize the profit he obtains from the production and sale of commodities.

Profit-maximizing firms must adhere to the following two decision rules: (1) the last unit of output must contribute as much to total revenue as it does to total costs and (2) the last, incremental unit of labor or capital must contribute as much to total revenue as it is paid. Conceptually, the theory of profit-maximizing firms, in microeconomics, resembles the theory of utility-maximizing households.[14] In William Hazlitt's words, corporations "feel neither shame, remorse, gratitude nor goodwill."

The assumption of profit-maximization compels economics to posit that the maximum amount of output is squeezed out of given amounts of labor, capital, and raw material inputs. This postulate holds universally for firms struggling in highly competitive markets and for monopolies who face no competition at all. In economic theory, since waste is in no one's interest, it does not exist. The chief critic of this postulate is Leibenstein (1976). He notes that firms purchase units of labor *time*. But the units critical for production are not work hours or days but *directed effort*. The individual is the main economic actor, Leibenstein claims, rather than the firm. All individuals decide how much effort to exert per labor hour. The psychology of motivation, drive, and achievement therefore becomes relevant and important. Tomer (1981) has argued that worker motivation is the most neglected element in microeconomic theory.

In the modern workplace, labor is done in small and large groups. Bureau of Labor Statistics reveal that for the United States, service workers are now more numerous than those in manufacturing; and services, perhaps even more than manufacturing, demand close interaction (e.g. Sutermeister, 1963). Industrial and social psychology therefore become increasingly relevant to labor economics. To cite one example, Latané, Williams, and Harkins (1979) have studied the phenomenon of "social

---

[14]"The well-known definition of a firm as an institution that makes internal decisions without the use of exchange does not distinguish firms from households, which also do not generally use exchange internally [Becker, 1971, p. 69]." Becker's economic theory of the family, discussed below, does analyze in detail the process of exchange among household members, in an interesting and perceptive manner.

loafing," where people exert less effort when they are part of a group than when they are alone, because each person thinks the other will bear the brunt. They refer to an early unpublished paper by Ringelmann who showed that individuals pulling on ropes each pull half as hard when in groups of eight than when pulling alone.

Microeconomic theory is concerned with economic efficiency and obstacles to achieving it, like monopoly. But its "maximum output per unit of input" assumption leads it to ignore perhaps the leading single cause of wasted resources, the failure of inputs to reach maximum productivity. Leibenstein (1976) estimates the resulting output loss at 20 percent for the economy as a whole. He has termed this waste "X-inefficiency." Ironically, while an entire branch of psychology—organizational behavior—focuses on the causes and nature of X-inefficiency, a major branch of economics denies its existence (Maital & Meltz, 1980).[15]

Capital is Knowledge

While workers' productivity depends to an important extent on how hard and how well they *choose* to work, it also depends on how well they are *capable* of working—on their knowledge, skill, and training. Long ago, Alfred Marshall wrote that "capital consists in a great part of knowledge and organization.... knowledge is our most powerful engine of production [1890/1962, p. 115]." This is the basis of the "human capital" approach pioneered by Schultz (1961) and Becker (1964). Anything that enhances the productiveness of people's labor is treated as investment, and the primary types of investment in human capital flow from acquisition of skills through education and through experience. If we treat a person's earnings as the return to his or her human capital, and compute the summed present value of those earnings to age 65, a dollar figure can be assigned to each individual's human capital. It is somewhat surprising but true that the average American's wealth in human capital exceeds his or her financial and physical capital (cars, insurance, securities, houses, etc.).

Human capital theory has traditionally centered around cognition—what people *know*. The huge literature on cognitive psychology could find here many useful applications. What people *feel*—affect, emotion, and personality—has not been assigned its rightful role in microeconomic theory in general, nor in human capital theory in particular. An important exception is Filer (1981), who defines and measures "affective" human

---

[15]For a comprehensive survey of organizational behavior and its application to economic productivity, see Arnold, Evans, and House (1980). The economic case against "The Xistence of X-efficiency" is best stated by Stigler (1976).

capital: the contribution of personality traits (measured by the Guilford-Zimmerman Temperament Survey) to monetary earnings. He found that "by far the most important personality trait appears to be general activity, or drive." Earlier, we argued that psychology can help explain how people spend their money. Filer's work opens up a new field, in which psychology is useful in explaining how much people can earn.

How Managers Behave

It ceased to be true long ago that owners of firms are also their managers. Gardner Means's 1929 study found that 44 percent of Fortune's top 500 companies were controlled by managers, as opposed to stockholders (Berle & Means, 1932). Recently, Galbraith (1973) cited studies showing that of the top 200 American nonfinancial corporations, 85 percent are controlled by their managers. The assumed concomitance of interest between those who run firms and those who receive the profits is by no means self-evident. Theories have been constructed based on the presumption that managers seek "satisfactory" profits (Simon, 1957), growth (Leibenstein, 1960; Marris, 1964), stability (Galbraith, 1967), size (Williamson, 1964), maximal lifetime incomes (Monsen & Downs, 1965), and maximal sales, subject to "acceptable" profit levels (Baumol, 1959). The latter theory is noteworthy, in that Baumol (1959) disputes the claim that sales maximization is "irrational" by defining rational behavior in a manner consistent with psychology, but at odds with mainstream economics:

> People's objectives are whatever they are. Irrationality must surely be defined to consist in decision patterns that make it more difficult to attain one's own ends, and not in choosing ends that, for some reason, are considered to be wrong. Unless we are prepared to determine other people's values, or unless they pursue incompatible objectives, we must class behavior as rational if it efficiently pursues whatever goals happen to have been chosen [p. 47].

On these grounds, managerial goals become a topic for empirical research, rather than philosophical debate (Cyert & March, 1963). Strikingly little has been done by microeconomic researchers to elicit these goals directly. Recent contributions of Hayes and Abernathy (1980) attribute the decline of American productivity, growth, and competitiveness to "managerial myopia"—excessive concentration on short-run profits and on the corporate equivalent of unwillingness to defer gratification. Whether or not this is true, American managers themselves tend to believe that managerial behavior is primarily responsible for lagging output and efficiency (Judson, 1982). A strong theoretical and empirical case exists for making managerial goals an endogenous variable, amenable to verification in the field, rather than an ironclad assumption of microeconomics.[16]

Do People Optimize?

A prevalent theme in microeconomics is that individuals—whether consumers, investors, producers, or managers—are optimizers. Their decisions are assumed to bring utility or profit functions to a global maximum, subject to existing technological constraints. Economists rightly argue that individuals *wish* to optimize. But their view of man does not admit constraints on their *ability* to do so—constraints on the ability to gather, sort, process, and use information. Schoemaker has recently noted that ". . . the failure to optimize appears to be cognitive, rather than motivational [1982, p. 553]." Psychologists have studied cognitive constraints for decades. Their results can steer economists toward more sensible, believable models of microeconomic behavior, in which economic agents behave as people really do, rather than as they might or as they should. As Exhibit A, we cite Akerlof and Dickens (1982), whose economic applications of Festinger's theory of cognitive dissonance yield valuable insights (Festinger, 1956; Festinger & Carlsmith, 1959).

Every person has several economic roles. As consumers, we decide how much to save and to spend, and on what. As producers, we choose how well and how hard to work. As investors, we pick from a variety of risks and returns. As managers, we organize the labor and capital of others to achieve complicated goals. Together, these roles form the substance of microeconomics. For each of them, there exists a substantial body of related results from psychology. Some of these results contradict conventional economics, and some complement it. Whichever case holds, tempering the logic of microeconomic theory with the findings of behavioral science deepens our understanding of how people earn, save, spend, and invest their own resources and those of other people.

INFLATION, RECESSION, AND GROWTH: MACROECONOMICS AND PSYCHOLOGY

"The historic terrain of macroeconomic theory," wrote James Tobin (1982, p. 171), "is the explanation of the levels and fluctuations of overall economic activity." Lately, there has been much to explain. Measured

---

[16] A survey by Spechler of "Organization and Economic Behavior" (1982) cites evidence that size, organizational form, and type of ownership influence corporate behavior. See also Maital (1978).

mid-year to mid-year, the annual rise in American consumer prices topped 10 percent three years in a row—1979, 1980, and 1981. This set a modern record; in the last bout of comparable inflation, double-digit inflation lasted only two years: 1918 and 1919. In July 1982, the rate of unemployment brushed close to double-digit levels; at 9.8 percent, it was the highest rate since 1941. By November, unemployment had reached 10.8 percent. In the bruising recession of Spring 1980, inflation-adjusted Gross National Product *declined* by nearly 10 percent in one quarter. Fewer than two years later, America found itself again mired in recession, stagnation, and unemployment, this time more prolonged.

From this dismal soil have sprung many pointed questions. What causes inflation? What causes unemployment? Why do they often occur together? Above all, what should be done? Economics has responded with several voices. The traditional macroeconomics of Keynes, born in the Great Depression, points to aggregate private and public spending as the proximate source of trouble. But the so-called "demand-side" theory has had difficulty explaining the coexistence of inflation (excess demand) and unemployment (inadequate demand). The "monetarist" school attributes inflation to excessive growth of money. Recent tight-money policies call into question the money-inflation causality, and they suggest the resulting "cure" (unemployment) may be worse than the illness. A third approach, "supply-side" economics, proposes to fight inflation not by curtailing demand but by boosting supply, mainly through tax cuts. Despite major reductions in personal and corporate taxes, American supply curves have remained intransigent.

The missing ingredient in these three approaches is human behavior. Keynes founded macroeconomics essentially as a search for stable relationships among aggregates such as consumer spending and disposable income. This methodology is not unlike that of physics, medicine, or psychology, whose big questions begin with phenomena that Nature tosses up. But unlike the exact or behavioral sciences, economics failed to establish precise micro underpinnings for its macro laws. Those macro laws are now crumbling, and, belatedly, explanations are being sought in the actions of individuals.

The Psychology of Inflation

We noted earlier that expected inflation plays an important role in modern macroeconomic theory. The psychology of inflation expectations is much more complex than economics is willing to assume. In the post-World War II era, fears of accelerated inflation have led people to spend *more,* in anticipation of price rises (the Vietnam War period) and to spend *less,* as jitters about the future foster the desire to build up a savings nest-egg (the Korean War period) (Katona, 1975). In general, surveys of consumer sentiment have proved useful in forecasting economic activity (e.g., Shapiro, 1972). But the links between what people *think* about the economy and what they themselves *do* are intricate and involved, and are not yet well understood (Behrend, 1974, 1977).

One approach to explicating those links is the interpretation of inflation as prisoner's dilemma. "Inflation is like a crowd at a football game," ex-President Carter once said. "No one is willing to be the first to sit down." An individual can forestall some of the impact of inflation by buying in advance of price rises, demanding large wage increases, or raising the price of things he or she sells. But when everyone engages in this behavior, the result is collective ruin. The clash between individual rationality and collective wellbeing is the crux of "prisoner's dilemma," a model used widely in psychology to study small-group interactions. This model of inflation traces its fundamental cause to people's perceptions and actions based on them (Maital & Benjamini, 1980). It is not a view of the world that ordinary people find appealing. Public opinion polls show consistently that the majority of Americans thinks government is responsible for inflation. Few believe they themselves are part of the cause—a phenomenon explained perhaps by cognitive dissonance. This perception itself becomes part of the problem, because it relieves individuals of both the need and the desire to engage in anti-inflationary behavior. The main economic policy implied by the prisoner's dilemma model is an incomes policy, a kind of social contract, in which, like a football crowd, every group (including government) "sits down" simultaneously by making agreed-upon sacrifices. It is significant that a large majority of economists opposes such a measure, while an equally large majority of the public supports it.

Psychology can illuminate not only the *causes* of inflation, but also its *effects*. Economics lacks a satisfactory theory about why inflation is bad and about why people dislike it. Despite rising prices, money incomes have in general risen faster than prices, leaving people better off in real terms. Yet there is widespread inflation aversion. Why? A possible behavioral explanation is provided by the theory of learned helplessness (Garber & Seligman, 1980). Seligman (1975) posits that a person or animal is helpless with respect to some outcome when the outcome occurs independently of all his voluntary responses. People come to learn that they are helpless to control a major determinant of their wellbeing: the purchasing power of their income and wealth over their lifetime. While they can control to some extent their dollar incomes, they cannot determine what their dollars can buy. The induced helplessness is strongly aversive (Maital, Maital, & Plaut, 1982).[17]

---

[17]Fried (1982, p. 12) cautions that learned helplessness "is one of the more ominous threats to our democratic society in view of the political passivity it induces."

Learned helplessness can in part explain a basic cause of inflation. Seligman argued that "if a person has learned in one place, his office for example, that he has control, and becomes helpless in a second place, a train for example, he will discriminate between the different controllability of the two contexts [1975, p. 60]." As consumers, people may learn to be helpless, accepting price rises with indifference. As suppliers of labor, people learn that in collective bargaining, immoderate wage demands, strike threats, and militancy bring results. This "learned efficacy" is further reinforced by "learned helplessness" on the part of employers, who find it easier to raise their own prices than to resist wage demands. Learned helplessness on the part of consumers of goods and of labor, and militancy on the part of sellers of goods and of labor, constitute a partial explanation of both the causes of rapid inflation and its psychological effects.

Recession and Depression

Between 1930 and 1939, economic activity in America fell sharply, leaving in its wake unemployment, hardship, and human suffering. Friedman and Schwartz (1963) called this "a tragic testimonial to the importance of monetary forces," specifically, a sharp contraction in the money supply during those years. Their view, supported by massive evidence, has become part of economics' conventional wisdom. A book by Temin (1976), however, proposes an alternate hypothesis: The main cause of the Depression was a large, autonomous drop in private spending. Whichever view is right—whether the quantity of money sets the level of output and employment, or how much of it people choose to spend—the importance of psychological perceptions and attitudes is undeniable. As if to remind us, came the 1980 recession.

On March 14, 1980, President Carter invoked the 1969 Credit Control Act to clamp down on inflation. His forty-page announcement of regulations restricting credit was highly complex. Experts debated its meaning. Ordinary people boiled it down to a simple message: Credit-card buying was to be penalized. In retrospect, the impact of the Carter measures on credit card buying was minimal. But people perceived it as drastic. In May and June, consumer debt declined sharply, and the mistaken perception left scorched earth in shopping centers, car showrooms, and department stores. Controls were dismantled in the summer, and by August, credit buying had returned to its January peak; the economy recovered nearly as rapidly as it had plummeted. The cost of this uncontrolled experiment in perception: $60 billion in lost output (about $300 per capita), equal to a 10 percent drop in G.N.P. for three months (Maital, 1982, p. 151). We conclude that how people *perceive* economic policy—

whose importance politicians and economists alike underestimate—is perhaps as important as the design of that policy itself.

Unemployment

A Gallup survey in January 1982 revealed that among those employed full-time or part-time, a full 15 percent think "it is at least fairly likely they will lose their jobs within the next 12 months." An unemployment rate of 8–10 percent implies that nearly one worker in four has either lost his or her job, or think they likely will. Economists measure the costs of unemployment in terms of lost output. But clearly, there are large psychological costs borne by those out of work, and by those who hold jobs but fear they soon will not (Fried, 1982). Psychologists in clinical practice can no doubt attest to this. A pathbreaking attempt at exploring the psychopathology of unemployment and major economic change is the conference volume edited by Ferman and Gordus (1979).

The causes, as well as the effects, of unemployment lie within the realm of psychology. Suppose two million people each undertake to buy a new car, who otherwise would not have done so. This would generate first-round increases of over $10 billion in output and in income. As auto workers, car dealers, and so on, spent their extra income, there would be second-, third-, and fourth-round expansions of employment, output, and income. Unemployment would fall substantially. Why, then, do not each of these two million persons buy a car, going into debt if necessary? Clearly, no individual is likely to take an action simply because, if everyone took that action, all would benefit (Baumol, 1952). This is a precise counterpart of the prisoner's dilemma model of inflation. Here, people *refrain* from spending, through uncertainty, doubt, and mistrust, causing inadequate demand and unemployment. Under inflation, people spend excessively for similar reasons. How can people be brought to spend more, or spend less, when their narrowly-defined immediate interest does not call for it? Searching for answers could lead to a social psychology of the business cycle.

In conclusion, throughout history great tides of economic activity have swept people into booms and busts, depression and prosperity, deflation and inflation. Macroeconomics strives to explain these fluctuations and at present is grappling with the deep recession which America and most other Western countries suffer from. There is growing recognition among economists that shifts in the pace of the national economy cannot be understood, let alone controlled, without reconstructing the micro underpinnings of macro behavior. Searching for these underpinnings will inevitably lead economists in the direction of psychology.

WHAT CAN ECONOMICS CONTRIBUTE TO PSYCHOLOGY?

Oscar Wilde once defined a cynic as someone who knows the price of everything, and the value of nothing. His quip has been revised to define "economist." There is considerable injustice in this. Much of economic theory comprises an intricate framework showing how individuals match objective prices with subjective values, and how such values find expression in marketplace exchanges of money and goods. For this section, we chose two areas of interest to psychologists, where the economics of prices and exchange has found interesting applications: operant psychology and family relationships.

Token Economies

Traditional reinforcement theories share economics' view of people as motivated by some form of hedonism, striving to maximize their reinforcements (Kagel & Winkler, 1972; Rachlin & Burkhard, 1978). Operant theorists, following Skinner, have been more concerned with relating reinforcement schedules to observable behavior than with the intervening variables that influence behavioral processes. This conforms with economics' methodology—outlined in a famous essay by Milton Friedman, and hence dubbed the "F-twist"—that tests theories not by examining the veracity of their assumptions but by their matching predictions with reality. Both economics and operant psychology share a willingness to let black-box utility functions remain tightly shut.

Lea (1978) has noted the similarity between assumptions underlying economics' demand curves and psychology's reinforcement schedules. Commodities are seen as reinforcers; reinforcement schedules parallel prices; and manipulation of reinforcement schedules in the laboratory is comparable to economic data matching prices and quantity demanded. Psychologists have borrowed the basic principle of demand theory—the quantity of some good we demand depends on that good's price and the price of goods that are close substitutes or complements—and tested it in animal experimental settings (Battalio, Kagel, & Rachlin, 1981; Kagel, Battalio, Rachlin, & Green, 1981). Their results generally confirm those of economics though, as Lea (1978) has noted, their demand curves are usually smoother. Research with human subjects in token economies suggests that demand is more price-sensitive and idiosyncratic than in animal studies, but overall, confirms economic theory.

Demand theory, borrowed from economics, has proven useful in planning token economies; it has helped provide a rational basis for decisions concerning management of prices, wages, and interest rates. This in turn has permitted testing of economic theories, and manipulation of economic variables under controlled conditions (Kagel & Winkler, 1972; Rachlin, Kagel, & Battalio, 1980). But for more open systems, with greater uncertainty and less experimental control over the range of choices, economic theory fares more poorly. In particular, for intertemporal choice, Lea (1978) concludes that economics and psychology diverge.

Application of economics to operant procedures and models occurs mainly with respect to individual behavior. For group behavior, where many options are simultaneously available and choices are interdependent, both traditional economic theory and operant theories appear to break down. In an attempt to explain behavior in its real-world, systems context, even rigidly behavioral psychologists have turned to social learning theories that include more phenomenological, interactive, and cognitive elements than the older, mechanistic operant and reinforcement theories. For example, Winkler and Winett (1982, p. 428) suggest that to understand human choices related to delay of gratification or resource conservation, we need knowledge of "the actions and perceptions of individuals interacting with their situational contexts, and other external systems". Psychology's eagerness to understand interpersonal perceptions, cognitive factors, and reciprocal relations may yield a double dividend for economics. It may elicit similar willingness on the part of economists to model group behavior realistically, and it may help explain complex economic behavior in social contexts using social and ecological models exemplified by Bandura (1982) and by Bronfenbrenner (1979).

Family Relationships

Perhaps the most determined, consistent, and original effort at exporting economics to social psychology, rather than importing psychology to economics, has been made by Becker (1976, 1981a, 1981b). Becker has applied the theory of utility maximization to explain such phenomena as love, marriage, divorce, and childbearing. His recent work (1981a, 1981b) is a challenging attempt to explain intra-family relationships with a hedonistic, "Economic Man" model.

The basis of market relationships is self-interest and selfishness, Becker notes, citing Adam Smith (1776/1937); it is this, he contends, which makes free markets work smoothly and efficiently. But in a family context, "the advantages of altruism in improving the wellbeing of children and parents are contrasted with its disadvantages in market transactions [1981, p. 1]."

Becker begins by assuming that at least one family member is altruistic; that is, his utility function is an increasing function of another family member's wellbeing, say, that of his spouse. Suppose the spouse is selfish; her utility function is independent of her husband's wellbeing. Assume that the husband gives part of his income to his wife. Will the wife do everything she can to maximize her own utility, even if it lowers that of her husband? The initial response is, yes, because we defined her as "selfish." No, Becker explains, citing what he calls his Rotten Kid theorem; "she is led by the 'invisible hand' of self-interest to act as if she is altruistic towards her benefactor [1981b, p. 5]." Consider the case where an increase in the wife's income causes the husband's income to fall by even more. Family income falls, and with it the optimal level of the wife's consumption. As a result, the husband will *reduce* the income he gives to his wife by *more* than the increase in her income. Both husband and wife are worse off. Though she is selfish, the wife will not undertake this action, because to do so is against her interest. She will *act* altruistically because it is not in her interest to harm her altruistic benefactor. "Since an altruist and his beneficiaries maximize family income, and do not shirk their responsibilities or otherwise increase their wellbeing at the expense of others," Becker argues, "altruism encourages the division of labor and an efficient allocation of resources in families [1981b, p. 10]."

It would be exceedingly interesting to read a critique of Becker's theory of the family by an experienced family therapist. The mathematics Becker uses—though fairly elementary compared with modern economic theory—may hamper such a confrontation.

Overall, economics' contribution to psychology has been quite limited. Relatively few economists have had the interest, knowledge, and courage to apply their tools to psychological phenomena. Whether this is because economists have little to contribute, or because few have tried, is an open question.

APPLYING PSYCHOLOGY TO ECONOMICS: FUTURE DIRECTIONS

Psychologists outnumber economists by two or three to one, an indication that the psyche is regarded as more important, or less tractable, than the fisc. The disproportion in scientific literature is likely weighted even more heavily in psychology's favor. From this massive body of knowledge, what can economics best appropriate to further its research aims?

The single most useful item in psychology's armory is not a particular model or theory—though we shall later list a few—but rather the method which emphasizes direct observation of people as individuals and as members of small and large groups. Economics has become topheavy with theory. When empirical tests are performed, they are predominantly based on aggregate data. Researchers themselves rarely generate their data, nor are they closely familiar with the accuracy of their data or the way the data were gathered and processed. As a result, economic theory has become isolated and insulated from the human beings it purports to understand. The predictive power of such theory is predictably poor.

In a letter to *Science,* Wassily Leontief, Nobel Laureate in Economics, recently published his tabulation of types of articles published over the past 10 years in economics' leading journal, the *American Economic Review* (Leontief, 1982). Two-thirds of the articles comprised mathematical or non-mathematical analysis, without data. Just over one article in four consisted of empirical analysis with data not generated by the author. For the period 1972–1976, 1.3 percent of all articles were empirical analyses based on simulations, experiments, or other data generated by the author; for 1977–1981, the comparable figure was 3.8 percent. The fraction of Ph.D. dissertations in economics based on author-generated data probably equals the fraction of psychology Ph.D. theses *not* based on such data.

If even a small percentage of economists would embrace the techniques of experimental psychology, this would constitute a major breakthrough. The important findings of economics' leading experimenter, Vernon Smith (1976, 1977, 1982) attest to this.

Much of economic behavior arises not from conscious, utility-maximizing decisions but from habit and social norms. Good use can be made of psychology's analysis of how norms emerge and change (see Opp, 1982).

Related to norms are social institutions, defined by Schotter (1981) as a regularity in social behavior agreed to by all members of society, which specifies behavior in specific recurrent situations, and is either self-policed or policed by some external authority. Conventional economic theory begins by assuming specific social institutions, i.e., the right to own property and appropriate income from it, and it analyzes markets and economies that result. This begs the key question of how particular social institutions arise in the first place. Researchers are tackling this problem by using game theory, invented by von Neumann and Morgenstern (1944). Social institutions *emerge* as part of the solution to games with given structures. The problem with this is that people do not always pick the optimal strategies that game theory posits. By using game theory to suggest particular social institutions, and then applying game-experiment methods drawn from psychology to observe actual behavior, economists can plant both their theory and measurement firmly in the soil of human behavior.

One of the aspects of economic choice least well understood is actions harmful to those who perform them, such as addiction to drugs, or, to some extent, smoking and excessive drinking and eating. Economic models of such behavior usually do not go beyond saying that the immediate gratification from such behavior must exceed the deferred pain (Stigler & Becker, 1977; but see Scitovsky, 1976, and Winston, 1980). In his 75th birthday address at Harvard, America's greatest economist Irving Fisher said he would like to see a study of how the human animal often misses his satisfactions instead of attaining them (Fisher, 1956, p. 77). He specifically mentioned narcotics. Such a study must await the extensive integration of cognitive psychology with the theory of economic behavior (see also Krautz & Glass, in Volume III).

In discussing the economics of uncertainty, we noted that the concept "mathematical expectation" is widely used. In social learning theory, the similar concept "expectancy" has a central role (Rotter, Chance, & Phares, 1972). Loosely speaking, expectancy is the subjective probability of an outcome multiplied by the subjective value of that outcome. Application of social learning theory to the economics of uncertainty and better to understand financial markets, risk aversion, etc. is inevitable; see, for example, Filer et al. (1982). Economists should find social learning theory sensible and appealing, falling as it does between the extremes of ephemeral psychoanalytic concepts and rigid stimulus-response models.

CONCLUSION

James Cicarelli's research on "The Future of Economics" asked economists to list areas where breakthroughs are most likely. At the top of his list is: "Explicit merger of economic theory with aspects of political science, psychology, sociology, sociobiology and law . . . [cited in Maital, 1982, p. 263]."

In this essay, we have mapped out research areas where psychology can fruitfully be applied to unsolved economic problems (as well as, to a lesser extent, psychological questions to which economics can be applied). For some of these areas, economics and psychology share common concepts (e.g., interest rates and deferred gratification), and only a common terminology is needed to help tear down artificial walls. For others, economics and psychology look upon the world with antithetical models and methods; here, cooperation will require radical changes in how economists think and work.

Two generations ago, Cambridge economics professor Arthur Pigou referred to economic theory as the commercial doings of a community of angels. He expressed the hope that this would be replaced by the actual world of men and women as they are found in experience to be. Pigou's desire has not yet been fulfilled. With the help of psychology, it can be. It has been said that there are no closed models; only the universe is closed.

Once opened to the vigorous influence of psychology, the sealed models of economics would gain immensely in realism and predictive power. This process has begun, and it will accelerate. Both economics and psychology share Pope's view about the proper study of mankind. One day, they will share a common perspective on the proper manner to engage in that study.

ACKNOWLEDGMENTS

Research for this paper was completed in part while the authors were visiting the Woodrow Wilson School of Public and International Affairs at Princeton University. The second author is grateful to the Social Sciences Research Council, the Ford Foundation (through the Israel Foundations Trustees), the Technion Vice-President's Fund, and the Neaman Institute for Advanced Studies in Science and Technology for financial support.

REFERENCES

Akerlof, G. A., & Dickens, W. T. The economic consequences of cognitive dissonance. *American Economic Review*, 1982, *72*, 307–319.
Allais, M. Le comportement de l'homme rationnel devant le risque: Critique des postulats et axiomes de l'école Americaine. *Econometrica*, 1953, *21*, 503–546.
Arnold, H. J., Evans, M. G., & House, R. J. Productivity: A psychological perspective. In S. Maital & N. Meltz (Eds.), *Lagging productivity growth: Causes and remedies*. Cambridge, MA: Ballinger, 1980.
Bandura, A. Self-efficacy mechanisms in human agency. *American Psychologist*, 1982, *37*, 122–147.
Barro, R., & Fischer, S. Recent developments in monetary theory. *Journal of Monetary Economics*, 1976, *2*, 133–167.
Battalio, R. C., Kagel, J. H., & Rachlin, H. Commodity-choice behavior with pigeons as subjects. *Journal of Political Economy*, 1981, *89*, 67–91.
Baumol, W. *Welfare economics and the theory of the state*. London: Longmans, 1952.
Baumol, W. *Business behavior, value and growth*. London: Macmillan, 1959.
Becker, G. S. Irrational behavior and economic theory. *Journal of Political Economy*, 1962, *70*, 1–13.
Becker, G. S. *Human capital*. New York: Columbia University Press, 1964.
Becker, G. S. *Economic theory*. New York: Knopf, 1971.
Becker, G. S. *The economic approach to human behavior*. Chicago, IL: University of Chicago Press, 1976.
Becker, G. S. *A treatise on the family*. Cambridge, MA: Harvard University Press, 1981. (a)
Becker, G. S. Altruism in the family and selfishness in the market place. *Economica*, 1981, *48*, 7–15. (b)
Behrend, H. *Attitudes to price increases and pay claims* (Monograph #4). London: National Economic Development Office, 1974.

Behrend, H. Research into inflation and conceptions of earnings. *Journal of Occupational Psychology*, 1977, *50*, 169–176.

Berle, A. A., Jr., & Means, G. C. *The modern corporation and private property*. New York: Macmillan, 1932.

Bronfenbrenner, U. *The ecology of human development: Experiments by nature and design*. Cambridge, MA: Harvard University Press, 1979.

Cyert, R. M., & March, J. G. *A behavioral theory of the firm*. Englewood Cliffs, NJ: Prentice-Hall, 1963.

Dobb, M. *An essay on economic growth and planning*. London: Routledge Kegan Paul, 1960.

Feather, N. Subjective probability and decision under uncertainty. *Psychological Review*, 1959, *66*, 150–164.

Fechner, G. *Elemente der Psychophysik* (Vol. 1). Leipzig: Breitkopf & Harterl, 1860.

Ferman, L. A., & Gordus, J. P. (Eds.). *Mental health and the economy*. Kalamazoo, MI: Upjohn Institute, 1979.

Festinger, L. *A theory of cognitive dissonance*. New York: Harper & Row, 1956.

Festinger, L., & Carlsmith, J. M. Cognitive consequences of forced compliance. *Journal of Abnormal & Social Psychology*, 1959, *28*, 203–210.

Filer, R. K. The influence of affective human capital on the wage equation. In R. Ehrenberg (Ed.), *Research in labor economics* (Vol. 3). Greenwich, CT: J.A.I. Press, 1981.

Filer, R., Maital, S., & Simon, J. *What do people bring to the stock market (besides money)?* Technion, Haifa, Israel: Faculty of Industrial Engineering & Management, 1982.

Fisher, I. N. *My father, Irving Fisher*. New York: Comet Press, 1956.

Freud, S. Formulations on the two principles of mental functioning. In S. Freud, *The complete psychological works of Sigmund Freud* (Vol. 13). London: Hogarth Press, 1946. (Originally published, 1911.)

Fried, M. Endemic stress; The psychology of resignation and the politics of scarcity. *American Journal of Orthopsychiatry*, 1982, *52*, 4–19.

Friedman, M., & Savage, L. The utility analysis of choices involving risk. *Journal of Political Economy*, 1948, *61*, 279–304.

Friedman, M., & Schwartz, N. *A monetary history of the United States, 1867–1960*. Princeton, NJ: Princeton University Press, 1963.

Galbraith, J. K. *The new industrial state*. Boston, MA: Houghton Mifflin, 1967.

Galbraith, J. K. *Economics and the public purpose*. Boston, MA: Houghton Mifflin, 1973.

Garber, J., & Seligman, M. E. P. *Human helplessness: Theory and applications*. New York: Academic Press, 1980.

Grether, D., & Plott, C. Preference reversal phenomenon. *American Economic Review*, 1979, *69*, 623–638.

Harrod, R. *Towards a dynamic economics*. London: Macmillan, 1948.

Hayes, R. H., & Abernathy, W. J. Managing our way to economic decline. *Harvard Business Review*, July-August 1980, 67–77.

Hayes, S. P. Some psychological problems of economics. *Psychological Bulletin*, 1950, *47*, 289–330.

Henderson, J. M., & Quandt, R. *Microeconomic theory: A mathematical approach*. New York: McGraw-Hill, 1958.

Hicks, J. R. *Value and capital*. Oxford: Oxford University Press, 1939.

Jevons, W. S. *Theory of political economy*. London: Macmillan, 1874.

Judson, A. S. The awkward truth about productivity. *Harvard Business Review*, September–October 1982, 93–97.

2

Kagel, J. H., Battalio, R. C., Rachlin, H., & Green, L. Demand curves for animal consumers. *Quarterly Journal of Economics*, 1981, *89*, 1–16.

Kagel, J. H., & Winkler, R. C. Behavioral economics: Areas of cooperative research between economics and applied behavioral systems. *Journal of Applied Behavioral Science*, 1972, *5*, 335–342.

Kahneman, D., & Tversky, A. Prospect theory: An analysis of decision under risk. *Econometrica*, 1979, *47*, 263–291.

Kahneman, D., Slovic, P., & Tversky, A. *Judgment under uncertainty: Heuristics and biases*. New York: Cambridge University Press, 1981.

Katona, G. *Psychological analysis of economic behavior*. New York: McGraw Hill, 1951.

Katona, G. Rational behavior and economic behavior. *Psychological Review*, 1953, *60*, 307–318.

Katona, G. *The powerful consumer*. New York: McGraw Hill, 1960.

Katona, G. *The mass consumption society*. New York: McGraw Hill, 1964.

Katona, G. Consumer behavior: Theory and findings on expectations and aspirations. *American Economic Review*, 1968, *58*, 19–30.

Katona, G. *Psychological economics*. New York: Elsevier, 1975.

Katz, D. Psychology and economic behavior. In B. Strumpel, J. N. Morgan, & E. Zahn (Eds.), *Human behavior in economic affairs*. Amsterdam: Elsevier, 1972.

Keynes, J. M. *The general theory of employment, interest and money*. London: Macmillan, 1936.

Kindelberger, C. P. *Manias, panics and crashes*. New York: Basic Books, 1978.

Knight, F. *The economic organization*. Chicago, IL: University of Chicago Press, 1933.(a)

Knight, F. *Risk, uncertainty and profit*. London: London School of Economics, 1933.(b)

Kogan, N., & Wallach, M. A. *Risk-taking: A study in cognition and personality*. New York: Holt Rinehart & Winston, 1964.

Kurz, M., Spiegelman, R. G., & West, R. W. The experimental horizon and the rate of time preference for the Seattle and Denver income maintenance experiments. Stanford, CA: Stanford Research Institute, 1973.

Laffont, J. J. *Essays in the economics of uncertainty*. Cambridge, MA: Harvard University Press, 1980.

Latané, B., Williams, K., & Harkins, S. Many hands make light the work: The causes and consequences of social loafing. *Journal of Personality and Social Psychology*, 1979, *37*, 822–832.

Lea, S. E. G. The psychology and economics of demand. *Psychological Bulletin*, 1978, *85*, 441–466.

Leibenstein, H. *Economic theory and organizational analysis*. New York: Harper & Row, 1960.

Leibenstein, H. *Beyond economic man*. Cambridge, MA: Harvard University Press, 1976.

Leibenstein, H. The missing link: Micro-micro theory? *Journal of Economic Literature*, 1979, *17*, 477–502.

Leontief, W. Letter. *Science*, 1982, *217*, 104.

Lipsey, R., & Steiner, P. *Economics*. New York: Harper & Row, 1972.

Maital, S. *The nature of man in conventional microeconomic theory*. Unpublished paper, Woodrow Wilson School of Public & International Affairs, Princeton University, 1978.

Maital, S. *Minds, markets and money: Psychological foundations of economic behavior*. New York: Basic Books, 1982.

Maital, S., & Benjamini, Y. Inflation as prisoner's dilemma. *Journal of Post Keynesian Economics*, 1980, *2*, 459–481.

Maital, S., & Maital, S. L. Time preference, delay of gratification and the intergenerational transmission of economic inequality: A behavioral theory of income distribution. In O.

Ashenfelter & W. Oates (Eds.), *Essays in labor market analysis, in memory of Yochanan Peter Comay*. New York: John Wiley, 1977.

Maital, S., & Maital, S. L. Individual-rational and group-rational inflation expectations. *Journal of Economic Behavior & Organization*, 1981, *2*, 179–186.

Maital, S., Maital, S. L., & Plaut, S. *Behavior toward uncertain inflation as learned help-lessness*. Technion, Haifa, Israel: Faculty of Industrial Engineering & Management, 1982.

Maital, S., & Meltz, N. M. *Lagging productivity growth: Causes and remedies*. Cambridge, MA: Ballinger, 1980.

Mandelbrot, B. Forecasts of future prices, unbiased markets, and martingale modes. *Journal of Business: Security Prices* (A Supplement), 1966, *39*, 242–255.

Marris, R. *The economic theory of managerial capitalism*. New York: Free Press, 1964.

Marshall, A. *Principles of economics*. London: Macmillan, 1962. (Originally published, 1890.)

Meyer, W. The research programme of economics and the relevance of psychology. *British Journal of Social Psychology*, 1982, *21*, 81–91.

Mischel, W. Preference for delayed reinforcement: An experimental study of a cultural observation. *Journal of Abnormal & Social Psychology*, 1958, *56*, 57–61.

Mischel, W. Delay of gratification, need for achievement, and acquiescence in another culture. *Journal of Abnormal & Social Psychology*, 1961, *63*, 543–552.

Mischel, W. Process in delay of gratification. In L. Berkowitz (Ed.), *Advances in experimental social psychology* (Vol. 7). New York: Academic Press, 1974.

Mischel, W., & Metzner, R. Preference for delayed reward as a function of age, intelligence and length of delay interval. *Journal of Abnormal & Social Psychology*, 1962, *64*, 425–431.

Modigliani, F., & Cohn, R. J. Inflation, rational valuation and the market. *Financial Analysts Journal*, March-April 1979, 24–44.

Monsen, R. J., Jr., & Downs, A. A theory of large managerial firms. *Journal of Political Economy*, 1965, *73*, 221–236.

Opp, K.D. The evolutionary emergence of norms. *British Journal of Social Psychology*, 1982, *21*, 139–149.

Plaut, S. *After silver and gold: Some sober thoughts on speculative bubbles*. Cleveland, OH: Federal Reserve Bank of Cleveland, 1980.

Pope, A. *An essay on man*. New York: Bobbs, 1965. (Originally published: 1733.)

Rachlin, H., & Burkhard, B. The temporal triangle: Response substitution in instrumental conditioning. *Psychological Review*, 1978, *85*, 22–47.

Rachlin, H., Kagel, J. H., & Battalio, R. C. Substitutability in time allocation. *Psychological Review*, 1980, *87*, 355–374.

Ramsay, F. A mathematical theory of saving. *Economic Journal*, 1928, *38*, 543–559.

Reder, M. *Studies in the theory of welfare economics*. New York: Columbia University Press, 1947.

Ricardo, D. *Principles of political economy taxation*. Harmondsworth, U.K.: Penguin, 1971. (Originally published, 1817.)

Robbins, L. *Essay on the nature and significance of economic science*. London: St. Martins, 1935.

Rotter, J. B., Chance, J. E., & Phares, E. R. *Applications of a social learning theory*. New York: Holt Rinehart & Winston, 1972.

Samuelson, P. Proof that properly anticipated prices fluctuate randomly. *Industrial Management Review*, 1965, *6*, 41–49.

Schoemaker, P. J. H. The expected utility model: Its variants, purposes, evidence and limitations. *Journal of Economic Literature*, 1982, *20*, 529–563.

Schotter, A. S. *The economic theory of social institutions*. Cambridge: Cambridge University Press, 1981.

Schultz, T. W. Investment in human capital. *American Economic Review*, 1961, *51*, 1–17.

Scitovsky, T. *The joyless economy*. New York: Oxford University Press, 1976.

Seligman, M. E. P. *Helplessness: On depression, development and death*. San Francisco: W. H. Freeman, 1975.

Sen, A. Rational fools: A critique of the behavioral foundations of economic theory. *Philosophy & Public Affairs*, 1977, *6*, 317–343.

Shapiro, H. T. The index of consumer sentiment and economic forecasting: A reappraisal. In B. Strumpel, J. N. Morgan, & E. Zahn (Eds.), *Human behavior in economic affairs*. Amsterdam: Elsevier, 1972.

Shefrin, H. M., & Statman, M. *Explaining investor preference for cash dividends*. Santa Clara, CA: School of Business, University of Santa Clara, 1982.

Simon, H. A. *Models of man*. New York: John Wiley, 1957.

Simon, H. A. Theories of decision-making in economics and behavioral science. *American Economic Review*, 1959, *49*, 253–283.

Simon, H. A., & Stedry, A. C. Psychology and economics. In G. Lindzey & E. Aaronson, (Eds.), *The handbook of social psychology* (Vol. 5). Reading, MA: Addison Wesley, 1969.

Slovic, P. Psychological study of human judgment: Implications for investment decision-making. *Journal of Finance*, 1972, *27*, 779–799.

Smith, A. *The theory of moral sentiments*. Oxford: Oxford University Press, 1976. (Originally published, 1759.)

Smith, A. *The wealth of nations*. New York: Random House, 1937. (Originally published, 1776.)

Smith, V. Experimental economics: Induced value theory. *American Economic Review*, 1976, *66*, 274–279.

Smith, V. The principle of unanimity and voluntary consent in social choice. *Journal of Political Economy*, 1977, *85*, 1125–1139.

Smith, V. *Microeconomic systems as an experimental science*. Tempe, AZ: Department of Economics, University of Arizona, 1982.

Spechler, M. Organization and economic behavior: An interpretation of recent findings. *Weltwirtschaftliches Archiv*, 1982, *118*, 366–380.

Stacey, B. G. Economic socialization in the pre-adult years. *British Journal of Social Psychology*, 1982, *21*, 159–173.

Stigler, G. J. The Xistence of X-efficiency. *American Economic Review*, 1976, *66*, 213–216.

Stigler, G. J., & Becker, G. S. De gustibus non est disputandum. *American Economic Review*, 1977, *67*, 76–90.

Stoner, J. A. F. *A comparison of individual and group decisions involving risk*. Unpublished Master's thesis. Cambridge, MA: M.I.T., School of Industrial Management, 1961.

Sutermeister, R. *People and productivity*. New York: McGraw Hill, 1963.

Temin, P. *Did monetary forces cause the Great Depression?* New York: Norton, 1976.

Thaler, R. Toward a positive theory of consumer choice. *Journal of Economic Behavior & Organization*, 1980, *1*, 39–60.

Thurstone, L. L. The indifference function. *Journal of Social Psychology*, 1931, *2*, 139–167.

Tobin, J. Money and finance in the macroeconomic process. *Journal of Money, Credit and Banking*, 1982, *14*, 171–204.

Tomer, J. Worker motivation: A neglected element in micro-micro theory. *Journal of Economic Issues*, 1981, *15*, 351–362.

Tversky, A. Intransitivity of preferences. *Psychological Review*, 1969, *76*, 31–48.

Van Raaij, W. F. *Consumer choice behavior: An information processing approach.* Unpublished Ph.D. dissertation. Netherlands: Tilburg University, 1977.

von Neumann, J., & Morgenstern, O. *Theory of games and economic behavior.* Princeton, NJ: Princeton University Press, 1944.

Walras, L. *Elements of pure economics.* London: Allen & Unwin, 1954. (Originally published, 1871.)

Williamson, O. *The economics of discretionary behavior.* Englewood Cliffs, NJ: Prentice-Hall, 1964.

Winkler, R., & Winett, R. A. Behavioral interventions in resource conservation. *American Psychologist,* 1982, *37,* 421–435.

Winston, G. C. Addiction & backsliding: A theory of compulsive consumption. *Journal of Economic Behavior & Organization,* 1980, *1,* 295–324.

4 Psychology and Education

Joanna P. Williams
Teachers College, Columbia University

INTRODUCTION

The relationship between psychology and education is complex. Psychology is one of the disciplines that most fundamentally and importantly influences education, but it is not the only one. Education is a social institution and as such is shaped and influenced by many forces, only some of which are scholarly disciplines; prominent among these is psychology. The relationship between psychology and education also goes the other way; that is, education influences psychology, sometimes in terms of influencing the development of theory, often in terms of specifying problems to be studied. This reciprocal relationship between psychology and education is the topic of this essay.

I show that psychology has had, and continues to have, a large and important influence on educational theory and on educational practice; that the degree of this influence has varied considerably over the years; and that the scope of this influence has always depended on a variety of factors, including social ones. In turn, education has put its own substantial demands on psychology. If these demands have not actually shaped psychological theory, they have certainly helped to select specific issues for study and to promote particular interpretations of findings by directing psychologists' attention to particular societal needs and goals.

The first part of this essay provides an overview of the relationship of psychology and education in the U.S. from the turn of the century to the present. This section will provide historical perspective. It also sets the stage for the second part of the essay, in which educational-psychological theories currently in vogue are examined. The issues that were raised

early in this century are, in large measure, the same issues that are important today. Moreover, many of the issues raised years ago were resolved
then, at least temporarily; thus, I tell a complete "story," which may help
us evaluate and interpret current theory and practice in psychology and
education.

AN HISTORICAL PERSPECTIVE

This section of the essay is divided into three parts. The first part describes the period 1900–1930, during which the fields of psychology and
education were closely entwined. E. L. Thorndike and John Dewey were
major figures in both fields, and their influence was felt in both for many
years. The second part covers the years 1930–1955. In these years, psychology and education were quite separate in their interests and their
development. Psychologists turned their attention to fundamental processes, especially learning, and their research was too basic and too detailed for useful application by educators. The third part covers the years
1955–1970. The middle 1950s marked an important turning point: In the
face of a new social climate, the schools began to be perceived as inadequate, and attempts to "reform" education led to a renewal of psychology's interest in educational problems. This third part deals with the
varied contributions of psychology to education during this period, many
of which remain important influences today.

1900–1930

Psychology was a very young discipline at the turn of the century. As a
laboratory science, it had barely reached its majority, dating from the
establishment of the first laboratory in 1879 by Wilhelm Wundt in Leipzig.
At that time many of the noted contemporary psychologists in the United
States, such as Titchener and Cattell, were working on psychophysics,
sensory psychology, and other related topics—not ones likely to influence
education. Other psychologists, however, like William James, expressed
serious interest in problems related to education. In his *Talks to Teachers*
(1900), for example, James used general psychological principles as a
basis for recommendations for educational practice.

It was G. Stanley Hall's (1893, 1911) influence on education that was
greatest during this period, however. Hall was a developmental psychologist and an evolutionist. He endorsed the general biogenetic law: ontogeny, the development of the individual, recapitulates phylogeny, the
evolution of the species (originally attributable to the biologist Haeckel).
The notion that the life and behavior of an individual develop through the

same stages that the species went through during the course of civilization led Hall to recommend that education should follow the same developmental pattern. His proposals focused on child-centered schools whose concern would be the nature and needs of the pupil and whose curriculum would not be narrowly academic but, rather, broad and varied.

One major aspect of Hall's theories was not easily accepted. Given the great press in this country to ameliorate social problems, especially in the cities, that had been caused by industrialization and massive immigration, one response was to use the school as a vehicle for change. The progressive education movement grew out of the larger Progressive political movement and was devoted to making the schools more democratic and useful to all. Hall's evolutionary point of view, with its emphasis on the importance of heredity, was difficult to reconcile fully with a conception of man as an organism that could be changed and bettered in this world, specifically through education.

This concern about the degree to which man's nature and abilities are determined through heredity as opposed to through the operation of environmental forces was an important one at this time, as it was before and has been since. It is, in fact, one of the persistent issues in educational psychology. The kind of attention given this question during the first two or three decades of the century illustrates the fact that there was not the sharp demarcation between psychology and education that appeared later. Indeed, there were strong ties between the two—psychology was interested in broad, molar questions that had direct relevance to the layman, and it also viewed applications to educational problems as centrally important to development of theory.

Two other major figures in psychology, E. L. Thorndike and John Dewey, took less extreme positions on this important issue, and they became intellectual leaders in psychology proper and in psychology applied to education. Thorndike represented the "hard scientist." He argued that true scientific method could be applied to education. Empirical studies, including experimental ones, would provide appropriate data for theory-building, and thus, Thorndike reasoned, questions concerning educational theory and practice could be answered on the basis of an objective, inductive science.

The list of Thorndike's specific contributions to psychology and education is long and impressive. His experiments with animals in a puzzle box were taken as a paradigm for the study of learning and provided an empirical base for Thorndike's enormously important *law of effect,* that is, that the bond or connection between a stimulus and a response is "stamped in" through the mechanism of reward. As expressed by Thorndike in his *Educational Psychology* (1913, Volume 2, p. 20), the basic principles of learning led to two fundamental rules for education: "(1) Put together what should go together and keep apart what should not go together. (2) Reward desirable *connections* and make undesirable *connections* produce discomfort."

In his work on the psychology of arithmetic, as well as other school subjects, Thorndike himself led the way in demonstrating how these basic principles could be applied. His analysis of the nature of arithmetic abilities and his application of learning theory to the teaching of this basic skill (Thorndike, 1922) led to enormous changes in the arithmetic curriculum between 1910 and 1930 (Gorman, 1931/1969). Indeed, according to Cronbach and Suppes (1969, p. 100) while by today's standards Thorndike's scientific analysis was rather imprecise, criticism should not be directed toward that imprecision but rather to the "lack of substantial inquiry at the same theoretical and experimental level in succeeding decades."

Thorndike's research on vocabulary provides an excellent example of his approach and of his far-reaching influence: The work began (Clifford, 1978) in order to establish the relationship among the vocabularies of listening, speech, reading, and writing. Thorndike's recommendation that schools address themselves to teaching high-frequency words (words common in adult usage) changed textbooks drastically. Texts now used a strictly limited vocabulary. Readability formulas were used to evaluate schoolbooks, and tests were constructed that used appropriate vocabulary. Such changes influenced texts, and therefore teaching, for several decades (Clifford, 1978).

Another major contribution was Thorndike's research on transfer of training, which argued that there was no significant gain in general thinking and problem solving ability from study of Latin and other such subject matter. Rather, Thorndike argued, specific training on the actual knowledge base that was of relevance to one's own life was desirable. Again, Thorndike's research had great impact: the earlier notion ("formal discipline") that gains in general thinking and problem-solving ability would come about through the study of Latin and Greek was repudiated, and the school curriculum was expanded.

Such modifications in school practice were fully in line with the nation's prevailing motivation to make the schools more democratic and socially useful. However, while Thorndike's psychology, focused as it was on learning, implied the ability to change and thus was much more palatable than Hall's ideas, Thorndike still emphasized the idea that much of man's nature was not modifiable by experience. Moreover, the basic idea of *connection* was rather mechanistic and seemed to be less applicable to acquiring higher-order reasoning than to acquiring simple skills. These factors, together with his rather conservative social views, kept Thorndike from becoming the most influential theorist of his time. That position belongs to John Dewey, whose influence on education was pervasive for almost half a century (Dewey, 1915, 1916).

Perhaps from today's perspective Dewey was less a psychologist and more a philosopher; certainly it is not easy to abstract his principles and generalizations from his empirical work, let alone evaluate them critically (Cremin, 1961). Indeed, Dewey had little influence on the development of psychology as a science; but he had enormous influence on education. In contrast to Thorndike, he had a more dynamic, holistic point of view. The prevailing conception of learning in terms of the bonding of stimulus and response was described by Dewey as "organic"; that is, the nature of the stimulus depended on the entire experience of the organism. Thus, the stimulus was "mediated" or interpreted in a very broad context. Dewey also emphasized motivation to a great extent: Individuals had basic aims or purposes and acted intelligently in terms of their intentions. Actions constituted the experiences and lead to consequences from which a further understanding of the world was gained. Effective education, therefore, must provide a child with problems that capture his intrinsic interest and that relate meaningfully to his overall intelligence and purpose.

The most important aspect of Dewey's thinking, however, and the one that made him the outstanding spokesman of his day was his focus on the role of education and the school within the current social movement of Progressivism. Dewey saw the school as the one social institution that could take on the educative role that, prior to the time of industrialism, had been carried out by the traditional agrarian family and community. The curriculum became liberalized; hygiene, manual arts, and other subjects were introduced, and, in traditional areas, the old emphasis on classical and literary studies was eliminated in favor of material deemed necessary to successful functioning in everyday life. Dewey's educational goals were fully in line with the aims of the larger society, and his *Democracy and Education* (1916) represents "the clearest, most comprehensive statement of the progressive education movement [Cremin, 1961, p. 120]."

MacDonald (1964) points to the inevitable simplistic comparison that was made between Thorndike and Dewey: Dewey's system was seen as picturing an "active" learning organism, and Thorndike's a "passive" learning organism. Few educators and no social planners, then or now, can accept the latter conception of man.

1930–1955

After 1930, the close relationship between psychology and education began to disintegrate. Academic psychology became more "scientific" and less applied; theorists took as their model the physical sciences (see Marks, in Volume III) and attempted to use the same philosophical bases in the development of comprehensive theories of learning. The formal nature of their theories and their attention to very basic learning processes led to empirical work far removed from most things of interest to educators. Since the nature of learning was assumed to be comparable for all animals, including man, psychologists could use lower organisms such as the rat and the pigeon in their experiments. This position virtually guaranteed that many of the phenomena they studied would be difficult to relate to problems of education. And even when they could be so related, many educators found unpalatable the basic assumption that rats and human beings were fundamentally alike.

Clark Hull, Edwin Guthrie, and B. F. Skinner represent the "big three" of the behavioristic movement. Hull's logico-deductive theory was perhaps the most representative of the ideal of stimulus-response theory in its formalism, its incorporation of widely accepted principles (e.g., the source of reinforcement was drive reduction), and its influence on the field as a whole (Hull, 1943). Guthrie's theory differed from Hull's on certain fundamental issues, such as whether reinforcement is necessary for learning to occur, and it was much less formal (Guthrie, 1952). However, Guthrie turned out to be the more influential forerunner of later developments in learning theory (e.g., of Estes's, 1960, statistical learning theory). Theorists within these traditions made some applications to education, but they were few. For example, Miller (1957) discussed the effective use of audiovisual techniques in terms of his neo-Hullian theory, and Sheffield (1961) analyzed instruction via films in light of his own Guthrian position, nicely anticipating, as a matter of fact, the later influential work of Gagné (1965) on the sequential organization of task units as a basis for teaching.

B. F. Skinner's early work (e.g., *The Behavior of Organisms*, 1938) placed him in the forefront of behavior theory. His approach is the only one of the behavior theories to have led to substantial and significant applications to education, though those came, as is characteristic, long after the basic research had been done.

Skinner rejected formal theory-building and concentrated on the discovery of simple laws relating environmental events to behavior. He emphatically denied the value of speculating about internal processes and focused instead on the analysis of observable events. He also rejected the need for reductionist explanations. Thus he described reinforcement solely in terms of its effect on behavior. There was no need, Skinner contended, to explain those effects in terms of drive-reduction or other such mechanisms.

One of Skinner's most important theoretical contributions was to distinguish between behavior that was "elicited" by a specific stimulus, as for example the Pavlovian conditional reflex, and behavior that was "emitted" in the absence of any specifically identifiable stimulus and whose probability of occurrence was increased by reinforcement. The rat pressing a bar or the pigeon pecking a key in a Skinner box is the prototypical experimental situation for studying emitted or operant behavior. Skinner was one of the first to make this distinction and the first to make it so clearly (Hill, 1964). Another of Skinner's major contributions involved the analysis of ways in which the schedule on which reinforcement occurs affect the pattern of responses. Intermittent reinforcement produces behavior highly resistant to extinction, that is, it will continue for a long time after reinforcement has been removed from the situation. Certain intermittent reinforcement schedules (such as a variable ratio schedule, in which a reinforcement follows every Nth-on-the-average response) produce very high response rates. The variable-ratio pattern has been likened to "highly motivated" behavior, and analogies to real-world situations have been drawn (e.g., paying on the basis of piecework in a factory). Finally, these principles were applied to complex behavior. To develop a complex behavior, one "shapes" it by reinforcing "successive approximations," that is, responses that are progressively more and more similar to the desired target behavior. According to Skinner, all organisms including human beings develop all of their highly complex behavior patterns through the same basic learning mechanisms.

The general approach taken by Skinner as well as by the other learning theorists was seen as basically mechanistic, and certainly too atomistic for use by education. Another theorist of this era, Edward Tolman (1932), proposed a behavior system that was much more cognitive and purposive in its approach than the others previously mentioned. Probably because of these very characteristics Tolman's theory did not attain the eminence of the other behavior theories. This theory, if it had had wider currency within psychology per se, might have come to the attention of someone who *might* have felt that it would be useful as a theoretical foundation for education. The fact that most of the data supporting it were generated by the white rat, however, probably helped to ensure that this would not happen.

During this period, other types of theories were adopted as the basis for educational planning and decision-making. For example, although the empirical work that Gestalt theory generated focused rather narrowly on problems of perception, that approach emphasized understanding and insight (e.g., Koffka, 1924; Kohler, 1929). Also, field theories, including Lewin's (1942) work on group dynamics, emphasized motivation and a

more global, purposive framework for psychology than did the mainstream learning theories. These approaches, consonant with the ideas of
Dewey, promised a basis for social amelioration, and so were highly
compatible with the view of education as a social institution.

One other major theory, psychoanalysis, also influenced education during this period (e.g., Freud, 1926/1959, 1930/1961). Although Freud had
done most of his major work early in the century, it took many years for
his influence to have an impact. Indeed, Freud's impact on education was
even slower to develop than that of other theories, probably because of
the revolutionary nature of his work. By the 1930s, however, ideas about
child development had been drastically permeated with Freudian concepts (mostly and directly through the popular press and general culture,
not via professional education). At first, the emphasis was on the
psychoanalytic method and the importance of the early years for later
development. Only in the mid-forties and later was much emphasis given
to other aspects of Freud's theory, such as infant sexuality (Suppes &
Warren, 1978).

Suppes and Warren have summarized Anna Freud's lectures to Vienna
teachers (A. Freud, 1935), which provide a general outline of those aspects of psychoanalytic theory most relevant for education. Schooling,
she says, is merely a continuation of general education, which starts at
birth. In all education, the instincts of the child must be taken into consideration, because learning to be a socialized human being means learning to repress certain instinctual drives (id) so that other aspects of the
personality (ego and superego) can develop and mature. Conflict in the
course of development (including formal education) is inevitable.

An important aspect of this theory for education is the notion of
psychosexual stages. At about 5 years of age, a child enters the latency
period, which is characterized by a repression of libidinal instincts; during
this period the child is unusually receptive to learning. (This theory thus
provides a strong rationale for starting schooling at 5 or 6, a traditional
time in Western societies.) With adolescence instinctual drives and increased conflict reappear. No specific recommendations for instruction
can be derived from psychoanalytic theory, but the emphasis on issues of
personality development and general adjustment, as well as on the potentially complex relationship between teacher and student, informs educators generally.

Again in the thirties, an important professional group arose that propa-
gated ideas similar to those of psychoanalysis and helped to ensure that
these ideas would be incorporated into our educational thinking. The
mental health movement, which earlier had focused primarily on improving the conditions of people who had been institutionalized because of
mental illness, began in the 1930s to be concerned with mental hygiene

and the importance of education in promoting mental health. The goal of promoting the development of more wholesome human relationships demanded a good understanding of human growth and development and of interpersonal relationships (Ryan, 1938). A book by E. K. Wickman, *Children's Behavior and Teachers' Attitudes,* published in 1928, showed that teachers had very little awareness of what mental health workers considered to be maladjusted behavior. Teachers were concerned about aggressiveness, sexual immorality, and dishonesty, whereas psychiatrists and other mental health workers considered that withdrawal, regressive behavior, and inability to get along with others were much more serious indicators of maladjustment. Wickman's book had an enormous impact and helped launch the mental hygiene movement. That the mental hygiene movement indeed itself had an effect is demonstrated in the results of later studies (Hunter, 1957; Mitchell, 1942) that found that teachers' attitudes had changed drastically over the years, becoming considerably closer to those of mental health workers.

In summary, although learning theory was the main preoccupation of academic psychology during the years 1930–1955, it did not provide any significant impetus at that time to educational theory or practice. Other theories and ideas did that. Or perhaps those other theories and ideas merely provided ad hoc justification for the changes in education that were going on anyway, thanks to the continuing strength of the Progressive Education movement. In any event, the role of the school in society continued to expand at this time. It became the societal institution that was responsible for social and emotional adjustment as well as for development of academic skills. The emphasis was on "the whole child," one whose total well-being must be considered. The curriculum was enlarged to include principles of growth and development as well as vocational training and such topics as music, art, and physical education. With less attention placed on traditional academic goals, there was less interest in specific methods and procedures for teaching subject matter. By 1955, psychology was fairly well divorced from education.

1955–1970

In the mid-fifties the educational establishment in America received a great amount of criticism. Progressive education, it was agreed, had failed; educational standards had been lowered, discipline in the schools was lacking, and children were not learning enough. Part of the impetus for the criticism came from the Sputnik launch in 1957 and anxiety lest the Soviet Union overtake the U.S. in space. Suddenly America was concerned about the dearth of scientists and technologists, and so the schools came under attack. Essentially, many of the changes that took place during the following decade-long reform period were not strictly tied to psychological theory, although in retrospect they can be justified in such terms. In truth, academic psychologists for the most part remained aloof from the schools and did not have much immediate influence (Woodring, 1964).

These modifications included an increased emphasis on organizational change in the schools. For example, team teaching was institutionalized on the grounds that individual differences among teachers preclude the possibility that any one teacher can perform all the diverse functions of teaching well. Thus, staffing ought to allow each teacher to do only what he or she did well. Other aspects of school reorganization were stressed, including the introduction of non-graded classes and of flexible arrangements of space and scheduling. New programs of teacher education were introduced that emphasized more rigorous preparation in the subject matter to be taught.

The one important area where there was substantial impact by psychological theory was curriculum. The content of the existing textbooks had begun to be criticized sharply, and a new movement to reform outmoded materials arose.

It is significant that these national curriculum-development projects (e.g., the School Mathematics Study Group, the University of Illinois Committee on School Mathematics, and the Physical Science Study Committee) involved both educators and psychologists, who were knowledgeable about the nature of learning and teaching, and subject-matter specialists, such as professional mathematicians and biologists, whose knowledge of content was deep enough so that, it was expected, they could abstract its underlying structure and formulate it effectively for children.

Bruner.   The influence of psychology in these ventures was strong. A landmark conference held in 1959 at Woods Hole, Massachusetts, led to J. S. Bruner's *The Process of Education* (1960), probably the earliest example of the use of cognitive psychology as a basis for the development of instruction. The Swiss psychologist Jean Piaget, whose writings had been largely ignored for many years in the United States, participated in the conference. (Piagetian theory has since then become highly influential in education; see pp. 106–111.)

The main theme of Bruner's approach is that it is the structure of a subject matter that must be emphasized in teaching. That is, what must be learned is the way in which things are related meaningfully; this is the basis for true understanding. If underlying structure is understood, new problems can be solved. This point of view marks a turning-point in the way the nature of transfer is perceived. Thorndike's dictum that transfer was highly specific had led to an emphasis on the direct training of specific skills—those skills and problems that, in themselves, were important beyond the school walls. Now Bruner pointed out that more general transfer could indeed be achieved through appropriate instruction: If a child initially learned a general idea (instead of a skill), that general idea could serve as the basis for recognizing later problems as further instances of the same idea. Thus, transfer of principles and also of attitudes could be taught. The implication was that the curriculum must stress the teaching of underlying principles and the structure of content. Though not made explicit, this was in some sense a reversion to a pre-Thorndike position on transfer, for it assumed that with an appropriate cognitive base there could be transfer to novel problems and situations.

Several other themes were also of importance. For example, Bruner recommended that teaching not be postponed too long—"the foundations of any subject may be taught to anybody at any age in some form [Bruner, 1960, p. 12];" the trick is to design early instruction appropriately and then to revisit the same basic ideas repeatedly throughout the school years (the "spiral curriculum"). Obviously, this represented a turning away from the then-still-prevalent idea that one should wait until the child is "ready" to learn. Also, Bruner emphasized the need for the school to preserve and to stimulate a child's intrinsic interest in learning.

According to Bruner, there are qualitative differences in cognitive abilities at different stages of development. The nature of these abilities provides the basis for the form of the instruction, which must be geared to particular developmental stages. One must present the content that is to be learned so that it is structured appropriately for a particular stage. The appropriate structure will be determined by the characteristic way in which knowledge is, at any given stage, represented in the mind. Very young children may represent a problem by a set of actions appropriate for achieving a certain result (enactive representation); at a later stage, by a set of summary images that stand for a concept without defining it fully (ikonic representation); and later still, by a set of symbolic or logical propositions drawn from a symbolic system that is governed by rules or laws for forming and transforming propositions (symbolic representation). Mathematics instruction, for example, might be sequenced so that the child begins with instrumental activity, through which he develops a "kind of definition of things by doing them [Bruner, 1964, p. 33]." These operations later become represented in the form of specific images. Finally, by means of a symbolic notation that remains invariant across variations in imagery, the child can grasp the abstract properties of mathematics. This stage progression suggests the form and sequence of examples and principles to be provided in instruction. In other words, curriculum development must capitalize on the young child's ability to grasp ideas intuitively and concretely, and indeed it should attempt to develop such intuitive thinking. Since the ability to comprehend formal descriptions and explanations appears only later in life, early instruction will be ineffective if it is formulated abstractly.

The overall message that was culled from this provocative new approach was that the goal of the schools should be to train intellectual inquiry starting right from the first grade. This was justified on the grounds that the intellectual activity of, say, a physicist is exactly the same as that of a young pupil who is learning physics.

These developments in curriculum reflected a new interest among psychologists in general in problems of cognition. Psychology had for many years concentrated on the basic questions put forth and shaped by behaviorism, and there had been very little significant research in areas such as thinking and language. The press for attention to the higher mental processes became strong. There was a serious attempt during the 1950s and early 1960s to extend classic learning theories to such issues. Within Hull's theory, for example, changes were made in order to incorporate cognitive phenomena (Hull, 1951). Hull as well as other theorists (e.g., Kendler & Kendler, 1962; Mowrer, 1960) developed the concept of "mediating responses" for this purpose, but S-R language proved much too cumbersome, and S-R behavior theories were abandoned by most psychologists whose main focus was on cognitive processes.

Mathematical models. Academic psychology did not abandon its efforts to develop formal theories, however. One of the important developments in the 1960s was the work on mathematical (stochastic) models of learning (e.g., Bush & Mosteller, 1955; Estes, 1960). Not only was there investigation of the problems (mainly from animal learning) that formed the main empirical bases of behaviorist theory, but, in addition, verbal learning also provided content for study. While there had been a great deal of activity in the field of rote verbal learning in the heyday of behaviorism, it was done within the functionalist tradition, and there was little elaborated theory in the area (except for a few forays such as Gibson's, 1940). Within statistical learning theory, work on verbal learning problems—paired-associate learning, list recall, concept identification— soon overtook analyses based on animal experimentation.

It is the general point of view, the fundamental assumptions, and only the simplest form of an empirical paradigm that provide the basis for adoption of a theory by education. What could mathematical modelers, with their emphasis on precise description and prediction of highly circumscribed behaviors, offer education? Not very much, it turned out.

An initial strong assertion of mathematical modeling (e.g., Estes, 1960) was that the learning of a simple association is an all-or-none matter; that is, an association is at any given time either not learned or it is learned. The traditional assumption that learning occurs gradually over trials was justified only because traditional analysis involved an artifact; namely, the traditional negatively-accelerated learning curve represented a conglomeration of many subjects and many discrete associations (e.g., word pairs) and therefore obscured the basic evidence. As is usually the case with such fundamental distinctions, a clear answer was not forthcoming: The hypothesis that learning was incremental and not all-or-none was supported in other studies (Postman, 1963; Williams, 1962).

In a less dramatic form, however, attempts to describe behavior in formal mathematical models were productive. Although additional processes had to be postulated for even simple learning tasks (because models more complicated than a two-state Markov model were needed to fit the data) and although different models were necessary for different tasks, this work in general led to an important modification in the way psychologists thought about learning. Instead of being characterized as a change in probability of response, learning came to be characterized as a discrete change between states of knowledge (Greeno, 1980). This new formulation helped set the stage for the new cognitive psychology, which, as will be seen below, does have genuine potential for educational applications.

The effort to describe behavior in terms of mathematical models died out after only a few years and obviously had little relevance to the problems of education. Psychology was attempting to elaborate and refine a model. In so doing, it became oriented toward matter far afield from any of those that education might deem useful.

Skinner and his legacy.   Meanwhile, the work of Skinner became known far beyond the confines of academic psychology. Skinner began to extend his analysis of behavior to a wide variety of social phenomena, from psychotherapy to religion. In 1953, he published *Science and Human Behavior,* which included a consideration of the field of education.

The notion of applying Skinner's principles, which were originally formulated on the basis of laboratory demonstrations using animals, to real-life problems of human beings turned out to be appealing, partly because of the simplicity and straightforwardness of the formulations. Many applied research programs were begun.

Because of Skinner's influence, the tradition of behaviorism is alive and strong today even though the current focus of theoretical work in psychology has moved away from this point of view. A new field, applied behavioral analysis, has developed. The ease with which Skinnerian techniques could be acquired, his preference for using positive rewards instead of punishment in training and for working with single subjects rather than groups, and, most important, the apparent success of the method encouraged more and more applications. The use of operant principles is now widespread in hospital and other clinical settings, for example, in the management of psychotic patients and autistic children as well as in therapeutic work on a variety of neurotic syndromes such as phobias.

Skinner's approach is extraordinarily widespread in educational settings. One area where such "behavioral management" has proved highly valuable is in dealing with inappropriate social behaviors. For example, a child who talks out of turn and otherwise disrupts classroom activity can be taught, by the application of simple reinforcement techniques, to raise his hand to get his teacher's attention before he speaks. Most teacher-training programs today acknowledge the value of the Skinnerian approach in this kind of situation, though its value in terms of intellectual activity is extremely controversial (Williams, 1979a).

Skinner's most dramatic contribution to the field of education was in programmed instruction. Visiting his daughter's arithmetic class, Skinner was struck by the teacher's violation of basic principles of learning, and in a 1954 paper "The Science of Learning and the Art of Teaching," he outlined the design of a "teaching machine."

The term "teaching machine" had been used by Sydney Pressey a generation earlier (1933), but Pressey's version, though it incorporated many of the same features as those of Skinner, did not become widely popular. The Zeitgeist was right when Skinner made the proposal, however, due in large measure to the previous acceptance of other applications of behavior theory.

In Skinner's teaching machine, the student, presented with only a small amount of text—one or two sentences—constructs a response, and immediately after his response he is given information as to whether or not he was correct. The contingencies of reinforcement must be immediate, according to the theory. The instructional material is designed in a carefully organized sequence of small steps, so that the student is "shaped" gradually through successive responses and their reinforcement to the final criterion behavior (or knowledge, in other terminology). The student must actively participate in the procedure, which should help to promote learning.

The development of an effective teaching program was the product not only of careful initial design but also of revisions based on the actual performance of students. If students made many errors, the program was modified. Theoretically, a program that had gone through this development and revision cycle could be relied on to teach effectively. Skinner argued that all students should learn equally well from a successful program, so that evaluation of school performance might be done on the basis of how many instructional programs a student had gone through, not in terms of how well he had mastered a particular portion of the curriculum.

Programmed instruction perhaps appealed to the educator too much, for schoolteachers, publishers, and others quickly began to produce programs, in a variety of formats ranging from cardboard boxes (to simulate a machine) to textbooks organized in accordance with the principles of programmed instruction, without the requisite care in applying the basic principles that Skinner had elaborated. Within a few years, as is to be expected in such situations, the early promise of the teaching machine had not materialized, and enthusiasm waned.[1]

There was one extremely important general outcome of the programmed instruction movement: a huge increase in the emphasis given to individualized instruction, which has remained almost unabated until very recently. While the many vehicles for ensuring individualization differ widely, the virtues accorded individualization in general derive directly from the Skinnerian principles of programmed instruction and, indeed, from the Skinnerian research paradigm as well.

There have been many other applications of Skinner's principles. For example, in accord with the basic tenet that in order to shape behavior (i.e., teach) or evaluate student performance or teaching effectiveness one must be able to state and recognize what it is that one is attempting to teach, there has been a movement toward writing educational objectives in behavioral terms, that is, to ensure clarity of purpose as well as ability to determine whether or not the objectives have been met. In a related movement, curricula have been designed around the concept of mastery-learning (Bloom, 1976; Carroll, 1963). In this "competency-based" instruction and assessment, there is a focus on how much an individual student has mastered and not on the evaluation of a student in relation to other students. These movements may have other reasons for their continued popularity, of course. For example, the need for integrating those segments of minorities that have poor preparation for school into mainstream education is another motivation for repudiating testing that emphasizes relative (normative) performance. However, mastery learning and testing and other related concepts became of interest originally because of behavior theory.

Glaser (1978) has discussed some of the most important counter-influences to the Skinnerian approach. Social learning theory extended traditional behavior theory to include the roles played by vicarious, symbolic and self-regulatory processes (Bandura, 1971). That is, one can learn not only through direct experience (as in the Skinner paradigm) but also

---

[1]One specific aspect of the programmed instruction movement still exists, however: computer-assisted instruction. In the beginning, such instruction followed closely the Skinnerian model. Later, programs that capitalized on the unique opportunities offered by computer-presentation were designed (e.g., "Plato" at the University of Illinois). Most recently, as will be seen later in this essay, cognitive psychologists have designed instruction for the computer in accordance with a set of principles quite different from those of Skinner.

through observation of others' behavior. Moreover, one's memory of what was observed can be used to regulate later behavior. As Glaser (1978, p. 252) points out, the fact that people can regulate their own behavior by "arranging environmental conditions and administering self-reinforcing consequences" suggests that the school should try to teach people to do this more effectively.

The great degree of acceptance of Skinnerian ideas notwithstanding, there has always been a substantial portion of the population—both professional and lay—who repudiate Skinner's stance. Interestingly, their concern comes not from a belief that operant methods are not effective but rather is often associated with a suspicion that they may indeed be too effective. There is an anxiety that we will be subject to someone else's manipulation and control, with all the attendant social and political ramifications of that state of affairs. There is another related but less extreme reaction as well; that is, that Skinner proposes an essentially mechanistic learning model and therefore a mechanistic teaching model which is faulty because it cannot encompass the rich emotional and aesthetic dimensions of man.

Summary and recent developments. In summary, the mid-fifties represent a very important turning-point: a halt to the tendency for the school to take over a greater and greater share of the socialization of the child. The ever-expanding responsibilities of schools were curtailed. For about ten years (1955–1965), emphasis was placed on academic content and the usual concomitant of this sort of emphasis, a concern for "standards," that is, a concern that there be adequate achievement of the academic goals.

By 1965 there was a small-scale shift back toward broader goals for education. This shift coincided with America's concern about the Vietnam War and, along with it, criticism of other aspects of American life such as big business and industrialism. Reformers seeking a more humane society emphasized individualism and the integrity of the self. There was strong criticism of public schools as oppressive institutions—not egalitarian and not sensitive to the rights of women, minorities, and the poor. Dramatic changes occurred, from seemingly rather trivial ones such as abolishing dress codes, all the way often to eliminating required courses of study, tests, and grades.

This revolution was clearly not motivated by psychological theory and research (or any other kind of academic scholarship), but of course it could and did find such support, as for example in humanistic psychology. Maslow is the most prominent theorist associated with humanistic psychology (Maslow, 1968a, 1968b). Maslow's needs-hierarchy theory of motivation identified uniquely human needs, such as to be competent, to be with others, and to be self-accepting, as well as the more typically postulated lower-order needs for physiological satisfactions and physical security. This theory also stressed the emotions and the interconnectedness of cognition and the emotions (called "the affective domain").

Maslow saw the goal of education as helping people toward self-actualization, which includes self-discovery, self-acceptance, and self-making. Education, he felt, should help one toward personal growth and life-enrichment. This point of view leads naturally to a broad curriculum, including attention to social knowledge and to interpersonal relations and to methods for self-development. Within humanistic education, learning through experience and teaching relevant material (i.e., related to what students themselves felt as their needs and interests) were stressed (Roberts, 1975).

This educational movement, however, relied even less than most others did on theory and research. Most people cited in support of humanistic education were critics of the educational establishment, such as John Holt (especially in *How Children Fail,* 1964), and educational "romantics" (Broudy's, 1979, term), such as Ivan Illich (1972). As expected, there was a substantial amount of criticism of the Skinnerian position among these humanists. The two schools of thought are well represented in the long-term debate between Skinner and Carl Rogers (see Rogers, 1969, and Roberts, 1975).

Often the most tangible manifestation of a change in psychological posture is a change in physical structure and organization. One important outcome of humanism was the "open classroom," modeled on the British Infant Schools. Physically, an open classroom in an elementary school meant a large, open space that contained a variety of settings suitable for a variety of simultaneous activities, in contrast to the traditional closed-off, one-activity-at-a-time classroom. Conceptually, it meant a situation in which children were given a greater opportunity to set their own educational goals and to work at them at their own pace.

The humanistic revolution was relatively short-lived, however. The Vietnam War ended, and American society returned to a more even keel. By the early 1970s, emphasis again focused on academic learning, now defined as "Basic Skills."

MODERN RELATIONSHIPS BETWEEN PSYCHOLOGY AND EDUCATION

At any given time in history, more than one psychological theory has influenced education. Moreover, since the ultimate impact of psychological theories on education is often long delayed, educational practice at a given time is likely to have derived not from the psychological theories popular at that time but from those that were of major intellectual interest at some earlier time. Thus today a great deal of the theory-based educational practice is still rooted in a Skinnerian model, and, to a lesser extent, some practices are theoretically based on humanism. These theories are no longer of great interest as theories, however, either within psychology proper or within educational psychology.

Today two very different theories vie for primacy in terms of potential future impact on educational practice. One, Piagetian theory, is not at all new: Piaget first published in the 1920s, and to some extent the curriculum reforms of the 1950s are based on Piaget's ideas. But the theory has been modified over the years, and now, in addition, there are "neo-Piagetian" formulations that serve as the basis for educational applications. The second theoretical position of importance today, information-processing, is newer. As the predominant paradigm within contemporary cognitive psychology, it has become the dominant theory of academic psychology. It has only recently begun to be tapped for its educational potential.

This section of the essay describes these theories and the educational applications that have been based on them and presents a critique of both theory and application. How long-lasting and pervasive the influence of these theories will be is, of course, unpredictable; that depends strongly on the social and cultural trends of the future—which in turn depend on unforeseen events of the future. An example is given later in the chapter of the way in which a new social phenomenon is justified after the fact by research evidence and by theory. As I pointed out earlier, such a pattern is not at all atypical.

Piaget

It took a considerable amount of time for Piagetian theory to attain its present, highly influential position. Piaget began his work in Geneva in the 1920s, but it was not until the late 1950s that that work had a major international impact. The theory is very complex, was modified greatly in the course of Piaget's long life, and has been elaborated and modified in recent years by others. Probably the most reasonable way to present the ideas of Piaget as they have influenced educational psychology is to do so chronologically.

One of Piaget's core ideas, which has been refined over the years but has not fundamentally changed, is that children think differently from adults (Piaget, 1926, 1928). An individual progresses through a series of developmental stages, each of which manifests a distinctly different way of understanding the world. The first is the sensorimotor stage, which lasts from birth to about 2 years of age; then comes the preoperational stage, from 2 to 8; the stage of concrete operations, from 8 to about 14; and, finally, the stage of formal operations, which represents the thinking of the adolescent and the adult. Piaget described these stages in terms of the logical processes that are characteristic of each stage.

Piaget's method consisted of observing the child performing simple tasks and interviewing him in depth to determine why the child performed the way he did in the task situation. This technique was often dubbed Piaget's "clinical" method, because there was no explicit way in which probe questions were formulated and sequenced. Piaget studied small numbers of children, and the many books he wrote presented long, carefully elaborated analyses of the performance of a few children in a wide variety of situations.

Both the notion that there were distinct developmental stages in how people think and the empirical approach that was taken to substantiate the theory were alien to American thinking. The latter, as we have seen, was dominated by an emphasis on learning as the central problem for psychology and by the pervasive assumption that learning and performance resulted from environmental, not developmental or maturational forces. Moreover, good scientific method demanded experiments that were rigorously derived from theory, easily replicable, and based on sufficient numbers of enough subjects so that statistical analyses could be used to indicate the generalizability of the results. For such reasons this early, simplified view of Piagetian theory, as it was first introduced to the United States, was not readily accepted.

In the 1950s and 1960s, however, as we have seen, there was an enormous shift of emphasis in psychological theory toward a concern for theoretical formulations that could better address complex behaviors. Some aspects of Piagetian theory became more attractive (e.g., the notion that complex tasks could be analyzed in terms of the logical operations required to solve them). Recall that according to Piaget, children of different ages operate with different logical structures and cognitive processes. If educational tasks could be analyzed in terms of their cognitive developmental requirements, then they could be appropriately classified and sequenced in the curriculum.

Piaget's theory, however, is so complex and his writing so voluminous and opaque that real popularization of his theory required interpretation and not merely translation. Books by Flavell (1963), Ginsburg and Opper (1969), and others appeared, and it was these works that provided the primary source material for American researchers and educationists. Americans, too, brought their own stamp to the Genevan theory. Although Piagetian scholars decried the enterprise, American psychologists focused intently on what seems always to have been a perennial concern: Could we, by suitable manipulation of environmental effects—that is, by training—modify the way children think and thereby speed up the transition from stage to stage? For example, one of the most commonly studied Piagetian phenomena has been conservation. (Indeed, conservation is one of the few empirical phenomena that demonstrates clear performance differences among children that can be interpreted unambiguously as manifesting different stages of development.) In the late sixties a rash of studies appeared that demonstrated that conservation was in fact "trainable" (e.g., Gelman, 1969).

Piagetian scholars derided these efforts, pointing out that the ages specified for transitions from one stage to another were among the least important aspects of the theory. However, this type of work has continued for a long period of time.

Current Piagetian scholars point out that the presentation in toto of the theory that had been brought to the United States reflected, actually, the less important aspects of Piaget's thinking. According to Groen (1978), Piaget really has developed a theory of knowledge (called *genetic epistemology*), and the psychological theory inherent in it is really only a minor part of the entire framework. Piaget's entire theory of intellectual development, according to Groen, focuses on the parallels in the development of the logical structure of knowledge and in the growth of psychological processes (Piaget, 1947/1950, 1957).

However true, this more sophisticated reading of Piaget is not the perspective that has provided the basis for educational applications of Piagetian theory. Rather, the general notion of developmental stages and the possibility of providing an environment that would help children move through these stages justified the early applications.

Many of the curriculum projects based on Piagetian ideas have focused on early childhood education. The reasons for this do not derive from strong implications of the theory but rather at least partly from the fact that these efforts were undertaken in the 1960s, when there was widespread emphasis on and funding for preschool educational programs. As might be expected, many applications emphasized the attainment of developmental stages as appropriate educational objectives. Thus preschool programs focused on the development of performances characteristic of the stage of concrete operations and chose, as content to teach, some of the tasks Piaget had used in his own research (e.g., Kamii & DeVries, 1977; Lavatelli, 1973). One of the few programs designed for older children and focused on the attainment of formal operational reasoning is that of Lawson (1975). This program centers around a series of activities, including experiments, that deal with scientific concepts. It uses the discovery method as a teaching technique. This method is designed to approximate, in an educational setting, the problem-solving activities that are required to promote cognitive development through the developmental stages in real life. How to use the discovery method has not been made very explicit; yet it represents the most specific teaching technique that is incorporated into these curricula. Indeed, according to Kuhn (1979), current Piagetian programs are even less structured today than they were 10 or 15 years ago. At present they tend to emphasize the necessity for children to direct their own cognitive activity. The "best" educational environment becomes one that is cognitively rich and supportive and which permits a child to choose his own activities. Presumably this promotes his own cognitive development, still, however, through the gradual development of more advanced cognitive structures.

These curricular applications of the theory have not met with universal approval, even among Piagetians. The controversy continues as to whether or not it is fruitful to try to speed up developmental progress by any kind of environmental manipulation. Moreover, there are other concerns that appear similar to questions posed about any theory-based curriculum: If the content of the curriculum focuses on a certain set of tasks chosen on the basis of theory, how certain is it that these tasks will prove a good foundation for the mastery of other important tasks? This is the familiar issue of transfer, although Piagetians themselves would not be likely to use this terminology. Indeed, the programs that emphasize self-directed activity refrain from specifying much content at all! Is this, then, content-free instruction that harks back to the turn of the century when Latin and Greek were taught not for their own sake but because such instruction was thought to enhance general thinking ability?[2]

It is difficult to set explicit criteria for evaluating the effectiveness of these programs, because (1) progress through Piagetian stages can only be evaluated as a long-term goal and (2) there is no consensus in the field even as to an appropriate way of evaluating whether someone has indeed reached the adult stage of formal operational thinking.

The emphasis on progress through the developmental stages as an educational goal has certain side-effects that are not logical concomitants of the theoretical formulations, yet are likely to occur. They include, first, a tendency to postpone instruction because of the assumed importance of the child's need to direct his own activities and also because of the theoretical emphasis on the gradualness of the development of cognitive structures, which lead one to expect slow transitions from one stage to the

---

[2] It is interesting to note that in 1900 languages and language-learning were more highly valued activities in their own right than they are today. Today's proponents of the teaching of skills in a content-irrelevant format concentrate on mathematics and science tasks. While the justification for such instruction is still stated in terms of developing cognitive processes in general, it is still the case that this choice of curriculum content reflects contemporary emphasis on mathematics and science as important areas of knowledge in their own right.

next. Even more important is a second side-effect, the de-emphasis of traditional curriculum offerings. Since at this point there is no validation of the Piagetian curriculum itself, there is some realistic concern that basic skills such as reading and arithmetic are sometimes given rather short shrift.

A more principled criticism of these programs also arises, namely that they may not be legitimate applications of Piagetian theory at all and that they are derived from the oversimplification of the theory when it was first imported from Geneva. According to Groen (1978), even the newer applications (e.g., of Kamii and DeVries) whose rationales are based on a modern interpretation of Piaget are deficient in their derivations of appropriate implications or in the actual design of materials and methods. Groen acknowledges that Piagetian theory in its entirety does not easily lend itself to concrete curricular application. Piaget himself wrote only a few very general essays on education, in which he emphasized a "balance between freedom and structure," which is of course a statement of such generality and obvious common sense that no reasonable person, whether theorist, educator, or layman, would disagree. Delving more deeply into the theory for more specific implications only reveals the ambiguities in the theory, which has led Kuhn (1979) to insist that further clarification of the theory itself is required before effective applications can be made. It is obvious that the curricula based on this developmental theory are only loosely justified in terms of the theory itself (a situation that is not restricted to educational programs based on Piagetian theory, of course). Recent research by the Genevans themselves (e.g., Inhelder, Sinclair, & Bovet, 1974) and by others (e.g., Kuhn, Ho, & Adams, 1979) focuses on observation of developmental processes under controlled situations that are designed to resemble naturally occurring ones. Whether or not a better understanding of the nature of developmental transition mechanisms will lead to better curricula is, of course, open to question.

Overall, the educational goals specified or assumed by these curriculum developers are unimpeachable, if overgeneral; that is, they include the development of intellectual curiosity and high-level cognitive strategies. A curriculum based on any psychological theory would have to incorporate these general goals in order to be acceptable. Framing these goals in terms of specific attainment of formal operational thinking, of course, puts a different light on the matter. But this last goal is the only one that seems to differentiate developmental curricula from the majority of up-to-date curricula that are based on a more general cognitive, information-processing approach (to be discussed below). After all, the techniques and methods do not differ very much at all. And if, in fact, there are no qualitative changes in cognitive structures and processes over the course of development, then there is nothing to make Piagetian curricula distinctive or particularly attractive. In fact, Piagetian curricula may actually retard educational progress, in one way, by insisting on the child's achievement of tasks that have little potential for transfer to traditionally important basic (or advanced) skills or, in another way, by inappropriately postponing instruction.

Information Processing

The emergence of today's central paradigm in psychology, information-processing, owes a great deal to the development of the digital computer (see Chapanis, in Volume III) and to developments in the field of artificial intelligence. Newell and Simon (1961, 1972; Newell, Shaw, & Simon, 1958) proposed that the human mind could be thought of as a system that manipulates symbols, just as a computer does, and that the workings of the mind, like those of any system, could be described in the form of a computer program. Such a program consists of sequences of basic information processing operations. The mind applies a series of cognitive operations to information, each time putting it into a form such that it can be further modified by the next operation in the sequence. Thus information is organized in different ways as it passes from *input* to *output* (or to *storage*).[3]

The simulation of human thinking by a computer requires a precise statement of each individual step of the thinking process. In this manner, a successful computer simulation can provide, essentially, a theory of thinking. This model easily lends itself to a consideration of "process" in the sense of understanding what goes on in the mind between input and output. Today's psychologists, unlike those of an earlier generation, are more willing to theorize about internal processes and to develop structural models, that is, descriptions of what knowledge a person has and what his mental processes are like.

Newell and Simon held a series of conferences in the late 1950s to promote their ideas, and their work has had a profound impact on the development of cognitive psychology since then (e.g., Lachman, Lachman, & Butterfield, 1979). The computer analogy is appealing because, indeed, it seems that a human being and a computer can do so many of the same things. Both can acquire information, manipulate it, store it, and use it in a wide variety of reasoning and problem-solving situations. The

---

[3]Note the change from the terms *stimulus* and *response;* psychologists have adopted the language of computer science. Such modifications in technical terminology reflect basic changes in theoretical conceptualizations and promote further advances that are consistent and productive within the theoretical framework. Moreover, the more pervasive the terminology, the more likely it is that the overall metaphor will be adopted by education.

power and complexity of the computer—its ability to deal with a great deal of information and to make decisions based not only on a great number of different variables but also on conditional states of individual or combined variables—seem to mirror the power and complexity of the human mind.

Much of the early basic research within this paradigm focused on analysis of the stages that are involved in information-processing and, as a means of identifying the stages, on the length of time that each one of them takes. Research by Neisser (1967) and Sternberg (1969) indicated, first, that it was possible to infer distinct information-processing stages and, second, that it was feasible to study mental processes using precise measures. This constituted an enormous advance for psychology. However, there is an emphasis on theoretical issues that can be studied using experimental situations that permit formal modeling. Often, this involves situations in which reaction-time differences of hundredths of seconds are important. This most likely means that the work is at too molecular a level to have great potential for educational applications.

A related area that does hold some such promise concerns the ways in which people use strategies to aid their thinking. Within the information-processing paradigm, these are considered techniques that involve control or executive processes. Early work in this area centered on simple strategies like rehearsal or classification, which were useful in rote-learning tasks. Contrary to the assumptions inherent in the stimulus-response paradigm, even simple paired-associate learning and other rote tasks seemed not to be the product of passive learning but rather of active cognition (see Miller, Galanter, & Pribram, 1960). Other executive strategies include self-monitoring (i.e., evaluating one's own thinking) and revising if necessary on the basis of the evaluation. The strategy of means-end analysis involves setting up subgoals within the context of the larger problem to be solved and then directing attention to solutions to those subgoals. These are sometimes called metacognitive strategies, and there has been some limited success in training children to use them, or at least in modifying performance by suggesting that they be used.

Simon's own research approach involves observing people "thinking aloud" as they solve problems. Computer programs are written to simulate the human performance, and the resulting "production systems" are taken as "an appropriate formalism for representing cognitive processes [Simon, 1979, p. 364]." A variety of different strategies is often found to be effective in solving problems. Some depend on attention to perceptual cues, for example, and others on the discovery of an effective sequence of actions.

One promising research strategy involves study of the nature of "expertness" in various tasks to determine the kinds of knowledge an expert has, how that knowledge is organized mentally, and how it is used. An analysis of the differences between expert and novice is particularly relevant for educational applications, in the sense that a detailed description of performance at various stages of expertise would provide the basis for work (as yet not extensively carried out) on the way in which performance changes from state to state and, it is hoped, on the ways in which such change might be promoted.

Analysis of problem-solving in school subjects became a popular research focus in the 1970s. Greeno (1978), for example, found similarities between problem-solving in geometry and the general process of making semantic inferences. Work in other content areas such as in physics also emphasized the close relationship between the knowledge that is specific to the problem domain on the one hand and strategies relevant to the general class of problem on the other (Greeno, 1980). This point of view has led Simon and Simon (1979) to recommend that instruction should incorporate both ambiguous and complex problems to simulate the poorly-defined problems of "real life." The principle is old, but the recent careful analysis of the potential sources of ambiguity and structural complexity may well help in designing classroom materials that truly follow the old principle. It is highly likely, in the light of recent work, that the older theories of learning proved unhelpful because they were "domain-independent," that is they were supposed to be generally applicable to all content areas (Collins & Rubin, 1980).

The careful and detailed description of knowledge in these school-relevant content areas has highlighted the fact that today's schools do *not* explicitly focus on certain important types of knowledge. For example, Greeno (1978) found that some of the strategic knowledge that is involved in constructing geometry proofs is not taught in most geometry courses. In the same vein, Simon and Simon (1979) pointed out that standard methods of science-instruction emphasize the development of circumscribed problem-solving skills within a narrow content domain but neglect the also-crucial development of general problem-solving skills. Thus both content-specific *and* general strategies seem to be important.

One type of research within the information-processing approach that is of high potential for education pertains to the work on the organization of verbal knowledge. Almost all previous research in verbal learning followed Ebbinghaus (1885/1964), whose development of the nonsense syllable for the study of memory was predicated on the assumption that it was important to remove all prior associations and knowledge from experimental material (stimuli) in order to discover basic laws of learning and memory. Modern cognitive psychology argues that prior knowledge cannot be removed from any task or situation without fundamentally changing that task or situation and that the effects of background knowledge are in fact one of the most interesting aspects of the problem. This point of view was taken by Bartlett (1932), who found that people who were asked to recall meaningful stories modified them in ways that made them fit with what they already knew. Bartlett interpreted this as demonstrating an active "effort after meaning."

Bartlett's work was largely ignored when it appeared, however, because it did not fit with the intellectual Zeitgeist of the earlier part of this century. Current cognitive psychology has resurrected his work and has emphasized his concept of *schema* as a cognitive structure that organizes knowledge. A central notion is that knowledge is *represented* in ways that align a given experience with past experience and make it useable in later experience. Hence, information must be organized coherently, which involves making those inferences that are necessary to relate it to other cognitive schemas. Methods of analyzing the information contained in a sentence (for example, Fillmore's, 1968, case grammar) have been a source for creating structural models of larger chunks of information. For example, investigators have developed story grammars on the assumption that a story can be parsed by the application of simple rules (Thorndyke, 1977). Presumably a person who has this knowledge of story structure will find it easier to remember and to comprehend stories that follow the grammars. The structure of expository text, which reflects to some extent school-relevant tasks, has been analyzed in the same way. A related idea is that of *scripts* (Schank & Abelson, 1977): A script consists of an outline of aspects of a specific type of situation (e.g., going to a restaurant) which provides a framework for expectations concerning—and therefore understanding—specific instances of that type of situation. Presumably, instruction could be designed that would provide for the development of such cognitive structures as tools to enhance comprehension. Or, at least, since memory and comprehension are related to the degree of correspondence of a given story to "ideal" structure, we could begin to specify more precisely guidelines for presenting information, i.e., for writing textbooks.

THE CONVERGENCE OF NEW THEORETICAL POSITIONS

Over the last 10 years there has been a serious effort to modify and extend Piagetian theory, and the resultant formulations (e.g., Case, 1978; Pascual-Leone, 1976) have been labeled "neo-Piagetian." One problem with the classic Piagetian approach was that, while at each developmental stage children's thinking has a characteristic logical form or structure, it has been difficult to describe many tasks, including school tasks, in terms of these logical structures. Another important problem lay in the lack of explicitness of explanation of the basic process by which a child moves from one stage to the next. Piaget described "equilibration" as a process that involves, first, a child's being faced with events and situations on which his current reasoning cannot operate successfully and, second, his resolution of this conflict by experimenting with new logical operations. This in turn leads to the gradual evolvement of a higher-order logical structure. The question of *how* this process actually works was not addressed. In terms of trying to determine how to apply the theory to instruction, this notion leads mainly to the idea that children must direct their own cognitive activity. The only available instructional method that seems not to contradict this dictum is the "discovery method," whose proponents claim that a child learns more effectively through an inductive method in which he discovers principles and problem solutions for himself.

A brief overview of aspects of Case's (1981) approach will illustrate the manner in which Piagetian theory has been modified. The notion that during development children manifest qualitatively different types of intellectual operation has been retained; the use of a model of logical structure to describe these stages, however, has been abandoned. Instead, the new theory describes cognitive development in terms of two factors. First, after the fashion of information-processing models (Newell & Simon, 1962), children are said to develop executive strategies. Second, use of these strategies depends on the capacity or size of a short-term or working memory store, and the capacity of this store increases with age. As any operation becomes more practiced, it requires less attention for its execution. This in turn provides more attentional resources that can be used for memory, and so more content can be dealt with at one time.

An attempt has been made to make the theory more amenable to empirical test by focusing more closely on performance. Also, the processes by which transitions occur between stages—as well as within stages—are described more clearly. These processes amount to active problem solving, exploration, and observation. Furthermore, an individual's active attention must be involved in order for any of these processes to add a new element to the repertoire of existing strategies. In an attempt to reconcile empirical evidence that, indeed, training does under some circumstances hasten the acquisition of certain Piagetian tasks, Case has spelled out the types of experiences that foster appropriate attentional processes. Among these are repeated exposure to a task and training that directs a child's attention to the aspects of the task that are relevant. The training must, of course, also be geared to the child's current developmental level if such experiences are to increase rate of intellectual development. Of course, maturation also plays a role: Biologically-determined changes, whatever these may be, presumably set an upper limit on the rate of intellectual growth.

The particular form of instructional theory that is offered as falling out of neo-Piagetian theory involves (1) structural analysis of the task to be learned; (2) assessment of the level of cognitive function of the children who are to be taught; and (3) the design of instruction in an effective sequence in which short-term storage demands are kept low, step-size small, and sufficient practice is provided at each step. This is not very different at all from recommendations based solely on information-processing models or, indeed, those based on earlier models that were developed initially from the perspective of neo-behaviorist theory (e.g., Gagné's, 1965, task analysis). Again, the particular value that a genuinely developmental theory would offer would be in terms of the validation of qualitatively different types of intellectual functioning at different ages. If this turns out to be true, then such a theory would provide a distinctly different model for instruction. At present, however, while neo-Piagetian theory does seem to allow a more serious consideration of the effects of environmental manipulation, that is, a class of events with which the educator can actually deal, there is not yet enough evidence to support the view that there are in fact qualitatively different developmental stages. The developmental processes that are postulated are classic ones and are described only generally. The instructional recommendations are also classic, with no distinctive elaborations to warrant considering them a contribution that arises specifically from Piagetian or neo-Piagetian theory.

At the beginning of this essay, I argued that educational trends, both in theory and in practice, were determined only partially by psychological theory and research. Often it is social needs and general cultural trends that actually determine which of several psychological theories is adopted and which research evidence is judged relevant and useful (Williams, 1979b).

It is foolhardy to try to predict the future, but it is probably fairly safe to suggest that rising costs may force re-assessment of many common educational practices. The value of individualized instruction, which for the last few years has been considered almost sacrosanct, is already being questioned. The influence of developing technology, especially if it is cost-effective, is always strong. Microcomputers are now becoming readily available both at school and at home. This means that educational games as well as computer-based instruction can and probably will be promoted widely. Such activities are likely to be designed in terms of current information-processing theory, although this is not necessary, of course.

How do social trends determine the educational questions that are

deemed relevant for study? The issue of the single-child family, currently
of interest, can serve as an example. The long-held stereotype of the only
child as lonely, self-centered, and unable to get along with others can be
traced to the turn of the century when children were needed for the work
force and when infant mortality was substantial. This view was accepted
for many years, and only recently has it been questioned. Faced with
today's smaller families and new social phenomena (such as more married
women in the work force, inflation, and concern in some quarters about
over-population) that suggest that the trend toward smaller families will
continue, there has been a new surge of interest in the topic. The results
of the new research have been used to support a different view: that only
children are, as a group, brighter, more ambitious and more mature than
children with siblings (e.g., Claudy, Farrell, & Dayton, 1979). These
studies do not contradict the observations of the earlier studies, that is,
they do not argue that only children are better at getting along with their
peers; rather, they choose to highlight other criteria that are pro-only-
children. (There seems to be no general current trend to look for
phenomena that lead to these particular criteria of brightness, ambition,
maturity, etc.)

A feature article on this topic appeared not long ago in the New York
Times (Moore, 1981). It emphasized the new positive findings; it did not
cite specific findings for the traditional, negative point of view; it presented the pictures of several "singular achievers." This type of interpretation and publicity about basic studies in child development play a major
role in promoting the acceptance of conclusions based on research as well
as in determining the conclusions that are to be drawn from recent
findings. In such instances—and they are many—the lack of a general
theory that encompasses the phenomenon seems to matter not at all.

CONCLUSIONS

It is often difficult to put a current situation into perspective; one may not
see the forest for the trees. Clearly, over the past decade psychology has
become more closely involved with educational issues than it has been
since the first quarter of the century, and this trend is likely to continue at
least into the next few years. In this light, valuable contributions to the
development of teaching techniques and to the design of curricula should
be forthcoming. As far as education is concerned, it appears that we are
still in a period of reaction against progressive education and that the
"Back-to-Basics" movement has not yet reached its peak. Whether there
will be a long-term trend toward delimiting the role of the school and a
consequent narrowing of concerns to strictly academic learning cannot be

predicted with certainty. It is virtually certain, however, that there will be further shifts between what William James referred to as "the soft and tender" and "the hard and tough" orientations of education; in fact, it has been suggested (Goodlad, 1979) that small-scale shifts between these two points of view occur every 12 years or so. Moreover, it is also virtually certain that education will continue to lean heavily on psychology, either before or after the fact, to determine and to justify its goals and practices.

ACKNOWLEDGMENTS

The preparation of this essay was supported by a contract (300-77-0491) with the Office of Special Education, Department of Education. The author thanks Sam Glucksberg for very helpful comments on an earlier version of the essay.

REFERENCES

Bandura, A. *Social learning theory*. New York: General Learning Press, 1971.
Bartlett, F. C. *Remembering: A study in experimental and social psychology*. London, England: Cambridge University Press, 1932.
Bloom, B. S. *Human characteristics and school learning*. New York; McGraw-Hill, 1976.
Broudy, H. S. Philosophical foundations of education. In H. J. Walberg (Ed.), *American education: Diversity and research*. Washington, DC: Voice of America, U.S. International Communication Agency, 1979.
Bruner, J. S. *The process of education*. Cambridge, MA: Harvard University Press, 1960.
Bruner, J. S. Some theorems on instruction illustrated with reference to mathematics. In E. R. Hilgard (Ed.), *Theories of learning and instruction*. Chicago, IL: National Society for the Study of Education, 1964.
Bush, R. R., & Mosteller, F. *Stochastic models for learning*. New York: Wiley, 1955.
Carroll, J. B. A model of school learning. *Teachers College Record, 1963, 64*, 723–733.
Case, R. Piaget and beyond: Toward a developmentally based theory and technology of instruction. In R. Glaser (Ed.), *Advances in instructional psychology* (Vol. 1). Hillsdale, NJ: Lawrence Erlbaum Associates, 1978.
Case, R. Intellectual development: A systematic reinterpretation. In F. H. Farley & N. J. Gordon (Eds.), *Psychology and education: The state of the union*. Berkeley, CA: McCutchan, 1981.
Claudy, J. G., Farrell, W. S., & Dayton, C. W. *The consequences of being an only child: An analysis of Project TALENT data*. (Final Report to the National Institute of Child Health and Human Development.) Palo Alto, CA: American Institutes for Research, 1979.
Clifford, G. J. Words for schools: The applications in education of the vocabulary researches of Edward L. Thorndike. In P. Suppes (Ed.), *Impact of research on education*. Washington, DC: National Academy of Education, 1978.
Collins, A., & Rubin, A. *How the cognitive sciences will impact education*. Paper presented at the meetings of the American Educational Research Association, Los Angeles, April, 1980.
Cremin, L. A. *The transformation of the school*. New York: A. A. Knopf, 1961.

Cronbach, L. J., & Suppes, P. (Eds.). *Research for tomorrow's schools: Disciplined inquiry for education*. London: Collier-Macmillan, 1969.

Dewey, J. *The school and society*. Chicago, IL: University of Chicago Press, 1915.

Dewey, J. *Democracy and education*. New York: Macmillan, 1916.

Ebbinghaus, H. [*Memory*.] New York: Dover, 1964. (Originally published, 1885.)

Estes, W. K. Learning theory and the new mental chemistry. *Psychological Review*, 1960, *67*, 207–223.

Fillmore, C. J. The case for case. In E. Bach & R. T. Harms (Eds.), *Universals in linguistic theory*. New York: Holt, Rinehart & Winston, 1968.

Flavell, J. H. *The developmental psychology of Jean Piaget*. Princeton, NJ: Van Nostrand, 1963.

Freud, A. [*Psychoanalysis for teachers and parents*] (B. Low, trans.). Boston, MA: Emerson Books, 1935.

Freud, S. [*The ego and the id*] In J. Strachey (Ed. and trans.), *The standard edition of the complete psychological works of Sigmund Freud* (Vol. 20). London: Hogarth, 1959. (Originally published, 1926.)

Freud, S. [*Civilization and its discontents*.] In J. Strachey (Ed. and trans.), *The standard edition of the complete psychological works of Sigmund Freud* (Vol. 21). London: Hogarth, 1961. (Originally published, 1930.)

Gagne R. M. *Conditions of learning*. New York: Holt, Rinehart, & Winston, 1965.

Gelman, R. Conservation acquisition: A problem of learning to attend to relevant attributes. *Journal of Experimental Child Psychology*, 1969, *7*, 167–187.

Gibson, E. J. A systematic application of the concepts of generalization and differentiation of verbal learning. *Psychological Review*, 1940, *47*, 196–229.

Ginsburg, H., & Opper, S. *Piaget's theory of intellectual development: An introduction*. Englewood Cliffs, NJ: Prentice-Hall, 1969.

Glaser, R. The contributions of B. F. Skinner to education and some counterinfluences. In P. Suppes (Ed.), *Impact of research on education*. Washington, DC: National Academy of Education, 1978.

Goodlad, J. Elementary education. In H. J. Walberg (Ed.), *American education: Diversity and research*. Washington, DC: Voice of America, U.S. International Communication Agency, 1979.

Gorman, F. H. Some facts concerning changes in the content and methods of arithmetic. In L. J. Cronbach & P. Suppes (Eds.), *Research for tomorrow's schools: Disciplined inquiry for education*. London: Collier-Macmillan, 1969. (Originally published, 1931.)

Greeno, J. G. A study of problem-solving. In R. Glaser (Ed.), *Advances in instructional psychology* (Vol. 1). Hillsdale, NJ: Lawrence Erlbaum Associates, 1978.

Greeno, J. G. Psychology of learning, 1960–1980. *American Psychologist*, 1980, *35*, 713–728.

Groen, G. J. The theoretical ideas of Piaget and educational practice. In P. Suppes (Ed.), *Impact of research on education*. Washington, DC: National Academy of Education, 1978.

Guthrie, E. R. *The psychology of learning*. New York: Harper, 1952.

Hall, G. S. *Contents of children's minds*. New York: Kellogg, 1893.

Hall, G. S. *Educational problems*. New York: Appleton, 1911.

Hill, W. F. Contemporary developments within stimulus-response learning theory. In E. R. Hilgard (Ed.), *Theories of learning and instruction*. Chicago, IL: The National Society for the Study of Education, 1964.

Holt, J. *How children fail*. New York: Pitman, 1964.

Hull, C. L. *Principles of behavior*. New York: Appleton-Century-Crofts, 1943.

Hull, C. L. *Essentials of behavior*. New Haven, CT: Yale University Press, 1951.

Hunter, E. C. Changes in teachers' attitudes toward children's behavior over the last thirty years. *Mental Hygiene*, 1957, *41*, 3–11.

Illich, I. *Deschooling society*. New York: Harrow Books, 1972.

Inhelder, B., Sinclair, H., & Bovet, M. *Learning and the development of cognition*. Cambridge, MA: Harvard University Press, 1974.

James, W. *Talks to teachers on psychology and to students on some of life's ideals*. New York: Holt, 1900.

Kamii, C., & DeVries, R. Piaget for early education. In M. C. Day & R. K. Parker (Eds.), *Preschool in action*. Boston, MA: Allyn & Bacon, 1977.

Kendler, H. H., & Kendler, T. S. Vertical and horizontal processes in problem-solving. *Psychological Review*, 1962, *69*, 1–16.

Koffka, K. [*The growth of the mind*] (R. M. Ogden, trans.). London: Kegan Paul, Trench, Trubner, 1924.

Kohler, W. *Gestalt psychology*. New York: Liveright, 1929.

Kuhn, D. The application of Piaget's theory of cognitive development to education. *Harvard Educational Review*, 1979, *49*, 340–360.

Kuhn, D., Ho, V., & Adams, C. Formal reasoning among pre- and late adolescents. *Child Development*, 1979, *50*, 1128–1135.

Lachman, R., Lachman, J. L., & Butterfiield, E. C. *Cognitive psychology and information processing: An introduction*. Hillsdale, NJ: Lawrence Erlbaum Associates, 1979.

Lavatelli, C. *Piaget's theory applied to an early childhood curriculum*. Boston, MA: American Science and Engineering, 1973.

Lawson, A. Developing formal thought through biology teaching. *American Biology Teacher*, 1975, *37*, 411–429.

Lewin, K. Field theory and learning. In N. B. Henry (Ed.), *The psychology of learning* (41st Yearbook of the National Society for the Study of Education, Part II). Chicago, IL: University of Chicago Press, 1942.

MacDonald, F. J. The influence of learning theories on education (1900–1950). In E. R. Hilgard (Ed.), *Theories of learning and instruction*. Chicago, IL: University of Chicago Press, 1964.

Maslow, A. H. *Toward a psychology of being*. Princeton, NJ: Van Nostrand, 1968. (a)

Maslow, A. H. Some educational implications of humanistic psychologies. *Harvard Educational Review*, 1968, *38*, 685–696. (b)

Miller, G. A., Galanter, E., & Pribram, K. *Plans and the structure of behavior*. New York: Holt, 1960.

Miller, N. E. Scientific principles for maximum learning from motion pictures. In N. E. Miller (Ed.), *Graphic communication and the crisis in education*. Washington, DC: National Education Associates, 1957.

Mitchell, J. C. A study of teachers' and mental hygienists' ratings of certain behavior problems of children. *Journal of Educational Research*, 1942, *36*, 292–307.

Moore, D. The only-child phenomenon. *The New York Times Magazine*, January 18, 1981, 26–48.

Mowrer, O. H. *Learning theory and behavior*. New York: Wiley, 1960.

Neisser, U. *Cognitive psychology*. New York: Appleton-Century-Crofts, 1967.

Newell, A., Shaw, J. C., & Simon, H. A. Elements of a theory of human problem solving. *Psychological Review*, 1958, *65*, 151–166.

Newell, A., & Simon, H. A. The simulation of human thought. In *Current trends in psychological theory*. Pittsburgh, PA: University of Pittsburgh Press, 1961.

Newell, A., & Simon, H. A. *Human problem solving*. Englewood Cliffs, NJ: Prentice-Hall, 1972.

Pascual-Leone, J. A view of cognition from a formalist's perspectives. In K. F. Riegel & J. Meacham (Eds.), *The developing individual in a changing world*. The Hague: Mouton, 1976.

Piaget, J. [*The language and thought of the child*] (M. Worden, trans.). New York: Harcourt, Brace & World, 1926. (Originally published, 1923.)

Piaget, J. [*Judgment and reasoning in the child*] (M. Worden, trans.). New York: Harcourt, Brace & World, 1928. (Originally published, 1924.)

Piaget, J. [*The psychology of intelligence*] (M. Piercy & D. E. Berlyne, trans.). London: Routledge and Kegan Paul, 1950. (Originally published, 1947.)

Piaget, J. *Logic and psychology.* New York: Basic Books, 1957.

Postman, L. One-trial learning. In C. N. Cofer (Ed.), *Verbal behavior and learning: Problems and processes.* New York: McGraw-Hill, 1963.

Pressey, S. L. *Psychology and the new education.* New York: Harper, 1933.

Roberts, T. B. (Ed.). *Four psychologies applied to education.* Cambridge, MA: Schenkman, 1975.

Rogers, C. *Freedom to learn.* Columbus, OH: Merrill, 1969.

Ryan, W. C. *Mental health through education.* New York: Commonwealth Fund, 1938.

Schank, R. C., & Abelson, R. P. *Scripts, plans, goals and understanding: An inquiry into human knowledge structures.* Hillsdale, NJ: Lawrence Erlbaum Associates, 1977.

Sheffield, F. D. Theoretical considerations in the learning of complex sequential tasks from demonstration and practice. In A. A. Lumsdaine (Ed.), *Student response in programmed instruction.* Washington, DC: National Academy of Sciences, National Research Council, 1961.

Simon, D. P., & Simon, H. A. A tale of two protocols. In J. Lockhead & J. Clement (Eds.), *Cognitive process instruction.* Philadelphia, PA: The Franklin Institute, 1979.

Simon, H. A. Information processing models of cognition. *Annual Review of Psychology,* 1979, *30,* 363–396.

Skinner, B. F. *The behavior of organisms: An experimental analysis.* New York: Appleton-Century, 1938.

Skinner, B. F. *Science and human behavior.* New York: Free Press, 1953.

Skinner, B. F. The science of learning and the art of teaching. *Harvard Educational Review,* 1954, *24,* 86–97.

Sternberg, S. Memory-scanning: Mental processes revealed by reaction-time experiments. *American Scientist,* 1969, *57,* 421–457.

Suppes, P., & Warren, H. Psychoanalysis and American elementary education. In P. Suppes (Ed.), *Impact of research on education.* Washington, DC: National Academy of Education, 1978.

Thorndike, E. L. *Educational psychology. Vol. 2: The psychology of learning.* New York: Teachers College Press, 1913.

Thorndike, E. L. *The psychology of arithmetic.* New York: Macmillan, 1922.

Thorndyke, P. W. Cognitive structures in comprehension and memory of narrative discourse. *Cognitive Psychology,* 1977, *9,* 77–110.

Tolman, E. C. *Purposive behavior in animals and men.* New York: Century, 1932.

Wickman, E. K. *Children's behavior and teachers' attitudes.* New York: Commonwealth Fund, 1928.

Williams, J. P. A test of the all-or-none hypothesis for verbal learning. *Journal of Experimental Psychology,* 1962, *64,* 158–165.

Williams, J. P. Educational psychology. In H. J. Walberg (Ed.), *American education: Diversity and research.* Washington, DC: Voice of America, U.S. International Communication Agency, 1979. (a)

Williams, J. P. Reading instruction today. *American Psychologist,* 1979, *34,* 917–922. (b)

Woodring, P. Reform movements from the point of view of psychological theory. In E. R. Hilgard (Ed.), *Theories of learning and instruction.* Chicago, IL: The National Society for the Study of Education, 1964.

5 Psychology and the Environmental Disciplines

Joachim F. Wohlwill
Pennsylvania State University

INTRODUCTION

Consider the following titles of three papers, chosen essentially at random from the field of research on relationships between environment and behavior: "The nature of perceived and imagined environments" (Lowenthal & Riel, 1972); "Personal construct theory and environmental evaluation" (Honikman, 1973); "Modeling and predicting human response to the visual recreation environment" (Peterson & Newmann, 1969). To judge from the titles of these papers—and many similar ones could have been cited—one might assume that we are dealing with excerpts from the table of contents of a psychological journal, referring to theoretical or empirical contributions by psychologists. As it happens, however, the authors involved represent, respectively, the disciplines of geography, architecture, and civil engineering. They illustrate the increasing tendency for workers in the environmental disciplines and professions to concern themselves with perceptual, attitudinal, and behavioral aspects of the problems they deal with, and thus to rub elbows with psychological theories, concepts, and methods, and with psychologists themselves.

Indeed, there appears to be general agreement that the new field of environmental psychology—or, to use a somewhat looser, but more apt term, "environment-and-behavior" (Epstein, 1976)—is inherently inter- or multi-disciplinary in character (e.g., Altman, 1976; Bell, Fisher, & Loomis, 1978; Ittelson, Proshansky, Rivlin, & Winkel, 1974). Let us take a closer look at this field, its history, and current status and examine in general terms the nature of its relationships both to other areas within the discipline of psychology and to other disciplines and professions.

The advent of environmental psychology can be pinpointed fairly precisely to the period between 1969 and 1970. These years saw the establishment of the journal *Environment and Behavior* and several graduate training programs in the field and the appearance of various articles (e.g., Wohlwill, 1970), anthologies (e.g., Proshansky, Ittelson, & Rivlin, 1970), and reviews (e.g., Craik, 1970) calling attention to it.

The psychologists who have identified themselves with this new field have come from several different directions. The first group, the largest group, and the one exerting the greatest impact on the field was made up of persons—primarily social psychologists—interested in people's behavior in and response to space and in the role of space in modulating interpersonal relationships. This area, which has come to be known under the generic name of "proxemics," covers four specific topics: personal space, territoriality, privacy, and crowding (Altman, 1975). While these topics are relevant to some fields outside of psychology, such as architecture, the concepts, theories, and research in this area fit fairly comfortably into the paradigms of interpersonal and social psychology. The significant point to be noted concerning this thematic emphasis is that it essentially treats environment as unfilled space; attributes of the environment itself have played a limited role at best in theorizing and in research in this area, except to the extent that they determine the nature of the space within which behavior is studied, e.g., through its size, layout of elements within the space, and the like (Epstein, 1976).

A second influence on environmental psychology has derived from ecological psychology, in the Barker-Wright tradition (Barker, 1968; Wicker, 1979). The "behavior setting" concept has found ready appeal among those, both inside and outside psychology, interested in conceptualizing environment-behavior relations of quite diverse sorts, without tying themselves to specific questions of process or mechanism. At the same time, ecological psychologists have tended to define behavior settings in predominantly institutional terms, rather than in terms of particular physical-environmental variables, which has limited the relevance of this concept to the problems dealt with by environmental psychologists.

To the above influences from within psychology one could add a scattering of others, such as that of the Skinnerians, who sensed an opportunity to apply behavior-modification principles to a new realm. Similarly, the human-factors school has contributed to the field, both through its attention to the relationships between specific dimensions of the stimulus environment (temperature, noise, gravity) and performance and through its interest in broader aspects of work environments (Parsons, 1976).

On the other hand, certain other branches of psychology have been conspicuous largely by their absence from the field as it has evolved thus far. Thus, considering the emphasis on the role of environmental influences in the development of the child that has been fueled by the controversies over heredity versus environment, and maturation versus learning, one might have expected a more active involvement on the part of child and developmental psychology in this field. Perhaps a major reason why this has not been the case, at least until very recently, is that while many child psychologists place great emphasis on the importance of the environment, it is most often the social environment (represented by parents, peers, school, and culture) that they have in mind. Only recently has some recognition been given to the potential importance of physical-environmental factors in the development of the child (e.g., Parke, 1978; Wachs, 1978).

But if we are to understand fully the directions in which environmental psychology has evolved, it is necessary to consider the forces impinging on it from outside psychology. Indeed, the rather diverse and to a large extent unrelated influences from within psychology would hardly, in themselves, have been effective in creating a new subdiscipline desig-nated as "environmental." It is in large part due to forces from outside of psychology that this interdisciplinary field of environment-and-behavior has come into existence; inevitably, they have played a highly selective role in shaping it as well. They have tended to support those emphases that were most congenial or relevant to the "foreigners" who have come to identify themselves with this area, to their problems, and to their concerns. Who, then, are these intruders, and what are the concerns they have brought with them?

ENVIRONMENTAL DISCIPLINES AND ENVIRONMENTAL PROFESSIONS

Before we can hope to answer this question, it is necessary to draw a distinction between two very different kinds of forces that have brought environmental psychologists into contact with individuals from other fields. The first involves cross-disciplinary relations, those with workers in other academic disciplines that have evolved an environmental focus within their own disciplines similar to that represented by environmental psychology. Foremost among these is the field of geography, which has in important respects become increasingly behavioral in its approach and interests. Geographers have formulated a series of questions that are intrinsically psychological in nature, making liberal use of such concepts as cognitive maps, personal constructs, adaptation levels, satisficing, etc.

Other social-science disciplines such as sociology, anthropology, eco-nomics, and political science have developed environmental foci along lines parallel to that represented by environmental psychology, but interaction and collaboration with workers in these disciplines on the part of psychologists has been rather more sporadic. Nevertheless, the emerging cross-disciplinary relations with these fields still bear consideration (see Back, Price-Williams, Maital & Maital, and Elms, in this volume).

It is environmental psychology's relationship to these other social-science disciplines that seems to correspond most closely to our usual conception of interdisciplinary fields, as exemplified by those of psychobiology (see Uttal, in Volume III), personality and culture (see Price-Williams, in this volume), etc. They represent essentially cases of two or more disciplines converging on problems that happen to lie on the boundaries between them. As we shall see when we examine the case of the geographer's interaction with psychologists, problems of communication, differences in methodological approach, evaluation of evidence, etc., may still need to be overcome. Yet basically the two disciplines are operating from similar epistemological bases and have similar purposes in the work they undertake. The matter is quite different, however, once we turn to environmentally oriented professions, notably architecture, landscape architecture, and planning, or similar to such fields as natural recreation, forestry, and natural resource management. The association of psychologists with members of these professional groups raises questions of a very different order, relating to the definition of problems, the conception of the research process, and the interpretation of information, that serve to differentiate this kind of transcending of disciplinary boundaries from the preceding case. Indeed the term "interdisciplinary" should probably be reserved for interrelations across academic disciplines and be differentiated from "interprofessional" relationships (treating the academic disciplines as a whole as one professional group).

There is, however, another side to this picture, as regards the relationship of the above-mentioned disciplines and professions to psychology. If we think of environmental psychology as the study of functional relationships between environmental and behavioral variables, we see that there is a direct link to the environmental professions: It amounts to analyzing the aspects of the environment that such professions deal with—the architect's buildings, the landscape architect's parks, the recreationist's wilderness areas—and translating them into the form of independent *variables* in terms that make them amenable to incorporation into statements of such functional relationships. ("Apartment" versus "single-family dwellings" may not be suitable for this purpose, but an analysis of the consequences associated with this characteristic may suggest different terms, such as "diversity," "territoriality," etc.) One might say, then, that these professions, which *qua* professions are not of course interested in studying functional relationships as such, provide the psychologist with the raw materials for their research, and in turn the psychologist provides the professional with important information concerning the behavioral effects of the structures or environmental features whose design, planning, or management is their concern.

In the case of other environmental-social science fields of interest to psychology, on the other hand, we are dealing with rival formulations of social-scientific aspects of environmental issues, varying in the conceptual and analytic frameworks used as the basis for the statement of functional relationships. For instance, economists may be interested in visitation of natural-recreation areas, as are some psychologists, but there will be differences in the aspects of recreational settings of interest to them and in the types of responses studied, based on a central difference in the formulation of the relationship between the park environment and the use made of it. Similarly, sociologists like psychologists are interested in the impact of urban environments on human well-being and behavioral pathology, but there are apt to be major differences in the source and type of data collected to bear on these issues that correspond to differences in the mode of conceptualizing the relationship between urban environments and behavior.

Thus we find a rather more complementary relationship between psychology and the professions, while that of psychology to the other disciplines tends to be more competitive in tone; a more positive, integrative relationship between them would presuppose a degree of subordination of intradisciplinal concerns and a readiness to synthesize aspects of each into some more comprehensive totality.

The preceding comments may seem highly general and abstract, but an examination of particular disciplines and professions will, hopefully, bring out their pertinence in concrete contexts. They should thus help bring into focus the following survey of the several fields that have provided points of contact for environmental psychologists and the examination of the particular relationship to psychology that has evolved in each case. Table 1 presents an overview, organized in terms of the differing role of each field in the scheme of environmental analysis as well as in terms of basic versus applied concerns. The subsequent discussion will be limited to those of the fields included in the table that have loomed of primary significance in their relationship to psychology.

INTERDISCIPLINARY TIES TO OTHER ENVIRONMENTAL SOCIAL SCIENCES

Behavior in its relation to the physical environment has been of interest to workers in all of the social sciences, including anthropology, sociology, political science, economics, and geography. Any of these could readily

TABLE 1
Overview of Environmental Disciplines and Professions and their Relation to Psychology

Field's Role in Relation to Environmental Analysis	Basic Disciplines		Applied Fields and Professions	
	Field	Relation to Psychology	Field	Relation to Psychology
Environmental Description and Taxonomy	Geography	Description and specification of the characteristics of the topographic and developed environment relevant to behavioral study and isolation of variables and dimensions for such study	Landscape Architecture Natural Resource Management Forestry Architecture Environmental Design and Planning	Description and isolation of attributes and dimensions of the natural and the man-man environment relevant to behavioral study
	Geology	Description and specification of characteristics and phenomena of the inanimate terrestrial environment relevant to behavior (weather; unusual geological formations and changes in them; natural hazards and cataclysmic events)		
Analysis of environmental influences on man	Physical Anthropology	Study of the response of the human organism to variation in environmental conditions, and of relationships between somatic and psychological aspects of such response	Environmental Health	Study of psychological consequences of environmental degradation and stress
	Cultural Anthropology	Relationship between individual behavior and cultural institutions as influences on environmental quality, use of land, etc.	Architecture Environmental Design and Planning Landscape	Study of relationships between particular features of the built and the natural environment and satisfaction and preference, mental health, indices of

Category	Discipline	Description
Analysis of Environmental and Ecological Processes	Environmental Biology; Ecology	Study of impact of environmentally relevant behaviors, and of individuals' use of an area, on eco-system quality and functioning
	Pollution Control Environmental Engineering	Role of behavior modification and behavioral engineering in coping with environmental problems
	Management Natural Recreation, etc.	
Societal Response to Environmental Issues	Environmental Sociology	Relationship between individual-behavioral and institutional, community-based and cultural factors in formation of environmental attitudes and response to environmental issues; Interaction of individual and societal processes in individual's response to environments (e.g., cities; suburbs)
	Social Impact Assessment	Study of individual and social consequences of intervention in and alteration of the environment (e.g., through urban renewal, highways, etc.)
	Geography	Individual and community response to natural and technological hazards, natural resource depletion, etc.
	Natural Resource and Recreation Management	Individual attitude and response related to management policies and decisions
	Environmental Political Science	Study of public attitudes and opinion relating to environmental issues and of environmental decision-making process
	Environmental Law	Determination of attitudinal and legislation on environmental matters affecting individual rights, freedoms, etc.
	Environmental Economics	Application of utility theory to and impact of pricing policies on individual and collective environmentally relevant behavior
	Environmental Health	Study of psychological consequences of environmental degradation and environmental stressors

129

130   WOHLWILL

be discussed in terms of its relationship to psychology, so as to bring out the point made in the preceding section of competing frameworks brought to bear on the same or similar phenomena. It will suffice, however, to refer to examples from two such disciplines, sociology and economics, and to add a more extensive examination of relationships with a third, geography, which occupies a somewhat special place in this regard.

Sociology

The linkage between sociology and psychology in the environmental area conforms to the prototype of associations among coordinate disciplines generally, such as those between psychology and physiology, as well as between psychology and sociology in such other areas as group and organizational behavior, population issues, and a broad array of socio-psychological issues that have been the shared province of the two disciplines. As Back notes in his chapter on sociology's relations to psychology in this volume, the distinction between them amounts primarily to one of levels of analysis, i.e., a focus on the individual as opposed to aggregate entities such as communities or institutions.

In the environmental area, a variety of problems could be cited that bring out this point, including the study of migration (Brody, 1969), the socio-psychological study of housing and residential satisfaction (Wedin & Nygren, 1979), and the impact of urban environments on psychological and social well-being and pathology. Let us consider briefly the last of these topics.

Treatments of urban life from the side of sociology, such as those of Michelson (1976) and of Fischer (1976), while sensitive to phenomena at the level of individual behavior, have understandably stressed social and institutional structure and organization as major determining variables, along with aggregate-level behavioral processes such as life-style and values as dependent variables. In contrast, psychologists have generally confined themselves to more specific problems of individual response to urban environments, as illustrated in Milgram's (1970; Bornstein & Bornstein, 1976) analysis of "social-stimulation overload" in the cities (an analysis whose debt to the sociologist Simmel is however explicitly acknowledged), Korte and Kerr's (1975) work on helping behavior in urban and rural settings, and Kohn's (1977) research on the evaluation of urban environments by newcomers (see also Wohlwill & Kohn, 1976).

A particularly apt illustration of the differing formulations of psychologists and sociologists comes from the study of a specific aspect of urban life, i.e., the effects of crowding. The psychologist is concerned with differentiating between density, as an environmental variable, and crowding, as an experiential variable (Stokols, 1972) and with extensive consideration of the determinants of negative as well as positive effects of an increase in density beyond some norm, much of it studied under experimentally controlled conditions (cf. Stockdale, 1978). Relevant variables have been predominantly couched in such psychologically relevant terms as stress, goal-blocking, personal space, etc., although other concepts that might link up with those of the sociologist, e.g., availability of resources and primary versus secondary environments (Stokols, 1976), have not been lacking. The sociologist, by contrast, engages in large-scale demographic field investigations of relationships between density and various indices of individual and social pathology and well-being (e.g., Booth, 1976; Galle, Gove, & McPherson, 1972). The study by Galle et al. is particularly notable for differentiating among diverse indices of density as they apply to urban residential settings. While the sociologist's perspective is maintained in this choice of essentially demographic indices of density, it is noteworthy that some of the indices chosen by Galle et al., notably number of persons per room, have a much more direct psychological import, as compared to such typical aggregate indices as persons per square mile. The authors themselves recognize this aspect of their work in their introduction of the concept of interpersonal press with reference to overcrowding at this interior scale. Indeed, one suspects that more refined and discerning use of density indices in the fashion of Galle et al. might well have led psychologists to a more satisfactory resolution of the density versus crowding issue, which as it stands has all too frequently been interpreted to warrant a rejection of an environmentally-defined measure such as density, and a preference for direct resort to the individual's experience.

A rather special case in the relations between sociology and psychology in the environmental area is represented by research into environmental attitudes. This area of research represents an obvious extension of the domain of attitude study and gives rise to many of the same questions that social psychologists have studied over many decades. These include such problems as attitude consistency, relationships between attitude and behavior, susceptibility of attitudes to change, and relationships between attitudes and broader values as well as personality dimensions.

The major impetus for research on this problem has come from sociologists, and more particularly rural sociologists (Buttel & Flinn, 1978; Dunlap & Van Liere, 1978; Heberlein, 1973), but their work has been complemented by a scattering of contributions from political science and geography, as well as from psychology (e.g., Bruvold, 1973; Maloney, Ward, & Braucht, 1975).

The significant point to be made about this area is that the actual theoretical and empirical work is largely *un*related to the auspices, psychological, sociological, or whatever, under which it has been carried out.

Thus we find a debate raging among the sociologists themselves over the question of how superficial or deep-rooted is the seeming shift in values that has occurred in regard to people's orientation toward the environment (Dunlap & Van Liere, 1977; Heberlein, 1972); similarly, we find a psychological level of analysis, along with the sociologist's more traditional focus on demographic-level variables, equally current among sociologists (e.g., Heberlein, 1973), while conversely psychologists (e.g., Tognacci, Weigel, & Wideen, 1972) have not been averse to analyzing environmental attitudes in terms of demographic correlates and such variables as political preference and social values. Yet the obvious opportunity for direct collaboration across the boundaries of the two disciplines that this problem area presents has not been realized, and as a result we are still lacking a comprehensive picture of the complex interplay of social and individual forces that determine people's attitudes towards such concerns as pollution and conservation.

Economics

Psychology and economics interface to a surprising degree in the analysis of diverse aspects of behavior. In the study of environmental concerns, however, the role of economics has generally been treated at an institutional level rather than at the level of individual behavior. But there are a few areas into which economists and psychologists have in fact come within shouting distance of one another, though to what extent they have succeeded in making themselves mutually understood remains a moot question. These problem areas include some of the major environmental issues that implicate individual behavior; two notable ones are natural resource conservation through recycling and choice of mode of transportation. Perhaps the most interesting, as well as complex example, however, is the evaluation and use of natural recreation areas; it is this topic that will be discussed to illustrate the relationship between psychology and economics in the environmental area.

The value attached to natural recreation areas can be approached from a strictly psychological standpoint through studies of aesthetic judgment, preferential choice, and similar techniques familiar to investigators in the areas of experimental aesthetics and of socio-psychological aspects of value (e.g., Becker & McClintock, 1967; Berlyne & Madsen, 1973). At the other extreme, it can be conceived according to the terms of economic theory, essentially as a commodity, like any other. These contrasting approaches were represented in a conference on natural environments (Krutilla, 1972). A paper by a psychologist (Craik, 1972) considers primarily the appraisal of landscapes through verbal ratings of aesthetic dimensions, in terms of their consistency across individuals and groups. In contrast, papers by the economists (Fisher & Krutilla, 1972; Fisher,

Krutilla, & Cicchetti, 1972) deal, respectively, with economic models for decisions on alternative uses for scenic natural areas (i.e., preservation versus exploitation) and with the concept of the "carrying capacity" of an area (i.e., the maximal density of use consonant with the preservation of the natural values and scenic quality attracting the user). Both papers make use of traditional cost-benefit models, although in the process of making them fit the case of the use of a recreation area, where "willingness to pay" is frequently a variable of at best peripheral relevance, the analysis becomes a bit strained.

The concept of "carrying capacity" represents a particularly interesting point of contact among diverse disciplines concerned with environmental quality of natural recreation areas, including not only economics and psychology, but ecology and sociology as well. Since it represents a central concept in the field of natural resource management, fuller discussion of it is reserved for the section to follow on relations between psychology and environmental professions, which includes a specific section on natural recreation. Suffice it to note at this point that a comparison between Fisher and Krutilla's paper and a psychological analysis of this problem in terms of the response to crowding in natural recreation areas (e.g., Becker, 1978) reveals the considerable gap between these alternative conceptions, suggesting some major obstacles to be overcome before an effective collaborative effort between the two disciplines on this problem can even be envisaged.

Geography

Geography appears, to an outsider, as virtually synonymous with the study of our environment in all its aspects. It would thus be natural for psychologists to look to geography for an analysis of the variables that make up the large-scale stimulus environment. This formulation would place geography closer to the environmental professions than to the rest of the environmental-social sciences in regard to the complementary rather than competitive character of its subject-matter, as discussed in the previous section. Such a view of geography would be eminently congenial to ecologically oriented behavioral systems like that of Brunswik (e.g., 1943), with its concern for the distal as contrasted to the proximal stimulus.[1] It might likewise seem potentially relevant to the work of the

---

[1] Brunswik showed little awareness of geography as a field of study, even when discussing psychology's relations to other disciplines (cf. Brunswik, 1956); where he used the phrase "geographic environment" (e.g., Brunswik, 1943), it was typically intended to refer to the physical, as contrasted to the psychological, environment in Lewin's sense of the psychological field. Yet his approach to the perception of size and distance suggests that he would have found in geography a congenial ally for the specification of distal variables.

ecological psychologists, although as noted above they have tended to define behavior settings in institutional rather than geographic terms. An attempt to construct such a "geographic psychology" in which behavior is related to geographically defined variables presupposes, however, some agreement on the terms in which these variables should be defined and on the units to be used. Should they be based on topographic categories, on categories of human settlements and their subdivision, or perhaps on the more fine-grained dimensions identified by the cartographer?

Yet this question has not been of primary concern to contemporary behavioral geographers—perhaps because it implicitly accords to geography the role of an essentially descriptive science. This may be the conception of this discipline that many of us still harbor from our high-school geography days, but in fact it bears little relationship to the discipline as it has evolved. Like psychology itself, geography is a diversified field, running the gamut from description to hypothesis-testing and mathematical modeling as well as from physiography to social science. Indeed, as geographers who have examined the recent history of the field and its relationships to other disciplines and to environmental concerns have shown (Burton, Kates, & Kirkby, 1974; Mikesell, 1969), the discipline has turned away from its earlier environmentalist stance and become both more formalized and more social-science oriented. Thus, the physio- and topographically directed branches of the field that might have dovetailed with the interests of perception- and stimulation-oriented psychologists have remained in the background, while it has been the social-science side of the field that has tended to dominate the points of contact between psychology and geography, leading to a number of quite distinct themes around which the two disciplines have converged.[2] Some of these, such as environmental decision making (e.g., O'Riordan, 1976), represent standard problems in applied environmental social science and need not concern us further. Two topics raise questions of greater interest: the study of cognitive maps and that of human response to natural hazards.

The study of mental maps.   A consistent favorite topic for a wide array of researchers in environment-and-behavior, from anthropology to architecture, has been the individual's mental representation of the geographic environment. Interest in this problem was sparked by the publication in 1960 of a small volume, *The Image of the City,* by Kevin Lynch (a planner), which analyzed the structure of urban environments in terms of the role of certain elements such as landmarks, edges, and nodes in enhancing the residents' ability to orient in the environment. This

---

[2] A comprehensive survey of the field of "behavioral geography" is J. R. Gold's (1980) *An Introduction to Behavioral Geography.*

feature of a city—its "imageability"—Lynch regarded as promoting the pleasure and satisfaction that a resident derives from an urban environment. As a planner, his main interest was in examining the role of the structural lay-out of a city in determining its imageability, a concern to which one might suppose geographers would have proved responsive. Yet, although geographers were at the forefront of those who became involved in research on this topic (see Downs & Stea, 1973, and Moore & Golledge, 1976, for major anthologies devoted to the topic), the interrelating of urban structure with measures of spatial representation or imaging has remained very much in the background in mental-mapping research.

The dominant mode of research, both on the part of geographers and others who took up the study of the problem, curiously veered away from a concern for such relationships between the cartographer's reality and the image or representation of the spatial environment by the individual, and focused on one of two much more purely psychological issues: that of differences among individuals and groups in the character of cognitive maps (e.g., Appleyard, 1970) and that of connotative non-spatial meanings attached to places (e.g., Downs, 1970). This led, for a while, to a proliferation of semantic-differential studies of urban images and subsequently to adaptation of personal-construct theory, via the Repertoire Grid technique (e.g., Harrison & Sarre, 1976; Honikman, 1973), used to study the concepts used by different people in differentiating among places—just as Kelley and his followers had done in their idiographical studies of an individual's interpersonal world. In the process, the role of actual properties of the physical environment became altogether obscured.

This focus on the person as an approach to the study of spatial cognition reflects the dominant orientation towards the subject on the part of those outside of psychology, such as geographers and planners, who have been drawn to it from an interest in the maps of their environment that people are thought to carry around with them in their heads. This focus has effectively permitted them to grapple with the internalization, at an ideational level, of the physical reality they had become accustomed to deal with *qua* geographers and planners. But the result of this subjectivist bias in the approach to this problem has been, rather paradoxically, to leave this area of research largely divorced from the domain of cognitive psychology proper—repeated obeisance to Tolman's (1948) paper on cognitive maps notwithstanding. More generally, interaction, let alone collaborative research between geographers and psychologists interested in this topic, has been little in evidence.

A notable exception to the preceding characterization of the geographer's stance is the work of Golledge and his associates (e.g., Golledge & Rushton, 1976), who have isolated primary cognitive dimensions of the urban environment, via the application of multidimensional scaling, and related these dimensions to characteristics of urban structure as defined by geographers. In so doing they have provided an effective bridge between the two disciplines. Conversely, from the side of psychology, the study of spatial cognition and its development is beginning to be extended to the large-scale environments of the geographer and the planner (e.g., Nagy & Baird, 1978; Siegel, Kirasic, & Kail, 1978), and a recent conference has even succeeded in bringing together persons from geography and psychology, if not in bridging the communications gap between them fully (Liben, Patterson, & Newcombe, 1981).

   Occupying a somewhat special place in this area is the work of Peter Gould (e.g., Gould & White, 1974), who has been interested in the spatial mapping of geographic preference and in relating such preference maps to the respondent's knowledge concerning a place, its distance from the respondent, etc. The preference maps that are the end-products of this research are not, however, obtained from the subjects directly, e.g., by asking them to draw maps, but are based on preference rankings of a set of states (in the case of the U.S.) or countries. The geographer's techniques of homomorphic mapping are then applied to these rankings, generating a surface that expresses the aggregate relative preference assigned to different areas. In contrast to most work on mental maps, this approach retains the real-world geographical map as a (two-dimensional) base, but it expresses the psychological variable of preference as a characteristic of a given locus, in much the same manner that the cartographer would indicate elevation above sea-level. There is here a true fusion of geography and psychology that goes well beyond most of the research in this area.

   Response to natural hazards.   One of the most vigorous and interesting developments in the behavioral-geography field, if not in geography generally, has been the work of a group of researchers on the perception of natural hazards and the assessment of and response to the risk of hazards on the part of inhabitants of areas prone to natural disasters, such as floods and hurricanes. This work is represented by such books and edited anthologies as those by Burton, Kates, and White (1978) and White (1974).

   Although this work relates to a class of natural phenomena that is properly the province of physical geography (as well as geology), it centers on individual and societal response to the hazard presented by the threat of such events as well as to the events themselves when they occur, and it thus falls squarely within the domain of psychological and sociological research. Indeed, the geographical or geophysical side of this problem has played a subsidiary role in the work of these researchers, who have conceptualized hazards in terms seemingly divorced from the context of natural events, as shown in the ready extension of the framework to response to technological hazards (Kates, 1978).

On the other hand, the psychological and sociological aspect of this problem has been extensively developed, in particular in relation to decision-theoretical frameworks and to such formulations as Simon's (1957) which stress the concepts of "bounded rationality" and of "satisficing" rather than maximizing as a basis for risk-taking decisions on the part of those subjected to the threat of floods, hurricanes, and the like (see, too, Slovic, Kunreuther, & White, 1974).

Needless to say, this observation does not represent a criticism of this line of work, since the non-environmental stance taken may be dictated by the nature of the phenomena under investigation. For instance, Sims and Baumann (1972), writing as a psychologist and a geographer, respectively, review diverse hypotheses concerning the differential response to the threat from tornados in the North and the South, based on characteristics of the tornados themselves, and of the geographic environments of the two areas. They wind up, however, rejecting either type of explanation in favor of one that centers on the characteristics of the inhabitants of the two areas and their individual and social needs and values. The area of the perception of natural hazards, then, emerges not so much as a subject for true interdisciplinary activity, but as one in which geographers, with the collaboration of a scattering of psychologists and sociologists, have become involved, undertaking essentially psychological and behavioral research.

Conclusion

The preceding review of relations between psychology and other social sciences in the realm of environment-behavior research leads one to the disquieting conclusion that such relations do not even qualify for the designation of multidisciplinary, let alone inter- or cross-disciplinary. In effect, in much of the work on problems in these areas, such as environmental decision-making or use of natural-recreation areas, the investigators have dealt with behavioral issues while remaining squarely planted on their own disciplinal base. Some research has been undertaken paralleling that of psychologists (e.g., on environmental attitudes and cognitive mapping) but without the active cross-fertilization of ideas or honing of more refined methodologies suited to the needs of the particular problem that a collaborative cross-disciplinary enterprise could have provided.

The reasons for this state of affairs are not obvious. Undoubtedly they reflect in part the more general well-known impediments to collaboration across disciplines. But they may plausibly entail differences in preferred methodologies and in conceptual models—specifically, a distrust of experimental approaches and of behavioristic formulations—that may have served as a block to more effective pooling of resources in attacking problems of mutual interest. The lack of an overarching framework that would allow one to interrelate concepts from these several disciplines, such as a systems-theoretical model might provide, has hampered more effective interaction at the level of theoretical formulation of problems and devising of broadly conceived interdisciplinary designs; an attempt at sketching the outlines of such a model is presented later in this essay. But whatever the reason, it is apparent that environmental social science has not as yet spawned the close integrative type of effort that has been seen in other interdisciplinary contexts in which psychologists have been involved, such as personality-and-culture or the diverse branches of psychobiology.

PSYCHOLOGY VIS-À-VIS THE ENVIRONMENTAL PROFESSIONS

As noted earlier, the distinction between environmentally oriented components of academic disciplines and professions concerned with the physical environment (such as the design professions, forestry and natural recreation, and natural resource conservation) is of central importance in considering psychology's ties to the environmental area. For here we are no longer dealing merely with interdisciplinary relations, but with relations across professions, which differ in their conceptions of a problem and of the research process, in their approaches to the evaluation of data, and more broadly in their values and goals. These issues are hardly new to psychologists. But they have emerged anew as psychologists have started to interact with architects, landscape architects, environmental managers, and natural-resource professionals. At the same time, the resolution of some of the problems has taken on rather different form for different professions, the comparison between architecture and design on the one hand and recreation and forestry on the other affording a particularly interesting contrast, with landscape architecture occupying a place somewhat intermediate between the two.

Architecture

It is not difficult to discern the diverse points of contact between psychology (environmental psychology specifically) and the field of architecture and design. Many questions that are in fact behavioral in nature must be faced, implicitly or explicitly, by those designing buildings. These include questions of the affective response to and aesthetic appeal of a particular design (see Bornstein's chapter on art in Volume I), the manner in which space in and around the periphery of the building will be used, the extent to which the building will meet needs for privacy and territoriality, the ease with which people will be able to find their way inside the building, etc.

In recent years designers have become increasingly aware of the tenuousness and at times invalidity of many of their assumptions about these and other aspects of behavior and of the potentially disastrous consequences resulting from their failure to take behavioral responses into account. A case in point—or so it was widely interpreted—was the fiasco of the Pruitt Igoe Public Housing project in St. Louis, which had won prizes for the felicity of its design when originally built, but wound up having to be demolished less than two decades later. By that time it had become virtually uninhabitable as a result of rampant vandalism, crime, and other manifestations of extreme social anomie, so that well before its final demise it had already been emptied of most of its tenants (see Yancey, 1972).

Experiences such as this one provided the impetus for members of the design professions to search for relevant behavioral knowledge and for psychologists and sociologists who could aid them in the design process. The tacit assumption behind this search was that psychology should be in a position to offer concrete, practical suggestions to designers that would help ensure that the end-products of their work would provide satisfaction to their users *and* prove behaviorally viable.

Yet the alliance thus forged turned out to be a problematical one. From the start it was beset with a variety of difficulties emanating from the rather different purposes and goals, and values and world views that each side brought with it. An excellent discussion of the problems of communication and collaboration between psychologists and designers and of their differing orientations towards problems and problem-solving has been provided by Altman (1973). He notes in particular the difference between a behavioral scientist's focus on matters of process and the practitioner's focus on a criterion (i.e., the behavior to be facilitated or elicited). Altman also points to a further differentiation between the behavioral scientist's interest in environmental phenomena as opposed to the designer's interest in specific types of places, locales, or institutions. That is to say, whereas a psychologist might be interested in territoriality as a phenomenon and in the psychological mechanisms governing territorial behavior and would choose a particular locale for study perhaps on pragmatic grounds of subject access, ease of observation, etc., the designer would start from a concern for effective use of space in some specific locale, such as an office building, and introduce the concept of territoriality so as to take account of problems of space use in that building.

Underlying these differences is presumably a more far-reaching one, relating to the different goals of the psychologist as opposed to the architect, and in particular the very different ways of defining a problem. For a behavioral scientist, a problem is a question to be answered through appropriate research data. For the practitioner, a problem is something in need of a concrete solution (typically within a very limited time-frame) through some form of intervention, which may involve an alteration of the environment or the design of a new one, the formulation of some policy or procedure, or the initiation of some program. These are very different and frequently incompatible goals, and the mismatch between them seems to have been at least in part responsible both for frequently voiced dissatis- faction with the kinds of information that psychologists have given the designer and for some impatience on the part of designers because of the typical difficulty of translating a research finding into a proposed solution to a problem.

This schism between the two fields is not complete—it would be easy to point to architects, particularly in academic settings, who have emulated the behavioral scientist's model of research (e.g., Appleyard, 1970). Con- versely, one finds some psychologists (e.g., Sommer, 1973) not only col- laborating very closely with architects, but in effect adopting their pragmatic, problem-solving orientation, and others (Stringer, 1970) dis- posed to minimize the differences between the two. Yet, in spite of the evident interest in psychology demonstrated by designers who became impressed with the need to take behavioral phenomena and dispositions into account in the design process, it does not seem that the very real glass-and-cement curtain separating the two groups has become notice- ably easier to penetrate. Not only has there been a dearth of collaborative research, but one senses a fundamental disillusion on the part of the designer with the abstractions of behavioral scientists, their hedged con- clusions, and their reluctance to offer specific recommendations for or solutions to design problems.

Landscape Architecture

To the extent that landscape architects represent a profession closely related to that of architecture and engaged in similar types of activities, it might be thought that what was said above about architecture could be readily extended to cover this field as well. But there are important differ- ences between the two professions that vitiate any such blithe generaliza- tion. To begin with, landscape architecture and practicing landscape architects in particular have not by and large had to face the urgent concerns relating to user satisfaction and behavioral efficacy of their designs that architects have. As an exception to this rule, one might cite the problems encountered in the design of public parks, particularly in urban areas, where landscape architects and other professional groups have had to confront the frequent pattern of underuse (Gold, 1977; Jacobs, 1961), ascribable to fear of crime, racial tensions, and manifestations of territorial behavior by one group towards another. But the primary point of contact between landscape architects and psychologists has been over questions of the aesthetic impact of the landscape on the person, and so the former have looked to the latter for information that might confirm or possibly challenge intuitions concerning the way people respond to landscapes and scenic areas.

These different orientations towards behavioral information on the part of architecture and landscape architecture appear to relate to rather broader differences in view point in regard to the role of behavior in their respective domains of work. At the risk of painting two extremes that are inevitably caricatures of the two fields being compared, one might put the differences as follows. Architects are inclined to draw a direct, quasi-deterministic link between the environmental variables over which they have control through their designs and the behavior of their clients or users. They are consequently intent on creating designs that will optimize behavioral functioning and conversely on avoiding design solutions that may lead to unwonted forms of behavior, dissatisfaction on the part of the user, etc. Perin (1970) has presented a particularly thoughtful and sophisticated statement of this conception of behavior on the part of the designer. The landscape architect, on the other hand, sees behavior in predominantly aesthetic terms, i.e., relating to the individual's affective response to the environment, which plays the role of one element among a much larger set to be considered, including topographical and biotic ones. The clearest formulation of this point of view has come from the influential work of McHarg (1969), who has argued eloquently for the consideration of ecological principles and of the topographical characteristics of the land in the formulation of plans for land use and development in a particular area, such as beach-front location or along the borders of a river. Behavioral science would seem to be of little direct relevance in this conception, but landscape architects would still wish to be sensitive to the individual's affective response to different forms of development introduced into an area (e.g., Steinitz & Way, 1969; Wohlwill, 1979) as a further factor meriting their attention.

This rather different "world-view" of the landscape architect may explain why the repeated plaints from architects concerning the shortcomings of the answers provided by behavioral scientists have not had a parallel in this profession. By and large, landscape architects in academe have related easily and effectively to behavioral scientists. Some have translated their interest in aesthetics into research on "perceived visual quality" or similar behavioral variables, as in Zube, Pitt, and Anderson's (1975) work on assessment and evaluation of scenes in a rivershed region or in Steinitz and Way's (1969) attempt to measure the visual impact of man-made development on a natural areas. Others have confined themselves to a systematic descriptive analysis of the visual resource (e.g., Fabos, 1971; Litton, 1972) that could serve as a starting point for behavioral study. To the extent that such work has had an applied component (as it has had in most instances), it has been directed more at planners and environmental managers, frequently working on a regional scale, rather than at the work of the individual practicing landscape architect. The latter, on the other hand, seems not to have experienced the need for behavioral information to the same degree and as acutely as have architects.

This does not, however, mean that the relationship between landscape architecture and psychology has been free of problems or difficulties. Perhaps the major and certainly the most interesting ones have centered around the approach to be taken to the definition and specification of the environmental dimensions that are to be related to behavioral measures. This issue arose previously in the discussion of geography's relation to environmental psychology, and of the place of topographically defined dimensions as opposed to the use of more abstracted dimensions of psychological relevance. Much of the work emanating from the direction of landscape architecture and related fields (e.g., Fabos, Hendrix, & Greene, 1975; Leopold, 1971; Zube et al., 1975) has taken an approach in this regard that could be termed eclectic and perhaps inconsistent. It has utilized a mixture of variables referring to physical and topographically defined properties on the one hand (e.g., amount of relief, topographical texture, amount of tree cover) along with others that are essentially properties of the landscape conceived in perceptual terms (amount of contrast, complexity, depth of view).

This point bears closer examination since it reflects a more pervasive source of difficulty in the confluence of environmental and behavioral disciplines, one that might be construed, in Brunswik's (1956) terms, as a difference between distal and proximal definitions of the environmental variables. A possible resolution of the problem might take the form of a two-phase approach that has in the past been inappropriately collapsed into a single one. A set of abstracted environmental dimensions is required that will be directly relatable to behavioral responses through their direct reference to psychologically relevant characteristics of the environment, such as brightness, diversity, contrast, openness, unity, etc. But if the work is to become relevant to the concerns of the landscape architect or the land-use planner, some prior translation scheme needs to be devised that will allow one to interrelate topographically defined characteristics with those of psychological relevance. It is this step that seems to have been generally ignored in this field, and yet it could represent a fruitful point of contact between the landscape architect, planner, or natural resource specialist and the behavioral scientist.[3]

Natural Recreation

Over the past decade, outdoor recreational behavior has come into the forefront of applied environmental-behavioral science as a flourishing, lively research area. This has occurred partly in response to the increasingly intractable problems of managing natural recreation areas under the pressure of ever-increasing numbers of visitors in such a way as to preserve the scenic and ecological qualities of those areas. Additionally, significant perceptual, motivational, and social phenomena of direct relevance to behavioral science were encountered in this domain. Thus, attention has been focused on such issues as whether visitation of wilderness areas is based on familiarity, as opposed to a "compensatory" principle, in terms of the relation between recreationists' home environment and their preferred recreational environments (Mercer, 1976), or whether mechanisms of response to "social overload" such as observed in cities (Milgram, 1970) apply to people's response to others encountered on trails (Lee, 1977). This type of concern has helped to deepen the theoretical interest in what otherwise has admittedly been a predominantly descriptive and narrowly applied field.

From the standpoint of interdisciplinary relations, however, perhaps work that has focused on the concept of "carrying capacity" is the most interesting, even though to date those who have concerned themselves with it have been drawn from economics (Greist, 1976), sociology (Heberlein, 1977), and natural resource management (Lime & Stankey, 1971) rather than psychology proper. Carrying capacity refers to the amount of use that a given place or area, such as a park, a riverbed, or a seashore strip, can tolerate. As Heberlein (1977) has noted, there are at least four separable uses of the term, each implying its own frame of reference, and set of criteria for determining such capacity. There is, first, the sheer physical space available, which sets upper bounds to the number of visitors that could be accommodated. This may be contrasted, second,

---

[3]This two-step process brings to mind Gibson's (1979) account of perception in terms of ecological properties of the environment that are conveyors of essential information for the perceiver.

with the area's ecological carrying capacity, i.e., the amount of use that an area can stand before the quality of its flora and fauna is seriously and irreversibly impaired. The facilities available (e.g., in terms of number of campsites, parking spaces, etc.) represent a third type of limitation on visitor use, this one being clearly relative to the users' demands for facilities (e.g., in a true wilderness area or a beach front, no facilities at all would be required). Finally, there is the social side of carrying capacity, that is, the number or density of encounters with other people that the user finds tolerable without detriment to enjoyment of the outdoor experience—clearly again a relative matter, depending on the user's frame of reference or expectations and obviously differing as between backpackers or riverrunners, as opposed to autocampers, skiers, etc.

A truly interdisciplinary attack on the determination of carrying capacity would entail a study of interrelationships among the various aspects that have been differentiated above. In particular the *reciprocal* relationship between the impact of human use and provision of increased facilities on the ecological quality of the area and the reverse effect of the changed appearance and condition of the area on the individual's response bears examining. (This suggests, incidentally, a fifth possible psychological aspect of carrying capacity, i.e., the amount of development imposed on the area and of change in its appearance that the user will accept.) Such a reciprocal analysis represents a special case of a systems-analytic approach that would tie together the state of an ecosystem or environment with the individual's response to the area and behavior within it. A rapprochement between environmental psychology and environmental science along these lines remains as yet purely ideal. It would presuppose, at the least, a much more effective mode of interrelating and much greater collaborative effort among the diverse disciplines involved in this problem area than has been witnessed to date.

Conclusion

The preceding review has focused on differences in the ways in which the fields of architecture, landscape architecture, and natural recreation relate to psychology. In spite of the differences in outlook, problem definition, views of the place of empirical evidence, etc., that separate such professional fields from the academic ones, it seems, somewhat paradoxically, that members of these professions have related much more closely and effectively to psychologists than have environmentally oriented workers in its sister social sciences. The fact is that it would be far easier to name psychologists who have worked in very close collaboration with professional groups (e.g., Bechtel, Canter, and Sommer for architecture and design; Craik and S. Kaplan for landscape architecture;

Daniel and R. Kaplan for natural resource management), than it would be to name environmental psychologists working closely with other social scientists. (The collaboration with geographers on problems of mental mapping represents but a very limited exception.)

There are probably several different reasons underlying this seeming greater rapport between environmentally oriented psychologists with those in applied fields and professions, as opposed to other environmental social sciences, including possible opportunities to contribute to applied, problem-solving directed efforts. Undoubtedly, however, a major factor at work here is that which was alluded to in comparing the two types of fields in the introduction to this essay: the intrinsically complementary nature of psychology's relation to environmental professions, as opposed to the more nearly competitive character of relations among different social sciences. For psychologists to collaborate with political scientists or economists in an attack on issues of environmental pollution, for instance, would presume a readiness to overcome barriers that derive from the very differing conceptual frameworks utilized by each in approaching problems. Some of these differences were noted at various points of the preceding review. Thus, this kind of collaboration would demand a readiness to transcend the limits of individual disciplinal perspectives and to integrate them into some overarching systemic framework. The final section of this essay will examine the possibilities for developing such a framework and of psychology's potential place in it.

THE PLACE OF PSYCHOLOGY IN THE STUDY OF ENVIRONMENTAL SYSTEMS

Psychology has traditionally placed a major emphasis on the role of the environment in behavior, and it has stressed the importance of environmental influences on behavior, as opposed, for example, to genetic or otherwise endogenous influences. To a certain extent the birth and growth of environmental psychology has served to give more explicit form to our recognition of this focal role accorded to the environment in our accounts of behavior, while at the same time extending our conception of environmental influences from its primary concern for the interpersonal, social, and cultural side to the physical domain. I have already considered some of the major forces that have been at work in determining the shape that the field has taken and the major trends discernible within it.

It remains apparent that psychology has to date played a minimal role in the study of environmental systems or the analysis of environmental problems. Thus, while such fields as economics, sociology, political science, and even history have spun off environmental specialties dealing with diverse social-science aspects of environmental issues, concern for such issues has played a minor role at best in environmental psychology.

This point was effectively documented by Cone and Hayes (1977) in a survey of the articles that appeared in the main journal in the field, *Environment and Behavior*. They showed that but a minute proportion dealt with environmental problems and with the effects of *behavior on the environment*, which they considered to be the proper subject of concern for an environmentally relevant field of environmental psychology. The balance has been redressed to some extent in more recent issues of the journal, which have increasingly included articles on the topic of environmental attitudes (though mostly from the direction of sociology and other, applied diciplines). Yet even these clearly fail to deal with the influence of human behavior on environmental quality that Cone and Hayes had in mind.

The reason for this state of affairs is apparent: Psychologists have been trained to look upon behavior as a dependent variable to be explained through functional relationships to independent variables, among which environmental factors have loomed prominent. The notion of reversing the direction of the B = f(E) formula probably appears strange and somehow as outside of the domain of psychology proper for many psychologists. Indeed, when seen in its simplest form, as for instance in a study of the environmental impact of visitor use of a wilderness area, there seems little of interest for the psychologist *qua* psychologist.

What, then, do Cone and Hayes consider to be the psychological relevance of this type of work? As exponents of the behavior-modification approach, they see here a possibility for the application of this technique in the service of improving environmental quality, and indeed their review presents extensive coverage of a considerable body of research dealing with behavior change applied to such diverse problems as energy use, transportation behavior, recycling, and noise abatement. Yet, if this were the main contribution that psychology had to make to environmental science, it would clearly remain of limited scope and would furthermore be confined to a purely intradisciplinary role. But there is no need to limit oneself to the rather narrow terms in which Cone and Hayes have conceived of the issue. By formulating the place of psychology in the study of environmental problems in a broader perspective, we arrive at a conception of the relationship between psychology and the environmental disciplines that, however idealized, will point to some potentially fruitful roles for psychology among these disciplines.

Consider the problem of noise. Noise can be studied as a type of environmental stimulus in terms of its impact on behavioral functioning, well-being, etc., that is as a standard problem for psychological research conforming to the B = f(E) paradigm. And so it has been studied, quite extensively, as part of the human factors branch of psychology (e.g., Kryter, 1970) as well as in research in social and personality psychology concerned with the individual's response to environmental stressors (e.g., Glass & Singer, 1972).[4] At the same time, noise has become identified as an environmental problem, akin to air and water pollution, toxic chemicals, and other hazards to our health. But, like at least some of these other problems, noise is also a *product of* our own behavior, and indeed we find it treated thus by Cone and Hayes, who cite a number of studies in which attempts have been made to reduce ambient noise levels through the application of behavior-modification techniques.

The circle has thus been closed, in a fashion that can be generalized to other environmentally relevant forms of behavior. That is, certain kinds of individual behavior produce noise, which in turn affects behavior in diverse ways—though, to be sure, not just the behavior of those making the noise but in some cases possibly excluding the originators of the noise (for instance, the operator of a power mower or the player of a radio going full blast may not be directly affected by it to the extent that those who are passively exposed to it are). Thus far, we have a situation that might be quite readily subsumed under other types of problems in psychology involving one person's behavior as a causal agent for another person's behavior—as in the study of aggression (e.g., Patterson, Littman, & Bricker, 1967). The treatment of the problem of noise as an environmental issue can, however, be considerably enlarged beyond the realm of psychology, even where it does not result from an individual's behavior, but serves as an aversive stimulus interfering with optimal behavioral functioning.

The point is effectively illustrated by reference to the problem of noise in the vicinity of airports. Such noise may affect the well-being of individuals residing in the neighborhood, the functioning of social groups and institutions such as schools (and thus the economy of the community), and even the biota in the area. The exposed individuals may respond to the situation with differing adaptive mechanisms, including attempts to adjust to the conditions (e.g., by sound-proofing their homes), to change their environment, or to take community action to lessen their exposure to noise. Depending on the relative predominance of these various responses, varying effects may result on the social and economic life of the communities affected, from virtual abandonment of the area by segments

---

[4]It is recognized that the B = f(E) formula is grossly oversimplistic, particularly in its failure to accord a role to the organism as a modulator of response to the environment. This is brought out clearly in Glass and Singer's own work, with its emphasis on the role of "perceived control" on the part of the subject as a factor that may mitigate the effects of environmental stressors.

of the population able to do so—as happened in the vicinity of the Los Angeles Airport—to unification of the community in resistance to plans for airport expansion that might intensify the problem—as in the case of Logan Airport in the Boston area.

It is significant, consequently, that the problem of noise has inspired some of the most wide-ranging interdisciplinary efforts in the environmental area in which psychologists have taken part. A good case in point at the level of research is the impressive project to study adaptation to ambient environmental noise levels carried out in the vicinity of a major airport in Germany (Deutsche Forschungsgemeinschaft, 1974), which included representatives from physiology, medicine, and sociology, along side experimental, personality, and social psychologists. Similarly, at the level of environmental problem-solving, there is the example of the multidisciplinary team of experts from the natural and social sciences, and from diverse environmental and engineering professions convened by the National Academy of Sciences (McGrath, 1971). This group was charged to formulate recommendations in regard to a proposed extension of the runways of a major urban airport; that development would have had a severe impact on neighboring residents as well as on the biota of a near-by Wildlife Refuge; and McGrath presents an interesting account of the manner in which the group fulfilled this objective.

Considering now environmental processes in a more general sense, what place should be accorded to psychology in their analysis? Since our discipline has only rarely been included in the discussion of such issues, let alone in research in a multidisciplinary context, the answer to this question must remain quite tentative and speculative at this point, and quite possibly idealized. Yet it seems worth attempting a preliminary analysis of the matter.

Such an analysis must necessarily take as a starting point a conception of psychology in which behavior plays neither the part of a dependent variable that varies as a function of environmental variables, as in most psychological research, nor that of an independent variable that exerts effects on the environment. Rather behavior must be treated as an element in a field of forces that interact with one another, standing in a relationship of partial reciprocity and mutual interdependence. It is worth noting that such a conception is implicit in socio-psychological work by Stern (1976) and Edney (1979), which attempts to use a gaming technique to simulate group behavior in the face of an exhaustable resource, based on Hardin's (1968) concept of the "dilemma of the commons." Although this research is modeled on the work of social psychologists on the "prisoner's dilemma" problem, it does entail a reciprocity between behavior and a resource, and it attempts to induce a behavior change on the basis of the participants' recognition of this reciprocity. As Stern (personal communication) notes, this work has a close parallel in work in political science and economics (as the economist's concept of "externalities"), though communication across disciplines on this basic issue of environment-behavior interaction is all too rare.

Expanding on this socio-psychological paradigm, a framework is needed that will bring individual behavior into relationship with processes operating within the physical environment at all levels, from that of the ecosystem as a biological system to that of institutional, societal, technological, and economic forces. This is admittedly a very tall order, and difficult conceptual and methodological issues will need to be resolved and institutional obstacles overcome if even a start in that direction is to be undertaken. Before considering these difficulties, however, it may be helpful to illustrate the conception of behavior and its role in the environmental context that is being proposed by reference to a prototype case taken from the domain of human activity in natural-recreation areas.

A phenomenon all too well known in the field of management of natural recreation areas is what might loosely be called the "Yosemite syndrome." A particular area of exceptional scenic attractiveness generates visitors at an accelerating rate; steps are taken to accommodate the increase and the demands made by the stream of users for services and facilities, resulting (1) in a marked alteration of the natural character of the area and deterioration of both its ecological quality and aesthetic values and at the same time (2) in further increases in visitor use, resulting from the improved facilities, etc. There is a more basic process underlying this phenomenon that is of major theoretical interest and deserving of attention on the part of behavioral-environmental scientists. The process in question clearly involves a positive feedback cycle, and the question arises as to its nature and origin, as well as its susceptibility to alteration.

Note, first, the direction of the feedback cycle. One might suppose that the relationship between environmental quality and visitor appeal of an area conforms to a *negative* feedback process: As use exceeds capacity and environmental quality start deteriorating, use will diminish (as a result of decreased satisfaction derived from it), and the area will have a chance to recover and revert to its earlier state of high appeal. Yet such an equilibrium process is not typically observed; rather, increase in use seems to result in increased development and provision of facilities, generating further increase in use, quite independent of its impact on the environment and appeal—until the problem of managing the area becomes so intractable as to demand deliberate counteraction, as has in fact happened in Yosemite. But how can such a positive feedback cycle operate, in seeming opposition to the declining qualities of the environment that served as the presumed reason for the popularity of the area for prospective users? The answer appears to lie in the role of a process of

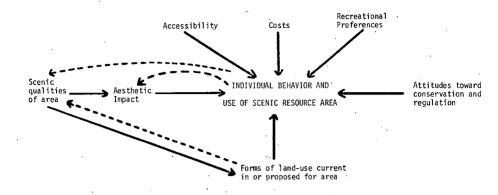

FIG. 1. Schema to represent individual behavior in and use of a scenic natural resource area as a function of environmental, attitudinal, economic, societal, and other variables.

self-selection whose effect is to replace visitors in search of an unde-veloped natural environment for their recreation surroundings with those with different expectations and motivations for their recreational experi-ence, and thus tolerating, or indeed demanding more services and facilities. There is good evidence for the operation of such self-selection (see Wohlwill & Heft, 1977).

The above example of the "Yosemite syndrome," illustrating the recip-rocal relationship between environmental and behavioral variables, is ad-mittedly fairly simplistic, and its analysis is limited to only a few disciplines: the ecological sciences, the behavioral sciences, and those in applied areas such as outdoor recreation, forestry, and natural resource management. But it is not difficult to expand on this scheme so as to model more complex cases that involve a much larger and diverse array of interdependent factors. Examples would be scenic areas (such as a sea-side or mountain resort) that are open to industrial and commercial de-velopment and to the provision of attendant services such as transportation, food, and housing for the tourist, etc. The situation is illustrated in Figures 1 and 2.

Figure 1 conforms to a paradigm typical of psychological analysis in-volving a relationship between a behavioral variable and others that co-determine it. Yet it is apparent even here that the variables represented by these determinants are of very different types. They include physical-environmental variables relating to the scenic quality of the area that are, in principle, grist for the mill of a psychological analysis based in princi-ples of environmental aesthetics, together with others that are themselves of a psychological kind, such as recreational preference and attitude toward conservation, and thus require a correlational model of analysis. Still others are more indeterminate or indirect in their influence on behavior, such as cost, access, and societal land use; they probably operate to a considerable extent through constraints placed on behavior.

Figure 2 has at its focus the variable of land-use—a concept that is not only non-behavioral, but mixed as to its disciplinary status, containing aspects of geography, political science, economics, and even ecology. Here we find psychological variables, notably attitudes toward development or conservation, and to a lesser extent individual behavior or use of the resource, contributing to the determination of the type of land use that might be made of a natural resource. In other words, behavior now takes on the role of a quasi-independent variable, alongside other, probably more potent non-behavioral variables.

Clearly the complexity of a system such as that represented in Figures 1 and 2 increases exponentially as additional variables are incorporated into it, suggesting the application of computer modeling along the lines of the Club-of-Rome population-environment projections (Meadows, Meadows, Randers, & Behrens, 1972). Precisely such an approach has been adopted to model the growth of a small Tyrolean winter-recreation resort (Ives & Stites, 1975), although individual-behavioral variables did not figure very prominently in that analysis. Nevertheless, this work, and more generally the type of problem conforming to the schemata shown in Figures 1 and 2,

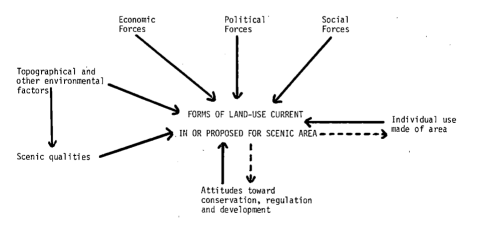

FIG. 2. Schema to represent influences on forms of land use in a scenic area, including environmental, economic-political-social, and attitudinal-behavioral factors.

clearly calls for broad-based interdisciplinary collaboration to do justice to the intricacies of behavioral analysis in the context of environmental systems.

In order to provide a viable conceptual underpinning for this type of systems analysis of the interaction of natural and social forces, it is necessary to come to grips with the fundamental issue of the nature of the relationship between an ecosystem and human behavior. Willems (1973, 1978) has persuasively argued that the type of phenomena characteristic of ecological systems (such as interdependence of elements, effects of intervention in one part of the system spreading throughout the system, etc.) operate at the level of environment-behavior interactions. He therefore suggests that the ecological perspective is fully relevant to the study of behavior. But he has been primarily interested in extending the framework of ecosystem analysis from the level of natural biological ecosystem functioning to that of human behavior. The question remains whether the interaction of man with the ecosystem is itself amenable to analysis in terms of ecosystem principles or whether human behavior must be considered as somehow external to such functioning. Writing from the perspective of anthropology, Bennett (1976) has presented a compelling analysis of both natural and cultural ecological systems, as well as of the impact of one on the other, and has pointed persuasively to fundamental differences between the two. These differences relate in part to the role of cognition, both at the level of individual behavior and as elaborated through cultural value systems and institutions, in modulating and even overriding the operation of natural ecological systems. Similarly, the instrumentalities of the food production system of a particular culture, and more especially of technological inventions, have radically altered the mode of operation of ecosystems and of the self-regulatory processes governing them.[5]

In a different vein, Klausner (1972) maintains that there is an unbridgeable conceptual gap between natural and social systems, i.e., that there is no way in which the physio-biological processes operating within an ecosystem can be brought into direct relationship with those of a social system; there is a basic discrepancy in the nature of the forces at work in each case such that there is no way of handling the interaction between

---

[5]This attempt to fit a highly detailed, thoroughly worked-through analysis of the complex interrelationships between behavioral and cultural mechanisms and ecological systems into a capsule-form statement inevitably fails to do justice to the subtleties of Bennett's theoretical argument. His book, *The Ecological Transition,* is strongly recommended to any reader interested in the problem of the interplay between environmental processes and social or cultural systems.

them. The point might be illustrated with reference to the concept of energy. This concept has a clear and readily operationalizable meaning at the physical level; it can at the same time be applied in a metaphorical extension to the functioning of social groups (cf. Odum, 1971). Yet, notwithstanding attempts such as Odum's to apply systems-theoretical analysis to encompass physical and human-social energy systems within a single framework, there does not seem to be any way of making the two energies interlock: There is no principle of energy conservation that would allow us to relate changes in the social structure to changes in the consumption of power.

These objections to incorporating human behavior into the analysis of biological ecosystems appear cogent enough in analyzing the changes occurring in natural recreation areas or in the natural niche occupied by small localized cultural groups. Yet they do not invalidate the rationale for examining the mode of interaction between individual behavior and the ecosystem, even if they suggest that we may have difficulty in analyzing the two as part of a single system. Indeed Klausner (1977) himself presents an interesting analysis of the relationship between social systems and mechanisms for the production and consumption of energy starting from the role of available energy in potentiating social institutions. He notes a variety of effects of an energy-based technology on social institutions including differentiation, dispersal, and shifts in the locus of power. Similarly, Bennett (1976) provides illuminating examples of the interrelationship between culture and natural-resource availability as a function in part of the food-production mechanisms devised by the culture. These writers give us reason to feel confident about the prospects of bringing behavior into relationship with environmental forces, since these represent the stimuli that instigate behavior.

CONCLUSIONS

The problems of interdisciplinary education and research in academic settings have received more than adequate attention in the literature (see Luszki, 1958; Nilles, 1976; Wolman, 1977) and thus need not be reviewed here in detail. There are, however, some issues that appear to apply more specifically to the relationship between environmental psychologists and those in other environmentally oriented fields that warrant closer scrutiny.

It is interesting, first, that collaborative research between psychologists and those in other disciplines in this avowedly interdisciplinary field is the exception rather than the rule. This point emerges clearly from a survey of the articles that have been published in the major journal in the field, *Environment and Behavior*. The papers published in this journal represent a broad array of disciplines, and psychology is quite prominently represented among them—out of the total of 224 papers published through Volume 10, 117 included a psychologist as either sole or joint author. Yet relatively few of these papers are co-authored by persons from some other discipline. Specifically, of the papers with psychologists as authors, 35% have but a single author. Another 47% have two or more psychologists writing jointly, leaving only 18% as instances of psychologists involved in interdisciplinary collaboration. Of the 21 papers in this group, most involve the two fields of geography (6) and architecture and urban systems or design (7), the remainder being scattered across such fields as civil engineering, science education, forestry, etc.

This result is not really surprising and probably not very different from the situation in other academic disciplines such as sociology and geography. Yet in psychology it may have a more deep-seated basis, one that raises a major question concerning the potential for future expansion and development of this field. For what we find is that individual psychologists have made forays into this area from most diverse directions—personality, social psychology, perception, motivation, human factors, etc.—to the extent of offering courses, undertaking sporadic research, and even writing textbooks (e.g., Bell et al., 1978) and theoretically oriented monographs (Mehrabian & Russell, 1974). But they have done so while remaining squarely identified not only with their parent discipline of psychology, but typically with their within-psychology specialty as well (e.g., child psychology, social psychology, personality), rather than that of environmental psychology. It is thus not surprising that they have made minimal efforts to relate to workers with relevant interests in other disciplines.

The other side of this coin is that formal programs in environmental psychology and even more than those outside of psychology departments, conceived of along interdisciplinary lines, such as those in man-environment relations, human or social ecology, etc., have remained few in number. Various factors may have contributed to this failure of the field to establish itself more securely, including the general retrenchment that universities are currently experiencing. Yet surely a more fundamental reason lies in the fact than an environmental focus has not as yet been generally accepted by psychology as a legitimate basis for the definition of a research problem, let alone the structuring of a program of graduate-level training. Ironically, part of the problem is probably that, as noted in the Introduction, the role of environmental influences on behavior is taken by most psychologists for granted, and as too generally applicable to a broad array of aspects of behavior to warrant choosing it as a topical focus for the definition of a program or a subspecialty. The result has been a position of benign neglect at best on the part of psychology generally towards environmental psychology and a corresponding mistrust of psychologists' involvement in this area under the auspices of some professionally oriented or interdisciplinary program focused on environmental issues.

This statement requires qualification to the extent that some environmental concerns are in and of themselves of relevance to psychology. The case of noise discussed above serves as a good example, but others could be cited, such as effects of pollution, etc., on behavior and mental health, affective and evaluative reactions to the physical environment, both natural and man-made, and effects of environmental stress on behavioral functioning. But, for reasons examined earlier, this type of psycho-centered formulation of an environmental problem is inadequate for attempts to incorporate behavioral concerns into an analysis of more broadly defined environmental issues, which presupposes a willingness, as pointed out, to allow behavior to assume the role of an element in a system, rather than treating it exclusively as an object of explanation.

Such obstacles to an involvement by psychologists in the study of environmental problems seem to be augmented by a definite reluctance on the part of the environmental disciplines to recognize the potential contribution of psychology to the analysis of such problems. In sharp contrast to other social sciences, such as geography, economics, political science, and sociology, psychology has not been represented on the staff of any of the major centers or institutes for environmental research or on the faculties of any of the various programs of environmental studies that have sprung up, particularly at the undergraduate level, in diverse institutions. The explanation must relate to the conception of psychology held by those outside of our field. Perhaps there is an assumption that, to the extent that environmental problems call for behavioral scientists at all, the environmental scientist should turn to those involved with behavior at the institutional, societal, or cultural level, rather than at the level of the individual and his or her motivations, expectations, etc.[6]

As a result, opportunities for environmentally focused teaching, re-

---

[6]The perception of psychology as quite divorced from the realm of environmental concerns seems somehow epitomized in the representation accorded to it in a volume dedicated to an overview of approaches to environmental issues from diverse disciplines, ranging from biology and chemistry to theology and literature (Utton & Henning, 1974). Psychology is represented by no more than an essay, conspicuous for its brevity, consisting of a psychiatrist's speculations on the individual's need for wilderness.

search, and consultation on the part of psychologists remain almost exclusively limited to certain of the professional fields, notably the design professions, which have recognized the potential contribution of psychology to their concerns and indeed have sought out the collaboration and assistance of psychologists to help them approach their problems more effectively. It is in this area that we may look for further active involvement on the part of psychologists, presumably to the benefit of both sides.

To conclude, then, what are the prospects for the development of a broadly integrative, conceptually-grounded behavioral science applied to environmental issues, or to an effective synthesis of behavioral and social sciences with environmental sciences? The prospects appear highly problematic for several reasons. One is that, while innovative teaching programs focused on environmental problems have managed to get some foothold, the academic establishment has remained consistently hostile to the development of graduate-level programs in this area, whether through Centers or Institutes for Environmental Studies or through the inauguration of new innovative programs or interdisciplinary academic units focused on environmental issues.

Yet an effective program of research converging on environmental problems from diverse directions, including both natural and social science perspectives, would seem to presuppose more formal, autonomous training programs for interdisciplinary research. Regrettably, those research-sponsoring institutions that have been interested in stimulating such a concentrated attack have at the same time done little to prod academic institutions to initiate training programs for the type of research that these problems demand. Thus the prospect is rather for a continuation of a pattern for particular individuals to collaborate on the study of some problem that happens to be of interest to them or because research funds happen to be available. This pattern rarely appears to straddle the boundary between the natural and social sciences and generally leaves psychology out of the picture altogether.

Thus, in the environmental arena, psychology is likely to play a peripheral role at best for some time to come. Paradoxically, the environment appears as a very distant star for psychology to link up with; it will take a major paradigmatic shift in the Kuhnian sense to bring such a linkage about.

ACKNOWLEDGMENT

The author is indebted to Paul Stern and Willem van Vliet for their helpful comments and criticisms of an earlier draft of this essay.

REFERENCES

Altman, I. Some perspectives on the study of man-environment phenomena. *Representative Research in Social Psychology*, 1973, *4*(1), 109–126.

Altman, I. *Environment and social behavior: Privacy, personal space, territoriality, crowding*. Monterey, CA: Brooks/Cole, 1975.

Altman, I. Environmental psychology and social psychology. *Personality and Social Psychology Bulletin*, 1976, *2*, 96–113.

Appleyard, D. Styles and methods of structuring a city. *Environment and Behavior*, 1970, *2*, 100–118.

Barker, R. G. *Ecological psychology: Concepts and methods for studying the environment of human behavior*. Stanford, CA: Stanford University Press, 1968.

Becker, G. M., & McClintock, C. G. Value: Behavioral decision theory. *Annual Review of Psychology*, 1967, *18*, 239–286.

Becker, R. H. Social carrying capacity and user satisfaction: An experiential function. *Leisure Sciences*, 1978, *1*, 241–258.

Bell, P. A., Fisher, J. D., & Loomis, R. J. *Environmental psychology*. Philadelphia, PA: Saunders, 1978.

Bennett, J. W. *The ecological transition: Cultural anthropology and human adaptation*. New York: Pergamon Press, 1976.

Berlyne, D. E., & Madsen, K. B. (Eds.). *Pleasure, reward, preference*. New York: Academic Press, 1973.

Booth, A. *Urban crowding and its consequences*. New York: Praeger, 1976.

Bornstein, M. H., & Bornstein, H. G. The pace of life. *Nature*, 1976, *259*, 557–559.

Brody, E. B. (Ed.). *Behavior in new environments*. Beverly Hills, CA: Sage, 1969.

Brunswik, E. Organismic achievement and environmental probability. *Psychological Review*, 1943, *50*, 255–272.

Brunswik, E. *Perception and the representative design of psychological experiments*. Berkeley, CA: University of California Press, 1956.

Bruvold, W. H. Belief and behavior as determinants of environmental attitudes. *Environment and Behavior*, 1973, *5*, 202–218.

Burton, I., Kates, R. W., & Kirkby, A. V. T. Geography. In A. E. Utton & D. H. Henning (Eds.), *Interdisciplinary environmental approaches*. Costa Mesa, CA: Educational Media Press, 1974.

Burton, I., Kates, R. w., & White, G. F. *The environment as hazard*. New York: Oxford University Press, 1978.

Buttel, F. H., & Flinn, W. L. The politics of environmental concern: The impact of party identification and political ideology on environmental attitudes. *Environment and Behavior*, 1978, *10*, 17–36.

Cone, J. D., & Hayes, S. Applied behavior analysis and the solution of environmental problems. In I. Altman & J. F. Wohlwill (Eds.), *Human behavior and the environment: Advances in theory and research* (Vol. 2). New York: Plenum, 1977.

Craik, K. H. Environmental psychology. In *New directions in psychology* (Vol. 4). New York: Holt, Rinehart & Winston, 1970.

Craik, K. H. Appraising the objectivity of landscape dimensions. In J. V. Krutilla (Ed.), *Natural environments*. Baltimore, MD: Johns Hopkins University Press, 1972.

Deutsche Forschungsgemeinschaft. *Fluglarmwirkungen: Eine interdisziplinare Untersuchung uber die Auswirkungen des Fluglärms auf den Menschen*. Boppard (Germany): B. Boldt, 1974.

Downs, R. M. The cognitive structure of an urban shopping center. *Environment and Behavior,* 1970, *2,* 13–39.

Downs, R. M. & Stea, D. (Eds.). *Image and environment.* Chicago, IL: Aldine, 1973.

Dunlap, R. E., & Van Liere, K. D. Land ethic or golden rule? Comment on "Land ethic realized" by Thomas A. Heberlein. *Journal of Social Issues,* 1977, *33,* 200–207.

Dunlap, R. E., & Van Liere, K. D. The 'new environmental paradigm'. *Journal of Environmental Education,* 1978, *9*(4), 10–19.

Edney, J. J. The nuts game: A concise commons dilemma analog. *Environmental Psychology and Nonverbal Behavior,* 1979, *3,* 252–254.

Epstein, Y. M. Comment on environmental psychology and social psychology. *Personality and Social Psychology Bulletin,* 1976, *2,* 346–349.

Fabos, J. G. An analysis of environmental quality ranking systems. In U.S. Forest Service, *Recreation Symposium Proceedings.* Upper Darby, PA: Northeastern Forest Experiment Station, 1971.

Fabos, J. G., Hendrix, W. G., & Greene, C. M. Visual and cultural components of the landscape resource assessment model of the METLAND study. In E. H. Zube, R. O. Brush, & J. G. Fabos (Eds.), *Landscape assessment.* Stroudsburg, PA: Dowden, Hutchinson & Ross, 1975.

Fisher, A. C., & Krutilla, J. V. Determination of optimal capacity of resource-based recreation facilities. In J. V. Krutilla (Ed.), *Natural environments.* Baltimore, MD: Johns Hopkins University Press, 1972.

Fisher, A. C., Krutilla, J. V., & Cicchetti, C. J. Alternative uses of natural environments: The economics of environmental modification. In J. V. Krutilla (Ed.), *Natural environments.* Baltimore, MD: Johns Hopkins University Press, 1972.

Fischer, C. S. *The urban experience.* New York: Harcourt, Brace, and Jovanovich, 1976.

Galle, O. R., Gove, W. R., & McPherson, J. M. Population density and pathology: What are the relationships for man? *Science,* 1972, *176,* 23-30.

Gibson, J. J. *The ecological approach to visual perception.* Boston, MA: Houghton-Mifflin, 1979.

Glass, D. C., & Singer, J. E. *Urban stress.* New York: Academic Press, 1972.

Gold, S. M. Neighborhood parks: The non-use phenomenon. *Evaluation Quarterly,* 1977, *2,* 319–327.

Golledge, R. G., & Rushton, G. (Eds.). *Spatial choice and spatial behavior: Geographic essays on the analysis of preference and perceptions.* Columbus, OH: Ohio State University Press, 1976.

Gould, P., & White, R. *Mental maps.* Baltimore, MD: Penguin, 1974.

Greist, D. A. The carrying capacity of public wild land recreation areas: Evaluation of alternative measures. *Journal of Leisure Research,* 1976, *8*(4), 123–128.

Hardin, G. The tragedy of the commons. *Science,* 1968, *162,* 1243-1248.

Harrison, J., & Sarre, P. Personal construct theory, the repertory grid, and environmental cognition. In G. T. Moore & R. G. Golledge (Eds.), *Environmental knowing.* Stroudsburg, PA: Dowden, Hutchinson, & Ross, 1976.

Heberlein, T. A. The land ethic realized: Some social psychological explanations for changing environmental attitudes. *Journal of Social Issues,* 1972, *28,* 79–87.

Heberlein, T. A. Social psychological assumptions of user attitude surveys: The case of the Wildernism scale. *Journal of Leisure Research,* 1973, *5,* 18–33.

Heberlein, T. A. Density, crowding, and satisfaction: Sociological studies for determining carrying capacities. In *Proceedings: River recreation management and research symposium.* St. Paul, MN: North Central Forest Experiment Station (U.S. Forest Service), 1977. (General Technical Report NC-28).

Honikman, B. Personal construct theory and environmental evaluation. In W. F. Preiser

(Ed.), *Environmental design research* (Vol. 1) (Fourth International EDRA Conference). Stroudsburg, PA: Dowden, Hutchinson & Ross, 1973.

Ittelson, W. H., Proshansky, H. M., Rivlin, L. G., & Winkel, G. H. *An introduction to environmental psychology.* New York: Holt, Rinehart, and Winston, 1974.

Ives, J. D., & Stites, A. (Eds.). *Program on man and the biosphere (MAB).* Project 6: Impact of human activities on mountain and tundra ecosystems. Proceedings of the Boulder Workshop, July 1974. Boulder, CO: Institute for Arctic and Alpine Research, University of Colorado, 1975.

Jacobs, J. *The death and life of great American cities.* New York: Random House, 1961.

Kates, R. W. *Risk assessment of environmental hazard.* New York: Wiley, 1978.

Klausner, S. Z. Some problems in the logic of current man-environment studies. In W. R. Burch, N. H. Cheek, Jr., & L. Taylor (Eds.), *Social behavior, natural resources and the environment.* New York: Harper & Row, 1972.

Klausner, S. Z. Energy and the structure of society: Methodological issues. In I. Altman & J. F. Wohlwill (Eds.), *Human behavior and environment* (Vol. 2). New York: Plenum, 1977.

Kohn, I. *The migrant's experience: An adaptation-level view.* (Doctoral dissertation, Pennsylvania State University, 1976.) *Dissertation Abstracts International,* 1977, *37,* 3328B. (University Microfilms No. 76–29,650.)

Korte, C., & Kerr, N. Responses to altruistic opportunities under urban and rural conditions. *Journal of Social Psychology,* 1975, *95,* 183–184.

Krutilla, J. V. (Ed.). *Natural environments: Studies in theoretical and applied analysis.* Baltimore, MD: Johns Hopkins University Press, 1972.

Kryter, K. D. *The effects of noise on man.* New York: Academic Press, 1970.

Lee, R. G. Alone with others: The paradox of privacy in wilderness. *Leisure Sciences,* 1977, *1,* 3–20.

Leopold, L. Landscape esthetics. In A. Meyer (Ed.), *Encountering the environment.* New York: Van Nostrand, 1971.

Liben, L., Patterson, A. H., & Newcombe, N. (Eds.). *Spatial representation and behavior: Developmental and environmental approaches.* New York: Academic Press, 1981.

Lime, D., & Stankey, G. H. Carrying capacity maintaining outdoor recreation quality. In *Proceedings, Forest Recreation Symposium* (U.S. Forest Service, Syracuse, N Y, 1971). Upper Darby, PA: Northeast Forest Experiment Station, 1971.

Litton, R. B., Jr. Aesthetic dimensions of the landscape. In J. V. Krutilla (Ed.), *Natural environments.* Baltimore, MD: Johns Hopkins University Press, 1972.

Lowenthal, D., & Riel, M. The nature of perceived and imagined environments. *Environment and Behavior,* 1972, *4,* 189–208.

Luszki, M. B. *Interdisciplinary team research: Methods and problems.* Washington, D C: The National Training Laboratories, 1958.

Lynch, K. *The image of the city.* Cambridge, MA: M.I.T. Press, 1960.

Maloney, M. P., Ward, M. O., & Braucht, C. N. A revised scale for the measurement of ecological attitudes and knowledge. *American Psychologist,* 1975, *30,* 787–790.

McGrath, D. C., Jr. Multidisciplinary environmental analysis: Jamaica Bay and Kennedy Airport. *Journal of The American Institute of Planners,* 1971, *37,* 243–252.

McHarg, I. *Design with nature.* Garden City, NY: Natural History Press, 1969.

Meadows, D., Meadows, H. D., Randers, J., & Behrens. W. W. *The limits to growth: A report on the Club of Rome's project on the predicament of mankind.* New York: Potomac Associates and University Books, 1972.

Mehrabian, A., & Russell, J. A. *An approach to environmental psychology.* Cambridge, MA: M.I.T. Press, 1974.

Mercer, D. C. Motivational and social aspects of recreational behavior. In I. Altman & J. F. Wohlwill (Eds.), *Human behavior and environment* (Vol. 1). New York: Plenum, 1976.

160   WOHLWILL

Michelson, W. *Man and his urban environment: A sociological approach.* Reading, MA: University of Toronto Press, 1976.
Mikesell, M. W. The borderlands of geography as a social science. In M. Sherif & C. W. Sherif (Eds.), *Interdisciplinary relationships in the social sciences.* Chicago, IL: Aldine, 1969.
Milgram, S. The experience of living in cities. *Science,* 1970, *167,* 1461–1468.
Moore, G. T., & Golledge, R. G. (Eds.). *Environmental knowing.* Stroudsburg, PA: Dowden, Hutchinson & Ross, 1976.
Nagy, J. N. & Baird, J. C. Children as environmental planners. In I. Altman & J. F. Wohlwill (Eds.), *Human behavior and environment* (Vol. 3). New York: Plenum, 1978.
Nilles, J. Interdisciplinary research and the American university. *Interdisciplinary Science Reviews,* 1976, *1,* 160–166.
Odum, H. T. *Environment, power and society.* New York: Wiley, 1971.
O'Riordan, T. Attitudes, behavior, and environmental policy issues. In I. Altman & J. F. Wohlwill (Eds.), *Human behavior and environment* (Vol. 1). New York: Plenum, 1976.
Parke, R. D. Children's home environments: Social and cognitive effects. In I. Altman & J. F. Wohlwill (Eds.), *Human behavior and environment* (Vol. 3). New York, Plenum, 1978.
Parsons, H. M. Work environments. In I. Altman & J. F. Wohlwill (Eds.), *Human behavior and environment* (Vol. 1). New York: Plenum, 1976.
Patterson, G. R., Littman, R. A., & Bricker, W. Assertive behavior in children: A step toward a theory of aggression. *Monographs of the Society for Research in Child Development,* 1967, *32* (5, Whole No. 113).
Perin, C. *With man in mind.* Cambridge, MA: M.I.T. Press, 1970.
Peterson, G. L., & Neumann, E. S. Modeling and predicting human response to the visual recreation environment. *Journal of Leisure Research,* 1969, *1,* 219–237.
Proshansky, H. M., Ittelson, W. H., & Rivlin, L. G. *Environmental psychology: Man and his physical setting.* New York: Holt, Rinehart & Winston, 1970.
Siegel, A. W., Kirasic, K. C., & Kail, R. V. Stalking the elusive cognitive map: The development of children's representations of geographic space. In I. Altman & J. F. Wohlwill (Eds.), *Human behavior and environment* (Vol. 3). New York: Plenum, 1978.
Simon, H. A. *Models of man.* New York: Wiley, 1957.
Sims, J. H. & Baumann, D. D. The tornado threat: Coping styles of the North and the South. *Science,* 1972, *176,* 1386–1392.
Slovic, P., Kunreuther, H., & White, G. F. Decision processes, rationality, and adjustment to natural hazards. In G. F. White (Ed.), *Natural hazards: Local, national, global.* New York: Oxford University Press, 1974.
Sommer, R. Evaluation, yes; research, maybe. *Representative Research in Social Psychology,* 1973, *4*(1), 127–134.
Steinitz, C., & Way, D. A model for evaluating the visual consequences of urbanization. In C. Steinitz & P. Rogers (Eds.), *Qualitative values in environmental planning: A study of resource use in urbanizing watersheds* (Section III). Washington, D C: Office of Chief of Engineers, U.S. Army, 1969.
Stern, P. C. Effects of incentives and education on resource conservation decisions in a simulated commons dilemma. *Journal of Personality and Social Psychology,* 1976, *34,* 1285–1292.
Stockdale, J. E. Crowding: Determinants and effects. *Advances in Experimental Social Psychology,* 1978, *11,* 197–247.
Stokols, D. On the distinction between density and crowding: Some implications for future research. *Psychological Review,* 1972, *79,* 275–277.

Stokols, D. The experience of crowding in primary and secondary environments. *Environment and Behavior,* 1976, *8,* 49–86.

Stringer, P. Architecture, psychology, the game's the same. In D. V. Canter (Ed.), *Architectural psychology.* London: RIBA Publications, 1970.

Tognacci, L. N., Weigel, R. H., Wideen, M. F., & Vernon, D. T. A. Environmental quality: How universal is public concern? *Environment and Behavior,* 1972, *4,* 73–86.

Tolman, E. C. Cognitive maps in rats and men. *Psychological Review,* 1948, *55,* 189–208.

Utton, A. E., & Henning, D. H. (Eds.). *Interdisciplinary environmental approaches.* Costa Mesa, CA: Educational Media Press, 1974.

Wachs, T. D. Proximal experience and early cognitive–intellectual development: The physical environment. *Merrill-Palmer Quarterly,* 1978, *24,* 3–42.

Wedin, C., & Nygren, G. L. *Housing perspectives: Individuals and families.* Minneapolis MN: Burgess Publishing Co., 1979.

White, G. F. (Ed.). *Natural hazards: Local, national, global.* New York: Oxford University Press, 1974.

Wicker, A. *An introduction to ecological psychology.* Monterey, CA: Brooks/Cole, 1979.

Willems, E. P. Behavioral ecology and experimental analysis: Courtship is not enough. In J. R. Nesselroade & H. W. Reese (Eds.), *Life-span developmental psychology: Methodological issues.* New York: Academic Press, 1973.

Willems, E. P. Behavioral ecology. In D. Stokols (Ed.), *Perspectives on environment and behavior: Theory, research and applications.* New York: Plenum, 1978.

Wohlwill, J. F. The emerging discipline of environmental psychology. *American Psychologist,* 1970, *25,* 303–312.

Wohlwill, J. F. What belongs where: Experimental research on fittingness of man-made structures in natural settings. In T. C. Daniel, E. Zube, & B. C. Driver (Eds.), *Assessing amenity resource values.* Ft. Collins, CO: Rocky Mountain Forest and Range Experiment Station, U.S.D.A., 1979. (General Technical Report RM-68).

Wohlwill, J. F., & Heft, H. A comparative study of user attitudes towards development and facilities in two contrasting natural recreation areas. *Journal of Leisure Research,* 1977, *9,* 263–280.

Wohlwill, J. F., & Kohn, I. Dimensionalizing the environmental manifold. In S. Wapner, S. B. Cohen, & B. Kaplan (Eds.), *Experiencing the environment.* New York: Plenum, 1976.

Wolman, M. Interdisciplinary education: A continuing experience. *Science,* 1977, *198,* 798–804.

Yancey, W. L. Architecture, interaction, and social control: The case of a large scale housing project. In J. F. Wohlwill & D. H. Carson (Eds.), *Environment and the social sciences: Perspectives and applications.* Washington, D C: American Psychological Association, 1972.

Zube, E. H., Pitt, D. G., & Anderson, T. W. Perception and prediction of scenic resource values of the Northeast. In E. H. Zube, R. O. Brush, & J. G. Fabos (Eds.), *Landscape assessment.* Stroudsburg, PA: Dowden, Hutchinson & Ross, 1975.

6 Psychology and History

Robert Jay Lifton
Yale University

in collaboration with

Charles B. Strozier
Sangamon State University

INTRODUCTION

Granted there is such a thing as a psychohistorical approach, can one then speak of a new psychohistory? If so, one had best be tentative. Historians know well—and psychologists should know—that anything now new will soon be old and that one often labels as new that which does not yet quite exist. Plato, for example, in Books VIII and IX of the *Republic,* makes some strikingly original psychological observations on the link between a tyrant's dream life and his behavior. Psychohistory is in one sense already old and in another sense hardly born.

None can deny the logic of a marriage between psychology and history. Many writers from both traditions have emphasized their common concern with narrative sequence and with the nature of human experience in the midst of that sequence. But a certain amount of skepticism about logical marriages and their offspring is always in order. And the greater one's commitment to that marriage, the more convinced one becomes of the impossibility—and undesirability—of an easy union.

PROBLEMS

Skepticism is as good a principle as any for approaching psychohistory. Most people involved in the project are not only critical of traditional psychoanalytic views of history but skeptical of the kind of pristine cause and effect—and, therefore, of the kind of knowledge—claimed by any monocausal and hyperreductive approach to history. A simple commitment to develop a psychological framework that takes historical currents seriously is itself an act of skepticism toward the ahistorical position of most psychological thought. But that kind of skepticism must be distinguished from the automatic dismissal of all psychological approaches to history and even from the more subtle dismissal of psychological efforts by insisting that one cannot really know anything significant about the minds of people (great or ordinary) of the past or about the ways in which current individual and collective ideas and emotions connect with wider historical currents.

There are, then, three levels of skepticism: immediate and total rejection (the assumption that the knowledge sought is unobtainable and the whole enterprise futile); anticipated rejection (the attitude, "You have to show me"; implicitly, "I don't expect or wish to be shown"); and a sense, which the authors share with a number of colleagues in the enterprise, that the kind of knowledge sought is extremely refractory and the methods of seeking it highly vulnerable. That third stance turns out to be in many ways the most skeptical of all.

It is tempting, especially for those with clinical experience, to speak of those forms of skepticism that dismiss out of hand or nearly so as "resistance." The term suggests the kind of psychological force and need that can accompany the rejection. But the temptation itself should be resisted because the word, whether used by classical psychoanalysts or Protestant evangelists or Chinese thought reformers, also implies that there is a true direction or intention that is ultimately to be accepted, even embraced, once the resistance has been overcome. That last assumption, dubious enough when applied to an individual person, can be disastrous when applied to history. Moreover, by invoking the term "resistance," one can all too readily fall into the psychologistic fallacy of explaining away criticism by examining the critics' involvement and needs, thereby avoiding any consideration of the weaknesses of what is being criticized.

Yet the psychological approach to history does cause discomfort because it entails formidable problems in method and because, for many working in both traditions and in other branches of social thought, it threatens to undermine explicit concepts and implicit images about how people behave, why societies change, and what constitutes an acceptable professional discipline or field. People are all, in other words, formatively bound by their own psychohistorical place and by their activity in that place. And so they should be, at least to a point, if their skepticism is to be rooted, as well as fertile.

But what are the impediments? Why is it so difficult for psychology and history to get together? Generally speaking, the two traditions often work

at cross-purposes: Worse each shows something of an impulse to eliminate the other. And that is so even if one limits his observations to depth
psychology and to human-centered history.

For instance, there is in classical psychoanalysis an implicit assumption
that the larger historical universe is nothing but a manifestation of the
projections or emanations of the individual psyche. Or, if not that, history
is seen as a kind of featureless background for those projections and
emanations, something out there that is given but that does not
significantly influence what is in here. The emergence, over the past few
decades, of a more developed ego psychology has somewhat altered the
situation by directing attention to the influence of the environment on the
development of the self. But, as Erikson (1968a) pointed out, the grudging
and impoverished terms used in the psychoanalytic approach to the environment reveal the approach itself to have remained grudging and impoverished. Moreover, ego psychology has had little to say about shifts in
social ethos central to historical change, especially those shifts related to
the new technological environment and its destructive capabilities.

Neo-Freudian psychoanalysis has been ahistorical in other ways. More
open to the influence of environment, it has for the most part failed to
evolve compelling general principles in the social sphere. And where it
has actively sought such principles, it has tended to view a culture or a
society as a more or less cross-sectional entity within which one can study
the relation of social institutions and basic personality but not as evolving
phenomena whose relationship is importantly defined by change. Neo-
Freudian psychoanalysis still finds itself—as much as or, at times, even
more than the Freudian tradition it rebelled against—bound by certain
limitations of the rationalistic and mechanistic imagery of the nineteenth-
century world view. And when psychoanalysis has moved in a
phenomenological or existential direction, its intrapsychic insights, however valuable, have tended to be insulated from historical issues.

Historical writing seems, perhaps somewhat analogously, to replace a
psychological perspective with common sense assumptions about human
motivation. Such an approach presumably is more methodologically
sound and firmly grounded in empirical evidence. Furthermore, the emphasis in the last generation of historical writing on the experience of
ordinary people—social history, broadly considered—tends to drown the
psychological person, that is, the inner life of the individual person, in a
sea of collectivity. That such drowning is not necessary is shown by the
recent work by Demos, *Entertaining Satan* (1982). More commonly, however, Fernand Braudel (1976), in his study of sixteenth-century Mediterranean life, creates the sea itself as a main character washing on the
shores of a complex topography that shapes human society but minimizes
the psychological experience of people within that society.

And yet there is much evidence of a longing from both psychology and history for some kind of union, a widely shared recognition that the psychological person lives in a history extending beyond himself and that history is bound up with conflicts and struggles within the minds of people. Indeed, those two simple principles form the basis for a contemporary psychohistory.

FREUDIAN MODELS

Freud's most fundamental historical model was not really historical at all but rather, a prehistorical paradigm: the primeval encounter between father and sons, in which the sons rebel against the father's authority and kill him, with the entire encounter psychologically centered on the Oedipus complex. That model was first put forward in *Totem and Taboo* as an explanation for the origins of society itself and then again in modified form toward the end of Freud's life in *Moses and Monotheism* (Freud, 1939) to account for the origins of Jewish religion and Jewish identity, for how, as Freud put it, the "one man, the man Moses . . . created the Jews." Freud saw Moses as a kind of foster father, an Egyptian who chose the Jews as his people and gave to them the gift of monotheism, only to be rejected and murdered by his chosen people, his symbolic sons.

As Rieff (1971) pointed out, the model is that of "a certain event, or events, necessarily in remote rather than near history—indeed, at the beginning—becom[ing] determinative of all that must follow [p. 26]."

Rieff suggested that Freud was influenced by certain facets of Judeo-Christian millennial thought and of German historicism, according to which one crucial event determines and explains all subsequent and even previous history. The principle is that of *kairos,* of the decisive moment, as opposed to that of *chronos,* the more orderly sequence of qualitatively identical units of mathematical time. Freud's historical event can be said to be a mythical one—the primeval murder of the father, as allegedly reenacted in the Jews' murder of Moses. But it is also individual-psychological, in the sense of being a product of the Oedipus complex, which is seen as the ultimate source of those decisive occurrences. Indeed, Rieff argued that Freud's overall historical method can be seen as a kind of apologia for the Oedipal event.

There are powerful insights in the two books expressed around that prehistorical encounter, insights that center on the psychological significance of the perceived historical past for both present and future and for the movement of history itself. And that model has nourished more recent psychohistorical approaches. But, since the model is a

mythical one that transcends history as such, it can be profoundly misleading when used to explain specific historical events.

There is a current vogue among psychoanalytic and psychoanalytically-
minded observers of viewing recent student rebellions as little more than
a repetition of the primeval rebellion of enraged sons against their fathers,
as a rebellion explained by and reducible to the Oedipus complex. The
explanation happens to be congenial to those in authority, the symbolic or
formative fathers involved, but it totally neglects the larger historical
currents that forcibly intrude on the psyches of young and old alike and,
therefore, misrepresents both the individual psychological and the group
processes at play.

Within Freud's prehistorical paradigm there is an iron mold of psychological repetition or repetition-compulsion, enveloping indiscriminately
the individual person and the undifferentiated collectivity. When that
principle of repetition is seen as the essence of historical experience,
there can be nothing new in history; indeed, if in Rieff's paraphrase of
Freud "history is predestination," then there is no history.

The second Freudian paradigm is perhaps the more obvious one, the
one most likely to come to mind when people think of a psychoanalytic
approach to history: that of individual psychopathology. The best known
example here is the Bullitt-Freud (1967) biography of Woodrow Wilson, a
work that Bullitt almost certainly wrote but that exemplified the Freudian
approach to history; that of individual psychopathology. The best known
would care to admit. In language and quality of thought, the Wilson
biography is a vulgarization of the Freudian paradigm; Freud himself
never wrote without elegance. Erikson's (1967) review of the book is itself
an important statement on psychohistorical method. The idea of interpreting the outcomes of major historical events as expressions of the individual psychopathology of a particular national leader, in that case
Wilson's struggles with masculinity and his need to fail, was prefigured in
Freud's own work—not only in his treatment of men like Leonardo and
Dostoyevsky as great artists, rather than political leaders, but also in his
general focus on individual psychopathology as existing more or less
apart from history. When that second paradigm dominates, psychopathology becomes a substitute for the psychohistorical interface. The
psychopathological idiom for individual development, so prominent in the
literature of psychoanalysis, becomes extended to the point where it
serves as the idiom for history or psychohistory. When that happens,
there is, once more, no history.

Those two Freudian paradigms, the prehistorical conformation and the
leader's individual psychopathology, come together in their assumption
that, in one way or another, history represents the intrapsychic struggles
of the individual person writ large—the same intrapsychic struggles that

can be observed by the psychoanalyst in his therapeutic work. For instance, the scenario of *Totem and Taboo* includes not only the murderous rebellion against the father and the consuming of the father in the totem feast but the subsequent remorse and residual guilt of the sons and of their sons and daughters ad infinitum, a guilt that reasserts itself periodically in the phenomenon of the return of the repressed. The entire argument derives from an individual psychological model, and the return of the repressed becomes the basis for Freud's view of history as psychological recurrence. And in the individual psychopathological model, it is the aberration of a specific person that is writ large as historical explanation.

No wonder, then, that Freudian models are frustrating to the historian. They interpret but avoid history. They are equally problematic for the historically-minded psychologist. On the one hand, Freud's clinical method, as many have pointed out, is entirely historical. It works on the assumption that a person automatically reveals his personal history if he merely lets his mind wander freely—that is, if he engages in free association. And Freud's fundamental discoveries of the significance of individual and collective past provide the basis for psychohistory. On the other hand, those same Freudian principles, when applied with closed system finality, tend to reduce history to nothing but recurrence or repetition-compulsion and, thereby, tend to eliminate virtually all that is innovative or even accumulative in the story of humans.

The Faustian intellectual temptation is to dismiss the paradox and to make things simple either by direct and uncritical application of classical Freudian terms to all manner of historical events or by pretending that neither Freud nor the emotional turmoil he described and stimulated has ever existed. One would do better to embrace the paradox, for it can be energizing.

ERIKSON AND THE GREAT MAN IN HISTORY

Erik Erikson retained a focus on the individual—the great man—and on the kinds of inner conflicts illuminated by the Freudian tradition. But he placed the great man and psychobiography itself within a specific historical context—hence, the model of the great man in history or, more generally and specifically, the prominent person in history. With Erikson's elaboration of that paradigm, something approaching a new psychohistory began to take shape.

Erikson's (1958) *Young Man Luther,* a pivotal work for the psychohistorical enterprise, has a direct historical relation to Freud's *Moses and Monotheism*. Apart from Erikson's connection as a young man with the Freudian circle in Vienna and his continuing identification of himself as a

Freudian, his title is meant to echo Freud's phrase "the man Moses." Freud used that same phrase as his original title for the book he later called *Moses and Monotheism*. Freud's original subtitle was, *A Historical Novel*, which suggests an interesting element of self-irony in relation to a historical method one must now view as highly dubious, especially in regard to the kind of evidence Freud used to develop his thesis that Moses was an Egyptian and that Moses was killed by the Jews. That subtitle has also found another recent echo, probably less intentional—*History as a Novel, the Novel as History*—the subtitle chosen by Norman Mailer for his book *The Armies of the Night*. The self-irony in juxtaposing history and fiction does not necessarily suggest that either Freud or Mailer lacked belief in his own views but, rather, suggests that each felt he was dealing with a kind of truth that took him beyond conventional historical description. Each was suggesting a form of fictionalized truth or, perhaps, fiction truer than truth, rather than truth stranger than fiction.

There are other ways in which Erikson's concept of the great man parallels Freud's. In *Moses and Monotheism,* Freud (1939) argued that the great man influences his contemporaries through his personality and through the idea(s) for which he stands. The impact of the great man rests on his resonance with an old group of repressed wishes that reside in the masses *or* his capacity to define a new aim for their wishes.

Freud saw Moses as having taken the Jews to a higher level of spirituality largely by dematerializing God and prohibiting worship of a visible form of God. Similarly, Erikson (1958) saw as Luther's fundamental achievement his new emphasis on man in inner conflict and his salvation through introspective perfection, an achievement and an emphasis Erikson compared with Kierkegaard's existentialism and Freud's psychoanalysis. Freud and Erikson both depicted the great man as a spiritual hero, as a man who achieves an intrapsychic break-through.

But Erikson also took several crucial steps away from Freud. Instead of an instinctual idiom—Freud's view of the great man as appealing to instinctual wishes, particularly aggressive ones, and possessing the ability to bring about in the masses a form of instinctual renunciation (control of aggression and subordination of sense perception to abstract ideas)—Erikson sought out more specifically historical ground, the intersection of individual and collective histories. Luther's achievement, then, depended not so much on instinctual renunciation as on a quality Erikson saw in Luther, Gandhi, and Freud: a grim willingness to do the dirty work of their ages (Erikson, 1958, p. 9).

That dirty work, although clearly involved with psychological universals, is historically specific. "We cannot lift a case history out of history," Erikson (1958, pp. 15–16) wrote. And he felt constrained to ask of himself and of his readers the kind of immersion he imagined Luther to have had in such early sixteenth-century matters confronting the young German aspirant to the priesthood as the contradictions between ideal Catholic spirituality and the "high spiritual finance" of monetary purchase of immortality through the practice of indulgences, the influence of Occamism in Catholic theology, the prevailing child-rearing practices and standards of family (especially father-son) relations, the discipline of monastic training, and the complexities of the Catholic response to the Renaissance. All that leaves behind Freud's concept of the traumatic historical event, followed by repression, and then by the return of the repressed in the form of guilt and conflict. Of concern, instead, is the great man's monumental struggle, at the border of religion and politics, with his simultaneous effort to remake himself and his world. For Luther to emerge from his own identity crisis, he had to bring about a shift in the historical identity of his epoch. He had to engage in a desperate effort (Erikson, 1958) "to lift his individual patienthood to the level of the universal one, and to try to solve for all what he could not solve for himself alone [p. 67]."

By "patienthood," Erikson, here following Kierkegaard, meant exemplar of ultimate alternatives. And one of the extraordinary qualities of Erikson's rendition of the young Luther is the book's painstaking exploration of the tenuous psychic boundaries between identity crisis, psychosis, theological innovation, and individual and historical revitalization. What Erikson demonstrated in that study of Luther, as in his book on Gandhi, is a combination of psychoanalytic sensitivity and historical imagination. The combination has been long in coming. Other contributions in relation to that model include Bromberg(1971, 1974), Waite (1977), Zeligs (1967), Mack (1976), and Mazlish (1972).

But the great man tends to be inaccessible, at least to direct interview, or, if accessible, not yet great. One must usually approach him through records or, if he belongs to recent history, through interviews with surviving friends and followers. That does not mean that the psychohistorian cannot say useful things on the basis of careful observations from a distance. But when he is centuries removed from the person he wishes to study in depth, problems of historical reconstruction are inevitable.

Freud faced those problems with the cavalier grandiosity of a genius, as one particularly memorable footnote in *Moses and Monotheism* makes clear (Freud, 1939):

> I am very well aware that in dealing so autocratically and arbitrarily with Biblical tradition—bringing it up to confirm my views when it suits me and unhesitatingly rejecting it when it contradicts me—I am exposing myself to serious methodological criticism and weakening the convincing force of my arguments. But this is the only way in which one can treat material of which one knows definitely that its trustworthiness has been severely impaired by

the distorting influence of tendentious purposes. It is to be hoped that I shall find some degree of justification later on, when I come upon the track of these secret motives. Certainty is in any case unattainable and moreover it may be said that every other writer on the subject has adopted the same procedure [p. 27].

Although one cannot but admire Freud's honesty and boldness, the method seems a somewhat dubious one for the aspiring psychohistorian.

Erikson was much more careful with his historical data, but he, too, ran into difficulties. For instance, he was forced to recreate certain psychological themes of Luther's early life on the basis of very limited evidence. Problems were also raised about events in Luther's adult life, notably his celebrated fit in the choir, during which he made his dramatic statement of negation of identity: "I am not!" Erikson himself pointed out that it was not known whether Luther roared in Latin or in German, and others have questioned whether he roared at all—that is, whether the episode actually took place.

Apart from specific problems of reconstruction, there is the larger question of the extent to which any person, great or otherwise, can exemplify an entire historical epoch or even, as in Erikson's treatment of Luther, its major collective psychological struggles. The question takes on special force during the unprecedentedly diverse and fickle twentieth century and no less so if raised in connection with the past.

SHARED THEMES MODEL

A recent approach is that of shared psychohistorical themes, as observed in men and women exposed to particular kinds of individual and collective experience. Examples here are Keniston's (1965, 1968) studies of alienated and then activist American students and Robert Coles's (1967–1971) work with children and adults in the midst of racial antagonism and social change. The authors have also been much concerned with the development of the method.

Over a number of years a group has met at Wellfleet, Massachusetts, to discuss questions of theory and method (Lifton & Olson, 1974). In that group—which includes Norman Birnbaum, Peter Brooks, Robert Coles, Erik Erikson, Stuart Hampshire, Kenneth Keniston, Bruce Mazlish, Alexander Mitscherlich, and Philip Rieff—and in psychohistorical work in general, the conceptual stress is somewhat one-sided, more psychological than historical. That one-sidedness is problematic but probably necessary, since psychological theories themselves require much renewal and replacement if they are to make genuine historical connections.

Lifton conducted interview studies of four specific groups of people whose historical exposures seem to have a bearing on important characteristics of the present era: Chinese and Westerners who underwent Chinese thought reform or brainwashing (Lifton, 1961); Japanese university students during the early 1960s (Lifton, 1970); Hiroshima survivors of the atomic bomb (Lifton, 1968a); and antiwar Vietnam veterans (Lifton, 1973). The focus was on themes, forms, and images that are in significant ways shared, rather than on the life of a single person as such.

The shared themes approach is based on a psychoanalytically derived stress on what goes on inside of people. But, as compared with Erikson's great-man paradigm, it moves still further from classical analytic tradition. That is, it moves outward from the individual person in the direction of collective historical experience. It explicitly rejects the nineteenth-century scientific model of a person as a mechanism propelled by quantities of energy—energy internally generated by means of instinctual drives, partially held in check by certain defense mechanisms, notably repression, but eventually erupting in the form of various actions of the person directed at his outer environment. That instinctual idiom and world view gave way to a symbolic, formative one.

The shared themes approach is based on a psychoanalytically-derived interview method. For more than 20 years Lifton struggled with modifications of the psychiatric and psychoanalytic interview in order to approach and understand various kinds of people who have not sought therapeutic help but, on the contrary, have been sought out by him, not because of particular experiences they have undergone—experiences that may be and usually have been disturbing—but because those experiences may have wider significance than any individual incapacities, psychological or otherwise. Lifton has developed a much freer interview style: It remains probing, encouraging the widest range of associations, and includes detailed life histories and explorations of dreams. But it focuses on the specific situation responsible for bringing interviewee and interviewer together—most of the interviews have been individual ones—and takes the form of something close to an open dialogue emerging from that tradition.

The relation these two develop is neither one of doctor and patient nor one of ordinary friends, although at moments it can seem to resemble either. The traditional term for the person in that situation, "research subject," seems increasingly unsatisfactory because it suggests someone merely studied or investigated in a more or less passive way. "Patient" is entirely inappropriate, and "client" is not much better. "Historical actor" and "pivotal person" come closer, but they have their own ambiguities. A number of new terms may be developed, as will new methods of investigation and interview—Lifton already depends on group interviews and a host of other informal approaches—to capture, in active ways, lived history. Progress in psychohistory depends on those innovations in method. Once developed in the study of contemporary matters, such innovations could also be applied to the study of the past, although mainly in relation to the search for and the interpretation of various kinds of records and documents.

The psychohistorical interview emphasizes shared exploration, mostly of the world of the person sought out but including a great deal of give and take and more than a little discussion of the author's own attitudes and interests. It requires, in other words, a combination of human spontaneity and professional discipline. One's way of combining the two is always idiosyncratic and always less than ideal.

The method is partly empirical, in its stress on specific data from interviews; partly phenomenological or formative, in its stress on forms and images that are simultaneously individual and collective; and partly speculative, in its use of interview data, together with many other observations, to posit relations between a person and his history and to suggest concepts that eliminate the artificial separation of the two. In that speculation the investigator has the advantage of beginning from concrete information that is a product of his own direct perceptions. Although subjective distortion can render the advantage a mixed one, exaggerated concerns with detached objectivity have too often caused investigators to undervalue what can be learned of history from their direct perception.

Within that perspective, all shared behavior is seen as simultaneously involved in a trinity of universality (that which is related to the psychological quests of all persons in all historical epochs), specific cultural emphasis and style (as evolved by a particular people over centuries), and recent and contemporary historical influences (the part of the trinity most likely to be neglected in psychological work). Any shared event is all of those. The weighting of the components may vary, but nothing is purely universal or cultural-historical or contemporary-historical; everything is all three. The over-all approach—or, at least, the authors' sense of it—is most fundamentally influenced by Freud and Erikson but also by Susanne Langer and Ernst Cassirer, Otto Rank, Albert Camus, Lancelot Law Whyte, David Riesman, R. G. Collingwood, Leslie Farber, Kenneth Keniston, Benjamin Schwartz, and Philip Rieff.

The shared themes approach was used in 6 months of research in Hiroshima in 1962 on the psychological effects of the atomic bomb. The work centered mainly on intensive interviews with 75 atomic bomb survivors, about half of them chosen at random from an official list, the other half specially selected because of their active involvement over the years in atomic bomb problems. Most of the interviews were tape recorded, and the book written about the work took shape mainly from those interviews and made extensive use of direct quotations to illustrate the death-haunted responses that were encountered. But in both the research and book Lifton (1968a) moved outward from interviews with individual survivors to groups they formed, leaders emerging from among them, and social currents in Hiroshima that they both created and were affected by. That approach required close attention to the post-atomic bomb history of the city and to the relation of that special history to the rest of Japan and to the world at large, as well as to the city's own earlier heritage. A significant part of that history consisted of creative struggles by writers, painters, and filmmakers from both within and without the city to come to terms with Hiroshima. Those historical and creative struggles were deeply bound up with issues of memorialization and commemoration, with efforts to move beyond the bomb while remaining true to its dead.

Through a detailed elaboration of the ethos of the survivor, Lifton was in some degree able to unite the individual psychological and historical currents observed. He compared survival of the atomic bomb to survival of other massive death immersions—Nazi persecutions, the plagues in the Middle Ages as revealed through records, natural disasters—and the deaths of close friends and family members. He could then in that and subsequent studies raise questions about the general importance of the survivor ethos of the present age, of the degree to which people have become historically prone to the survivor's retained death imprint, to his death guilt and his psychic numbing or desensitization to death-dominated images, and to his struggle for significance or what the author calls, after Langer, his "formulation." Those questions now intrude into virtually all of Lifton's work, and they haunt the contemporary imagination.

Thus, in *Revolutionary Immortality,* Lifton, (1968b) discussed Mao Tse-tung's relation to the Chinese cultural revolution in terms of his many experiences of individual and revolutionary survival. His creative use of the survivor state was related to his extraordinary accomplishments as a leader, and the general relevance of death symbolism was considered in the broadest historical perspective to the Chinese cultural revolution. By connecting certain psychological characteristics of Mao's personal and revolutionary style with the predominant themes of the cultural revolution, the author attempted to combine the great-man and shared themes approaches.

The central thesis of the book revolved around Mao's anticipation of his own impending death and his and his followers' fear of the death of the revolution. What Lifton saw as the overwhelming threat Mao faced was not so much death itself as the suggestion that his revolutionary works would not endure. By revolutionary immortality, then, was meant a shared sense of participating in permanent revolutionary ferment and of transcending individual death by living on indefinitely within that continuing revolution. Some such vision has been present in all revolutions and was directly expressed in Trotsky's principle of permanent revolution: That vision took an unprecedented intensity in Chinese Communist experience. That quest for revolutionary immortality provided a general framework within which the political and economic struggles and antibureaucratic and antirevisionist assaults of the cultural revolution could be examined, without being reduced to a particular psychological or psychopathological trait of any one person.

Also related to that quest was a pattern that reflected the excruciating Maoist struggles with technology. The author called that pattern "psychism," by which was meant an exaggerated reliance on psychic power as a means of controlling the external environment, an attempt to replace the requirements of technology with pure revolutionary will. Technology was desperately sought, but feelings were cultivated. In that pattern of psychism, there was once more a coming together of Mao's personal revolutionary style, including what Chinese Communist commentators themselves referred to as his revolutionary romanticism, and a number of larger currents surrounding the cultural revolution. The concept of psychism, like that of revolutionary immortality, was an attempt to say something about precisely that psychohistorical interface.

The Mao book was not based on the kind of detailed interview approach described in relation to Lifton's Hiroshima work. Rather, it was a brief, interpretive essay that drew heavily on documents and observations by others of the cultural revolution and on the writings of Mao and only on a very limited number of interviews with participants and observers of the events described. As compared with the Hiroshima study, the Mao study was more tenuous and more vulnerable. Nevertheless, the themes and concepts developed in it shed light on a mysteriously explosive social upheaval, and it represents a useful experiment in the pursuit of psychohistory.

SEARCH FOR IMMORTALITY

The post-Freudian paradigms, like the Freudian ones, do not make clear exactly what they explain, and they fall short of providing coherent theories of historical causation. The Freudian paradigms lean heavily on instinctual energies and struggles that inevitably reduce themselves to the Oedipal event, whether in connection with a prehistorical generational conflict or with the psychopathology of a leading historical actor. If broadened, that principle of the Oedipal event could be made to connect with more inclusive versions of generational impasse, in keeping with

Ortega y Gasset's (1960) belief that the concept of the generation is the most important one in all of recorded history. Ortega y Gasset, however, had in mind a specificity of the timing of generational transition that Freudian models have tended to ignore.

Erikson's great-man paradigm looks for historical causation in the leader's singular capacity and absolute need to carry history with him as he breaks out from and transcends his own demonic intrapsychic conflicts. Since those conflicts are rooted in the leader's historical period and his solution affects a great collectivity of his contemporaries, as well as subsequent generations, the great-man approach is relatively more specific than the other paradigms in its causal explanations. But one still senses a theoretical gap between the individual person and the collectivity that none of the paradigms has fully bridged.

The shared themes approach is the most diffuse of the four paradigms but in many ways the most attuned to historical complexity. Within it, effect can become virtually indistinguishable from cause. A group understood to be created by a particular historical event (the Hiroshima survivors) or by an evolving set of historical vicissitudes (dissident Japanese or American youth) is also seen simultaneously to act on and affect history by epitomizing, exacerbating, and suggesting something beyond the immediate conflicts and visions of large numbers of contemporaries. If that kind of explanation, strictly speaking, deals more with historical flow than with cause, it at least leaves open many possibilities for more subtle theoretical explorations that relate cause and effect to evolving patterns and directions. Among those future possibilities are additional combinations of the shared themes and great-man approaches and new ways of conceptualizing radical historical shifts—the breakdown and re-creation of the forms of human culture (biological, experiential, institutional, technological, aesthetic, and interpretive)—or what Lifton (1969) called a new history.

In both of the post-Freudian paradigms, the social theory necessary to bridge the gap between individual and collectivity remains fragmented, implicit, unclear, or nonexistent. One solution would be to graft onto either of the two paradigms relatively established and comprehensive social theory such as the neo-Marxist concepts of alienation and overspecialization. The authors' own views are that much of the necessary theory will have to be constructed anew. When approaching intellectual traditions of all kinds, one may do better to draw on them partially and critically, sometimes even fragmentally, as one constructs new combinations of ideas from the continuing investigation of shared psychohistorical themes. Most of all, one should avoid that form of professional territoriality that insists that psychological, sociological, and historical realms remain categorically discrete, each holding fast to an explanatory principle claimed to subsume or exist independently of all else.

The concept of revolutionary immortality is part of a more general theory of symbolic immortality: Lifton has developed a theory that concerns man's need, in the face of inevitable biological death, to maintain an inner sense of continuity with what has gone on before and what will go on after his own individual existence. From that standpoint, the sense of immortality is much more than mere denial of death, although it can certainly be bound up with denial. Rather, it is part of compelling, life-enhancing imagery binding each person to significant groups and events removed from him in place and time. The sense of immortality may be expressed biologically, by living on through or in one's sons and daughters and their sons and daughters; theologically, in the idea of a life after death or in other forms of spiritual conquest of death; creatively, through works and influences perceived as persisting beyond biological death; through identification with nature and its infinite extension into time and space, the idea of eternal nature; or experientially, through a feeling state—experiential transcendence—so intense that, at least temporarily, time and death are eliminated, the mode classically used by mystics.

That sense of immortality serves as the person's inner perception of his involvement in the historical process. Much of human history consists of the struggle to achieve, maintain, and reaffirm a shared or collective sense of immortality under constantly changing psychic and material conditions.

Generally speaking, imagery of immortality has shifted, over the course of history, from the magical to the supernatural to the natural and human-centered—from literal promise of eternal life to more symbolic expressions of human continuity. However, the emerging discussion and practice of cryonics, the freezing of bodies from the time of death in the hope of later restoring life, return one to the most literal kind of quest for direct bodily immortality. In any case, the shifting and recombining of modes of immorality mark great turning points in human history. The Darwinian revolution, for instance, epitomized the shift from the theological to the biological mode and did so in relation to both human origins and human destiny. A shift of that kind can be neither total nor unopposed, and the world is still in the midst of its reverberations.

Hiroshima and the subsequent development of nuclear weapons can be viewed as another major shift, perhaps more in the undermining of existing modes of immortality than in any clear suggestion of new combinations. Indeed, one way of viewing the present world-wide crisis in terms other than political is as a form of radical psychohistorical dislocation associated with the breakdown of viable modes of symbolic immortality. What has broken down is the sense of connection people have long felt with the vital and nourishing symbols of their cultural traditions, the sense of connection with their own history. The human sense of historical continuity or of a symbolic immorality is now being profoundly threatened by simple historical velocity—which subverts the imagery, notably the theological imagery, in which it has been traditionally maintained—and by nuclear and other ultimate weapons that, by their very existence, call into question all modes of immortality. When one considers, more often unconsciously or preconsciously than with clear awareness, the possibility of nuclear or bacteriological warfare, one can hardly be certain of living on in his children or grandchildren, in his works or influences on others, in some form of theological conquest of death, or even in nature, which is now known to be vulnerable to human weapons. The striking contemporary reliance on the fifth mode of symbolic immortality, that of experiential transcendence, whether through drugs or other forms of turned-on psychic states, may well be a reflection of precisely that decline in the belief in the other four modes. People hunger for both connection and transcendence, and they have need to experiment with the historical and antihistorical boundaries of both.

In America one feels that kind of dislocation profoundly, so much so that Americans may well be in the vanguard of two specific responses to it. The first, which can have highly malignant consequences, entails an embrace—even deification—of technology as a new mode of immortality through which people seek to perpetuate themselves. That embrace of technology can be associated with great adventure and with other forms of imaginative transcendence, as in the case of the space program. But it takes on grotesque contours when the technology involved is that of weaponry. One then witnesses the development, not only in America but throughout the world, of the religion of nuclearism, an attitude of worship toward weapons of destruction and a dependence on them to solve otherwise baffling human problems—ultimately, the investment in them of the sense of immortality that has been lost.

A second response to historical dislocation is the emergence of protean man (Lifton, 1968b), by which is meant a relatively new life style, characterized by interminable exploration and flux, by a self-process capable of relatively easy shifts in belief and identification, a life style that is postmodern and in some ways post-Freudian. Protean man has been created not only by the dislocations mentioned but by the revolution in mass media. A flooding of imagery is produced by the extraordinary flow of postmodern cultural influences over mass communications networks. Each person can be touched and at times significantly affected by virtually everything and presented with endless partial alternatives in every sphere of life, whether superficial messages, undigested cultural elements, or moving evocations.

THE NEW PSYCHOHISTORY

The theory of symbolic immortality can hardly resolve the many-sided dilemmas of historical causation. But it does seem to be a potentially useful way of looking at humans in history, most specifically as a framework for the study of revolutions and a variety of related problems of historical continuity and discontinuity. The general point of view seems also to be given force by the death-dominated times in which it emerges: History does much to create the ways in which people, at any particular moment, decide to study it.

Since the protean style in some degree inhibits everyone, it affects relations to ideas—the ways in which one responds to them, believes them, and attaches them to one's sense of self. Protean man is continuously open to new ideas and can move among them rather freely. His difficulty lies in giving lasting allegiance to any particular idea or idea system. Nor are scholars immune to that pattern. Hence, the intellectual restlessness within most disciplines—the dissatisfaction with established concepts and the failure of new concepts of equal authority to appear.

Those working in the area of psychohistory, where established concepts hardly exist, are especially likely to encounter such restlessness in both their readers and themselves. It will not be easy to discover and then collectively maintain the kind of authoritative conceptual principles one has come to expect and depend on with an intellectual tradition. Moreover, there is a sense in which psychohistory adds to the burdens of a historical discipline already immersed in difficult struggles to replace no longer acceptable nineteenth-century versions of history as clear narrative or epic or inevitable destiny, struggles to come to grips with the convoluted, opaque, and deadly actualities of the twentieth century. Psychohistory, at least in the version described here, tends to complicate, rather than simplify, which is as it should be. Moreover, protean tendencies among scholars can render them receptive to the new principles of psychohistory and yet cautious in granting them intellectual authority, which is also as it should be.

Within those uncertainties lie extraordinary possibilities. They, too, are protean, and one can observe in contemporary humans an increasing capacity for coming to what would previously have been viewed as impossible intellectual combinations and innovations. Compared with their predecessors, they are not only less bound by tradition but much more fluid in their potential integration of diverse conceptual elements. And the new psychohistory emerges as itself a radical investigative response to a radically dislocated historical epoch.

Despite the protean possibilities and what some perceive as an exotic aura surrounding the idea of psychohistory, all that the authors have said here and experienced in investigation militates strongly against facile intellectual efforts or the creation of instant psychohistorians. On the contrary, the approach seems to require not only a central commitment to one of the disciplines or a related one and a considerable knowledge of the other but something more—a considerable ethical concern with the problems of being investigated. As he explained in his essay on psychohistorical evidence, Erikson (1968b) was hardly neutral in his feelings about Luther's achievements or about what Gandhi's legacy may mean for the world. Nor was Keniston neutral about student radicals, Coles about minority group aspirations, or Lifton about Hiroshima and its legacy. Rather, all have been struggling toward ways of acknowledging their involvements and exploring their relation to the findings, toward making conceptual use of those very involvements.

CONCLUSIONS

Although the developments discussed here have for the most part come from psychology, psychohistory borrows theories and methods from anthropology, sociology, and literature. The need for theories and methods that will help the historian understand complex social and psychological elements of collective activity and address phenomena around change has stimulated the movement toward the social sciences and the humanities.

Problems in psychohistorical method are an effect of its hybrid status. Psychohistory cannot easily fulfill many of the rigorous demands of historiography, including implicit requirements for external verification for interpretation, for precise meaning of language, for clearly defined rationales for the commonly accepted social science technique of comparing a series of phenomena to other series. The problems of cause and effect and of the relationship of external events to mental life are of concern both to theoreticians and to the practicing researcher and writer of psychohistory. The ambiguity of many historical texts and the cultural and psychological biases of the historian-interpreter of those texts create further obstacles for the psychohistorian. It is difficult, for example, to sort out commonplace patterns of language usage as opposed to fantasy if there is no clear-cut or thorough understanding of the precise social or historical context in which the language occurs. It is also difficult to reconstruct discontinuities and breaks in culture or mass behavior when the theory used denies the potential for profound social change. Whatever their origin, those transformations cut across social classes, profoundly altering the psychological functions, both conscious and unconscious, of masses of persons.

Scholarly detachment is a myth in historical studies, in which subjective bias plays an active role in the interpretation of texts and in attitudes toward historical figures and events. What classical psychoanalytic theory does offer to the historian is an opportunity to ferret out those less explicit or arcane allusions in historical data, to uncover relationships between seemingly unrelated events, to explore the taboos and biases of a society, to find pattern and order in chaotic phenomena, and to be sensitized to his own and others' unconscious distortions. The schematicism and antihistoricism of Freudian theory and the ambiguity and metaphorical quality of psychoanalytic language are dangers and pitfalls that the historian must avoid while he seeks out the convergences of his documents, establishes patterns of behavior or experience, and seeks verification for his findings by using other analyzing constructs. Saul Friedländer's (1978) monograph on psychohistory, *History and Psychoanalysis,* described psychoanalytic theory as a valuable systematized explanation of human behavior differing from traditional historiography only by degree. Friedländer reviewed many psychohistorical works and set up criteria for the validation of psychoanalytic hypotheses applied to historical figures or events. A recent work by Loewenberg (1983) amplifies the observations of Friedländer.

An important approach to collective phenomena was formulated by Weinstein and Platt (1973), who integrated psychoanalytic understanding of the mechanisms of internalization with social theory for use in historical studies. They reflected on the impact of massive social change as it moves from group process to individual internalization. They did not find the study of infantile experience or family process to be useful in understanding the function of social institutions. Those trends in psychohistory are bolstered as well by the ability to approach historical and sociological data quantitatively—that is, through the use of computers. Such methods can approach and identify pattern and trend but not causes or certain phenomena of collective behavior. Taken together with individual studies enriched by sensitivity to language and psychoanalytic theory, such research efforts can provide a convergence of data from which the psychohistorian is able to construct coherent interpretation. Persons and groups may then be viewed in the largest context of cultural life, as well as within the life of the family.

The work of Kohut (1971, 1977, 1978) on self psychology and of Kernberg (1976) on object relations has been used to probe affective states within historical groups. Kohut himself wrote extensively on historical issues and his influence on historians has been extensive; see, for example, Strozier (1982).

It is often difficult for historians using psychoanalytic theory to feel comfortable with psychohistorical studies of living figures. In their view, historical materials must gain a certain patina that only time and distance from the subject can furnish. Those historians argue that it is not possible to distinguish polemic and propaganda from historical scholarship when the subject of a psychobiography is alive. Further, there is a strong likelihood of factual error and confusion, resulting from lack of documentation and the relative sparsity of sensitive data. Ethical questions about psychohistory have been raised by the American Psychiatric Association (1976). The Task Force on Psychohistory argued that considerations of confidentiality and questions of ethics must be dealt with in regard to the release of privileged information relating to the intimate details and fantasy lives of prominent persons. They cautioned that the lack of training in historical theory and methods makes psychiatric practitioners of psychohistory particularly vulnerable to errors of fact, and they lamented the lack of grounding in historical methods and the sophisticated use of source materials among some psychiatrist-historians, while citing the lack of clinical experience or finesse among historians writing psychohistory. The latter leads to wild analysis, and the former creates a historiography without social or cultural context.

Particularly relevant to recent writing in psychohistory is the structuralist approach to language, symbol, and institutions and their relationships to the social-cultural matrix. The writings of French historians Michel Foucault (1965, 1973, 1975, 1976) and Alain Besançon (1967, 1968) reflect the structuralist's concern to unearth the quality and the texture of a society by examining the meaning of its symbols, particularly in their linguistic manifestations. Besançon used a comparative method to identify a common unconscious theme in Russian law, literature, and social institution; Foucault poetically reconstructed the cultural life of a whole society by examining its institutions, laws, and use of language.

Psychohistory is experiencing a growth spurt. More than 200 courses in the field are listed in United States college catalogues. Many of those courses are conducted by teachers with formal psychoanalytic training. The Group for the Use of Psychology in History, founded in 1972 as an affiliate of the American Historical Association, publishes *Psychohistory Review,* a quarterly that serves as a clearinghouse for information about the field—publishing articles, reviews, essays, syllabuses, research notes, and bibliographic information. *The Journal of Psychohistory* has also had some importance, although it is mixed in the quality of its papers. Journals, anthologies, and autobiographies that match family and social histories with psychoanalysis or with developmental psychology abound.

Developmental theory in particularly historical context, with careful analysis of cultural and social matrices, is reflected in the works by Demos (1971). Although many sins have been committed in the name of psychohistory, the approach remains crucial to improving one's grasp on the ever more confusing psychological universe.

REFERENCES)

Besançon, A. *La Tsarevitch immolee.* Paris; Plon, 1967.
Besançon, A. A psychoanalysis: Auxiliary science or historical method? *Contemporary History,* 1968, *3,* 149.
Binion, R. *Hitler among the Germans.* New York: Elsevier, 1976.
Braudel, F. *The Mediterranean and the Mediterranean world in the age of Philip the Second.* New York: Harper & Row, 1976.
Bromberg, N. Hitler's childhood. *International Review of Psychoanalysis,* 1974, *34,* 19.
Bullitt, W. D., & Freud, S. *Thomas Woodrow Wilson, Twenty-Eighth President of the United States: A psychological study.* Boston, MA: Houghton-Mifflin, 1967.
Coles, R. *Children of crisis.* Boston, MA: Atlantic-Little Brown, 1967–1971.
Demos, J. *Little commonwealth: Family life in Plymouth Colony.* New York: Oxford University Press, 1971.
Demos, J. *Entertaining Satan: Witchcraft and the culture of early New England.* New York: Oxford University Press, 1982.
Erikson, E. H. *Young man Luther: A study in psychoanalysis and history.* New York: W. W. Norton, 1958.
Erikson, E. H. Book review: *Thomas Woodrow Wilson. International Journal of Psychoanalysis,* 1967, *48,* 462–468.
Erikson, E. H. *Identity: Youth and crisis.* New York: W. W. Norton, 1968. (a)
Erikson, E. H. On the nature of psychohistorical evidence: In search of Gandhi. *Daedalus,* 1968, *97,* 695–730. (b)
Foucault, M. *Madness and civilization.* New York: Pantheon Books, 1965.
Foucault, M. *The order of things: An archaeology of the human sciences.* New York: Vintage Books, 1973.
Foucault, M. *The birth of the clinic: An archaeology of medical perception.* New York: Vintage Books, 1975.
Foucault, M. *The archaeology of knowledge and the discourse on language.* New York: Harper, 1976.
Freud, S. *Moses and monotheism. In Standard edition of the complete psychological works of Sigmund Freud* (Vol. 23). London: Hogarth Press, 1939.
Friedlander, S. *History and psychoanalysis.* New York: Holmes & Meier, 1978.
Gay, P. *Freud, Jews, and other Germans: Masters and victims in modernist culture.* New York: Oxford University Press, 1978.
George, A. L., & George, J. L. *Woodrow Wilson and Colonel House: A personality study.* New York: Day, 1956.
Kardiner, A. *The individual and his society.* Westport, CT: Greenwood Press, 1939.
Keniston, K. *The uncommitted.* New York: Harcourt, Brace and World, 1965.
Keniston, K. *Young radicals.* New York: Harcourt, Brace and World, 1968.
Kernberg, O. *Borderline conditions and pathological narcissism.* New York: Jason Aronson, 1976.

Kohut, H. *The analysis of the self.* New York: International Universities Press, 1971.

Kohut, H. *The analysis of the self.* New York: International Universities Press, 1977.

Kohut, H. *The search for the self: Selected writings* (P. H. Ornstein, Ed.). New York: International Universities Press, 1978.

Lifton, R. J. *Thought reform and the psychology of totalism: A study of "brainwashing" in China.* New York: W. W. Norton, 1961.

Lifton, R. J. *Death in life: Survivors of Hiroshima.* New York: Random House, 1968. (a)

Lifton, R. J. *Revolutionary immortality: Mao Tse-tung and the Chinese cultural revolution.* New York: Random House, 1968. (b)

Lifton, R. J. *History and human survival.* New York: Random House, 1970.

Lifton, R. J. *Home from the war: Vietnam veterans: Neither victims nor executioners.* New York: Simon & Schuster, 1973.

Lifton, R. J., & Olson, E. (Eds.). *Explorations in psychohistory: The Wellfleet papers.* New York: Simon & Schuster, 1974.

Loewenberg, P. *Decoding the past: The psychohistorical approach.* New York: Knopf, 1983.

Mack, J. *A prince of our disorder: The life of T. E. Lawrence.* New York: Little Brown, 1976.

Mazlish, B. *In search of Nixon: A psychohistorical inquiry.* New York: Basic Books, 1972.

Meyerhoff, H. On psychoanalysis and history. *Psychoanalytic Review, 1962, 49,* 27.

Ortega y Gasset, J. *What is philosophy?* New York: W. W. Norton, 1960.

Rieff, P. The meaning of history and religion in Freud's thought. In B. Mazlish (Ed.), *Psychoanalysis and history.* New York: Grosset & Dunlap, 1971.

Strozier, C. *Lincoln's quest for union: Public and private meanings.* New York: Basic Books, 1982.

Waite, R. G. L. *The psychopathic god: Adolf Hitler.* New York: Basic Books, 1977.

Weinstein, F., & Platt, G. *Psychoanalytic sociology: An essay on the interpretation of historical data and the phenomena of collective behavior.* Washington, DC: Johns Hopkins, 1973.

Zeligs, M. A. *Friendship and fratricide: An analysis of Whitaker Chambers and Alger Hiss.* New York: Viking Press, 1967.

7 Psychology and Political Science

Alan C. Elms
University of California, Davis

INTRODUCTION

Psychology and political science are natural bedfellows. The study of politics demands attention to the beliefs, attitudes, values, motives, and personalities of political participants. A thorough study of psychological processes should encompass humans as they experience their most intense commitments and as they act creatively to limit their individual impulses and to attain their goals through cooperation and conflict with others. One might assume that the two fields, from their beginnings as formal disciplines, would have developed with continuing interchanges of ideas, techniques, and data. Instead, many political scientists have through much of their field's history rejected psychology as either corrupting or irrelevant. Many psychologists have done their best to avoid dealing with any aspects of human functioning that carry the remotest hint of emotional involvement—let alone politics, with its dismaying complexity of high-minded idealism and low ambition, anger and love, charismatic leadership and back-alley brawls.

Yet a strain of psychologically informed theorizing and research has steadily grown within political science over the past several decades, while an increasing number of psychologists have become concerned with aspects of individual political participation. In the 1980s, "political behavior" is a recognized subdiscipline within political science, and social scientists of diverse disciplinary backgrounds have developed their own organizations and journals concerned explicitly with political psychology. The International Society of Political Psychology (ISPP) has already sponsored several annual conventions with extensive scholarly programs and has established a journal, *Political Psychology*. Of the Society's more than 200 founding members, approximately one-third are political scientists, one-third are psychologists, and the remainder come from sociology, psychiatry, history, anthropology, and several related fields. The International Psychohistorial Association, founded at about the same time as the ISPP, is not limited to the consideration of political topics, but often deals with case-history research on political figures and with psychodynamic interpretations of political phenomena (see Lifton and Strozier, in this volume). The Society for the Psychological Study of Social Issues (Division 9 of the American Psychological Association) is concerned in part with explicitly political research topics. The American Psychiatric Association has a "special interest group" concerned with political behavior. The other major journals in the area, *Political Behavior* and *Micropolitics*, define their scope to include political sociology and other disciplines as well as political psychology, but much of their proposed and actual coverage of topics is similar to that of *Political Psychology*. A new journal, *Political Communication and Persuasion*, focuses on international politics, but its papers often apply to domestic political phenomena as well. Other specialized journals with a substantial proportion of papers relevant to political psychology include *Psychohistory Review*, *Public Opinion Quarterly*, and *Experimental Study of Politics*. Much of the political psychology literature, of course, appears in the standard journals in political science, psychology, and other fields.

This essay will survey the field of political psychology as it has grown out of psychology's contributions to and borrowings from political science. Conceptually and methodologically, the field's origins are largely traceable to the work of Harold Lasswell, though other influences will also be discussed. Major research areas may be categorized conveniently as focusing on either the political audience or the political actor. The political audience has been studied in terms of how its members acquire political orientations, seek political satisfaction of basic motives, express their personalities through political attitudes, and undergo persuasive attempts to change those attitudes. Political actors (i.e., professional politicians) have been examined mainly in terms of the psychological functioning and personality patterns of chief executives, lower-level office-holders, and political advisers. Finally, the future of the field will be discussed as dependent on training arrangements designed to promote continued interdisciplinary cross-fertilization and improvements in research quality.

THEORETICAL AND METHODOLOGICAL ORIGINS

History and Theory

Historically, political science and the more social-scientific aspects of psychology developed from a common ancestry in political philosophy. From Plato and Aristotle onward, political philosophers combined their concepts of how political systems should or do operate with assumptions about the essential nature of human character. Bentham, Comte, Hegel, Hobbes, Marx, Mill, Nietzsche, Adam Smith, Rousseau, and Spencer each made early and important contributions to the conceptualization of political systems; all can likewise be seen as having helped to lay the groundwork for current theoretical structures in psychology (Allport, 1968). Twentieth-century political scientists have continued the tradition of blending political and characterological hypotheses (see, for instance, Lasswell's, 1951, discussion of "democratic character"), while psychologists as disparate as Maslow (1961) and Skinner (1948) have developed models of the ideal society based on specific conceptualizations of personality.

When political science and psychology began to acquire distinct identities and separate empirical bases, each field had reasons to reject the lures of the other. For early twentieth-century academic psychologists, political science still looked too philosophical and not sufficiently empirical to meet the criteria of "true science" or to satisfy disciplinary identity needs. For political scientists, psychological methodologies often appeared to involve an unnecessary descent from abstraction to crude "hands-on" contacts with real people, while the adoption of psychological theories or perspectives seemed to threaten the abandonment of political science's distinctively system-oriented approach. Occasional political scientists protested their field's predominantly "intellectualist" or "rationalist" assumptions about human nature (e.g., Wallas, 1908/1962), while occasional psychologists made armchair forays into political matters (e.g., Münsterberg, 1914). But empirical research on psychological aspects of political behavior was minimal in quantity and quality until the end of the 1920s.

In 1930, Harold Lasswell published a book titled *Psychopathology and Politics*. Lasswell's training as a political scientist came largely from Charles E. Merriam, whose orientation was unusually empirical and who advocated research on "new aspects of politics," including psychological issues (Smith, 1969). Lasswell also underwent a training analysis with Theodor Reik, one of Freud's most prominent nonmedical disciples. That combination of influences in Lasswell's research preparation—empirical political science and psychoanalysis—proved fateful for the development of political psychology.

In *Psychopathology and Politics,* Lasswell offered a general formula for the creation of "political man":

$$p\}d\}r = P.$$

The formula looks vaguely mathematical, but it is in fact a shorthand version of basic psychoanalytic theory as applied to politics: The individual's private and largely unconscious motives *(p)* are transformed through displacement *(d)* onto public objects. These displaced motives are then further transformed through rationalizations *(r)* in terms of the public interest, and it is these rationalized displacements of private motives that become visible as the political man *(P).* Lasswell supported this formula with depth-psychological interviews of a number of politically-oriented individuals, some of them institutionalized or in psychotherapeutic treatment. His analysis of their behavior dealt largely with Oedipal issues, sibling rivalry, and other psychodynamic constructs. From such material he identified several basic political types, each associated with a general pattern of psychological development and symptomatology.

Lasswell's political types were not absorbed into the research mainstream either of political science or of psychology. But his vigorous arguments for the political importance of unconscious and irrational motives, in this and later books and papers (e.g., Lasswell, 1948, 1951), established a beachhead for psychoanalytic ideas in political science; and psychoanalytic theory has since remained one of the most important conceptual approaches in political psychology. Lasswell's use of that conceptual approach, in combination with his application of depth interviewing techniques and symbolic interpretation, might alone have been sufficient to establish the utility of psychoanalysis in this area, but other researchers have independently introduced various facets of psychoanalytic thought and research. The several authors of *The Authoritarian Personality* (Adorno, Frenkel-Brunswik, Levinson, & Sanford, 1950), for instance, brought diverse but psychoanalytically-informed orientations and methodological skills to bear upon a personality type of particular concern to political psychologists. When political psychobiography began to emerge as a distinct specialty, it too offered support for Lasswell's formula for "political man" and for psychoanalytic theory's place in political psychology, though Lasswell's own work had exerted little direct influence on the psychobiographers. (One important exception is the Georges' application of Lasswellian constructs to the case of Woodrow Wilson; see, for example, George, 1971.)

Though Freudian psychoanalytic theory has played a major role in political psychology, other broad theories have been employed usefully as well. Several variants of psychoanalytic theory, including Adlerian psychology (Broh, 1979; Lasswell, 1948) and ego psychology (Erikson, 1969, 1974), have been applied directly or indirectly to questions of political socialization (Renshon, 1977) and elsewhere. Maslow's humanistic approach has been applied with some success to questions of political recruitment (Knutson, 1974). A variety of more limited theories and constructs has been borrowed from developmental, social, and personality psychology for occasional use (see, for instance, Post, 1980).

Theories originating within political science have, on the other hand, gained few converts in psychology. As previously indicated, the many centuries of pre-scientific political philosophy contributed Marxist, utilitarian, and other broad perspectives to psychology. But most modern political-scientific theories have been too concerned with institutions and systems to carry much appeal for psychologists, except perhaps to those within cognate specialties such as organizational psychology.

Research Methods

The research methods as well as the principal theories of political psychology derive to a considerable extent from psychological sources rather than from political science. They have, however, often been modified and refined for the specific purposes of political research. The major methodological approaches of political psychology include case history, content analysis, surveys, and experimentation, with cross-cultural comparisons as an added perspective that may include any or all of the others.

The case history approach, as pioneered by Lasswell (1930), involves assembling a detailed account of an individual's personality and life history as related to political issues. It often utilizes depth interviews, as in Lasswell's study; but it may rely solely on archival or secondary data (e.g., Barber, 1977). It may involve a case study of a single individual (e.g., Kramnick, 1977) or comparisons of numbers of individuals falling into discrete categories (e.g., Elms, 1969). It may be concerned with the individual's political life in broad perspective (e.g., Lane, 1962, 1969) or with the relevance of individual psychological patterns to specific political issues (e.g., Smith, Bruner, & White, 1956). It may be applied to individuals who represent a particular demographic or geographic grouping (e.g., Lamb, 1974) or to individuals deliberately chosen for their diversity (e.g., Adorno et al., 1950). It may include the administration of projective tests and quantifiable questionnaires as well as interviews; and it usually involves psychoanalytically-inspired symbolic interpretations of at least portions of the data.

Content analysis is another approach whose application to political psychology was pioneered by Lasswell (1927). Most broadly, *"Content analysis is any technique for making inferences by systematically and objectively identifying specified characteristcs of messages* [Holsti, 1968, p. 601; italics in the original]." It is a useful technique for examining patterns of psychological appeals in political propaganda (as in Lasswell's work), for identifying national motivational trends (McClelland, 1975), and for quantifying aspects of individual personality patterns (Winter & Stewart, 1977). With antecedents in communications research, sociology, and anthropology as well as in psychology and political science, content analysis techniques have probably benefited more from interdisciplinary contributions than has any other methodological approach (see Back and Price-Williams, in this volume).

Survey research is nearly as interdisciplinary in its origins. One of the earliest successes in quantification of social-psychological processes was attitude measurement (Likert, 1932; Thurstone & Chave, 1929). The development of survey research followed Lippman's (1925/1965) influential argument for achieving a better understanding of the foundations of public opinion, and the development of reliable attitude measurement techniques paved the way for mass opinion surveys as practiced by the Gallup and Roper polling organizations. In the intervening years, professional pollsters, along with political scientists, sociologists, and other psychologists, have elevated public opinion assessment from a rather imprecise art to a fairly precise science. Accurate opinion polling made possible the correlation of voter attitudes with voting behavior and with a number of psychologically meaningful variables. The effects of political propaganda were measured, and changes in political attitudes over time were related to nonpolitical events or to changes in the characteristics of the electorate.

Techniques of psychological experimentation have seldom been applied to political phenomena, either in the laboratory or in the field. Twenty years ago, Robert E. Lane (1963, pp. 625-626) could state that "political scientists have never, to our knowledge, attempted a controlled laboratory experiment to ascertain the relation between relevant variables." Though there is now a journal titled *Experimental Study of Politics,* Lane's statement does not need much revision. Most genuinely relevant political variables do not lend themselves to direct experimentation, except in some evil kingdom beyond the ken of ethical researchers. Simulation studies have been exploited in certain subdisciplines, principally those concerned with international politics (e.g., Semmel & Minix, 1978). More realistic laboratory experiments dealing indirectly with variables of political-scientific interest appear occasionally in the social-psychological literature (e.g., Milgram, 1974). But as experimentation becomes increasingly problematic for social and personality psychologists, because of increases in theoretical complexity and in government regulations, it becomes still less likely ever to gain a solid foothold in political psychology. (See, however, an interesting collaboration between a political scientist and an experimental psychologist in Tanenhaus & Foley, 1981.)

One final methodological approach has been paid much more lip service than honest tribute in psychology generally, but it is growing in importance in political psychology. That approach is a cross-cultural one, and it can be applied—albeit with considerable difficulty—to studies otherwise stressing case-historical, content analysis, survey, or experimental techniques. The cross-cultural approach lends itself most readily to comparisons of survey data (Nathan & Remy, 1977) and to content analysis (McClelland, 1961). But studies of national character, for instance, may be validly based on case-historical data, treated carefully and at least in part quantitatively (LeVine, 1973); and cross-cultural experiments on such psychological variables as conformity behavior (Milgram, 1961) are at least suggestive of political insights. Research on the psychology of international relations, which will not be explicitly reviewed in this essay, has at times used all of these approaches in a necessarily cross-cultural context (deRivera, 1968; Kelman, 1965).

RESEARCH AREAS

In the organization of political science textbooks, courses, and professional societies, research on political psychology usually falls under the heading either of "political behavior" or of "personality and politics." Neither term is particularly useful for organizing a review of topics within political psychology. The first includes research that is not in any meaningful sense psychological (e.g., voter trends measured over time without reference to psychological variables). The second typically excludes material that is quite psychological and that may in fact be very much concerned with personality, though not exclusively so (e.g., political socialization). Instead, I have organized major research topics in this essay in terms of the psychology of the political *audience* and the psychology of the political *actor*. Even these terms are relative, since members of the political audience (i.e., voters and potential voters) intermittently engage in consequential political actions, if only by refusing to vote in an election, while political actors (office-holders, political advisers, committed party workers, and activists) are often members of the political audience when other political actors take the stage.

Psychology of the Political Audience

Political socialization. When Robert E. Lane wrote his 1963 survey of
the interdisciplinary connections between political science and psychology, he could reasonably include child psychology among the "somewhat
less fruitful" areas of psychology for political scientists—along with
physiological psychology and sensory perception (p. 593). Lane did cite
two recent publications on political socialization in another part of his
paper (p. 619) while discussing the social environment of political acts.
But at that time the subdiscipline of political socialization was only beginning to develop a distinct identity, and its rapid elevation to one of the
most active research areas in political psychology was impossible to anticipate.

   Political socialization is, most centrally, the process by which the child
learns about politics and develops his or her own political orientation
(though some recent research has dealt with similar processes in later life
as well; see Dawson, Prewitt, & Dawson, 1977). It might seem that
knowledge about political socialization should stand as a cornerstone of
political science. It might also seem that developmental psychologists
would be keenly interested in how children come to understand and respond to the political world, particularly in a democracy where 18-year-
olds are expected to be able to cast a rational vote. But developmental
psychologists, outside of those directly involved in political research,
continue to give such matters remarkably little attention; and prior to
1959, most political scientists appear to have assumed, as did Victorians
concerning sexual motives, that political attitudes emerge fullblown in the
young adult without prior gestation.

   In 1959, Hyman introduced the term *political socialization* and laboriously assembled the extant literature that was at least vaguely relevant to
it. At about the same time, Greenstein in New Haven and Easton and
Hess in Chicago initiated original research projects designed to study the
process of political socialization in schoolchildren as broadly as possible.
Publication of their papers and books (Easton & Dennis, 1969; Greenstein, 1965; Hess & Torney, 1967) firmly established the field and
stimulated a massive outpouring of research papers from others. Most
often, studies of political socialization have utilized forced-choice survey
instruments, though "semi-projective techniques" have occasionally been
employed as well (Renshon, 1977, pp. 96–97). These studies have been
limited mainly to asking children of specified ages what they know or
believe about various political figures, institutions, and issues and, perhaps, to inquiring about the sources of children's information and opinions. Rarely has any detailed observation been conducted longitudinally
to obtain direct evidence about such sources of information and influence.

In one important line of early research on these issues, children were found to hold largely benevolent views of the government and of its principal spokespersons (e.g., the U.S. President). Such views were often attributed to a transference or displacement of the child's attitudes toward the parents onto political figures (much in the Lasswellian psychodynamic tradition). More recent research, however, has found that the political attitudes of children—particularly older children—shift considerably under the pressure of external events such as the Watergate scandal (e.g., Arterton, 1974). A more active, integrative, and developmentally complex model of the child's information processing with regard to politics is therefore suggested (Dawson et al., 1977, pp. 63–72). Direct parental transmission of political attitudes and party allegiances, also regarded as of great importance in the initial socialization research, has recently undergone considerable questioning by researchers (Beck, 1977). The complexity of political socialization has been further underlined by studies of this process in various U.S. subcultures and in a number of national groups (e.g., Torney, Oppenheim, & Farnen, 1975).

Motives for political participation. Political socialization research has been concerned mainly with how children learn about politics and how they acquire attitudes toward political objects. Political psychologists who study adults, assuming that the knowledge and attitudes already exist, have been much more interested in why people are motivated to participate in the political system. Beliefs and attitudes have not usually been seen as sufficient to move an individual to argue vehemently in favor of a political position, to visit a polling booth, or to send money to a candidate. The initial assumption was that people engaged in such activities for purely "rational" reasons, i.e., on the basis of economic self-interest or of civic duty. Lasswell's (1930) formula for political man, $p \} d \} r \} = P$, was a direct challenge to that assumption, asserting instead that irrational motives generally hold sway in politics.

Subsequent formulations of the motives for political participation have tended toward a middle position. One of the most influential, the functional approach of Smith, Bruner, and White (1956; Smith, 1973), postulates three major foundations for political attitudes and behaviors: *object appraisal,* referring to rational attempts to assess external reality and to act advantageously upon it; *social adjustment* (or, in Smith's revised terminology, mediation of self-other relationships), involving the role of attitudes and behavior in promoting satisfactory social relationships; and *externalization,* the Lasswellian process of dealing with one's repressed psychological conflicts by displacing them onto political objects. Smith, Bruner, and White, as well as other researchers who use similar formulations (e.g., Katz, 1960), have developed empirical evidence for the importance of each general motivational category in political involvement. From an extensive set of case-history studies, Lane (1969) derived a more detailed list of needs expressed in politics, including various constructs (e.g., consistency needs, autonomy needs) much studied by psychologists in other contexts. Other researchers have dealt with specific needs rather than trying to encompass the entire range; for instance, Renshon (1974) has provided support for the importance of a need for personal control in motivating political involvement.

Psychologists as well as political scientists have readily recognized political involvement as a major channel for the expression of diverse needs. (In addition to Smith, Bruner, and White's works, see the research on political activism cited below.) Perhaps political involvement is so useful in this regard because it appears to the average citizen to provide a potential link to a variety of possible goals while not being closely linked to any of them. Jobs, marital relationships, participation in narrowly focused voluntary organizations, or hobbies all carry specific and fairly immediate outcomes, while a modest level of political involvement may promise long-term payoffs ranging from chickens in the pot to the most elaborate personal and ideological paradises. Thus an individual's political position can be—and, in various empirical studies, has been shown to be—an expression of virtually any possible psychological motive. That being the case, one might wish to know at least which motives are *most* important in propelling the ordinary citizen into political involvement; but no one has done the necessary research. Research on the relative importance of several major motives for office-seeking is reviewed below.

Political attitudes and personality. During the first flurry of interest in attitude measurement in the 1930s, a favorite research topic was political attitudes. The topic was usually reduced to measuring liberal versus conservative attitudes, and correlating something else with them—most often I.Q. or a personality variable. The measures were crude, and the research designs were usually cruder, so nothing particularly useful came of these early efforts. But interest in relating personality variables to political attitudes, particularly at the extreme ends of the liberal-conservative continuum, was renewed soon after World War II and again in the 1960s.

Postwar research efforts focused on the concepts of fascism, anti-semitism, and authoritarianism. Authoritarianism is by now perhaps the most heavily researched concept in the entirety of political psychology. The first major publication in the area (Adorno et al., 1950) was formidable: a thousand pages of psychoanalytically-based theory, individual case studies, projective test results, and elaborate attempts to devise quantifiable questionnaires that simultaneously assessed psychological defensive maneuvers and extreme political positions. This initial publication was quickly followed by an avalanche of critical studies (e.g., Christie & Jahoda, 1954), complaining about everything from the wording of specific questionnaire items to the philosophical underpinnings of the entire enterprise.

The concept of authoritarianism as a politically expressed psychological variable has proven more robust than its early critics expected. The individual who treats social relationships mainly in hierarchical terms, is prejudiced against outgroups, tends toward conservative political views, and displays various problems with anxiety and impulse control has reappeared in two successive decades of empirical research employing substantially different methodologies (Rokeach, 1960; Wilson, 1973). Further, authoritarianism and related concepts have exhibited unusual appeal for psychologists, many of whom think of political psychology only in terms of ideology-and-personality relationships.

Such relationships were explored in the late 1960s and early 1970s largely in terms of whether political activists of right and left display distinctive personality patterns—and even, reverting to the concerns of the 1930s, whether an individual's political position is correlated with intelligence level. For a while, it appeared from the empirical data that leftist activists were on the average smarter than rightist activists. By the time more basic and reliable findings emerged, showing instead that activists in general are usually smarter than nonactivists (Kerpelman, 1972), both the activists and research interest in them had begun to subside. Nonetheless, the intense psychological interest in activism over a decade has left a heritage of interesting questions and some increasingly complex answers concerning the psychological origins of political extremism (e.g., Kraut & Lewis, 1975; Schoenberger, 1969).

A related set of questions, increasingly salient during the 1970s, concerned the psychological origins of political alienation. These questions were of more interest to political scientists and to some sociologists, schooled as they were in classical theories of alienation, than to psychologists. Easy psychological diagnoses of the origins of alienation proved increasingly irrelevant as alienated attitudes spread throughout the U.S. populace. Explanations taking into account interactions among personal motives, political events, and peer relationships appeared more useful (Elms, 1976, pp. 20–24).

Influencing political attitudes. "Public opinion and propaganda" has long been a standard course offering in political science departments, and attitude change is a major research topic within social psychology. But the psychological study of political attitude change has so far not been as productive a research area as its antecedents would lead one to hope. Meaningful experimentation is again seriously limited by ethical considerations, though it may be possible under certain circumstances to generalize from laboratory effects to actual campaign phenomena (Grush, McKeough, & Ahlering, 1978). The use of extensive public opinion survey data has enabled researchers to identify a number of variables associated with holding particular political attitudes, but these variables often hold no obvious psychological implications.

Political learning, viewed as antecedent to the development of political attitudes, has been studied in adults as well as in children (Chaffee, 1977; Kraus & Davis, 1976). Once an individual has learned something about politics and about particular politicians, the process by which he or she arrives at a voting position has again come to be seen by recent researchers, from both political science and psychology, as largely a rational choice (Ajzen & Fishbein, 1980; Kelley & Mirer, 1974). This assumption is in odd contrast to those of earlier researchers who examined attitudes through case-historical methods (Lane, 1962, 1969; Lasswell, 1930; Smith et al., 1956) and who perceived attitudes as often expressing irrational motives. Perhaps the more quantitative approaches of the recent researchers produced a greater appearance of rationality; perhaps differences in subject samples and the kinds of political topics subjects were asked about skewed the results in one direction or another. (But a thoroughly quantitative, nationally representative survey of voters by other researchers has found little support for the rational-choice model; see Sears, Lau, Tyler, & Allen, 1980.) It should be noted in any case that by including a detailed theoretical and empirical consideration of political attitudes and voting behavior in their most recent book, Ajzen and Fishbein (1980) have considerably expanded the range of content considered in psychological texts on attitude change, and their work may be leading the way toward greater involvement by psychologists in this area.

Much of the research on political attitude change has concerned mass media influence on voters' final choice of presidential candidates. But some research suggests that the media may be less important in producing specific persuasive effects than in "agenda-setting"—that is, in telling voters not what attitudes to take about particular candidates and issues, but which issues are most important (Graber, 1980, pp. 132–134). Such agenda-setting may make the issue positions and personal characteristics of certain candidates more salient to voters than those of other candidates, who appear ill-attuned to the issues judged as major by the media. Media judgments may also directly establish for voters an agenda of candidates, particularly in presidential campaigns—by communicating early in the primary campaign which candidates are worth the voters' attention and which may be ignored (Barber, 1978, 1980a). Such agenda-setting or salience-increasing functions of persuasive communications have not been much attended to in mainstream attitude change research; this may be an area where further study of political persuasion can contribute significantly to attitude theory and research in general.

Psychology of the Political Actor

Lower-level office holders. As I turn to research on the psychology of the professional politician, I shall refrain from looking first at the highest office-holders, who have also received the bulk of research attention. Office-holders lower in the hierarchy come in large enough numbers to make quantitative data analysis relatively easy, and they may also be more accessible to the researcher who wants to collect personality or life-history data firsthand. Several researchers have indeed managed to persuade substantial numbers of office-holders to fill out standard personality questionnaires—most notably Costantini and Craik (1972, 1980), who have obtained Adjective Check List responses from California legislators and party officials for over a decade. The time span and the number of respondents in their studies are large enough to enable these investigators to make reliable comparisons of personality constellations among various subgroups (e.g., Republican and Democratic male and female party leaders) and to find evidence of reliability in these personality constellations over time. Other studies have been less ambitious but have provided data on an interesting variety of characteristics, including self-actualizing tendencies (Knutson, 1974), self-esteem levels (Sniderman, 1975), and power, achievement, and affiliation motives (Browning & Jacob, 1964).

A particularly intriguing study of lower-lever office-holders, using both quantitative data and case-history materials, was carried out by Barber (1965) on the Connecticut State Legislature. Barber identified four major characterological types of legislators. *Lawmakers* work hard and enjoy their legislative work enough to want to return to office repeatedly; they are achievement-oriented, relatively free of repressed conflicts, and unusually empathic. *Advertisers* are also quite active in the legislature but do not particularly enjoy it, seeing it instead as a stepping-stone to higher or more lucrative positions. They appear to be high both in achievement motivation and in fear of failure; much of their intense activity is defensive in nature. *Spectators* are low in legislative activity, enjoying the job mainly for its social status and its satisfaction of their need for approval. *Reluctants* neither enjoy being legislators nor do very much once in office; they serve from a sense of duty to parents and community and tend not to remain in office if another competent candidate can be found. The first two categories appear likely to be found in most legislative chambers, though Barber's study has not been replicated elsewhere. The latter categories seem likely to occur frequently only in states where being a legislator is a part-time and fairly low-visibility pursuit. Barber has since revised the categories and applied them to U.S. Presidents (see below and Barber, 1977, as well as criticisms by Qualls, 1977).

Chief executives. U.S. Presidents are highly visible individuals, not only to the child going through the early phases of political socialization but to political psychologists. (Chief executives of other nations have been studied to a much more limited degree, but see Hermann's, 1980a, b, resourceful content-analytic research on heads of government.) Because the total number of Presidents has been small and because only one serves at a time, most of the psychological research on them has employed a case-history approach. However, Winter and Stewart (1977), Barry (1979), and Simonton (1981) have conducted quantitative analyses of certain psychologically relevant variables associated with Presidents, while Wendt and Muncy (1979) have conducted a quantitative personality study of U.S. Vice-Presidents, a number of whom have become Presidents. Barber (1977), too, has used a semi-quantitative comparative case–history approach to the study of a substantial number of Presidents.

Barber's quadripartite categorization scheme as applied to Presidents involves essentially the same two variables as in his study of legislators: level of political activity and enjoyment of the office. Beginning with the nation's first four Presidents and including all twentieth-century Presidents, Barber has found certain regularities in the character and behavior of Presidents in each of his four categories. His greatest concern is reserved for the "active-negative" Presidents, including Wilson, Hoover, Johnson, and Nixon. They are compulsive, using the job to reduce their own anxiety and guilt. When failure threatens, they typically become rigid rather than adaptive. Active-positive Presidents, on the other hand, are flexible and learn from their mistakes; they are basically high in self-esteem and do not respond defensively to threats of defeat. FDR, Truman, and John Kennedy all fall in this category, as do—somewhat more tentatively—Gerald Ford and Jimmy Carter. Passive-positive Presidents are compliant, affection-seeking, easily swayed by cronies or by admired pressure groups; Taft, Harding, and Reagan are examples. Passive-negatives serve dutifully but with little intiative or true leadership; the category includes Coolidge and Eisenhower.

Barber advocated using his schema and other information to make predictions about the performance in office of potential Presidents, but he avoided making any explicit predictions in 1976, and in 1980 he made only the most general speculation that, as President, Reagan might "cave in to pressure" (Barber, 1980b). Other researchers have not been remiss about

making both psychological diagnoses and behavioral predictions concerning candidates and incumbent Presidents. The pressures of publication
deadlines during campaigns (as with Mazlish & Diamond, 1976) and the
intensity of personal feelings toward incumbent Presidents (as in deMause
& Ebel, 1977) have so far rendered such attempts at predictive political
psychobiography less than satisfactory. The current level of activity in
political psychobiography and in psychobiographical methodology generally, however, suggests the possibility of substantial improvements in the
near future.

Of available presidential psychobiographies, the Georges' (1956) work
on Woodrow Wilson is usually cited as the best. Though their model of
analysis was basically psychoanalytic, they avoided the personal excesses of the Wilson psychobiography by Freud and Bullitt (1967). However,
they by no means provided a conclusive psychological characterization of
Wilson. Tucker (1977), for example, suggested applying Karen Horney's
theory of neurotic personality as an alternative, while Weinstein, Anderson, and Link (1978; see also Weinstein, 1981) proposed that a neurologi-
cally-based developmental dyslexia, rather than repressed Oedipal
hostilities, formed the partial origin of Wilson's personality problems.
(Beyond this explanatory variety, the interdisciplinary scope of this single
limited controversy is noteworthy, as it has involved scholars from the
fields of political science, psychoanalysis, history, neurology, and clinical
psychology.)

Psychobiography is a method of such complexity and immaturity that
multiple studies of a single figure, particularly at such a high level of
discourse and involving such diverse approaches as the Wilson controversy, should be welcomed. Of other U.S. Presidents, only Nixon and
Carter have received so much attention. Psychobiographical studies of
Nixon have run the gamut from the scurrilous and unreliable to the reasonably responsible but not altogether persuasive (Brodie, 1981; Mazlish,
1973). Psychobiographies of Carter have displayed much the same range,
with studies by Mazlish and Diamond (1980) and by Glad (1980) being the
best so far among an array that will surely increase in number and objectivity with the passage of time. Kearns's (1976) psychobiography of Lyndon Johnson is of interest for its use of first-hand data and its examination
of Johnson's psychological functioning within various governmental
roles.

The psychobiographical study of political leaders appears to be a potentially powerful approach. It requires, however, unusual investments of
time as well as unusual skills in more than one field—at a minimum,
clinical or personality theory plus political biography or history. Further,
methodological guidelines and evidential criteria are still being developed
(see Anderson, 1981a, 1981b; Crosby & Crosby, 1981; Glad, 1973; Green-

stein, 1975; Runyan, 1982; Tetlock, Crosby, & Crosby, 1981). It remains to be seen whether the approach will attain the general utility in political psychology that it has already displayed in so different a field as literary criticism (see Lindauer, in Volume I).

Political advisers. Elected officials are by no means the only individuals to attain positions of political power, even in a democracy. The higher the level of office and the more complex the political issues to be faced, the more important an elected official's appointed or informally selected advisers are likely to be. The Georges (1956) recognized this in writing their book not about Wilson alone, but (as the title says) about *Woodrow Wilson and Colonel House.* The book's personality assessments principally concern Wilson rather than House, but the relationship with House is crucial in understanding Wilson's behavior as President and the roots of that behavior in his earlier life.

Political advisers have not yet been subjected to extensive study by political psychologists, but research interest in them has been increasing. Henry Kissinger has stimulated several psychobiographical studies (e.g., Mazlish, 1976; Ward, 1975). Kissinger provides an example of an individual whose psychological functioning may at present be better understood by applying psychological constructs of limited scope—in this case, Machiavellianism—than by speculating about early events and unconscious processes in psychoanalytic terms (Elms, 1976, pp. 136–148). In attempting psychobiographical research on individuals whose lives are not as much a matter of public record as Presidents, or who (even in the case of Presidents) have become well-known too recently for detailed life-history data to become available, political psychologists may do well to employ empirically derived psychological constructs that can be applied to the subject's recent political behavior, such as Machiavellianism, internal versus external control, and tendencies toward groupthink.

Groupthink tendencies were initially identified within the context of interactions between U.S. Presidents and their foreign policy advisers (Janis, 1972). Under circumstances where members of a cohesive in-group are highly motivated to maintain the group's unanimity and its very existence, they may interact in ways that discourage independent critical thinking. Such patterns of interaction appear to have been present during the planning of what became major foreign policy failures (such as the Bay of Pigs invasion), and they may also have contributed to such domestic policy disasters as the Watergate affair. Political leaders with certain personality characteristics may tend toward recurrent groupthink-induced failures; others may under certain circumstances be likely to appoint advisers who are themselves prone to groupthink. Psychological aspects of small-group interactions have received less attention from political psychologists than they deserve, given the ubiquity of small groups in politics (Golembiewski, 1978, 1981). Janis's concepts concerning groupthink have been one stimulus for renewed interest in small group processes, as observed in the deliberations of political leaders and their advisers (Tetlock, 1979).

Like legislators, political advisers come in large enough numbers to be studied quantitatively by the persevering researcher. Etheredge (1978) has studied relationships between personality variables and decision-making processes in a sample of 126 career foreign service officers in the U.S. State Department. Measures of such variables as dominance-submission, affection-hostility, self-esteem, and neuroticism were correlated with foreign policy perceptions and attitudes and with the officers' choice of various policy options concerning actual or hypothetical international incidents. Etheredge has also found evidence for the contribution of consistent personality patterns to disagreements between U.S. Presidents and their foreign policy advisers over a 70-year period. Those scoring relatively high on quantitative indices of dominance behavior in interpersonal interactions were more likely to advocate the threat or use of military force to achieve national aims, while those scoring relatively high on measures of extraversion were more likely to advocate international cooperation and negotiation. (Hermann's, 1980b, research on Soviet Politburo members yields somewhat similar findings.) Such a combination of standardized psychological questionnaire data, policy advisers' quantifiable responses to policy choice situations, and psychologically relevant archival data, all brought to bear on a single set of hypotheses, is unusual in political psychology and offers a model to be emulated.

CONCLUSIONS

Political psychology has never been wholeheartedly embraced by either of its disciplinary parents. It has thus had to develop its own identity and is perhaps the better for that. Its parents are perhaps the poorer. Substantial portions of "orthodox" political science could still benefit from greater use of psychological constructs and methods, while those areas of psychology from which such constructs and methods have come remain in large part untouched by the serious real-world concerns, the subsequent conceptual and methodological innovations, and the relevant findings of political psychology.

The further development of political psychology as a coherent research area and as a source of contributions to the parent disciplines is seriously hampered by current training arrangements. With rare exceptions, graduate training in political psychology is not available in formal programs but is dependent on the availability of two or three interested faculty members in either a political science or a psychology department. Failing that, the would-be political psychologist must, like most other interdisciplinary scholars, jerry-build the "political" part of his or her training onto an orthodox psychological base, or vice versa, at some time after leaving graduate school. The result is often a notably weaker control of the skills and concepts of the secondary field than of the primary one, with deleterious effects upon the final research product.

Degree-granting departments or institutes of political psychology are not the best answer to such problems. Psychology and political science will both continue to benefit—and will benefit to an even greater degree in the future, one hopes—from the contributions of intermediaries between the two fields. Political psychology itself has much to gain from a continuing close association with its parent fields. Perhaps as political psychology's own methodological practices become more sophisticated, as its conceptual underpinnings gain in originality, and as its data base expands, the parents will more fully recognize its worth and will be willing to give more time and attention to the appropriate training of its practitioners. Perhaps at that point we will begin to see a greater *rapprochement* between the parent disciplines, with a larger number of joint degree programs and structured postdoctoral training opportunities as a result. It is likely in any case that the initiative for such advances in training and practice will have to come from within political psychology itself.

REFERENCES

Adorno, T. W., Frenkel-Brunswik, E., Levinson, D. J., & Sanford, R. N. *The authoritarian personality.* New York: Harper & Row, 1950.

Ajzen, I., & Fishbein, M. *Understanding attitudes and predicting behavior.* Englewood Cliffs, NJ: Prentice-Hall, 1980.

Allport, G. W. The historical background of modern social psychology. In G. Lindzey & E. Aronson (Eds.), *Handbook of social psychology* (2nd ed.). Reading, MA: Addison-Wesley, 1968.

Anderson, J. W. The methodology of psychological biography. *Journal of Interdisciplinary History,* 1981, *11,* 455–475. (a)

Anderson, J. W. Psychobiographical methodology: The case of William James. *Review of Personality and Social Psychology,* 1981, *2,* 245–272. (b)

Arterton, F. C. The impact of Watergate on children's attitudes toward political authority. *Political Science Quarterly,* 1974, *89,* 269–288.

Barber, J. D. *The lawmakers.* New Haven, CT: Yale University Press, 1965.

Barber, J. D. *The presidential character* (2nd ed.). Englewood Cliffs, NJ: Prentice-Hall, 1977.

Barber, J. D. (Ed.). *Race for the Presidency: The media and the nominating process.* Englewood Cliffs, NJ: Prentice-Hall, 1978.

Barber, J. D. *The pulse of politics: Electing Presidents in the media age.* New York: Norton, 1980. (a)

Barber, J. D. Worrying about Reagan. *New York Times,* September 8, 1980. (b)

Barry, H. Birth order and paternal namesake as predictors of affiliation with predecessor by Presidents of the United States. *Political Psychology,* 1979, *1,* 61–66.

Beck, P. A. The role of agents in political socialization. In S. A. Renshon (Ed.), *Handbook of political socialization.* New York: Free Press, 1977.

Brodie, F. M. *Richard Nixon: The shaping of his character.* New York: Norton, 1981.

Broh, C. A. Adler on the influence of siblings in political socialization. *Political Behavior,* 1979, *1,* 175–200.

Browning, R. P., & Jacob, H. Power motivation and the political personality. *Public Opinion Quarterly,* 1964, *28,* 75–90.

Chaffee, S. H. Mass communication in political socialization. In S. A. Renshon (Ed.), *Handbook of political socialization.* New York: Free Press, 1977.

Christie, R., & Jahoda, M. (Eds.). *Studies in the scope and method of "The authoritarian personality."* Glencoe, IL: Free Press, 1954.

Costantini, E., & Craik, K. W. Women as politicians: The social background, personality, and political careers of female party leaders. *Journal of Social Issues,* 1972, *28,* 217–236.

Costantini, E., & Craik, K. W. Personality and politicians: California party leaders, 1969–1979. *Journal of Personality and Social Psychology,* 1980, *38,* 641–661.

Crosby, F., & Crosby, T. L. Psychobiography and psychohistory. In S. Long (Ed.), *Handbook of political behavior.* New York: Plenum, 1981.

Dawson, R. E., Prewitt, K., & Dawson, K. S. *Political socialization* (2nd ed.). Boston, MA: Little, Brown, 1977.

deMause, L., & Ebel, H. (Eds.). *Jimmy Carter and American fantasy: Psychohistorical explorations.* New York: Psychohistory Press, 1977.

deRivera, J. *The psychological dimension of foreign policy.* Columbus, OH: Merrill, 1968.

Easton, D., & Dennis, J. *Children in the political system.* New York: McGraw Hill, 1969.

Elms, A. C. Psychological factors in right-wing extremism. In R. A. Schoenberger (Ed.), *The American right wing.* New York: Holt, Rinehart, & Winston, 1969.

Elms, A. C. *Personality in politics.* New York: Harcourt, Brace, Jovanovich, 1976.

Erikson, E. H. *Gandhi's truth.* New York: Norton, 1969.

Erikson, E. H. *Dimensions of a new identity.* New York: Norton, 1974.

Etheredge, L. S. *A world of men: The private sources of American foreign policy.* Cambridge, MA: MIT Press, 1978.

Freud, S., & Bullitt, W. C. *Thomas Woodrow Wilson: A psychological study.* Boston, MA: Houghton Mifflin, 1967.

George, A. L. Some uses of dynamic psychology in political biography: Case materials on Woodrow Wilson. In F. I. Greenstein & M. Lerner (Eds.), *A source book for the study of personality and politics.* New York: Markham, 1971.

George, A. L., & George, J. L. *Woodrow Wilson and Colonel House.* New York: John Day, 1956.

Glad, B. Contributions of psychobiography. In Knutson, J. N. (Ed.), *Handbook of political psychology.* San Francisco, CA: Jossey-Bass, 1973.

Glad, B. *Jimmy Carter: In search of the great white house.* New York: Norton, 1980.

Golembiewski, R. T. (Ed.). *The small group in political science: The last two decades of development.* Athens, GA: University of Georgia Press, 1978.

Golembiewski, R. T. Small-group analysis in political behavior: Perspectives on significance and stuckness. *Micropolitics,* 1981, *1,* 295–319.

Graber, D. A. *Mass media and American politics.* Washington, DC: Congressional Quarterly Press, 1980.

Greenstein, F. I. *Children and politics.* New Haven, CT: Yale University Press, 1965.

Greenstein, F. I. *Personality and politics* (2nd ed.). Chicago, IL: Markham, 1975.

Grush, D. E., McKeough, K. L., & Ahlering, R. F. Extrapolating laboratory exposure research to actual political elections. *Journal of Personality and Social Psychology,* 1978, *36,* 257–270.

Hermann, M. G. Explaining foreign policy behavior using personal characteristics of political leaders. *International Studies Quarterly,* 1980, *24,* 7–46. (a)

Hermann, M. G. Assessing the personalities of Soviet Politburo members. *Personality and Social Psychology Bulletin,* 1980, *6,* 332–352. (b)

Hess, R. D., & Torney, J. V. *The development of political attitudes in children.* Chicago, IL: Aldine, 1967.

Holsti, O. R. Content analysis. In G. Lindzey & E. Aronson (Eds.), *Handbook of social psychology* (Vol. 2). Reading, MA: Addison-Wesley, 1968.

Hyman, H. *Political socialization.* Glencoe, IL: Free Press, 1959.

Janis, I. L. *Victims of groupthink.* Boston, MA: Houghton Mifflin, 1972.

Katz, D. The functional approach to the study of attitudes. *Public Opinion Quarterly,* 1960, *24,* 163–204.

Kearns, D. *Lyndon Johnson and the American dream.* New York: Harper & Row, 1976.

Kelley, S., & Mirer, T. W. The simple act of voting. *American Political Science Review,* 1974, *68,* 572–591.

Kelman, H. C. (Ed.). *International behavior: A social-psychological analysis.* New York: Holt, Rinehart & Winston, 1965.

Kerpelman, L. C. *Activists and nonactivists: A psychological study of American college students.* New York: Behavioral Publications, 1972.

Knutson, J. N. *Psychological variables in political recruitment: An analysis of party activists.* Berkeley, CA: Wright Institute, 1974.

Kramnick, I. *The rage of Edmund Burke.* New York: Basic Books, 1977.

Kraus, S., & Davis, D. *The effects of mass communication on political behavior.* University Park, PA: The Pennsylvania State University, 1976.

Kraut, R. E., & Lewis, S. H. Alternate models of family influence on student political ideology. *Journal of Personality and Social Psychology,* 1975, *31,* 791–800.

Lamb, K. A. *As orange goes.* New York: Norton, 1974.

Lane, R. E. *Political ideology.* Glencoe, IL: Free Press, 1962.

Lane, R. E. Political science and psychology. In S. Koch (Ed.), *Psychology: A study of a science* (Vol. 6). New York: McGraw-Hill, 1963.

Lane, R. E. *Political thinking and consciousness.* Chicago, IL: Markham, 1969.

Lasswell, H. D. *Propaganda technique in the World War.* New York: Knopf, 1927.

Lasswell, H. D. *Psychopathology and politics.* Chicago, IL: University of Chicago Press, 1930.

Lasswell, H. D. *Power and personality.* New York: Norton, 1948.

Lasswell, H. D. Democratic character. In H. D. Laswell, *The political writings of Harold D. Lasswell.* Glencoe, IL: Free Press, 1951.

LeVine, R. A. *Culture, behavior, and personality.* Chicago, IL: Aldine, 1973.

Likert, R. A technique for the measurement of attitudes. *Archives of Psychology,* 1932, *22,* 1–55.

Lippman, W. *Public opinion.* New York: Free Press, 1965. (Originally published, 1925.)

McClelland, D. C. *The achieving society.* Princeton, NJ: Van Nostrand, 1961.

McClelland, D. C. *Power: The inner experience.* New York: Irvington, 1975.

Maslow, A. H. Eupsychia—The good society. *Journal of Humanistic Psychology,* 1961, *2,* 1–11.

Mazlish, B. *In search of Nixon.* Baltimore, MD: Penguin, 1973.

Mazlish, B. *Kissinger: The European mind in American policy.* New York: Basic Books, 1976.

Mazlish, B., & Diamond, E. Thrice-born: A psychohistory of Jimmy Carter's "rebirth." *New York,* 1976, *9*(35), 26–33.

Mazlish, B., & Diamond, E. *Jimmy Carter: An interpretive biography*. New York: Simon & Schuster, 1980.

Milgram, S. Nationality and conformity. *Scientific American*, 1961, *205*(6), 45–51.

Milgram. S. *Obedience to authority*. New York: Harper & Row, 1974.

Münsterberg, H. *Psychology and social sanity*. Garden City, NY: Doubleday, Page & Co., 1914.

Nathan, J. A., & Remy, R. C. Comparative political socialization: A theoretical perspective. In S. A. Renshon (Ed.), *Handbook of political socialization*. New York: Free Press, 1977.

Post, J. M. The seasons of a leader's life: Influences of the life cycle on political behavior. *Political Psychology*, 1980, *2*, 35–49.

Qualls, J. H. Barber's typological analysis of political leaders. *American Political Science Review*, 1977, *71*, 182–211.

Renshon, S. A. *Psychological needs and political behavior*. New York: Free Press, 1974.

Renshon, S. A. Assumptive frameworks in political socialization theory. In S. A. Renshon (Ed.), *Handbook of political socialization: Theory and research*. New York: Free Press, 1977.

Rokeach, M. *The open and closed mind*. New York: Basic Books, 1960.

Runyan, W. M. *Life histories and psychobiography*. New York: Oxford, 1982.

Schoenberger, R. A. (Ed.). *The American right wing*. New York: Holt, Rinehart & Winston, 1969.

Sears, D. O., Lau, R. R., Tyler, T. R., & Allen, H. M. Self-interest vs. symbolic politics in policy attitudes and presidential voting. *American Political Science Review*, 1980, *74*, 670–684.

Semmel, A. K., & Minix, D. Group dynamics and risk-taking: An experimental examination. *Experimental Study of Politics*, 1978, *6*, 1–33.

Simonton, D. K. Presidential greatness and performance: Can we predict leadership in the White House? *Journal of Personality*, 1981, *49*, 306–323.

Skinner, B. F. *Walden two*. New York: MacMillan, 1948.

Smith, B. L. The mystifying intellectual history of Harold D. Lasswell. In A. A. Rogow (Ed.), *Politics, personality, and social science in the twentieth century*. Chicago, IL: University of Chicago Press, 1969.

Smith, M. B. Political attitudes. In J. N. Knutson (Ed.), *Handbook of political psychology*. San Francisco, CA: Jossey-Bass, 1973.

Smith, M. B., Bruner, J., & White, R. W. *Opinions and personality*. New York: Wiley, 1956.

Sniderman, P. *Personality and democratic politics*. Berkeley, CA: University of California Press, 1975.

Tanenhaus, J., & Foley, M. A. Separating objects of specific and diffuse support: Experiments on Presidents and the Presidency. *Micropolitics*, 1981, *1*, 345–367.

Tetlock, P. E. Identifying victims of groupthink from public statements of decision makers. *Journal of Personality and Social Psychology*, 1979, *37*, 1314–1324.

Tetlock, P. E., Crosby, F., & Crosby, T. L. Political psychobiography. *Micropolitics*, 1981, *1*, 191–213.

Thurstone, L. L., & Chave, E. J. *The measurement of attitude*. Chicago, IL: University of Chicago Press, 1929.

Torney, J. V., Oppenheim, A. N., & Farnen, F. F. *Civic education in ten countries: An empirical study*. New York: Wiley, 1975.

Tucker, R. C. The Georges' Wilson reexamined: An essay on psychobiography. *American Political Science Review*, 1977, *71*, 606–618.

Wallas, G. *Human nature in politics*. Lincoln, NB: University of Nebraska Press, 1962. (Originally published, 1908.)

Ward, D. Kissinger: A psychohistory. *History of Childhood Quarterly,* 1975, *2,* 287–348.

Weinstein, E. A. *Woodrow Wilson: A medical and psychological biography.* Princeton, NJ: Princeton University Press, 1981.

Weinstein, E. A., Anderson, J. W., & Link, A. S. Woodrow Wilson's political personality: A reappraisal. *Political Science Quarterly,* 1978, *93,* 585–598.

Wendt, H. W., & Muncy, C. A. Studies of political character: Factor patterns of 24 U.S. Vice-Presidents. *Journal of Psychology,* 1979, *102,* 125–131.

Wilson, G. D. (Ed.). *The psychology of conservatism.* New York: Academic Press, 1973.

Winter, D. G., & Stewart, A. J. Content analysis as a technique for assessing political leaders. In M. G. Hermann (Ed.), *A psychological examination of political leaders.* New York: Free Press, 1977.

8 Psychology and Sociology

Kurt W. Back
Duke University

INTRODUCTION

The paradox of the relationship between psychology and sociology is even reflected in their etymology. In the dictionary definition (American Heritage Dictionary, 1969), psychology is the science of mental processes and behavior, and sociology is the study of interpersonal patterns and relationships. The whole psychological-social complex can be visualized as a network, psychology being concerned with the nodes of the network, and sociology with the links. This division shows the interdependence and complementarity of the two sciences. Neither nodes nor links have independent meaning, but they can be discussed separately. However, looking at the origin of the terms we find very different sources. Psychology, the older science, was defined in its seventeenth and eighteenth century origins as a branch of anthropology (the study of man), which is divided into anatomy—the study of the body—and psychology—the study of the mind (Oxford English Dictionary, 1933). Sociology, on the other hand, originated in the nineteenth century, and the term was used first as equivalent to social ethics, or criticism and evaluation of society (Oxford English Dictionary, 1933). These different sources, one in understanding the human organism, the other in the search for a utopian society, have led to an enduring contrast between the two sciences.

Further, this uneasy combination of complementarity and contrast has colored the whole relationship between these two fields. On the one hand, the division between psychology and sociology is a purely conceptual artifact: All individual processes and actions are determined to some degree by social conditions; even the most individualistic sensory experiment is made possible by a culture which has legitimized laboratory research and the relations among subject, experimenter, and other persons involved. On the other hand, large-scale social changes and patterns are influenced by individual capacities, needs, and desires. For these reasons one would expect a considerable overlap in the work of these two fields, with a great proportion of the work and workers not clearly identified with either. But historical conditions of the rise of the two sciences led to disparity in the way scientists in the two fields actually work, think, and present their results; that is, they have developed different cultures and are clearly distinct. The interplay of these two kinds of relations forms the framework of the investigation.

HISTORICAL BACKGROUND

Psychology and sociology, like all sciences, developed by emancipation from philosophy, and in both fields metaphysical questions continued to motivate research. Psychology studied topics such as the mind-body problem, freedom of the will, and the essence of human nature; sociology, the natural state of society or the ultimate aim of social evolution. In both fields, as in other sciences, these questions gradually retreated, not being considered proper for empirical investigation, though they are periodically resurrected. However, psychology and sociology differ in the circumstances accompanying their origins as independent sciences. Psychology sprang from the laboratory sciences, as an extension of biological research; sociology's origin was based in concern about social problems and instigation of social change.

Psychology

Even in its early concerns with philosophical questions, the biological model of understanding was predominant in psychology, not the search for an ideal. For example, the classic psychological study in education and in the construction of test materials, the wild boy of Aveyron, was supported mainly because of interest it inspired in discovering ultimate factors of raw human nature and the modification of human nature through modern civilization (Shattuck, 1980), and not by a desire to help the handicapped. The main concern was whether the essence of a modern Frenchman of the revolutionary period was present in the animal-like creature. When the experiment to find the essential human nature—Rousseau's "natural man"—failed, concern with the fate of the boy vanished too. A systematic construction of a different human being, taking into account previous experiences, was not considered: The aim was understanding of human essence and not its improvement. Striving toward the aim of perfection of humanity through individuals was condemned, as in cautionary tales such as the Golem and Mary Shelley's *Frankenstein;* by contrast, sociology had a long early history with favorable views of the complete reconstruction of society, starting with Thomas More's *Utopia*.

Scientific psychology itself developed as an offspring of physiological research. Wilhelm Wundt's laboratory is conventionally taken as its birthplace (Boring, 1950). Wundt investigated sensory process in a way analogous to the current state of biological research. He compared applications of physical stimuli with subjective reports of sensory impressions and tried to establish regularities in relations between the two—stimuli and response. The program was to continue this procedure for all human faculties, sensations, perceptions, and emotions to complete a description of the functioning of a normal human being. In effect, Wundt was applying in the laboratory Kant's (1781) principles, distinguishing between things as they really are, outside of human experience *(Ding an sich),* and the categories which organize them in the world. Psychology investigated systematically the ways in which the human soul and universe could interact or face each other. The earliest psychological laboratories out of which scientific psychology arose were devoted to this understanding, an expansion of the scientific study of nonliving and living organisms.

The historical link between psychology and the biological laboratory sciences has been maintained through many deviations. By and large the aim of psychology has stayed within this framework, despite criticism from inside and outside the field and despite many successful forays into different settings. The basic orientation has remained: Tackle a problem by controlling the situation and limit irrelevant factors in a way that only the functionally important features remain. In general, a psychologist will look at any research question by first determining which variables are strongly represented, whether in a sensory laboratory experiment, a clinical setting, or some other approximation to the ideal. Coming from a different tradition, the sociologist will look first at the situation as it exists and then try to use descriptive or analytic techniques until a theoretical framework can be justified; this framework, to be sure, may have been in the investigator's mind from the beginning. The difference is not that one is deductive and the other inductive, but that the psychologist is more comfortable with physical manipulation and the sociologist with symbolic arrangements.

Looking at the heritage of biological research, we note that many advances there have been achieved by combining laboratory research and ethology. Psychology, however, has deemphasized human ethology, the study of man in his natural habitat, placing its emphasis mainly on the laboratory side of the inquiry.

This choice has not gone without controversy. From time to time new departures have been made to drop or relax controls and search for insight in the raw environment. In psychology, these new techniques usually evolved into a return to more controlled procedures. A few examples may suffice: Explorations of problem-solving and classroom learning gave way to the rigorous disciplines of mental testing and conditioning and learning experiments; the gestalt psychologists' insistence on studying perception in natural conditions led to laboratories for the study of cognition; attempts, such as Moreno's, to add different actors to a limited clinical situation led back to a change from individual to group therapy using equivalent frameworks; work in organizational and industrial psychology tends to leave the work site and become a model for ingenious experiments. The same trend may be one of the reasons for the decline of the community mental health movement.

A case closer to sociology shows this trend fully, namely the work in group dynamics (Back, 1979a, in press; Cartwright & Zander, 1968). Group dynamics were based on Lewinian psychology; Lewin (1918/1981) tried originally to distinguish sensory psychology, the classical laboratory science, from a psychology devoted to investigating human action and thought. In individual psychology these studies have come to look more and more like traditional experiments with novel types of variables. In transforming these approaches to social situations, the aim of group dynamics was to study group functioning in society, combining laboratory and field studies. Again, however, laboratory studies took over; group dynamics became experimental social psychology. In trying to impose even greater control, psychological researchers decreased the size of the groups studied to dyads and then to single individuals with programmed partners. The sociologist Borgatta (1954) suggested (sarcastically) that the future of this research belonged to no-person groups in which computers talked to computers, and *Time* magazine's "Man of the Year" for 1982 was the computer. Incredibly, the rise in simulation has almost surpassed Borgatta's seemingly preposterous claim.

These highlights do not constitute a comprehensive history of psychological research, but serve to document norms which are part of the identity of psychologists. Psychologists perceive research questions about relations between theoretically founded variables as appropriately reproducible to study under controlled conditions.

Sociology

By contrast, the tradition of sociology is bound intimately to the search for social betterment. Its origins lie in the dislocations of the industrial revolution and the disintegration of feudalism, an order in which a multitude of pre-established ranking and privileges persisted through super-natural sanctions. The eighteenth century questioned these premises, and the nineteenth superseded them. Early thinkers on sociological problems faced these questions and tried to find new forms to substitute for out-dated feudalism and new ways to justify and perpetuate new social ar-rangements. The construction of a new world requires, of course, understanding how the social world is put together. The heritage of pro-posing ideal solutions, that is to play at being a social reformer, is as strong in sociology as the laboratory tradition is in psychology. Con-versely, just as the dabbling of Dr. Frankenstein is the cautionary exam-ple for the psychologist, Machiavelli's cold, dissecting approach to society is a warning for the sociologist's reputation. Again, some high-lights can document this enduring cultural norm among sociologists.

The original group of protosociologists, the "prophets of Paris" (Manuel, 1962), first stressed a utopian tradition in sociology. The five authors whom Manuel discusses—Turgot, Condorcet, Saint-Simon, Fourier, and Comte—all proposed programs for social reform and looked to the future in their theoretical statements; the last three devised elabo-rate schemes of creating new societies with all their paraphernalia. Comte is often called the father of sociology, but he also founded the positivist church. The Frankenstein monster of a created society becomes apparent in the twentieth century; a new cautionary tale, dystopia instead of utopia, belongs in this century: Zamyatin's *We,* Huxley's *Brave New World,* and Orwell's *1984* were written between 1921 and 1948. But soci-ologists did not flinch from planning new societies.

The recognized modern founders of sociological theory, Durkheim, Weber, and Marx, added analysis to their normative concerns. They did this to varying degrees, Marx preferring to change the world rather than explain it, while Weber advocated teaching value-free sociology. Durk-heim ostensibly dealt with analysis of social structure; but his aim was to establish a foundation for the secular French Third Republic, substituting for the Catholicism and traditional loyalties of the monarchic tradition (Tiryakian, 1965).

Even the start of systematic research in sociology was motivated by welfare concerns. The survey of the poor in London by Charles Booth (1892–1897) was the earliest major interview study of an appreciable sam-ple of the population. Booth's aim was not to study the urban system as ecology or organization but to document a plight in order to help agitate for remedies. The question of improving method arose from this possible interference into the collection and analysis of research data. An illustra-tive anecdote is an early study by Rice (1929); Rice found a prohibitionist interviewer collecting reports from respondents who blamed drink for their poverty, while a socialist interviewer found that respondents blamed social conditions. It is significant that the controversy about value-free science originated in sociology, which has never been able to steer clear of value commitment. Sociology has long been plagued with abstract discussion of the possibility and desirability of value-free science, an assertion of the separation of values and empirical science. Max Weber (1949) demonstrated the need for objectivity in analysis of social data, but he did not deny necessity for the sociologist to acknowledge the role of values in the selection of problems and in the implications of research. He distinguished between value-free science, which he advocated, and science without values, which he condemned (Etzioni, 1965).

Weber's defense of value-free science must be seen in the context in which he stated it (see Marianne Weber's note in Weber, 1949, p. 51). He wanted to assert the independence of his work from political pressure. The general issue is, however, still alive among sociologists and gives occasion for animated discussion (Becker, 1967; Gouldner, 1965, 1968). At issue is not only the question of whether scientists can, but whether they should, be objective. Among psychologists one finds little general discussion of the issue, although in specific issues controversy about value presuppositions has not been absent.

Just as many subdisciplines in psychology have converged in the end on the experimental paradigm, so even the most abstract sociological designs seem to be pulled toward their effects on current social problems. For instance, Parsons's (Parsons & Smelser, 1956) structural-functionalist position, which is based on the analysis of a set of variables, such as ascription-achievement or particularist-universalist, has been attacked as being conservative: This is incorrect but it does lead to a certain political position which might inhibit social change (Gouldner, 1970). Correspondingly, new fields in sociology open when interest groups propose a new problem in society; thus, today, we have new specialties such as sociology of aging, sociology of sex roles, sociology of war and peace, or of ecology. Psychologists also become engaged in these fields, but they usually include them in traditional subfields, such as subject selection in experimental, developmental, or social psychology.

Research Strategy

The methods favored by psychology and by sociology follow the same pattern. Sociologists tend to shy away from physical control of a situation and prefer to impose statistical controls on natural events. This leads, of course, to a different kind of reasoning from that of psychologists. The importance of variables is inferred from their contribution to an effect in a naturalistic situation; the effect of each variable may be actually very weak because of the presence of a variety of other factors, which are

controlled only by mathematical procedures. Each type of control—
actual and experimental or virtual and statistical—has its well-known
virtues and defects. It is important to stress here that exerting physical
control changes the object studied, at least for a time. Sociologists are
reluctant to do so, unless the change takes a direction which they favor
for ideological reasons. In the language of many sociologists, physical
control is called intervention, and it is only to be used for a desired end.
At an extreme, in Marxist sociology, empirical work is called "praxis"
(the German or Greek term giving a more mystical effect than the English
"practice"), and it signifies the application of theory for socially acceptable ends. To a less extreme degree, the search for Utopia is still considered to be a valid aim and technique for sociology (Moore, 1966).
    The culture of sociologists continues their tradition of wanting to alter
and to improve society. In each period, different terms are used to justify
this aim in its scientific context. A recent instance of this tradition has
been the use of the term "policy research," the insistence of policy relevance for sociology. Sociologists tend to feel excluded from this primary
purpose if their results contribute only to understanding and knowledge
and have no effect on changes in society. This orientation, the greater
desire of sociologists to "get a piece of the action," leads to a greater
differentiation between sociology and psychology than their subject matter may suggest.
    The persistence in modern times of the historical accident of the differ-
ent origins and development of sociology and psychology may, however,
signify a fundamental difference between the two, which, to be sure, has
become exaggerated. This difference lies equally in the natural or real unit
of study for sociology and psychology, and the question of the unit of
analysis has different impact on the two sciences.

LEVELS OF DISCOURSE

The Hierarchy of Sciences: The Naive View

The whole human individual is the obvious standard for human sciences.
Everything below the individual—organs, cells, and responses—are fragments that get meaning only from their part in the whole organism. On the
other hand, units larger than the individual—groups, organizations,
classes, nations—seem to be either abstract constructions whose real
units are persons or voluntaristic creations by individual actors. The reality of larger units is asserted and established in a reasoned argument. To
naive perception, the individual is the reality, and all else is theory or
faith.
    In this sense there is psychological truth in the maxim "man is the

measure of all things," and psychology would be the natural base to start human sciences. This science would then make the study of the individual the basis for all other sciences dealing with humans; indeed, their autonomy from psychology is still not universally accepted. Originally, psychology had the same problem: The objects of nature appear as immediately given—there are stars, rocks, plants, and animals with whom people must deal; the problem of the actor or the perceiver as a topic of science came later, and so psychology followed astronomy, physics, and chemistry in different cycles of scientific progress. When both the individual and society came to be accepted as objects of study, the relation of their study to each other and to other sciences was placed into a hierarchy.

Comte (1858, pp. 38–50) was among the first modern scientists to arrange such a hierarchy. But he combined scientific and utopian ways, affirming that only the arrangement of a scientific pyramid with sociology at the apex and psychology just below it would make an ideal society possible. This arrangement included the ethical division of egoism and altruism, terms that Comte invented and that have since come to express moral values in social science.

The hierarchical arrangement of sciences has persisted in diverse schematics, though emphasis has veered from moral worth to a scientific base. Currently the most influential approach is that of systems theory. Here a set of principles is established which could apply to any self-organizing unit, from cells to nations. There are principles such as communication, energy exchange, boundary, differentiation, integration, and power. Continuity is established among these principles, hierarchy by the fact that each higher level must repeat the principle of each lower level—for instance, physiology cannot contradict the principles of biochemistry, and psychology not those of physiology. The laws of each higher level include the lower levels, but add their own principles. Human action cannot contradict the laws of physiology but is not completely determined by them; social life cannot contradict the principles of psychology, but is not completely determined by them.

A most comprehensive theory of living systems is that proposed by Miller (1977). Miller's model shows a hierarchy based on complexity, each higher level implying the lower one and adding its own influence to the principal variables of the lower one. Miller's hierarchy includes seven steps: cell, organ, organism, group, organization, society, and supranational system. Neither psychology nor sociology corresponds exactly to one of these levels, but, to a degree, psychology is centered on the organism, with some interest in its relationship to organs on the one hand, and to groups and even organizations on the other. Sociology is basically a science of organizations and society, but also treats groups and the supranational system; sociology has the additional characteristic that much of its data are derived from the organism and sometimes described in terms of the organism. This tension arises from the human tendency to refer to the individual as the natural unit.

Reality of the Social Realm

From this perspective, the reality of social levels, the existence of groups and societies, has to be justified. It can be looked at purely as a research question and defined in an operational way. D. T. Campbell (1958) has used this procedure in defining larger units by using the idea of commonality of fate; two particles (or individuals) have commonality of fate if we can improve our prediction of what happens to one particle by knowing what happens to the other one. This definition creates physical bodies out of particles, organisms out of organs, and groups and societies out of individuals. While there has been little trouble in the first steps, the last step seems artificial at first glance. Campbell explained this by a general perceptual bias in favor of time as against space in the social sphere; this leads to the preference of the individual over society. Immediate perceptions lead us to accept the persistence of the same person over time—we speak of the life course of "one" organism—but we cannot as easily perceive the links in space to other individuals who compose a contemporaneous social unit. However, in the actual methodology of prediction and explanation, the position is easily reversed. Frequently we can predict actions more precisely by taking into account synchronous social conditions than we can by considering the history of an individual. Political activity and economic actions (see Elms and Maital & Maital, in this volume), to give just two examples, are better explained by contemporary social conditions and group membership than by individual histories: The relative proportions of explained variance vary with the particular problem.

Evolution

The systems hierarchy does not necessarily include a value judgment. However, even within the systems approach a normative process has been preserved. This may happen, for instance, if an evolutionary perspective is accepted. If evolution has an aim at all it is toward ever larger units, as up to now biological systems have evolved from smaller to larger ones. In addition, in large-scale human history, the same sequence has prevailed from tribe to the world community. Thus, it could be supposed that the direction of human evolution would be toward ever larger units, that is toward the supranational unit, and that this larger unit would become more integrated and interdependent, just as unicellular colonies have progressed toward multicellular organisms. The most prominent proponent of this kind of systems theory has been Teilhard de Chardin (1969), who sees a—probably supernaturally inspired—progression toward a unity in the whole biosphere.

Perhaps even more significant is the not quite so literal claim of evolution toward a social unity which gives collective action superiority over individual achievement. Theories of social evolution and progress in history lead to assumptions of collective future and individual quests; current applications are exaltations of group and communal action and lend such terms as "collective," "commune," or "group action" an aura of the futuristic.

Here the reformist origins of sociology and the assertion of social reality combine to overwhelm not only psychology as a science but even the legitimacy of the individual. The contrast need not be all or none; ideologies can prefer individual solutions in one area of life and collective solutions in another: E.g., the radical feminist may prefer collectives in work and individual competition in the family. The relation of the two sciences is thus transformed from a question of intellectual understanding to an ideological contrast of which level of discourse should concern the future of humanity.

The Autonomy of Sociology

The distinction in theory and subject matter between psychology and sociology seems therefore to depend on autonomous concepts in sociology. The autonomy of psychology is less problematic because the idea of a known action is generally acceptable. The idea of social reality, of forces and laws which rule society *qua* society—without a reductionist recourse to individuals—seems even to many social scientists quite artificial, and this idea has constituted a recurrent obstacle to sociological thinkers. Some more important recurrences in the classical theories of Durkheim, Marx, and Weber can be sketched.

Durkheim. Early sociological theorists attempted purposively to exclude individual variables from their list of causes. Durkheim, for example, promulgated rules of the sociological method, which explicitly required only sociological conditions without recourse to psychology. In his main empirical work, *Suicide* (1897/1932), he attempted to derive suicide rates from social conditions, and he proposed social integration or lack of it as the determining condition for variations in suicide rates. Normlessness or "anomie" was for him the principal cause of suicide. He thus compared two characteristics of society—normlessness and suicide rate—in his research. Anomie was not the characteristic of an individual, and suicide could not be predicted for a person; assigning a degree of anomie to an individual did not make sense. A drawback of this approach is that it leaves many issues unexplained; Durkheim tried to justify this position by using ever finer categories, accounting for season, sex, religion, and culture, defining each as leading to more or less anomie. He even took excess of integration as a special cause of suicide, occurring, for instance, in army groups, and called it altruistic suicide. Throughout this detailed analysis Durkheim refrained from discussing any individual decision or personal event as a precondition of suicide of a certain person. He used suicide rates as a means of diagnosing society, not as a means of solving individual problems. In contrast, psychologists used a corresponding concept, "anomia," as an individual trait of powerlessness (Seeman & Evans, 1962). Anomia can be measured on a scale of attitudes, and individual degrees of anomia will be related to other attitudes and to behavior.

Durkheim's principal disciple, Mauss (1979), published a series of addresses on the relationship of the two sciences, discussing the consequences of such an extreme distinction. Mauss devoted special attention to what each science can expect from the other, and all he asked of psychology was more detailed studies of the concept of expectation—what we may call "set"—which would represent an individual correlate of a social condition. Mauss's own field of research was magic, for which individual set—or socially produced expectations—would be crucial to acceptance. Reciprocally, Mauss offered to psychology the help of sociology in integrating individual processes into a whole, showing the reflection of the whole individual gestalt (he did not use the term) within the social context.

Marx. Other early theorists in sociology sought each in his own way to reconcile the elusiveness of the individual to social theory. Marx kept changing from the early, humanistic theory (1844/1964), which stressed the alienation of workers and the loss of human dignity in capitalistic, industrialized society, to the later, economic determinist theory (Marx & Engels, 1942), which counted social classes as the units of discourse and derived much of individual actions and feelings from class position (Althusser, 1969; Gouldner, 1980). In this latter theory, consciousness which does not correspond to the concept of class position is called "false consciousness," thus relegating much of psychology to the study of an illusion. In later Marxist history, this rejection of psychology was rarely absolute. However, its extreme was reached in the Chinese cultural revolution, which regarded teaching and research in psychology as dealing with pseudo-problems if not worse. In its longer history in the Soviet

Union, psychology, like any intellectual endeavor, had its vicissitudes. It could resist complete extinction, at times retreating to a physiological model, as in Pavlov's work on conditioning. Its greatest achievements have been in determining the social conditions of perception and learning, as in Luria's (1976) work. Luria's pathbreaking research and thinking on the development of perception was motivated by the problems of education among non-Russian minorities. Under the Marxist regime psychology fell between physiological or "material" research and sociological or problem-oriented work. Individual psychological problems could not be recognized as being autonomous, but people could be changed by social conditions. Hence a new Soviet man could emerge (Bauer, 1952). Apart from promoting the sociological interpretations of class position as all-important, the general trend to producing a complete social and personal change would lead the Soviet scientific establishment toward emphasis on changeable social conditions. The Soviet abuse of psychiatric treatment for political ends can be seen in this light.

Western neo-Marxists have, by contrast, tried in varying degrees to keep individual concerns within the bounds of Marxist analysis. In fact, "humanist Marxism" has become the slogan for such an assorted group as Gramsci (1971), Merleau-Ponti (1973), Lukacz (1923), and Goldman (1970). Their emphasis is on varying ways for individual development to occur under different class systems and for members of different classes. The role of individual traits and the relationship between individual and society, with the society taken as the more important reality, have preoccupied these Marxist thinkers, and paradoxically have forced them to treat individual conditions in great detail. Thus, a Marxist psychologist, like Merleau-Ponti, could write a book justifying torture and terrorism (1967) by exalting social ends over individual suffering. He denied the importance of the latter, although in his own research he would present phenomenological analysis of individual consciousness. This exaltation of social aims while running roughshod over individuals has led to severe internal contradictions. Attempts to transcend it, as in the "Prague Spring" of 1968 or the Polish Solidarity movement of 1980–81, have given hope of "socialism with a human face," but they were quickly suppressed. That is, the social emphasis overwhelmed the human one. Moreover, this condition has led some philosophers, especially the French "new philosophers," to deny all possibility of combining socialism and human concern, and to call Marxist humanism "barbarism with a human face" (Levy, 1979). In fact, Western Marxists were not limited in their own work to subordinate science to ideology and could work independently of the Marxist views. Thus one can find Marxist psychologists whose own work is little influenced by ambivalence of the role of the person.

One incident, however, can be used to demonstrate the tension between humanism and socialism in current social events. This is the French social revolt of 1968. During the few days in which a coalition of students and workers lasted, the movement centered as much on individual release as on social change. People tried to express their problems and their feelings to each other, even to strangers, and it seemed that the ideology of encounter groups and group therapy would take over together with a socialist philosophy (Turkle, 1981). Of course, the rapid breakdown of the revolt prevents any knowledge of what might have happened; the victory of the Left thirteen years later proceeded along conventional political lines. In the interval, the psychoanalyst Lacan (1977) has tried to combine detached close readings of Freud with a social interpretation of mental health and illness. For this he was both expelled from psychoanalytic associations and attacked by radical student groups.

Weber. Another main trend in sociological theory, started by Max Weber, stressed organizational features as well as the importance of belief systems in attempts to understand the necessary and sufficient conditions for industrialization. Weber acknowledged the influence of individual leaders; thus, he originated the concept of "charisma" in its popular meaning (1963). In general, though, Weber tried to find the types of society in which an economic system could occur, defining different types of religious faiths and organizations: Within-the-world asceticism and rationality would lead to modern industrial society (1930). This led to a theoretical construction of the individual derived in his method of ideal types (1949). Ideal types are theoretical constructs of societies and individuals in them which would represent best their important features. It is not asserted that these people exist or, if they do, how many exist. Again, we find sociological theory trying to create individuals, to change man. Adherence to these ideas can still be found in studies of national character.

These three classical theorists showed three different ways of eliminating the individual from social analysis: by concentrating on characteristics of a social unit, as Durkheim did, by assuming human nature as infinitely pliable to social influence, as in the classical Marxist position, or by constructing individuals to conform to social theories, as in Weber's ideal type.

Parsons. A more recent compromise among these positions and the claims of the individual may be found in the work of Talcott Parsons. Parsons (1949) tried first to combine the work of Durkheim and Weber with other theorists to arrive at the social conditions of human action. In later theory he distinguished individual, social, and cultural levels, which worked on analogous principles but interacted to produce human action.

Parsons worked with psychologists Edward Tolman, Gordon Allport, Henry Murray, and Robert Sears, and anthropologists Clyde Kluckhohn and Richard Sheldon to describe systems which would fit into recognized theories in each field (Parsons & Shils, 1951). In psychology he was especially influenced by psychoanalysis and Tolman's behavioral gestalt theory. Out of this work he developed four functional requirements which would be found in every system: goal attainment, adaptation, integration, and latency (Parsons & Smelser, 1956).

Toward the end of his life Parsons expanded this theory to include not only the personal, cultural, and social levels, but other levels of existence as well, from the four elements of the Greeks to the organic system of the individual (1978). Parsons's oeuvre shows all the strengths and weaknesses of distinguishing levels and describes their interaction at our present state of knowledge. It is exciting in its attempt to show the similarities and distinctions in the subject matters of different sciences, but it also threatens to force recalcitrant facts neatly into patterns, and, unfortunately, it retreats easily into empty formalism.

Summary

Although the subject matter of psychology and that of sociology overlap to a great degree—some might even say they are indistinguishable—two factors have led to a contrast between the two. One has been the unit of study: Psychologists concentrate on the human organism, while sociologists deal with supra-human units. Such units are conceptually as acceptable as individuals, but not available to immediate perception. The other factor is the origin of the sciences: Psychology derived from the biological laboratory, sociology from utopian reformism and concern with social problems. Both of these differences led to problems for sociologists, from which psychologists were spared: Sociologists had to justify their unit of study and became self-conscious about separating scientific, objective study from advocacy.

The work of the founders and theorists of sociology—Durkheim, Marx, Weber, Parsons—shows the varied treatment of these problems and a continuing dialogue with psychology, accepting and rejecting the place of the individual in society at the same time. The history of sociology shows a series of ingenious solutions to this problem.

METHODS

The essential tension between the similarity and contrast of these two sciences emerges strongly in the collection and interpretation of research data. In essence, both sciences deal with the same data. But different perspectives lead to different procedures and interpretations; the raw data acquire different meanings.

The basic elements with which the psychologist as well as the sociologist deals are human actions or their residuals. Psychologists in general prefer to collect data in a way which they can control materially, while sociologists prefer symbolic control after the data are collected. These preferences derive from the different aspects of the situation with which the two are concerned. Psychologists can deal directly with the subject of their science, the human individual, and try therefore to obtain facts about a person. Sociologists can use data collected from individual actions to infer something about a large supra-individual unit: The data have to be transformed into measures of a social reality.

The task of the psychologist looks like the easier one. The individual seems to be the natural unit, and data obtained from interviews and observations of individuals can be combined in certain ways. But the manner of combination depends, to a great extent, on the systems level dealt with. If the social order is seen simply as a sum of individuals, then simple distributional measures or descriptive statistics can be used to summarize data; data can even be analyzed individually without regard to social membership. For instance, attitude changes induced by different messages in separate experimental groups can be analyzed as attitude changes of individuals and correlated with other factors such as initial attitudes, individual by individual. Or, if the influence of different experimental conditions is called for, the mean of the changes can be taken as representing different individuals, and variability, as expressed by variance, is then a way of expressing unmeasured individual differences.

A different approach is necessary if data about social units are required. Each particular measure is then only an indicator of a social property; values derived from different individuals give different measures of the same facts (Back & Cross, 1982). Analysis according to this principle would look at each measure as a more or less imperfect representation of the underlying social reality. All individuals may have equal access to the information, and thus the set of data from all individuals can be divided into information and error by normal statistical techniques; this would not be very different from the methods used on individual models. But if individuals have differential access, then other models are more effective. In the extreme, one person may, by reason of training and skill, be able to give the best picture of the social events. This possibility justifies the use of scientific, literary, or artistic productions as measures of social facts. In accepting a skewed distribution of insight sociologists are led to selection of informants who may have especially good insights; this, again, may depend on ability, training, or special position in the social structure (Back, 1956).

Besides different sampling criteria the search for social facts leads to a variety of combinations of measures. For some purposes, such as possibilities for group action, only the values of extremes would be important. For example, a group might act if nobody is strongly opposed. Variability within the group, for instance the differences between subsocieties, can show measures of strain, segmentation, or hierarchy. These too are characteristics of units larger than individuals. These cannot be defined for individuals, but only for social units, although the data may be collected from individuals. For instance, hierarchy may be measured from information obtained from each person on relationships between members of an organization, but hierarchy can only be defined for a social unit.

Transformation of individual measures into those of social conditions demands both conceptual and methodological skills. Conceptually one wants to decide whether data collected from individuals are to be used at the individual or social level, and if the latter, how the individual measures should be processed for their use as measures of social units. Even in the smallest unit, the dyad, several strategies are possible, such as the average of the two members, the higher score, or the difference between the two. For such a situation, the marital couple, Klein (in press) has distinguished five different strategies which have been used, and he has suggested their appropriate use for specific conditions. In establishing relationships between these measures, one must be careful of the level to which they are supposed to refer. For instance, for some purposes one could take the husband as representative of the family and relate his responses to another social variable, such as conflict. This would give a relationship between two social variables. On the other hand, the husband's responses could be measured for their own sake, and then they would assess the effect of conflict on one individual. Here psychological and social research are felicitously combined in social psychology, though it becomes important at each point on what level information is desired.

Again, the difference between orientations of psychology and sociology becomes sharper if the aim is more applied. The psychological interview becomes in this case the clinical interview, the intensive personality study in which a wealth of data on an individual can be combined and interpreted; frequently this interpretation can be used to change or help the individual. By contrast, a popular use of survey data in recent years has been toward construction of social indicators, collective measures taken regularly to assess the success of some (e.g., government) activity. They do not indicate any inferred variable which will help in understanding and predicting social structure. Their meaning depends on values given to public goals, whether to increase education, further equality, or provide a sanitary environment.

Summary

Differences in unit of discourse have led to different cultures in the two sciences psychology and sociology, and in their conduct of research. Psychologists were able to study the object of their interest, the individual, directly, but sociologists have to infer their facts from indirect measures, sometimes even the psychologists' measures of the individual. Thus both scientists construct different facts from the same or similar data, guided by their trained reasoning.

PURE VERSUS APPLIED SCIENCE

Data collection methods can loosely be arranged along a continuum of control by the investigator: from laboratory experiments, through field experiments, formal interviews, informal interviews, and participant observation, to content analysis, and analysis of cultural artifacts. While psychological methods lean toward the first-mentioned pole and sociological toward the second, there is a considerable region of overlap. This leads to a paradoxical situation because the need for control and interference derived from the conceptual needs of the two sciences leads to the opposite preferences. Thus, the origins and interests in analysis as opposed to reform of these two sciences stands in contrast to their methodology: Although sociologists want to produce change eventually, their preferred methods of research are non-invasive; by contrast, psychologists try to control the organism in research for the ultimate aim of understanding it. This contrast leads to several distinctions in the methodologies of the two sciences.

One distinction that has been discussed heatedly in both fields is between basic and applied science. For emphasis sake, put the case that, originally, all psychology tended to be basic, and all sociology applied. This origin had the effect that psychologists seem to know much more easily than sociologists when they are working on theory or applications. Psychologists in general have stepped from a set of general principles and techniques of a special topic to found new applied subfields: Examples of these are clinical, industrial, school, or military psychology. The area where application is most problematic is the one which is closest to sociology, namely social psychology. By contrast, sociology has encountered trouble spinning off any specific applied field; the subfields of the science define areas in which application could be possible such as urban, family, economic development, or stratification. This has led to the paradoxical development that the majority of psychologists work in applied fields, while sociology is principally an academic discipline; sociologists even find it difficult to characterize the members of their profession who do applied research. One very frequent term is purely negative, namely "non-academic sociologists." Even among professional organizations, the difference is pronounced: The American Psychological Association has divisions clearly earmarked for the applied fields mentioned above, while the American Sociological Association has sections devoted to topics on theoretical and ideological approaches, and one section with the ambiguous title "Sociological Practice." These observations notwithstanding, the ideological direction of some of the sections, e.g., Marxist sociology, may still betray the real thrust of utopianism in sociology's origins.

SOCIAL PSYCHOLOGY

The principal field in which the content of psychology and sociology overlap is, of course, social psychology. This discipline, which treats the relations of persons toward each other and with the social structure, must accept the interdependence of both; it cannot submerge the individual in the social structure, nor does it assess linkages without considering the individual nodes of the structure in their own right.

In spite of this common concern, the term social psychology covers distinct traditions, methods, and substance. Early speculations and grand theories of social psychology concerned themselves on one side with the determination of a principle of human nature which could account for social behavior, such as imitation or the herd instinct (McDougall, 1920; Tarde, 1903; Trotter, 1916). From the point of society grand theories tried to link history, e.g., wars and revolution, with individual behavior (Le-Bon, 1896; Woolf, 1953). Empirical work, eschewing grand theory, started more modestly. It is significant that the first use of the term in a textbook was in Ross's *Social Psychology* (1908); the term experimental social psychology appeared much later in a psychologically oriented volume (Murphy, Murphy, & Newcomb, 1937). Their work summarized well the concerns out of which the psychologist's early research in social psychology developed: measurement of attitudes, social influences on productivity, and individual development of social behavior. Speculation and theory in the field extended to theories of attitude formation, influence, and socialization. Sociologists concerned themselves mainly with the way individuals adapt to society and how social structures can persist; they worked especially on the self, and its development, continuity, and change. This difference led to a separation of time perspectives which permeates research in both fields: Psychologists look upon social phenomena as temporary influences on human behavior, as one set of changing stimuli which must be studied, while sociologists look at social conditions as an essential setting, almost as a definition of human nature.

Because of these distinctions one can speak of two parallel sciences. Rosenberg and Turner (1981) have defined sociological social psychology (SSP) and psychological social psychology (PSP) as having differences in theory, method, and substance, and they have edited a text which represents the sociological approach. Inspecting the selections and comparing them with the standard subject matter in psychological social psychology texts, one is impressed by the differences in all three respects.

Theory

The sociologists prefers two theories—exchange theory and symbolic interaction. Both of them are general perspectives of human behavior, seeking a general principle for all human action in the social sphere; the SSP interpretation follows as corollaries from this general perspective. In fact, the background for these theories lies in theories of psychology current at the time that their original protagonists flourished, namely conditioning and learning theory: Symbolic interaction was influenced by G. H. Mead's work on conditioning and the transfer of responses to conditioned stimuli, which then become symbols (1934). In this way Mead derived language acquisition and the importance of the symbolic base of human action. Similarly, exchange theory was developed on the basis of theories of reinforcement, an adaptation of Skinner's perspective by G. C. Homans (1950, 1961), later formalized by Thibaut and Kelley (1959; Kelley & Thibaut, 1978). Mutually reinforcing actions eventuate as social norms and become the foundations of social structures. However, these theories are extended far beyond their origins in conditioning and learning theory and try to give a basis to social life which is compatible with other psychological theories of human behavior. Theories in psychological works, even in general books, are more eclectic: They are miniature models, neat and conceptually tight, which are applicable to certain topics or sequences of research. Examples of social perception, learned helplessness, cognitive dissonance, and reactance—theories which are typically derived from research on the topic itself, although they have some link with general psychological theories. Thus, the preferred theories of psychologists as well as sociologists are typically linked to a foundation in general psychology, not one in sociology: There is no Marxist social psychology. A recent attempt to construct one ended in self-confessed failure (Israel, 1979).

Method

These theoretical differences conform to the differences in the favorite methods of sociologists and psychologists, which they may reflect. The issue here is whether one wants an explanation of the action of variables or an investigation of the impact of social situations. Experimental methods are suited to the study of variables and to assessing precisely results of their actions. They lead easily therefore to miniature theories which deal with abstract principles of interpersonal actions. Sociologists prefer methods which try to disturb actually occurring situations as little as possible, thus leading to inferences of the actor's motives and perceptions in a social process. Even criticism of sociological methods, like survey research and participant observation, is based on claims that they do not represent the situation as it actually exists, not that they do not isolate relevant variables. The questioning by an interviewer and presence of an observer may distort the situation by emphasizing the variables in which the researcher is interested, exactly the effect which an experimenter would try to produce.

Content

The substantive distinctions between sociology and psychology are compatible with theory and method, but also derive from each science's source of reality. Psychologists will return eventually to the individual as the ultimate unit and organize the area of social psychology by the topics of general psychology: social learning, social perception, cognition, attitudes and attitude change, stereotyping, emotions and contagion, motivations and specific motives. Sociologists organize the field according to events which they can see and describe: socialization, reference groups, deviance and control, collective behavior, mass communication, roles, and the self concept. Some of the topics are quite similar though they may have different names: socialization and social learning, identity and self, social roles. On the other hand, some topics may look similar, but the approach is very different; psychologists study attitudes in their own right, improving techniques of measurement and of defining change, while sociologists are more concerned with the value of attitudes in predicting appropriate action. Similarly, the study of communication means for psychologists mainly the conditions and interpretations of interpersonal communication, e.g., patterns of behavior in small group observation or the study of communication networks; sociologists study the management of control and effect of mass media, as well as their link with interpersonal communication.

The tensions in social psychology pull it toward either the individual or toward society. This dilemma will be illustrated by looking at the locus of research, field or laboratory, and at a crucial content area, the study of small groups.

Field and Laboratory

One of the problems plaguing social psychology has been that of contradictory results. The structure of opinion in society is steady and quite recalcitrant to any change. Advertisers and political action committees have to spend millions of dollars to influence the public to a small degree or to reinforce current beliefs, but in attitude change experiments considerable changes can be measured within thirty minutes by carefully contrived communications and corresponding manipulations. In fact, experiments have been so spectacularly successful that a recent summary of research has claimed that much attitude change can be induced in the absence of communication (Aronson, 1980). This does not mean, of course, that all the messages in mass media are useless and advertising would cease.

This question hits directly at the validity of social psychological experiments or, alternatively, at the conceptual value of field studies. It is unlikely that different relations hold according to the method of research employed or that investigations could so consistently contradict the common experiences in social life. However, the difference lies mainly in the extent and permanence of the effect and not in the mechanics themselves. The results of short-range investigations may be valid, and the laws derived from them function also in large-scale situations. But in a real situation additional variables become important, such as long-range trends in beliefs and values, which can only be ascribed to social units and which overwhelm interpersonal effects over the long run. To give a simple example, position of a name on a ballot shows a primary effect in voting studies; but strong political trends will overcome these effects. One cannot imagine seriously that a voter with strong ideological polarization would change a vote in an election simply because of the position of a lever. Similar considerations can then apply to campaign tactics. Political observers are continually surprised that superior tactics do not translate into electoral victories. They are important, to be sure, but larger social trends which can only be measured by assessing the whole social system will counteract these techniques over the long run. This contrast strongly exhibits the autonomy of the social level which is assessed only indirectly by individual measures.

Group Dynamics

As a final example of the interdependence of psychology and sociology in social psychology, consider the study of small groups. Group dynamics burst on the scene in the years following World War II as a new field

which would study groups as units. This would be done for several purposes, to use small groups as tractable models for large social groups, to
study groups in their own right, and to determine the selection between
groups and the individuals. Besides its other functions, the study of small
groups was to form a bridge between the individual and social levels
(Cartwright & Zander, 1968).

Understanding of group action has benefitted greatly by the activities of
social psychology. Possible major achievements, however, have been
stymied recently by the ambiguity of individual and social variables, so
much so that activity has been slowed down appreciably and questions
have been asked about the reasons for this sudden decline (Lakin, 1979).
It can be reasonably argued that the main stumbling blocks consisted of
conceptual and methodological difficulties caused by the intermediate
position. Experimental methods using small groups, which had been a
great achievement in group dynamics, proved cumbersome in execution
and in analysis. Experiments attacked questions of group functioning as
well as the influence of group conditions on individuals. The latter were,
in fact, the early studies and led to group study's early successes: the
influence of group conditions on conformity (Asch, 1956), the studies of
group atmosphere on individual productivity and morale (Lippitt, 1940),
or the role of group structures (Leavitt, 1951). However, later work in the
opposite direction, attempting to derive group actions from individual
characteristics, proved to be an almost insurmountable challenge; people
do not necessarily act consistently according to previous test scores when
put into a social situation. Many researchers in effect gave up on social
conditions to focus only on single aspects of individuals involved. An
example of this trend is the neo-behavioral approach, initiated by Skinner
(1953) and Homans (1961); but this tendency is also shown in strict social
psychological work, such as that of Thibaut and Kelley (1959). In many
current experiments, attention is paid to only one individual subject, the
remainder of the group being programmed or simulated by tapes. The
tradition of small group research has been overwhelmed by the pressure
of individuals and has retreated from a consideration of "social" factors.

The theory of small groups has had a similar fate. An initial question
was the reality of groups, an argument which followed the general argument on the reality of social units (Warriner, 1956). But even if that reality
were accepted, theorists would still have trouble dealing with groups
without considering aspects of the individuals who compose them. As
individuals are included it becomes extremely difficult to define emergent
qualities of groups in their own right, however. Thus in research as well as
in theory, group dynamics has leaned heavily toward psychology,
threatened by extreme psychological reductionism. In the same way, ap-

plied group dynamics has become mainly a technique for individual self development (Back, 1972).

The sociological counterweight to excessive individual concerns lies less in stressing group qualities as autonomous from individuals, and more in studying the social setting and conditions of groups. A sociology of groups can deal with such questions as: Under which conditions do groups of a certain type arise? Does social change involve change in groups? Which forms of groups are persistent and which occur only under special conditions? Abstracting over a variety of situations, the variables which are most significant can be determined, and groups can be studied without reference to individuals. One fruitful example has been Mary Douglas's (1973) definition of two variables, *group*, the strength of group boundaries, and *grid*, the strength of norms of behavior within the group. Cross-classifying these variables, a typology of groups has been constructed which has shown itself valuable in interpreting a variety of conditions. The existence of group dynamics as a discipline seems to lie in explicit recognition of both psychological and sociological perspectives and their application. Here may be a lesson for the relationship of these two sciences.

Summary

The content of social psychology links individual and social levels. Different approaches to this field, namely individual actions as they are affected by other individuals or social conditions, show the distinctive styles of psychology and sociology in theory, method, and locus of research. Psychologists look for exact miniature theories, supported by precise laboratory experiments or their equivalents, limiting the action to a few well-defined individuals. They then extend the application of the theorems to the larger social sphere. Sociologists start from theories which have already had success in other fields of sociology and infer their applicability to social psychological problems by data collection and measurement techniques, which they can abstract from disturbing, purely situational, conditions. Psychologists can then work toward a pure theory with possible applications, and sociologists toward theories which are applicable to certain aspects of social reality and to social action.

CONCLUSIONS

Considering social psychology as an entity forces the question of the division between psychology and sociology. Are the two really only one field? We cannot imagine man as a species or individual without society; nor can we consider society without attending to individual men. Perhaps the division is only artificial, and instead of the conventional division into two fields, there ought to exist autonomy for social psychology or for group dynamics; that is, one could divide the unified science of man-in-society into many arbitrary segments.

This argument may look like pedantic quibbling or a parochial effort to stake out one's turf. But history and the identification of these two disciplines have led to diverging and converging paths which have given meaning to the differing terms beyond what could be strictly reasoned from a pure definition of content.

In this chapter, I have stressed two circumstances which have historically divided psychology and sociology: their historical origins and their levels of discourse. These two issues have been influential in the self-identification, actions, and organization of each science. Together they form a definition of human nature, and relationships between them lead to basic questions of philosophy and ethics.

One question is the ethical legitimacy of the work in both fields. Do we go beyond what should be known? Is it dangerous to go beyond some boundaries? The dread of knowledge is ancient, and it is expressed in such myths as the apple from the tree of knowledge and the box of Pandora. This general fear seems to be more individual than social. Basic understanding of human nature and of its manipulation has threatened psychological research with the picture of the mad scientist controlling people or making them less than human (Back, 1979b). Fear of excessive knowledge of social facts is less widespread, but still present in extreme conditions. Threats loom that too great knowledge of social processes can maintain positions of power, and they engender reactions against support of activities which further acquisition of this knowledge. Such reactions are usually mitigated by the tradition that sociology works to change society, not to explain it.

The fear of interference beyond acceptable boundaries of person and society has manifested itself in anti-scientific attacks against both sciences. Psychology has suffered in this way from the politically-insired rejection of Mesmerism and hypnosis to the 1982 referendum in Berkeley outlawing psychosurgery. Attacks on social interference have also found a ready audience. Applications of social knowledge to counterinsurgency and riot control are easily made uncanny as actions of dangerous scientists' hidden hands. Sociologists bear the additional burden of their origin in advocacy of social change, and opponents of change may oppose work in the field purely for that reason.

Psychology and sociology differ strongly in application, a good example of which is the treatment of deficiency and of normality: The difference between defective and normal individuals is quite clear, in spite of some recent doubts based mainly on the influence of social norms. In general, though, clients are referred to a psychologist because they are troublesome to themselves or to others. The legitimacy of psychologists' interference cannot be questioned in principle, although its limits may be controversial; examples would be questions on involuntary commitment or psychosurgery. On the other hand, questions are asked immediately if functioning individuals are treated: The legitimacy of widespread use of psychoactive drugs or encounter groups for well-functioning persons has been questioned on ethical grounds. Sociological interventions, however, can be questioned from the beginning. In special cases defects in the society may give rise to problems, especially with subgroups in need of intervention; criminology or the sociology of poverty are usually recognized as ethically acceptable as warranted interventions. However, the general thrust of sociology has been to accept that current society is not perfect—not "normal"—and therefore the task of the study of society is to produce changes in functioning which would correspond to therapy for normals in psychology. Thus, sociologists frequently feel bound to give policy recommendations, that is to intervene in the society which they study. They are therefore vulnerable to questions of the ethics of their intervention, especially if their advice leads to questionable results (e.g., Kelman & Warwick, 1978). The controversies on busing and of the Coleman Reports on education (1966, 1977) are recent cases in point. Sociologists look at individual well-being as a function of social conditions and therefore will seek sources of human problems as well as their cures in social malfunctions. This goes sometimes even so far as saying that people who should be in need of intervention but resist it are sick for that reason; an example is the Marxist claim of false consciousness of the happy proletarian. Psychologists use the medical intervention model of representing the client and thus look at needs for therapy from the client's point of view. They generally do not want to wait for the millenium to make a client adapted to a perfect society, but define the problem within present imperfections.

The ideal of human perfectibility has been a dominant theme in Western society since Homer. The philosopher Passmore (1970) has traced its course over 3000 years and has shown how it has changed from a theological and philosophical problem to a scientific one. Thus, biologists, psychologists, and social scientists have taken over from the priest. Assumption of this position involves privileges, but also responsibilities.

Social control over research procedures is one expression of these responsibilities. It is different in our two fields. Psychological research is easily characterized as interference with free action by individuals and questioned by the public and higher authorities. Social experiments are more elusive. Social reforms have been called social experiments (Campbell, 1969), but they are experiments conducted without the informed consent of subjects. When the experiment fails, the participants may be harmed for life, such as having insufficient schooling in busing reforms or experiments. Here, the advantage lies with the experimenters who can call a study a "policy" which stands outside the ethical controls of experimentation. The sociological tradition which built a science on reformist sentiments has little ethical problems with large-scale experiments, but it may share in the general opprobrium if a policy, or experiment, fails. Psychologists, who by tradition distinguish clearly among science, experiment, and intervention, are less prone to be attacked by a general broadside, but individual pieces of work are extremely vulnerable. Here, different approaches even to the same situation, as in mental health, are distinct because of the divergent culture and experience of the two sciences.

A challenging question, though probably moot at the present time, is how far the distinctive patterns of the two sciences result from differences in focus on subject matter and how far they derive from historical accident.

In example after example I have raised, a distinction between levels of the subject matter of psychology and sociology recurs. Treatment of the relation of the individual to society leads almost automatically to considerations of ethics or values, while discussion of treating individuals will stay on a more detached level. While Catholics and Communists may oppose the use of specific therapeutic techniques, such as psychoanalysis, hardly anybody will oppose therapy as such. Some ideologists, however, may oppose any social change. This results from a deep-rooted belief that it may be all too easy to change society while the structure of the organism is predetermined and relatively impervious to capricious change.

Finally, what is natural in social aggregates arises as an important question in the relation of psychology and sociology. As far as social structure, from interpersonal relationships to global organization, is seen as a voluntary arrangement created by individual will, study of these structures will be reduced to personal control and will be seen as ethical problems. As far as society and the individual are seen as subject to natural or systemic laws, we can find agreement on dispassionate analysis of both.

REFERENCES

Althusser, L. *For Marx*. London: Allen Lane, 1969.
American Heritage Dictionary of the English Language. (P. Davies, Ed.). New York: Dell, 1969.

Aronson, E. Persuasion via self-justification: Large commitments for small rewards. In L. Festinger (Ed.), *Retrospections in social psychology.* New York: Oxford University Press, 1980.

Asch, S. E. Studies of independence and conformity: A minority of one against a unanimous majority. *Psychological Monographs,* 1956, *70* (9, Whole No. 416).

Back, K. W. The well-informed informant. *Human Organization,* 1956, *14,* 30–33.

Back, K. W. *Beyond words.* New York: Russell Sage, 1972.

Back, K. W. The small group—Tightrope between sociology and personality. *Journal of Applied Behavioral Science,* 1979, *15,* 283–294. (a)

Back, K. W. Secrecy and the individual in sociological research. In K. Wulff (Ed.), *Regulation of scientific inquiry.* Boulder, CO: Westview Press (AAAS Series), 1979. (b)

Back, K. W. Group dynamics. In R. J. Corsini (Ed.), *Encyclopedia of psychology.* New York: Wiley, in press.

Back, K. W., & Cross, T. S. Response effects of role-restricted respondent characteristics. In W. Dijkstra & J. van der Zouwen (Eds.), *Response behaviour in the survey-interview.* London: Academic, 1982.

Bauer, R. *The new man in Soviet psychology.* Cambridge, MA: Harvard University Press, 1952.

Becker, H. S. Whose side are we on? *Social Problems,* 1967, *14,* 239–247.

Booth, C. *Life and labour of the people of London* (17 Vols.). London: MacMillan, 1892–1897.

Borgatta, E. F. Sidesteps toward a nonspecial theory. *Psychological Review,* 1954, *61,* 343–352.

Boring, E. G. *A history of experimental psychology.* New York: Appleton-Century-Crofts, 1950.

Campbell, D. T. Common fate, similarity and other indices of the status of aggregates of persons as social entities. *Behavioral Science,* 1958, *3,* 14–27.

Campbell, D. T. Reforms as experiments. *American Psychologist,* 1969, *24,* 409–429.

Cartwright, D., & Zander, A. *Group dynamics.* New York: Harper & Row, 1968.

Coleman, J. S., et al. *Equality of educational opportunity.* Washington, DC: U.S. Government Printing Office, 1966.

Coleman, J. S. (Ed.). *Parents, teachers and children: Prospects for choice in American education.* San Francisco: Institute for Contemporary Studies, 1977.

Comte, A. *The positive philosophy.* New York: Calvin Blanchard, 1858.

Douglas, M. *Natural symbols.* London: Penguin, 1973.

Durkheim, E. *Suicide.* New York: Free Press, 1932. (Originally published, 1897.)

Etzioni, A. Social analysis as a sociological vocation. *American Journal of Sociology,* 1965, *70,* 613–622.

Goldman, L. *Marxisme et sciences humaines.* Paris: Gallimard, 1970.

Gouldner, A. W. Anti-minotaur: The myth of a value-free sociology. *Social Problems,* 1965, *9,* 42–44.

Gouldner, A. W. The sociologist as partisan: Sociology and the welfare state. *American Sociologist,* 1968, *3,* 103–116.

Gouldner, A. W. *The coming crisis in Western sociology.* New York: Basic Books, 1970.

Gouldner, A. W. *The two Marxisms.* New York: Seabury, 1980.

Gramsci, A. *Prison notebooks.* New York: International Publishing, 1971.

Homans, G. C. *The human group.* New York: Harcourt, Brace & World, 1950.

Homans, G. C. *Social behavior: Its elementary forms.* New York: Harcourt, Brace & World, 1961.

Israel, J. *The language of dialectics and the dialectics of language.* Copenhagen: Munksgaard, 1979.

Kant, I. *Kritik der reinen Vernunft* (M. Muller, trans.). Oxford: Oxford University Press, 1881. (Originally published, 1781.)

Kelley, H. H., & Thibaut, J. W. *Interpersonal relations: A theory of interdependence.* New York: Wiley, 1978.

Kelman, H. C., & Warwick, D. P. The ethics of social intervention: Goals, means and consequences. In G. Bermant, H. C. Kelman, & D. P Warwick (Eds.), *The ethics of social intervention.* Washington, DC: Hemisphere, 1978.

Klein, D. M. The problem of multiple perception in family research. In L. Larson & J. White (Eds.), *Interpersonal perception in families.* (In press)

Lacan, J. *Ecrits.* New York: Norton, 1977.

Lakin, M. (Ed.). What's happened to the small group? *Journal of Applied Behavioral Science,* 1979, *15.*

Leavitt, H. J. Some effects of certain communication patterns on group performance. *Journal of Abnormal & Social Psychology,* 1951, *46,* 38–50.

LeBon, G. *The crowd.* London: T. Fisher Unwin, 1896.

Levy, B-H. *Barbarism with a human face.* New York: Harper & Row, 1979.

Lewin, K. Psychologische und sinnespsychologische Beariffsbildung. In A. Métraux (Ed.), *Kurt Lewin Werkausgabe. (Vol. 1.) Wissenschaftslehre.* Bern: Huber, 1981. (Originally published, 1918.)

Lippitt, R. An experimental study of autocratic and democratic group atmospheres: Studies in topological and vector psychology (Vol. 1). *University of Iowa Studies in Child Welfare,* 1940, *16,* 44–193.

Lukacz, G. *Geschichte und Klassenbewusstsein.* Berlin: Malik, 1923.

Luria, A. R. *Cognitive development: Its cultural and social foundations.* Cambridge, MA: Harvard University Press, 1976.

McDougall, W. *The group mind.* New York: G. P. Putnam's Sons, 1920.

Manuel, F. G. *The prophets of Paris.* Cambridge, MA: Harvard University Press, 1962.

Marx, K. Economic and philosophical manuscripts. In T. B. Bottomore (trans.), *Karl Marx: Early writings.* New York: McGraw Hill, 1964. (Originally published, 1844.)

Marx, K., & Engels, F. *Selected correspondence: 1846–1895* (D. Torr, trans.). New York: International Publishers, 1942.

Mauss, M. *Sociology and psychology: Essays.* London: Routledge & Kegan Paul, 1979.

Mead, G. H. *Mind, self and society.* Chicago: University of Chicago Press, 1934.

Merleau-Ponti, M. *Humanism and terror.* Boston: Beacon Press, 1967.

Merleau-Ponti, M. *Adventures of the dialectic.* Evanston, IL: Northwestern University Press, 1973.

Miller, J. G. *Living systems.* New York: McGraw Hill, 1977.

Moore, W. E. The utility of utopias. *American Sociological Review,* 1966, *31,* 765–773.

Murphy, G., Murphy, L. B., & Newcomb, T. *Experimental social psychology.* New York: Columbia University Press, 1937.

Oxford English Dictionary. (J. A. H. Murray, Ed.). Oxford: Clarendon Press, 1933.

Parsons, T. *The structure of social action.* Glencoe, IL: Free Press, 1949.

Parsons, T. A paradigm for the human condition. In T. Parsons (Ed.), *Action theory and the human condition.* New York: Free Press, 1978.

Parsons, T., & Shils, E. A. (Eds.). *Toward a general theory of action.* Cambridge, MA: Harvard University Press, 1951.

Parsons, T., & Smelser, N. J. *Economy and society.* London: Routledge & Kegan Paul, 1956.

Passmore, J. *The perfectibility of man.* New York: Scribners, 1970.

Rice, S. A. Contagious bias in the interview: A methodological note. *American Journal of Sociology,* 1929, *35,* 420–423.

Rosenberg, M., & Turner, R. H. *Social psychology: Sociological perspectives*. New York: Basic Books, 1981.

Ross, E. A. *Social psychology*. New York: MacMillan, 1908.

Seeman, M., & Evans, J. W. Alienation and learning in a hospital situation. *American Sociological Review*, 1962, *27*, 772–783.

Shattuck, R. *Forbidden experiment: The story of the wild boy of Aveyron*. New York: Farrar, Straus & Giroux, 1980.

Skinner, B. F. *Science and human behavior*. New York: MacMillan, 1953.

Tarde, G. *The laws of imitation*. New York: Henry Holt, 1903.

Teilhard de Chardin, P. *Future of man*. New York: Harper & Row, 1969.

Thibaut, J. W., & Kelley, H. H. *The social psychology of groups*. New York: Wiley, 1959.

Tiryakian, E. A. *Sociologism and existentialism*. Englewood Cliffs, NJ: Prentice-Hall, 1965.

Trotter, W. *Instincts of the herd in peace and war*. New York: MacMillan, 1916.

Turkle, S. *Psychoanalytic politics: Freud's French revolution*. Cambridge, MA: M.I.T. Press, 1981.

Warriner, C. K. Groups are real: A reaffirmation. *American Sociological Review*, 1956, *21*, 549–551.

Weber, M. *The protestant ethic*. London: Allen & Unwin, 1930.

Weber, M. *The methodology of the social sciences*. Glencoe, IL: Free Press, 1949.

Weber, M. *The sociology of religion*. Boston: Beacon Press, 1963.

Woolf, L. S. *Principia politica: A study of communal psychology*. London: Hogarth Press, 1953.

Biographical Notes

KURT W. BACK is James B. Duke Professor of Sociology at Duke University. He received his B.S. from New York University, his M.A. from the University of California, Los Angeles, and his Ph.D. in Group Psychology from Massachusetts Institute of Technology. He is coauthor (with L. Festinger and S. Schachter) of *Social Pressures in Informal Groups* and (with R. Hill and J. M. Stycos) of *The Family and Population Control;* author of *Slums, Projects and People: Social Psychological Problems of Relocation in Puerto Rico* and *Beyond Words: The Story of Sensitivity Training and the Encounter Movement;* and editor of *In Search for Community: Encounter Groups and Social Change* and *The Life Course: Integrative Theories and Model Populations.*

ALAN C. ELMS is Professor of Psychology at the University of California, Davis. He received his B. A. from the Pennsylvania State University and his Ph.D. from Yale University. He is a founding member of the International Society of Political Psychology and is currently on the editorial boards of *Political Psychology, Political Behavior,* and *Micropolitics.* He is the author of *Social Psychology and Social Relevance* and *Personality in Politics,* and he is now conducting psychobiographical research on personality theorists, imaginative writers, and politicians.

HANS JURGEN EYSENCK is Professor of Psychology in the University of London at the Institute of Psychiatry, Maudsley Hospital. He has received B.A., Ph.D., and D.Sc. degrees from the University of London. He has published over 600 articles and three dozen books, some in collaboration, and is editor of the journals *Behaviour Research & Therapy* and *Personality and Individual Differences;* he is also on the editorial board of a dozen other journals. His main interests are in personality, behavior therapy, behavioral genetics, intelligence, social attitudes, and learning theory.

ROBERT JAY LIFTON holds the Foundation's Fund for Research in Psychiatry Professorship at Yale University. He is the author of *Indefensible Weapons* (with Richard Falk), *The Broken Connection,* and *Death in Life*. Lifton is currently completing a study, tentatively titled, "Medicalized Killing in Auschwitz."

SHARONE L. MAITAL is School Psychologist for Haifa Public Schools. She received B.A. and M.A. degrees from Tel Aviv University and a Ph.D. from Temple University. Her published research has focused on social aspects of schooling and, together with Shlomo Maital, on the application of psychological models and methods to economic behavior.

SHLOMO MAITAL is Associate Professor and Chairman, Economics Department, at the Faculty of Industrial Engineering & Management at the Technion-Israel Institute of Technology, in Haifa, Israel. His B.A. and M.A. degrees are from Queen's University, Canada, and Ph.D. from Princeton. He is co-editor of *Lagging Productivity Growth: Causes & Remedies* (with Noah M. Meltz) and author of *Minds, Markets & Money: Psychological Foundations of Economic Behavior.* Together with Sharone L. Maital, he has authored a book on economics, psychology, and game theory.

DOUGLASS R. PRICE-WILLIAMS is currently Professor in the Departments of Psychiatry and Anthropology at the University of California, Los Angeles. He received his B.A. and Ph.D. degrees in psychology from the University of London, Price-Williams has focused his research and thinking on cross-cultural psychology and psychological anthropology for the last twenty years. He was co-editor of *Ethos* for five years, and he serves on the editorial board of the *Journal of Cross-Cultural Psychology.* His book, *Explorations in Cross-Cultural Psychology,* deals in detail with much of the subject matter covered in his chapter for this volume.

CHARLES B. STROZIER is Professor of History at Sangamon State University and holds a visiting appointment in the Department of Psychiatry, Rush Medical School. He is the editor of *The Psychohistory Review* and author of *Lincoln's Quest for Union,* as well as many articles on history and psychohistory.

JOANNA P. WILLIAMS is Professor of Psychology and Education at Teachers College, Columbia University. She received an A.B. degree from Brown, a M.Ed. from Harvard, and a Ph.D. in experimental psychology from Yale. She has served as President of the Educational Psychology Division of the American Psychological Association and is past editor of the *Journal of Educational Psychology*. Williams is interested in the processes that underlie both beginning and skilled reading and in the development of effective instruction.

JOACHIM F. WOHLWILL is Professor of Human Development at the Pennsylvania State University. He received his B.A. in Social Relations from Harvard and his Ph.D. in Experimental Psychology from the University of California, Berkeley. He has been a Fellow at the Center for Advanced Study in the Behavioral Sciences and at the Educational Testing Service. Wohlwill is the author of *The Study of Behavioral Development*. Before 1970, he was a developmental psychologist at Clark University; since then he has been associated with the Programs in Man-Environment Relations and Individual and Family Studies at Pennsylvania State University, working in the areas of environmental aesthetics, environmental attitude, adaptation to environmental stimulation, and the role of the physical environment in behavioral development, and more recently on problems of exploration and play in children.

PSYCHOLOGY AND ITS ALLIED DISCIPLINES
Volume III: Psychology and the Natural Sciences

1
Psychology and Biology

William R. Uttal
Institute for Social Research
University of Michigan

Biology:	The science of the processes and structure of living organisms.
Mental Process:	A kind of information manipulation that has so far been identified only in living organisms.
Psychology:	The science that deals with mental processes and, *ipso facto,* a subfield of biology.

INTRODUCTION

The three brief definitions that serve as the header to this essay are intended to make a particular point concerning the relationship between the science of psychology and the science of biology. My thesis is that these two fields of science are related in the most intimate manner—psychology is as much an integral part of biology as are anatomy, ecology, or physiology: Mental processes are as much biological processes as are endocrine secretions and spike action potentials. The student of mental processes who loses sight of this basic fact does so at the peril of losing sight of the most fundamental premise of psychobiology—psychoneural equivalence—the idea that mind is a brain function—and exposes himself to cultism, mysticism, and inconsistency outside the body of modern scientific thinking. To assert this premise so strongly is not to say that the emphases of psychology are not different from the emphases of anatomy for example, but rather to note that scientific psychology's origins and

1

goals are no more different from any of the other biological sciences than they are from each other. Psychologists typically find themselves in a separate department or institute from other biological scientists, but mainly because their *methods* and the specific *objects* of their research attention differ from those of other biological sciences, not because there is any fundamental distinction to be made between the intellectual or conceptual bases of the biological and psychological fields of inquiry. To propose a contrary view is implicitly to accept a kind of dualistic thinking that has decreasing acceptability in today's scientific thought.

The methodological distinction that does exist between psychology and biology exists for the simplest of practical reasons—psychologists are dealing with a particular type of biological process that is considerably more complicated than are most other outcomes of physiological processes. Consciousness and most interesting preconscious mentation are the outcomes of unimaginably (and perhaps uncomputably and unanalyzably) complicated interactions among neurons. Most biologists, on the other hand, whether they study the secretory function of endocrine glands or the ionic mechanisms of membrane permeability (or, better, semipermeability), are dealing with mechanisms and processes that are much simpler in both principle and practice than those encountered in psychology. We do know quite a bit about the chemistry of ionic transport across a membrane, or of digestion; we know virtually nothing about the myriad interactions that occur among neurons to produce even the simplest thought.

Although it is not always the case in conceptual discussions of this kind, in this particular context what we mean by simplicity is relatively easily appreciated. Ionic transport is a process that can be fully understood in terms of individual molecular mechanisms at a single point in space; the response of the aggregate of all points on the membrane is not, in principle, different from the response of the single point. In the context of the mind, however, aggregation introduces problems that are not evident in the responses of the individual neuron. In fact, from one point of view, the mind can be thought of as totally a function of aggregation, of concatenation, and of interaction: In this case, the study of individual neurons tells us virtually nothing about the function of the aggregate. Indeed, extrapolations from the recent history of computer science clearly show that the particular "technology" (i.e., the particular materials from which the elements of an information system are made) is really of little consequence. Minds, according to this point of view, would emerge regardless of the nature of the material (e.g., relays, vacuum tubes, transistors, integrated circuits, neurons, jelly beans) as soon as the appropriate level of interactive complexity was reached.

This practical problem—complexity—in no way mitigates the most fundamental metaphysical premise—psychoneural equivalence—of the very biological science that is contemporary psychology. That premise asserts that all psychological processes are equivalent to, or identifiable with, some state or set of states of the great neural networks of our brain. Mind is a brain (and thus a biological) process; it is no more nor no less than that; the functioning brain is both necessary, at least at the present level of technology, and sufficient to account for all psychological processing. No nonbiological, nonbrain process must be invoked to account for any aspect of mind. This neuroreductionistic monism, while asserted in a dogmatic and radical form in the preceding sentences, is implicit in a somewhat more subtle form in most modern psychological research. The very act of carrying out a controlled experiment using the "method of detail" of John Stuart Mill (1806–1873) or René Descartes (1596–1650) or, even more germanely, any excursion into a laboratory dedicated to "physiological psychology" implicitly attests to a belief in this same monistic physicalism, even if the scientist should somewhat inconsistently adhere to an immaterialistic dualism in some other aspect of his life.

We do not know all of the details of this physicalism yet, of course, but clearly the main goal of modern psychobiology is to understand the exact nature of the relationship between the brain and the mind. This is the main theme unifying not only the widely diverse activities of this science, but also this essay. In the following sections, I expand upon these general points. First, I shall present a history of the mind-brain (body) problem. Then, I shall identify what seem to be the major scientific and philosophical issues currently guiding research in the field of psychobiology. Next, I shall discuss the major theoretical approaches that have been proposed as solutions to these problems. A cautious look at the future constitutes the next section, and, finally, a few brief conclusions will be drawn. The raisons d'être for this excursion into interpretation are to consider in a more precise fashion the present relationship of psychology and biology and to speculate about the future prospects of that association.

A HISTORY

We do not have to delve too deeply into the history of modern scientific psychology to see the exceedingly close relationship between its historical evolution and that of experimental physiology—the name of the more general science of organic function. (Physiology, of course, is a rubric that should encompass psychology as well as certain other subject matters, if one adhered to some logical taxonomy of the biological sciences.)

Like other fields of biological science, physiology grew out of the needs to control agriculture and animal husbandry and to solve medical problems that have plagued humanity. The first psychologists must have found the origins to their speculations about the nature of mind in similar practical problems—the question of how we felt, learned, enjoyed, etc., the obvious difference between the living and the dead, the problem of pain, and the question of the personalization of the objects and causal forces of nature—to mention only a few of the most obvious. At first, the solutions posed to these great human problems, all of which are involved with the issue of mind in one way or another, were framed in dualistic terms. An air of mystery was generated to help explain why we seemed to know so little—there were "unknowable things," it was asserted, and thus we *could* not know everything. Later, when the search for scientific and intellectual understanding became more respectable, the scientific method evolved under the stimulation of Grossteste (1168–1253), Bacon (1214?–1292), and Hobbes (1508–1679). As the applicability of the scientific method to the study of biological processes, in general, and then psychological processes, in particular, became acceptable, there was almost a simultaneous explosion in both physiology and psychology. Harvey's (1578–1657) demonstration of the circulation of the blood, Vesalius's (1514–1564) remarkable anatomical discoveries, and Descartes's physiological (though dualistic) interactionistic theory of the mind were all nearly contemporaneous.

The subsequent histories of physiology and of psychology were also intimately intertwined. By the middle of the nineteenth century when, among other notable works, Bain (1855) wrote his milestone text on *The Senses and the Intellect,* the framework of a biological psychology was well developed and firmly rooted in the anatomical, physiological, and physical discoveries of the previous decades. Although the pictures and language in the books of that time are somewhat quaint and the details have changed over the years, neither Bain's nor, similarly, Ferrier's (1886) views of physiological psychology are different in fundamental principle from those expressed in contemporary texts. Both Bain and Ferrier, as well as their contemporaries, were aware of the sensory-integration-effector organization of the brain, the Bell-Magendie law,[1] the gross anatomy of the brain, the idea of primary sensory projection regions, topographic mapping, and many other modern concepts.

The twin facts that physiological psychology has existed as a more or less respectable science for a couple of centuries and that mind has been accepted as but another function of the brain for at least as long do not

---

[1]Dorsal spinal roots are sensory pathways, and ventral roots are motor pathways (Editor's note).

dispute the equally solid fact that a more phenomenological and molar psychology is also necessary for a complete description of mental events. The complexities of the great neural networks of the central nervous system are of sufficient magnitude to guarantee that there will be, in practice, no neuroreductive theory of most psychological processes no matter how valid the monistic philosophy or the neuroreductionistic metaphysics. Looking backward, we can see that psychology has of necessity turned again and again to mentalistic vocabularies and methods. The present rise of cognitive or "human information processing" psychology is but another example of this mentalistic revival. It was only in the most dismal of days of a radical positivistic behaviorism that this science went so far as actually to reject the existence of mind and thus to change the content of the science from *rich mind* to interesting, but *sterile* (in the context of the study of mind) *behavior*. However extreme and whatever the momentarily aberrant view of what constitutes the "proper content" of psychological science, mental processes do not lose their fundamental biological origins. Even the most positivistic behaviorist did not deny the biological origins of mind. Behaviorism did, however, lead to a dark age in the history of scientific research in the field then called physiological psychology.

Other biological themes than neuroreductionism also permeate psychological research. The evolutionarisms of Lamarck (1744-1829), Darwin (1809-1882), Wallace (1823-1913), and many others throughout history, regardless of the specific mechanisms each theoretician invoked, all speak to the problem of change, not only in anatomic form, but also in mental process. All of these intellectual innovators are as much in the line of psychology's history as they are in that of anatomy. To support this argument, consider the following. It is not well known, but Darwin wrote on the developmental psychology of his own son (Darwin, 1877); it is much better known that he studied the expression of human emotions (Darwin, 1872).

The enormous developments in biochemical genetics in recent times, stimulated initially by Mendel's (1822-1884) work, have provided putative mechanisms for the transmission of traits from generation to generation and have detailed our knowledge of how the structure of the DNA double helix permits the introduction of random changes into the heritage of a species. Contemporary work by psychobiologists such as Jerison (1973) relating the evolution of the brain to the evolution of mental processes is in exactly this same intellectual tradition. The evolution of behavior is in its own right a topic that has a rich history dating at least from Romanes's (1848-1894) pioneering studies of animal intelligence up through the impressive work of contemporary behavioral geneticists (see Fuller, in this volume).

Just as evolutionary theory has contributed to psychological thinking, psychology has both been enriched by and enriched other patently biological areas of study. The anatomical discoveries concerning the structure of the brain by such illuminaries as Willis (1621-1675), Bell (1774-1842), Megende (1783-1855), and Flourens (1794-1867), among many others, also contributed to the ideas of cerebral localization, first embodied in the now rejected theories of Gall (1758-1828) and Spurzheim (1776-1832) concerning the localization of psychological "faculties." Subsequently, these theories have been accepted as a major conceptual building block of modern studies of the localization of psychological function in the brain.

Furthermore, it is interesting to note that the electrical activity of the nervous system was not only an early physiological topic, but also, in the hands of Volta (1745-1827) and Galvani (1737-1798), the impetus to the discovery of the physical aspects of electricity. The development of modern electrical, and subsequently electronic, equipment went hand in hand with the development of the techniques used in electrophysiology until the most recent times (see Chapanis and Marks, in this volume).

Today we see psychology paying electrical engineering back for this help; psychology provides models for new developments in artificial intelligence and robotics. The influence of ecology, the analysis of the biological systems including both flora and fauna as interacting entities, can also be discerned in the motivating forces behind modern field studies of a wide variety of animals in their natural habitats carried out by such workers as Schaller (1963, 1972) and Van Lawick-Goodall (1971). The biochemical sciences have also contributed to our understanding of the mechanisms underlying psychological processes, but I shall not deal with such issues, as they are covered in greater detail by Kornetsky (in this volume).

In summary, psychology is an integral and inseparable part of biological science. This contention is supportable from several different points of view. From a basic metaphysical point of view, all psychological processes, most psychobiologists assert nowadays, are nothing but the expression of one set of functions of the neural substrate—the brain. From an innovative and conceptual point of view, psychology is stimulated by developments in the other biological sciences and in turn stimulates them. No matter how dedicated to his neurons or electron microscopes, any scientist specializing in the study of the central nervous system must be in at least some not-so-small part motivated by the hope that his discoveries will ultimately contribute to the alleviation of psychological maladies or to the understanding of the still inscrutable relationship between the mind and the brain. With this contention in hand, let me now turn to a consideration of the issues, theories, and prospects of biological psychology.

THE ISSUES

In the Introduction, I expressed a radical psychoneural monism. This assertion, however, should not be interpreted to mean that the field of psychobiology has matured to a point at which the major issues of brain-mind relationships have even begun to be resolved. In fact, it may not be incorrect to assert equally strongly that we probably know less (with a high degree of certainty) now than we did a decade ago about the relationship between mind and brain. Many of the experimental findings that were the fundamental building blocks of psychobiological theory in the 1960s are now appreciated to be equivocal.

There is, however, an even more fragile relationship between data concerning neurons and theory purporting to explain mind in neural terms. It must not be forgotten that neurophysiological facts obtained in the laboratory become theories when applied to the mind-brain problem; and theories (as well as facts) can change their meaning as the years go by. Methodological difficulties (e.g., the uncertainty associated with microsurgery on the very small brains of typical laboratory animals), sampling difficulties (e.g., the modest number of experimental animals or individual cells that can be subjected to complex procedures) as well as the variability in even the best controlled procedures, and the enormous adaptability and flexibility of nervous tissue in response to surgical insults make animal research "noisy" at best. All of these practical difficulties are superimposed on the enormous conceptual complexity of the problem, both at a macroscopic and a microscopic level. Give this interacting mesh of difficulties, it becomes quite understandable why such modest progress has been made towards solving major issues in biological psychology.

In spite of the indisputable fact that psychobiologists are dealing with an exceedingly messy set of problems, it is nevertheless possible to identify many of the major intellectual and scientific issues that engage their attention. Although the fundamentally significant motivating forces driving the activities of this science are rarely stated explicitly in research publications, an examination of the experimental literature makes clear what are the implicit conceptual guides to and goals of contemporary research in psychobiology. In the following paragraphs I briefly summarize one possible set of major issues. In doing so, I do not intend to cover the entire span of the field. Some other matters will be more completely covered in other chapters in this volume, and others are of insignificant theoretical import (in my opinion) to warrant inclusion. At the outset of this exercise, it is important to note that there is no particular order of priority or importance associated with the sequence in which I present the issues here. There are many scholars who would give priority to one or the other, but I see these issues as essentially existing in parallel with each other. The reader will note only a slight tendency for me to deal with the more general issues first.

The Mind-Brain Problem

The most general intellectual theme of psychobiology—and the one I shall emphasize here—is the one encompassed under the great perplexity known as the mind-body (or more properly in the context of modern psychobiology—the mind-brain) problem. How is it that the processes of the brain are transformed into the phenomena of the mind? This is what Schopenhauer (1788–1860) referred to as the "world knot," a phrase that gives this issue center stage in the playing out of this particular scientific drama. No matter how great the difficulties and complexities surrounding this conundrum may be, most contemporary theoreticians would agree that this issue is central and that it is not only of great theoretical significance, but that in one guise or another, the issue has had practical implications throughout history. Currently, it is *the* reason we psychobiologists do what we do. However, this great question must be considered to be a concatenation of a number of other philosophical and scientific subquestions rather than a researchable problem itself. From a modern perspective, the mind-brain question can be expressed in the form of a more specific corollary—How can a global self-awareness arise as the result of the action and interaction of a large aggregation of elemental neuronal components, themselves capable of only the most primitive logical functions? As I have indicated earlier, the answer to this question that seems most plausible and most generally accepted by most of my psychobiological colleagues is that consciousness (and all of the attendant psychological processes) must be, at some level of analysis, *equivalent* to the state of some as yet unidentified neuronal network that has reached an appropriate level of complexity. This is a neuroreductionist version of the radical monism that Feigl (1958) referred to as the psychoneural identity hypothesis. However, for reasons noted above, the great global mind-brain question and the consensus answer are probably meaningless as specific guides to detailed experimental research. Therefore, from a more practical view, the following issues must be considered to be the proximal and specific motivating forces behind particular kinds of psychobiological theory and empirical research.

Motivating Issues in Psychobiological Research

Are neuroreductive explanations possible in practice? In spite of the broad base of agreement concerning the intimate relationship between brain and mind that must exist in principle, there remains a great deal of uncertainty whether that monistic metaphysics can be the basis of a practical epistemology. The optimistic hope for the ultimate development of a practical neuroreductionistic theory is mitigated by constraints emerging from logical, mathematical, and computational theory. The problem raised here is an insidious one. Even if we accept the limits of current technology and knowledge, and thus the practical fact that presently we have no means to bridge the gap between the neuron and the mind, a superficial and unduly optimistic open-mindedness might lead us to believe that there can be no limits to the accomplishments of psychobiology in the long run and that "ultimately" a true neuroreductionism must necessarily emerge. Simply to make this bald assertion, however, is to ignore the fact that there are very real physical, informational, and conceptual limits on measurement, analysis, and understanding that have been demonstrated in many other scientific areas. Among the most notable is Heisenberg's uncertainty principle—the physical *law* that states that the position and momentum of subatomic particles can never be simultaneously known to a precision better than the limit of 6×10^{-34} joule-seconds, a value known as Planck's constant. Though small, this constant is not infinitessimal and thus the uncertainty principle places a specific limit on measurement, determinism, and ultimately on scientific understanding and achievement. Another limit is the speed of propogation of light (3×10^{10} m/sec) and of all other physical or informational entities. This too is a limit imposed by nature, not of man's current ingenuity or available technology. Continued pursuit of either finer joint measurements of position and momentum or higher velocities, along with the search for a perpetual motion machine (a putative violation of the second law of thermodynamics), would be futile.

The question now confronted is—Do similar constraints on future developments in psychobiology also exist? In partial answer to this question, we should note that there are other limits that are somewhat closer to the mind-brain problem that may also restrict this science's "ultimate" accomplishment. For example, Gödel's (1930) theorem, a major foundation of modern mathematics, conjectures that no system can be shown to be internally consistent using only the premises and axioms of that system. Some philosophers have suggested that the constraint implied by this theorem may also be extrapolated to the mind-brain problem by defining the brain as such a system and internal tests of consistency to be equivalent to "understanding" the mechanisms of the brain by the brain. This would be a fundamental logical limit, if the argument is valid.

In a more practical vein, other authors such as Knuth (1976) and Stockmeyer and Chandra (1979) have raised the question of the "computability" of problems posed by systems much less complex than the great neural networks of the brain. Very simply stated problems, they assert, can produce computational requirements so great that, even though they are not infinite, they may require for their solution a computer with as many logical units as there are elementary particles in the universe operating for as long as the universe has existed.

While not all of these limits, practical or logical, may turn out to be applicable to the mind-brain perplexity, their very existence in fields so closely related to the combinatorics of neurons should alert us to the fact that there is at least a possibility of similar limits on the analyzability of the brain and its manifold interacting parts. Neuroreductionism, like any other kind of reductionism in science (including the equivalently perplexing issue of whether or not life itself can be reduced to chemical and thence to physical principles), cannot be accepted a priori as a practically achievable goal no matter how strongly we believe, in principle, that the only plausible scientific solution to the problems posed by life and mind is based on materialistic and monistic premises.

What is the proper level of neural analysis in the search for the basis of mind? Even though I have asserted a radical monism based on a neural network model, it must not be overlooked that the attribution of mind to this particular level of analysis is but a conjecture. The psychobiologist faces a myriad of possible levels of analysis at which he could examine neural mechanisms in his search for the basis of mind. He could concentrate on the molecular aspects of the neuron's plasma membrane, the electrophysiological indications of the function of the entire neuron, the interconnections and interactions among networks of neurons, the function and/or organization of gross anatomical nuclei, or even on the compound signals (such as the electroencephalogram or evoked brain potential) coming from the brain as a whole. Which of these levels of analysis is the valid one, or indeed if any one is uniquely appropriate, is, of course, still moot. There are psychobiologists working at all levels. This uncertainty arises from the fact that there is a curious paradox implicit in the mind-brain problem—the action of a network of neurons, each individually capable of responding only with responses of a highly limited number of degrees of freedom and of a highly localized nature, somehow produces singular, global, molar mental responses that exhibit extremely powerful cognitive capabilities. What in the molecule-neuron-nucleus hierarchy is critical and what is merely metabolic and supportive, or epiphenomenal? And as an important corollary, if we accept the neural network level as the proper one, how do molar mental properties emerge from the microproperties of neurons? These are some of the most perplexing questions confronting the psychobiologist involved in the search for the relationship between brain and mind, and, clearly, they are not trivial.

Are psychological processes localizable to specific regions of the brain and, if so, in which specific regions should particular psychological processes be localized? One of the major efforts of experimental research in psychobiology has been to determine the behavioral effects of neurosurgical or neurostimulative procedures in order to determine the locus in the brain of some psychological function. This is a hoary issue in psychobiology, but it also has its roots as far back as classic Greek medicine where it was known that specific head injuries produced specific behavioral aberrations. The localization of function hypothesis embodies the implicit concepts that psychological processes (faculties?) are discrete or separable and that they can be localized in equally discrete or separable regions of the brain. Such premises, though not totally confirmed, provide virtually the only plausible current basis for therapy, as well as a seductively simple solution to one aspect of the mind-brain problem. There is, therefore, a compelling pressure towards a radical localization theory, whether or not the evidence supports such a perspective.

The explosion of knowledge of the nuclear anatomy of the brain in the 1800s and the rise (and then collapse) of the radical faculty psychobiology championed by Gall and Spurzheim (1808) left a particular experimental paradigm as its intellectual legacy. That paradigm is: cut brain-observe behavior-attribute change to localized function in the insulted region. This paradigm, stressing localization of mental processes in major nuclei, dominated psychobiology for most of the last century, up until the great developments in single cell recordings that followed Ling and Gerard's (1949) development of the intracellular microelectrode. The localization paradigm is, however, based on a conceptualization of the brain that is fraught with logical, conceptual, and empirical difficulties. Both of the key premises—separable psychological function and precise localizability—are open to question. It is now becoming clear that behavior may be modified in exactly the same way by vastly different neurological manipulations. It is possible to produce a gross hyperphagia by disrupting some motivational system, but it is also possible to produce an indistinguishable disruption in normal eating behavior by interrupting the sensory pathways conveying information concerning satiation from the blood or the stomach. It is also possible, in a highly interconnected system, that a surgically ablated nucleus may produce a deficit by virtue of either its inhibitory or excitatory effect on some other center without actually being the specific locus of the function under investigation. Thus, correlation between a behavioral deficit and a surgical procedure does not necessarily imply a sharply demarcated functional localization. Indeed, we are beginning to read reports of the *recovery* of some functions as a result of further surgical *removal* of tissue—an outcome that raises serious questions about the role of the original areas that were ablated and produced deficits. The fragility of this kind of interpretation reminds us that putative localizations of particular functions are theories, conjections, or hypotheses in much the same way as is any other kind of theory. We must conclude that brain ablation experiments are conceptually much more complicated and inconclusive than is usually appreciated.

Further confounding this issue is that the anatomical complexity is embedded in an equally obscure semantic matrix in which the psychological or behavioral constructs under investigation are very poorly, if at all, defined. The situation is not even stable. Vast amounts of adaptive reorganization of redundant representation almost certainly occurs after injury to the nervous system. In short, the hypothesis of the specific localization of psychological phenomena is beset with a host of technical and logical difficulties, not all of which have been considered in sufficient detail to allow its easy acceptance.

How does the brain mediate language? Another major psychobiological research issue, closely related to the problem of localization of function but somewhat more specific, concerns the means through which the brain mediates language. Some of the earliest reports associating specific brain regions with particular intellectual skills were those describing the regions now known (after their discoverers) as Broca's and Wernicke's areas. Lesions of these areas, either through trauma or tumor usually only appreciated in post mortem situations, are more likely than other regions to produce aphasias (language difficulties). It has, therefore, long been fashionable to attribute language to these regions in particular. However, similar, if not equivalent aphasias can often result from damage to the motor areas of the prefrontal motor cortex among many other regions. Indeed, some authorities (e.g., Lenneberg, 1974; Penfield & Roberts, 1959) argued that damage to virtually any area of the dominant hemisphere has at least some probability of producing some kind of aphasia. It is thus difficult to define a unique "speech center". As with so many other molar psychological functions, sensory, integrative, and motor area lesions can all mimic the behavioral difficulties generated by damage to a putative speech center.

It does seem, however, that the hemisphere opposite the preferred hand is much more intimately involved in the speech process than is the other hemisphere. Recent studies (Sperry, 1966) of individuals with transections of the corpus callosum and the anterior comissures ("split brain preparations") have suggested that each hemisphere is specialized, with regard to the speech function, to at least a partial degree. The dominant (usually) left hemisphere seems to be better at language-type skills; the right hemisphere seems to excel at spatial and other nonverbal activities. But the right hemisphere is not semantically deaf and mute, as sometimes suggested—it can at least comprehend simple sentences (Zaidel, 1973).

The intrinsically exciting nature of the recent work on split brains as well as some of the anecdotal extravagances (e.g., two minds in a single head) have raised this issue to a high level of attention in psychobiology. There are, however, many questions and difficulties in any analysis of language, and most evident are the problems associated with the neurophysiological basis of language. This issue will obviously be a rich source of experimental challenges for many years to come.

How is stimulus information represented by individual neurons and the network within which they interact? The problem of representation or coding in afferent nerves, for example, is prototypical of the more general problem of representation of mind by the states of centrally-located neuronal nets. However, the former problem is far simpler than the latter since it deals with well-defined and relatively simple dimensions of both the stimulus and the perceptual response and since it is anchored to the physical world through a virtually monodirectional (afferent) flow of information. In the central nervous system, the problem is conceptually identical, just more difficult to unravel because specific stimulus equivalents for "thoughts" are more elusive and because simple directionality is lost. The flow of information changes from a predominantly monodirectional and well-ordered one to something more akin to what Sherrington termed an "enchanted loom." In the central nervous system, information flows backward and forward, hither and thither, and is confounded by feedforward, feedbackward, and other even more complex spatiotemporal interactions. It is clear that decoding the language of the central nervous system will be nowhere nearly as simple a job as decoding the DNA molecule. In the domain of the gene, there is also an overt order—linearity—and thus also a conceptually simple mono-dimensionality, whereas in the domain of the brain there is a nonlinearity and a three-dimensionality that are orders of magnitude more complex. Nevertheless, determining the ways in which ideas are represented in the brain by the great networks of neurons must be considered to be one of the major challenges in the agenda of psychobiology, if it does not turn out to be an unobtainable goal.

What is the nature of the plastic changes in the brain that underlie learning? Lashley (1950) set the tone for a major portion of contemporary psychobiological research when he asked—"What is the engram?" and "Where is it located?" "Engram" is the word we now use to denote the neuroanatomical equivalent of a stored memory—the changes in the nervous system that occur as a result of experience, subsequently to be reflected in behavioral variation. Lashley's major conclusion, and one to which we still adhere, was that the engram's nature is not yet established, but that whatever it is, it appears to be distributed over widely spaced portions of the brain. Lashley also spoke to the likelihood that synaptic conductivity changes underlay learning. We also still adhere to this tenet. Indeed, it is continuously surprising to reread his 30-year-old paper and to find in it a neural theory of memory that differs hardly at all from the currently generally accepted view. Three decades of additional research has changed virtually nothing of significance in this area of psychobiology, only added to the conceptual framework invented by Lashley. We still agree that there must be some distinct physical change corresponding to the various kinds of memory in the central nervous system and that both transient (probably associated with temporary changes in conductivity) and semipermanent (probably associated with growth) synaptic changes are the most likely correlates of short- and long-term memory, respectively. Nor is there any substantial doubt currently expressed that the engram must be widely distributed throughout the central nervous system. While there are loci in the hippocampus, for example, that clearly are related to the control and regulation of learning and memory (particularly the consolidation of short-term into long-term memory), no one has yet located any particular brain site in which a particular engram seems to be localized. Indeed, neurophysiological studies such as those of Olds, Disterhoft, Segal, Kornblith, and Hirsch (1972) continue to support Lashley's conclusion of a widely dispersed engram. The conclusion is that learning is a general property of neurons and not a function of only one part of the brain. This is a highly important, if peculiar, result.

The issue is deeper than is connoted by such neurophysiological results, however. We do not look at memory alone when we behaviorally study memorial processes. Rather, our estimates of the underlying plastic mechanisms must always be indirect and mediated by a complex of processes including sensory inputs, central integrations, and both covert and overt responses. The overall learning process may, therefore, be interfered with or modified by insults to neural mechanisms that have little if any direct relationship to the actual storage process.

Can the mind affect the body? Despite popular conviction that the mind is capable of exerting an influence over the brain and other parts of the body, a logical argument can be presented that this may be a fallacious conclusion. The monistic argument against this "nonsensical" question goes as follows: If the mind is equivalent to an information state of a selected set of neurons in the brain, and consciousness emerges simply as a matter of informational complexity, then one might legitimately be concerned about how that state can be modified by itself. Since mind is a pattern of organization, from what source does it draw the energy that it must have to alter the state of the material system in which it is embodied? The issue is semantically complex, and in the few words that I dedicate to it here, it is obvious that I cannot resolve the matter. However the reader may want to consider as an alternative that it may not be the mental process nor any illusory "free will" that influences the body, but rather the neural network state's elicitation of associated somatic and behavioral responses that is the specific causal agent in "psychosomatic" or any other kind of "mind over matter" response. In other words, mind does not influence anything in any physical sense; it only reflects or indicates the state of the nervous system. The putative impact of "mental phenomena" is, according to this point of view, better attributed to the changes in the external and internal environment that are simultaneously produced by internal or external responses. Mind is but one of these responses; motor twitches, glandular secretions, and vascular contractions are others, and it is these others that are the real effective agents, not the indicator—mind—in affecting the material of the body. Thus, for example, our brain may send signals that change the concentration of some gastric juice or modulate the input pattern of some external stimulus by some inhibitory action. These kinds of responses can and do exert the physical forces necessary to modify the material states of the body. On the other hand, this argument goes on, the mind as pattern exerts no physical force—the idea of a measuring instrument (the mind) of brain states affecting those states obviously raises serious questions about the language that is used in formulating the mind over matter concept.

Some Additional Problems that Motivate Research

So far I have concentrated on issues that are associated with unraveling the nature of the specific relationship between the brain and the mind. While these issues constitute a major portion of the motivation behind psychobiological research, there are other biological issues, falling into a somewhat different category that are also of considerable contemporary interest. These other major issues can generally be included within the single rubric of *evolution* and *development*. Whether this generic issue is made explicit or not by individual investigators, meaning becomes attached to some very curious kinds of scientific activity only when we consider them as probes towards answers to the following additional questions.

Are adult mentation and behavior the results of innate mechanisms that have evolved over the millenia of organic evolution, or are they predominantly determined by experiences during the early development of the organism? Obviously, no brief comment could begin to do justice to all of the ramifications of this classic and grand issue of biological psychology. Thus stated, this issue is none other than the nature-nurture controversy clothed in somewhat different verbiage. Controversy concerning the relative contributions of genetic heritage and experience to such high-level mental processes as personality, intelligence, and even social interaction is vigorous, even vitriolic, in both scientific and lay circles currently. However, it is probably not too much of a leap of logic to assert eclectically that in fact both heritage and experience must contribute to mental properties of these levels of complexity. However confident of this broad generalization one may be, it is also self-evident that the degree to which each factor contributes remains not only one of the most challenging areas of psychobiology, but also a matter of deep concern for practical social reasons. Do different ethnic or racial subgroups of humans have any major genetic differences that determine their respective mental properties to an extent comparable to that by which their physical properties are so obviously affected? Or, to the contrary, is the adaptability of the human brain so great that any slight genetic differences in mental ability within our species would be submerged by the general ability to respond flexibly to a wide variety of information processing tasks? The degree to which environment directs and heritage constrains intelligence, for example, is an issue whose significance transcends the laboratory, but ultimately it seems highly likely that it is a scientifically resolvable question. That resolution obviously will be of immense importance to the kind of life we lead outside of the laboratory in the years to come.

The nature-nurture issue has taken a somewhat new form in recent years since the publication of Wilson's (1975) seminal book *Sociobiology*. Wilson proposed that it is not only the individual's behavior and mental properties that are defined by genetic heritage, but also the social interactions in which it takes part (see Fuller, in this volume). Wilson's ideas are based on his background as a zoologist and his years of study of the behavior of infrahuman species. And, indeed, there is little doubt that insect societies at least are rigidly programmed by their genetic heritage to respond in predetermined social patterns. There is considerably more doubt about the role that genetic preprogramming plays in mammalian behavior and downright violent controversy about its application to the social behavior of *homo sapiens* in particular.

On a somewhat less controversial level, the enormous growth of developmental psychology in the last few years can be attributed in large part to interest in exactly this same issue. To determine what aspects of behavior are innate and which are the result of experience, we must trace the development of the organism over its life course. Is a particular be-havior pattern available to the organism at birth, or does it emerge at some later stage of development? Does it emerge spontaneously, or does it depend upon some triggering experiential event? These are some of inherently biological questions concerning the nature-nurture issue that guide and motivate the research program of developmental psychology.

How has behavior changed over the millenia, in particular with regard to the concomitant evolution of the brain? The nature-nurture issue concerns individual ontogeny and is related to but distinguishable from the question of the phylogenetic modification of the brain and the mind during the course of organic evolution. The fossil record makes it certain that man's brain is the result of millions of years of gradual modification just as is any other organ of the body. We are but one stage in a continuum ranging from the most simple neural networks of the coelenterates at one extreme to the elaborate neural networks of cetaceans and primates at the other. Jerison (1973) in his distinguished book on the evolution of the brain brings this exciting field of paleoneuroanatomy up to date. There are, however, no fossils of mind (unless one wishes to let this role be played by cultural artifacts), and thus modern psychobiologists have turned to a distinctly different methodology—that of a comparative psy-chology—to compare the mental capacities of the different species (see Beer, 1980). Though there is considerable controversy concerning the validity of some of the most fundamental assumptions involved when one compares intelligence in different species, even more so when one crosses the boundaries of phyla—all animals are not necessarily evolved to solve the same ecological challenges and thus may differ in the kinds rather than the quantity of intelligence—it does seem likely that some evidence of the past evolution of human behavior may be discernible in the behavior of infrahuman species. Hodos and Campbell's (1969) paper on this important topic is essential reading for any comparatively oriented psychologist.

These then are the issues that guide and direct the course of psychobiological research. It is not always possible, of course, to discern these profound issues in the day to day activities of laboratory scientists, but they are there nevertheless, however deeply embedded in the precon-sciousness of empirical psychobiologists. It would be a reductio ad absur-dum to ascribe what we do in the laboratory to reasons other than these.

It is not my intention here to review the enormous variety of empirical data and findings that have resulted from what amounts to a surprisingly large expenditure of national effort. Despite protestations, psychobiology is now a rich science and its role assured by an appreciation of the mag-nitude and importance of the scientific task. The literature spills out over many journals, within and without psychology, and the data base is enormous. The only hope to bring some order to this mass of data (and to meet the goals of this volume) is to find general principles and guiding universals. That is the purpose of theory (not idle speculation, as some seem to believe).

THE THEORETICAL PERSPECTIVES

In this section I consider some of the theoretical stances taken by various members of the psychobiological community concerning the mind-brain relationship. These perspectives are samples of the answers now current concerning the issues just presented. There is no consensus yet, however; fortunately this science has not arrived at that stage. In fact many of these "theories" deal with less global matters than do the issues just presented. The assertion that psychology is a part of the biological sciences is itself a theoretical statement. This assertion derives from the monistic hypothesis that mind and brain are so intimately linked together that the destruction of the brain—the mechanism—inevitably leads to the destruction of the mind—the process. This hypothesis then leads to the corollary that psychobiology is meaningful only when interpreted within the context of a group of solutions to the mind-body problem that are clustered together under the rubric of physicalisms. However, it must be acknowledged, this is not the only class of solutions to the mind-brain problem, and, indeed, it is possibly only a minority view even among scholars. It is sometimes startling to discuss this issue with deeply concerned psychobiologists and to discover embedded in their professional physicalistic theories and experiments a serious and fervent commitment to the alternative view—a dualistic or even pluralistic philosophy.

Perhaps the most explicit pluralistic psychobiological philosophy expressed today can be found in the writing of Eccles, Nobel laureate for his work in neurophysiology (Eccles, 1970, 1979; Popper & Eccles, 1977). Greatly influenced by the eminent philosopher Popper, Eccles has propounded a pluralism in which each of three levels of reality (physical, mental, and cultural-informational) has its own separate though interacting existence.

The main logical deficiency in this modern pluralistic argument, from my point of view, is its lack of an appreciation of the meaning of organization and information. The brain, composed as it is of miniscule electrochemical engines (neurons), must of course carry out its functions on the basis of that particular physiochemical "technology." However, that does not mean that neural impulses are what the brain is all about. Rather, it can be asserted that impulses are only a means to an end and simply reflect the specific "technological implementation" of a pattern of activity that represents an idea or a concept. Whether the information that is being processed is represented in electrochemical impulses, electronic transients, or optical inference patterns is beside the question we are concerned with here. The real issue is—What is the nature of the changing *information patterns* of the brain?—What is the content of the message, not the particular coded language in which it is represented?

The purpose of the brain is not to generate impulses (this is the misperception of the neurophysiologist), rather it is to integrate and synthesize information (this is the emphasis of the psychobiologist). The derivative science in the case of mind happens to be information theory—not chemistry or physics. It does not matter of what a brain is constructed, only how those parts are hooked together.

Eccles's solution to the mind-body problem is to classify it a dualism (or more correctly a trialism). This approach fits well into the company of such related philosophies as parallelism and vitalism, as well as those aspects of the classic theologies that deal with the soul. Modern identity theory as professed by Feigl (1958), a physicalistic monism, on the other hand, fits well into the company of such philosophies as double aspect theory, automata theory, epiphenomenalism, and neutral monism. Though recorded controversy over which of these two points of view— monism or pluralism—is correct has been continuous for two and a half millenia, both points of view still are very evident in modern discussions.

The persistence of the two opposed philosophies—monism and dualism—is attributable to the fact that the issue over which they are divided is probably not resolvable by empirical means. An internally consistent, logical, and theoretical structure can be built based on either a monistic or dualistic premise. In the final analysis, it usually turns out that it is a personal value judgment that leads each of us to his own decision. Elegance, parsimony, consistency, personal value, and simplicity are the criteria to which all involved in this controversy ultimately turn. For an eloquent and comprehensive review of the subtle distinctions among the various theories that have been proposed as solutions to the mind-body problem, the reader could do no better than to read Bunge (1980). I deal briefly with similar matters in one chapter of an earlier work (Uttal, 1978).

Because of personal bias, because of their somewhat greater susceptibility to experimental analysis, and because of their greater fertility for new ideas, only materialistic and monistic theories of the nature of the relationship between the mind and the brain will be considered in the remainder of this essay. Dualistic theories are excluded from further consideration. I also eschew any further discussion of the philosophical points of view and consider only those specifically neurobiological theories that deal directly with the relationship between the processes of the brain and of the mind.

In general, the most significant theoretical approaches towards modeling the ways in which individual neurons represent psychological processes have been formulated for sensory and perceptual processes on the one hand and developmental and learning processes on the other. Other psychological processes are more often interpreted theoretically in terms of localization theory; that is, at a more macroscopic level of analysis than that of microscopic neurons. Emotion, motivation, and speech, for example, are of such great subtlety, both in terms of specification of what they are psychologically and in terms of their neural substrates, that their analysis at the level of neuronal interactions must, of necessity, be impossible at the present time. Thus, it is primarily learning and perception that are studied at the level of detail that seems comparable to the neuronal level at which they are likely to be coded, and it is to these areas of research that we must turn for examples of the best contemporary psychobiological theories. The theories that I shall consider here can be classified as: (1) Single Cell Theories, (2) Neural Network Theories, (3) System Interaction Theories, and (4) Field Theories.

Theories of Representation in the Brain

Single cell theories.   The basic postulate of single cell theoretical interpretations of (primarily, but not exclusively) perceptual processes is that more and more complex aspects of the stimulus pattern are encoded by the responses of individual neurons as one ascends higher and higher into the nervous system. The basic neural process operating to produce this increasing complexity of concept coding in single neurons is proposed to be a convergent interaction of the cellular responses representing the more elemental features of the stimulus in the periphery onto more central neurons, central neurons that progressively encode or represent more macroscopic aspects of the stimulus. To make this hypothesis more concrete, remember that we do know that the visual system has evolved in a way that peripheral neurons encode simple features like lines and corners. The output of these peripheral neurons then, it is proposed, hierarchically converge on more central neurons whose activation is in some way psychoneurally equivalent to the wholistic property of squareness qua squareness, rather than merely to the elements of which the square is composed.

This hierarchical convergence hypothesis evolved mainly from the early interpretations of the data collected by Hubel and Wiesel (e.g., 1959, 1962, 1965) who suggested that there were several different kinds of neuron types (simple, complex, hypercomplex) in the visual system of cats and monkeys. Initially these various cell types were thought to be sequential steps in a hierarchy of neuronal "types". It is now known that the idea of a neural hierarchy is not, in fact, likely to be valid. Simple cells, for example, do not necessarily feed into complex; nor do the out-puts of complex cells necessarily feed into hypercomplex cells. Rather, it is now believed that these cell types themselves are the result of different *patterns* of neural organization. In spite of this change in interpretation, the notion of a hierarchy of neurons (representing a hierarchy of more and more complex single cell encodings) is still current among many psychobiologists. The most extreme version of such a single cell hypothe-sis was proposed by Konorski (1967) some years ago. He suggested that individual neurons could encode the most global of concepts. Konorski's idea of such "gnostic neurons" is no longer taken very seriously, but it takes no great effort to find the theoretical vestiges of such a concept in current issues of journals dealing with visual perception.

The essential premise of single cell theories—complex concepts or properties can be represented by the activity of single cells or small groups of cells—has evolved in another direction. The new idea is the one proposed by Campbell and Robson (1968) whose main premise is that single neurons do not encode the particular features of the stimulus in terms of the explicit details of their geometry such as lines and corners, but rather in a more elaborate fashion based on a two-dimensional Fourier (spatial frequency) analysis. Campbell and Robson, and many others in recent years, have argued that perception is tantamount to the activation, not of a single neuron sensitive to a particular geometrical form, but rather of groups of neurons (or very loosely defined "channels") that represent the relative proportion of the spatial frequency components into which that stimulus may be analyzed by some kind of a neurobiological Fourier analyzer. That is, it is assumed that there exists a set of neural components that are each selectively sensitive to one frequency of the two-dimensional Fourier components into which any pattern can be ana-lyzed. Different stimuli are represented by different spectral patterns across this set.

There is a rich variety of criticisms that can be made against any single cell or Fourier channel theory that links perception (or, for that matter, thought of any kind) to the action of individual units in the brain. Some of these arguments are logical and some empirical. They include: the diver-gence (rather than convergence) of neural signals as information ascends the sensory pathways; the difference in time scale between single neuron response and molar behavior; the phenomena of stimulus equivalence; cognitive effects on many perceptual experiences putatively associated with single cell responses; the fact that specific feature sensitivity is more a characteristic of the peripheral portions of the brain and sensory pathways than of the region more likely to be the psychoneural equivalents of perception; the breakdown in the hierarchical neuron hypothesis; and, finally, the profound effect of configuration and global form on visual perception.

   In the brief space that I have to consider these theories it is not possible to develop these counter arguments directly (see Uttal, 1981, for a complete discussion), but it might be well to simply note the words of Hubel (1978) regarding this matter:

> Of course, this information [Hubel and Wiesel's findings] concerning feature specificity of single neurons by no means tells us how we recognize a hat, or a boat, or a face. The information from cells at this stage is fed onto subsequent stages, and at some point sense must be made of it. *We have no idea how it is done* (Emphasis added) [p. 25].

Neural network theories.   Single cell or channel theories assert that the activity of individual neurons or channels represents psychological experience. At the base of such an idea lies the necessary implication that the individual units have achieved their selective sensitivities on the basis of the way in which they are hooked up to other neurons. The emphasis in such theories, however, is on the single neuron's activities, rather than those interneuron interactions. Neural network theories, on the other hand, minimize the role played by the individual neuron and stress the integrative interaction among many neurons as the essential aspect of sensory coding or psychoneural equivalence. To the neural network theorist, it is the global pattern of action and interaction in the entire network that is the essential aspect. And, indeed, when one begins to consider the network and its properties, there is a far richer range of capabilities and functions that can be imagined to be the basis of mental experience than ever could be attributed to single neurons.

   The major difficulty with the neural network theory, of course, is that the networks that are plausible equivalents of human psychological processes are probably so complex as to preclude any mathematical or neurophysiological analysis. Therefore, it has become fashionable to deal with model systems of a lower level of intricacy, composed of a smaller number of neurons. For example, some researchers (Hartline & Ratliff, 1957; Kandel, 1974; Willows, 1969) have utilized the naturally occurring simpler model neural systems found in invertebrates to develop ideas about the logic of neural networks.

   One of the most popular neural network approaches invokes the concept of lateral inhibitory interaction, a ubiquitous interactive process occurring among neural elements at the same anatomical level. A group of neurons (either receptors or higher-level units) of equivalent function are horizontally interconnected by a system of inhibitory fibers. No neuron is specialized for any particular function; the system operates by virtue of the reticulum of interconnections to produce a transformation of the signal passing through it. The most familiar application in the psychobiology of this model is to the explanation of the Mach Band—the illusory accentuation of contours between stimulus areas of different luminance (see Ratliff's, 1965, book for the best possible discussion of this topic). However, lateral inhibitory interaction has also been applied to the problem posed by geometric illusions and metacontrast (Bridgemen, 1975; Weisstein, 1968).

More sophisticated neural net models have also been developed that involve other more complex forms of neural interaction than simple lateral interaction. Among the first to study the interactions of more complicated neuronal networks was Rashevsky (1948), and the line of research he pioneered has branched off in several directions. One direction has culminated in digital computer simulations of large scale neural networks. As one notable example, Pellionisz and Szentágothai (1973) have simulated a network in which as many as 30,000 neurons were repetitively connected together in a way that simulated the organization and function of the cerebellar cortex. The output of the simulation program was subsequently photographed on motion picture film to illustrate the dynamic pattern of the simulated "neural activity." They discovered that the behavior of large networks of this sort can be stable, yet vary in systematic ways depending on the manner in which the interconnections are defined. Indeed, simulated experiments can be carried out with this model that allow inferences to be made with regard to the effects of specific patterns of interaction. Because of the ease with which programming changes can be introduced, it is easy to test the effects of a wide variety of overall interconnection patterns in rapid order.

However, the success that Pellionisz and Szentágothai had with their simple neurons and repetitive patterns of interaction may not be generalizable to more realistic neural simulations in which the neurons are more complicated and the interconnections less repetitive. Another direction that the neural net simulation paradigm has taken is to use electronic rather than mathematically simulated logical elements as surrogates for neurons. The major conclusion at which studies of this sort have arrived is that an enormous amount of functional complexity arises even when as few as two or three electronic neurons are connected together in other than a repetitive network. For example, Gollub, Brunner, and Danly (1978) have shown that if only two simple electronic circuits with nonlinear properties (a feature they share with real neurons) are connected together, they are likely to produce chaotic and virtually unpredictable patterns of response. The important points that emerge from this demonstration are that only a very few neurons are necessary to produce highly complicated patterns of responses and that these patterns of responses, so easily generated by so few neurons, may be virtually unanalyzable or noncomputable in any practical sense of the word. Consider, then, the complexities of response that could result if the number of elements in the simulated network approached the number of neurons involved in any practical psychological situation. Then raise that number many orders of magnitude higher because of the tens of thousands of possible synaptic interconnections to each of those many neurons. Having arrived at that stupendous number, the difficulty of actually crossing the conceptual gap between the actual microscopic details of the elements of a realistic neural net and the macroscopic psychological process becomes crystal clear.

Other neural net models take a somewhat different tack than did either of the two approaches just described. Anderson, Silverstein, Ritz, and Jones (1977), for example, have proposed a mathematical model based on neural net principles that they believe describes both categorical perception and probability learning. However, their model involves only a very few neurons and a kind of mathematical formularization that is more descriptive of the psychological processes involved than specifically linked to any particular hypothesis of neural implementation. It is also an important general, but often unappreciated, outcome of this kind of theorizing that the mathematical assumptions of a neural net theory are often quite distinct from the neurophysiological ones.

System interaction theories.   Another major theme of neuroreductionism in psychobiology—system interaction—operates at a more macroscopic level than do either the single cell or neural network interaction models. This alternative approach deals with the nervous system as a set of interconnected functional blocks. The blocks are conceptually comparable to the major anatomic nuclei or to some hypothetical functional units that have not yet been anatomically or physiologically demonstrated but, on the basis of some behavioral evidence, seem to be necessary for the system to function. The elements in this type of model are usually proposed to be heavily interconnected by means of feedforward and feedback links, and it is the cybernetic system (as defined by Wiener, 1948) that constitutes the typical form of the model. Arbib's (1972) cybernetic theory of visual information processing is of this category, but so also are the many information processing systems proposed by cognitive psychologists in the last few years. The latter are not at all physiological; the blocks in their flow diagrams are rarely associated with any neuroanatomical structure but are much more likely to be inferred on the basis of psychological observations. However, the basic conceptual similarity between theoretical structures such as Shiffrin and Atkinson's (1969) model of human memory and Arbib's explicitly cybernetic structure, or Pribram and McGuinness's (1975) neuroanatomic model of the attention system, for example, are self evident.

The major premise underlying those empirical studies in which the effects of brain lesions on behavior are determined also falls under this same rubric. Psychobiologists dealing with the effects of, for example, a lesion of a certain hypothalamic nucleus obviously conceptualize their experiments and their models of mind from this same system interaction point of view. Their stress is also on the possible interconnections that a given nucleus may have with other nuclei and on the valence (inhibition or excitation) of the influence that is exerted by any surgical ablation. That mental processes may be attributable to a particular macroscopic *region* of the brain is the key element of this kind of system-interaction theory.

Field theories. The final class of neuroreductionistic theories of mental processes has undergone a radical transformation in recent years. During the heyday of the Gestalt movement, and in spite of the major accomplishments of that school of psychology in calling attention to the influence of the configuration of the elements of a stimulus (as opposed to their individual nature) on perception, the Gestalt neuroreductionistic theory was an abysmal failure. That theory asserted that there were isomorphic electrotonic fields of electrical activity in the brain that directly corresponded to the perceptual experiences. Such a theory fell victim in the 1950s to a series of experiments that demonstrated that these putative "fields" could not be short-circuited by the insertion of pins or foils into the brain (Lashley, Chow, & Semmes, 1951; Sperry, Miner, & Myers, 1955). Animals that had such metallic objects in the cerebral cortices behaved indistinguishably from those that did not. Though this strong evidence against the existence of passively spreading fields of electrical activity laid to rest Gestalt neuroreductionistic field theories, this idea has recently been resurrected in a modified form that is now consistent with what we know of the neuronal and synaptic organization of the cerebral cortex. The main proponent of this modern type of field theory has been Pribram (e.g., Pribram, Nuwer, & Baron, 1974). Pribram, who was a student of Lashley, was stimulated by the developments in holography to notice the analogies that existed between the hologram and brain processes. (The hologram—a form of lensless photography— produces a three-dimensional image from two-dimensional photographic plates consisting only of interference patterns produced by interactions between the light directly from a laser and the same light bounced off the object being photographed.) Pribram and his colleagues were aware that a number of psychobiologists, including Lashley, had proposed that interference patterns among electrical waves on the surface of the cerebral cortex produced interference patterns of a similar kind. The important link between the two ideas was that all parts of the image in a hologram are distributed over the entire photographic plate, much as the engram in Lashley's classic psychobiological experiments appeared to be. It is not appropriate to go deeper into the details of the optics of holograms here— they are explained in detail both in Pribram, Nuwer, and Baron's paper and in Uttal (1978)—and, in fact, there is a danger in carrying the metaphor too far (one might be tempted to look for a physical implementation of the hologram in neural tissue rather than just an analogous process). The point that is relevant to the present discussion is that the mathematics that describe the holographic process also seems to be applicable to the brain in general and to the storage of the engram in particular.

Although I have classified Pribram, Nuwer, and Baron's model as a field theory (because it uses a continuous type of mathematics and is associated by that mathematics with a continuous optical process), in fact, this particular field theory does not invoke continuous fields in the same way that Gestalt theorists did. Rather, these modern "field theorists" are well aware of the fact that the neurons in the brain are actually discrete entities and do not function merely as passive media for the spread of electrotonic fields. Quite to the contrary, Pribram and his colleagues state emphatically that the actual implementation of their model is based on a discrete network of interacting neural elements that is not in conflict with any of the neural net theories so far discussed. Nor does their network model (or their mathematical analysis) differ substantially from the one invoked in an autocorrelation theory of form detection (Uttal, 1975) which is also a network model. Thus, classic field theories seem to have evolved into versions that are hardly distinguishable from the other network theories described above.

An Interim Conclusion

The message of this brief review of theoretical developments concerning the mind-brain problem is this: Not only can modern field type theories be considered to be implemented in terms of the action of a discrete neural network, but so also can the single cell and the system interaction theories be considered to be consistent with such an approach. Though the emphasis on the single cell in the former class of theory is extreme, the specific sensitivities of those feature selective neurons are now appreciated to result from the network of neural interactions feeding into them. Similarly, the latter control system models, while emphasizing a much more macroscopic level of neural organization than do the cellular models, do not invoke any concepts that are necessarily inconsistent with the idea of a network of discrete neurons. Indeed, if one digs below the superficial aspects of all of these theories, it becomes clear that there is virtual unanimity among psychobiologists that interactions in a vast network of neurons represent *the essential level of representation* of mind. The consensus, therefore, seems to be that mind is a manifestation of neural networks; that is, there is a psychoneural identity between mind and the state of some network. However close to being universally accepted this view may be, it should not be overlooked that this is a speculative hypothesis based on virtually no directly relevant empirical evidence. No one has ever synthesized mental or quasimental processes by concatenating a number of neuron-like elements. No one has ever teased apart a neural network and shown that it progressively loses those functional properties that we would call mental. Thus, mind has never been either analyzed into its elements nor synthesized from them, nor do we know anything about the internal logic of the network that is likely to lead to the kind of self-awareness to which we are all individually witness. Clearly, whatever goes on in the brain, it is quite different from conventional computer logic. What we do know is a considerable amount about the coding of sensory and motor communication messages; we are learning how information is transmitted to and from the central nervous system; and we have achieved a deep appreciation of how the individual neuron and synapse execute their functions. The problem that remains, however, is the essential one—the mind-brain problem. Though most psychobiologists believe that mind is embodied in the action and interaction occurring in neural networks, all frankly accept the fact that this problem remains totally refractory. This is the current state of affairs. The future is another matter, and it is at this point that we leave history, philosophy, and interpretation of the state of current experimentation and theory and turn briefly to speculations about the future of the psychobiological sciences to conclude this essay.

FUTURE TRENDS

This essay asserts that psychobiology—a subfield of scientific biology—has many unanswered questions and must, therefore, remain highly flexible in its choice of tools, approaches, and realistic goals. The problems that have been posed over the centuries continually raise new challenges to our techniques and research paradigms. It is especially fascinating to note the rapid change in the techniques used and the specific research problems tackled by the various psychobiological subdisciplines as new instruments became available over the last few decades, even within the context of persisting historical issues. Many of the tools now routinely used did not even exist even a few years ago. Perhaps, even more important than the change in methodology, however, is the change that has occurred in our thinking about the mind-brain problem. The advent of electronic logical engines (i.e., computers) only 40 years ago stimulated a whole new kind of theoretical approach in psychobiology. Many of the words and phrases used in earlier parts of this essay were not a part of anyone's vocabulary prior to that time. Along with new words, new concepts have arisen in which traditional biological theorizing has been enriched and broadened by an infusion of ideas from electrical engineering and computer science. No more can we say that the derivative sciences of psychobiology are only chemistry and physics—we now have to emphasize information science.

The end product of the change in technology and concept, of course, is that there will also be a change in the kind of research that will be done in psychobiology in the future. There will be (in my view, but certainly not in that of all of my colleague psychobiologists) a substantial reduction in the kind of work that involves ablative surgery of various portions of the brain and the observation of the resulting behavioral changes. I believe this reduction in ablative psychobiology will result from an emerging realization that the complexity of the brain at this level is far greater than we had thought. To observe the impairment of some behavior following the destruction of some nucleus does not necessarily, we now appreciate, localize that behavior in that particular nucleus. I believe that there is an increasingly large body of evidence that asserts that a large portion of the brain is involved in most psychological processes, and that earlier ideas of precisely and uniquely localized mental functions may not be correct.

Closely related to this paradigmatic change in the psychobiological laboratory is a reemergence of a wholistic view in psychological research itself. A trend is discernible, perhaps not yet fully evident but embryonic, towards a more molar approach to some of the problems that heretofore had often been approached in a more neuroreductionistic manner. The emergence of contemporary cognitive psychology is an example of this change in perspective. Psychology, in the light of this new emphasis, will never be supplanted by some kind of super-neurobiological science in which all mental subject matters are explained in terms of neurobiological mechanisms. The trend towards a more molar psychology is largely attributable to the practical problem of complexity to which I previously alluded.

Thus, there are portents of a reawakening psychology as the science of mind and an emerging appreciation that neuroscientific tools alone can never replace psychophysical methodology. Only in the simplest of instances, and mainly for percepts that are constrained, determined, or transformed by the most peripheral neural mechanisms, does the kind of neural model so popular a few years ago still seem to be generally acceptable. What I am suggesting is that neural models of illusions, constancies, contrasts, and even more so, of thought, intelligence, and personality may be forever beyond the abilities of biological science to analyze, no matter how assured we may be that that is the domain from which they actually arise. Cellular neurophysiologists, I expect, will become more and more concerned with cellular neurophysiology and less and less with some of the absurd analogies that have previously been proposed as explanations of molar mental phenomena. I do not believe that simplistic single cell theories of pattern recognition, aftereffects, or contrast are likely to survive this reevaluation. Furthermore, since in my opinion the detailed spatial temporal patterning of the interactions within the neural network are the essential correspondents of the mental process, I also suspect that the statistical "sums" of neural response ensembles recorded in the form of electroencephalograms or evoked brain potentials are also not likely to give us deep insights in the mind-brain relationship.

CONCLUSION

The theses of this essay are that psychology is an integral part of biology and that there has been a two-way interaction between these two sciences. Biology has profoundly influenced psychological thinking, and it takes no great imagination to see how contemporary neurophysiological research is often guided by psychological concepts. Modern psychobiology, in particular, stands as a fusion of ideas from both fields—neither being intellectually dominant over the other, even if one or the other enjoys a momentary advantage in popularity.

A variety of physicalistic theoretical approaches exists in the field, not any one of which necessarily excludes the others. These physicalistic approaches are, however, in profound conflict with pluralistic theories, which seem to have fallen out of favor. In the laboratory, however, many psychobiologists behave as if they believe mind is a brain process.

It is critically important to make the distinction between the metaphysics of mind-brain unity on the one hand, and the practical potential of neuroreductionistic theory to explain mind on the other. However deeply convinced in principle one may be of a psychoneural identity, the practical reductive solution of the mind-brain problem will probably remain elusive and subject to well-determined limits to analysis because of the twin constraints of its great complexity and our inadequate computing power. Perhaps a totally neuroreductionistic explanation of mind is a chimera, for which we may search forever without success. Certainly, few psychobiologists see in current strategies the germ of the complete solution to the question of how it is that the action of a myriad of neurons in the brain can be transmuted from a complex pattern of electrochemical actions to that most precious of human possessions—the awareness of one's own existence.

REFERENCES

Anderson, J. A., Silverstein, J. W., Ritz, S. A., & Jones, R. S. Distinctive features, categorical perception, and probability learning: Some applications of a neural model. *Psychological Review,* 1977, *84,* 413–451.

Arbib, M. A. *The metaphorical brain: An introduction to cybernetics as artificial intelligence and brain theory.* New York: Wiley-Interscience, 1972.

Bain, A. *The senses and the intellect.* London: John W. Parker and Son, 1855.

Beer, C. G. Perspectives on animal behavior comparisons. In M. H. Bornstein (Ed.), *Comparative methods in psychology.* Hillsdale, NJ: Lawrence Erlbaum Associates, 1980.

Bridgeman, B. Correlates of metacontrast in single cells of the cat visual system. *Vision Research,* 1975, *15,* 91–99.

Bunge, M. *The mind-body problem: A psychobiological approach.* Oxford: Pergamon Press, 1980.

Campbell, F. W., & Robson, J. G. An application of Fourier analysis to the visibility of gratings. *Journal of Physiology,* 1968, *197,* 551–566.

Darwin, C. *The expression of the emotions in man and animals.* London: Murray, 1872.

Darwin, C. A biographical sketch of an infant. *Mind,* 1877, *2,* 285–294.

Eccles, J. C. *Facing reality.* Berlin: Springer-Verlag, 1970.

Eccles, J. C. *The human mystery.* Berlin: Springer International, 1979.

Feigl, H. The mental and the physical. In H. Feigl, M. Scriven, & G. Maywell (Eds.), *The Minnesota studies in the philosophy of science* (Vol. 2): *Concepts, theories and the mind-body problem.* Minneapolis, MN: University of Minnesota Press, 1958.

Ferrier, D. *The functions of the brain.* New York: Putnam's Sons, 1886.

Gall, F. J., & Spurzheim, J. C. Recherches sur le système nerveux en général, et sur celui du cerveau en perticulier. Paris: Académie de Sciences, 1808.

Gödel, K. Einige metamathematische resultate uber entscheidungsdefinitheit and widerspruchsfreiheit. *Anzeiger der Akademie der Wissenschaften, Vienna Mathematisch-naturwissenschaftliche Klasse,* 1930, *67,* 214–215.

Gollub, J. P., Brunner, T. O., & Danly, B. G. Periodicity and chaos in coupled nonlinear oscillators. *Science,* 1978, *200,* 48–50.

Hartline, H. K., & Ratliff, F. Inhibitory interaction of receptor units in the eye of *Limulus. Journal of General Physiology,* 1957, *40,* 357–376.

Hodos, W., & Campbell, C. B. G. Scala naturae: Why there is no theory in comparative psychology. *Psychological Review,* 1969, *76,* 337–351.

Hubel, D. Vision and the brain. *Bulletin of the American Academy of Arts and Sciences,* 1978, *31,* 17–28.

Hubel, D. H., & Wiesel, T. N. Receptive fields of single neurons in the cat's striate cortex. *Journal of Physiology,* 1959, *148,* 574–591.

Hubel, D. H., & Wiesel, T. N. Receptive fields, binocular interaction and functional architecture in the cat's visual cortex. *Journal of Physiology,* 1962, *160,* 106–154.

Hubel, D. H., & Wiesel, T. N. Receptive fields and functional architecture in two nonstriate visual areas (18 and 19) of the cat. *Journal of Neurophysiology,* 1965, *28,* 229–289.

Jerison, H. J. *Evolution of the brain and intelligence.* New York: Academic Press, 1973.

Kandel, E. R. An invertebrate system for the cellular analysis of simple behaviors and their modifications. In F. O. Schmitt & F. G. Worden (Eds.), *The neurosciences: Third study program.* Cambridge, MA: M.I.T. Press, 1974.

Knuth, D. E. Mathematics and computer science: Coping with finiteness. *Science,* 1976, *194,* 1235–1242.

Konorski, J. *Integrative activity of the brain.* Chicago, IL: University of Chicago Press, 1967.

Lashley, K. S. In search of the engram. Society of Experimental Biology Symposium No.

4: Physiological Mechanisms in Animal Behavior. Cambridge University Press, 1950, 454–482.

Lashley, K. S., Chow, K. L., & Semmes, J. An examination of the electrical field theory of cerebral integration. *Psychological Review,* 1951, *58,* 123–136.

Lenneberg, E. H. Language and brain: Developmental aspects. *Neurosciences Research Program Bulletin,* 1974, *12,* 511–656.

Ling, G., & Gerard, R. W. The normal membrane potential of frog sartorius fibers. *Journal of Cellular and Comparative Physiology,* 1949, *34,* 383–385.

Olds, J., Disterhoft, J. F., Segal, M., Kornblith, C. L., & Hirsch, R. Learning centers of rat brain mapped by measuring latencies of conditioned unit responses. *Journal of Neurophysiology,* 1972, *35,* 202–219.

Pellionisz, A., & Szentagothai, J. Dynamic single unit simulation of a realistic cerebellar network model. *Brain Research,* 1973, *49,* 83–99.

Penfield, W., & Roberts, L. *Speech and brain mechanisms.* Princeton, NJ: Princeton University Press, 1959.

Popper, K. R., & Eccles, J. C. *The self and its brain.* Berlin: Springer-Verlag, 1977.

Pribram, K. H., & McGuinness, D. Arousal, activation, and effort in the control of attention. *Psychological Review,* 1975, *82,* 116–149.

Pribram, K. H., Nuwer, M., & Baron, R. J. The holographic hypothesis of memory structure in brain function and perception. In D. H. Krantz (Ed.), *Contemporary developments in mathematical psychology* (Vol. 2). San Francisco, CA: Freeman, 1974.

Rashevsky, N. *Mathematical biophysics.* Chicago, IL: The University of Chicago Press, 1948.

Ratliff, F. *Mach bands: Quantitative studies on neural networks in the retina.* San Francisco, CA: Holden-Day, 1965.

Schaller, G. B. *The mountain gorilla: ecology and behavior.* Chicago, IL: University of Chicago Press, 1963.

Schaller, G. B. *The Serengeti lion: A study of predator-prey relations.* Chicago, IL: University of Chicago Press, 1972.

Shiffrin, R. M., & Atkinson, R. C. Storage and retrieval processes in long-term memory. *Psychological Review,* 1969, *76,* 179–193.

Sperry, R.W. Brain bisection and mechanisms of consciousness. In J. C. Eccles (Ed.), *Brain and conscious experience.* New York: Springer-Verlag, 1966.

Sperry, R. W., Miner, R., & Myers, R. E. Visual pattern perception following subpial slicing and tantalum wire implantations in the visual cortex. *Journal of Comparative and Physiological Psychology,* 1955, *48,* 50–58.

Stockmeyer, L. J., & Chandra, A. K. Intrinsically difficult problems. *Scientific American,* May 1979, *240,* 140–159.

Uttal, W. R. *An autocorrelation theory of form detection.* Hillsdale, NJ: Lawrence Erlbaum Associates, 1975.

Uttal, W. R. *The psychobiology of mind.* Hillsdale, NJ: Lawrence Erlbaum Associates, 1978.

Uttal, W. R. *A taxonomy of visual processes.* Hillsdale, NJ: Lawrence Erlbaum Associates, 1981.

Van Lawick-Goodall, J. *In the shadow of man.* Boston, MA: Houghton-Mifflin, 1971.

Weisstein, N. A Rashevsky-Landahl neural net: Simulation of metacontrast. *Psychological Review,* 1968, *75,* 494–521.

Weiner, N. *Cybernetics.* New York: Wiley, 1948.

Willows, A. O. D. Neuronal network triggering a fixed action pattern. *Science,* 1969, *166,* 1549–1551.

Wilson, E. O. *Sociobiology: The new synthesis.* Cambridge, MA: Belknap Press, 1975.

Zaidel, E. *Linguistic competence and related functions in the right hemisphere of man following cerebral commissurotomy and hemispherectomy.* Unpublished Ph.D. dissertation, California Institute of Technology, Pasadena, CA, 1973.

2 Psychology and Engineering

A. Chapanis
Communications Research Laboratory
The Johns Hopkins University

INTRODUCTION

Psychology and engineering owe much more to each other than is generally recognized for the two disciplines are linked in many ways: by the men who have moved from engineering to psychology, by the engineering technology that makes possible most psychological research, by the problems that each field presents to the other, and by the ideas from one that enrich the other. This essay begins with a characterization of the engineering profession and follows with a discussion of some contributions of engineering to psychology. The next section reverses orientation to look at some contributions from psychology to engineering. In the final section, I speculate about future relations between psychology and engineering.

THE ENGINEERING PROFESSION

Like psychology, engineering has a short history but a long past.[1] Canals, bridges, roads, tunnels, aqueducts, fortifications, ships, and monuments dating back thousands of years bear mute and, in many cases, awe-inspiring testimony to the engineering skills of our ancient forefathers. For the most part these works were constructed under the supervision of

---

[1] Paraphrase of a remark attributed to Ebbinghaus by Boring (1929).

craftsmen and architects who had available only simple machines such as the wheel and the lever. What these builders lacked in machinery they compensated with manpower and time. The architect-builders of ancient times were able to command immense pools of raw labor. Even so, many projects took so long that they were never completed during the lifetimes of their original designers.

As civilization advanced, machines became more complicated but the men who designed and built them were still master craftsmen and not engineers. For example, of those men who are now credited with inventing the steam engines that brought in the industrial revolution, Newcomen was an ironmonger and blacksmith, Crompton and Hargreaves were weavers, Smeaton and Watt were instrument makers, and Stephenson was a fireman. For centuries, training in the engineering arts and crafts was by apprenticeship or, later, by pupilage, a system that was at a slightly higher level than apprenticing.

Engineering as an academic discipline did not emerge until about the middle of the eighteenth century. The impetus for this development came from the special skills needed in military engineering to cope with the complicated problems of the ordnance of that time and to design fortresses capable of withstanding siege by that ordnance. To fill his almost insatiable need for military engineers, Napoleon established special schools that subsequently developed into the *grandes écoles* of France, those exclusive institutions that still produce an intellectual elite of that country.

Something similar happened in America. The United States Military Academy at West Point, which graduated its first student in 1802, was in its early years a corps of engineer cadets. The first civilian school of engineering was established either at the American Literary, Scientific, and Military Academy (later Norwich University) in 1819 or at the Rensselaer School (later Rensselaer Polytechnic Institute) in 1824. What is certain is that the first four degrees in civil engineering were granted by Rensselaer in 1835. Less than 50 years later, G. Stanley Hall founded the first psychological laboratory in America at The Johns Hopkins University.

Since then, both engineering and psychology have experienced phenomenal growth, engineering more so than psychology. Although engineering and the engineering profession are often described in the singular, engineering today is not a unitary and circumscribed activity, but is rather practiced in many apparently unrelated ways. There are at least 50 clearly defined specialties in engineering (see Table 1), most of which are offshoots of approximately a dozen familiar branches such as aeronautical, chemical, civil, electrical, industrial, and mechanical engineering. The *Dictionary of Occupational Titles* (1965) lists 16 occupational groups

TABLE 1
Some Engineering Specialties

Acoustical engineering	Mechanical engineering
Aeronautical engineering	Metallurgical engineering
Architectural engineering	Mining engineering
Automotive engineering	Municipal engineering
Biomedical engineering	Nuclear engineering
Ceramic engineering	Optical engineering
Chemical engineering	Petroleum engineering
Civil engineering	River engineering
Electrical engineering	Safety engineering
Environmental engineering	Sales engineering
Hydraulic engineering	Salvage engineering
Illumination engineering	Sanitary engineering
Industrial engineering	Systems engineering
Management engineering	Telephone engineering
Marine engineering	Traffic engineering

specifically concerned with engineering under *Occupations in Engineering*. These 16 occupational groups contain a total of 237 so-called *base job titles*, a figure that contrasts sharply with the total of 15 *base job titles* in the single occupational group headed *Occupations in Psychology*. In a less quantitative, but more engaging style Florman (1976) describes ". . . this vast, motley group. . ." of engineers in these words:

> . . . the approximately one million American engineers exhibit an enormous variety of professional specialties ranging from designing electronic circuits to building dams, from devising theoretical models for systems analysis to testing new plastics, from conceiving new means of utilizing solar energy to selling machine parts. There are solitary geniuses working on discoveries that will amaze the world; and there are thousands of quasi-engineers seated like galley slaves in huge drafting rooms. There are teachers and deans, brilliant teams in "think tanks," advisers to presidents, titans of industry, rugged individualists heading their own consulting firms; and there are thousands of frustrated inspectors for government agencies, and checkers of quality control in factories [pp. 148–149].

Although it might seem impossible to find a single satisfactory definition for this melange of activities, the Engineers' Council for Professional Development (ECPD)[2] encompasses them all in the following way:

> Engineering is the profession in which a knowledge of the mathematical and natural sciences gained by study, experience, and practice, is applied with

---

[2] The ECPD is now the ABET, Accreditation Board for Engineering and Technology.

judgment to develop ways to utilize, economically, the materials and forces of nature for the benefit of mankind [p. 114].

As we shall see, the last five words of that definition form a bridge between the professions of psychology and engineering. Still, the ECPD's definition is considerably more restricted than some engineers themselves use. Florman, for example, says that engineering is "the art or science of making practical application of the knowledge of pure sciences [1976, p. x]." He goes on to say that engineers ". . . study the sciences and use them to solve problems of practical interest, most typically by the process that we call creative design [ibid.]" and that "the engineer uses the logic of science to achieve practical results [p. xi]." With the change of only a few words Florman's definition of engineering describes accurately what some psychologists do. And that is a good starting point for the substance of this essay.

SOME CONTRIBUTIONS OF ENGINEERING TO PSYCHOLOGY

Three classical works on the history of psychology (Boring, 1942, 1950; Murphy, 1949) document in great detail the debt that psychology owes to such disciplines as philosophy, medicine, physiology, and physics. Yet the words *engineer* and *engineering* do not appear in any of these books. By implication engineering has had nothing to do with the history and development of modern psychology, an implication that is very strange because Boring himself started out as an engineer. In any case, it is time to challenge that implication.

Engineering has had, and continues to have, a major (though heretofore largely unrecognized) impact on psychology through four distinct kinds of contributions:

(1)   men;
(2)   technology;
(3)   problems; and
(4)   ideas.

Men

Most of us can easily identify the names of physicians who have contributed to the development of psychology (see, for example, Krantz & Glass, in this volume): Thomas Young, Wilhelm Wundt, Arnold Gesell, Sigmund Freud, and Hermann Rorschach are among the more prominent ones. Philosophers have also figured prominently in the history of psychology, and John Dewey, G. Stanley Hall, and Edward B. Titchener are some of the more eminent of those (see, for example, Block & Alston, in Volume I). But what engineers have become famous psychologists? Although few come readily to mind, psychology is indebted to the engineering profession for some of its most illustrious exponents.

Clark Hull started out as an engineer and had been employed for only two months as a mining engineer with the Oliver iron mines in Hibbing, Montana, when he was struck with polio that left him seriously crippled and debilitated for life. Forced to make a new career for himself, he became a psychologist. How much of Hull's later work as a psychologist was colored by his early engineering background? We shall never know, but we can speculate. For example, while he was a graduate student he designed and constructed a logic machine on which he could set up all the syllogism types and formal fallacies. Upon manipulation, the machine would examine and display all the implications, both universal and particular, of each syllogism and fallacy. Later, as an instructor at Wisconsin, Hull designed and constructed the first machine to compute correlation coefficients from raw data. Was this because of his engineering background? Probably so.

Knowing Hull's early background gives us a new perspective on his choice of words for the presidential address he delivered to the American Psychological Association in 1937, *Mind, Mechanism, and Adaptive Behavior*. The published version of his talk, unfortunately, makes no mention of the model he used to illustrate it. The model was an impressive collection of wires, lights, switches, and chemicals, which, under Hull's skillful hand, simulated simple stimulus substitution and forgetting, the effect of the order of stimulation on conditioning, experimental extinction, spontaneous recovery, secondary extinction, irradiation, summation, differentiation, external inhibition, and the redintegration of compound stimuli (see Chapanis, 1961, p. 125). Although Hull seems never to have referred to his model as such, it is easy to recognize the device as an engineer's model of behavior. Was Hull's dedication to the construction of a rigorous, formal theory of behavior also the result of his early engineering background? Probably. Whatever the dynamics, there can be no doubt that Hull, the engineer turned psychologist, had a profound influence on American psychology.

Consider next Louis Thurstone, an instructor in engineering at the University of Minnesota when he first became interested in psychology. His lifelong pursuit of the quantification of psychological phenomena and his choice of words for the title of one of his books, *The Vectors of Mind* (1935), suggest the influence of his early engineering experience. Indeed, as he says in his autobiography, "Ever since my undergraduate days I have been interested in the psychological aspects of machine design, especially as regards human limitations in visual motor coordination in the controls [Thurstone, 1952, p. 298]."

Other well-known psychologists who started out in engineering include C. Lloyd Morgan, Edward Chace Tolman, and Walter S. Hunter. Still, we should not put undue stress on famous personages. No less important, in my opinion, is the steady trickle of engineering students who have gone into graduate schools of psychology, especially schools offering programs in management, industrial psychology, engineering psychology, and human factors. Psychology has been and will continue to be enriched so long as such cross-fertilization is allowed and encouraged.

Technology

Advances in science depend in part on the *Zeitgeist*—the knowledge and habits of thought that make new knowledge possible. But scientific advancement is equally dependent on technology—technical advances that make possible discoveries that would have been impossible without that technology. We have only to look around any psychological laboratory with a discerning eye to appreciate the enormous debt that psychology owes to engineering in this respect.

Where do we start in the long list of technological achievements that have fostered the growth of modern psychology? Everyone will have his or her own idea. In compiling such a list, however, we need to keep in mind that modern definition of engineering given earlier in this essay. Technological accomplishments that today are made by professional engineers were, up to a hundred or so years ago, made by brilliant men, Renaissance men, who were sometimes philosophers, sometimes physicians, sometimes physicists, and sometimes just tinkerers. So in looking at technical advances of the past we must classify them by what they do, not by whom they were invented.

My own list of technological achievements important to psychology begins with the invention of printing and of the printing press around 1440. Psychologists, after all, produce more words than anything else. We have only to look at the flood of journals and books published each year to appreciate how much psychology owes to printing. Next on my list would be the harnessing of electricity because it powers the thousands of devices and machines—such as pursuit rotors, tachistoscopes, amplifiers, tape recorders, and computers—that populate psychological laboratories. In addition, the detailed understanding we now have of the intimate action of nerve cells, of the eye and ear, and of the brain could never have been attained without the many elaborate stimulating, measuring, and recording devices powered by electricity. My list of important inventions for

psychology continues with timing devices—chronoscopes and chrono-
graphs—whose invention in the 1840s paved the way for studies of reaction time and related phenomena.

After timing devices, my list becomes jumbled, and I am no longer able
to sort out and attach priorities to the thousands of gadgets that psychologists have come to use routinely in their work. Is photography next?
Maybe, maybe not. One thing is certain: From the beginning of our science as an experimental discipline, psychologists have been ingenious in
adapting, modifying, or constructing the mechanical, electrical, and
chemical contrivances they needed for their work. Hering's indirect-
vision color mixer (built of the parts of an old sewing machine), his stereo-
scope, and his binocular color mixer are examples of the beautiful devices
of German manufacture that filled his laboratory in the late 1800s. These
and other gadgets earned for our discipline the name "brass-instrument
psychology," a name that persevered until about the 1960s.

Although there may be a great deal of uncertainty about the technological advances that aided psychology most during its first hundred years, a
poll among psychologists would almost certainly be unanimous in identifying one device as the most important engineering contribution to contemporary psychology. That device is the electronic computer. In some
fields of psychology, for example sensory and information processing,
one would be hard pressed to find any research that has not been done,
either directly or indirectly, with the help of computers (see, for example,
Mayzner & Dolan, 1978). Computers are standard items of hardware in
almost every experimental psychology department in the country, and
they are used in virtually every aspect of psychological work from physiological research to modelling abnormal behavior. They are used for: the
analysis of data; experimentation, including stimulus control and presentation, and response recording and timing; the administration and tabulation of interviews and questionnaires; the administration, scoring, and
interpretation of psychological tests; education and training; modelling of
human behavior; communication; information storage and retrieval; and
text processing and report preparation.

Problems

Ever since the Industrial Revolution, engineering and technology have
provided a never-ending list of topics for psychological research. To
understand the reasons it may be helpful to make a brief historical excursion. Before the Industrial Revolution, the technology of civilization was
relatively primitive, and economic systems were simple and predominantly localized. Agriculture was feudal and based on traditional methods
handed down from father to son over generations. Overland travel was

difficult and hazardous because the few existing roads were usually in a miserable state of disrepair. Manufacturing was performed by skilled artisans and craftsmen who laboriously started with raw materials and cut, molded, wove, carved, polished, and decorated each product into its final form. Communication over extended distances was painfully slow and unreliable. In most cases animal power—by man, beast, or both—provided the energy needed for these various activities.

The Industrial Revolution changed all that. The invention of the steam engine supplanted and greatly augmented the work that could be done by animal power. The discovery of crop rotation and other soil improvement techniques so increased agricultural productivity that it was possible for many farmers to move from the land to the cities where they provided the manpower needed in the factories that were the creations of the Industrial Revolution. Transportation of heavy goods was facilitated by the invention of the steam locomotive and steamboat. Manufacturing was taken out of the home and centralized in factories where new power-driven machines could be better accommodated and controlled. The discovery of electricity was followed by the invention of the telegraph which made possible the transmission of information almost instantaneously over vast distances.

These and other innovations transformed the essential fabric of society. As a result of them, man changed his way of working, the tools he worked with, the tempo at which he worked, and the organizations in which he worked. In the long run, these changes have allowed the peoples of the earth to enjoy far better health, more comfortable lives, more leisure time, and much greater mobility than their ancestors did. These benefits, however, did not come without costs. To the simple kinds of accidents that befell our ancestors were now added a whole new class of industrial accidents and hidden hazards. Factory environments were often unhealthy, lighting was usually bad, hours of work were too long, sanitary facilities were primitive, ventilation was insufficient to expel noxious vapors, and the work itself was frequently so repetitive and constraining that it virtually deformed workers.

Improving working conditions.   Although working conditions have improved greatly over the decades, national laws have often been required to bring about needed improvements. An American law that has special relevance for psychology is the Occupational Safety and Health Act of 1970 (OSHA). This is the first law to mention specifically *psychological factors* that might be involved in occupational safety and health. Moreover, it set up as one of its goals the "general welfare" of workers and the establishment of "criteria which will assure insofar as practicable that no employee will suffer diminished health, functional capacity, or life expectancy as a result of his work experience [U.S. Government Printing Office, 1971, p. 1590]." This is a law with far-reaching implications for psychology, and a law that will provide psychologists with researchable problems for decades to come.

A contemporary example of the operation and effect of this law concerns an almost explosively-expanding segment of our economy, namely, the increasing use of computers and, more generally, office automation. In 1979 the National Institute of Occupational Safety and Health (NIOSH), the research arm of OSHA, received from a consortium of unions in the U.S. a bill of complaints from workers using visual display terminals (VDTs). The general nature of these complaints was that employees using VDTs experienced a variety of symptoms including headaches, general malaise, eyestrain, and other visual and musculoskeletal problems. In response to these complaints NIOSH conducted an extensive investigation of computer workstations in three companies in the San Francisco Bay area (Murray, Moss, Parr, Cox, Smith, Cohen, Stammerjohn, & Happ, 1981). The study consisted of four phases: (1) radiation measurements, (2) industrial hygiene sampling, (3) a survey of health complaints and psychological mood states, and (4) ergonomics and human factors measurements.

Although radiation and chemical airborne contaminants have long been suspected as potential health hazards, the NIOSH study found that radiation and chemical contamination in and around all workstations were either not detectable or well below all occupational standards. Indeed, these levels were not appreciably different from what one would find in an ordinary living environment.

The results of the survey of health complaints were quite different, however. VDT operators experienced a greater number of health complaints, particularly related to emotional and gastrointestinal problems, than did comparable operators who did not work with VDTs. These findings, according to the NIOSH report, demonstrate a level of emotional distress for the VDT operators that could have potential long-term health consequences. The NIOSH study concludes that it is quite likely that the emotional distress shown by the VDT operators is more related to the type of work activity than to the use of VDTs per se. With the growing number of computers and VDTs in our society, it is clearly of considerable importance to establish how much of worker complaints can be traced to VDTs and how much to other factors (Ketchel, 1981; Smith, 1981). This is a research question that needs urgently to be further investigated.

The NIOSH report has more to say about the ergonomic and human factors aspects of the computer workplace than about any other aspect of computer work. Keyboard heights, table and chair designs, viewing distances, viewing angles, copy holders, and other aspects of workstation design all come in for criticism. In short, many computer workstations in America force operators to adopt strained postures, to contend with glare and generally substandard viewing conditions, and to engage in repetitive, uninspiring tasks that almost literally require the operator to be "chained" to his workstation.

Although these problems have not been solved, they have stimulated a great deal of research and will continue to do so. More important, however, is that this whole area of research would probably never come so forcefully to the attention of designers, manufacturers, and researchers if it had not been for OSHA which provided the channel through which problems could be translated into action.

The nature of factory work. Before the Industrial Revolution the worker made products slowly and painstakingly, from beginning to end. He was his own boss, and he worked according to his own schedule. The factory system, on the other hand, was designed for the mass production of standardized products. To do that, the manufacturing process was divided into many small operations, each performed by workers routinely and repetitively. Since the work was machine-paced, rather than operator-paced, workers became almost literally cogs in the machine. Finally, to insure that the production of goods went smoothly, the worker was supervised and controlled by rules that specified when he would work, what work he would do, and exactly how he would do it. "Efficiency" and "productivity" became the catch-words of the new system. They are still with us.

Some of the earliest research on improving the efficiency of industrial operations was conducted by engineers, not by psychologists. It was in 1898 that Frederick W. Taylor, the founder of "scientific management," conducted his classic study of pig-iron handling for the Bethlehem Iron Company, a study that is widely cited by industrial psychologists today. Although the principles of scientific management, time and motion study, and piece work that Taylor espoused are generally accepted today, the Hawthorne studies conducted by Roethlisberger and Dickson (1939) showed dramatically that social psychological factors in the work situation were more powerful determiners of productivity than early engineers had ever imagined. Now, almost 50 years later, psychologists have incorporated "the Hawthorne effect" into their everyday vocabularies.

The realizations that the worker was an individual, a person, and that he could not be treated as a cog in the machine were the foundations of modern industrial psychology. Walter Dill Scott (1911) and Hugo Münsterberg (1913) had, to be sure, published their pioneering works before World War I, but they were virtually alone among psychologists.

Industrial psychology did not mushroom until after the results of the Hawthorne studies were assimilated. Now, of course, it comprises a large and important part of the psychological scene. Thumbing through the contents of any book on industrial psychology shows the enormously wide range of topics with which psychologists are now concerned: job analysis, interviewing, personnel testing, performance appraisal, training, attitudes and morale, motivation and job satisfaction, financial incentives and job evaluation, working conditions, equipment and work design, accidents and safety, leadership and supervision, decision making, organizational structure, job enrichment, and union-management relations. All this is the heritage of the Industrial Revolution and the engineering and technology that produced it.

Human factors. Related to industrial psychology, but still distinct from it, is the area of human factors, or *ergonomics* as it is generally called throughout much of the world. Whereas industrial psychology has traditionally been more concerned with the worker in his working situation, human factors is more concerned with the products of our industrial enterprise and how these products can be best designed to match the abilities, limitations, and other characteristics of the people who use them. Human factors deals not only with the tools and machines that workers use, but with the thousands of products—stoves, washing machines, typewriters, computers, recreational equipment, automobiles, aircraft—that consumers buy and use by choice or by necessity.

There is nothing really revolutionary about the idea of designing for man's needs. Man has always done that, ever since he first started making tools and implements. Stone Age man fashioned his axe and his spear to fit his hand and his arm. Chairs and chariots, scissors and scythes were designed and built to suit man's physique, his strength, and the way he moves naturally. And, if we look around us, we see lots of things that work, and that work well, even though they have not had the benefit of any formal human factors work.

World War II, however, forced into our awareness that common sense and intuition were no longer dependable guidelines for design. The war needed and produced new machines—radar, sonar, high-flying aircraft—that created serious mismatches between the requirements these machines placed on their human operators and the actual abilities of those operators. Bombs and bullets often missed their targets, friendly planes were sometimes shot down, whales instead of submarines were depth charged, and many men needlessly lost their lives because the men in uniform could not manage the machines they were given to operate.

The machines produced for that war were also qualitatively different from those of earlier times in that they used the operator not primarily as a

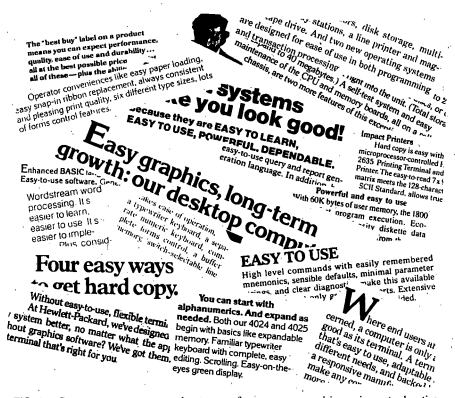

FIG. 1.   Contemporary concerns about ease of use as expressed in equipment advertisements.

source of muscular power, but as a perceiver and a decision maker. The jobs of a radar operator or sonar operator, for example, do not require much muscular effort, but do require that operators perceive and interpret information displayed for them and arrive at correct decisions about what they perceive. These are psychological capacities, capacities that are more complicated than the simple motion economy principles that had been developed by Taylor and by the Gilbreths after him. So it was that biological and psychological scientists were called in to consult on the design of equipment.

After the war, human factors moved gradually into industry to help increase the efficiency and safety of industrial operations, and after that into the design of consumer products, architecture, and environmental design (see Wohlwill, in Volume II). Several events during the past decade have powerfully influenced and promoted human factors. One has been the enactment of the Consumer Product Safety Act of 1972 (CPSA)[3]

[3] An act and commission which are, at the time of this writing, in some danger of being abolished.

by the Federal Government. Whereas OSHA was concerned with the protection of workers at their jobs, the CPSA was designed to protect consumers against the hidden hazards in products that are created by our technology. Among other things it states that:

(1) "an unacceptable number of consumer products which present unreasonable risks of injury are distributed in commerce";
(2) "complexities of consumer products and the diverse nature and abilities of consumers using them frequently result in an inability of users to anticipate risks and to safeguard themselves adequately"; and
(3) "the public should be protected against unreasonable risks of injury associated with consumer products [U.S. Government Printing Office, 1972, p. 1207]."

The purposes of the CPSA are to develop uniform standards for consumer products and to promote research and investigation into the causes and prevention of product-related deaths, illnesses, and injuries. It is a powerful law, and it has provided an almost endless series of research problems for psychology (for a small sample, see Chapanis, 1980; Grandjean & Vigliani, 1980; Kaminaka, Rehkugler, & Gunkel, 1981; Lhuede, 1980; and Olson, Halstead-Nusslock, & Sivak, 1981).

The enactment of the CPSA was in part the response to a growing number of accidents that stimulated public inquiries and product-liability law suits. In many cases, the central issue was a human factors one: Was the product defective in design, defective in the sense that it contained a hazard that should have been anticipated by the engineer, designer, and manufacturer? Products that have been involved in such accidents and that have been investigated by the Consumer Product Safety Commission, the action agency of the CPSA, include swimming pool slides, ladders, stoves, power lawn mowers, matches, and toys. Even if Federal support for this kind of activity were decreased or eliminated, public and private awareness and expectations about the design of consumer products have greatly changed in the last decade. Courts of law are now shifting responsibility for the safe design of products on to designers and manufacturers. "Caveat emptor" or "human error" are no longer acceptable excuses for poor or inadequate design.

Designing for "ease of use." It would be a mistake to infer from the foregoing that human factors is only, or even primarily, concerned with designing against accidents. Designing equipment so that it can be used safely is, to be sure, an important goal of human factors. Depending on the product, however, other goals are equally or even more important. One of them is expressed in contemporary concerns for "ease of use."

Technology, especially computer technology, has created devices that are beyond the comprehension of many potential users. Banking terminals, word-processing systems, and computers of all kinds are constantly being misused or not used at all because they are too complicated. This realization has forced many designers and manufacturers to place greater emphasis on the design of products to be more usable, or easier to use by occasional or casual users. Evidence of these concerns appears in Figure 1.

Today, the field of human factors lists the following among its major goals: reducing errors, increasing safety, increasing the reliability of man-machine systems, reducing training requirements, improving maintainability, increasing efficiency, increasing productivity, improving the working environment, increasing human comfort, reducing boredom and monotony, increasing convenience of use, increasing user acceptance, enlarging the job, and improving the quality of life.

The field is now represented in the United States most importantly by the Human Factors Society and, somewhat less so, by the Society of Engineering Psychologists, Division 21 of the American Psychological Association. Although the Human Factors Society is multi-disciplinary, about half of its membership is made up of psychologists. The psychologist members of the human factors profession are not merely experimental or academic psychologists, for the field has developed its own unique methodologies, principles, and language. Because engineering and technology are inventing new products at an accelerating rate, the demand for human factors specialists trained in the field exceeds the supply. This situation is not likely to change in the foreseeable future.

Devices as objects of psychological study. A somewhat different class of problems includes studies of the way machines and other devices are used, not so much because of a desire to improve them, but rather because they are interesting objects of study in their own right. The classic studies of telegraphy by Bryan, a psychologist, and Harter, an expert railway telegrapher who at the age of 35 became a student in psychology under Harter, (Bryan & Harter, 1897, 1899) were conducted because the two were interested in knowing more about this activity. (As an aside, they spent the first five pages of their 1899 article justifying the study of an occupation as a legitimate area of psychological science. Over 80 years later many of us in applied areas still have to feel defensive about our work!)

One of the findings that came out of those studies is that learning telegraphy consists of acquiring a hierarchy of habits: The telegrapher first learns to recognize letters, then progresses to words, and then to phrases. Indeed, the expert telegrapher may copy behind by 6 to 12 words. Bryan and Harter also found that this learning did not progress smoothly. There were level areas—plateaus—in the learning curve, and those plateaus appeared to coincide with periods when lower-order habits were being consolidated and made almost automatic. Still other findings concerned the magnitude of individual differences, the importance of rhythm in telegraphy, and the effects of emotion and stress on performance.

Today those old findings are still being cited in textbooks of psychology, and the concepts they enunciated—hierarchies of habits and plateaus—have been incorporated into our everyday psychological language. For purposes of this essay, however, it is important to note that those classical studies were motivated by a device—the telegraph. If the telegraph had never been invented and put to commercial use, those studies might never have been done.

Since Bryan and Harter, technology has created hundreds of devices that have provided problems for psychological inquiry. Indeed, it is not a long step from the study of telegraphy to contemporary studies of sophisticated telecommunication and teleconferencing devices (see Chapanis, 1981, for example). Telephones, radios, television, typewriters, computers, lathes, drill presses, automobiles, and aircraft are only a few of the technological inventions that have stimulated psychological research, because among other things, they have provided the occasion for natural experiments on otherwise latent or untested capacities and limitations of man. We can assert with confidence that we have not seen the end of such stimulation.

Ideas

To a greater extent than most psychologists probably realize, psychology is indebted to engineering for some of its most important models, concepts, and ideas (see, for example, Marks, in this volume). The history of this fertilization goes back many centuries. Descartes, inspired by the hydraulically operated moving figures in vogue in public gardens in seventeenth-century France, wrote in 1650:

> It is to be observed that the machine of our bodies is so constructed that all the changes which occur in the motion of the spirits may cause them to open certain pores of the brain rather than others, and, reciprocally, that when any one of these pores is opened in the least degree more or less than is usual by the action of the nerves which serve the senses, this changes somewhat the motion of the spirits, and causes them to be conducted into the muscles which serve to move the body in the way in which is commonly moved on occasion of such action; so that all the movements which we make without our will contributing thereto . . . depend only on the conformation of our

> limbs and the course which the spirits, excited by the heat of the heart, naturally follow in the brain, in the nerves, and in the muscles, in the same way that the movement of a watch is produced by the force solely of its mainspring and the form of its wheels . . . [Rand, 1912, pp.172f].

This was followed almost exactly a century later by La Mettrie's (1748) *L'Homme Machine,* a title that in turn was reincarnated exactly two centuries later in an edition of Carlson and Johnson's *The Machinery of the Body* (1948). Newton's mechanics brought forth models of man as a machine made up of levers and similar linkages. Watt's steam engine and the development of thermodynamics produced models of man as a complicated heat engine.

More contemporary models and ideas begin with World War II. For example, the speed of World War II aircraft rendered obsolete all traditional methods of air-to-air combat. Much more sophisticated control apparatus was needed to compute how to shoot a missile, not at where a target is now, but at where the target would be in the future. This involved not only the instantaneous solution of complicated mathematical equations, but also the development of servosystems that could immediately sense and respond to the states and conditions of the aircraft. In this connection control engineers invoked the term *feedback,* a term that has since been incorporated into the language of psychology. The technology of these new servosystems came to be called *cybernetics,* or the science of control and communication (Wiener, 1948). Cybernetic principles have been found useful not only in the design of machines, but also in our understanding of the mechanism and behavior of the human body.

Almost coincidentally in time, telephone engineers were working on a comprehensive set of principles to explain and deal with the complicated switching networks that were the products of the communication industry. Those principles and the theory behind them are described in a book by Shannon and Weaver, *The Mathematical Theory of Communication* (1949). The general communication system that Shannon and Weaver described (Figure 2) was taken over almost without modification by psychologists and such commonplace psychological terms as *bits, channel capacity, redundancy, noise,* and *information* trace their origins to that work (see, for example, Quastler, 1955). Somewhat later, some of the terms were changed (e.g., Garner, 1962) as the ideas were more thoroughly assimilated by psychologists.

Meanwhile, computer technology was developing rapidly and not entirely independently of communication theory. *Giant Brains* was the title of an important book at the time, not about living brains, but about computing machines (Berkeley, 1949). The model of the computing machine has been much more successful in telling us about the living brain, than

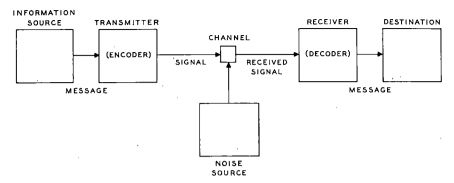

FIG. 2.   The communication model (From Shannon & Weaver, 1949).

living brains have been successful in telling us about the design of computing machines. Indeed, some psychologists believe that trying to program a computer to carry out some complicated function, for example, pattern recognition, tells us more about how humans probably perform that function than decades of basic psychological research have been able to tell us. In any case, this heritage of computer technology has given psychology concepts such as *information processing, parallel-processing, time-sharing, heuristics,* and *algorithms* now incorporated into its professional language.

Finally, psychologists are indebted to engineering for many basic measurements that make it possible to quantify the phenomena that we study. The need to measure and specify light and color for practical purposes led to the development of our fundamental measures of light by illuminating engineers. When telephone engineers had to cope with the transmission of speech, they developed not only fundamental acoustical measures but speech articulation test methods as well. Even the new psychophysics, signal detection theory, was initially a development by electrical engineers and mathematical statisticians who were concerned with the transmission of signals in the presence of random noise. Psychologists later adopted, studied, and contributed to the refinement of all these measures, but the beginnings were made by practical men who had engineering problems to solve.

SOME CONTRIBUTIONS OF PSYCHOLOGY TO ENGINEERING

To reverse perspectives and turn to what psychology has contributed to engineering is to look at the other side of the same coin we have already been examining. Historically, applied psychology originated in relation to business and industry, and the term *applied psychology* has been most closely identified with those areas ever since. For example, most of the articles in the *Journal of Applied Psychology,* founded in 1917, have been concerned with some aspect of industrial psychology. Over the years, however, what used to be called simply industrial psychology has separated into seven more or less distinct areas of specialization, including personnel selection and classification, personnel training, employee relations and management problems, human performance and worker efficiency, consumer psychology, engineering psychology, or, more broadly, human factors, and environmental psychology.

The contributions that psychology has made in some of these areas have already been discussed in the preceding section in which it was shown how psychology and engineering have interacted to benefit each other. The Industrial Revolution led to the design of factories that required workers with specialized skills; psychology provided the measurement techniques for selecting and classifying workers according to their abilities so that workers could be better matched to jobs. Engineering provided man with complicated machines and systems; psychology provided the principles and methods for training people to use those machines and systems. Without minimizing the contributions that psychology has been able to make in these several ways, the greatest and most direct impact of psychology on engineering has come from engineering psychology, or, as it is more commonly referred to, human factors.

Human Factors and Systems Engineering

Machines come in all sizes, and the larger ones are usually called systems. In general terms, systems are made up of machines, components, or subsystems all of which are linked together and work for some common goal, e.g., transporting people or goods over long distances; creating, manipulating, storing, and transferring information; or manufacturing and distributing electric power over large regions. Examples are large aircraft, large ships, computer systems, office automation systems, telephone systems, power plants, large factories, and missile systems. The smaller units that make up systems are generally called subsystems. A commercial aircraft, for example, has a propulsion subsystem, a guidance subsystem, an electrical subsystem, a pressurization subsystem, and still others. A subsystem that is of particular concern to us here is what is often called the personnel subsystem: the people who use, operate, interact with, direct, and maintain the system. Although most large systems are automated to some extent, even the most highly automated systems use people to monitor, check, and service the system. It is now generally accepted that the people who use, operate, or maintain systems—the personnel subsystem—are vital to the successful operation of those systems.

Large systems offer substantial advantages over small ones, "economies of scale" being one of them. A large commercial aircraft can transport people more efficiently, faster, and at a lower cost per passenger mile than smaller aircraft. Against this major advantage are some serious disadvantages. Large systems are very expensive, they take a long time to design and construct, and when they fail, or do not operate properly, the consequences can be catastrophic. Oftentimes the reason systems fail or do not operate properly is what for years was called "human error". One of the most widely-publicized accidents of this kind was the one that occurred at the Three-Mile Island nuclear power plant in 1979. This accident brought the problem of human error to the attention of the public as no other accident had been able to do. What human factors has taught us, however, is that the ways some systems are designed almost literally invite people to commit errors, and Three-Mile Island is a case in point. Conversely, many common sources of so-called "human error" can be reduced or even eliminated by proper design. As has already been stated, however, human factors has goals other than the reduction of errors.

The system design process. The design and construction of large systems generally go through a series of steps (Chapanis, 1970a). First is a planning stage that is at a conceptual level. Eventually blueprints and drawings are prepared. This is often followed by mockup design after which the system is "breadboarded", that is loosely constructed of components that can be easily moved around, manipulated, and changed. A prototype, the first working model, is then generally constructed and tried out. After modifications are made to the prototype, the first working system may be constructed and subjected to further evaluations and tests. If these are successful, the system is then put into service. As the system goes through these, or a comparable series of steps, the design becomes more and more "frozen." Major changes are easy to make at the planning or conceptual stage. They are still relatively easy to make at the blueprint stage. By the time the first prototype has been constructed, however, it is usually impossible to make major changes in the design of the system. Since personnel considerations are often involved at the planning or conceptual stage of system design, it is now generally recognized that human factors specialists need to be contributing members of systems design teams so that they can work with engineers in the entire design process.

Defining user characteristics. One of the first things the human factors specialist can do is to prepare a thorough "user-characteristics analysis."

This is a description of the user population in terms of such things as age, sensory and motor abilities, anthropometric dimensions, general intellectual capabilities, education, training, and experience. These are then translated into specific design implications. A system to carry astronauts into outer space is designed for highly selected individuals who are physically superb, intelligent, and well trained. Such a system can place greater demands on the user than systems such as automobiles or telephones that are designed for a broad cross-section of the general population.

Function allocation. At the initial but important conceptual stage of system design, decisions are made about the functions that will be assigned to people and those that will be assigned to machines. To illustrate, although mail sorting and distribution are now generally done by automated systems, people are still used in these systems because of their remarkable perceptual capacities. People are needed to read the zip codes on letters and to verify that the correct postage is on the envelope. We do not yet have machines that are capable of performing these functions. It would be possible, of course, to design a mail handling system now in which postage could be verified by machine, but this would require some major changes in our entire postal system, for example, the design and use of special stamps whose values could be read by machine. It would also require replacing thousands of postage meters with completely redesigned ones. In any case, decisions about the allocation of functions are basic to the subsequent design of the system. Moreover, these decisions need to be made early in the system design process because once made they influence virtually all subsequent design and determine the ultimate form of the system.

Other contributions. In later stages of system design, human factors specialists may be involved in the design of specific hardware components, which often require short-cut, "quick-and-dirty" experiments to decide about alternative designs. The human factors specialist may then be called on to establish staffing and training requirements so that people will have been selected and trained to operate the system when it is finally put into place (Chapanis, 1970b). Human factors specialists may also be called on to prepare job aids and user manuals to accompany the system. Finally, such experts are almost invariably involved in tests and evaluations of the entire system—the system as it is actually used by the people for whom it was designed (Van Cott & Chapanis, 1972).

This highly abbreviated description of system design is perhaps sufficient to show the immediate, direct, and multi-faceted contributions

that human factors can make to engineering practice. For a fuller description of these and still other functions see De Greene (1970).

Some Great Ideas from Psychology to Engineering

In closing this section, I review briefly four great ideas that psychology
has contributed to engineering.

Individual differences. The first great idea is obvious but is sufficiently
important to warrant comment. That idea simply is that people differ and
that there are ways of dealing with individual differences. Engineers are
used to uniformity, standardization, and interchangeability. However,
people vary. Indeed, the diversity of human shapes, sizes, intellects, and
temperaments is enormous and bewildering. Although this fact may be
obvious to everyone, engineers find it difficult to cope with and to fit into
their engineering equations. Psychologists, on the other hand, are constantly faced with individual differences. They are inescapable, and psychologists have devised ways of dealing with them. The statistics that we
take for granted to quantify and measure individual differences are oftentimes the single most important contribution psychologists make when
they work with engineers. One important consequence of these ideas is
that engineers now accept that they cannot design for themselves, or for
an "average" user, but must rather design for a range of users.

Changes over time. The second great idea is that man changes with
time. His capacities increase as he grows from infancy into adulthood and
then decline slowly as he moves into later maturity and old age. More
rapid changes occur when his performance increases as he learns and
adapts, or when his performance decreases as he becomes fatigued,
bored, or uninterested. The distinctive psychological contribution is to
have identified, measured, and quantified these changes so that they can
be accommodated in engineering design.

Man is a thinking, feeling being. The development of the factory
system during the Industrial Revolution meant a substantial change in the
way workers were organized and labored. Efficiency and productivity
were the goals of the new regime, and the best way to achieve those goals
was through specialization, uniformity, replaceability, and impersonality.
Some characteristics of the new work organization were enunciated in the
late nineteenth century by the influential theorist, Max Weber, who held,
among other things, that:

(1) all tasks should be broken down into the smallest possible units, and the division of labor should insure that each unit is done by qualified experts;

(2) all tasks should be carried out according to a consistent set of abstract rules to assure uniformity and coordination so that individual differences are thereby eliminated or at least reduced; and

(3) business should be conducted in an impersonal, formalistic manner with a social distance between superiors and subordinates to insure that personalities do not interfere with the efficient conduct of business.

Ideas similar to these underlie the principles of "scientific management" and the principles of motion economy that have been used to increase efficiency by analyzing operations into their elemental components. The worker was supposed to do what he was told in exactly the way he was told to do it. He became, in essence, just another cog in the machine.

The Hawthorne studies provided the first scientific inkling that things were not quite that simple. Those studies were followed by the equally-significant experiments by Kurt Lewin on such human characteristics as motivation, interaction, and leadership in real-life situations. Lewin was an inspiring teacher, and his students have been powerful influences in American psychology. Their research and writings have shown that simplistic, mechanistic theories fail to account for a large proportion of behavior in the workplace.

Psychologists in particular accept as axiomatic that men in general, and working men in particular, cannot be fragmented or segmented. People take their attitudes, motivations, aspirations, and problems with them wherever they are. Although we do not know very much about ways of harnessing and directing these subjective forces, we have at least been able to measure some of them and to convey some indication of their importance to our engineering colleagues.

Measurement of man at work. The last great contribution that psychologists have made and continue to make to engineering and technology derives from techniques for measuring man at work, that is, for measuring the performance of man interacting with machines. Some of these methods have been devised from familiar methods of controlled experimentation, but a great many, such as critical incident studies, activity analyses, task analyses, simulation studies, and fault-free reliability analyses, have been developed specifically for studying man-machine interactions. The application of these techniques to engineering problems is very often one of the most important contributions that psychologists can make to engineering design and practice (see, for examples, Chapanis, 1959, and Van Cott & Chapanis, 1972).

FUTURE DIRECTIONS

What does the future hold for relations between psychology and engineering? Some trends seem sufficiently clearcut and robust that we can probably extrapolate from them safely at least into the near future.

Contributions from Engineering to Psychology

Engineering today appears to be more vigorous than it has ever been. Indeed, the pace of technological invention seems to be constantly accelerating. At the same time, new technological inventions are creating human and social problems in such profusion that the social sciences in general, and psychology and human factors in particular, cannot keep up with them. Moreover, there seems to be no likelihood that the number, variety, and complexity of these problems will decrease, or even reach an asymptote in the near future. That may be good or bad or anything in between. The practical result is that engineering is creating more than enough problems to occupy fully those psychologists who want to be concerned with the applications of their science.

Inevitably, new technological inventions are also certain to contribute to psychology directly by providing new and sophisticated mechanisms for use in research. Stimulating, measuring, recording, and computing devices these days are almost outmoded by the time they are purchased, set up, and put into use in psychological laboratories. Each new major advance in technology seems to open up such new vistas for psychological research that it is exciting to speculate about what the future will bring.

As engineering technology advances, it creates and needs new ideas, concepts, and principles. Although it is less certain how many of these will eventually find their way into psychology, we may expect at least some to be integrated into psychological thought.

Finally, those engineers who occasionally switch professions to become psychologists are sure to enrich the field because of their distinctive backgrounds, interests, and temperaments.

The Impact of Engineering on Psychology

One effect that engineering has had on psychology has been to contribute to a separation between those parts of psychology that are most relevant to engineering and the rest of psychology. Some evidence for this is that engineering psychology seems to be losing ground to the much broader, interdisciplinary field of human factors. Somewhat more than half of all educational programs in human factors are now located in engineering departments, generally industrial engineering, systems engineering, management engineering, or operations research. Only about 40 percent of human factors programs are in psychology departments. What seems to be happening is that psychologists are migrating into engineering departments to staff the human factors programs in those departments. Whether that trend will continue is hard to say. One thing that is true is that most psychologists who have become human factors engineers no longer talk and think like their more traditional colleagues.

Human factors has developed into a highly technical discipline with its own data, concepts, methods, and jargon. Although at the time of this writing the *Human Engineering Guide to Equipment Design* (Van Cott & Kinkade, 1972) is nearly ten years old, it is still the "bible" of the human factors profession. Most psychologists who thumb through that volume think of it as an engineering book, and not a psychological one. Yet 13 of the 18 authors who contributed chapters to that volume are psychologists. What happens to psychologists who work with engineers? In what ways do they see the world differently from their more academic colleagues?

The stimuli and responses. The human factors psychologist who works with engineering problems faces much more complicated problems than those faced by the typical experimental psychologist. First, the stimuli and responses are generally so much more complex in applied work that it is sometimes difficult to identify exactly what those stimuli and responses are. Figure 3 shows six stimuli that are representative of those used in experimental work. They derive from well-known and authoritative books of general psychology and perception. Note how simple they are. In the experiments for which these stimuli were used, responses were correspondingly simple. Generally, the subject was required to do no more than to make a verbal response or to push a simple button. Contrast that with some typical stimuli and responses that the human factors psychologist faces. Figure 4 shows a part of the control room in a nuclear power plant. Note the complexity of the stimulus situation. This picture also allows you to imagine the complexity of the operator's monitoring task. Figure 5 shows the cockpit of a simulator for the 747 aircraft. What exactly is the stimulus here? What are the relevant parts of it?

A second important difference between the stimulus-response situation of the experimental psychologist and that faced by the engineering psychologist is that in laboratory work stimuli and responses are generally discrete. The experimenter presents a stimulus, the subject responds. The experimenter presents the next stimulus, the subject responds again. In practical engineering work, by contrast, the operator is faced with a continually changing series of stimuli and responses. In the control room situation (Figure 4), electricity constantly flows, the demand is constantly

FIG. 3.   Some representative stimuli used in basic experimental work in psychology.

changing, and the generation of electricity—whether by coal, oil, or nuclear power—is also constantly changing. The same is true for flying,
driving, or, indeed, operating a haying machine or power lawn mower.
The world of work is dynamic and not static.

Still another consideration contrasts the ways the general psychologist
and human factors psychologist look at stimuli and responses. For the
general psychologist stimuli and responses are sort of incidental. His
interest in stimuli and responses is confined to what they can tell him
about what goes on in the head when the organism is stimulated this way
or that. If the psychologist were more behavioristically inclined, he may
say that he is interested in what relationships hold between the stimuli and
responses. The human factors psychologist, on the other hand, views
stimuli and responses themselves as more important than what goes on
between them because the stimuli and responses are identified with dis-

FIG. 4.   Part of the control room in the Nine Mile Point Nuclear Power Plant (Courtesy of
the Niagara Mohawk Power Corporation).

plays and controls. One of the goals of engineering design is to select and
design displays and controls so that they best suit the people who need to
use them.

All of the foregoing mean that the human factors psychologist views
stimuli and responses quite differently than the general psychologist does.
These are not trivial differences for they represent fundamentally different ways of looking at the world.

Dependent measures.   Psychologists worry a great deal about independent variables, but they seem to be largely unconcerned with the dependent ones. Even most textbooks of experimental design pay scant
attention to dependent variables. Perhaps for that reason most psycholo-

gists seem to pick dependent variables for their convenience, that is, they pick dependent variables that are most likely to give significant results. Table 2 illustrates the importance of this problem. In the left-hand column is a baker's dozen of important systems criteria. These are the kinds of criteria that apply to many, if not most, man-machine systems. Some of them are what a consumer might use when thinking about buying a new automobile or washing machine. The criteria are mostly self-explanatory. Other things being equal, the better of two systems is the one that (1) has a/ longer anticipated life, (2) has the more pleasing appearance, (3) is more comfortable for the people who use it, (4) is more convenient, (5) is easier to operate and use, (6) is more familiar, that is, more similar to systems in existence, (7) is cheaper to buy, (8) is quicker to repair, (9) requires fewer operators, (10) is cheaper to operate, (11) breaks down less often, (12) is safer, and (13) can be used with less highly trained people.

The right-hand column of the table lists an equal number of dependent variables or experimental criteria extracted from research studies. This, of course, is a highly abbreviated list. But it constitutes a set of dependent variables being used over and over again in research.

There is little correspondence between the two columns. It is difficult to see what some of the experimental criteria in the right-hand column have to do with the systems criteria in the left-hand column. Part of the problem is that systems criteria are complex. Even when there seem to be some connections between some of the experimental criteria and systems criteria, it turns out that the latter are much more complex than the

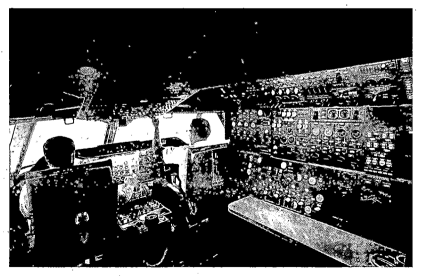

FIG. 5. Cockpit of a 747 aircraft simulator (Courtesy of American Airlines).

TABLE 2
Some General Systems Criteria and
Some Common Dependent Measures, or Criteria,
used in Experimental Work.*

Systems criteria	Experimental criteria
Anticipated life of the system	Accuracy (or, conversely, errors)
Appearance	Cardiovascular responses
Comfort	Critical flicker fusion
Convenience	EEG
Ease of operation or use	Energy expenditure
Familiarity	Muscle tension
Initial cost	Psychophysical thresholds
Maintainability	Ratings
(e.g., mean time to repair)	(e.g., of annoyance, comfort, etc.)
Manpower requirements	Reaction time
Operating cost	Respiratory responses
Reliability	Spare mental capacity
(e.g., mean time to failure)	
Safety	Speed
Training requirements	Trials to learn

*From Chapanis (1971).

former. Safety, for example, comprises much more than the accuracy of doing some particular task. Safety involves not only the design of equipment but it also involves signs, selection, training, attitudes, motivations, rewards, and punishments. The same is true for other systems criteria in this list. Furthermore, a number of systems criteria do not seem to be measured by any of the experimental criteria. The question that the applied researcher must continually ask is: "Of all the dependent variables that I could study, which ones will have the greatest transfer to the criteria that the world is really interested in?"

Methodological orientation. Finally, there is a potpourri of differences between the human factors psychologist and the general psychologist originating from the methodologies used in applied work, the ways research findings are used in applied work, and other considerations that enter into the application of psychology to engineering.

The great physicist Percy Bridgman once wrote that science is "doing one's damndest with one's mind, no holds barred." That quotation is particularly true in applied areas. In fact, for applied work, controlled laboratory experimentation has a number of serious limitations (reviewed in Chapanis, 1967). The literature and the guide books of human factors contain an enormous body of dependable and useful information that has been collected by techniques other than controlled experimentation.

Some of these are: accident studies, activity analyses, critical incident studies, field studies, human error analyses, link analyses, mission simulations, mock-up studies, system safety analyses, task-equipment analyses, and time-line function analyses. The list is impressive not only because of the highly technical content of topics in it, but also because so much of it seems unrelated to the content of academic psychology and the methods of controlled experimentation.

The practical psychologist also learns quickly that the world mostly does not care about psychological theories. What it wants to know is what we can do for it. It also turns out that you do not need a theory to have useful principles and generalizations that can be applied to practical engineering problems. Moreover, statistical significance in itself is of little importance to engineering design. Practical significance—the actual size of the difference that can be expected from the deliberate manipulation of variables—is much more important.

Finally, in practical work, the psychologist soon learns that everything involves compromises and that psychological findings cannot necessarily be applied without modification. There are always trade-offs involved, and these are trade-offs of time, costs, and benefits.

All of the foregoing lead to the conclusion that the world outside the laboratory is complicated, messy, untidy, and cluttered. Working in that world requires different perspectives from those embraced by academic psychologists. In short, engineering realities have forced a significant part of psychology away from the mainstream of psychological theory and practice. Those same engineering realities will almost certainly cause perspectives to diverge rather than to converge in the years to come.

CONCLUSIONS

Engineering contributions to psychology have been rich and varied, though largely unrecognized. Psychologists are quick to acknowledge their debt to the biological and physical sciences, but appear to have overlooked the important debt that they owe to engineering. This oversight may perhaps reflect a preoccupation with demonstrations that psychology is a science. In so doing, psychology has disassociated itself from engineering because engineers are so intensely practical and are much more concerned with solving problems than they are with the discovery of knowledge for knowledge's sake. Yet it is to some extent ironic that in arriving at solutions to the problems of the world, engineering has provided many of the stimuli, methods, models, and ideas that have greatly furthered basic psychological science. That realization may perhaps be the greatest contribution that engineering has to offer psychology.

In looking to the future, the impact of engineering on psychology is almost certain to continue and to increase in importance as the pace of technological invention creates new human and social problems.the search for solutions to these problems has resulted in a split between the kind of applied psychology that can help solve them and the rest of psychology. The gap seems likely to increase rather than decrease in the years to come. One thing is certain: An important segment of psychology is hitched to an engineering star and the destiny of one is inextricably linked to the other.

REFERENCES

Berkeley, E. C. *Giant brains*. New York: Wiley, 1949.

Boring, E. G. *A history of experimental psychology*. New York: Century, 1929.

Boring, E. G. *Sensation and perception in the history of experimental psychology*. New York: Appleton-Century, 1942.

Boring, E. G. *A history of experimental psychology*. New York: Appleton-Century-Crofts, 1950.

Bryan, W. L., & Harter, N. Studies in the physiology and psychology of the telegraphic language. *Psychological Review*, 1897, *4*, 27–53.

Bryan, W. L., & Harter, N. Studies on the telegraphic language: The acquisition of a hierarchy of habits. *Psychological Review*, 1899, *6*, 345–375.

Carlson, A. J., & Johnson, V. *The machinery of the body*. Chicago, IL: University of Chicago Press, 1948.

Chapanis, A. *Research techniques in human engineering*. Baltimore, MD: The Johns Hopkins University Press, 1959.

Chapanis, A. Men, machines, and models. *American Psychologist*, 1961, *16*, 113–131.

Chapanis, A. The relevance of laboratory studies to practical situations. *Ergonomics*, 1967, *10*, 249–255.

Chapanis, A. Human factors in systems engineering. In K. B. De Greene (Ed.), *Systems psychology*. New York: McGraw-Hill, 1970. (a)

Chapanis, A. Systems staffing. In K. B. De Greene (Ed.), *Systems psychology*. New York: McGraw-Hill, 1970. (b)

Chapanis, A. The search for relevance in applied research. In W. T. Singleton, J. G. Fox, & D. Whitfield (Eds.), *Measurement of man at work*. London: Taylor and Francis, 1971.

Chapanis, A. Mensch-machine-systeme im Alltag. In F. C. Stoll (Ed.), *Die Psychologie des 20. Jahrhunderts. Vol. 13: Anwendungen im Berufsleben*. Zürich: Kindler Verlag, 1980.

Chapanis, A. *Interactive human communication: Some lessons learned from laboratory experiments*. In B. Shackel (Ed.), *Man-computer interaction: Human aspects of computers and people*. Alphen aan den Rijn, the Netherlands: Sijthoff and Noordhoff, 1981.

De Greene, K. B. (Ed.). *Systems psychology*. New York: McGraw-Hill, 1970.

Engineer's Council on Professional Development. *Annual Report, 1977–1978* (Vol. 46). New York: Author, 1978.

Florman, S. C. *The existential pleasures of engineering*. New York: St. Martin's Press, 1976.

Garner, W. R. *Uncertainty and structure as psychological concepts*. New York: Wiley, 1962.

Grandjean, E., & Vigliani, E. (Eds.). *Ergonomic aspects of visual display terminals*, London: Taylor and Francis, 1980.

Hull, C. L. Mind, mechanism, and adaptive behavior. *Psychological Review*, 1937, *44*, 1–32.

Kaminaka, S., Rehkugler, G. E., & Gunkel, W. W. Visual monitoring in a simulated agricultural machinery operation. *Human Factors*, 1981, *23*, 165–173.

Ketchel, J. Visual display terminal research—the opportunity and the challenge. *Human Factors Society Bulletin*, 1981, *24*, 2–3.

La Mettrie, J. O. de. *L'homme machine*. Leyde: Elie Luzac, 1748.

Lhuede, E. P. Ear muff acceptance among sawmill workers. *Ergonomics*, 1980, *23*, 1161–1172.

Mayzner, M. S., & Dolan, T. R. (Eds.). *Microcomputers in sensory and information-processing research*. Hillsdale, NJ: Lawrence Erlbaum Associates, 1978.

Münsterberg, H. *Psychology and industrial efficiency*. Boston: Houghton Mifflin, 1913.

Murphy, G. *An historical introduction to modern psychology*. New York: Harcourt, Brace, 1949.

Murray, W. E., Moss, C. E., Parr, W. H., Cox, C., Smith, M. J., Cohen, B. F. G., Stammerjohn, L. W., & Happ, A. *Potential health hazards of video display terminals*. Washington, DC: U.S. Government Printing Office, 1981.

Olson, P. L., Halstead-Nussloch, R., & Sivak, M. The effect of improvements in motorcycle/motorcyclist conspicuity on driver behavior. *Human Factors*, 1981, *23*, 237–248.

Quastler, H. (Ed.). *Information theory in psychology: Problems and methods*. Glencoe, IL: The Free Press, 1955.

Rand, B. *The classical psychologists*. New York: Houghton Mifflin, 1912.

Roethlisberger, F. J., & Dickson, W. J. *Management and the worker*. Cambridge, MA: Harvard University Press, 1939.

Scott, W. D. *Increasing human efficiency in business*. New York: Macmillan, 1911.

Shannon, C. E., & Weaver, W. *The mathematical theory of communication*. Urbana, IL: University of Illinois Press, 1949.

Smith, M. J. Job stress, and VDT work. *Human Factors Society Bulletin*, 1981, *24*, 4–5.

Thurstone, L. L. *The vectors of mind*. Chicago, IL: University of Chicago Press, 1935.

Thurstone, L. L., L. L. Thurstone. In E. G. Boring, H. Werner, R. M. Yerkes, & H. S. Langfeld (Eds.), *A history of psychology in autobiography* (Vol. 4). Worcester, MA: Clark University Press, 1952.

U. S. Department of Labor. *Dictionary of occupational titles, Vol. 2: Occupational classification*. Washington, DC: U. S. Government Printing Office, 1965.

U. S. Government Printing Office. *United States statutes at large*. 1971, 84 (Part 2), 1590–1620.

U. S. Government Printing Office. *United States statutes at large*. 1972, 86, 1207–1233.

Van Cott, H. P., & Chapanis, A. Human engineering tests and evaluations. In H. P. Van Cott & R. G. Kincade (Eds.), *Human engineering guide to equipment design*. Washington, DC: U. S. Government Printing Office, 1972.

Van Cott, H. P., & Kincade, R. G. (Eds.) *Human engineering guide to equipment design*. Washington, DC: U. S. Government Printing Office, 1972.

Wiener, N. *Cybernetics*. New York: Wiley, 1948.

3
Psychology and Genetics

John L. Fuller
State University of New York at Binghamton

INTRODUCTION

A commonly accepted ordering of the sciences is: physics, chemistry, biology, psychology, and sociology. Reductionists affirm that the phenomena studied by each science can be explained by the laws established for the sciences preceding it in this list. All phenomena in a final analysis must conform to physical principles. Actually, reduction beyond a single step has not been pursued very far although there are fields known as pharmacology and psychophysics (see Kornetsky and Marks, in this volume). Psychology's connections with biology are closer; those with physiology at the cellular and organ-system level are discussed by Uttal (in this volume). I shall concentrate on organismic biology, which includes ecology, genetics, and evolution.

The ordering of the sciences presented here is one of ascending complexity of the units studied, from the fundamental particles of matter and energy to human societies. There is one exception. Organismic biology and psychology both center on living organisms as wholes, although they are often concerned with different features. Both sciences are interested in the physiological underpinnings of behavior and in the relationships between individuals and groups. They share another characteristic. Organismic biology, particularly genetics, and psychology deal primarily with transfers of information among organisms and between organisms and their physical environment. The physical and physiological sciences are also concerned with transfer of information, but the transfer of energy plays a larger role in their theories.

Transfer of biological information is based on DNA molecules (genes) that are passed from generation to generation in the nuclei of specialized cells. Psychological information is transmitted through physical agents—sound, light, pressure, molecular configuration—that are collectively called stimuli. In both types of transfer the amount of information conveyed by a message is related more to the pattern of the components than to their energy content. Psychologists have some interest in the relation between the energy of a stimulus and the vigor of the response, but often there is no correlation. The energy expended in saying "yes" and "no" is equal, but the responses to these words are very different. The same is true of a gene mutation. It may have trivial effects on structure and function, or it may be lethal to the organism carrying it. The difference is not ascribable to the chemical toxicity of the new gene, but to the faulty instructions it provides to the developing organism.

In a formal sense, genetics (the organismic as distinguished from the molecular variety) and psychology stand on the same rung of the hierarchial ladder, and some psychologists are moving closer to biology as they adopt an evolutionary perspective. The rapprochement is not without its strains, largely, I believe, because the two sciences have rival theories of information transfer between individuals. The coexistence and interplay of two systems in the shaping of behavior produces problems for both geneticists and psychologists. Both groups may be expected to emphasize their own theories and, to some extent, defend their territories. This essay reviews the history of relations between genetics and psychology, considers some current issues, and looks towards the future.

From one point of view, genetics has had a minimal effect upon contemporary psychological theorizing. None of the articles in the two-volume *Theories in Contemporary Psychology* (Marx, 1963; Marx & Goodson, 1976) deals even peripherally with genetics or heredity. This is not as surprising as it might seem. A collection of papers on theoretical population genetics would not include a chapter on the structural chemistry of DNA, even though it is the material from which genes are made. Nevertheless, I believe that the omission of reference in a collection of essays on psychological theory to such issues as the heritability of behavior, the plasticity of behavioral development, and the evolutionary forces that have shaped human and animal nature, indicates a restricted view of the range of theory. The impact of genetics on psychology touches four major areas:

(1) the relationship between the psychological studies of individuals (the idiographic approach) and the search for universal laws of behavior (the nomothetic approach);

(2) the relative importance of genes and environment in producing individual differences;

(3) the degree to which the plasticity of psychological development is constrained by biological characteristics that have been shaped by natural selection; and,

(4) the use of gene-produced phenotypic variation as a tool for exploring the relations between biological and psychological characteristics.

The first three areas relate particularly to theories of psychological development, and they will be emphasized in this chapter. The fourth is of special interest to physiological psychologists.

HISTORICAL BACKGROUND

Historians ascribe the origins of psychology to philosophy, dating back at least to Aristotle's *De Anima,* and continuing more recently in the works of Hobbes, Locke, and Hume (Thompson, 1968). In the early nineteenth century an essentially mentalistic approach was supplemented by the new knowledge of sensory and neural psychology. The first important impact of genetics upon psychology was the publication in 1859 of Darwin's *Origin of the Species.* This work challenged the view of man as a special creation in the image of God, and it placed man among the primates, the descendant of an extinct ape-like ancestor. The transformation of ape to human had been accomplished by the impersonal, unplanned force of natural selection.

Darwin's theory of evolution by natural selection involved four postulates: (1) members of a species vary with respect to important physical and behavioral characteristics; (2) the high natural rate of increase of all species leads inevitably to competition for limited resources; (3) individuals best able to compete leave more progeny; and, (4) characteristics favoring success in competition are heritable.

Darwin's ideas of the mechanisms of heredity were completely wrong. It remained for Mendel, Morgan, and Watson and Crick, among many others, to establish modern genetics as a science in its own right. But the Darwinian postulates are still the basis of evolutionary theory and of such recent twentieth century specialties as sociobiology. The major difference is that we now interpret Huxley's description of evolution as "survival of the fittest" as a progressive, systematic change in gene frequencies within a breeding population.

Early Applications of Genetics to Psychology

McClearn (1962) has presented an excellent account of important post-Darwinian inputs of genetics to psychology. The major trends are summarized here. In 1869 Galton published *Hereditary Genius: An Inquiry into its Laws and Consequences.* Today, we are rightly skeptical of Galton's conclusion that eminence should be ascribed to hereditary (in the genetic sense) qualities rather than to the advantages of being reared in a well-to-do home, of superior educational opportunities, and of bearing the name of an eminent relative. Actually Galton was aware of these alternative possibilities and attempted to disprove their importance. His efforts seem ingenuous in the late twentieth century, but we have the advantage of more than a hundred additional years of experimentation and theorizing.

The rediscovery of Mendel's (1865) papers in 1900 led to an explosion in genetic research, some of which involved human and animal behavior. One of the major areas of investigation in humans was mental defect. Many projects were designed to demonstrate a simple Mendelian basis for retardation, presumably with the objective of developing a workable eugenics program. McClearn points out that workers at this period tended to overgeneralize from limited data. Pearson (1904) correctly noted that there was no sharp break between "normal" and "abnormal" intelligence, but he erred in rejecting all Mendelian explanations for mental defect. Pearson's papers sparked a debate between geneticists and biometricians that lasted until Fisher (1918) demonstrated that quantitative variation could be explained by Mendelian principles if one postulated that many independently transmitted genes were involved in the development of complex traits like intelligence or height.

Supporting the Mendelian position, Goddard (1914) analysed several pedigrees of mental retardation and showed that they were compatible with the assumption that afflicted individuals had received two recessive genes, one from each parent, both of whom though normal were carriers. He was wrong, however, in concluding that the dominant form of the gene produced normal intelligence. Tredgold (1937) came close to the modern view that either "bad" genes or "bad" environments could produce similar syndromes of mild retardation. His notion of a progressive degeneration of germ plasm in socially inadequate families, however, was nonsense.

Discarding the errors, one is left with the view generally held by modern geneticists. Low intelligence, as measured by psychologists, may arise from inheriting a single dominant gene, a pair of recessive genes, or a large number of genes with individually undetectable but cumulative deleterious effects. Retardation may also, regardless of genotype, be caused by chemical, viral, bacterial, or traumatic damage to the nervous system, or from extreme experiential deprivation.

From Eugenics to Social and Evolutionary Biopsychology

This brief history shows that much early research in human genetics was directed at a social problem, the origin and prevention of mental deficiency. Implicit in the research was the potential application of genetic findings to negative and positive eugenics programs. Haller (1963) gives a good account of the eugenics movement that flourished between 1910 and the 1930s and declined thereafter. Fear that the gene pool was degenerating led many scientists to advocate management of human reproduction by involuntary sterilization of defectives and the prohibition of interracial marriage. Edward Lee Thorndike, Professor of Psychology at Columbia University, believed that a weakness of the American public school system was that it rested "on a total disregard of hereditary differences between the classes and the masses [cited in Haller, 1963, p. 165]."

The objective of the eugenics movement, that every child should be well born, is praiseworthy. The excesses of the movement stemmed from two sources. The first, which is not restricted to any continent or ethnic group, is the tendency of high-status social and racial groups to attribute their good fortune to innate superiority. The second was widespread ignorance, even among scientists, of such subjects as population genetics, genotype-environment interactions (GEIs), the nature of gene action, and the psychological processes involved in the development of competence.

There is more humility today. Geneticists admit that they do not know enough about human genetics to manage an eugenics program, even if agreement could be reached on its objectives and ethical implications. The *Eugenics Society* has become the *Society for the Study of Social Biology* and is no longer an advocacy organization. Genetic counseling has taken the place of eugenics programs. Individuals voluntarily refer problems of potentially transmittable defects, physical or mental, to professionals. Genetic counseling is closely associated with medical practice, but it has an important psychological component (Lappé & Brody, 1976). There is a place for genetically trained psychologists in this complex and important field.

The disillusionment with eugenics, a form of artificial selection of humans, does not mean that our species has become immune to natural selection. In fact, the intensity of selection may actually be increasing. The two essential features for evolutionary change in a population are: (1) genetic heterogeneity among its members, and (2) differences in reproductive rate correlated with genotype. Variance in family size has increased in all societies where contraception is regularly practiced (Crow, 1961). The choice by individuals to refrain or participate in reproduction has, in many areas, replaced disease and famine resistance as the major factor in natural selection. We do not know, however, whether fecundity is correlated with genotype. The evolutionary significance of voluntary withdrawal from the breeding population cannot be predicted.

The decline of the eugenics movement and its replacement by social biology and genetic counseling are not only social phenomena. They represent a shift in evolutionary thought as Darwin's insights have been supplemented by data from paleontology, taxonomy, biochemistry, ecology, population biology, and psychology. Evolutionary studies are now flourishing after a period in which the biophysical aspects of biology threatened to supplant them. Since so much of evolutionary theory is based on genetics, it is desirable here to describe what Huxley (1942) called the "modern synthesis." Although much has been learned since Huxley coined the term, the idea of synthesis is still strong. One of its major features is that it views behavior as both a product of, and a directing force in, biological evolution (Dobzhansky, 1962; Mayr, 1970).

PHYLOGENESIS, EPIGENESIS, PSYCHOGENESIS

The selective process that has led to the differentiation of species, genera, and higher taxonomic groups is called *phylogenesis*. It depends upon random gene mutations that are rejected or accepted for retention in the gene pool dependent upon their effects on the reproductive fitness of their carriers. A species is characterized by a pool of genes that are compatible enough to permit free interbreeding among its members. Natural selection operates on all phenotypic characteristics from enzymes, through complex structures, to reflexes, fixed action patterns, and even learned behavior.

The direction of phylogenesis is determined by environmental changes with restrictions set by the difficulty of adjusting the gene pool rapidly to meet new challenges. The genes needed for an adaptive response may not be present in the gene pool. The pool cannot change too rapidly without reducing the probability of fertile matings. The result is phylogenetic inertia. Except for inertia, the direction of evolution is generally considered to depend upon exogenous factors, rather than those endogenous to the organism. An exception is Piaget (1978) who advocates a drive for incorporating learned adaptations into the genotype, but his ideas have not been widely accepted by geneticists.

Each phylogenetic path leads to a species-specific genotype that provides information necessary for development, but the metaphor of a genetic blueprint is completely misleading. Unlike a building plan there is no physical congruence between genotype and phenotype. The DNA triplets of the genetic code are more like letters in a sentence. Their meaning depends upon their position in relation to other letters that form words and sentences.

Genes need not carry all the information needed to specify the course of development. Environment, as well as being a source of energy, provides additional information along the way. This coactive process is called *epigenesis*. The environment may be regarded as a broad-band transmitter; the organism as a selectively tuned receiver. The kinds of signals accepted and the developmental response to them are species-specific, the product of phylogenesis (Plotkin & Odling-Smee, 1979). Characteristically an organism's sensitivity to a specific input varies with its developmental stage. This phenomenon has led to the concept of critical or sensitive periods (Bateson, 1979; Scott, 1978). Epigenesis might be considered a type of learning and, thus, could be subsumed under psychogenesis. Both processes are dependent upon information that is not encoded in DNA. A stimulus-response relationship is present in epigenesis and in learning, but there is no clearly recognizable reinforcement in the former. Learned behavior can be extinguished though sometimes with difficulty. An epigenetically induced deviation in development persists through life.

   Psychogenesis, as used in this essay, is an inclusive term for the acquisition of habits, skills, knowledge, and attitudes through learning. It requires neural circuits that can filter, store, and organize information streaming in from the environment. The neural traces that accompany learning in an individual organism have no effects upon its genes. Nevertheless, an individual who learns well has a better change of leaving offspring. Thus natural selection has an opportunity to shape the neural apparatus that makes learning possible, and fit it to the specific challenges that a species is most likely to encounter. The following section deals with relationships among the three kinds of genesis and with their evolution, based largely on an important paper by Plotkin and Odling-Smee (1979).

The Limits of Phylogenesis

Natural selection operates impartially on the outcomes of the phylogenetic, epigenetic, and psychogenetic systems. Phylogenesis is primary since all biological evolution is, in simplest terms, a process of directional change in gene frequencies. A purely phylogenetic strategy requires that all adaptive mechanisms, behavioral and otherwise, be programmed in the genotype. All individual variation is associated with genetic heterogeneity, and there is no room for developmental flexibility.

   The disadvantages of dependence on an inflexible genetic program become apparent when an animal is exposed to conditions that differ from those that shaped its ancestor's genomes. The phototactic moth is consumed in the candle flame. A species restricted to the phylogenetic process for coping with change has two alternatives: (1) avoid change or (2) track change. Some habitats have changed little over long periods. The horse-shoe crab of the Atlantic coast scarcely differs from its Devonian ancestors who lived 300 million years ago. By simply staying on the sandy beaches these animals have prospered while most of their Devonian contemporaries are known only as fossils. The same fate will befall the horse-shoe crab if its environment changes and the crab does not.

Phylogenesis copes with environmental threats by differential repro-duction. In a changing environment individuals whose genotypes lie out-side the central range may be able to survive and propagate more successfully than the typical members of the species. This is evolution by natural selection. The difficulties of tracking change through phylogenetic processes alone are formidable. The environment may fluctuate so much that there is no consistent direction to the selection pressure. Phy-logenetic inertia has already been mentioned. Above all, at best phy-logenesis is a slow process. The survival of a species depending exclusively on a phylogenetically programmed behavioral repertoire is dependent upon stability in an unpredictable future world.

Nevertheless, most of the world's animals (here are included hosts of small invertebrates) have managed to get by with largely preprogrammed, automatic responses to stimuli. Many more species have become extinct. Even "higher" animals have retained responses for respiration, digestion, withdrawal from nocuous agents, and other "housekeeping" functions.

Selection for Adaptiveness

Natural selection for adaptiveness in an unstable environment requires a different strategy. In the epigenetic mode, organisms are programmed to take different paths of development dependent upon the conditions to which they are exposed. A striking example from biology is the interpola-tion of sexual reproduction at certain seasons in species (aphids, micro-crustacea, rotifers) that reproduce parthenogenetically under favorable conditions. As conditions deteriorate, sexual reproduction replaces asex-ual, and zygotes are produced that are resistant to dryness, cold, and other unfavorable factors. The genetic structure does not fluctuate sea-sonally, but the same genotype can direct development along different paths dependent upon an environmental signal. Once committed, there is no turning back.

Imprinting in birds can be classified as an epigenetic process since it occurs during a particular phase of the life cycle and is long-lasting. Under natural conditions, it is presumed to be adaptive and a result of natural selection. However, epigenetic control has the disadvantage of limited reversibility. Male zebra finches who see only Bengalese finch females in early life prefer them at sexual maturity to their own species (Immelmann, 1972). The requirements for a suitable mate are not coded in the zebra finch male's genes, but the rules for acquiring that information from the environment at a particular age are. In nature, the male zebra finch sees females of its own species, and its epigenetic strategy is adaptive. In an ethologist's aviary it malfunctions.

An evolutionary strategy based on psychogenesis involves selection of mechanisms for accepting and organizing a variety of information inputs in a way that is adaptive. For psychologists there is one such mechanism, learning, but in a broader sense such phenomena as acquired immunity and drug tolerance follow the same evolutionary rules. Natural selection is still the force that is behind the evolution of neural systems capable of learning. In order to be favored by natural selection learning must result in improved adaptation. It is not enough to set up machinery to modify the response to a stimulus by selective reinforcement. The modified response must be adaptive.

Compared with adaptation to change through phylogenesis, learning is more rapid by many orders of magnitude. But it has limitations. To depend upon learning for the perfection of the eye-blink reflex is less efficient than coding its neural base into the genotype. Learned behavior may be resistant to extinction to a degree that is maladaptive. Addictions to drugs and to gambling are examples. Learning permits animals and humans to adapt quickly and flexibly, but it also allows them to be deceived to their disadvantage. Fortuitous reinforcement can lead to superstitious behavior that is at best nonadaptive and, at worst, fatal.

Relations of the Three Processes

Since the epigenetic and psychogenetic processes require an organism, their evolution is ultimately dependent upon phylogenesis. The relationships are, however, reciprocal. Every species shapes or chooses its environment by its own activities, and it is this altered environment that exerts selective pressure in its turn. The selective pressure for learning arises when irregular, unpredictable challenges arise regularly. Under these conditions natural selection favors adaptability through learning rather than through phylogenesis. However, there is no necessary reason that species phylogenetically separated for millions of years should have evolved the same anatomical and physiological bases for learning, except to the degree imposed on all living systems by physical principles.

What gives direction to the behavioral evolution of a species? Only its own phylogenetic history. Of the three adaptive processes, learning alone has the potential of adjusting responses rapidly to radically new conditions. But is learning completely emancipated from the phylogenetic history of a species? Many psychologists doubt that it is. Do remnants of phylogenetic and epigenetic modes of adaptation place constraints on learning? Are the phylogenetic histories of species different enough to negate the possibility of deriving general laws of learning that apply equally well to humans, rats, and octopuses? Since interspecific differences in behavior are strongly influenced by genetic differences, are intraspecific differences determined likewise? If so, how much? These are some of the questions to which behavior-genetic analysis is addressed.

Before addressing these questions it will be useful to consider the relation between general psychological principles and individual psychological differences. It will also be helpful to review briefly the techniques that geneticists apply in their behavioral researches.

UNIVERSALITY, INDIVIDUALITY, AND GENETICS

There are two significant aspects to the evolutionary genetics of behavior. Genetic variability among individuals of a population is essential if natural selection is to be effective. At the same time the members of the population must be similar enough genetically to produce viable offspring. Genetic uniformity ensures that members of the population will behave predictably. There is a parallel here to Windelband's (1894; summarized in MacKinnon & Maslow, 1951, p. 616) distinction between two competing approaches to science. Windelband designated the natural sciences, seeking laws of universal generality, as *nomothetic*. The social sciences, attempting to explain unique occurrences through historical analysis, he termed *idiographic*. He urged that psychology should not become a completely natural science; instead, it should try to understand the characteristics of individuals. Windelband's distinction is too sharp. A clinical psychologist, working with a client, does not abandon the "laws of learning" as he endeavors to solve a personal, possibly unique, problem.

Individual variability is universal within species, although only a dedicated biologist may recognize it in a cloud of fruit flies hovering over an over-ripe banana. Much of genetic variability is not expressed phenotypically but is manifest when the flies are inbred or artificially selected. With respect to behavior, humans are undoubtedly the most variable of species, due in great measure to cultural diversity. Humans are also very diverse genetically. It is improbable that, except for identical twins, any two individuals in human history have had duplicate genotypes. Using some simplifying assumptions that result in underestimation, it is interesting to calculate the number of genetically different offspring that a given human couple could produce. Each parent has 23 pairs of chromosomes that assort independently in the formation of ovum and sperm. Thus each parent has the capability of forming 8,388,609 types of gametes. Any one of these can combine with any one of the mate's gametes, yielding over 70 trillion genetically distinguishable types of offspring.

Views differ as to how important genetic variability is to the science of psychology. The behaviorist tradition plays down its significance. Acknowledging that the basic behavioral repertoire of a species is gene dependent, Skinner (1953) wrote:

> Among members of a species the extensive differences (in reinforcing events) are unlikely to be due to hereditary endowment, and to that extent may be traced to circumstances in the history of the individual. . . . Organisms inherit capacity to be reinforced by certain events . . . [this is] no help in predicting the effect of an untried stimulus [p. 75].

For Skinner, genetic differences may produce some noise in experiments designed to demonstrate behavioral laws, but they are not of major interest to psychology.

Skinner's devaluation of genetic influences has been challenged. Hirsch (1967) pitted "behavior-genetic-analysis (science)" against the "lure of technology (behaviorism)." He charged that the typological approach of many experimental psychologists leads to postulation of abstract, idealized principles that do not apply to any individual. There is merit in this statement; smooth learning curves based on group averages obscure the irregularities in the progress of individuals. A complete experimental psychology must deal with populations of diverse individuals as well as with an idealized type. Fortunately, there is no fundamental conflict between accepting general laws and special laws that consider individuality. Such a program must embrace genetic as well as environmental sources of differences (Vale & Vale, 1969).

BEHAVIOR GENETICS

Fundamental to all genetic study is the distinction between genotype and phenotype. The genotype is the assortment of DNA molecules that is found in the nuclei of cells; the phenotype includes all other characteristics ranging in complexity from enzyme molecules to the anatomy of the brain and personality characteristics. When phenotypes can be separated clearly into categories (e.g., albino vs. pigmented), it is often possible to explain differences in terms of alternate forms of a gene. When variation is continuous (e.g., height, IQ scores) statistical techniques are needed to determine the genetic situation. Even though individual genes are not identified, it is possible to explain inheritance patterns quantitatively in terms of additive and dominant effects of genes (Falconer, 1960; Mather & Jinks, 1971; Roberts, 1967).

Geneticists, as basic scientists, naturally prefer experimental material in which an easily observed and measured phenotype is a reliable guide to genotype. Psychological characteristics do not qualify. The reason for studying behavior genetics is interest in the phenotype. Behavioral phenotypes differ from those studied by most geneticists in being processes rather than structures. Fuller and Wimer (1973) proposed the terms, *psychophene* for processes and *somatophene* for structures. Fuller (1979) distinguished two varieties of psychophenes: (1) *ostensible,* acts that are recognizable by any qualified observer (e.g., number of avoidance responses, score on a psychological test) and (2) *inferred,* postulated general attributes of an individual (e.g., fearfulness, extraversion). In distinguishing psychophenes from somatophenes, there is no implication that behavior is independent of physical structure. There must be an organism to behave.

If the motivation for behavior-genetic research is its potential contribution to psychology, it is fair to ask what can be learned from it. At a 1961 symposium on behavior genetics sponsored by the American Psychological Association, a discussant commented that he had just listened for two hours to talk about another variable to be added to schedule of reinforcement and degree of deprivation. Topoff (1974) argued that, though genes probably influence behavior, "behaviorists may do well to reconsider, not only the feasibility of quantifying genetic and environmental factors, but also the utility of distinguishing between them in the future [p. 40]." Fuller (1976) objected to this conclusion on the grounds that, "among the manifold factors that contribute to the behavioral characteristics of an individual, only its genes can be transmitted in a consistent and lawful pattern to its offspring [p. 13]." This still seems to be a sufficient reason for maintaining the distinction.

Research Techniques: Animals

Animal researchers have a wide variety of procedures for controlling genotypes. Inbred strains whose members are as similar as identical twins are widely used. With such specialized animals a researcher is essentially working with replicates of a single genotype. All of the variability among the replicates can be ascribed confidently to the environment. Also available are congenic, inbred lines with two classes of members that differ only at a single genetic locus. Thus, the effects of that one locus can be identified (Fuller, 1967a; Henry & Haythorn, 1975). Inbred lines have disadvantages. They are less vigorous, and doubts are often expressed about the legitimacy of extending conclusions based on such specialized creatures to their species as a whole.

Selected lines are obtained by breeding like with like using a behavioral criterion such as errors in a maze or aggression against a companion. After a number of generations the groups are usually well separated, evidence for a genetic contribution to the behavioral variation present in the base stock. Well-designed selection programs include unselected controls and replicated high-score and low-score lines. Even when conscious selection is not practiced, animals from closed breeding populations are likely to differ from those in another closed population. Thus the practice has arisen of identifying animal subjects as Sprague-Dawley or Fischer rats. When looked at closely, it is common to find that such stocks differ significantly on behavioral criteria.

For some purposes, such as starting a selection program or measuring heritability, a population with maximal genetic variability is desired. For this purpose heterogeneous, synthesized stocks assembled from a mix of inbred strains are available. Captive animals of recent wild ancestry are useful for testing evolutionary hypotheses. Except for the requirement to control genetic variables in some way, there is no restriction on the nature of behavior-genetic experiments with animals. Particular interest has been given to learning, emotionality, and social behavior (Ehrman & Parsons, 1976; Fuller & Thompson, 1978; McClearn & DeFries, 1973). In a later section, the behavior-genetic analysis of animal learning will be reviewed.

Research Techniques: Humans

The behavior-geneticist who works with humans cannot control the genotypes of his subjects and must make the most of the material at hand. All methods involve comparing the similarity of related individuals with that of a random sample of their population. The most familiar techniques are: (1) comparisons between monozygotic (MZ, identical) and dizygotic (DZ, fraternal, sororal) cotwins; (2) comparisons between MZ twins reared together and apart; (3) correlations between parents and offspring; (4) comparisons between the correlations of adopted children with their biological and foster parents; (5) comparisons between siblings and half-siblings; (6) correlations between the offspring of monozygotic twins; and, (7) behavioral assessment of individuals with chromosomal anomalies or inherited metabolic defects. The last procedure is generally of greater interest to medicine (see Krantz & Glass, in this volume) than to psychology.

Problems with these procedures on the psychological side include the validity, stability, and precision of phenotypic measures and of measures of the environment. Psychology also lacks a quantitative theory for measuring environmental variables on a quantitative scale. Genetics is ahead in having a sound theoretical basis for determining the degree of relationship between pairs of individuals. However, there are plenty of problems on the genetic side including: errors in distinguishing MZ and

DZ twin pairs; errors in the assignment of paternity; genotype-environment correlations; and genotype-environment interactions. These issues are discussed extensively by Eaves, Last, Young, and Martin (1978) who point to a growing flexibility in the formulation of models for analysing the sources of human behavioral variation. Much of the advance in data analysis stems from new statistical and computing procedures that permit more complex and imaginative models that allow the effects of interfamilial environment, genetic relationship, age changes, and the like to be factored in. The new wave is not particularly concerned with the heritability of a trait for its own sake. However, the debate over heritability of human traits has been so vigorous that the meaning of the term requires attention.

Heritability

The concept of heritability originated from efforts to improve procedures for breeding plants and animals for the benefit of humans. Only if a desired trait were reliably transmitted from parents to offspring would selection be practical. In measuring heritability, the total phenotypic variance (V_p) of a population is divided between a genetic (V_g) and an environmental (V_e) component. Broad heritability, better called *degree of genetic determination,* is an indicator of the relative contribution of gene differences to phenotypic variation in a population. The relationship is symbolized as: $h_b^2 = V_g/(V_g + V_e)$. Narrow heritability, h_n^2, is a measure of the predictability of an individual's phenotype given knowledge of the phenotypes of close relatives. Narrow heritability is much more meaningful for predicting the efficacy of selection. In its computation V_g is divided into an additive component V_a and a dominant component V_d (Falconer, 1960; Roberts, 1967). Heritability in the narrow sense is: $V_a/(V_a + V_d + V_e)$. It can be measured in a number of ways: the regression of offspring on parents, sibling correlations, and differences between MZ-cotwin and DZ-cotwin correlations. Each method has problems, but the most important fact about heritability is not the methods of measurement, but the recognition that it is not an attribute of a trait with a fixed value which will be defined with greater precision by more and more refined data and procedures. Heritability is a characteristic of a defined population in a specified environment.

Genotype-Environment Correlation

The assumptions involved in measuring heritability are basically the same for animal and human populations. Geneticists working with animals have the advantage of control over the breeding and environment of their subjects. Human geneticists cannot control mating patterns, but this limitation is less serious than the problem of evaluating the effects of genotype-environment correlations and interactions. Interactions are considered later. Difficulties arise when "better" genotypes are found in "better" environments. Observations on adopted children have the potential to detect the effects of G-E correlations. Although the matter is still controversial, there is considerable evidence that the effects of selective placement in foster homes are not great enough to invalidate genetic analyses based on comparisons of children with foster and biological parents (Ho, Plomin, & DeFries, 1979; Horn, Loehlin, & Willerman, 1979; Munsinger, 1975). Granting that G-E correlations exist, there are ambiguities in interpreting them in an analysis of variance. Plomin, DeFries, and Loehlin (1977) distinguished three types of these correlations. In the passive type, an individual's environment is independent of his genotype. In the reactive variety, other persons' social responses to an individual depend on his phenotype which is shaped in part by his genotype. The third type of G-E correlation, the active type, results from individuals seeking the environments for which they are best fitted by their genotypes.

We can apply these ideas to children growing up together in a natural family. None of these children has any control over the parents' economic status, education, or life style and must accept them passively, just as they must accept their genotypes. But children are individuals, and parents react to them differently. The genetically hyperactive child is treated differently from the timid withdrawn sibling; a reactive G-E correlation is generated. Finally, the home has athletic and indoor games, musical instruments, and books. One child opts for baseball, another for chess, and a third for the piano. Once committed, their environments are altered. Folk belief ascribes such special interests and skills to innate predispositions, and it may be correct. A committed behaviorist looks for a history of selective reinforcement, but positive reinforcement from such activities is dependent on early success. To the extent that there is a genetic factor for success, an active G-E correlation is produced. Parental influences on personality development are conventionally considered to be very important. However, the results of a large-scale twin study that included data on parental attitudes and child-rearing practices led Loehlin and Nichols (1976) to conclude:

> In the personality domain we seem to see environmental effects that operate almost randomly with respect to the sort of variables that psychologists (and other people) have traditionally deemed important in personality development. What can be going on? [p. 92]

Behavior geneticists cannot neatly separate the effects of nature and nurture and quantify their input to the phenotype by calculating heritabilities. But despite harsh criticism (e.g., Feldman & Lewontin,

1975; Layzer, 1974), heritability can still tell us where it might be useful to look for functional relationships between genes and psychological characteristics. Something can be learned from the sophisticated models discussed by Eaves et al. (1978), and even the failure to find a significant h^2 is helpful if it turns attention to nongenetic factors. Vale (1973) is skeptical of quantitative behavior genetics and model-fitting techniques because the results are limited to the population and environment studied. He overlooks the implications of such approaches for unravelling non-genetic contributions to the variability of complexly determined phenotypes. Vale's recommendation that behavior geneticists place more emphasis on genotype-environment interaction is excellent and ought to be heeded.

GENES AND LEARNING DIFFERENCES

Numerous psychophenes have been studied by behavior geneticists. This section will concentrate on animal learning and human intelligence testing. Emphasis is placed on the role of genotype in producing individual differences. Animal research is considered first followed by an account of human studies.

Genetics and Animal Learning

Learning, a central concern of experimental psychologists, has also been a dominant interest of behavior geneticists. Successful selection of rats for good and poor learning in a multiple T-maze was reported by Tryon (1929, 1940). The animals became familiarly known as the Tryon Bright and Dull strains. The appelation is inaccurate. Searle, a student of Tryon, found that rapid learning in the Tryon maze did not correlate well with performance on dissimilar tests (Searle, 1949). Apparently there is no general intelligence factor in rats.

Hereditary transmission of good maze performance was confirmed by other selection experiments at the University of Minnesota (Heron, 1935) and at McGill (Thompson & Bindra, 1952). The two McGill strains (maze-bright and maze-dull) were later reared under three conditions in order to observe the effects of early environment on their development (Cooper & Zubek, 1958). Reared in a standard animal room, with open cages and moderate stimulation, the maze-brights continued to show their superiority. Members of neither strain learned well when reared in an unstimulating, restricted environment. Rats reared in large cages with the opportunity to explore and manipulate learned well irrespective of their genotype.

Current research on genetics and animal learning has turned away from complex mazes to simple T-mazes (useful for reversal problems) and to various forms of escape and avoidance from shock or other nocuous stimuli. A few of the findings are noted here; additional examples are described in Fuller and Thompson (1978). Strains of mice that quickly learned active avoidance of scheduled, unsignaled shock were slow in acquiring a passive-avoidance strategy in the identical apparatus. The poor active-avoiders were superior in passive avoidance (Fuller, 1970). Rats from strains that made frequent anticipatory running responses to a signal warning of unescapable shock (classical conditioning) were also superior in shock avoidance (instrumental conditioning) under the same conditions (Katzev & Mills, 1974). It is doubtful that the good avoidance learners were superior in the rapidity of forming a CS-US association. They did differ in the nature of their classically conditioned emotion response: running in the "good learners" and freezing in the "poor learners."

Wahlsten (1972) tested several strains of mice for avoidance learning using a constant shock-intensity and found substantial differences between them. He then determined the threshold for an unconditioned flinch response in all strains. When new subjects were tested with the shock levels adjusted to equalize the unconditioned response, learning differences among the strains were greatly attenuated.

The results of these and other experiments justify the following conclusions: (1) genetic differences in rate of learning are widespread in animals and (2) factors other than the rapidity of forming S-S and S-R associations contribute to these differences.

Genetics and Human Intelligence

A survey of current introductory psychology texts shows that most devote a few pages to the variability of human intelligence as measured by standard IQ tests. Reference is made to findings that: (1) MZ twins are more similar than DZ twins on test scores; (2) identical twins separated at birth are only slightly less similar at maturity than those reared together; (3) children's IQs are correlated with those of their parents and regress towards the mean as predicted by genetic theory; and, (4) the IQs of adopted children correlate more strongly with their biological than with their foster parents. These data come from several countries and are consistent in showing that the mean correlations in IQ between different classes of relatives are remarkably close to those predicted from their degree of relationship (Erlenmeyer-Kimling & Jarvik, 1963).

Not everyone accepts the "hereditarian" explanation of the twin, family, and adopted children data. Kamin (1974) contends that the facts can be explained equally well by environmental factors. He admits that genetic interpretations cannot be logically disproved in some cases, but he finds them less attractive than his own "environmentalist" views. Kamin's arguments are based on assumptions regarding the magnitude of environmental effects that many geneticists consider to be ad hoc and overestimated. Urbach (1974), a philosopher and a strong supporter of the hereditarian research program, criticizes the environmentalists for accounting for anomalies in data by untested, and perhaps untestable, improvised explanations. A comparison of Kamin's and Urbach's views is convincing evidence that the nature-nurture debate still thrives.

Geneticists, though they may have a vested interest in hereditarian explanations of individual differences, are aware of the problems associated with G-E correlations and regularly include estimates of them in their calculations (Eaves et al., 1978; Jencks, 1972; Jinks & Fulker, 1970). However, the identification and quantification of specific environmental variables remain more empirical than the quantification of genetic relationships.

Most psychologists are familiar with the results of adoption studies where G-E correlations are attenuated, if not eliminated. A relatively new technique, the "twin kinship method" is less well known and will be used as an example of current family research which embraces both genetic and environmental variables (Rose, Harris, Christian, & Nance, 1979). The experimental design is shown diagramatically in Figure 1. Individuals shown by shaded symbols are identical twins (B, C is a female pair; I, L, a male pair). The coefficients of relationship (r), the proportion of genes shared by descent, are represented by the nature of the lines connecting related individuals. Unrelated individuals are not connected, but an $\times$ between a pair connotes mating. Important points are: (1) The children, E and F, are related equally to their mother, B, and to their aunt, C and (2) E and F are related to their cousins, G and H, as half-siblings $(r = .25)$ instead of as ordinary cousins $(r = .125)$. Similar relationships hold for the male identical-twin kinships.

Children and parents were given the Wechsler Block-Design Test. Finger-ridge counts were also obtained since they are known to be highly heritable and unaffected by known environmental factors. Results are shown in Table 1. As predicted, ridge counts of the children were more accurately predicted from parental counts than were Block Design scores. The important point is that the children's resemblance on the Block Design Test to a twin uncle/aunt does not differ significantly from their resemblance to their twin-parent. The children's scores are not correlated with those of their twin-spouse uncles/aunts.

In another study using the same material and method, Rose, Boughman, Corey, Nance, Christian, and Karg (1980) found a higher correlation on the information subtest of the Wechsler Intelligence Scales for maternally related half-sibs (E,F:G,H) than for paternal half-sibs (M,N: O,P). Similar results (not quite reaching the .05 level of significance) were found for the vocabulary subtest. Children's verbal development seems to be

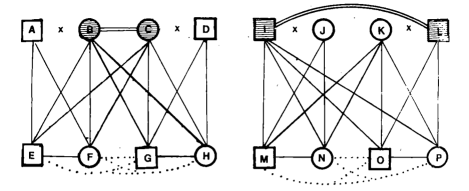

FIG. 1.   Genetic correlations in identical-twins kinships. □, Male; ○, Female. Twin pairs
are shaded. The coefficients of relationship are indicated by the lines.   Cotwins, 1.0;
parent-offspring, child, twin aunt/uncle, siblings, 0.5; ...., cousins from twin aunt/
uncle families. Note the absence of relationship between children and their spouse uncle or
aunt.

influenced much more by their mothers than by their fathers. On the basis
of extensive data on family life-styles, the investigators rejected a number
of plausible general environmental variables as explanations for the similarity of the maternally-related biological half-sibs, most of whom had
little contact with their sociological cousins. Since the paternally-related
half-sibs, though equally correlated genetically, were uncorrelated
phenotypically, we must conclude that a mother's influence is ascribable
to her nurturance rather than to her genes.

Genetics and Group Differences

The hypothesis that the demonstrated differences in the mean IQ of social
classes and racial groups are of genetic origin has aroused even more
controversy than the assertion that individual differences are heritable.
The vigor of this controversy flared up after the publication of Jensen's
(1969) paper, *How much can we boost IQ and scholarly achievement?* A
section of this somewhat innocuously titled paper suggested that the in-
feriority of Negroes vis-à-vis Caucasians on IQ tests was genetic and
could not be removed by compensatory education. The generally negative
reactions can be sampled in Cancro (1971), Richardson and Spears (1972),
and Kamin (1974). Other geneticists and psychologists do not reject Jensen's hypothesis, and a sampling of their views can be found in Osborne,
Noble, and Weyl (1978). Perhaps the most balanced review of racial differences in intelligence comes from a collaboration between two psychologists competent in genetics and an anthropologist (Loehlin,
Lindzey, & Spuhler, 1975). They concluded that as long as two racial

TABLE 1
Regression and Correlation Analyses of Wechsler Block-Design Scores and
Finger Ridge Counts in Monozygotic Twin Kinships.*

	Regressions			
	Block Design		Ridge Count	
Relationship	N	Coefficient	N	Coefficient
Son, daughter / father, mother	572	.28 ± .04	564	.42 ± .05
Nephew, niece / twin aunt, uncle	318	.23 ± .04	310	.37 ± .05
Nephew, niece / spouse & aunt, uncle	241	−.01 ± .06	247	−.06 ± .07
Child / midparent	254	.54 ± .07	254	.82 ± .07
	Correlations			
Monozygotic twins	65	.68 ± .06	60	.96 ± .03
Full siblings	297	.24 ± .08	296	.36 ± .08
Half-siblings	318	.10 ± .12	310	.17 ± .12
Father-Mother	102	.06 ± .10	98	.05 ± .10

*From R. J. Rose, E. L. Harris, J. C. Christian, and W. E. Nance, *Science,* 1979, *205,* 1153–1155. By permission of The American Association for the Advancement of Science.

groups live under widely different social and economic conditions, it is not possible either to accept or reject genetic or environmental explanations for differences in average IQ test scores.

This may seem to be a feeble outcome of extensive research on racial differences in intelligence, but the heritability of this difference has restricted significance for genetics and psychology as sciences. Differing beliefs do arouse emotional reactions, but I see no great relevance of the issue to a humane social policy based on individuals rather than categories. The chief contribution of genetic differences to racial tension is the inheritance of external physical traits that are used to classify the social status of an individual. When social classes are not so labelled, as was the case in Europe in the middle ages, class barriers were more easily broken down, and gene pools were more easily mixed (Van den Berghe, 1979, p. 214).

CONSTRAINTS ON PHENOLABILITY

Up to this point we have dealt with the contribution of genetic diversity to psychological diversity. Going beyond the hackneyed statement that genotype and environment coact in development, I argued that efforts to confirm theories of psychological development, especially those centering on the family, must consider both experiential history and genetic background. When the results of such a research program are expressed in a partition of variance into V_g and V_e components, we learn relatively little about the nature of the gene actions and specific environmental factors contributing to individual differences. Comparing the behavior of genetically identical individuals with unlike life histories is one way of identifying the important environmental variables. To a degree this is possible with MZ twins. For example, Gottesman and Shields (1972) compared the biographies of MZ twins who were concordant or discordant for schizophrenia. No reliable differences were found between the number of stressors in the families of the concordant and discordant pairs. In some discordant pairs the affected member was alcoholic. Discordance was most common when the affected twin had mild symptoms, suggesting that susceptibility varies quantitatively and that, when individuals are near the manifestation threshold, chance factors determine the expression of a psychotic vulnerability. Studies of this kind may lead to the rejection of some etiological hypotheses, but the lack of control and the rarity of suitable pairs restrict their value. In a sense, each MZ pair is a separate experiment with two subjects.

Animal researchers have an advantage since they can work with selected lines and inbred strains that are composed of genetically similar individuals. With such material one can try to determine the plasticity of the phenotypic expression of a given genotype. Traits that are readily altered can be called *phenolabile;* those resistant to change are *phenostable*. Almost all psychology students have been exposed to Watson's (1930) statement that, given a dozen healthy infants, he could train any one of them to become any type of specialist, doctor, lawyer to beggarman and thief. Watson never carried out this ambitious program, and observations on the propensity of adolescents to deviate from the goals set for them by their parents suggest that he would have failed. Nevertheless, he was correct in rejecting genetic predestination.

The concept of phenostability, which implies a degree of genetic determinism, is sometimes carelessly confused with high heritability. Actually they are very different. Consider a trait, $T,$ in a population of inbred mice. None of the differences in T within the strain is heritable since there is no genetic variance, yet T could not exist without a particular complement of genes. Now consider the same trait in a genetically heterogeneous population, all of whose members share the same environment. In this situation a geneticist would feel comfortable in partitioning the variance of T into genetic and environmental components and calculating h^2. Since, in this experiment, environmental differences are reduced, and genetic ones are maximized, we expect h^2 to be high. The fact that h^2 was zero in one population and high in the other does not mean that the role of genes in shaping development differed between them.

To obtain information on the phenostability of *T,* we perform two experiments. In the first, we start with a supply of genetically identical animals (inbred mice or rats would be a good choice), rear them under conditions as identical as possible, and look at the variation among them. The smaller the variation; the greater the phenostability. In an experiment of this type there is no way to identify the causes of variation because all individuals were treated alike. All we can be sure of is that the causes of variation were environmental. However, if we carry out the same experiment with two different genotypes and find that one is much more variable than the other, it is safe to conclude that the degree of phenostability is genetically influenced.

In a second type of experiment, we expose genetically similar subjects to a variety of environments and observe their behavior. We may find that some traits are affected more than others by our treatments. Thus environmentally impoverished beagles do not differ significantly from controls in final performance on a reversal-learning task. They were, particularly in the early stages of training, more timid than controls (Fuller, 1966). In an experiment of this kind the environmental variable is identifiable, and hypotheses of its mode of action can be tested.

A third type of experiment compares two or more genotypes in two or more environments. The Cooper-Zubek experiments with McGill "bright" and "dull" rats are an example. The phenolability of learning ability was demonstrated for both strains, but "dull" rats needed more stimulation during development. Similar strain differences in the effects of experiential deprivation have been found in dogs (Fuller, 1967b).

Early experience research can involve enrichment as well as impoverishment. We expect that as the variety of environments to which a genotype is exposed increases its phenotypic variability will also increase. The ultimate reaction range of a particular rat strain cannot be defined. Some new drug or rearing procedure might produce a genius. However, evolutionary theory predicts that there should be constraints on phenolability. There is no point in selecting a species to cope with challenges that are outside its phylogenetic experience.

Constraints on Learning

The literature of constraints on learning has been reviewed by Shettleworth (1972a), Seligman and Hager (1972), and Hinde and Stevenson-Hinde (1973). I shall illustrate such restrictions by two examples: temporal aspects of song learning in white-crowned sparrows (Marler, 1970) and stimulus relevance in avoidance conditioning of chicks (Shettleworth, 1972b). Neither of these experiments involves direct genetic manipulation, but both have implications for understanding the phylogenetic history of a species.

Song learning in white–crowned sparrows. The white-crowned sparrow (WCS) is a common inhabitant of North America, particularly west of the Rocky Mountains. As in most perching birds, singing is exclusively a male activity and is limited to the breeding season. It functions as an advertisement of territory occupation and possibly as an attractant to females. The song is basically the same everywhere, but regional dialects are recognized. Marler's objective was to determine whether the song was acquired by imitative learning or by maturation independent of experience.

Procedures included isolation of male nestlings at various ages, sometimes with controlled exposure to recorded WCS or other bird songs. Males isolated at five days of age (the earliest feasible time) who never heard the WCS song sang at sexual maturity in a disorganized, uncharacteristic manner. Males whose isolation began 5 weeks after hatching heard the WCS song in their natural habitat and sang normally at maturity. Playbacks of WCS songs to very young nestlings and to 5-day isolates at maturity were ineffective for inducing normal song. However, playbacks to birds between 7 and 100 days post-hatching lead to typical WCS song at maturity. Clearly there is a limited period during which a WCS male can acquire and store information on his species song. He learns the dialect that he hears; not the one of his parent. The learning process is selective. WCS males did not acquire song-sparrow songs played during the sensitive period for learning their own song.

By some definitions the WCS song is learned down to the details of the regional dialects, but the time elapsed from stimulus to response is so long that conventional ideas of contiguity among stimulus, response, and reinforcement are not applicable. Furthermore, the WCS system for storing vocal information is available for an extremely limited set of signals and for a period of only 90 days. The process might better be characterized as epigenesis than as learning.

The WCS findings are not applicable to song birds in general. Song sparrows isolated from social contact as nestlings sing their species-typical song as adults, even though it is considerably more complex than the WCS song. Male chaffinches have a critical period for song-learning when they first become sexually mature. Evolutionary doctrine postulates that such differences are not ascribable to chance but reflect different selection pressures.

Stimulus-response relevance in chicks. Some biological constraints on learning are so obvious that they are of trivial interest to psychologists. Every species is limited in the scope of its learning by its sensory and motor equipment and by the size and complexity of its neural network. A matter of greater interest is the degree to which the nervous system is constructed so that some stimulus-response conditions are more readily established than others.

Shettleworth (1972b) reported that chicks readily associate sound stimuli with foot shock and develop a conditioned emotional response (CER). Under similar conditions visual stimuli were ineffective in producing a CER. In contrast, chicks learned to discriminate an electrified from a safe water source from visual, but not from auditory, cues. Control experiments led Shettleworth to reject the hypotheses that these differences were ascribable to relations between the aversiveness of shock in the two situations, or to relations between the conditioned stimulus and the reinforcer. She proposed that relations between stimulus and response determine the effectiveness of the former as a controller of behavior. Some S-R connections are readily made because making them quickly was advantageous in the past, and genes biasing the nervous system to form these associations readily were passed on. Chicks employ vision extensively in feeding and drinking where they must select between edible and unpleasant objects. They are warned of predators by maternal clucks. Shettleworth argued that these predispositions for linking certain classes of stimuli with certain classes of responses carry over into the laboratory.

Learning Constraints and Behaviorism

The idea of specific restraints on learning is not necessarily incompatible with behaviorism. Few geneticists would quarrel with the following statement by Skinner (1974):

> It is no doubt true that early behaviorists were unduly enthusiastic about the learning processes they were discovering and neglected the subject of behavioral genetics. . . . In an important sense all behavior is inherited, since the organism that behaves is a product of natural selection. Operant conditioning is as much a part of the genetic endowment as digestion or gestation. The question is not whether the human species has a genetic endowment, but how it is to be analysed [pp. 43–44].

I would add that the possibility of discovering the laws governing environmental effects on behavior depends on the assumption that genotypes place rather strict limits on phenolability. A degree of genetic determinism, at least at the species level, is essential for every psychological school from radical behaviorism to cognitive humanism. All must assume that the members of a species which interests them have some common characteristics. The real problems arise with respect to intraspecies differences in reaction to environmental stimuli. The extent and importance of genotype-environment interaction is perhaps the most central issue in the relations between psychology and genetics.

GENOTYPE-ENVIRONMENT INTERACTION

For the sake of clarity, I define *genotype-environment interaction* (GEI) in a statistical sense, the presence of nonadditive effects of a genetic and an environmental variable upon a phenotype. For the universal mutual involvement of genotype and environment in development, I use the word *coaction*. Interest in GEIs arises from the fact that they make it difficult to predict the effects of a treatment on a specific individual.

GEIs: Animal Studies

Henderson (1967) reported great genetic variability in the effects of mild (buzzer) or strong (shock) stress in an open field upon later emotionality in the same field. Control groups were unstressed but treated similarly otherwise. Observations were made on four inbred mouse strains and on their 12 reciprocal hybrids. Regarding the study as 16 separate experiments, identical except for the genotypes of the subjects, and using defecation as the index of emotionality, the following hypotheses were supported (N times): no effects of stress (6); emotion increases montonically with the amount of stress (2); controls less emotional than the two stressed groups which do not differ (3); strongly stressed animals are most emotional, mildly stressed are least, controls are intermediate (2); controls most emotional, buzzer group least, shocked intermediate (2); and, shocked most emotional, buzzer and controls the same (1). Critics might challenge the validity and generalizability of the emotionality test, but the important point is that any theory of the relation between prior stress and temperament could be supported by choosing the right subjects. What happens to general laws?

Striking breed differences in the effects of early experiential deprivation on dogs were found by Fuller and Clark (1968). Beagles and wirehaired terriers were either raised as laboratory pets or isolated for 12 weeks without contact with humans or other dogs. At 15 weeks of age they were observed in an arena where they could react to humans, to other dogs, and to toys. Composite indices of activity level and response intensity were computed for each subject over a 5-week "rehabilitation" period. Compared with pets, isolated beagles were initially inactive, but they eventually caught up. Isolated terriers responded in the opposite direction by becoming hyperactive and remaining so. The response indices of the pet-reared beagles and terriers were the same. They were initially reduced in isolates of both breeds, but terriers soon recovered and were indistiguishable from controls. In beagles the depression lasted to the end of the observation period, and later check-ups suggested that it might be permanent.

GEIs: Human Implications

Genotype-environment interactions are readily found in animals, and experiments to demonstrate them are popular. Do the results of these experiments have implications for human development? The answer is of more than theoretical interest with respect to child-rearing, education, and psychotherapy (Henderson, 1975). Unfortunately, knowledge of interactions in our own species is scanty, and progress is likely to be difficult and slow. Such evidence as we have indicates that common assumptions about the influence of family and cultural factors on personality are likely to be wrong. After analyzing data from a very large twin study, Loehlin and Nichols (1976) wrote:

> In the personality domain we seem to see environmental effects that operate almost randomly with respect to the sorts of variables that psychologists (and other people) have traditionally deemed important in personality development. What can be going on? [p. 92]

It is easy to share their sense of frustration. But since so few data on GEIs in humans are available, it may be worthwhile to consider the implications of accepting the hypothesis that they exist. Let us start by looking at the evidence for genetic differences in early infancy, before parental practices have had time to shape a child's personality. The few infant twin studies give evidence that behavioral differences at an early age are heritable, although the samples are small and personality changes are rapid over the first three years (Freedman, 1965; Rutter, Korn, & Birch, 1963).

A more comprehensive longitudinal twin study is being carried on in Louisville, Kentucky (Wilson, 1977). A most interesting finding of this project is that MZ cotwins are much more similar than DZ cotwins in their developmental profiles, based on the timing of periods of accelerated and decelerated acquisition of new competencies. Some of the correspondence may be attributable to greater similarity of parental treatment of the MZ pairs, but most efforts to measure such effects in this and other studies indicate that they must be small, if indeed they exist (Loehlin & Nichols, 1976; Scarr, 1968).

Types of GEIs

It is possible to identify likely patterns of GEIs and to deduce their psychological consequences. Figure 2 shows some possibilities. In each of the four parts of the figure two genotypes, G_1 and G_2, are exposed to one of two environments, E_1 and E_2, and evaluated for phenotypic quality. Quality may be defined genetically in terms of fitness, or psychologically in terms of individual welfare. Except for D, phenotypic quality improves with increased stimulation. Figure A shows no interaction since the phenotypic difference between G_1 and G_2 is the same in both environments. In B, G_2's superiority increases with a high level of stimulation. In C, a high level equalizes the two genotypes. Finally, in D, the interaction is disordinal; strain ranks reverse as the environment changes.

The situations depicted in A, B, and C present no problems to a parent, educator, or psychotherapist. Provided that the characteristics of a favor-

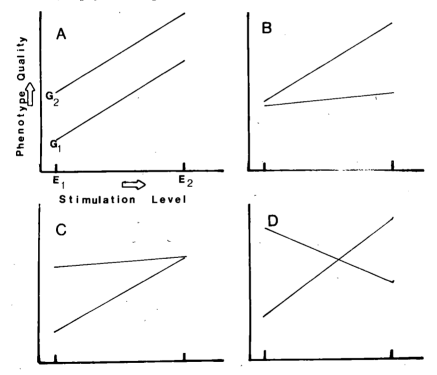

FIG. 2.   Types of genotype-environment interaction. G_1 and G_2 represent two genotypes observed under two conditions or after two different treatments, E_1 and E_2. (A) no interaction; (B) divergence; (C) convergence; (D) disordinal. In this figure increased stimulation (except for G_2 in D) is assumed to improve phenotypic quality. The opposite assumption is allowable when appropriate.

able environment are known, there is no need to match genotypes with treatments. Some individuals may benefit more than others, but no one loses by being transferred form E_1 to E_2. Disordinal interactions are another matter and have disturbed some geneticists. Feldman and Lewontin (1975) imply that such interactions are common enough to make worthless any estimation of the heritability of IQ, for example. This would be no great loss, but the import of the Feldman-Lewontin model (their figure is similar to D) is that any intervention is as likely to damage as to improve the phenotype. Three ways of handling the problem of disordinal interactions exist: (1) find a way to distinguish G_1 and G_2 and assign them appropriately to E_1 and E_2; (2) show that one genotype, say G_1, is so rare that treating everyone as a G_2 will do little harm; or, (3) put everyone in an environment intermediate to E_1 and E_2, thus eliminating the highest and the lowest quality phenotypes.

GEIs and Applied Psychology

Is there a risk in neglecting the possibility of GEIs in applied psychology, admitting that we know less than we ought to about them? Many geneticist-psychologists believe that there is and that a combination of genetic analysis with learning theory is necessary to advance our knowledge of individual differences (e.g., Henderson, 1975). Crawford (1979) believes that mistakenly attributing individual differences to environmental rather than genetic factors could lead to as many inequities as errors in the opposite direction. Eaves et al. (1978) insist that understanding of familial influences on development will come only when both genetic and environmental components are incorporated into research designs. These geneticists are essentially saying that an overcommitment to purely environmental hypotheses is likely to be as socially damaging as the excessive hereditarian views espoused by the eugenicists.

The geneticists' views have made only modest inroads among social scientists. A special issue of *American Psychologist* (1979, Vol. 34) entitled *Psychology and Children: Current Research and Practice,* includes 41 papers. Only two mention hereditary factors. Schwartz (1979) suspects "that all forms of psychopathology that are not clearly due to traumatic, toxic or infectious conditions of the brain are significantly influenced . . . not only by environmental factors but also by genetic variation." Willerman (1979), noting that a large part of IQ variance is within rather than between families, concludes that social measures to reduce inequity among families are unlikely to lessen differences between siblings.

Social scientists are not unaware of human diversity, and its importance for education is argued forcefully in another paper from the same collection (Gordon & Shipman, 1979). Their statement that individuality transcends membership in a social, economic, or ethnic group could be viewed as recognition of the genotype-environment-coaction concept. However, genetic influences are absent from Gordon and Shipman's list. They do postulate *attribute-treatment-interaction* which might be viewed as a *phenotype-treatment-interaction,* related in a degree to the geneticists' GEI. This is an advance over neglecting individuality, but it is not likely to advance our understanding of why children vary in rate and timing of development and in their level of attainment on specific skills.

SOCIOBIOLOGY: AN EVOLUTIONARY APPROACH TO THE GENETICS OF BEHAVIOR

Sociobiology is neither a new word nor a new concept, but it was brought to the attention of psychologists, sociologists, anthropologists, and the general public by the publication of *Sociobiology: The New Synthesis* (Wilson, 1975). Most of this massive volume is a scholarly presentation of social behavior in animals from the viewpoint of evolutionary biology. Its stated purpose was to give ultimate, that is phylogenetic, explanations of sociology in contrast with the proximate explanations of ethology and comparative psychology. The last chapter, which applied similar explanatory concepts to humans, evoked strong scientific criticism and harsh, personal attacks upon the author (see Wade, 1976).

There are similarities to the attacks on Wilson and those on Darwin which followed the appearance of *Origin of the Species* when it was first published. Darwin challenged orthodox religion; Wilson challenges the view that man may have descended from apes but is now emancipated from phylogenetic controls with respect to group behavior and organization. No attempt is made here to detail challenges and rebuttals. Evaluations of the theory by natural and social scientists and by philosophers are contained in books edited by Barlow and Silverberg (1980) and by Gregory, Silvers, and Sutch (1978). Ruse (1979) subjects the claims of sociobiologists and their critics to a logical and entertaining analysis. Those wishing to read for themselves about sociobiology will find it described in popular fashion by Dawkins (1976). Alcock (1979) and Barash (1977) present the theory in more formal, but readable, fashion.

Fundamentally, sociobiological explanations for social behavior do not differ from Shettleworth's (1972a) ideas of why her chicks, when a feeding response was involved, conditioned better to a visual than to an aural cue. Sociobiology, however, goes far beyond the concept of phylogenetically induced biases in favor of specific stimulus-response connections. Evolution is considered to have shaped complex strategies that are used to obtain scarce resources in competition with conspecifics.

Since sociobiology and behavior genetics make use of the same body of genetic knowledge and theory, we might expect a close relationship between them. Actually this has not developed. Sociobiology places major influence on population genetics in formulating its theories of the evolution of behavior. The ultimate cause of evolutionary changes in behavior is changes in gene frequency that improve adaptation to existing environments. Sociobiologists are rather casual concerning the way in which a gene substitution actually alters mating behavior or the tendency to form dominance hierarchies. Behavior geneticists are concerned with empirical demonstration that a gene difference is responsible for variation in a specific type of behavior. Such a demonstration strengthens an evolutionary hypothesis. Behavior geneticists are also interested in *how* genes operate within individuals as proximate causes of behavioral differences. A gene cannot code for aggression, but it could affect the hormonal sensitivity of neurones that play a key role in the integration of attack and defense.

Sociobiological Concepts and Applications

The major principles of sociobiology are relatively simple. Essentially they attempt to explain the prevalence of cooperative and altruistic behavior in animals through the process of selection of individuals. Cooperative social behavior evolved because it was advantageous to individuals to behave in a cooperative manner. Tendencies to act in this way are, to a degree, inherited. Cooperative individuals on the average have outbred noncooperators, and the frequency of their genes increases relative to the genes of selfish, asocial individuals. In the language of evolutionary genetics cooperators are more *fit* than noncooperators. Viewed in this manner sociobiology seems to predict that the unbiased process of natural selection should lead to an earthly paradise free from selfish competition.

But sociobiology is more realistic. Resources are finite and successful species expand in numbers until a limit is reached. The result is competition for food, habitats, and mates. In competitive social interactions some individuals receive a smaller share of resources and usually lose fitness. Even in cooperative social interactions, such as courtship, mating, caring for offspring, and association for defense, the participants have different interests. Some of these differences, as in male-female collaboration in rearing young, are biologically based. But in any cooperative enterprise there is an opportunity to cheat and obtain the benefits of sociality without paying the full cost. Thus there might be counter selection for "cheater genes" proceding at the same time as selection for altruism. Presumably the two opposing forces would achieve a stable balance at some point. In the following sociobiological theory is applied to a specific topic—human sexuality and family dynamics.

Sexuality and Family Structure in Humans

The ideas in this example have been expounded by a number of authors and have been summarized by Wilson (1975) and by Barash (1977). The concept of parental investment was explicated by Trivers (1972); the evolution of human sexuality by Symons (1979, 1980), of family structure by Van den Berghe (1979), and of general human social behavior by Lockard (1980).

Many studies have been made of social behavior and group organization in invertebrates and vertebrates (Kleiman, 1977; Orians, 1969; Short, 1979). The general conclusion from such analyses is that the social structure of a species is adaptive with respect to its biological capacities and its preferred habitat. Here I apply conventional sociobiological reasoning to outline a series of hypotheses related to human sexual behavior and family structure. The ideas are not original but are derived from the previously cited sources.

In humans, as in mammals generally, a male's investment of time and energy in reproduction is smaller than a female's. She has fewer gametes to invest, a shorter period of fertility, the stress of pregnancy and parturition, and usually the energy costs of caring for her infant over several years. Human infants achieve maturity only very slowly, and their period of dependence often overlaps the birth of siblings. Human females are unique in not having periods of estrus and nonestrus. Although the menstrual cycle affects the probability of conception, females can participate in intercourse from puberty to postreproductive ages. These biological parameters play an important role in shaping human sexuality and child-rearing.

Both sexes have common interests in finding a mate who appears likely to pass on good genes to any offspring, and who seems likely to give them good care. Females are more discriminating in the courtship game since their investment in child-bearing is much greater than a male's. Males are more likely to take multiple sexual partners (or at least fantasize about them) since they can thereby increase their genetic contribution to the next generation at little cost. A male's philandering may be tolerated by his partner, provided he does not desert her, since she can be certain that any infant she conceives carries her genes. A cuckolded male cannot be certain that a new addition to his family is a true relative. Hence males are generally less forgiving of a mate's infidelity.

Continuous sexual receptivity in human females is a counterploy to induce husbands to tolerate monogamy instead of increasing their fitness by polygyny. This strategy is not necessarily injurious to male fitness. Infants are likely to be more vigorous if both parents participate in their care. Stable monogamous marriages are energy efficient in providing sexual and other social satisfaction along with a good environment for child development. But even here the sexes do not have exactly the same biological investments and marital tension may result.

An individual's fitness is obviously dependent on the number of his or her offspring who survive to maturity and reproduce in turn. However, fitness may be increased by giving aid to close relatives, particularly to siblings and their offspring, who share a large proportion of genes, one-half for siblings, one-fourth for nieces and nephews. The sum of individual fitness plus that based on close kin yields *inclusive fitness*. Natural selection, therefore, favors genes that promote close contact with and mutual support of relatives. Such genes need not code for a mystical bond of kinship. During most of human history children grew up in small communities or migratory bands where most of their social contacts were with close relatives. One need only postulate selection for the facilitation at an early age of social bonding with familiars. The result would be kin selection. In some present-day societies where families are widely dispersed the same process of affiliation would occur, but it would not result in kin selection. Instead, the same genetic substrate would facilitate the development of reciprocal altruism (Trivers, 1971).

The period of child dependency in humans is longer than the natural interval between sibling births. Each child to insure his or her welfare is seeking a maximal share of parental nuturance which may be in short supply. This situation favors selection for assertiveness and intersibling competition. Sibling conflicts would be expected to decrease later when nuturance is not as strongly dependent on parents. The interests of parents and offspring with respect to maximizing individual fitness often conflict. A parent, particularly a mother, must weigh the benefits, in terms of her fitness, of bearing another child or in further nuturance of a nearly self-sufficient one. Clearly the existing child calculates (emotionally, not logically) that it might be better off without the extra sibling.

Natural selection might even be responsible for the extension of the human life-span beyond the age of reproduction. In most free-living mammalian species postreproductive individuals are extremely rare. In many human societies they are common. One explanation is that nonfertile elder humans contribute enough to the survival of grandchildren, nieces, and nephews to favor the increase of genes that promote longevity.

The above account is greatly simplified, but it follows the general rationale of a number of sociobiological explanations for human social behavior and organization. The hypothesis provides a rationale for either a monogamous or a polygynous mating system depending on cultural and environmental factors. It predicts the wide occurence of extended families whose members cooperate with each other. It also explains perturbations even within stable family groups arising from sibling and parent-offspring conflicts over the distribution of resources. Plausibility is not proof, and some anthropologists (e.g., Sahlins, 1976; Washburn, 1978) assert that the sociobiological and comparative approaches are not useful for understanding human social behavior. For a rejoinder to this type of criticism see Ruse (1979, pp. 104 *ff*.).

Variability in Humans and Nonhumans

The evolutionary approach to the social behavior of animals has been widely accepted. Ethograms (descriptions of species-typical behavior) have been constructed for many species: Foxes and most perching birds are described as monogamous, chimpanzees as promiscuous, and red deer as seasonally polygynous. Although such characteristics of social organization are generally accurate, some species have been shown to alter their mating patterns according to circumstances. Acorn woodpeckers, who generally form mixed, communally mating, static colonies, will break up into migratory male-female pairs when the acorn harvest is poor and dispersion is advantageous (Stacey & Beck, 1978). There is no evidence that communal birds differ genetically from pairs. A reasonable hypothesis is that all acorn woodpeckers have the potential of adopting group or pair mating dependent on circumstances. Natural selection has provided discriminatory mechanisms that enable the birds to choose the most adaptive mode for a particular situation.

Human societies are much more variable than those of acorn woodpeckers. They seem to be governed by rules that are transmitted culturally, rules that are subject to selection in somewhat the same manner as genes are. Anthropologists are right when they prefer cultural to phylogenetic explanations for wide variations in social organization. But this rejection does not pose a threat to evolutionary hypotheses. Sociobiologists and behavior geneticists are well aware of acculturization and developmental plasticity. The objective of evolutionary analysis of human cultures is to determine the environmental and biological factors that have shaped characteristics shared among them.

A common criticism of sociobiology and behavior genetics is that they are deterministic (e.g., Gould, 1976). Actually scientific theories in general are deterministic. It is axiomatic in experimental sciences that there are causes and effects. Since behavior has multiple causes, often unrecognized or difficult to measure, the predictive value of behavioral hypotheses is less than that of physical sciences. The precision of the physical sciences stems from the ability of experimenters to control a few relevant factors on a small scale in a laboratory. If we look at physical science outside the laboratory, meterology for example, its predictions are not noticeably better than those of psychology and sociobiology. The issue of determinism is more important to philosophers of science than it is to present-day behavior geneticists and sociobiologists who are well aware of genotype-environment coactions and interactions. The hypothesis that sexual and family relationships have biological underpinnings does not contradict the hypothesis that a considerable amount of learning is required to play mating and parental games effectively. The objectives are the same in all societies, the rules fundamentally similar, but success requires the ability to learn the fine points of play and to follow the variations sanctioned by the arbiters of one's group. Thus in Western societies we observe changes in sex roles associated with reliable, cheap methods of contraception, the mechanization of housework, and the availability of day-care facilities. The success of women in formerly masculine occupations supports the belief that many traditional gender differences are culture-based.

Such developments do not completely settle the question of whether the extreme plasticity of human behavioral development made possible by a large brain, a prolonged period of infantile dependence, and a rich assortment of traditions that must be learned, has led to the disappearance of all constraints on human social behavior and organization. Is the complete abolition of gender differences in social roles, other than the essential biological ones, possible? If possible, does it have deleterious effects on fitness? Is it possible to alter the propensity for human groups above a critical size to form hierarchies and split into tribes or social classes? Would individual and group conflict disappear if economic systems were altered? Perhaps, but if some of our problems result from inherent qualities of human nature, some social problems may be permanent aspects of the human condition (Sarason, 1978).

The belief that aggressive behavior has been subjected to positive selection and thus indirectly coded in our genotypes does not imply that humans have need to be violent, or even to release aggressive impulses through redirection and catharsis. It simply means that phylogenesis has put the machinery there, ready to be used in times of danger, because aggressive responses were important in the survival and reproductive success of our ancestors. Despite pessimistic views of our species as inordinately violent, we may be less so than other species that have been carefully observed over long periods of time (Wilson, 1975, p. 247). Perhaps natural selection has been eliminating aggression facilitating genes, or perhaps ethical indoctrination has been beneficial. But, even if social interdictions result in the suppression of overt violence, will they eliminate the internal emotional state that we call anger or rage? Relying on introspection, I doubt it. One learns that in our society violence is usually less effective than other tactics in settling conflicts, but remaining peaceful can be difficult and stressful.

An Appraisal of Sociobiology

I personally disagree with the idea that the ultimate, evolutionary explanations of behavior espoused by sociobiologists have a higher status than the proximate explanations of anthropologists, behavior geneticists, ethologists, psychologists, and sociologists. The question, *How?* is as important as *Why?* But in spite of some wild hypothesizing (mostly with regard to humans) and tendencies for anthropomorphism and zoomorphism, sociobiology has made a stimulating contribution to the behavioral sciences. Rather than viewing the evolutionary approach as a threat, it can be considered as a source of hypotheses. When they can be tested, fine. When they cannot, thinking concurrently about *how* and *why* organisms behave the way they do is a splendid intellectual game. Psychology can gain from closer relations with the phylogenetic approach of sociobiology and the developmental approach of behavior genetics.

THE INFLUENCE OF PSYCHOLOGY ON GENETICS

The influence of psychology on genetics might be characterized by one word—*none*—but that would be an overstatement. It is true that psychology has had little influence on basic biological genetics, the transmission of genes, their biochemistry, and their distribution in populations. Psychophenes are too pliable to serve as markers for the genes that are the proper study of geneticists. Behavioral phenotypes are not congruent with genotypes in the way that biochemical phenotypes are. To be sure, having two recessive phenylketonuria genes always leads, if not treated, to some degree of mental retardation. But one does not detect the genetic condition by an IQ test. Phenylketonuria is diagnosed by the excessive level of phenylalanine in blood or urine.

Evolutionary genetics is an exception to the general trend. Evolutionary geneticists and sociobiologists believe that the effect of genes on behavior is a very important factor in natural selection. Structural modifications may follow rather than precede behavioral innovations. To understand the evolutionary process it is necessary to know a great deal about all factors influencing social behavior. The scientists who study the genetics of mating choice, aggression and dominance hierarchies, and cooperative behavior must draw on psychology for the methodology of measuring and scaling these complex and elusive phenotypes. It is not surprising that a large proportion of behavior geneticists were trained in psychology departments. They are the channels for the transfer of ideas between disciplines.

SUMMARY AND CONCLUSIONS

Major Points of Contact

This account of the relation between psychology and genetics has traced its history from Darwin to twentieth-century biopsychology and sociobiology. An early concentration on eugenics programs has waned, and is nearly dormant. The renewed interest in evolution has lead to recognition of three levels of gene involvement in an individual's development: phylogenesis, epigenesis, and psychogenesis. The latter is the prime interest of psychology, but epigenetic and phylogenetic history place constraints on it.

The two major problems that have occupied behavior geneticists are: (1) the contribution of genetic differences to individual behavioral variation and (2) the degree to which a specified genotype constrains or extends the developmental potential of its possessor. Sociobiologists are interested in a related problem: (3) the remote environmental conditions that have shaped the genotypes and the behavioral repertoire of present-day species. Research on the first two problems involves the idiographic approach; the third problem requires a nomothetic approach.

A variety of genetic techniques has been applied to psychological traits (inferred psychophenes) and specific behaviors (ostensible psychophenes). A high degree of experimental sophistication has been attained in animal research. With humans, geneticists must make use of natural experiments such as identical and fraternal twins, and adopted versus biological children. The widely used term *heritability* refers to the proportion of variance in a population attributable to genetic differences within that population. It should not be confused with phenostability, the degree to which an individual's phenotype is constrained by its genotype.

In humans, the major interests of behavior geneticists have been intelligence, personality, and psychopathology. In animals, research has concentrated on physiological regulation, sensory preferences, learning, emotionality, and social behavior. Genetic effects are readily found when they are looked for. Interpretation of data requires, particularly in human studies, that genotype-environment correlations be recognized and evaluated. Genotype-environment interactions are of particular interest when attempts are made to fit instructional or remedial procedures to individuals.

The sociobiological approach to behavior stresses the relation between environmental demands and the direction of individual natural selection based on behavior. The shaping of behavior by natural selection is assumed to operate thrdugh changes in gene frequency from generation to generation. Sociobiologists postulate a strong association between genes and behavior, but have done little to demonstrate how this association operates. Judged from current literature, the sociobiological thesis has been warmly received by animal behaviorists. As applied to humans it is more controversial. Nevertheless, the evolutionary approach to human social behavior and organization is a fertile source of hypotheses, some of which appear to be testable.

Nature and Nurture: Still an Issue

Throughout this essay the nature-nurture issue has recurred; sometimes explicitly, sometimes covertly. It is common to read that the distinction is "useless," "sterile," or "obsolete." At one time I believed that it would wither away as scientists discovered how genes worked and how organisms developed. It is true that extremism on both the hereditarian and the environmentalist sides has decreased, but I am now convinced that the nature-nurture issue has a long life expectancy.

The reason for this is inherent in the nature of the science hierarchy described at the beginning of this chapter. The relation of nature to nurture is not hierarchial and is not conducive to reductionist explanations. The relation is one of coaction and interaction at the same level of organization. When a neurophysiologist demonstrates that the formation of a stimulus-response bond in a classical conditioning experiment is associated with a change in synaptic potentials at a specific locus in the brain, we have a reductionist explanation for conditioning. Accepting this explanation has no effect on the validity of laws of conditioning based on overt responses.

The situation is different when we look at nature and nurture as causes of schizophrenia, a psychological syndrome that is known to run in families. Its occurrence has been explained by a gene or genes predisposing to the disorder, or by pathogenic features of child rearing such as the double-bind (Weakland, 1960). I shall not review the data presented in favor of these two hypotheses but shall consider some general features of competition between explanations based on nature vs. nurture. In all such instances the phenotypes are complex, usually variable in manifestation, and not clearly associated with an identifiable gene.

The double-bind hypothesis is psychological, the genetic hypothesis is biological, but the psychological hypothesis cannot be reduced to biology. Either hypothesis is compatible with explaining schizophrenia in

102   FULLER

neurochemical terms, but demonstrating that the disorder was based on neurotransmitter imbalance would have no impact on the validity of the competing genetic and double-bind hypotheses. There are a number of types of relationships between a genetic and an environmental hypothesis depending on the way in which each is expressed. Any hypothesized cause can be considered as sufficient, necessary, or irrelevant. As an example let us look at the prospects for conflict and conciliation between the double-bind and the genetic hypotheses for the etiology of schizophrenia.

Either condition might be sufficient in itself. In this situation no conflict occurs. Both might be necessary. A child could inherit vulnerability to schizophrenia so that it could not tolerate the double-bind. The genetic vulnerability might be enhanced if the child's behavior evoked double-bind behavior in the parents. This would be an example of a reactive genotype-environment correlation. If either hypothesized cause is considered sufficient, the other is automatically excluded as necessary. If genetics is found irrelevant, an environmental cause must be assumed, but it need not be a double–bind. If the double-bind is found irrelevant, the case for genetics is not affected. It is neither supported nor disproved.

The coactive model that implies synergism between genetic dispositions and the environment seems to be the most reasonable model to explain schizophrenia but even here the possibility of conflict is still present. In an analysis of variance context, assigning more weight to nurture means less weight for nature. Perhaps we can learn to look at interactions and correlations of genotypes and environments as entities in their own right, but to do so will require accommodation on all sides. Genes and environments are physical things that can be visualized; interactions and correlations are relationships, one step away from the physical world. Despite the inevitable tension between genetic and environmental hypotheses, the relations of genetics with psychology have become closer over the past thirty years. The existence of a degree of tension has resulted in a sharpening of research designs in both disciplines. The move towards an evolutionary approach to the nature of behavioral diversity between and within species should help to answer questions as to why humans and nonhumans behave the way they do, as well as questions on how they behave.

REFERENCES

Alcock, J. *Animal behavior: An evolutionary approach.* Sunderland, MA: Sinauer, 1979.
Barash, D. P. *Sociobiology and behavior.* New York: Elsevier, 1977.
Barlow, G. W., & Silverberg, J. (Eds.). *Sociobiology: Beyond nature/nurture.* Boulder, CO: 1980.

Bateson, P. How do sensitive periods arise and what are they for? *Animal Behaviour*, 1979, *27*, 470–486.

Cancro, R. (Ed.). *Intelligence: Genetic and environmental influences*. New York: Grune & Stratton, 1971.

Cooper, R. M., & Zubek, J. P. Effects of enriched and restricted early environments on the learning ability of bright and dull rats. *Canadian Journal of Psychology*, 1958, *12*, 159–164.

Crawford, C. George Washington, Abraham Lincoln and Arthur Jensen. Are they compatible? *American Psychologist*, 1979, *34*, 664–672.

Crow, J. F. Mechanisms and trends in human evolution. *Daedalus*, 1961, *90*, 416–431.

Darwin, C. *Origin of the species*. New York: Macmillan, 1927. (Originally published, 1859.)

Dawkins, R. *The selfish gene*. New York: Oxford University Press, 1976.

Dobzhansky, T. *Mankind evolving*. New Haven: Yale University Press, 1962.

Eaves, L. J., Last, K. A., Young, P. A., & Martin, N. G. Model-fitting approaches to the analysis of human behaviour. *Heredity*, 1978, *41*, 249–320.

Ehrman, L., & Parsons, P. A. *The genetics of behavior*. Sunderland, MA: Sinauer, 1976.

Erlenmeyer-Kimling, L., & Jarvik, L. F. Genetics and intelligence: A review. *Science*, 1963, *142*, 1477–1478.

Falconer, D. S. *Introduction to quantitative genetics*. New York: Ronald Press, 1960.

Feldman, M. W., & Lewontin, R. C. The heritability hang-up. *Science*, 1975, *190*, 1163–1168.

Fisher, R. A. The correlation between relatives on the supposition of Mendelian inheritance. *Transactions of the Royal Society of Edinburgh*, 1918, *52*, 399–433.

Freedman, D. G. An ethological approach to the genetical study of human behavior. In S. G. Vandenberg (Ed.), *Methods and goals in human behavior genetics*. New York: Academic Press, 1965.

Fuller, J. L. Transitory effects of experiential deprivation upon reversal learning in dogs. *Psychonomic Science*, 1966, *4*, 273–274.

Fuller, J. L. Effects of the albino gene upon behavior of mice. *Animal Behaviour*, 1967, *15*, 467–470. (a)

Fuller, J. L. Experiential deprivation and later behavior. *Science*, 1967, *158*, 1645–1652. (b)

Fuller, J. L. Strain differences in the effects of chlorpromazine and chlordiazepoxide upon active and passive avoidance in mice. *Psychopharmacologia*, 1970, *16*, 261–271.

Fuller, J. L. Nature vs. nurture: The dead issue is resurrected. *Contemporary Psychology*, 1976, *21*, 12–13.

Fuller, J. L. The taxonomy of psychophenes. In J. R. Royce & L. P. Mos (Eds.), *Theoretical advances in behavior genetics*. Alphen aan den Rijn, Netherlands: Sijthoff & Noordhoff, 1979.

Fuller, J. L., & Clark, L. D. Genotype and behavioral vulnerability to isolation in dogs. *Journal of Comparative and Physiological Psychology*, 1968, *66*, 151–156.

Fuller, J. L., & Thompson, W. R. *Foundations of behavior genetics*. St. Louis, MO: Mosby, 1978.

Fuller, J. L., & Wimer, R. E. Behavior genetics. In D. A. Dewsbury & D. A. Rethlingshafer (Eds.), *Comparative psychology*. New York: McGraw Hill, 1973.

Galton, F. *Hereditary genius*. London: Macmillan, 1869.

Goddard, H. H. *Feeble mindedness: Its causes and consequences*. New York: Macmillan, 1914.

Gordon, E. W., & Shipman, S. Human diversity, pedagogy, and educational equity. *American Psychologist*, 1979, *34*, 1030–1036

Gottesman, I. I., & Shields, J. *Schizophrenia and genetics: A twin vantage point*. New York: Academic Press, 1972.

Gould, S. J. Biological potential vs. biological determinism. *Natural History*, 1976, *85*, 1–22.

Gregory, M. S., Silvers, A., & Sutch, D. *Sociobiology and human nature*. San Francisco, CA: Jossey-Bass, 1978.

Haller, M. H. *Eugenics*. New Brunswick, NJ: Rutgers University Press, 1963.

Henderson, N. D. Prior treatment effects on open field behavior of mice—a genetic analysis. *Animal Behaviour*, 1967, *15*, 364–376.

Henderson, N. D. Gene-environment interaction in human behavioral development. In K. W. Schaie, V. E. Anderson, G. E. McClearn, & J. Money (Eds.), *Developmental human behavior genetics*. Lexington, MA: Heath, 1975.

Henry, K. R., & Haythorn, M. M. Albinism and auditory function in the laboratory mouse: I. Effects of single gene substitutions on auditory physiology, audiogenic seizures, and developmental processes. *Behavior Genetics*, 1975, *5*, 137–149.

Heron, W. T. The inheritance of maze learning ability in rats. *Journal of Comparative Psychology*, 1935, *19*, 77–89.

Hinde, R. A., & Stevenson-Hinde, J. *Constraints on learning*. London: Academic Press, 1973.

Hirsch, J. Behavior-genetic or "experimental" analysis: The challenge of science vs. the lure of technology. *American Psychologist*, 1967, *22*, 118–130.

Ho, H., Plomin, R., & DeFries, J. C. Selective placement in adoption. *Social Biology*, 1979, *26*, 1–6.

Horn, J. M., Loehlin, J. C., & Willerman, L. Intellectual resemblance among adoptive and biological relatives: The Texas adoption project. *Behavior Genetics*, 1979, *9*, 177–207.

Huxley, J. *Evolution, the modern synthesis*. New York: Harper, 1942.

Immelman, K. Sexual and other long-term aspects of imprinting in birds and other species. In D. S. Lehrman, R. A. Hinde, & E. Shaw (Eds.), *Advances in the study of behavior* (Vol. 4). New York: Academic Press, 1972.

Jencks, C. *Inequality*. New York: Basis Books, 1972.

Jinks, J. L., & Fulker, D. W. Comparison of the biometrical, genetical, MAVA and classical approaches to the analysis of human behavior. *Psychological Bulletin*, 1970, *73*, 311–349.

Jensen, A. R. How much can we boost IQ and scholastic achievement? *Harvard Educational Review*, 1969, *39*, 1–123.

Kamin, L. J. *The science and politics of IQ*. Potamac, MD: Lawrence Erlbaum Associates, 1974.

Katzev, R. D., & Mills, S. K. Strain differences in avoidance conditioning as a function of the classical CS-US contingency. *Journal of Comparative and Physiological Psychology*, 1974, *87*, 661–671.

Kleiman, D. G. Monogamy in mammals. *Quarterly Review of Biology*, 1977, *52*, 39–69.

Lappé, M., & Brody, J. A. Genetic counseling: A psychotherapeutic approach to automony in decision making. In M. A. Sperber & L. F. Jarvik (Eds.), *Psychiatry and genetics*. New York: Basic Books, 1976.

Layzer, D. Heritability analyses of IQ: Science or numerology? *Science*, 1974, *183*, 1259–1266.

Lockard, J. S. *The evolution of human social behavior*. New York: Elsevier, 1980.

Loehlin, J. C., Lindzey, G., & Spuhler, J. N. *Race differences in intelligence*. San Francisco, CA: Freeman, 1975.

Loehlin, J. C., & Nichols, R. C. *Heredity, environment and personality: A study of 850 sets of twins*. Austin, TX: University of Texas Press, 1976.

MacKinnon, D. W., & Maslow, A. H. Personality. In H. Helson (Ed.), *Theoretical foundations of psychology*. New York: Van Nostrand, 1951.

Marler, P. A comparative approach to vocal learning: Song development in white-crowned sparrows. *Journal of Comparative and Physiological Psychology Monograph*, 1970, *71*(2), 1–25.

Marx, M. H. *Theories in contemporary psychology*. New York: Macmillan, 1963.

Marx, M. H., & Goodson, F. E. *Theories in contemporary psychology*. New York: Macmillan, 1976.

Mather, K., & Jinks, J. L. *Biometrical genetics: The study of continuous variation*. London: Chapman-Hall, 1971.

Mayr, E. *Populations, species and evolution*. Cambridge, MA: Harvard University Press, 1970.

McClearn, G. E. The inheritance of behavior. In L. Postman (Ed.), *Psychology in the making*. New York: Knopf, 1962.

McClearn, G. E., & DeFries, J. C. *Introduction to behavioral genetics*. San Francisco, CA: Freeman, 1973.

Mendel, G. [Experiments in plant hybridization.] In J. A. Peters (Ed.), *Classic papers in genetics*. Englewood Cliffs, NJ: Prentice-Hall, 1959. (Originally published, 1865.)

Munsinger, H. The adopted child's IQ: A critical review. *Psychological Bulletin,* 1975, *82,* 623–659.

Piaget, J. *Behavior and evolution*. New York: Random House, 1978.

Orians, G. H. On the evolution of mating systems in birds and mammals. *American Naturalist*, 1969, *103,* 589–604.

Osborne, R. T., Noble, C. E., & Weyl, N. (Eds.). *Human variation*. New York: Academic Press, 1978.

Pearson, K. On the laws of inheritance of man: II. On the inheritance of the mental and moral characters in man and its comparison with the inheritance of physical characters. *Biometrika*, 1904, *3,* 131–190.

Plomin, R., DeFries, J. C., & Loehlin, J. C. Genotype-environment interaction and correlation in the analysis of human behavior. *Psychological Bulletin*, 1977, *84,* 309–322.

Plotkin, H. C., & Odling-Smee, F. J. Learning, change and evolution: An enquiry into the teleonomy of learning. In J. S. Rosenblatt, R. A. Hinde, C. Beer, & M. C. Busnel (Eds.). *Advances in the study of behavior* (Vol. 10). New York: Academic Press, 1979.

Richardson, K., & Spears, D. *Race and intelligence*. Baltimore, MD: Penquin, 1972.

Roberts, R. C. Some concepts and methods in quantitative genetics. In J. Hirsch (Ed.), *Behavior-genetic-analysis*. New York: McGraw-Hill, 1967.

Rose, R. J., Boughman, J. A., Corey, L. A., Nance, W. E., Christian, J. C., & Kange, K. W. Data from the kinships of monozygotic twins indicating maternal effects on verbal intelligence. *Nature,* 1980, *283,* 375–377.

Rose, R. J., Harris, E. L., Christian, J. C., & Nance, W. E. Genetic variance in non-verbal intelligence: Data from the kinships of identical twins. *Science*, 1979, *205,* 1153–1155.

Ruse, M. *Sociobiology: Sense or nonsense?* Boston, MA: D. Reidel, 1979.

Rutter, M., Korn, S., & Birch, H. G. Genetic and environmental factors in the development of primary reactions pattern. *British Journal of Social and Clinical Psychology*, 1963, *2,* 161–173.

Sahlins, M. *The use and abuse of biology*. Ann Arbor, MI: University of Michigan Press, 1976.

Sarason, S. The nature of problem solving in social action. *American Psychologist*, 1978, *33,* 370–380.

Scarr, S. Environmental bias in twin studies. In S. G. Vandenberg (Ed.), *Progress in human behavior genetics*. Baltimore, MD: Johns Hopkins Press, 1968.

Schwartz, J. C. Childhood origins of psychopathology. *American Psychologist*, 1979, *34,* 879–885.

Scott, J. P. (Ed.). *Critical periods*. Stroudsburg, PA: Dowden, Hutchinson and Ross, 1978.

Searle, L. V. The organization of hereditary maze-brightness and maze-dullness. *Genetic Psychology Monographs*, 1949, *39*, 279–325.

Seligman, M. E. P., & Hager, J. L. (Eds.). *Biological boundaries of learning*. New York: Appleton-Century-Crofts, 1972.

Shettleworth, S. J. Constraints on learning. In D. S. Lehrman, R. A. Hinde, & E. Shaw (Eds.). *Advances in the study of behavior* (Vol. 4). New York: Academic Press, 1972. (a)

Shettleworth, S. J. Stimulus relevance in the control of drinking and conditioned fear responses in domestic chicks. *Journal of Comparative and Physiological Psychology*, 1972, *80*, 175–198. (b)

Short, R. V. Sexual selection and its component parts, somatic and genital selection as illustrated by man and the great apes. In J. S. Rosenblatt, R. A. Hinde, C. Beer, & M. C. Busnel (Eds.), *Advances in the study of behavior* (Vol. 9). New York: Academic Press, 1979.

Skinner, B. F. *Science and human behavior*. New York: Free Press, 1953.

Skinner, B. F. *About behaviorism*. New York: Knopf, 1974.

Symons, D. *The evolution of human sexuality*. New York: Oxford University Press, 1979.

Symons, D. The evolution of human sexuality-precis. *Behavioral and Brain Sciences*, 1980, *3*, 171–181.

Thompson, R. *The Pelican history of psychology*. Harmonsworth, England: Penguin Books, 1968.

Thompson, W. R., & Bindra, D. Motivational and emotional characteristics of "bright" and "dull" rats. *Canadian Journal of Psychology*, 1952, *6*, 116–122.

Topoff, H. R. Genes, intelligence and race. In E. Tobach (Ed.), *The four horsemen: Racism, sexism, militarism and social darwinism*. New York: Behavioral Publications, 1974.

Tredgold, A. F. *Mental deficiency (amentia)*. London: Balliere, Tindall & Cox, 1937.

Trivers, R. L. The evolution of reciprocal altruism. *Quarterly Review of Biology*, 1971, *46*, 35–57.

Trivers, R. L. Parental investment and sexual selection. In B. Campbell (Ed.), *Sexual selection and the descent of man*. Chicago, IL: Aldine, 1972.

Tryon, R. C. The genetics of learning ability in rats: Preliminary reports. *University of California Publications in Psychology*, 1929, *4*, 71–89.

Tryon, R. C. Genetic differences in maze learning in rats. *39th Yearbook of the National Society for Study of Education, 2*. Bloomington, IL: Public School Publishing Company, 1940.

Urbach, P. Progress and degeneration in the 'IQ debate'. *British Journal of the Philosophy of Science*, 1974, *25*, 99–135.

Vale, J. R. Role of behavior genetics in psychology. *American Psychologist*, 1973, *28*, 871–882.

Vale, J. R., & Vale, C. A. Individual differences and general laws in psychology: A reconciliation. *American Psychologist*, 1969, *24*, 1093–1108.

van den Berghe, P. L. *Human family systems: An evolutionary view*. New York: Elsevier, 1979.

Wade, N. Sociobiology: Troubled birth for a new discipline. *Science*, 1976, *191*, 1151–1155.

Wahlsten, D. Phenotypic and genetic relations between initial response to electric shock and rate of avoidance learning in mice. *Behavior Genetics*, 1972, *2*, 211–240.

Washburn, S. L. Animal behavior and social anthropology. In M. Gregory, A. Silvers, & D. Sutch (Eds.), *Sociobiology and human nature*. San Francisco, CA: Jossey-Bass, 1978.

Watson, J. B. *Behaviorism*. New York: Norton, 1930.

Weakland, J. H. The "double-bind" hypothesis of schizophrenia and three-party interaction. In D. D. Jackson (Ed.), *The etiology of schizophrenia*. New York: Basic Books, 1960.
Willerman, L. Effects of families on intellectual development. *American Psychologist*, 1979, *34*, 923–929.
Wilson, E. O. *Sociobiology: The new synthesis*. Cambridge, MA: Belknap, 1975.
Wilson, R. S. Mental development in twins. In A. Oliverio (Ed.), *Genetics, environment and intelligence*. New York: Elsevier, 1977.
Windelband, W. *Geschichte und Naturwissenschafte*. Strassburg, Germany: J. H. E. Heitz, 1894.

4 Psychology and Mathematics

Clyde H. Coombs
The University of Michigan

INTRODUCTION

To some people the thought of a close and rewarding relationship between
psychology and mathematics is accompanied by amusement or indignation, as if one were attempting the impossible or intruding where one
should not. To some the very thought of such a blend is a contradiction.
Though there may be contradiction, that is not where it lies.

The same people who perceive a relationship between mathematics and
psychology as a contradiction will discriminate between two books in
selecting a gift for a friend or will recommend a movie to one friend but
not another. This indicates that they perceive some kind of consistency in
the behavior of each of their friends which they have abstracted, generalized, and applied to new situations. But such a capability on their part
requires a belief in rules and principles and reason; and this differs from
mathematical psychology only in form and self-awareness.

There are many ways in which mathematics is used in an empirical
science like psychology, and most of them will be beyond the scope of
this essay. It is not my intention to survey mathematical psychology or its
history (see Grier, 1980, and Miller, 1964), but rather to concentrate on its
modern role in theory construction. This is a small part of mathematical
psychology and a small part of theoretical psychology, but it is an area of
substantial achievements. For this reason I have chosen only a few cases
to discuss in detail. They have been chosen in part because they illustrate
a variety of ways in which mathematics is useful in theory construction

and also because the interrelations among these cases illustrate the power of mathematics in building a cumulative science.

I shall seek in this essay to abstract and to distinguish the symbiotic roles of mathematics on the one hand and behavioral observations on the other hand. Most of these things have been said before and by many others,[1] but their interrelations are complex, with many facets that appear differently to different observers. So, at the risk of stating some obvious things, I shall first review the role of mathematics in an empirical science. To a certain extent my purpose will be to clarify the meaning to be associated with certain words as they are used in this essay. I discuss the nature of mathematical and empirical systems, their complementary relation, and the role of deductive and inductive reasoning. I shall illustrate this paradigm with a discussion of a theory of preference behavior. I then use measurement theory to illustrate the use of mathematical analysis in the search for and detection of empirical regularities and probabilistic choice behavior to illustrate the anticipation and explanation of empirical regularities, the development of general principles of behavior, and the cumulative character of the mathematical analysis of behavior. In the last sections, I discuss the relation between the power and generality of theories, and I compare mathematics with other theory languages for psychology.

A SCHEMA FOR MATHEMATICAL MODELS IN BEHAVIORAL SCIENCE

The discussion that follows is an elaboration of an earlier paper by Coombs, Raiffa, and Thrall (1954) but with a more personal orientation. The discussion is organized in terms of the schema shown in Figure 1.

Mathematical Systems

A mathematical system begins with a set of abstract objects, such as elements of one or more sets, and a set of assertions about these objects. By a process of logical reasoning, one or more consequences of the original assertions are derived (see right-hand side of Figure 1). The abstract objects are called *primitives,* and the set of assertions with which the system begins may be called an *axiom system.* The consequences that are

---

[1] See, for example, Campbell (1920/1957), Cohen and Nagel (1954), Medawar (1969a, 1969b), Miller (1964), Newell and Simon (1955), Popper (1957), Quine and Ullian (1970), and Stevens (1951).

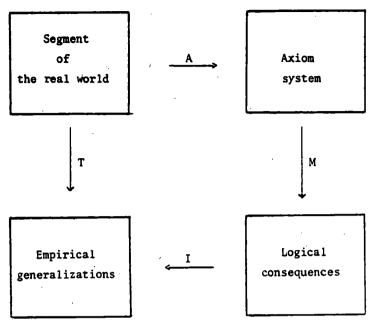

FIG. 1.   A schema for discussing the interaction between a mathematical system and an empirical system.

derived from the axiom system are called *theorems*.The process of derivation is labelled M in the figure, for mathematical reasoning.[2]

The most important part of a mathematical system for our purposes is the axiom system, and it deserves some discussion. Words or terms that are undefined are also primitives in the axiom system. Such terms as "element," "belong to," "set," "point," "and," "or" often are undefined to avoid circularity of definition. A dictionary that defines a dollar as a hundred cents and a cent as the hundredth part of a dollar leaves both terms, cent and dollar, undefined unless it is assumed that the reader knows what either a cent or a dollar is, in which case that term becomes a primitive and would not be defined.

In an analogous manner, axioms are unproven assertions and thereby avoid circularity of reasoning. An axiom system also includes the laws of logic, though these are usually taken for granted and not made explicit. Examples of these laws[3] are the law of contradiction (a statement and its

---

[2]Axioms in a mathematical system are treated "as if" true, and their consequences, deductively arrived at, are true. Truth in a mathematical (logical) system is a matter of deduction. "Logic neither observes, nor invents, nor discovers; . . . [Mill, 1843/1973, p. 10]."

[3]These statements of the laws usually require some qualification of context or domain. Here, the context is that of a mathematical system (cf. Wilder, 1965).

negation cannot both be true) and the law of the excluded middle (a statement and its negation cannot both be false).

Simple nontrivial examples of mathematical systems in behavioral theory are in the area of psychological measurement. The axioms of such systems can be classified on the basis of their logical form as, for example, universal axioms, technical, existential, etc. But axioms capturing empirical regularities are potential laws of behavior. So testability is an important property from the point of view of the empirical scientist. But the logical form of an axiom does not uniquely determine its testability, that depends on the empirical domain in which the primitives are interpreted; this issue is discussed further below. I turn next to the real world of nature and to the role of the empirical behavioral scientist.

Empirical Systems

On the left-hand side of Figure 1 is the world of the empirical scientist. Beginning with some segment of the real world, for example kinship systems, language development, attitude measurement, illusions, etc., the scientist proceeds through observation or experiment, labelled T for testing, to draw conclusions from the data about the existence of empirical regularities and to form generalizations about the domain of interest.

It is not unusual for these generalizations to be expressed in mathematical form, and these would be instances of what Miller (1964) calls the descriptive use of mathematics. For example, the Weber ratio, $\triangle R/R = k$, is familiar as an expression of Weber's generalization that fixed proportionate changes in the intensity of a stimulus are equally often detected. It is not unusual for such generalizations to be called laws or rules of behavior, and quite legitimately so. Some behavioral scientists believe that such rules are the only ones that have legitimacy. We shall see that that is not the case.

The uses of mathematics for descriptive purposes and in the routine analysis of data are well known. These uses can be very valuable, if for no other reason than economy: A simple mathematical equation is a substitute for a table. But it has its limitations, and they are severe. Extrapolation of such an equation beyond the bounds of the observations is unjustified. There is an infinite variety of equations that will fit any set of data equally well, but will extrapolate differently. If a particular equation is chosen for reasons of mathematical convenience and not for theoretical soundness, then its application to situations not previously observed is without justification.

My interest in this essay is in the process by which the prediction of future observations, in situations not yet encountered, is achieved. This interest is aroused because descriptions of observations are not explanatory and hence cannot safeguard inferences about situations not previously observed.

Inference depends on explanation, that is, inferences are consequences of a theory based on assertions assumed to be true about the real world. Some of these assertions may be laws and principles of behavior, based on empirical observation. But drawing logical consequences may involve additional assertions, and the validity of the conclusions is dependent on the validity of all the assertions. We can see that there is an interplay here between an empirical system and a logical structure. It is this interplay I examine next.

Reciprocity of Empirical and Mathematical Systems

The mere description of empirical laws, whether in mathematical form or not, would be an endless cookbook. The empiricist goes beyond descriptive generalizations when he seeks to explain them. Explanation means theory, and for this purpose the two systems, the empirical and the mathematical, are brought into interactive roles by the processes labelled A and I in Figure 1, for abstraction and interpretation, respectively. The process A refers to a mapping of a segment of the real world into a mathematical system where the postulates of the mathematical system have been selected to characterize the properties and relations that are proposed to hold in the real world domain. The logical process M yields conclusions that must be true if the postulates are true. Then, by the inverse process I in Figure 1, the mathematical conclusions can be interpreted as real world conclusions. The mathematical system is called a "model" and the real world system a "realization" or an "instance" of the model. The process A makes the model a theory about the real world system.

It is not uncommon to identify the model with the theory, and usually there is no harm in this. For some purposes, however, it is important to distinguish between them, as in this chapter, because a theory can be false when the model is not, a point that will be illustrated later.

There are then here two routes for drawing conclusions about the real world. One is by the way of the processes AMI and the other by way of the process T; one is through reasoning, the other is through observation.

Conclusions drawn by way of AMI are based on beliefs because the axiom system contains unproven assertions. In that sense, conclusions based on such a route are authoritative (doctrinaire), but they are useful because this route can always provide an answer, which may be all one asks for. To paraphrase J. B. S. Haldane, AMI is good science fiction in that every such system is a possible world, a hypothetical world which may exist in the sense of being logically consistent, i.e. free of internal contradictions. The variety of such worlds—such systems—is limited only by our imagination.

When someone says that something about the real world is true, that it can be proven mathematically, AMI is what is being referred to. If one accepts the premises, one must accept the conclusions. Most people implicitly recognize this, when arguing politics or economics, by attacking premises and definitions. Unfortunately the difficulty may sometimes lie in the undefined terms, the primitives, in which case real communication ceases.[4]

The other route for drawing conclusions about the real world is by way of the process T. This is the route of pure empiricism. One of its virtues is that it is safer, in that the conclusions are based on experience; given exactly the same circumstances, what happened before is expected to happen again.

But what happened before does not tell you what will happen when the circumstances are changed, as they inevitably are in the world of the behavioral scientist. There is no known limit to the number of ways to explain the past; such explanations are *post hoc,* and to be interesting they have to anticipate the future. This requires abstraction of the real world system and logical reasoning.

The conclusion is obvious: AMI and T are both necessary to any science. The strengths and weaknesses of these two systems for drawing conclusions about the real world are complementary. By the process M one seeks logical consistency and hence truth. By the process T one seeks reality and meaningfulness. In brief, there is no certainty of meaningfulness in the process M; there is no certainty of truth in the process T. The empirical world is rich; the mathematical world is powerful. The matchup is fruitful.

In a broad sense, science is merely a confrontation between reason and nature, the essence of which I have tried to capture in the two processes AMI and T, and nature is the final arbiter. Thomas à Kempis expressed it in fewer words in the fifteenth century: Man proposes, God disposes.

Deductive and Inductive Reasoning

The processes by which explanation is arrived at via the two routes, that of AMI and of T, are different and deserve discussion. In a mathematical system, conclusions are reached deductively. The sequences of logical

---

[4]The following anecdote is from Medawar (1969b, p. 48). "The Rev. Sydney Smith, a famous wit, was walking with a friend through the extremely narrow streets of old Edinburgh when they heard a furious altercation between two housewives from high-up windows across the street. 'They can never agree,' said Smith to his companion, 'for they are arguing from different premises.'"

steps in deduction are open to scrutiny, they are visible and repeatable, and errors of omission or commission are detectable. The process AMI embeds the observations in an explanatory framework which permits one to perceive structure in the midst of empirical detail in a way which T does not. Indeed, T in the absence of AMI may obscure structure; I shall illustrate this below.

The empiricist, by way of T, must reach explanation (theoretical conclusions) inductively. Inductive reasoning is not a (known) logical process but an insightful leap, a discontinuity in logical reasoning. The process by which an inductive conclusion is reached is not visible or subject to verification. Inductive empirical generalization is fallible, but it is the only process by which new knowledge comes into the world. Inductive inference is as crucial to science as creativity. Inductive inference, like creativity, is not the exclusive province of either the tough or tender minded, as William James might have put it.

An inductive inference is not a necessary consequence of the data. Equivalently, data cannot imply a theory. The belief that there can be only one explanation for a set of observations is not accepted. We may, of course, sometimes be convinced that an explanation is valid beyond reasonable doubt, but we cannot be certain that there are no other assumptions possible which would explain the observations. This is the only sense in which science is not reasonable—there is no such thing as being "beyond a reasonable doubt." Truth in an empirical system is an empirical question and cannot be achieved until the results of all future experiments are known.

John Stuart Mill (1843/1973) was much concerned with the distinction between deductive and inductive inference. He says, speaking of deductive reasoning, "our assent to the conclusion being grounded on the truth of the premises, we never could arrive at any knowledge by reasoning . . . [p. 7]" and, of inductive inference, ". . . all knowledge consists of generalizations from experience . . . [p. xxii]." I shall first offer two examples to clarify the relation between the roles of inductive and deductive inference in science; then, after, I shall take up an example of a behavioral science theory and illustrate the interacting roles of mathematics and empirical observations in detail.

An empirically minded (and bright) shepherd, while tending sheep, keeping track of their number, and diverting himself by fiddling with pebbles, might build a naive arithmetic. He might even come to the conclusion that "equals added to equals are equal" because he always found this principle to hold.

The trouble with this principle is that all the possible situations to which it may be applied have not been observed, and there is no way of knowing that it will always be found to hold. Indeed, it probably would not.

Consider, for example, an individual who is planning to give each of two grandchildren a gift of stock. To one he plans to give shares in company A, which is engaged in offshore oil exploration, and to the other he plans to give shares in company B, which is an established high-grade retail chain. He regards the two gifts as equal in desirability.

Suppose now that the individual also considers dividing his AT&T stock equally between the two children. Here, he would be adding the same amount to each portfolio, but it is quite possible that he would no longer regard the two portfolios that resulted as equal in desirability. The AT&T stock might appear to him to form a better balanced portfolio in conjunction with one company than with the other company. Another way of putting it is that the principle would require that *any* two portfolios matched in preference could have all the shares common to both deleted, and what remained would still be matched in preference. The advice of investment counselors contradicts that principle.

If a mathematician had conjectured that "if equals are added to equals the results are equal," he would have directed his attention to formulating a set of abstract conditions (postulates) under which it would necessarily, invariably, and inevitably be true. In deduction, the truth of the conclusion is certified by the truth of the premises.

Note that the logical system of the mathematician says nothing about the real world, and the empirical generalization of the shepherd is not necessarily true. To put it somewhat differently, the mathematician does not give a real world interpretation to the things being added on, and the shepherd does not characterize the domain to which the principle applies. The application of the principle to preference for portfolios of stock may or may not be justified.

Another example is that of Darwin's theory of the origin of species. This theory does not follow logically from observations made during the voyage of the Beagle. I repeat: There is no unique explanation for data. The insight from data is a creative step with no known logical basis. To achieve the status of a theory it needs support from more elemental empirical regularities, also supported by data: in this case, elemental generalities as genetic variation, survival of the fittest, and the law of divergence.

It most instances, mathematicians have a pretty good idea where they are trying to get to and seek a deductive route that will get them there. Most empirical scientists also have some idea of what generalizations they wish to reach, and they seek a set of observations that will support or disconfirm the generalization. Their insights are the result of inductive processes; there is no known way to program the process of arriving at generalizations. Equivalently, the detection of empirical regularities is not insured by the deductive process.

In this first part of this essay, I have distinguished between the *descriptive* and the *explanatory* role of mathematics. The descriptive use of mathematics does not seek to explain an empirical generalization by deducing it from basic (axiomatic) properties of the empirical system. In its explanatory role, mathematics can be used to show that an empirical generalization must necessarily hold, provided that the postulates of the mathematical systems are true of the empirical system.

A theory seeks to explain empirical generalizations, as distinguished from describing them. If a theory is arrived at by induction, as is usually the case, the object of mapping a theory into a model is to replace the inductive leap with a deductive link. A well-founded theory is merely a logical linkage between empirical invariances, in contrast to a law, which is a statement of an invariance (see also Nagel, 1961). A model is a (demonstrably) logically consistent system. If a theory language is used that is not demonstrably logically consistent, then the theory is on the side of T in Figure 1. There are many other possible theory languages besides mathematics that are demonstrably logically consistent, and these are discussed later. This chapter is mostly concerned with the role of mathematics as a theory language.

SOME CONTEMPORARY ISSUES IN PSYCHOLOGY AND MATHEMATICS

In this section of the essay, I discuss three examples or representative domains where psychology and mathematics contemporarily meet. The first is *preference behavior,* where empirical generalization in psychology interacts with logical reasoning in mathematics. In discussing a general theory of preference behavior (Coombs & Avrunin, 1977a, 1977b), I limit myself to those aspects of the theory that serve to illustrate mutually supporting strengths of the real and the logical perspectives of scientific theory. The second domain is *measurement theory,* which as it is developed in behavioral science illustrates that mathematical analysis of even commonplace empirical regularities can be the key to an explosive advance. The third domain is *probabilistic choice behavior,* an area of mathematical psychology which illustrates still further important aspects of the interrelations between mathematics and behavior theory.

The Case of Preference Behavior

Preferential choice behavior reflected in decisions is ubiquitous. As a wise philosopher once said, the most universal problem is what to do next. It is an important source of data, not only in psychology, but in economics, political science, sociology, and in applied sciences like operations research, marketing, decision analysis, policy sciences, and conflict resolution. So the theory of such behavior is of general relevance.

One could begin the study of preference behavior by building a mathematical theory. But without its being motivated by an empirical structure in the real world, it is pure mathematics, of interest in its own right, perhaps, as new mathematics, but not as scientific theory. So I shall begin with the real world of preferential choice.

What is there to explain? In view of the importance of preference behavior, it is surprising how little understanding there is of the psychology of preference. The first question to be asked, of course, is what is there to explain? Common as it is and intimately familiar with it as we are, it is not obvious what empirical invariances there might be. The fact that Johnny likes chocolate more than vanilla and the fact that Mary would rather go to the seashore than to the mountains seem to have very little in common. And for a theory of preference, or of anything else, to be very interesting it needs to have relevance to more than an isolated event.

The recognition of a regularity is the abstraction of a property which is to some degree common. Most interesting regularities are usually somewhat irregular. They are rarely universal and rarely obvious. The perception of regularities is the creative insight of inductive reasoning. There is no known way to deduce them; this was Darwin's genius, his creative leap.

The first to have had such an insight with respect to preference behavior may have been Joseph Priestley, the discoverer of oxygen, who described the flow of pleasure and pain with temperature in the following words: ". . . a moderate degree of warmth is pleasant, and the pleasure increases with the heat to a certain degree, at which it begins to become painful; and beyond this the pain increases with the degree of heat, just as the pleasure had done before [1775, p. xvi]."

In more modern times, we would say that the course of preference for warmth may be described by a single-peaked function, a function that increases monotonically to a maximum and then decreases monotonically. By 1870, such a curve appears in Wundt's psychology textbook (see Figure 2) to describe the course of pleasantness/unpleasantness (hedonic tone) as a function of stimulus intensity. Beebe-Center refers to this curve in the following words, quoting a later edition of Wundt: "The reader is warned not to take the figure too seriously: 'As feelings, unlike sensations, are not subject to exact measurement, nothing can be said concerning the detailed form of this curve' [Beebe-Center, 1932/1966, p. 167]."

The experimental study of hedonic tone evolved into the study of preference behavior in the following 100 years, and single peakedness was recognized as occurring sometimes, but not all the time. It tended to occur with simpler stimuli rather than with more complex stimuli, but exactly when and why was not apparent.

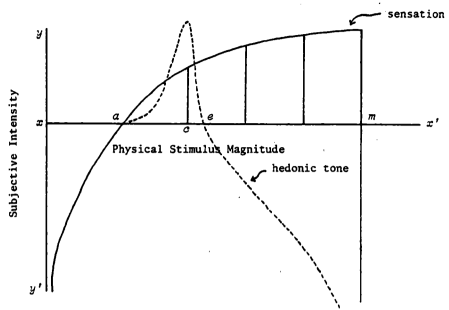

FIG. 2.   Figure 121 with English labels from Wundt (1880).

If we wish to look on single peakedness as an empirical regularity of preference behavior, then it is necessary to account not only for its occurrence but also for its failure to occur. And it is not very satisfactory to account for the failure of single peakedness by attributing it to random fluctuations in choice behavior, but rather we must specify precisely the circumstances in which it should not occur, so that the failure of single peakedness can itself be an empirical invariant. I am distinguishing here between single peakedness as a *description* of an empirical regularity and the *explanation* of single peakedness as a necessary consequence of more basic processes, in this case, hedonic processes.

As an aside, a guiding principle which might be useful in the construction of theory is that any process described by a function whose first or second derivative changes sign must require at least two elemental processes. It seems intuitively reasonable that any process described by a function with an inflection point or with a finite maximum or minimum must be the resultant of at least two underlying processes.[5] Any process

---

[5]This "insight" is nothing more than an analogy with the laws of motion in physics, in that it takes another force to change the smooth monotone path of an object in motion (see Marks, in this volume). It seems a reasonable hypothesis that the process of learning or of development reveals the influence of more than one elemental process whenever the course is changed.

described by a smoothly increasing or decreasing function may, of course, also be the joint effect of a multiplicity of processes, but without evidence the assumption of their existence is gratuitous.

Elemental hedonic processes for pleasure and pain. A simple mathematical system that could account for a single-peaked function is one in which that function is the joint effect of two elemental functions, one of which is increasing (has positive slope) the other decreasing (has negative slope) and both are negatively accelerated (concave downward) as a function of increasing stimulus magnitude. Simplicity of the mathematical postulates (Occam's razor) has something to recommend it, but better yet is direct support from behavioral science. In this case we can formulate two further empirical generalities from behavioral science in support of the mathematical assumptions that elemental utility functions are concave. One is that *good things satiate,* and the other is that *bad things escalate.*[6]

The earlier discussion of the paradigm set forth in Figure 1 was idealized (i.e., oversimplified) in that the two sides of Figure 1, the empirical and the logical, were described as if they were separate and distinct in execution, but that is rarely the case. Because there is never just one way to account logically for empirical structure, a theory becomes more interesting if the postulates in its model receive empirical support. As a consequence, theory construction is a continuous interplay between the empirical and the logical structure, and either system has veto power.

To return to single-peaked functions, one simple example is offered as an illustration. Consider an individual's preference for number of children. If a woman is asked how many children she would like to have, she usually says some modest number in preference to more or less. A preference order, for example, might be 3, 4, 2, 5, 6, 1, 0, indicating a preference for three children, with four next preferred, then two, etc., with "no children" least preferred. Note that preference is increasing from zero to three children and then decreases from three to six. How might we account for this single-peaked function?

On the one hand, children are a delight. With more children there is increased involvement, more loving, more excitement and stimulation. But the increased pleasure from each additional child tends to diminish,

[6]Aschenbrenner (1980) has pointed out the close relation between this theory and that proposed by Edgeworth (1881) for the effect of competition on the economic behavior of two individuals with contrasting goals as in the case of two contracting parties. Edgeworth proposed a "law of diminishing utility" and a "law of increasing labour" as his first two axioms. The mathematical definitions of these correspond exactly to our definitions for satiation of the good and escalation of the bad. (See, too, Maital & Maital, in Volume II.)

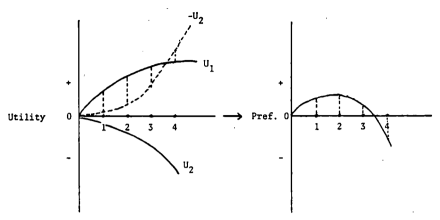

FIG. 3.   A single-peaked preference function as a consequence of optimizing good versus bad.

the novelty wears off, good things satiate. At the same time there are bad things associated with children. There are increased demands, loss of freedom and mobility, more conflict and trouble; and the magnitude of these things escalates. The joint effect of these two elemental functions is a single-peaked function as illustrated in Figure 3.

In the figure, u_1 and u_2 are the two functions representing satiation of the good and escalation of the bad, respectively; differences between them are represented by dotted lines between u_1 and $-u_2$; and these differences are represented by the single-peaked function over number of children assuming the individual optimized the differences between good and bad.

Of course what is considered good and bad in the first place is in the eyes of the beholder, and the particular shapes of the two functions u_1 and u_2 depend on numerous factors like social and economic circumstances, health, attitudes of the spouse, personal values, etc., but the hypothesis is that the general shape of the two elemental functions will be as postulated. It is easy to show mathematically that, given elemental utility functions for good and bad of the kind postulated and simple stimuli like these (in a sense to be defined), an individual's preference function will necessarily be single-peaked (Coombs & Avrunin, 1977b).

In this example, the stimulus intensity is number of children, which is one-dimensional, although, as was suggested in the example, there are any number of psychological dimensions on which children may be evaluated. Are single-peaked functions necessarily restricted to stimuli that may be described in only one dimension? Suppose, for example, that our options were some resort hotels in the mountains which differed in price and comfort. We would like to know what, if any, conditions there might be under which these options would guarantee that every individual's preference function over them would be single-peaked. This is a difficult problem to solve on an empirical or verbal level, and a logical analysis is very helpful (see Coombs, 1983). Briefly, a third principle, that *dominated options are neglected,* must be postulated; it asserts that if any resort is both more expensive and less comfortable than some other it will be neglected. Exercising this principle screens the set of options available and leaves as viable options only those which are not dominated, i.e., for every two options, each is better than the other in some respect, any option that is more expensive than another must also be more comfort- able. Such a set is illustrated in Figure 4 by the options a, b, c, and d and will be called a Pareto optimal set.

If this third principle eliminates all options but one, there is no further decision problem. If, however, two or more options survive this screening process, then the individual has a choice to make which involves a tradeoff; any gain is achieved at some cost. Unfortunately, our third principle for screening options does not insure a common ordering if there are three or more components, and hence single peakedness is not as- sured with complex stimuli.

We have seen that even in two dimensions, concave functions for the subjective effects of good and evil and an elimination principle for the screening of options to provide an ordering are not sufficient to insure that all preference functions over such options will be single-peaked. To in- sure single peakedness, then, we need stronger assumptions. The one found necessary and sufficient, given concave utility functions, is the property that the increments in the bad components from one option to another must increase as fast or faster than the increments in the good components. Such a set is called an efficient set and is illustrated in Figure 4 in the case of two components by the set of options labelled e, f, g, and h.

The distinction between requirements for an efficient set and the re- quirement for a set that is only Pareto optimal may be described in verbal terms loosely as follows. A Pareto optimal set of options is one in which increased quality is more expensive; if you pay more you get more. An efficient set is Pareto optimal and also satisfies the further condition that successive increments in quality are increasingly expensive.

The interaction of empirical generalities and mathematical reasoning. Let us review the roles that empirical structure and mathematical rea- soning play. In order to account for single-peaked preference functions in terms of more elemental processes, I proposed that an individual has negatively accelerated utility functions for the good and bad aspects of options and that he optimizes the difference between them. There is em-

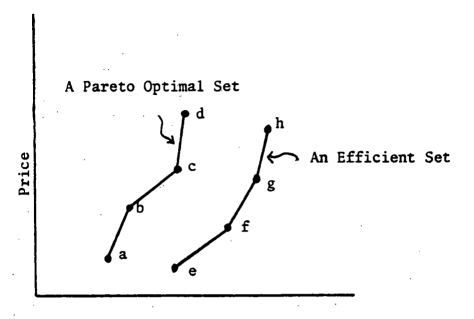

Comfort

FIG. 4.   Pareto optimal and efficient sets.

pirical support for such utility functions from two empirical generalities
which were formulated as behavioral principles, that good things satiate
and bad things escalate.

The mathematical postulates imply that preference will inevitably be
single-peaked over options that differ on only one dimension. If options
differ in two or more dimensions, however, preference functions will, in
general, not be single-peaked. What further mathematical conditions
might be imposed which would insure single peakedness over options
which differed in any number of dimensions? These are the conditions
that characterize what I called efficient sets.

There are no obvious (to me) empirical generalities in behavioral science which would insure that the mathematical conditions for efficient
sets would be satisfied, so I conclude that in the case of complex stimuli
(i.e., more than one dimension) single-peaked preference functions will
not be insured unless contrived in the laboratory. However, if an individual utilizes a suitable elimination process for screening options, the
result will be what was called a Pareto optimal set. These are sets of
options in which, of every pair of options, each is better than the other in
some respect. There is support for this elimination process in the behavioral principle that dominated options are neglected, a kind of rationality
principle.

If the options differ in exactly two dimensions, then a Pareto optimal set is ordered the same (or reversed) on both dimensions and approximates an efficient set in somewhat the same sense that an interval scale is approximated by any arbitrary transformation that preserves the rank order. Such an approximation can range from poor to excellent. In general, the better the approximation, the higher the proportion of single-peaked preference functions. So in the case of two dimensions, single-peaked functions are not insured because an efficient set of options is not insured naturally; however, a Pareto optimal set can be insured naturally, in which case single-peaked preference functions will be common.

The theory is eminently testable because an experimenter can control the selection of options. Hence, an experimenter can insure single peakedness in any dimensionality by constructing a set of options which are efficient; or avoid it in two dimensions by constructing a set of options which are not Pareto optimal. To avoid single peakedness with options in one dimension would require violating concave utility functions.

As a psychological theory in ordinary language, the three behavioral principles above might be offered to account for the occurrence of single-peaked preference functions. The theory at that level is plausible, is testable experimentally, and would sometimes, even often, appear to be right, but sometimes would be clearly false. Explanations for why it failed when it did might also be plausibly contrived; but no amount of verbal elaboration would provide a convincing analysis of why it worked when it did and why it sometimes did not.

Of course, the assumptions about the processing of pleasure and pain (concave functions) are not invariably true. In particular, the assumption that bad things escalate is false if one adapts. Mathematical analysis reveals, however, that there are conditions under which adaptation to bad will also yield single-peaked functions; this will occur when the adaptation (deceleration) proceeds more slowly than satiation.

There is more that could be said here about the theory of preference that would illustrate some other aspects of the process of building formal theory in psychology, but this has been sufficient to illustrate the interplay of AMI and T in the schema of Figure 1 at a more than trivial level. We have seen the distinction between the *description* of single peakedness as an empirical phenomenon and the *explanation* of single peakedness as a consequence of the nature of hedonic processes.

A simpler example could certainly have been found, but it might also leave the reader with the impression that the use of mathematics is all well and good on simple problems, but that it cannot be used on complex or substantial problems. Behavioral theory seeks to explain observed behavior in terms of more elemental components. This is not to say that complex behavior may not be derived from equally or more complex behavior, but to avoid circularity of reasoning there must be a more elemental level from which the more complex behavior may be derived. So, also, the theorems of a mathematical system may become the postulates of another system, forming a hierarchy of theorems.

It is time to begin to see mathematical modeling in a larger perspective. It should be evident that exploration and development of a theory is not the exclusive task of the mathematician nor the empiricist. Either path of the schema of Figure 1 could lead to new insight, and neither path is ultimately sufficient. Indeed, even the path of the model builder, the AMI of Figure 1, does not belong exclusively to the mathematician. Biological explanations for these empirical generalities are as desirable as mathematical ones (see Uttal, in this volume). This aspect of model building is discussed later.

The Case of Measurement Theory

Empirical measurement structures surely have been with us ever since the first men started trading with each other. The systems worked very well and did not attract a great deal of intellectual attention. It is only when a difficulty arises, as when one wants to measure attention or intention or other psychological or sociological variables, and the conventional measurement structures are not effective or are impossible to apply, that it becomes important to understand just why the familiar procedures work so well. A previously unmotivated and esoteric line of research becomes valuable and goes public.

The empirical structures of measurement are among the simplest in nature and are now well understood. As Margeneau put it, measurement is the first contact between reason and nature. Although some of the ideas go back to Grassmann (1854) and Helmholtz (1887), the period from Norman Campbell's book of 1920/1957 to the volume by Krantz, Luce, Suppes, and Tversky in 1971 essentially spans the era of what might be called sophisticated measurement theory, and it continues to develop more deeply and more widely. This work is perhaps the deepest use of mathematics in psychology, and its influence is pervasive and will probably become more so. Many psychological theories, when reduced to their logical structure and stripped of their real world vocabulary, are measurement systems, and closely interrelated ones at that.[7]

Measurement theory in psychology is behavior theory. In psychological measurement, the individual is the measuring device; he plays the role of the pan balance, the meter stick, or the thermometer. Psychological measurement theory is concerned with the empirical regularities in his

---

[7] See Coombs and Lehner (1981) for a number of instances of psychological theories which have the same mathematical structure, in this case the bilinear model.

behavior which justify numerical assignments to the stimuli he is responding to and/or justify numerical assignments to him.

We recognize immediately that a psychological measurement theory is
a behavioral theory (see Marks, in this volume). Certain of the axioms of a
mathematical system for measurement are principles of behavior which
are assumed to describe and characterize that behavior. Many psychological measurement procedures or devices, however, assign numbers
with no known theoretical basis to justify them. To the extent that they
"work," that they exhibit consistencies, both internal and external, they
are important. Stevens's (1946) work with the methods of magnitude and
ratio estimation and the power law is a case in point. It may be put in
perspective in terms of the schema of Figure 1. This work, although very
mathematical, is for the most part, an instance of the process T, involving
empirical regularities, laws, and the descriptive use of mathematics. Such
work is exceedingly important to psychological science because it is
knowledge about behavior. Its limitation, as is always the case for knowledge obtained through the process T, is that explanation is reached inductively and is fallible.

Without secure knowledge of what makes a system work there is no
deep understanding of its limitations, of when it can be expected not to
work, or of how to improve it. Some of the skepticism and resistance to
the use of magnitude and ratio estimation is due in large part to the
absence of testable conditions which would provide a logical justification
for the use of such numbers. The application of the methods to social
psychophysics (Steven, 1966) strains even further what one is asked to
believe without being able to test.

Krantz (1972) attacked the problem of justifying magnitude and ratio
estimation by contrasting the views of two possible theories; one is that a
subject's judgments are mediated by sensations evoked by the stimuli,
and the other is that the judgments are mediated by perceived relations
between stimuli. His axiomatic development of the two theories provides
a deeper analysis than is available anywhere else in the literature of the
concept of sensation and its numerical representation.

Measurement theorists will approach a problem from their knowledge
of what makes a measurement system work, and they will look for an
empirical structure which will assure a measurement system. Unfortunately, there is no reason to expect that such a search will always be
successful. Not everything that one would like to measure is measurable,
and not all possible measurement systems are known.

The historical pattern in the development of measurement theory can
teach us something of the interrelation of the two approaches, one approach being that through empirical relations and invariances and the
other through what we know of the logical structures of measurement

systems, T and AMI respectively (Figure 1). Discussion of the development of measurement theory will be in the context of Figure 5,
which is merely a restatement of the beginning of chapter 1 of Krantz et
al. (1971).

Measurement systems. Measurement systems can be classified in
terms of two dichotomies. One dichotomy is that of an ordinal relation or
a counting process. The other is whether the elements (units) are objects
or differences between objects.
, Most all measurement before measurement theory was based on the
counting process. A person's fortune could be expressed by counting
ducats and an interval of time by swings of a pendulum, well known as
ratio scales and interval scales, respectively. Such measurements also
satisfy ordinal scales, of course, but a weaker scale is a poor relation
when the counting process is available with a constant unit.
    The beginning of measurement theory was the recognition of the depen-
dency of the counting process on an empirical structure which includes a
concatenation operation. This takes us back to our shepherd who was
counting piles of stones and clusters of sheep. Let us suppose he also has
a pan balance and observes that one stone is heavier than another, and he
places it on his left and the other on his right. Then suppose he does the
same for another pair of stones. We know from experience that if the two
stones on his left are placed together on the left side of the pan balance
and the two lighter ones on his right are placed on the other side of the pan
balance, then the pan will dip to the left. An incredibly trivial observation
and seemingly not worthy of the attention given it here, but, as we shall
see, the contrary is the case.
    The real world operation is "empirical addition," and for such a system
to justify an additive numerical assignment (the weight of the stones) this
concatenation operation must be compatible with the order relation, i.e.,
it must be order preserving. If, for example, we let $x > y$ signify that the
pan balance indicates that x is heavier than y, then $x > y$ and $v > w$
together imply that $x \oplus v > y \oplus w$, where $\oplus$ indicates the concatenation
operation of putting two stones together on the same side of the pan
balance. This is a necessary prerequisite for what Campbell (1920/1957)
called "extensive measurement," an example of "fundamental measurement," which is measurement not dependent on the prior assignment
of numbers, but on qualitative empirical relations.
    This requirement clearly raises serious difficulties for psychology. The
inability in general to achieve empirical addition in psychology led a committee of the British Association for the Advancement of Science to the
conclusion that fundamental measurement is not possible in psychology
(Pfanzagel, 1959; Stevens, 1946). The committee was appointed in 1932

	Ordinal Relation	Counting Process
Objects as Units	**(1)** Ranking athletic teams, Election systems. Ordinal Scales	**(2)** Campbellian fundamental measurement Ratio Scales
Differences as units	**(4)** Preference theory, Similarity data analysis, Finite conjoint measurement Ordered metric scales	**(3)** Time and Temperature, Luce and Tukey con-joint measurement Interval scales

FIG. 5.   A classification of measurement systems.

and directed its attention to Stevens's sone scale of loudness. The committee had 19 members drawn from mathematics, physics (including N. R. Campbell), and psychology; it issued a final report in 1940. Stevens's account of the report was that the committee was split widely, but in the final report one member said, "I submit that any law purporting to express a quantitative relation between sensation intensity and stimulus intensity is not merely false, but is in fact meaningless, unless and until a meaning can be given to the concept of addition as applied to sensation [Stevens, 1946, p. 677]."

Because quantification and the development of science have gone hand in hand, the outlook for psychology appeared dismal. Today, with the development of conjoint measurement theory, there is new life in psychological measurement. Conjoint measurement theory literally restored the operation of empirical addition to behavioral science, with the recognition that it was there all the time. This recognition was the insightful interpretation of an experimental design as a concatenation of differences. This interpretation, as far as I know, was first made by Adams and Fagot (1956, 1959), and it played a seminal role in the formal development of conjoint measurment theory by Luce and Tukey (1964), who recognized the generality and the importance of the insight for behavioral science.

Let us see how this interpretation comes about. Consider the 3 × 3 design presented in Figure 6. There are two factors, A and P, with three levels of each, and their effect on the dependent variable increasing in the direction of the vertical and horizontal arrows as shown.

We could, of course, make this example real and concrete by referring to A as incentive and P as probability of success, and ask an individual to order his preferences on the nine combinations corresponding to the nine cells in the figure. Or we could let A and P be wines and cheeses, or food and water deprivation, or speed and difficulty of a task, etc. As soon as we make the experiment concrete, however, many issues irrelevant at this point may arise, such as whether the data are individual or group data, the control of other relevant variables, and so on. By keeping the example abstract, we keep it general and simple, and we can concentrate on what is essential.

In this example, then, we assume that the experimenter has observed the behavior, the dependent variable, induced by each combination of a level of A and a level of P, the independent variables, and that the cells may be ordered in that for any two cells, say 2 and 4 in the figure, it has been observed that the performance in cell 4 is superior to the performance in cell 2, as indicated by the arrow between the two cells. The recognition of what the direction of that arrow means, and the exploitation of that meaning is what set off the modern view of fundamental measurement in behavioral science; so let's take a close look at it.

The experimenter, in going from cell 2 to cell 4, has increased the effect of factor A from A_1 to A_2 and at the same time has decreased the effect of factor P from P_2 to P_1. The joint effect of these two changes was to improve performance.

If performance is an increasing function of A and of P, then to increase one and decrease the other will have a joint effect that depends on the relative magnitude of the two changes. In this case, the indication is that the effect of the increase in factor A has overcome the depressing effect of the decrease in P. Analogously, a specific change in one factor has been placed on one side of a pan balance and "weighed" against a specific change in another factor, and the pan balance has indicated which is greater in their respective effects on the performance.

The comparison between cells 6 and 8 is similar. Here the change from cell 6 to 8 is an increase in A from A_2 to A_3, and a decrease in P from P_3 to P_2, and here the performance indicates that this particular change in A is greater than that particular change in P.

Fundamental measurement, however, requires a concatenation operation and that it be compatible with the ordering. If we compare cell 3 with

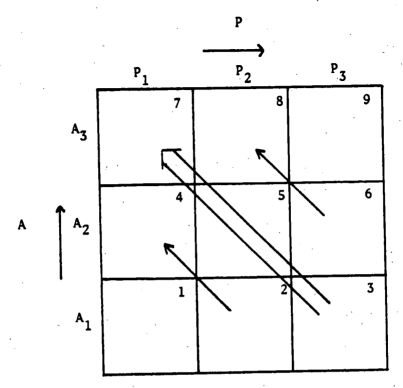

FIG. 6.   A 3 × 3 design and the comparison of differences.

cell 7, we see that we have the change from A_1 to A_3 on one side of the pan balance and the change from P_3 to P_1 on the other side. The comparison of those two cells, 3 and 7, is a comparison of the joint effect of the two changes in A pitted against the joint effect of the two changes in P.

This comparison, we see, has in it the implicit concatenation of two differences in A and also of two differences in P. Clearly, for the concatenation operation to be order preserving, the performance in cell 7 must be superior to that in cell 3, and so the two previous comparisons require that this comparison go in the direction indicated by the double arrow in the figure. If this fails to be the case, then these two factors cannot be measured on scales which add up to provide a measurement of the performance.

This condition is called a *cancellation condition* and is a necessary condition for additivity of A and P. If this condition is violated it means that the independent variables interact and that the interaction is inherent in the sense that it cannot be removed by monotone transformations of the scales. Interaction that is scale dependent is, in general, of little interest in theoretical psychology.

There is much that has been left out, and the story is far from finished. Conjoint measurement may be said to begin with R. A. Fisher (1935) with the development of analysis of variance. But it was not until after World War II that a clear statement of the interpretation described above was made and not until 1964 that conjoint measurement became an entity. After that, development was exceedingly rapid, and by 1971 the theory had been extensively developed both in breadth and depth (Krantz et al., 1971).

Conjoint measurement as Luce and Tukey (1964) originally developed it falls in the third cell of Figure 5, the counting of differences. They added sufficient mathematical structure to the cancellation condition (illustrated by Figure 6) to insure that equal units existed and could be counted and thereby yield an additive representation. This meant that numerical assignments would exist for the factors A and P which would add to yield numerical assignments to the cells that would preserve the empirically observed ordering.

If all the conditions are satisfied, then interval scale measurement of the independent variables and the dependent variable simultaneously is justified in principle. The Luce and Tukey conditions are called a set of sufficient conditions because they imply (guarantee) the existence of such measures.

In conjoint measurement it is intervals, changes, differences, that are on the two sides of the pan balance or are being laid end to end; and it is differences, then, that are being counted and hence measured on a ratio scale. But a ratio scale of differences is preserved under translation, and so our uniqueness level in such a system is reduced to that of an interval scale.

A set of sufficient conditions, not all of which are necessary, is not as desirable as a set of conditions that are both necessary and sufficient. Both Scott (1964) and Tversky (1964) independently provided axiomatic conditions which were both necessary and sufficient for the finite case. With such a system the existence of an additive representation proves that the axioms are satisfied, so even if the axioms are not directly testable they are indirectly testable by showing that an additive representation does exist. The uniqueness of an additive representation, if one exists, is that of an ordered metric scale and falls in the fourth cell of Figure 5 involving order relations between differences (see Lehner & Noma, 1980; McClelland & Coombs, 1975).

The role of AMI in the discovery of empirical addition in behavior. This account has singled out the role of concatenation in the development of measurement theory. It was first explicitly recognized by Campbell as an essential ingredient in fundamental measurement. Its apparent absence in social science and psychology seemed to render fundamental measurement impossible. Then it was recognized that it did exist, but in modified form. We see that mathematical reasoning and the search for empirical structure play mutually dependent roles, but it is not always so easy to separate them so clearly.

We note, in this account of the development of the fundamental measurement of behavior, that new experimental findings and observable behavior have not changed, but rather new insights have arisen in particular the interpretation of a certain kind of behavior as relations on differences. An understanding of the role of such relations in measurement has led to the generalization of fundamental measurement as found in the physical sciences to a weaker form applicable in behavioral science, from ratio scales to interval and ordered metric scales.

Fundamental measurement of mass and distance, for example, was possible on the real world level long before it was understood. Then, when the logical structure of such measurement came to be understood, this made possible the recognition of a concatenation operation in factorial designs, and from that came the generalization of fundamental measurement to behavioral science. The point here is that the empirical structure that could justify fundamental measurement in behavioral science was not recognized, or even looked for, until the logical analysis of the empirical structure that supported conventional measurement provided guidance. This development was a product of the human intellect, a result of both deductive and inductive reasoning, leading to the recognition and use of empirical structure that was there all the time.

Knowing something of the logical structure necessary for a system to operate is a guide to the kind of empirical invariances to look for. Much, if not most, of psychological research is devoted to a search for empirical regularities, and as a science advances the empirical regularities that are the substance for theory become more and more subtle, and more and more difficult to detect. Monotonic relationships are always the most obvious, but are not diagnostic of fine structure. This point is basic to Dawes and Corrigan's (1974) explanation for the robustness of linear models. When dependent variables are a monotone function of independent variables, it is the tradeoffs between the variables that are diagnostic and discriminate between theories; and the tradeoffs can be easily obscured by the overwhelming impact of the linear fit to monotonicity.

This account of the history of measurement illustrates another aspect of the interrelation between psychology and mathematics. Sometimes the mathematics can be ahead of empirical knowledge and sometimes the reverse. There is a continuous flow back and forth. If the mathematics is not there, the behavioral system requires the creation of new mathematics. An example of this is the stimulus given to the development of graph theory by the collaboration between Cartwright and Harary (1956) in applying graph theory to social interaction, an instance in which mathematical development and empirical research proceeded together. (See also Roberts, 1976, for a number of specific instances of this cyclic inter-relation.)

I remarked at the beginning of this section on measurement theory that a measurement theory is a behavior theory. In the abstract, of course, it is not a theory about a particular behavior, but when it is applied to a data matrix then it becomes a theory about the behavior that generated that data matrix.

Conjoint measurement is simply an extension of measurement theory to a dependent variable that is a function of more than one independent variable, simultaneously contributing to or affecting the behavior. It is, for the most part, limited to models in which the joint effect of two or more variables can be expressed in terms of addition and multiplication. It is striking how adequately these mathematical operations capture our deepest thoughts about behavior.

It is the extension of measurement theory to dependent variables that are a function of several independent variables which makes abstract measurement theory of so much value to theoretical psychologists. Although mathematical psychologists are a diverse lot, they have in common a commitment to a common language for disciplined thinking. Substantively they go many different ways, but the abstract language of mathematics makes communication and cross–fertilization easy and stimulating.

The Case of Probabilistic Choice Behavior

In the following examples, aspects of the schema in Figure 1 will be brought out to emphasize the use of mathematical models to guide experimental design and to anticipate and explain invariances. Important as these aspects are, a perhaps greater one is the capability which theory cast in mathematical form has for integrating and unifying apparently incompatible empirical regularities.

There are many substantive areas from which examples could be drawn to serve these purposes. For instance, the literature on stimulus sampling theory, initiated and largely developed by Estes (1950), could be used to illustrate these same aspects of mathematical psychology, especially in the detection of unsuspected regularities and its richness in inspiring new experiments. The stochastic approach is of particular value in the modelling of dynamic processes and when introduced opened up the study of learning and forgetting, for example, to a finer grain analysis than ever before possible. At our current level of knowledge, the ability of a theory to generate new experiments leading to new empirical regularities is probably its greatest asset.

Another area is that of signal detectability theory (SDT), which is an application of statistical decision theory. SDT is a mathematical theory built by engineers to detect submarines underwater using sonar (Peterson, Birdsall, & Fox, 1954). Its potential for psychology was recognized early by Tanner and Swets (1954) and was translated into a theory of psychophysical discrimination and decision making in a noisy environment. This is an instance in which a ready-made mathematical system was transported into an empirical domain completely unrelated to that which gave rise to it and provided significant theory—a quite rare event. One very important aspect of signal detectability theory is the distinction it is able to make between the individual as a sensory device and as a decision maker. The one involves his sensitivity as a discriminator, and the other involves his tradeoff between costs and benefits.

The impact of these two theories—stochastic learning theory and signal detectability theory—on psychological research has never been assessed; however, I would not be surprised if they would rate among the top half-dozen in the history of scientific psychology.

Both of these theories are also examples of the important role probabilistic models play in mathematical psychology. In this section I shall confine my examples to some other models of probabilistic choice behavior, in part because they provide some continuity with what has been discussed in previous sections and because they reveal something of the cumulative strength of mathematics in psychological theory.

Intransitivity of preference and weak stochastic transitivity. I begin this discussion of probabilistic models with Tversky's (1969) study of intransitivity of preference. A fundamental property necessary for all measurement theory and scaling algorithms is algebraic transitivity. It is not entirely uncommon, however, for an experimental subject to say he prefers option A to B at one moment, to prefer B to C at another moment, and then to say he prefers C to A at still another moment. Such behavior appears even in the apparent absence of changes in the course of the experiment in conditions which could affect preferences.

It is not unreasonable that the occurrence of an intransitivity could reflect momentary fluctuations in the choice process. This leads rather naturally to the concept of defining choice behavior probabilistically.

The probabilistic version of x being preferred at least as much as y is defined as the probability of choosing x over y being at least as great as one-half,

$$x \geq y \text{ iff } p(x,y) \geq \tfrac{1}{2}.$$

The probabilistic version of algebraic transitivity then becomes:

$$p(x,y) \geq \tfrac{1}{2} \text{ and } p(y,z) \geq \tfrac{1}{2} \rightarrow p(x,z) \geq \tfrac{1}{2},$$

a condition or property called weak stochastic transitivity (WST). In words, if x is usually chosen over y, and y is usually chosen over z, then x will be usually chosen over z.

With choice behavior assumed to be probabilistic, intransitive choice would be expected to occur in the normal course of events, but be unpredictable. Tversky (1969, p. 32), in reviewing the literature, reports that "no conclusive violations of WST have been demonstrated in studies of preferences, although Morrison (1962) provided some evidence for predictable intransitivities in judgments of relative numerosity." In his paper Tversky reports two experiments in which he obtained systematic violations of WST for probabilistic choice. The problem, then, is what type of choice theory can explain and predict systematic violations.

Tversky developed and contrasted two models, originally suggested by Morrison, for evaluating alternatives which are multidimensional. In the first model, the utility of an alternative is a simple (weighted) sum of the individual's utility for each of its components. This is called the additive model, and if each alternative is evaluated in this fashion, then the utilities associated with them would necessarily lead to transitive choice. The second model involves a different processing strategy. Here the individual is assumed to compare two alternatives on one component at a time, assess the advantage in utility of one alternative over the other on that component, and then sum up these component-wise differences over all the components. This is called the additive difference model.

Tversky showed that under certain conditions the additive difference model could yield systematic intransitivities. This theoretical analysis has shifted the emphasis from an interest in intransitive preference per se to an interest in the decision process more generally. This analysis of processing strategies suggests how to run an experiment so that systematic intransitivities can be observed and how they may be avoided. If probabilities need to be assessed, for example, the display and instructions to the subject need to be carefully controlled in a manner that is now understood. It would have been difficult to have reached this understanding inductively, from observation alone.

Intransitive preference, before Tversky (1969), was a very irregular phenomenon and seriously doubted to be more than random fluctuation in probabilistic choice. Tversky's paper made it an empirical regularity, the causes of which could be studied experimentally in their own right or removed from concern, depending on experimental procedures and the objectives of the experimenter.

Transitivity of preference and moderate stochastic transitivity. In the next example, a model implied the existence of an empirical regularity not previously suspected. The best known and most widely used models of probabilistic choice for scaling stimuli are Thurstone's (1927) Law of

Comparative Judgment (Case V) and Luce's (1959) BTL model (in defer-ence to Bradley & Terry, 1952, who had proposed a relation of pairwise probabilities to stimulus scale values that Luce derived from basic princi-ples and generalized).

Principles common to both of these models are that pairwise prob-abilities are transformed in a strictly monotone fashion into distances between stimuli on a scale and that two stimuli are assigned the same scale value if and only if the probability of choosing one over the other is one half, i.e., $v(x) = v(y)$ iff $p(x,y) = \frac{1}{2}$.

The magnitude of a pairwise choice probability would seem to have a natural interpretation as a strength of choice, i.e., if $p(x,y) > p(v,w) > \frac{1}{2}$ then x is more strongly preferred over y than v is over w. This interpreta-tion goes back to Fechner and was also made by Thorndike in 1915 when he was building scales for educational evaluation, such as a scale for assessing the quality of handwriting. He used teachers' pair-comparison judgments on specimens of handwriting and assumed that equally often noticed differences are equal (unless always or never noticed).

The property of probabilistic choice behavior described above is known as strong stochastic transitivity (SST) and is defined as follows:

$$p(x,y) \geqslant \tfrac{1}{2} \text{ and } p(y,z) \geqslant \tfrac{1}{2} \rightarrow p(x,z) \geqslant \max\,[p(x,y),\,p(y,z)].$$

In words, if x is usually chosen over y, and y is usually chosen over z, then x will usually be chosen over z at least as often as x over y or as y over z, whichever is larger.

The psychological idea behind SST is that if $p(x,y)$ is a measure of the strength of choice of x over y, then it should be reflected in the scale values of x and y, the greater the probability the greater the difference between the scale values—a most reasonable idea. This is one of the conditions that is a necessary condition for Thurstone's Case V, as well as for the BTL model.

It comes then as something of a shock that SST is not necessarily true empirically and, indeed, that it is a reasonable idea that SST should not hold. The unfolding theory model for preferential choice is based on the existence of single-peaked preference functions, the theory of which was discussed above. In exploring the possibility of a probabilistic version of unfolding theory, it became evident that SST should, in general, be vio-lated by probabilistic preferential choice under a theory of singled-peaked preference functions and a Thurstonian type of discriminal process theory (see below). A full explanation of this implication is provided in Coombs (1958, 1964/1976).

Psychophysical choice theory and strong stochastic transitivity. A final example from probabilistic choice behavior is one which brings out the power of abstraction to clarify what is and what is not distinguishable in the conceptualization behind different theories and which illustrates the role of general principles. Here I shall try to convey the implications of some of the work of several mathematical psychologists on Thurstonian models of psychophysical choice and to demonstrate the cumulative character of this work.

The conceptualization behind Thurstone's Law of Comparative Judgment was that each stimulus, when presented, drew a sample (of size one, in Thurstone's original conceptualization) from a distribution of discriminal processes (levels of possible sensation magnitude) on each trial. The individual then compared the discriminal processes aroused by the two stimuli on a given trial, and his response indicated which was greater. Thurstone assumed that the distribution of the discriminal processes for each stimulus was normal and (for Case V) that they had equal variances and were uncorrelated.

Of course, distributions other than the normal are possible, and arguments might be made for choosing one or another, but the important characteristic here is that the Thurstone Case V model calls for independently identically–distributed discriminal processes (except for translation) as a conceptual structure underlying psychophysical discrimination. Accordingly, I shall follow Yellott (1977) and call a model a Thurstone model if the distribution of discriminal processes is any of a very large class of distributions and the model satisfied these Case V conditions otherwise.

The BTL model as developed by Luce comes out of a completely different conceptual structure. What Luce did was simply to assume that probabilistic choice behavior obeyed the axioms of probability including the axiom of conditional probability interpreted in real world terms. In simple language, he assumed that the probability of choosing an alternative out of a larger set of alternatives is independent of the (sequence of) partitionings of the larger set.

So we have two theories of psychophysical choice. The Thurstonian Case V type theory conceives of discrimination behavior as a result of a process comparing discriminal processes independently and randomly chosen from their respective distributions which differ only in a single parameter, the mean. And Luce's individual choice model conceives of discrimination as probabilistic behavior that satisfies the axioms of probability. They both are psychological theories about behavior and not purely mathematical theories. The theories are conceptually quite different. In fact, the Thurstonian type model has been described (Luce & Suppes, 1965) as a random utility model and Luce's as a constant utility model: the idea being that in a Thurstonian model, the relation between the discriminal processes associated with each stimulus determines the judgment of which is greater, but the discriminal processes are random variables and so the judgment is probabilistic, i.e., the uncertainty is in the utilities; in

Luce's model the utilities associated with the stimuli are constants but the relation between them merely determines the probability of the judgment of which is greater, i.e., the uncertainty is in the decision process.

The complete story of the interrelations of these models is an interesting one in its own right but complicated and technical, and again I shall omit the details. Three steps reveal that the BTL model for data from certain kinds of experiments is indistinguishable from a random utility model that satisfied Thurstonian Case V conditions. So the conceptualization that led Luce to his constant utility model is equivalent to a conceptualization in the form of a random utility model in certain kinds of experiments.

The difficulty of discriminating between the models experimentally and their closely related conceptualizations as random utility theories discourages discrimination between them by making it appear unnecessary and unimportant. From the point of view of the objective of obtaining scale values, i.e. getting numbers which can serve some useful purpose, the attitude is well founded. But to many psychologists, such difficulties are merely obstacles in the search for truth. When measurement theories are recognized as behavior theories, then choosing between them takes on a different aspect than merely goodness-of-fit.

I shall digress here for a paragraph. Two different points of view are being contrasted which in their extreme form may be distinguished in terms of whether the end justifies the means or whether the means justifies the end. For practical purposes the end may justify the means. For theoretical purposes, this is unacceptable; the means justifies the end. If a scale is desired to serve some useful purpose we have the former case, which may be well served by goodness-of-fit tests. When behavioral principles are at issue then we have the latter case in which the numbers that may be obtained are less important than their justification. Although measurement may sometimes be justified by the purpose it serves, this principle is so subject to abuse that it must never be the sole justification. Thus, these conceptually different theories are difficult to distinguish by conventional tests of goodness-of-fit, and mathematical analysis reveals why certain kinds of experiments are futile in attempting to distinguish between them.

Yellott (1977), pursuing a question raised by Luce, constructed a behavioral principle that distinguishes the random utility conceptualization of the BTL model from all other Thurstonian models. He showed that, under the assumption that some Thurstonian model must be true, then a general principle of probabilistic choice that implies Luce's choice axiom and all the equivalent alternatives to it is the following: that the choice probabilities must be invariant under uniform expansion of the choice set. Paraphrasing Yellott's example, this is to say that the probability of choosing a cup of coffee out of a set that consists of a cup of coffee, a cup of tea, and a glass of milk, must be invariant over expansion of the set to any number n of cups of coffee, cups of tea, and glasses of milk. In other words, if there were a hundred of each type, the probability of picking an alternative of any one type would be unchanged. This work of Yellott provides an explanation for an empirical regularity, the constant ratio rule, and a possible experimental test for assessing whether probabilistic behavior would satisfy the axioms of probability. This is another instance of the deeper pursuit of basic principles of behavior which have consequences for both application and cumulative theory, a necessary part of any science.

We recognize that it is always the deductive implications of a model that are tested and not the conceptualization behind it. If a model is rejected the conceptualization that led to it is thereby rejected, but to whatever degree a model is supported, the support for the conceptualization is always weaker. So a conceptualization is never as well supported by the data as the model is.

This helps to make clear why the axiom system is so useful to the behavioral theorist. To axiomatize a theory ideally is to dissect it into independent pieces which can be tested to see which pieces are safe to preserve in projections, extensions, and modifications. When a mathematical system is unacceptable it may only require modification in part of the axiom system. With testable postulates it is easier to diagnose the incorrect assumptions and build on what is not rejected. For peace of mind, however, it is probably necessary to keep in mind that ideals may be impossible to achieve.

One of the values of the mathematical analysis of a theory is that it may direct attention away from what is futile, e.g. trying to discriminate between different theories on the basis of experiments that cannot distinguish.

POWER AND GENERALITY OF THEORIES

From time to time I have used the term domain with reference to a theory without any indication of the importance of the role it plays. The domain of a mathematical model is its set of elements. The axiom system and what follows from it deductively are, then, what is true of that domain.

When a segment of the real world is mapped into that model, the model becomes a theory about that segment of the real world and that segment is the domain of the theory. The domain is the set of experiments for which the theory is true; so the domain of a theory is a matter of empirical research and inductive generalization.

A theory, A, is said to be less general than another, B, if the domain of A is a proper subset of the domain of B, that is, its domain is included in that of B but does not exhaust it. Another attribute which every theory possesses is its strength or power. We say that a theory B is weaker than a theory A if all of B's implications are a proper subset of A's; that is, if A says everything B does and more, we would say that A is a more powerful theory.

Both *power* and *generality* are desirable, so one theory may dominate another if it is at least as general and at least as powerful and exceeds the other in one of these. But two theories in which one is more powerful and the other has a broader domain are Pareto optimal in the sense discussed above and so both are viable theories.[8]

It is inevitable and natural that this should be. Any implication that a theory has for a domain must be true of all its instances. A theory of paired-associate learning is going to have a different domain from a theory of concept formation, but a theory that covers both domains will inevitably be less powerful than either of them. Otherwise, it would dominate one of them, and the dominated theory would cease to be viable. So a theory builder faces a tradeoff between saying more about less or saying less about more.

Consider, for example, the plight of an experimenter who has just confirmed a theory. What is there left for him to do? He can either seek to strengthen the theory so that it says more about the same domain or seek to widen the domain of the theory so that it says the same but about more things.

The experimenter who has just done an experiment that rejects a theory is in an analogous plight. He can weaken the theory so that it says less about the same domain or reduce the domain to exclude the instances in which the theory does not hold.

It is not uncommon to disparage theory that is weak and general and to disparage theory that is powerful but has a very limited domain. Although understandable, in my opinion neither evaluation is always justified. As domains get more inclusive, there are fewer significant things to say. For example, the more integrative an elementary text, the more trite and

---

[8] An instance of the value of both general theories and powerful ones, and a very practical instance, is medical diagnosis. Peter Politser (personal communication) has pointed out that a diagnosis (a disease) is a theory about a set of empirical observations (the symptoms). Generality is important in the initial stages to rule out general categories (such as infectious versus metabolic diseases) and to avoid missing important ones; and power is terribly important in the later stages (such as viral versus bacterial pneumonia) so that treatment can be most effective.

obvious it must inevitably be. On the other hand, the more it wants to say, the narrower the domain becomes and hence the less popular it will be as an introductory text. However, both texts have an audience.

At one extreme is the generalist who can speak in global terms about everything to anyone but says very little. And at the other extreme is the specialist who has his own language, speaks to very few, and has a great deal to say about very little. The goal of the search for knowledge is to say a great deal about everything, but at any point in time the state of the art makes it possible to say more only about less.

An example of this tradeoff is found in some of the issues that I have already discussed. In Thurstone's Case V and the BTL model, we have powerful theories leading, for example, to interval or ratio scale representations of stimuli, so that the scale differences between stimuli will reflect strength of choice. But the domain of those theories does not include strength of preferential choice because the laterality effect on pairwise probabilities results in the violation of SST and hence removes preference behavior from their domain. To expand the domain to include preference behavior may reduce the strength of the scales to ordered metric scales and a corresponding weakening of interpretation in terms of strength of preference. A stronger interpretation is equivalent to assuming existence of empirical regularities which have not been demonstrated.

Another example is found in the measurement of attitudes. A set of attitude statements may be ordered the same from pro to con for people with certain demographic characteristics, but if the differences between statements were also assessed for these individuals, there would be fewer who would also agree on the ordering of the differences. The ordered metric scale is stronger than the ordinal and cannot be more general.

One may increase the value of a theory by either increasing its power or its generality, if it can be done without cost to the other. The discussion of single-peaked functions for preference was in the context of resolving an approach-avoidance conflict in choosing among alternatives. That theory is readily extended to include approach-approach and avoidance-avoidance conflicts which expand the domain with no loss of power, and the increased generality increases the value of the theory.

It is not uncommon for a behavioral theory to be somewhat ambiguous about its domain. The result is that an experiment usually can be performed which will support it and another experiment will disconfirm it. The value of such experiments is to be found in the implications they may have for the boundaries of the domain rather than an overall acceptance or rejection of the theory.

The problem of how to define the boundaries of a domain, especially in social and behavioral science, is subtle and complex. Guttman's facet theory (see Shye, 1978) is, I believe, the only substantial attempt to pro-vide a general theory for characterizing domains; in this sense, it is a metatheory. As behavioral science advances so will the need for such theory.

The ambiguity about the domain of a theory is the source of some of the criticism levelled at the use of mathematical models. Slatkin in reviewing a book on genetics of altruism refers to a fault of many mathematical models in evolutionary theory which he calls an "hourglass effect":

> First, a problem of real evolutionary importance is presented and discussed. Second, a model or class of models, which are very special and restrictive in their assumptions, is introduced. This is the point at which the mathematics takes over . . . finally, the results from the narrow models are expanded into conclusions of grand importance with respect to the problem originally pro-posed [Slatkin, 1980, pp. 633–634].

This criticism is not restricted to mathematical models in evolutionary theory but mathematical models for any empirical system. Indeed, it is by no means peculiar to mathematical models. Overgeneralization is a com-mon fault or danger in the application of any theory. Perhaps mathe-matical models are especially vulnerable to such criticism because of the visibility and precision of the assumptions; when they are misused it is readily detected. It would be unfortunate if this became a fault rather than a virtue.

THEORY LANGUAGES IN PSYCHOLOGY

Models are as important and as inevitable in psychology as logical con-sistency is in science. A model, whether it is mathematical or otherwise, is an analogy for another system, and by virtue of knowing something about the analogy we presume we know something about the other sys-tem. Reasoning by analogy is probably the most common form of rea-soning there is, in spite of being generally recognized as risky. One reason for its riskiness lies in the lack of precision in the correspondence that is drawn between the two systems, as represented by process A in Figure 1, and the correspondence may be inaccessible or incomplete. Some analogies are so poorly drawn as to be worthless except as Sunday sup-plement psychology, e.g. the aphorisms "as the twig is bent so grows the tree" and "like father like son" may be contradictory[9], so as analogies

---

[9]"Absence makes the heart grow fonder" and "out of sight, out of mind" are another pair, suggested by Marc Bornstein (personal communication).

they may be used to account for anything. One of the strengths of a good model lies in the precision with which the correspondence is drawn.

Any system in the real world can serve as an analogy—a model—for another system; mathematics is not the only theory language. Assuming that any real world system that works is inherently logically consistent, then it can serve as a model and do our reasoning for us. The "behavior," i.e. events in the model, play the same role as the theorems of the mathematical model. For example, an electrical wiring diagram or an hydraulic system with pumps, pipes, reservoirs, and filters might be designed as a model for a theory of motivation or a model of the galvanic skin response (see Chapanis, in this volume).

Generally speaking, physical models like these are not taken seriously as literal behavioral models, but are used as an intermediate step for illustrating or clarifying subsequent mathematical analysis or to make it more readily imaginable. A computer program is another case in point, and for complex systems involving many variables it is preeminently practical. A limitation of such models is that one does not always know the principles (axioms, laws, postulates, empirical regularities) from which the behavior of the system is derived, in which case one does not have explanation but description. Axioms permit localizing weaknesses and strengths in an explanatory model.

Psychology, however, has a natural affinity for biological models because they have the great advantage of feeling closer to the reality of what must be "going on," at least for individual behavior. Examples may be found in the study of sensory, neural, and humoral mechanisms for such psychological processes as audition, chemoreception, cognition, and conation (see Uttal, in this volume). Such mechanisms, also, are very compatible with the cumulative character of science. Acceptable models in either biological or mathematical language are stepping stones to further knowledge. But even when biological models are most eminently called for, mathematical analysis can play a significant role.

A good example of this interaction between theory languages may be found in the theory of color vision. On any a priori grounds it would seem that this is one empirical system that calls for explanation and understanding in terms of a biological system. The value of mathematical analysis, however, in its interaction with a biological theory is exemplified by the work of Krantz (1975a, 1975b) in color vision. I shall do no more than suggest the kind of interaction that has occurred here. In Krantz's words,

Since the work of Helmholtz, most work in color theory has been concerned with discovering a special set of coordinates in color space, which would constitute the three "fundamental sensations" of color. Such spatial coordinates have been devised to attempt to fit various bodies of data. Hurvich and

Jameson (1957) gave the first really comprehensive attempt to encompass all the major data on discrimination, perceptual attributes, color defects, and adaptation into a single theory. They used three coordinates corresponding to opponent-processes [1975a, p. 9].

The empirical world of color vision consists of two physical operations, which are mixing lights and changing the energy level of a wavelength, and one behavioral relation, which is a perceptual response such as matching colors or judgments of similarity or discrimination. The mathematical structure of the color space is enriched (made more unique) with more empirical structure (observable relations), to which Krantz added color matching relations typical of various kinds of dichromatic color vision (color blindness) as well as that of normal color matching. The idea is that each kind of dichromacy involves the loss of one coordinate of the color space.

Krantz developed the mathematical structure using the two physical operations on light and Grassmann's laws (1854) proposed for color matching. Interestingly enough, the mathematical structure that results for dichromatic vision is almost identical with that for a force table, sometimes used in teaching elementary physics, which involves a system of weights attached by long lines to a ring sitting in the center of a round table with the weights hung over pulleys at the edge of the table with the pulleys set at various angles and the entire system in equilibrium. The force table is used in physics to demonstrate vector representation. As a model of dichromatic color matching the angles between pulleys are mapped into (differences between) wavelengths, and the weights are mapped into energy levels at particular wavelengths. Equilibrium of the force vectors corresponds to the subjective matching of mixtures of lights of different wavelengths. In this case we have a physical model that works like dichromatic color vision and although it does not serve all the purposes of the mathematical structure, yet it is directly observable and provides another source of insight in understanding color vision.

There are a number of useful mathematical results on color codes that mediate color discrimination. These results are logical consequences of Grassmann's laws, and most are well-known empirical relations in normals and dichromats. But the mathematical analysis goes much further than this, showing that the isomorphism that holds between the force table and dichromacy does not exist between a three-dimensional force field and a three-dimensional color structure and that red/green cancellation and blue/yellow cancellation have linearity properties in the cancellation of mixtures which no other bases do, which suggests that "they depend on codes readily computed in the nervous system [Krantz, 1975b, p. 326]."

The rich interaction between mathematical modelling and a biological system in the case of color vision is far too extensive to be pursued further here. Suffice it to say that one can see in this interaction numerous instances in which biological theorizing is advanced by mathematical modelling, and in a manner for which there is essentially no substitute.

Psychology seems to have two preferred theory languages: One is biological, and the other is mathematical. The biological is valuable because of its content; the mathematical is valuable because of its lack of content and hence wide applicability by virtue of its reduction to more elemental principles which provide the basis for transfer, systemization, and integration. The former language provides realism for the model and the latter exposes principles and logical structure. In social psychology it would seem that mathematics would be the preeminent language.

. Perhaps the greatest fault of mathematics might be said to be its elitism, though this may be no more than cultural artifact. The technological level of each new generation is impressively greater, and there is no well-supported empirical generalization to the effect that intellectual capability of man or woman is bounded, much less a theory that makes it a logical consequence of other empirical generalities.

A student once said to me that we had solved all the easy problems and only the difficult ones remained. He's now a professor solving new problems. All unsolved problems are difficult, but their solutions in retrospect are often simple.

CONCLUSION

This essay represents a singular view rather than a balanced account of the relation between psychology and mathematics in all its many facets. I have focused on the use of mathematics in theoretical psychology, a most important usage and perhaps not as well understood as the wide use of statistics at the junction of the processes T and I in Figure 1—the ultimate point in the confrontation between reason and nature.

The applications of mathematics in data reduction, in the search for empirical regularities, and in statistical testing are probably far greater than any other use of mathematics in psychology. Multivariate methods, like psychometric theory (Lord & Novick, 1968; Nunnally, 1978), factor analysis (Mulaik, 1972), LISREL (a structural equation approach to causal modelling of Jöreskog, 1978), and the development of functional measurement (Anderson, 1974), are all in that tradition. The application of the latter to information integration reveals the potential of that approach, like that of conjoint measurement, for theoretical modelling.

I have, perhaps, put more emphasis on the role of mathematics in modelling than may seem deserved to some, but the rapid growth of mathematics in theoretical psychology calls for discussion of its values and limitations. The development of theory depends on empirical structure; theory provides the *why* for the *what*. The invariances that are the basis of theory naturally become less obvious and more subtle as a science develops. The interpretation of invariances becomes more obscure and their interrelations more difficult to observe. One needs to know what to look for and where to look for it. This will be an increasingly important role of mathematics and will come, in my view, from an increasing use of mathematics in psychological theory. The danger that it faces is that it may become mathematical game playing in search of a trivial application. Unfortunately, it is an exceedingly difficult line to draw. As a case in point, Hölder (1901) proved a theorem in abstract algebra that was not recognized as a foundation stone of behavioral measurement for over sixty years. That is not, however, as serious a danger in mathematical modelling as overgeneralization, or as the overconfidence that a mathematical formulation might engender, exemplified by what Postman (1975) calls "premature precision" referring to taking too seriously and literally the numerical estimates obtained in fitting a model.

Much is already written about methodology and scaling and data analysis but not much that is useful can be said of a "how to do it" nature about theory construction. I thought that perhaps some examples of theoretical developments, pointing out principles or rules that they suggested or illustrated and putting the whole process into a schematic framework would be one way to go about conveying a picture of how and why mathematics is becoming increasingly used in psychological theory. The literature that I selected was chosen with that purpose in mind.

I close with a quotation from Goodman and Ratti:

> In recent times the term "mathematical model" has been used. . . . By using the term *model* the author is deliberately calling attention to the fact that his "model" is only a crude approximation to the true explanation. Thus the author sounds a subtle warning for the reader that he should examine the model (or theory) with the proper mixture of respect, belief, and suspicion [1971, p. 340].

Models are not necessarily more veridical or more to be believed by virtue of being mathematical.

ACKNOWLEDGMENTS

This essay is an outgrowth of many years of interaction with students and colleagues, and my indebtedness can never be fully expressed. Insofar as the immediate preparation of this manuscript is concerned however, I, if not the reader, owe a debt of gratitude to K. Michael Aschenbrenner, Mark Batell, Robyn Dawes, William Goldstein, Stephen Hirtle, Cornelis Hoede, Keith Levi, David Krantz, R. Duncan Luce, Alexander MacRae, Wilbert McKeachie, John Miyamoto, John Palmer, Peter Schönemann, Nicholas Steneck, Amos Tversky, John Yellott, and Joseph Zinnes. It is to be understood, of course, that these people do not necessarily agree with what is said here. Indeed, they don't always agree with each other, but fortunately (?) the author was the final arbiter. This essay is abbreviated from *Psychology and Mathematics* (Coombs, 1983); preparation and some of the research discussed was supported in part by NSF research grant BNS 78-09101 and BNS 81-20299.

REFERENCES

Adams, E. W., & Fagot, R. F. *A model of riskless choice*. Technical Report #4, Stanford University: Institute for Mathematical Studies in the Social Sciences, 1956.

Adams, E. W., & Fagot, R. F. A model of riskless choice. *Behavioral Science*, 1959, *4*, 1–10.

Anderson, N. H. Information integration theory: A brief summary. In D. H. Krantz, R. C. Atkinson, R. D. Luce, & P. Suppes (Eds.), *Contemporary developments in mathematical psychology* (Vol. 2). San Francisco: W. H. Freeman, 1974.

Aschenbrenner, K. M. Efficient sets, decision heuristics, and single-peaked preferences. *Journal of Mathematical Psychology*, 1981, *23*, 227–256.

Beebe-Center, J. G. *The psychology of pleasantness and unpleasantness*. New York: Russell and Russell, 1966. (Originally published, 1932.)

Bradley, R. A., & Terry, M. E. Rank analysis of incomplete block designs. I. The method of paired comparisons. *Biometrika*, 1952, *39*, 324–345.

Campbell, N. *Physics: The elements*. Cambridge University Press, 1920. Reissued as *The foundations of science: The philosophy of theory and experiment*. New York: Dover Press, 1957.

Cartwright, D., & Harary, F. Structural balance: A generalization of Heider's theory. *Psychological Review*, 1956, *63*,277–293.

Cohen, M. R., & Nagel, E. *An introduction to logic and scientific method*. New York: Harcourt and Brace, 1954.

Coombs, C. H. On the use of inconsistency of preferences in psychological measurement. *Journal of Experimental Psychology*, 1958, *55*, 1–7.

Coombs, C. H. *Psychology and mathematics*. Ann Arbor, MI: University of Michigan Press, 1983.

Coombs, C. H., & Avrunin, G. S. Single-peaked functions and the theory of preference. *Psychological Review*, 1977, *84*, 216–230. (a)

Coombs, C. H. & Avrunin, G. S. A theorem on single-peaked preference functions in one dimension. *Journal of Mathematical Psychology*, 1977, *4*, 497–512. (b)

Coombs, C. H., & Lehner, P. E. The conjoint analysis of the bilinear model, illustrated with a theory of risk. In I. Borg (Ed.), *Multidimensional data representations: When and why*. Ann Arbor, MI: Mathesis Press, 1981.

Coombs, C. H., Raiffa, H., & Thrall, R. M. Some views on mathematical models and measurement theory. *Psychological Review*, 1954, *61*, 132–144.

Davidson, R. R. On a relationship between two representations of a model for paired comparisons. *Biometrics*, 1969, *25*, 597–599.

Dawes, R. M., & Corrigan, B. Linear models in decision making. *Psychological Bulletin*, 1974, *81*, 95–106.

Edgeworth, F. Y. *Mathematical psychics*. London: Kegan Paul, 1881.

Estes, W. K. Toward a statistical theory of learning. *Psychological Review*, 1950, *57*, 94–107.

Fisher, R. A. *The design of experiments*. London: Oliver and Boyd, 1935.

Goodman, A. W., & Ratti, J. S. *Finite mathematics with applications*. New York: MacMillan Company, 1971.

Grassmann, H. On the theory of compound colours. *Philosophical Magazine* (London), 1854, *4*, 254–264.

Grier, J. B. *Mathematical psychology: The first 2000 years*. An invited address presented at the meeting of the Society for Mathematical Psychology, University of Wisconsin, August 30, 1980.

Helmholtz, H. Zählen and Messen erkenntnis-theoretisch betrachtet. In *Philosophische Aufsätze Eduard Zeller gewidmet*. Leipzig: np, 1887.

Hölder, O. Die Axiome der Quantität und die Lehre vom Mass. *Berichte über die Verhandlungen der Königlich Sachsischen Gesellschaft der Wissenschaften, Zu Leipzig, Mathematisch-Physische Classe*, 1901, *53*, 1–61.

Hurvich, L. M., & Jameson, D. An opponent-process theory of color vision. *Psychological Review*, 1957, *64*, 384–404.

Jöreskog, K. G. Structural analysis of covariance and correlation matrices. *Psychometrika*, 1978, *43*, 443–477.

Krantz, D. H. A theory of magnitude estimation and cross-modality matching. *Journal of Mathematical Psychology*, 1972, *9*, 168–199.

Krantz, D. H. Color measurement and color theory: I. Representation theorem for Grassmann Structures. *Journal of Mathematical Psychology*, 1975, *12*, 283–303. (a)

Krantz, D. H. Color measurement and color theory: II. Opponent-colors theory. *Journal of Mathematical Psychology*, 1975, *12*, 304–327. (b)

Krantz, D. H., Luce, R. D., Suppes, P., & Tversky, A. (Eds.). *Foundations of measurement (Vol. 1) Additive polynomial representation*. New York: Academic Press, 1971.

Lehner, P. E., & Noma, E. A new solution to the problem of finding all numerical solutions to ordered metric structures. *Psychometrika*, 1980, *45*, 135–137.

Lord, F. M., & Novick, M. R. *Statistical theories of mental tests*. Reading, MA: Addison-Wesley, 1968.

Luce, R. D. *Individual choice behavior: A theoretical analysis*. New York: Wiley, 1959.

Luce, R. D., & Suppes, P. Preference, utility, and subjective probability. In R. D. Luce, R. B. Bush, & E. Galanter (Eds.), *Handbook of mathematical psychology* (Vol. 3). New York: Wiley, 1965.

Luce, R. D., & Tukey, J. W. Simultaneous conjoint measurement: A new type of fundamental measurement. *Journal of Mathematical Psychology*, 1964, *1*, 1–27.

McClelland, G. H., & Coombs, C. H. ORDMET: A general algorithm for constructing all numerical solutions to ordered metric structures. *Psychometrika*, 1975, *40*, 269–290.

Medawar, P. B. *The art of the soluble*. London: Penguin, 1969. (a)

Medawar, P. B. *Induction and intuition in scientific thought*. Philadelphia: American Philosophical Society, 1969. (b)

Mill, J. S. *A system of logic*. Toronto: Routledge and Kegan Paul, 1973. (Originally published, 1843.)

Miller, G. A. *Mathematics and psychology*. New York: Wiley, 1964.

Morrison, H. W. *Intransitivity of paired comparison choices*. Unpublished doctoral dissertation, University of Michigan, 1962.

Mulaik, S. A. *The foundations of factor analysis*. New York: McGraw-Hill, 1972.

Nagel, E. *The structure of science*. New York: Harcourt, Brace and World, 1961.

Newel, A., & Simon, H. A. Models: Their uses and limitations. In L. D. White (Ed.), *The state of the social sciences*. Chicago, IL: University of Chicago Press, 1955.

Nunnally, J. C. *Psychometric theory*. New York: McGraw-Hill, 1978.

Peterson, W. W., Birdsall, T. G., & Fox, W. C. The theory of signal detectability. *Institute of Radio Engineers Transactions*, 1954, *P.G.I.T.-4*, 171–212.

Pfanzagel, J. A general theory of measurement-applications to utility. *Naval Research Logistics Quarterly*, 1959, *6*, 283–394.

Popper, K. *Poverty of historicism*. London: Routledge and Kegan Paul, 1957.

Postman, L. Verbal learning and memory. *Annual Review of Psychology*, 1975, *26*, 291–335.

Priestley, J. *Introductory essays to Hartley's theory of the human mind*. London: np, 1775.

Quine, W. V., & Ullian, J. S. *The web of belief*. New York: Random House, 1970.

Robert, F. S. *Discrete mathematical models with applications to social, biological, and environmental problems*. Englewood Cliffs, NJ: Prentice–Hall, 1976.

Scott, D. Measurement structures and linear inequalities. *Journal of Mathematical Psychology*, 1964, *1*, 233–247.

Shye, S., (Ed.). *Theory construction and data analysis in the behavioral sciences*. San Francisco: Jossey-Bass, 1978.

Slatkin, M. Altruism in theory. *Science*, 1980, *210*, 633–634.

Stevens, S. S. On the theory of scales of measurement. *Science*, 1946, *103*, 677–680.

Stevens, S. S. Mathematics, measurement, and psychophysics. In S. S. Stevens (Ed.), *Handbook of experimental psychology*. New York: Wiley, 1951.

Stevens, S. S. A metric for the social concensus. *Science*, 1966, *151*, 435–541.

Tanner, W. P., Jr., & Swets, J. A. A decision making theory of visual detection. *Psychological Review*, 1954, *61*, 401–409.

Thorndike, E. L. *Handwriting*. New York: Teachers College Press, 1915.

Thurstone, L. L. A law of comparative judgment. *Psychological Review*, 1927, *38*, 368–398.

Tversky, A. *Additive choice structures*. Unpublished dissertation, University of Michigan, 1964.

Tversky, A. Intransitivity of preference. *Psychological Review*, 1969, *76*, 31–48.

Wilder, R. L. *The foundations of mathematics*. New York: Wiley, 1965.

Wundt, W. *Grundzüge der Physiologischen Psychologie*. Leipzig: Verlag von Wilhelm Engelmann, 1880.

Yellott, J. I., Jr. The relationship between Luce's choice axiom, Thurstone's theory of comparative judgment, and the double exponential distribution. *Journal of Mathematical Psychology*, 1977, *15*, 109–144.

5 Psychology and Medicine

David S. Krantz
Uniformed Services University of the Health Sciences

David C. Glass
State University of New York at Stony Brook

INTRODUCTION AND HISTORICAL BACKGROUND

The behavioral sciences are developing an increasingly significant relationship with medicine. This interdisciplinary contact has matured and
expanded beyond one area of mental health to a far broader area called
"behavioral medicine", which is concerned with behavioral factors in
physical disease. At the same time, old disciplinary boundaries are being
erased; behavioral and biomedical scientists alike are studying the joint
influence of psychosocial and biological factors on somatic health and
illness.

The interface between psychology and medicine has its historical roots
in pre-Cartesian philosophy (Alexander, 1950; Mcmahon, 1976). Early
physicians believed that intense emotions had the potential to produce
acute imbalances in bodily function which culminated in various forms of
organ pathology. Western medical thinking was radically altered in the
late seventeenth century when the biomedical model, based on the Cartesian dualism of mind and body, became the accepted basis for explaining
health and illness (McMahon & Hastrup, 1980). According to this model,
disease was viewed as a purely biological phenomenon, that is a product
of specific agents or pathogens and bodily dysfunction.

Psychological variables regained some legitimacy in the explanation of
physical disorders with the emergence of the field of psychosomatic
medicine in the first half of the twentieth century. Psychoanalytic theories
of disease etiology were proposed, emphasizing the role of characteristic

personality traits or types in the development and course of disorders such as coronary disease, peptic ulcer, arthritis, and asthma (Alexander, 1950; Dunbar, 1947; Lipowski, 1977). However, this field was frequently characterized by attempts to correlate or describe psychological factors that were associated with disease states. Few attempts were made to advance understanding beyond the correlational level by exploring basic mechanisms linking behavioral processes to disease states.

In recent years, there has been renewed interest from both behavioral and biomedical communities in a broader model of health and illness, encompassing psychological and social variables and their interaction with biological processes (e.g., Engel, 1977; Matarazzo, 1980; Miller, 1976). This interest arose because the traditional biomedical model has not accounted for all illness states, nor has it sufficiently explained selective susceptibility to disease. Changing patterns of health and illness also contributed to a broadening of the interface between psychology and medicine. In the United States at the turn of the century, the greatest contributors to morbidity and mortality were the infectious diseases. Today, the leading causes of mortality are chronic diseases, including the cardiovascular disorders and cancer. These disease states are caused by a confluence of social, environmental, behavioral, and biological factors (Institute of Medicine, 1978; U.S.D.H.E.W., 1979a), including habits of living (e.g., smoking, diet, and exercise) and what has been termed psychosocial stress (Levi, 1979; Selye, 1956). For example, epidemiologists studying lung cancer have considered many causal variables, including heredity and the physical environment (particularly air pollution), but the strongest risk factor turns out to be a behavioral variable, namely, cigarette smoking.

Considerable research has documented important associations between psychosocial variables and physical disease outcomes. Of greater significance perhaps for the interplay of psychology and medicine is the fact that a biobehavioral paradigm has emerged from this work in an effort to advance scientific understanding beyond the descriptive level. In contrast to a purely correlational approach, biobehavioral research explores basic mechanisms linking behavioral processes to disease states. This research involves integration of behavioral science principles and methods with biomedical knowledge of the disease being studied. An example is provided by recent evidence linking psychosocial factors (e.g., emotional stress) to the development of cardiovascular disease. Behavioral scientists working in this area are devoting increasing attention to physiological processes (e.g., neuroendocrine activity) implicated in the development of coronary heart disease in order to determine how these processes are influenced by behavioral events.

In this essay, it is impossible to represent fully the broad spectrum of health-related behavioral research. Therefore, we shall not attempt to discuss mental illness categories (see Eysenck, in Volume II) or substance abuse disorders (see Kornetsky, in this volume), except insofar as they are related to physical disease endpoints (e.g., cigarette smoking leading to cancer and heart disease). We begin by conceptualizing the mechanisms and processes by which psychology and medicine are linked. Next, we consider the literature on behavioral and social factors in the etiology and pathogenesis of selected physical diseases such as cancer, psychosomatic disorders (e.g., ulcers), and infectious disease. Because considerable progress has been made in understanding the relationship between behavior and the major cardiovascular disorders (the leading cause of death in the United States), emphasis will be directed to this area as an exemplar of biobehavioral approaches to physical illness. Consideration will then be given to treatment and rehabilitation of physical disease. This discussion will not be limited to any one disorder but, instead, will emphasize themes that have relevance to a variety of somatic illnesses. We shall conclude with an overview of research directions projected for the next few years.

MECHANISMS LINKING PSYCHOLOGY AND MEDICINE

The processes and mechanisms linking behavior to physical illness of various kinds may be grouped into three broad categories. These include direct physiological effects, health impairing lifestyles, and reactions to illness.

Direct Psychophysiological Effects

The first category involves alterations in tissue function via neuroendocrine and other physiological responses to psychosocial stimuli. This mechanism encompasses bodily changes without the intervention of external agents such as cigarette smoking or dietary risk factors, although the two sets of variables may produce interactive effects (e.g., stress and smoking might increase, synergistically, the risk of coronary heart disease).

Central to this process is the concept of stress, which was originally described by Selye (1956) as a nonspecific response of the body to external demands that are placed upon it. According to Selye, the stress response proceeds in a characteristic three-stage pattern which involves a variety of physiological systems (neural, hormonal, and metabolic) in complex interrelation with each other. The term "stress" is also used in a psychological sense (Cox, 1978; Lazarus, 1966) to refer to an internal state of the individual who is perceiving threats to physical and/or psychic well-being. This broader use of the term places emphasis on the organism's perception and evaluation of potentially harmful stimuli and considers the perception of threat to arise from a comparison between the demands imposed upon the individual and the individual's felt ability to cope with these demands. A perceived imbalance in this mechanism gives rise to the experience of stress and to the stress response, which may be physiological and/or behavioral in nature.

Physiological responses to stress include neural and endocrine activity, which, in turn, can influence a wide range of bodily processes including metabolic rate, cardiovascular and autonomic nervous system functioning, and altered immune reactions (Levi, 1979; Mason, 1971). Short-term stress responses include hormonal and cardiovascular reactions (e.g., increased heart rate and blood pressure) which may precipitate clinical disorders (e.g., stroke, cardiac instabilities and pain syndromes, psychosomatic symptoms, etc.) in predisposed individuals. If stimulation becomes pronounced, prolonged, or repetitive, the result may be chronic dysfunction in one or more systems (e.g., gastrointestinal, cardiovascular, etc.).

Early stress research (Selye, 1956) emphasized the generality or non-specificity of responses to a wide variety of stimuli, but subsequent research has recognized that the link between stress and disease is not simple; instead, it depends upon the context in which the stressful agent occurs, how individuals appraise it, and the social supports and personal resources available (Cohen, Horowitz, Lazarus, Moos, Robins, Rose, & Rutter, 1981; Lazarus, 1966; Mason, 1971). There are wide individual differences in physiological responses to stressors, which depend not only on biological predispositions (Levi, 1979), but also on the individual's felt ability to cope with or master conditions of harm, threat, or challenge. For example, stressful events (e.g., failure, loss of loved ones, divorce, etc.) are inevitable throughout the life cycle, yet only a minority of individuals suffers lasting adverse effects. Research has shown that a variety of social and psychological factors (e.g., styles of coping and social supports provided by others) act to modify or buffer the impact of stressful events on illness (Cohen et al., 1981).

It should be emphasized that since the processes in this category involve functional alterations brought about, in part, by exposure to psychosocial stimuli, adequate scientific understanding requires a specification of mediating physiological processes (e.g., sympathetic-adrenomedullary and pituitary-adrenocortical axes). It is not enough to establish correlations between disease end-points and behavioral variables.

Health-Impairing Habits and Lifestyles

A second means by which behavior leads to physical illness occurs when individuals engage in habits and styles of life that are damaging to health. Personal habits play a critical role in the development of many serious diseases, as amply documented by the recent Surgeon General's reports on smoking and health and on health promotion and disease prevention. Cigarette smoking is probably the most salient behavior in this category, for it has been implicated as a risk factor for three leading causes of death in the United States—coronary heart disease, cancer, and stroke. However, poor diet, lack of exercise, excessive alcohol consumption, and poor hygienic practices also have been linked to disease outcomes. These habits may be deeply rooted in cultural practices or initiated by social influences (e.g., smoking to obtain peer group approval). They may be maintained as part of an achievement-oriented lifestyle as well as by the interaction of biological and behavioral mechanisms of addiction. Therefore, a major focus of behavioral medicine research has been on the role of socio-cultural systems, lifestyles, and psychophysiological processes in the etiology and pathogenesis of the chronic diseases. Considerable attention also has been directed toward the development of techniques to modify those behaviors that constitute risk factors for illnesses.

Reactions to Illness and the Sick Role

A third process through which behavior leads to physical illness occurs when individuals minimize the significance of symptoms, delay in seeking medical care, or fail to comply with treatment and rehabilitation regimens. One prominent example is the sizable number of heart attack patients who procrastinate in seeking help, thereby diminishing their chances of survival. These actions are representative of a larger area of study concerned with the way people react to the experience of organ dysfunction (illness behavior) as well as to the experience of being in the role of a sick person (patienthood). To succeed, medical therapies require that the patient follows the physician's advice, but an extensive literature reports disturbingly low rates of compliance with health and medical care regimens (e.g., Sackett & Haynes, 1976). Accordingly, there has been considerable research on social and psychological processes involved in patients' reactions to pain and illness, the decision to seek medical care, and medical compliance. This research has led to the development of interventions that have been applied in treatment and rehabilitation settings.

BEHAVIORAL FACTORS IN THE ETIOLOGY AND PATHOGENESIS OF PHYSICAL DISEASE

In 1900, the leading causes of death in the United States were pneumonia, influenza, and tuberculosis. Changing patterns of illness since that time have been marked by the ascendancy of cardiovascular disease as the chief cause of mortality in this country. The cardiovascular disorders, including coronary heart disease and high blood pressure, now account for more than half of all deaths. A large percentage of these would be classified as "premature," for they occur during the middle years of 35 to 50 (National Science Foundation, 1980).

Atherosclerosis, Coronary Heart Disease, and Sudden Death

Coronary atherosclerosis is a symptomless condition characterized by narrowing and deterioration of the arteries, including the coronary arteries, that is blood vessels that nourish the heart. An excess accumulation of cholesterol and related lipids forms a mound of tissue, or atherosclerotic plaque, on the inner wall of one or more of the coronary arteries (Hurst, Logue, & Schlant, 1978). The formation of atherosclerotic plaques may proceed undetected for years, affecting cardiac functioning only when they cause a degree of obstruction sufficient to diminish blood supply to the heart. Once this occurs, coronary atherosclerosis has evolved into coronary heart disease (CHD).

In one form of CHD, angina pectoris, occasional instances of inadequate blood supply (ischemia) cause the individual to experience attacks of chest pain. Although ischemia per se does not cause permanent tissue damage, angina is a painful condition that can lead to more serious complications. A more severe and frequently fatal consequence of CHD is myocardial infarction (MI), or heart attack, in which a prolonged state of ischemia results in death or damage to a portion of the heart tissue. Other manifestations of CHD include congestive heart failure, conditions secondary to MI (e.g., ventricular failure and heart rupture), and disturbances of the conductive or beat-regulating portion of the heart, i.e., the arrhythmias (Hurst et al., 1978).

Standard risk factors for cardiovascular disease. Individuals who are likely to develop coronary heart disease may be identified with a modest degree of accuracy. This is possible because a set of "risk factors" has been recognized in recent years. A CHD risk factor is an attribute of the population of interest, or of the environment, which appears to increase the likelihood of developing one or more of the clinical manifestations of cardiovascular disease. The following risk factors have been identified: (1) aging; (2) sex (being male); (3) elevated serum cholesterol and related low-density lipoproteins; (4) dietary intake of animal fats and cholesterol; (5) high blood pressure; (6) heavy cigarette smoking; (7) diabetes mellitus; (8) specific diseases such as hypothyroidism; (9) family history of coronary disease; (10) obesity; (11) sedentary life-style; and (12) specific anomalies of the electrocardiogram, such as evidence of left ventricular hypertrophy (Kannel, McGee, & Gordon, 1976).

The risk-enhancing effects of the standard risk factors have been viewed in terms of their physiological influence (e.g., toxic effects of tars and nicotine, the role of salt intake in regulating blood pressure levels, and the relationship between diet and serum cholesterol). Note, however, that many of these variables are determined, at least partially, by behavioral factors. For example, cigarette smoking is a preventable behavior undoubtedly brought about by psychosocial forces (Leventhal & Cleary, 1980). Cultural, racial, and social class groups differ in serum cholesterol levels, independently of dietary practices (McDonough, Hames, Stulb, et al., 1965). Enhanced risk due to sex and age may also derive from non-biological correlates of these variables, such as occupational pressure, stressful life events, and behavior patterns (Eisdorfer & Wilkie, 1977; Riley & Hamburg, 1981). At least two implications follow from these observations: (1) analysis of the etiology and pathogenesis of coronary disease must be extended into the domain of psychosocial factors and (2) psychosocial factors should be considered important targets in the prevention and treatment of CHD.

Psychosocial risk factors for coronary disease. The best combinations of the standard risk factors fail to identify most new cases of heart disease (Jenkins, 1971). Some variable or set of variables appears to be missing from the predictive equation. This limitation in knowledge has led to a broadened search for influences and mechanisms contributing to coronary risk, which now includes social indicators, such as socioeconomic status and social mobility, and psychological factors, such as anxiety and neuroticism, psychological stress, and overt patterns of behavior. The results have been encouraging, though not uniformly so. The two most promising psychosocial risk factors to emerge in recent years are psychological stress and the Type A coronary-prone behavior pattern (Jenkins, 1971).

1. Psychological stress. As noted earlier, Selye (1956) first popularized the notion of stress, which he defined as the body's non-specific physiological reaction to noxious agents or stressors. More recently, psychological investigators, such as Lazarus (1966) and Mason (1971), have taken exception to this view, arguing that the body's response varies with the particular type of stressor and the context in which the stressor occurs (Glass & Singer, 1972; Lazarus, 1966).

Several indices of psychological stress have been studied in relation to the development of coronary disease. Research suggests that excessive work and job responsibility may enhance coronary risk, especially when they approach the limits of the individual's capacity to control his work environment (Haynes, Feinleib, & Kannel, 1980; House, 1975). Another job-related stressor that appears to be related to coronary disease is reported work dissatisfaction, such as lack of recognition by superiors, poor relations with co-workers, and inferior work conditions (House, 1975). Other life dissatisfactions, including problems and conflicts in areas of finance and family, have been correlated with the presence and future development of coronary disease (Haynes et al., 1980; Medalie, Snyder, Groen, Newfeld, Goldbourt, & Riss, 1973).

The experience of a single, traumatic life event has long been suspected as a cause of clinical CHD (e.g., Cannon, 1942). More recently, it has been suggested that the cumulative effects of repeated adjustments required by life changes drain the adaptive resources of the individual and increase susceptibility to a variety of diseases. To test this, an objective instrument, the Social Readjustment Rating Scale (SRRS), was developed by Holmes and Rahe to assess the impact of such events as the death of spouse, a change to a different line of work, and a son or daughter leaving home (Holmes & Rahe, 1967).

Several retrospective studies have used this technique in an effort to link the accumulation of life events with the occurrence of coronary disease (see Garrity & Marx, 1979). For example, survivors of myocardial infarction show a pattern of increased life changes during the period approximately 1½ years before the MI, whereas healthy control subjects reported a relatively stable number of life events during the same period. Other research, in which information regarding life events prior to sudden cardiac death was obtained from a survivor of the deceased (usually the spouse), revealed an accumulation in the intensity of life events in the six months prior to death (Garrity & Marx, 1979).

Despite replication of the foregoing findings, negative results have been reported as well (e.g., Hinkle, 1974). Reviewers point to defects in the methodology of retrospective designs that might account for the positive findings (Dohrenwend & Dohrenwend, 1978). However, such explanations cannot explain significant associations obtained in prospective studies in which data concerning psychosocial stressors were obtained prior to the development of disease (e.g., Haynes et al., 1980; Medalie et al., 1973).

The relation of stress to pathological outcomes depends on both the adaptive capacity of the individual before the stressor occurs and the resources marshalled in response to its occurrence (Cohen et al., 1981). It follows that variables moderating the impact of stress must be taken into account in order to gauge the predictive validity of stress as a risk factor for coronary disease. These moderators include biological factors (e.g., genetic susceptibility and general state of health), psychological attributes (e.g., felt ability to cope), aspects of the immediate context in which the stressor occurs (e.g., whether the stressor is perceived as controllable), various sociocultural variables (e.g., amount of social support from other people and/or the health care system), and factors related to the life course (e.g., the expectedness of events at a certain stage of life). For example, there is evidence that individuals who have social supports may live longer, have a lower incidence of somatic illness, and possess higher morale and more positive mental health (Cohen et al., 1981).

2. Type A coronary-prone behavior pattern.   Perhaps the most thoroughly investigated psychosocial risk factor for coronary disease is the Type A behavior pattern (Rosenman & Friedman, 1974). Type A (or Pattern A) is characterized by extreme competitiveness and achievement striving, a strong sense of time urgency and impatience, hostility, and aggressiveness. The relative absence of these traits is designated as Type B.

The Type A concept does not refer simply to the conditions that elicit Pattern A behavior, or to the responses per se, nor to some hypothetical personality trait that produces them. It refers, instead, to a set of behaviors that occur in susceptible individuals in appropriately stressful and/or challenging conditions. Pattern A is, therefore, the outcome of a person-situation interaction. It is not a typology, but a behavior *pattern,* which is displayed in varying degrees, at one time or another, by everyone.

Although several studies have documented an association between Pattern A and CHD, the most convincing evidence comes from the WCGS, or Western Collaborative Group Study (Rosenman, Brand, Jenkins, Friedman, Straus, & Wurm, 1975). In this prospective, double-blind study, more than 3,000 initially healthy men, 39 to 59 years of age, were assessed for a comprehensive array of social, dietary, biochemical, clinical, and behavioral variables. An 8½ year follow-up showed that subjects exhibiting Type A behavior at the study's inception were about twice as likely as Type B individuals to develop coronary disease (i.e., angina pectoris or myocardial infarction). This two-fold differential in risk remained when statistical procedures were used to control for the influence of other risk factors such as cigarette smoking, serum cholesterol, and high blood pressure. This research also linked Pattern A to sudden cardiac death (Friedman, Manwaring, Rosenman, Donlon, Ortega, & Grube, 1973) and recurrent MI. Similar results were obtained from an 8-year follow-up of data from the Framingham Study, a large-scale prospective study of heart disease undertaken by the National Institutes of Health. Results indicated that Pattern A is predictive of CHD in both men and women, although for male subjects the enhanced risk appeared only among white-collar workers (Haynes et al., 1980).

3. Pathophysiological mechanisms linking stress and behavior Pattern A to coronary disease. It is not enough to demonstrate a relationship between CHD risk factors—whether biomedical or psychosocial in nature—and the occurrence of cardiovascular disease. The precise mechanisms mediating the association must be specified. Although the pathogenesis of coronary disease is not completely understood, several factors are believed to play a major contributing role. These include a variety of physiological and biochemical states which may enhance coronary risk by influencing the initiation and progression of atherosclerosis and/or by precipitating clinical CHD (Herd, 1978; Ross & Glomset, 1976). Many of these physiological states have been observed in human and animal experimental studies of psychological stress. For example, hemodynamic effects, such as elevated heart rate and blood pressure, and biochemical changes, such as increased levels of serum cholesterol, are produced in animals under prolonged or severe stress (Schneiderman, 1978). It has been observed, in addition, that a reduction in blood-clotting time occurs under conditions of stress, and in some cases, degeneration of heart tissue has been reported as well. Other animal research has linked laboratory stressors to a lowered threshold for ventricular arrhythmia and for ventricular fibrillation (e.g., Lown, Verrier, & Corbalan, 1973), a state which leads to sudden cardiac death unless immediate treatment is given. In studies of psychological stress in healthy humans, stressors such as occupational pressure have been shown to produce biochemical changes such as elevated levels of serum cholesterol (Friedman, Rosenman, & Carroll, 1958) and blood pressure (Herd, 1978).

A notable feature of the foregoing research is the measurement of physiological reactivity in response to stress, as distinct from the observation of basal or resting levels of physiological variables. These changes in functioning, which are not detected by basal risk-factor measurement, are believed to yield a better index of the pathogenic processes involved in coronary disease. In addition, by observing such changes in response to real-life or laboratory-induced stressors, pathogenic states may be detected within the context of their psychosocial antecedents.

The physiological concomitants of psychological stress are believed to result from activation of the sympathetic-adrenal medullary system (SAM) and the pituitary-adrenocortical axis (PAC). Interest in the impact of SAM activation on bodily reactions to emergency situations may be traced to Walter Cannon's work on the fight or flight response (e.g., Cannon, 1942). This neuroendocrine response appears to be elicited in situations demanding effortful coping with threatening stimuli (Frankenhaeuser, 1971). The hormonal responses of the PAC axis were emphasized by Selye in his notion of a generalized physiological response to aversive stimulation. The PAC secretions include a number of hormones (e.g., cortisol) that influence bodily systems of relevance to the development of coronary disease.

The same pathophysiological mechanisms linking stress and coronary disease may apply, a fortiori, to Type A individuals thereby accounting, in part, for their enhanced coronary risk. Research has shown greater urinary catecholamine secretion during the working day and greater plasma catecholamine responses to competition and stress among Type As compared to Type Bs (Rosenman & Friedman, 1974). Recent studies by Glass, Krakoff, Contrada, et al. (1980) also have demonstrated higher elevations in plasma catecholamines among Type A individuals in situations of hostile competition. These cardiovascular and neuroendocrine changes are consistent with the findings of other investigators indicating greater cardiovascular reactivity among As than Bs in challenging situations (Dembroski, MacDougall, Shields, Petitto, & Lushene, 1978; Herd, 1978).

High Blood Pressure

High blood pressure (also called "essential" hypertension) is a condition of unclear etiology in which blood pressure shows chronic elevations. When the disorder becomes developed fully, increased pressure is usually ascribable to a constriction or contraction of blood vessels throughout the body (Page & McCubbin, 1966). Although high blood pressure (HBP) is a symptomless disorder, there is epidemiologic evidence that even mild blood pressure elevations are associated with a shortening of life expectancy (Kannel & Dawber, 1971) and increased risk of coronary heart disease and stroke. As is the case with CHD, the causes of HBP are believed to involve complex interactions among genetic, sociocultural, behavioral, and physiological processes.

Heterogeneity of the disorder and physiological mechanisms. Essential hypertension is not a single homogeneous disease. In the development of the disorder, blood pressure is thought to progress over a period of years from moderately elevated or "borderline" levels to more appreciably elevated levels, called "established" hypertension. Several pathogenic mechanisms may bring about blood pressure elevations, and different physiological and/or behavioral mechanisms are implicated at various stages of the disorder. For example, individuals with borderline hypertension are commonly observed to have an elevated cardiac output (i.e., amount of blood pumped by the heart) but little evidence of increased resistance to the flow of blood in the body's vasculature (Julius & Esler, 1975). As noted earlier, this physiological pattern is consistent with increased activation of the sympathetic nervous system, which is the body's initial reaction to psychological stress. However, in older individuals with more established high blood pressure, cardiac output is either normal or depressed, while the vascular resistance is elevated. Although psychological stimuli such as emotionally stressful events have been shown to correlate highly with the exacerbation of hypertension episodes in diagnosed patients (see Weiner, 1977), recent research on behavioral influences has focused increasingly on earlier stages, rather than on the culmination of the disease.

In addition to cardiovascular adjustments and changes, the physiological mechanisms of high blood pressure probably involve the interaction of the central and autonomic nervous systems, the endocrine-hormonal system, and the kidneys. Accordingly, behavioral factors (in particular, psychological stress), might play a role in the etiology of HBP via a number of physiological pathways (Kaplan, 1980). Stress leads to discharge of the sympathetic nervous system and to increases in catecholamines. High levels of blood and tissue catecholamines have been found in some hypertensive humans and animals (Julius & Esler, 1975). Such elevations could lead to increased blood pressure via increased heart rate and force of heart action, constriction of peripheral blood vessels, and/or activation of a hormonal mechanism in the kidney that constricts the vasculature (Kaplan, 1980) and regulates the volume of blood.

Genetic-environment interactions. The prevalence of essential hypertension in the U.S. usually increases with age, and below the age of 50 years it occurs with less frequency in women than in men (Weiner, 1977). Evidence from animal research and studies of human twins indicates the genetic factors play a role in the etiology of the disease (Pickering, 1967). This evidence suggests that many genes are involved in the susceptibility of HBP, and it is likely that in humans, sustained elevations in blood pressure are produced by an interaction of a variety of environmental and genetic factors. Epidemiological studies reveal a difference in the prevalence of HBP among various social and cultural groups, a difference which cannot be accounted for by genetic factors alone (Henry & Cassel, 1969). For example, in the United States, hypertension is more common among blacks than among whites, but the prevalence of high blood pressure is greater in poor than in middle class black Americans (Harburg, Erfurt, Hauenstein, Chape, Schull, & Schork, 1973). Animal research similarly reveals examples where environmental factors (such as dietary salt intake or environmental stress) lead to sustained blood pressure elevations only in certain genetic strains (e.g., Dahl, Heine, & Tassinari, 1962). Closely related to this observation is the finding that family members tend to have similar blood pressures. Although the prevalent view attributes this solely to a genetic source, there is emerging evidence suggesting joint genetic and environmental factors. A possible environmentally-determined behavioral factor, family social interaction, is illustrated by a recent study which observed more negative nonverbal behavior (e.g., grimacing and gaze aversion) among families with a hypertensive father compared to families with a normotensive father (Baer, Vincent, Williams, Bourianoff, & Bartlett, 1980).

Behavioral factors. Sociocultural and psychological studies of humans, in conjunction with animal research, have identified some environmental factors related to behavior that might play a role in the initiation of HBP. These factors include dietary intake of salt, obesity, and psychological stress.

1. Dietary salt intake. Much has been written about the role of salt in essential hypertension, largely because excessive intake of sodium is thought to increase the volume of blood. However, studies indicate that high salt intake may be associated with high blood pressure levels only in some cultures and population groups. The relationship between salt intake and HBP appears to be complex, and salt intake may result in sustained blood pressure elevations only in genetically predisposed individuals. At present, the human craving for salt intake in excess of physiological needs is not fully understood, but evidence suggests that it may, in part, be a habit that is learned.

2. Obesity. Obesity is another cultural and behavioral phenomenon that plays an important role in hypertension, although the precise reasons for the higher prevalence of high blood pressure in obese patients have not been determined. In the case of obesity, recent studies have determined that weight loss can result in significant decreases in blood pressure (see Shapiro, 1982). As is the case with all non-pharmacologic approaches involving lifestyle alterations, effective treatment outcomes depend not only on producing transitory changes in behavior but also on the maintenance of these changes and sustained compliance with prescribed regimens. We will discuss these issues more fully in a later section of this chapter.

3. Psychosocial stress. Stress deriving from psychosocial causes is yet another factor implicated in the etiology and maintenance of high blood pressure. As previously described, psychological stimuli that threaten the

organism result in cardiovascular and endocrine responses that can play an important role in the development of hypertension (Julius & Esler, 1975). The brain and central nervous system, which are involved in determining whether situations are harmful or threatening, thus play a role in physiological mechanisms mediating the impact of noxious stimuli. On a societal level, there is some evidence that blood pressure elevations can occur under conditions of rapid cultural changes and socioeconomic mobility. Moreover, there are many studies in which "primitive" populations living in small cohesive societies were found to have low blood pressure that did *not* increase with age. When members of such societies migrated to areas where they were suddenly exposed to Western culture, they were found to have high levels of blood pressure that increased with age. This suggested some cumulative effect of the new living conditions that became evident over the course of the life span (Henry & Cassel, 1969). However, the strength of epidemiologic association between stressful conditions and the prevalence of high blood pressure in population groups has been challenged (e.g., Syme & Torfs, 1980).

While such studies can attempt to rule out confounding factors, (e.g., diet, sanitation, etc.) by using carefully matched control groups and by employing statistical control techniques, there are inherent limits to conclusions that can be reached from correlational research. Experimental techniques for inducing HBP in animals offer the ability to control both genetic and environmental variables by manipulating separate variables relevant to the course of this disorder (Campbell & Henry, 1983). Accordingly, various animal models of experimental high blood pressure indicate that the brain participates at some stage or another in the development or maintenance of increases blood pressure levels. The role of stress in the etiology of hypertension is supported by experimental studies demonstrating that sustained and chronic blood pressure elevations can be produced in animals exposed to environmental events such as fear of shock, social isolation followed by crowding, and experimentally produced conflict (see Campbell & Henry, 1983). Thus, there is the possibility that learning and conditioning processes might be involved in the development of the hypertensive state. In accord with our earlier discussion of genetic-environment interaction, studies have demonstrated that strains of animals that are genetically susceptible to hypertension are also susceptible to stress-induced pressure elevations (e.g., Friedman & Iwai, 1976).

Associations between emotional and behavioral stimuli and the development and/or maintenance of high blood pressure receive additional support from human studies indicating that techniques such as biofeedback and relaxation training can be used to modify the stress-induced components of high blood pressure (Shapiro, 1983). These techniques, to be discussed in more detail in a later section, are designed to counteract pressure-increasing stimuli that operate through the central and autonomic nervous systems.

Personality correlates. The traditional psychosomatic approach to HBP proposed that one's emotional dispositions or personality traits play a causal role in the development of chronic blood pressure elevations (Harrell, 1980). The individual susceptible to HBP has been described as one with inhibited and poorly expressed anger (suppressed hostility), and it has been suggested that inhibited anger expresses itself in stimulation of the autonomic nervous system leading to acute and eventually chronic HBP. Although emotional states such as anger do lead to cardiovascular adjustments resembling HBP, and although identifiable traits have been observed in patients with high blood pressure (Weiner, 1977), on balance, the search for a hypertensive personality has not yielded conclusive results. Patients with high blood pressure are not homogenous in terms of either physiological or psychological characteristics. A recent study showed convincingly that 30% of a sample of young male patients with HBP (namely, with mild pressure elevations and high plasma renin levels) displayed *both* elevations in sympathetic nervous system activity and higher levels of suppressed hostility (Esler, Julius, Zweifler, Randall, Harburg, Gardner, & DeQuattro, 1977), a behavioral trait independently linked to increased nervous system activity. These results might be explained by suppressed hostility leading to blood pressure elevations, by increased nervous system activity as the initial event, or by some other underlying factor(s). This issue may be resolved with studies of families of patients with HBP and the social interaction patterns that could have a bearing on the personality development of offspring, or by animal research which looks at behavioral characteristics associated with the development of high blood pressure in susceptible strains.

Behavioral-cardiac interactions. Experimental work has sought to identify individuals who are at risk of developing HBP and the types of situations that might activate genetic predispositions to high blood pressure. Since the aim is to understand mechanisms in the *cause* of the disorder, research has focused increasingly on the beginning stage, rather than the culmination or the disease.

Given the borderline high blood pressure is characterized by heightened responsiveness of the cardiovascular and sympathetic nervous systems to psychological stimuli such as mental stress (Julius & Esler, 1975), recent research has examined the tendency toward large episodic or acute increases in heart rate, blood pressure, and sympathetic nervous system hormonal (catecholamine) activity as possible mechanisms involved in etiology. Several groups of investigators (e.g., Manuck & Schaefer, 1978; Obrist, 1981) have found that cardiovascular responsiveness is a stable and persistently evoked response that can be measured reliably in a laboratory situation. Cardiovascular responsiveness to certain psychological stimuli has also been related consistently to family history of high blood pressure (a hypertension risk factor), even among individuals who have normal resting blood pressure levels and display no overt signs of the disorder (Falkner, Obrist, 1981; Onesti, Angelakos, Fernandes, & Langman, 1979). For example, in one representative study (Falkner et al., 1979), adolescents with normal blood pressure and at least one parent with HBP displayed greater diastolic blood pressure, heart rate, and plasma catecholamine responses to a stressful mental arithmetic task compared to a control group of adolescents with no family history of HBP.

In summary, these studies represent several approaches currently being used by social and behavioral scientists to understand the etiology of high blood pressure. They represent an attempt to move from the symptom-oriented and purely descriptive level to a focus on mechanisms. These early findings justify further experimental, longitudinal, and naturalistic studies.

Psychosomatic Diseases

While there is evidence that several physical disorders are, to some degree, caused or exacerbated by psychological or emotional factors, the terms "psychosomatic" or "psychophysiological" refer to those physical conditions that appear to be *initiated* primarily by psychological factors (American Psychiatric Association, 1968). It should be noted that these conditions involve actual organ pathology, often due to activity of the autonomic nervous system initiated by psychosocial stimuli. Common examples of physical conditions that may be subsumed under this category include, but are not limited to, tension and migraine headache, ulcer, asthma, and rheumatoid arthritis.

Predispositions for specific disorders. The field of psychosomatic research has provided medicine with a basis for predicting who might be at risk for a specific illness as well as knowledge of the conditions under which the predisposed individual is most likely to develop that disorder. At one time, psychosomatics overemphasized the role of individual differences or dispositions, without taking into account the physiological, genetic, and situational factors that interact in predisposing an individual to a particular illness (cf. Weiner, 1977). Today, this perspective has changed, and researchers have become aware of genetically and environmentally-determined physiologic response patterns that might predispose particular individuals to one disorder rather than another. (This is commonly referred to as the "specificity problem.") For example, studies have shown that individuals differ in secretion of pepsinogen (a precusor of the stomach enzyme pepsin which is under neural control) and that the tendency to secrete this substance, which is related to ulcer susceptibility, may be genetically transmitted (Weiner, 1977).

It should be emphasized that a single predisposing factor may not be enough to result in physical disease. A variety of activating situations is necessary to produce organ dysfunction. This is amply demonstrated by studies of gene-environment interactions in the etiology of high blood pressure and ulcers (see Fuller, in this volume); it is also shown by the importance of environmental challenge and/or stress in activating Type A behavior. Further investigation of factors leading to the expression of predispositions for specific disorders should contribute to basic knowledge concerning mechanisms of mind-body interaction and provide greater understanding of physiological disease processes.

Cancers

Cancers are the second leading cause of death in the United States, accounting for about 20% of the overall mortality rate, or nearly 400,000 deaths annually. Despite improvements in rate of cure, total cancer mortality has risen substantially over the past several decades. This may be attributable, in part, to the growing proportion of older people in the population, since the risk of developing cancer increases with age. Another reason for increased mortality is the dramatic rise in the incidence of lung cancer: Cancer of the lung is the leading cause of death from cancer among men (National Science Foundation, 1980; U.S.D.H.E.W., 1979b) and may soon have a similar dubious distinction for women.

Cancers are not a single disease; instead, the term is used for more than 100 conditions characterized by unrestrained multiplication of cells and abnormal forms of cell growth (Fraumeni, 1975). One significant attribute of cancers is their ability to spread beyond the site of origin. They may invade neighboring tissue by direct extension or disseminate to more remote locations through the blood stream or through the lympathic system, which controls fluid transport between body tissues. It is believed that some or all cancers arise from a single abnormal or transformed cell, triggered in different ways to produce unrestrained multiplication (Levi, 1979). A complementary view is that cancer cells multiply and spread when a breakdown occurs in a portion of the immune system that performs the function of recognizing transformed cells and eliminating them before a detectable tumor can result.

The known risk factors for cancer include a variety of environmental agents, such as tobacco, X- and UV-radiation, alcohol, viruses, drugs,

asbestos, and many chemicals. Personal attributes, including genetic predispositions, congenital defects, precancerous lesions, and aging, have
also been implicated (Fraumeni, 1975). Tobacco is the exogenous substance for which data demonstrate a strong association with cancer:
Smoking increases the risk of lung cancer about 10-fold, increasing with
duration of smoking and number of cigarettes smoked per day
(U.S.D.H.E.W., 1979b). In addition, tobacco use enhances the effects of
other carcinogens. For example, exposure to asbestos carries some risk
to non-smokers; however, this is of a low order of magnitude compared to
the risks experienced by cigarette smokers. It has been estimated that
asbestos workers who smoked cigarettes had eight times the lung cancer
risk of smokers without this occupational exposure (U.S.D.H.E.W.,
1979a). This is 92 times the risk of non-smokers who did not work with
asbestos.

While cigarette smoking represents a specific behavior with known
pathogenic consequences, three other classes of psychological variables
have been suspected as risk factors for cancer: (1) stressful life events,
particularly those involving loss (e.g., bereavement); (2) lack of closeness
to parents; and (3) inability to express emotions, especially negative ones
(Fox, 1978; Schmale, 1981). The research designs used in most of these
studies are retrospective. Various methodological flaws tend to render
their results as suggestive only.

A related area holding some promise concerns the relationship of psychological factors to cancer growth and progression. This research is a
subset of a larger area of study dealing with determinants of successful
coping with chronic illness (e.g., Hamburg et al., 1980; Krantz, 1980).
Clinicians have often commented on the psychological differences between those cancer patients who do well or survive longer and those who
do poorly or succumb rapidly to the disease. Characteristics such as low
denial, depression, and anxiety have been related to poor cancer prognosis, and the experience of emotional stress has been observed in patients some months prior to relapse after long remission periods (see
Miller & Spratt, 1979).

Research attempting to link psychosocial variables to cancer may be
criticized for lacking a theoretical basis. Except for vague reference to the
possibility that emotional stress may decrease bodily resistance to malignant growth, little attention has been given to the pathophysiological
mechanisms underlying an association between psychosocial variables
and the development of cancer. However, experimental work has now
provided the groundwork for an investigation of such mechanisms. Advanced techniques for measuring immunological functions show that,
rather than existing as an autonomous defense agency, the immune system is integrated with other physiologic processes. Moreover, it is subject

to the influence of the central nervous system and endocrine responses that accompany psychological stress.

A new interdisciplinary research area, psychoneuroimmunology, examines the interrelationships among central nervous system, endocrine, behavioral, and immunologic processes (Ader, 1981). For example, laboratory stressors tend to decrease the responsiveness of the immune system in animals, and stress-responsive hormones, including corticosteroids, can alter directly and indirectly components of the immune response (Ader, 1981; Amkraut & Solomon, 1977). Animal and human studies demonstrate that laboratory and naturalistic stressors can reduce the number of lymphocytes (cells important in the immune process), lower the level of interferon (a substance which may prevent the spread of cancer), and cause damage in immunologically-related tissue (Ader, 1981).

Of particular relevance to cancer are other studies demonstrating that stress can inhibit the body's defenses against malignancy. For example, Riley (1975) reported markedly different latencies for mammary tumor development as a function of stress exposure in mice injected with a virus that induces tumors. Those animals housed under conditions of chronic environmental stress (e.g., crowding and noise) develop tumors with a median latency of 358 days, compared to a latency of 566 days in animals housed under protective conditions.

It should be emphasized that the relationship between stress and the immune system is by no means a simple one. Under certain conditions, enhanced immunity and increased resistance to cancers in response to stressors have been reported. Appropriate levels of hormones (e.g., corticosteroids) released under stressful conditions are essential for normal development and functioning of the immune system (Amkraut & Solomon, 1977). This suggests that the direction of stress-effects on the immune system—that is, whether imnunocompetence is enhanced or depressed—may depend on the level of stress experienced and resultant changes in hormonal levels.

The exploration of psychosocial influences on immune function constitutes an important area of biomedical research with implications for understanding cancer, as well as a variety of infectious diseases (see below). Further psychoneuroimmunological investigation in needed to isolate the variables that moderate the impact of stress on immunologic activity. There is also the possibility that certain groups of individuals (e.g., the elderly) may be particularly susceptible to psychosocially-induced alterations in immune response. This might occur because documented changes in the immune system (Makidonan & Yunis, 1977) or psychosocial changes, such as decreased financial security and reduced mobility (Eisdorfer & Wilkie, 1977) that accompany aging.

Infectious Diseases

Exposure to contagious microorganisms does not invariably lead to disease. In fact, only a small percentage of infected persons actually become ill during disease epidemics. There is evidence that psychosocial factors can influence the acquisition, course, and recovery from infectious diseases via at least three mechanisms. These mechanisms parallel the processes linking behavior and physical illness outlined above.

Direct psychophysiological effects on immunity. As noted in the section on cancer, there is evidence that psychosocial factors affect the functioning of the immune system. This leads to increased susceptibility to immunologically-mediated diseases and increased expression of the disease among those who are infected. Biobehavioral research has specified certain immunologic changes (e.g., reduced production or level of antibodies) which mediate these relationships.

With regard to infections, the immune system can be divided into three functional components: processes involved in transporting the invading microorganisms to the immune system, processes leading to the production of antibodies or immunologically active cells, and processes involving interaction between immunologically active substances and invading microorganisms. Neurohumoral factors can influence each of these immune mechanisms (Amkraut & Solomon, 1977). As with cancer, stress-related influences on susceptibility to infectious disease depend on a complex of factors. These include the type of stress, type and number of invading microorganisms, mode of infection (e.g., air, contact, or bloodstream), and the species of animal and its immunologic state at the time of inoculation (Ader, 1981; Amkraut & Solomon, 1977).

Psychoneuroimmunological research with animals has demonstrated that behavioral conditioning with noxious stimuli increases susceptibility to viral infections. In one study, neither exposure to a stressor nor inoculations with a virus was alone sufficient to induce disease in adult mice, but the combination of stress and inoculation with a virus elicited symptoms of viral disease (Friedman & Glasgow, 1966). In other studies, rats handled for brief periods of time early in life showed more vigorous antibody response to bacteria than did non-handled controls (Amkraut & Solomon, 1977). The impact of psychosocial stimulation on the immune response appears to be related to the dose of pathogen administered, as well as to the timing of exposure to the stressor (Amkraut & Solomon, 1977).

In humans, much of the evidence linking psychosocial stress to increased susceptibility to infectious diseases is derived from retrospective clinical studies, although there has been some promising prospective research. For example, Meyer and Haggerty (1962) studied the influence of family crises on factors that might modify susceptibility to streptococcal disease. In subjects observed over a l-year period, each family member was followed with periodic throat cultures and measures of immunologic function. Clinical ratings of chronic stress were positively related to streptococcal illness rate and levels of streptococcal antibodies in the blood. While close contact with infected family members and the season of the year influenced acquisition of a streptococcal organism, several respiratory illnesses were considerably more frequent after family episodes judged to be stressful.

A prospective study of infectious mononucleosis (Kasl, Evans, & Niederman, 1979) used a class of military cadets—a population subjected to the simultaneous rigors of military training and academic pressure. Among subjects susceptible to infectious mononucleosis (i.e., those without Epstein-Barr virus antibodies at matriculation), about 20% became infected each year with the virus, and 25% of this group went on to develop the clinical disease. Psychosocial factors that increased the risk of clinical disease among those infected included having a high level of motivation, doing poorly academically, and having "overachieving" fathers.

Health-impairing habits and lifestyles. An individual's behavior can influence exposure to infection and the dose of pathogen. Poor nutrition and/or poor personal hygiene obviously increase illness susceptibility and delay recovery. In this regard, various behavioral and social factors (e.g., low socioeconomic status) are associated with increased incidence of infectious illness. Individuals in these categories are more likely to be exposed to harmful microorganisms, suffer from known health hazards at home and at work, and have poor training in prudent, healthy ways of living. They may also have less access to quality medical care and are less likely to engage in preventive health practices (Institute of Medicine, 1978).

Behavioral reactions to illness. A third process linking behavior to the course of infectious illness involves treatment-seeking behavior and response to treatment. For example, a study of individuals in Maryland who had contracted Asian influenza during 1957–1958 revealed that clinical disease characteristics (e.g., serological response, height of fever, and symptom severity) failed to distinguish those who recovered quickly from those who retained symptoms for longer periods of time. However, subjects with delayed recovery scored as more "depression–prone" on psychological tests given in advance of the outbreak of illness. This finding was interpreted to indicate that depression-prone individuals exhibit

greater concern over illness, which increased and prolonged their physical complaints and reports of illness. A prospective follow-up study measured actual frequency of infection via assays for rises in serum antibody
titers. Among those who were infected, depression-prone subjects tended
to develop the disease (thus suggesting a possible role of immunologic
factors) but increased concern over the illness seems the most likely
explanation for these findings (Cluff, Canter, & Inboden, 1966).

Summary

The first portion of this chapter has highlighted the mechanisms implicat-
ing behavioral factors in the etiology and pathogenesis of physical disease. Three such mechanisms were identified: direct psychophysiological
effects, health-impairing habits and behaviors, and reactions to illness and
the sick role. These processes were discussed as they apply to cardiovascular disorders, cancers, infectious diseases, and other psychosomatic
disorders. In the following section we consider the role of behavioral
factors in the treatment and rehabilitation of physical illness.

TREATMENT AND REHABILITATION OF PHYSICAL ILLNESS

The Prospective Patient and the Medical Encounter

The provision of medical care depends, to a very considerable extent, on
the social, psychological, and cultural processes that lead people to define
themselves as requiring care (Mechanic, 1968). Many factors unrelated to
the biological severity of illness combine to determine who receives care;
persons requiring medical attention do not always seek out medical help
and are not always seen by health care providers. These variables must be
considered by practitioners and policy planners in the formulation and
delivery of health care service.

   Recognition of symptoms and resultant use of health care services are
influenced by situational factors, such as life difficulties and psychological
stress (Mechanic, 1968). Also important are learned patterns of behavior
such as social roles and cultural norms: For example, females are more
likely than males to visit health care professionals. Social class and cultural background influence patients' evaluations of symptoms and doctors' responses to patients' complaints. Age is another factor that
determines reactions to symptoms and use of medical facilities. For example, the elderly take aches and pains for granted and place little faith in

medical science, even though the frequency of use of medical facilities and concern with health increase with age (Riley & Foner, 1968).

Psychological and Physiological Aspects of Pain and Illness

Much progress has been made in identifying sociopsychological corre-lates of pain and psychophysiological pain mechanisms and in developing research-based techniques for pain control. Pain is more than a sensory experience. It is not a necessary consequence of injury or tissue damage. Definitions that imply that pain can be stopped simply by interrupting neural pathways are not adequate to account for clinically-related phenomena. For example, surgical interventions indicate a rather disap-pointing record of success (Weisenberg, 1977). People without known organic pathology suffer pain (Fordyce, 1976), and even when an organic basis for pain is established, psychological factors continue to affect the experience of pain.

A range of cultural, sociopsychological, and situational factors in-fluence pain perception and tolerance (see Weisenberg, 1977). Different cultural groups have different views of appropriate pain reactions, includ-ing the circumstances under which it is permissible to cry or ask for help. Moreover, the influences of the social context and meaning of the pain experience produce differences between clinical and experimentally-induced pain. Pain in clinical situations involves anxiety associated with the disease process and fear of death (Beecher, 1959; Weisenberg, 1977) whereas experimentally-induced pain does not.

The placebo effect. A pervasive phenomenon in the pain literature is the placebo effect, that is the reduction of pain or the removal of symp-toms via medication or therapeutic treatment which has no identifiable active component (Shapiro, 1971). It has been estimated that placebo medication (e.g., use of pharmacologically inert substances) and other non-specific treatment factors reduce pain successfully in about 35% to 40% of patients (Beecher, 1959). Although the placebo response in medicine has been widely recognized, until recently it had been regarded as a nuisance variable. In pharmacological research, the routine inclusion of a control group receiving an inert medication has been considered an essential methodological control, particularly in evaluating psychoactive drugs (see Kornetsky, in this volume). Mechanisms of the placebo re-sponse as a component of various therapeutic interventions have now come under study in their own right. Contrary to the popular belief that placebo effects are confined to psychological changes, there are data showing that placebos can produce a variety of changes on a physiological level, for example, significant blood pressure reductions among persons with HBP (Shapiro, 1983).

Psychosocial variables that enhance the effectiveness of placebos have been identified, thereby shedding light on the mechanisms of placebo action in pain relief. Person-centered approaches aimed at identifying the patient responsive to placebos have not proven valuable. However, there is evidence that situational factors, which influence a patient's motivational and attentional processes, as well as a host of variables relating to doctor-patient interaction (e.g., expectations of relief and the patient's confidence in the physician and the procedures) can heighten placebo effects (Shapiro, 1971). Stress and anxiety-reduction also seem to be important facets of placebo effectiveness (Beecher, 1959). It is likely that placebo-related factors, when fully understood, will provide a powerful tool in clinical practice.

Psychophysiological models. The influential "gate control" theory of pain (Melzack & Wall, 1965) was proposed in order to integrate physiological and psychological factors in pain perception. This theory proposes that noxious stimuli activate selective central nervous system processes, which act to exert control over incoming messages. Influenced by this trigger mechanism, cells at each level of the spinal cord act as a gate-control system, increasing or decreasing their receptivity to incoming pain signals traveling along the nerves. This system makes it possible for higher mental processes, which underlie attention, emotion, and memories of prior experience, to alter transmission of pain signals (Weisenberg, 1977).

The posited physiological and anatomical bases for the gate-control theory have been subject to considerable criticism (e.g., Liebeskind & Paul, 1977; Nathan, 1976). However, a wide assortment of clinical and experimental findings has been interpreted as supporting the theory—or at least certain aspects of it (Liebeskind & Paul, 1977)—and the theory has led to the development of a technique for artificially stimulating the nervous system to relieve pain. Although subsequent work on endorphins calls into question some key details of the gate-control theory, the original theory and subsequent modifications have been influential in highlighting the importance of motivational and cognitive factors in pain experience.

The recent discovery of endogenous, opiate-binding receptors and substances in the brain (endorphins) which bind with these receptors has led to a new interest in central nervous system mechanisms of pain control. It has been demonstrated that a pain-suppression system exists in the brain which can be activated by psychophysiological procedures such as electrical stimulation (Liebeskind & Paul, 1977) and by environmental and psychological manipulations such as exposure to stress. Recent research (Levine, Gordon, & Fields, 1978; Mayer, Price, Rafii, & Barber, 1976) suggests that mechanisms of action of heretofore poorly understood phenomena of pain relief (e.g., accupuncture and placebo response) may involve this endogenous system.

Compliance with Medical Regimens

In recent years, there has been a growing awareness that the failure of patients to adhere to prescribed medical regimens is probably the single greatest problem in bringing effective medical care to the individual patient. This problem also contributes in a major way to the economic and social costs of illness (Cohen, 1979; Sackett & Haynes, 1976). Although adherence varies, it is not uncommon to find compliance rates as low as 50% in many situations. It was estimated recently that about 33% of patients adhere correctly, that 33% are noncompliant because they adhere to a misunderstood regimen, and that 33% are knowingly noncompliant (Cohen, 1979).

The medication compliance problem may be most pronounced for chronic illnesses, such as high blood pressure, where effective therapy requires regular, long-term taking of medications that may produce unpleasant side-effects (Sackett & Haynes, 1976). However, noncompliance is a problem in areas of the treatment process other than adherence to regimens. Substantial numbers of patients who do not have painful symptoms fail to come for scheduled appointments, and the problem of inducing and maintaining change of unhealthful habits (such as diet and smoking) is particularly formidable.

A good deal of attention has been given to isolating factors that influence or predict compliance (Becker, 1979; Sackett & Haynes, 1976). Surprisingly, common demographic variables such as age, sex, and marital and socioeconomic status have little independent influence. The crux of the problem is often poor doctor-patient communication, rather than the patient's behavior alone. Two sets of variables deriving from the physician-patient encounter—satisfaction with care and comprehension of treatment regimen—appear to affect compliance.

Aspects of the doctor-patient relationship determine satisfaction, and satisfaction determines the degree to which medical advice is accepted. For example, a study of a pediatric setting (Korsch & Negrete, 1972) found that a major source of mothers' dissatisfaction was the failure of physicians to answer questions and provide clear explanations of illness. More than 80% of those who thought the physician had been understanding were satisfied, as compared to only 33% of those who did not feel that the doctor tried to understand their problems. If mothers were dissatisfied with the communicator (i.e., the doctor) or the content of the consultation, they were less likely to comply with the physician's advice.

A second aspect of the compliance problem is the patient's ability to comprehend and recall details of the treatment regimen. Much of the failure to follow a doctor's orders is attributable to genuine problems in understanding and remembering what is told (Ley & Spelman, 1967). Often, the material presented by the doctor is too difficult to understand, the treatment regimen itself is overly complicated, or patients hold misconceptions about illness or human physiology which lead to confusion.

The crucial challenge for medical compliance, as with the modification of other health-impairing behaviors, is to maintain people on prescribed regimens for sustained periods. This problem is illustrated by the remarkably similar relapse rates among subjects treated in programs aimed at weight reduction, smoking cessation, and reduction of alcohol consumption (Hunt, Matarazzo, Weiss, & Gentry, 1979). About 66% of such patients abandon the regimen and backslide by the end of 3 months, and only about 25% of the individuals maintain changed behavior at the end of a 1-year period.

One technique used to help maintain long-term adherence to treatment regimens is a focus on the immediate rewards and consequences of compliance or noncompliance. A range of "behavior modification" procedures, based on principles of operant learning, has proven the most effective (Pomerleau & Brady, 1979). Interventions to increase adherence must also recognize those characteristics of the social interactions of physicians and patients that foster noncompliance.

Most of the research on medical compliance has been designed to solve practitioners' everyday clinical problems, rather than to develop a comprehensive theory that may apply across a broad range of medical situations, illnesses, and behaviors. However, one conceptual approach that has received some support in explaining medically-related behaviors (including compliance) is the Health Belief Model. This model centers on the patient's views about the appropriate paths of action in the presence of health disturbances, perceptions of barriers to action, and subjective interpretations of symptoms (Becker, 1979). Still more effective approaches are needed, which encompass the physician-patient communication process and suggest ways of making the rewards of long-term medical compliance more salient to patients.

The Smoking Problem: An Exemplar of Health-Impairing Behavior

The cigarette smoking habit has been described as the single most preventable cause of death in the United States (U.S.D.H.E.W., 1979b). By virtue of this fact, it provides an important basis for the involvement of psychology in medicine. Yet, despite the fact that knowledge of the health risks of smoking has reduced the percentage of adults who regularly use cigarettes, there are still over 50 million smokers in the U.S. today. Moreover, in recent years there has been an alarming increase in the proportion of teenagers (particularly females) who are acquiring the smoking habit. With regard to the modification of smoking behavior, the problem is not that the public is unaware of the negative health consequences, but that the great majority of smokers are unable to quit or stay off cigarettes for *prolonged* periods (Bernstein & Glasgow, 1979; Leventhal & Cleary, 1980).

Cigarette smoking is a behavior whose initiation, maintenance, and cessation are determined by a mixture of social, psychological, and physiological factors. Many of the problems faced in attempts to prevent and modify the smoking habit are also associated with the correction of other health-impairing habits, lifestyles, and dependencies (e.g., poor diet, alcoholism, and lack of exercise). We will give considerable attention to the smoking problem to illustrate behavioral science approaches to these health-impairing behaviors.

Initiation and prevention of smoking. Cigarette smoking can be viewed as the product of a multi-stage process that begins with initial experimentation with cigarettes and leads to the acquisition of a habit and/or addictive process (Pomerleau, 1979). Data suggest that even limited adolescent experimentation with smoking may lead to habitual smoking (Leventhal & Cleary, 1980). Psychosocial factors related to initiation of smoking include social pressure from peers, imitation of adult behavior, adolescent rebellion and antisocial tendencies, and personality factors such as extraversion—a biologically-based dimension related to arousal or simulation-seeking. A social learning explanation of smoking initiation (Bandura, 1977) assumes that the habit is acquired through imitation and social reinforcement, typically under the influence of peer pressure, media stereotypes, etc.

The inhalation of smoke is initially somewhat aversive, but after sufficient practice, pharmacological habituation (or tolerance) occurs, and the behavior produces enough satisfaction or reward in its own right to maintain the habit (Pomerleau, 1979). The delayed negative health consequences, but immediate social and biological rewards of smoking, may account for many of the difficulties in modifying the habit once it becomes established (Jarvik, 1979).

Early efforts to prevent smoking assumed that this could be accomplished by teaching young people the health consequences of this habit. But the results were largely disappointing (see McAlister, Puska, Koskela, Pallonen, & Maccoby, 1980). However, several projects have obtained encouraging results by employing sociopsychological techniques of communication and attitude change to deter smoking in adolescents. A pioneering effort in the area, The Houston Project, is a 3-year longitudinal study (Evans, Rozelle, Maxwell, Raines, Dill, Guthrie, Henderson, & Hill, 1981). This project created persuasive films and posters to teach young teens (grades 7–9) about peer and media pressures to smoke and about effective techniques for resisting pressures. Other films demonstrated the immediate physiological consequences of smoking (e.g., carbon monoxide in the breath). Hundreds of students in matched experimental and control groups were compared for cigarette smoking rates at the start of the project and during the 3-year follow-up. The results indicated a significant impact of the films and posters: Experimental subjects smoked less frequently and expressed less intention to smoke compared to a control group receiving no intervention (Evans et al., 1981).

Maintenance of the smoking habit. Once smoking is established, both psychological and biological factors contribute to its persistence and resistence to change. Learning mechanisms, possibly in conjunction with physiological satisfactions derived from smoking, play a considerable role in maintaining the habit (Hunt & Matarazzo, 1970). The use of cigarettes becomes part of a chain of behaviors: taking out the package, lighting the cigarette, getting tobacco smoke, etc. As a result, the aforementioned stimuli *associated* with smoking come to elicit pleasurable responses by themselves. In addition, the avoidance of unpleasant withdrawal effects (e.g., craving) becomes rewarding, thus helping to maintain the habit (Russell, 1979). These observations receive more systematic support from animal research which demonstrates that drug responses (e.g., morphine tolerance) can become conditioned reactions and that withdrawal symptoms can be conditioned to external cues (Siegel, 1979).

Learning or conditioning mechanisms alone are not sufficient to explain the maintenance of smoking, since many smokers will increase intake to regulate or achieve a particular level of nicotine in their system (Schachter, Silverstein, Kozlowski, Perlick, Herman, & Liebling, 1977). Biological factors figure prominently in the maintenance of the habit and nicotine is the chemical in tobacco that is most likely responsible for these effects (Jarvik, 1979). However, the question of whether cigarette smoking can be considered an addiction comparable to heroin or alcohol addiction remains a subject of scientific debate (Russell, 1979).

Tobacco has the capacity to elicit many of the defining characteristics of an addictive process, and there has been recent biobehavioral research on the complex interplay of psychological and pharmacological processes leading to smoking behavior. For example, a *nicotine-regulation* hypothesis asserts that heavy smokers adjust their smoking rate to keep nicotine at a roughly constant level and that the rate of smoking depends on the rate of nicotine excretion and breakdown by the body. The rate of nicotine excretion depends, in part, on the acid/base balance (pH) of the urine, which, in turn, can be altered by psychological stress or anxiety. Thus, it is argued that the links between psychological processes, the craving for cigarettes, and increased smoking are mediated by a physiological addiction mechanism involving the pH of urine (Schachter et al., 1977). A series of programmatic studies (Schachter et al., 1977) provides support for this hypothesis.

However, there remain several exceptions to the nicotine-regulation model. There are different types of smokers, some of whom do not appear to smoke for nicotine content (Schachter et al., 1977). In addition, the nicotine-regulation model suggests that lowered nicotine content of cigarettes will increase the number of cigarettes smoked, and data in this regard are, at best, contradictory (Garfinkel, 1979). Nevertheless, the nicotine-regulation hypothesis has identified a possible biobehavioral mechanism for cigarette addiction.

Withdrawal. Because of the addictive component of smoking, it is crucial to understand the withdrawal process in order to develop effective intervention strategies that modify the habit. However, most research efforts have concentrated on the effects of cigarette smoking, rather than on the effects of cessation, i.e., irritability, sleep disturbances, inability to concentrate, and weight gain (Schachter, 1978).

Recent research by Grunberg (1983) suggests that weight gain accompanying withdrawal from nicotine may result from increased preferences for sweet-tasting foods. In humans and animals, it was demonstrated that cessation of nicotine was accompanied by marked increases in body weight and concomitant increases in consumption of sweet foods. Moreover, these effects could not be explained by changes in total food consumption or activity level. Ability to put up with the withdrawal syndrome is crucial to the maintenance of smoking cessation. Therefore, further investigation of mechanisms responsible for symptoms accompanying withdrawal may suggest techniques for controlling the high recidivism rate among those who quit smoking.

Modification of smoking behavior. Most of the effort in research on smoking has been directed toward the development of smoking-cessation strategies. Many of the earlier intervention studies suffered from problems of experimental design (e.g., lack of adequate control groups) and difficulties in measuring smoking-cessation objectively. There was also a high drop-out rate, sometimes reaching 50% of subjects included in the initial sample, which may spuriously inflate the initial success rate (Leventhal & Cleary, 1980; Pomerleau, 1979). More recent work has enabled some systematic evaluation of the long-term efficacy of smoking-cessation programs and techniques.

Research indicates that most therapy techniques (e.g., individual and medical counseling, hypnosis, behavioral therapies) are effective in promoting short-term cessation of smoking, but usually fail to keep more than 50% of exsmokers off cigarettes for long periods of time (Bernstein & Glasgow, 1979). Systematic study of the important area of maintenance of nonsmoking is just beginning, and strategies such as long-term group support and behavioral techniques for coping with anticipated withdrawal symptoms are promising. A number of the public health studies described below incorporate components of behavioral therapy approaches. Successful long-term smoking-cessation results obtained by these studies are attributable in part to therapy techniques.

Public health approaches have also been used to modify the smoking habit. It appears that significant reductions in adult smoking, especially among middle-aged males and certain professional groups, can be attributed to information and educational campaigns initiated after the first Surgeon General's Report on Smoking in 1964 (Pomerleau, 1979). In recent years, several large scale media-based projects have been undertaken in the United States and Europe to change attitudes and behavior related to smoking.

The Stanford Heart Disease Prevention Project was designed to reduce a broad range of risk factors including smoking (Farquhar, Maccoby, Wood, et al., 1977; Meyer, Nash, McAlister, Maccoby, & Farquhar, 1980.) Three communities were studied. One served as a control; a second was exposed to a mass media campaign on heart disease risk factors, including smoking; and a third received the mass media campaign and face-to-face behavioral therapy for selected high-risk persons. The media campaign alone produced some reductions in smoking at long-term follow-up. More substantial reductions occurred when the media campaign was supplemented by face-to-face therapeutic instruction. These findings are encouraging, but must be evaluated cautiously because of several methodological problems inherent in risk factor studies of this sort—namely, the high drop-out rate and/or other difficulties encountered when subjects do not adhere to the randomly assigned interventions involving life-style changes (Kasl, 1980).

Another ambitious study, in Finland (Puska et al., 1978), introduced a nationwide multiple-component program, including televised counseling sessions. These were designed to prevent relapse by educating participants in behavioral techniques for coping with anticipated relapse problems (e.g., stress and weight gain). About 40,000 adult smokers participated in the study; as a result of the program a small but significant percentage achieved sustained abstinence from smoking at 6-month and 1-year follow-ups (McAlister et al., 1980).

The Stanford and Finnish programs represent impressive and, perhaps, cost-effective efforts to induce large numbers of people to abandon the cigarette habit on a long-term basis. These and related studies, however, have not produced unequivocally successful outcomes (Kasl, 1980; Leventhal & Cleary, 1980). Nonetheless, they do suggest that meaningful changes in smoking behavior via public health approaches are possible, but only when the risks of smoking are made immediate and salient and both skills and support to change smoking behavior are provided (Pomerleau, 1979). The more important question of whether risk factor (e.g., smoking) reduction will lower morbidity and mortality, particularly from cardiovascular diseases, is being studied directly by large-scale intervention trials now underway. These projects will be discussed in the last section of this essay.

Other Behavioral Therapies in Health Care

The increasing importance of behavioral and social sciences in medicine has derived, in part, from the development of effective procedures for changing illness-related behaviors. Several of these behavior modification techniques, which were designed and evaluated for the prevention, management, and treatment of physical disease (Pomerleau & Brady, 1979), have already been alluded to in the discussions of medical compliance and cigarette smoking. Other health-care applications are in the areas of pain control, childhood disorders, adult psychosomatic disorders, rehabilitation of the disabled and physically ill, and geriatric problems (Melamed & Siegel, 1980). Four representative behavioral techniques are described presently.

Operant control of chronic pain. Pain reactions can persist long after the original physiological sensation and tissue damage have been remediated. Fordyce (1976) and others have developed a successful technique for treatment of chronic pain through the application of operant conditioning procedures. Many pain-related behaviors become established and maintained by the particular rewards they provide for the patient, for example, attention from family, staying home from work, as well as pain relief. Environmental rewards (e.g., attention from family and/or hospital staff) are therefore manipulated so that the value of undesirable pain behaviors is reduced or removed.

Cognitive-behavioral interventions. These techniques are designed to reduce pain and the aversiveness of medical procedures (e.g., surgery) by diminishing perceived threat and the psychological stress associated with medical procedures (Turk & Genest, 1979). Since the physiological and/or behavioral components of the stress response (e.g., excessive sympathetic nervous system activity, lowered motivation or ability to comply with medical regimens, etc.) also may interfere with the recovery process (see Krantz, 1980), there is some indication that stress-reduction procedures can speed recovery. Some of these procedures (e.g., psychological preparation of children for hospitalization) are being applied routinely (Melamed & Siegel, 1980).

Biofeedback. Until recently, it was believed that the responses of the autonomic nervous system were involuntary and that an individual could exert little or no control over these processes. However, visceral responses such as heart rate, blood pressure, and skin temperature can be controlled voluntarily when feedback is provided to the individual for altering these responses (Miller, 1969). Biofeedback training teaches the individual to monitor physiological responses through the use of electronic instruments. When a subject alters a physiological state (e.g., heart rate, muscle tension, or electrical activity of the brain), he or she is provided with auditory, visual, or other feedback indicating that the correct response has been made. The feedback is effective in teaching subjects to control the physiological response because it tells them that their motivated attempts to alter the response are effective. Thus, the feedback serves as a reinforcer (reward), which leads to learned control of the physiological response (Miller, 1969).

Recent research has explored the clinical utility of biofeedback techniques for such disorders as high blood pressure, migraine headache, seizure disorders, sexual dysfunctions, and muscular paralysis (Gatchel & Price, 1979; Ray, Racynski, Roger, & Kimball, 1979). A particularly effective clinical application has been in the treatment of neuromuscular disorders. For example, through the use of feedback for activity of muscle units (cells), paralyzed or damaged muscles may one again come under voluntary control. Dysfunctions such as cerebral palsy, muscular spasms, and various paralyses have been successfully treated by biofeedback. Often, these dysfunctions were previously unresponsive to traditional physiotherapies and medical or surgical treatment (Ray et al., 1979).

The initial enthusiasm for biofeedback probably exaggerated its therapeutic effectiveness. Further research has revealed limitations in the use of this technique. For example, it must still be established that training in laboratory or clinic generalizes to real-life settings, and there is need for more research evaluating the relative effectiveness of biofeedback versus other therapeutic techniques.

Relaxation training. Relaxation therapies are procedures designed to elicit physical and emotional calmness in order to decrease autonomic nervous system arousal, muscular tension, and other physiological correlates of psychic trauma. The most common technique is deep muscle relaxation (Jacobson, 1938), which involves supervised practice in the systematic relaxation of major skeletal muscle groups. Relaxation therapy is effective in the treatment of a variety of psychophysiologic disorders, including high blood pressure, migraine headache, and chronic pain syndromes (Melamed & Siegel, 1980).

Summary

The preceding portion of this essay has highlighted the role of behavioral factors in the treatment and rehabilitation of physical illness. We considered the role of psychological and cultural processes in the definition of and response to "illness" and the use of health care facilities. Our discussion continued with reviews of psychophysiological aspects of pain, medical compliance, and the smoking problem. We concluded this section with a discussion of behavioral therapies currently applied to the treatment of physical disorders. Having completed the main portions of our review documenting the linkages between psychology and medicine, we conclude the essay with a discussion of future directions for research on the interface between these two disciplines.

FUTURE DIRECTIONS

An important priority for research interfacing psychology and medicine is the integration of behavioral and biomedical knowledge in a way that elucidates mechanisms underlying the interplay among behavior, physiological processes, and somatic dysfunctions. Accordingly, the key issues for biobehavioral inquiry include further study of features of the behavioral context and of the individual (e.g., coping styles, biologic predispositions, and availability of social supports), which may determine the outcome of exposure to stressful events. Also suggested are further studies of psychophysiological mechanisms that mediate behavior-disease linkages, particularly those involving neuroendocrine and immune responses. Other priorities are the development and evaluation of techniques to produce sustained changes in behavioral risk factors. This includes research on mechanisms of smoking addiction and withdrawal and the prevention of health-impairing habits. The important area of medical compliance requires more theoretically-based research taking into account doctor-patient communication and the cognitive and motivational factors that sustain adherence to treatment regimens.

Biobehavioral Paradigm for Research into the Etiology and Pathogenesis of Physical Disease

Psychosocial stress. As noted earlier, stress has been implicated as a central factor in the etiology of cardiovascular illness and also may play a role in the development of peptic ulcer, cancers, and infectious diseases. The association of psychological stress with somatic disorders underscores the importance of research aimed at understanding when and under what conditions stress becomes translated into physical diseases, specifying the physiological and neuroendocrine pathways through which stress-reactions potentiate illness, and identifying factors which predispose individuals to one stress-related disorder rather than another (Graham, 1972).

Research on the psychophysiological pathways linking stress to disease will require continued technological improvements to facilitate the measurement and identification of neuroendocrine, central-neural, and related processes. Animal models will play an important role in such research (e.g., Ader, 1976; Campbell & Henry, 1983). The study of pathophysiological mechanisms often relies on procedures that cannot be used with human subjects. These procedures include the use of surgical interventions and electrical stimulation as means of identifying sites that regulate bodily reactions to stressful events. Drugs that selectively stimulate (or block) the activity of suspected mediating structures, such as the receptor sites of the sympathetic nervous system, provide a direct means of assessing the impact of stress-related physiologic processes upon target organs whose dysfunction is suspected to be of psychogenic origin (e.g., Obrist, 1981).

Human research models will, however, remain indispensable, especially in the study of cognitive and perceptual variables that initiate and regulate physiological reactions to stressful stimuli. Experimental research is essential and justifiable for making progress in this area where no demonstratable damage to subjects can be discerned. Where ethical and practical concerns limit the applicability of laboratory methodologies in studying a problem area, it is frequently possible to conduct studies of populations who are exposed to the variable of interest under natural conditions. Recent developments in psychophysiological measurement have also made it possible to measure the influence of behavioral variables on physiological processes in naturalistic settings, such as home or work-place. These techniques have opened new frontiers in biobehavioral research.

A focus on mechanisms linking behavior and health is required in order to translate historical and epidemiological descriptors, such as age, personality, genetics, or nutritional history, into psychophysiological processes that can be modified or altered (Schwartz, Shapiro, Redmond, Ferguson, Ragland, & Weiss, 1979). To influence medical practice, behavioral and social science research must identify modifiable variables involved not only in the etiology of disease, but also in the progression of illness after symptoms have appeared (Stachnik, 1980).

Type A behavior pattern. One illustration of a developing area of mechanism-oriented biobehavioral research is the study of the Type A "coronary-prone" behavior pattern. Having demonstrated its association with coronary disease, researchers now are addressing issues similar to those discussed in the section on psychological stress: isolation of aspects of the behavior pattern that confer enhanced risk, identification of the psychological mechanisms that produce and sustain coronary-prone behavior, specification of the physiological processes that account for the enhanced risk of individuals displaying coronary-prone behavior (Glass, 1981). Subsequent studies (probably with animal models) might be undertaken to elucidate cause-and-effect. That is, do animals bred or trained to exhibit Type A behavioral characteristics show elevated physiological reactivity, or are the behavioral responses caused by physiological reactivity? Indeed, both behavioral and physiological reactions may be consequences of a third variable located elsewhere in the nervous system.

Psychoneuroimmunology. The emerging field of psychoneuroimmunology also holds great promise (see Ader, 1981). Exploration of basic mechanisms of immune changes produced by psychological simuli will continue to be an active area of research. In addition to controlled laboratory experimentation with animals, there is a need to determine if reliable, replicable, and clinically meaningful alterations in immune function in humans are associated with psychosocial variables (e.g., certain life stressors, coping styles, or both of these acting together). Other research priorities for this field include the study of correlated changes in neuroendocrine and immune functions across the life span (developmental immunology), studies of possible learning and conditioning effects on the immune system, and prospective studies relating behavior to processes of immunologically-mediated diseases (Ader, 1981).

Methodological issues. The complexities involved in integrating behavioral and biomedical knowledge will require multifaceted research strategies. What is needed is a continual exchange between laboratory and field methodologies. This interaction may take several forms. For example, an effect can be established as reliable with controlled laboratory experimentation, where causal links can be inferred. The generality of the relationship can then be established in subsequent research in natural settings, e.g., home or workplace (e.g., Cohen et al., 1981). Similarly, by first conducting field studies, it is possible to isolate important dimensions of a particular research area. At that point, laboratory studies may be useful to rule out alternative explanations often inherent in naturalistic research. A vivid example of this methodological dynamic is provided by data on biobehavioral factors in the etiology of high blood pressure. Naturalistic and clinical evidence suggested that psychosocial stress plays a role in this disorder. Accordingly, laboratory studies were undertaken to isolate the psychophysiological mechanisms involved in behavioral responses to environmental stressors. Further naturalistic work (e.g., Rose, Jenkins, & Hurst, 1978) extended the laboratory findings by demonstrating that exaggerated blood pressure responses to high work loads were predictive of sustained hypertension (Herd, 1978).

Risk Factor Modification and Prevention

Associations between major chronic diseases and seemingly modifiable behavioral factors have spurred interest in relating behavioral knowledge to health promotion and the prevention of disease (Breslow, 1978; Matarazzo, 1980). The present body of research in this area constitutes only a promising beginning, and it is wise to be cautious about making unequivocal claims of success based on existing evidence. However, this emerging research area does raise important challenges and questions.

Maintaining abstinence. While there are encouraging indications that established patterns of behavior can be changed in the short-term, a major difficulty has been maintaining these changes in substantial numbers of individuals over sustained periods of time (Bernstein & Glasgow, 1979; Hunt et al., 1979). There is also a high early drop-out rate in various treatment programs (e.g., Leventhal & Cleary, 1980). Research in these areas by behavioral scientists will intensify in the near future and must focus on understanding factors that initiate and maintain health-impairing habits and not just on techniques to modify and prevent them.

For some habits, such as smoking or drug abuse, biological factors are intimately involved at all stages of the problem. Considerable attention must be given to the psychobiological and psychosocial aspects of the withdrawal and behavior change processes themselves (Leventhal & Cleary, 1980). Smoking, dietary, and exercise habits, and other health-endangering practices such as failure to use seat belts, alcohol abuse, and poor hygiene, also must be studied as sociocultural phenomena. Decisions to engage in or modify health-impairing habits and the incorporation of changed behaviors as part of an overall lifestyle all occur in a social context (Syme, 1978).

Antecedents of habits and risk factors. Habits and lifestyles develop in the context of family and society; hence, more research is needed on the socialization of health-related habits. Such longitudinal and cross-cultural research is expensive, but it may be conducted in a cost-effective manner in conjunction with ongoing longitudinal studies of the development of disease risk factors in children. For example, a number of projects are being carried out among populations of school-age children (e.g., the Bogalusa Heart Study by Voors, Foster, Frerichs, Weber, & Berenson, 1976) to track the distribution and time course of heart disease risk factors such as blood pressure and serum lipids. Behavioral and social variables, including family health values and habits, could be incorporated into such projects. A behavioral interface with bio-medical research would also provide an excellent opportunity to examine the processes involved in the socialization of healthful lifestyles.

Prevention. "Primary" prevention (i.e., before disease develops) of health impairing habits and the promotion of healthy lifestyles for people of all ages are cost-effective approaches to health. For in the long term, the potential costs in lives and dollars of treating disease are likely to outweigh the costs of preventing unhealthful habits. Social learning approaches to smoking prevention have yielded promising results in the Houston school-based intervention (Evans et al., 1981). Further work with children and adolescents might expose other habits to social learning interventions. More systematic research with adults also is needed. The work place has proven to be a promising setting for such efforts. People spend considerable time at work, and many employers sponsor such programs because of the benefits that accrue from healthier employees.

The terms "secondary prevention" and "tertiary prevention" refer, respectively, to interventions taken to arrest the progress of illness already in early asymptomatic stages and to interventions to stop the progression of a clinically manifest disease (Institute of Medicine, 1978). Secondary and tertiary prevention activities involving behavioral factors may be more feasible than primary prevention, given the present state of knowledge. Advantages of such interventions are that target groups can be easily recognized and are motivated to change their behavior (Institute of Medicine, 1978).

Determining the impact of behavior change on morbidity and mortality. The presumably causal associations between behavioral factors and chronic diseases imply that effective modification of habits and behavior patterns will reduce the incidence of and mortality from these disorders. The assumption is complex and requires further evidence before it can be accepted. In the case of cigarette smoking, epidemiological data reveal that former cigarette smokers experience declining overall mortality rates as the years of discontinuance of the habit increase (U.S.D.H.E.W., 1964). Data on morbidity are more complex, and they indicate that the benefits of being an exsmoker are not as high as the benefits of never having smoked. Similarly, the data on the effects of reduced blood lipids on CHD are not conclusive (Kasl, 1980). Indeed, they suggest that factors such as the age at which reductions occur and the underlying mechanisms for lipid elevations make a difference in the benefits that accrue.

Convincing evidence that risk factor modification reduces disease incidence and mortality can be obtained only from experimental or clinical trials. Several primary prevention trials (selecting subjects free of disease at entry into the study) are underway to determine if altering diet, smoking, and controlling high blood pressure will lower the incidence of coronary heart disease.

Clinical trials of lifestyle interventions face the problems of behavioral measurement and of maintaining continued adherence to regimens (Kasl, 1980; Syme, 1978). Despite these disadvantages, such studies are major field trials of therapeutic and preventive measures which are relevant to the formation of public policy regarding behavior and health.

CONCLUSION

The previous sections of this essay have highlighted the more promising research areas in behavior and health. Foremost among these are studies of psychosocial stress and the mechanisms linking stress and illness; psychoneuroimmunology; the challenge of maintaining abstinence from health-impairing behaviors; and techniques for enhancing medical compliance. In our overview of the historical interface between psychology and medicine, we noted that important behavior-health associations have been documented for years. However, a significant recent development—the biobehavioral approach—is characterized by an emphasis on basic mechanisms linking behavioral processes to disease states. Three broad categories of such mechanisms were described: direct psychophysiological effects, health-impairing habits and behaviors, and reactions to illness and the sick role. We have structured our review around these three behavioral mechanisms and have provided illustrative examples of the important role these categories of behavior play in health and illness.

The biobehavioral approach to somatic health and illness is by definition an interdisciplinary venture between psychology and medicine. It requires the contributions of researchers and practitioners with a wide variety of skills and perspectives. The benefits of this approach promise increasing collaborative efforts between these two disciplines.

· ACKNOWLEDGMENTS

This essay is adapted from *Behavior and Health* (co-authored with Richard Contrada and Neal E. Miller) which was commissioned by the Social Science Research Council for the National Science Foundation's *Five Year Outlook on Science and Technology: 1981*. Preparation of the earlier report was supported by NSF Contract No. PRA-8017924. Preparation of this essay was assisted by USUHS Grant C07214.

REFERENCES

Ader, R. Psychosomatic research in animals. In C. Hill (Ed.), *Modern trends in psychosomatic medicine*. London: Butterworths, 1976.

Ader, R. (Ed.). *Psychoneuroimmunology*. New York: Academic Press, 1981.

Alexander, F. *Psychosomatic medicine*. New York: Norton, 1950.

American Psychiatric Association. *Diagnostic and statistical manual of mental disorders (DSM-II)*. Washington, DC: American Psychiatric Association, 1968.

Amkraut, A., & Solomon, G. F. From the symbolic stimulus to the pathophysiologic response: Immune mechanisms. In S. J. Lipowski, D. R. Lipsitt, & P. C. Whybrow (Eds.), *Psychosomatic medicine: Current trends and clinical applications*. New York: Oxford University Press, 1977.

Baer, P. E., Vincent, J. P., Williams B. J., Bourianoff, G. G., & Bartlett, P. C. Behavioral response to induced conflict in families with a hypertensive father. *Hypertension*, 1980, 2, 170–177.

Bandura, A. *Social learning theory*. Englewood Cliffs, NJ: Prentice-Hall, 1977.

Becker, M. H. Understanding patient compliance: The contributions of attitudes and other psychological factors. In S. J. Cohen (Ed.), *New directions in patient compliance*. Lexington, MA: D. C. Heath, 1979.

Beecher, H. K. *Measurement of subjective responses: Quantitative effects of drugs*. New York: Oxford University Press, 1959.

Bernstein, D. A., & Glasgow, R. E. Smoking. In O. F. Pomerleau & J. P. Brady (Eds.), *Behavioral medicine: Theory and practice*. Baltimore, MD: Williams and Wilkins, 1979.

Breslow, L. Risk factor intervention for health maintenance. *Science*, 1978, *200*, 908–912.

Campbell, R. J., & Henry, J. P. Animal models of hypertension. In D. S. Krantz, A. Baum, & J. E. Singer (Eds.), *Handbook of psychology and health: Cardiovascular disorders and behavior*. Hillsdale, NJ: Lawrence Erlbaum Associates, 1983.

Cannon, W. B. Voodoo death. *American Anthropologist*, 1942, *44*, 169–181.

Cluff, L. E., Canter, A., & Inboden, J. B. Asian influenza: Infection, disease, and psychological factors. *Archives of Internal Medicine,* 1966, *177,* 159–163.

Cohen, F. Personality, stress, and the development of physical illness. In G. C. Stone, F. Cohen, & N. E. Adler (Eds.), *Health psychology—A handbook.* San Francisco: Jossey-Bass Publishers, 1979.

Cohen, F., Horowitz, M. J., Lazarus, R. S., Moos, R. H., Robins, L. N., Rose, P. M., & Rutter, M. *Report of the subpanel on psychosocial assets and modifiers.* Prepared for Committee to Study Research on Stress in Health and Disease, Institute of Medicine, National Archives, National Academy of Sciences, 1981.

Cox, T. *Stress.* Baltimore, MD: University Park Press, 1978.

Dahl, L. K., Heine, M., & Tassinari, L. Role of genetic factors in susceptibility to experimental hypertension due to chronic excess salt ingestion. *Nature,* 1962, *194,* 480–482.

Dembroski, T. M., MacDougall, J. M., Shields, J. L. Petitto, J., & Lushene, R. Components of the Type A coronary-prone behavior pattern and cardiovascular responses to psychomotor performance challenge. *Journal of Behavioral Medicine,* 1978, *1,* 159–176.

Dohrenwend, B. S., & Dohrenwend, B. P. Some issues in research on stressful life events. *Journal of Nervous and Mental Disease,* 1978, *166,* 7–15.

Dunbar, F. *Mind and body: Psychosomatic medicine.* New York: Random House, 1947.

Eisdorfer, C., & Wilkie, F. Stress, disease, aging, and behavior. In J. E. Birren & K. W. Schaie (Eds.), *Handbook of the psychology of aging.* New York: Van Nostrand Reinhold, 1977.

Engel, G. L. The need for a new medical model: A challenge for biomedicine. *Science,* 1977, *196,* 129–136.

Esler, M., Julius, S., Zweifler, A., Randall, A., Harburg, E., Gardner, H., & DeQuattro, V. Mild high-renin essential hypertension: Neurogenic human hypertension? *The New England Journal of Medicine,* 1977, *296,* 405–411.

Evans, R. I., Rozelle, R. M., Maxwell, S. E., Raines, B. E., Dill, C. A., Guthrie, T. J., Henderson, A. H., & Hill, P. C. Social modeling films to deter smoking in adolescence: Results of a three year field investigation. *Journal of Applied Psychology,* 1981, *66,* 399–414.

Falkner, B., Onesti, G., Angelakos, E. T., Fernandes, M., & Langman, C. Cardiovascular response to mental stress in normal adolescents with hypertensive parents. Hemodynamics and mental stress in adolescents. *Hypertension,* 1979, *1,* 23–30.

Farquhar, J. W., Maccoby, N., Wood, P. D., et al. Community education for cardiovascular health. *Lancet,* 1977, *1,* 1192–1195.

Fordyce, W. E. *Behavioral methods for chronic pain and illness.* Saint Louis: C. V. Mosby, 1976.

Fox, B. H. Premorbid psychological factors as related to cancer incidence. *Journal of Behavioral Medicine,* 1978, *1,* 45–133.

Frankenhaeuser, M. Behavior and circulating catecholamines. *Brain Research,* 1971, *31,* 241–262.

Fraumeni, J. F. *Persons at high risk of cancer: An approach to cancer etiology and control.* New York: Academic Press, 1975.

Friedman, M., Manwaring, J. H., Rosenman, R. H., Donlon, G., Ortega, P., & Grube, S. Instantaneous and sudden death: Clinical and pathological differentiation in coronary artery disease. *Journal of the American Medical Association,* 1973, *225,* 1319–1328.

Friedman, M., Rosenman, R. H., & Carroll, V. Changes in the serum cholesterol and blood-clotting time in men subjected by cyclic variation of occupational stress. *Circulation,* 1958, *17,* 852–861.

Friedman, R., & Iwai, J. Genetic predisposition and stress-induced hypertension. *Science,* 1976, *193,* 161–162.

Friedman, S. B., & Glasgow, L. A. Psychologic factors and resistance to infectious disease. *Pediatric Clinics of North America,* 1966, *13,* 315–335.

Garfinkel, L. Changes in the cigarette consumption of smokers in relation to changes in tar/nicotine content of cigarettes smoked. *American Journal of Public Health,* 1979, *69,* 1274–1276.

Garrity, T. F., & Marx, M. B. Critical life events and coronary disease. In W. D. Gentry & R. B. Williams, Jr. (Eds.), *Psychological aspects of myocardial infarction and coronary care.* Saint Louis, MO: C. V. Mosby, 1979.

Gatchel, R. J., & Price, K. P. (Eds.). *Clinical applications of biofeedback: Appraisal and status.* New York: Pergamon Press, 1979.

Glass, D. C. Type A behavior: Mechanisms linking behavioral and pathophysiologic processes. In J. Siegrist & M. J. Halhuber, (Eds.), *Myocardial infarction and psychosocial risks.* New York: Springer-Verlag, 1981.

Glass, D. C., Krakoff, L. R., Contrada, R., Hilton, W. C., Kehoe, K., Mannucci, E. G., Collins, C., Snow, B., & Elting, E. Effect of harassment and competition upon cardiovascular and plasma catecholamine responses in Type A and Type B individuals. *Psychophysiology,* 1980, *17,* 453–463.

Glass, D. C., & Singer, J. E. *Urban stress: Experiments on noise and social stressors.* New York: Academic Press, 1972.

Graham, D. T. Psychosomatic medicine. In N. S. Greenfield & R. A. Sternbach (Eds.), *Handbook of psychophysiology.* New York: Holt, Rinehart and Winston, 1972.

Grunberg, N. E. The effects of nicotine and cigarette smoking on food consumption and taste preferences. *Addictive Behaviors* 1983, *7,* 317–331.

Hamburg, B. A., et al. Executive summary. In B. A. Hamburg, L. F. Lipsett, G. E. Inoff, & A. L. Drash (Eds.), *Behavioral and psychosocial issues in diabetes: Proceedings of a national conference.* U.S. Department of Health and Human Services, U.S. Public Health Service Publication No. 80-1993. Washington, DC: U.S. Government Printing Office, 1980.

Harburg, E., Erfurt, J. C., Hauenstein, L. S., Chape, C., Schull, W. J., & Schork, M. A. Socio-ecological stress, suppressed hostility, skin color, and black-white male blood pressure: Detroit. *Psychosomatic Medicine,* 1973, *35,* 276–296.

Harrell, J. P. Psychological factors and hypertension: A status report. *Psychological Bulletin,* 1980, *87,* 482–501.

Haynes, S. G., Feinleib, M., & Kannel, W. B. The relationship of psychosocial factors to coronary heart disease in the Framingham Study. III. Eight-year incidence of coronary heart disease. *American Journal of Epidemiology,* 1980, *3,* 37–58.

Henry, J. P., & Cassell, J. C. Psychosocial factors in essential hypertension. Recent epidemiology and animal experimental evidence. *American Journal of Epidemiology,* 1969, *90,* 171–200.

Herd, A. J. Physiological correlates of coronary-prone behavior. In T. M. Dembroski, S. M. Weiss, J. L. Shields, S. G. Haynes, & M. Feinleib (Eds.), *Coronary-prone behavior.* New York: Springer-Verlag, 1978.

Hinkle, L. E. The effect of exposure to culture change, social change and changes in interpersonal relations on health. In B. S. Dohrenwend & B. P. Dohrenwend (Eds.), *Stressful life events: Their nature and effects.* New York: Wiley, 1974.

Holmes, T. H., & Rahe, R. H. The social readjustment rating scale. *Journal of Psychosomatic Research,* 1967, *11,* 213–218.

House, J. S. Occupational stress as a precursor to coronary disease. In W. D. Gentry & T. B. Williams, Jr. (Eds.), *Psychological aspects of myocardial infarction and coronary care.* Saint Louis, MO: C. V. Mosby, 1975.

Hunt, W. A., & Matarazzo, J. D. Habit mechanisms in smoking. In W. A. Hunt (Ed.), *Learning mechanisms in smoking.* Chicago, IL: Aldine, 1970.

Hunt, W. A., Matarazzo, J. D., Weiss, S. M., & Gentry, W. D. Associative learning, habit and health behavior. *Journal of Behavioral Medicine,* 1979, *2,* 111–124.

Hurst, J. W., Logue, R. B., & Schlant, R. C. (Eds.). *The heart.* New York: McGraw-Hill, 1978.

Institute of Medicine. *Perspectives on health prevention and disease prevention in the United States.* Report to National Academy of Sciences, 1978.

Jacobson, E. *Progressive relaxation.* Chicago, IL: University of Chicago Press, 1938.

Jarvik, M. E. Biological influences on cigarette smoking. In Surgeon General's report, *Smoking and health,* DHEW Publication No. 79-50066. Washington, DC: U.S. Government Printing Office, 1979.

Jenkins, C. D. Psychologic and social precursors of coronary disease. *The New England Journal of Medicine,* 1971, *284,* 244–255, 307–317.

Julius, S., & Esler, M. Autonomic nervous cardiovascular regulation is borderline hypertension. *American Journal of Cardiology,* 1975, *36,* 685–696.

Kannel, W. B., & Dawber, T. R. Hypertensive cardiovascular disease. In G. Onesti, K. E. Kim, & J. Hayer (Eds.), *The Framingham study: Hypertension: Mechanisms and management.* New York: Grune and Stratton, 1971.

Kannel, W. B., McGee, D., & Gordon, T. A general cardiovascular risk profile: The Framingham study. *American Journal of Cardiology,* 1976, *38,* 46–51.

Kaplan, N. M. The control of hypertension: A therapeutic breakthrough. *American Scientist,* 1980, *68,* 537–545.

Kasl, S. V. Cardiovascular risk reduction in a community setting: Some comments. *Journal of Consulting and Clinical Psychology,* 1980, *48,* 143–149.

Kasl, S. V., Evans, A. S., & Niederman, J. C. Psychosocial risk factors in the development of infectious mononucleosis. *Psychosomatic Medicine,* 1979, *41,* 445–467.

Korsch, B., & Negrete, V. Doctor-patient communication. *Scientific American,* 1972, *227,* 66–78.

Krantz, D. S. Cognitive processes and recovery from heart attack: A review and theoretical analysis. *Journal of Human Stress,* 1980, *6,* 27–38.

Lazarus, A. S. *Psychological stress and the coping process.* New York: McGraw-Hill, 1966.

Leventhal, H., & Cleary, P. D. The smoking problem: A review of the research and theory in behavioral risk modification. *Psychological Bulletin,* 1980, *88,* 370–405.

Levi, L. Psychosocial factors in preventive medicine. In *Surgeon General's background papers for healthy people report,* DHEW Publication #79-55011A. Washington, DC: U. S. Government Printing office, 1979.

Levine, J. D., Gordon, N. C., & Fields, H. L. The mechanism of placebo analgesia. *The Lancet,* 1978, *2,* 654–657.

Ley, P., & Spelman, M. S. *Communicating with the patient.* London: Staples Press, 1967.

Liebeskind, J. C., & Paul, L. A. Psychological and physiological mechanisms of pain. *Annual Review of Psychology,* 1977, *28,* 41–60.

Lipowski, Z. J. Psychosomatic medicine in the seventies: An overview. *American Journal of Psychiatry,* 1977, *134,* 233–244.

Lown, B., Verrier, R., & Corbalan, R. Psychologic stress and threshold for repetitive ventricular response. *Science,* 1973, *184,* 834–836.

McAlister, A., Puska, P., Koskela, K., Pallonen, U., & Maccoby, N. Mass communication and community organization for public health education. *American Psychologist,* 1980, *35,* 375–379.

McDonough, J. R., Hames, C. G., Stulb, S. C., et al. Coronary heart disease among Negroes and whites in Evans County, Georgia. *Journal of Chronic Disease,* 1965, *18,* 443–468.

Mcmahon, C. E. The role of imagination in the disease process: Pre-Cartesian medical history. *Psychological Medicine*, 1976, *6*, 179–184.

Mcmahon, C. E., & Hastrup, J. L. The role of imagination in the disease process: Post-Cartesian history. *Journal of Behavioral Medicine*, 1980, *3*, 205–207.

Makidonan, T., & Yunis, E. (Eds.). *Immunology and aging*. New York: Plenum, 1977.

Manuck, S. B., & Schaefer, D. C. Stability of individual differences in cardiovascular reactivity. *Physiology and Behavior*, 1978, *21*, 675–678.

Mason, J. W. A re-evaluation of the concept of "non-specificity" in stress theory. *Journal of Psychiatric Research*, 1971, *8*, 323–333.

Matarazzo, J. D. Behavioral health and behavioral medicine: Frontiers for a new health psychology. *American Psychologist*, 1980, *35*, 807–817.

Mayer, D. J., Price, D. D., Rafii, A., & Barber, J. Acupuncture hypalgesia: Evidence for activation of a central control system as a mechanism of action. In J. J. Bonica & D. Albe-Fesard (Eds.), *Recent advances in pain research and therapy: Proceedings of the First World Congress on pain*. New York: Raven, 1976.

Mechanic, D. *Medical sociology*. New York: Free Press, 1968.

Medalie, J. H., Synder, B., Groen, J. J., Newfeld, H. N., Goldbourt, U., & Riss, E. Angina pectoris among 10,000 men: 5 year incidence and univariate analysis. *American Journal of Medicine*, 1973, *55*, 583–594.

Melamed, B. G., & Siegel, L. J. *Behavioral medicine: Practical application in health care*. New York: Springer, 1980.

Melzack, R., & Wall, P. D. Pain mechanisms: A new theory. *Science*, 1965, *150*, 971–979.

Meyer, A. J., Nash, J. D., McAlister, A. L., Maccoby, N., & Farquhar, J. W. Skills training in a cardiovascular education campaign. *Journal of Consulting and Clinical Psychology*, 1980, *48*, 129–142.

Meyer, R. J., & Haggerty, R. J. Streptococcal infections in families: Factors altering individual susceptibility. *Pediatrics*, 1962, *29*, 339–349.

Miller, N. E. Learning of visceral and glandular responses. *Science*, 1969, *163*, 434–445.

Miller, N. E. Behavioral medicine as a new frontier: Opportunities and dangers. In S. M. Weiss (Ed.), *Proceedings of the national heart and lung institute working conference on health behavior* (DHEW Publication No. 76-868). Washington, DC: U.S. Government Printing Office, 1976.

Miller, T., & Spratt, J. S. Critical review of reported psychological correlates of cancer prognosis and growth. In B. A. Stoll (Ed.), *Mind and cancer prognosis*. London: Wiley, 1979.

Nathan, P. W. The gate-control theory of pain: A critical review. *Brain*, 1976, *99*, 123–158.

National Science Foundation. Health of the American people. In *Science and technology: A five-year outlook*. Report from the National Academy of Sciences. Washington, DC: U.S. Government Printing Office, 1980.

Obrist, P. A. *Cardiovascular psychophysiology: A perspective*. New York: Plenum, 1981.

Page, I. H., & McCubbin, J. W. The physiology of arterial hypertension. In W. F. Hamilton & P. Dow (Eds.), *Handbook of physiology: Circulation* (Volume 1, Section 2). Washington, DC: American Physiological Society, 1966.

Pickering, G. W. The inheritance of arterial pressure. In J. Stamler, R. Stamler, & T. N. Pullman (Eds.), *The epidemiology of hypertension*. New York: Grune and Stratton, 1967.

Pomerleau, O. F. Why people smoke: Current psychobiological models. In P. O. Davidson & S. M. Davidson (Eds.), *Behavioral medicine: Changing health life styles*. New York: Brunner/Mazel, 1980.

Pomerleau, O. F., & Brady, J. P. *Behavioral medicine; Theory and practice*. Baltimore, MD: Williams and Wilkins, 1979.

Puska, P., et al. *Changing cardiovascular risk in an entire community: The North Karelia project.* Paper presented at the International Symposium on Primary Prevention in Early Childhood or Atheroschlerotic and Hypertensive Diseases, Chicago, October 1978.

Ray, W. J., Racynski, J. M., Rogers, T., & Kimball, W. H. (Eds.). *Evaluation of clinical biofeedback.* New York: Plenum, 1979.

Riley, M. W., & Foner, A. *Aging and society.* New York: Russell Sage Foundation, 1968.

Riley, M. W., & Hamburg, B. A. *Report of the subpanel on stress, health, and the life course.* Prepared for Committee to Study Research on Stress in Health and Disease, Institute of Medicine, National Academy of Science, 1981.

Riley, V. Mouse mammary tumors: Alteration of incidence as apparent functions of stress. *Sciences,* 1975, *189,* 465–467.

Rose, R. M., Jenkins, C.D., & Hurst, M. W. *Air traffic controllers health change study.* FAA Contract No. DOT-FA73WA-3211, Boston University, 1978.

Rosenman, R. H., Brand, R. J., Jenkins, C. D., Friedman, M., Straus, R., & Wurm, M. Coronary heart disease in the Western Collaborative Group Study: Final follow-up experience of 8½ years. *Journal of the American Medical Association,* 1975, *233,* 872–877.

Rosenman, R. H., & Friedman, M. Neurogenic factors in pathogenesis of coronary heart disease. *Medical Clinics of North America,* 1974, *58,* 269–279.

Ross, R., & Glomset, J. A. The pathogenesis of atherosclerosis. *The New England Journal of Medicine,* 1976, *295,* 369–377, 420–425.

Russell, M. A. H. Tobacco dependence: Is nicotine rewarding or aversive? In N. A. Krasnegor (Ed.), *Cigarette smoking as a dependence process* (NIDA Research Monograph 23). DHEW Publication No. (ADM) 79-800. Washington, DC: U. S. Government Printing Office, 1979.

Sackett, D. L., & Haynes, R. E. *Compliance with therapeutic regimens.* Baltimore, MD: Johns Hopkins University Press, 1976.

Schachter, S. Pharmacological and psychological determinants of smoking. *Annals of Internal Medicine,* 1978, *88,* 104–114.

Schachter, S., Silverstein, B., Kozlowski, L. T., Perlick, D., Herman, C. P., & Liebling, B. Studies of the interaction of psychological and pharmacological determinants of smoking. *Journal of Experimental Psychology: General,* 1977, *106,* 3–40.

Schmale, A. Stress and cancer. In *Research on Stress in Health and Disease.* Washington, DC: National Academy of Sciences, Institute of Medicine, 1981.

Schneiderman, N. Animal models relating behavioral stress and cardiovascular pathology. In T. M. Dembroski, S. M. Weiss, J. L. Shields, S. G. Haynes, & M. Feinleib (Eds.), *Coronary-prone behavior.* New York: Springer-Verlag, 1978.

Schwartz, G. E., Shapiro, A. P., Redmond, D. P., Ferguson, D. C. E., Ragland, D. R., & Weiss, S. M. Behavioral medicine approaches to hypertension: An integrative analysis of theory and research. *Journal of Behavioral Medicine,* 1979, *2,* 311–364.

Selye, H. *The stress of life.* New York: McGraw-Hill, 1956.

Shapiro, A. K. Placebo effects in medicine, psychotherapy, and psychoanalysis. In A. E. Bergin & S. L. Garfield (Eds.), *Handbook on psychotherapy and behavioral change.* New York: Aldine, 1971.

Shapiro, A. P. The non-pharmacologic treatment of hypertension. In D. S. Krantz, A. Baum, & J. E. Singer (Eds.), *Handbook of psychology and health: Cardiovascular disorders and behavior.* Hillsdale, NJ: Lawrence Erlbaum Associates, 1983.

Siegel, S. Pharmacological learning and drug dependence. in D. J. Oborne, M. M. I. Gruneberg, & J. R. Eiser (Eds.), *Research in psychology and medicine* (Vol. 2). London: Academic Press, 1979.

Stachnik, T. Priorities for psychology in medical education and health care delivery. *American Psychologist,* 1980, *35,* 8–15.

Syme, S. L. Lifestyle intervention in clinic-based trials, *American Journal of Epidemiology,* 1978, *108,* 87–91.

Syme, S. L., & Torfs, M. S. Epidemiological research in hypertension: A critical appraisal. *Journal of Human Stress,* 1980, *4,* 43–48.

Turk, D. C., & Genest, M. Regulation of pain: The application of cognitive and behavioral techniques for prevention and remediation. In P. C. Kendall & S. D. Hollon (Eds.), *Cognitive-behavioral interventions: Theory, research and procedures.* New York: Academic Press, 1979.

U.S. Department of Health, Education, and Welfare. *Smoking and health: A report of the Surgeon General* (U.S. Public Health Service Publication No. 1103). Washington, DC: U.S. Government Printing Office, 1964.

U.S. Department of Health, Education, and Welfare. *Healthy people: A report of the Surgeon General on health promotion and disease prevention* (U.S. Public Health Service Publication No. 79-55071). Washington, DC: U.S. Government Printing Office, 1979.(a)

U.S. Department of Health, Education, and Welfare. *Smoking and health: A report of the Surgeon General* (U.S. Public Health Service Publication No. 79-50066) Washington, DC: U.S. Government Printing Office, 1979.(b)

Voors, A. W., Foster, T. A., Frerichs, R. R., Weber, L. S., & Berenson, G. S. Studies of blood pressure in children, ages 5-14 years, in a total biracial community. *Circulation,* 1976, *54,* 319–327.

Weiner, H. *Psychobiology and human disease.* New York: Elsevier, 1977.

Weisenberg, M. Pain and pain control. *Psychological Bulletin,* 1977, *84,* 1008–1044.

6 Psychology and Pharmacology

Conan Kornetsky
Laboratory of Behavioral Pharmacology
Boston University School of Medicine

INTRODUCTION

Although pharmacology and psychology are two disciplines that for the most of their history have developed in separate ways, the discovery of drugs that were effective in the treatment of mental illness in the early 1950s placed them juxtaposed in pursuit of a common goal. This common goal spawned another discipline or disciplines called psychopharmacology and/or behavioral pharmacology. Prior to this revolution in the chemotherapeutic treatment of the mentally ill, there were pharmacologists who studied the effects of *their* drugs on behavior and psychologists who studied the effects of drugs on *their* behavior.

In this essay I discuss aspects of the interplay between psychology and pharmacology. In their early history the two were geographically and conceptually close, yet they did not interact. Early interests of psychologists (physiologists) in the physical intensity-response relationship and of pharmacologists in the drug dose-response relationship suggested a closeness in thinking that was not explicitly stated by either group. The discovery that certain compounds had hallucinogenic properties also fostered mutual interests but not joint endeavors. The specific early contributions of both Freud and Pavlov to a science that was later to be called psychopharmacology will be discussed. The interaction of social psychology and pharmacology was facilitated relatively early by the social and legal problems engendered by the non-medical use of drugs and by the passing of punitive penalties for such use. Finally, I discuss the impact of the discovery of psychotherapeutic drugs in the 1950s on the disciplines of psychology and pharmacology. In the space available I do not attempt to present an inclusive review of the interactions of the two disciplines. This emphasis reflects biases that I have developed as a participant who has been trying to relate to both of these disciplines for more than 30 years.

EARLY HISTORY

The First Laboratories

Until the middle of the nineteenth century, the history of pharmacology was mainly rooted in the history of materia medica (the drugs used for medical treatment), while the history of psychology was rooted for the most part in philosophy. However in the middle of that century both experimental psychology and experimental pharmacology were commonly related to the discipline of physiology.

Credit for establishing the first laboratory for the experimental study of pharmacology is generally given to Rudolph Buchheim (1820–1879) who, in 1846 accepted the chair of materia medica, diethetics, and history and encyclopedia at the University of Dopat in Estonia. Although Estonia was at that time governed by Russia, the University was for the most part German (Holmstedt & Liljestrand, 1963, p. 76). The laboratory that Buchheim established was in the cellar of a private house, and in 1860 the University officially created a laboratory of pharmacology. This was 19 years before the establishment of what is considered to be the first laboratory of psychology by Wilhelm Wundt (Boring, 1929, p. 318) in 1879 at Leipzig. Although Wundt is given credit for establishing the first laboratory of psychology, the beginning of formal experimental psychology started with Gustav Theodor Fechner (1801–1887) who published his major work in psychology in 1860 (Boring, 1929, p. 266) two years before Wundt's first psychological studies.

Psychophysics and the Dose-effect Relationship

Fechner's major contribution was his work in psychophysics. Earlier interest in the relationship between the psychological and physical world was explored by Ernst Heinrich Weber (1795–1878) who discovered that there was not a simple one-to-one relationship between the magnitude of the difference in weight between two objects and the ability of an observer to perceive the difference (Heidbreder, 1933, p. 77). Fechner gave this empirical relationship mathematical form and named it "Weber's Law" (Boring, 1929, p. 271). Subsequently it has been called the "Weber-Fechner Law." The work started with Weber and culminated with Fechner's 1860 text, *Elemente der Psychophysik.* Of interest is that Buchheim was an assistant in the anatomy and physiology department under the direction of Weber. Although it is reasonable to assume that Buchheim was aware of Weber's work in psychophysics and possibly of the early work of Fechner, the scaling of dose-effect relationships awaited the publication of J.W. Trevan's 1927 paper, "The Error of Determination of Toxicity."

Despite the similarity between a dose-effect relationship and psychophysics, Trevan and later pharmacologists do not mention it. Also, psychologists working in psychophysics seemed to be unaware that similar types of maneuvers were being carried out by pharmacologists and toxicologists. Stevens's (1975) *Psychophysics* does not mention the dose-effect relationship except in the context of the psychophysical scaling of some chemicals on taste and smell (p. 15).

The similarity between the dose-effect relationship and psychophysics is shown in the two sigmoid curves depicted in Figure 1. On the left is an adaptation of a figure from Trevan's (1927) paper showing percent mortality (in mice) as a function of dose of cocaine. On the right is an adaptation of a figure from a paper by Hill, Kornetsky, Flanary, and Wikler (1952a) showing the percent of stimuli judged to be stronger than a standard as a function of electrical stimulus delivered to the hand of the subject. Figure 2 shows the same data plotted with log units on the abscissa and z-scores on the ordinate. Pharmacologists and toxicologists usually employ a standard score transformation called "probit" in which the mean is equal to 5 with a standard deviation of 1.

The Experimental Psychologist

Although psychopharmacology was not a significant current of the mainstream of either pharmacology or psychology until the latter part of the 1950s, there was a significant history of related research by psychologists.

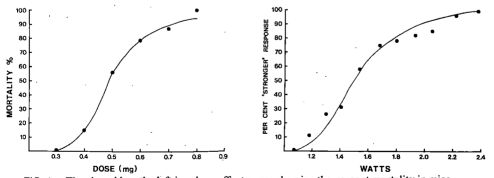

FIG. 1.   The sigmoid on the left is a dose-effect curve showing the percent mortality in mice as a function of dose of cocaine (adapted from Trevan, 1927), and on the right is a sigmoid showing the mean percent of "stronger" responses as a function of stimulus intensity in watts (adapted from Hill et al., 1952).

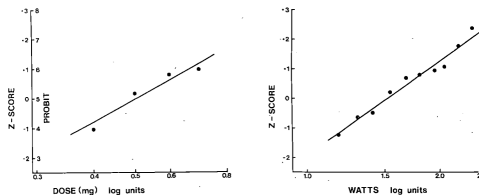

FIG. 2. Data from Figure 1 replotted with the percent scores converted to z-scores and the intensity of dose and watts, respectively, plotted in log units. Equivalent probit scores are given on the right.

This research was not reflected in texts prior to the middle 1950s. The 1938 edition of Woodworth's *Experimental Psychology* has only four entries in the index on the effects of drugs on behavior. Even the second edition which was published in 1954 (Woodworth & Schlosberg, 1954) had only nine entries. There certainly was a more extensive bibliography of the effects of drugs on behavior prior to 1954, but before this time psychopharmacology had not yet achieved an identity of its own. This early history was reviewed in 1957 by Brady. The early experiments studied the effects of drugs on behaviors that were of interest to the psychologist of the period. Some investigated the effects of drugs on learning (e.g., Lashley, 1917; Macht & Mora 1920) and others motor activity (e.g., Searle & Brown, 1937; Shirley, 1929). In the 1940s there arose an interest in the effects of seizures, especially those caused by pentylenetetrazol (Metrazol®), on learning (e.g., Heron & Carlson, 1941; Rosen & Gantt, 1943). Physiological psychologists focused on the effects of hormones on innate behavioral patterns such as sex and aggression (e.g., Beach, 1942; Koster, 1943; Stone, 1938). Starting with Pavlov interest grew in developing animal models of conflict and neurosis and the effects of drugs on this experimentally produced abnormal behavior (e.g., Masserman & Yum, 1946; Wikler & Masserman, 1943).

In his review, Brady (1957) pointed out that there are many conflicting reports of drug effects, and this was especially true in regard to the CNS stimulants amphetamine and caffeine. He argued that disparate results were primarily ascribable to the lack of precise definitions of behavioral variables being examined. However, much of the variability in results in these early experiments, as well as in current experiments, may be the result of pharmacological variables that have not been addressed, such as dose, method of drug administration, vehicle, time after drug that testing took place, and tolerance. Also such factors as different species and strains of animals tested must have contributed to some conflicting reports.

The Hallucinogens

In addition to the study of the effects of drugs on various techniques, experimental psychologists expressed early interest in hallucinogens. These drugs no doubt created excitement because of the love affair that man has had since early times with mystical and religious implications of altered states of consciousness. Mescaline is one of the many alkaloids found in the peyote cactus, an indigenous plant of northern Mexico and southwestern United States. The term "peyote" is derived from the Aztec work "peyotl" ("divine messenger") (del Pozo, 1967). Mescal buttons or beans are the dried tops cut from the peyote cactus.

In the 1920s the physiological psychologist Heinrich Klüver published a paper on the effects of mescaline entitled "Mescal Visions and Eidetic Visions" (Klüver, 1926), and in 1928 he published a monograph on mescaline that was reprinted in 1966. In the monograph, Klüver described his own experiences with mescaline: Klüver was a man before his time.

> We refer now to our personal observation to demonstrate some other aspects of mescal visions. 23 g. of the powdered buttons were taken in doses of 13 and 10 g. Half an hour after taking the second dose vomiting occurred. Soon hereafter phenomena of the following kind could be observed with closed eyes: 'Clouds from left to right through optical field. Tail of a pheasant (in center of field) turns into bright yellow star; star into sparks. Moving scintillating screw; 'hundreds' of screws. A sequence of rapidly changing objects in agreeable colors. A rotating wheel (diameter about 1 cm.) in the center of a silvery ground. Suddenly in the wheel a picture of God as represented in old Christian paintings.—Intention to see a homogeneous dark field of vision: red and green shoes appear. Most phenomena much nearer than reading distance.—The upper part of the body of a man, with a pale face but red cheeks, rising slowly from below. The face is unknown to me.—While I am thinking of a friend (visual memory-image) the head of an Indian appears.— Beads in different colors. Colors always changing: red to violet, green to bright gray, etc. Colors so bright that I doubt that the eyes are closed.— Yellow mass like saltwater taffy pierced by two teeth (about 6 cm. in length).—Silvery water pouring downward, suddenly flowing upward.— Landscape as on Japanese pictures: a picture rather than a real landscape.— Sparks having the appearance of exploding shells turn into strange flowers which remind me of poppies in California.—(Eyes open): streaks of green and violet on the wall. Then a drawing of a head changing into a mushroom (both of natural size). Then a skeleton (natural size) in lateral view turned

about 30° to the left. Head and legs are lacking. Try to convince myself that there are only shadows on the wall, but still see the skeleton (as in X-ray).— (Eyes closed). Soft deep darkness with moving wheels and stars in extremely pleasant colors.—Nuns in silver dresses (about 3 cm. height) quickly disappearing.—Collection of bluish ink-bottles with labels.—Red, brownish and violet threads running together in center.—Autumn leaves turning into mescal buttons.—Different forms emitting intense greenish light.—Forms in different colors; contours often dark.—Strange animal (length perhaps 10 cm.) rapidly turns into arabesques.—Gold rain falling vertically. On stationary background rotating jewels revolving around a center. Then, with a certain jerk, absence of all motion.—Regular and irregular forms in irridescent colors reminding me of radiolaria, sea urchins and shells, etc., in symmetrical or asymmetrical arrangement.—Shells illuminated from within radiating in different colors, moving towards the right, turned about 45° towards the right and somewhat towards me. A little piece in every shell is broken out.— Slowly majestic movements along differently shaped curves simultaneously with 'mad' movements.—Feeling there is motion per se.—Man in greenish velvet (height about 7-8 cm.) jumping into deep chasm.—Strange animal turns into a piece of wood in horizontal position [Klüver, 1928/1966, pp. 17– 18].

Report of the discoveries of the hallucinogenic properties of lysergic acid diethylamide (LSD) in 1943 by the Swiss pharmacologist Hofmann (1959), who originally synthesized the drug in 1938, is of related interest, for like the Klüver self-report it is a first-person account that gives the essence of the effect in a most colorful manner. A portion of Hofmann's account follows:

At the height of the experience, the following symptoms were most marked: Visual disturbances, everything appearing in impossible colours, objects out of proportion. At times the floor seemed to bend and the walls to undulate. The faces of the persons present changed into colourful grimaces.

Marked motor restlessness alternating with paralysis. Limbs and head felt heavy as if filled with lead and were without sensation. My throat felt dry and constricted.

Occasionally I felt as if I were out of my body. I thought I had died. My ego seemed suspended somewhere in space, from where I saw my dead body lying on the sofa [Hofmann, 1959, p. 156].

A more recent first-person report of the effects of a number of drugs is given by the psychologist Bennett (1960); he studied not only LSD, but chlorpromazine, phenobarbital, iproniazid, d-amphetamine, and alcohol. This report was unique in that not only were different drugs compared but a placebo was used and Bennett's performance after the drug was tested on a number of simple psychomotor tests. Although the reports of his experiences after taking LSD have an objectivity and a level of systematic assessment not found in Klüver or Hofmann, Bennett's description lacks the colorful prose of his predecessors.

No review of the early beginnings of psychopharmacology, no matter how brief, can ignore the work of Louis Lewin (1850-1929). Lewin wrote extensively about the social, psychological, and pharmacological actions of drugs that alter behavior. His 1924 book, first published in English in 1931 and reprinted in 1964, *Phantastica: Narcotic and Stimulating Drugs* is a classic. Most of his observations are relevant today; however, he at times stressed the degradation of drug use. For example, in commenting on cocaine use he said,

> During recent years I have seen among men of science frightful symptoms due to the craving for cocaine. Those who believe they can enter the temple of happiness through this gate of pleasure purchase their momentary delights at the cost of body and soul. They speedily pass through the gate of unhappiness into the night of abyss [Lewin, 1964, p. 88].

Even though psychopharmacology was not a significant part of the mainstream of psychology until the middle 1950s, a number of psychologists whose reputations were earned in other areas of psychology published papers on the effects of drugs on behavior. For example, Neal Miller published with W.R. Miles in 1935 and 1936 on the effects of caffeine and alcohol on running speed and maze behavior, respectively, in the rat; likewise, B.F. Skinner published a paper on the effects of caffeine and benzedrine on conditioning and extinction with W.T. Heron in 1937.

Pavlov and Freud

Even earlier than the studies described above was of course the psychopharmacological work of Pavlov and of Freud. Although Pavlov's fame is based on his work on the conditioned reflexes which was begun about 1900, prior to that (1890-1895) he held the professorship in pharmacology at the Military Medical Academy in St. Petersburg (Holmstedt & Liljestrand, 1963, p. 213). Pavlov and his students studied the effects of such drugs as alcohol, bromides, caffeine, and cocaine on the process of stimulation and inhibition in conditioned reflexes. It was suggested that drugs that alter the central nervous system could be classified by either their ability to heighten or inhibit stimulating processes.

Laties (1979) recently published a translation of a 1908 paper by Igor Vladimirovich Zavadskii, who worked in Pavlov's laboratory from 1907 through 1909; in this paper effects of alcohol, morphine, cocaine, and caffeine on conditioned reflexes are reported. After Zavadskii completed his doctoral dissertation, Pavlov asked him to study the behavioral effects of a number of drugs on the conditioned salivary responses of animals that were originally trained for other experiments. Both Pavlov and Zavadskii indicated that these were only preliminary experiments but they allowed a method for study of the effects of drugs on the "function of the higher regions of the central nervous system." The work was presented to the medical society in St. Petersburg in 1908, and during the discussion a leading Russian pharmacologist of the period, N. P. Kravkov, stated ". . .I salute this new method and its introduction in the study of pharmacologic problems. It is precisely because of the lack of strictly objective method that pharmacologic knowledge in the domain of the central nervous system is still so sketchy." Laties (1979), in his discussion of Zavadskii's work, asked the question, "Is this the first paper in *behavioral pharmacology*?" By behavioral pharmacology, Laties probably meant behavioral analysis of the effects of drugs on behavior by means of emitted responses of instrumental conditioning rather than elicited responses of classical Pavlovian conditioning. Also, although Pavlov and his students were developing an objective science of behavior, they interpreted their results on the bases of putative intervening physiological variables such as inhibition and excitation, and therefore their work does not fit Laties definition of behavioral pharmacology.

While Laties asks whether Zavadskii's 1908 paper was the first publication in behavioral pharmacology, objective evaluation of behavioral effects of a drug was carried out by Freud in 1884 and published in 1885. Although the subject in these experiments was Freud himself, Freud systematically studied the effects of cocaine on "motor power" and "psychic reaction time." In these experiments, Freud used a dynamometer and a simple instrument for measuring reaction time. This latter device consisted of a metal strip that vibrated 100 times/second. As soon as the subject heard the tone caused by starting the vibration of the metal strip, he stopped its movement. The number of vibrations, recorded directly on a pen writer allowed for the measurement of reaction time to .01 seconds. Of interest is that Freud recognized that the improvement he observed in psychomotor performance under stimulants may have been a secondary effect. He stated:

> I often noticed that under cocaine my reaction times were shorter and more uniform than before taking the drug; but sometimes, in a more cheerful and efficient mood, my psychic reactions were just as good. Change in reaction time is then a characteristic of cocaine euphoria to which I have also ascribed the increase in muscular strength [in Byck, 1974, p. 104].

This was not Freud's first paper on cocaine. His earliest article was on the coca plant "Über Coca" published in July 1884. In this paper Freud gave a history of the use of coca in South America and its spread to western Europe. He described its effects on animals and humans and discussed its believed therapeutic uses. There are hints in this paper concerning its local anesthetic properties. Freud was enthusiastic about the potential uses of this drug. (For an interesting description of Freud's near miss in discovering the use of cocaine as a local anesthetic and specifically in ophthalmological procedures, see Byck, 1974.) In the introduction to *Cocaine Papers—Sigmund Freud,* Byck stated: "When I first read the papers, I at once realized that they established Sigmund Freud as one of the founders of psychopharmacology [1974, p. xviii]."

The Addiction Research Center

Despite many early experiments on the effects of drugs on behavior, prior to the 1950s there was no single laboratory dedicated to the study of psychopharmacology, with the possible exception of the Addiction Research Center (ARC) at the U.S. Public Health Service Hospital in Lexington, Kentucky. In 1929, Congress authorized the establishment of two hospitals for the treatment of narcotic addicts, one in Lexington, Kentucky and one in Fort Worth, Texas. The Lexington hospital was the first to open (in 1935) and became the primary center in the U.S. and probably the world for the study of addictive narcotics and other drugs. (For a history of research at the USPHS Hospital, see Martin & Isbell, 1978.)

The earliest research at the ARC was concerned with the quantification of the narcotic abstinence syndrome (Himmelsbach, 1978). However, clinical psychologists at the institution embarked on a number of research problems that by present standards may be considered quite naive but by the accepted beliefs of the 1930s and 1940s constituted important research questions. For example, it was determined that narcotic addicts were anthropometically and intellectually normal (Brown, 1940). Questions asked then and still not satisfactorily solved today included, for example, Why do people abuse narcotic drugs? In 1943, Brown reported the findings of a Rorschach study in post-addicts and concluded that morphine tends to reduce neurotic responses and to facilitate introversion and fantasy and that it seems to reduce reactions to stress (Brown, 1943). In studies employing the galvanic skin response, Andrews (1943) reported that morphine exerted a greater effect on human's reaction to pain than the perception of pain per se, an effect of morphine that has been rediscovered a number of times since.

Although the ARC is still active, the Fort Worth hospital closed in 1971 and the Lexington hospital in 1974. The Lexington research building remains part of the National Institute of Drug Abuse, and research at the ARC continues.

Prior to the mid-1950s, the ARC carried out many clinical research studies that drew on the talents of psychologists. Two of these investigations had major impact on our understanding of the problems of barbiturate (Isbell, Altshul, Kornetsky, Eisenman, Flanary, & Fraser, 1950; Kornetsky, 1951) and alcohol abuse (Isbell, Fraser, Wikler, Belleville, & Eisenman, 1955). These two clinical experiments clearly demonstrated physical dependence to barbiturates and alcohol and that the withdrawal syndrome for each is far more severe and dangerous to life than the withdrawal syndrome associated with narcotic use.

During this early period, the ARC also carried out systematic studies on pain and analgesia. These experiments showed in both animals and man the role of psychological and environmental factors on the perception of pain (Hill, Belleville, & Wikler, 1954, 1955; Hill, Kornetsky, Flanary, & Wikler, 1952a, 1952b; Kornetsky, 1954). Experimental animal models of drug abuse were carried out by a neuropsychiatrist, Abraham Wikler. (For a review of this early work including a comprehensive treatise on problems of opioid dependence, see Wikler, 1980.)

THE CHEMOTHERAPEUTIC REVOLUTION

The extensive use of drugs for the treatment of the mentally ill began in the 1950s with the introduction of reserpine and chlorpromazine for the treatment of psychoses. The use of these drugs completely changed the course of psychiatry and has had major impact on psychology. For example, these drugs altered the picture of what happened to most patients diagnosed as schizophrenic. Until 1955 the number of resident patients in public mental hospitals was on a continuous increase. However, since then the number of patients in mental institutions has continually declined (Kline, 1968). In recent years this change has been further facilitated by the public policy of deinstitutionalization. Prior to the use of antipsychotic drugs returning patients to the community in large numbers would have not been possible.

Although reserpine was used in the early 1950s as an antipsychotic medication, this use was short lived, and its use today is primarily as an anti-hypertensive agent. Reserpine is an alkaloid derived from the plant *Rawolfia serpentina,* and it is primarily responsible for the pharmacological effects of powdered preparations made from the root of this plant. Powdered Rawolfin has been used by Hindu physicians for centuries in the treatment of a variety of physical and mental conditions.

Chlorpromazine, the first of the phenothiazine class of antipsychotic drugs, has continued to be used extensively in the treatment of the schizophrenic patient despite the introduction of many other effective drugs.

The history of the discovery of the antipsychotic properties of chlor-promazine is well documented by Swazey (1974). In 1950, chlorpromazine was introduced as an adjunct medication in anesthesia. It seemed to potentiate the anesthetic action of the anesthesia, and also because of its anticholinergic action it reduced the possibility for respiratory complication. The first report of the use of chlorpromazine in a psychiatric patient was given by Delay, Deniker, and Harl (1952).

Despite some use in mental patients in late 1951 and early 1952, credit for the clinical use of chlorpromazine in psychotic patients is usually given to Delay and Deniker who first published with Harl (see Swazey, 1974, pp. 111–141). Lehmann and Hanrahan (1954) reported the first clinical experiment with chlorpromazine conducted in North America and published in English. Also it was the first report in which clinical psychological tests were used to evaluate the drug. Although Lehmann and Hanrahan were impressed with its therapeutic usefulness in the schizophrenic patient, they were most enthusiastic with its usefulness in the treatment of the manic patient.

A few years after the discovery of the clinical usefulness of phenothiazine drugs in the treatment of schizophrenia, Kline (1958) reported that the monamine oxidase (MAO) inhibitor, iproniazid, was effective in the treatment of depression. Introduced shortly after the discovery of the clinical efficacy for depression of iproniazid was imipramine, a tricyclic drug with less toxicity than the MAO inhibitors (Kuhn, 1958).

The antianxiety drug meprobamate was introduced for clinical use in 1955 (Harvey, 1980), and its trade name (Miltown) has become part of our modern culture. Other, more effective antianxiety drugs have quickly followed, such as chlordiazepoxide (Librium®) and diazepam (Valium®) (Randall & Shallek, 1968). Thus, in the short span of about 10 years a potpourri of pharmaceuticals appeared for the treatment of mental problems and mental disease.

This tremendous growth of pharmacotherapy would lead one to believe that there was no future for clinicians except as psychological testers. For a number of reasons this has turned out not to be the case. First, these drugs have been most effective with the severely psychotic or depressed patient, and this group of patients was never particularly amenable to psychotherapy. Second, although a large portion of the population is using antianxiety drugs, the use of behavioral methods still seems to be needed for amelioration of many problems associated with anxiety.

Of more importance to psychology is that this revolution in the treatment of mentally ill people has led to focused research, by large numbers of psychologists on the effects of drugs on behavior of both animals and man. In clinical psychopharmacological research, psychologists have mainly developed the techniques and experimental designs that allowed for the systematic clinical study of these new therapeutic agents. It was not that there was no clinical pharmacology prior to the 1950s, but for the most part it lacked sophistication in statistical and experimental design that psychology brought to the field. Also the dependent variables that were being observed not only included blood pressure changes and body temperature but subjective estimates of behavior and mood made both by observers and by patients. Psychologists have also attempted systematically to scale subjective clinical states, as for example by the Inpatient Multidimentional Psychiatric Scale (Lorr, Klett, McNair, & Lasky, 1962).

Both the Veterans Administration (Casey, Bennett, Lindley, Hollister, Gordon, & Springer, 1960) and the National Institute of Mental Health Collaborative Study Group (1964) have sponsored clinical studies of the efficacy of these new compounds, and psychologists have played prominent roles in these studies. For example, Fisher, Cole, Rickels, and Uhlenhuth (1964) pointed out the importance of non-drug factors in clinical psychopharmacology. Similarly, Goldberg, Schooler, Hogarty, and Roger (1977) demonstrated that relapse (return to the hospital) in schizophrenic patients is less likely in those who continue on maintenance doses of drugs after discharge from the hospital than patients who continue on either psychotherapy or no therapy. Patients receiving drugs plus psychotherapy do not differ from drug-alone groups for the first year after discharge but at the end of two years show a slight but significantly lower relapse rate than drug–alone groups. These are only a few examples of the many contributions that psychologists have made to clinical pharmacology. If there was not a cadre of trained clinical psychologists knowledgeable in statistics and experimental design during the past three decades then the clinical pharmacologist would have had to invent psychology.

BEHAVIORAL PHARMACOLOGY

Animal Models of Pathological States

Most psychologists conducting experiments on the effects of drugs on behavior prior to the 1950s studied alcohol or stimulants such as caffeine or amphetamine. Other investigators studied the effects of hormones on natural consummatory and motivational states. The effects of testosterone and other hormones were detailed by Beach (1948). However, the field that is currently called "behavioral pharmacology," a term perhaps first used by Brady (1957), finds its origins in the discovery of psychotherapeutic drugs and the emergence of operant conditioning methodology in psychology at about the same time. The techniques of this neobehaviorism were well described in 1953 by Skinner. The operant model had many advantages over other behavioral techniques that were utilized for the study of drug effects. Investigators such as Brady (1957) and Dews (1958) argued strongly for a behavioral pharmacology that defined the action of drugs only in objective behavioral terms. In a 1957 symposium of the American Society for Pharmacology and Experimental Therapeutics, Dews (1958) argued for a behavioral pharmacology that would discard assumptions of what the animal was thinking or feeling. He stated,

> It may well be that many "obvious" features of behavior for which neurophysiological explanations are currently being sought will turn out to be chimera; for example, some of the "emotions" may prove to be as useless as scientific concepts as the humors of the ancients are to the biochemists of today. The neurophysiologist may be misled by what he supposes to be incontrovertible psychology. On the other hand, neuropharmacologists and psychopharmacologists can pursue their rigorous studies independently; though, being good friends, they watch one another's progress with interest. The mere fact that they study the same drugs inevitably provides points of correspondence between the two systems; and one may confidently expect that clear and unforced correlations will emerge of an altogether higher order of generality than the ad hoc fragmentary hypotheses of today [Dews, 1958, p. 1030].

The difference between the humors of the ancients and constructs such as "emotion" is that there was no possibility to define a humor. Humor was an intervening variable; whereas emotion may be treated as an intervening variable, it may, however, also be defined in behavioral terms as an independent or dependent variable. Of course, the difficulty with operational definitions is that calling something so does not make it so. However, if drug effects are defined only in terms of the schedule of reinforcement used then the "inevitable . . . points of correspondence" may be long in coming.

Despite Dews's plea to avoid terms like "emotion", many of the early behavioral pharmacologists were not adverse to using "emotion" or "anxiety" if they could operationally define what was meant in terms of specific measurable independent or dependent variables. In the early 1950s Hunt and Brady (1951) and Brady (1951) published on the effects of electroconvulsive shock "therapy" on a conditioned emotional response ("anxiety"). Their procedure superimposed a classical conditioning paradigm on an operant model. This combination of classical and operant conditioning was described by Estes and Skinner in 1941 in an experiment designed to quantify "anxiety" in an animal.

The procedure consisted of pairing a signal (the conditioned stimulus, CS) with a brief, unavoidable electric shock (the unconditioned stimulus, UCS) to the feet of the animal. The CS is presented for 3 to 5 minutes before it is terminated at the onset of the UCS. The onset of the CS often results in complete termination of the animal's responding for food or water on the operant schedule. This cessation of lever pressing until after the termination of the UCS is the "conditioned emotional response" (CER). During the CER period the animal will crouch or freeze, and this behavior is often accompanied by defecation. This early work gave promise as an animal model for the study of pathological behavioral conditions of man, and thus the model was an obvious choice for the study of the effects of the new tranquilizing drugs.

In 1956 Brady published in the journal *Science* a paper assessing the effects of reserpine on the CER. This drug produced an effect similar to that of an animal treated with convulsive "therapy." At proper doses reserpine suppressed the emotional response, and the animal would continue to press the lever for the food reinforcement throughout the CER period.

Independent of Brady and Hunt, Hill et al. (1954) demonstrated that morphine would also alter the CER in a manner similar to that seen with reserpine. Hill et al. did not call the procedure the "CER" but referred to it as "pain conditioned anxiety." They concluded that their results supported the hypothesis that a major component of morphine's analgesic action was the reduction of anxiety associated with the anticipation of the noxious stimulus.

Despite the apparent potential of the CER method in the study of drug effects, it was replaced by two other animal model systems, the conditioned avoidance response for evaluating antipsychotic drugs and the approach-avoidance conflict technique for evaluating anti-anxiety drugs.

The earliest studies of the effects of an antipsychotic drug on a conditioned avoidance response (CAR) was an experiment by Courvoisier, Fournel, Ducrot, Kolsky, and Koetschet (1953) who demonstrated in the rat that chlorpromazine suppressed a rope-climbing response elicited by an auditory signal that had previously been paired with an electric shock. A somewhat simpler procedure was described by Cook, Weidley, Morris, and Mattis (1955) at a meeting of the American Society for Pharmacology and Experimental Therapeutics. A detailed description was published in 1957 by Cook and Weidley. In their original work, the experimental animal was placed in a small chamber with a grid floor in which a pole was suspended from the ceiling. A trial consisted of the onset of a buzzer and electrifying the grid floor. The rat could escape by jumping onto the suspended pole. After approximately 10 to 15 such exposures the animal would jump onto the pole at the onset of the buzzer only. Cook and Weidley referred to the procedure as a conditioned avoidance-escape response. Since the CS and UCS were delivered simultaneously, they stated that one ". . . cannot define the response as a pure conditioned-avoidance response." This is also true of the Courvoisier et al. (1953)

report. In these experiments, Cook and Weidley found that of the drugs they tested only chlorpromazine and morphine would block the response to the buzzer without also blocking the response to the shock. The hypnotics and the minor tranquilizer meprobamate only blocked the response to the CS at doses that affected the response to the UCS.

The first study of the effects of an antipsychotic drug on the CAR in which there was a time delay between the onset of the CS and the UCS was reported by Miller, Murphy, and Mirsky (1957). Their report was immediately followed by a paper by Ader and Clink (1957). In both of these experiments a two-compartment conditioning chamber allowed the animal to move to the "safe" compartment at the onset of an auditory signal (CS). Ader and Clink studied the effects of chlorpromazine on the acquisition and extinction of the avoidance response. Prior to their 1957 paper, Murphy and Miller (1955) published a report on the effects of ACTH on the acquisition and extinction of an avoidance response in the rat. Even earlier, this group studied avoidance behavior in the monkey treated with ACTH (Mirsky, Miller, & Stein, 1953).

Mirsky et al. as well as Ader and Clink interpreted the avoidance response as a model for anxiety and reasoned that the effect of chlorpromazine in blocking the avoidance response could be ascribed to the drug's ability to attenuate anxiety. Subsequent investigators have concluded that attenuating anxiety was not the critical factor in the effects of antipsychotic drugs on the CAR. Poslun (1962) argued for an effect of the drugs on motor systems. Low, Eliasson, and Kornetsky (1966) and Lipper and Kornetsky (1971) have since argued that the drug's effect on CAR is probably the result of its reducing arousal necessary for responding.

In addition to the CAR procedure in which a specific CS is presented, Sidman (1953) described a non-discriminated avoidance procedure, or a postponement schedule. In this procedure, the animal avoids shock to the feet by responding at least once every 15 seconds (this time will vary depending on the specific experiment). Each time the animal responds it postpones the foot shock for a programmed amount of time. Despite the fact that this nondiscriminated avoidance gives steady rates of responding and that antipsychotic drugs seem to have effects similar to those seen with the discriminated avoidance (Fielding & Lal, 1978), the procedure has not found much favor.

Recently, Fielding and Lal (1978) reviewed the effects of neuroleptics (antipsychotic drugs) on avoidance behavior and reported that 21 drugs tested in the rat inhibited avoidance behavior. However, in an experiment from their own laboratory they reported as well that the inhibition of avoidance behavior for haloperidol and spiroperidol is seen only at doses in which there were undesirable side effects in the animal, e.g., muscle tremors. Since the details of this experiment have not been published it is difficult to evaluate the significance of these findings. Haloperidol and spiroperidol are both potent antipsychotic drugs, and both have marked extrapyramidal side effects in man.

In addition to the models described above for the study of antipsychotic drugs, Kornetsky and Eliasson (1969) proposed an animal model for the postulated overarousal state of the schizophrenic. This model was based on the hypothesis that there was a malfunction in the midbrain or brain-stem reticular formation which resulted in an altered arousal system. This malfunction is manifested in much of the psychological impairment seen in schizophrenic patients and specifically in an attentional impairment (Kornetsky & Mirsky, 1966; Mirsky & Kornetsky, 1964). The model con-sists of a simple attention task for the rat which could be disrupted by electrical stimulation to the mesencephalic reticular formation through implanted electrodes. Chlorpromazine also impaired performance on this task, however, and when the two treatments were combined the perform-ance of the animal returned to baseline levels.

The behavioral procedure used to predict possible anti-anxiety effect of drugs is a simple conflict test first proposed by Geller and Seifter (1960). This technique has many of the elements of the conditioned emotional response originally described by Estes and Skinner (1941) in that there is a second schedule superimposed on a simple operant schedule. However, in the CER the delivery of the foot shock to the animal is not contingent on the response of the animal. In the conflict procedure, animals working on either an interval- or a ratio-reinforcement schedule for positive rein-forcement (usually food) are switched at predetermined intervals to con-tinuous reinforcement. Unfortunately for the animal, each response not only brings food but also foot shock. As in the CER procedure, lever pressing is suppressed during the second schedule, and if the intensity of the foot shock is properly titrated animals will make a small number of responses even though they receive foot shock. However, anxiolytic drugs such as chlordiazepoxide (Librium®) and diazepam (Valium®) allow the animal to continue to press for food despite the contingent foot shock (Sepinwall & Cook, 1978). With few exceptions, most drugs that are not useful in the treatment of anxiety will suppress responding during the foot shock interval.

Other Scheduled Behavior

In addition to adopting procedures that attempt to mimic psychopatholog-ical conditions in man, behavioral pharmacologists have made use of a variety of operant reinforcement schedules. These techniques are power-ful tools for the study of behavior and the effects of drugs on these behaviors. As previously mentioned, the operant methodology with its emphasis on rate of response became part of mainstream of behaviorism at about the same time as the introduction of the new psychotherapeutic drugs. Dews and DeWeese (1977, p. 123) stated, "Before the early 1950s there was no behavioral pharmacology as such; that is, there was no corps of workers dedicated to studying systematically the behavioral effects of drugs, although of course there were certain prescient experiments (e.g., Macht and Mora, 1920; Skinner and Heron, 1937)." If Dews and DeWeese mean that there was no corps of investigators studying the effects of drugs on operant schedules they are correct. However, as mentioned there was the group at the USPHS Hospital in Lexington, Kentucky, whose contribution to understanding behavioral effects of drugs was of significance. This group published a number of systematic investigations prior to Dews's (1955) paper on the effects of pentobarbital on scheduled behavior.

In his 1955 paper, Dews compared the effects of various doses of pentobarbital on rate of responding on FR50 and FI15' reinforcement schedules. The results clearly showed that a drug could have different effects at similar doses depending on the reinforcement schedule. At doses that decreased rate of responding on the FI schedule, responding rate increased on the FR schedule. This experiment by Dews as well as many other operant schedule experiments with drugs have demonstrated that the topography of the experiments will, within limits of dose, affect the outcome. However, investigators not employing operant technology both prior to and after the introduction of operant procedures have demonstrated that the effect of a drug can be manipulated by the topography of the experiment (e.g., Hill et al., 1952a, 1952b).

DRUGS AS REINFORCERS

The only research group with a clear focus on the behavioral and pharmacological effects of drugs prior to the 1950s was the Addiction Research Center Group at Lexington, Kentucky. One of the major problems in the study of drug abuse at this time was the failure to develop an animal model. Investigators had hoped that animals would spontaneously self-administer (by drinking) abuse substances. The desire was to make taking the drug the operant and the drug itself the reinforcer. Although water-deprived animals could be trained to drink weak solutions of morphine or alcohol, both these drugs at effective doses were aversive to animals. Wikler, Green, Smith, and Pescor (1960) and Wikler, Martin, Pescor, and Eades (1963) investigated whether or not etonitazene could be used as an oral reinforcer in rats previously made physically dependent without prior water deprivation. Etonitazene is a benzimidazole derivative that has morphine-like properties and is about 1,000 times more potent than morphine. Although Wikler found that animals could not distinguish a solution of etonitazene from water, if previously made physically dependent by means of injections of morphine, animals would prefer the etonitazene solution. Although this line of research looked promising, a simpler conceptual model developed by a cardiovascular pharmacologist working at Upjohn Company in Kalamazoo, Michigan, changed the course of much animal behavior work with abuse substances.

In the spring of 1961 at the meeting of the American Society for Pharmacology and Experimental Therapeutics as part of the Federation of American Societies for Experimental Biology meeting, James Weeks (1961) presented a 10-minute paper that was a clear methodological breakthrough. It was surprising that no one had tried his experiment before. Weeks demonstrated that unrestrained rats can be trained to emit lever pressing responses to receive intravenously infused morphine. Although Weeks seemed to believe at that time that every response the animal emitted needed to be reinforced, he varied the magnitude of injections and demonstrated that if the dose/injection was decreased the rate of responding increased. A table from Weeks (1962) summarizes the results of his original experiment (see Table 1).

This work was quickly followed by other investigators. Thompson and Schuster (1964) reported that physically dependent rhesus monkeys would also self-administer morphine. At the present time, this technique is the major animal model used for determining the possible abuse liability of drugs.

Although research on the use of drugs as reinforcement has generally had the same form as the effects of drugs on scheduled behavior, there are some important differences. When drugs are used as reinforcers the drug itself may have a direct effect on the ability of the animal to press the lever resulting in a confounding of independent and dependent variables. Also, with drugs that cause physical dependence it is difficult to determine if the animal is pressing the lever to avoid the withdrawal effects or is pressing for some primary effect of the drug. For a recent review, see Woods (1978).

STATE DEPENDENT LEARNING AND DRUG DISCRIMINATION

State dependent learning (SDL) occurs when the performance of a learned response by an animal is conditional upon the drug state present when the response was learned, i.e., an animal trained to make a simple discrimination while always under the influence of a barbiturate will make

TABLE 1
Responses Per Hour for Self-Administered Morphine by Addict Rats
on Continuous (1:1) reinforcement (Adapted from Weeks, 1962).

Condition		Responses per hour						Daily
Reinforce-ment ratio	Dose (mg/kg)	Rat 95	Rat 224	Rat 255	Rat 261	Rat 402	Ave.	intake (mg/kg)
1:1	10	2.4	2.0	1.3	0.9	1.2	1.6	384
1:1	3.2	5.5	3.1	2.9	2.5	2.1	3.2	240
Withdrawal*		33	11	21	27	17	22	

*Calculations on first 3 hours only.

errors when tested under non-drug conditions. Drug discrimination is a related phenomenon in which animals are trained to perform one response in one drug state (e.g., turn left in T-maze) and a second response in another drug state (turn right).

The first report of SDL was by Girden and Culler in 1937, although this early paper had little impact probably because it did not employ centrally acting drugs and because there was not a great deal of interest in such phenomena at that time. In 1958, Richard Belleville submitted a Ph.D. Dissertation to the Graduate School, University of Kentucky, on SDL based on work done at the Addiction Research Center in Lexington, Kentucky. Unfortunately the work was not published until six years later (Belleville, 1964). Based on previous work of Hull (1933) and Leeper (1935) in which animals were trained to make different responses depending on a particular drive state, Belleville reasoned that the use of drugs would provide a relatively rapid way of changing the internal state of the animal, a situation analogous to the changing of drive state. Rats were trained on a variable interval schedule under four experimental conditions (saline, morphine, amphetamine, and no treatment) and then compared for the number of extinction trials when the treatment was held constant and when the conditions were changed. Although all comparisons did not reach statistical significance, they were all in the predicted direction. Extinction was more rapid when conditions were changed than when extinction trials were under conditions of training.

The same year that Belleville published, Donald Overton published a report on state dependent learning (Overton, 1964) based on his 1962 Ph.D. thesis. Overton using a T-maze found that a response learned while the animal was drugged with pentobarbital was not elicited when the animal was tested under non-drug conditions. The extent of transfer from treatment to no-treatment conditions was inversely proportional to the magnitude of the dose of the drug used during the training period.

The use of drugs as discriminative stimuli, however, was reported as early as 1960 by Cook, Davidson, Davis, and Kelleher in an experiment in which the effects of epinephrine, norepinephrine, and acetylcholine were used as conditioned stimuli for avoidance behavior. The success of this area of research for the most part must be attributed to its continuous pursuit by Overton so that by the 1970s the technique was one of the major procedures used for the prediction of therapeutic effects or abuse liability. Unfortunately, like the other models discussed these procedures will, by the nature of the generalization gradient, only select drugs like ones that we already have. However, the technique has unexploited potential as a tool for the study of physiological influences on learning. For a recent review, see Colpaert and Rosecrans (1978).

BRAIN-STIMULATION REWARD

Olds (1977) in describing the discovery of electrical self-stimulation stated, "A new window on the brain was opened in 1953 when a rat fortuitously evidenced a neural rewarding effect by returning to the place in an open field where it had been when an electrical stimulus was applied to the brain via chronically implanted electrodes [Olds, 1977, p. 4]." The first publication describing the phenomenon had been 20 years earlier (Olds & Milner, 1954). Considering the explosion in the development of drugs for the treatment of the mentally ill at that time it was not surprising that the technique was applied to study the effects of drugs. This first work was published by Olds, Killam, and Bach-y-Rita (1956).

By means of drug studies on this "window on the brain," the technique lent itself to the development of theories concerning etiological factors of various mental illnesses. In a paper that reported the effects of a number of centrally active drugs, Olds and Travis (1960) postulated that psychotic behavior may be the result of an "excess of the positive feedback process subserving reinforcement mechanisms."

In a similar vein, Stein (1962) postulated that depression may be associated with a hypoactivity of this reward system. There is certain face validity to this model of depression for one of the major characteristics of the depressed patient is a failure to appreciate the normal reinforcers of life. Later, Stein and Wise (1971) hypothesized that the "anhedonia" behavior of some chronic schizophrenic patients may be the result of a selective loss of the neurons of the noradrenergic reward pathways. This hypothesis was based on experiments in which they produced progressive damage to the noradrenergic system by the administration of 6-hydroxydopamine and on the early observation of Bleuler that the behavior of some schizophrenics can be characterized by a lack of interest and initiative. In a series of papers, Crow (1979) also implicated the reward system in schizophrenia. As opposed to Stein and Wise, he argued that the critical transmitter system is dopaminergic and more specifically that there is a super-sensitivity of the post-synaptic dopamine receptor. More recently, Stein and Belluzzi (1979), still making the point that dysfunction in the reward system is an etiological factor in both affective disorders and schizophrenia, postulated that "endorphins may serve as transmitters or modulators in neural systems for the mediation of satisfaction and reward."

Brain-stimulation reward has in recent years been suggested as a useful method for the study of the euphorigenic effects of abuse substances (e.g., Bush, Bush, Miller, & Reid, 1976; Kornetsky, Esposito, McLean, & Jacobson, 1979; Marcus & Kornetsky, 1974; Wise, 1980). A variety of abuse substances lowers the threshold for self-stimulation (Kornetsky & Esposito, 1979). Recent research suggests that despite a variety of pharmacological actions by various abuse substances, the self-stimulation threshold lowering effects of cocaine (Kornetsky, Bain, & Riedl, 1981), amphetamine (Esposito, Perry, & Kornetsky, 1980), and phencyclidine (Kornetsky, Markowitz, & Esposito, 1981), in addition to morphine, are all reversed by the narcotic antagonist naloxone. These findings suggest that the underlying neurochemical basis of the euphoric effects of these clinically diverse substances may be related to a common effect on the opiate receptor.

TOXICOLOGY

Behavioral Toxicology

The term behavioral toxicology is used to describe the adverse effects of drugs on psychological functioning in man and animals. Certainly when Freud (1885/1974) determined the effect of cocaine on strength of hand grip and reaction time he was determining the behavioral toxicity of the drug. It must be remembered that toxic effects of a drug are only those effects that are not necessary for its main (or putative) therapeutic effect. Thus, somnolence caused by a barbiturate is not a side effect of one using the drug for its hypnotic effect, while the same degrees of somnolence caused by an antihistamine is considered a toxic side effect.

Much of what is called behavioral pharmacology constitutes the study of behavioral toxicity. Thus, the decrease in avoidance behavior in animals caused by antipsychotic drugs, although predictive of clinical efficacy, is an effect that could lead to non-survival of the animal in a natural environment.

In addition to the study of therapeutic and abuse substances, there has been increased involvement by psychologists in recent years in the effects of environmental pollutants on behavior. Among these pollutants are carbon monoxide, lead, and methylmercury. A detailed review of the methodology is provided in *Behavioral Toxicology* edited by Weiss and Laties (1975). Behavioral toxicology was one of the early interests of psychologists. In 1912, Hollingsworth carried out a study on the possible adverse effects of caffeine. However, he found that in normal subjects there was slight improvement in psychological functioning.

Researchers at the Addiction Research Center focused much of their early work on behavioral toxicology. In 1948, it was still not known whether or not there was physical dependence to barbiturates. The experimental study of chronic barbiturate intoxication included a major section on the psychological effects (Isbell et al., 1950; Kornetsky, 1951).

Discovery of the hallucinogenic properties of lysergic acid diethylamide (LSD) in 1944 (Hofmann, 1959) led to a series of experiments at Mt. Sinai Hospital in the early 1950s on the behavioral toxicity of LSD by Jarvik, Abramson, and Hirsch (1955a, 1955b). With the introduction of various tranquilizing drugs a number of investigators looked at the behavioral effects of these agents in normal subjects (e.g., Kelly, Miller, Marquis, Gerard, & Uhr, 1958; Kornetsky, Humphries, & Evart, 1957; Loomis & West, 1958; Nowlis & Nowlis, 1956; Primac, Mirsky, & Rosvold, 1957). All of these investigators found that commonly used psychotherapeutic drugs caused significant impairment in functioning at therapeutically effective doses. Also some experiments found that effects could be demonstrated relatively selectively. For example, it was demonstrated that although barbiturates and chlorpromazine both made subjects sleepy there was a relatively greater effect of the barbiturates on cognitive functioning while chlorpromazine more selectively altered attention (Mirsky & Kornetsky, 1964).

Behavioral Teratology

One area of behavioral toxicology that has become a major focus of research is behavioral teratology. Until the last 10 to 15 years, teratology was primarily concerned with the development of gross structural malformations. The most well known teratological effect was the thalidomide induced tragedy of the 1960s. Within the past few years awareness that prenatal exposure to drugs and chemicals may lead to teratological effects and/or subsequent development of various types of neoplastic disease has developed.

In addition to morphological changes, a large number of behavioral disorders and learning disabilities in children have been reported that may be attributable to prenatal or perinatal exposure to drugs or chemicals (see review by Hutchings, 1978). The growth of research in behavioral teratology not only reflects public awareness of the milieu of toxic chemicals and drugs to which the pregnant female is exposed but interesting findings coming out of psychological studies in animals indicating that functional behavioral alterations are produced at much lower levels of exposure than are required to cause morphological effects. For a review of this important commingling of branches of pharmacology and psychology, see Buelke-Sam and Kimmel (1979).

FORMAL JOINING

During the three decades in which psychopharmacology became a major area of investigation and of teaching in both pharmacology and psychology, a number of journals and societies were established whose main purpose was to develop forums for the large amount of research relevant to both. In 1959 the first such journal was published, *Psychopharmacologia*. This international journal had two managering editors, Rothlin from Basal and Wikler from Lexington, Kentucky. The editorial advisory board was divided into sections, including neuropharmacology, psychiatry, etc. The section of psychology listed seven people: Brady, Dews, Eysenck, Hunt, Klüver, Pribram, and Zangwill. The first paper in the first issue was a review by Murray Sidman of behavioral pharmacology. In 1975 the name of the journal was changed to *Psychopharmacology*, and several psychologists have edited it, including Murray Jarvik, Conan Kornetsky, Herbert Barry III, and Roger Russell.

A number of societies were also formed during the same period with psychopharmacology or behavioral pharmacology as their primary focus. In 1957 the Collegium Internationale Neuro-Psychopharmacologicum was organized and in 1961 the American College of Neuropsychopharmacology. In both of these groups, psychology was well represented. In 1962 the Behavioral Pharmacology Society was formed. In 1966 Division 28, Psychopharmacology, of the American Psychological Association was founded, and Murray Jarvik was elected as its first president. The recognition by pharmacologists that behavior is a relevant and important aspect of the pharmacology of any drug that affected the CNS came early in the acceptance of behavioral papers in the official journal of the American Society of Pharmacology and Experimental Therapeutics, the *Journal of Pharmacology and Experimental Therapeutics*.

220 · KORNETSKY

SUMMARY

This essay has not attempted a comprehensive review of the relationship between psychology and pharmacology. There are many important points of contact between psychology and pharmacology not discussed here. For example, psychologists have been involved intimately in recent years in research involving the psychobiological implications of the relief of pain by the endogenous morphine-like substances, endorphins, that have been found in brain (e.g., Mayer & Price, 1976) and the use of drugs as tools in the study of the neuronal bases of memory (e.g., Agranoff, Burrell, Dokas, & Springer, 1978).

Although the major converging of the two disciplines did not occur until the 1950s, there were a great many, but for the most part unrelated, psychopharmacologic experiments prior to that time. Major research only appeared when critical questions arose concerning the mechanism of action and the toxicological effects of the new psychotherapeutic agents and with citizens' concern with drug abuse and later with the large number of toxic chemicals in the environment.

At times mutually relevant research suffered because of the failure of each discipline to take the complexity of the other discipline seriously. Pharmacologists counted fecal boli after giving a drug and believed that they had discovered a way to quantify behavior in the rat. Psychologists also counted fecal boli and believed that they were studying the pharmacology of the drug. The literature is replete with studies that do not take into account the fact that the environment could change a drug's biological effect or that the pharmacokinetics of a drug could change its behavioral effect.

Many departments of psychology and pharmacology now offer courses in behavioral pharmacology or psychopharmacology. A clinical psychologist cannot really be considered well trained without a basic understanding of the pharmacology of drugs used in the treatment of the mentally ill or of abuse substances. Pharmacologists no longer blink at national meetings when a slide showing a cumulative record is presented; they have heard of Skinner, and they understand the complexities of rating scales and the need for the double-blind experiment. Indeed, today, the integration of pharmacology and psychology has progressed to a point where the primary discipline identification of an investigator often cannot be discerned.

It is intriguing to contemplate a possible conversation in 1840 or 1846 between Weber, the first psychophysicist, and his assistant Buchheim, who established the first experimental laboratory of pharmacology. Weber: "When you give a certain amount of a drug to an animal or to a man, is it not similar to applying a physical stimulus to the subject? Do you not determine the minimum drug necessary to cause a change in the subject?" Buchheim: "That is an interesting question, but I am busy translating *The Elements of Materia Medica and Therapeutics* by Pereria, and I plan to accept the chair in materia medica at Dorpat in Estonia." Thus we see that a century and one-half ago a great opportunity was lost for pharmacology and psychology to begin to work on mutually important problems.

REFERENCES

Ader, R., & Clink, D. W. Effects of chlorpromazine on the acquisition and extinction of an avoidance response in the rat. *Journal of Pharmacology and Experimental Therapeutics,* 1957, *121,* 144–148.

Agranoff, P. W., Burrell, H. R., Dokas, L. A., & Springer, A. D. Progress in biochemical approaches to learning and memory. In M. A. Lipton, A. DiMascio, & K. F. Killam (Eds.), *Psychopharmacology: A generation of progress.* New York: Raven Press, 1978.

Andrews, H. L. Skin resistance changes and measurement of pain threshold. *Journal of Clinical Investigation,* 1943, *22,* 517–520.

Beach, F. A. Effects of testosterone propionate upon the copulatory behavior of sexually inexperienced male rats. *Journal of Comparative Psychology,* 1942, *33,* 227–247.

Beach, F. A. *Hormones and behavior.* New York: Hoeber, 1948.

Belleville, R. E. Control of behavior by drug-produced internal stimuli. *Psychopharmacologia* (Berlin), 1964, *5,* 95–105.

Bennett, C. C. The drug and I. In L. Uhr & J. G. Miller (Eds.), *Drugs and behavior.* New York: Wiley, 1960.

Boring, E. G. *A history of experimental psychology.* New York: Appleton-Century, 1929.

Brady, J. V. The effect of electro-convulsive shock on conditioned emotional response: The permanence of the effect. *Journal of Comparative and Physiological Psychology,* 1951, *44,* 507–511

Brady, J. V. The assessment of drug effects on emotional behavior. *Science,* 1956, *123,* 1033–1034.

Brady, J. V. A review of comparative behavioral pharmacology. *Annals of the New York Academy of Sciences,* 1957, *66,* 719–732.

Brown, R. R. The relation of body build to drug addiction. *Public Health Service Reports,* 1940, *55,* 1954–1963.

Brown, R. R. The effect of morphine upon Rorschach pattern in postaddicts. *American Journal of Orthopsychiatry,* 1943, *13,* 339–342.

Buelke-Sam, J., & Kimmel, C. A. Development and standardization of screening methods for behavioral teratology. *Teratology,* 1979, *20,* 17–29.

Bush, H. D., Bush, M. F., Miller, M. A., & Reid, L. D. Addictive agents and intracranial stimulation: Daily morphine and lateral hypothalamic self-stimulation. *Physiological Psychology,* 1976, *4,* 79–85.

Byck, R. *Cocaine papers—Sigmund Freud.* New York: Meridan Books, 1974.

Casey, J. F., Bennett, I. F., Lindley, C. F., Hollister, L. E., Gordon, M. H., & Springer, N. M. Drug therapy in schizophrenia: A controlled study of the relative effectiveness of chlorpromazine, promazine, phenobarbital and placebo. *Archives of General Psychiatry,* 1960, *2,* 210–220.

Colpaert, F. C., & Rosecrans, J. A. (Eds.). *Stimulus properties of drugs: Ten years of progress*. Amsterdam: Elsevier/North-Holland, Biomedical Press, 1978.

Cook, L., Davidson, A., Davis, D. J., & Kelleher, R. T. Epinephrine, norepinephrine, and acetylcholine as conditioned stimuli for avoidance behavior. *Science*, 1960, *131*, 990–991.

Cook. L., & Weidley, E. Behavioral effects of some psychopharmacological agents. *Annals of the New York Academy of Sciences*, 1957, *66*, 740–752.

Cook, L., Weidley, E., Morris, R., & Mattis, P. Neuropharmacological and behavioral effects of chlorpromazine. *Journal of Pharmacology and Experimental Therapeutics*, 1955, *113*, 11.

Courvoisier, S., Fournel, J., Ducrot, R., Kolsky, M., & Koetschet, P. Propierties pharmacodynamiques du chlorhydrate de chloro-3 (dimethyl-amino-3' propyl)-10 phenothiazine (4560 RR). *Archives Internationales de Pharmacodynamie et de Therapie*, 1953, *92*, 305–367.

Crow, T. J. Catecholamine reward pathways and schizophrenia: The mechanism of the antipsychotic effect and the site of the primary disturbance. *Federation Proceedings*, 1979, *38*, 2462–2467.

Delay, J., Deniker, P., & Harl, J. M. Utilisation en thérapeutique psychiatrique d'une phénothiazine d'action centrale elective. *Annales Médico-Psychologique*, 1952, *110*, 112–131.

del Pozo, E. C. Empiricism and magic in Aztec pharmacology. In D. H. Efron, B. Holmstedt, & N. S. Kline (Eds.), *Ethnopharmacologic search for psychoactive drugs*. (U.S. Public Health Service Publication, No. 1645.) Washington, DC: U.S. Government Printing Office, 1967.

Dews, P. B. Studies on behavior. I. Differential sensitivity to pentobarbital of pecking performance in pigeons depending on the schedule of reward. *Journal of Pharmacology and Experimental Therapeutics*, 1955, *113*, 393–401.

Dews, P. B. Analysis of effects of psychopharmacological agents in behavioral terms. *Federation Proceedings*, 1958, *17*, 1024–1030.

Dews, P. B., & DeWeese, J. Schedules of reinforcement. In L. L. Iversen, S. D. Iversen, & S. H. Snyder (Eds.), *Handbook of psychopharmacology* (Vol. 7). New York: Plenum Press, 1977.

Esposito, R. U., Perry, W., & Kornetsky, C. Effects of d-amphetamine and naloxone on brain stimulation reward. *Psychopharmacology*, 1980, *69*, 187–191.

Estes, W. K., & Skinner, B. F. Some quantitative properties of anxiety. *Journal of Experimental Psychology*, 1941, *29*, 390–400.

Fielding, S., & Lal, H. Behavioral actions of neuroleptics. In L. L. Iversen, S. D. Iversen, & S. H. Snyder (Eds.), *Handbook of psychopharmacology* (Vol. 10). New York: Plenum Press, 1978.

Fisher, S., Cole, J. O., Rickels, K., & Uhlenhuth, E. H. Drug Set interactions: The effect of expectations on drug response in outpatients. *Neuropsychopharmacology*, 1964, *3*, 149–156.

Freud, S. Uber Coca. *Centralblatt für die ges. Therapie*, 1884, *2*, 289–314. [Translated by R. S. Potash in R. Byck, Cocaine papers—Sigmund Freud, New York: Meridan Books, 1975.]

Freud, S. Betrag zur Kenntniss der Cocawirkung. *Wiener Mediziniche Wochenchrift*, 1885, *35*, 130–133. [Translated by R. S. Potash in R. Byck, *Cocaine papers—Sigmund Freud*, New York: Meridan Books, 1975.]

Geller, J., & Seifter, J. The effects of meprobamate, barbiturates, d-amphetamine and promazine on experimentally induced conflict in the rat. *Psychopharmacologia* (Berlin), 1960, *1*, 483–492.

Girden, E., & Culler, E. A. Conditioned responses in curarized striate muscle in dogs. *Journal of Comparative Psychology,* 1937, *23,* 261–274.

Goldberg, S. C., Schooler, N. R., Hogarty, G. E., & Roger, M. Prediction of relapse in schizophrenic outpatients treated by drug and sociotherapy. *Archives of General Psychiatry,* 1977, *34,* 171–184.

Harvey, S. C. Hypnotics and sedatives. In A. G. Gilman, L. S. Goodman, & A. Gilman (Eds.), *Goodman and Gilman's the pharmacological basis of therapeutics.* New York: MacMillan, 1980.

Heidbreder, E. *Seven psychologies.* New York: Appleton-Century, 1933.

Heron, W. T., & Carlson, W. S. The effects of Metrazol shock on retention of the maze habit. *Journal of Comparative Psychology,* 1941, *32,* 307–309.

Hill, H. E., Belleville, R. E., & Wikler, A. Reduction of pain-conditioned anxiety by analgesic doses of morphine in rats. *Proceedings of the Society for Experimental Biology and Medicine,* 1954, *86,* 881–884.

Hill, H. E., Belleville, R. E., & Wikler, A. Studies on anxiety associated with anticipation of pain. II. Comparative effects of pentobarbital and morphine. *Archives of Neurology and Psychiatry,* 1955, *73,* 602–608.

Hill, H. E., Kornetsky, C. H., Flanary, H. G., & Wikler, A. Effects of anxiety and morphine on discrimination of intensities of painful stimuli. *Journal of Clinical Investigation,* 1952, *31,* 473–480. (a)

Hill, H. E., Kornetsky, C. H., Flanary, H. G., & Wikler, A. Studies on anxiety associated with anticipation of pain. I. Effects of morphine. *Archives of Neurology and Psychiatry,* 1952, *67,* 612–619. (b)

Himmelsbach, C. K. Summary of chemical, pharmacological, and clinical research, 1929–44. In W. R. Martin & H. Isbell (Eds.), *Drug addiction and the U.S. public health service,* Washington, DC: DHEW, 1978.

Hofmann, A. Psychomimetic drugs: chemical and pharmocological aspects. *Acta Physiologica et Pharmacologica Neerlandica,* 1959, *8,* 240–258.

Hollingworth, H. L. The influence of caffeine on mental and motor efficiency. *Archives of Psychology,* 1912, *3,* 22.

Holmstedt, B. & Liljestrand, G. *Readings in pharmacology.* New York: Pergamon, 1963.

Hull, C. L. Differential habituation to internal stimuli in the white rat. *Journal of Comparative Psychology,* 1933, *16,* 255–273.

Hunt, H. F., & Brady, J. V. Some effects of electro-convulsive shock on conditioned emotional response ("anxiety"). *Journal of Comparative and Physiological Psychology,* 1951, *44,* 88–98.

Hutchings, D. E. Behavioral teratology: Embryopathic and behavioral effects of drugs during pregnancy. In G. Gottleib (Ed.), *Studies on the development of behavior and the nervous system: Early influences.* New York: Academic Press, 1978.

Isbell, H., Altshul, S., Kornetsky, C. H., Eisenman, A. J., Flanary, H. G., & Fraser, H. F. Chronic barbiturate intoxication: An experimental study. *Archives of Neurology and Psychiatry,* 1950, *64,* 1–28.

Isbell, H., Fraser, H. F., Wikler, A., Belleville, R. E., & Eisenman, A. J. An experimental study of the etiology of "rum fits" and delirium tremens. *Quarterly Journal of Studies on Alcohol,* 1955, *16,* 1–33.

Jarvik, M. E., Abramson, H. A., & Hirsch, M. W. Lysergic acid diethylamide (LSD-25): V. Effect on attention and concentration. *Journal of Psychology,* 1955, *39,* 373–383. (a)

Jarvik, M. E., Abramson, H. A., & Hirsch, M. W. Comparative subjective effects of seven drugs including lysergic acid diethylamide (LSD-25). *Journal of Abnormal and Social Psychology,* 1955, *51,* 657–662. (b)

Kelly, E. L., Miller, J. G., Marquis, D. G., Gerard, R. W., & Uhr, L. Effects of continued meprobamate and prochlorperazine administration on behavior of normal subjects. *Archives of Neurology and Psychiatry*, 1958, *80*, 247–252.

Kline, N. S. Clinical experience with iproniazid (Marsalid). *Journal of Clinical and Experimental Psychopathology*, 1958, *19*, 72–78.

Kline, N. Presidential address. In D. Efron (Ed.), *Psychopharmacology: A review of progress 1957–1967*. (Public Health Service Publication, No. 1936.) Washington, DC: U.S. Government Printing Office, 1968.

Klüver, H. Mescal visions and eidetic visions. *American Journal of Psychology*, 1926, *37*, 502–515.

Klüver, H. *Mescal and mechanisms of hallucinations*. Chicago, IL: University of Chicago Press, 1966. (Originally published, 1928.)

Kornetsky, C. Psychological effects of chronic barbiturate intoxication. *Archives of Neurology and Psychiatry*, 1951, *65*, 557–567.

Kornetsky, C. Effects of anxiety and morphine on the anticipation and perception of painful radiant thermal stimuli. *Journal of Comparative and Physiological Psychology*, 1954, *47*, 130–132.

Kornetsky, C., Bain, G., & Riedl, M. Effects of cocaine and naloxone on brain-stimulation reward. *The Pharmacologist*, 1981, *23*, 192.

Kornetsky, C., & Eliasson, M. Reticular stimulation and chlorpromazine: An animal model for schizophrenic over-arousal. *Science*, 1969, *165*, 1273–1274.

Kornetsky, C., & Esposito, R. U. Euphorigenic drugs: Effects on the reward pathways of the brain. *Federation Proceedings*, 1979, *38*, 2473–2476.

Kornetsky, C., Esposito, R. U., McLean, S., & Jacobson, J. O. Intracranial self-stimulation thresholds: A model for the hedonic effects of drugs of abuse. *Archives of General Psychiatry*, 1979, *36*, 289–292.

Kornetsky, C., Humphries, O., & Evarts, E. V. Comparison of psychological effects of certain centrally acting drugs in man. *Archives of Neurology and Psychiatry*, 1957, *77*, 318–324.

Kornetsky, C., Markowitz, R., & Esposito, R. U. Phencyclidine and naloxone: Effects on sensitivity to aversive and rewarding stimulation in the rat. In E. F. Domino (Ed.), *PCP (Phencyclidine): Historical and current perspectives*. Ann Arbor, MI: NPP Books, 1981.

Kornetsky, C., & Mirsky, A. On certain psychopharmacological and physiological differences between schizophrenics and normal persons. *Psychopharmacologia* (Berlin), 1966, *14*, 309–318.

Koster, R. Hormone factors in male behavior of the female rat. *Endocrinology*, 1943, *33*, 337–348.

Kuhn, R. The treatment of depressive states with G 22355 (imipramine hydrochloride). *American Journal of Psychiatry*, 1958, *115*, 459–464.

Lashley, K. S. Effect of strychnine and caffeine upon rate of learning. *Psychobiology*, 1917, *I*, 141–170.

Laties, V. G. I.V. Zavadaskii and the beginning of behavioral pharmacology: An historical note and translation. *Journal of the Experimental Analysis of Behavior*, 1979, *32*, 463–472.

Leeper, R. The role of motivation in learning: A study of the phenomenon of differential motivational control of the utilization of habits. *Journal of Genetic Psychology*, 1935, *46*, 3–40.

Lehmann, H. E., & Hanrahan, G. E. Chlorpromazine, a new inhibiting agent for psychomotor excitement and manic states. *Archives of Neurology and Psychiatry*, 1954, *71*, 227–257.

Lewin, L. *Phantastica: Narcotic and stimulating drugs, their use and abuse*. London: Routledge & Kegan Paul, 1964.

Lipper, S., & Kornetsky, C. Effect of chlorpromazine on conditioned avoidance as a function of CS-US interval length. *Psychopharmacologia* (Berlin), 1971, *22*, 144–150.

Loomis, T. A., & West, T. C. Comparative sedative effects of a barbiturate and non–tranquilizer drugs on normal subjects. *Journal of Pharmacology and Experimental Therapeutics,* 1958, *122*, 525–537.

Lorr, M., Klett, C. J., McNair, D. M. & Lasky, J. J. *Inpatient multi-dimensional psychiatric scale (IMPS) manual.* Copyright Maurice Lorr, 1962.

Low, L. A. Eliasson, M., & Kornetsky, C. Effect of chlorpromazine on avoidance acquisition as a function of CS-US interval length. *Psychopharmacologia* (Berlin), 1966, *10*, 148–154.

Macht, D. I., & Mora, C. F. Effect of opium alkaloids on the behavior of rats in the circular maze. *Journal of Pharmacology and Experimental Therapeutics,* 1920, *16*, 219–235.

Marcus, R., & Kornetsky, C. Negative and positive intracranial reinforcement thresholds: Effects of morphine. *Psychopharmacologia* (Berlin), 1974, *38*, 1–13.

Martin, W. R., & Isbel, H. *Drug addiction and the U.S. Public Health Service.* (DHEW Publication No. 77-434.) Washington, DC: U.S. Government Printing Office, 1978.

Masserman, J. H., & Yum, K. S. Analysis of influence of alcohol on experimental neurosis in cats. *Psychosomatic Medicine,* 1946, *8*, 36–52.

Mayer, D. J., & Price, D. D. Central nervous system mechanisms of analgesia. *Pain,* 1976, *2*, 374–404.

Miller, N. E., & Miles, W. R. Effect of caffeine on running speed of hungry, satiated and frustrated rats. *Journal of Comparative Psychology,* 1935, *20*, 397–412.

Miller, N. E., & Miles, W. R. Alcohol and removal of reward: An analytical study of rodent maze behavior. *Journal of Comparative Psychology,* 1936, *21*, 179–204.

Miller, R. E., Murphy, J. V., & Mirsky, I. A. The effect of chlorpromazine on fear motivated behavior in rats. *Journal of Pharmacology and Experimental Therapeutics,* 1957, *120*, 379–387.

Mirsky, A. F., & Kornetsky, C. On the dissimilar effects of drugs on the digit symbol substitution and continuous performance tests. *Psychopharmacologia* (Berlin), 1964, *5*, 161–177.

Mirsky, I. A., Miller, R., & Stein, M. Relation of adrenocortical activity and adaptive behavior. *Psychosomatic Medicine,* 1953, *15*, 574–588.

Murphy, J. V., & Miller, R. E. The effect of adrenocorticotrophic hormone (ACTH) on avoidance conditioning in the rat. *Journal of Comparative and Physiological Psychology,* 1955, *48*, 47–49.

National Institute of Mental Health Psychopharmacology Service Center Collaborative Study Group. Phenothiazine treatment in acute schizophrenia: Effectiveness. *Archives of General Psychiatry,* 1964, *10*, 246–261.

Nowlis, V., & Nowlis, H. H. The description and analysis of mood. *Annals of the New York Academy of Sciences,* 1956, *65*, 345–355.

Olds, J. *Drives and reinforcements.* New York: Raven Press, 1977.

Olds, J. Killam, K. F., & Bach-y-Rita, P. Self-stimulation of the brain used as a screening method for tranquilizing drugs. *Science,* 1956, *124*, 265–266.

Olds, J., & Milner, P. Positive reinforcement produced by electrical stimulation of septal area and other regions of rat brain. *Journal of Comparative and Physiological Psychology,* 1954, *47*, 419–427.

Olds, J., & Travis, R. P. Effects of chlorpromazine, meprobamate, pentobarbital and morphine on self-stimulation. *Journal of Pharmacology and Experimental Therapeutics,* 1960, *128*, 397–404.

Overton, D. A. State-dependent or "dissociated" learning produced with pentobarbital. *Journal of Comparative and Physiological Psychology,* 1964, *57*, 3–12.

Poslun, D. An anlysis of chlorpromazine-induced suppression of the avoidance response. *Psychopharmacologia* (Berlin), 1962, *3*, 361–373.

Primac, D. W., Mirsky, A. F., & Rosvold, H. E. Effects of centrally acting drugs on two tests of brain damage. *Archives of Neurology and Psychiatry*, 1957, *77*, 328–332.

Randall, L. O., & Shallek, W. Pharmacological activity of certain benzodiazepines. In D. Efron (Ed.), *Psychopharmacology: A view of progress 1957–1967*. (Public Health Service Publication No. 1936.) Washington, DC: U.S. Government Printing Office, 1968.

Rosen, V. H., & Gantt, W. H. Effect of metrazol convulsives on conditioned reflexes in dogs. *Archives of Neurology and Psychiatry*, 1943, *50*, 8–17.

Searle, L. V., & Brown, C. W. The effect of injections of benzedrine on the activity of white rats. *Journal of Comparative Psychology*, 1937, *36*, 143–155.

Sepinwall, J., & Cook, L. Behavioral pharmacology of antianxiety drugs. In L. L. Iversen, S.D. Iversen, & S.H. Snyder (Eds.), *Handbook of psychopharmacology* (Vol. 13). New York: Plenum Press, 1978.

Shirley, M. Spontaneous activity. *Psychological Bulletin*, 1929, *26*, 341–365.

Sidman, M. Avoidance conditioning with brief shock and no exteroceptive warning signal. *Science*, 1953, *118*, 157–158.

Skinner, B. F. Some contributions of an experimental analysis of behavior to psychology as a whole. *American Psychologist*, 1953, *8*, 69–78.

Skinner, B. F., & Heron, W. T. Effects of caffeine and benzedrine upon conditioning and extinction. *Psychological Record*, 1937, *1*, 340–346.

Stein, L. Effects and interactions of imipramine, chlorpromazine, reserpine, and amphetamine on self-stimulation: Possible neurophysiological basis of depression. In R. Heath (Ed.), *Recent advances in biological psychiatry*. New York: Plenum Press, 1962.

Stein, L., & Belluzzi, J. D. Brain endorphins: Possible role in reward and memory formation. *Federation Proceedings*, 1979, *38*, 2468–2472.

Stein, L., & Wise, C. D. Possible etiology of schizophrenia: Progressive damage to the noradrenergic reward system by 6-hydroxydopamine. *Science*, 1971, *171*, 1032–1036.

Stevens, S. S. *Psychophysics*. New York: Wiley, 1975.

Stone, C. P. Activation of impotent male rats by injections of testosterone propionate. *Journal of Comparative Psychology*, 1938, *25*, 445–450.

Swazey, J. *Chlorpromazine in psychiatry: A study of therapeutic innovation*. Cambridge, MA: MIT Press, 1975.

Thompson, T., & Schuster, C. R. Morphine self-administration, food-reinforced and avoidance behavior in rhesus monkeys. *Psychopharmacologia* (Berlin), 1964, *5*, 87–94.

Trevan, J. W. The error of determination of toxicity. *Proceedings of the Royal Society of Biology*, 1927, *101*, 483–514.

Weeks, J. R. Self-maintained morphine "addiction": A method for chronic programmed intravenous injection in unrestrained rats. *Federation Proceedings*, 1961, *20*, 397.

Weeks, J. Experimental morphine addiction: Method for automatic intravenous injections in unrestrained rats. *Science*, 1962, *138*, 143–144.

Weiss, B., & Laties, V. G. *Behavioral toxicology*. New York: Plenum Press, 1975.

Wikler, A. *Opioid dependence mechanisms and treatment*. New York: Plenum Press, 1980.

Wikler, A., Green, P. C., Smith, H. D., & Pescor, F. T. Use of a benzimidazole derivative with potent morphine-like properties orally as a presumptive reinforcer in conditioning of drug-seeking behavior in rats. *Federation Proceedings*, 1960, *19*, 22.

Wikler, A., Martin, W. R., Pescor, F. T., & Eades, C. G. Factors regulating oral consumption of an opioid (etonitazene) by morphine-addicted rats. *Psychopharmacologia* (Berlin), 1963, *5*, 55–76.

Wikler, A., & Masserman, J. H. The effects of morphine on learned adaptive response and experimental neurosis in cats. *Archives of Neurology and Psychiatry*, 1943, *50*, 401–404.

Wise, R. Action of drugs of abuse on brain reward systems. *Pharmacology, Biochemistry and Behavior,* 1980, *13,* 213–224.

Woods, J. H. Behavioral pharmacology of drug self-administration. In M.A. Lipton, A. DiMascio, & K.F. Killam (Eds.), *Psychopharmacology: A generation of progress.* New York: Raven Press, 1978.

Woodworth, R. S. *Experimental psychology.* New York: Henry Holt, 1938.

Woodworth, R. S., & Schlosberg, H. *Experimental psychology.* New York: Henry Holt, 1954.

7 Psychology and Physics: An Historical Perspective

Lawrence E. Marks
John B. Pierce Foundation Laboratory
Yale University

INTRODUCTION

Physics, like mathematics, is often hailed as a "Queen of the Sciences." For physics (including astronomy) is not only the oldest, but commonly estimated to be the most advanced, the most rigorous, and the most precise of human scientific endeavors, readily cast into rational quantitative form. After all, "Nature," Galileo said, "is written in mathematical language." And in many respects physics is the most successful of the sciences, both because of its power to make theoretical predictions and because of its applications in the technology that surrounds us. Perhaps it is not surprising, then, for many psychologists to view physics as the instantiation of the scientific method itself, and thus as a model for scientific psychology. A colleague once inquired of me whether, in my opinion, psychology would ever become a science like physics. Not "a science, like physics," but "a science like physics." Not a co-equal in a dominion of sciences, but perhaps at best a consort to Her Majesty.

Psychology's connections to physics have been long in duration and close in intimacy. The pursuit of fundamental physical elements of the universe, and especially the pursuit of unifying and simplifying principles, has continued to be one of the main themes of physics—from the aquacentrism of Thales through the unification of electricity and magnetism by Maxwell to the modern theories of quarks—a pursuit that has not been lost on some psychological thinkers:

> The scientist is usually looking for invariance whether he knows it or not. Whenever he discovers a functional relation between two variables, his next

question follows naturally: under what conditions does it hold? In other
words, under what transformations is the relation invariant? The quest for
invariant relations is essentially the aspiration toward generality, and in psychology, as in physics, the principles that have wide application are those we
prize [Stevens, 1951, p. 20].

One would doubtless classify Stevens among psychology's
hedgehogs—to use Isaiah Berlin's (1953) well-known dichotomy—among
those who seek unity rather than the diversity so welcomed by the foxes.
Although it would be an overstatement to say that physics is a discipline
wholly dominated by hedgehogs (unification, suggests Holton, 1975, is
just one of physics' themata)[1], nonetheless the search for simple, universal principles has been the hallmark of physicists like Newton, Maxwell,
and Einstein. It does not seem unreasonable to distinguish those psychologists who, like many if not most physicists, seek a small number of
general principles from those psychologists who, perhaps better compared to some biologists, seek to describe the myriad of forms and functions.

Physics touches base with psychology in several ways. Physical science exerted influence because it embodies so well the scientific method:
through its emphasis on control of pertinent variables and elimination of
extraneous ones, on precise measurement and quantification, and on
public verifiability; physics has also provided the impetus to the scientific
tradition of reductionism, which sees statements of all scientific disciplines as in principle reducible to statements invoking laws of physics.
Ultimately, according to one idealized point of view, the universe reduces
to matter and energy, or matter in motion: Macroscopic, deterministic
laws of physics can account in full for the plethora of reactions in chemistry, for diverse forms in biology, and for overt and covert behaviors in
psychology.

One need not be a reductionist to ask about the role that physical
processes play in psychological descriptions. When biological organisms
interact with their environment, it is, after all, a physical environment that

[1]By one of the quirks of historical fate, the psychology of individual differences—by
definition a haven for foxes—received a strong impetus from astronomy. Boring relates with
gusto the well-known story of how in 1796 the astronomer "Maskeleyne . . . dismissed
Kinnebrook, his assistant, because Kinnebrook observed the times of stellar transits almost
a second later than he did [Boring, 1957, p. 134]"; the observation of stellar transits required
a complex perceptual judgement of the spatial position of a star with reference both to visual
markers and to audible ticks of a clock. A published account of Kinnebrook's perceptual
"error"—more accurately, of the discrepancy between his judgments and Maskeleyne's—
was discovered around 1816 by Bessel, who then developed the concept that each observer
has his own "personal equation."

they interact with, an environment whose energies impinge upon the organisms to activate their sensory systems. Hence physics has played a direct role in those branches of psychology, notably sensation and perception, that deal directly with responses to configurations of stimulus energies in the environment. For generations, students of sensory psychology have had to learn not only about the psychology of color, sound, and temperature, and about the receptors of the eye, ear, and skin, but also about the physics of light, sound, and heat. In this substantive way, physics finds itself incorporated into the very body of psychological knowledge. To understand behavior means, in part, to understand physics.

Of course, physics has influenced psychology in many other ways, by means of form as well as substance: in form, as a guide to methodology and quantification (positivism, operationism, mathematical laws); in substance, as one part of what must eventually be a complete psychological system, as a source of general models like mechanism, materialism, and elementarism, and as a source of specific models for particular psychological phenomena. Perhaps one of the most important reasons why physics has influenced psychology so strongly is that great scientists like Newton, Helmholtz, and Maxwell contributed to both physics and psychology in their quest to understand Nature.

Psychology's relationship to physics can be best understood—indeed, perhaps can only be fully understood—within its historical development. Experimental psychology is a discipline only about one century old, while experimental physics dates about three and one-half centuries, if Wundt and Galileo are used as "temporal landmarks." The early experimental and theoretical successes of physics emerged in the seventeenth century while psychological analysis was still speculative. Despite this gap in maturity, the early physics bore clear implications for psychology, in part because Newton's science incorporated psychophysics as well as physics, but more significantly because the successes of Galilean-Newtonian mechanics induced others to try to incorporate the physicist's view of nature into accounts of behavior. An experimental mechanics of physical processes led to a speculative mechanics of mental processes. To be sure, speculative analysis of physics and psychology (and some experimental research, notably in topics like optics) existed before the seventeenth century, and often this speculation consisted of an integrated philosophy of nature that incorporated physics, psychology, and indeed virtually all of what were to become the separate sciences. But it was the demonstrated success of experimental physics that helped to inspire the speculative analysis of mind that in turn became the basis of much modern experimental psychology.

OVERVIEW

The goal of this essay is to show, in historical perspective, how physics has influenced psychology, in what ways modern psychology has been molded by a steady inflow of currents from physical science. Psychology in the twentieth century is very much the grandchild of its philosophical and scientific ancestors, including physics. Of course, to speak of psychology is really to speak of a host of smaller component disciplines, for psychology itself comes in many colors and flavors. Some of these disciplines much more than others have witnessed the influence of physics, experimental psychology having witnessed the most. For it is the experimental investigation of sensation, perception, learning, cognitive processes, and so forth that exhibit most clearly the undercurrents of (1) materialism, (2) mechanism, (3) elementarism, and (4) psychophysics described in this essay.

The roots of this quadrumvirate took hold in preexperimental science, when atomistic materialism and psychophysics first appeared in pre-Socratic thought. Materialism, mechanism, elementarism, and psychophysics all established themselves with the development of experimental mechanics beginning in the seventeenth century.

(1) Materialism derives directly from the view that all processes and phenomena of the universe reduce to processes and phenomena described by the laws of physics. The chemical, the biological, and the psychological all derive ultimately from the qualities of matter; and matter is physical in nature.

(2) The success of mechanics—and with this success the plausible view that the universe is a vast, complicated machine—engendered one of the recurrent themes in psychology: that mind and behavior are machine-like or mechanical. The embodiment of this theme at any point in time has depended on the kinds of machines available to serve as models—clocks in the seventeenth century, computers in the twentieth.

(3) Early physics was corpuscular, treating matter as composed of fundamental elements—the atoms. Just as physics had its unit, the atom, so psychology had its unit, the idea (Locke) or reflex (Descartes).

(4) Psychophysics is an intersection of psychology and physics, properly considered part of both—the study of the relationships between sensations and perceptions on the one hand and physical stimuli on the other. To ask psychophysical questions is, implicitly at least, to recognize two major philosophical questions: "What is?" and "What can be known?" Physics and psychology both grew

out of the earliest attempts to answer these questions of ontology and epistemology.

ANCIENT ATOMISM AND MATERIALISM

Speculations about the physical make-up of the inanimate world and about the psychological make-up of the human (and animal) world coexisted even in pre-Socratic thought. More importantly, speculations on both interpenetrated. The speculative atomism and materialism of Democritus, Epicurus, and Lucretius provided an intellectual framework that would take hold and flourish many centuries later. From the seventeenth century onward, a corpuscular view of nature predominated. Galileo, Boyle, Newton, and their followers were atomists, and, as will be made clear, the corpuscular view of the physical universe heavily influenced the beginnings of psychology in the seventeenth and eighteenth centuries.

The roots of atomistic materialism appear in the work of Socrates's contemporary Democritus (ca. 460–370 B.C.), who believed that all matter comprises tiny, indivisible corpuscles (atoms) separated by empty space (the void). According to this doctrine—passed down in fragments of Democritus's own writings and in the works of Plato and Theophrastus—all physical phenomena reduce to the behavior of these atoms, which can take on a variety of shapes, sizes, and motions. Of special significance to psychology was Democritus's claim that the spatial characteristics of the atoms determine the qualities of our sensory and perceptual responses. In his primitive psychophysics—transmitted largely through the *De Sensu* of Theophrastus—every color, every pitch, every taste quality results from the character of the stream of atoms entering the channels of each sense. Smooth particles excite whiteness in the eye, and sweet and bitter tastes in the tongue (depending on whether the smooth atoms are large, as in the case of sweet, or small and with hooks, as in bitter). Rough particles produce black colors and sour tastes.

Democritus's psychology was materialistic. For the soul that appreciates the sensory qualities is itself material, consisting of fine, round atoms no different in their essential make-up from the atoms that form the remainder of the physical universe. In Democritus, then, mind is in principle a matter of physics, and we find a thoroughgoing materialism in which psychology and physics unite. In developing his corpuscular psychophysics, Democritus promoted an early version of the doctrine of secondary qualities, a doctrine that from the time of Locke was to govern much of the thinking about sensory psychology. According to Democritus, the attributes of sensation are not at all like their physical causes. The names given to sensations are conventions, not physical specifications: "Sweet exists by convention, bitter by convention, color by convention; atoms and void *(alone)* exist in reality [Freeman, 1948, p. 93]."

The atomistic psychology and physics of Democritus was extended by Epicurus (ca. 342–270 B.C.) and later adopted by the Roman poet Lucretius (ca. 96–55 B.C.). Lucretius elaborated atomism in his long poem *De Rerum Natura,* which provides what is perhaps the best single source of ancient materialist philosophy. An interesting addition that Epicurus and Lucretius made to this philosophy was the doctrine of "swerve" of the atoms: The natural downward motion of the atoms could be modified, for "if the atoms do not swerve and cause a certain beginning of action that may break the chains of Fate . . . whence comes this power of free will . . . .? *[De Rerum Natura,* Book II, lines 251–256]." Thus the psychological as well as the physical determinism of Democritus was partially repealed by modifying the atomistic doctrine to permit voluntary changes in the *direction* of physical motion. This view reappeared 1700 years later in the philosophical psychology of Descartes.

Ancient atomism set the stage for the new corpuscular physics that emerged in the seventeenth century, when physics burst forth as an experimental science. Preceded by such astronomical work as Copernicus's (1472–1543) theory and Tycho Brahe's (1546–1601) observations, the seventeenth century of Galileo, Kepler, and Newton brought a revolution to the conception of the workings of the physical universe.

How could the conception of man not be radically altered by the developments of the seventeenth century? The motions of celestial bodies in the sky, the motions of mundane bodies on earth, all fell to the mathematical equations of the new physics: "The construction of Newton's corpuscular world machine completes the conceptual revolution that Copernicus had initiated a century and a half earlier [Kuhn, 1957, p. 261]." The success in describing mechanical motion (Galileo, Newton), the invention of instruments (Galileo's telescope, Torricelli's barometer), even the implementation of mechanics into engineering (for instance, mechanical figures powered by fountains of water, that could simulate human motion, (see Chapanis, in this volume) portended the eighteenth-century view of the universe as an enormous machine—and of the human mind as a smaller one.

GALILEO'S IMPACT: PHYSICS AND PSYCHOLOGY

Galileo Galilei (1564–1642) is a seminal source and central figure, both in physics and in the relation of physics to psychology. Galileo was not the first to conduct experiments in physics; nor did he analyze physical phenomena with the theoretical power of Newton. Nonetheless Galileo was significant because, among other things, his physics transcended mere descriptive science (often attributed to the empiricism of Francis Bacon) to seek quantification through general physical laws. Where Aristotle and perhaps Bacon are to be considered among the foxes of physics, Galileo stands as one of the first major hedgehogs.

The following aspects of Galileo's work had special import for psychology: scientific method, kinematics (analysis of motion), and psychophysics.

Scientific method. Galileo's approach combined both empirical and hypothetical-deductive methods. Though Galileo may not often have used experiment as a discovery procedure, he almost certainly used the experimental method to confirm the quantitative laws he had deduced. From this point of view, Galileo far superseded the relatively simple inductionism of Francis Bacon's (1561–1626) *Novum Organum* (1620) and made possible the fuller expression of induction and deduction found in Isaac Newton's (1642–1727) *Principia* (1686) and *Opticks* (1704). To say this is not to diminish the importance of Bacon's scientific philosophy, with its emphasis on empirical observation. Controlled observation and induction are cornerstones of scientific method; and empiricism, both as a method and as a theory of the contents of the human mind, exerted its own powerful influence on psychology (notably through the so-called British empiricist school of Locke and others), providing a main tenet of psychological science as it emerged in the nineteenth century. But the hypothetical-deductive model of Galilean-Newtonian physics has often been a special goal, though it has tended to remain for psychology just that, a consummation mostly to be wished.

Kinematics. Kinematics refers to the motions of bodies and the laws of motion. Galileo's discovery (perhaps his best known discovery) of the law of falling bodies, his analyses of uniform motion, of uniform acceleration, and of suddenly imparted motion (leading to the parabolic law of projectiles, which made important use of the principle of inertia), all formed the groundwork upon which Newton (1686) developed the axioms and theorems of motion in the *Philosophia Naturalis Principia Mathematica*.

Galileo's kinematics was not only a landmark achievement, but provided a significant new perspective. The very lawfulness of mechanical behavior—the success in describing and predicting mechanical events in terms of matter and the efficient causes of motion—profoundly influenced subsequent thinking, including psychological thinking. For if mechanical explanations can describe the activity of inanimate objects, why not also the activity of animate objects?

Biological systems too are subject to the laws of mechanics, as illustrated by William Harvey's (1628) discovery of the circulation of blood and Giovanni Borelli's (1680) application of Galilean mechanics to the movements of animals, for instance to the flight of birds. The body is a physical system; and while the vitalistic view—that some special force, a *vis viva,* distinguishes living from nonliving matter—still prevailed in the minds of many, it was only a matter of time before physics would in principle account for biology (see Uttal, in this volume). Such was the credo of the *iatrophysical* school of biology and medicine. Among the most significant statements in the seventeenth century of this reductionist dogma appear in the writings of Descartes, who described structure and function of human and animal bodies as if they were machines.

And if the body is a machine, a matter of matter in motion, why not also the mind? Certainly sensation and perception could be conceived in such terms. After a quick glance back to the materialism of Democritus, we can look forward to the early visual theory of Newton's *Opticks* (1730/1952):

> . . . when a Man views any Object . . . . the Light which comes from the several Points of the Object is so refracted by the transparent skins and humours of the Eye . . . as to converge and meet again . . . in the bottom of the Eye, and there to paint a Picture of the Object upon [the retina] . . . . And these Pictures, propagated by Motion along the Fibres of the Optick Nerves into the Brain, are the cause of Vision [p. 15].

A line runs from Galileo to Hobbes as well as to Newton, and through both Galileo and Newton to Locke, to Berkeley, to Hume, and especially to Hartley, with a branch to Herbart, to Fechner, to Freud. The view that the mind operates according to mechanical principles (whether or not wholly materialistic, based on the activity of matter; and whether couched in the language of eighteenth-century physics or twentieth-century computer science) has its roots in the work of Galileo.

Psychophysics and sensation. Finally, I will mention an observation and a theoretical distinction, both of which were made by Galileo and both of which bore important consequences for psychological thought. In the course of his observations on mechanical properties of strings, Galileo (1638) discovered that the pitch of a sound is directly related to its frequency of vibration. Pitch is a psychological dimension, an attribute of the sensation of sound, whereas frequency is a physical measure, a characteristic of the stimulus, defined as the reciprocal of the time for one complete wave motion. Thus, the relationship that Galileo noted is what is now termed a *psychophysical relationship,* a functional relationship between a psychological attribute and a physical dimension.

Galileo's empirical observation, said by Boring to be the "great acoustic event of the seventeenth century [Boring, 1942, p. 323]," is closely tied to a distinction that Galileo (1623) noted in *Il Saggiatore* and that was subsequently affirmed by Newton and proposed more formally by Locke: Whereas there are some psychological attributes of sensation that may resemble the physical qualities that cause them, there are other attributes that do not resemble their qualities or causes and must be distinguished from them. In modern terminology, an object that is 2 meters in length appears longer to perception than an object 1 meter in length. But a light of wavelength 510 nanometers doesn't look longer (wavelength) or slower (frequency) than a light of 460 nanometers; instead, the one looks green, the other blue. Locke called these two kinds of physical qualities *primary* and *secondary,* respectively. While the spatial and temporal properties of sensations may be like their objects and events, the modality-specific qualities—such properties as color, pitch, and taste—are not: "I do not believe that for exciting in us tastes, odors, and sounds there are required in external bodies anything but sizes, shapes, numbers, and slow or rapid movements; and I think that if ears, tongues, and noses were taken away, shapes, numbers, and motions would remain, but not odors or tastes or sounds [Galileo, 1623/1960, p. 311]." The study of the relationships between the sensory appearances and the physical properties is essentially what the discipline of sensory psychophysics is all about.

MECHANISM AND THE ROOTS OF MATERIALISM

Beginnings of Mechanistic Psychology

Thomas Hobbes (1588–1679) visited Galileo in 1636 and, after returning to England, subsequently developed and published his major works (*Human Nature* in 1650; *Leviathan* in 1651). In both works, Hobbes incorporated a materialistic, mechanistic psychology. Hobbes saw Galilean motion as a central concept with which to explain psychological phenomena, including sensation and imagination. Physical motions in external objects arouse the senses, and they do this by exciting motions within sensory nerves: "All which qualities, called *sensible,* are in the object, that causeth them, but so many several motions of the matter, by which it presseth our organs diversely. Neither in us that are pressed, are they any thing else, but divers motions; for motion produceth nothing but motion [Hobbes, 1651/1946, pp. 7–8]."

Sensation is the outcome of matter in motion, ever obedient to the physical principles of inertia and uniform motion as stated by Galileo.

Sensation and perception consist of the transfer of motion from the external world to the sense organs. Imagination is decayed sensory motion, impeded by other physical motions; dreams are the outcome of the imagination in sleep, consisting of the restorations in the sense organs of motions that sleep had benumbed. The physically smaller motions of imagination and dreams, as compared to the motions of sensations, turn up a century later as the little vibrations, or vibratiuncles, in David Hartley's (1749) version of psychophysical parallelism.

Hobbes's rather simplistic, mechanistic psychology (which formed a prolegomenon to his political theory) represented a primitive attempt to use laws of physics as a model for laws of psychology. Looking backward, it is easy to dismiss Hobbes's psychology by saying that it represented the laws of physics misapplied. However, the seeming naïveté of Hobbes's theory should not obscure the historical importance of what Hobbes did—he tried to exlain psychological phenomena in the best physical (physiological) terms he had available.

Physical motions serve as more than just a model in Hobbes's theory; they form a reduction of psychological processes to physical ones. Such reductionism, whether implicit or explicit, was already finding experimental success in biology—in, as already noted, Harvey's discovery of blood circulation.

In René Descartes (1596-1650) is perhaps the first clear statement of the reductionist dogma that physiological processes reduce to physical ones (though the battle against vitalism in biology continued for at least two more centuries). According to Descartes, all bodies—whether animate or inanimate—whether planets or trees, rocks or dogs—are like machines and can be fully described in terms of the laws of physics.

Descartes is perhaps best known to psychologists for his metaphysical dualism—for the view that mind and body are distinct substances, interacting primarily through the pineal gland—but his mechanistic physiology and reflexology played important roles in the development of scientific psychology. Indeed, Descartes came exceedingly close to proposing a wholly mechanistic psychology. The 36th of his *Principles of Philosophy,* Part 2 (1644), declared that the amount of motion (that is, momentum) in the universe was originally established by God and thereafter remained constant. This fundamental ontological rule set limits on the possible laws of both physics and psychology. The bodies of human and nonhuman animals alike behave like machines, he wrote in the *Discourse on Method* of 1637/1931, for "the laws of Mechanics, which are identical with those of Nature [p. 115]" are also the laws of biological systems. Muscular activity occurs when the muscles are inflated by animal spirits (themselves a material substance), in accord with principles just like those governing automata: "And this will not seem strange to those, who, knowing how many different *automata* or moving machines can be made by the industry of man, without employing in doing so more than a very few parts in comparison with the great multitude of bones, muscles, nerves, arteries, veins, or other parts that are found in the body of each animal. From this aspect the body is regarded as a machine [pp. 115–116]." Humans however have language, which, Descartes argued, distinguishes us from mere machines.

What, then, can the mind (rational soul, for Descartes) do? In animals, nothing, since only humans have souls. In humans, the mind can be the source of rational thought, of plans for actions. But the possible effects of mind are limited by physical laws. Given that the total amount of motion in the universe is constant (the principle described in the paragraph above), the mind cannot spawn action, cannot create motion; all the mind can do is change the directions of ongoing movements. This function, reminiscent of the "swerve" of atoms postulated by Epicurus and Lucretius, is allocated by Descartes primarily to the pineal gland, where the Cartesian mind or soul may modify the automatic or reflex activity of the body.

Descartes provided detailed descriptions of what is now called reflex behavior (in his *Treatise on Man,* 1664), and he used the word "reflected" (*réfléchis*) in Article 36 of Part 1 of *Passions of the Soul* (1650). The notion of a reflex—of reflection, as light from a mirror—comes, of course, directly from physics. In Cartesian doctrine, the animal spirits aroused by some potentially dangerous object in the environment are conveyed through the nerves to the pineal gland "in such a way that the spirits reflected from the image thus formed on the gland, proceed thence to take their places partly in the nerves which serve to turn the back and dispose the legs for flight [Descartes, 1650/1931, p. 348]." The reflex was seen as a small part of a grander causal sequence of motions, ultimately describable in terms of physical laws—and was to be seen as such for nearly three centuries until, again partly under the influence of physics (here the positivism of Mach and the operationism of Bridgman—see below), the reflex was reinterpreted by B. F. Skinner (1931) in terms of correlation rather than causation.

Despite the small role of *l'âme* in the human psychology of Descartes, it is still a step, though a relatively little one, from Descartes's basically mechanical psychology to Julien Offray de La Mettrie's (1709–1751) wholly mechanical one a century later—from the animal as machine to the human as machine (see Rosenfield, 1941). For La Mettrie's *Man: A Ma-*

chine (1748) there is no rational Cartesian soul distinct from body; soul there may be, but the soul is itself the body, itself matter as in Democritus, needing only materialistic laws for its explanation.

Materialism and the Experimental Analysis of Animal Behavior

The experimental embodiment of this materialistic approach came a century and a half later in the work of Jacques Loeb (1859-1924), a zoologist whose mechanistic analysis of animal behavior at once recalled the tradition of Descartes and La Mettrie and anticipated the new movement of behaviorism. Striving to describe animal behavior in purely physical and chemical terms and without resource to concepts like "purpose" that might smack of vitalism, Loeb latched onto the tropism, or environmentally forced movement, as a unit and model for behavior. From "the assumption that all [the] motions are determined by internal or external forces [1918, p. 13]," Loeb extended the domain of the tropism—not only would it refer to orientations made by plants under the influence of external sources of energy, but now also to movements made by animals. Light, heat, chemicals can all induce tropistic movements.

One of the best examples is the way winged aphids (and other organisms) move toward a source of light (positive heliotropism). According to Loeb, "Heliotropic animals are . . . in reality photometric machines [1912, p. 41]," behaving much as a light meter does in response to visible electromagnetic radiation. Heliotropism obeys the cosine law of photometry—the response, whether the behavior of an organism or the pointer on a light meter, depends on the cosine of the angle of incidence of the light. Loeb wrote, with obvious pleasure, that his mechanistic interpretation of forced movements was strengthened by the fact that J. H. Hammond had constructed an artificial heliotropic machine—an automaton whose behavior paralleled that of moths. A strange circle this: The argument that certain behaviors are machine-like, because they obey the same mathematical laws that certain machines obey, is supported by the building of another such machine!

It is tempting to include Loeb's work under the rubric of animal psychophysics, for Loeb sought to relate behavior to the various physical energies in the environment: All behaviors consist of responses to stimulus events. Loeb clearly perceived his analysis of forced movements as providing the framework to a comprehensive scheme for even the most complex of behaviors:

> Our wishes and hopes, disappointments and sufferings have their source in instincts which are comparable to the light instinct of the heliotropic animals. The need of and the struggle for food, the sexual instinct with its poetry and

its chain of consequences, the maternal instincts with the felicity and the suffering caused by them, the instinct of workmanship, and some other instincts are the roots from which our inner life develops. For some of these instincts the chemical basis is at least sufficiently indicated to arouse the hope that their analysis, from the mechanistic point of view, is only a question of time [1912, p. 30].

One of the most significant features of Loeb's theoretical stance was his conception of forced movements as a single, unifying theme in understanding behavior. In this regard, Loeb belongs among the hedgehogs of biological and behavioral science:

The progress of natural science depends upon the discovery of rationalistic elements or simple natural laws. We find that there are two classes of investigators in biology, grouped according to their attitude toward such simple laws or rationalistic elements. One seems to aim at the denial of the existence of such simple laws and every new case which does not fall at once under such a law offers an opportunity for them to point out the inadequacy of the latter. The other group of investigators aims to discover and not to disprove laws [1912, p. 59].

To Loeb, the model for the scientific analysis of the behavior of inanimate matter became the model for the scientific analysis of the behavior of living organisms.

Loeb's approach continued in the experimental research program of William J. Crozier, a biologist who like Loeb recognized physics as his scientific ancestor. Crozier and Hoagland (1934) introduced their review of "The Study of Living Organisms" by quoting Santayana's statement that "scientific psychology is a part of physics"; then they went on to provide a quantitative account of animal behavior—an "animal psychophysics" of functional relations between behavior and physical stimuli based on the tropism as a fundamental unit.

Loeb spent several years on the faculty of the University of Chicago, overlapping there with John Watson (1878–1958)—then a graduate student—who was later to announce, identify, and lead the new movement, behaviorism (Watson, 1913). To the behaviorist, psychology treats what is observable and observed, the behaviors of animals and humans. Although the principles of behaviorism do not require a mechanistic science, nevertheless mechanistic it has been—from the simple stimulus-response reflexology of Watson through the more complicated reflexology of Hull and the operant conditioning of Skinner to the information-processing psychology currently in vogue. Each is heir, in its own way and to a greater or lesser extent, to the marriage of physical science and behavior found in Descartes and Loeb.

Materialism, Mechanism, and Associationism

The materialistic dogma—the view, like La Mettrie's, that there is only
"base matter"—lies at the heart of physiological thinking in psychology.
Physiological mechanisms become an intermediary between behavioral
processes and physical laws. Physics begets (bio)chemistry, biochemistry
begets physiology, and physiology begets psychology. The proximity of
physics and physiology to each other as well as to psychology is especially clear in Descartes, who was an important forerunner of modern
physiological psychology.

A second forerunner of physiological psychology was the Scottish physician David Hartley (1705–1757), whose writings, like those of Descartes, clearly evidence the impact of physical science. By the
eighteenth century, it had become rather easy to see the universe as a vast
mechanical system ever obedient to the laws of God and Newton. The
metaphor of the universe as a clock—a precisely organized physical system set into perpetual motion in accord with quantitative laws—soon
expanded into a metaphor of two clocks, one physical and the other
mental; perhaps the best known of these is embodied in Leibniz's (1705/
1951) psychophysical parallelism:

> Souls follow their laws, which consist in a certain development of percep-
> tions, according to goods and evils; and bodies also follow their laws, which
> consist in the laws of motion; and nevertheless these two beings of entirely
> different kind are in perfect accord, and correspond like two clocks perfectly
> regulated on the same basis, although perhaps of an entirely different con-
> struction. This is what I call Pre-established Harmony [p. 192].

Such a system appears in Hartley's *Observations on Man, His Frame,
His Duty, and His Expectations* (1749). Initially trained for the clergy but
subsequently a physician by profession, Hartley developed a speculative
system in which physiological events, described in terms of matter and
motion, paralleled the corresponding mental events. Though mechanistic
it certainly is, Hartley's system should not properly be called materialistic
or reductionistic, for he did not reduce sensation to mechanical events.
Technically speaking, each is the concomitant of the other. Still, the
material aspect to psychological events is always close at hand.

The first chapter of *Observations on Man* opens as follows:

> My chief design in the following chapter, is, briefly, to explain, establish,
> and apply the Doctrines of *Vibrations* and *Association*. The First of these
> Doctrines is taken from the Hints concerning the Performance of Sensation
> and Motion, which Sir *Isaac Newton* has given at the End of his *Principia*,
> and in the Questions annexed to his *Optics;* the Last, from what Mr. *Locke,*

and other ingenious Persons since his Time, have delivered concerned the influence of *Association* . . . .
.The proper Method of Philosophizing seems to be, to discover and establish the general Laws of Action, affecting the Subject under Consideration, from certain select, well-defined, and well-attested Phaenomena, and then to explain and predict the other Phaenomena by these Laws. This is the Method of Analysis and Synthesis recommended and followed by Sir *Isaac Newton* [Hartley, 1749, Vol. 1, pp. 5–6].

Thus Hartley attempted to incorporate Newtonian (as well as Lockean) thinking into both the form and substance of his psychophysiology. Sensations consist of vibrations in the nerves and brain, the to-and-fro motion of fine particles. Sensations differ in quality as these vibrations differ in their physical properties—in frequency, location, and direction. With repetition of stimuli, the sensations that are aroused leave remnants, which we would now call memory images, and which have their physiological counterparts, according to Hartley, in miniature vibrations or what he called vibratiuncles. At this point Hartley tapped Locke's doctrine of association; by means of temporal contiguity, sensations gain the capacity to bring forth ideas, and, correspondingly, vibrations gain the capacity to bring forth vibratiuncles.

Hartley helped turn associationism into a physiological psychology. But Hartley's psychology—like Descartes's—could just as easily be called a physical psychology, being as much physics as physiology. Both men conceived of behavior in terms of machines they were familiar with, just as many contemporary psychologists do. Where automata and vibrating strings provided physical analogues to behavior and mind in the seventeenth and eighteenth centuries, more complex machines, notably computers, provide models in the twentieth. But if it is easy, from the perspective of this century, to smile and dismiss Hartley's speculations of 250 years ago, what of psychologists a quarter of a millenium from now? Will they gaze with similarly bemused eyes on currently popular physical models of mind?

Materialistic Roots of Psychoanalysis

Materialism took hold in the nineteenth century. Much biological and psychological science operated under the aegis of the known laws of physics. And sometimes the influence of physics appeared in unexpected places:

The intention of this project is to furnish us with a psychology which shall be a natural science; its aim, that is, is to represent psychical processes as quantitatively determined states of specifiable material particles and so to

make them plain and void of contradictions. The project involves two principal ideas:
  1.   That what distinguishes activity from rest is to be regarded as a quantity (Q) subject to the general laws of motion.
  2.   That it is to be assumed that the material particles in question are the
  neurones.

  Thus, perhaps surprisingly, begins the *Project for a Scientific Psychology* (1954b, p. 355) of Sigmund Freud (1856–1939), written in 1895 but not
published by Freud in his lifetime. The *Project* clearly represents an early
strain in Freud's thought—coming as it does right around the time of his
publication with Josef Breuer of their studies on hysteria, and half a
decade before the less blatantly physico-physiological *The Interpretation
of Dreams* (1900). Indeed, later Freudian writings only rarely evidence
the physicalistic physiology that Freud postulated in the *Project*. Instead,
the physics of Freud's subsequent psychoanalytical theory is of a more
metaphorical sort, appearing largely in the use of terminology appropri-
ated from physics—in *mental energy* (a concept absorbed from the psychologist Herbart and the physicist-psychophysicist Fechner), in the
notion of *force* as applied to psychological concepts, and in the determinism of psychic forces. In short, Freud's psychoanalysis began with a
strong current of physical science and later maintained some of the trappings of physics even when the theory became more psychological in
spirit—more hermeneutic than reductionistic.
  Yet Freud's roots were in natural science, in biology and physiology—
and most relevant here, in a physiology that was especially well-
connected to physics. For during the eight years of his medical studies in
Vienna, Freud spent the six-year period 1876–1882 at the Physiological
Institute of Ernst Brücke (1819–1892), the eminent physiologist who with
Emil du Bois-Reymond (1818–1896) and Hermann von Helmholtz (1821–
1894) took an oath to uphold the view that all processes within an organism can be described in terms of the laws of physics and chemistry. (This
the pledge of three former students of Johannes Müller, himself a vitalist.)
Biology was to be purged of vitalism, to be reduced to physics in fact as
Descartes and La Mettrie could only propose to do in theory.
  And to Freud, psychology was to be put on a similar material-science
basis. Helmholtz himself—physicist, physiologist, psychophysicist—was
to Freud an idol (Jones, 1956). That most important rule of the conservation of energy—first formulated in 1842 by Robert Mayer—worked its
way from Helmholtz's paper read in 1847 at the Berliner Physikalische
Gesellschaft (which Brücke helped found two years earlier) to Brücke's
physiology and Freud's psychology.
  In the *Project,* Freud begins in the paragraph quoted above by proposing that psychological processes are reducible to the physical properties

of matter and motion in the underlying physiological (neural) substrate. Following this, he brings forth a "principle of neuronic inertia," which he defines as the tendency for neurones to "divest themselves of quantity (Q)," and which he then uses to explain phenomena that range from reflexes to hysteria (the ridding of excess excitation through the muscular system). This discharge of excess quantity appears in later writings without the specific physical-physiological baggage, more purely psychological in its content, though still physicalistic in its structure. The mechanical flavor remained as Freud then elaborated a spatial model of the mind (Conscious, Preconscious, Unconscious, as in *The Interpretation of Dreams*), and as he subsequently modified the theory to engage the three psychic agents id, ego, and superego (*The Ego and the Id,* 1923).

Central to Freud's theorizing was the conception of psychic determinism: the determinism of physical science translated into the psychological realm, where it signifies that behavior—all behavior, even the apparently trivial and unintentional—has its causes. At the discovery of these causes Freud tried his hand, and a reader of the *Psychopathology of Everyday Life* can only marvel at his attempts to account for the bases of seemingly haphazard verbal behaviors, as when Freud tried to explain exactly why he chose the number 2,467 when he wrote to a friend that "I had finished reading the proof sheets of *The Interpretation of Dreams,* and that I did not intend to make any further changes in it, 'even if it contained 2,467 mistakes' [(1907/1938, p. 152]."[2] Even the dubious reader will doubtless be impressed by Freud's Sherlockian travails.

Beyond mere determinism are the physicalistic models and analyses that continued to pervade Freud's theory of the mind—the mind a psychic machine powered by psychic energy. Only a précis is possible here, covering a few of the basics. Psychic energy is, according to Freud, one of the most significant components of the libido, "a force of variable quantity," as he called it (*Three Contributions to the Theory of Sex,* 1905). Libido makes itself apparent when it is directed toward (cathected on) a sexual object; the process of cathexis *(Besetzung)* proves to be a psychological analogue to the charging of a capacitor with electrical potential.

In *The Interpretation of Dreams,* the general process of cathexis is incorporated into a mechanical model: An Unconscious primary process (homeostatic) seeks to avoid the accumulation of excess excitation (akin to the "principle of neuronic inertia" described in the *Project*), and a Preconscious secondary process directs the psychic energy toward exter-

---

[2]The explanation was that Freud had just then (in 1899, at the age of 43) read of the retirement of an ordinance inspector whom Freud had seen on his own 24th birthday. Freud's interpretation rested on the projection of his own retirement to *24* years thence, when he would be *67*.

nal objects. As to the underlying model itself, again Freud's words serve best:

> The mechanics of these processes is entirely unknown to me; anyone who seriously wishes to follow up these ideas must address himself to the physical analogies, and find some way of getting a picture of the sequence of motions which ensues on the excitation of the neurones. Here I do no more than hold fast to the ideas that the activity of the first ψ-system aims at the *free outflow of the quantities of excitation,* and that the second system, by means of the cathexis emanating from it, effects an *inhibition* of this outflow, a transformation into dormant cathexis, probably with a rise in potential. . . . After the second system has completed its work of experimental thought, it removes the inhibition and damming up of the excitations and allows them to flow off into motility [Freud, 1900/1938, p. 534].

Freud also had exposure to the psychophysics popular in experimental psychology of the later nineteenth and early twentieth century—not just to the work of Helmholtz, but also to Gustav Fechner (1801–1887), whom Freud cited in several places; to Brücke himself, known to visual scientists for the Brücke effect (enhanced brightness of flashing light) and the Bezold-Brücke effect (changes in hue due to changes in brightness); and to Ernst Mach (1838–1916), in whose work Freud saw at least some kinship: "But when I read the latest psychological books (Mach's *Analyse der Empfindungen,* second edition, Kroell's *Aufbau der Seele,* etc.) all of which have the same kind of aims as my work, and see what they have to say about dreams, I am as delighted as the dwarf in the fairy tale because 'the princess doesn't know' [Freud, 1954a, p. 322]."

Freud was not a physicist, and it would be difficult to argue that, in the end, Freud's psychoanalytic theory was in any fundamental sense a physicalistic psychology. Still, even in his anthropological and linguistic writings, his mythological and artistic speculations, there is a real sense in which Freud sought to be a Natural Philosopher of the human mind.

Routes of Materialism

As I have already mentioned, the routes from physics to materialistic psychology were twofold—besides a direct one, there was an indirect one through physiology.[3] Throughout the eighteenth, nineteenth, and twen-

---

[3] No attempt will be made to document this indirect relationship of physics to psychology through biology, for this pathway would lead too wide afield (but see Uttal, in this volume). Clearly, to take but one example, Darwin's biology—with its implications for adaptation by species and for continuity among species—influenced psychology enormously.

tieth centuries, as the biological sciences have progressed their success has fostered the materialist dogma that living systems can be explained by (reduced to) physical terms and physical laws.[4] Still, the battle was not easily won: Some biological scientists of note (even some of the present century, like Haldane, 1914) have argued against materialism. It is worth mentioning that when Forbes wrote his chapter on "The Mechanism of Reaction" in 1934 for Murchison's *Handbook,* he felt it necessary to begin by rejecting vitalism and averring that materialistic laws suffice to explain all biological activity. However, the controversy between materialism and vitalism in biology and physiology and the encroachment of this controversy into psychology fall outside the scope of the present essay.

Two points need to be made here. First, though the explication of psychology (or of biology, see Uttal, in this volume) by physics is by its nature a reductionism, reductionism need not entail a physical materialism—one may also attempt to reduce psychology to sociology, as did Comte (see Back, in Volume II), or to a socioeconomic dialectical materialism, as did Lenin. Nevertheless, the blatant success of the physical sciences undoubtedly encourages the kind of reductionism that seeks physicalistic explanation.

Second, physical explanations of psychological phenomena tend to be mechanistic ones, though they need not be; similarly, mechanistic models need not be materialistic or reducible to physics, though they tend to be: The materialistic view of nature takes the physical properties of the world as they are, whether or not these properties are explicable in terms of mechanical action; Newton's theory of gravitation was, to some, distressingly nonmechanistic, in that the theory relied on the notion of "action at a distance"—the force of gravity acting without direct contact between bodies. In this sense, the mechanistic view is the more reductionistic (Schofield, 1970). Indeed, it is the extended notion of mechanisms— extended in application beyond physical systems, beyond machines, and thus metaphorized—that has become a dominant, reductive mode of thinking in modern scientific psychology (see Chapanis, in this volume). This mode of explanation has its origins in the speculative psychologies of the eighteenth and nineteenth centuries. Hartley's psychology and physiology were both mechanistic; it is not easy to disentangle the influence of physics on his conception of neural processes as vibratory from the indirect influence of physics on his conception of association of ideas. But the notion of association of ideas per se is not materialistic, though it is mechanical.

---

[4]Though not without digressions, for instance in the second half of the eighteenth century, which saw "an escape from mechanical reductionism" (Schofield, 1970).

MECHANISM OF MIND: ASSOCIATIONISM AND ITS ELEMENTS

Hartley obtained the doctrine of association from John Locke (1632–1704), who in turn was strongly influenced by the physical and biological science of his time, especially through his good friend Robert Boyle (1627–1691). In Locke's hands, the doctrine of association was thoroughly psychological, for he declared in the first chapter of the *Essay Concerning Human Understanding* (1690) that he "shall not meddle with the physical consideration of mind." Instead, with the epistemological goal of explaining the sources of knowledge, Locke tried to account for the ideas of the mind, their origin and synthesis. Although connections among ideas play a major role, the chapter on "Association of Ideas" did not appear until the fourth edition of the *Essay* (1700). Fuller treatment of the doctrine of association awaited David Hume's (1711–1776) *Treatise of Human Nature* (1739), where association became the fundamental principle of the operation of the mind. Hume elaborated three principles by which he claimed association operated, namely by means of resemblance, contiguity in time or place, and cause and effect. For Hume more than for Locke, the principle of association appears as a psychological counterpart to a principle of physics, for Hume described association as an *attraction* of ideas, his model clearly being the gravitational attraction between bodies that Newton had described in the *Principia.*[5]

To return to Locke, the influence of physics appears less significant to his doctrine of association than to his elementaristic analysis. Locke's friend Boyle, like many of his contemporary physical scientists, held a corpuscular view of nature—that the material universe is composed of microscopic particles, elements, in a plethora of combinations. The psychology of Locke, transmitted to Berkeley, Hume, and Hartley, contained by analogy its elements, the atoms of the mind. All ideas, said Locke, come from sensation or from reflection: The *Essay* is largely an epistemological account of how knowledge reduces to these ideas. In Hume's *Treatise* the elementarism is even more apparent, for Hume attempted to analyze and describe the mind much as Newton did the physical universe. Indeed, though he did not conduct experiments in the modern sense, Hume subtitled his *Treatise* "An Attempt to Introduce the Experimental Method of Reasoning into Moral Subjects" (see Klein, 1970).

---

[5]To be accurate, it should be noted that in the "mechanism" of mind—the "mechanical" association of ideas—psychology uses the conception of mechanics in a somewhat broader way than does physics. For mechanical action in physics implies direct contact between bodies (Newton's gravitational "action at a distance" being, therefore, nonmechanical). Often, however, to be mechanical in psychology means simply to be lawful and automatic.

It is clear that principles of physics and physical models of nature were never far from the minds of the eighteenth- and nineteenth-century psychologists of mechanism, elementalism, and associationism. This tradition passed from Locke and Hume to (notably) James Mill (1773-1836) and Alexander Bain (1818-1903), who may be considered the last major figures of the British empiricist-associationist school of speculative psychologists—and from there on into the twentieth century, where it found expression in the connectionism of E. L. Thorndike's principles of learning, in the stimulus-response psychology of John Watson and the later behaviorists, and even in contemporary theoretical analysis of thought and language (most notable in this respect is the theory of knowledge and memory, discussed later, of Anderson & Bower, 1973):[6]

Let me select for special mention at this point the systematic behavioristic psychology of Clark Hull (1884–1952), whose work culminated in A Behavior System, published a few months after his death. Hull's psychology evidences as clearly as any a mechanistic and elementalistic scheme to account for behavior. But perhaps most striking about Hull's system is his attempt to use in a formal way the hypothetical-deductive model, couching as he did the principles of psychological analysis of behavior in a format of postulates, corollaries, and theorems much like the axioms, corollaries, and theorems of Newton's physics. Starting with unconditioned reflexes and a general principle of conditioning through reinforcement (derived from Pavlov), the system details the acquisition of learned responses—describing, in terms of quantitative laws, how performance depends on the strength of learned association (habit strength), the degree of motivation (drive), the magnitude of the reinforcer, and the intensity of the behavior-eliciting stimulus in the environment. In A Behavior System (1952), Hull used a set of 17 postulates and 15 corollaries to derive theorems about trial-and-error learning, maze learning, problem solving, and other complex behaviors, thereby combining a mechanistic psychology in which the organism is a "completely automatic entity [p. 347]" with the quantitative formalism of a hypothetical-deductive system.

Now, more than a quarter century since Hull's death, one cannot help being struck by an arresting contrast: On the one hand, the form of

---

[6]Begetting can be a strange thing. If physics helped to engender associationism—the epitome of mechanistic and elementaristic psychology—physics also helped spawn Gestalt psychology, which developed largely in opposition to associationism. Wertheimer, Köhler, and Koffka all felt the impact of physics, and with them the field theory of physics became a model for a field theory of perception. Miller (1975) has documented the relationship between Wertheimer and Einstein: In his posthumous Productive Thinking, Wertheimer (1945) strove to show how Gestalt theory could describe the way Galileo came to uncover the law of inertia, Einstein to propound the special theory of relativity.

Galileo's and Newton's laws of motion resembles the form of many of Hull's quantitative laws (which consist by and large of multiplicative relations between variables); and on the other hand, the eminent success of the physical theory stands out against the essential failure of the psychological one.

Mechanism, like its cousin materialism, continues to underpin much scientific analysis of mind and behavior—and in particular to generate "physicalistic" models and theories of psychological phenomena. (Some are described later in this essay.) It is likely that theories proximally or distally derived from physics—as well as theories derived from other disciplines—will continue in the foreseeable future to infiltrate psychology. A significant question is the following: Is the infiltration of physical theory into psychology an enriching immigration that should be embraced, or an unwarranted invasion that should be repelled? Perhaps psychology, a young and immature science still unsure of itself, is merely showing its vulnerability to undue influence when it emulates a science seen as superior; if this is so, then insidious infiltration from other disciplines probably will continue up to such time that psychology matures and "finds itself."

There is considerable truth, in my view, to this appraisal, though I do not think it tells the whole story. To be sure, there is the risk of being dazzled by the trappings of physics' formalism or its methodology. Even more serious is the risk of seeing, as they come off assembly lines, every era's machines as the models for behaving, thinking organisms. Formalism has its place, once the empirical concepts are ready for it; methodology always matters, but to suit its subject a method must be tailored to the questions being asked; and mechanical or other physical analogies are fine in models today, as long as one remembers how each generation pushes the previous generation's devices into dusty corners of museums—and sometimes into junkyards. Yet despite all of these reservations, I suspect that physical theory will continue to imburse and invigorate psychology with stimulating ideas, ideas engendered by the view that the universe of physics and the universe of behaving organisms are actually one universe. To be sure, good physics can make bad psychology. But good science of physical nature can also spur good science of human nature.

PHYSICS, PSYCHOLOGY, AND THEIR INTERSECTION

Physics and Psychology Distinguished

Psychophysics serves at once as a bridge to merge its two namesake components—psychology and physics—and as a border to distinguish them. One of the notable places where this occurs, historically, is in the doctrine of qualities. Although the distinction between qualities as primary and secondary (and tertiary) is usually attributed to Locke (1690), who perhaps made the earliest full statement about it, the distinction is found in Locke's predecessors as well as his contemporaries—in the writings, for example, of physical scientists like Galileo, Boyle, and Newton.

Qualities are properties of physical objects in the universe—of objects as physicists study them. Primary qualities are macroscopic physical properties like size, shape, and location; they are the large-scale spatio-temporal properties of things. According to Locke's theory, these qualities are perceived "veridically," as they really are. Secondary qualities, by contrast, are spatio-temporal physical properties on a smaller scale—microscopic properties that today we would refer to in the language of chemical structure, of frequency or wavelength of light or sound. Locke claimed that these qualities are not perceived "veridically" but instead are ascribed phenomenally distinct psychological properties like sweetness or sourness, redness or greenness, high pitch or low pitch.

The doctrine of qualities has been a source of controversy both in philosophy and psychology, but what I want to accent here are two of its important roles in shaping psychological thought. First, Locke's view of secondary qualities formed the basis for Müller's (1838) doctrine of "specific nerve energies," a doctrine that headed the major subsequent tradition in sensory psychophysiology. According to Locke, our perceptions of secondary qualities are wholly unlike the qualities themselves; there is nothing in greenness that makes that sensation resemble certain wavelengths of light. According to Müller, the reason for this dissimilarity is that sensations depend directly on the specific nerves that are activated and not directly on the qualities of the stimuli that produce nerve activity. To speak crudely yet succinctly, the mind looks at the nervous system, not at the external world. In one form or another, Müller's doctrine lies at the heart of investigations into the ways that the nervous system codes such attributes of sensation as taste, color, and pitch.

A second role of the doctrine of qualities has been to help delineate the disciplines of psychology and physics. Physics is, in a manner of speaking, the science that deals with qualities—with the macroscopic and microscopic properties of the natural world. The perceptual effects of these qualities are part of the subject matter of psychology—at least, to the extent that psychology deals with phenomenological aspects of sense-perception. Pitch depends on sound frequency, as Galileo showed, but pitch is not the same as frequency; pitch is a psychological measure, frequency a physical measure.

Similarly light and color. White light is not simple, but of "the most surprising, and wonderful composition . . . . There is no one sort of Rays which alone can exhibit this [whiteness]. 'Tis ever compounded, and to its composition are requisite all the . . . primary Colours, mixed in a due proportion," as Newton (1672, p. 3083) wrote. Later he qualified this by pointing out that all the colors, white, red, blue, green, and so forth, are effects produced by rays of light themselves not colored:

> And if at any time I speak of Light and Rays as coloured or endued with Colours, I would be understood to speak not philosophically and properly, but grossly, and according to such Conceptions as vulgar People in seeing all these Experiments would be apt to frame. For the Rays to speak properly are not coloured. In them there is nothing else than a certain Power and Disposition to stir up a Sensation of this or that Colour [Newton, 1730/1952, pp. 124–125].

To study the qualities of light (such as the refraction of the rays) is to do physics; to study the colors aroused by the light rays is to do psychology (or psychophysics as it would come to be called a little more than a century later).

Yet, it must be pointed out, to do physics is at least partly to observe phenomena in the world—to describe its objects and events. And observations are perceptual (see Ziman, 1979). The scientist observing the world may be doing physics, but the scientist's observations of the world are perceptions, are themselves objects for scrutiny by psychologists.

Psychology of Physics

The science of physics marks its origin in observations that people make of phenomena in the world around them. These observations—which themselves are perceptions of objects and events—formed the starting point for Mach's attempt to define and delimit the domains of physics and psychology. Mach argued that sensory experience provides the basic data for both disciplines, that the elements of the physical world "out there" and the psychological world inside the head both derive from the analysis of sensations, as he entitled his book (1906/1914):

> There is but one kind of elements out of which this supposed inside and outside are formed—elements which are themselves inside or outside, according to the aspect in which . . . they are viewed.
> The world of sense belongs to both the physical and psychical domains alike [p. 310].

According to Mach's brand of positivism, whether one does psychology or physics depends on the viewpoint one takes toward the data:

> A color is a physical object as soon as we consider its dependence, for instance, upon its luminous source, upon other colors, upon temperatures, upon spaces, and so forth. When we consider, however, its dependence upon the retina . . . , it is a psychological object, a sensation. Not the subject

· matter but the direction of our investigation, is different in the two domains [pp. 17–18].

Influential as Mach's position was on experimental psychology, steeped as it was in a positivistic reliance on data, nevertheless it was limited by its introspective bent—by its view of phenomenological sensation as the cornerstone of psychology. In fact, it is difficult to see how Mach's position fails to lead to the view that the psychological perspective is the primary one—a view that developed out of the subsequent version of positivism known as operationism. Stevens (1936), for example, wrote of psychology as "the propaedeutic science," by which he meant that "psychology differs from and is propaedeutic to physics in that it . . . inquires into the laws of behavior under which men spin hypotheses, observe events, and construct generalizations [pp. 97–98]." Stevens's argument is a psychological solipsism reminiscent of Skinner's suggestion that science, mathematics, and other disciplines reduce to the activity of doing science: "Scientific knowledge is verbal behavior [Skinner, 1974, p. 235]."

When pushed to the limit, this approach implies that there is no physics, no mathematics—no bodies of knowledge that exist outside the realm of human activity, certainly no Platonic truths—only the behavior of scientists measuring or calculating. Of course, this same logic leads to the conclusion that there is no psychology either, only the behavior of those who study the behavior of organisms.

Without succumbing to so extreme a reductionistic view, it is nonetheless perfectly proper to include scientists among the subjects of psychology and to ask about the behavior of scientists:—to perform a psychological analysis of the processes by which, for example, people do, or try to do, physics. In this regard, it is notable that the basic laws of motion that Galileo and Newon formulated three centuries ago apparently continue to elude the grasp of college students, even many who have studied physics (McCloskey, Caramazza, & Green, 1980). College students often fail to understand the basic principle of physical inertia (that an object set into motion but not subject to external forces will continue in uniform motion); in addition, many of them hold a similar, incorrect view—for instance, many believe that an object spun at the end of a string, then suddenly released, will continue in curvilinear motion, as if some "force" maintains the curved path. McCloskey et al. note that this erroneous view resembles the medieval "impetus" theory of motion (see Clagett, 1959; Piaget, 1972), which also assumed the existence of a force continuing after mechanical contact has ceased.

Perhaps most notable here is the work of Jean Piaget (1896-1980), whose forays into what he called "genetic epistemology" in large measure consist of investigations into the ways that children come to understand the physical world. Piaget traced from infancy to adolescence the development of concepts like mass and volume (and their conservation), causality, space, time, velocity, and acceleration, arguing that the child's comprehension of these physical concepts develops through a series of relatively fixed stages, starting with intial action-based schema, working through perceptual schema based on the salience of certain stimulus characteristics, and ending with an understanding that can be described in terms of formal logical operations (1946/1970, 1954).

A good example is velocity. Piaget (1957) recounts how Albert Einstein once raised the question whether the psychological conception of velocity chronologically precedes or succeeds the conception of its components—distance and time—these components being clearly differentiated in physics. When presented an object moving in a straight line, young children may interpret velocity, distance, and time all in the same way, as a function of the end point the object reaches (Siegler & Richards, 1979). Piaget's own research suggests that in the young child a primitive conception of velocity (based on the perception of one object overtaking another) precedes the conception of velocity as the ratio of distance to time (the Galilean definition). Not until age 10–11 or so (Stage IV in Piaget's scheme) does the child formalize the proportionality of ratios among velocity, distance, and the inverse of time (Piaget, 1946/1970). It is only at this stage that the child can separate these three variables, that is that the child can decide whether one velocity is equal or unequal to another even when both the distances and the durations are unequal.[7] In a basic way, the fundamental criterion is conservation or invariance, the determination of those conditions under which the child can discern that one physical parameter remains constant though other parameters vary. This is an

---

[7]Two interesting points to note: First, parallel to Piaget's work has been a long-standing question in psychophysics whether *perceived* velocities, distances, and durations obey a psychological law isomorphic to the physical law of motion: Does perceptual velocity equal perceptual distance divided by perceptual duration? Much of the research dealing with this topic has used sparse stimuli (for instance, spots of light in a dark room) rather than the real objects in more natural environments that Piaget employed. Results of the psychophysical studies are inconclusive, sometimes supporting the existence of a psychological analogue (Svenson, 1971), other times rejecting it (Rachlin, 1966).

Second, although the Stage-IV children in Piaget's studies function as if they treat velocity as equal to distance divided by time, they generally do not achieve understanding of the metric relationship for acceleration. Perhaps this should not surprise, for Galileo (1638) gave considerable attention to the question of acceleration and the appropriate rule to describe uniform acceleration in nature (as produced by gravity). It is one thing to learn by being told that uniform acceleration consists of constant increments of velocity in equal intervals of time, but quite another thing to discover this rule for oneself, as Galileo had to do (and, for example, to reject the possibility that uniform acceleration consists of equal increments of velocity with equal increments of distance).

example of the invariance that Stevens (1951), quoted earlier, cited as a fundamental principle of both physics and psychology.

Physics of Psychology

Specification of the environment in which an organism operates often entails description in physical terms.[8] Stevens (1951) argued that the primary problem for psychology is the specification of the stimulus, by which he meant specification of those characteristics of stimuli that determine or control behavior. Such specification typically uses physicalistic terms (for example, spatial-temporal characteristics of objects and events); sometimes, it even requires analysis of the stimulus as a physicist would do it.

One branch of psychology—the study of sensation and perception—has seen physics and physicists play a special role. Indeed, much of the early experimental research on vision, hearing, and other sensory processes was carried out by physicists—by individuals like Galileo, Newton, Maxwell, and Mach. Sensory processes mark a domain in science where the bodies of knowledge in physics and psychology intersect, for the study of the senses requires an assessment of how sensory systems operate on configurations of stimulus energies that impinge on an organism. To understand vision means, in part, to understand the physics of light: to treat the properties of reflection, refraction, and transmission of energy from light sources to the eye, and through the cornea, lens, and ocular media to the receptor surface; to understand the mechanisms by which photons or quanta of light are absorbed by visual photopigment. To understand hearing requires, in part, to understand the physics of sound (some of these analogous to physical properties of light), including diffraction of sound waves at the head and transmission of sound energy through the ear canal and tympanum to the bony ossicles of the middle ear, and thence to the cochlea of the inner ear. To understand temperature perception requires one to understand processes of thermodynamics, of heat production in the body, convection and conduction of heat to and from the skin, and absorption of radiant energy in the skin. Some divisions within sensory psychology recognize their intersection with physics by their names, as in *psychoacoustics* (see Deutsch, in Volume I).

It is impossible in this essay to give even a comprehensive overview of what could be called sensory physics. What I shall do here is try to give, by means of a few examples, a flavor of the range and nature of physics' role vis-à-vis sensory psychology.

---

[8]The qualifier "often" appears in this sentence because other descriptions besides physical ones (e.g., sociological ones) are also possible.

An example, from hearing. Consider sounds in the environment and what happens to them by the time they activate sensory receptors in the cochlea of the inner ear. The initial pathway for sound is appropriately described in the language of mechanics: Indeed, physical principles are useful in accounting for many phenomena of hearing. Localization of a sound source, for instance, depends importantly on the difference in the time of the sound's arrival at the two ears, and this time difference, in its turn, depends on geometric considerations: the location of the source with respect to the head, the distance between the ears, and the speed of sound in air. Once sound reaches the ear, its frequency spectrum is modified by the shapes and sizes of the external ear (pinna) and the external ear canal and by the mechanical properties of the series of three bones (ossicles) of the middle ear, which transmit the vibration to the cochlear partition and thereby to the auditory receptors—the hair cells on the basilar membrane.

One more example from hearing: Georg Simon Ohm (1787-1854)—a physicist best known for his law relating voltage, current, and resistance in electrical circuits—also gave a law to psychology. Known as Ohm's acoustical law, it states that the auditory system behaves as if it breaks down complex sound waves into their simple sine-wave components. That is, the ear acts as if it performs something like a Fourier analysis. Fourier analysis is one of the main tools used by acousticians and psychoacousticians to analyze sound. Ohm's acoustical law implies that Fourier analysis is also a useful model for the way the auditory system works. In fact, it paved the way to Helmholtz's (1863) resonance theory of hearing: that the basilar membrane of the cochlea might contain a spatial array of tuned strings, each one corresponding to a distinct sine-wave frequency, hence making it possible for the ear to ascribe a distinct pitch to each of very many sound frequencies. Though now known to be incorrect, Helmholtz's theory of pitch perception had enormous influence for many decades, eventually in its turn paving the way for Georg von Békésy's (1960) Nobel-Prize winning studies of the mechanical properties of the cochlea.

A second example, from vision. The human eye is a remarkably acute instrument, with enormous capacity to detect minute amounts of light when its sensitivity is measured under appropriate conditions. A classical experiment, conducted by Hecht, Schlaer, and Pirenne (1942), demonstrated that the ultimate factor limiting our ability to detect very weak lights comes from physical processes—from the probabilistic nature of the absorption of packets of light or photons, as described by quantum physics.

It is well known that a very weak stimulus (a light or sound or other form of stimulus energy) is detected on only a fraction of the stimulus presentations. Quantum physics teach us that even with a supposedly constant stimulus, it is quite impossible for the receptors to absorb a fixed number of light quanta every time the stimulus is flashed. This is so because the absorption of light quanta is quintessentially uncertain—that is, the absorption of any given quantum can only be given a probability. A light that on the average produces absorption of 10 quanta will produce, from one trial to another, a fluctuating number of absorptions (often 10, sometimes 11 or 9, less often 12 or 8), the exact frequencies defined by the Poisson distribution of mathematics. What this boils down to is that a large measure of the moment-to-moment fluctuations in perception results not from variable sensitivity of a physiological state within the sense organ, or from the lack of attention, but from fluctuations that characterize the physical properties of elementary particles.

SOME THOUGHTS ON PSYCHOLOGY AND PHYSICS IN THE TWENTIETH CENTURY

Modern experimental psychology is characterized by its dedication to a style of research that emphasizes precise and objective measurement, quantification, and scrupulous control of the potentially relevant stimuli; in short, it is a discipline that emphasizes the style closely associated with physical science. I have already discussed how measurement, especially measurement of the stimulus, is crucial to psychophysics. But psychophysics is not alone in its emphasis on exact stimulus measurement. Research on learning and conditioning, for instance, demonstrates how reinforced behaviors come under the control of discriminative or conditioned stimuli; the study of discrimination thus becomes as much the domain of animal learning as of psychophysics, where one descendant of physics (psychophysics) weds another (associationist learning) in contemporary research on animal psychophysics.

The emphasis on precision and control is a rather general characteristic of physical science and long-standing in its influence on psychology. Often in this century, specific developments in physics have blended with developments in psychology. I shall mention three briefly.

(1) The process of measurement, and the mathematical theory behind measurement, is a metascientific concern—a concern of all quantitative science. This concern led Stevens (1946), a psychologist much influenced by physical science, to develop a hierarchical system of scales of measurement: Stevens's system shows, for each type of scale, its mathematical properties and permissible statistical manipulations.

(2) Quantum theory helps explain fluctuations in perception. More could be said about quantum theory—and in particular about its implications for the question of determinism (the unpredictability of individual

quantal events seems to deny strict causality at the microscopic level) and for the question of limits on possible knowledge (Heisenberg's uncertainty principle gives limits to possible specification of simultaneous measurements of position and momentum, limits that are most apparent in elementary particles.) Superficially, to question strict determinism in this way has seemed to some, erroneously, to open a door to "free will," with strong consequences for a science of behavior.

Although questions about determinism bear importantly on general scientific issues—determinism is a concern of all the sciences—they edge over too far into philosophy to receive detailed attention here. It is sufficient to note that even among physicists there has not been unanimity of interpretation: Some (e.g., Bohr) have concluded that quantum theory implies a fundamental indeterminancy in the natural world; others (e.g., Einstein) have argued that all events may be subject to an underlying, though unknown, determinism (hidden variables), and therefore that the indeterminancy is surely epistemological, not ontological (see Block & Alston, in Volume I).

(3) The theory of relativity has captured much of the scientific imagination, including that of psychology. Although the theme of "relativism" has several roots—another is anthropological research on primitive societies, demonstrating the relativity of cultural traditions and mores (see Price-Williams, in Volume II)—still, Einstein's theory of 1905 meant something special. It was remarked recently, for example, that Helson's adaptation-level theory (a mathematical theory that predicts behavior in the presence of current stimulation as a function of the adaptation level—this determined from current context and prior stimulation) "brought relativity to psychology [Guilford, 1979, p. 629]."

Operationism

Perhaps the most pervasive influence of relativity theory has come by way of operationism, which provided a new sort of reductionism. Operationism is itself a movement that came directly from physics, in the wave of the Einsteinian revolution at the turn of this century. The special theory of relativity demanded new conceptions of space and time, which thereafter had to be defined in terms of the observer making the measurements. Are two events at different locations simultaneous? To answer such a question requires one to specify the observer's (human's or machine's) frame of motion. Two events can occur simultaneously to one observer but successively to another if the observers differ in their relative motions. Percy Bridgman's (1927) *The Logic of Modern Physics* proposed that physical quantities be defined in terms of the operations used to measure them, and the "operational definition" soon became a credo to

psychology. Ambiguity could henceforth be resolved, and psychology
would be set on a plane just like that of physics—to the extent that both
disciplines rest their fundamental concepts on operational definitions.

Operationism is, in its own way then, another sort of reductionism.
Psychology, physics, indeed all of the sciences reduce to a single common
denominator—the set of rules by which empirical observations underlying
scientific data are to be described. Operationism joined with logical
positivism—a philosophical movement that began in Vienna in the 1920s
and is closely associated with the names Moritz Schlick, Rudolph Carnap,
and Otto Neurath, among others, a movement that sought to clarify
scientific language and determine the kinds of statements that are
scientifically meaningful. Operationism and logical positivism formed a
groundwork for attempts at the unification of science: "The primary advantage of operational definitions," wrote Boring in 1945, "lies in the
unification of science and the resolution of controversy [p. 243]." This is
a view of science dear to the hearts of psychologists who see physics as
the ideal model. Boring continued, "The purpose of science is the
simplification of our knowledge of nature under a set of broad generalizations, and the simplification is greatest when laws are stated in a single
language, which inevitably turns out to be 'physicalistic'."

According to this vantage point, the language of physics is the language
of psychology as well. This is Physicalism with a capital "P" (as expressed
by Neurath, 1931), to be distinguished from the physicalism with a small
"p" that characterizes the reduction of psychological processes and
phenomena themselves to processes and phenomena in the realms of
physiology, physical chemistry, and physics, that is to say, from the
physicalism that seeks to uncover the physical basis of behavior and
mind.

The Human Machine

To return to small-p physicalism, the notion of the human machine has
undergone considerable change in the past three centuries; this change
entailed an enormous evolution in our conception of what human beings
are like, an evolution tailored at least in part by an enormous evolution in
our conception of what machines can be like. Descartes observed relatively simple automata in royal gardens of Germany; Loeb knew of tropistic machines that incorporated feedback; and today even young children
are familiar with robots and digital computers. As times change, and
psychology's fads and fancies shift, Köhler's (1920) physical Gestalts give
way to Pribram's (1971) holograms in the brain. Physical models of psychological phenomena, whether they be electrostatic fields or holograms
in the brain theorized to represent perceptions and memories, exemplify a

materialism and reductionism that is heir to the traditions of Descartes and Hartley.

What kind of machines are people (or what kinds of machines are they like, as Descartes asked)? The answers that psychology gives at any time seem to reflect the kinds of machines that psychologists find around them (Chapanis, in this volume).

In their seminal work on *Plans and the Structure of Behavior* (1960), Miller, Galanter, and Pribram argued that a prime characteristic of complex modern machines—servomechanisms, computers—is that they display purpose. Purposes, goals, values, intentions, all of these can characterize the behavior of complex machines: These psychological concepts are fully compatible with mechanisms and need not be relegated to the dustbins of fuzzy-minded subjectivism. To say that people are like machines is not necessarily to denigrate humanity, but to appreciate the rich potential of "mere" machinery.

The mind (or, at least, the brain that presumably lies behind the mind) *as a computer* represents one of the strongest metaphors in modern psychology. Much of contemporary cognitive psychology calls itself "information processing," thereby implying that human sensory-perceptual-cognitive systems do what computers do—or perhaps that computers do what human sensory-perceptual-cognitive systems do. To the extent that *mind-as-computer* proposes to be a model of the hardware of the brain—for instance, by the analogy between digitized processes of individual logical circuits and the on-off characteristics of neurons—it is even a physical model of the brain. But perhaps more importantly, the metaphor of the mind-as-computer is a psychological model. The physical model is relevant mainly to the extent that a model requires some sort of physical embodiment—in this case a computer for the machine, a brain for the human. But the crux of the computer's role as a model for mind and behavior lies not in its hardware but in its program, and the program is a series of symbols.

An elegant example is the theory of human associative memory presented by Anderson and Bower (1973)—a hierarchical theory in which the elements (ideas, concepts) associate with one another to form propositions, which then in turn also associate with one another. Formalized in the mathematical notation of set theory and couched in the form of a computer model, the theory tries to account for the acquisition, storage, and retrieval of verbal knowledge. And the historical roots that Anderson and Bower acknowledge are those of reductionism, connectionism, sensationism, and mechanism—the very tradition that experimental psychology has inherited from physics.

Has technology in the modern computer finally caught up to the technology of the brain and mind? Perhaps the next century will see an answer.

SUMMARY: WITH SOME SPECULATIONS ON
PSYCHOLOGY IN THE TWENTY-FIRST CENTURY

Psychology today is the grandchild of its philosophical and scientific ancestors, including physics. And, lineage being difficult simply to disavow, psychology tomorrow will almost certainly bear evidence of the same heritage. To those who see physics as the science ne plus ultra, psychology does and will use rigorous methodology, does and will precisely control stimulus variables, and above all does and will formulate results into quantitative laws. Even those psychologists who eschew the materialistic bent and the mechanistic models that so clearly represent the traditional influence of physics, even they may nonetheless see the need for a behavioral science that can stand with physical science in attaining these metascientific standards.[9]

How is physics likely to influence psychology over the next hundred years? It would be foolhardy to try to predict specific developments in either discipline. It is almost certain that some future findings or theories in physics would surprise contemporary physicists. And it is hard enough to appraise the position of psychology today, to say nothing of predicting where it will be a century, a decade, or even a year from now.

Yet if the past is at all a map to the present, it may be a guide to the future as well, at least in suggesting some general trends. Three present themselves:

(1) Accoutrements of physics such as quantification and precise control of variables will continue to be important. So too will physical specification itself, where physical description and analysis are necessary and appropriate. It takes little hindsight or foresight to prognosticate continuous development in the psychophysics of sensory and perceptual processes.

(2) Certainly, new and unpredicted developments will emerge in physics. Despite not knowing what these will be, it is reasonable to suppose that some of the new developments will be picked up and applied to psychology—perhaps as the next generation's passing fads, perhaps as the basis for important and original insights into mind and behavior.

(3) What will happen to the conception of the "human machine"? What in particular will become of the conception of the brain/mind-as-computer? Will psychologists a century from now look at computer theories of cognition as old curiosities, much as some today see the automata theory of Descartes, the vibration theory of Hartley, or the tropistic theory of Loeb? Or will it become so much a part and parcel of standard psychological theory that—like the notion of a reflex—the metaphor of

---

[9]For an alternate aspiration, see Wolman (1971).

the mind as computer will be a metaphor no more? As is so often the case, the outcome here probably will fall somewhere in between these extremes. My suspicion, though, is that this in-between will lie somewhat closer to the former than to the latter: Although some aspects of the computer model will doubtless find themselves incorporated into the psychology of the future, the digital computer will be seen largely as one further step in the development of machines that more and more closely approach, but still do not fully realize, the richness of human behavior.

REFERENCES

Anderson, J. R., & Bower, G. H. *Human associative memory*. New York: Wiley, 1973.
Bacon, F. *Novum organum*. London: Billium, 1620.
Békésy, G. von *Experiments in hearing*. New York: McGraw-Hill, 1960.
Berlin, I. *The hedgehog and the fox*. New York: Simon and Schuster, 1953.
Borelli, G. *De motu animalium*. Rome: Bernabò, 1680.
Boring, E. G. *Sensation and perception in the history of experimental psychology*. New York: Appleton-Century-Crofts, 1942.
Boring, E. G. The use of operational definitions in psychology. *Psychological Review*, 1945, *52*, 243–245.
Boring, E. G. *A history of experimental psychology*. New York: Appleton-Century-Crofts, 1957.
Bridgman, P. W. *The logic of modern physics*. New York: MacMillan, 1927.
Clagett, M. *The science of mechanics in the middle ages*. Madison, WI: University of Wisconsin Press, 1959.
Crozier, W. J., & Hoagland, H. The study of living organisms. In C. Murchison (Ed.), *A handbook of general experimental psychology*. Worcester, MA: Clark University Press, 1934.
Descartes, R. *Discours de la méthode pour bien conduire la raison, & chercher la verité dans les sciences*. Leyden: Maire, 1637. In *The philosophical works of Descartes* (Vol. 1) (E. S. Haldane & G. R. T. Ross, trans.). Cambridge, England: Cambridge University Press, 1931.
Descartes, R. *Principia philosophiae*. Amsterdam: Elzevier, 1644.
Descartes, R. *Les passions de l'âme*. Amsterdam: Elzevier, 1650. In *The philosophical works of Descartes* (Vol. 1) (E. S. Haldane & G. R. T. Ross, trans.). Cambridge, England: Cambridge University Press, 1931.
Descartes, R. *L'homme*. Paris: LeGras, 1664.
Forbes, A. The mechanism of reaction. In C. Murchison (Ed.), *A handbook of general experimental psychology*. Worcester, MA: Clark University Press, 1934.
Freeman, K. *Ancilla to the pre-Socratic philosophers*. Oxford: Blackwell, 1948.
Freud, S. *Die Traumdeutung*. Leipzig and Wien: Deuticke, 1900. In *The basic writings of Sigmund Freud* (A. A. Brill, trans.). New York: Random House, 1938.
Freud, S. *Drei Abhandlungen zur Sexualtheorie*. Leipzig: Deuticke, 1905.
Freud, S. *Zur Psychopathologie des Alltagslebens*. Berlin: Karger, 1907. In *The basic writings of Sigmund Freud* (A. A. Brill, trans.). New York: Random House, 1938.
Freud, S. *Das Ich und das Es*. Leipzig: Internationaler Psychoanalytischer Verlag, 1923.
Freud, S. Letter to Fliess of June 12, 1900. In M. Bonaparte, A. Freud, & E. Kris (Eds.), *The origins of psychoanalysis. Letters to Wilhelm Fliess, drafts and notes: 1887–1902*. New York: Basic Books, 1954. (a)

Freud, S. Project for a scientific psychology. In M. Bonaparte, A. Freud, & E. Kris (Eds.), *The origins of psychoanalysis. Letter to Wilhelm Fliess, drafts and notes: 1887–1902.* New York: Basic Books, 1954. (b)

Galilei, G. *Il saggiatore.* Rome: Mascardi, 1623. In *The controversy on the comets of 1618* (S. Drake & C. D. O'Malley, trans.). Philadelphia, PA:. University of Pennsylvania Press, 1960.

Galilei, G. *Discorsi e dimostrazioni matematiche, intorno à due nuove scienze attenenti alla mecanica e i movimenti locali.* Leyden: Elsevier, 1638.

Guilford, J. P. Obituary: Harry Helson (1898–1977). *American Psychologist,* 1979, *34,* 628–630.

Haldane, J. S. *Mechanism, life, and personality.* New York: Dutton, 1914.

Hartley, D. *Observations on man, his frame, his duty, and his expectations.* London and Bath: Leake and Frederick, and Hitch and Austen, 1749.

Harvey, W. *De motu cordis et sanguinis in animalibus.* Frankfurt: Fitzer, 1628.

Hecht, S., Schlaer, S., & Pirenne, M. H. Energy, quanta, and vision. *Journal of General Physiology,* 1942, *25,* 819–840.

Helmholtz, H. L. F. von. *Die Lehre von den Tonempfidungen als physiologische Grundlage für die Theorie der Musik.* Braunschweig: Vieweg, 1863.

Hobbes, T. *Humane nature: or, The fundamental elements of policie. Being a discoverie of the faculties, acts, and passions of the soul of man, from their original causes; according to such philosophical principles as are not commonly known or asserted.* London: Bowman, 1650.

Hobbes, T. *Leviathan; or The matter, forme, and power of a common-wealth, ecclesiasticall or civill.* Oxford: Blackwell, 1946. (Originally published, 1651.)

Holton, G. On the role of themata in scientific thought. *Science,* 1975, *188,* 328–338.

Hull, C. L. *A behavior system: An introduction to behavior theory concerning the individual organism.* New Haven, CT: Yale University Press, 1952.

Hume, D. *A treatise of human nature: Being an attempt to introduce the experimental method of reasoning into moral subjects.* London: Noon, 1739.

Jones, E. *The life and work of Sigmund Freud* (Vol. 1). New York: Basic Books, 1956.

Klein, D. B. *A history of scientific psychology: Its origins and philosophical backgrounds.* New York: Basic Books, 1970.

Köhler, W. *Die physische Gestalten in Ruhe und im stationären Zustand.* Braunschweig: Vieweg, 1920.

Kuhn, T. S. *The Copernican revolution.* Cambridge, MA: Harvard University Press, 1957.

La Mettrie, J. O. de *L'homme machine.* Leyden: Luzac brothers, 1748.

Leibniz, G. W. von. Considérations sur le principe de la vie, et sur les natures plastiques, par l'auteur de l'Harmonie Preétablie. *Histoire des Ouvrages des Savans,* 1705. In P. Weiner (Ed.), *Leibniz selections.* New York: Scribners, 1951.

Locke, J. *An essay concerning human understanding.* (Fourth Edition) London: Bass, 1690.

Locke, J. *An essay concerning human understanding.* London: Awnsham and Churchill, 1700.

Loeb, J. *The mechanistic conception of life.* Chicago, IL: University of Chicago Press, 1912.

Loeb, J. *Forced movements, tropisms, and animal conduct.* Philadelphia, PA: Lippincott, 1918.

Lucretius. *[On nature]* (R. M. Geer, trans.). Indianapolis, IN: Bobbs-Merrill, 1965.

Mach, E. *[The analysis of sensations]* (C. M. Williams & S. Waterlow, trans.). Chicago, IL: Open Court, 1914. (Originally published, 1906.)

McCloskey, M., Caramazza, A., & Green, B. Curvilinear motion in the absence of external forces: Naive beliefs about the motion of objects. *Science,* 1980, *210,* 1139–1140.

Miller, A. I. Albert Einstein and Max Wertheimer: A Gestalt psychologist's view of the genesis of special relativity theory. *History of Science*, 1975, *13*, 75–103.

Miller, G. A., Galanter, E., & Pribram, K. H. *Plans and the structure of behavior.* New York: Holt, 1960.

Müller, J. *Handbuch der Physiologie des Menschen* (Vol. 5). Coblenz: Hölscher, 1838.

Neurath, O. Physicalism: The philosophy of the Vienna Circle. *Monist*, 1931, *41*, 618–623.

Newton, I. New theory about light and colors. *Philosophical Transactions of the Royal Society* (London), 1672, *80*, 3075–3087.

Newton, I. *Philosophia naturalis principia mathematica.* London: Streater, 1686.

Newton, I. *Opticks; or, A treatise of the reflexions, refractions, inflexions and colours of light.* London: Smith and Walford, 1704.

Newton, I. *Opticks; or, A treatise of the reflexions, refractions, inflexions and colours of light* (fourth edition). New York: Dover, 1952. (Originally published, 1730.)

Piaget, J. *The child's conception of movement and speed.* London: Routledge and Kegan Paul, 1970. (Originally published, 1946.)

Piaget, J. *The construction of reality in the child.* New York: Basic Books, 1954.

Piaget, J. The child and modern physics. *Scientific American*, 1957, *196*, 46–51.

Piaget, J. Physical world of the child. *Physics Today*, 1972, *25*, 23–27.

Pribram, K. H. *Languages of the brain: Experimental paradoxes and principles in neuro-Psychology.* Englewood Cliffs, NJ: Prentice-Hall, 1971.

Rachlin, H. C. Scaling subjective velocity, distance, and duration. *Perception & Psychophysics*, 1966, *1*, 77–82.

Rosenfield, L. C. *From beast-machine to man-machine.* New York: Oxford University Press, 1941.

Schofield, R. E. *Mechanism and materialism: British natural philosophy in an age of reason.* Princeton, NJ: Princeton University Press, 1970.

Siegler, R. S., & Richards, D. D. Development of time, speed, and distance concepts. *Developmental Psychology*, 1979, *15*, 288–298.

Skinner, B. F. The concept of the reflex in the description of behavior. *Journal of General Psychology*, 1931, *5*, 427–458.

Skinner, B. F. *About behaviorism.* New York: Knopf, 1974.

Stevens, S. S. Psychology: The propaedeutic science. *Philosophy of Science*, 1936, *3*, 90–103.

Stevens, S. S. On the theory of scales of measurement. *Science*, 1946, *103*, 677–680.

Stevens, S. S. Mathematics, measurement, and psychophysics. In S. S. Stevens (Ed.), *Handbook of experimental psychology.* New York: Wiley, 1951.

Svenson, O. Interrelations and structure of judgments of velocity, time, and displacement in relative movement. *Reports from the Psychological Laboratories*, The University of Stockholm, 1971, No. 325.

Theophrastus. *De sensu.* In G. M. Stratton, *Theophrastus and the Greek physiological psychology before Aristotle.* London: Allen and Unwin, 1917.

Watson, J. B. Psychology as the behaviorist views it. *Psychological Review*, 1913, *20*, 158–177.

Wertheimer, M. *Productive thinking.* New York: Harper, 1945.

Wolman, B. B. Does psychology need its own philosophy of science? *American Psychologist*, 1971, *26*, 877–886.

Ziman, J. The eyes have it. *The Sciences*, 1979, *19*, 13–15, 18.

Biographical Notes

ALPHONSE CHAPANIS is professor of psychology and director of the Communications Research Laboratory at The Johns Hopkins University, Baltimore, Maryland. He received his Ph.D. from Yale. He is past president of the Human Factors Society, The Society of Engineering Psychologists, and the International Ergonomics Association, and the recipient of six major awards, among them the Distinguished Contribution for Applications in Psychology Award of the American Psychological Association. Senior author of the first textbook in human factors, *Applied Experimental Psychology: Human Factors in Engineering Design* published in 1949, he is also author or editor of four other major books in the field.

CLYDE H. COOMBS is Professor of Psychology at the University of Michigan. He received both a B.A. and an M.A. from the University of California at Berkeley and a Ph.D. from the University of Chicago. He has been President of the Psychometric Society and of Division 5 of the American Psychological Association and Chairman of the Society for Mathematical Psychology; he is a member of the U.S. National Academy of Sciences. Coombs is author of *Theory of Data* and co-author of *Mathematical Psychology*. His research interests are in measurement, scaling, choice behavior, preference, and decision making and in methodology in the behavioral sciences in general.

JOHN L. FULLER is Emeritus Professor of Psychology, State University of New York at Binghamton. His Ph.D. in Biology was awarded at The Massachusetts Institute of Technology. For many years Fuller was associated with the behavior studies program at the Jackson Laboratory, Bar Harbor, Maine. He has been a Guggenheim Fellow, is a past-president of the Behavior Genetics Association, and presently president of The Society for the Study of Social Biology. Fuller's research has concentrated on behavior genetics and developmental psychology in animals. With W. R. Thompson he published *Behavior Genetics* in 1960 and *Foundations of Behavior Genetics* in 1978.

DAVID C. GLASS is Vice-Provost for Graduate Studies and Research and Professor of Psychology at the State University of New York at Stony Brook. He received his Ph.D. from New York University in 1959 where he did post-doctoral work in experimental social psychology and psychophysiology. He was staff Social Psychologist at Russell Sage Foundation (New York City) and has held positions at Ohio State University, Columbia University, Rockefeller University, New York University, University of Texas at Austin, and the Graduate Center of the City University of New York. Dr. Glass is a past President of the Academy of Behavioral Medicine Research and is author or co-author of over 85 articles and reviews in professional journals and technical books. He is co-author of *Urban Stress: Experiments on Noise and Social Stressors,* which won the AAAS Socio-Psychological Prize for 1971, and author of *Behavior Patterns, Stress and Coronary Disease.*

CONAN KORNETSKY is Professor of Psychiatry (Psychology) and Pharmacology and Director of the Laboratory of Behavioral Pharmacology at Boston University School of Medicine. He received his B.A. degree from the University of Maine and his M.S. and Ph.D. from the University of Kentucky. His early research was at the Addiction Research Center in Lexington, Kentucky. He was a research scientist at the NIMH, Bethesda, before joining the faculty at Boston University. His published work has been primarily in psychopharmacology and has relevance to schizophrenia and drug abuse. He is author of *Pharmacology: Drugs Affecting Behavior.*

DAVID S. KRANTZ is Associate Professor of Medical Psychology at the Uniformed Services University of the Health Sciences in Bethesda, Maryland. He received his Ph.D. from the University of Texas at Austin in 1975 and further training in psychophysiology at Harvard Medical School. Krantz is a co-editor of the *Handbook of Psychology and Health.* He is the recipient of the 1981 Annual Award for Outstanding Contributions to Health Psychology and a 1982 Scientific Award for an Early Career Contribution to Psychology from the American Psychological Association. His scientific publications are concerned with cardiovascular disorders and behavior, and psychosocial and environmental influences on health.

LAWRENCE E. MARKS is at the John B. Pierce Foundation Laboratory and Yale University. He received his A.B. from Hunter College, City

University of New York, and his Ph.D. from Harvard. The founding editor of *Sensory Processes*, Marks has written *Sensory Processes: The New Psychophysics, The Unity of the Senses: Interrelations among the Modalities*, and many papers and chapters on psychophysics, on processes of sensation and perception, and on language.

WILLIAM R. UTTAL is Professor of Psychology in the Department of Psychology and Program Director at the Institute for Social Research of The University of Michigan. He was awarded a Ph.D. from The Ohio State University, and then spent six years at IBM's Thomas J. Watson Research Center before going to the University of Michigan in 1963. Uttal has been an NIMH special post-doctoral fellow and a recipient of an NIMH research scientist award. He has held a James McKeen Cattell award, a Japanese Society for the Promotion of Sciences senior scientist fellowship, and was the MacEachran Lecturer at the University of Alberta in 1982. His experimental work has focused primarily on sensory processes, but he has also written extensively on more general topics of scientific psychology. Among other books, Uttal has completed a major trilogy consisting of *The Psychobiology of Sensory Coding, The Psychobiology of Mind*, and *A Taxonomy of Visual Processes*.

Author Index

AUTHOR INDEX

AUTHOR INDEX

Finnegan, R., II: 6, *27*
Firth, R., II: 8, *26*
Fischer, C. S., II: 130, *158*
Fischer, E., I: 61, *67*
Fischer, S., II: 61, *82*
Fishbein, M., I: 258, *279;* II: 196, *202*
Fisher, A. C., II: 132, *158*
Fisher, D. F., I: 31, *71*
Fisher, I. N., II: 81, *83*
Fisher, J. D., II: 123, 154, *157*
Fisher, R. A., III: 68, *103,* 131, *148*
Fisher, S., III: 208, *222*
Fiske, D. W.,II: 5, *26*
Flanary, H. G., III: 199, 206, 213, 218, *223*
Flavell, J. H., II: 107, *119*
Flesch, R., I: 133, *148*
Flinn, W. L., II: 131, *157*
Florman, S. C., III: 35, 36, *62*
Fodor, J., I: 209, *234*
Fodor, J. A., I: 88, 91, 93, *109, 110,* 199, 205, 206, 207, 208, 209, 220, 221, 222, 223, 226, 227, 228, 233, *236*
Fodor, J. D., I: 93, 103, *109*
Foley, M. A., II: 191, *205*
Foner, A., III: 173, *194*
Forbes, A., III: 247, *262*
Fordyce, W. E., III: 173, 181, *190*
Forster, K. I., I: 88, *109*
Forte, A., I: 185, *191*
Fortes, M., I: 48, 50, *67*
Foss, D. J., I: 88, *109*
Foster, T. A., III: 187, *195*
Foucault, M., II: 182, *183*
Fournel, J., III: 210, *222*
Fowler, R. D., Jr., I: 129, *152*
Fox, B. H., III: 168, *190*
Fox, W. C., III: 134, *149*
Francès, R., I: 33, *67*
Frankenhaeuser, M., III: 161, *190*
Frankfurt, H., I: 213, *236*
Fraser, H. F., III: 206, 218, *223*
Fraumeni, J. F., III: 167, 168, *190*
Frazer, J. G., I: 249, *279*
Frazier, L., I: 103, *109*
Freedman, B. J., I: 142, *149*
Freedman, D. G., III: 90, *103*
Freedman, M. B., I: 262, *278*
Freeman, D., II: 33; *53*
Freeman, K., I: 156, *191;* III: 234, *262*
Freeman, N. H., I: 43, 44, *67*
Frege, G., I: 76, 94, 95, *109*
Frenkel-Brunswick, E., I: 251, *277;* II: 188,

189, 194, *202*
Frerichs, R. R., III: 187, *195*
Freud, A., II: 96, *119*
Freud, S., I: 4, 8, 11, 12, 13, 15, 40, *67, 68,* 115, *149,* 247, *279;* II: 7, *26,* 65, *83,* 96, *119,* 166, 167, 169, 170, *183,* 199, *203;* III: 204, 217, *222,* 244, 245, 246, *262, 263*
Fried, M., II: 74, 76, *83*
Friedländer, M. J., I: 4, 15, *68*
Friedlander, S., II: 181, *183*
Friedman, A. J., I: 146, *149*
Friedman, M., II: 67, 75, *83;* III: 159, 160, 161, *190, 194*
Friedman, N., I: 116, *149*
Friedman, R., III: 164, *190*
Friedman, S. B., III: 170, *191*
Friedman, S. T., I: 133, *149*
Fritz-Bailey, S., I: 146, *149*
Fromkin, V., I: 222, *236*
Fry, R., I: 23, 26, *68*
Fulker, D., II: 33, *52*
Fulker, D. W., III: 82, *104*
Fuller, J. L., III: 76, 77, 81, 86, 89, *103*

G

Gablik, S., I: 56, *68*
Gagne, R. M., II: 94, 116, *119*
Galanter, E., I: 82, *111,* 184, *192;* II: 112, *120;* III: 260, *264*
Galbraith, J. K., II: 71, *83*
Galilei, G., III: 236, 237, 254, *263*
Gall, F. J., III: 11, *30*
Gallagher, C. E., I: 259, *279*
Galle, O. R., II: 131, *158*
Galton, F., I: 122, *149;* III: 67, *103*
Gantt, W. H., III: 200, *226*
Garber, J., II: 74, *83*
Gardner, H., I: 38, 46, 48, 51, 52, 53, 61, *66, 68,* 125, 146, *149;* III: 165, *190*
Gardner, J., I: 51, *68*
Garey, M. R., I: 102, *109*
Garfinkel, L., III: 179, *191*
Garner, W. R., I: 181, *191;* III: 48, *62*
Garrett, M. F., I: 88, 93, *109,* 222, *236*
Garrity, T. F., III: 158, *191*
Gatchel, R. J., III: 182, *191*
Gay, J., II: 22, 24, *25*
Gay, P., II: *183*
Gazdar, G., I: 101, *110*
Geach, P., I: 204, *236*
Geertz, C., II: 10, 13, *26*

AUTHOR INDEX

H

Haber, R. N., I: 3, *72*
Habicht, J. P., II: 16, *28*
Haddon, A. C., II: 21, *26*
Hagen, M. A., I: 31, *69*
Hager, J. L., III: 86, *106*
Haggerty, R. J., III: 171, *193*
Haimowitz, M. L., I: 128, *149*
Haimowitz, N. R., I: 128, *149*
Halasz, L., I: 120, *149*
Haldane, J. S., III: 247, *263*
Hall, C. S., I: 215, *236*
Hall, G. S., I: 247, 248, *279;* II: 90, *119*
Halle, M., I: 78, 103, *109*
Haller, M. H., III: 69, *104*
Halliday, M. A. K., I: 105, *110*
Hallowell, A. I., II: 4, 6, 10, *26*
Halstead-Nussloch, R., III: 45, *63*
Hamburg, B. A., III: 157, 168, *191, 194*
Hames, C. G., III: 157, *192*
Hammond, W. A., I: 25, *69*
Hanrahan, G. E., III: 207, *224*
Hanson, A. R., I: 184, *192*
Happ, A., III: 41, *63*
Harary, F., III: 132, *147*
Harburg, E., III: 163, 165, *190, 191*
Hardin, G., II: 148, *158*
Haring, D. G., II: 3, *26*
Harkins, S., II: 69, *84*
Harl, J. M., III: 207, *222*
Harman, G., I: 225, *236, 237*
Harré, R., I: 211, *237*
Harrell, J. P., III: 165, *191*
Harrington, C., II: 22, *26*
Harris, E. L., III: 82, 84, *105*
Harrison, J., II: 135, *158*
Harrod, R., II: 65, *83*
Harter, N., III: 46, *62*
Hartley, D., III: 238, 242, 243, *263*
Hartline, H. K., III: 22, *30*
Harvey, S. C., III: 207, *223*
Harvey, W., III: 236, *263*
Hassenger, R., I: 261, *279*
Hastrup, J. L., III: 151, *193*
Hattwick, L. W., I: 53, *65*
Hauenstein, L. S., III: 163, *191*
Haugeland, J., I: 200, 220, *236, 237*
Hauser, A., I: 56, *69*
Hawkins, Sir J. A., I: 158, *192*
Hay, D.,I: 114, 135, 145, *149*
Hayes, R. H., II: 71, *83*

Hayes, S., II: 146, *157*
Hayes, S. P., II: 55, *83*
Haynes, R. E., III: 155, 175, *194*
Haynes, S. G., III: 158, 159, 160, *191*
Haythorn, M. M., III: 76, *104*
Heberlein, T. A., II: 131, 132, 143, *158*
Hecht, S., III: 256, *263*
Heft, H., II: 150, *161*
Heidbreder, E., III: 198, *223*
Heiman, M., I: 15, *69*
Heine, M., III: 163, *190*
Helmholtz, H. L. F. von, I: 161, 165, 167,
  168, *192;* III: 125, *148,* 256, *263*
Helson, R., I: 118, *149*
Hempel, C. G., I: 204, 205, *237*
Henderson, A. H., III: 178, 187, *190*
Henderson, J. M., II: 63, 69, *83*
Henderson, N. D., III: 89, 90, 92, *104*
Hendrix, W. G., II: 142, *158*
Henning, D. H., II: 155, *161*
Henry, A. F., II: 19, *26*
Henry, E. R., I: 249, *279*
Henry, J. P., III: 162, 164, 184, *189, 191*
Henry, K. R., III: 76, *104*
Henry, W. E., I: 262, 263, *279*
Herd, A. J., III: 160, 161, 186, *191*
Herman, C. P., III: 178, 179, *194*
Hermann, M. G., II: 198, 201, *204*
Heron, W. T., III: 80, *104,* 200, 203, 213,
  223, 226
Herrnstein, R. J., I: 230, *237*
Hersh, H. M., I: 104, *110*
Hess, R. D., II: 192, *204*
Hevener, K., I: 119, 120, *150*
Hewitt, E. C., I: 264, 269, *281*
Hicks, J. R., II: 61, *83*
Hill, H. E., III: 199, 206, 210, 213, *223*
Hill, P. C., III: 178, 187, *190*
Hill, W. F., II: 95, *119*
Hills, D., I: 219, *237*
Hilton, W. C., III: 161, *191*
Himmelsbach, C. K., III: 205, *223*
Hinde, R. A., III: 86, *104*
Hinkle, L. E., III: 158, *191*
Hirsch, J., III: 75, *104*
Hirsch, M. W., III: 218, *223*
Hirsch, R., III: 14, *31*
Hirsh, I. J., I: 169, *192*
Ho, H., III: 79, *104*
Ho, V., II: 110, *120*
Hoagland, H., III: 241, *262*
Hobbes, T., III: 237, *263*

AUTHOR INDEX

Lewin, K., II: 95, *120,* 210, *234*
Lewin, L., III: *203, 224*
Lewis, D., I: 207, 209, *237*
Lewis, I., II: 2, *27*
Lewis, M. H., I: 128, *148*
Lewis, S. H., II: 195, *204*
Lewontin, R., I: 230, *237*
Lewontin, R. C., III: 79, 92, *103*
Ley, P., III: 176, *192*
Lhuede, E. P., III: 45, *63*
Liben, L., II: 136, *159*
Lieberman, D. A., I: 138, *150*
Liebert, R. S., I: 15, *70*
Liebeskind, J. C., III: 174, *192*
Liebling, B., III: 178, 179, *194*
Lifton, R. J., II: 171, 172, 174, 178, *184*
Likert, R., II: 190, *204*
Liljestrand, G., III: 198, 203, *223*
Lime, D., II: 143, *159*
Lindauer, M. S., I: 114, 119, 120, 121, 129, 131, 133, 134, 138, 143, 146, *147, 150, 151*
Lindley, C. F., III: 208, *221*
Lindzey, G., I: 215, *236;* II: 17, *27;* III: 83, *104*
Ling, G., III: 11, *31*
Link, A. S., II: 199, *206*
Linton, R., I: 254, *280;* II: 7, *27*
Lipowski, Z. J., III: 152, *192*
Lipper, S., III: 211, *225*
Lippit, R., II: 228, *234*
Lippman, W., II: 190, *204*
Lipsey, R., II: 64, *84*
Littman, R. A., II: 147, *160*
Litton, R. B., Jr., II: 142, *159*
Loar, B., I: 225, *237*
Lockard, J. S., III: 95, *104*
Locke, J., I: *237;* III: 248, 251, *263*
Loeb, J., III: 240, 241, *263*
Loehlin, J. C., III: 79, 83, 90, *104, 105*
Loewenberg, P., II: 181, *184*
Lofland, J., II: 24, *27*
Logue, R. B., III: 156, *192*
Lohman, W., I: 125, *149*
Lonner, W., II: 23, *27*
Loomis, R. J., II: 123, 154, *157*
Loomis, T. A., III: 218, *225*
Lord, F. M., III: 145, *148*
Lorr, M., III: 208, *225*
Low, L. A., III: 211, *225*
Lowenthal, D., II: 123, *159*
Lowenthal, L., I: 132, *151*

Lowie, R. H., II: 10, *27*
Lown, B., III: 160, *192*
Lucas, F. L., I: 116, *151*
Luce, R. D., III: 125, 127, 129, 131, 136, 137, *148*
Lucretius, III: 234, *263*
Lukacz, G., II: 218, *234*
Luria, A. R., I: *70;* II: 218, *234*
Lushene, R., III: 161, *190*
Luszki, M. B., II: 153, *159*
Lycan, W., I: 208, 210, *237*
Lynch, K., I: 186, *192;* II: 134, *159*
Lyons, J., I: 60, *70*

M

Maccoby, N., III: 177, 180, 181, *190, 192, 193*
MacDonald, F. J., II: 93, *120*
MacDonell, A. J., I: 261, *280*
MacDougall, J. M., III: 161, *190*
Mach, E., III: 252, *263*
Machlis, J., I: 175, *192*
Machotka, P., I: 51, *70*
Macht, D. I., III: 200, 213, *225*
Mack, J., II: 170, *184*
MacKenzie, D. M., I: 261, *281*
MacKinnon, D., I: 17, *70*
MacKinnon, D. W., I: 113, 117, *151;* III: 74, *104*
Mackworth, N. H., I: 29, *70*
Maddi, S. R., I: 128, *151,* 215, *237*
Madsen, K. B., II: 132, *157*
Magill, D. W., I: 261, *278*
Magnusson, D., II: 24, *27*
Maier, N. R. F., I: 114, *151*
Maital, S., II: 55, 62, 65, 66, 67, 68, 70, 72, 74, 75, 81, *83, 84, 85*
Maital, S. L., II: 62, 66, 74, *84, 85*
Makidonan, T., III: 169, *193*
Malcolm, N., I: 205, *237*
Mâle, E., I: 34, *70*
Malinowski, B., II: 8, *27*
Maloney, M. P., II: 131, *159*
Malony, H. N., I: 258, 263, *280, 281*
Manaster, G., I: 133, *149*
Mandelbrojt, J., I: 34, *70*
Mandelbrot, B., II: 68, *85*
Mannucci, E. G., III: 161, *191*
Manuck, S. B., III: 165, *193*
Manuel, F. G., II: 211, *234*

AUTHOR INDEX

AUTHOR INDEX

AUTHOR INDEX

Waite, R. G. L., II: 170, *184*
Wall, P. D., III: 174, *193*
Wallace, A. F. C., I: 243, 276, *282;* II: 3, 17, 28
Wallace, R., I: 92, *111*
Wallach, M. A., II: 68, *84*
Wallas, G., I: 122, 126, *153;* II: 187, *205*
Walras, L., II: 58, *87*
Walsh, D., I: 114, 131, *153*
Walters, R., I: 214, *234*
Wanner, E., I: 89, 103, *112*
Ward, D., II: 200, *206*
Ward, M. O., II: 131, *159*
Ward, W. D., I: 162, 182, *194*
Warren, A., I: 114, *153*
Warren, H., II: 96, *121*
Warren, R. M., I: 167, 169, *194*
Warren, R. P., I: 169, *194*
Warrick, P., I: 128, *150*
Warriner, C. K., II: 228, *235*
Warwick, D. P., II: 231, *234*
Washburn, S. L., III: 97, *106*
Watson, J. B., I: 77, *112,* 247; *282;* III: 85, *106,* 241, *264*
Way, D., II: 141, 142, *160*
Weakland, J. H., III: 101, *107*
Weaver, W., III: 48, 49, *63*
Weber, L. S., III: 187, *195*
Weber, M., II: 212, 219, *235*
Wedin, C., II: 130, *161*
Wedin, L., I: 166, *194*
Weeks, J. R., III: 214, 215, *226*
Weidley, E., III: 210, *222*
Weigel, R. H., II: 132, *161*
Weil-Malherbe, H., II: 36, *53*
Weiner, H., III: 162, 165, 166, 167, *195*
Weiner, N., III: 24, *31*
Weinstein, E. A., II: 199, *206*
Weinstein, F., II: 181, *184*
Weisenberg, M., III: 173, 174, *195*
Weiss, B., III: 218, *226*
Weiss, S. M., III: 176, 185, 186, *192, 194*
Weisstein, N., III: 23, *31*
Wellek, R., I: 114, *153*
Wells, R. S., I: 86, *112*
Wendt, H. W., II: 198, *206*
Werner, E. E., II: 22, *28*
Werner, H., I: 46, *73,* 183, *194;* II: 12, *28*
Werner, O., II: 6, *29*
Wertheimer, M., I: 176, *194;* III: 249, *264*
Wessel, D. L., I: 166, 167, *193, 194*
West, R. W., II: 65, *84*

West, T. C., III: 218, *225*
Westergaard, P., I: 185, *194*
Wexler, K., I: 197, *239*
Weyl, H., I: 25, 26, *73*
Weyl, N., III: 83, *105*
Wheeler, G. C., II: 13, *26*
Wheeler, O. A., I: 143, *153*
White, B., I: 181, 183, *194*
White, G. F., II: 136, 137, *157, 160, 161*
White, L., I: 122, *154;* II: 18, *29*
White, R., II: 136, *158*
White, R. K., I: 123, *154*
White, R. W., II: 189, 193, 196, *205*
Whitehead, A. N., I: *238*
Whiting, B. B., II: 14, 22, *29*
Whiting, J. W. M., II: 4, 9, 14, 22, 23, *26, 27, 29*
Wicker, A., II: 124, *161*
Wickman, E. K., II: 97, *121*
Wideen, M. F., II: 132, *161*
Wiener, N., III: 48, *63*
Wiesel, T. N., III: 20, *30*
Wijsen, L. M. P. T., I: 140, *154*
Wikler, A., III: 199, 200, 206, 210, 213, *223, 226*
Wilder, R. L., III: 111, *149*
Wilkie, F., III: 157, 169, *190*
Willats, J., I: 44, 45, *73*
Willems, E. P., II: 152, *161*
Willerman, L., III: 79, 92, *104, 107*
Williams, B. J., III: 163, *189*
Williams, C., I: 133, *147*
Williams, E. D., I: 122, *154*
Williams, J. P., II: 101, 102, 116, *121*
Williams, K., II: 69, *84*
Williamson, O., II: 71, *87*
Willows, A. O. D., III: 22, *31*
Wilson, B. R., I: 261, *282*
Wilson, E. O., III: 16, *31,* 93, 95, 98, *107*
Wilson, G. D., II: 32, *52,* 195, *206*
Wilson, G. T., II: 44, *53*
Wilson, J. J., I: 48, *71*
Wilson, R. C., I: 133, *154*
Wilson, R. N., I: 132, 135, 142, 146, *154*
Wilson, R. S., III: 90, *107*
Wilson, T., II: 34, 43, 50, *53*
Wimer, R. E., III: 76, *103*
Windelband, W., III: 74, *107*
Winett, R. A., II: 78, *87*
Winkel, G. H., II: 123, *159*
Winkler, R. C., II: 55, 77, 78, *84, 87*
Winner, E., I: 125, *149*

Subject Index

SUBJECT INDEX

SUBJECT INDEX

SUBJECT INDEX

II, 208
III, 3, 8, 10, 11, 18–19, 26–29
Model, *see also* Theory,
xxix–xxx
III, 117, 37, 47–48, 142–146
Models,
  econometric,
II, 58
Monism,
III, 5, 7–10, 14, 19
Morality, *see* Religion
Mortality,
xl
III, 152, 156, 167, 181, 188
Motivation,
I, 3, 5, 31, 130, 132, 199, 211–215, 245
II, 69, 93, 95–96, 104–105, 185–186, 188–190,
      193–197, 226
III, 20
Multidimensional scaling,
I, 175
II, 136
Music,
xxvi–xxvii, xxxiv–xxxv, xxxix, xli, xliii
I, 119–120, 134–135, 155–194
II, 97
Music,
  hierarchical structure,
I, 184–187
Music,
  overtone series,
I, 160
Music,
  principle of proximity
I, 176–179, 189
Music,
  spatial aspects, *see also* Musical shape
    analysis,
I, 170–176, 179–180, 189
Music theory,
I, 155, 157
Musical shape analysis,
I, 179–184
Myth,
I, 247, 256
II, 3–4, 11

N

Narrative,
II, 163
Natural resources,
II, 128–129, 143, 145, 150

Natural selection, *see also* Darwinism,
III, 67, 71–73, 94, 96–98, 101
Nature-nurture controversy,
I, 46, 56, 123, 202, 231–234
III, 16–17, 79, 82, 101–102
Neuroendocrine activity,
III, 152–153, 161
Neurons,
III, 2, 6, 18, 20–21
Neurons,
  neural models,
III, 20–27
Neurons,
  neural network model,
III, 10, 13, 15, 22–24
Neuroreductionistic theory,
III, 3, 9–10, 24–25, 29
Neuroses,
I, 15, 17, 128, 257
II, 33, 36–44, 47–49, 102, 201
III, 200, 205
Noise,
II, 146–148, 155
Nomothetic,
xxiv, xxxii
III, 74
Novel,
I, 113, 119–120, 123–124, 127

O

Object relations theory, *see also* Ego
    psychology,
I, 257
Observation,
III, 113
Operationalism,
xlii, xliv
I, 2, 197, 260
Operationism,
III, 231, 239, 253, 258–259

P

Pain,
III, 173–175, 181, 205, 206, 210, 220
Painting, *see also* Art,
xxvii
I, 134
II, 174
Parsing,
I, 100–103

SUBJECT INDEX

SUBJECT INDEX

SUBJECT INDEX

SUBJECT INDEX

SUBJECT INDEX

Therapies,
  psychological,
I, 252–253
II, 31–53, 101, 188, 231
III, 207–208
Therapies,
  rehabilitation,
III, 156, 172, 183
Therapies,
  relaxation,
III, 183
Thinking, *see* Cognition
Timbre,
I, 164, 169–170, 172
Timbre,
  harmonics,
I, 165–167, 189
Tonality,
I, 163
Toxicology,
  behavioral,
III, 217–218
Trait, *see also* Personality,
I, 215–218
II, 5, 14, 19, 62, 71, 218
Treatment, *see* Therapies
Tropism,
III, 240–241, 259, 261
Twelve-tone composition,
I, 179–184

Twelve-tone system,
I, 163
Twins,
II, 46
III, 76–79, 81–82, 85, 90, 162
Type A (Pattern A) behavior,
III, 159–160, 167, 185

U

Unemployment,
II, 56, 59, 73, 76
Urban life,
II, 134–136, 154
User characteristics,
III, 51–52
Utopia,
II, 209, 211, 213–214, 220, 224

V

Value-free science,
II, 211–212
Vitalism,
III, 19

W

Working conditions,
III, 40–42